Welcome to

Holt Science & Technology Earth Science

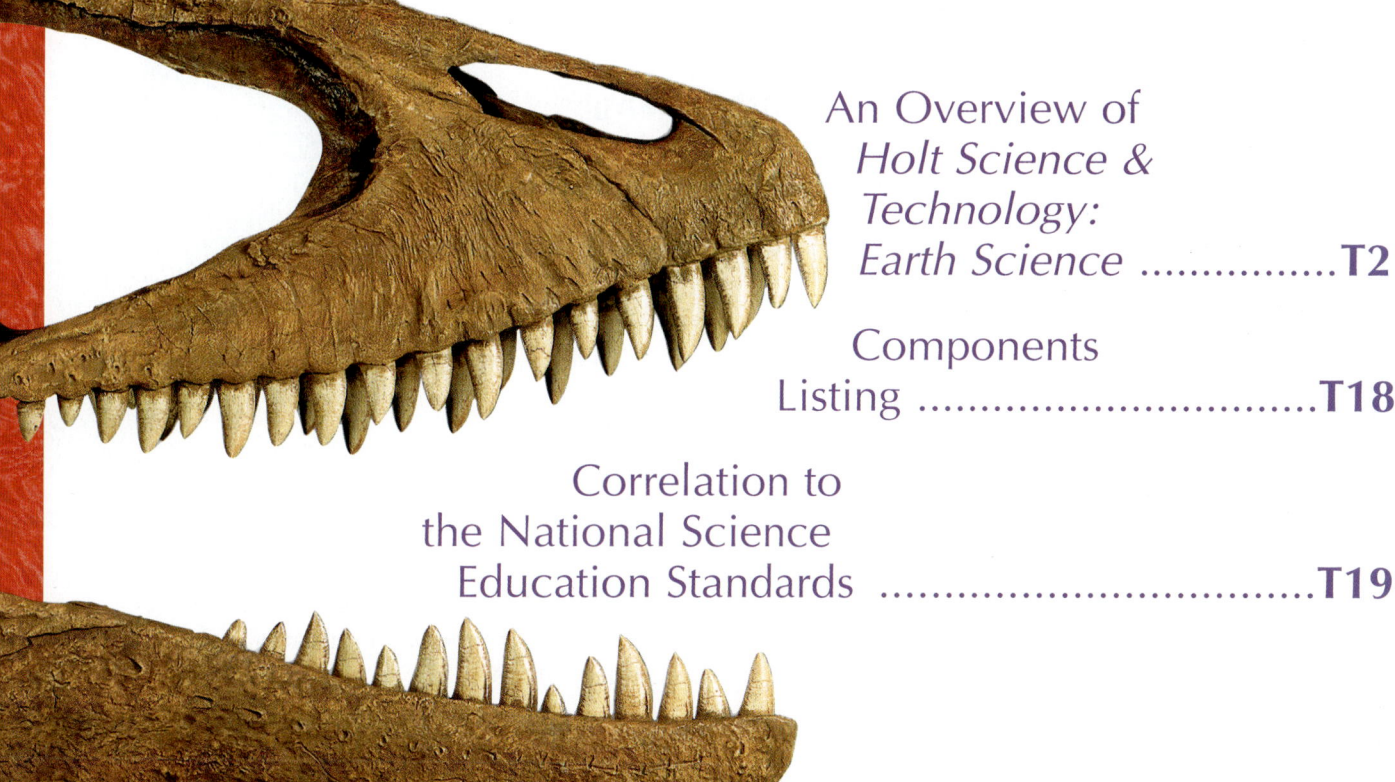

An Overview of *Holt Science & Technology: Earth Science* T2

Components Listing T18

Correlation to the National Science Education Standards T19

**EXPECT EXCITEMENT!
EXPECT RESULTS!**

HOLT SCIENCE & TECHNOLOGY

A Text that Grabs and Holds Your Students' Attention

Begins with a bang!
Each chapter begins with a brief introduction designed to pique your students' interest. Pre-Reading Questions are included so you can check students' prior understanding.

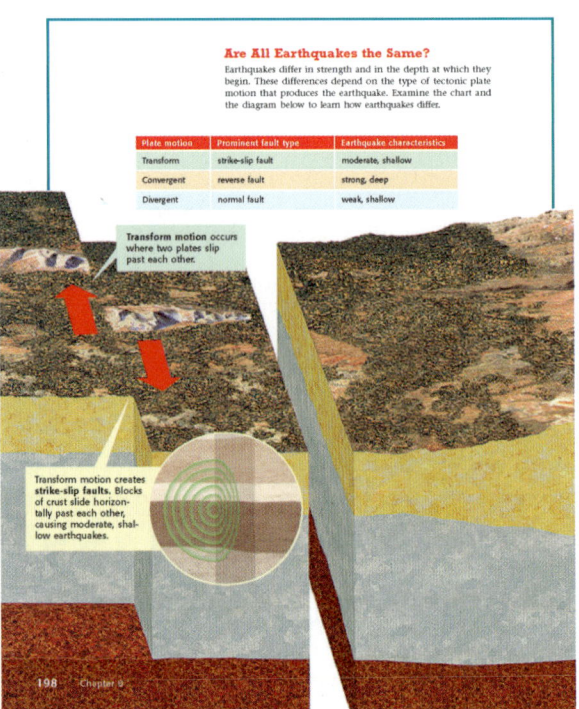

A text that motivates
Holt Science & Technology motivates your students in a variety of ways.

Visuals
- are integrated into the narrative
- clearly reveal macro-to-micro relationships
- support English-language learners and reluctant readers
- are functional, accurate, and understandable

Narrative
- contains concise, outline-style headings to help students find information easily
- presents content in a clear, logical sequence
- contains friendly language to make reading accessible and enjoyable
- incorporates analogies to help students relate concepts to the real world

Student Edition

T2   HOLT SCIENCE & TECHNOLOGY

"I need a textbook that will engage and excite my students while they're learning."

Applies to real life

Some of your students may ask you why they are studying science. *Holt Science and Technology* provides answers with motivating features:

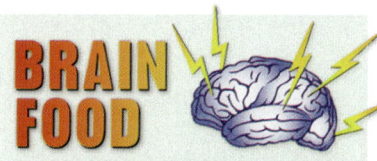

Violent volcanic eruptions sometimes produce a porous rock called pumice. Pumice is full of small holes once filled with trapped gases. Depending on how much space is taken up by these holes, some types of pumice can even float!

- **Start-Up Activity** stimulates your students' curiosity about upcoming chapter concepts with a hands-on activity.
- Tidbits to feed the mind are presented in small captions called **Brain Food**. There's nothing better than a fun fact to captivate a young audience!
- **Apply** poses real-world questions and asks your students to answer them by applying what they have just learned.
- **Activity** gives your students the opportunity to use their imaginations and to expand their learning.

Brings focus to the Internet

SciLinks—a National Science Teachers Association-sponsored Web service—links you and your students to interactive activities and current information directly related to chapter content. (see page T17)

The first middle school program with SciLinks

Ends with enrichment

Weird Science, **Health Watch**, **Careers**, **Scientific Debate**, and other end-of-chapter features extend chapter content with real-world examples, articles, and motivating activities.

Student Edition

HOLT SCIENCE & TECHNOLOGY

Focus on Reading and Understanding

Holt Science & Technology makes instruction accessible to all your students—English-language learners, special needs students, those having difficulty mastering content, students who need more practice or hands-on experience, and advanced learners.

Read for understanding
Each lesson gives you suggestions to help your students read for understanding.

- **Pre-Reading Questions** assess your students' prior knowledge and serves as a reading warm-up.
- **Reading Check-Up** allows students to see how their understanding has changed.
-  highlights activities that help English-language learners grasp content.
- **READING STRATEGY** emphasizes key concepts in order to guide reading and ensure comprehension.
- *Directed Reading Worksheets* makes reading an active process. A variety of strategies and fun activities help your students identify the main idea, then organize and synthesize supporting information.
- *Reinforcement & Vocabulary Review Worksheets* makes reviewing and reinforcing chapter content easy. Students have opportunities to examine issues in each section from different perspectives or to benefit from a different instructional approach.
- *Holt Science Skills Workshop: Reading in the Content Area* contains activities and exercises that target the reading skills specific to the comprehension of science texts.

READING STRATEGY
Prediction Guide Before students read the passage describing the three...
ask...
cau...
oce...
ans...
Sect...

READING STRATEGY
Activity As students read about map projections, have them write down the name of each type of projection and a brief description of what the projection represents. Have students list the advantages or disadvantages of each type of projection.

Reading Check-up — Take a minute to review your answers to the Pre-Reading Questions found at the bottom of page 568. Have your answers changed? If necessary, revise your answers based on what you have learned since you read the chapter.

Pre-Reading Questions
1. Why do stars shine?
2. What is a galaxy?
3. How did the universe begin, and how will it end? or will it?

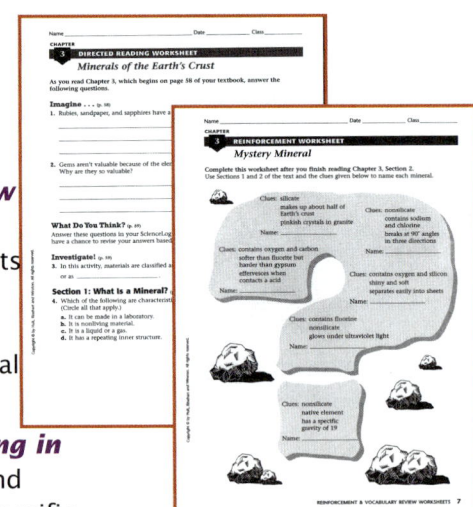

> "I need a program that helps me teach **today's students**."

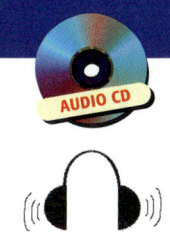

Guided Reading Audio CD Program

This audio program provides students with a direct reading of each chapter using instructional visuals as guideposts. Auditory learners, students with limited reading proficiency, and Spanish-speaking students receive the explanation they need from this alternative text format.
Available in English and Spanish.

Provide universal access

Holt Science & Technology helps all your students learn science.

- **Meeting Individual Needs** in the teacher's wrap provides engaging demonstrations and hands-on activities to help learners of all levels.
- **Reteaching** gives you alternate methods of instruction for those students who need it.
- **Homework** options use a variety of teaching strategies to complement diverse learning styles.
- *Critical Thinking & Problem Solving Worksheets* provides challenging activities connecting science concepts to the "real world." Your students learn to think through a problem and to use the scientific method and other strategies to find a solution.

MEETING INDIVIDUAL NEEDS

Advanced Learners

MEETING INDIVIDUAL NEEDS

Learners Having Difficulty Have students copy descriptive phrases about the three types of volcanoes in their ScienceLog. Beside the entries, have them draw a cross section of each type of volcano. Students should find an example of each volcano type and write three paragraphs about each one. The paragraphs should describe how the volcano fits its category, detail its last eruption, and explain how the volcano's shape is linked to the way it erupted. **Sheltered English**

Universal Access

Approach learning from different angles

with these in-text features and ancillaries. You can make sure your students understand science concepts no matter what their learning styles.

 **HOLT SCIENCE POSTERS**

REAL-WORLD CONNECTION   **HOLT ANTHOLOGY OF SCIENCE FICTION**

GROUP ACTIVITY   **COOPERATIVE LEARNING**

HOLT SCIENCE & TECHNOLOGY   T5

Labs to Make Learning Active and Meaningful

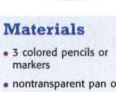

Holt Science & Technology provides a strong yet flexible lab program that meets lab science requirements, regardless of limited lab equipment or time restrictions. Labs include clear procedures, demonstrate scientific concepts, and develop students' understanding of scientific methods. **Using Scientific Methods**

These labs have been classroom-tested, and also reviewed by an independent laboratory, for reliability, safety, and efficiency.

Terry Rakes
Elmwood Junior High School
Rogers, Arkansas

To try your hand at using the scientific method, turn to page 486 in the LabBook.

In-text LabBook

LabBook, in the back of the *Student Edition*, allows for
- more labs and activities,
- greater flexibility in lesson planning,
- a wider variety of labs,
- more detailed lab procedures and explanations,
- an uninterrupted chapter narrative, and includes
- separate *Datasheets for LabBook*.

> "I need a variety of **fun** yet **meaningful** lab activities that are **cost effective**."

Additional, in-text labs and activities

LABS AND ACTIVITIES FOR EVERY LESSON

- **QuickLabs** are easy to execute and require minimal time and materials—great for quick in-class activities, teacher demonstrations, or group presentations.
- **Start-Up Activity** stimulates your students' curiosity about scientific concepts in the upcoming chapter.
- **Activity** gives your students the opportunity to use their imaginations and expand their learning.
- **Apply** poses real-world questions and asks your students to answer them by applying what they have just learned.
- **Demonstration** and **Activity** in the Teacher's Edition give you options to demonstrate labs and procedures to the whole class or provide fun, hands-on activities.

QuickLab

Reaction to Stress

1. Make a pliable "rock" by pouring 60 mL (1/4 cup) of **water** into a **plastic cup** and adding 150 mL of **cornstarch**, 15 mL (1 tbsp) at a time. Stir well after each addition.
2. Pour half of the cornstarch...

Activity

...w far do you think the ice-...rg that struck the *Titanic* ...fted before the two met ...t fateful night in 1912? ...t on a map of the North Atlantic Ocean the route of the *Titanic* from Southampton, England, to New York. Then plot a possi-...

Lab Ratings make choosing labs easy

Lab Ratings, for all labs, make it easy for you to determine, at a glance, which labs are most appropriate for your class.

Time Required
One 45-minute class period

Lab Ratings

EASY ———→ HARD

TEACHER PREP — 1
STUDENT SET-UP — 2
CONCEPT LEVEL — 2
CLEAN UP — 1

Science Kits, available in both consumable and nonconsumable packages, offer you all the materials you need for in-text labs and will cut your prep time significantly. Replacement materials can be ordered directly through Science Kit at www.sciencekit.com.

For a complete materials list, see page xxiv in the Annotated Teacher's Edition

HOLT SCIENCE & TECHNOLOGY T7

HOLT SCIENCE & TECHNOLOGY

Lab Manuals Extend Your Options

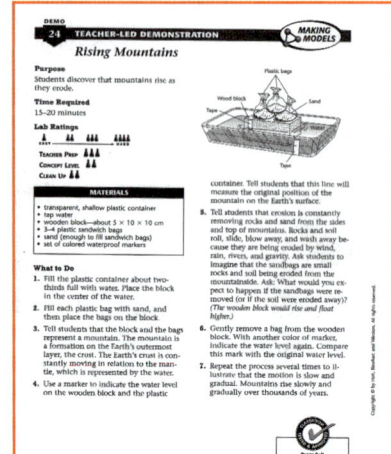

Whiz-Bang Demonstrations gives you a rousing way to get your students' attention at the beginning of a lesson. **65 in all!**

Labs You Can Eat safely incorporates food into the classroom to provide a fun inquiry-based learning tool. **25 in all!**

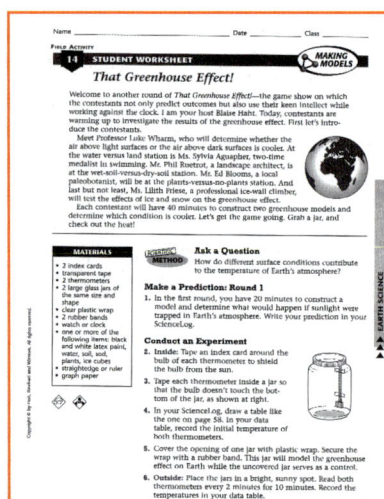

EcoLabs & Field Activities includes activities that address specific ecological questions and increase environmental awareness. **23 in all!**

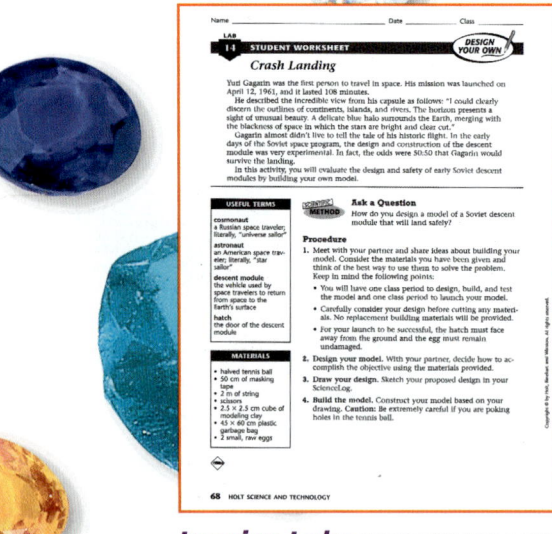

Inquiry Labs encourages your students to ask questions and investigate problems in order to find solutions. **23 in all!**

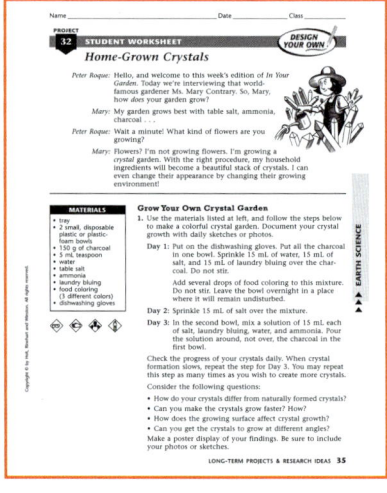

Long-Term Projects & Research Ideas extends and enriches chapter content with experiments, activities, inquiry-based projects, and Internet and library research. **2 for every chapter!**

T8   HOLT SCIENCE & TECHNOLOGY

Comprehensive Skill Development

Science skills ensure future success

Holt Science & Technology gives your students ample opportunities to master the skills necessary for future success in science. Science skills are developed in a variety of ways:

- The in-text **LabBook**, activities, and lab booklets provide lots of practice using scientific methods.
- The **Appendix** helps your students refresh their measuring and data-analysis skills, as well as their understanding of the **scientific method**.
- **Apply** and **Activity** allow your students to develop science skills in fun and motivating ways.

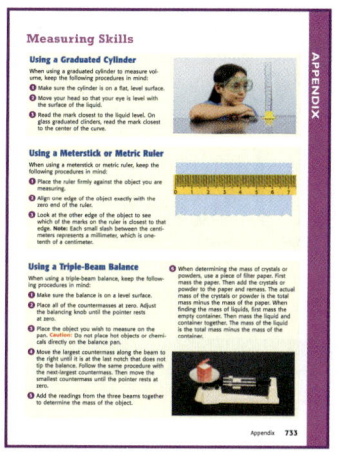

In addition, your students can find plenty of skill-building practice in *Science Skills Worksheets*. These worksheets help your students hone important science skills, such as thinking objectively, conducting research, designing investigations, keeping accurate records, and creating and analyzing graphs.

Math is covered everywhere you look!

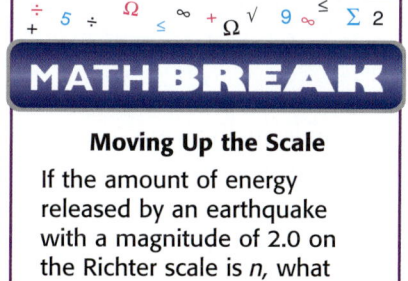

Moving Up the Scale

If the amount of energy released by an earthquake with a magnitude of 2.0 on the Richter scale is *n*, what are the amounts of energy

Holt Science & Technology also strengthens your students' math skills. From practice problems to reviews, math skills are continually developed:

- **MathBreak** provides practice with direct application to the science concepts being taught.
- **Math Concepts** reviews the math lessons presented in the chapter.
- **Math Refresher**, found in the Appendix, reviews basic math skills, such as averages, ratios, percentages, and more.

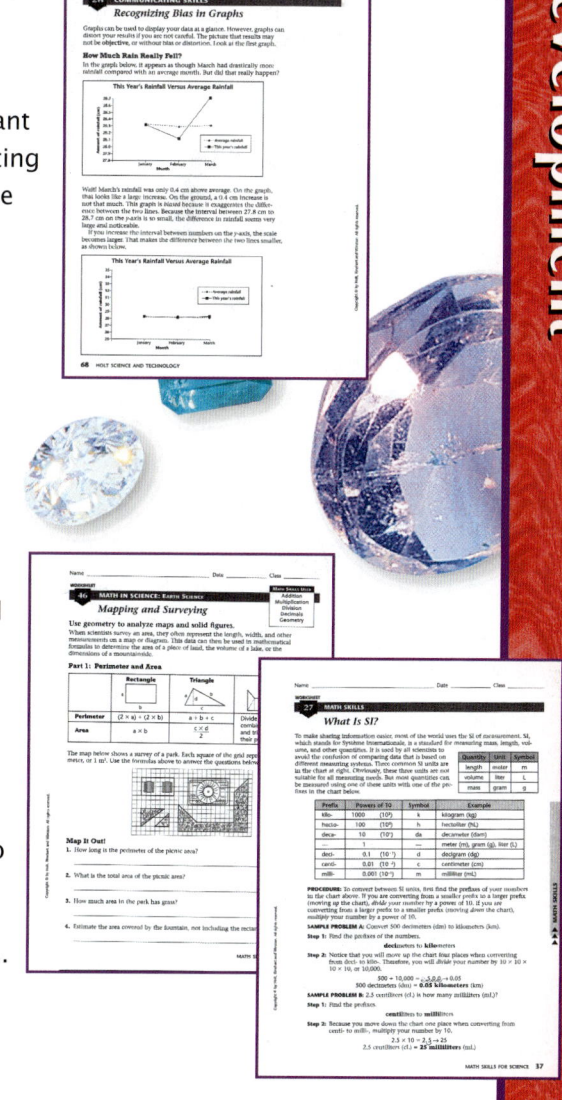

Math Skills for Science helps your students develop and apply basic math skills to scientific problems with two types of worksheets.

- **Math Skills Worksheets** provide a brief introduction to a relevant math skill, a step-by-step explanation of the math process, and example and practice problems.
- **Math in Science Worksheets** give your students practice using math in real-life science situations.

HOLT SCIENCE & TECHNOLOGY T9

HOLT SCIENCE & TECHNOLOGY

A Versatile Teacher's Edition that is Easy-to-Use

The Chapter Organizer— your easy-to-follow road map

With such a wealth of program resources, you'll be glad to know we've included a convenient, timesaving guide suggesting how and when to use them. The **Chapter Organizer**
- integrates all labs, technology, and print resources
- is organized according to time requirements
- includes National Standards correlated by section
- Activities are leveled by ability level to help you choose which ones are appropriate.

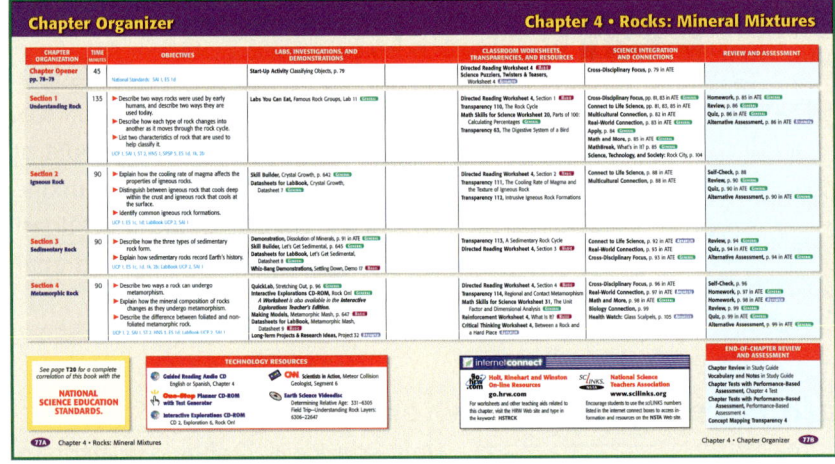

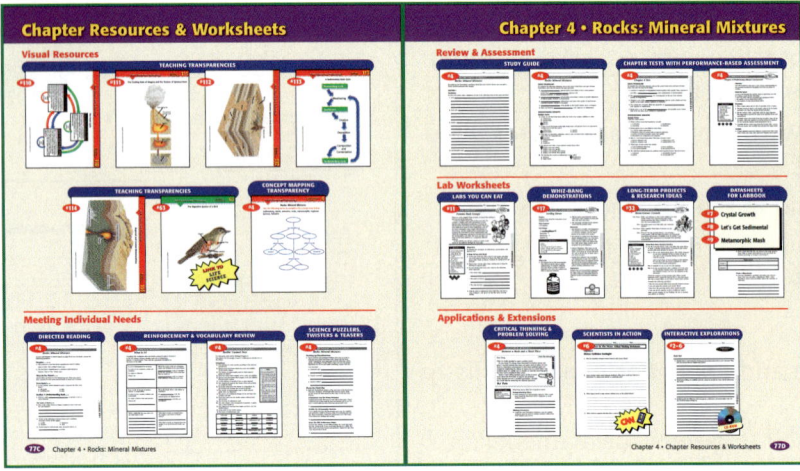

Chapter Resources & Worksheets makes choosing teaching resources easy by showing them as reduced pages. Available resources are categorized by
- Visual Resources
- Meeting Individual Needs
- Review and Assessment
- Lab Worksheets
- Applications & Extensions

The **Chapter Background** provides additional information to help you enrich upcoming lessons.

T10 HOLT SCIENCE & TECHNOLOGY

> "A teacher's edition should be **well-organized** and provide **effective** tips and techniques."

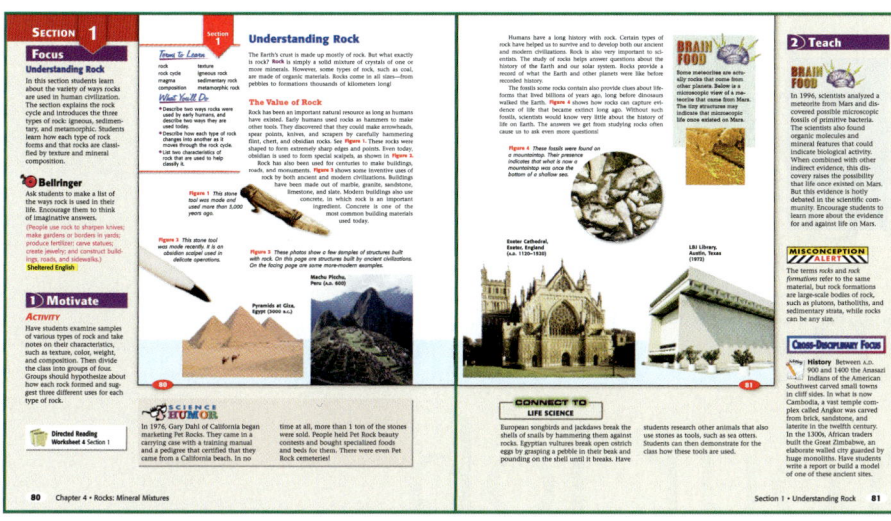

Keep the focus on the lesson

The complete lesson cycle helps you keep your students interested and involved. An array of both traditional and new teaching strategies, creative reinforcement, and thought-provoking extensions help you teach to a wide variety of learning styles, ability levels, and interests.

Fuel your presentation

Found on almost every page, fun features and intriguing stories ignite class discussion and get your students thinking.

Q: What do you get when a cow is caught in an earthquake?

A: a milkshake

IS THAT A FACT!

The largest expanse of exposed metamorphic rock in the world is the Canadian Shield, a huge horseshoe-shaped region encircling Hudson Bay. Covering about half of Canada, it is about 4,586,900 km² and is the source of more than 70 percent of the minerals mined in Canada.

MISCONCEPTION ALERT

People often assume that humid air is heavier than dry air. Actually, humid air rises like a balloon because it is less dense than dry air at the same pressure and temperature. The reason is that water molecules are lighter than N_2 and O_2, the main constituents of air.

Science Bloopers

During a World War I naval engagement off the Falkland Islands, British gunners were astonished to see that their artillery shells were landing 100 yd to the left of German ships. The gunners had made corrections for the Coriolis effect at 50° north latitude, not 50° south of the equator. Consequently, their shells fell at a distance from the target equal to twice the Coriolis deflection!

Engineers have devised giant shock absorbers for buildings. The shock absorbers contain a ferrofluid solution that becomes rigid in a magnetic field. When an earthquake occurs, a computer controls electromagnets in the shock absorbers to dampen the vibrations!

Teacher's Edition

HOLT SCIENCE & TECHNOLOGY T11

HOLT SCIENCE & TECHNOLOGY

Teaching Support that Makes Your Job Easier

Teaching Resources

Point-and-Click Planning

One-Stop Planner CD-ROM

with Exam-View® Test Generator

The *One-Stop Planner® CD-ROM with Exam-View® Test Generator* is a timesaving, all-in-one planning tool that contains everything you need on a single disc!

- **customizable** lesson plans, tests, assessment checklists, and rubrics
- a **powerful** test generator
- **printable** resources, including
  - worksheets
  - transparencies
  - Spanish transcripts
  - assessment materials
  - rubrics
  - National Standards Correlation
  - Science Fair Guide
  - Parent Letters
  - and much more!

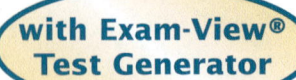

Includes student worksheets

*"I would love to **streamline planning** so I can spend more time on what I do best—teaching."*

Sharpen your saw

The *Professional Reference for Teachers* provides current information about pertinent issues in science education today. In professional articles, you can learn more about the National Science Education Standards, block scheduling, classroom management, and more. A bibliography of books, lectures, magazines, and Web sites is included.

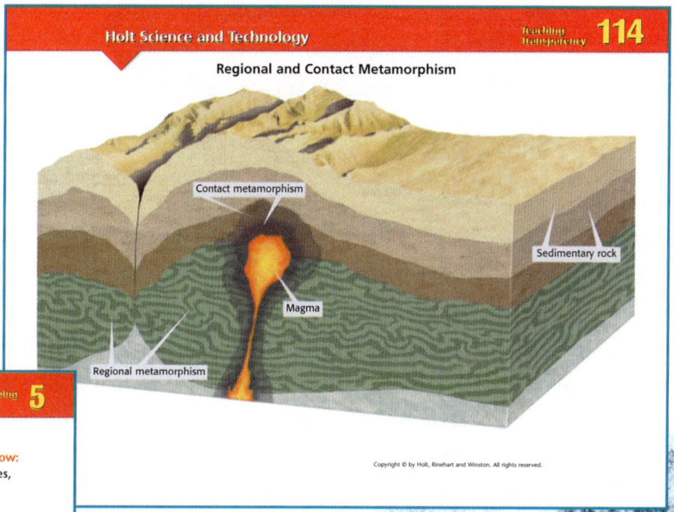

Visualize science concepts

Teaching Transparencies, many with images taken directly from the text, reinforce important science concepts and processes.

Two *Concept Mapping Transparencies* are included for each chapter—a partial map transparency to use with your students as they progress through the chapter and a completed concept map to serve as an answer key.

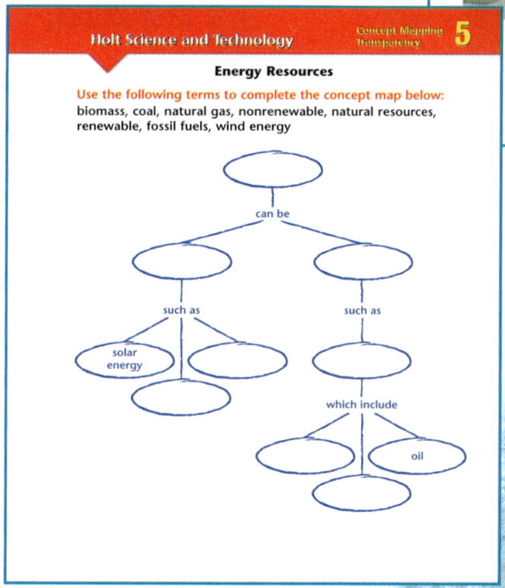

Bellringer Transparency Masters (found on the *One-Stop Planner CD-ROM*) help you focus your students' attention quickly at the beginning of class while you are dealing with administrative demands.

Teaching Resources

HOLT SCIENCE & TECHNOLOGY

HOLT SCIENCE & TECHNOLOGY

Assessment that Accurately Measures Mastery of Content

Check progress

Self-Check encourages your students to evaluate their own learning by answering questions found intermittently within the chapter. A page reference allows them to check their own answers. After reading each lesson, your students explore, evaluate, and extend what they've learned by answering questions in the section **Review**. In the teacher's wrap, a **Quiz** provides an objective assessment of each lesson.

> ✓ **Self-Check**
>
> Would a large wave or a small wave have more erosive energy? Why? *(See page 726 to check your answer.)*

Chapter Highlights lists vocabulary and provides content summaries in a concise, visual format. This helps your students organize their thoughts and synthesize information.

Study Guide contains blackline masters for Chapter Highlights and Chapter Reviews that help your students gear up for tests and quizzes.

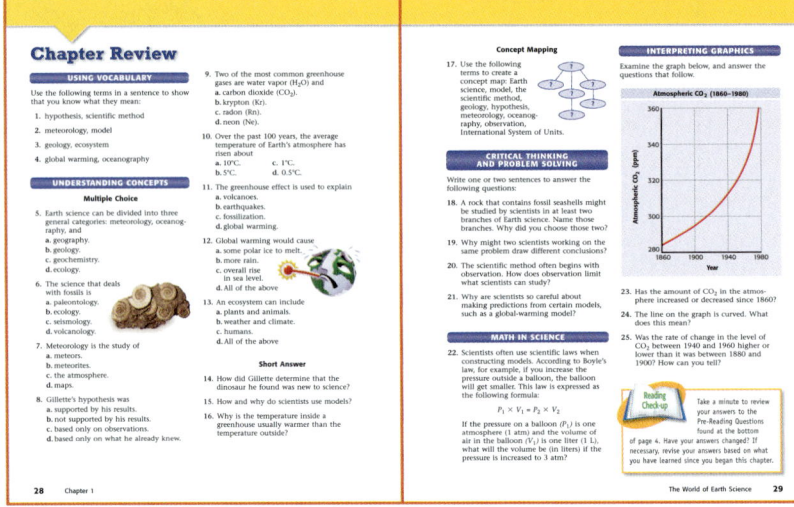

Chapter Review question types are identical to those found on the chapter tests, making the Chapter Review an excellent resource for pretest practice.

> "I want to **make sure** my students are **learning.**"

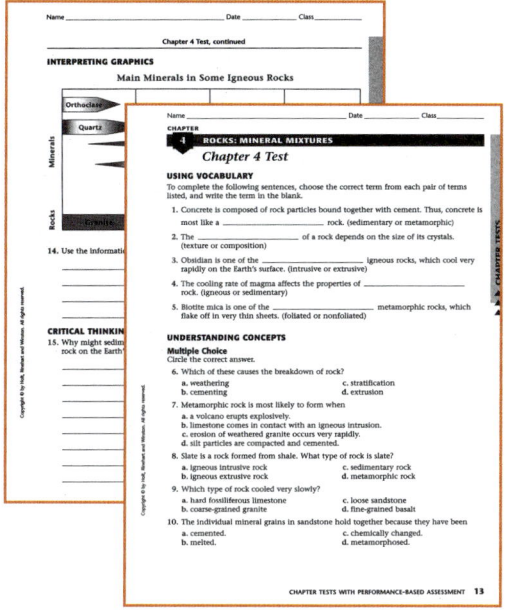

Chapter Tests with Performance-Based Assessment includes multiple-choice, concept-mapping, critical-thinking, interpreting graphics, math-in-science, and alternative assessment questions, to name a few.

Alternative Assessment in the teacher's wrap provides you with different evaluation options, such as expository writing and concept mapping, to ensure a thorough assessment.

Create your own assessments

One-Stop Planner CD-ROM

With the *One-Stop Planner CD-ROM with Test Generator*, you can create, revise, and edit quizzes, section and chapter reviews, and chapter tests, drawing from thousands of questions organized by chapter and linked to chapter objectives. Performance-based assessment is also included.

The *Test Generator: Test Item Listing* provides a printed copy of thousands of assessment items on the *One-Stop Planner CD-ROM*. This handy guide allows you to preview test items before making selections.

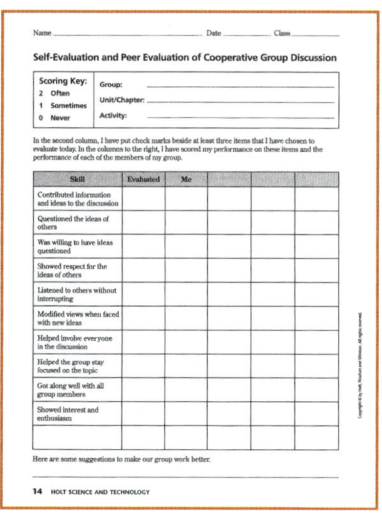

Assessment Checklists & Rubrics, available on the *One-Stop Planner CD-ROM* or as blackline masters, gives you guidelines for evaluating your students' progress, including performance and portfolio assessment tools. You can also create a customized checklist for each class, helping you gather daily scores and determine grades.

Assessment

HOLT SCIENCE & TECHNOLOGY T15

HOLT SCIENCE & TECHNOLOGY

Technology That Expands Your Options

Holt Science & Technology provides the right combination of fully integrated technology resources—including CD-ROMs, videos, and Internet products—to make your teaching more effective, efficient, and creative.

Technology Resources

Guided Reading Audio CD Program provides a direct reading for each chapter, in English and Spanish, to help struggling readers and English-language learners better understand the text.

Interactive Explorations CD-ROM Program turns a computer into a virtual laboratory where your students act as lab assistants in solving 24 real-world problems.

Science Tutor CD-ROM serves as a personal tutor for helping students practice what they've learned in their textbooks and in class by offering immediate feedback.

Student Edition, CD-ROM Version provides students with the entire textbook on CD-ROM so they have less to carry home.

Lesson Presentation CD-ROM provides you with a media-based presentation of core concepts to engage your students.

One-Stop Planner CD-ROM with Test Generator makes planning and managing lessons easier than ever with the following resources:
- printable worksheets and resources
- customizable lesson plans
- powerful ExamView® Test Generator

One-Stop Planner CD-ROM

Earth Science Videotape contains 60 minutes of Earth science footage.

CNN Presents Science in the News: Video Library allows students to see the impact of science on their everyday lives with the following videos: Multicultural Connections, Science Technology & Society, Scientists in Action, and Eye on the Environment.

> "I don't have time to **find** and **evaluate** the **technology** resources out there."

Internet Resources

Online Edition is portable, expandable, and interactive, and yet it weighs nothing at all! This online learning resource gives you and your students the following:
- the Student Edition online
- interactive exercises and feedback
- presentation materials
- homework help

SciLinks is an Online service developed and maintained by NSTA that links you to the best and most up-to-date Web sites directly related to the textbook.

cnnstudentnews.com is the ultimate news and information Web site for students and teachers and includes news as it happens, classroom resources, activities, and lesson plans.

go.hrw.com enriches student learning with chapter activities and resources.

EXPECT EXCITEMENT!
EXPECT RESULTS!

HOLT SCIENCE & TECHNOLOGY

Earth Science Components Listing

Student Edition

Annotated Teacher's Edition

Earth Science Teaching Resources

- Study Guide
- Study Guide Answer Key
- Critical Thinking & Problem Solving Worksheets
- Reinforcement & Vocabulary Review Worksheets
- Science Puzzlers, Twisters & Teasers
- Chapter Tests with Performance-Based Assessment
- Directed Reading Worksheets
- Directed Reading Worksheets Answer Key
- Datasheets for LabBook
- Datasheets for LabBook Answer Key
- Test Generator: Test Item Listing

LabBank

- Labs You Can Eat
- Whiz-Bang Demonstrations
- Inquiry Labs
- EcoLabs & Field Activities
- Long-Term Projects & Research Ideas

Program Teaching Resources

- Science Skills Worksheets
- Math Skills for Science
- Professional Reference for Teachers
- Holt Anthology of Science Fiction
- Assessment Checklists & Rubrics
- Science Fair Guide
- Holt Science Posters
- Holt Science Skill Workshop: Reading in the Content Area

Technology Resources

Online Edition

Student Edition, CD-ROM Version

Science Tutor CD-ROM

Lesson Presentation CD-ROM

Teaching Transparencies with Concept Mapping Transparencies

Guided Reading Audio CD Program

Guided Reading Audio CD Program, Spanish

One-Stop Planner CD-ROM with Test Generator for Mac® and Win®

Interactive Explorations CD-ROM Program for Mac® and Win®

CNN Presents Science in the News: Video Library
- Scientists in Action
- Multicultural Connections
- Science, Technology & Society
- Eye on the Environment

Earth Science Videotape

HOLT SCIENCE & TECHNOLOGY Earth Science

National Science Education STANDARDS CORRELATIONS

The following lists show the chapter correlation of **Holt Science & Technology: Earth Science** with the *National Science Education Standards* (grades 5–8).

The chapter correlations for the Earth Science Content Standards begin on page T22.

Unifying Concepts and Processes

Standard	Chapter Correlation		
Systems, order, and organization Code: UCP 1	**Chapter 3** 3.1, 3.2 **Chapter 4** 4.1, 4.2, 4.3, 4.4 **Chapter 6** 6.2, 6.3, 6.5 **Chapter 11** 11.1	**Chapter 14** 14.3 **Chapter 19** 19.1 **Chapter 20** 20.1, 20.2, 20.3 **Chapter 21** 21.1, 21.2, 21.3, 21.4	
Evidence, models, and explanation Code: UCP 2	**Chapter 1** 1.2, 1.3 **Chapter 2** 2.1, 2.2, 2.3 **Chapter 4** 4.2, 4.3, 4.4 **Chapter 5** 5.3 **Chapter 6** 6.1, 6.2, 6.5 **Chapter 7** 7.1, 7.2, 7.3, 7.4 **Chapter 8** 8.1, 8.3	**Chapter 10** 10.1 **Chapter 11** 11.1, 11.4 **Chapter 12** 12.2, 12.3 **Chapter 13** 13.2 **Chapter 14** 14.1, 14.3 **Chapter 15** 15.2 **Chapter 16** 16.1	**Chapter 17** 17.2, 17.3 **Chapter 18** 18.1, 18.2 **Chapter 19** 19.1, 19.3 **Chapter 20** 20.2 **Chapter 21** 21.1, 21.2, 21.4 **Chapter 22** 22.1, 22.4
Change, constancy, and measurement Code: UCP 3	**Chapter 1** 1.4 **Chapter 2** 2.1, 2.2, 2.3 **Chapter 5** 5.3 **Chapter 6** 6.2, 6.3, 6.4, 6.5 **Chapter 8** 8.2, 8.3 **Chapter 9** 9.3	**Chapter 11** 11.4 **Chapter 12** 12.1, 12.2, 12.3 **Chapter 13** 13.2 **Chapter 14** 14.2 **Chapter 15** 15.3 **Chapter 16** 16.1, 16.4	**Chapter 17** 17.2, 17.3 **Chapter 18** 18.2 **Chapter 20** 20.1, 20.2 **Chapter 21** 21.1, 21.2, 21.4 **Chapter 22** 22.1, 22.2
Evolution and equilibrium Code: UCP 4	**Chapter 6** 6.1, 6.2, 6.5 **Chapter 19** 19.1, 19.3 **Chapter 22** 22.1, 22.2, 22.3, 22.4		
Form and function Code: UCP 5	**Chapter 2** 2.1, 2.2, 2.3 **Chapter 3** 3.1, 3.2, 3.3 **Chapter 5** 5.3	**Chapter 8** 8.3 **Chapter 11** 11.1 **Chapter 21** 21.2, 21.3, 21.4	**Chapter 22** 22.1, 22.3, 22.4

SCIENCE AS INQUIRY

Standard	Chapter Correlation		
Abilities necessary to do scientific inquiry Code: SAI 1	Chapter 1 1.1, 1.2, 1.4 Chapter 2 2.1, 2.2, 2.3 Chapter 3 3.2, 3.3 Chapter 4 4.1, 4.2, 4.3, 4.4 Chapter 5 5.1, 5.2, 5.3 Chapter 6 6.1, 6.2, 6.3, 6.5 Chapter 7 7.1, 7.3, 7.4 Chapter 8 8.1, 8.2, 8.3	Chapter 9 9.1, 9.2, 9.3 Chapter 10 10.1, 10.2 Chapter 11 11.1, 11.3, 11.4 Chapter 12 12.1, 12.2, 12.3, 12.4 Chapter 13 13.2, 13.4 Chapter 14 14.1, 14.2, 14.3 Chapter 15 15.1, 15.2, 15.3, 15.4 Chapter 16 16.1, 16.4	Chapter 17 17.1, 17.2, 17.3 Chapter 18 18.1, 18.2, 18.3 Chapter 19 19.1, 19.2, 19.3 Chapter 20 20.1, 20.2, 20.3 Chapter 21 21.1, 21.2, 21.3, 21.4 Chapter 22 22.1, 22.2, 22.4
Understandings about scientific inquiry Code: SAI 2	Chapter 1 1.2, 1.3 Chapter 6 6.2 Chapter 8 8.2 Chapter 15 15.2 Chapter 17 17.3 Chapter 18 18.1		

SCIENCE AND TECHNOLOGY

Standard	Chapter Correlation		
Abilities of technological design Code: ST 1	Chapter 2 2.1, 2.3 Chapter 5 5.3 Chapter 7 7.3 Chapter 8 8.3 Chapter 13 13.2	Chapter 14 14.3 Chapter 15 15.1, 15.2, 15.3 Chapter 16 16.4 Chapter 17 17.2 Chapter 18 18.1, 18.3	Chapter 20 20.1, 20.2 Chapter 21 21.3 Chapter 22 22.1, 22.4
Understandings about science and technology Code: ST 2	Chapter 1 1.1, 1.2 Chapter 2 2.1, 2.2, 2.3 Chapter 4 4.1, 4.4 Chapter 5 5.3 Chapter 6 6.4 Chapter 9 9.2, 9.3	Chapter 11 11.4 Chapter 12 12.2 Chapter 13 13.2, 13.4, 13.5 Chapter 16 16.4 Chapter 17 17.3 Chapter 18 18.1, 18.2, 18.3	Chapter 19 19.1, 19.2 Chapter 20 20.1 Chapter 21 21.3 Chapter 22 22.1, 22.2, 22.3, 22.4

SCIENCE IN PERSONAL AND SOCIAL PERSPECTIVES

Standard	Chapter Correlation	
Personal health Code: SPSP 1	Chapter 1 1.4 Chapter 5 5.2 Chapter 8 8.3 Chapter 11 11.4	Chapter 15 15.1, 15.4 Chapter 17 17.1 Chapter 19 19.1
Populations, resources, and environments Code: SPSP 2	Chapter 2 2.3 Chapter 3 3.3 Chapter 5 5.1, 5.2, 5.3 Chapter 10 10.4 Chapter 11 11.3, 11.4	Chapter 12 12.1, 12.2 Chapter 13 13.4, 13.5 Chapter 15 15.2, 15.4

SCIENCE IN PERSONAL AND SOCIAL PERSPECTIVES (CONT'D)

Standard	Chapter Correlation		
Natural hazards Code: SPSP 3	**Chapter 1** 1.1, 1.3 **Chapter 8** 8.2, 8.3 **Chapter 9** 9.2 **Chapter 11** 11.2 **Chapter 12** 12.1, 12.3, 12.4	**Chapter 14** 14.2 **Chapter 15** 15.1, 15.2, 15.4 **Chapter 16** 16.1, 16.3 **Chapter 17** 17.1, 17.3	
Risks and benefits Code: SPSP 4	**Chapter 1** 1.1, 1.3 **Chapter 3** 3.3 **Chapter 5** 5.1, 5.2, 5.3 **Chapter 7** 7.3 **Chapter 8** 8.2, 8.3 **Chapter 9** 9.2	**Chapter 10** 10.4 **Chapter 11** 11.2 **Chapter 12** 12.4 **Chapter 13** 13.4, 13.5 **Chapter 14** 14.2 **Chapter 15** 15.1, 15.2, 15.4	**Chapter 16** 16.3 **Chapter 17** 17.3 **Chapter 18** 18.3 **Chapter 19** 19.1
Science and technology in society Code: SPSP 5	**Chapter 2** 2.1, 2.2, 2.3 **Chapter 4** 4.1 **Chapter 5** 5.2, 5.3 **Chapter 6** 6.4 **Chapter 7** 7.1, 7.3 **Chapter 8** 8.3	**Chapter 9** 9.2, 9.3 **Chapter 10** 10.4 **Chapter 11** 11.4 **Chapter 13** 13.4, 13.5 **Chapter 15** 15.4 **Chapter 16** 16.4	**Chapter 17** 17.3 **Chapter 18** 18.1, 18.2, 18.3 **Chapter 19** 19.1, 19.2 **Chapter 20** 20.1 **Chapter 21** 21.1, 21.3 **Chapter 22** 22.1, 22.2, 22.3, 22.4

HISTORY AND NATURE OF SCIENCE

Standard	Chapter Correlation		
Science as a human endeavor Code: HNS 1	**Chapter 1** 1.1 **Chapter 2** 2.1, 2.3 **Chapter 4** 4.1 **Chapter 6** 6.1 **Chapter 7** 7.2, 7.3 **Chapter 8** 8.1, 8.2	**Chapter 9** 9.2 **Chapter 12** 12.2 **Chapter 13** 13.2 **Chapter 14** 14.1, 14.3 **Chapter 16** 16.4 **Chapter 17** 17.2, 17.3	**Chapter 18** 18.1, 18.2, 18.3 **Chapter 19** 19.1, 19.2 **Chapter 20** 20.1, 20.2 **Chapter 21** 21.1, 21.3 **Chapter 22** 22.1, 22.2, 22.3, 22.4
Nature of science Code: HNS 2	**Chapter 1** 1.2, 1.3 **Chapter 6** 6.1 **Chapter 8** 8.4	**Chapter 9** 9.1 **Chapter 12** 12.2 **Chapter 18** 18.1	**Chapter 19** 19.1, 19.2 **Chapter 21** 21.1, 21.3
History of science Code: HNS 3	**Chapter 1** 1.4 **Chapter 2** 2.1, 2.2 **Chapter 4** 4.4 **Chapter 6** 6.1 **Chapter 7** 7.3 **Chapter 8** 8.2	**Chapter 9** 9.2 **Chapter 12** 12.2 **Chapter 13** 13.2 **Chapter 14** 14.1, 14.3 **Chapter 16** 16.2 **Chapter 17** 17.2	**Chapter 18** 18.1, 18.3 **Chapter 19** 19.1, 19.2 **Chapter 20** 20.1, 20.2 **Chapter 22** 22.1, 22.2, 22.3, 22.4

Earth Science
CONTENT STANDARDS

STRUCTURE OF THE EARTH SYSTEM

Standard	Chapter Correlation	
The solid earth is layered with a lithosphere; hot, convecting mantle; and dense metallic core. **Code: ES 1a**	Chapter 1 1.3 Chapter 7 7.1 Chapter 8 8.4	
Lithospheric plates on the scales of continents and oceans constantly move at rates of centimeters per year in response to movements in the mantle. Major geological events, such as earthquakes, volcanic eruptions, and mountain building result from these plate motions. **Code: ES 1b**	Chapter 7 7.3, 7.4 Chapter 8 8.1 Chapter 9 9.3	Chapter 13 13.1, 13.2 Chapter 14 14.2
Land forms are the result of a combination of constructive and destructive forces. Constructive forces include crustal deformation, volcanic eruption, and deposition of sediment, while destructive forces include weathering and erosion. **Code: ES 1c**	Chapter 4 4.2, 4.3 Chapter 7 7.4 Chapter 9 9.1, 9.2, 9.3 Chapter 10 10.1, 10.2, 10.3	Chapter 11 11.1, 11.2, 11.3, 11.4 Chapter 12 12.1, 12.2, 12.3, 12.4 Chapter 13 13.2 Chapter 20 20.1
Some changes in the solid earth can be described as the "rock cycle." Old rocks at the earth's surface weather, forming sediments that are buried, then compacted, heated, and often recrystallized into new rock. Eventually, those new rocks may be brought to the earth's surface by the forces that drive plate motions, and the rock cycle continues. **Code: ES 1d**	Chapter 4 4.1, 4.2, 4.3, 4.4 Chapter 13 13.1	
Soil consists of weathered rocks and decomposed organic material from dead plants, animals, and bacteria. Soils are often found in layers, with each having a different chemical composition and texture. **Code: ES 1e**	Chapter 10 10.3	
Water, which covers the majority of the earth's surface, circulates through the crust, oceans, and atmosphere in what is known as the "water cycle." Water evaporates from the earth's surface, rises and cools as it moves to higher elevations, condenses as rain or snow, and falls to the surface where it collects in lakes, oceans soil, and in rocks underground. **Code: ES 1f**	Chapter 11 11.1, 11.3 Chapter 13 13.1 Chapter 16 16.1	

Structure of the Earth System (cont'd)

Standard	Chapter Correlation
Water is a solvent. As it passes through the water cycle it dissolves minerals and gases and carries them to the oceans. Code: ES 1g	**Chapter 11** 11.1, 11.3 **Chapter 13** 13.1
The atmosphere is a mixture of nitrogen, oxygen, and trace gases that include water vapor. The atmosphere has different properties at different elevations. Code: ES 1h	**Chapter 13** 13.1 **Chapter 15** 15.1
Clouds, formed by the condensation of water vapor, affect weather and climate. Code: ES 1i	**Chapter 16** 16.1, 16.3
Global patterns of atmospheric movement influence local weather. Oceans have a major effect on climate, because water in the oceans holds a large amount of heat. Code: ES 1j	**Chapter 13** 13.1 **Chapter 16** 16.2, 16.3 **Chapter 14** 14.1 **Chapter 17** 17.1 **Chapter 15** 15.3
Living organisms have played many roles in the earth system, including affecting the composition of the atmosphere, producing some types of rocks, and contributing to the weathering of rocks. Code: ES 1k	**Chapter 4** 4.1, 4.3 **Chapter 10** 10.1, 10.3 **Chapter 5** 5.2 **Chapter 15** 15.2, 15.4 **Chapter 6** 6.4 **Chapter 17** 17.3

Earth's History

Standard	Chapter Correlation
The earth processes we see today, including erosion, movement of lithospheric plates, and changes in atmospheric composition, are similar to those that occurred in the past. Earth history is also influenced by occasional catastrophes, such as the impact of an asteroid or comet. Code: ES 2a	**Chapter 6** 6.1 **Chapter 15** 15.2, 15.4 **Chapter 7** 7.2, 7.4 **Chapter 17** 17.3 **Chapter 11** 11.1 **Chapter 20** 20.3 **Chapter 12** 12.2, 12.3 **Chapter 13** 13.1
Fossils provide important evidence of how life and environmental conditions have changed. Code: ES 2b	**Chapter 4** 4.1, 4.3 **Chapter 6** 6.2, 6.4, 6.5 **Chapter 19** 19.3

HOLT SCIENCE & TECHNOLOGY

Earth in the Solar System

Standard	Chapter Correlation
The earth is the third planet from the sun in a system that includes the moon, the sun, eight other planets and their moons, and smaller objects, such as asteroids and comets. The sun, an average star, is the central and largest body in the solar system. **Code: ES 3a**	**Chapter 19** 19.1, 19.2 **Chapter 20** 20.1, 20.2, 20.3
Most objects in the solar system are in regular and predictable motion. Those motions explain such phenomena as the day, the year, phases of the moon, and eclipses. **Code: ES 3b**	**Chapter 18** 18.1, 18.2 **Chapter 19** 19.1 **Chapter 20** 20.1, 20.2, 20.3
Gravity is the force that keeps planets in orbit around the sun and governs the rest of the motion in the solar system. Gravity alone holds us to the earth's surface and explains the phenomena of the tides. **Code: ES 3c**	**Chapter 14** 14.3 **Chapter 18** 18.1 **Chapter 19** 19.1 **Chapter 20** 20.2
The sun is the major source of energy for phenomena on the earth's surface, such as growth of plants, winds, ocean currents, and the water cycle. Seasons result from variations in the amount of the sun's energy hitting the surface, due to the tilt of the earth's rotation on its axis and the length of the day. **Code: ES 3d**	**Chapter 5** 5.2, 5.3 **Chapter 14** 14.1 **Chapter 15** 15.3 **Chapter 17** 17.1 **Chapter 18** 18.2

Earth Science

HOLT, RINEHART AND WINSTON

A Harcourt Classroom Education Company

Austin • New York • Orlando • Atlanta • San Francisco • Boston • Dallas • Toronto • London

Annotated Teacher's Edition

Acknowledgments

Contributing Authors

Kathleen Meehan Berry
Science Chairman
Canon-McMillan School District
Canonsburg, Pennsylvania

Robert H. Fronk, Ph.D.
Chair of Science and Mathematics Education Department
Florida Institute of Technology
West Melbourne, Florida

Mary Kay Hemenway, Ph.D.
Research Associate and Senior Lecturer
Department of Astronomy
The University of Texas
Austin, Texas

Kathleen Kaska
Life and Earth Science Teacher
Lake Travis Middle School
Austin, Texas

Peter E. Malin, Ph.D.
Professor of Geology
Division of Earth and Ocean Sciences
Duke University
Durham, North Carolina

Karen J. Meech, Ph.D.
Associate Astronomer
Institute for Astronomy
University of Hawaii
Honolulu, Hawaii

Robert J. Sager
Chair and Professor of Earth Sciences
Pierce College
Lakewood, Washington

Lab Writers

Kenneth Creese
Science Teacher
White Mountain Junior High School
Rock Springs, Wyoming

Linda A. Culp
Science Teacher and Dept. Chair
Thorndale High School
Thorndale, Texas

Bruce M. Jones
Science Teacher and Dept. Chair
The Blake School
Minneapolis, Minnesota

Shannon Miller
Science and Math Teacher
Llano Junior High School
Llano, Texas

Robert Stephen Ricks
Special Services Teacher
Department of Classroom Improvement
Alabama State Department of Education
Montgomery, Alabama

James J. Secosky
Science Teacher
Bloomfield Central School
Bloomfield, New York

Academic Reviewers

Mead Allison, Ph.D.
Assistant Professor of Oceanography
Texas A&M University
Galveston, Texas

Alissa Arp, Ph.D.
Director and Professor of Environmental Studies
Romberg Tiburon Center
San Francisco State University
Tiburon, California

Paul D. Asimow, Ph.D.
Assistant Professor of Geology and Geochemistry
Department of Physics and Planetary Sciences
California Institute of Technology
Pasadena, California

G. Fritz Benedict, Ph.D.
Senior Research Scientist and Astronomer
McDonald Observatory
The University of Texas
Austin, Texas

Russell M. Brengelman, Ph.D.
Professor of Physics
Morehead State University
Morehead, Kentucky

John A. Brockhaus, Ph.D.
Director—Mapping, Charting, and Geodesy Program
Department of Geography and Environmental Engineering
United States Military Academy
West Point, New York

Michael Brown, Ph.D.
Assistant Professor of Planetary Astronomy
Department of Physics and Astronomy
California Institute of Technology
Pasadena, California

Wesley N. Colley, Ph.D.
Postdoctoral Fellow
Harvard-Smithsonian Center for Astrophysics
Cambridge, Massachusetts

Andrew J. Davis, Ph.D.
Manager—ACE Science Data Center
Physics Department
California Institute of Technology
Pasadena, California

Peter E. Demmin, Ed.D.
Former Science Teacher and Department Chair
Amherst Central High School
Amherst, New York

James Denbow, Ph.D.
Associate Professor
Department of Anthropology
The University of Texas
Austin, Texas

Roy W. Hann, Jr., Ph.D.
Professor of Civil Engineering
Texas A&M University
College Station, Texas

Frederick R. Heck, Ph.D.
Professor of Geology
Ferris State University
Big Rapids, Michigan

Richard Hey, Ph.D.
Professor of Geophysics
Hawaii Institute of Geophysics and Planetology
University of Hawaii
Honolulu, Hawaii

John E. Hoover, Ph.D.
Associate Professor of Biology
Millersville University
Millersville, Pennsylvania

Copyright © 2004 by Holt, Rinehart and Winston

All rights reserved. No part of this publication may be reproduced or transmitted in any form or by any means, electronic or mechanical, including photocopy, recording, or any information storage and retrieval system, without permission in writing from the publisher.

Requests for permission to make copies of any part of the work should be mailed to the following address: Permissions Department, Holt, Rinehart and Winston, 10801 N. MoPac Expressway, Building 3, Austin, Texas 78759.

SciLinks is owned and provided by the National Science Teachers Association. All rights reserved.

Printed in the United States of America

ISBN 0-03-073174-7

1 2 3 4 5 6 7 048 06 05 04 03 02

Acknowledgments (cont.)

Robert W. Houghton, Ph.D.
Senior Staff Associate
Lamont-Doherty Earth Observatory
Columbia University
Palisades, New York

Steven A. Jennings, Ph.D.
Assistant Professor
Department of Geography & Environmental Studies
University of Colorado
Colorado Springs, Colorado

Eric L. Johnson, Ph.D.
Assistant Professor of Geology
Central Michigan University
Mount Pleasant, Michigan

John Kermond, Ph.D.
Visiting Scientist
NOAA–Office of Global Programs
Silver Spring, Maryland

Zavareh Kothavala, Ph.D.
Postdoctoral Associate Scientist
Department of Geology and Geophysics
Yale University
New Haven, Connecticut

Karen Kwitter, Ph.D.
Ebenezer Fitch Professor of Astronomy
Williams College
Williamstown, Massachusetts

Valerie Lang, Ph.D.
Project Leader of Environmental Programs
The Aerospace Corporation
Los Angeles, California

Philip LaRoe
Professor
Helena College of Technology
Helena, Montana

Julie Lutz, Ph.D.
Astronomy Program
Washington State University
Pullman, Washington

Duane F. Marble, Ph.D.
Professor Emeritus
Department of Geography and Natural Resources
Ohio State University
Columbus, Ohio

Joseph A. McClure, Ph.D.
Associate Professor
Department of Physics
Georgetown University
Washington, D.C.

Frank K. McKinney, Ph.D.
Professor of Geology
Appalachian State University
Boone, North Carolina

Joann Mossa, Ph.D.
Associate Professor of Geography
University of Florida
Gainesville, Florida

LaMoine L. Motz, Ph.D.
Coordinator of Science Education
Department of Learning Services
Oakland County Schools
Waterford, Michigan

Barbara Murck, Ph.D.
Assistant Professor of Earth Science
Erindale College
University of Toronto
Mississauga, Ontario
CANADA

Hilary Clement Olson, Ph.D.
Research Associate
Institute for Geophysics
The University of Texas
Austin, Texas

Andre Potochnik
Geologist
Grand Canyon Field Institute
Flagstaff, Arizona

John R. Reid, Ph.D.
Professor Emeritus
Department of Geology and Geological Engineering
University of North Dakota
Grand Forks, North Dakota

Gary Rottman, Ph.D.
Associate Director
Laboratory for Atmosphere and Space Physics
University of Colorado
Boulder, Colorado

Dork L. Sahagian, Ph.D.
Professor
Institute for the Study of Earth, Oceans, and Space
University of New Hampshire
Durham, New Hampshire

Peter Sheridan, Ph.D.
Professor of Chemistry
Colgate University
Hamilton, New York

David Sprayberry, Ph.D.
Assistant Director for Observing Support
W.M. Keck Observatory
California Association for Research in Astronomy
Kamuela, Hawaii

Lynne Talley, Ph.D.
Professor
Scripps Institution of Oceanography
University of California
La Jolla, California

Glenn Thompson, Ph.D.
Scientist
Geophysical Institute
University of Alaska
Fairbanks, Alaska

Martin VanDyke, Ph.D.
Professor of Chemistry Emeritus
Front Range Community College
Westminister, Colorado

Thad A. Wasklewicz, Ph.D.
Assistant Professor of Geography
University of Memphis
Memphis, Tennessee

Hans Rudolf Wenk, Ph.D.
Professor of Geology and Geophysical Sciences
University of California
Berkeley, California

Lisa D. White, Ph.D.
Associate Professor of Geosciences
San Francisco State University
San Francisco, California

Lorraine W. Wolf, Ph.D.
Associate Professor of Geology
Auburn University
Auburn, Alabama

Charles A. Wood, Ph.D.
Chairman and Professor of Space Studies
University of North Dakota
Grand Forks, North Dakota

Safety Reviewer

Jack Gerlovich, Ph.D.
Associate Professor
School of Education
Drake University
Des Moines, Iowa

Teacher Reviewers

Barry L. Bishop
Science Teacher and Dept. Chair
San Rafael Junior High School
Ferron, Utah

Yvonne Brannum
Science Teacher and Dept. Chair
Hine Junior High School
Washington, D.C.

Daniel L. Bugenhagen
Science Teacher and Dept. Chair
Yutan Junior & Senior High School
Yutan, Nebraska

Kenneth Creese
Science Teacher
White Mountain Junior High School
Rock Springs, Wyoming

Linda A. Culp
Science Teacher and Dept. Chair
Thorndale High School
Thorndale, Texas

Alonda Droege
Science Teacher
Pioneer Middle School
Steilacom, Washington

Laura Fleet
Science Teacher
Alice B. Landrum Middle School
Ponte Vedra Beach, Florida

Susan Gorman
Science Teacher
Northridge Middle School
North Richland Hills, Texas

C. John Graves
Science Teacher
Monforton Middle School
Bozeman, Montana

Janel Guse
Science Teacher and Dept. Chair
West Central Middle School
Hartford, South Dakota

Gary Habeeb
Science Mentor
Sierra–Plumas Joint Unified School District
Downieville, California

Dennis Hanson
Science Teacher and Dept. Chair
Big Bear Middle School
Big Bear Lake, California

Acknowledgments (cont.)

Norman E. Holcomb
Science Teacher
Marion Local Schools
Maria Stein, Ohio

Tracy Jahn
Science Teacher
Berkshire Junior-Senior High School
Canaan, New York

David D. Jones
Science Teacher
Andrew Jackson Middle School
Cross Lanes, West Virginia

Howard A. Knodle
Science Teacher
Belvidere High School
Belvidere, Illinois

Michael E. Kral
Science Teacher
West Hardin Middle School
Cecilia, Kentucky

Kathy LaRoe
Science Teacher
East Valley Middle School
East Helena, Montana

Scott Mandel, Ph.D.
Director and Educational Consultant
Teachers Helping Teachers
Los Angeles, California

Kathy McKee
Science Teacher
Hoyt Middle School
Des Moines, Iowa

Michael Minium
Vice President of Program Development
United States Orienteering Federation
Forest Park, Georgia

Jan Nelson
Science Teacher
East Valley Middle School
East Helena, Montana

Dwight C. Patton
Science Teacher
Carroll T. Welch Middle School
Horizon City, Texas

Joseph Price
Chairman—Science Department
H. M. Brown Junior High School
Washington, D.C.

Terry J. Rakes
Science Teacher
Elmwood Junior High School
Rogers, Arkansas

Steven Ramig
Science Teacher
West Point High School
West Point, Nebraska

Helen P. Schiller
Science Teacher
Northwood Middle School
Taylors, South Carolina

Bert J. Sherwood
Science Teacher
Socorro Middle School
El Paso, Texas

Larry Tackett
Science Teacher and Dept. Chair
Andrew Jackson Middle School
Cross Lanes, West Virginia

Walter Woolbaugh
Science Teacher
Manhattan Junior High School
Manhattan, Montana

Alexis S. Wright
Middle School Science Coordinator
Rye Country Day School
Rye, New York

Gordon Zibelman
Science Teacher
Drexel Hill Middle School
Drexel Hill, Pennsylvania

Staff Credits

Editorial
Robert W. Todd, Associate Director, Secondary Science
Debbie Starr, Managing Editor
Robert V. Tucek, Senior Editor

Annotated Teacher's Edition
Jim Ratcliffe

Copyeditors
Dawn Spinozza, Copyediting Manager

Editorial Support Staff
Jeanne Graham, Mary Helbling, Kenneth G. Raymond, Tanu'e White

Editorial Permissions
Cathy Paré, Permissions Manager
Jan Harrington, Permissions Editor

Art, Design, and Photo
Book Design
Richard Metzger, Design Director
Marc Cooper, Senior Designer
Jose Garza, Designer
David Hernandez, Designer
Alicia Sullivan, Designer (ATE), **Cristina Bowerman**, Design Associate (ATE), **Holly Whittaker**, Traffic Coordinator

Image Acquisitions
Elaine Tate, Art Buyer Supervisor
Erin Cone, Art Buyer
Jeannie Taylor, Photo Research Supervisor
Andy Christiansen, Photo Researcher
Jackie Berger, Assistant Photo Researcher

Photo Studio
Sam Dudgeon, Senior Staff Photographer
Victoria Smith, Photo Specialist
Lauren Eischen, Photo Coordinator

Production
Mimi Stockdell, Senior Production Manager
Adriana Bardin Prestwood, Senior Production Coordinator
Beth Sample, Production Coordinator
Suzanne Brooks, Sara Carroll-Downs

Contents in Brief

Unit 1 **Introduction to Earth Science**   **2**
- **Chapter 1** The World of Earth Science 4
- **Chapter 2** Maps as Models of the Earth 32

Unit 2 **Earth's Resources**   **56**
- **Chapter 3** Minerals of the Earth's Crust 58
- **Chapter 4** Rocks: Mineral Mixtures 78
- **Chapter 5** Energy Resources 106
- **Chapter 6** The Rock and Fossil Record 132

Unit 3 **The Restless Earth**   **162**
- **Chapter 7** Plate Tectonics 164
- **Chapter 8** Earthquakes 194
- **Chapter 9** Volcanoes......................... 220

Unit 4 **Reshaping the Land**   **242**
- **Chapter 10** Weathering and Soil Formation......... 244
- **Chapter 11** The Flow of Fresh Water 268
- **Chapter 12** Agents of Erosion and Deposition 296

Unit 5 **Oceanography**   **326**
- **Chapter 13** Exploring the Oceans 328
- **Chapter 14** The Movement of Ocean Water......... 362

Unit 6 **Weather and Climate**   **388**
- **Chapter 15** The Atmosphere 390
- **Chapter 16** Understanding Weather............... 420
- **Chapter 17** Climate 450

Unit 7 **Astronomy**   **478**
- **Chapter 18** Observing the Sky.................. 480
- **Chapter 19** Formation of the Solar System 508
- **Chapter 20** A Family of Planets 536
- **Chapter 21** The Universe Beyond 568
- **Chapter 22** Exploring Space 596

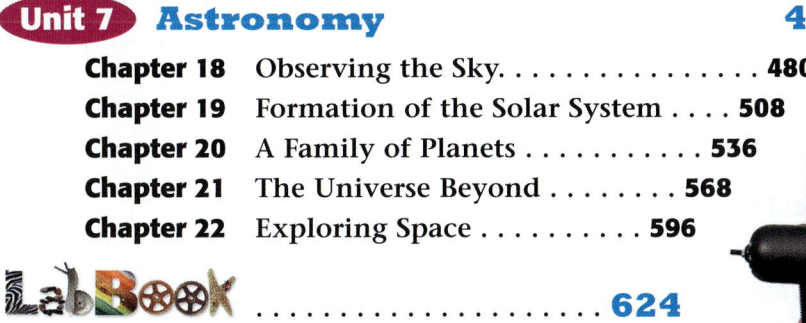 624

Contents

Master Materials List xxiv
Science & Math Skills Worksheets xxx

Unit 1 — Introduction to Earth Science

Timeline 2

CHAPTER 1

Chapter Organizer 3A
Chapter Resources & Worksheets 3C
Chapter Background 3E

The World of Earth Science 4

Section 1 Branches of Earth Science 6
Section 2 The Scientific Method in Earth Science 12
Section 3 Life in a Warmer World—An Earth Science Model 18
Section 4 Measurement and Safety 22

Chapter Highlights/Review 26

Feature Articles
Across the Sciences: All the Earth's a Magnet 30
Careers: Geophysicist 31

LabBook
- Safety First! 626
- Using the Scientific Method 630

CHAPTER 2

Chapter Organizer 31A
Chapter Resources & Worksheets 31C
Chapter Background 31E

Maps as Models of the Earth 32

Section 1 You Are Here 34
Section 2 Mapping the Earth's Surface 40
Section 3 Topographic Maps 46

Chapter Highlights/Review 50

Feature Articles
Science, Technology, and Society: The Lost City of Ubar 54
Careers: Watershed Planner 55

LabBook
- Round or Flat? 632
- Orient Yourself! 634
- Topographic Tuber 636

Contents

Unit 2 — Earth's Resources

Timeline 56

CHAPTER 3

Chapter Organizer 57A
Chapter Resources & Worksheets 57C
Chapter Background 57E

Minerals of the Earth's Crust 58

Section 1 What Is a Mineral? 60
Section 2 Identifying Minerals 64
Section 3 The Formation and Mining of Minerals 68

Chapter Highlights/Review 72

Feature Articles

Weird Science: Lightning Leftovers 76
Science Fiction: "The Metal Man" 77

LabBook

- Mysterious Minerals 638
- Is It Fool's Gold?—A Dense Situation 640

CHAPTER 4

Chapter Organizer 77A
Chapter Resources & Worksheets 77C
Chapter Background 77E

Rocks: Mineral Mixtures 78

Section 1 Understanding Rock 80
Section 2 Igneous Rock 87
Section 3 Sedimentary Rock 91
Section 4 Metamorphic Rock 95

Chapter Highlights/Review 100

Feature Articles

Science, Technology, and Society: Rock City 104
Health Watch: Glass Scalpels 105

LabBook

- Crystal Growth 642
- Let's Get Sedimental 645
- Metamorphic Mash 647

Contents

CHAPTER 5
Chapter Organizer 105A
Chapter Resources & Worksheets 105C
Chapter Background 105E

Energy Resources 106
Section 1 Natural Resources 108
Section 2 Fossil Fuels 111
Section 3 Alternative Resources 118

Chapter Highlights/Review 126

Feature Articles
Eye on the Environment: Sitting on Your Trash 130
Eureka!: Oil Rush! 131

LabBook
- Make a Water Wheel 648
- Power of the Sun 650

CHAPTER 6
Chapter Organizer 131A
Chapter Resources & Worksheets 131C
Chapter Background 131E

The Rock and Fossil Record 132
Section 1 Earth's Story and Those Who First Listened .. 134
Section 2 Relative Dating: Which Came First? 137
Section 3 Absolute Dating: A Measure of Time 142
Section 4 Looking at Fossils 146
Section 5 Time Marches On 151

Chapter Highlights/Review 156

Feature Articles
Science, Technology, and Society:
CAT Scanning Fossils 160
Careers: Paleontologist 161

LabBook
- How DO You Stack Up? 652

viii Contents

Unit 3 · The Restless Earth

Timeline 162

CHAPTER 7

Chapter Organizer 163A
Chapter Resources & Worksheets 163C
Chapter Background 163E

Plate Tectonics 164

Section 1 Inside the Earth 166
Section 2 Restless Continents 173
Section 3 The Theory of Plate Tectonics 177
Section 4 Deforming the Earth's Crust 181

Chapter Highlights/Review 188

Feature Articles
Science, Technology, and Society:
  Living on the Mid-Atlantic Ridge 192
Scientific Debate: Continental Drift 193

LabBook

- Convection Connection 656
- Oh, the Pressure! 657

CHAPTER 8

Chapter Organizer 193A
Chapter Resources & Worksheets 193C
Chapter Background 193E

Earthquakes 194

Section 1 What Are Earthquakes? 196
Section 2 Earthquake Measurement 202
Section 3 Earthquakes and Society 205
Section 4 Earthquake Discoveries Near and Far 211

Chapter Highlights/Review 214

Feature Articles
Weird Science: Can Animals Predict Earthquakes? ... 218
Eye on the Environment:
  What Causes Such Destruction? 219

LabBook

- Quake Challenge 660
- Earthquake Waves 662

Contents

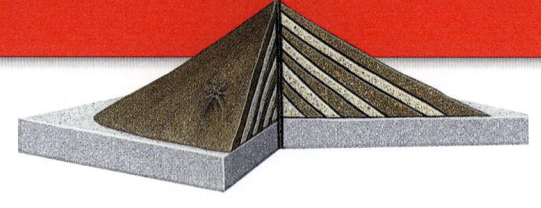

CHAPTER 9

Chapter Organizer 219A
Chapter Resources & Worksheets 219C
Chapter Background 219E

Volcanoes 220

Section 1 Volcanic Eruptions 222
Section 2 Volcanoes' Effects on Earth 227
Section 3 What Causes Volcanoes? 230

Chapter Highlights/Review 236

Feature Articles
Science, Technology, and Society:
  Robot in the Hot Seat 240
Across the Sciences: Europa: Life on a Moon? 241

LabBook
- Some Go "Pop," Some Do Not 664
- Volcano Verdict 666

Unit 4 ··· Reshaping the Land
Timeline 242

CHAPTER 10

Chapter Organizer 243A
Chapter Resources & Worksheets 243C
Chapter Background 243E

Weathering and Soil Formation 244

Section 1 Weathering 246
Section 2 Rates of Weathering 252
Section 3 From Bedrock to Soil 255
Section 4 Soil Conservation 259

Chapter Highlights/Review 262

Feature Articles
Across the Sciences: Worms of the Earth 266
Eye on the Environment: Losing Ground 267

LabBook
- Great Ice Escape 668
- Rockin' Through Time 669

Contents

CHAPTER 11
- Chapter Organizer 267A
- Chapter Resources & Worksheets 267C
- Chapter Background 267E

The Flow of Fresh Water 268
- **Section 1** The Active River 270
- **Section 2** Stream and River Deposits 277
- **Section 3** Water Underground 280
- **Section 4** Using Water Wisely 285

Chapter Highlights/Review 290

Feature Articles
- **Weird Science:** Bubble, Boil, & Squirt 294
- **Eye on the Environment:** Disaster Along the Delta 295

LabBook
- Water Cycle—What Goes Up... 670
- Clean Up Your Act 672

CHAPTER 12
- Chapter Organizer 295A
- Chapter Resources & Worksheets 295C
- Chapter Background 295E

Agents of Erosion and Deposition 296
- **Section 1** Shoreline Erosion and Deposition 298
- **Section 2** Wind Erosion and Deposition 304
- **Section 3** Erosion and Deposition by Ice 309
- **Section 4** Gravity's Effect on Erosion and Deposition 316

Chapter Highlights/Review 320

Feature Articles
- **Science, Technology, and Society:** Boulder Boogie 324
- **Eye on the Environment:** Beach Today, Gone Tomorrow 325

LabBook
- Dune Movement 676
- Gliding Glaciers 677
- Creating a Kettle 679

Contents

Unit 5 ··· Oceanography

Timeline 326

CHAPTER 13
Chapter Organizer 327A
Chapter Resources & Worksheets 327C
Chapter Background 327E

Exploring the Oceans 328
Section 1 Earth's Oceans 330
Section 2 The Ocean Floor 337
Section 3 Life in the Ocean 342
Section 4 Resources from the Ocean 346
Section 5 Ocean Pollution 351

Chapter Highlights/Review 356

Feature Articles
Across the Sciences: Exploring Ocean Life 360
Eye on the Environment: Putting Freshwater
   Problems on Ice 361

LabBook
- Probing the Depths 680
- Investigating an Oil Spill 682

CHAPTER 14
Chapter Organizer 361A
Chapter Resources & Worksheets 361C
Chapter Background 361E

The Movement of Ocean Water 362
Section 1 Currents 364
Section 2 Waves 372
Section 3 Tides 378

Chapter Highlights/Review 382

Feature Articles
Careers: Seismologist 386
Health Watch: Red Tides 387

LabBook
- Up from the Depths 684
- Turning the Tides 686

xii Contents

Unit 6 ··· Weather and Climate
Timeline 388

CHAPTER 15

Chapter Organizer 389A
Chapter Resources & Worksheets 389C
Chapter Background 389E

The Atmosphere 390

Section 1 Characteristics of the Atmosphere 392
Section 2 Heating of the Atmosphere 398
Section 3 Atmospheric Pressure and Winds 402
Section 4 The Air We Breathe 408

Chapter Highlights/Review 414

Feature Articles
Health Watch: Particles in the Air 418
Scientific Debate: A Cure for Air Pollution? 419

LabBook

- Boiling Over! 688
- Go Fly a Bike! 690
- Under Pressure! 692

CHAPTER 16

Chapter Organizer 419A
Chapter Resources & Worksheets 419C
Chapter Background 419E

Understanding Weather 420

Section 1 Water in the Air 422
Section 2 Air Masses and Fronts 430
Section 3 Severe Weather 434
Section 4 Forecasting the Weather 440

Chapter Highlights/Review 444

Feature Articles
Careers: Meteorologist 448
Science Fiction: "All Summer in a Day" 449

LabBook

- Watching the Weather 694
- Let It Snow! 697
- Gone with the Wind 698

Contents xiii

Contents

CHAPTER 17
Chapter Organizer 449A
Chapter Resources & Worksheets 449C
Chapter Background 449E

Climate 450
Section 1 What Is Climate? 452
Section 2 Climates of the World 458
Section 3 Changes in Climate 467

Chapter Highlights/Review 472

Feature Articles
Across the Sciences: Blame "The Child" 476
Science, Technology, and Society:
  Some Say Fire, Some Say Ice 477

LabBook
- Global Impact 700
- For the Birds 701
- Biome Business 704

Unit 7 · · · Astronomy

⋮ **Timeline** 478

CHAPTER 18
Chapter Organizer 479A
Chapter Resources & Worksheets 479C
Chapter Background 479E

Observing the Sky 480
Section 1 Astronomy—The Original Science 482
Section 2 Mapping the Stars 489
Section 3 Telescopes—Then and Now 496

Chapter Highlights/Review 502

Feature Articles
Science, Technology, and Society: Planet or Star? 506
Eye on the Environment: Eyes in the Sky 507

LabBook
- Create a Calendar 706
- The Sun's Yearly Trip Through the Zodiac 708
- Through the Looking Glass 710

CHAPTER 19

Chapter Organizer 507A
Chapter Resources & Worksheets 507C
Chapter Background 507E

Formation of the Solar System 508

Section 1 A Solar System Is Born 510
Section 2 The Sun: Our Very Own Star 519
Section 3 The Earth Takes Shape 524

Chapter Highlights/Review 530

Feature Articles
Science, Technology, and Society:
  Don't Look at the Sun! 534
Scientific Debate: Mirrors in Space 535

LabBook
 How Far Is the Sun? 712

CHAPTER 20

Chapter Organizer 535A
Chapter Resources & Worksheets 535C
Chapter Background 535E

A Family of Planets 536

Section 1 The Nine Planets 538
Section 2 Moons 549
Section 3 Small Bodies in the Solar System 557

Chapter Highlights/Review 562

Feature Articles
Scientific Debate: Is Pluto Really a Planet? 566
Science Fiction: "The Mad Moon" 567

###
- Why Do They Wander? 714
- Eclipses 716
- Phases of the Moon 717

Contents **xv**

Contents

CHAPTER 21
Chapter Organizer 567A
Chapter Resources & Worksheets 567C
Chapter Background 567E

The Universe Beyond 568
Section 1 Stars 570
Section 2 The Life Cycle of Stars 577
Section 3 Galaxies 582
Section 4 Formation of the Universe 586

Chapter Highlights/Review 590
Feature Articles
Weird Science: Holes Where Stars Once Were 594
Careers: Astrophysicist 595

LabBook
- Red Hot, or Not? 718
- I See the Light! 720

CHAPTER 22
Chapter Organizer 595A
Chapter Resources & Worksheets 595C
Chapter Background 595E

Exploring Space 596
Section 1 Rocket Science 598
Section 2 Artificial Satellites 602
Section 3 Space Probes 606
Section 4 Living and Working in Space 612

Chapter Highlights/Review 618
Feature Articles
Across the Sciences: International Space Station 622
Science Fiction:
"Why I Left Harry's All-Night Hamburgers" 623

LabBook
- Water Rockets Save the Day! 722
- Reach for the Stars 724

Contents

LabBook 624

Self-Check Answers 726

Appendix 729
- Concept Mapping 730
- SI Measurement 731
- Temperature Scales 732
- Measuring Skills 733
- Scientific Method 734
- Making Charts and Graphs 737
- Math Refresher 740
- Periodic Table of the Elements 744
- Physical Science Refresher 746
- Physical Laws and Equations 748
- Properties of Common Minerals 750
- Sky Maps 752

Glossary 754

Spanish Glossary 765

Index 780

Answers to Concept Mapping Questions 800

Contents

The more labs, the better!
Take a minute to browse the **LabBook** located at the end of this textbook. You'll find a wide variety of exciting labs that will help you experience science firsthand. But please don't forget to be safe. Read the "Safety First!" section before starting any of the labs.

Safety First! **626**

CHAPTER 1 The World of Earth Science
Using the Scientific Method 630

CHAPTER 2 Maps as Models of the Earth
Round or Flat? 632
Orient Yourself! 634
Topographic Tuber 636

CHAPTER 3 Minerals of the Earth's Crust
Mysterious Minerals 638
Is It Fool's Gold?—A Dense Situation 640

CHAPTER 4 Rocks: Mineral Mixtures
Crystal Growth 642
Let's Get Sedimental 645
Metamorphic Mash 647

CHAPTER 5 Energy Resources
Make a Water Wheel 648
Power of the Sun 650

CHAPTER 6 The Rock and Fossil Record
How DO You Stack Up? 652

CHAPTER 7 Plate Tectonics
Convection Connection 656
Oh, the Pressure! 657

CHAPTER 8 Earthquakes
Quake Challenge 660
Earthquake Waves 662

CHAPTER 9 Volcanoes
Some Go "Pop," Some Do Not 664
Volcano Verdict 666

CHAPTER 10 Weathering and Soil Formation
Great Ice Escape 668
Rockin' Through Time 669

CHAPTER 11 The Flow of Fresh Water
Water Cycle—What Goes Up... 670
Clean Up Your Act 672

CHAPTER 12 Agents of Erosion and Deposition
Dune Movement 676
Gliding Glaciers 677
Creating a Kettle 679

CHAPTER 13 Exploring the Oceans
Probing the Depths 680
Investigating an Oil Spill 682

CHAPTER 14 The Movement of Ocean Water
Up from the Depths 684
Turning the Tides 686

CHAPTER 15 The Atmosphere
Boiling Over! 688
Go Fly a Bike! 690
Under Pressure! 692

CHAPTER 16 Understanding Weather
Watching the Weather 694
Let It Snow! 697
Gone with the Wind 698

CHAPTER 17 Climate
Global Impact 700
For the Birds 701
Biome Business 704

CHAPTER 18 Observing the Sky
Create a Calendar 706
The Sun's Yearly Trip Through
  the Zodiac 708
Through the Looking Glass 710

CHAPTER 19 Formation of the Solar System
How Far Is the Sun? 712

CHAPTER 20 A Family of Planets
Why Do They Wander? 714
Eclipses 716
Phases of the Moon 717

CHAPTER 21 The Universe Beyond
Red Hot, or Not? 718
I See the Light! 720

CHAPTER 22 Exploring Space
Water Rockets Save the Day! 722
Reach for the Stars 724

Contents

Start your engines with an activity!
Science is an activity in which investigation leads to information and understanding. The **Start-Up Activity** at the beginning of each chapter helps you gain scientific understading of the topic through hands-on experience.

Mission Impossible 5
Follow the Yellow
   Brick Road 33
Riding a Mineral 59
Classifying Objects 79
What Is the Sun's
   Favorite Color? 107
Making Fossils 133
Continental Collisions . . . 165
Bend, Break, or Shake? . . . 195
Anticipation 221
What's the Difference? . . . 245
Stream Weavers 269
Making Waves 297
Exit Only? 329
When *Whirls* Collide 363
Air—It's Massive 391
A Meeting of the Masses . . 421
What's Your Angle? 451
Indoor Stargazing 481
Strange Gravity 509
Measuring Space 537
Exploring Galaxies
   in the Universe 569
Rocket Fun 597

QuickLab

How Hot Is 300°C? 7
Finding Directions
   with a Compass 36
Scratch Test 66
Stretching Out 96
Rock Sponge 113
Make a Time Scale 155
Floating Mountains . . . 171
Modeling Seismic
   Waves 201
Bubble, Bubble,
   Toil and Trouble 224
Reaction to Stress 230
Acids React! 250
Degree of
   Permeability 281
Making Desert
   Pavement 305
Angle of Repose 316

How Much Fresh
   Water Is There? 349
Do the Wave 376
Full of "Hot Air" 404
Out of Thin Air 425
A Cool Breeze 455
Using a Sky Map 490
Staying in Focus 516
Mixing It Up 525
Clever Insight 552
Not All Thumbs! 575
Plotting Pairs 577

Not all laboratory investigations have to be long and involved.
The **QuickLabs** found throughout the chapters in this book require only a small amount of time and limited equipment. But just because they are quick, don't skimp on the safety.

MATH BREAK

Science and math go hand in hand.
The **MathBreaks** in the margins of the chapters show you many ways that math applies directly to science and vice versa.

Lots of Zeros! 9
Counting Contours 47
How Pure Is Pure? 70
What's in It? 85
Miles per Acre 124
Get a Half-Life! 143
Using Models 168
Moving Up the Scale . . . 204
How Hot Is Hot? 232
The Power of 2 253
Calculating a
   Stream's Gradient . . . 273
Counting Waves 299
Speed of a Glacier 311
Depths of the Deep . . . 340
Wave Speed 373

Calculating
   Groundspeed 407
Relating Relative
   Humidity 423
The Ride to School 470
Understanding
   Scale 494
Kepler's Formula 516
Orbits Within Orbits . . . 553
Starlight, Star Bright . . . 573
It's Just Rocket
   Science 601

Contents

Making Hypotheses 15	
Reading a Map 45	
Classifying Objects 84	
Renewable or Nonrenewable? 110	
Making Assumptions 135	
Tectonics and Natural Gas 184	Timing a Tsunami 377
	UV and SPFs 395
Earthquake Safety Plan 210	Reducing Pollution 471
Calling an Evacuation? ... 235	Newton's Law and Satellites 517
Wasting Water? 288	Surviving Space 547
Describing the Dust Bowl 306	Graphing Expansion 588
Ocean Treaty 354	Anything GOES 603

Science can be very useful in the real world.
It is interesting to learn how scientific information is being used in the real world. You can see for yourself in the **Apply** features. You will also be asked to apply your own knowledge. This is a good way to learn!

Connections

One science leads to another.
You may not realize it at first, but different areas of science are related to each other in many ways. Each **Connection** explores a topic from the viewpoint of another science discipline. In this way, areas of science merge to improve your understanding of the world around you.

Astronomy CONNECTION
Finding North Without a Compass 37
Rivers on Mars 278
Storms on Jupiter 439

Physics CONNECTION
Magnetism and Floating Frogs 176
Understanding Waves ... 200
The Pull of Gravity 317
The Sun and Ocean Currents 367
Why You See Lightning Before You Hear Thunder 435
Climate on the Roof 466
Car Horns and Starlight .. 493
Boiling Away 543
Falling Attraction 550
Tracing the Culprit 571

Biology CONNECTION
A Magnetic Sense of Direction 62
Metamorphic Animals 99
Filling Your Tank with Solar Energy 120
Making an Impact 135
Going Separate Ways 151
Biosphere: The Layer of Life 169
Fertile Ground Around Volcanoes 226
A Snake in the Sand 308
Coral Reefs 343
The Speed of Growing Nails 401
Escaping the Heat Underground 460
Life in the Comets? 512
A Different Frame of Mind 521
The Stars at Night 572
Clues on Titan 611
Gravity's Effects on the Body 614

Chemistry CONNECTION
Fossil Fuels Share a Common Bond 112
Water as Ice 246
Water: A Unique Substance 393
Titan's Air 526

Environment CONNECTION
Rain Forests and the Greenhouse Effect 20
Mapping Endangered Species 49
Caves and Bats 283
Using Sludge in the Garden 352
Harnessing the Wind 405
Frozen in Time 465
Hidden CO_2 527
Sky Pollution 574
Space Pollution 604

Feature Articles

Feature articles for any appetite!
Science and technology affect us all in many ways. The following articles will give you an idea of just how interesting, strange, helpful, and action-packed science and technology are. At the end of each chapter, you will find two feature articles. Read them and you will be surprised at what you learn.

CAREERS

Geophysicist	31
Watershed Planner	55
Paleontologist	161
Seismologist	386
Meteorologist	448
Astrophysicist	595

ACROSS THE SCIENCES

All the Earth's a Magnet	30
Europa: Life on a Moon?	241
Worms of the Earth	266
Exploring Ocean Life	360
Blame "The Child"	476
International Space Station	622

Science, Technology, and Society

The Lost City of Ubar	54
Rock City	104
CAT Scanning Fossils	160
Living on the Mid-Atlantic Ridge	192
Robot in the Hot Seat	240
Boulder Boogie	324
Some Say Fire, Some Say Ice…	477
Planet or Star?	506
Don't Look at the Sun!	534

EYE ON THE ENVIRONMENT

Sitting on Your Trash	130
What Causes Such Destruction?	219
Losing Ground	267
Disaster Along the Delta	295
Beach Today, Gone Tomorrow	325
Putting Freshwater Problems on Ice	361
Eyes in the Sky	507

Eureka!

Oil Rush!	131

Health WATCH

Glass Scalpels	105
Red Tides	387
Particles in the Air	418

SCIENTIFIC DEBATE

Continental Drift	193
A Cure for Air Pollution?	419
Mirrors in Space	535
Is Pluto Really a Planet?	566

Science Fiction

"The Metal Man"	77
"All Summer in a Day"	449
"The Mad Moon"	567
"Why I Left Harry's All-Night Hamburgers"	623

WEIRD SCIENCE

Lightning Leftovers	76
Can Animals Predict Earthquakes?	218
Bubble, Boil, & Squirt	294
Holes Where Stars Once Were	594

How to Use Your Textbook

Your Roadmap for Success with Holt Science & Technology

Study the Terms to Learn
Key Terms are listed for each section. Learn the definitions of these terms because you will most likely be tested on them. Use the glossary to locate definitions quickly.

STUDY TIP If you don't understand a definition, reread the page where the term is introduced. The surrounding text should help make the definition easier to understand.

Read What You'll Do
Objectives tell you what you'll need to know.

STUDY TIP Reread the objectives when studying for a test to be sure you know the material.

Take Notes and Get Organized
Keep a science notebook so that you are ready to take notes when your teacher reviews the material in class. Keep your assignments in this notebook so that you can review them when studying for the chapter test. In addition, you will be asked to keep a *ScienceLog*, in which you will write your answers to certain questions. Your *ScienceLog* may be a section of your science notebook.

Section 1

Terms to Learn

crust
mantle
core
lithosphere
asthenosphere
mesosphere
outer core
inner core
tectonic plate

What You'll Do

- Identify and describe the layers of the Earth by what they are made of.
- Identify and describe the layers of the Earth by their physical properties.
- Define *tectonic plate*.
- Explain how scientists know about the structure of Earth's interior.

Inside the Earth

The Earth is not just a ball of solid rock. It is made of several layers with different physical properties and compositions. As you will discover, scientists think about the Earth's layers in two ways—by their *composition* and by their *physical properties*.

Earth's layers are made of different mixtures of elements. This is what is meant by differences in composition. Many of the Earth's layers also have different physical properties. Physical properties include temperature, density, and ability to flow. Let's first take a look at the composition of the Earth.

The Composition of the Earth

The Earth is divided into three layers—the *crust*, *mantle*, and *core*—based on what each one is made of. The lightest materials make up the outermost layer, and the densest materials make up the inner layers. This is because lighter materials tend to float up, while heavier materials sink.

The Crust The **crust** is the outermost layer of the Earth. Ranging from 5 to 100 km thick, it is also the thinnest layer of the Earth. And because it is the layer we live on, we know more about this layer than we know about the other two.

There are two types of crust—continental and oceanic. *Continental crust* has a composition similar to granite. It has an average thickness of 30 km. *Oceanic crust* has a composition similar to basalt. It is generally between 5 and 8 km thick. Because basalt is denser than granite, oceanic crust is denser than continental crust.

Figure 1 *Oceanic crust is thinner but denser than continental crust.*

166 Chapter 7

Be Resourceful, Use the Web

Internet Connect boxes in your textbook take you to resources that you can use for science projects, reports, and research papers. Go to **scilinks.org** and type in the SciLinks code to get information on a topic.

Visit go.hrw.com Find worksheets and other materials that go with your textbook at **go.hrw.com**. Click on the textbook icon and the table of contents to see all of the resources for each chapter.

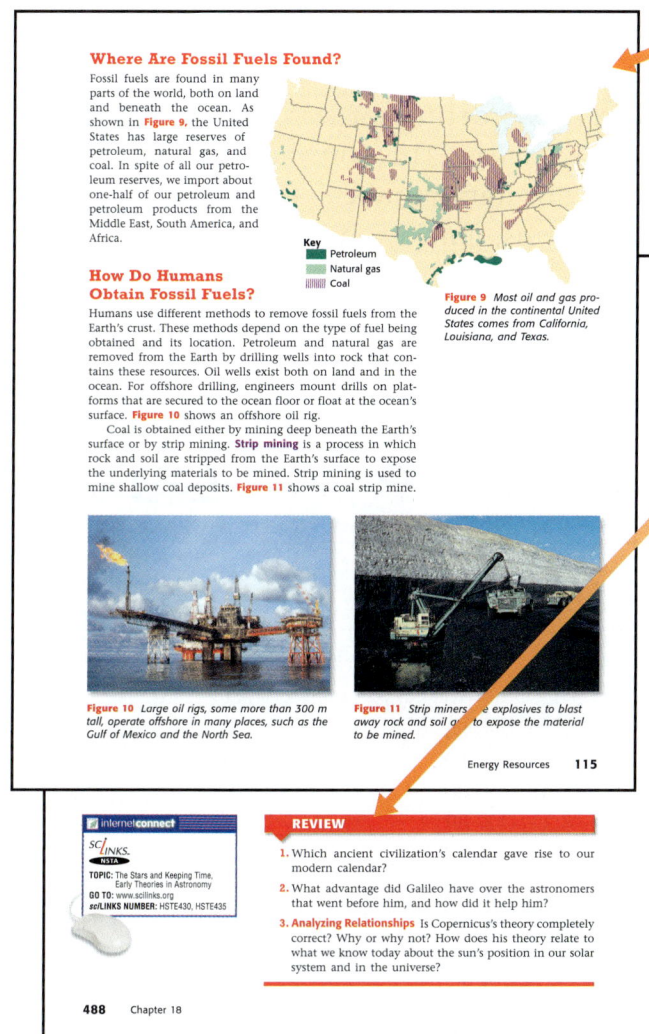

Use the Illustrations and Photos
Art shows complex ideas and processes. Learn to analyze the art so that you better understand the material you read in the text.

Tables and graphs display important information in an organized way to help you see relationships.

A picture is worth a thousand words. Look at the photographs to see relevant examples of science concepts you are reading about.

Answer the Section Reviews
Section Reviews test your knowledge over the main points of the section. Critical Thinking items challenge you to think about the material in greater depth and to find connections that you infer from the text.

STUDY TIP When you can't answer a question, reread the section. The answer is usually there.

Do Your Homework
Your teacher may assign worksheets to help you understand and remember the material in the chapter.

STUDY TIP Don't try to answer the questions without reading the text and reviewing your class notes. A little preparation up front will make your homework assignments a lot easier. Answering the items in the Chapter Review will help prepare you for the chapter test.

Visit Holt Online Learning
If your teacher gives you a special password to log onto the **Holt Online Learning** site, you'll find your complete textbook on the Web. In addition, you'll find some great learning tools and practice quizzes. You'll be able to see how well you know the material from your textbook.

Visit CNN Student News
You'll find up-to-date events in science at **cnnstudentnews.com**.

Master Materials List

The following chart provides a comprehensive list of all the materials you would need in order to teach all of the labs and investigations in *Holt Science and Technology, Earth Science*.

For added convenience, Science Kit® provides materials-ordering software on CD-ROM designed specifically for *Holt Science and Technology*. This software allows you to create an electronic materials list, complete with item numbers. Using this software, you can order complete kits or individual items, quickly and efficiently.

For more information about this software, contact your HRW representative, call Science Kit® directly at 1-800-828-7777, or visit the Web site: www.sciencekit.com.

As you can see from the listings, *Holt Science and Technology* is designed around readily available materials and equipment, with an emphasis on economy. More specific materials lists and information can be found with the lab or investigation in this *Annotated Teacher's Edition*.

MATERIALS AND EQUIPMENT CONSUMABLE	AMOUNT*	QuickLab PAGE NO.	Start-Up Activity PAGE NO.	LabBook PAGE NO.
Adhesive note	4		481	
Aluminum foil, 2 × 8 cm	1			650
Aluminum foil, approx. 5 × 5 cm	1			712
Aluminum foil, approx. 20 × 40 cm	1			642
Bag, plastic sealable sandwich	1			672
Baking soda	15 mL			666
Baking soda	10 mL		221	
Balloon	1		597	692
Balloon, black	1		107	
Balloon, colored (not black or white)	3		107	
Balloon, white	1		107	
Battery, D-cell	2			718
Battery, D-cell, weak	1			718
Bottle, soda, 2 L, with cap	1			672, 722
Bottle, soda, 3 L (or jar)	1			645
Box, cardboard, large	1			708, 724
Candle, birthday	1		391	
Card, index, 3 × 5 in.	1		5	648, 688, 692, 698, 712
Card, index, large	12			708
Cardboard, 1 × 1 cm	1			686
Cardboard, corrugated, 15 × 15 cm	4			701
Cardboard, corrugated, 20 × 20 cm	2			686
Cardboard, corrugated, 20 × 20 cm (or plywood)	2			647
Cardboard, approx. 20 × 40 cm	1		165	
Cardboard toilet-paper tube	1			710
Cardboard wrapping-paper tube	1			710
Charcoal, activated	½ lb			672
Clay, modeling	1 stick			710, 716, 722
Clay, modeling	2 sticks		133	647
Clay, modeling (3 colors)	2 sticks of each			630
Clay, modeling, (4 colors)	1 stick of each			657
Clothes hanger, plastic	1		195	
Clothes hanger, wire	1		195	
Container, empty milk, 1 gal	1			648
Cork	1			648
Cornstarch	150 mL	230		
Craft sticks	2			656

* Amount is for one group of students.

Master Materials List

MATERIALS AND EQUIPMENT		QuickLab	START-UP Activity	LabBook
CONSUMABLE (CONTINUED)	**AMOUNT***	PAGE NO.	PAGE NO.	PAGE NO.
Cup, clear plastic, 9 fl oz	1			666
Cup, paper	5			690
Cup, plastic-foam	5	281		
Cup, plastic-foam	1		269	
Cup, plastic-foam, large	2			688
Detergent, dishwashing (powder or liquid)	40 mL			672
Detritus (cut up leaves and grass)	40 mL			672
Dowel, wood, approx. 20 cm	1		195	
Dowel, wood, $\frac{1}{4}$ in. diam, 36 cm	1			686
Epsom salt	15 mL			642
Filters, coffee, cone-shaped (or plastic funnel)	1			688
Flashlight bulb	1			718
Foam board	1 sheet			722
Food coloring, any color	1 bottle			656
Food coloring, blue	1 bottle		363	684
Food coloring, red	1 bottle	404	221, 363	684, 688
Gelatin square, 8 × 8 cm	1			660
Gloves, protective	1			638, 682
Glue, white	1 bottle			648, 686
Gravel	2 lb		269	
Gravel	250 mL			645
Honey	1 jar	224		
Ice, shaved	150 mL			697
Limewater	1 L			666
Marker, colored	1			642, 690
Marker, permanent black	1			648, 650, 676, 706
Marker, transparency	1			636
Marshmallow	10			660
Mask, disposable filter	1	305		676
Napkin, paper	6		165	
Oil, cooking	50 mL	525		
Oil, cooking,	500 mL		421	
Oil, light machine	1 small can	113		
Oil, light machine	15 mL			682
Paint, black tempera	1 container			701
Paint, light blue tempera	1 container			701
Paint, white tempera	1 container			701
Paper, adding machine, approx. 50 cm	1		165	
Paper, construction	1 sheet			710
Paper, heavy white	1 sheet	552		
Paper, graph	1 sheet			664
Paper, tracing	1 sheet			636, 704
Paper brad	2			724
Paper clip	1		195, 481	
Paper clip, jumbo	2			724
Pencil, assorted colored	1 box		33	706
Pencil, colored	3			630
Pencil, colored	4			657, 700
Pencil, colored (or marker)	2			634
Pencil, colored (red, blue, green)	3			714
Pencil, colored (red, orange, yellow)	3			664
pH test strips	6			672
Plastic tubing, 5 mm diam, 30 cm long (or clear inflexible plastic straws)	1			688
Plastic wrap, 30 × 20 cm	4			684

* Amount is for one group of students.

Master Materials List

Master Materials List

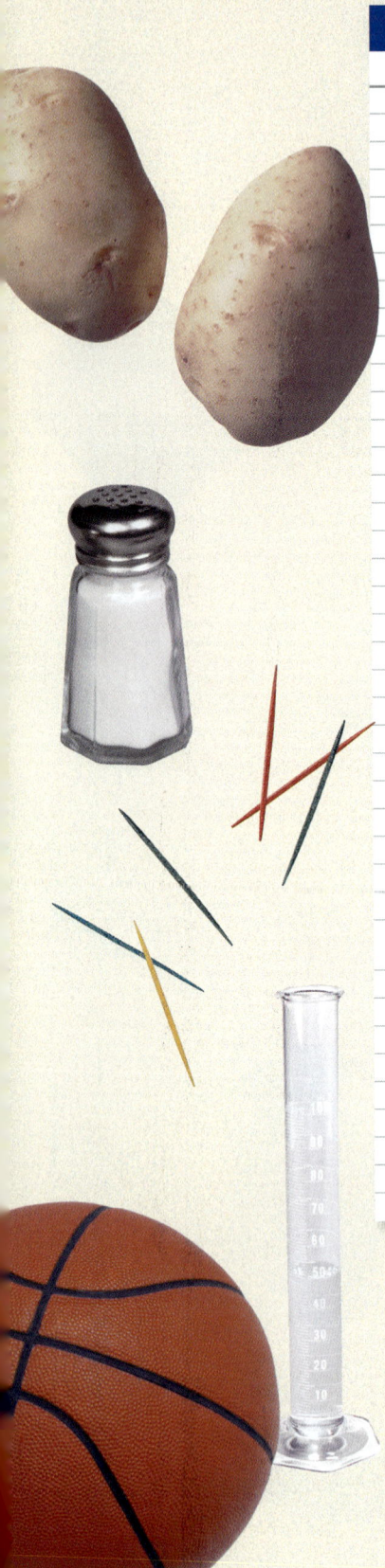

MATERIALS AND EQUIPMENT CONSUMABLE (CONTINUED)	AMOUNT*	QuickLab PAGE NO.	START-UP Activity PAGE NO.	LabBook PAGE NO.
Plate, paper	1			660, 698
Poster board	1 sheet			706, 712
Poster board, square, 5 × 5 cm	2			657
Poster board strip, 5 × 15 cm	1			657
Poster board, square, 16 × 16 cm	1			720
Potato	1			636
Rope, approx. 3 m long	1	376		
Rope, approx. 30 cm long	1		195	
Rubber band	1			692
Salt	approx. 1 tbsp			684
Sand	4 oz	281		
Sand	250 mL			645
Sand	800 mL	316		
Sand	$\frac{1}{2}$ lb			672
Sand	1 lb	305		676, 677
Sand	10 lb			679
Sand	15 lb		269, 297	
Skewer, wooden	2			648
Soap, liquid dishwashing	1 small bottle		221	
Soil	250 mL			645
Soil, clay	40 mL			672
Soil, potting	4 oz	281		
Spoon, plastic	1	525	195	
Straw	1			692
Straw, flexible	1			666
Straw, straight plastic	1		481, 597	698
Straw, straight plastic	2	224		690
String	1 ball	404, 516	481, 597	632, 640, 686, 720
Tape, duct	1 roll			722
Tape, electrical, 20–30 cm	1			718
Tape, masking	1 roll		165, 481, 597	632, 642, 690, 692, 708, 710, 712
Tape, transparent	1 roll			648, 688, 712, 720
Thread, white, 20 cm	1 spool			648
Tissue, bathroom	1 sheet		221	
Tissue, bathroom	2 sheets			666
Toothpick	10			660
Vinegar	40 mL			672
Vinegar	50 mL		221	
Vinegar	140 mL			666
Wire, uninsulated	50 cm			724

* Amount is for one group of students.

MATERIALS AND EQUIPMENT NONCONSUMABLE	AMOUNT*	QuickLab PAGE NO.	Start-Up Activity PAGE NO.	LabBook PAGE NO.
Balance, triple-beam, metric	1		391	640
Ball, large	1		391	708
Ball, styrene, 3–4 cm diam.	1			724
Ball, styrene, 7–8 cm diam.	1			717
Basketball	1			632
Beaker, 100 mL	1			697
Beaker, 150 mL	1	525		
Beaker, 250 mL	1		221	
Beaker, 400 mL	1			640, 642, 672
Beaker, 400 mL	1			670
Beaker, 400 mL	5			684
Beaker, 400 mL (or container)	1	316		
Beaker, 1000 mL	1	349		
Beaker, 1000 mL	2			672
Bottle, 16 fl oz	1			666
Bottle, small (vitamin)	1	404		
Bottle, soda, 2 L	1			648
Bowl, clear plastic, 3 gal	1	230	329	
Bowl, mixing, 3 L	1			645
Box, cardboard, shallow (or lid)	1			676
Box, nontransparent (or pan), approx. 30 × 50 cm	1			630
Brick	3			677
Bucket, 5 gal	1			684, 722
Calculator, scientific	1			650, 662, 706, 720
Can, coffee	1			692
Clay, modeling	1 lb			688, 690
Clay, modeling	1 stick		221	632, 648, 650, 666
Clay, modeling	2 lb			677, 680
Clothespin	1		269	
Coin	1			648, 666
Compass, drawing	1			662, 698, 714
Compass, magnetic	1	36		634, 698
Container, clear plastic storage	1	171, 404		
Container, clear plastic storage with lid	1			636
Container, empty large margarine	3			677
Container, plastic (or jar or glass)	1	425		
Convex lens, 3 cm diam. (different focal lengths)	2			710
Cup, plastic	1	230, 455	329	
Cup, plastic	2	224		
Dropper	1	113		
Dropper pipet	1			645, 682
Erlenmeyer flask	1			672
Fan, electric	1	305		
Flashlight	1			632, 716
Funnel, plastic	1		221	
Globe, world	1		451	717
Gloves, heat-resistant	2			642, 650, 656, 670, 672, 682, 684, 688, 697
Graduated cylinder, 50 mL	1	349		677
Graduated cylinder, 100 mL	1	349		666, 670, 697
Graduated cylinder, 1000 mL	1	349		
Gravel	$\frac{1}{2}$ lb			672
Gravel	1 lb	305		677
Hair dryer	1			676

* Amount is for one group of students.

Master Materials List

Master Materials List

MATERIALS AND EQUIPMENT NONCONSUMABLE (CONTINUED)	AMOUNT*	QuickLab PAGE NO.	START-UP ACTIVITY PAGE NO.	LabBook PAGE NO.
Hammer	1			672
Hole punch	1			648, 690, 724
Hot plate	1			642, 670, 672, 684, 688, 697
Hot plate	2			656
Iron filings	$\frac{1}{4}$ cup			638
Jar with 2 lids (one lid with a hole in its center), approx. 16 oz	1			650
Knife, plastic	1			630, 647, 657
Laboratory scoop, pointed	1			642
Lamp, with removable shade and 100 W bulb	1			650
Lamp, goose-neck	1	552		710, 717
Lamp, goose-neck with 60 W bulb	1		451	
Magnifying lens	1			642, 645, 672
Measuring tape, metric	1			632
Meterstick	1			632, 712, 720
Mineral, biotite sample	1			638
Mineral, feldspar (pink) sample	1			638
Mineral, galena sample	1			638, 640
Mineral, graphite sample	1			638
Mineral, gypsum sample	1			638
Mineral, hematite sample	1			638
Mineral, hornblende sample	1			638
Mineral, magnetite sample	1			638
Mineral, muscovite sample	1			638
Mineral, pyrite sample	1			640
Mineral, quartz sample	1			638
Nail, approx. 1 in.	1			672
Pan, aluminum pie	1		221, 391	682, 688
Pan, aluminum rectangular	1			656
Pan, aluminum rectangular	3			677
Penny	1	66		
Petri dish	3	113		
Pin, bobby	2		165	
Pipe, PVC, 1.3 cm diam, approx. 20 cm long	1			630
Pitcher	1			688
Plastic tubing, 5 mm diam, 1.5 m long	1			672
Protractor	1	316	195, 481	632, 698, 720
Putty, adhesive	1 package		451	
Putty, plastic toy	1 ball	96		
Razor, safety	1			648
Ribbon, approx. 30 cm long	1	376		
Ring stand	1			640
Ring stand with ring	1			672
Rock, basalt sample	1			642
Rock, granite sample	1			642
Rock, limestone sample	1	113		
Rock, pumice sample	1			642
Rock, sandstone sample	1	113		
Rock, shale sample	1	113		
Rock, small, approx. $\frac{1}{4}$ lb	1			698
Rocket launcher	1			722
Rolling pin, wood	1			657, 677

* Amount is for one group of students.

MATERIALS AND EQUIPMENT NONCONSUMABLE	AMOUNT*	QuickLab PAGE NO.	START-UP Activity	LabBook PAGE NO.
Rubber square, tan, approx. 15 × 15 cm	1			701
Ruler, metric	1		569	632, 634, 636, 648, 650, 656, 662, 664, 676, 677, 679, 680, 682, 688, 690, 697, 698, 700, 706, 710, 712, 714, 716, 720, 724
Scale, spring	1			640
Scissors	1		165, 481	645, 648, 672, 680, 690, 692, 698, 710, 712, 720, 722, 724
Sequin	1 small package			647
Shoe box with lid	1			680
Slides, microscope	10			638
Spoon, plastic	1	230		
Spoon, plastic	2			672, 684
Spring toy, coiled	1	201	195	
Stake, tent-style	10		537	
Stapler	1			686, 698
Stapler (mini)	1			690
Stopper, rubber, 1 hole, with glass tube	1			672
Stopwatch	1	113		642, 648, 650, 676, 677, 684
Streak plate	1			638
Tape measure, metric	1			720
Test tube, medium	1			642
Thermometer, Celsius	1	7, 455		642, 650, 688
Thermometer, Celsius	2		451	
Thermometer, Celsius	3			656
Thermometer, Celsius	4			701
Thumbtack	1			690, 712
Thumbtack	2	516		
Thumbtack	5			648
Thumbtack (or pushpin)	1			698
Tissue box	1			666
Tongs	1			670
Tongs, test-tube	1			642
Towel, small hand	1			677
Washtub, plastic	1		269, 297, 363	
Washtub, small plastic	1			679
Watch glass	1			670
Wire, insulated copper, with ends stripped, approx. 20 cm	2			718
Wood square, approx. 15 × 15 cm	1			701
Wood, block, approx. 5 × 10 × 20 cm	1	171		
Wood, block, approx. 5 × 10 × 20 cm	4			656
Wood, block, approx. 8 × 3 × 3 cm	2		165	
Wood, block, approx. 35 × 10 × 5 cm			297	

* Amount is for one group of students.

Master Materials List

Science & Math Skills Worksheets

The *Holt Science and Technology* program helps you meet the needs of a wide variety of students, regardless of their skill level. The following pages provide examples of the worksheets available to improve your students' science and math skills whether they already have a strong science and math background or are weak in these areas. Samples of assessment checklists and rubrics are also provided.

In addition to the skills worksheets represented here, *Holt Science and Technology* provides a variety of worksheets that are correlated directly with each chapter of the program. Representations of these worksheets are found at the beginning of each chapter in this Annotated Teacher's Edition.

Many worksheets are also available on the HRW Web site. The address is **go.hrw.com**.

Science Skills Worksheets: Thinking Skills

#1 BEING FLEXIBLE
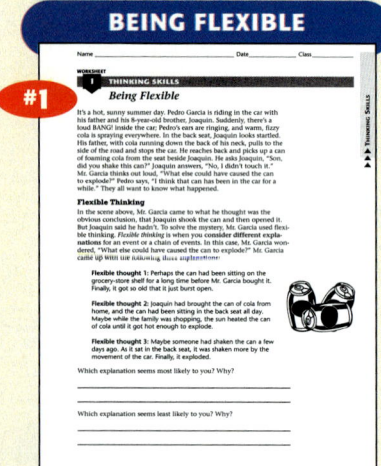

#2 USING YOUR SENSES
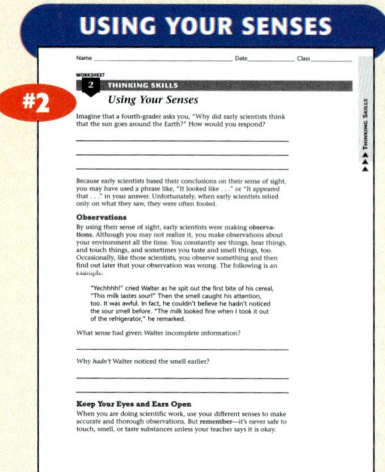

#3 THINKING OBJECTIVELY
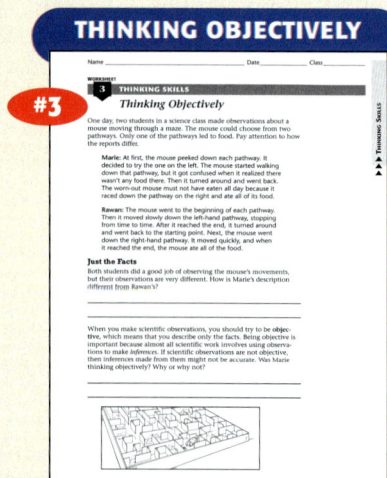

#4 UNDERSTANDING BIAS
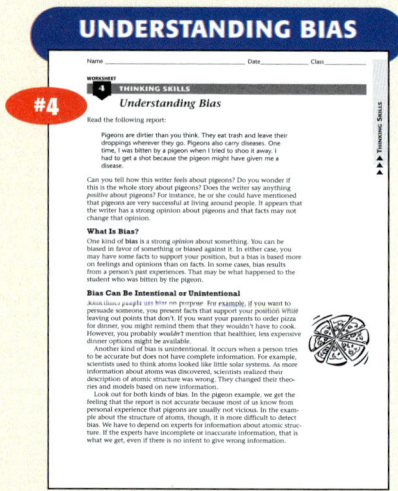

#5 USING LOGIC
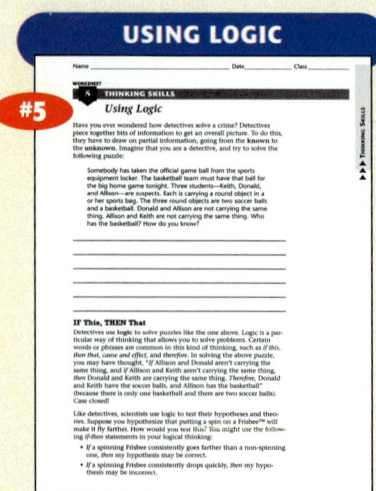

#6 BOOSTING YOUR MEMORY
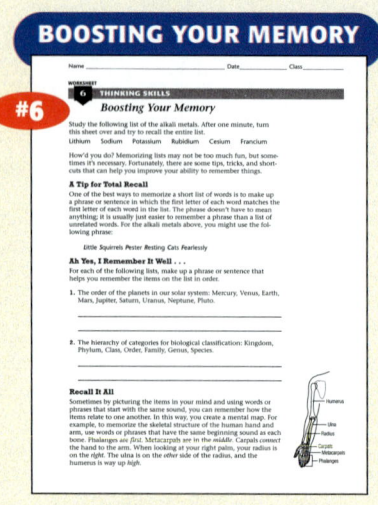

#7 IMPROVING YOUR STUDY HABITS
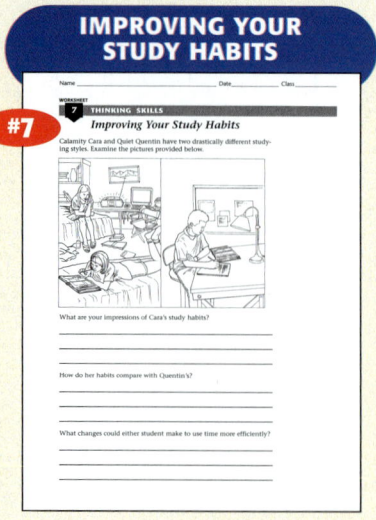

#8 READING A SCIENCE TEXTBOOK
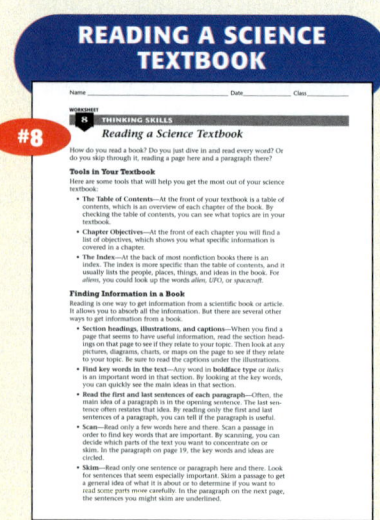

Science Skills Worksheets: Experimenting Skills

SAFETY RULES!
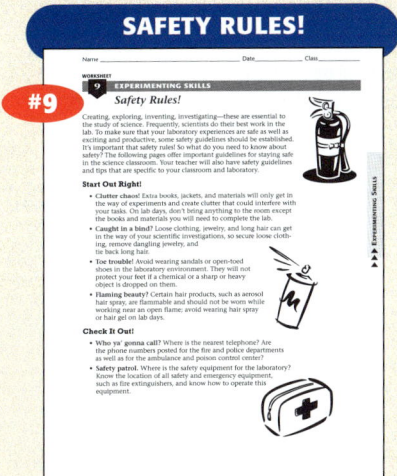
#9 — Safety Rules!

DOING A LAB WRITE-UP
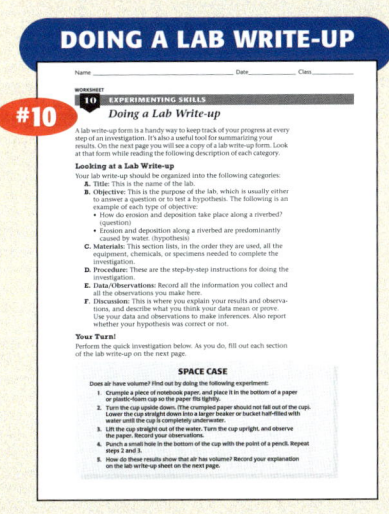
#10 — Doing a Lab Write-up

UNDERSTANDING VARIABLES
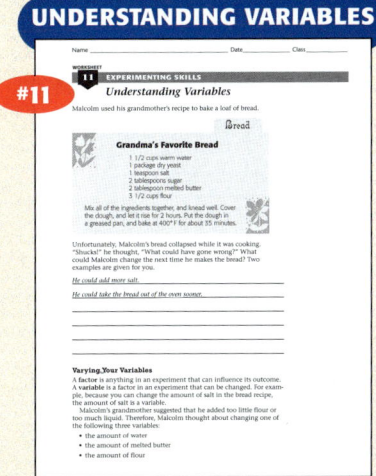
#11 — Understanding Variables

WORKING WITH HYPOTHESES
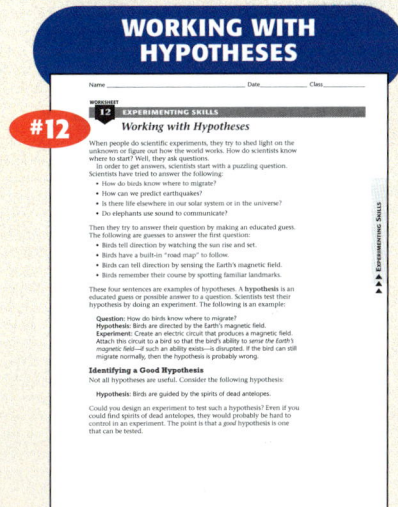
#12 — Working with Hypotheses

DESIGNING AN EXPERIMENT
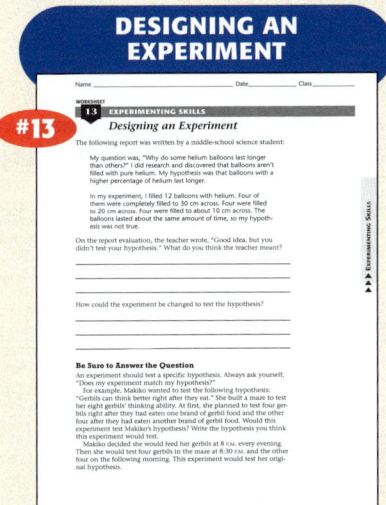
#13 — Designing an Experiment

USING THE INTERNATIONAL SYSTEM OF UNITS (SI)
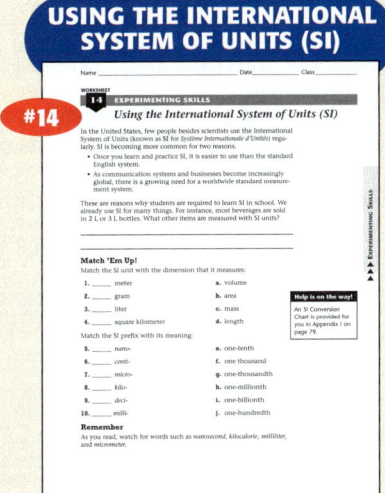
#14 — Using the International System of Units (SI)

MEASURING
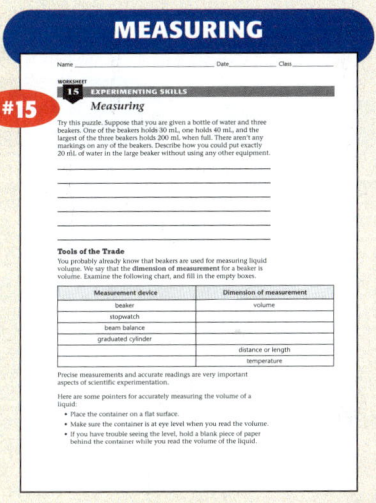
#15 — Measuring

Science Skills Worksheets: Researching Skills

CHOOSING YOUR TOPIC
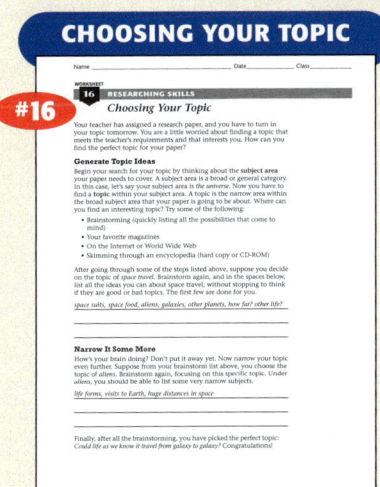
#16 — Choosing Your Topic

ORGANIZING YOUR RESEARCH
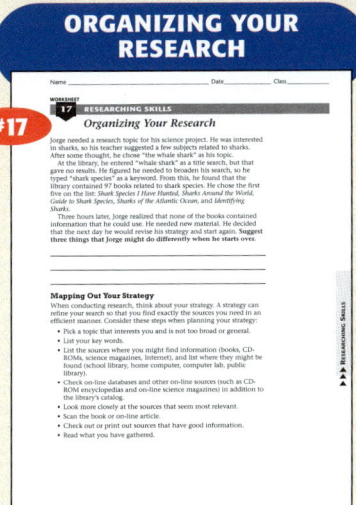
#17 — Organizing Your Research

FINDING USEFUL SOURCES
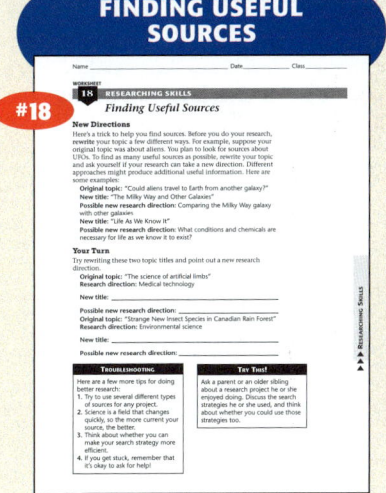
#18 — Finding Useful Sources

RESEARCHING ON THE WEB

#19 — Researching on the Web

Science & Math Skills Worksheets

Science & Math Skills Worksheets (continued)

Science Skills Worksheets: Researching Skills (continued)

IDENTIFYING BIAS
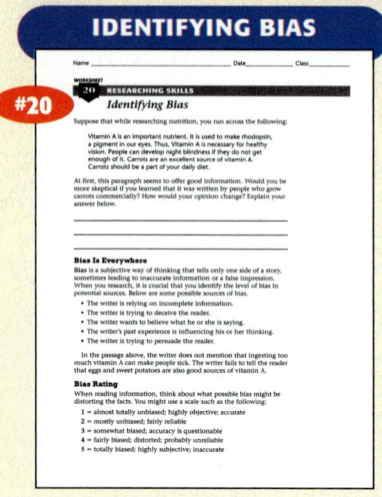
#20

TAKING NOTES
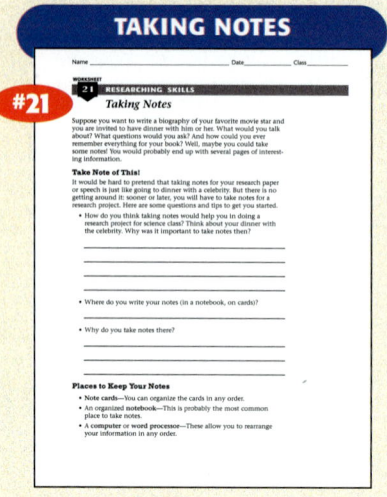
#21

SCIENCE WRITING
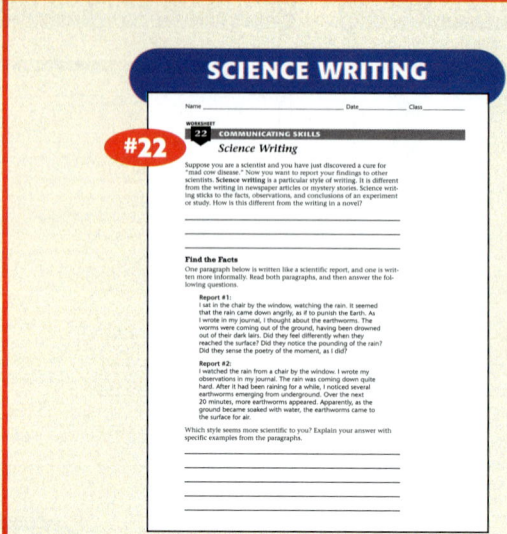
#22

Science Skills Worksheets: Communicating Skills

SCIENCE DRAWING
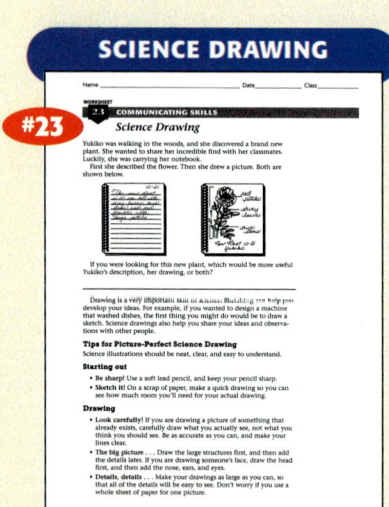
#23

USING MODELS TO COMMUNICATE
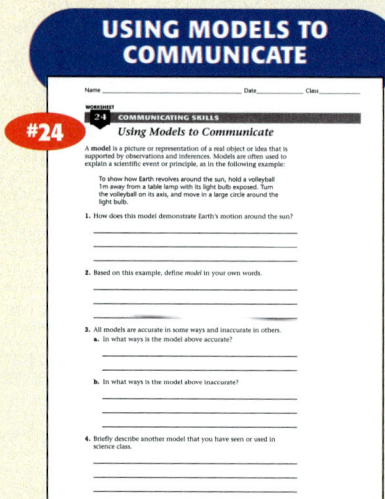
#24

INTRODUCTION TO GRAPHS
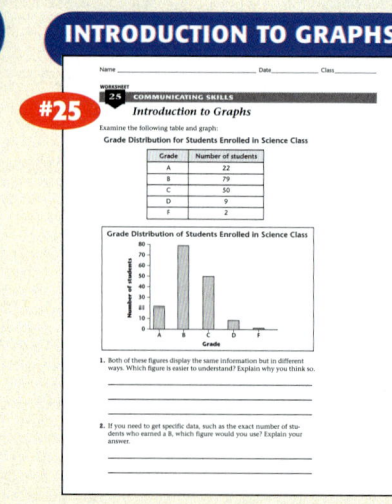
#25

GRASPING GRAPHING
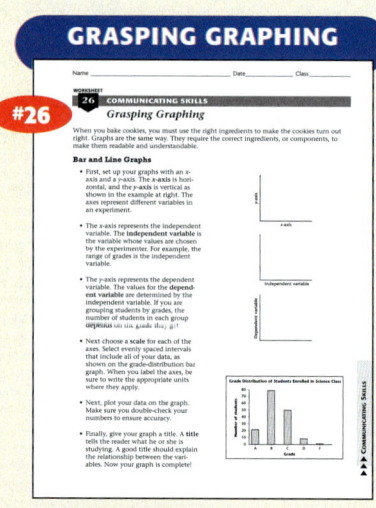
#26

INTERPRETING YOUR DATA
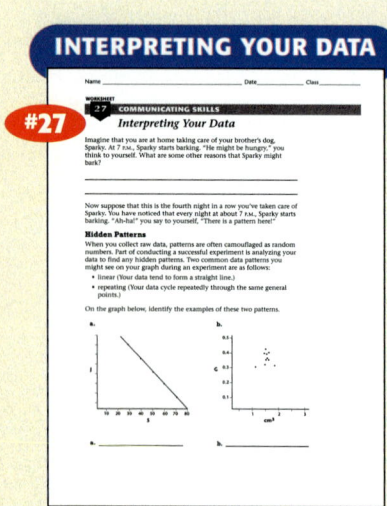
#27

RECOGNIZING BIAS IN GRAPHS
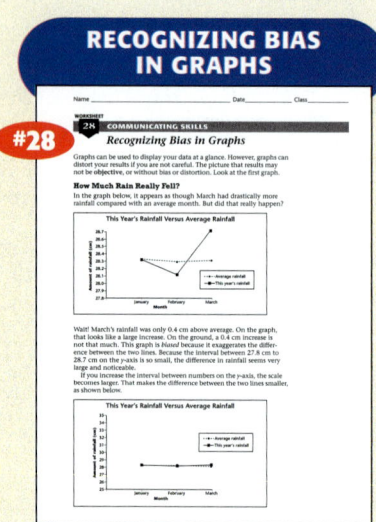
#28

MAKING DATA MEANINGFUL
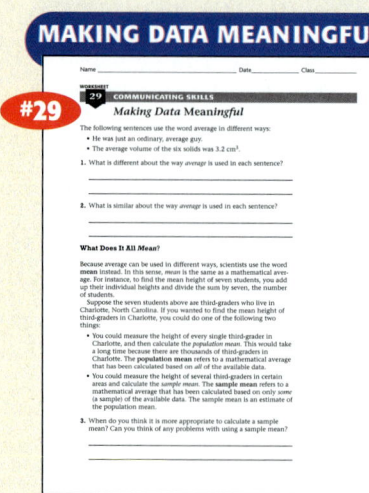
#29

HINTS FOR ORAL PRESENTATIONS
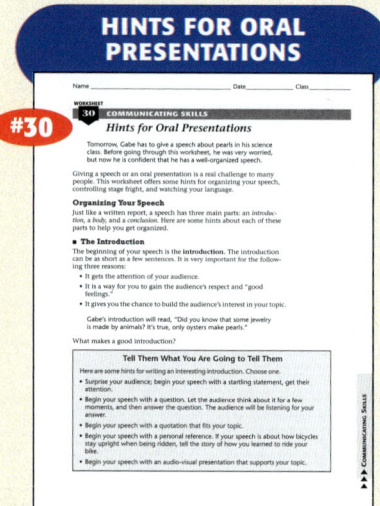
#30

Science & Math Skills Worksheets

Math Skills for Science

ADDITION AND SUBTRACTION
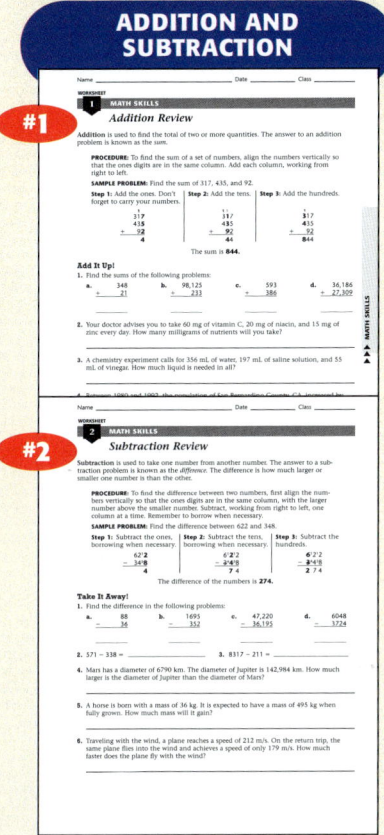

MULTIPLICATION
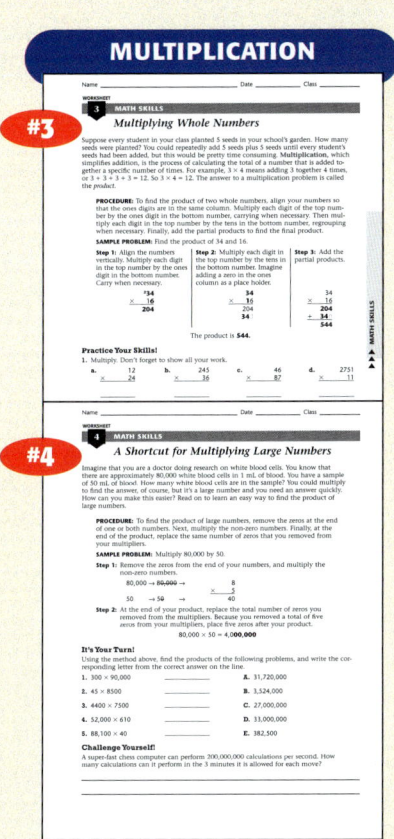

DIVISION
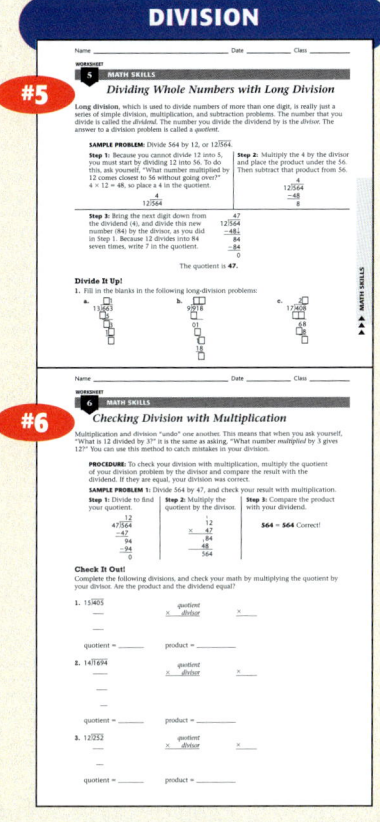

AVERAGES
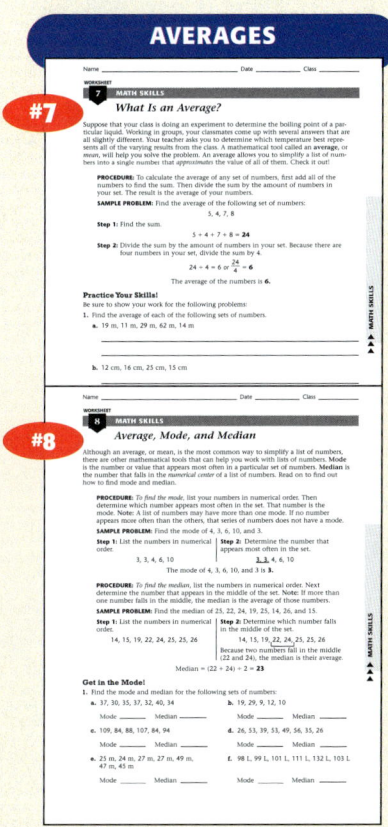

POSITIVE AND NEGATIVE NUMBERS
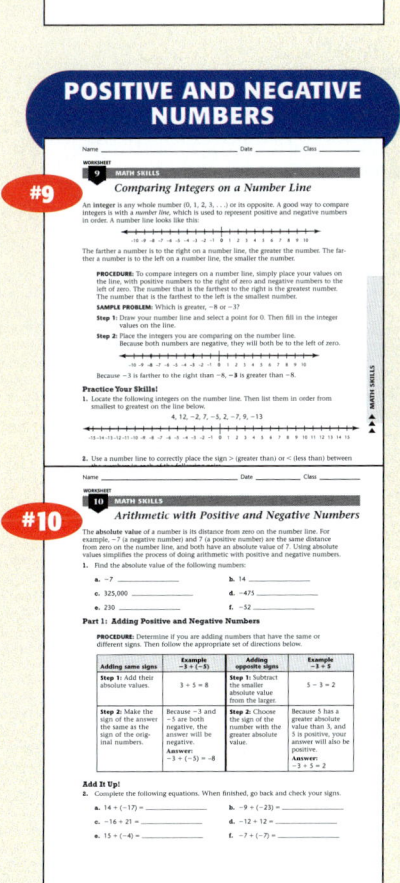

FRACTIONS
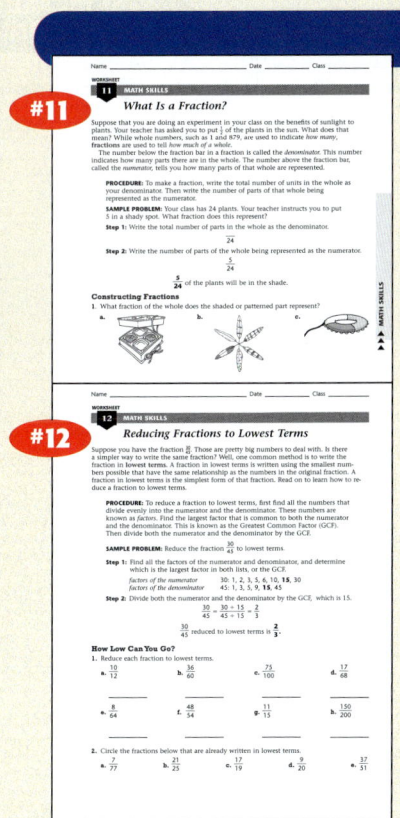
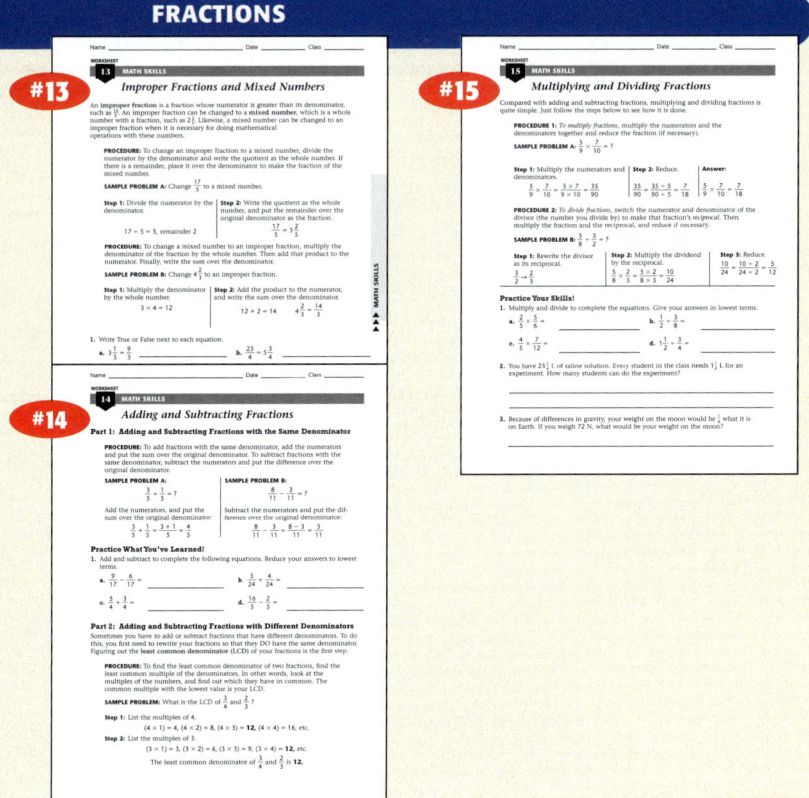

Science & Math Skills Worksheets

Science & Math Skills Worksheets (continued)

Math Skills for Science (continued)

RATIOS AND PROPORTIONS

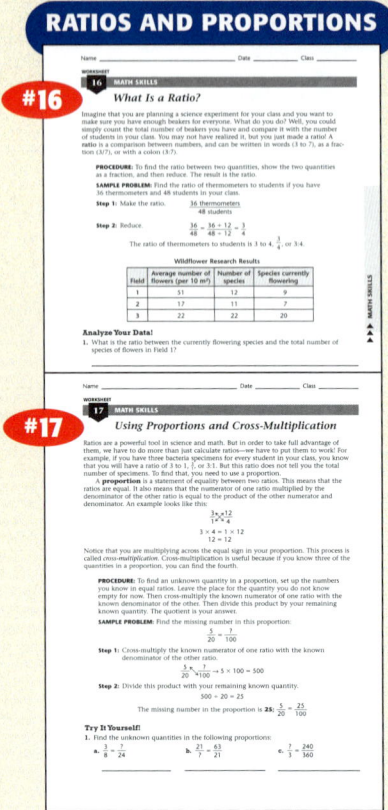

- #16 — What Is a Ratio?
- #17 — Using Proportions and Cross-Multiplication

DECIMALS

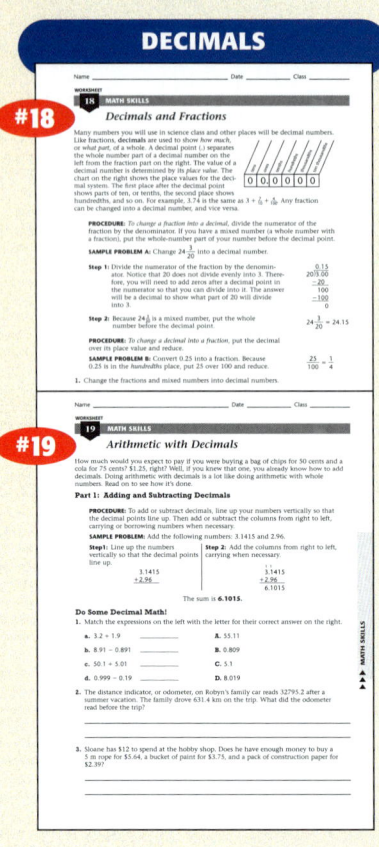

- #18 — Decimals and Fractions
- #19 — Arithmetic with Decimals

PERCENTAGES

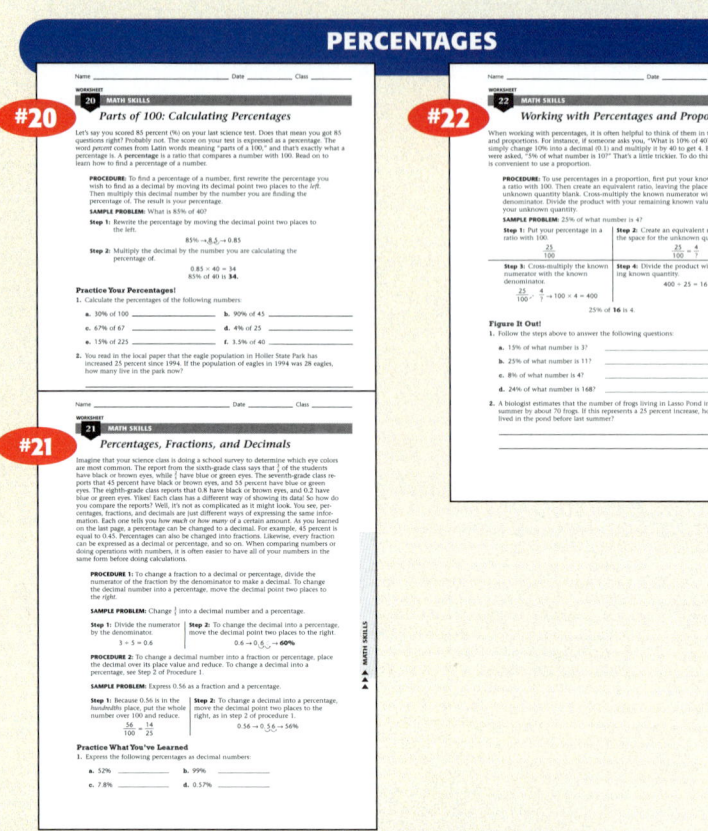

- #20 — Parts of 100: Calculating Percentages
- #21 — Percentages, Fractions, and Decimals
- #22 — Working with Percentages and Proportions

POWERS OF 10

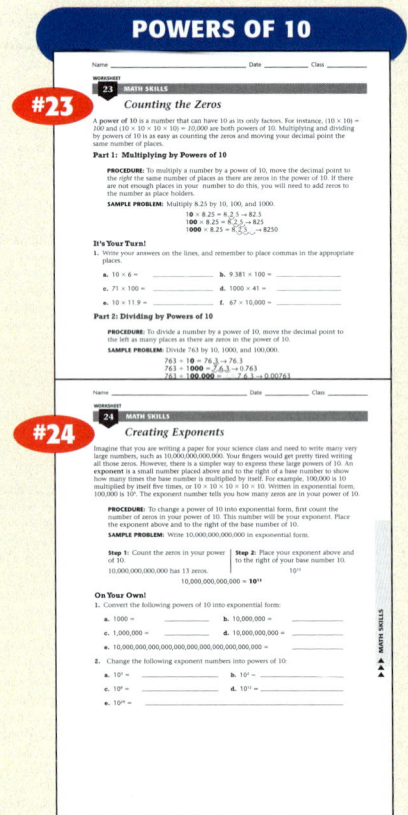

- #23 — Counting the Zeros
- #24 — Creating Exponents

SCIENTIFIC NOTATION

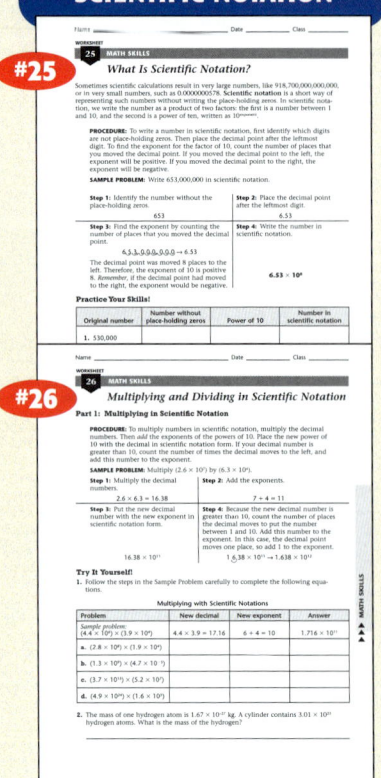

- #25 — What Is Scientific Notation?
- #26 — Multiplying and Dividing in Scientific Notation

SI MEASUREMENT AND CONVERSION

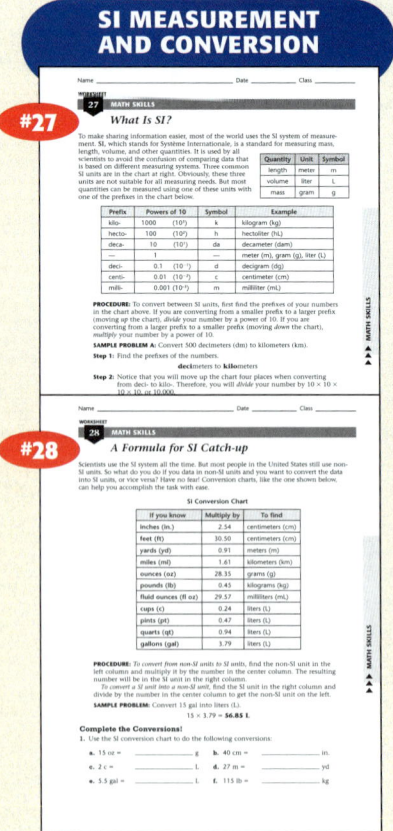

- #27 — What Is SI?
- #28 — A Formula for SI Catch-up

Math Skills for Science (continued)

GEOMETRY

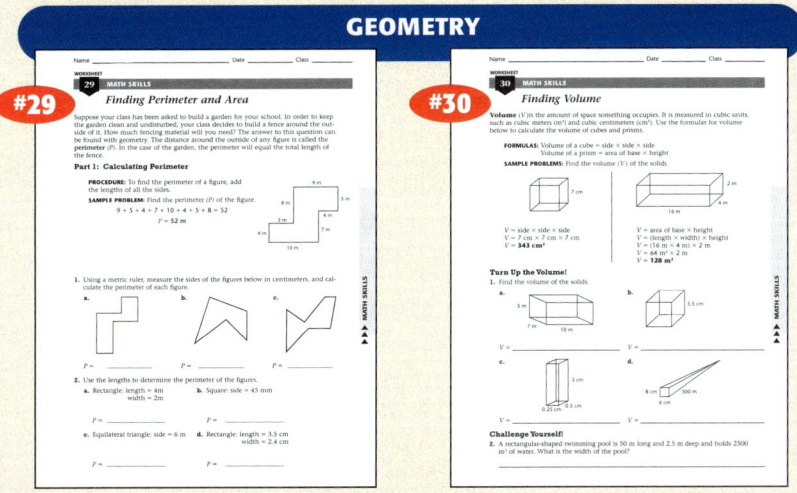

THE UNIT FACTOR AND DIMENSIONAL ANALYSIS

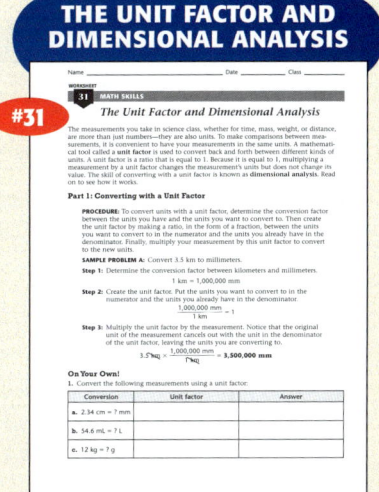

MATH IN SCIENCE: INTEGRATED SCIENCE

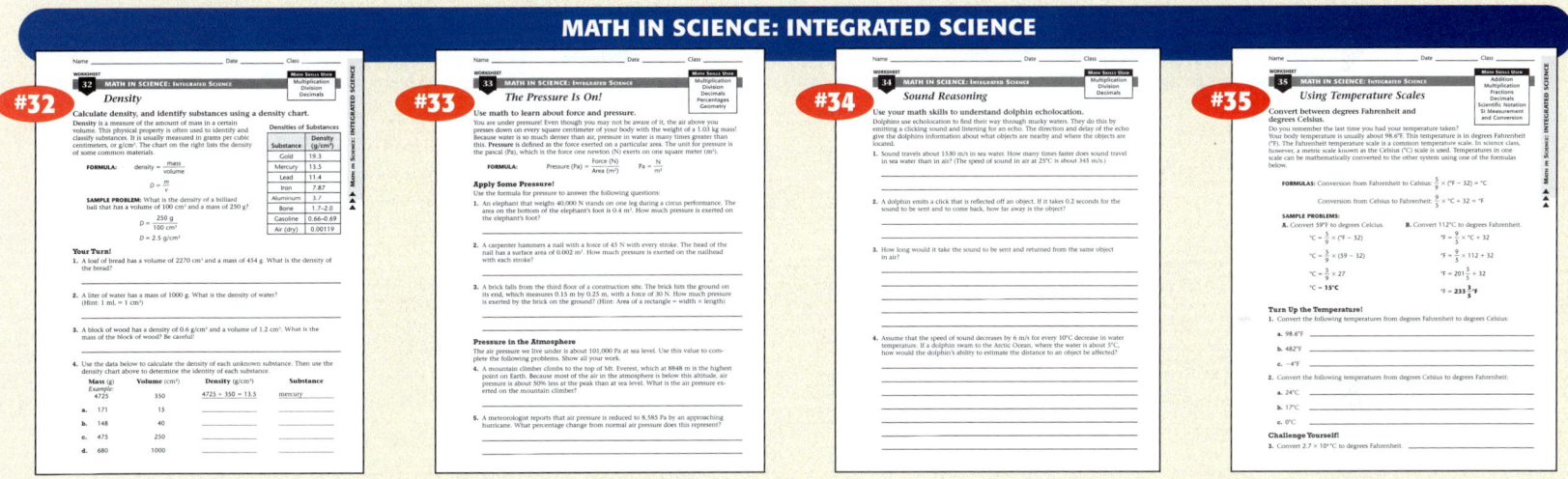

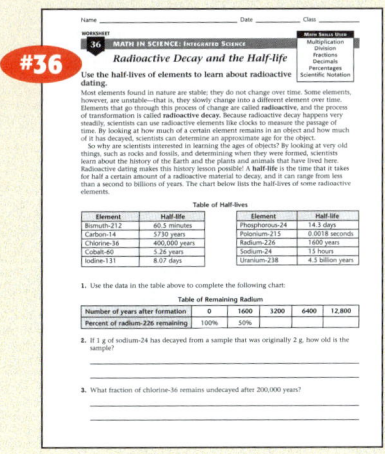

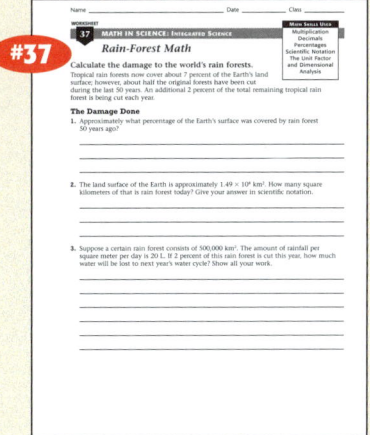

Science & Math Skills Worksheets

Science & Math Skills Worksheets (continued)

Math Skills for Science (continued)

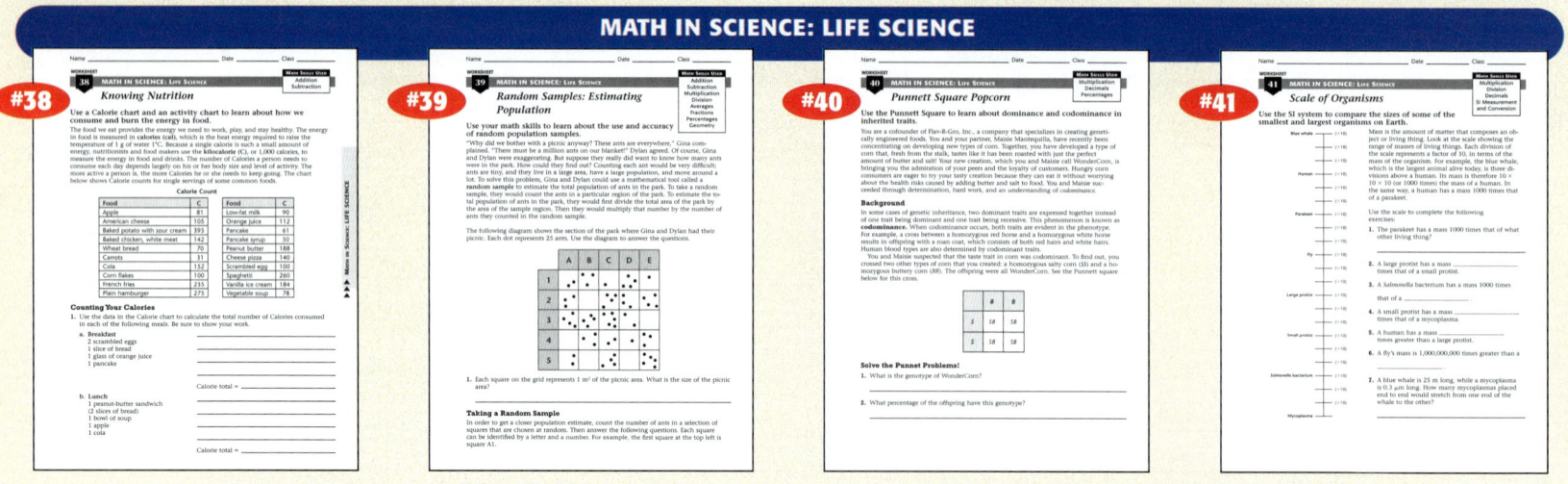

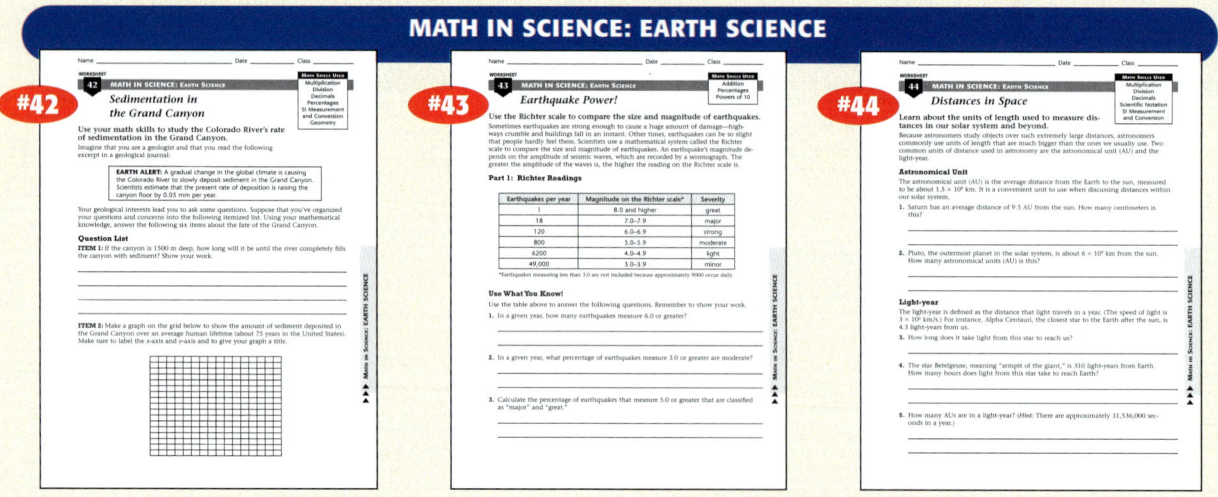

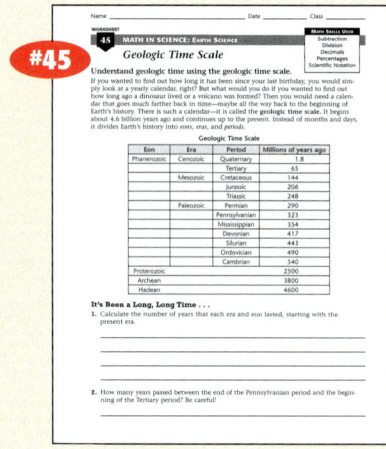
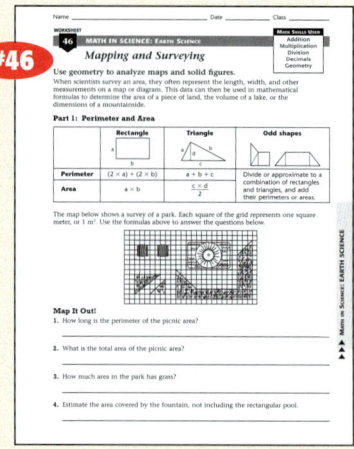

Math Skills for Science (continued)

MATH IN SCIENCE: PHYSICAL SCIENCE

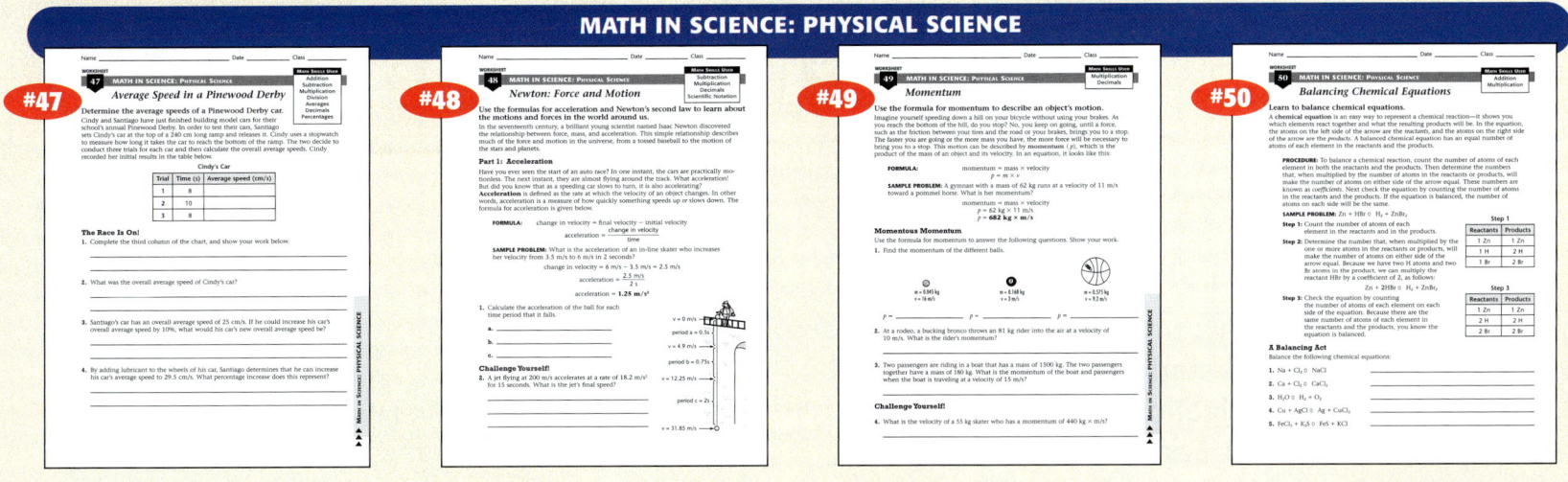

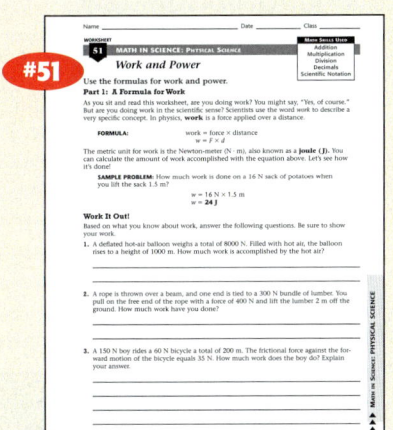
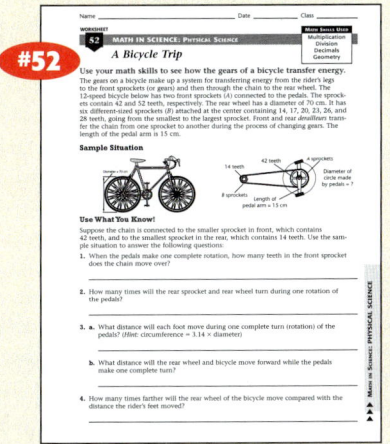
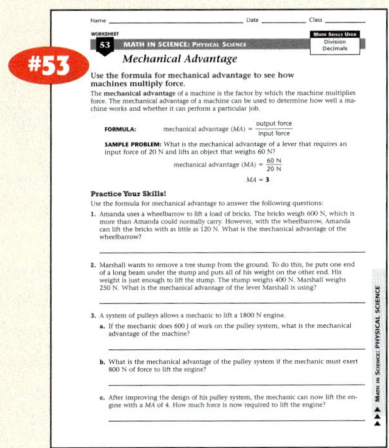
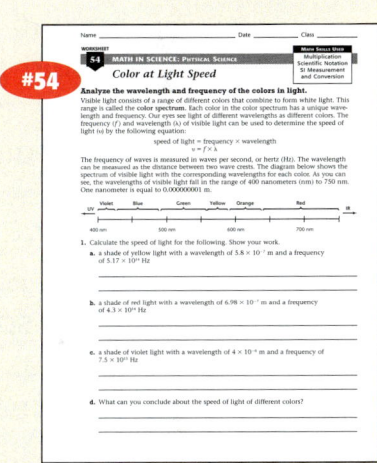

Assessment Checklist & Rubrics

The following is just a sample of over 50 checklists and rubrics contained in this booklet.

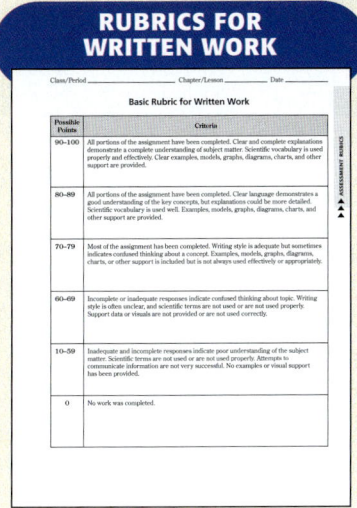
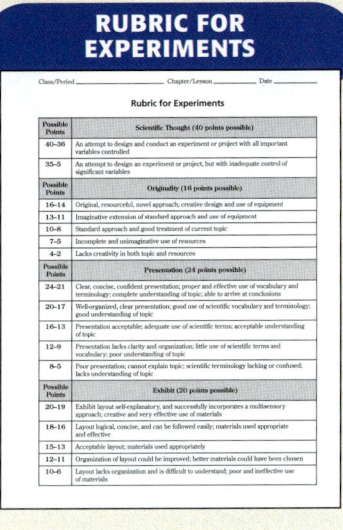
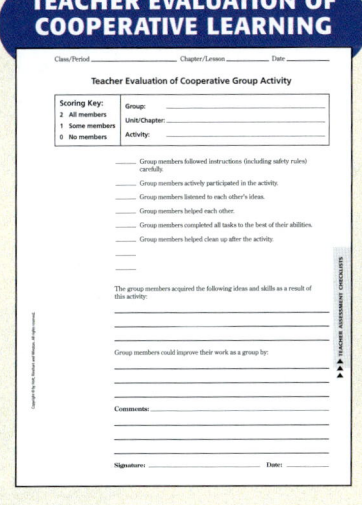
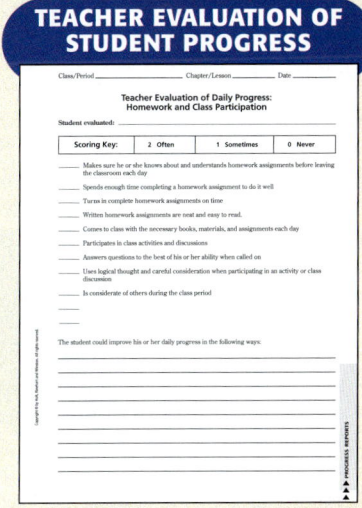

Science & Math Skills Worksheets

UNIT 1

TIMELINE

Introduction to Earth Science

In this unit, you will start your own investigation of the planet Earth and of the regions of space beyond it. But first you should prepare yourself by learning about the tools and methods used by Earth scientists. As you can imagine, it is not easy to study something as large as the Earth or as far away as Venus. Yet that is what Earth scientists do. The timeline shown here identifies a few of the events that have helped shape our understanding of Earth.

1669
Nicolaus Steno accurately describes the process by which living organisms become fossils.

1758
Halley's comet makes a reappearance, confirming Edmond Halley's 1705 prediction. Unfortunately, the comet reappeared 16 years after his death.

1943
The volcano *Paricutín* grows more than 150 m tall during its first six days of eruption.

1960
The first weather satellite, *Tiros I*, is launched by the United States.

1962
By reaching an altitude of 95 km, the *X-15* becomes the first fixed-wing plane to reach outer space.

1896
The first modern Olympic Games are held in Athens, Greece.

1899
The Rosetta stone is discovered in Egypt. It enables scholars to decipher Egyptian hieroglyphics.

1906
Roald Amundsen determines the position of the magnetic north pole.

1922
Roy Chapman Andrews discovers fossilized dinosaur eggs in the Gobi Desert. They are the first such eggs to be found.

1997
China begins construction of Three Gorges Dam, the world's largest dam. Designed to control the Yangtze River, the dam will supply 84 billion kilowatt-hours of hydroelectric power per year.

1970
The United States holds its first Earth Day on April 22. More than 20 million people participate in peaceful demonstrations to show their concern for the environment.

1990
The Hubble Space Telescope is launched into orbit. Three years later, faulty optics are repaired during a space walk.

Introduction to Earth Science

Chapter Organizer

CHAPTER ORGANIZATION	TIME MINUTES	OBJECTIVES	LABS, INVESTIGATIONS, AND DEMONSTRATIONS
Chapter Opener pp. 4–5	45	National Standards: HNS 2, SAI 1	**Start-Up Activity** Mission Impossible, p. 5
Section 1 Branches of Earth Science	45	▶ List major branches of Earth science. ▶ Identify branches of Earth science that are linked to other areas of science. ▶ Describe careers associated with different branches of Earth science. SAI 1, ST 2, SPSP 3, 4, HNS 1	**QuickLab,** How Hot is 300°C? p. 7 GENERAL
Section 2 The Scientific Method in Earth Science	120	▶ Explain the scientific method and how scientists use it. ▶ Apply the scientific method to an Earth science investigation. ▶ Identify the importance of communicating the results of a scientific investigation. ▶ Describe how scientific investigations often lead to new investigations. SAI 1, 2, HNS 2; LabBook UCP 2, SAI 1, ST 2	**Making Models,** Using the Scientific Method, p. 630 GENERAL **Datasheets for LabBook,** Using the Scientific Method, Datasheet 1 GENERAL **Whiz-Bang Demonstrations,** Tubby Terra, Demo 16 GENERAL
Section 3 Life in a Warmer World—An Earth Science Model	120	▶ Demonstrate how models are used in science. ▶ Compare mathematical models with physical models. ▶ Determine limitations of models. UCP 2, SAI 2, SPSP 3, 4, HNS 2, ES 1a	
Section 4 Measurement and Safety	120	▶ Explain the importance of the International System of Units. ▶ Determine appropriate units to use for particular measurements. ▶ Identify lab safety symbols and determine what they mean. UCP 3, SAI 1, SPSP 1, HNS 3	**Long-Term Projects & Research Ideas,** Project 29 ADVANCED

See page T20 for a complete correlation of this book with the

NATIONAL SCIENCE EDUCATION STANDARDS.

TECHNOLOGY RESOURCES

 Guided Reading Audio CD English or Spanish, Chapter 1

 One-Stop Planner CD-ROM with Test Generator

 CNN Scientists in Action, Exploring a Watery Cave, Segment 2

Multicultural Connections, Hopi Science, Segment 1

Chapter 1 • The World of Earth Science

CLASSROOM WORKSHEETS, TRANSPARENCIES, AND RESOURCES	SCIENCE INTEGRATION AND CONNECTIONS	REVIEW AND ASSESSMENT
Science Puzzlers, Twisters & Teasers, Worksheet 1 `ADVANCED` **Directed Reading Worksheet 1** `BASIC` **Science Skills Worksheet 8,** Reading a Science Textbook `GENERAL`		
Directed Reading Worksheet 1, Section 1 `BASIC` **Math Skills for Science Worksheet 23,** Counting the Zeros `GENERAL` **Math Skills for Science Worksheet 25,** What Is Scientific Notation? `GENERAL` **Reinforcement Worksheet 1,** Scenes from the Earth `BASIC`	**Cross-Disciplinary Focus,** p. 7 in ATE `GENERAL` **Real-World Connection,** p. 8 in ATE **Multicultural Connection,** p. 8 in ATE **MathBreak,** Lots of Zeros! p. 9 `GENERAL` **Math and More,** p. 9 in ATE `GENERAL` **Connect to Environmental Science,** p. 10 in ATE `ADVANCED` **Careers:** Geophysicist—Bob Grimm, p. 31 `GENERAL`	**Homework,** p. 9 in ATE `GENERAL` **Review,** p. 11 `GENERAL` **Quiz,** p. 11 in ATE `GENERAL` **Alternative Assessment,** p. 11 in ATE `BASIC`
Directed Reading Worksheet 1, Section 2 `BASIC` **Transparency 101,** The Scientific Method **Problem Solving Worksheet 1,** Kryptonite! `ADVANCED`	**Cross-Disciplinary Focus,** p. 12 in ATE `ADVANCED` **Connect to Life Science,** p. 14 in ATE **Apply,** p. 15 `GENERAL` **Connect to Physical Science,** p. 15 in ATE **Cross-Disciplinary Focus,** p. 16 in ATE `GENERAL`	**Homework,** p. 13 in ATE `GENERAL` **Review,** p. 17 `GENERAL` **Quiz,** p. 17 in ATE `GENERAL` **Alternative Assessment,** p. 17 in ATE `GENERAL`
Directed Reading Worksheet 1, Section 3 `BASIC` **Transparency 102,** A Model of Global Warming **Math Skills Worksheet 17,** Using Proportions and Cross-Multiplication `GENERAL` **Science Skills Worksheet 15,** Measuring `GENERAL`	**Connect to Life Science,** p. 18 in ATE **Math and More,** p. 19 in ATE `BASIC` **Environment Connection,** p. 20 **Cross-Disciplinary Focus,** p. 20 in ATE **Across the Sciences:** All the Earth's a Magnet, p. 30	**Homework,** p. 19 in ATE `BASIC` **Review,** p. 21 `GENERAL` **Quiz,** p. 21 in ATE `GENERAL` **Alternative Assessment,** p. 21 in ATE `GENERAL`
Directed Reading Worksheet 1, Section 4 `BASIC` **Math Skills for Science Worksheet 27,** What Is SI? `GENERAL` **Transparency 103,** Common SI Units **Transparency 204,** Differences Between Mass and Weight **Science Skills Worksheet 9,** Safety Rules! `GENERAL`	**Multicultural Connection,** p. 23 in ATE **Math and More,** p. 24 in ATE `BASIC` **Connect to Physical Science,** p. 24 in ATE	**Homework,** p. 24 in ATE `BASIC` **Review,** p. 25 `GENERAL` **Quiz,** p. 25 in ATE `GENERAL` **Alternative Assessment,** p. 25 in ATE `GENERAL`

END-OF-CHAPTER REVIEW AND ASSESSMENT

Chapter Review in Study Guide
Vocabulary and Notes in Study Guide
Chapter Tests with Performance-Based Assessment, Chapter 1 Test
Chapter Tests with Performance-Based Assessment, Performance-Based Assessment 1
Concept Mapping Transparency 1

internet connect

Holt, Rinehart and Winston On-line Resources
go.hrw.com

For worksheets and other teaching aids related to this chapter, visit the HRW Web site and type in the keyword: **HSTWES**

National Science Teachers Association
www.scilinks.org

Encourage students to use the sciLINKS numbers listed in the internet connect boxes to access information and resources on the **NSTA** Web site.

Chapter Resources & Worksheets

Visual Resources

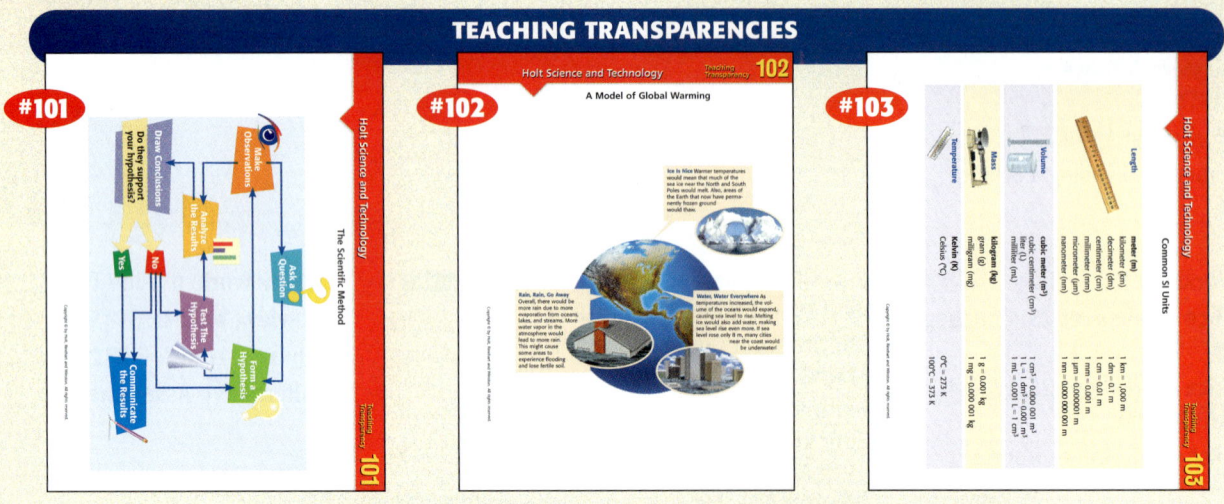

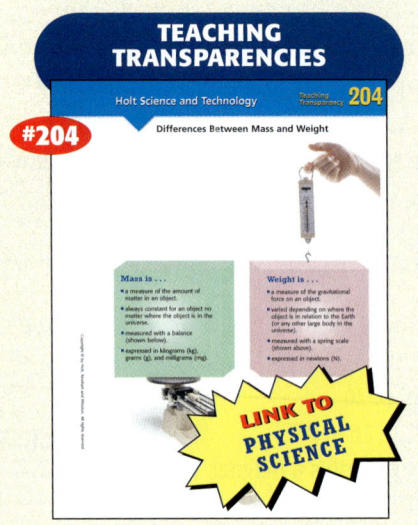

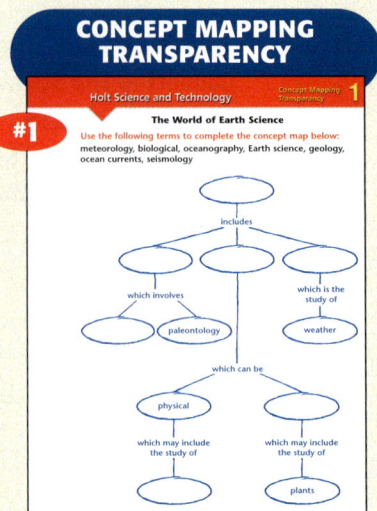

Meeting Individual Needs

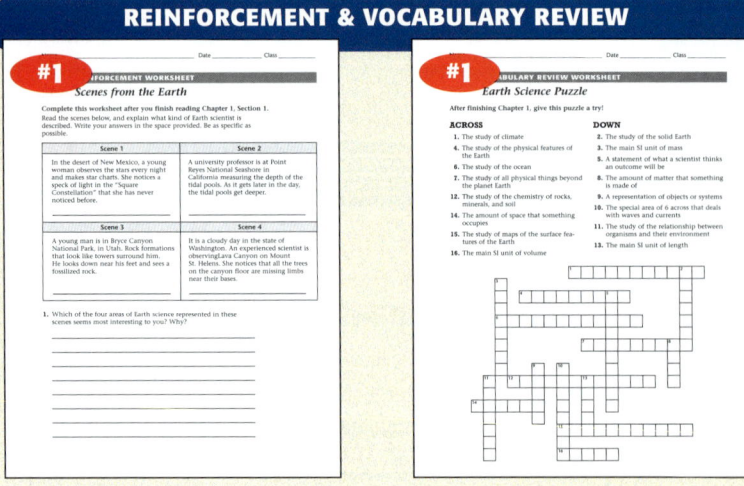

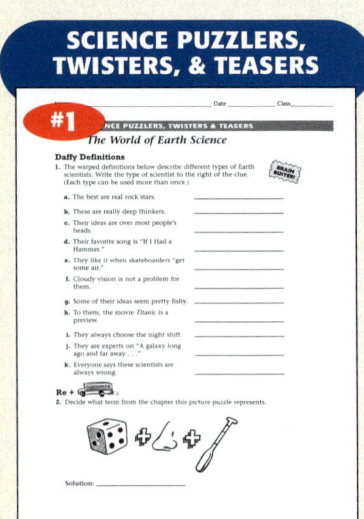

Chapter 1 • The World of Earth Science

Chapter 1 • The World of Earth Science

Review & Assessment

STUDY GUIDE
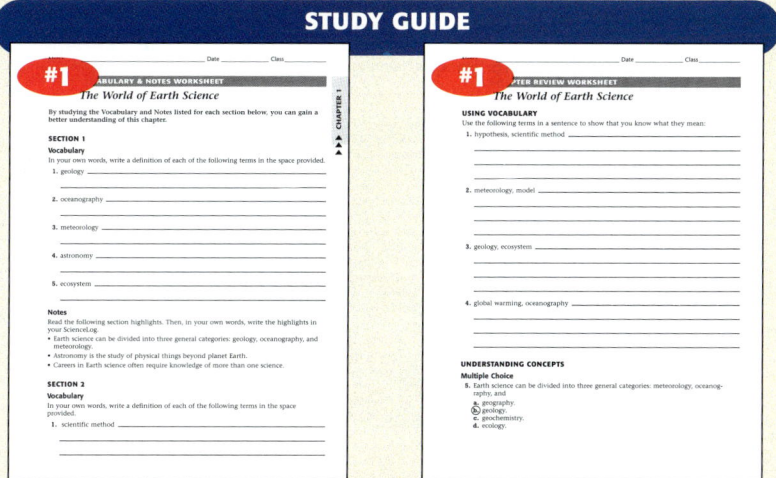

CHAPTER TESTS WITH PERFORMANCE-BASED ASSESSMENT
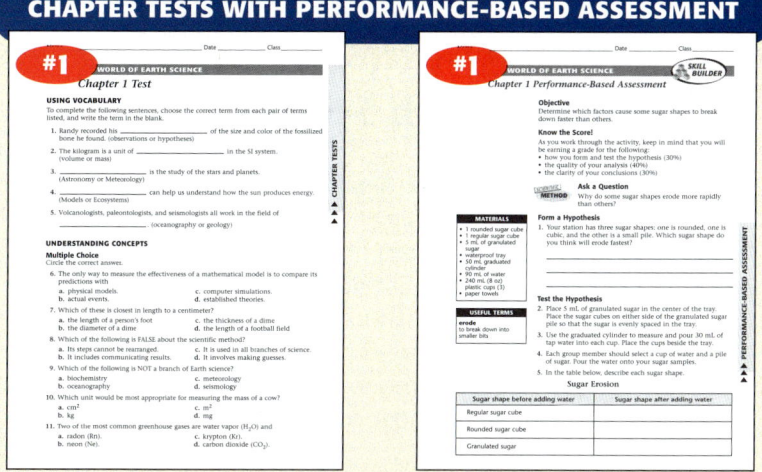

Lab Worksheets

WHIZ-BANG DEMONSTRATIONS
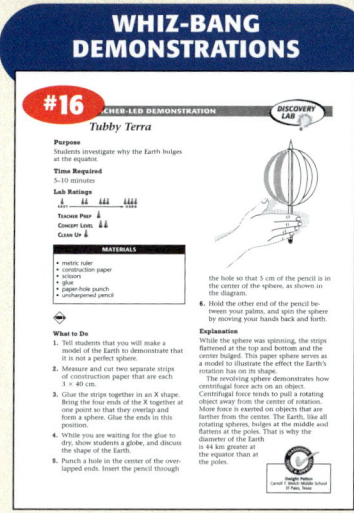

LONG-TERM PROJECTS & RESEARCH IDEAS
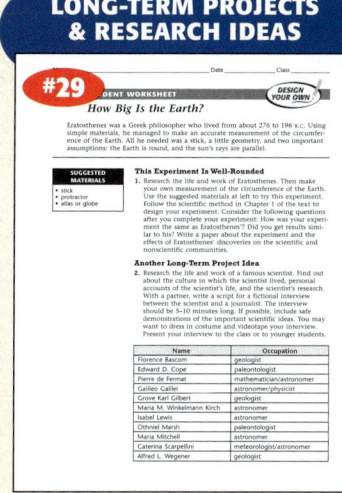

DATASHEETS FOR LABBOOK
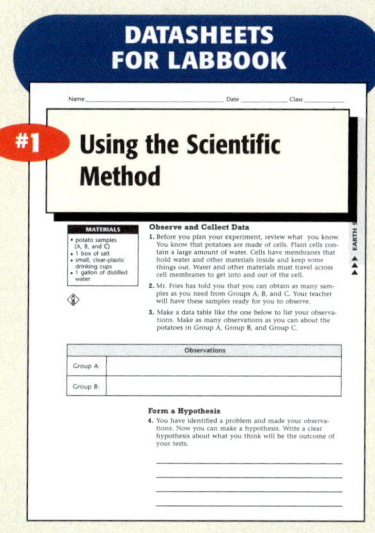

Applications & Extensions

CRITICAL THINKING & PROBLEM SOLVING
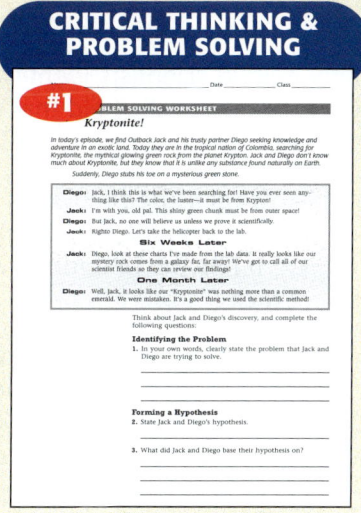

MULTICULTURAL CONNECTIONS
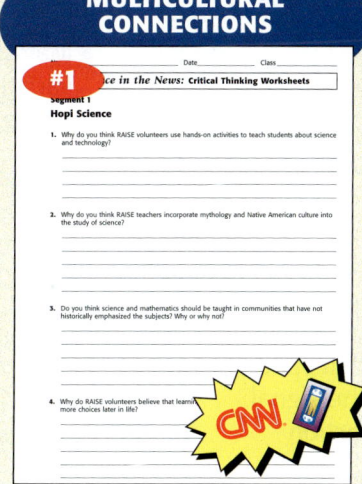

SCIENTISTS IN ACTION
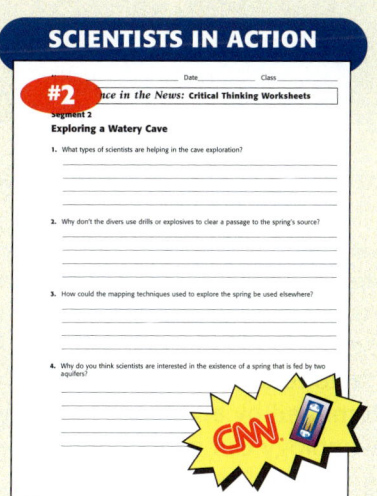

Chapter 1 • Chapter Resources & Worksheets   **3D**

Chapter Background

SECTION 1

Branches of Earth Science

▶ **Volcanology and Seismology**
Seismology and volcanology are separate branches of Earth science, but they are often studied together under the heading of geology. Earthquakes and volcanic activity are often connected. Earthquakes may give clues to impending eruptions, and movements of magma sometimes produce tremors. A volcanic eruption is accompanied by an almost continuous tremor.

▶ **Paleontology**
From movies and TV, students might have the idea that there is a high demand for paleontologists. In truth there are currently relatively few positions available in the field. Most paleontologists work in related jobs, such as education. This allows them to pursue their research interests in the field.

▶ **Oceanography**
Research organizations and industrial firms with interests in the ocean employ many oceanographers. These scientists must have at least a bachelor's degree with emphasis in geology, physics, chemistry, and biology. Most also have some specialized postgraduate training.

▶ **Meteorology and Doppler Radar**
The National Weather Service has greatly improved the quality and reliability of forecasting with the use of Doppler weather surveillance radar. The radar bounces an electromagnetic signal off particles of water, ice, or dust in the atmosphere and measures the time it takes for the signal to return. If objects are moving, their speed can be determined by analyzing variations in the signal. Doppler technology can calculate both the direction and speed of severe storms. It also can identify the conditions leading to severe weather.

SECTION 2

The Scientific Method in Earth Science

▶ **Cooperation Between the Sciences**
Before David Gillette and his team broke ground on their historic *Seismosaurus* dig, they used exhaustive high-tech sensing and mapping technology to locate the best places to dig. Gillette's team was helped by the technology and expertise of the Los Alamos National Laboratory, in New Mexico. The Los Alamos technology was developed for use in other fields of science, but paleontologists and physicists cooperated to make Gillette's dig a success.

- The ground-penetrating radar that helped paleontologists locate the bones of *Seismosaurus* was originally developed to locate 55 gal drums of hazardous waste beneath the soil.

- Magnetometry helped scientists identify the subtle variations in Earth's magnetic field that could be caused by buried bone.

- Radiation detectors measured radiation levels below the surface. Dinosaur bone can have as much as 100,000 times the uranium content of the surrounding rock.

- The underground location of the dinosaur bones was mapped using seismic waves. First a shotgun was fired into the Earth, and then the time it took for the waves to reach a receiving station was recorded.

Chapter 1 • The World of Earth Science

IS THAT A FACT!

- A dowser also visited the site and tried his hand with a low-tech version of remote sensing.

SECTION 3

Life in a Warmer World— An Earth Science Model

▶ **Revising the Model of the Solar System**
Ptolemy (second century A.D.) is credited with developing the solar system model with Earth at its center. The sun, moon, and five visible planets moved around Earth in circular orbits. This model worked so well that astronomers used it to predict the positions of the known planets for many centuries.

- Nicolaus Copernicus (1473–1543) challenged Ptolemy's theory that the Earth was the center of the solar system and developed a model with the sun at the center. In this model, only the moon orbited Earth. Copernicus first presented his theory to friends in 1513. Only 30 years later, at the very end of his life, did Copernicus publish his complete theory.

IS THAT A FACT!

- Although Copernicus's model made it easier to explain the observed changes in the positions of the sun, moon, and planets, many people resisted the idea the model represented. They would not believe that Earth was not the center of *everything*.

▶ **Early Flying Models**
Some of the earliest pioneers in flight attempted to model the flight of birds. In the thirteenth century, Roger Bacon (c. 1220–1292) suggested that people could use wings like those of birds to fly. Two hundred years later, following Bacon's suggestions, Leonardo da Vinci (1452–1519) drew plans for a craft with flapping wings that would be operated by hand. The machine was referred to as an ornithopter. No one, including da Vinci, ever developed a successful ornithopter.

- Sir George Cayley (1773–1857) noticed that some birds could remain aloft for long periods of time without flapping their wings, so he took a different approach to human flight. He made a number of gliders with wings modeled after the wings of birds.

- The first successful glider flight was made in 1855 by Jean-Marie le Bris. The glider he designed was inspired by the albatross, a bird capable of soaring over the ocean for many hours without flapping its wings.

SECTION 4

Measurement and Safety

▶ **Early Systems of Measurement**
For many centuries, measurement was based on the human body. Egyptians defined a cubit as the distance between the elbow and the tip of the middle finger. A yard was the distance from the nose to the middle fingertip of an extended arm. The standard yard, still used today, was based on a measurement established by England's King Henry I (1068–1135).

▶ **The International System of Units**
In 1840, the metric system was established as the legal system of measurement in France. In 1960, the International System of Units, which is based almost entirely on the metric system, was adopted by the General Conference on Weights and Measures.

For background information about teaching strategies and issues, refer to the *Professional Reference for Teachers*.

CHAPTER 1

The World of Earth Science

 Pre-Reading Questions

Students may not know the answers to these questions before reading the chapter, so accept any reasonable response.

Sample Answers

1. Scientific methods are the ways in which scientists answer questions and solve problems.
2. A model is a representation of an object or system. The limitations of models include that they do not look or act exactly like the things they model.
3. A balance is used to measure mass, and a graduated cylinder is used to measure volume.

 Directed Reading Worksheet 1

 Science Puzzlers, Twisters & Teasers Worksheet 1

 Guided Reading Audio CD English or Spanish, Chapter 1

 Science Skills Worksheet 8 "Reading a Science Textbook"

CHAPTER 1

The World of Earth Science

Sections

1. **Branches of Earth Science** 6
   - QuickLab 7
   - MathBreak 9
   - Internet Connect 11
2. **The Scientific Method in Earth Science** 12
   - Apply 15
   - Internet Connect 17
3. **Life in a Warmer World— An Earth Science Model** 18
   - Environment Connect 20
   - Internet Connect 21
4. **Measurement and Safety** 20
   - Internet Connect 25

Chapter Review 28
Feature Article 30, 31
LabBook 630–631

 **Pre-Reading Questions**

1. What are scientific methods?
2. What is a model, and what are the limitations of models?
3. What tools are used to measure mass and volume?

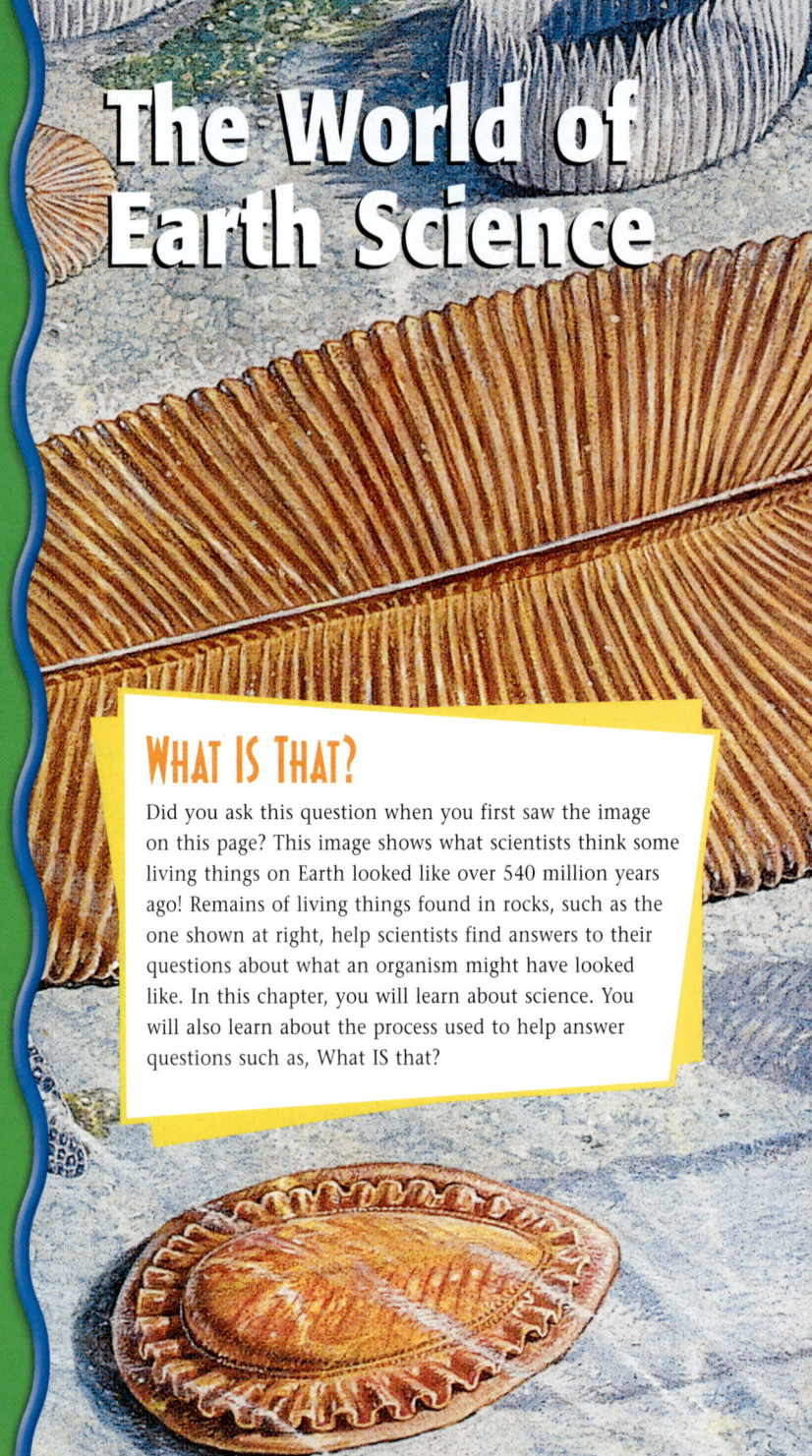

What Is That?

Did you ask this question when you first saw the image on this page? This image shows what scientists think some living things on Earth looked like over 540 million years ago! Remains of living things found in rocks, such as the one shown at right, help scientists find answers to their questions about what an organism might have looked like. In this chapter, you will learn about science. You will also learn about the process used to help answer questions such as, What IS that?

internetconnect

 **HRW On-line Resources**
go.hrw.com
For worksheets and other teaching aids, visit the HRW Web site and type in the keyword: **HSTWES**

 www.scilinks.com
Use the *sci*LINKS numbers at the end of each chapter for additional resources on the **NSTA** Web site.

 www.cnnfyi.com
Visit the CNN Web site for current events coverage and classroom resources.

These are thought to be the remains of one of the first large multicellular living things on Earth!

START-UP Activity

MISSION IMPOSSIBLE?

In this activity, you will do some creative thinking to solve what might seem like an impossible problem.

Procedure

1. Examine an **index card.** Take note of its size and shape. Your mission is to fit yourself through the card.
2. Brainstorm with a partner about ways to complete your mission. Keep the following rules in mind: You can only tear and fold the card. You cannot use tape, glue, or anything else to hold the card together.
3. When you and your partner have a plan, write your procedure in your ScienceLog.
4. Test your plan. Did it work? If necessary, get another index card and try again. Record your new plan and results in your ScienceLog.
5. Share your plans and results with other groups in your class.

Analysis

6. Why was it helpful to come up with a plan in advance?
7. How did testing your plan help you complete your mission?
8. How did sharing your ideas with your classmates help you complete your mission? What did your classmates do differently?

START-UP Activity

MISSION IMPOSSIBLE?

MATERIALS

FOR EACH PAIR OF STUDENTS:
Use a 3 × 5 in. or larger index card. If you choose to let students use scissors to cut the card, be sure to review proper safety precautions.

Teacher's Note: If students need a hint, suggest that they consider using a combination of folds and tears to accomplish their task.

(The solution: Fold the card in half lengthwise. Tear a slit along the fold that doesn't quite reach either end of the card. Fold the card along the slit. Make tears in the card that alternate direction, as shown below.)

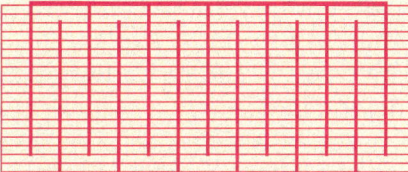

Answers to START-UP Activity

6. Responses should say that a plan made students more efficient and helped prevent mistakes.
7. Responses should indicate a cursory understanding of testing a hypothesis.
8. Responses will vary but should indicate that sharing ideas leads to greater understanding of a problem.

Chapter 1 • The World of Earth Science

SECTION 1

Focus

Branches of Earth Science

This section shows how the branches of Earth science help us to understand and protect the Earth, survive its upheavals, and comprehend its place in the universe. It examines the fields of geology, oceanography, meteorology, and astronomy. Students also learn about ecology, geochemistry, environmental science, geography, and cartography, which combine Earth science and other disciplines.

Bellringer

Tell students the following:

Imagine you are an Earth scientist, and you can travel wherever you want to on Earth. Name the aspects or features of Earth you would like to study. Explain where you would go and what you would do.

Have students write and illustrate their answers in their ScienceLog.

1 Motivate

ACTIVITY

Have students use dictionaries to determine the meaning of the following:

geo-
volcan-
paleo-
meteor-
ocean-
astro-

Ask students to build scientists' names by adding suffixes such as -nomer, -ologist, and -ographer. Have students describe what they think each scientist does based on the name. Sheltered English

---

Section 1

Terms to Learn

geology
oceanography
meteorology
astronomy
ecosystem

What You'll Do

- List major branches of Earth science.
- Identify branches of Earth science that are linked to other areas of science.
- Describe careers associated with different branches of Earth science.

Branches of Earth Science

Planet Earth! How can anyone study something as large and complicated as our planet? One way is to divide the study of Earth into smaller areas of study. The most common areas of study are *geology, oceanography,* and *meteorology.* However, Earth science does not stop at our planet. *Astronomy* is the study of all physical things beyond planet Earth. Let's take a look at each of these four sciences and at some of the people who work within them.

Geology—Science that Rocks

Geology is the study of the solid Earth. Anything and everything that has to do with the solid Earth is part of geology. Most geologists specialize in a particular aspect of the Earth.

Would you like to put on an insulated suit and walk to the edge of a 1,000°C pool of lava? If so, you could be a *volcanologist,* a geologist who studies volcanoes. Are earthquakes more to your liking? Then you could be a *seismologist,* a geologist who studies earthquakes. How about digging up dinosaurs? You could be a *paleontologist,* a geologist who studies fossils. These are only a few of the careers you could have as a geologist.

Figure 1 *Stalagmites grow upward from the floors of caves, and stalactites grow downward from the ceilings of caves.*

Specialized Exploration Some geologists become highly specialized. For instance, geologist Robert Fronk, at the Florida Institute of Technology, explores the subsurface of Earth by scuba-diving in underwater caves in Florida and the Bahamas. Underwater caves often contain evidence that sea level was once much lower than it is now. They contain *stalagmites* and *stalactites,* as shown in **Figure 1.** These formations develop from minerals in dripping water in air-filled caves. When Fronk sees these kinds of geologic formations in underwater caves, he knows that the caves were once above sea level.

Directed Reading Worksheet 1 Section 1

IS THAT A FACT!

Earth is estimated to be 4.6 billion years old. It travels around the sun at 29.79 km/s (18.5 mi/s). The Earth is not round; it is an oblate spheroid—flattened at the poles and bulging at the equator.

Oceanography—Water, Water Everywhere

Oceanography, which is the study of the ocean, is often divided into special areas. Physical oceanographers study things like waves and ocean currents. Biological oceanographers study the plants and animals that live in the ocean. Geological oceanographers study the ocean floor. Chemical oceanographers study natural chemicals and chemicals from pollution in the ocean.

Not long ago, people studied the ocean only from the surface. But as technology has advanced, scientists have worked with engineers to build miniature research submarines. Now oceanographers can go practically anywhere in the oceans. Below, oceanographer John Trefry talks about a trip he took in the minisub *Alvin.*

"We move through the darkness of the Pacific Ocean at a depth of almost one and a half miles with the lights of the submersible shining on the glassy black rock that is new ocean crust. Then, in a magic moment, we can peer ahead through a small porthole at a 300°C black smoker surrounded by an oasis of beautiful and exotic life-forms. The feeling of exhilaration inspires renewed wonderment and makes the many years of study in oceanography seem so satisfying and worthwhile."

Exploring the Ocean Floor Trefry and other oceanographers have discovered the world of the black smokers. *Black smokers* are rock chimneys on the ocean floor that spew black clouds of minerals. Black smokers are a type of *hydrothermal vent,* which is a crack in the ocean floor that releases very hot water from beneath the Earth's surface. The minerals and hot water from these vents support a biological community that includes blood-red tube worms that are 3.5 m long, clams that are 30 cm in diameter, and blind white crabs.

QuickLab

How Hot Is 300°C?

1. Use a **thermometer** to measure the air's temperature in the room in degrees Celsius. Record your reading.
2. Hold the thermometer near a **heat source** in the room, such as a light bulb or a heating vent. Be careful not to burn yourself. Record your reading.
3. How do the temperatures you recorded compare with the 300°C temperature of the water from a black smoker?

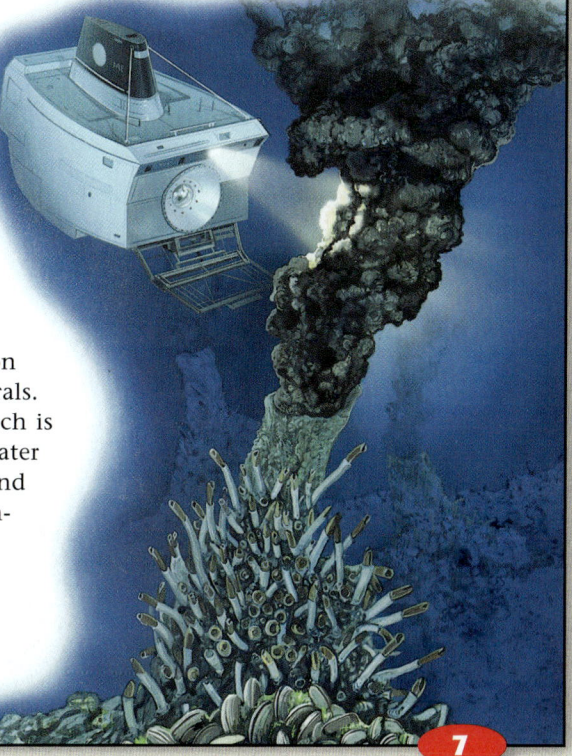

2 Teach

DISCUSSION

Invite students to speculate about what kind of scientist might answer each of the following questions. Discuss ways that scientists find answers to these questions.

- How can you tell when a volcano is going to erupt?
- What life-forms dwell on the ocean floor, 9.5 km down?
- Is Earth's atmosphere becoming warmer? How will this affect us?
- Are there deposits of oil, gas, gold, and silver still undiscovered in Earth's crust? How can they be reached?
- How many stars are there? Is there life on other planets?

Have students add their own questions to the discussion.

CROSS-DISCIPLINARY FOCUS

History Help students research the lives and contributions of the following Earth or space scientists:

- Hipparchus (developed the first system for identifying stars)
- James Hutton (father of modern geology)
- Galileo Galilei (refined the scientific method, astronomy)
- Inge Lehman (discovered the Earth's inner core)
- Robert Goddard (rocket science)
- Johannes Kepler (discovered elliptical orbits in the solar system)
- Marie Curie (studied radioactive decay)
- George E. Hale (developed the Hale reflecting telescope)
- Florence Bascom (a distinguished American geologist)

QuickLab

Answers to Quicklab

3. Answers will vary, but students should realize that the temperature of the water around a black smoker is much hotter than the temperatures they measured. Encourage students to speculate why the water temperature is 200°C above the boiling point of water at sea level. Students might conclude that the tremendous pressure at that depth raises the boiling point of water.

Section 1 • Branches of Earth Science   **7**

2) Teach, continued

REAL-WORLD CONNECTION

Ask students to describe their experiences with severe weather, such as tornadoes, hurricanes, or severe thunderstorms. What preparations did they make before the storm? What safety measures did they take during the storm? How did weather forecasters influence their behavior? What was the result of the storm in their community? Finally, discuss the information students get from meteorologists every day and how they use it.

MEETING INDIVIDUAL NEEDS

Learners Having Difficulty
Have students create concept-map posters for the four branches of Earth and space science and their subdivisions. Have them add illustrations, symbols, and photographs or headlines clipped from articles to provide visual information about each field.

Multicultural CONNECTION

Cultures all over the world observe animal behavior to predict the weather. Chinese farmers use this formula: If frogs croak on a fine day, it will rain in 2 days. If frogs croak after rain, there will be fine weather. It will continue to rain if frogs do not croak after many overcast days. Other cultures observe insect behavior: It will rain if ants travel in a straight line; it will be clear if the ants are scattered. Students may be surprised to learn that counting cricket chirps is an accurate way to measure ambient temperature. Have students find out how other cultures observe animal behavior to predict the weather and use these methods for 1 week.

Figure 2 *This satellite photo traces Hurricane Andrew's path from the Atlantic Ocean (right) to the Gulf of Mexico (left).*

Figure 3 *These meteorologists are risking their lives to gather data about tornadoes.*

Meteorology—It's a Gas!

The study of the entire atmosphere is called **meteorology**. When you ask, "Is it going to rain today?" you are asking a meteorological question. One of the most common careers in meteorology is weather forecasting. Sometimes knowing what the weather is going to be like makes our lives more comfortable. And occasionally our lives depend on these forecasts.

Hurricanes In 1928, a major hurricane hit Florida and killed 1,836 people. In comparison, a hurricane of similar strength—Hurricane Andrew, shown in **Figure 2**—hit Florida in 1992, killing only 48 people. Why were there far fewer deaths in 1992? Two major reasons were hurricane tracking and weather forecasting.

Meteorologists began tracking Hurricane Andrew on Monday, August 17. By the following Sunday morning, most South Floridians had left the coast because the National Hurricane Center had warned them that Andrew was headed their way. Hurricane Andrew hit southern Florida early on Monday morning, August 24. The hurricane caused a lot of damage, but it killed very few people thanks to meteorologists' warnings.

Tornadoes Another dangerous weather element is tornadoes. An average of 780 tornadoes touch down each year in the United States. What do you think about a meteorologist who chases tornadoes as a career? Howard Bluestein does just that. Bluestein predicts where tornadoes are likely to form and then drives to within a couple of kilometers of the site to gather data, as shown in **Figure 3.** By gathering data this way, scientists like Bluestein hope to understand tornadoes better. The better they understand them, the better they can predict how these violent storms will behave.

IS THAT A FACT!

Our planet has some extreme temperatures. A world record high temperature of 58°C (136°F) was recorded in El Azizia, Libya, in 1922. In 1983 in Vostok, Antarctica, a world record low temperature of −89°C (−129°F) was recorded.

Astronomy—Far, Far Away

How do you study things that are far away in space? That's a question that astronomers can answer. **Astronomy** is the study of all physical things beyond Earth. Astronomers study stars, asteroids, planets, and everything else in space.

Because most things in space are too far away to sense directly, astronomers depend on technology to help them study objects in space. Optical telescopes have been used for hundreds of years—Galileo built one in 1609. Astronomers still use optical telescopes to look into space, but they also use other types of telescopes. For example, the radio telescopes shown in **Figure 4** allow astronomers to study objects that are too far away to be seen using optical telescopes or that do not give off visible light.

Figure 4 These radio telescopes receive radio waves from space.

Star Struck Astronomers spend much of their time studying stars. Astronomers estimate that there are 100 billion billion stars in the sky. That's a lot of stars! Try the MathBreak at right to get an idea of how many stars there are. The most familiar star in the universe is the sun, which is the closest star to Earth. Astronomers have studied the sun more than any other star. Astronomers have also studied planets that are close to Earth. **Figure 5** illustrates the sun, the Earth, and some nearby planets. Can you name these planets?

Figure 5 Astronomers have spent more time studying objects near Earth than objects that are farther away in space.

MATH BREAK

Lots of Zeros!
Astronomers estimate that there are more than 100 billion billion stars in the sky! One billion written out in numerals looks like this:

1,000,000,000

1. How many zeros do you need in order to write 100 billion billion in numerals? To find out, multiply 1 billion by 1 billion, then multiply your answer by 100. Count the zeros in the final answer.
2. Now time how long it takes you to count to 100. How long would it take you to count to 100 a billion billion times?

USING THE FIGURE

Students are asked to name the planets shown in **Figure 5**. Moving away from the sun, they are: Mercury, Venus, Earth, Mars, Jupiter, and Saturn. Note that an asteroid belt is between Mars and Jupiter and that Uranus, Neptune, and Pluto lie beyond the orbit of Saturn.

MATH and MORE

Explain that space science involves measuring extremely large distances. To express these enormous numbers, scientists use *scientific notation*, or powers of 10. Write the following on the board:

10 = 10^1
100 = 10^2
1000 = 10^3

Have students continue the table and explain the pattern. Ask students to express the following numbers using this type of notation:

1. 10,000°C (1.0×10^4°C)
2. 1,497,000 km (1.497×10^6 km)
3. 4,600,000,000 years (4.6×10^9 years)

 Math Skills Worksheet 23 "Counting the Zeros"

 Math Skills Worksheet 25 "What Is Scientific Notation?"

Homework

Finding Out About Telescopes Ask students to learn about optical telescopes, liquid mirror telescopes, X-ray telescopes, or radio telescopes. Have students draw the telescope and show its working parts. Ask them to write a brief explanation of how the telescope works and how it is used.

Answers to MATHBREAK

1. 20 zeros
2. Answers will vary, but counting one number per second, it will take more than 3 trillion years! The universe is thought to be only 10 billion to 15 billion years old.

Section 1 • Branches of Earth Science

3) Extend

CONNECT TO ENVIRONMENTAL SCIENCE

Many of the world's grassland ecosystems are endangered due to overgrazing. If too many animals graze the land, topsoil may dry out and erode. The result may be desertification—the dry grassland becomes a desert. Have students research how the Peace Corps and other organizations attempt to control desertification around the world.

GOING FURTHER

 Ask students to imagine an exciting day in the life of an astronomer, a volcanologist, a meteorologist, or an oceanographer. Have them write a ScienceLog entry from the perspective of the scientist describing what happened to make the day exciting and why the scientist enjoys his or her job.

INDEPENDENT PRACTICE

 Have students create an Earth Science Current Events scrapbook. Encourage creativity as they incorporate articles, illustrations, photographs, and original entries. The book can be organized by category in a three-ring binder, and students can add pages throughout the school year.
Sheltered English

---

internet connect

SC**L**INKS
NSTA

TOPIC: Branches of Earth Science
GO TO: www.scilinks.org
*sci*LINKS NUMBER: HSTE005

TOPIC: Careers in Earth Science
GO TO: www.scilinks.org
*sci*LINKS NUMBER: HSTE010

Special Branches of Earth Science

In addition to the main branches of Earth science, there are branches that depend more heavily on other areas of science. Earth scientists often find themselves in careers that rely on life science, chemistry, physics, and many other areas of science. Let's take a look at some Earth science careers with strong ties to other sciences.

Ecology It is difficult to understand the behavior of certain organisms without studying the relationships between these organisms and their surroundings. Ecologists study ecosystems, like the one in **Figure 6.** An **ecosystem** is a community of organisms and their nonliving environment. The principles of ecology are useful in many related fields, such as wildlife management, agriculture, forestry, and conservation. The science of ecology requires people trained in many disciplines, such as biology, geology, chemistry, climatology, mathematics, and computer technology.

Figure 6 *Because beavers spend time in water as well as on land, they share their ecosystem with many plants and other animals.*

Is there water on Mars? Turn to page 31 to see how one geophysicist is finding out.

Geochemistry As the name implies, geochemistry combines the studies of geology and chemistry. Geochemists, like the one in **Figure 7,** specialize in the chemistry of rocks, minerals, and soil. They study the chemistry of these materials to determine their economic value, interpret what the environment was like when they formed, and learn what has happened to them since they first formed.

Figure 7 *This geochemist is taking rock samples from the field so she can perform chemical analyses of them in her laboratory.*

MISCONCEPTION ALERT

Many people think that ecosystems exist somewhere "out there"—in open fields, quiet woods, and national parks. In fact, anywhere living things form a network of feeding, reproduction, and survival systems, an ecosystem exists. Ecosystems are found in cities and small towns, on school playgrounds, in backyards, and even in your body. Students who learn to observe with care and patience can learn a great deal about the ecosystems around them.

Environmental Science Humans have recently begun to examine their relationship with their surroundings, or *environment,* more closely. The study of how humans interact with the environment is called *environmental science.* As shown in **Figure 8,** one common task of an environmental scientist is trying to find out whether humans are damaging the environment. Pollution of the air, water, and land can harm natural resources, such as wildlife, drinking water, and soil. Environmental science, which relies on life science, chemistry, physics, and geology, is helping us to preserve Earth's resources and to use them more wisely.

Figure 8 *This environmental scientist is testing the effects of industry on the environment.*

Geography and Cartography Geographers, who are educated in geology, life science, and physics, study the surface features of the Earth. Cartographers make maps of those features. Have you ever wondered why our cities are located where they are? Often, the location of a city is determined by geography. Many cities, such as the one in **Figure 9,** were built near rivers, lakes, or oceans because boats were used for transporting people and items of trade. Rivers and lakes also provide communities with plenty of water for drinking and for raising crops and animals. We make maps to record the geography of our world. Maps help us keep track of natural resources and navigate the surface of the Earth.

Figure 9 *The easily accessible Mississippi River helped St. Louis become the large city it is today.*

REVIEW

1. List three major branches of Earth Science.
2. Name two branches of Earth science that rely heavily on other areas of science. Explain how the branches rely on the other areas of science.
3. List and describe three Earth-science careers.
4. **Inferring Relationships** If you were a *hydrogeologist,* what kind of work would you do?

internet connect

SC/**INKS**
NSTA

TOPIC: Branches of Earth Science
GO TO: www.scilinks.org
*sci***LINKS NUMBER:** HSTE005

SECTION 2

Focus

The Scientific Method in Earth Science

This section introduces the scientific method by following an actual paleontologist's discovery of a new type of dinosaur. The section also discusses the importance of sharing discoveries and information among scientists.

🔔 Bellringer

Pose the following question to your students:

How can paleontologists know what a dinosaur looked like, how it behaved, and what it ate based only on its fossilized skeleton?

Ask students to write their answers in their ScienceLog. Discuss their ideas.

1) Motivate

DISCUSSION

Ask students to think about "discoveries" they have made in their lives. Students may be surprised to learn that they make scientific discoveries every day. A student might say, for example, "I found out that if my brother sat on the seesaw opposite from me, I would go flying off." Tell students that discoveries are often made by accident but that a controlled experiment using the scientific method is necessary to explain observations. Have students identify the steps of the scientific method in the discoveries they have made.
Sheltered English

Directed Reading Worksheet 1 Section 2

Section 2

The Scientific Method in Earth Science

Terms to Learn
scientific method
observation
hypothesis

What You'll Do
- Explain the scientific method and how scientists use it.
- Apply the scientific method to an Earth science investigation.
- Identify the importance of communicating the results of a scientific investigation.
- Describe how scientific investigations often lead to new investigations.

Imagine that you are standing in a thick forest on the bank of a river. The sun is shining through the needles of the trees. Insects are buzzing, but no birds are flying because they don't yet exist. It is the Jurassic period, 150 million years ago.

Wading in the shallow water, several long-necked dinosaurs quietly munch on vegetation. As you peer through the trees, you spot a different type of dinosaur on the prowl for prey. It is an allosaur, the most common meat-eating predator of this time.

Suddenly you feel the ground begin to shake. You begin to hear a booming noise that accompanies the tremors. The allosaur stops and looks in the direction of the sound. The booming gets louder, and the tremors get stronger.

Suddenly you notice a creature's head looming over the treetops. The creature's head is so high that its neck must be 20 m long! Then the entire animal comes into view. You understand why the ground is shaking. The animal is *Seismosaurus hallorum* (SEIZ moh SAWR uhs hah LOHR uhm), the "earth shaker." You are looking at one of the largest dinosaurs known.

Seismosaurus hallorum

CROSS-DISCIPLINARY FOCUS

Writing — Language Arts As students read the description of a Jurassic period environment, have them pay particular attention to the language used to describe the scene. Ask them to analyze the description and hypothesize how scientists discovered what this environment was like. For example, what parts of the description could be learned from the fossil record? What parts are inferred from observations of living things today? Have students record their observations in their ScienceLog and write their own description of a Jurassic environment.

The scene you just witnessed is not based on imagination alone. Scientists have been studying dinosaurs for years. From the bits and pieces of information they gather about dinosaurs and their environment, scientists re-create what the Earth might have been like 150 million years ago. But how do scientists tell one dinosaur species from another? How do they know if they have discovered a new species? The answers to these questions are related to the methods that scientists use.

Steps of the Scientific Method

When scientists make observations about the natural world, they are often presented with a question or problem. But scientists don't just throw out random answers. Instead, they follow a series of steps called the *scientific method*. The **scientific method** is a series of steps that scientists use to answer questions and solve problems. The most basic steps are illustrated in **Figure 10.**

Although the scientific method has several distinct steps, it is not a rigid procedure. Scientists may use all of the steps or just some of the steps of the scientific method. They may even repeat some of the steps or do them in a different order. The goal of the scientific method is to come up with reliable answers and solutions. As long as scientists use the scientific method effectively, the overall result is the same—they gain more insight into the problems they investigate.

Several species of dinosaurs are claimed to be the largest known. So which is the largest? Good scientists look carefully at the information available and judge for themselves.

Figure 10 *The scientific method is illustrated in this flowchart. Notice that there are several ways to follow the paths.*

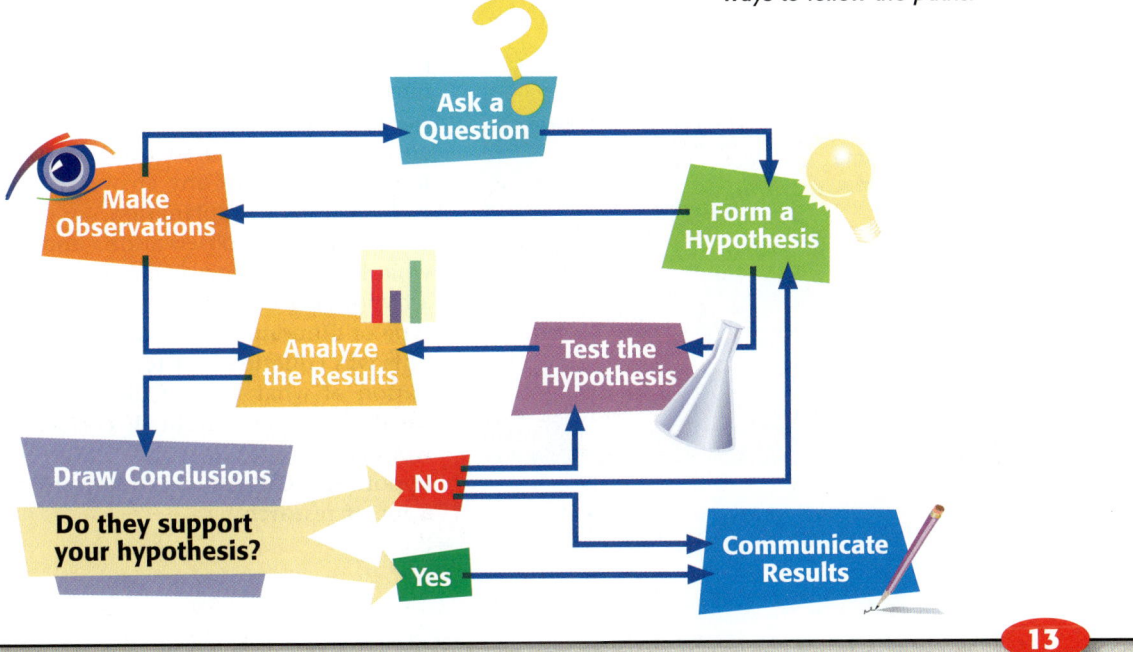

2) Teach

GROUP ACTIVITY

Have students work in small groups to solve an everyday problem using the scientific method. For example, students might devise a way to keep sandwiches in a sack lunch from being squashed in a backpack. Ask students to report on how they followed the six steps, and have them record their experimental processes and conclusions. Write the steps of the scientific method on the board, and point out different ways groups approached each step. Sheltered English

Homework

 **Using the Scientific Method** Ask students to think of a question or a problem in their daily lives that they can answer by making observations, forming a hypothesis, testing the hypothesis, and analyzing the results. Set a time limit for students' observations, and have them share their results in a poster or written report.

 **Teaching Transparency 101** "The Scientific Method"

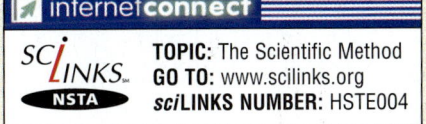
TOPIC: The Scientific Method
GO TO: www.scilinks.org
sciLINKS NUMBER: HSTE004

Ask students to define *observations*. Many may assume that observations only include phenomena they can see. In fact, observations are made using all the senses. Point out that many scientific observations must be made indirectly, for example, when studying Earth's deep interior, faraway stars, and magma chambers inside volcanoes.

2 Teach, continued

CONNECT TO LIFE SCIENCE

Fossils can tell a scientist many more things besides an animal's height or weight. In addition to bones, Gillette found many *gastroliths*—large stones found in the digestive system of some animals, particularly birds. *Seismosaurus* apparently swallowed the stones; once inside the digestive system, the stones ground up plant material that otherwise would have been too hard for *Seismosaurus* to digest!

DISCUSSION

How is the scientific method like detective work? Have students list the stages they think occur in a robbery investigation and match them to steps in the scientific method.

- Determine what happened, when it happened, and where it happened (state the problem).
- Gather clues (make observations).
- Determine suspects (form a hypothesis).
- Interrogate suspects (test the hypothesis).
- Analyze clues (analyze the results).
- Solve the crime (draw conclusions).
- Arrest the alleged perpetrator (communicate the results).

Dino Discovery—A Case for the Scientific Method

One of the first things a scientist does, even before starting an investigation, is make observations. An **observation** is any use of the senses to gather information. Observations are made throughout scientific investigations.

Remember the hikers at the beginning of this chapter and their discovery of dinosaur bones in the desert? Those hikers may have been the first to examine the bones, but they weren't the last. In May 1985, paleontologist David D. Gillette visited the site and began to wonder what type of dinosaur these huge bones came from. This started him on the path to using the scientific method.

Ask a Question

Ask a question that needs a scientific answer.

Ask a Question When scientists make observations, they often have questions that they would like answered. Gillette may have asked, "What type of dinosaur did these bones come from?" Gillette knew that in order to answer this question, he would have to use the scientific method. So Gillette moved to the next step.

Form a Hypothesis

Propose a possible answer to the question.

Form a Hypothesis When scientists want to investigate a question, they form a *hypothesis*. A **hypothesis** is a possible explanation or answer to the question. Sometimes called an *educated guess*, the hypothesis represents a scientist's best answer to the question. But it can't be just any answer. It has to be a testable explanation.

Based on his observations and on what he already knew, Gillette formed a hypothesis—the bones came from a type of dinosaur unknown to science. This was Gillette's best testable explanation of what type of dinosaur the fossil bones came from. If correct, it would answer his question. To test his hypothesis, Gillette would have to do a lot of research.

SCIENTISTS AT ODDS

Paleontologist David Gillette named the dinosaur *Seismosaurus*, or earth shaker, because of its great size. No one doubts that *Seismosaurus* was very heavy, weighing more than 15 elephants. But there is debate about its length. Some paleontologists believe that it was the longest land animal that ever lived, measuring 45 to 50 m long. But other paleontologists say that *Seismosaurus* was only about 30 m long. Have students find out more about this controversy and write a paragraph stating their own conclusions.

Making Hypotheses

Scientists exploring the Texas Gulf Coast have discovered American Indian artifacts that are thousands of years old. The odd thing about it is that the artifacts were buried in the sea floor several meters below sea level. These artifacts were in-place, meaning that they had not been moved since they were originally buried. The *observation* is that there are American Indian artifacts several meters below sea level, and the *question* is, "Why are they there?" Your job is to *form a hypothesis* that answers this question. Remember, your hypothesis must be stated in such a way that it can be tested using the scientific method.

Answer to APPLY
Answers will vary. The most accepted hypothesis is that sea level has risen since the artifacts were originally placed. This hypothesis is testable through the analysis of other evidence that suggests sea level was once lower. For example, old river channels have been found below sea level in the same area as the artifacts.

Test the Hypothesis

Once a hypothesis is established, it must be tested. Scientists test hypotheses by gathering data that can help determine whether the hypotheses are valid or not. Often a scientist will run experiments to test a hypothesis.

To test a hypothesis, a scientist may conduct a controlled experiment. *A controlled experiment* is an experiment that tests only one factor at a time. By changing only one factor (the *variable*), scientists can see the results of just that one change. Earth scientists, however, usually rely more heavily on observations to test their hypotheses. Instead of trying to control nature, Earth scientists more often observe nature and collect large amounts of data to test their hypotheses.

To test his hypothesis, Gillette took hundreds of measurements of the bones and compared his measurements with those of bones from known dinosaurs. He visited museums and talked with other paleontologists. His testing took more than a year to complete.

Analyze the Results

Once scientists finish their tests, they must analyze the results. In this step, scientists often create tables and graphs to organize their data. When Gillette analyzed the results of the bone comparisons, he found that the bones of the mystery dinosaur were either too large or shaped too differently to have belonged to any of the dinosaurs he used for comparison.

Test the Hypothesis

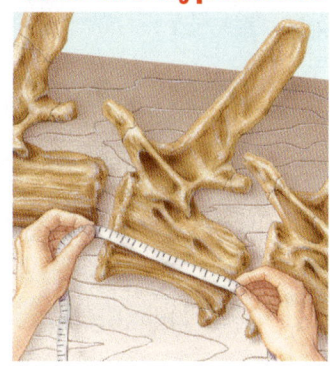

Test the hypothesis with observations or experiments.

Analyze the Results

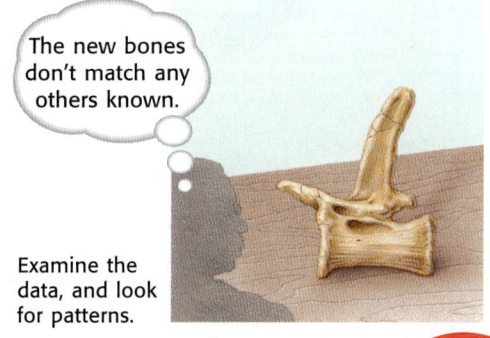

The new bones don't match any others known.

Examine the data, and look for patterns.

BRAIN FOOD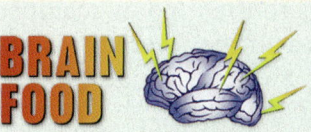

Just because experimental results do not match your hypothesis does not mean that the experiment was a failure. Emphasize to students that unexpected results are often more useful than proving a hypothesis correct. Sometimes scientists make new observations or discoveries while testing a hypothesis. These discoveries might require scientists to start over and rethink their original hypothesis. Ask students whether the scientific method is a linear process or a complex circular one and discuss how different steps could be connected.

CONNECT TO PHYSICAL SCIENCE

Unearthing *Seismosaurus* took 7 years. The bones were so deeply embedded in sandstone that Gillette asked for help from the Los Alamos National Laboratory. The lab staff devised an experimental way to use ground-penetrating radar and magnetometers to pinpoint the location of bone inside solid rock. Although the laboratory helped locate the dinosaur, Gillette's team still put in many hard hours excavating the fossil with hammers, picks, and shovels.

MISCONCEPTION ALERT

Most people think of laboratories, bubbling test tubes, flashing screens, and white coats when they hear the word *experiment*. In Earth science, though, the laboratory is most often outdoors. Often, Earth science phenomena cannot be observed under controlled conditions—you can't make a volcano erupt at will. In these cases, Earth scientists make many observations and use statistics and long-term records to predict when an event, such as an eruption, will occur.

Section 2 • The Scientific Method in Earth Science

3) Extend

CROSS-DISCIPLINARY FOCUS

Language Arts Communicating results is an important part of science. Have students choose an important scientific discovery and then present those findings to their fellow scientists in class as if they were the discoverer. Students should write and read a brief speech describing their accomplishment. Encourage students to be creative as well as concise and clear. Other students should prepare questions relating to the discovery.

MEETING INDIVIDUAL NEEDS

Advanced Learners Austrian-born philosopher Karl Popper once said, "A scientific idea can never be proven true, because no matter how many observations seem to agree with it, it may still be wrong." Discuss this statement and ask students to explain why they agree or disagree.

DEBATE

Have students research the ways that the scientific method is applied by agribusinesses to increase the yield of their harvests. Suggest that students find out about tests in experimental plots and the genetic engineering of seeds. Students should also research the potential risks to human health and the environment that genetically engineered crops pose. Ask them to consider whether or not genetically engineered seeds should be patented and owned by private companies and what the rights of small farmers should be. Have student groups outline their positions and debate these topics in class.

Draw Conclusions Finally, after carefully analyzing the results of their tests, scientists must draw conclusions. Scientists must conclude whether the results supported the hypothesis. If the hypothesis was not supported, scientists may repeat the investigation to check for errors. Or they may ask new questions and form a new hypothesis.

Based on all his analyses, Gillette concluded that the eight bones found in New Mexico were indeed from a newly discovered dinosaur species that was probably 45 m long and weighed at least 100 tons. The creature certainly fit the name Gillette gave it—*Seismosaurus hallorum,* the "earth shaker."

Decide if the original hypothesis is supported.

Communicate Results Upon completing an investigation, scientists communicate their results. In this way, scientists share what they have learned with other scientists, who may want to repeat the investigation to see if they get the same results. Science depends on the sharing of information.

Scientists share information by publishing reports in scientific journals. Scientists also give lectures on the results of their scientific investigations at professional meetings.

Gillette announced his discovery of *Seismosaurus* at a press conference at the New Mexico Museum of Natural History and Science. He later submitted a report to the *Journal of Vertebrate Paleontology* that summarized his investigation.

Share your discoveries with other scientists.

Figure 11 This reconstruction of the skeleton of *Seismosaurus hallorum* is based on Gillette's research. The bones shown in the darker color are those that have so far been identified.

Science Bloopers

In 1989, two scientists from the University of Utah held a press conference to announce that they accomplished nuclear fusion using a method called *cold fusion.* They claimed this would offer the world cheap, clean, and unlimited energy. Their press release went directly to the public, and their work was not first reviewed by other scientists. Within five weeks, scientists around the world discredited their work because the results could not be duplicated. Unable to provide data on how their apparatus created cold fusion, the two scientists were forced to withdraw their paper from a prestigious journal.

Case Closed?

All of the *Seismosaurus* bones that Gillette found have been dug up, but the *Seismosaurus* project continues in a laboratory phase as the remains of one of the largest dinosaurs ever discovered are still being studied. Like so many other scientific investigations, Gillette's work led to new problems to be explored using the scientific method.

To try your hand at using the scientific method, turn to page 630 in the LabBook.

Figure 12 *David Gillette continues to study the bones of Seismosaurus for new insights into the past.*

REVIEW

1. What is the scientific method? How do scientists use it?
2. After observing eight tailbones, Gillette hypothesized that they were from a newly discovered dinosaur species. What was his hypothesis based on?
3. Why do scientists communicate the results of their investigations?
4. **Applying Concepts** Why might two scientists develop different hypotheses based on the same observations?

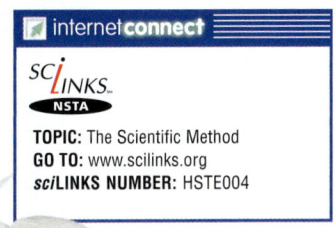

internet connect

SCILINKS NSTA
TOPIC: The Scientific Method
GO TO: www.scilinks.org
sciLINKS NUMBER: HSTE004

Using the Scientific Method

4) Close

Quiz

1. Why is a hypothesis called an educated guess? Why must it be testable? (A hypothesis is a solution based on previous knowledge, so it is an educated guess. No conclusion can be reached if the hypothesis cannot be tested.)
2. What options does a scientist have if an experiment does not support a hypothesis? (A scientist could repeat the investigation to check for errors, ask new questions and form a new hypothesis, or simply communicate the results of the experiment.)
3. What would happen if scientists kept their experimental results secret? (Efforts and mistakes would be duplicated; there would be less scientific progress.)

ALTERNATIVE ASSESSMENT

Have students write a detective story in which the detective solves a mystery using the scientific method. Encourage them to make the story flow naturally and to avoid merely listing steps in the process. Have students exchange stories and identify each of the steps used.

Problem Solving Worksheet 1 "Kryptonite!"

Answers to Review

1. The scientific method is a series of steps that scientists use to answer questions and solve problems. Scientists follow the steps of the scientific method to gain insights into the problems they investigate.
2. He based his conclusion on the observation that the bones did not match tailbones of any known dinosaur.
3. It is important that scientists communicate because science depends on the exchange of information.
4. Answers will vary. Interpretations are influenced by a number of factors, including previous studies the scientist has conducted.

SECTION 3

Focus

Life in a Warmer World—An Earth Science Model

This section discusses the importance of models in science and defines physical, mathematical, and conceptual models. Students will explore how a mathematical model is used to predict global warming. Students also see how models may be a limited but important tool for prediction.

🔔 Bellringer

Ask students to answer the following questions:

- Why is an airplane flight simulator a kind of model?
- What are some advantages to training pilots in a flight simulator rather than in a real airplane?

1 Motivate

ACTIVITY

Modeling a Human Leg On a table, place two half-meter lengths of lightweight wood, a metal hinge, screws, a screwdriver, and several large rubber bands. Ask students to help you use these materials to make a model of the human leg and to show how it works. Pose questions such as the following:

- In what ways would your model be like an actual leg?
- In what ways would it differ?
- For what purpose might you use the model?

 Directed Reading Worksheet 1 Section 3

Section 3

Terms to Learn

global warming
model
theory

What You'll Do

- Demonstrate how models are used in science.
- Compare mathematical models with physical models.
- Determine limitations of models.

Life in a Warmer World— An Earth Science Model

There has been a lot of talk lately about changes in Earth's climate. Some people think the world is getting dangerously warm; others say it is only a natural cycle. But what would happen if Earth's average surface-air temperature rose only a few degrees? Look at **Figure 13;** the answers might surprise you.

A worldwide increase in temperature is called **global warming.** Is global warming really happening? What would cause global warming? To answer these questions, many scientists are studying the concept of global warming. One way they study global warming is by making a model of it.

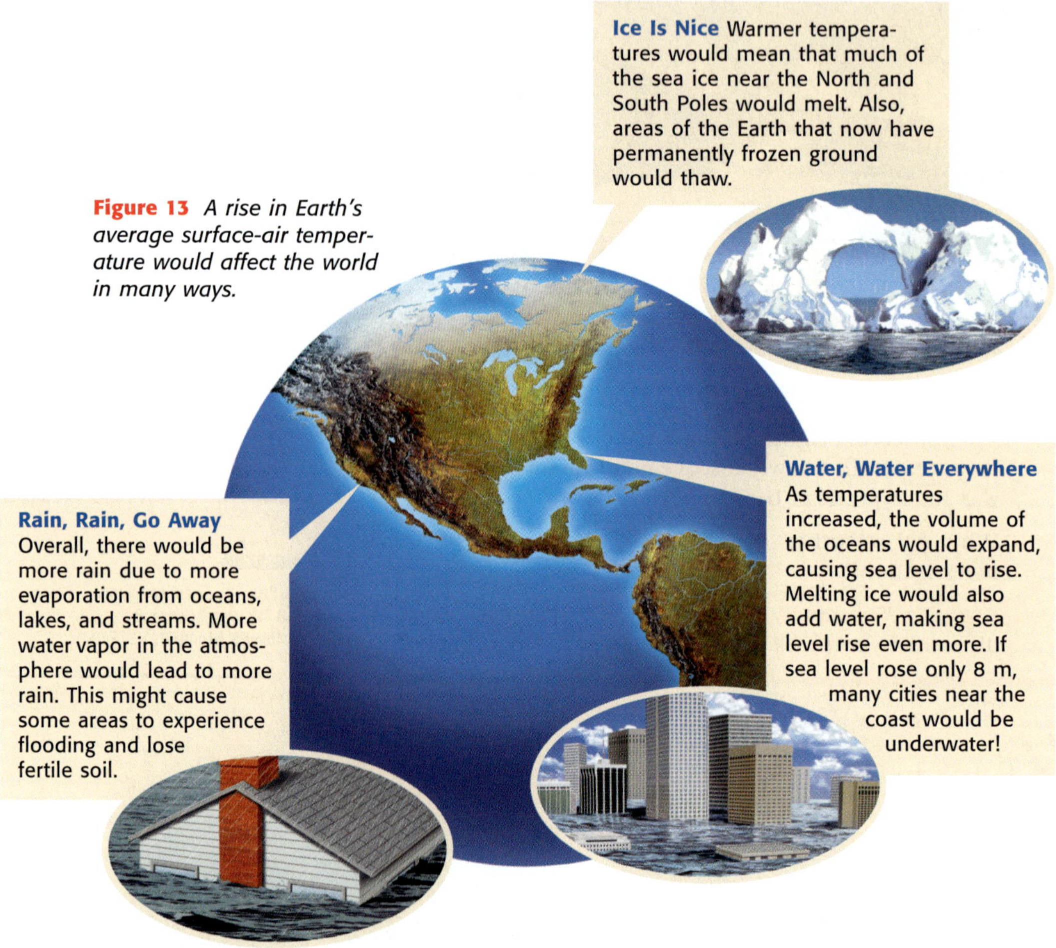

Ice Is Nice Warmer temperatures would mean that much of the sea ice near the North and South Poles would melt. Also, areas of the Earth that now have permanently frozen ground would thaw.

Figure 13 A rise in Earth's average surface-air temperature would affect the world in many ways.

Rain, Rain, Go Away Overall, there would be more rain due to more evaporation from oceans, lakes, and streams. More water vapor in the atmosphere would lead to more rain. This might cause some areas to experience flooding and lose fertile soil.

Water, Water Everywhere As temperatures increased, the volume of the oceans would expand, causing sea level to rise. Melting ice would also add water, making sea level rise even more. If sea level rose only 8 m, many cities near the coast would be underwater!

18

CONNECT TO LIFE SCIENCE

Point out to students that all of Earth's systems are closely linked. For example, if the Earth's temperature rose as a consequence of global warming, the rate of decay of plant and animal remains would increase. This would contribute even more CO_2 to the atmosphere, further exacerbating global warming. One possible indicator of global warming is shorter winters. Scientists study plants in the Northern Hemisphere to see when their springtime growing season begins. Today, trees and grasses begin to sprout new leaves a full week earlier than they did just 20 years ago.

Types of Scientific Models

You are probably familiar with many types of models—models of ships, cars, planes, buildings, and other objects. **Models** are representations of objects or systems. Models are used to represent things that are too small to see, such as atoms, or too large to completely see, like the Earth or the solar system. Models can also be used to explain the past and present as well as to predict the future. Scientific models come in three major types.

Figure 14 *Models of airplanes are tested in models of wind, as shown here by a prototype jet inside a wind tunnel.*

Physical Models Physical models are models that you can touch. Model airplanes, car kits, and dolls are all physical models. Physical models should look and act just like the real thing. For example, engineers put very accurate models of new airplanes in wind tunnels, as shown in **Figure 14,** to see how aerodynamic they are. It is safer and less expensive to discover problems with models than with real planes.

Mathematical Models Every day, people try to predict the weather. One way they do this is by using mathematical models. A mathematical model is made up of mathematical equations and data. Some mathematical models are so complex that only supercomputers can handle them. These models are complicated, but then so is trying to predict the weather!

Conceptual Models The third type of model is a conceptual model, or system of ideas. These take the form of theories. A **theory** is a unifying explanation for a broad range of hypotheses and observations that have been supported by testing. Atomic theory and the big bang theory can be thought of as conceptual models. Conceptual models are composed of many hypotheses, each of which has found support through the scientific method.

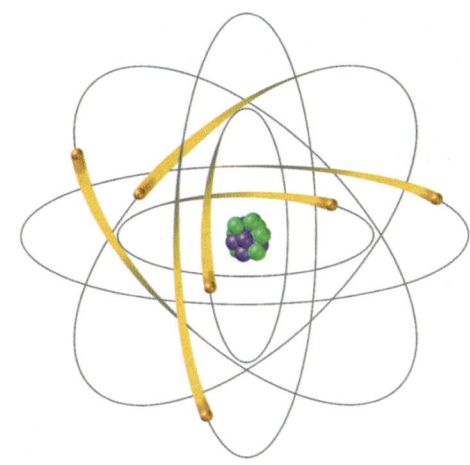

Figure 15 *Atoms are not really made up of tiny colored balls, but using a model like this helps scientists understand atoms.*

Homework

Identifying Models Have students use the weather section of the newspaper to identify uses of physical, mathematical, and conceptual models. For example, a mathematical model may be used to predict how likely it is that it will rain on a certain day. A physical model, specifically a map, may be used to show the locations of pressure fronts or storms. A conceptual model may be used to explain long-term trends in the weather.

2) Teach

ACTIVITY

Display a variety of models of Earth, such as globes, political maps, satellite photos, and weather maps. Invite volunteers to describe each model, suggest uses for it, and compare and contrast it to another model. Sheltered English

DISCUSSION

Use a model car and a map to discuss with students what a scale model is. A unit of measure in the model is equivalent to a larger or smaller unit of measure in the original. For example, in a model car, 1 cm might equal 15 cm on the actual vehicle. Point out the legend on the map, and ask students to explain how distance on the map relates to actual miles or kilometers.

MATH and MORE

Assign students to groups. Have each group select a large object to measure and record its dimensions. Have them plan a scale model of the object (suggest a one-tenth scale). Ask them to calculate the dimensions of their scale model and draw it. After the groups finish their drawings, discuss the methods they used to create their scale drawings. Have students devise strategies for creating more-accurate scale models, and have them work individually to create their own scale drawings.

Math Skills Worksheet 17
"Using Proportions and Cross-Multiplication"

Science Skills Worksheet 15
"Measuring"

Section 3 • Life in a Warmer World—An Earth Science Model

3 Extend

CROSS-DISCIPLINARY FOCUS

History From about A.D. 800 to 1250, Europe's climate was much milder than it is today. The milder climate could explain why Norse settlers migrated to Iceland, Greenland, and possibly even North America. Have students find out about the Norse expansion and the climatic changes that may have ended it.

COOPERATIVE LEARNING

Ask students to create skits demonstrating the greenhouse effect, using the four stages in **Figure 16.** Students can choose to model the following:

- sunlight traveling to Earth
- heat radiating from Earth's surface
- greenhouse gases
- heat radiating back toward Earth

Sheltered English

GROUP ACTIVITY

Poster Project Have students work with partners to create posters illustrating the factors that contribute to global warming. They will first need to research the effects of deforestation and air pollution on the carbon cycle. Stress that this visual aid will be a model that shows how the greenhouse effect works and how human activity contributes to it.

TOPIC: Using Models in Earth Science
GO TO: www.scilinks.org
sciLINKS NUMBER: HSTE015

Environment CONNECTION

The destruction of rain forests has been linked to increases in the greenhouse effect. Trees play a vital role in taking in carbon dioxide from the air, storing it, and releasing oxygen into the air. Without trees, more carbon dioxide would remain in the air, which would increase the greenhouse effect and possibly contribute to global warming.

The Global-Warming Model

All models have pieces. A model ship, for example, may contain hundreds of pieces that are glued together. Mathematical models also contain pieces. The pieces are numbers representing information that describe real events. The global-warming model is a mathematical model designed to help scientists predict future temperature changes of the Earth's atmosphere. One of the pieces used in the global-warming model is the *greenhouse effect*.

Greenhouse Effect
A greenhouse is a building made mostly of glass in which plants are grown. If you have been in a greenhouse, you know that it is usually warmer inside than outside. This is because sunlight not only heats the greenhouse directly after passing through the glass, but the glass also traps thermal energy inside the greenhouse. The greenhouse effect, shown in **Figure 16,** works a lot like a greenhouse made of glass.

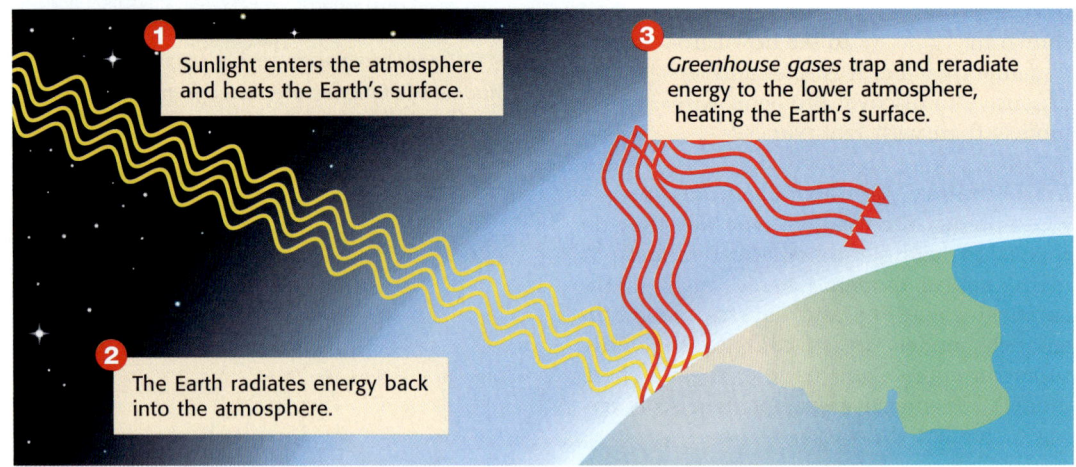

Figure 16 The greenhouse effect is partly responsible for the Earth's moderate temperatures, which are suitable to support life.

1. Sunlight enters the atmosphere and heats the Earth's surface.
2. The Earth radiates energy back into the atmosphere.
3. Greenhouse gases trap and reradiate energy to the lower atmosphere, heating the Earth's surface.

Testing the Global-Warming Model

Models are used to try to explain the present. But how do we know if models are accurate? Physical, mathematical, and conceptual models can be tested. For instance, we can compare the model of a car with the real car. Similarly, we can compare our global-warming model's prediction of Earth's temperature changes with Earth's actual temperature changes. If the model can accurately explain the present, then we can be more confident that the model will be able to accurately predict the future.

Teaching Transparency 102 "A Model of Global Warming"

SCIENTISTS AT ODDS

Some scientists fear that human actions, such as deforestation and the burning of fossil fuels, are causing Earth's temperatures to rise at an abnormally fast rate. Other scientists believe that Earth is simply in a normal temperature fluctuation (from colder to warmer temperatures) that lasts thousands of years. Ask students to find evidence for both theories.

Scientists have estimated the amount of carbon dioxide that has been added to the atmosphere over the last 100 years. The model should therefore be able to predict how much warmer the atmosphere is today than it was 100 years ago. Most global-warming models tell us that overall temperature change due to increased greenhouse gases during the last 100 years should be between 0.5°C and 1.5°C. Now comes the test: How much global warming has actually taken place? The answer is 0.5°C. So far so good!

Using the Global-Warming Model

Models are used to predict the future and are good for answering, "What if?"

Because trees take in CO_2, what will happen if we reduce the number of trees we cut down each year?

What will happen if people use more-fuel-efficient engines?

What will happen if we cut our CO_2 emissions in half over the next 50 years?

These are the kinds of questions that many scientists are asking as they enter the new millennium. The global-warming model can give them answers, but will these answers be accurate? The more complicated models are, the more careful scientists must be when using them to make predictions. The global-warming model is extremely complicated, so scientists often use words like *possible* and *probable* when making predictions. The only certain test of this model is the test of time.

REVIEW

1. How might a scientist use a model to test a new airplane design?
2. How are astronomers limited when they design models of the universe?
3. **Analyzing Relationships** Name one advantage of physical models and one advantage of mathematical models.

TOPIC: Using Models in Earth Science
GO TO: www.scilinks.org
*sci*LINKS **NUMBER:** HSTE015

4) Close

Quiz

1. What do scientists use models for? (to test hypotheses, explain events or behaviors, or predict future events or conditions)

2. What is the difference between the greenhouse effect and the global-warming model? (The greenhouse effect is a phenomenon that has been observed and can be explained using many different models. The greenhouse effect makes life on Earth possible. The global-warming model is a hypothesis used to predict the consequences of an increase in the greenhouse effect.)

3. How does a model help scientists predict that Earth's climate will continue to get warmer? (They measure changes in climate and other factors, such as global temperatures and CO_2 levels. Over time, they integrate the information into their model, see how the model compares with reality, and then make their predictions.)

ALTERNATIVE ASSESSMENT

Making Models
Have students construct a physical model. It could be a model of a room, a living thing, or a phenomenon, such as wave motion. Students should explain in writing what the model is and describe how it works and how it was constructed. They should also describe how the model can be used and what its limits are.

▼ Answers to Review

1. Sample answer: Scientists could make a scale model of the proposed airplane and test it in a wind tunnel.
2. They cannot base everything in their model on what they can observe. The universe extends far beyond the limits of human perception.
3. Answers will vary. Physical models can often be more easily understood because they can be seen and touched. Mathematical models often better represent complex, large-scale phenomena.

SECTION 4

Focus

Measurement and Safety

This section introduces the International System of Units (SI), a unified global measurement system. Students explore the units and methods used to measure length, volume, mass, and temperature. Students also learn about lab safety and safety symbols and their meanings.

Bellringer

Ask students the following questions:

- What kinds of things would be best measured in millimeters? in meters? in kilometers?
- What kinds of things would be best measured in liters? in milliliters?
- What kinds of things would be best measured in milligrams? in metric tons? in kilograms?

Ask students to write their responses in their ScienceLog. Discuss their answers.

1) Motivate

DISCUSSION

Tell students that the SI system is based on the decimal system, just like our monetary system. Ask students the following questions:

How many pennies are in a dime? How many dimes are in a dollar? How many pennies are in 10 dollars?

Explain to students that the SI system uses different prefixes to signify larger or smaller units. Have students look at **Figure 17** and identify the prefixes and what they stand for.

Section 4

Terms to Learn

meter
volume
mass
temperature

What You'll Do

- Explain the importance of the International System of Units.
- Determine appropriate units to use for particular measurements.
- Identify lab safety symbols and determine what they mean.

Figure 17 *Prefixes are used with SI units to convert them to larger or smaller units. The prefix used depends on the size of the object being measured.*

Measurement and Safety

Hundreds of years ago, different countries used different systems of measurement. At one time in England, the standard for an inch was three grains of barley placed end to end. Other standardized units were based on parts of the body, such as the foot. Such units were not very accurate because they were based on objects that varied in size.

Eventually people recognized that there was a need for a global measurement system that was simple and accurate. In the late 1700s, the French Academy of Sciences set out to develop that system. Over the next 200 years, the metric system, now called the International System of Units (SI), was refined.

Using the SI System

Today most scientists and almost all countries use the International System of Units. One advantage of using SI measurements is that it helps all scientists to share and compare their observations and results. Another advantage of SI is that all units are based on the number 10, which is a number that is easy to use in calculations. The table in **Figure 17** contains the commonly used SI units for length, volume, mass, and temperature.

	Common SI Units	
Length	meter (m)	
	kilometer (km)	1 km = 1,000 m
	decimeter (dm)	1 dm = 0.1 m
	centimeter (cm)	1 cm = 0.01 m
	millimeter (mm)	1 mm = 0.001 m
	micrometer (μm)	1 μm = 0.000001 m
	nanometer (nm)	1 nm = 0.000 000 001 m
Volume	cubic meter (m^3)	
	cubic centimeter (cm^3)	1 cm^3 = 0.000 001 m^3
	liter (L)	1 L = 1 dm^3 = 0.001 m^3
	milliliter (mL)	1 mL = 0.001 L = 1 cm^3
Mass	kilogram (kg)	
	gram (g)	1 g = 0.001 kg
	milligram (mg)	1 mg = 0.000 001 kg
Temperature	Kelvin (K)	
	Celsius (°C)	0°C = 273 K
		100°C = 373 K

Directed Reading Worksheet 1 Section 4

Math Skills Worksheet 27 "What Is SI?"

IS THAT A FACT!

If Earth were the size of a golf ball, the sun would be as large as a 3 m ball and would be located a football field's distance from Earth.

22 Chapter 1 • The World of Earth Science

Measuring Length How thick is the ice sheet in **Figure 18**? To describe this length, an Earth scientist would probably use meters (m). A **meter** is the basic unit of length in the SI system. A meter is divided or multiplied by powers of 10 to produce the other SI units of length. If you divide 1 m into 100 parts, for example, each part equals 1 cm. In other words, 1 cm is one-hundredth of a meter. Some objects are so tiny that even smaller units must be used. To describe the length of microscopic objects, micrometers (µm) or nanometers (nm) are used. Going the other way, 1,000 m is equal to one kilometer. **Figure 19** shows how the units of length relate to various objects.

Figure 18 *This scientist is measuring the thickness of an ice sheet.*

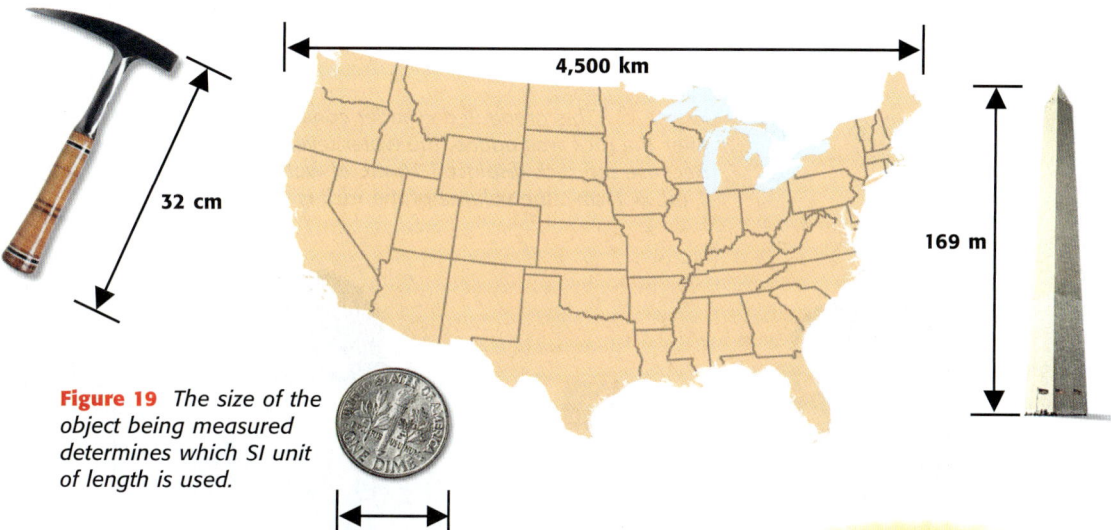

Figure 19 *The size of the object being measured determines which SI unit of length is used.*

Measuring Volume Imagine that you're a scientist who needs to move some fossils to a museum. How many fossils will fit into a crate? That depends on the volume of the crate and the volume of each fossil. **Volume** is the amount of space that something occupies, or, as in the case of the crate, the amount of space that something contains.

The volume of a liquid is often given in liters (L). Liters are based on the meter. A cubic meter (m^3) is equal to 1,000 L. In other words, 1,000 L of liquid will fit into a box 1 m on each side. Just like the meter, the liter can be divided into smaller units. A milliliter (mL) is one-thousandth of a liter and is equal to one cubic centimeter (1 cm^3). A microliter (µL) is one-millionth of a liter. Graduated cylinders are used to measure the volume of liquids.

Activity

Measure the width of your desk, but do not use a ruler or a tape measure. Pick an object to use as your unit of measurement. It could be a pencil, your hand, or anything else. Find how many units wide your desk is, and compare your measurement with those of your classmates. In your ScienceLog, explain why it is important to use standard units of measurement.

Science Bloopers

The meter was originally defined as one ten-millionth of the distance along the meridian running from the North Pole to the equator through Dunkirk, France, and Barcelona, Spain. French surveyors determined this length in 1798 after working for 6 years. Almost 100 years later, it was discovered that the surveyors had made an error of about 3.2 km in their measurement. Today, a meter is defined as the distance light travels in 1/299,792,458 of a second in a vacuum.

3) Extend

MATH and MORE

Give students the following dimensions for the crate in **Figure 20:**

volume: 40,392 cm³

length: 51 cm

width: 33 cm

Test their comprehension of volume by asking them to calculate the height.

$$\frac{40{,}392 \text{ cm}^3}{(51 \text{ cm} \times 33 \text{ cm})} = 24 \text{ cm}$$

CONNECT TO PHYSICAL SCIENCE

Students often confuse mass and weight. Point out to students that mass is a measure of the amount of matter that makes up an object. Weight is expressed in newtons and measures the gravitational force between objects. If a given object has not lost or gained matter, its mass will be the same anywhere in the universe. The weight of an object, however, varies with gravitational attraction. Use the Teaching Transparency below to discuss this distinction with students.

Teaching Transparency 204 "Differences Between Mass and Weight"

 **TOPIC:** Systems of Measurement
GO TO: www.scilinks.org
sciLINKS NUMBER: HSTE020

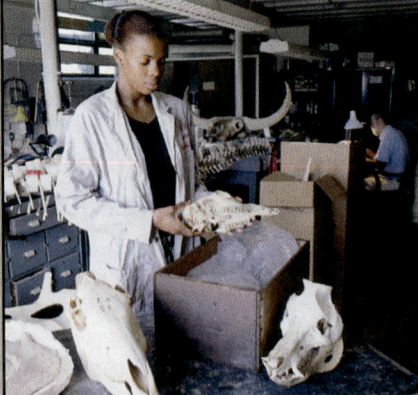

Figure 20 The volume of the crate can be calculated by multiplying its length by its width by its height.

Measuring Volume of Solids The volume of a large solid object is given in cubic meters (m³). The volumes of smaller objects, such as the crate in **Figure 20,** can be given in cubic centimeters (cm³) or cubic millimeters (mm³). To calculate the volume of a box-shaped object, multiply the object's length by its width by its height.

Objects like fossils and rocks have irregular shapes. If you multiplied only their length, width, and height, you would not get a very accurate measure of their volume. One way to determine the volume of an irregularly shaped object is to measure how much liquid the object displaces. The student in **Figure 21** is measuring the volume of a rock by placing it in a graduated cylinder that contains a known quantity of water. The student can find the volume of the rock by subtracting the volume of the water alone from the volume of the water and the rock.

Figure 21 This graduated cylinder contains 70 mL of water. After the rock was added, the water level moved to 80 mL. Because the rock displaced 10 mL of water, and because 1 mL = 1 cm³, the volume of the rock is 10 cm³.

Mass How large of a boulder can a rushing stream move? That depends on the energy of the stream and the mass of the boulder. **Mass** is the amount of matter that something is made of. The kilogram (kg) is the basic unit for mass and is used to describe the mass of things like boulders. Many common objects are not so large, however. Grams are used to describe the mass of smaller objects, such as an apple. The mass of large objects, such as an elephant, is given in metric tons. A metric ton equals 1,000 kg.

Homework

Finding Safety Risks Have students choose five photographs from magazines and label each with appropriate safety cautions. Students should use the safety symbols shown in this section. Ask students to explain to the class how each photo depicts a safety risk. <mark>Sheltered English</mark>

Q: What happened when the inchworm went metric?

A: It became a centipede!

Temperature How hot is a lava flow? To answer this question, an Earth scientist would need to measure the temperature of the lava. **Temperature** is a measure of how hot (or cold) something is. You are probably used to describing temperature with degrees Fahrenheit (°F). Scientists use degrees Celsius (°C) and kelvins, which is the SI unit for temperature. The thermometer at right shows the relationship between °F and °C. Degrees Celsius is the unit you will most often see in this book.

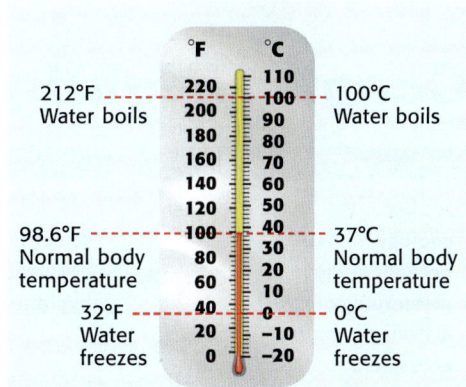

Safety Rules!

Earth science is exciting and fun, but it can also be dangerous. So don't take any chances! Always follow your teacher's instructions, and don't take short-cuts—even when you think there is little or no danger.

Before starting any science investigation, get your teacher's permission and read the lab procedures carefully. Pay particular attention to safety information and caution statements. The table below shows the safety symbols used in this book. Get to know these symbols and what they mean. Do this by reading the safety information starting on page 626. **This is important!** If you are still unsure about what a safety symbol means, ask your teacher.

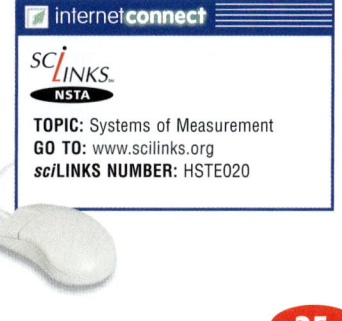

Stay on the safe side by reading the safety information on page 626. **This is a must before doing any science activity!**

Safety Symbols

- Eye protection
- Clothing protection
- Hand safety
- Heating safety
- Electric safety
- Sharp object
- Chemical safety
- Animal safety
- Plant safety

REVIEW

1. What are two benefits of using the International System of Units?
2. Which SI unit best describes the volume of gasoline in a car?
3. **Doing Calculations** What is the minimum length and width (in meters) of a box that can contain an object 56 cm wide and 843 mm long?

TOPIC: Systems of Measurement
GO TO: www.scilinks.org
sciLINKS NUMBER: HSTE020

Answers to Review

1. It helps all scientists to share and compare observations and results, and all units are based on the number 10, which is a number that is easy to use in calculations.
2. liters
3. length = 0.843 m, width = 0.56 m

Chapter Highlights

VOCABULARY DEFINITIONS

SECTION 1

geology the study of the solid Earth

oceanography the study of the ocean

meteorology the study of the entire atmosphere

astronomy the study of all physical objects beyond Earth

ecosystem a community of organisms and their nonliving environment

SECTION 2

scientific method a series of steps that scientists use to answer questions and solve problems

observation any use of the senses to gather information

hypothesis a possible explanation or answer to a question

 Science Skills Worksheet 7 "Improving Your Study Habits"

Chapter Highlights

SECTION 1

Vocabulary
- geology (p. 6)
- oceanography (p. 7)
- meteorology (p. 8)
- astronomy (p. 9)
- ecosystem (p. 10)

Section Notes
- Earth science can be divided into three general categories: geology, oceanography, and meteorology.
- Astronomy is the study of physical things beyond planet Earth.
- Careers in Earth science often require knowledge of more than one science.

SECTION 2

Vocabulary
- scientific method (p. 13)
- observation (p. 14)
- hypothesis (p. 14)

Section Notes
- The scientific method is essential for proper scientific investigation.
- Scientists may use the scientific method differently.
- The discovery of *Seismosaurus hallorum* as a new kind of dinosaur was made using the scientific method.
- When scientists finish investigations, it is important that they communicate the results to other scientists.

Labs
Using the Scientific Method (p. 630)

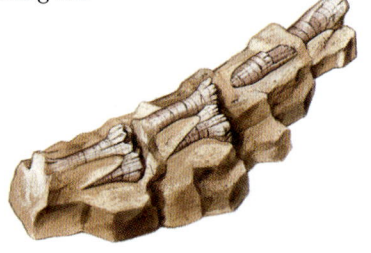

✓ Skills Check

Math Concepts

CONVERTING SI UNITS Take another look at the SI chart on page 22. The SI units for most categories of measurement, such as length and mass, are all expressed in terms of a single unit. For example, the unit *centimeter* is expressed in terms of the unit *meter*. To write 50 cm in terms of meters, divide 50 by 100 (there are 100 cm in 1 m).

$$50 \text{ cm} \times \frac{1 \text{ m}}{100 \text{ cm}} = 0.5 \text{ m}$$

Visual Understanding

WHICH PATH SHOULD YOU FOLLOW? Review the flowchart on page 13. The scientific method can follow many paths. For example, a scientist may make observations before asking a question or after forming a hypothesis.

Lab and Activity Highlights

Using the Scientific Method **PG 630**

 Datasheets for LabBook (blackline masters for this lab)

26 Chapter 1 • The World of Earth Science

SECTION 3

Vocabulary
global warming *(p. 18)*
model *(p. 19)*
theory *(p. 19)*

Section Notes
- Models are used in science to represent physical things and systems.
- Typically, physical models represent objects, and mathematical models represent systems.
- The global-warming model is a mathematical model.
- The greenhouse effect is an important part of the global-warming model.
- Scientists use models to explain the past and present as well as to predict the future.
- The only way to measure the accuracy of a model is to compare predictions based on the model with what actually occurs.

SECTION 4

Vocabulary
meter *(p. 23)*
volume *(p. 23)*
mass *(p. 24)*
temperature *(p. 25)*

Section Notes
- The International System of Units (SI) helps all scientists share and compare their work.
- The basic SI units of measurement for length, volume, and mass are the meter, cubic meter, and kilogram, respectively.
- To describe temperature, scientists use degrees Celsius (°C) and kelvins (K), which is the SI unit for temperature.

VOCABULARY DEFINITIONS, continued

SECTION 3

global warming a rise in average global temperatures

model a representation of an object or system

theory a unifying explanation for a broad range of hypotheses and observations that have been supported by testing

SECTION 4

meter the basic unit of length in the SI system

volume the amount of space that something occupies or the amount of space that something contains

mass the amount of matter that something is made of; its value does not change with the object's location

temperature a measure of how hot (or cold) something is

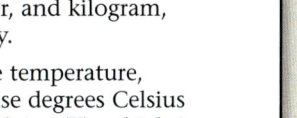

internetconnect

GO TO: go.hrw.com

Visit the **HRW** Web site for a variety of learning tools related to this chapter. Just type in the keyword:

KEYWORD: HSTWES

SC**iLINKS**
N S T A
GO TO: www.scilinks.org

Visit the **National Science Teachers Association** on-line Web site for Internet resources related to this chapter. Just type in the *sci*LINKS number for more information about the topic:

TOPIC: Branches of Earth Science	*sci*LINKS NUMBER: HSTE005
TOPIC: Careers in Earth Science	*sci*LINKS NUMBER: HSTE010
TOPIC: The Scientific Method	*sci*LINKS NUMBER: HSTE004
TOPIC: Using Models in Earth Science	*sci*LINKS NUMBER: HSTE015
TOPIC: Systems of Measurement	*sci*LINKS NUMBER: HSTE020

Vocabulary Review Worksheet 1

Blackline masters of these Chapter Highlights can be found in the **Study Guide.**

Lab and Activity **Highlights**

LabBank

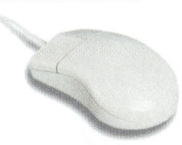
Whiz-Bang Demonstrations, Tubby Terra, Demo 16

Long-Term Projects & Research Ideas, How Big Is the Earth? Project 29

Chapter Review Answers

USING VOCABULARY

1. The scientific method involves forming a hypothesis that must be tested.
2. Models are used in meteorology to predict weather.
3. Studying geology can be part of studying an ecosystem.
4. Part of oceanography involves studying global warming because global warming may cause a rise in sea level.

UNDERSTANDING CONCEPTS

Multiple Choice

5. b
6. a
7. c
8. a
9. a
10. d
11. d
12. d
13. d

Short Answer

14. He compared the bones he found with similar bones from known dinosaurs. He could not find a match.
15. Answers may vary. Scientists use models to represent things that are too small or too large to see, to test designs and hypotheses, to explain the past, and to predict the future.
16. Sunlight passes through the greenhouse glass and is absorbed by the Earth's surface. This energy is then reradiated and warms the greenhouse.

Chapter Review

USING VOCABULARY

Use the following terms in a sentence to show that you know what they mean:

1. hypothesis, scientific method
2. meteorology, model
3. geology, ecosystem
4. global warming, oceanography

UNDERSTANDING CONCEPTS

Multiple Choice

5. Earth science can be divided into three general categories: meteorology, oceanography, and
   a. geography.
   b. geology.
   c. geochemistry.
   d. ecology.

6. The science that deals with fossils is
   a. paleontology.
   b. ecology.
   c. seismology.
   d. volcanology.

7. Meteorology is the study of
   a. meteors.
   b. meteorites.
   c. the atmosphere.
   d. maps.

8. Gillette's hypothesis was
   a. supported by his results.
   b. not supported by his results.
   c. based only on observations.
   d. based only on what he already knew.

9. Two of the most common greenhouse gases are water vapor (H_2O) and
   a. carbon dioxide (CO_2).
   b. krypton (Kr).
   c. radon (Rn).
   d. neon (Ne).

10. Over the past 100 years, the average temperature of Earth's atmosphere has risen about
    a. 10°C.   c. 1°C.
    b. 5°C.   d. 0.5°C.

11. The greenhouse effect is used to explain
    a. volcanoes.
    b. earthquakes.
    c. fossilization.
    d. global warming.

12. Global warming would cause
    a. some polar ice to melt.
    b. more rain.
    c. overall rise in sea level.
    d. All of the above

13. An ecosystem can include
    a. plants and animals.
    b. weather and climate.
    c. humans.
    d. All of the above

Short Answer

14. How did Gillette determine that the dinosaur he found was new to science?
15. How and why do scientists use models?
16. Why is the temperature inside a greenhouse usually warmer than the temperature outside?

Concept Mapping

17. Use the following terms to create a concept map: Earth science, model, the scientific method, geology, hypothesis, meteorology, oceanography, observation, International System of Units.

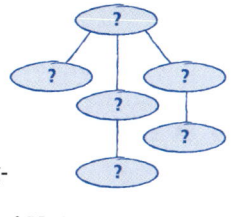

CRITICAL THINKING AND PROBLEM SOLVING

Write one or two sentences to answer the following questions:

18. A rock that contains fossil seashells might be studied by scientists in at least two branches of Earth science. Name those branches. Why did you choose those two?
19. Why might two scientists working on the same problem draw different conclusions?
20. The scientific method often begins with observation. How does observation limit what scientists can study?
21. Why are scientists so careful about making predictions from certain models, such as a global-warming model?

MATH IN SCIENCE

22. Scientists often use scientific laws when constructing models. According to Boyle's law, for example, if you increase the pressure outside a balloon, the balloon will get smaller. This law is expressed as the following formula:

$$P_1 \times V_1 = P_2 \times V_2$$

If the pressure on a balloon (P_1) is one atmosphere (1 atm) and the volume of air in the balloon (V_1) is one liter (1 L), what will the volume be (in liters) if the pressure is increased to 3 atm?

INTERPRETING GRAPHICS

Examine the graph below, and answer the questions that follow.

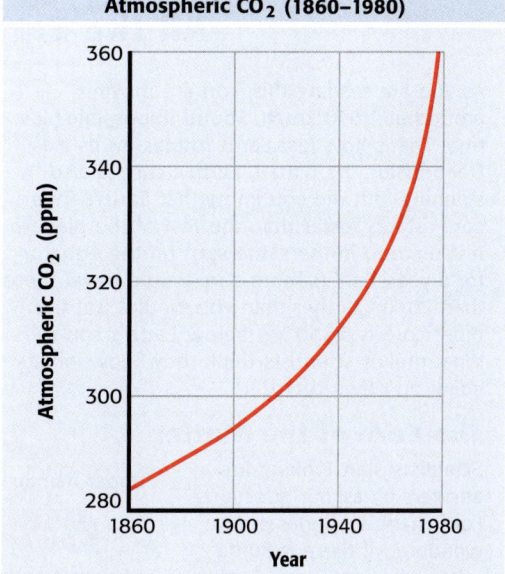

23. Has the amount of CO_2 in the atmosphere increased or decreased since 1860?
24. The line on the graph is curved. What does this mean?
25. Was the rate of change in the level of CO_2 between 1940 and 1960 higher or lower than it was between 1880 and 1900? How can you tell?

 Take a minute to review your answers to the Pre-Reading Questions found at the bottom of page 4. Have your answers changed? If necessary, revise your answers based on what you have learned since you began this chapter.

Concept Mapping

17. 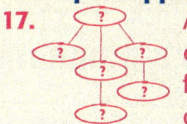 An answer to this exercise can be found at the end of this book.

CRITICAL THINKING AND PROBLEM SOLVING

18. Geology and oceanography; it relates to geology because it is a rock and it contains fossils. It relates to oceanography because it is a rock formed in the ocean and it contains fossils of marine animals.
19. They may make different observations, form different hypotheses, test the same hypothesis differently, or analyze the results of their tests differently.
20. Observation limits what scientists can study because hypotheses can be supported only by observable phenomena.
21. They are careful because models such as the global-warming model are based on very complex sets of data. In addition, the global-warming model predicts change over a long period of time, so it is not immediately testable. For a model to be reliable, it must remain accurate during repeated testing.

MATH IN SCIENCE

22. $\frac{1}{3}$ L

INTERPRETING GRAPHICS

23. The amount of CO_2 has increased.
24. The rate at which the amount of CO_2 in the atmosphere increases has changed over time.
25. higher; The graph's line curves more steeply between 1940 and 1960.

Concept Mapping Transparency 1

Blackline masters of this Chapter Review can be found in the **Study Guide.**

Chapter 1 • Chapter Review

ACROSS THE SCIENCES
All the Earth's a Magnet

Background
Geologists have known for a long time that a magnetic field surrounds the planet. Scientists suspected that the solid inner core had something to do with creating the magnetic field, but until recently they could only guess about the connection: the Earth is a huge electromagnet because the core rotates at a different speed than the mantle. The core rotates faster for the following reasons:

- The solid inner core, which is mostly iron, is surrounded by a liquid outer core, which means that it is possible for the inner core to rotate inside the outer core (not much friction exists between a solid and a liquid).

- Iron in the inner core is a conducting material, so it transmits billions of amps of electrical energy. This also drives the core to rotate slightly faster than the mantle.

ACROSS THE SCIENCES

EARTH SCIENCE • PHYSICAL SCIENCE

All the Earth's a Magnet

As you are reading this, you are moving around at 1,670 km/h. Sound impossible? It's true. That's how fast Earth rotates on its axis. Deep inside the planet, Earth's core is also spinning. But did you know that Earth's inner core rotates *faster* than the rest of the planet? If you stood in the same spot on the equator for a year, Earth's inner core would travel more than 20 km farther than you would! But the inner core is 5,150 km below Earth's surface. What makes scientists think they know what's going on down there?

The Core of the Matter
Scientists start looking for answers by asking questions. For instance, scientists have wondered if there is some relationship between Earth's core and Earth's magnetic field. To build their hypothesis, scientists started with what they knew: Earth has a dense, solid inner core and a molten outer core. They then created a computer model to simulate how Earth's magnetic field is generated. The model predicted that Earth's inner core spins in the same direction as the rest of the Earth but slightly faster than the surface. If that theory is correct, it might explain how Earth's magnetic field is generated. But how could the researchers test the theory?

Because scientists couldn't drill down to the core, they had to get their information indirectly. They decided to track seismic waves created by earthquakes.

Catch the Waves
Scientists analyzed 30 years' worth of earthquake seismic data. They knew that seismic waves traveling through the inner core along a north-south path travel faster than waves passing through it along an east-west line. Scientists searched seismic data records to see if the orientation of the "fast path" for seismic waves changed over time. They found that in the last 30 years, the direction of the "fast path" for seismic waves had indeed shifted. This is strong evidence that Earth's core does travel faster than the surface, and it strengthens the theory that the spinning core creates Earth's magnetic field.

Now That We Know . . .
This discovery will lead to more research into how Earth's magnetic field changes and how the north and south poles "wander" and even occasionally reverse. The new information may also lead to a better understanding of the role that heat plays in moving tectonic plates on Earth's surface.

Write About It
▶ Imagine what would happen if the magnetic poles were suddenly reversed or if magnetism disappeared completely. How would you be affected personally? How would it affect our civilization? Write a funny story describing a world with no magnetism.

Answers to Write About It

Stories will vary but could include the following information:

The Earth's magnetic field helps create the aurora borealis, or northern lights; makes compasses point north; and helps migratory animals keep their bearings. It also shields us from harmful solar radiation. Without a magnetic field, Earth probably could not support life as we know it.

CAREERS

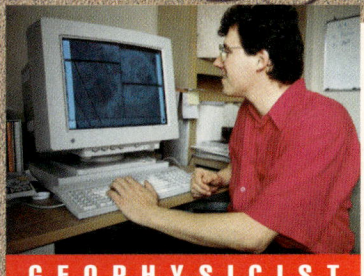

GEOPHYSICIST

Bob Grimm is looking for water on Mars. Grimm is a geophysicist, a scientist who uses the science of physics to study Earth, its structure, and its atmosphere. Some geophysicists try to answer questions about the origin and history of Earth, while others use their knowledge of Earth to answer questions about other planets. One of those questions is whether there is water on Mars.

It isn't likely that humans will be living on Mars anytime soon, so why try to find water there? Bob Grimm explains the importance of his work this way: "The search for water on Mars really is the search for life. Are there microorganisms, algae, or other primitive life-forms beneath the surface? By finding liquid water, we will know where to look for life."

Probing Mars

Grimm isn't going to Mars in person. Instead, he and others are developing instruments to send to Mars to try to locate water beneath that planet's surface. These instruments work by reading patterns of electromagnetic waves reflected by formations beneath the surface. When electromagnetic waves hit something under the surface that conducts electricity, the pattern of the waves changes. By looking at the patterns in the waves as they are reflected back to the equipment, Grimm and others will be able to "see" what lies beneath Mars's surface. If there is underground water on Mars, it should show up as a change in the wave patterns.

Meanwhile, Back on Earth

The same procedures Grimm is using to find water on Mars can be used to locate objects, such as land mines, buried beneath the ground here on Earth. Standard metal detectors are useful, but they can't tell the difference between a mine and a piece of scrap metal. Along with electromagnetic pulses, Grimm uses imaging technologies similar to medical scanners to create images of objects buried beneath the ground. Once their location is pinpointed, mines can be safely removed or detonated.

An Interesting Career

Being a geophysicist has been rewarding for Grimm. "The sense of exploration really appeals to me," he explains. "It's like a hunt—I try to figure something out to bring some relationships together, and soon I have a story to tell!"

Think It Over

▶ Think of ways to locate objects buried more than 2 m below the surface. Could you use sound, light, X rays, or something else? What problems would you have to solve to make a useful detector to send to Mars?

▲ *The surface of Mars*

31

CAREERS
Geophysicist— Bob Grimm

Background
Geophysics involves seismology, meteorology, and hydrology. Planetary geophysicists study many topics, from the shape of a planet's surface to the processes at work deep in its interior. They also study a planet's temperature variations, climatic patterns, volcanic activity, gravitational field, and magnetic field.

Sample Answer to Think It Over
Answers will vary. Students should discuss how wave energy can travel through a medium without disturbing it. A useful detector for the Martian surface would have to be lightweight. It would also need to withstand very cold temperatures and navigate on rugged terrain.

Chapter 1 • Careers **31**

Chapter Organizer

CHAPTER ORGANIZATION	TIME MINUTES	OBJECTIVES	LABS, INVESTIGATIONS, AND DEMONSTRATIONS
Chapter Opener pp. 32–33	45	National Standards: SAI 1, SPSP 5, HNS 1, 3	**Start-Up Activity** Follow the Yellow Brick Road, p. 33
Section 1 You Are Here	90	▶ Explain how a magnetic compass can be used to find directions on the Earth. ▶ Distinguish between true north and magnetic north. ▶ Distinguish between lines of latitude and lines of longitude on a globe or map. ▶ Explain how latitude and longitude can be used to locate places on Earth. UCP 2, 3, 5, SAI 1, ST 2, SPSP 5, HNS 1, 3; LabBook UCP 2, 3, SAI 1, ST 1, HNS 1	**QuickLab,** Finding Directions with a Compass, p. 36 GENERAL **Skill Builder,** Round or Flat? p. 632 ADVANCED **Datasheets for LabBook,** Round or Flat? Datasheet 2 ADVANCED **Design Your Own,** Orient Yourself! p. 634 GENERAL **Datasheets for LabBook,** Orient Yourself! Datasheet 3 GENERAL
Section 2 Mapping the Earth's Surface	90	▶ Compare a map with a globe. ▶ Describe the three types of map projections. ▶ Describe recent technological advances that have helped the science of mapmaking progress. ▶ List the parts of a map. UCP 2, 3, 5, SAI 1, ST 2, SPSP 5, HNS 3	
Section 3 Topographic Maps	135	▶ Describe how contour lines show elevation and landforms on a map. ▶ List the rules of contour lines. ▶ Interpret a topographic map. UCP 2, 3, 5, SAI 1, ST 2, SPSP 2, 5, HNS 1; LabBook UCP 2, 3, SAI 1, ST 1	**Skill Builder,** Topographic Tuber, p. 636 GENERAL **Datasheets for LabBook,** Topographic Tuber, Datasheet 4 GENERAL **Inquiry Labs,** Looking for Buried Treasure, Lab 9 ADVANCED **Long-Term Projects & Research Ideas,** Project 30 ADVANCED

*See page **T20** for a complete correlation of this book with the*

NATIONAL SCIENCE EDUCATION STANDARDS.

TECHNOLOGY RESOURCES

 Guided Reading Audio CD English or Spanish, Chapter 2

 One-Stop Planner CD-ROM with Test Generator

 Multicultural Connections, Mapping Asian Temples from Space, Segment 2

Chapter 2 • Maps as Models of the Earth

Chapter 2 • Maps as Models of the Earth

CLASSROOM WORKSHEETS, TRANSPARENCIES, AND RESOURCES	SCIENCE INTEGRATION AND CONNECTIONS	REVIEW AND ASSESSMENT
Directed Reading Worksheet 2 BASIC **Science Puzzlers, Twisters & Teasers,** Worksheet 2 ADVANCED	**Cross-Disciplinary Focus,** p. 33 in ATE	
Transparency 104, Finding Direction on Earth **Directed Reading Worksheet 2,** Section 1 BASIC **Transparency 105,** Lines of Latitude **Transparency 105,** Lines of Longitude **Reinforcement Worksheet 2,** Where on Earth? BASIC	**Multicultural Connection,** p. 34 in ATE **Connect to Life Science,** p. 35 in ATE **Multicultural Connection,** p. 37 in ATE **Astronomy Connection,** p. 37	**Self-Check,** p. 36 **Homework,** p. 38 in ATE GENERAL **Review,** p. 39 GENERAL **Quiz,** p. 39 in ATE GENERAL **Alternative Assessment,** p. 39 in ATE GENERAL
Directed Reading Worksheet 2, Section 2 BASIC **Transparency 106,** Mercator Projection **Transparency 106,** Conic Projection **Transparency 106,** Azimuthal Projection **Transparency 291,** The Electromagnetic Spectrum **Math Skills for Science Worksheet 17,** Using Proportions and Cross-Multiplication GENERAL **Critical Thinking Worksheet 2,** Shaping the World ADVANCED	**Cross-Disciplinary Focus,** p. 42 in ATE BASIC **Cross-Disciplinary Focus,** p. 43 in ATE **Connect to Physical Science,** p. 43 in ATE **Math and More,** p. 44 in ATE GENERAL **Multicultural Connection,** p. 44 in ATE **Apply,** p. 45 GENERAL **Science, Technology, and Society:** The Lost City of Ubar, p. 54 ADVANCED	**Homework,** p. 42 in ATE GENERAL **Review,** p. 45 GENERAL **Quiz,** p. 45 in ATE GENERAL **Alternative Assessment,** p. 45 in ATE GENERAL
Directed Reading Worksheet 2, Section 3 BASIC **Reinforcement Worksheet 2,** Interpreting a Topographic Map BASIC **Math Skills for Science Worksheet 46,** Mapping and Surveying GENERAL	**MathBreak,** Counting Contours, p. 47 GENERAL **Connect to Oceanography,** p. 48 in ATE BASIC **Environment Connection,** p. 49 **Careers:** Watershed Planner—Nancy Charbeneau, p. 55 GENERAL	**Self-Check,** p. 47 **Homework,** p. 47 in ATE ADVANCED **Review,** p. 49 GENERAL **Quiz,** p. 49 in ATE GENERAL **Alternative Assessment,** p. 49 in ATE GENERAL

END-OF-CHAPTER REVIEW AND ASSESSMENT

Chapter Review in Study Guide
Vocabulary and Notes in Study Guide
Chapter Tests with Performance-Based Assessment, Chapter 2 Test
Chapter Tests with Performance-Based Assessment, Performance-Based Assessment 2
Concept Mapping Transparency 2

 Holt, Rinehart and Winston On-line Resources
go.hrw.com
For worksheets and other teaching aids related to this chapter, visit the HRW Web site and type in the keyword: **HSTMAP**

 **National Science Teachers Association**
www.scilinks.org
Encourage students to use the sciLINKS numbers listed in the internet connect boxes to access information and resources on the **NSTA** Web site.

Chapter Resources & Worksheets

Visual Resources

TEACHING TRANSPARENCIES

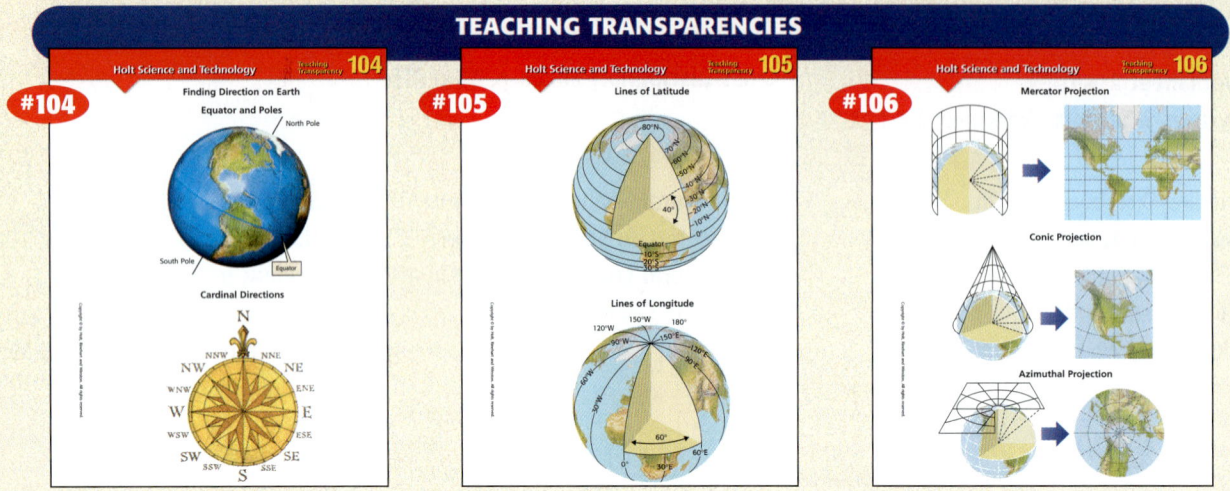

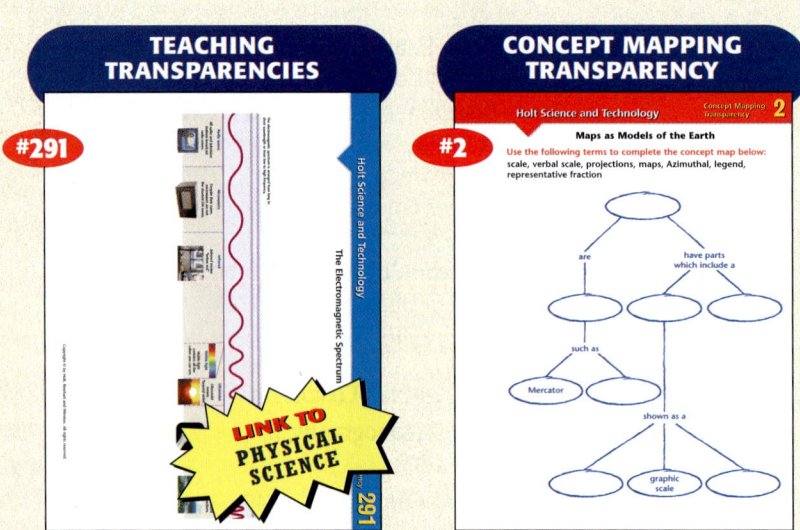

Meeting Individual Needs

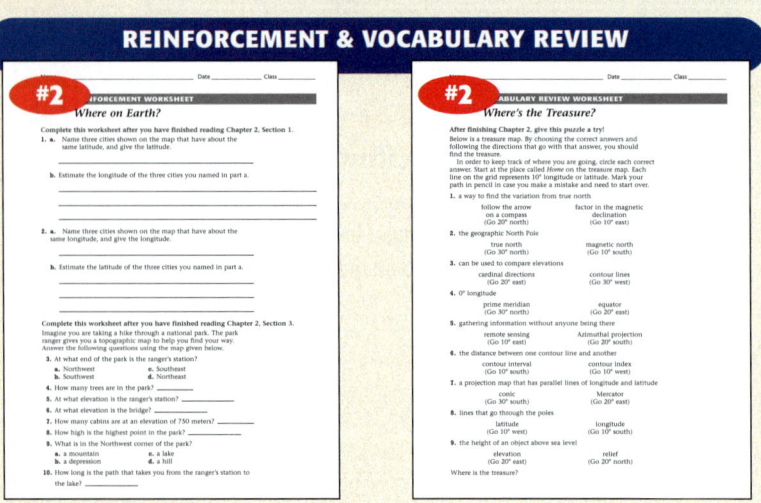

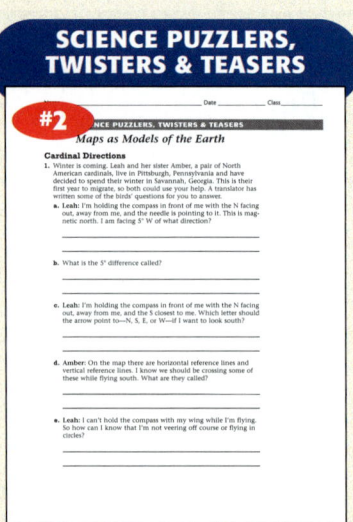

Chapter 2 • Maps as Models of the Earth

Chapter 2 • Maps as Models of the Earth

Review & Assessment

STUDY GUIDE

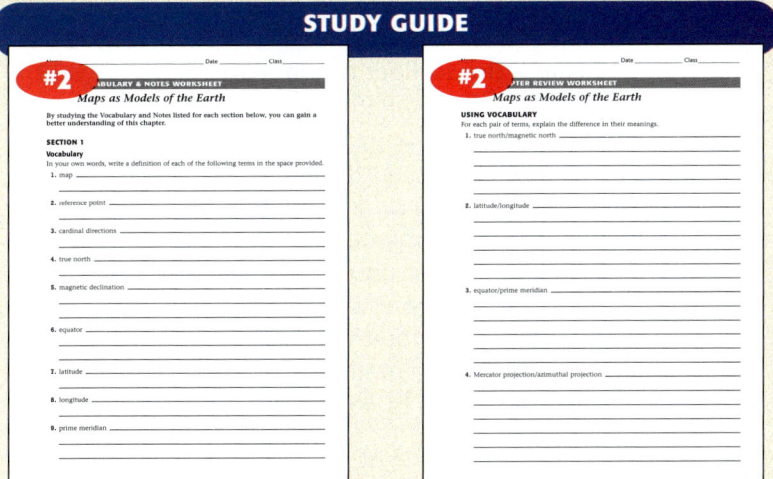

CHAPTER TESTS WITH PERFORMANCE-BASED ASSESSMENT

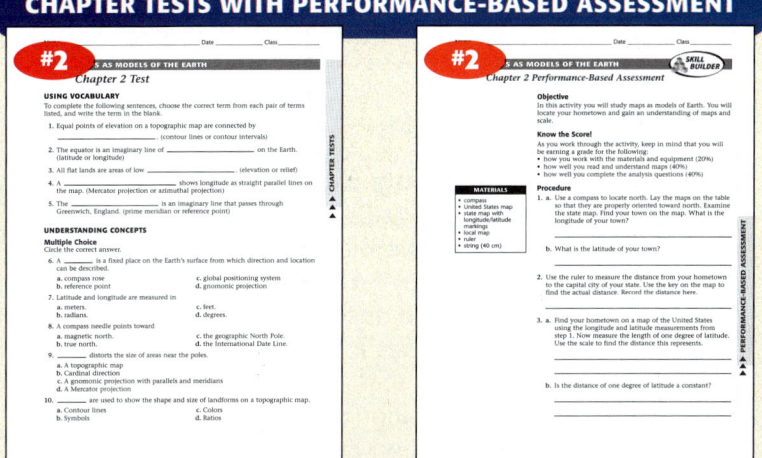

Lab Worksheets

INQUIRY LABS

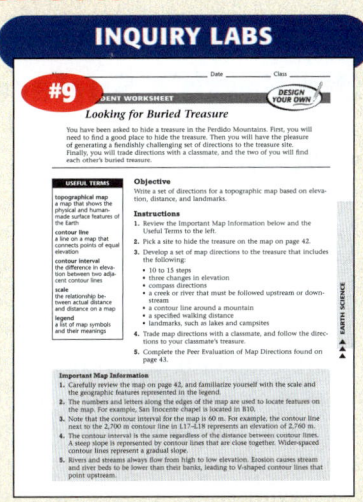

LONG-TERM PROJECTS & RESEARCH IDEAS

DATASHEETS FOR LABBOOK

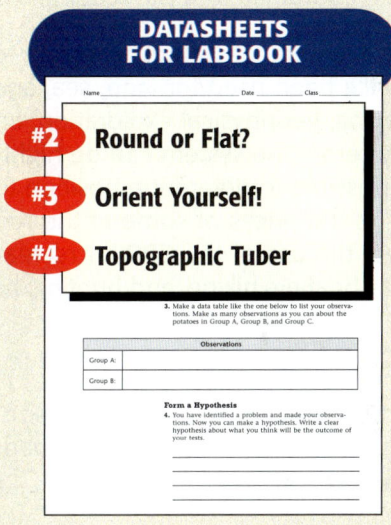

Applications & Extensions

CRITICAL THINKING & PROBLEM SOLVING

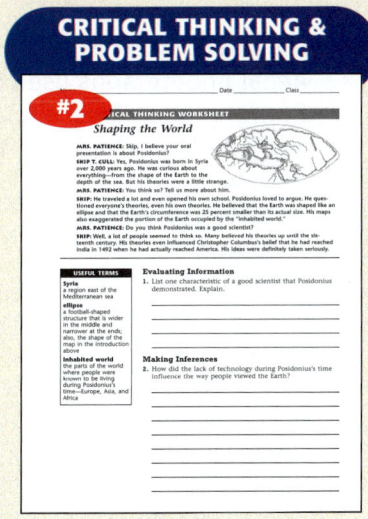

MULTICULTURAL CONNECTIONS

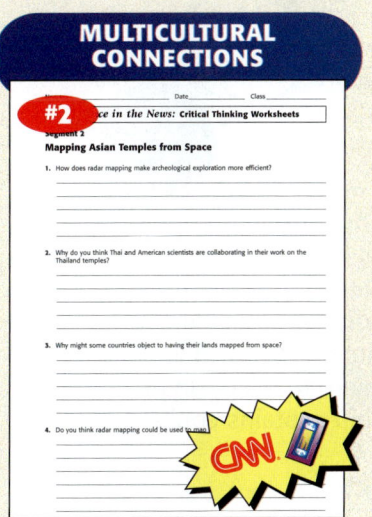

Chapter 2 • Chapter Resources & Worksheets

Chapter Background

SECTION 1

You Are Here

▶ **Global Positioning Systems**
During the 1970s, the U.S. Department of Defense developed the Global Positioning System (GPS) for use in aircraft navigation and missile guidance. The system uses a network of 25 satellites that continually transmit positioning information to receivers on Earth. The distance between a receiver and at least three satellites is used to compute the latitude and longitude coordinates of the receiver's position.

- In 1983, the system was made available to the public and has since been used for land, sea, and air navigation, surveying, geophysical exploration, and vehicle-location systems. The system can be highly accurate, making it possible to determine position to within less than 1 m. As the prices of some of the receivers have plummeted, the use of the GPS for recreational activities, such as boating, hiking, and hunting, has increased.

IS THAT A FACT!

▰ The first GPS receiver was about the size of a filing cabinet, but by 1989, manufacturers had perfected hand-held versions.

▶ **Longitude**
Because Earth rotates 360° every 24 hours, it turns 15° every hour. It is therefore possible to determine longitude at any place on the globe if the local time and the time at the prime meridian are known. Before the mid-eighteenth century, however, the unreliability of clocks—especially those aboard ships, where motion, temperature variation, and moisture could wreak havoc with a timepiece's workings—thwarted calculations of longitude. Many shipwrecks were caused because the ship captains could not accurately calculate their location.

- In 1707, inaccurate longitudinal information caused four ships in a British fleet to run aground, and 2,000 sailors died. The British Parliament addressed the problem by offering a large reward to anyone who could develop a method to accurately calculate longitude within half a degree. John Harrison (1693–1776), a self-taught clockmaker, developed a chronometer that remained accurate on rough seas and won the prize in 1763. More than 200 years later, astronaut Neil Armstrong gave credit to Harrison for the role he played in enabling exploration of Earth and in inspiring future generations to venture toward exploration of the moon.

SECTION 2

Mapping the Earth's Surface

▶ **Gerardus Mercator**
Gerardus Mercator was born Gerhard Kremer in 1512, in Rupelmonde, Flanders (present-day Belgium). At age 24, Mercator was a highly skilled engraver, calligrapher, and scientific-instrument maker. With two of his teachers, he made the first globe of Earth, in 1536–1537. A true Renaissance man, Mercator was a highly esteemed cartographer who also published a treatise on italic lettering, designed a grammar-school curriculum, taught mathematics, and conducted genealogical research for his patron, Duke Wilhelm of Cleve. He even attempted to write a chronology of the history of the world from the formation of Earth to 1568.

▶ **Aerial Photographs**
Aerial photographs used for mapping have been taken from mountaintops, airplanes, hot-air balloons, rockets, and satellites. Originally, the photographs were taken from various angles. Today, specialized cameras take pictures straight down, in sequences, and along predetermined lines. Each picture overlaps parts of the pictures taken before and after it. This is done because the least amount of

31E Chapter 2 • Maps as Models of the Earth

Chapter 2 • Maps as Models of the Earth

distortion is at the center of each photo. Together these photos produce an image with very little distortion. When used with specialized instruments, these photos can be used to produce a three-dimensional view of an area. From the three-dimensional model, land contours are plotted.

▶ Landsat

Since the Landsat program began in 1972, a number of satellites have been deployed that carry remote sensing equipment. The equipment is designed to detect radiation in different bands of the electromagnetic spectrum. *Landsats 4* and *5* orbit Earth from pole to pole at an altitude of 705 km every 16 days. Landsat data are particularly useful for thematic mapping. For example, data from the blue-green spectral region are useful for distinguishing between coniferous and deciduous plants, while data from the thermal infrared range supply information about soil moisture.

SECTION 3

Topographic Maps

▶ Inuit Relief Maps

The Inuit of Baffin Island were skilled mapmakers. They made permanent relief maps by carving coastal features into pieces of wood and walrus ivory. The Inuit also sewed small pieces of fur or driftwood to sealskin to represent islands. They measured distance on their maps not by miles but by "sleeps." This distance to a hunting ground, for example, would be measured by how many rest stops would be taken before reaching it.

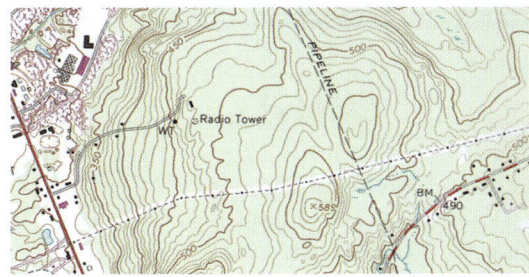

▶ John Wesley Powell (1834–1902)

American geologist and surveyor John Wesley Powell headed an official expedition to the Grand Canyon in 1871. His purpose was to conduct a topographic survey to map "as broad a belt of country as it was possible" on both sides of the Colorado and Green Rivers. The expedition yielded meticulously detailed topographic maps for an area that had previously been described as the "great unknown." Those maps were instrumental to Powell's appointment in 1881 as director of the U.S. Geological Survey (USGS). As director, Powell aimed to create topographic maps for the entire country using very large scales, ranging from 6.4 km/2.5 cm for desert regions to 1.6 km/2.5 cm for densely populated areas. Powell insisted on including data concerning soils, springs, and other natural resources, which he felt were essential for making land-use decisions. The high-quality topographical maps created during Powell's administration set the standard for published topographic maps in the United States for many years to come.

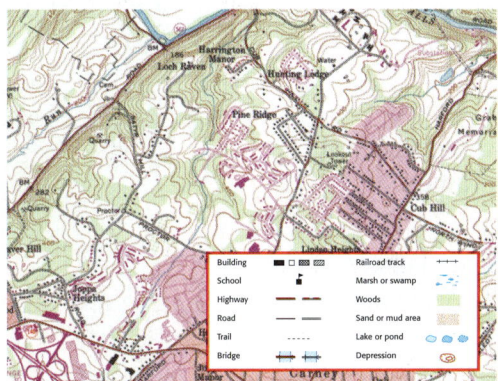

IS THAT A FACT!

▶ By the time Powell retired from the USGS in 1894, about one-fifth of the United States had been mapped according to his standards. Powell told Congress that he expected the remainder of the task (excluding the mapping of Alaska) could be completed in 24 years. However, he vastly underestimated the undertaking; it was not until the 1980s that a full set of topographic maps was finally completed.

For background information about teaching strategies and issues, refer to the *Professional Reference for Teachers*.

Chapter 2
Maps as Models of the Earth

Pre-Reading Questions

Students may not know the answers to these questions before reading the chapter, so accept any reasonable response.

Suggested Answers

1. No; maps do not represent the world accurately because all maps are distorted.
2. Answers may vary. Sample answer: Symbols are used to show information on maps.
3. Every map must have a title, legend, scale, date, and north arrow.

 Directed Reading Worksheet 2

 Science Puzzlers, Twisters & Teasers Worksheet 2

 Guided Reading Audio CD English or Spanish, Chapter 2

Chapter 2
Maps as Models of the Earth

Sections

1. You Are Here 34
   QuickLab 36
   Astronomy Connection 37
   Internet Connect 39
2. Mapping the Earth's Surface 40
   Apply 45
   Internet Connect 45
3. Topographic Maps 46
   MathBreak 47
   Environment Connection 49
   Internet Connect 49

Chapter Review 52
Feature Articles 54, 55
LabBook 632–637

 **Pre-Reading Questions**

1. Do all maps picture the world accurately?
2. How is information shown on maps?
3. What information must every map have?

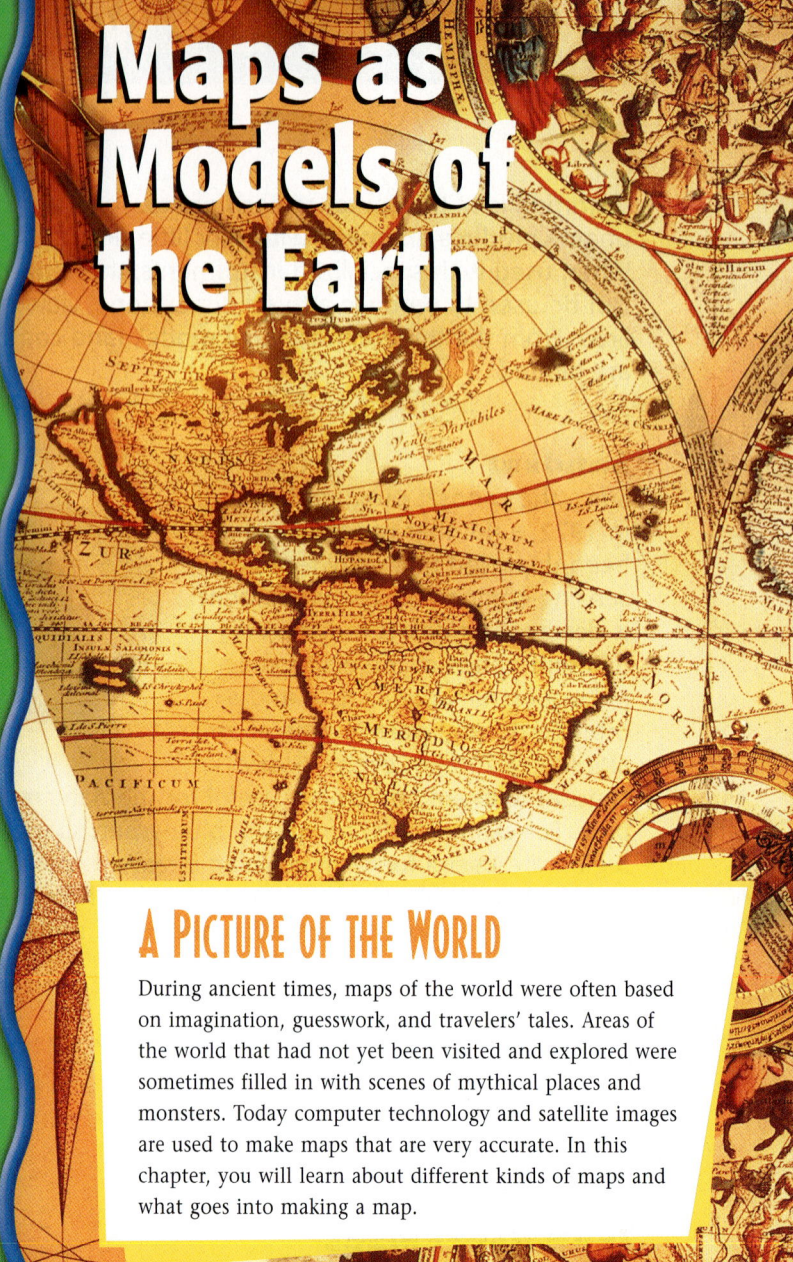

A Picture of the World

During ancient times, maps of the world were often based on imagination, guesswork, and travelers' tales. Areas of the world that had not yet been visited and explored were sometimes filled in with scenes of mythical places and monsters. Today computer technology and satellite images are used to make maps that are very accurate. In this chapter, you will learn about different kinds of maps and what goes into making a map.

 **go.hrw.com**
For worksheets and other teaching aids, visit the HRW Web site and type in the keyword: **HSTMAP**

 **www.scilinks.com**
Use the sciLINKS numbers at the end of each chapter for additional resources on the **NSTA** Web site.

 **www.cnnfyi.com**
Visit the CNN Web site for current events coverage and classroom resources.

START-UP Activity

FOLLOW THE YELLOW BRICK ROAD

In this activity, you not only will learn how to read a map but also make a map that someone else can read.

Procedure

1. With a **computer drawing program** or **colored pencils** and **paper,** draw a map showing how to get from your classroom to another place in your school, such as the gym. Make sure you include enough information for someone unfamiliar with your school to find his or her way.
2. After you finish drawing your map, switch maps with a partner. Examine your classmate's map, and try to figure out where the map is leading you.

Analysis

3. Is your map an accurate picture of your school? Explain your answer.
4. How do you think your map could be made better? What are some limitations of your map?
5. Compare your map with your partner's map. How are your maps alike? How are they different?

START-UP Activity

FOLLOW THE YELLOW BRICK ROAD

MATERIALS
- computer drawing program
- colored pencils
- paper

Teacher's Notes

Before students start their maps, have them brainstorm to make a list of school landmarks and suggest that they use the location of these landmarks as reference points in their maps.

Answers to START-UP Activity

3. Answers will vary. Accept all reasonable responses.
4. Answers will vary. Accept all reasonable responses.
5. Answers will vary.

Chapter 2 • Maps as Models of the Earth

SECTION 1

Focus

You Are Here
This section opens with a discussion of the history of mapmaking. Students learn how to find directions on a globe by using reference points such as the North and South Poles and the equator. Students learn how a compass is used to find directions and how true north differs from magnetic north. The section closes with a discussion of lines of latitude and longitude and how they can be used to locate points on Earth's surface.

🔔 Bellringer
Ask students to draw a map from their homes to one of their favorite places. Have them clearly label all landmarks and include information that might be useful to someone using the map.

1 Motivate

GROUP ACTIVITY
Making Compasses This activity will work best when it is performed outside. Supply each group with a small bowl of water, a steel sewing needle, a magnet, and a 1 × 3 cm piece of tissue paper. Have students carefully rub the needle against the magnet in the same direction 40 times. Then have them float the paper on the surface of the water and place the needle on the paper. After a minute, allow students to observe other groups' bowls; all of the needles should be oriented in a north-south direction. Explain that they have all just created a simple compass, a device that changed the course of human history.

Section 1

Terms to Learn
map magnetic declination
true north longitude
equator prime meridian
latitude

What You'll Do
- Explain how a magnetic compass can be used to find directions on the Earth.
- Distinguish between true north and magnetic north.
- Distinguish between lines of latitude and lines of longitude on a globe or map.
- Explain how latitude and longitude can be used to locate places on Earth.

You Are Here

When you walk across the Earth's surface, the Earth does not appear to be curved. It looks flat. In the past, beliefs about the Earth's shape changed. Maps reflected the time's knowledge and views of the world as well as the current technology. A **map** is a model or representation of the Earth's surface. If you look at Ptolemy's world map from the second century, as shown in **Figure 1,** you probably will not recognize what you are looking at. Today satellites in space provide us with true images of what the Earth looks like. In this section you will learn how early scientists knew the Earth was round long before pictures from space were taken. You will also learn how to determine location and direction on the Earth's surface.

What Does the Earth Really Look Like?
The Greeks thought of the Earth as a sphere almost 2,000 years before Christopher Columbus made his voyage in 1492. The observation that a ship sinks below the horizon as it sails into the distance supported the idea of a round Earth. If the Earth were flat the ship would appear smaller as it moved away.

Figure 1 This map shows what people thought the world looked like 1,800 years ago.

🌍 Multicultural CONNECTION
The Chinese invented the magnetic compass in the third century B.C. The magnetic properties of lodestone, known today as magnetite, were well known to many ancient cultures. Lodestone was thought to have magical properties because it could attract metal. Early compasses consisted of a piece of lodestone on a card that was balanced on a pivot. The scale of the compass was marked with compass points at 15° increments. By the tenth century, the compass was standard equipment on Chinese sailing ships.

34 Chapter 2 • Maps as Models of the Earth

Eratosthenes (ER uh TAHS thuh NEEZ), a Greek mathematician, wanted to know how big the Earth was. In about 240 B.C., he calculated the Earth's circumference using geometry and observations of the sun. We now know his estimation was off by only 6,250 km, an error of 15 percent. That's not bad for someone who lived more than 2,000 years ago, in a time when computer and satellite technology did not exist!

Finding Direction on Earth

How would you give a friend from school directions to your home? You might mention a landmark, such as a grocery store or a restaurant, as a reference point. A *reference point* is a fixed place on the Earth's surface from which direction and location can be described.

Because the Earth is round, it has no top, bottom, or sides for people to use as reference points for determining locations on its surface. The Earth does, however, turn on its axis. The Earth's axis is an imaginary line that runs through the Earth. At either end of the axis is a geographic pole. The North and South Poles, as shown in **Figure 2**, are used as reference points when describing direction and location on Earth.

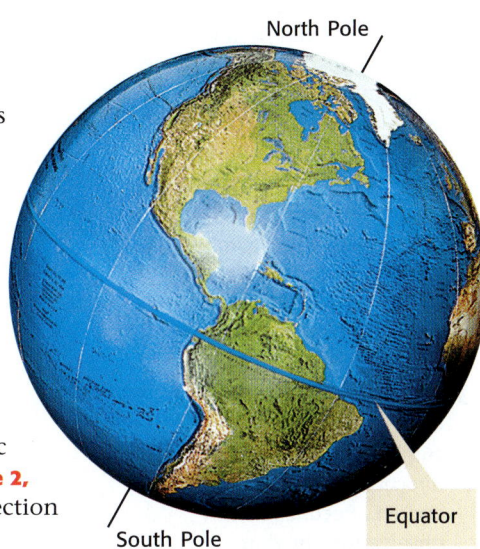

Figure 2 *Like the poles, the equator can be used as a reference.*

Cardinal Directions North, south, east, and west are called *cardinal directions*. **Figure 3** shows these basic cardinal directions and various combinations of these directions. Using these directions is much more precise than using directions such as turn left, go straight, and turn right. Unfortunately for most of us, using cardinal directions requires the use of a compass.

Figure 3 *A compass rose helps you orient yourself on a map.*

2) Teach

GROUP ACTIVITY

Have students write a description of the route they take as they travel between home and school. Then have them rewrite the description using cardinal and intercardinal directions. Have pairs of students trade route descriptions and use a community map to check the accuracy of each other's maps.
Sheltered English

MISCONCEPTION ALERT

Students may be under the impression that Christopher Columbus discovered that Earth was round only after he safely made his voyage in 1492 without sailing off the edge of the world. In fact, Columbus, like most other educated people of his time, was well aware that Earth was not flat before he set out.

CONNECT TO LIFE SCIENCE

Magnetotactic bacteria use magnetic particles in their cytoplasm to align themselves with the Earth's magnetic field. North of the equator, the bacteria are north-seeking travelers. South of the equator, they are south-seeking travelers. At the equator, where the magnetic fields are at their weakest, the populations are mixed between north- and south-seeking bacteria.

 Teaching Transparency 104 "Finding Direction on Earth"

 Directed Reading Worksheet 2 Section 1

IS THAT A FACT!

The orientation of maps with north at the "top" is arbitrary. For many centuries European maps placed east at the top to stress the importance of Jerusalem to their faith. The Chinese put the south at the top of their maps because nothing of interest to them was to the north.

 SCIENCE

Although globes are round, Earth is not a perfect sphere. Because Earth is a rotating body, it bulges at the equator and is slightly flattened at the poles. Earth's circumference measured pole to pole is 40,008 km, while its circumference around the equator is 40,075 km.

Section 1 • You Are Here

2) Teach, continued

READING STRATEGY

Prediction Guide Before students read the following two pages, have them answer these true/false statements:

- Earth has four poles. (true)
- A compass is the only thing you need to find a location. (false)
- Imaginary lines drawn around Earth can be used to pinpoint locations. (true)

Sheltered English

 PG 632
Round or Flat?

Answer to Self-Check

The Earth rotates around the geographic poles.

Explain that magnetic attraction occurs between the opposite poles of magnets. The north-seeking pole of a compass needle actually points to the south pole of Earth's magnetic field. What we call the Earth's magnetic north pole is actually the south pole of Earth's magnetic field. This can be easily demonstrated by placing the south pole of a bar magnet next to a compass. The compass needle will point toward the south pole of the bar magnet in the same way it tends to point toward the south pole of Earth's magnetic field, what we call magnetic north.

Orient Yourself!

Finding Directions with a Compass

1. This lab should be done outside. Hold a **compass** flat in your hand until the needle stops moving. Rotate the dial of the compass until the letter *N* on the case lines up with the painted or colored end of the needle.

2. While holding the compass steady, identify objects that line up with each of the cardinal points. List them in your ScienceLog.

3. See if you can locate objects at the various combinations of cardinal directions, such as SW and NE. Record your observations in your ScienceLog.

It's better than a scavenger hunt! Interested? Turn to page 634 of your LabBook.

36

Using a Compass One way to determine north is by using a magnetic compass. The compass uses the natural magnetism of the Earth to indicate direction. A compass needle points to the magnetic north pole. The Earth has two different sets of poles—the geographic poles and the magnetic poles. As you can see in **Figure 4**, the magnetic poles have a slightly different location than the geographic poles.

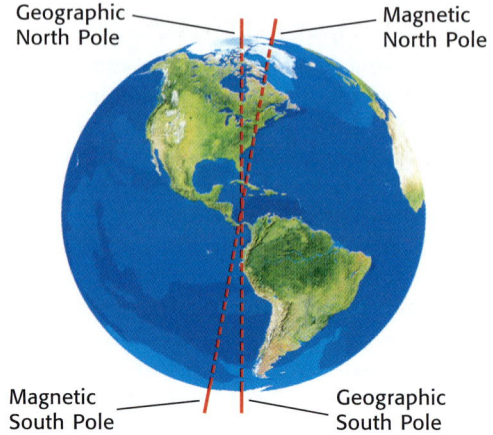

Figure 4 Unlike the geographic poles, which are always in the same place, the magnetic poles have changed location throughout the history of the Earth.

 Self-Check

Does the Earth rotate around the geographic poles or the magnetic poles? *(See page 726 to check your answer.)*

True North and Magnetic Declination Because the geographic North Pole never changes, it is called **true north**. The difference between the location of true north and the magnetic north pole requires that one more step be added to using a compass. When using a compass to map or explore the Earth's surface, you need to make a correction for the difference between geographic north and magnetic north. This angle of correction is called **magnetic declination**. Magnetic declination is measured in degrees east or west of true north.

Magnetic declination has been determined for different points on the Earth's surface. Once you know the declination for your area, you can use a compass to determine true north.

SCIENCE HUMOR

Before the seventeenth century, many sailors refused to transport onions and garlic because they believed they would destroy a compass's magnetic properties. In 1600, English physician and scientist William Gilbert set about testing the belief. He ate a quantity of garlic and then belched on a compass needle, which he had also rubbed with garlic juice. The compass's magnetic properties remained intact, and Gilbert proved, at least to himself, that the notion was unfounded.

36 Chapter 2 • Maps as Models of the Earth

This adjustment is like the adjustment you would make to the handlebars of a bike with a bent front wheel. You know how much you have to turn the handlebars to make the bike go straight.

As **Figure 5** shows, a compass needle at Pittsburgh, Pennsylvania, points about 7° west of true north. Can you determine the magnetic declination of San Diego?

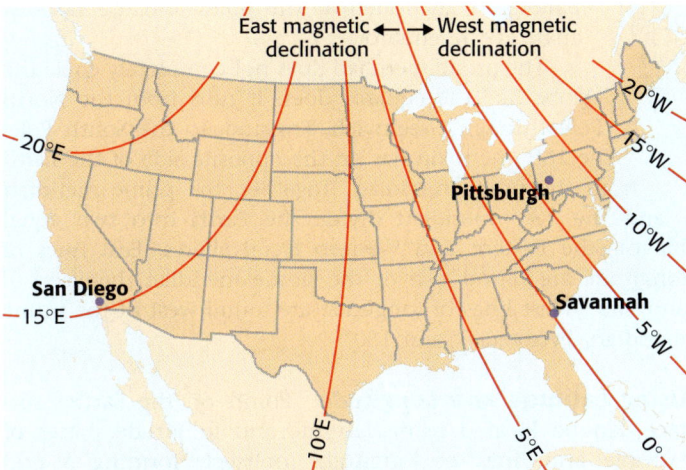

Figure 5 *The red lines on the map connect points with the same magnetic declination.*

Finding Locations on the Earth

The houses and buildings in your neighborhood all have addresses that identify their location. But how would you find the location of something like a city or an island? These places can be given an "address" using *latitude* and *longitude*. Latitude and longitude are intersecting lines on a globe or map that allow you to find exact locations. They are used in combination to create global addresses.

Latitude Imaginary lines drawn around the Earth parallel to the equator are called lines of latitude, or *parallels*. The **equator** is a circle halfway between the poles that divides the Earth into the Northern and Southern Hemispheres. It represents 0° latitude. **Latitude** is the distance north or south, measured in degrees, from the equator, as shown in **Figure 6**. The North Pole is 90° north latitude, and the South Pole is 90° south latitude.

Astronomy CONNECTION

There are ways you can find north without using a compass. In the morning, the sun rises in the east. In the evening, it sets in the west. If you point your right hand toward where you saw the sun rise in the morning and your left hand to where it sets at night, you will be facing north.

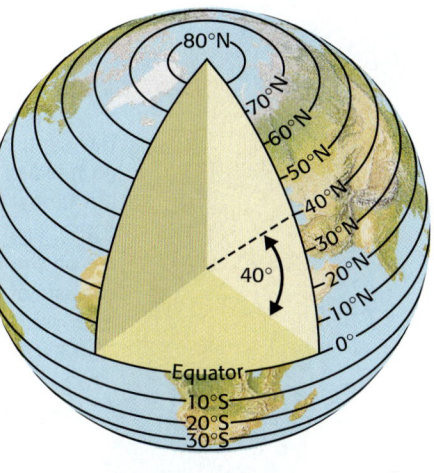

Figure 6 *The degree measure of latitude is the angle created by the equator, the center of the Earth, and the location on the Earth's surface.*

GROUP ACTIVITY

Finding True North For thousands of years, people have used the sun to determine true north. This activity is most accurate at midday, when the sun is at its southernmost point.

- At 11:30 A.M., have students insert a ruler in the ground and a pencil at the tip of the ruler's shadow.
- After 1 hour, have students insert another pencil where the tip of the ruler's shadow is now.
- Have students place a piece of string between the two pencils. The string will be an east-west line. Viewed with your back to the sun, the first pencil indicates west and the second indicates east.

Students can then use a protractor to position a north-south string perpendicular to the east-west string.

Multicultural CONNECTION

Matthew Henson (1866–1955), an African-American member of Robert Peary's North Pole exploration team, was one of the first people believed to have reached the geographic North Pole in 1909. Henson's knowledge of Arctic regions also helped him gain a position as an exhibit preparator at the American Museum of Natural History, in New York City. In 1944, Congress recognized Henson's contributions to polar exploration. Interested students may want to read Henson's autobiography, *A Negro Explorer at the North Pole*.

Teaching Transparency 105 "Lines of Latitude"

As the Earth rotates, both the geographic North Pole and the magnetic north pole move constantly. The geographic North Pole moves about 6 m on a 435-day cycle. This movement results from a wobble in the Earth's rotation. The magnetic north pole wanders because of changes in Earth's rotating iron core. The magnetic pole is currently moving northwest at an average rate of 10 km per year.

3) Extend

GOING FURTHER
Ask students to find out why the meridian passing through Greenwich, England, serves as the prime meridian. They should find that Greenwich was chosen as 0° by an international committee in 1884 in part because it was the site of Britain's Royal Greenwich Observatory, which had been important in developing time-keeping methods necessary for ship navigation. In addition, most of the world's shipping lines were already using Greenwich as the longitudinal baseline.

Before 1884, when Greenwich was established by international agreement as the prime meridian, there were no fewer than 13 "prime meridians" in use. Countries simply selected a meridian in their own country as the prime meridian; for example, Italy's prime meridian passed through Rome, and France's prime meridian passed through Paris. Discuss with students the benefits of the international standardization of the prime meridian.

Homework
Research Explain to students that longitude is directly related to time. Earth rotates 360° every 24 hours, turning 15° every hour. Earth can be divided into 24 meridians of 15° each. Have students find out how time in different parts of the world can be determined using lines of longitude and the local time at Greenwich.

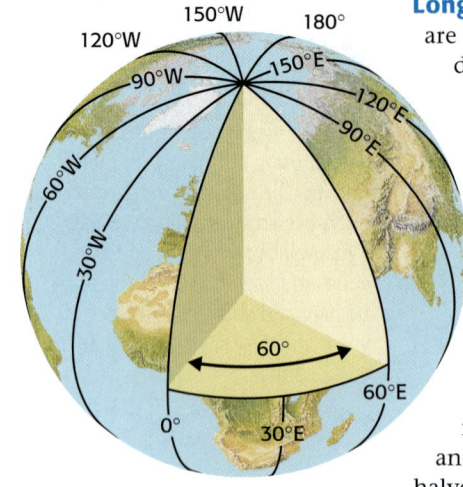

Figure 7 The degree measure of longitude is the angle created by the prime meridian, the center of the Earth, and the location on the Earth's surface.

Longitude Imaginary lines that pass through the poles are called lines of longitude, or *meridians*. **Longitude** is the distance east and west, measured in degrees, from the prime meridian, as shown in **Figure 7**. By international agreement, one meridian was selected to be 0°. The **prime meridian**, which passes through Greenwich, England, is the line that represents 0° longitude. Unlike lines of latitude, lines of longitude are not parallel. They touch at the poles and are farthest apart at the equator.

The prime meridian does not completely circle the globe like the equator does. It runs from the North Pole through Greenwich, England, to the South Pole. The 180° meridian lies on the opposite side of the Earth from the prime meridian. Together, the prime meridian and the 180° meridian divide the Earth into two equal halves—the Eastern and Western Hemispheres. East lines of longitude are found east of the prime meridian, between 0° and 180°. West lines of longitude are found west of the prime meridian, between 0° and 180°.

Using Latitude and Longitude Points on the Earth's surface can be located using latitude and longitude. Lines of latitude and lines of longitude intersect, forming a grid system on globes and maps. This grid system can be used to find locations north or south of the equator and east or west of the prime meridian.

Finding Your Way

Have you ever been lost? There's no need to worry anymore. With the Global Positioning System (GPS), you can find where you are on the Earth's surface. GPS consists of 25 orbiting satellites that send radio signals to receivers on Earth in order to calculate a given location's latitude, longitude, and elevation.

GPS was invented in the 1970s by the United States Department of Defense for military purposes. During the last 20 years, this technology has made its way into many people's daily lives. Today GPS is used in a variety of ways. Airplane and boat pilots use it for navigation, and industry uses include mining and resource mapping as well as environmental planning. Even some cars are equipped with a GPS unit that can display the vehicle's specific location on a computer screen on the dashboard.

Teaching Transparency 105
"Lines of Longitude"

MISCONCEPTION ALERT

Students may believe that a compass is all you need to keep from getting lost outdoors. Point out that compasses are useful only when combined with the ability to read maps and to observe land features. Compasses can be used for orienting oneself and for taking bearings on landmarks for map triangulation.

Chapter 2 • Maps as Models of the Earth

Figure 8 shows you how latitude and longitude can be used to find the location of your state capital. First locate the star symbol representing your state capital on the appropriate map. Find the lines of latitude and longitude closest to your state capital. From here you can estimate your capital's approximate latitude and longitude.

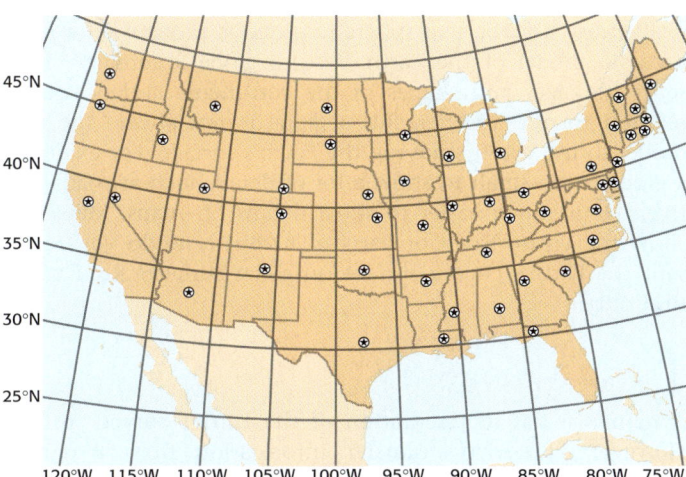

Figure 8 *The grid pattern formed by lines of latitude and longitude allows you to pinpoint any location on the Earth's surface.*

Activity

Use an atlas or globe to find the latitude and longitude of the following cities:
New York, New York
Sao Paulo, Brazil
Sydney, Australia
Madrid, Spain
Cairo, Egypt

TRY at HOME

REVIEW

1. Explain the difference between true north and magnetic north.
2. When using a compass to map an area, why is it important to know an area's magnetic declination?
3. In what three ways is the equator different from the prime meridian?
4. How do lines of latitude and longitude help you find locations on the Earth's surface?
5. **Applying Concepts** While digging through an old trunk, you find a treasure map. The map shows that the treasure is buried at 97° north and 188° east. Explain why this is impossible.

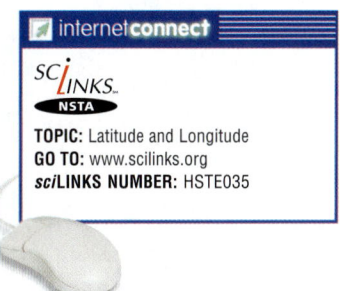

internet connect
sciLINKS
NSTA
TOPIC: Latitude and Longitude
GO TO: www.scilinks.org
*sci*LINKS NUMBER: HSTE035

Answers to Activity

New York, New York: 40°N, 74°W
Sao Paulo, Brazil: 23°S, 46°W
Sydney, Australia: 33°S, 151°E
Madrid, Spain: 40°N, 3°W
Cairo, Egypt: 30°N, 31°E

4) Close

Quiz

1. Name three references that can be used to describe direction and location on Earth.
 (possible answers: North Pole, South Pole, the equator, lines of latitude and longitude)
2. What are lines of latitude and lines of longitude?
 (Lines of latitude are imaginary lines around Earth parallel to the equator, and they are used to measure a location's distance north or south of the equator. Lines of longitude are imaginary lines that run between the Earth's poles, and they are used to measure a location's distance east or west of the prime meridian.)

ALTERNATIVE ASSESSMENT

Have students use a world map to plan an around-the-world trip in which they give their various destinations only in degrees of latitude and longitude. Have students trade their itinerary with a partner, and have each "decode" the other's trip.

Answers to Review

1. Because the geographic North Pole never changes, it is called true north. Magnetic north refers to the magnetic north pole, which has changed throughout history.
2. Because the compass points to magnetic north, it is important to know the magnetic declination at your location. This will help you make corrections to adjust for the difference between true north and magnetic north.
3. Answers will vary.
4. Lines of latitude and lines of longitude form a grid system that can be used to find locations on the Earth's surface.
5. This is impossible because the greatest measure of latitude is 90° and the greatest measure of longitude is 180°.

Reinforcement Worksheet 2
"Where on Earth?"

internet connect
sciLINKS
NSTA
TOPIC: Latitude and Longitude
GO TO: www.scilinks.org
*sci*LINKS NUMBER: HSTE035

Section 1 • You Are Here

SECTION 2

Focus

Mapping the Earth's Surface

In this section, students compare the uses of maps and globes and explore the features of three common map projections. In addition, they learn the parts of a map and discover some of the technological advances that have influenced recent trends in cartography.

Bellringer

Display a world map, a map of your state, and a map of your community. Have students make a chart in which they list the similarities and differences between each map. Then have students suggest three uses for each map.

1) Motivate

DISCUSSION

Have students examine a globe and a Mercator projection of a world map. Point out to students that both are representations of Earth. Then challenge students to find examples of ways in which the two representations differ. If necessary, point out the relative difference in the size and shape of Greenland. Ask students how they might account for the discrepancies. Record students' ideas on the chalkboard, and tell them that in this section they will learn about some of the difficulties involved in making flat representations of Earth's curved surface.

 Directed Reading Worksheet 2 Section 2

40   Chapter 2 • Maps as Models of the Earth

Section 2

Terms to Learn
Mercator projection
conic projection
azimuthal projection
aerial photograph
remote sensing

What You'll Do
◆ Compare a map with a globe.
◆ Describe the three types of map projections.
◆ Describe recent technological advances that have helped the science of mapmaking progress.
◆ List the parts of a map.

Mapping the Earth's Surface

Models are often used to represent real objects. For example, architects use models of buildings to give their clients an idea of what a building will look like before it is completed. Likewise, Earth scientists often make models of the Earth. These models are globes and maps.

Because a globe is a sphere, a globe is probably the most accurate model of the Earth. Also, a globe accurately represents the sizes and shapes of the continents and oceans in relation to one another. But a globe is not always the best model to use when studying the Earth's surface. For example, a globe is too small to show a lot of detail, such as roads and rivers. It is much easier to show details on maps. Maps can show the entire Earth or parts of it. But how do you represent the Earth's curved surface on a flat surface? Read on to find out.

A Flat Sphere?

A map is a flat representation of the Earth's curved surface. However, when you transfer information from a curved surface to a flat surface, you lose some accuracy. Changes called distortions occur in the shapes and sizes of landmasses and oceans. These distortions make some landmasses appear larger than they really are. Direction and distance can also be distorted. Consider the example of the orange peel shown in **Figure 9.**

Figure 9 *If you remove the peel from an orange and flatten the peel, it will stretch and tear. Notice how shapes are distorted, as well as distances between points on the peel.*

40

Q: What do you get when you cross a cowboy with a mapmaker?

A: a cowtographer

Map Projections Mapmakers use map projections to transfer the image of Earth's curved surface onto a flat surface. No map projection of the Earth can represent the surface of a sphere exactly. All flat maps have some amount of distortion. A map showing a smaller area, such as a city, has much less distortion than a map showing a larger area, such as the entire world.

To understand how map projections are made, imagine the Earth as a transparent globe with a light inside. If you hold a piece of paper up against the globe, shadows appear on the paper that show markings on the globe, such as continents, lines of latitude, and lines of longitude. The way the paper is held against the globe determines the kind of projection that is made. The most common projections are based on three geometric shapes—cylinders, cones, and planes.

Mercator Projection A **Mercator projection** is a map projection that results when the contents of the globe are transferred onto a cylinder of paper, as shown in **Figure 10.**

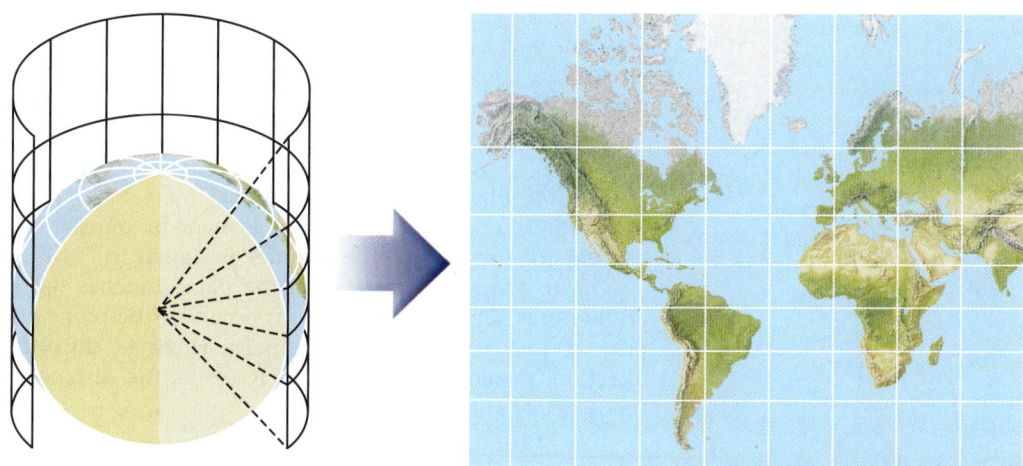

Figure 10 A Mercator projection is accurate near the equator but distorts distances and sizes of areas near the poles.

The Mercator projection shows the Earth's latitude and longitude as straight, parallel lines. Lines of longitude are plotted with an equal amount of space between each line. Lines of latitude are spaced farther apart north and south of the equator. Making the lines parallel widens and lengthens the size of areas near the poles. For example, on the Mercator projection in the map shown above, Greenland appears almost as large as Africa. Actually, Africa is 15 times larger than Greenland.

2) Teach

READING STRATEGY

Activity As students read about map projections, have them write down the name of each type of projection and a brief description of what the projection represents. Have students list the advantages or disadvantages of each type of projection. Sheltered English

MISCONCEPTION ALERT

The distortions of landmasses are not the only inaccuracies that occur on maps. When making maps for popular use, such as road maps, mapmakers routinely generalize them for both practical and aesthetic reasons. For example, when the size of a map's scale is reduced, two features (such as two lakes or two towns) might appear to be adjacent to each other. In this case, the mapmaker might move them slightly apart. Mapmakers sometimes also add details that may not really exist; for instance, meander loops might be added to a river or stream to make it look more realistic. Topographic maps, however, are made from aerial photographs and are extremely accurate.

 Teaching Transparency 106 "Mercator Projection"

IS THAT A FACT!

In 1544, Gerardus Mercator was imprisoned on charges of treason. Apparently, his frequent absences from Flanders (now Belgium) to gather map data aroused the suspicions of authorities. He remained imprisoned for 7 months before his friends succeeded in clearing his name.

2 Teach, continued

READING STRATEGY

Mnemonics Have students think of some rhymes to help them remember key points about the projections discussed in the text. You might suggest the following to help students get started:

"If you're traveling to the equator, you'll do well with Mercator"; "for east to west, conic is best"; "for a stroll at a pole, an azimuthal will help you stay in control." **Sheltered English**

CROSS-DISCIPLINARY FOCUS

History One of the earliest known maps was made by the Babylonians. It shows Babylon at the center, with Syria and other territories represented as a circular area surrounded by the Persian Gulf. This type of map is called a "wheel map." Many cultures in Arabian and European countries used wheel maps. Wheel maps reinforced the idea that a civilization was at the center of the universe. Ask students to draw a wheel map of the area where they live.

Teaching Transparency 106
"Conic Projection"
"Azimuthal Projection"

Conic Projection A **conic projection** is a map projection that is made by transferring the contents of the globe onto a cone, as shown in **Figure 11.** This cone is then unrolled to form a flat plane.

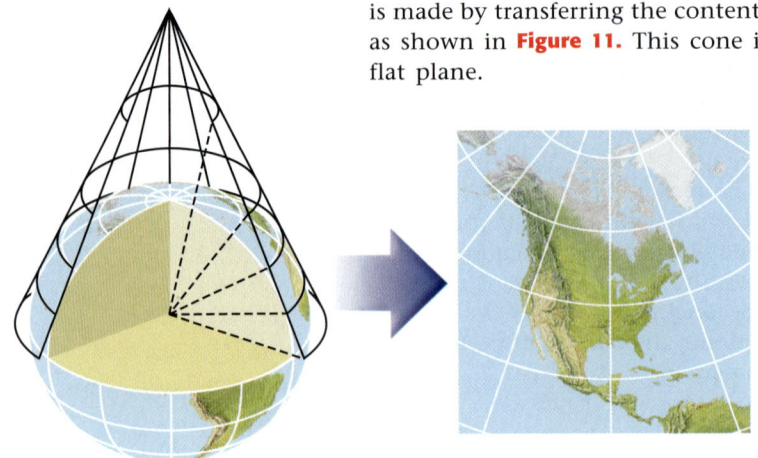

Figure 11 A series of conic projections can be used to map a large area. Because each cone touches the globe at a different latitude, it reduces distortion.

The cone touches the globe at each line of longitude but only one line of latitude. There is no distortion along the line of latitude where the globe comes in contact with the cone. Areas near this line of latitude are distorted the least amount. Because the cone touches many lines of longitude and only one line of latitude, conic projections are best for mapping landmasses that have more area east to west, such as the United States, than north to south, such as South America.

Azimuthal Projection An **azimuthal** (AZ i MYOOTH uhl) **projection** is a map projection that is made by transferring the contents of the globe onto a plane, as shown in **Figure 12.**

On an azimuthal projection, the plane touches the globe at only one point. Little distortion occurs at the point of contact, which is usually one of the poles. However, distortion of direction, distance, and shape increases as the distance from the point of contact increases.

Figure 12 On this azimuthal projection, distortion increases as you move further away from the North Pole.

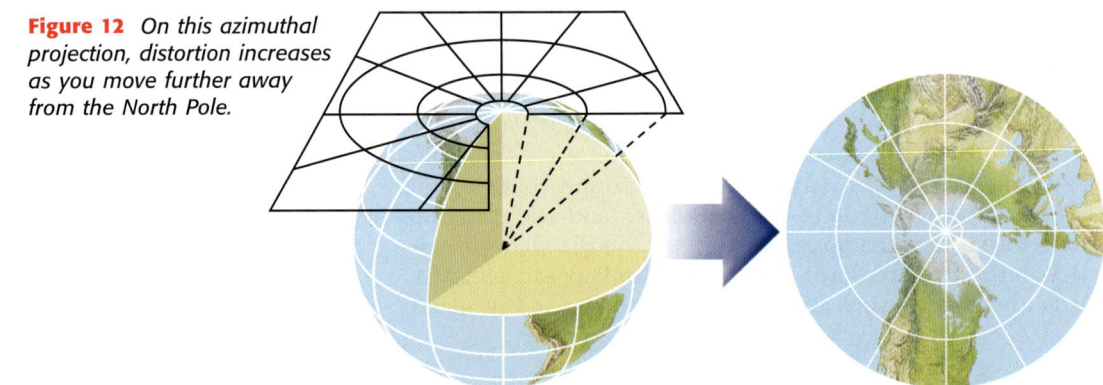

Homework

Map Projections Have students make a chart listing the strengths and weaknesses of each of the three projections studied in this section. Then have them also research another projection, such as the Robinson projection. Have them add the strengths and weaknesses of that projection to their charts. At the bottom of the chart, have them explain why none of the projections is entirely free of distortions and inaccuracies.

Modern Mapmaking

The science of mapmaking has changed more since the beginning of the 1900s than during any other time in history. This has been due to many technological advances in the twentieth century, such as the airplane, photography, computers, and space exploration.

Airplanes and Cameras The development of the airplane and advancements in photography have had the biggest effect on modern mapmaking. Airplanes give people a bird's-eye view of the Earth's surface. Photographs from the air are called **aerial photographs.** These photographs are important in helping mapmakers make accurate maps.

Remote Sensing The combined use of airplanes and photography led to the science of remote sensing. **Remote sensing** is gathering information about something without actually being there. Remote sensing can be as basic as cameras in planes or as sophisticated as satellites with sensors that can sense and record what our eyes cannot see. Remotely sensed images allow a mapmaker to map the surface of the Earth more accurately.

Our eyes can detect only a small part of the sun's energy. The part we see is called visible light. Remote sensors on satellites can detect energy that we cannot see. Satellites do not take photographs with film like cameras do. A satellite collects information about energy coming from the Earth's surface and sends it back to receiving stations on Earth. A computer is then used to process the information to create an image we can see, like the one shown in **Figure 13.**

The first major use of aerial photography was to seek out information about enemy positions during World War I.

Figure 13 Satellites can detect objects the size of a baseball stadium. The satellite that took this picture was 220 km above the Earth's surface!

Science Bloopers

During the complex process of compiling vast amounts of data from a number of different maps and sources, mistakes are sometimes made. Cartographers have wiped entire cities off maps accidentally! Canada's capital, Ottawa, for example, was once omitted from a Canadian tourist-office map. An official explanation that there was no direct air service between New York City and Ottawa failed to satisfy one Ottawa tourist bureau executive, who remarked irately, "Ottawa should be shown in any case, even if the only point of entry was by two-man kayak."

3 Extend

MEETING INDIVIDUAL NEEDS

Learners Having Difficulty
Show students two maps with different representative fraction scales, such as a map of North America and a map of your community. Point out that the larger the denominator in a representative fraction scale, the smaller the scale of the map. You might clarify this by pointing out that $\frac{1}{4}$ of a pie is smaller than $\frac{1}{2}$ of a pie. Maps that show a large area, such as a continent, use a smaller scale and show less detail. Maps that show a smaller area, such as a town, can have a larger scale and show more detail. Discuss with students cases in which large-scale maps are the most useful and cases in which small-scale maps are most useful. **Sheltered English**

MATH and MORE

Have students suppose that they want to use a map with a scale of 1:24,000 to estimate the length of a hike. On the map, the route measures 20 cm. Have students calculate the length of the hike in kilometers.

(20 cm × 24,000 = 480,000 cm;
480,000 cm ÷ 100 cm/m = 4,800 m;
4,800 ÷ 1,000 m/km = 4.8 km)

Math Skills Worksheet 17
"Using Proportions and Cross-Multiplication"

Critical Thinking Worksheet 2
"Shaping the World"

Information Shown on Maps

As you have already learned, there are many different ways of making maps. It is also true that there are many types of maps. You might already be familiar with some, such as road maps or political maps of the United States. But regardless of its type, each map should contain the information shown in **Figure 14**.

Figure 14 Road Map of Connecticut

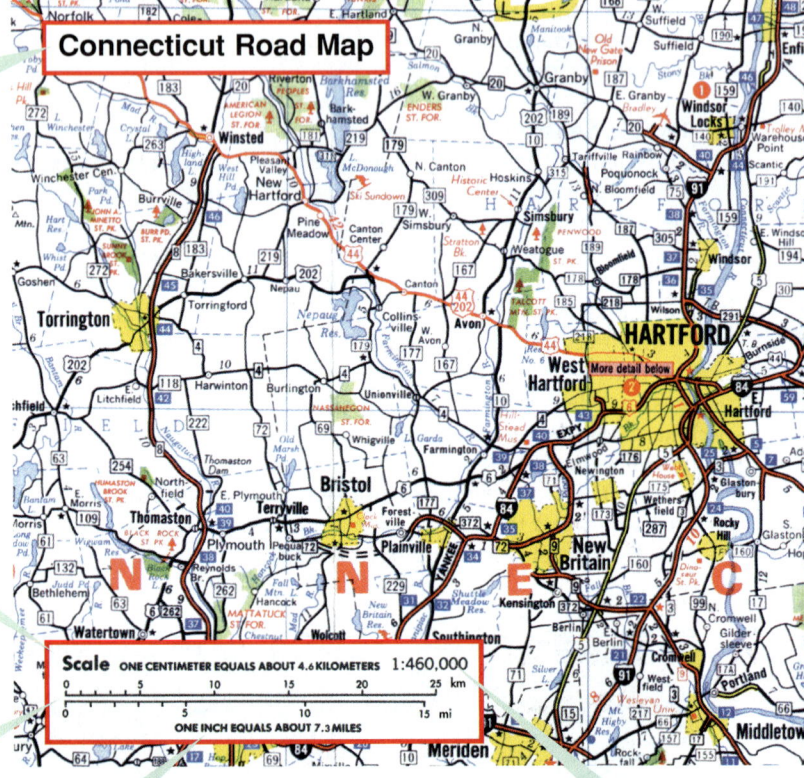

The **title** tells you what area is being shown on the map or gives you information about the subject of the map.

A **map's scale** shows the relationship between the distance on the Earth's surface and the distance on the map.

A **graphic scale** is like a ruler. The distance on the Earth's surface is represented by a bar graph that shows units of distance.

A **verbal scale** is a phrase that describes the measure of distance on the map relative to the distance on the Earth's surface.

A **representative fraction** is a fraction or ratio that shows the relationship between the distance on the map and the distance on the Earth's surface. It is unitless, meaning it stays the same no matter what units of measurement you are using.

Multicultural CONNECTION

Maps made by Native Americans were similar to maps made by Europeans in that they included not only geographic information but also elements of their history, traditions, and mythology. Native American mapmakers also used standardized symbols to indicate roads, villages, rivers, and other physical features. The Aztec of central Mexico, for example, used rows of footprints to represent roads and swirling lines to indicate water. Aztec maps and mapmaking techniques were adapted by the Spanish, who explored and conquered the region.

Reading a Map

Imagine that you are a trip planner for an automobile club. A couple of people come in who want to travel from Torrington, Connecticut, to Bristol, Connecticut. Using the map in Figure 14, describe the shortest travel route you would suggest they take between the two cities. List the roads they would take, the direction they would travel, and the towns they would pass through. Use the map scale to determine approximately how many miles there are between Torrington and Bristol.

A **compass rose** shows you how the map is positioned in relation to true north.

A **legend** is a list of the symbols used in the map and their explanations.

The **date** gives the time at which the information on the map was accurate.

REVIEW

1. A globe is a fairly accurate model of the Earth, yet it has some weaknesses. What is one weakness?
2. What is distortion on a map, and why does it occur?
3. What is remote sensing? How has it changed mapmaking?
4. **Summarizing Data** List five items found on maps. Explain how each item is important to reading a map.

TOPIC: Mapmaking
GO TO: www.scilinks.org
sciLINKS NUMBER: HSTE040

Answers to APPLY
Answers may vary. Sample answer: The people would take State Road 8 south to U.S. Route 6 east to travel between Torrington and Bristol. This route would take them through Plymouth and Terryville before reaching Bristol. The trip is approximately 27 km.

4) Close

Quiz

1. Where is distortion found in a Mercator projection map? (near the poles)
2. How have photography and air travel contributed to the science of mapmaking? (Aircraft and satellites allow people to view Earth's surface from above; photography has improved the accuracy of maps.)
3. Why is it important for maps to have scales? (Map scales explain the relationship between distances as measured on the map and corresponding distances on Earth's surface.)

ALTERNATIVE ASSESSMENT

Desktop publishing software makes it easier for the noncartographer to create maps. Such maps often omit crucial elements, such as a scale, a date, or a compass rose. Have students bring in a map from a newspaper, a magazine, or an advertisement, and have them write a critique of the map's strengths and its shortcomings. Students may post the maps and critiques on a bulletin board.

TOPIC: Mapmaking
GO TO: www.scilinks.org
sciLINKS NUMBER: HSTE040

Answers to Review

1. Answers will vary. Sample answer: A globe is too small to show details such as roads and rivers.
2. Distortions are changes in direction, distance, and the size and shape of landmasses that occur when information is transferred from a curved surface to a flat surface.
3. Remote sensing is the gathering of information about something without actually being there. Remote sensing has allowed mapmakers to map the surface of the Earth more accurately.
4. title, scale, north arrow, legend, and date; Answers may vary.

Section 2 • Mapping the Earth's Surface

SECTION 3

Focus

Topographic Maps

In this section, students investigate how contour lines are used to show elevation and landforms on a topographic map. In addition, they learn how to read and interpret the features of a topographic map.

 **Bellringer**

Have students examine the topographic map shown in **Figure 15.** Have them imagine that they are standing on the top of Campbell Hill. Students should describe in their ScienceLog what they see in each direction. Tell students that they will learn to read topographic maps, such as the ones in this section.

1 Motivate

ACTIVITY

Investigate Your Area If possible, obtain topographic maps of your area from the USGS. Display the maps for students to study. As a class, locate different landforms, such as lakes, mountains, and valleys. Discuss with students how contour intervals indicate changes in elevation. If possible, take a class field trip to an area shown on a topographic map. Students will enjoy comparing the map with the topography they observe.
Sheltered English

Directed Reading Worksheet 2 Section 3

Section 3

Terms to Learn
topographic map
elevation
contour lines
contour interval
relief
index contour

What You'll Do
- Describe how contour lines show elevation and landforms on a map.
- List the rules of contour lines.
- Interpret a topographic map.

Topographic Maps

Imagine that you are on an outdoor adventure trip. The trip's purpose is to improve your survival skills by having you travel across undeveloped territory with only a compass and a map. What kind of map will you be using? Well, it's not a road map—you won't be seeing a lot of roads where you are going. You will need a topographic map. A **topographic map** is a map that shows surface features, or topography, of the Earth. Topographic maps show both natural features, such as rivers, lakes and mountains, and features made by humans, such as cities, roads, and bridges. Topographic maps also show elevation. **Elevation** is the height of an object above sea level. The elevation at sea level is 0. In this section you will learn how to interpret a topographic map.

Elements of Elevation

The United States Geological Survey (USGS), a federal government agency, has made topographic maps for all of the United States. Each of these maps is a detailed description of a small area of the Earth's surface. Because the topographic maps produced by the USGS use feet as their unit of measure rather than meters, we will follow their example.

Contour Lines On a topographic map, contour lines are used to show elevation. **Contour lines** are lines that connect points of equal elevation. For example, one contour line would connect points on a map that have an elevation of 100 ft. Another line would connect points on a map that have an elevation of 200 ft. **Figure 15** illustrates how contour lines appear on a map.

Figure 15 *Because contour lines connect points of equal elevation, the shape of the contour lines reflects the shape of the land.*

internet connect

TOPIC: Topographic Maps
GO TO: www.scilinks.org
sciLINKS NUMBER: HSTE045

IS THAT A FACT!

The Ordnance Survey of Great Britain produces topographic maps with very large scales, ranging from 1:10,000 to 1:1,250. Such large scales permit a level of detail that extends to showing the location of public telephones, windmills, and large boulders!

Contour Interval The difference in elevation between one contour line and the next is called the **contour interval**. For example, a map with a contour interval of 20 ft would have contour lines every 20 ft of elevation change, such as 0 ft, 20 ft, 40 ft, 60 ft, and so on. A mapmaker chooses a contour interval based on the area's relief. **Relief** is the difference in elevation between the highest and lowest points of the area being mapped. Because the relief of a mountainous area is high, it might be shown on a map using a large contour interval, such as 100 ft. However, a flat area has low relief and might be shown on a map using a small contour interval, such as 10 ft.

The spacing of contour lines also indicates slope, as shown in **Figure 16.** Contour lines that are close together, with little space between them, usually show a steep slope. Contour lines that are spaced far apart generally represent a gentle slope.

Index Contour On many topographic maps, the mapmaker uses an index contour to make reading the map a little easier. An **index contour** is a darker, heavier contour line that is usually every fifth line and that is labeled by elevation. Find an index contour on both of the topographic maps.

Counting Contours

Calculate the contour interval for the map shown in Figure 15 on the previous page. (Hint: Find the difference between two bold lines found next to each other. Subtract the lower marked elevation from the higher marked elevation. Divide by 5.)

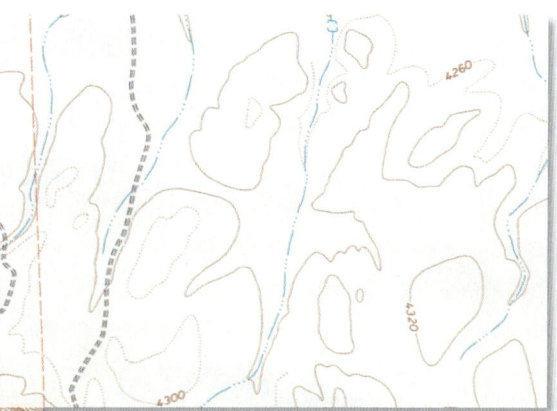

Figure 16 *The portion of the topographic map on the left shows Pikes Peak, in Colorado. The map above shows a valley in Big Bend Ranch State Park, in Texas.*

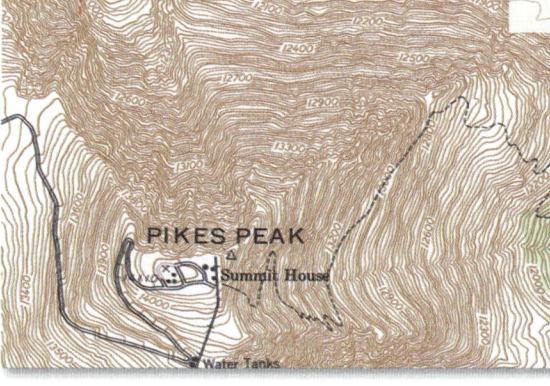

✓ Self-Check

If elevation is not labeled on a map, how can you determine if the mapped area is steep or not? *(See page 726 to check your answer.)*

Homework

Expedition Journal Have students write a fictitious journal from the perspective of a member of an expedition team. Every journal entry should include a description of the topography they encountered. Students should include a map in which they use the appropriate symbols and contour lines to show their route. This activity will take several days to complete. After the student explorers have "returned" from their expedition, they should present their map and read their journal entries to the class.

2) Teach

Answers to MATHBREAK

Sample answer:
500 ft − 450 ft = 50 ft
50 ft ÷ 5 = 10 ft
contour interval = 10 ft

DISCUSSION

Reproduce on the chalkboard a mountainous portion of one of the contour maps shown in the text. Discuss with students where the steepest slopes are (where the lines are closest together). Then change the contour interval by erasing every other contour line. Point out to students that the contour interval is now twice as large. Discuss with students the advantages and the disadvantages of a map with a larger contour interval. (The map may seem easier to read, but detail is lost.)

RETEACHING

If students are having trouble understanding contour lines, use some modeling clay to make a landform. Ask a volunteer to hold a ruler vertically next to the landform while you use a plastic knife to mark off contour intervals around the landform. When you are finished, have students view the landform from the side so that they can see the uniformity of the contour intervals and from above so they can see how the intervals would appear on a topographic map. Then give pairs of students some modeling clay and invite them to try the same activity themselves. **Sheltered English**

Answers to Self-Check

If the lines are close together, then the mapped area is steep. If the lines are far apart, the mapped area has a gradual slope or is flat.

Section 3 • Topographic Maps

3) Extend

GUIDED PRACTICE

Display a portion of a topographic map and point to the following features. Have students identify them and describe what they indicate.

- **index contour line** (identifiable from its color and its label elevation; index contours make reading the map easier)
- **steep slope** (identifiable by the close spacing of the contour lines)
- **gentle slope** (identifiable because the contour lines are relatively far apart)
- **river, lake, or pond** (identifiable by shape and color)

Sheltered English

GROUP ACTIVITY

Have groups put together a contour map reading presentation for another class. Encourage them to make some handouts for the class about topographic maps and their uses and to include visual elements, such as a poster or a diagram, that highlight the features of topographic maps. Groups might finish their presentation with a quiz to assess how well they've explained the material.

MEETING INDIVIDUAL NEEDS

Advanced Learners Have students research orienteering and learn some of the techniques involved. Encourage students to explain or demonstrate for classmates such skills as how to set a map with a compass, how to determine bearings, and how to reconcile the differences between magnetic north, grid north, and true north.

Reading a Topographic Map

Topographic maps, like other maps, use symbols to represent parts of the Earth's surface. The legend from the USGS topographic map in **Figure 17** shows some of the common symbols used to represent certain features in topographic maps.

Different colors are also used to represent different features of the Earth's surface. In general, buildings, roads, bridges, and railroads are black. Contour lines are brown. Major highways are red. Cities and towns are pink. Bodies of water, such as rivers, lakes, and oceans, are shown in blue, and wooded areas are represented by the color green.

Figure 17 *All USGS topographic maps use the same legend to represent natural features and features made by humans.*

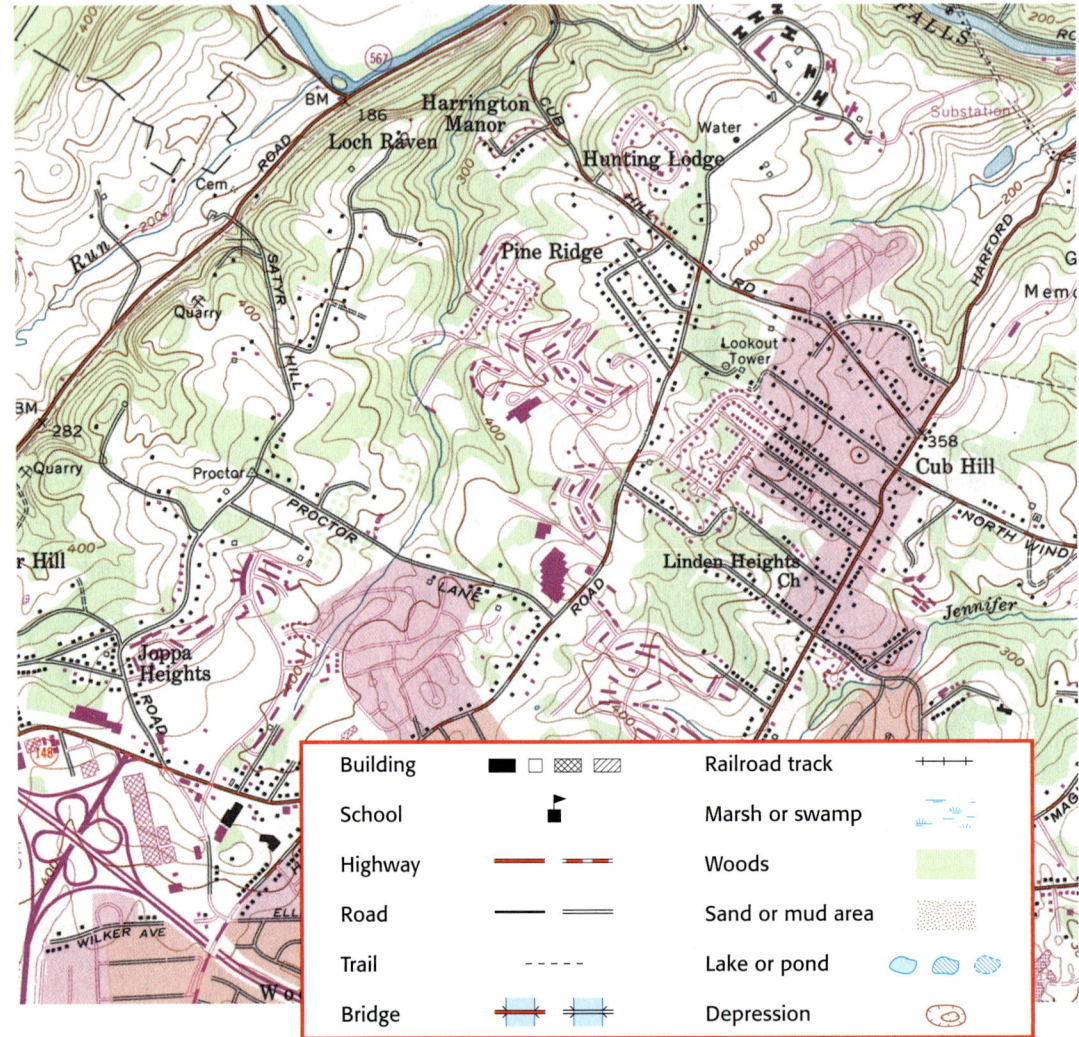

48

CONNECT TO OCEANOGRAPHY

Oceanographers use contour maps to map the topography of the ocean floor. Traditionally, darker colors represent deeper depths, while lighter colors represent areas closer to the surface of the water. If possible, display an oceanographic map, and have students apply what they have learned about topographic maps to create a profile of a section of the ocean floor. Students should find similarities between the topography of the ocean floor and that of continental landmasses.

The Golden Rules of Contour Lines Contour lines are the key to interpreting the size and shape of landforms on a topographic map. When you first look at a topographic map, it might seem confusing. Accurately reading a topographic map requires training and practice. The following rules will help you understand how to read topographic maps:

1. Contour lines never cross. All points along a contour line represent a single elevation.

2. The spacing of contour lines depends on slope characteristics. Closely spaced contour lines represent a steep slope. Widely spaced contour lines represent a gentle slope.

3. Contour lines that cross a valley or stream are V-shaped. The V points toward the area of higher elevation. If a stream or river flows through the valley, the V points upstream.

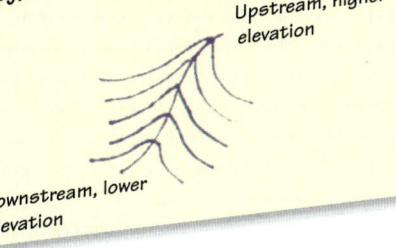

4. Contour lines form closed circles around the tops of hills, mountains, and depressions. One way to tell hills and depressions apart is that depressions are marked with short, straight lines inside the circle, pointing downslope toward the center of the depression.

 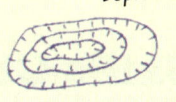
Hill   Depression

Environment CONNECTION

State agencies, such as the Texas Parks and Wildlife Department, use topographic maps to plot the distribution and occurrence of endangered plant and animal species. By marking the location of endangered species on a map, these agencies can record and protect these habitats.

REVIEW

1. How do topographic maps represent the Earth's surface?
2. If a contour map contains streams, can you tell where the higher ground is even if all of the numbers are removed?
3. Why can't contour lines cross?
4. **Inferring Conclusions** Why isn't the highest point on a hill or mountain represented by a contour line?

internet connect
TOPIC: Topographic Maps
GO TO: www.scilinks.org
sciLINKS NUMBER: HSTE045

Chapter Highlights

VOCABULARY DEFINITIONS

SECTION 1

map model or representation of the Earth's surface

true north the geographic North Pole

magnetic declination the angle of correction for the difference between geographic north and magnetic north

equator a circle halfway between the poles that divides the Earth into the Northern and Southern Hemispheres

latitude the distance north or south from the equator; measured in degrees

longitude the distance east or west from the prime meridian; measured in degrees

prime meridian the line of longitude that passes through Greenwich, England; represents 0° longitude

SECTION 2

Mercator projection a map projection that results when the contents of the globe are transferred onto a cylinder

conic projection a map projection that is made by transferring the contents of the globe onto a cone

azimuthal projection a map projection that is made by transferring the contents of the globe onto a plane

aerial photograph a photograph taken from the air

remote sensing gathering information about something without actually being nearby

Chapter Highlights

SECTION 1

Vocabulary
- map (p. 34)
- true north (p. 36)
- magnetic declination (p. 36)
- equator (p. 37)
- latitude (p. 37)
- longitude (p. 38)
- prime meridian (p. 38)

Section Notes
- The North and South Poles are used as reference points for describing direction and location on the Earth.
- The cardinal directions—north, south, east, and west—are used for describing direction.
- Magnetic compasses are used to determine direction on the Earth's surface. The north needle on the compass points to the magnetic north pole.
- Because the geographic North Pole never changes location, it is called true north. The magnetic poles are different from the Earth's geographic poles and have changed location throughout the Earth's history.
- The magnetic declination is the adjustment or difference between magnetic north and geographic north.
- Latitude and longitude are intersecting lines that help you find locations on a map or a globe. Lines of latitude run east-west. Lines of longitude run north-south through the poles.

Labs
Round or Flat? (p. 632)
Orient Yourself! (p. 634)

SECTION 2

Vocabulary
- Mercator projection (p. 41)
- conic projection (p. 42)
- azimuthal projection (p. 42)
- aerial photograph (p. 43)
- remote sensing (p. 43)

Section Notes
- A globe is the most accurate representation of the Earth's surface.
- Maps have built-in distortion because some information is lost when mapmakers transfer images from a curved surface to a flat surface.

✓ Skills Check

Math Concepts

REPRESENTATIVE FRACTION One type of map scale is a representative fraction. A representative fraction is a fraction or ratio that shows the relationship between the distance on the map and the distance on the Earth's surface. It is unitless, meaning it stays the same no matter what units of measurement you are using. For example, say you are using a map with a representative fraction scale that is 1:12,000. If you are measuring distance on the map in centimeters, 1 cm on the map represents 12,000 cm on the Earth's surface. A measure of 3 cm on the map represents 12,000 × 3 cm = 36,000 cm on the Earth's surface.

Visual Understanding

THE POLES The Earth has two different sets of poles—the geographic poles and the magnetic poles. See Figure 4 on page 36 to review how the geographic poles and the magnetic poles differ.

INFORMATION SHOWN ON MAPS Study Figure 14 on pages 44 and 45 to review the necessary information each map should contain.

Lab and Activity Highlights

Round or Flat? PG 632

Orient Yourself! PG 634

Topographic Tuber PG 636

Datasheets for LabBook (blackline masters for these labs)

SECTION 2

- Mapmakers use map projections to transfer images of the Earth's curved surface to a flat surface.
- The most common map projections are based on three geometric shapes—cylinders, cones, and planes.
- Remote sensing has allowed mapmakers to make more accurate maps.
- All maps should have a title, date, scale, legend, and north arrow.

SECTION 3

Vocabulary
topographic map (p. 46)
elevation (p. 46)
contour lines (p. 46)
contour interval (p. 47)
relief (p. 47)
index contour (p. 47)

Section Notes
- Topographic maps use contour lines to show a mapped area's elevation and the shape and size of landforms.
- The shape of contour lines reflects the shape of the land.
- The contour interval and the spacing of contour lines indicate the slope of the land.
- Like all maps, topographic maps use a set of symbols to represent features of the Earth's surface.
- Contour lines never cross. Contour lines that cross a valley or stream are V-shaped. Contour lines form closed circles around the tops of hills, mountains, and depressions.

Labs
Topographic Tuber (p. 636)

VOCABULARY DEFINITIONS, continued

SECTION 3

topographic map a map that shows the surface features of the Earth

elevation the height of an object above sea level; the height of surface landforms above sea level

contour lines lines that connect points of equal elevation

contour interval the difference in elevation between one contour line and the next

relief the difference in elevation between the highest and lowest points of an area being mapped

index contour a darker, heavier contour line that is usually every fifth line and is labeled by elevation

 Vocabulary Review Worksheet 2

 Blackline masters of these Chapter Highlights can be found in the **Study Guide.**

internet connect

GO TO: go.hrw.com

Visit the **HRW** Web site for a variety of learning tools related to this chapter. Just type in the keyword:

KEYWORD: HSTMAP

GO TO: www.scilinks.org

Visit the **National Science Teachers Association** on-line Web site for Internet resources related to this chapter. Just type in the *sci*LINKS number for more information about the topic:

TOPIC: Finding Locations on the Earth   *sci*LINKS NUMBER: HSTE030
TOPIC: Latitude and Longitude   *sci*LINKS NUMBER: HSTE035
TOPIC: Mapmaking   *sci*LINKS NUMBER: HSTE040
TOPIC: Topographic Maps   *sci*LINKS NUMBER: HSTE045

Lab and Activity Highlights

LabBank

 Inquiry Labs, Looking for Buried Treasure, Lab 9

Long-Term Projects & Research Ideas, Globe Trotting, Project 30

Chapter Review Answers

Using Vocabulary

1. True north is the geographic North Pole. Magnetic north refers to the magnetic north pole, which changes.
2. Latitude is the distance north and south from the equator. Longitude is the distance east and west from the prime meridian. Both latitude and longitude are measured in degrees.
3. The equator is the imaginary circle halfway between the poles that divides the Earth into Northern and Southern Hemispheres and represents 0° latitude. The prime meridian represents 0° longitude.
4. A Mercator projection is a map projection made by transferring the contents of the globe onto a cylinder of paper. An azimuthal projection is a map projection made by projecting the contents of the globe onto a plane.
5. Contour interval is the difference in elevation between one contour line and the next. An index contour is a darker, heavier contour line that usually occurs every fifth line and is labeled.
6. Elevation is the height of an object above sea level. Relief is the difference in elevation between the highest and lowest points of the area being mapped.

Understanding Concepts

Multiple Choice

7. b
8. c
9. d
10. b
11. b
12. a
13. d
14. b
15. b
16. b

Chapter Review

USING VOCABULARY

Explain the difference between the following sets of words:

1. true north/magnetic north
2. latitude/longitude
3. equator/prime meridian
4. Mercator projection/azimuthal projection
5. contour interval/index contour
6. elevation/relief

UNDERSTANDING CONCEPTS

Multiple Choice

7. A point whose latitude is 0° is located on the
   a. North Pole.
   b. equator.
   c. South Pole.
   d. prime meridian.

8. The distance in degrees east or west of the prime meridian is
   a. latitude.
   b. declination.
   c. longitude.
   d. projection.

9. The needle of a magnetic compass points toward the
   a. meridians.
   b. parallels.
   c. geographic North Pole.
   d. magnetic north pole.

10. The most common map projections are based on three geometric shapes. Which of the following geometric shapes is not one of them?
    a. cylinder
    b. square
    c. cone
    d. plane

11. A Mercator projection is distorted near the
    a. equator.
    b. poles.
    c. prime meridian.
    d. date line.

12. What kind of scale does not have written units of measure?
    a. representative fraction
    b. verbal
    c. graphic
    d. mathematical

13. What is the relationship between the distance on a map and the actual distance on the Earth called?
    a. legend
    b. elevation
    c. relief
    d. scale

14. The latitude of the North Pole is
    a. 100° north.
    b. 90° north.
    c. 180° north.
    d. 90° south.

15. Widely spaced contour lines indicate a
    a. steep slope.
    b. gentle slope.
    c. hill.
    d. river.

Concept Mapping Transparency 2

Blackline masters of this Chapter Review can be found in the **Study Guide**.

16. __?__ is the height of an object above sea level.
    a. Contour interval
    b. Elevation
    c. Declination
    d. Index contour

Short Answer

17. How can a magnetic compass be used to find direction on the Earth's surface?
18. Why is a map legend important?
19. Why does Greenland appear so large in relation to other landmasses on a map with a Mercator projection?
20. What is the function of contour lines on a topographic map?

Concept Mapping

21. Use the following terms to create a concept map: maps, legend, map projection, map parts, scale, cylinder, title, cone, plane, date, north arrow.

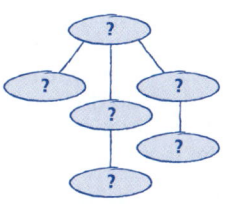

CRITICAL THINKING AND PROBLEM SOLVING

Write one or two sentences to answer the following questions:

22. One of the important parts of a map is its date. Why is this so important?
23. A mapmaker has to draw one map for three different countries that do not share a common unit of measure. What type of scale would this mapmaker use? Why?
24. How would a topographic map of the Rocky Mountains differ from a topographic map of the Great Plains?

MATH IN SCIENCE

25. A map has a verbal scale of 1 cm equals 200 m. If the actual distance between two points is 12,000 m, how far apart will they appear on the map?
26. On a topographic map, the contour interval is 50 ft. The bottom of a mountain begins on a contour line marked with a value of 1050 ft. The top of the mountain is within a contour line that is 12 lines higher than the bottom of the mountain. What is the elevation of the top of the mountain?

INTERPRETING GRAPHICS

Use the topographic map below to answer the questions that follow.

27. What is the elevation change between two adjacent lines on this map?
28. What type of relief does this area have?
29. What surface features are shown on this map?
30. What is the elevation at the top of Ore Hill?

Take a minute to review your answers to the Pre-Reading Questions found at the bottom of page 32. Have your answers changed? If necessary, revise your answers based on what you have learned since you began this chapter.

53

INTERPRETING GRAPHICS
27. 20 ft
28. It has very high relief.
29. Answers will vary. Sample answer: Two hills are shown on this map.
30. The elevation at the top of Ore Hill is 2,025 ft.

Short Answer
17. The needle on a magnetic compass points to magnetic north, indicating the direction of the magnetic north pole. If you know an area's magnetic declination, you can determine true north.
18. A map legend is important because it defines the set of symbols used in the map.
19. Greenland appears large on a map with a Mercator projection because of distortion. Maps with a Mercator projection are increasingly distorted as the distance from the equator increases.
20. Contour lines on a topographic map show the elevation, the relief, and the shape of landforms.

Concept Mapping
21. 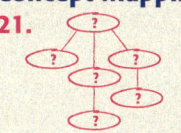 An answer to this exercise can be found at the end of this book.

CRITICAL THINKING AND PROBLEM SOLVING

22. A date on a map is important because the Earth is constantly changing. The date shows you how old the information is. It might also indicate what the landscape was once like.
23. The mapmaker should use a representative fraction. A representative fraction is unitless and could be used by all three countries. Furthermore, the countries could find out distances on the map using their own unit of measure.
24. A topographic map of the Rocky Mountains would show contour lines close together, indicating steep slopes, while a contour map of the Great Plains would show contour lines spaced far apart, indicating a flat or gradual slope.

MATH IN SCIENCE
25. 60 cm
26. above 1,650 ft

Chapter 2 • Chapter Review   53

SCIENCE, TECHNOLOGY, AND SOCIETY

The Lost City of Ubar

Background

According to legend, Allah became displeased with the wickedness of the citizens of Ubar and buried the city under a wave of sand. Ubar remained lost for thousands of years until the coordinated efforts of filmmaker Nicholas Clapp, NASA scientist Dr. Ronald Blom, and a team of explorers uncovered the ruins in 1991.

Science, Technology, and Society

The Lost City of Ubar

Can you imagine tree sap being more valuable than gold? Well, about 2,000 years ago, a tree sap called frankincense was just that! Frankincense was used to treat illnesses and to disguise body odor. Ancient civilizations from Rome to India treasured it. While the name of the city that was the center of frankincense production and export had been known for generations—Ubar—there was just one problem: No one knew where it was! But now the mystery is solved. Using remote sensing, scientists have found clues hidden beneath desert sand dunes.

▲ *Trails and roads appear as purple lines on this computer-generated remote-sensing image.*

Using Eyes in the Sky

The process of remote sensing uses satellites to take pictures of large areas of land. The satellite records images as sets of data and sends these data to a receiver on Earth. A computer processes the data and displays the images. These remote sensing images can then be used to reveal differences unseen by the naked eye.

Remote-sensing images reveal modern roads as well as ancient caravan routes hidden beneath sand dunes in the Sahara Desert. But how could researchers tell the difference between the two? Everything on Earth reflects or radiates energy. Soil, vegetation, cities, and roads all emit a unique wavelength of energy. The problem is, sometimes modern roads and ancient roads are difficult to distinguish. The differences between similar objects can be enhanced by assigning color to an area and then displaying the area on a computer screen. Researchers used differences in color to distinguish between the roads of Ubar and modern roads. When researchers found ancient caravan routes and discovered that all the routes met at one location, they knew they had discovered the lost city of Ubar!

Continuing Discovery

Archaeologists continue to investigate the region around Ubar. They believe the great city may have collapsed into a limestone cavern beneath its foundation. Researchers are continuing to use remote sensing to study more images for clues to aid their investigation.

Think About It!

▶ Do modern civilizations value certain products or resources enough to establish elaborate trade routes for their transport? If so, what makes these products so valuable? Record your thoughts in your ScienceLog.

Answer to Think About It!
Students' answers will vary but may include the value modern civilizations place on paper currency, fossil fuels, or spices.

CAREERS

WATERSHED PLANNER

Have you ever wondered if the water you drink is safe or what you could do to make sure it stays safe? As a watershed planner, **Nancy Charbeneau** identifies and solves land-use problems that may affect water quality.

Nancy Charbeneau enjoys using her teaching, biology, and landscape architecture background in her current career as a watershed planner. A watershed is any area of land where water drains into a stream, river, lake, or ocean. Charbeneau spends a lot of time writing publications and developing programs that explain the effects of land use on the quality of water.

Land is used in hundreds of ways. Some of these land uses can have negative effects on water resources. Charbeneau produces educational materials to inform the public about threats to water quality.

Mapping the Problems

Charbeneau uses Geographic Information System (GIS) maps to determine types of vegetation and the functions of different sections of land. GIS is a computer-based tool that allows people to store, access, and display geographic information collected through remote-sensing, field work, global positioning systems, and other sources. Maps and mapping systems play an important role in identifying land areas with water problems.

Maps tell Charbeneau whether an area has problems with soil erosion that could threaten water quality. Often the type of soil plays an important role in erosion. Thin or sandy soil does not hold water well, allowing for faster runoff and erosion. Flat land with heavy vegetation holds more water and is less prone to erosion.

Understanding the Importance

Charbeneau's biggest challenge is increasing understanding of the link between land use and water quality. If a harmful substance is introduced into a watershed, it may contaminate an aquifer or a well. As Charbeneau puts it, "Most people want to do the right thing, but they need information about land management practices that will protect water quality but still allow them to earn a decent living off their land."

Reading the Possibilities

▶ Map out your nearest watershed. Can you find any potential sources of contamination?

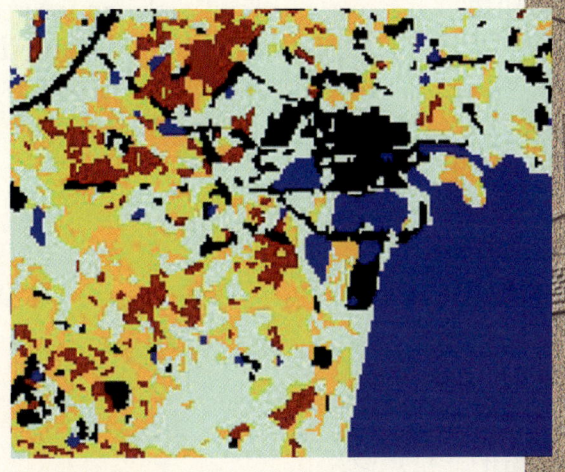

▲ *This GIS map shows the location of water in blue.*

CAREERS
Watershed Planner— Nancy Charbeneau

Background

Nancy Charbeneau has undergraduate degrees in elementary education and biology and a master's degree in landscape architecture.

Charbeneau's experience as a teacher prepared her for the production of educational materials that alert the public to water quality issues. Her degree in landscape architecture exposed her to the sophisticated mapping systems she uses as a watershed developer.

Answer to Reading the Possibilities

Answers will vary, depending on the topography and degree of urbanization of your region. Industrialized areas may have problems with groundwater pollution, while mountainous areas may have problems with erosion. Aerial photography, GIS, and infrared maps can reveal additional information about the vegetation and land use in a region.

UNIT 2

TIMELINE
Earth's Resources

In this unit, you will learn about the basic components of the solid Earth—rocks and the minerals from which they are made. The ground beneath your feet is a treasure-trove of interesting materials, some of which are very valuable. Secrets of the past are also hidden within its depths. This timeline shows some of the events that have occurred through history as scientists have come to understand more about our planet.

1533
Nicolaus Copernicus argues that the sun is the center of the universe rather than the Earth, as was commonly believed, but does not publish his findings for another 10 years.

1680
The dodo, a flightless bird, is driven to extinction by hunters. It is the first extinction of a species in recorded history.

1955
Using 1 million pounds of pressure and temperatures of more than 3,000°F, General Electric creates the first artificial diamonds from graphite.

1969
Apollo 11 astronauts Neil Armstrong and Edwin "Buzz" Aldrin bring 20 kg of moon rocks back to Earth.

1975
Junko Tabei becomes the first woman to successfully climb Mount Everest, 22 years after Edmund Hillary and Tenzing Norgay first conquered the mountain in 1953.

Unit 2

1848
Gold is discovered in California. Prospectors during the gold rush of the following year are referred to as "forty-niners."

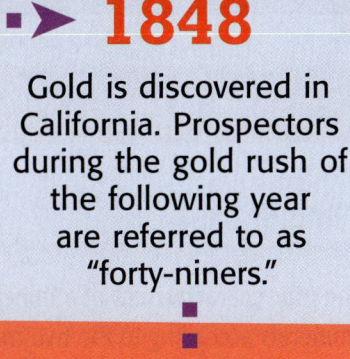

1735
George Brandt identifies a new element and names it cobalt. This is the first metal to be discovered since ancient times.

1861
Fossil remains of *Archaeopteryx*, a possible link between reptiles and birds, are discovered in Germany.

1936
Hoover Dam is completed. This massive hydroelectric dam, standing more than 72 stories high, required 450,000 cement-truck loads of concrete to build.

1946
Willard F. Libby develops a method of dating prehistoric objects by using radioactive carbon.

1997
Sojourner, a roving probe on Mars, investigates a Martian boulder nicknamed Yogi.

1984
Russian engineers drill a borehole 12 km into the Earth's crust, three times deeper than the deepest mine shaft.

Earth's Resources

Chapter Organizer

CHAPTER ORGANIZATION	TIME MINUTES	OBJECTIVES	LABS, INVESTIGATIONS, AND DEMONSTRATIONS
Chapter Opener pp. 58–59	45	National Standards: UCP 5, SAI 1	**Start-Up Activity** Riding a Mineral, p. 59
Section 1 What Is a Mineral?	90	▶ Explain the four characteristics of a mineral. ▶ Classify minerals according to the two major compositional groups. UCP 1, 5	
Section 2 Identifying Minerals	90	▶ Classify minerals using common mineral-identification techniques. ▶ Explain special properties of minerals. ▶ Describe what makes a mineral crystal a gem. UCP 1, 5, SAI 1; LabBook SAI 1	**QuickLab,** Scratch Test, p. 66 **GENERAL** **Skill Builder,** Mysterious Minerals, p. 638 **BASIC** **Datasheets for LabBook,** Mysterious Minerals, Datasheet 5 **BASIC** **Skill Builder,** Is It Fool's Gold?—A Dense Situation, p. 640 **GENERAL** **Datasheets for LabBook,** Is It Fool's Gold?—A Dense Situation, Datasheet 6 **GENERAL**
Section 3 The Formation and Mining of Minerals	90	▶ Describe the environments in which minerals are formed. ▶ Compare and contrast the different types of mining. UCP 5, SAI 1, SPSP 2, 4	**Long-Term Projects & Research Ideas,** Project 31 **ADVANCED**

See page T20 for a complete correlation of this book with the

NATIONAL SCIENCE EDUCATION STANDARDS.

TECHNOLOGY RESOURCES

 Guided Reading Audio CD English or Spanish, Chapter 3

 CNN Eye on the Environment, Greening Sudbury, Segment 12

 One-Stop Planner CD-ROM with Test Generator

Chapter 3 • Minerals of the Earth's Crust

CLASSROOM WORKSHEETS, TRANSPARENCIES, AND RESOURCES	SCIENCE INTEGRATION AND CONNECTIONS	REVIEW AND ASSESSMENT
Directed Reading Worksheet 3 BASIC **Science Puzzlers, Twisters & Teasers,** Worksheet 3 ADVANCED		
Directed Reading Worksheet 3, Section 1 BASIC **Transparency 107,** Gold Crystal Structure	**Connect to Life Science,** p. 60 in ATE **Biology Connection,** p. 62 **Connect to Chemistry,** p. 62 in ATE **Multicultural Connection,** p. 62 in ATE **Holt Anthology of Science Fiction,** The Metal Man ADVANCED	**Homework,** p. 62 in ATE GENERAL **Review,** p. 63 GENERAL **Quiz,** p. 63 in ATE GENERAL **Alternative Assessment,** p. 63 in ATE GENERAL
Directed Reading Worksheet 3, Section 2 BASIC **Reinforcement Worksheet 3,** Mystery Mineral GENERAL **Transparency 108,** Mohs' Hardness Scale **Transparency 109,** Special Properties of Some Minerals **Reinforcement Worksheet 3,** The Mineral Quiz Show BASIC	**Multicultural Connection,** p. 66 in ATE **Real-World Connection,** p. 67 in ATE	**Review,** p. 67 GENERAL **Quiz,** p. 67 in ATE GENERAL **Alternative Assessment,** p. 67 in ATE GENERAL
Directed Reading Worksheet 3, Section 3 BASIC **Transparency 210,** The Three Major Categories of Elements **Math Skills for Science Worksheet 21,** Percentages, Fractions, and Decimals GENERAL **Critical Thinking Worksheet 3,** Mineral Hunt ADVANCED	**Connect to Life Science,** p. 69 in ATE **Cross-Disciplinary Focus,** p. 69 in ATE **Multicultural Connection,** p. 69 in ATE **MathBreak,** How Pure is Pure? p. 70 GENERAL **Math and More,** p. 70 in ATE GENERAL **Connect to Physical Science,** p. 70 in ATE **Multicultural Connection,** p. 70 in ATE **Weird Science:** Lightning Leftovers, p. 76	**Self-Check,** p. 69 **Review,** p. 71 GENERAL **Quiz,** p. 71 in ATE GENERAL **Alternative Assessment,** p. 71 in ATE GENERAL

internet connect

 Holt, Rinehart and Winston On-line Resources
go.hrw.com

For worksheets and other teaching aids related to this chapter, visit the HRW Web site and type in the keyword: **HSTMIN**

 **National Science Teachers Association**
www.scilinks.org

Encourage students to use the *sci*LINKS numbers listed in the internet connect boxes to access information and resources on the **NSTA** Web site.

END-OF-CHAPTER REVIEW AND ASSESSMENT

Chapter Review in Study Guide
Vocabulary and Notes in Study Guide
Chapter Tests with Performance-Based Assessment, Chapter 3 Test
Chapter Tests with Performance-Based Assessment, Performance-Based Assessment 3
Concept Mapping Transparency 3

Chapter Resources & Worksheets

Visual Resources

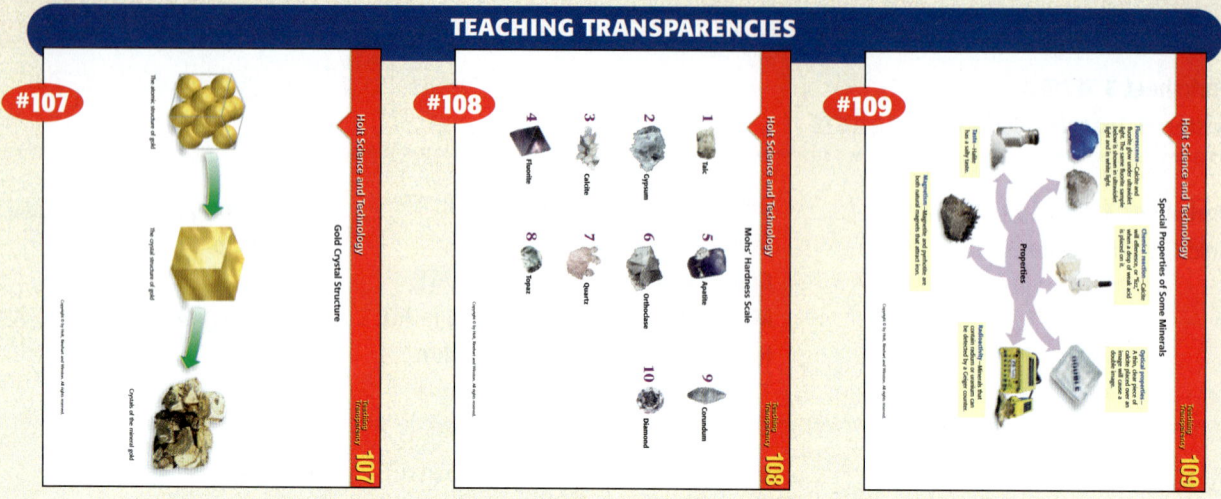

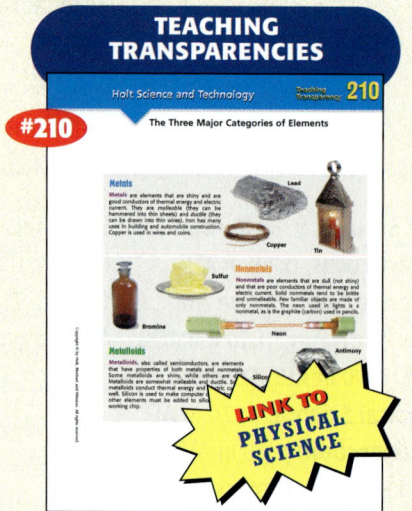

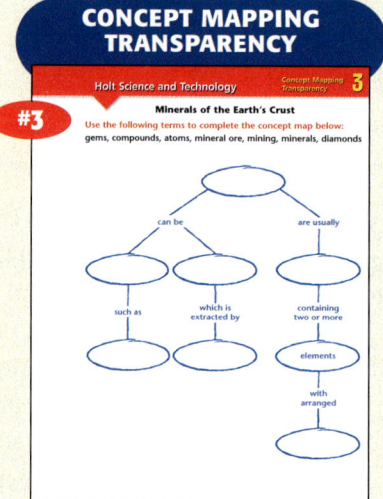

Meeting Individual Needs

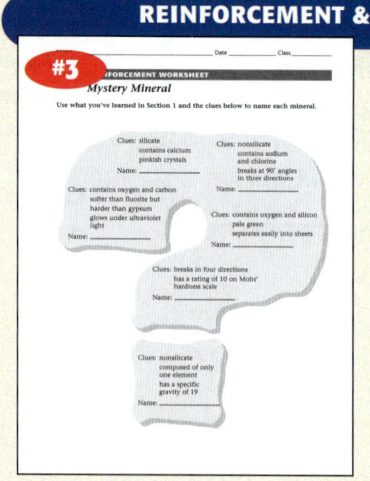

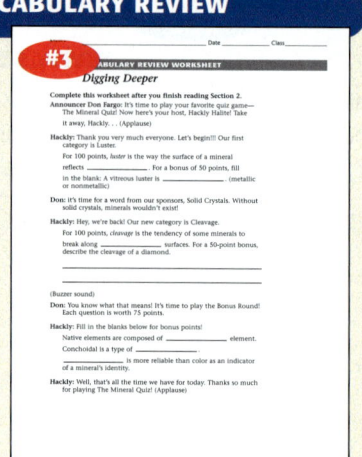

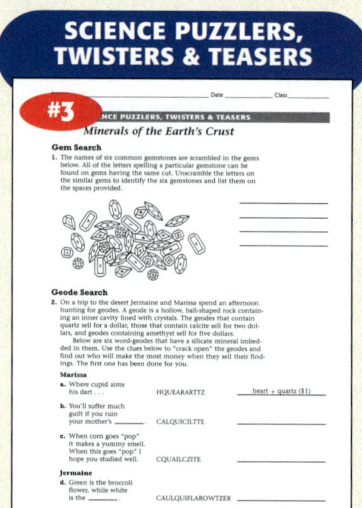

Chapter 3 • Minerals of the Earth's Crust

Chapter 3 • Minerals of the Earth's Crust

Review & Assessment

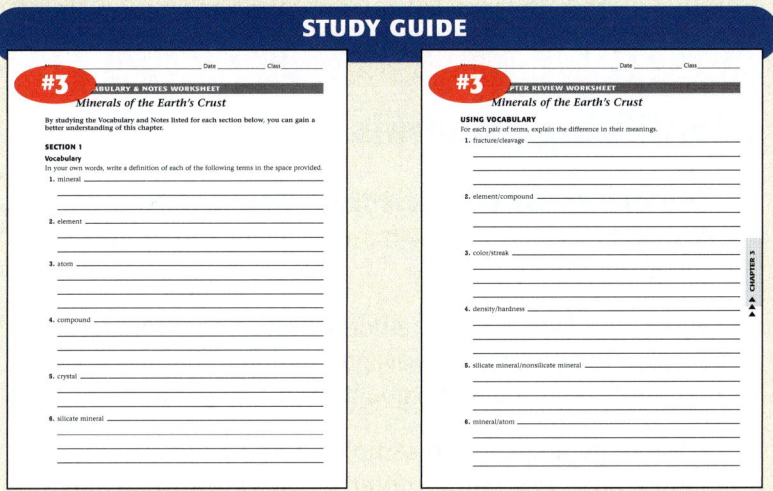

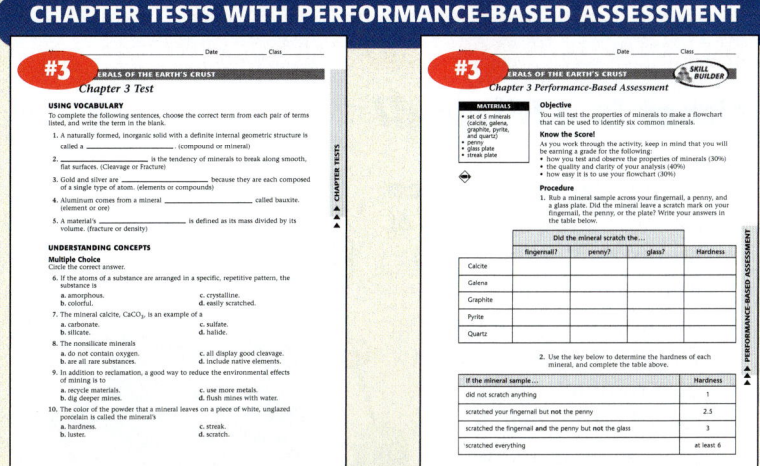

Lab Worksheets

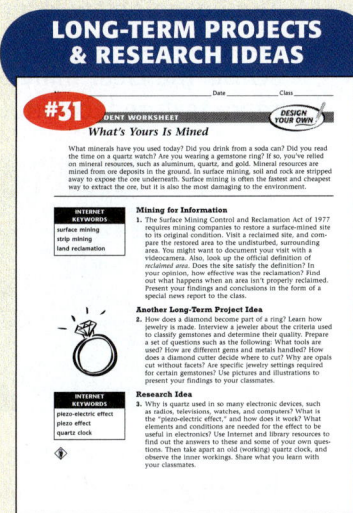

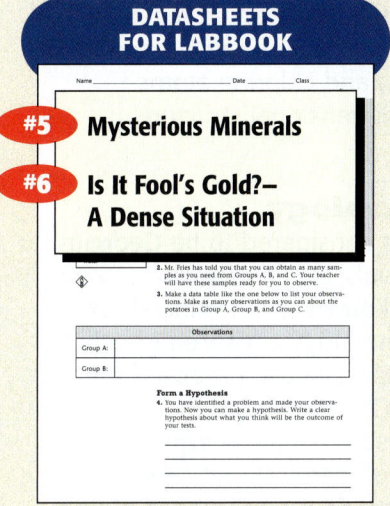

Applications & Extensions

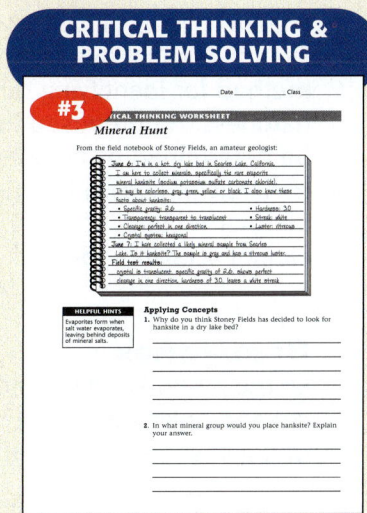

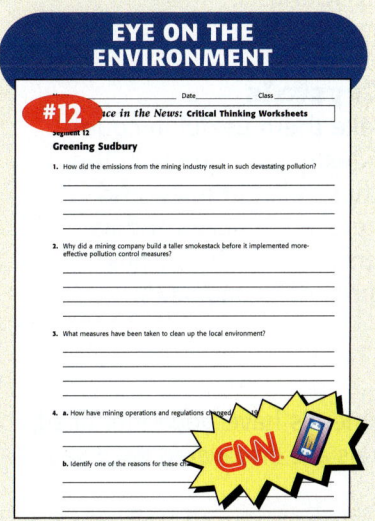

Chapter Background

SECTION 1
What Is a Mineral?

▶ **Crystal Structures**
Minerals are composed of atoms that are arranged in repeating three-dimensional patterns. The basic building block of a mineral crystal is called a unit cell. A unit cell is the smallest three-dimensional arrangement of atoms that displays the basic form, or symmetry, of the crystal. Many unit cells stacked together form a crystal. For example, a crystal of halite is composed of unit cells of sodium and chlorine atoms arranged in a unique three-dimensional structure.

▶ **The Origins of Mineralogy**
The founder of mineralogy is considered to be Georgius Agricola. His treatise on minerals, *De Re Metallica* (1556), recorded most of what was known about minerals at that time. The science of mineralogy advanced greatly when Rome de l'Isle, a French scientist, proposed the concept of the unit cell in 1772. He argued that the characteristics of mineral crystals could be explained only if they were composed of identical unit cells organized in a predictable way. Crystals are composed of unit cells much like a wall might be composed of bricks. After that discovery, the composition of mineral crystals was actively studied by many scientists.

▶ **Industrial Uses of Crystals**
The properties of crystals make them useful in countless ways. The electronics industry uses quartz in the manufacture of radios, watches, microphones, and sonar transducers. Rubies are used in lasers and as ball bearings in record players and watches, while diamonds are used in industrial drills and saws.

IS THAT A FACT!
▪ Currently about 3,600 minerals have been identified, and about 50 new minerals are discovered each year.

SECTION 2
Identifying Minerals

▶ **Methods of Identifying Minerals**
Scientists usually identify minerals using one of the following three methods.

- The *hand-specimen* method involves determining the color, luster, streak, cleavage, hardness, fluorescence, density, and magnetic qualities of a mineral.

- When geologists take samples back to the lab, they often use *petrographic microscopes* to identify minerals. These microscopes make it easier to identify minerals by the optical properties of their crystals. The image below is a photograph taken with a petrographic microscope of a metamorphic rock called *schist*. The clear mineral grains are quartz, and the more textured, colorful ones are muscovite mica.

- Geologists can analyze minerals at the atomic level by using *X-ray diffraction,* which measures the way crystal structures diffract X rays.

▶ **Mohs' Hardness Scale**
Friedrich Mohs (1773–1839) was a mineralogist who lived in Vienna, Austria. In 1812, Mohs developed a method for identifying minerals based on their relative hardness. He proposed that a mineral's identity can be determined by comparing the mineral with several minerals of known hardness. A mineral can scratch another mineral of equal or lesser hardness, but it cannot scratch a mineral of greater hardness.

▶ **Gemstones**
Of the 3,600 known minerals, only about 100 can be cut and polished to become gemstones. The definition of a gemstone is any naturally occurring mineral, rock,

Chapter 3 • Minerals of the Earth's Crust

or organic material that, when cut and polished, is suitable for use as jewelry. Diamonds, emeralds, rubies, and topazes are usually referred to as precious stones. Amethysts, garnets, and jades are considered semiprecious. Materials such as coral, pearls, and amber are also considered gemstones, even though they form by organic processes.

- Many gems used in jewelry are imitations. For example, glass can be colored green to look like an emerald. Scientists also create some gems artificially. Synthetic rubies, for example, have the same chemical structure as natural rubies. However, a gemologist can identify synthetic rubies by the presence of curved growth striations and air pockets, which do not occur in natural rubies.

IS THAT A FACT!

- The largest gold nugget ever found had a mass of 71 kg! It was found in Australia on February 5, 1869.
- One of the world's largest rubies has a mass of 8,500 carats and is cut to resemble the Liberty Bell.

SECTION 3
The Formation and Mining of Minerals

▶ Ancient Mines
The earliest evidence of mining dates to a 43,000-year-old iron mine in South Africa. Early iron miners were probably interested in the pigments associated with iron ores. The earliest metals used by neolithic people were gold and copper. Archaeological evidence indicates that the Egyptians mined copper and turquoise around  3400 B.C. Although most of the earliest mining was conducted on the surface, underground mining did occur by 1300 B.C. in Africa.

▶ Intrusions and Mineral Formation
Plutons are bodies of igneous rock that cooled beneath the Earth's surface. They are composed of coarse-grained, interlocking crystals. A large area of exposed intrusive rock (greater than 100 km^2) is called a batholith. Large batholiths occur in British Columbia, Alaska, and in the Sierra Nevada.

- A pegmatite is a very coarse-grained intrusive rock formed from the fluid-rich magma that remains after the rest of a pluton has solidified. Pegmatites may contain minerals such as tourmaline, topaz, or beryl.

▶ The Hope Diamond
The Hope diamond is a 45.5 carat blue diamond owned by the Smithsonian Institution since 1958. The gem was thought to be cursed because it was allegedly stolen from a statue of the Hindu goddess Sita. Misfortune and tragedy seemed to befall those who came in contact with the stone. The fabled gem was originally 112 carats. It was sold to King Louis XIV in 1668, and named the French Blue. The French Blue was stolen in 1792 from Louis XVI and may have been depicted in an 1800 portrait of a Spanish queen. In 1830, a 45.5 carat cut diamond surfaced in London. Experts declared that it was the French Blue recut to hide its identity. The American Henry Hope bought it, and it has since been called the Hope diamond.

IS THAT A FACT!

- The Wieliczka Salt Mine, in Poland, has more than 200 km of tunnels and is carved entirely out of halite (rock salt). Rock salt has been mined there since the late thirteenth century. The mine contains a number of sculptures, statues, altars, and even a chapel—all carved from salt!

For background information about teaching strategies and issues, refer to the *Professional Reference for Teachers*.

Minerals of the Earth's Crust

 Pre-Reading Questions

Students may not know the answers to these questions before reading the chapter, so accept any reasonable response.

Suggested Answers

1. A mineral is a naturally occurring inorganic solid that has a crystalline structure.
2. Minerals form when salt water evaporates; they can crystallize out of a solution; and they form when magma solidifies.

 Directed Reading Worksheet 3

 Science Puzzlers, Twisters & Teasers Worksheet 3

 Guided Reading Audio CD English or Spanish, Chapter 3

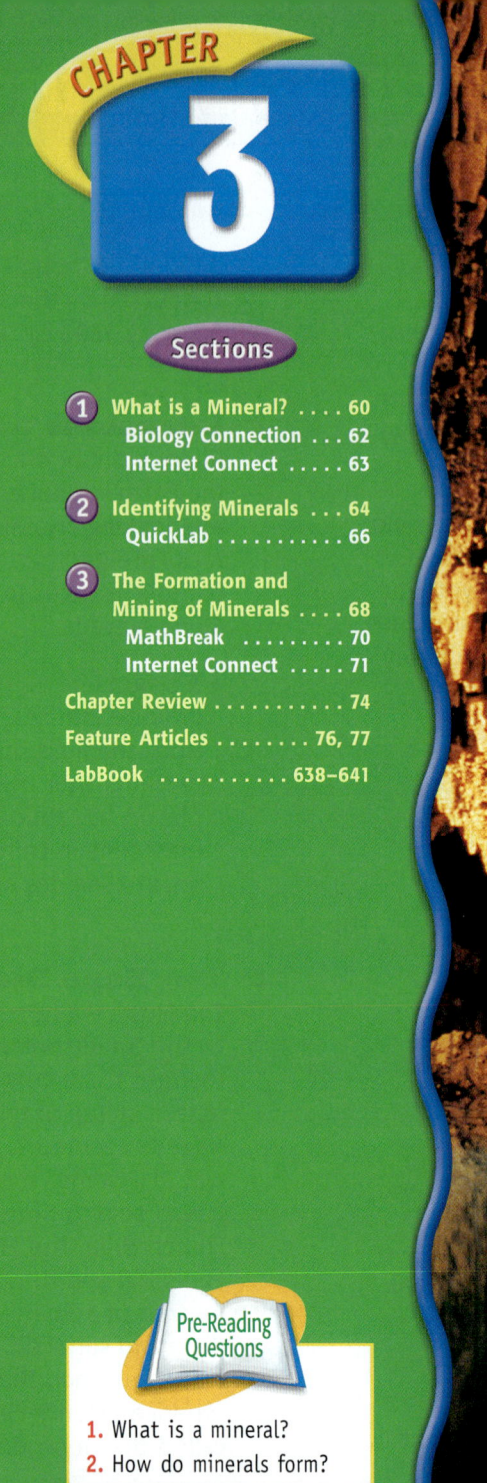

CHAPTER 3

Minerals of the Earth's Crust

Sections

1. What is a Mineral? 60
   Biology Connection ... 62
   Internet Connect 63
2. Identifying Minerals ... 64
   QuickLab 66
3. The Formation and Mining of Minerals 68
   MathBreak 70
   Internet Connect 71

Chapter Review 74
Feature Articles 76, 77
LabBook 638–641

Pre-Reading Questions

1. What is a mineral?
2. How do minerals form?

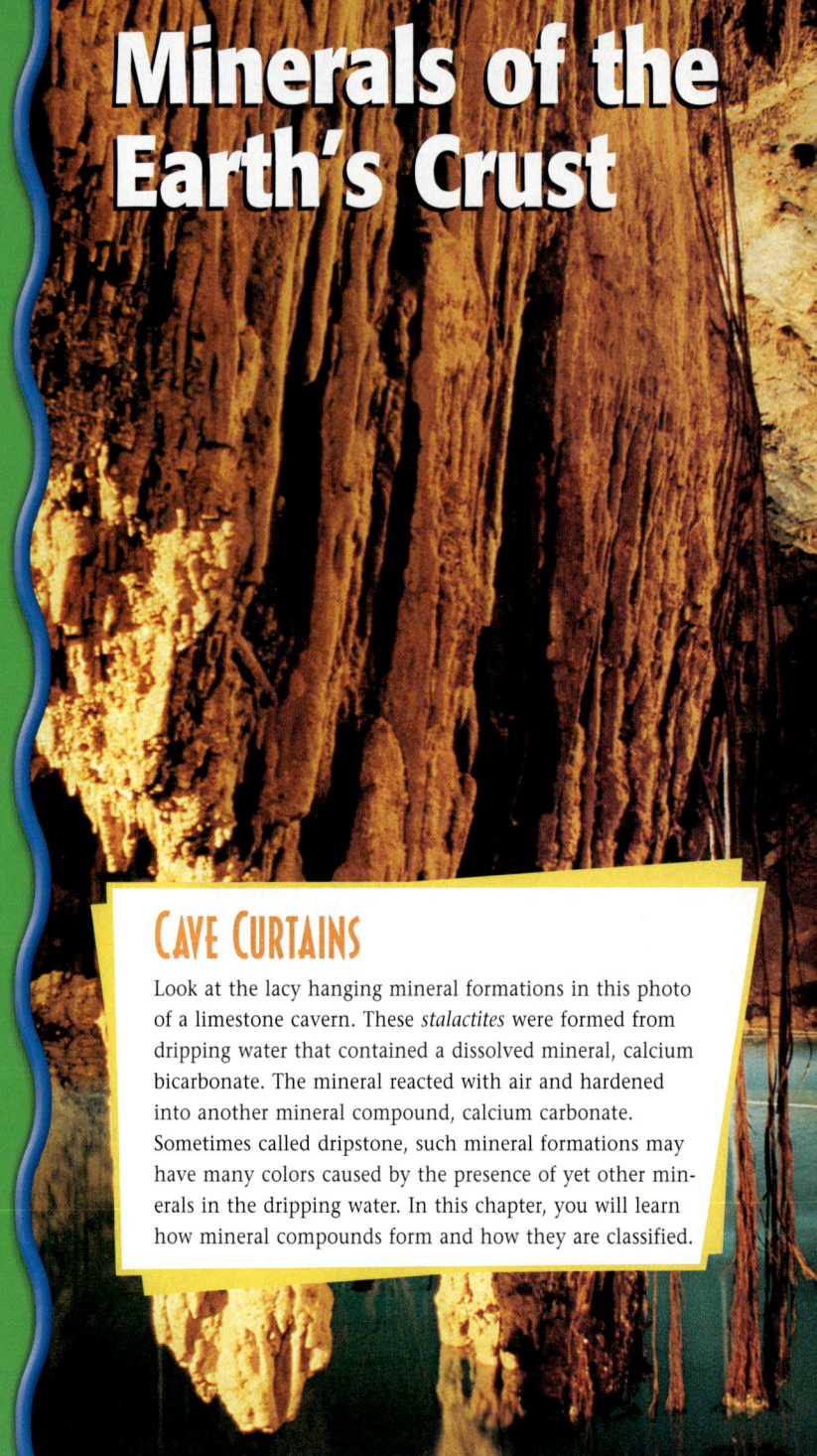

Cave Curtains

Look at the lacy hanging mineral formations in this photo of a limestone cavern. These *stalactites* were formed from dripping water that contained a dissolved mineral, calcium bicarbonate. The mineral reacted with air and hardened into another mineral compound, calcium carbonate. Sometimes called dripstone, such mineral formations may have many colors caused by the presence of yet other minerals in the dripping water. In this chapter, you will learn how mineral compounds form and how they are classified.

 **go.hrw.com**
For worksheets and other teaching aids, visit the HRW Web site and type in the keyword: **HSTMIN**

 **www.scilinks.com**
Use the *sci*LINKS numbers at the end of each chapter for additional resources on the **NSTA** Web site.

 **www.cnnfyi.com**
Visit the CNN Web site for current events coverage and classroom resources.

58 Chapter 3 • Minerals of the Earth's Crust

START-UP Activity

RIDING A MINERAL?

More than 3,000 different minerals occur naturally on Earth. What is a mineral? Do the following activity, and see if you can figure it out.

Procedure

1. In your ScienceLog, make two columns—one for minerals and one for nonminerals.
2. Ask your classmates what ideas they have about the materials that make up a motorcycle. Take notes as you gather information.
3. Based on what you already know about minerals, classify the materials in a motorcycle into things that come from minerals and things that come from nonminerals.

Analysis

4. Based on your list, is most of a motorcycle made of minerals or nonminerals?
5. Where do you think the minerals that make a motorcycle come from?

START-UP Activity

RIDING A MINERAL
Teacher's Notes

Display some photos of different types of motorcycles from magazines or books to help students make their classifications. Encourage them to take notes.

Materials that are minerals or are derived from minerals include glass headlights and any metal objects. Plastic and rubber objects are not minerals.

Answers to START-UP Activity

4. Most of the materials are metals, which come from minerals.
5. Answers will vary. Metals come from metal ore minerals, such as hematite, magnetite, beryl, and cuprite.

Chapter 3 • Minerals of the Earth's Crust

SECTION 1

Focus

What Is a Mineral?

This section explores the nature of minerals by describing their four characteristics. Students learn that mineral crystals are generated by atomic structures, and they learn how to classify minerals in two major compositional groups—silicates and nonsilicates.

Display a piece of pencil lead (graphite) and a photograph of a diamond. Explain that both substances are composed of carbon. Ask students to brainstorm about how two substances with such different properties can form from atoms of the same element.

1) Motivate

GROUP ACTIVITY

Identifying Minerals Place an assortment of objects on a table. Possibilities include a piece of wood, a fossil, a piece of bone, a piece of granite, and a quartz crystal. Divide the class into groups of two or three students. Tell the students to examine the objects and to determine which ones are minerals by using the four questions on this page. **Sheltered English**

 Directed Reading Worksheet 3 Section 1

Section 1

Terms to Learn

mineral
element
atom
compound
crystal
silicate mineral
nonsilicate mineral

What You'll Do

- Explain the four characteristics of a mineral.
- Classify minerals according to the two major compositional groups.

What Is a Mineral?

Not all minerals look like gems. In fact, most of them look more like rocks. But are minerals the same as rocks? Well, not really. So what's the difference? For one thing, rocks are made of minerals, but minerals are not made of rocks. Then what exactly is a mineral? By asking the following four questions, you can tell whether something is a mineral:

Is it a solid? Minerals can't be gases or liquids.

Is it formed in nature? Crystalline materials made by people aren't classified as minerals.

Does it have a crystalline structure? Minerals are crystals, which have a repeating inner structure that is often reflected in the shape of the crystal. Minerals generally have the same chemical composition throughout.

Is it nonliving material? A mineral is inorganic, meaning it isn't made of living things.

A **mineral** is a naturally formed, inorganic solid with a crystalline structure. If you cannot answer "yes" to all four questions above, you don't have a mineral.

Minerals: From the Inside Out

Three of the four questions might be easy to answer. The one about crystalline structure may be more difficult. In order to understand what crystalline structure is, you need to know a little about the elements that make up a mineral. **Elements** are pure substances that cannot be broken down into simpler substances by ordinary chemical means. All minerals contain one or more of the 92 elements present in the Earth's crust.

How many elements does it take to "set" the periodic table? Find out by turning to page 744.

CONNECT TO LIFE SCIENCE

Guide students in a discussion of the importance minerals have to life on Earth. Display a bone, a bottle of mineral supplements, and a plant. Ask students to brainstorm about how these objects are related to minerals. Explain to students that minerals, which are inorganic, provide essential nutrients to living things and are the building blocks of organisms.

- Bones are largely made of microscopic apatite crystals.
- Diatoms, which are microscopic organisms, have silica crystals in their cell walls.

60 Chapter 3 • Minerals of the Earth's Crust

Atoms and Compounds Each element is made of only one kind of atom. An **atom,** as you may recall, is the smallest part of an element that has all the properties of that element. Like all other substances, minerals are made up of atoms of one or more elements.

Most minerals are made of compounds of several different elements. A **compound** is a substance made of two or more elements that have been chemically joined, or bonded together. Halite, for example, is a compound of sodium and chlorine, as shown in **Figure 1.** A few minerals, such as gold and silver, are composed of only one element. For example, pure gold is made up of only one kind of atom—gold.

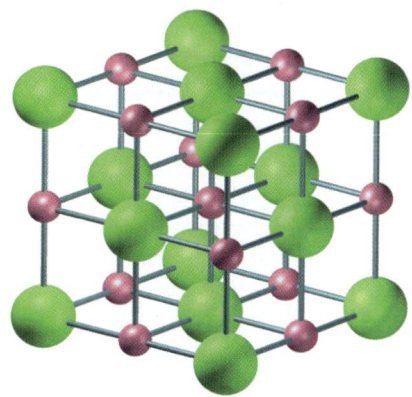

Figure 1 Atoms of sodium and chlorine are joined together in a compound commonly known as rock salt, or the mineral halite.

Crystals A mineral is also made up of one or more crystals. **Crystals** are solid, geometric forms of minerals produced by a repeating pattern of atoms that is present throughout the mineral. A crystal's shape is determined by the arrangement of the atoms within the crystal. The arrangement of atoms in turn is determined by the kinds of atoms that make up the mineral. Each mineral has a definite crystalline structure. All minerals can be grouped into crystal classes according to the kinds of crystals they form. **Figure 2** shows how the atomic structure of gold gives rise to cubic crystals.

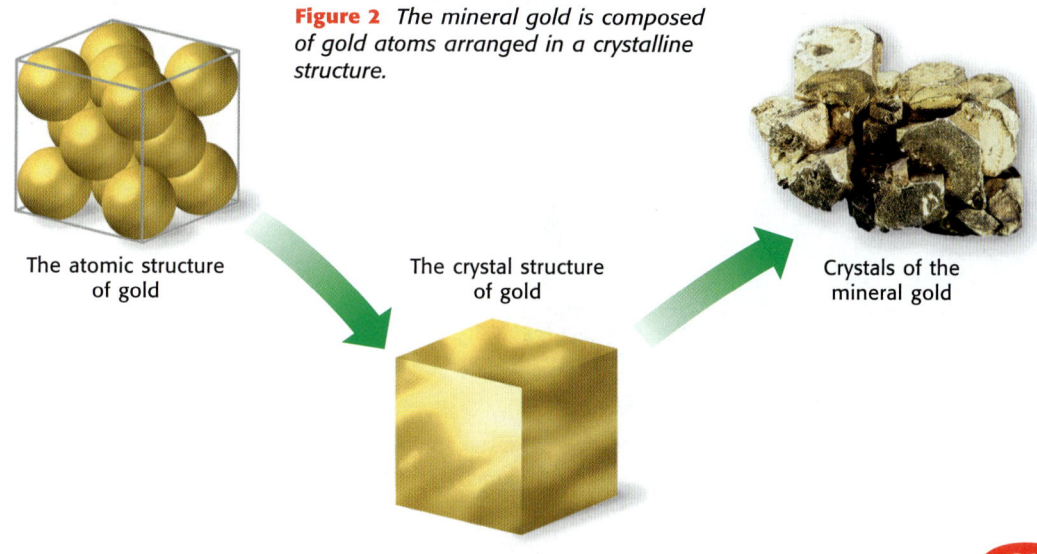

Figure 2 The mineral gold is composed of gold atoms arranged in a crystalline structure.

The atomic structure of gold → The crystal structure of gold → Crystals of the mineral gold

MISCONCEPTION ALERT

In much the same way that color is a deceptive guide to identifying minerals, crystal form is often a misleading physical property. The crystal structures of halite and gold shown on this page are atomic structures. When different unit cells are combined, however, they can generate crystal forms that look nothing like their atomic structure. A large variety of complex crystal shapes can be generated by starting with a simple polyhedron, such as a cube. For example, the mineral fluorite belongs in the isometric (cubic) class but commonly forms octahedral-shaped crystals.

2) Teach

DISCUSSION

Rocks and Minerals Students may benefit from a discussion of the differences between rocks and minerals. Stress that rocks are composed of minerals, but minerals are not composed of rock. It is possible for a rock to be made of just one mineral or many. Minerals should also not be confused with mineraloids. Mineraloids are similar to minerals, but they have no crystalline structure. Some common mineraloids are obsidian, limonite, flint, and opal. **Sheltered English**

USING SCIENCE FICTION

Have students read "The Metal Man" by Jack Williamson in *The Holt Anthology of Science Fiction*. As you discuss the story in class, tell students that the story was written in the 1920s when the phenomenon of radioactivity was poorly understood. Have students consider how our knowledge of radioactivity has increased since that time.

GROUP ACTIVITY

Writing At the beginning of this section, give pairs of students an unknown mineral. Tell students that their goal will be to identify the mineral by the end of the chapter and to present a short report on it. Their reports should include the chemical formula of the mineral, detail the mineral's uses and properties, and explain what type of rock the mineral occurs in.

Teaching Transparency 107 "Gold Crystal Structure"

Section 1 • What Is a Mineral? **61**

2) Teach, continued

ACTIVITY

Microscope Work Sand forms from the breakdown of rock over many years. Most sand is composed of the mineral quartz. Distribute magnifying lenses or microscopes to student groups, and invite them to examine samples of sand, rock salt, granulated salt, and sugar to compare the crystalline structure of each. Have students record what they see in their ScienceLog.

USING THE FIGURE

After students study the examples shown in **Figure 3,** distribute samples of granite, feldspar, quartz, and mica to students for close examination. Encourage students to record their observations in their ScienceLog and to note differences and similarities.
<mark>Sheltered English</mark>

CONNECT TO CHEMISTRY

The way atoms bond together gives a mineral its properties. For example, carbon atoms that are bonded in one way form graphite, which is commonly used for pencil lead, while carbon atoms that are bonded in another way form diamonds. Have students research the chemical composition and structure of different minerals and find out how the minerals are used. Ask students to make a model that shows the atomic structure of a unit cell of a simple mineral, such as halite, pyrite, galena, or quartz.

Biology CONNECTION

Several species of animals have a brain that contains the mineral magnetite. Magnetite has a special property—it is magnetic. Scientists have shown that certain fish can sense magnetic fields because they have magnetite in their brain. The magnetite gives the fish a sense of direction.

Types of Minerals

Minerals can be classified by a number of different characteristics. The most common classification of minerals is based on chemical composition. Minerals are divided into two groups based on the elements they are composed of. These groups are the silicate minerals and the nonsilicate minerals.

Silicate Minerals Silicon and oxygen are the two most common elements in the Earth's crust. Minerals that contain a combination of these two elements are called **silicate minerals.** Silicate minerals make up more than 90 percent of the Earth's crust—the rest is made up of nonsilicate minerals. Silicon and oxygen usually combine with other elements, such as aluminum, iron, magnesium, and potassium, to make up silicate minerals. Some of the more common silicate minerals are shown in **Figure 3.**

Feldspar Feldspar minerals make up about half the Earth's crust, and they are the main component of most rocks on the Earth's surface. They contain the elements silicon and oxygen along with aluminum, potassium, sodium, and calcium.

Biotite Mica Mica minerals are shiny and soft, and they separate easily into sheets when they break. Biotite is but one of several varieties of mica.

Quartz Quartz (silicon dioxide, SiO_2) is the basic building block of many rocks. If you look closely at the piece of granite, you can see the quartz crystals.

Figure 3 *Granite is a rock composed of various minerals, including feldspar, mica, and quartz.*

Multicultural CONNECTION

The first recorded use of sandpaper dates to thirteenth-century China, when crushed seashells were bound to parchment with a natural adhesive from trees. Today sandpaper is commonly made from aluminum oxide, garnet, or quartz. Interested students can make their own sandpaper at home and share it with the class.

Homework

At Home With Minerals Ask students to find four items in their home that are derived from minerals. Have them share their findings with the class on the following day. (Examples include table salt, composed of halite; pencil lead, composed of graphite; cooking pots, composed of iron, copper, or aluminum; and jewelry.)

Nonsilicate Minerals Minerals that do not contain a combination of the elements silicon and oxygen form a group called the **nonsilicate minerals.** Some of these minerals are made up of elements such as carbon, oxygen, iron, and sulfur. Below are several categories of nonsilicate minerals.

Classes of Nonsilicate Minerals

Native elements are minerals that are composed of only one element. About 20 minerals are native elements. Some examples are gold (Au), platinum (Pt), diamond (C), copper (Cu), sulfur (S), and silver (Ag).

Native copper

Carbonates are minerals that contain combinations of carbon and oxygen in their chemical structure. Calcite ($CaCO_3$) is an example of a carbonate mineral. We use carbonate minerals in cement, building stones, and fireworks.

Calcite

Halides are compounds that form when atoms of the elements fluorine, chlorine, iodine, or bromine combine with sodium, potassium, or calcium. Halite (NaCl) is better known as rock salt. Fluorite (CaF_2) can have many different colors. Halide minerals are often used to make fertilizer.

Fluorite

Oxides are compounds that form when an element, such as aluminum or iron, combines chemically with oxygen. Corundum (Al_2O_3) and magnetite (Fe_3O_4) are important oxide minerals. Oxide minerals are used to make abrasives and aircraft parts.

Corundum

Sulfates contain sulfur and oxygen (SO_4). The mineral gypsum ($CaSO_4 \cdot 2H_2O$) is a common sulfate. It makes up the white sand at White Sands National Monument, in New Mexico. Sulfates are used in cosmetics, toothpaste, and paint.

Gypsum

Sulfides are minerals that contain one or more elements, such as lead, iron, or nickel, combined with sulfur. Galena (PbS) is a sulfide. Sulfide minerals are used to make batteries, medicines, and electronic parts.

Galena

REVIEW

1. What are the differences between atoms, compounds, and minerals?
2. Which two elements are most common in minerals?
3. How are silicate minerals different from nonsilicate minerals?
4. **Making Inferences** Explain why each of the following is not considered a mineral: a cupcake, water, teeth, oxygen.

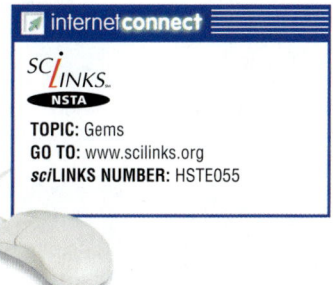

internet connect

SC/**INKS**
NSTA

TOPIC: Gems
GO TO: www.scilinks.org
sci/LINKS NUMBER: HSTE055

---

3) Extend

RESEARCH

Writing From about 200 B.C. to A.D. 1700, alchemists explored the boundaries of chemistry and philosophy. They dedicated their lives to discovering a chemical reaction that would change common metals into precious gold and silver. Despite their unscientific methods, alchemists contributed a great deal to the development of the science we now call chemistry. Even Sir Isaac Newton devoted much of his life to pursuing alchemy. Challenge interested students to research the history of alchemy and to present a report to the class.

4) Close

Quiz

1. What is a mineral? (a naturally formed, inorganic solid with a crystalline structure)
2. What does a crystal's shape depend on? (the arrangement of the atoms within the crystal)

ALTERNATIVE ASSESSMENT

Write the following mineral-group names on the board: silicates, native elements, carbonates, halides, oxides, sulfates, and sulfides. Have students match the following items with the mineral group from which they are derived: a copper penny (native elements); cement (carbonates); rock salt (halides); oxide sandpaper (oxides); toothpaste (sulfates); batteries (sulfides); sand (silicates).

▼ **Answers to Review**

1. Compounds are composed of two or more atoms of different elements that are chemically bonded. Minerals consist of atoms or compounds arranged in a crystalline structure.
2. oxygen and silicon
3. Silicate minerals are made of combinations of the elements silicon and oxygen, and nonsilicate minerals are not.
4. A cupcake is not a mineral because it does not have a crystalline structure and it does not form in nature. Liquid water is not a mineral because it does not have a crystalline structure and it is a liquid, not a solid. (Water ice can be considered a mineral.) Teeth are not minerals because they are a living part of your body. Oxygen is not a mineral because oxygen atoms by themselves do not have a crystalline structure.

SECTION 2

Focus

Identifying Minerals

In this lesson, students will learn some of the common techniques used to identify minerals. The section also examines some of the interesting properties of minerals, such as fluorescence, radioactivity, and magnetism.

🔔 Bellringer

Ask students to consider the question posed at the beginning of this section. Students should list as many phrases as they can to describe each mineral shown. Have students organize these phrases into different catagories, such as *color, shape,* and *luster*. Students can use these comparisons to determine whether or not the samples are actually the same mineral. **(The mineral on the left is a yellow variety of garnet. The mineral on the right is a "diamond in the rough.")**

1) Motivate

COOPERATIVE LEARNING

Ask students to work in small groups to determine a classification system for minerals based on observable physical properties. Give groups a number of minerals or photographs of a variety of minerals. Students should create a classification system based on observable differences and similarities among the samples. After groups have developed a classification system, give them several new samples, and have them place the samples in their classification scheme.

Directed Reading Worksheet 3 Section 2

Section 2

Terms to Learn
luster fracture
streak hardness
cleavage density

What You'll Do
- Classify minerals using common mineral-identification techniques.
- Explain special properties of minerals.
- Describe what makes a mineral crystal a gem.

Identifying Minerals

If you found the two mineral samples below, how would you know if they were the same mineral?

By looking at these minerals, you can easily see physical similarities. But how can you tell whether they are the same mineral? Moreover, how can you determine the identity of a mineral? In this section you will learn about the different properties that can help you identify minerals.

Color

Minerals come in many different colors and shades. The same mineral can come in a variety of colors. For example, in its purest state quartz is clear. Quartz that contains small amounts of impurities, however, can be a variety of colors. Rose quartz gets its color from certain kinds of impurities. Amethyst, another variety of quartz, is purple because it contains other kinds of impurities.

Besides impurities, other factors can change the appearance of minerals. The mineral pyrite, often called fool's gold, normally has a golden color. But if pyrite is exposed to weather for a long period, it turns black. Because of factors such as weathering and impurities, color usually is not a reliable indicator of a mineral's identity.

Luster Chart

Metallic   **Submetallic**

Nonmetallic

Vitreous   **Silky**
glassy, brilliant   swirly, fibrous

Resinous   **Waxy**
plastic   greasy, oily

Pearly   **Earthy**
creamy   rough, dull

Luster

The way a surface reflects light is called **luster.** When you say an object is shiny or dull, you are describing its luster. Minerals have metallic, submetallic, or nonmetallic luster. If a mineral is shiny, it may have either a glassy or a metallic luster. If the mineral is dull, its luster is either submetallic or nonmetallic. The different types of lusters are shown in the chart at left.

 **SCIENCE**

How can you tell a real diamond from a fake? A gem specialist uses specialized tools to distinguish real diamonds from impostors. But there are some tests that even an untrained person can conduct.

One of the simplest is to try to pick up the stone in question with a moistened fingertip. Diamonds can be picked up this way; most other stones cannot.

64 Chapter 3 • Minerals of the Earth's Crust

Streak

The color of a mineral in powdered form is called the mineral's **streak**. To find a mineral's streak, the mineral is rubbed against a piece of unglazed porcelain called a streak plate. The mark left on the streak plate is the streak. The color of a mineral's streak is not always the same as the color of the mineral sample, as shown in **Figure 4**. Unlike the surface of a mineral sample, the streak is not affected by weathering. For this reason, streak is more reliable than color as an indicator of a mineral's identity.

Figure 4 The color of the mineral hematite may vary, but its streak is always red-brown.

Cleavage and Fracture

Different types of minerals break in different ways. The way a mineral breaks is determined by the arrangement of its atoms. **Cleavage** is the tendency of some minerals to break along flat surfaces. Gem cutters take advantage of natural cleavage to remove flaws from certain minerals, such as diamonds and rubies, and to shape them into beautiful gemstones. **Figure 5** shows minerals with different cleavage patterns.

Fracture is the tendency of some minerals to break unevenly along curved or irregular surfaces. One type of fracture is shown in **Figure 6**.

Once you've learned about the properties of minerals, put your knowledge to the test! To find out how, turn to page 638 in your LabBook.

Figure 5 Cleavage varies with mineral type. Mica breaks easily into distinct sheets. Halite breaks at 90° angles in three directions. Diamond breaks in four different directions.

Figure 6 This sample of quartz shows a curved fracture pattern called conchoidal (kahn KOYD uhl) fracture.

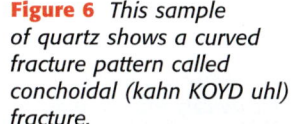

IS THAT A FACT!

During the black plague of the fourteenth century, opals developed a reputation for being unlucky gems. People thought that opals became brilliant when the wearer caught the plague and dulled when the person died!

Mysterious Minerals PG 638

TOPIC: Identifying Minerals
GO TO: www.scilinks.org
sciLINKS NUMBER: HSTE065

2) Teach

ACTIVITY

Applying the Scientific Method
Before allowing students to test minerals themselves, go through the process with them to demonstrate how each identification step is performed. Use a few common minerals that have distinctly different characteristics, such as talc and quartz. Show students how each test is conducted, and discuss with them why every step is necessary to correctly identify a mineral. When students test the minerals, stress a systematic approach. Students should perform the same steps, in order, to each unknown sample. Caution students not to taste mineral samples. To satisfy their curiosity, provide table salt and explain that it is the mineral halite. With a magnifying glass, they should be able to see halite's cubic crystal form. **Sheltered English**

MISCONCEPTION ALERT

Students may believe that a specific mineral is always the same color. Explain to students that a mineral can occur in a range of colors. Labradorite can be yellow or dull gray. Quartz crystals range from clear to purple or brown to rose. Purple quartz is the gemstone known as *amethyst*, while yellow quartz is the gemstone *citrine*. Remind students that they must test all of a mineral's characteristics—color, luster, hardness, streak, cleavage, density, and fluorescence to determine its identity.

Reinforcement Worksheet 3
"Mystery Mineral"

3 Extend

QuickLab

MATERIALS

FOR EACH STUDENT:
- penny
- pencil

Answer to QuickLab

3. The penny is the hardest material of the three, followed by the fingernail and then the mineral graphite.

READING STRATEGY

Mnemonics Have students create a mnemonic device that will help them learn Mohs' hardness scale. One example is **T**errible **G**iants **C**an **F**ind **A**lligators **O**r **Q**uaint **T**igers **C**onveniently **D**igestible. This will help students remember the minerals in order of hardness: **t**alc, **g**ypsum, **c**alcite, **f**luorite, **a**patite, **o**rthoclase feldspar, **q**uartz, **t**opaz, **c**orundum, and **d**iamond. Ask students to brainstorm for several mnemonic devices and share them with the class. Sheltered English

Jade is a mineral that has great importance in China. According to Chinese mythology, jade is a symbol of life and it possesses protective powers. Jade is actually the name given to two minerals—jadeite and nephrite—that rank between 6.5 and 7 on Mohs' hardness scale. Have students find out about the cultural significance of jade and how it was carved without metal tools.

Scratch Test

1. You will need a **penny**, a **pencil**, and your **fingernail**. Which one of these three materials is the hardest?
2. Use your fingernail to try to scratch the graphite at the tip of a pencil.
3. Now try to scratch the penny with your fingernail. Which is the hardest of the three?

Hardness

Hardness refers to a mineral's resistance to being scratched. If you try to scratch a diamond, you will have a tough time because diamond is the hardest mineral. Talc, on the other hand, is one of the softest minerals. You can scratch it with your fingernail. To determine the hardness of minerals, scientists use *Mohs' hardness scale*, shown below. Notice that talc has a rating of 1 and diamond has a rating of 10. Between these two extremes are other minerals with progressively greater hardness.

To identify a mineral using Mohs' scale, try to scratch the surface of a mineral with the edge of one of the 10 reference minerals. If the reference mineral scratches your mineral, it is harder than your mineral. Continue trying to scratch the mineral until you find a reference mineral that cannot scratch your mineral.

Density

Figure 7 *Because a golf ball has a greater density than a table-tennis ball, more table-tennis balls are needed to balance the scale.*

If you pick up a golf ball and a table-tennis ball, which will feel heavier? Although the balls are of similar size, the golf ball will feel heavier because it is denser, as shown in **Figure 7**. **Density** is the measure of how much matter there is in a given amount of space. In other words, density is a ratio of an object's mass to its volume. Density is usually measured in grams per cubic centimeter. Because water has a density of 1 g/cm^3, it is used as a reference point for other substances. The ratio of an object's density to the density of water is called the object's *specific gravity*. The specific gravity of gold, for example, is 19. This means that gold has a density of 19 g/cm^3. In other words, there is 19 times more matter in 1 cm^3 of gold than in 1 cm^3 of water.

 Teaching Transparency 108 "Mohs' Hardness Scale"

Teaching Transparency 109 "Special Properties of Some Minerals"

Comparative Hardness Scale

Hardness	Common material
Less than 2.5	mineral that marks paper
2.5	fingernail
3	copper penny
5	steel knife blade
6.5	steel file

Chapter 3 • Minerals of the Earth's Crust

Special Properties

Some properties are particular to only a few types of minerals. The properties below can quickly help you identify the minerals shown. To identify some properties, however, you will need specialized equipment.

Fluorescence—Calcite and fluorite glow under ultraviolet light. The same fluorite sample below is shown in ultraviolet light and in white light.

Chemical reaction—Calcite will effervesce, or "fizz," when a drop of weak acid is placed on it.

Optical properties—A thin, clear piece of calcite placed over an image will cause a double image.

Special Properties of Some Minerals

Taste—Halite has a salty taste.

Radioactivity—Minerals that contain radium or uranium can be detected by a Geiger counter.

Magnetism—Magnetite and pyrrhotite are both natural magnets that attract iron.

REVIEW

1. How do you determine a mineral's streak?
2. What is the difference between cleavage and fracture?
3. How would you determine the hardness of an unidentified mineral sample?
4. **Applying Concepts** Suppose you have two minerals that have the same hardness. Which other mineral properties would you use to determine whether the samples are the same mineral?

For a list of minerals and their properties, see page 750.

Is It Fool's Gold?—A Dense Situation

REAL-WORLD CONNECTION

Invite a jeweler to visit the class, and ask the jeweler to explain how gemstones are made into jewelry. The jeweler could bring in visual aids to help students understand how gems are located, mined, and prepared for commercial use.

4) Close

Quiz

1. Why is color not always a reliable way of identifying a mineral? (Factors such as weathering and the inclusion of impurities can affect the mineral's color.)
2. What property do minerals that glow under ultraviolet light display? (fluorescence)

ALTERNATIVE ASSESSMENT

Have students prepare mineral identification cards for some of the most common minerals. They can list the words *color, luster, hardness, streak, cleavage and fracture,* and *density* on each card. For each card, ask them to fill in the properties of a common mineral. Students should write the name of the mineral on the back of the card and use the cards as study aids or assessment tools. Sheltered English

Reinforcement Worksheet 3 "The Mineral Quiz Show"

Answers to Review

1. Scrape the mineral across a ceramic streak plate. The color of the material that rubs off the mineral sample is the mineral's streak.
2. If a mineral has cleavage, it breaks along flat surfaces. Fracture is the way a mineral breaks along curved or irregular surfaces.
3. To determine the hardness of an unknown mineral sample, take a material of known hardness and try to scratch the unknown mineral with it. If the unknown mineral is scratched, try to scratch it with a material that has a lower hardness. Continue with this process until you know which materials are harder and which are softer than the unknown mineral sample. The hardness of the unknown mineral is between these two.
4. Answers will vary but should not include color.

Section 2 • Identifying Minerals

SECTION 3

Focus

The Formation and Mining of Minerals

This section discusses how minerals form deep within Earth's crust as well as close to the surface. Students will learn about different techniques used to mine minerals. This section concludes with a discussion of the value of mineral resources and the importance of ecologically responsible mining and reclamation.

🔔 Bellringer

Ask students to write briefly on this statement:

"The meek shall inherit the Earth but not the mineral rights."

Discuss students' responses, and ask them what they would do if valuable minerals were discovered on property they owned.

1 Motivate

DISCUSSION

Simulate the Gold Rush To simulate the excitement of the gold rush of 1849, make up a flyer that tells of a rich gold deposit found in a nearby area. Make copies and pass them out to students to read. Discuss with students what their reactions are to such an announcement. Then discuss the chaotic enthusiasm of the gold rush: from 1848 to 1860, the population in California grew from 14,000 to 380,000!

Directed Reading Worksheet 3 Section 3

Section 3

Terms to Learn
ore
reclamation

What You'll Do
◆ Describe the environments in which minerals are formed.
◆ Compare and contrast the different types of mining.

The Formation and Mining of Minerals

Almost all known minerals can be found in the Earth's crust. They form in a large variety of environments under a variety of physical and chemical conditions. The environment in which a mineral forms determines the mineral's properties. Minerals form both deep beneath the Earth's surface and on or near the Earth's surface.

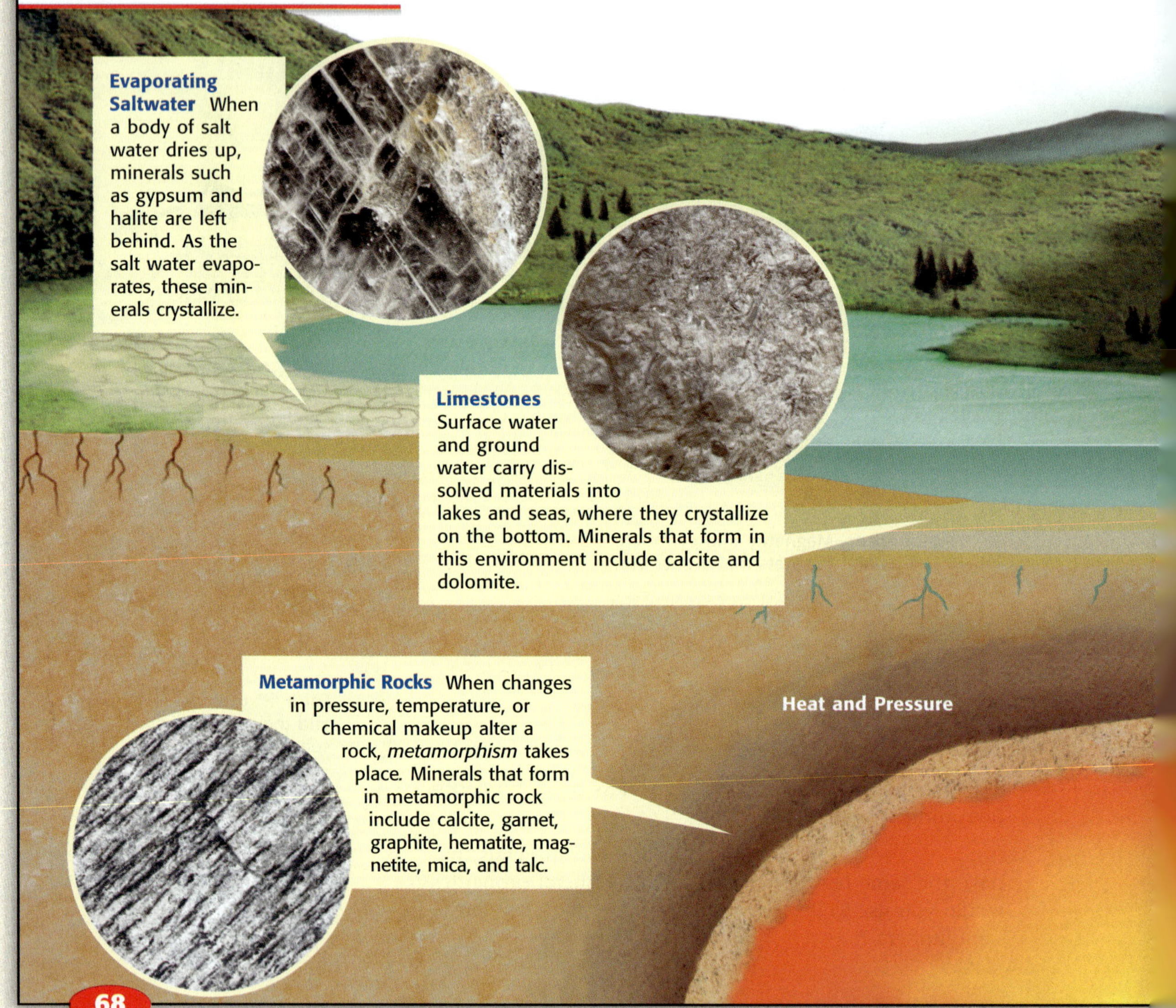

Evaporating Saltwater When a body of salt water dries up, minerals such as gypsum and halite are left behind. As the salt water evaporates, these minerals crystallize.

Limestones Surface water and ground water carry dissolved materials into lakes and seas, where they crystallize on the bottom. Minerals that form in this environment include calcite and dolomite.

Metamorphic Rocks When changes in pressure, temperature, or chemical makeup alter a rock, *metamorphism* takes place. Minerals that form in metamorphic rock include calcite, garnet, graphite, hematite, magnetite, mica, and talc.

Heat and Pressure

68

WEIRD SCIENCE

Some of the greatest untapped sources of minerals are hydrothermal vents deep under the sea. These hydrothermal vents are called black smokers because they spew out hot, mineral-rich water that is almost black. As the hot water mixes with the cool ocean water, minerals crystallize and form nodules on the ocean floor. These mineral deposits contain significant amounts of manganese, copper, zinc, gold, and silver, but no one has figured out an economical way to mine them yet.

68   Chapter 3 • Minerals of the Earth's Crust

Hot-water Solutions Ground water works its way downward and is heated by magma. It then reacts with minerals to form a hot liquid solution. Dissolved metals and other elements crystallize out of the hot fluid to form new minerals. Gold, copper, sulfur, pyrite, and galena form in such hot-water environments.

✓ Self-Check

Where do minerals such as gypsum and halite form? *(See page 726 to check your answer.)*

Pegmatites As magma moves upward it can form teardrop-shaped bodies called *pegmatites*. The presence of hot fluids causes the mineral crystals to become extremely large, sometimes growing to several meters across! Many gems, such as topaz and tourmaline, form in pegmatites.

Plutons As magma rises upward through the crust, it sometimes stops moving before it reaches the surface and cools slowly, forming millions of mineral crystals. Eventually, the entire magma body solidifies to form a *pluton*. Mica, feldspar, magnetite, and quartz are some of the minerals that form from magma.

Magma

69

Multicultural CONNECTION

Halite, or rock salt, is perhaps the most important mineral to human civilization. The word *salt* is derived from the Latin word *sal*. Instead of money, Roman soldiers were paid their salary, or *salarium*, in salt. Have students research the Tibetan salt trade or the use of iodized salt to correct thyroid deficiencies.

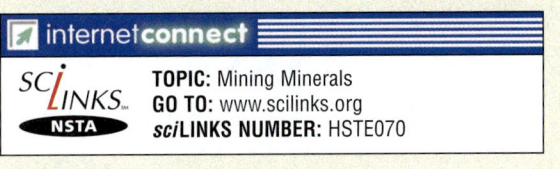
internetconnect
SCI LINKS
NSTA
TOPIC: Mining Minerals
GO TO: www.scilinks.org
*sci*LINKS NUMBER: HSTE070

2) Teach

Answer to Self-Check
These minerals form wherever salt water has evaporated.

CONNECT TO LIFE SCIENCE

The Surface Environment and Mining (SEAM) program was established by the U.S. Forest Service in 1973 to address the issue of land reclamation in the wake of mining operations. Since then, this highly successful program has returned vast areas of land formerly used for mining to its original condition. The most recent SEAM projects can be researched on the Internet. To research local reclamation efforts, students could contact local conservation groups listed in the phone directory.

CROSS-DISCIPLINARY FOCUS

History Encourage students to learn more about the social and environmental effects of mining by having each student create a scrapbook detailing the history of a mining community. Students should research the history of a community from the discovery of ore to the present. Students' scrapbooks should include drawings and photographs showing changes in the community as well as text describing the history of the area. Have students focus on the types of ore extracted, the use and value of the ore in the world market, and the impact mining has had on the people and environment of the area. Possible communities include: Leadville, Colorado; Butte, Montana; and the Yanomami Indian tribes of Brazil and Venezuela. Have students share their scrapbooks with the class.

Section 3 • The Formation and Mining of Minerals   **69**

3) Extend

MATH and MORE

To produce 1 metric ton of coal, up to 30 metric tons of earth must first be removed or stripped. Some strip mines produce up to 50,000 metric tons of coal a day. How many metric tons of earth could be removed in order to mine 50,000 metric tons of coal? **(1,500,000 metric tons)**

Answer to MATHBREAK

$\frac{18}{24} = \frac{3}{4} = 75\%$ pure

CONNECT TO PHYSICAL SCIENCE

Referring to the chart on the following page, discuss with students that minerals are valuable because of the properties of the elements that are in them. Elements can be divided into three major groups: *metals, nonmetals,* and *metalloids*. Use the Teaching Transparency below to discuss how the characteristics of each element group make the minerals they are found in useful to human cultures.

Teaching Transparency 210
"The Three Major Categories of Elements"

LINK TO PHYSICAL SCIENCE

Math Skills Worksheet 21
"Percentages, Fractions, and Decimals"

MATH BREAK

How Pure Is Pure?

Gold classified as 24-karat is 100 percent gold. Gold classified as 18-karat is 18 parts gold and 6 parts another, similar metal. It is therefore 18/24 or 3/4 pure. What is the percentage of pure gold in 18-karat gold?

MISCONCEPTION ALERT

The mass of gems is measured using a unit called the *carat*. This should not be confused with the *karat* used to measure the purity of gold. A 1-carat diamond crystal has a mass of 200 mg. This is approximately the same as the mass of one children's aspirin. A one karat gold nugget is one twenty-fourth pure gold.

Mining

Many kinds of rocks and minerals must be mined in order to extract the valuable elements they contain. Geologists use the term **ore** to describe a mineral deposit large enough and pure enough to be mined for a profit. Rocks and minerals are removed from the ground by one of two methods—surface mining or deep mining. The method miners choose depends on how far down in the Earth the mineral is located and how valuable the ore is. The two types of mining are illustrated below.

Surface mining is the removal of minerals or other materials at or near the Earth's surface. Types of surface mines include open pits, strip mines, and quarries. Materials mined in this way include copper ores and bauxite, a mixture of minerals rich in aluminum.

Deep mining is the removal of minerals or other materials from deep within the Earth. Passageways must be dug underground to reach the ore. The retrieval of diamonds and coal commonly requires deep mining.

Multicultural CONNECTION

The mining of gold, copper, and iron in southeastern Africa helped build the empire of Great Zimbabwe, which arose during the mid-thirteenth century and lasted until about the middle of the fifteenth century. Invite students to find out more about mining techniques in Great Zimbabwe and about the Karanga people who ruled then.

The Value of Minerals

Many of the metals you are familiar with originally came from mineral ores. You may not be familiar with the minerals, but you will probably recognize the metals extracted from the minerals. The table at right lists some mineral ores and some of the familiar metals that come from them.

As you have seen, some minerals are highly valued for their beauty rather than for their usefulness. Mineral crystals that are attractive and rare are called gems, or gemstones. An example of a gem is shown in **Figure 8.** Gems must be hard enough to be cut and polished.

Common Uses of Minerals

Mineral	Metal	Uses
Chalcopyrite	copper	coins, electrical wire
Galena	lead	batteries, paints
Beryl	beryllium	bicycle frames, airplanes
Chromite	chromium	stainless steel, cast iron, leather tanners

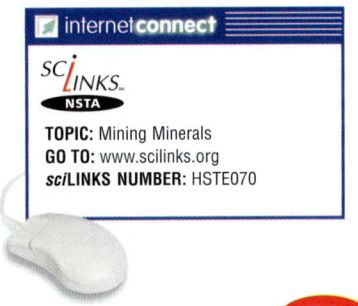

Figure 8 The Cullinan diamond, at the center of this scepter, is part of the largest diamond ever found.

Responsible Mining

Mining gives us the minerals we need, but it also creates problems. Mining can destroy or disturb the habitats of plants and animals. The waste products from a mine can get into water sources, polluting both surface water and ground water.

One way to reduce the harmful effects of mining is to return the land to its original state after the mining is completed. This process is called **reclamation.** Reclamation of mined public land has been required by law since the mid-1970s. But reclamation is an expensive and time-consuming process. Another way to reduce the effects of mining is to reduce our need for minerals. We do this by recycling many of the mineral products we currently use, such as aluminum and iron. Mineral ores are *nonrenewable resources;* therefore, the more we recycle, the more we will have in the future.

REVIEW

1. Describe how minerals form underground.
2. What are the two main types of mining?
3. **Analyzing Ideas** How does reclamation protect the environment around a mine?

internetconnect
SC*i*LINKS.
NSTA
TOPIC: Mining Minerals
GO TO: www.scilinks.org
*sci*LINKS NUMBER: HSTE070

Answers to Review

1. Answers will vary. Minerals form when magma cools and solidifies. Changing temperature and pressure conditions inside the Earth can cause the formation of new minerals from pre-existing rock. Minerals can also form underground when dissolved solids crystallize out of heated ground water.
2. surface mining and deep mining
3. Reclamation reduces the harmful effects of mining by returning the land to its original state.

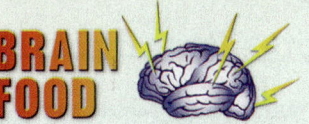

Scientists know that there are valuable deposits of minerals on other bodies in our solar system. Ask students to think about what issues should be considered before staking claims and mining other planets.

4) Close

Quiz

1. Name three minerals that form in metamorphic rock. (possible answers: calcite, muscovite, chlorite, garnet, graphite, hematite, magnetite, and talc)
2. What is ore? (mineral deposits large enough and pure enough to be mined for profit)
3. How can mining cause water pollution? (The waste products from a mine can introduce toxic concentrations of elements in rivers, lakes, and ground water.)

Alternative Assessment

Concept Mapping Have students make a concept map in their ScienceLog of one mining process discussed in this section. Make sure students include each step in the process of mining. The first should be the search for the mineral or ore deposits. The final step should include information about the products that are manufactured with the mineral and the cleanup of the mine wastes.

Critical Thinking Worksheet 3 "Mineral Hunt"

Chapter Highlights

VOCABULARY DEFINITIONS

SECTION 1

mineral a naturally formed, inorganic solid with a crystalline structure

element a pure substance that cannot be separated or broken down into simpler substances by ordinary chemical means

atom the smallest part of an element that has all of the properties of that element

compound a pure substance made of two or more elements that have been chemically joined, or bonded together

crystal the solid, geometric form of a mineral produced by a repeating pattern of atoms

silicate mineral a mineral that contains a combination of the elements silicon and oxygen

nonsilicate mineral a mineral that does not contain compounds of silicon and oxygen

SECTION 2

luster the way the surface of a mineral reflects light

streak the color of a mineral in powdered form

cleavage the tendency of a mineral to break along flat surfaces

fracture the tendency of a mineral to break along curved or irregular surfaces

hardness the resistance of a mineral to being scratched

density the amount of matter in a given space; mass per unit volume

Chapter Highlights

SECTION 1

Vocabulary
- mineral *(p. 60)*
- element *(p. 60)*
- atom *(p. 61)*
- compound *(p. 61)*
- crystal *(p. 61)*
- silicate mineral *(p. 62)*
- nonsilicate mineral *(p. 63)*

Section Notes
- A mineral is a naturally formed, inorganic solid with a definite crystalline structure.
- An atom is the smallest unit of an element that retains the properties of the element.
- A compound forms when atoms of two or more elements bond together chemically.
- Every mineral has a unique crystalline structure. The crystal class a mineral belongs to is directly related to the mineral's chemical composition.
- Minerals are classified as either silicates or nonsilicates. Each group includes different types of minerals.

SECTION 2

Vocabulary
- luster *(p. 64)*
- streak *(p. 65)*
- cleavage *(p. 65)*
- fracture *(p. 65)*
- hardness *(p. 66)*
- density *(p. 66)*

Section Notes
- Color is not a reliable indicator for identifying minerals.
- The luster of a mineral can be metallic, submetallic, or nonmetallic.
- A mineral's streak does not necessarily match its surface color.
- The way a mineral breaks can be used to determine its identity. Cleavage and fracture are two ways that minerals break.

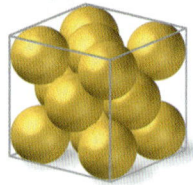  

✓ Skills Check

Math Concepts

THE PURITY OF GOLD The karat is a measure of the purity of gold. Gold that is 24 karats is 100 percent gold. But gold that is less than 24 karats is mixed with other elements, so it is less than 100 percent gold. If you have a gold nugget that is 16 karats, then 16 parts out of 24 are pure gold—the other 8 parts are composed of other elements.

24 karats = 100% gold
16 karats = 24 karats − 8 karats
$\frac{16}{24} = \frac{2}{3} = 0.67 = 67\%$ gold

Visual Understanding

ATOMIC STRUCTURE This illustration of the atomic structure of the mineral halite shows that halite is made of two elements—sodium and chlorine. The large spheres represent atoms of chlorine, and the small spheres represent atoms of sodium. The bars between the atoms represent the chemical bonds that hold them together.

Lab and Activity Highlights

Mysterious Minerals PG 638

Is It Fool's Gold?— A Dense Situation PG 640

 Datasheets for LabBook
(blackline masters for these labs)

SECTION 2

- Mohs' hardness scale provides a numerical rating for the hardness of minerals.
- The density of a mineral can be used to identify it.
- Some minerals have special properties that can be used to quickly identify them.

Labs
Mysterious Minerals (p. 638)
Is It Fool's Gold?—A Dense Situation (p. 640)

SECTION 3

Vocabulary
ore (p. 70)
reclamation (p. 71)

Section Notes
- Minerals form in both underground environments and surface environments.
- Two main types of mining are surface mining and deep mining.
- Minerals are valuable because metals can be extracted from them and because some of them can be cut to form gems.
- Reclamation is the process of returning mined land to its original state.

VOCABULARY DEFINITIONS, continued

SECTION 3
ore a mineral deposit large enough and pure enough to be mined for a profit

reclamation the process of returning land to its original state after mining is completed

 Vocabulary Review Worksheet 3

 Blackline masters of these Chapter Highlights can be found in the **Study Guide**.

---

internet connect

 **GO TO:** go.hrw.com

Visit the **HRW** Web site for a variety of learning tools related to this chapter. Just type in the keyword:

KEYWORD: HSTMIN

 **GO TO:** www.scilinks.org

Visit the **National Science Teachers Association** on-line Web site for Internet resources related to this chapter. Just type in the sciLINKS number for more information about the topic:

TOPIC: Gems — *sci*LINKS NUMBER: HSTE055
TOPIC: Birthstones — *sci*LINKS NUMBER: HSTE060
TOPIC: Identifying Minerals — *sci*LINKS NUMBER: HSTE065
TOPIC: Mining Minerals — *sci*LINKS NUMBER: HSTE070

Lab and Activity Highlights

LabBank

 Long-Term Projects & Research Ideas,
What's Yours Is Mined, Project 31

Chapter Review Answers

USING VOCABULARY

1. If a mineral breaks along a curved or irregular surface, it has fracture. If a mineral breaks along flat surfaces, it has cleavage.
2. Elements are made of only one kind of atom, while compounds are made of two or more elements that are chemically bonded.
3. Streak is the color of a mineral in powdered form. The color of a mineral may change, but the mineral's streak is always the same.
4. The hardness of a mineral is its resistance to being scratched, while the density of a mineral is a measure of the amount of matter in a given space.
5. Silicate minerals are made of silicon and oxygen compounds, while nonsilicate minerals are made of other compounds.
6. A mineral is made up of a particular arrangement of different kinds of atoms.

UNDERSTANDING CONCEPTS

Multiple Choice

7. d
8. a
9. d
10. d
11. d
12. b
13. b

Chapter Review

USING VOCABULARY

For each pair of terms, explain the difference in their meaning.

1. fracture/cleavage
2. element/compound
3. color/streak
4. density/hardness
5. silicate mineral/nonsilicate mineral
6. mineral/atom

UNDERSTANDING CONCEPTS

Multiple Choice

7. On Mohs' hardness scale, which of the following minerals is harder than quartz?
   a. talc
   b. apatite
   c. gypsum
   d. topaz

8. A mineral's streak
   a. is more reliable than color in identifying a mineral.
   b. reveals the mineral's specific gravity.
   c. is the same as a luster test.
   d. reveals the mineral's crystal structure.

9. Which of the following factors is **not** important in the formation of minerals?
   a. heat
   b. volcanic activity
   c. presence of ground water
   d. wind

10. Which of the following terms is **not** used to describe a mineral's luster?
    a. pearly
    b. waxy
    c. dull
    d. hexagonal

11. Which of the following is considered a special property that applies to only a few minerals?
    a. color
    b. luster
    c. streak
    d. magnetism

12. Which of the following physical properties can be expressed in numbers?
    a. luster
    b. hardness
    c. color
    d. reaction to acid

13. Which of the following minerals would scratch fluorite?
    a. talc
    b. quartz
    c. gypsum
    d. calcite

Short Answer

14. Using no more than 25 words, define the term *mineral*.
15. In one sentence, describe how density is used to identify a mineral.
16. What methods of mineral identification are the most reliable? Explain.

Concept Mapping

17. Use the following terms to create a concept map: minerals, oxides, nonsilicates, carbonates, silicates, hematite, calcite, quartz.

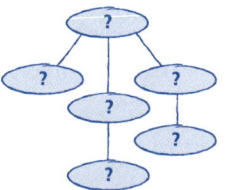

Short Answer

14. A mineral is a naturally occurring inorganic solid with a crystalline structure.
15. Each mineral has its own unique density.
16. Answers will vary. Cleavage, hardness, and density are very reliable because they can be measured and do not change. Color and fracture are less reliable.

Concept Mapping

17. 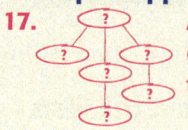 An answer to this exercise can be found at the end of this book.

74 Chapter 3 • Minerals of the Earth's Crust

CRITICAL THINKING AND PROBLEM SOLVING

Write one or two sentences to answer the following questions:

18. Suppose you have three rings, each with a different gem. One has a diamond, one has an amethyst (purple quartz), and one has a topaz. You mail the rings in a small box to your friend who lives five states away. When the box arrives at its destination, two of the gems are damaged. One gem, however, is damaged much worse than the other. What scientific reason can you give for the difference in damage?

19. While trying to determine the identity of a mineral, you decide to do a streak test. You rub the mineral across the plate, but it does not leave a streak. Does this mean your test failed? Explain your answer.

20. Imagine that you work at a jeweler's shop and someone brings in some "gold nuggets" that they want to sell. The person claims that an old prospector found the gold nuggets during the California gold rush. You are not sure if the nuggets are real gold. How would you decide whether to buy the nuggets? Which identification tests would help you decide the nuggets' identity?

21. Suppose that you find a mineral crystal that is as tall as you are. What kinds of environmental factors would cause such a crystal to form?

MATH IN SCIENCE

22. Gold has a specific gravity of 19. Pyrite's specific gravity is 5. How much denser is gold than pyrite?

23. In a quartz crystal there is one silicon atom for every two oxygen atoms. That means that the ratio of silicon atoms to oxygen atoms is 1:2. If there were 8 million oxygen atoms in a sample of quartz, how many silicon atoms would there be?

INTERPRETING GRAPHICS

Imagine that you had a sample of feldspar and analyzed it to find out what it is made of. The results of your analysis are shown below.

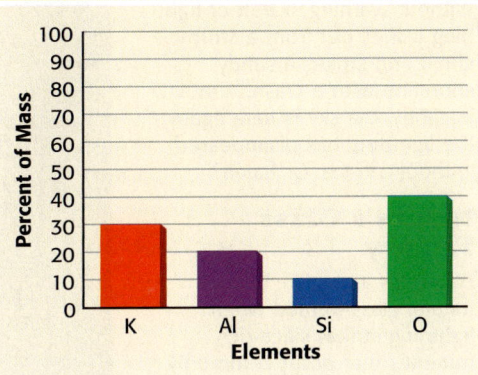

24. Your sample consists of four elements. What percentage of each one is your sample made of?

25. If your mineral sample has a mass of 10 g, how many grams of oxygen does it contain?

26. Make a circle graph showing how much of each of the four elements the feldspar contains. (You will find help on making circle graphs in the Appendix of this book.)

 Take a minute to review your answers to the Pre-Reading Questions found at the bottom of page 58. Have your answers changed? If necessary, revise your answers based on what you have learned since you began this chapter.

CRITICAL THINKING AND PROBLEM SOLVING

18. Each mineral has a different hardness. The hardest mineral was damaged the least. (The diamond will not be damaged, the topaz will be slightly damaged, and the amethyst will sustain the most damage.)

19. No; the test was actually successful. You learned that the unknown mineral has no streak and that it is harder than the streak plate. This clue will help you classify the mineral.

20. Students should suggest performing several tests to see whether the mineral is gold or not. Gold is very dense and soft, so one would start with density and hardness tests.

21. Answers will vary. When magma contains a lot of hot fluids and cools slowly, very large crystals can grow.

MATH IN SCIENCE

22. Gold is $\frac{19}{5} = 3\frac{4}{5}$, or 3.8 times as dense as pyrite.

23. $\frac{8 \text{ million}}{2}$ = 4 million silicon atoms

INTERPRETING GRAPHICS

24. K: 30 percent
    Al: 20 percent
    Si: 10 percent
    O: 40 percent
25. 4 g
26. Answers will vary.

Concept Mapping Transparency 3

Blackline masters of this Chapter Review can be found in the **Study Guide.**

Weird Science
Lightning Leftovers

Background
Silica, also known as silicon dioxide, SiO_2, is a compound of the two most common elements in the Earth's crust, silicon and oxygen. Silica can take a variety of forms. Crystalline forms include quartz, agate, and amethyst. Noncrystalline forms include obsidian, flint, and opal. Silica is the primary ingredient of most commercial glasses and ceramics and is also used in cements and mortars.

LIGHTNING LEFTOVERS

Without warning, a bolt of lightning lashes out from a storm cloud and strikes a sandy shoreline with a crash. Almost instantly, the sky is dark again—the lightning has disappeared without a trace. Or has it?

Nature's Glass Factory
Fulgurites are a rare type of natural glass formed when lightning strikes silica-rich minerals that occur commonly in sand, soil, and some rocks. *Tubular fulgurites* are found in areas with a lot of silica, such as beaches or deserts. Lightning creates a tubular fulgurite when a bolt penetrates the sand and melts silica into a liquid. The liquid silica cools and hardens quickly, leaving behind a thin glassy tube, usually with a rough outer surface and a smooth inner surface. Underground, a fulgurite may be shaped like the roots of a tree. It branches out with many arms that trace the zigzag path of the lightning bolt. Some fulgurites are as short as your little finger, while others stretch 20 m into the ground.

Underground Puzzles
So should you expect to run across a fulgurite on your next trip to the beach? Don't count on it. Scientists and collectors search long and hard for the dark glass formations, which often form with little or no surface evidence pointing to their underground location. Even when a fulgurite is located, removing it in one piece is difficult. They are quite delicate, with walls no thicker than 1–2 mm. Some of the largest fulgurites are removed from the ground in many pieces then glued back into their original shape.

Rock Fulgurites
Rock fulgurites are extremely rare, usually occurring only on high mountains. These oddities are created when lightning strikes the surface of a silica-rich rock. A rock fulgurite often looks like a bubbly glass case 1–3 mm thick around the rock. Lightning travels around the outside of the rock, fusing silica-rich minerals on its surface. Depending on which minerals melt, a rock fulgurite's color can range from glassy black to light gray or even bright yellow.

Find Out More
▶ Investigate how scientists studying the formation of fulgurites try to make lightning bolts strike a precise location to create a new fulgurite. You may also want to do some research to find out about companies that will *create* a fulgurite just for you!

◀ *A Tubular Fulgurite*

Sample Answer to Find Out More
To learn more about how fulgurites form, scientists have to get lightning to strike where they can observe it. To attract lightning, scientists attach long metal wires to a rocket that is then shot into storm clouds, triggering a huge electrical spark. The bolt of lightning travels down the wire and into the ground. There, it comes in contact with silica, forming a fulgurite, which scientists then study. But scientific study is not the only reason to create a fulgurite: some companies sell custom-made fulgurites as natural works of art. You provide the sand, and they will fire the rocket and reel in a bolt of lightning, forming a fulgurite made just for you!

Science Fiction

"The Metal Man"
by Jack Williamson

In a dark, dusty corner of Tyburn College Museum stands a life-sized statue of a man. Except for its strange greenish color, the statue looks pretty ordinary. But if you look closely, you will marvel at the perfect detail of the hair and skin. You will also see a strange mark on the statue's chest, a dark crimson shape with six sides.

No one knows how the statue ended up in the dark corner. Everyone believes that the Metal Man is, or once was, Professor Thomas Kelvin of the Geology Department. Professor Kelvin had for many years spent his summer vacations along the Pacific coast of Mexico, prospecting for radium. Then at the end of one summer, Kelvin did not return to Tyburn. He had been more successful than he ever dreamed, and he had become very rich. But high in the mountains, he had also found something else . . .

Now there is only one person who knows what really happened to Professor Kelvin, and he tells the professor's story in "The Metal Man," by Jack Williamson. The tale involves Kelvin's expedition to search for the source of El Rio de la Sangre, the River of Blood, and the radium that makes the river radioactive. Did he find it? Is that what made Kelvin so rich? And what else did Professor Kelvin find there in the remote mountain valley?

Read for yourself the strange story of Professor Kelvin and the Metal Man in the *Holt Anthology of Science Fiction.*

Further Reading

Wonder's Child: My Life in Science Fiction, Bluejay, 1985

The Best of Jack Williamson, Ballantine, 1978

The Pandora Effect, Ace Books, 1969

SCIENCE FICTION
"The Metal Man"
by Jack Williamson

The Metal Man stands tall in the Tyburn College Museum, but it is no ordinary statue . . .

Teaching Strategy

Reading Level This compelling story will be a challenge for many students, but with some vocabulary help, they will enjoy this inventive work.

Background

About the Author Few people have had as long-lasting an impact on science fiction as Jack Williamson (1908–). This story, "The Metal Man," was first published in 1928—over 70 years ago! Although it was his very first short story, it is still a classic. Since then, Williamson has written dozens of science fiction novels, short-stories, other novels, and books about writing.

The term *science fiction* was not even around when Williamson began writing. Known as one of the great pioneers of science fiction, Williamson was the first to write about antimatter. In addition, he coined the terms *terraform* (in 1941) and *genetic engineering* (in 1951).

Williamson is also credited for legitimizing science fiction as a field worthy of literary attention. For this accomplishment, Williamson has received several awards. In 1976, he became the second person to win the Grand Master Nebula Award. In 1994, Williamson earned a lifetime achievement award from World Fantasy.

Chapter 3 • Science Fiction

Chapter Organizer

CHAPTER ORGANIZATION	TIME MINUTES	OBJECTIVES	LABS, INVESTIGATIONS, AND DEMONSTRATIONS
Chapter Opener pp. 78–79	45	National Standards: SAI 1, ES 1d	**Start-Up Activity** Classifying Objects, p. 79
Section 1 Understanding Rock	135	▶ Describe two ways rocks were used by early humans, and describe two ways they are used today. ▶ Describe how each type of rock changes into another as it moves through the rock cycle. ▶ List two characteristics of rock that are used to help classify it. UCP 1, SAI 1, ST 2, HNS 1, SPSP 5, ES 1d, 1k, 2b	**Labs You Can Eat,** Famous Rock Groups, Lab 11 `GENERAL`
Section 2 Igneous Rock	90	▶ Explain how the cooling rate of magma affects the properties of igneous rocks. ▶ Distinguish between igneous rock that cools deep within the crust and igneous rock that cools at the surface. ▶ Identify common igneous rock formations. UCP 1, ES 1c, 1d; LabBook UCP 2, SAI 1	**Skill Builder,** Crystal Growth, p. 642 `GENERAL` **Datasheets for LabBook,** Crystal Growth, Datasheet 7 `GENERAL`
Section 3 Sedimentary Rock	90	▶ Describe how the three types of sedimentary rock form. ▶ Explain how sedimentary rocks record Earth's history. UCP 1, ES 1c, 1d, 1k, 2b; LabBook UCP 2, SAI 1	**Demonstration,** Dissolution of Minerals, p. 91 in ATE `GENERAL` **Skill Builder,** Let's Get Sedimental, p. 645 `GENERAL` **Datasheets for LabBook,** Let's Get Sedimental, Datasheet 8 `GENERAL` **Whiz-Bang Demonstrations,** Settling Down, Demo 17 `BASIC`
Section 4 Metamorphic Rock	90	▶ Describe two ways a rock can undergo metamorphism. ▶ Explain how the mineral composition of rocks changes as they undergo metamorphism. ▶ Describe the difference between foliated and non-foliated metamorphic rock. UCP 1, 2, SAI 1, ST 2, HNS 3, ES 1d; LabBook UCP 2, SAI 1	**QuickLab,** Stretching Out, p. 96 `GENERAL` **Interactive Explorations CD-ROM,** Rock On! `GENERAL` A **Worksheet** is also available in the **Interactive Explorations Teacher's Edition.** **Making Models,** Metamorphic Mash, p. 647 `BASIC` **Datasheets for LabBook,** Metamorphic Mash, Datasheet 9 `BASIC` **Long-Term Projects & Research Ideas,** Project 32 `ADVANCED`

*See page **T20** for a complete correlation of this book with the* **NATIONAL SCIENCE EDUCATION STANDARDS.**

TECHNOLOGY RESOURCES

 Guided Reading Audio CD English or Spanish, Chapter 4

 One-Stop Planner CD-ROM with Test Generator

 CNN. Scientists in Action, Meteor Collision Geologist, Segment 6

 Interactive Explorations CD-ROM CD 2, Exploration 6, Rock On!

Chapter 4 • Rocks: Mineral Mixtures

Chapter 4 • Rocks: Mineral Mixtures

CLASSROOM WORKSHEETS, TRANSPARENCIES, AND RESOURCES	SCIENCE INTEGRATION AND CONNECTIONS	REVIEW AND ASSESSMENT
Directed Reading Worksheet 4 BASIC **Science Puzzlers, Twisters & Teasers,** Worksheet 4 ADVANCED	**Cross-Disciplinary Focus,** p. 79 in ATE	
Directed Reading Worksheet 4, Section 1 BASIC **Transparency 110,** The Rock Cycle **Math Skills for Science Worksheet 20,** Parts of 100: Calculating Percentages GENERAL **Transparency 63,** The Digestive System of a Bird	**Cross-Disciplinary Focus,** pp. 81, 83 in ATE GENERAL **Connect to Life Science,** pp. 81, 83, 85 in ATE **Multicultural Connection,** p. 82 in ATE **Real-World Connection,** p. 83 in ATE GENERAL **Apply,** p. 84 GENERAL **Math and More,** p. 85 in ATE GENERAL **MathBreak,** What's in It? p. 85 GENERAL **Science, Technology, and Society:** Rock City, p. 104	**Homework,** p. 85 in ATE GENERAL **Review,** p. 86 GENERAL **Quiz,** p. 86 in ATE GENERAL **Alternative Assessment,** p. 86 in ATE ADVANCED
Directed Reading Worksheet 4, Section 2 BASIC **Transparency 111,** The Cooling Rate of Magma and the Texture of Igneous Rock **Transparency 112,** Intrusive Igneous Rock Formations	**Connect to Life Science,** p. 88 in ATE **Multicultural Connection,** p. 88 in ATE	**Self-Check,** p. 88 **Review,** p. 90 GENERAL **Quiz,** p. 90 in ATE GENERAL **Alternative Assessment,** p. 90 in ATE GENERAL
Transparency 113, A Sedimentary Rock Cycle **Directed Reading Worksheet 4,** Section 3 BASIC	**Connect to Life Science,** p. 92 in ATE ADVANCED **Real-World Connection,** p. 93 in ATE **Cross-Disciplinary Focus,** p. 93 in ATE GENERAL	**Review,** p. 94 GENERAL **Quiz,** p. 94 in ATE GENERAL **Alternative Assessment,** p. 94 in ATE GENERAL
Directed Reading Worksheet 4, Section 4 BASIC **Transparency 114,** Regional and Contact Metamorphism **Math Skills for Science Worksheet 31,** The Unit Factor and Dimensional Analysis GENERAL **Reinforcement Worksheet 4,** What Is It? BASIC **Critical Thinking Worksheet 4,** Between a Rock and a Hard Place ADVANCED	**Cross-Disciplinary Focus,** p. 96 in ATE **Real-World Connection,** p. 97 in ATE ADVANCED **Math and More,** p. 98 in ATE GENERAL **Biology Connection,** p. 99 **Health Watch:** Glass Scalpels, p. 105 ADVANCED	**Self-Check,** p. 96 **Homework,** p. 97 in ATE GENERAL **Homework,** p. 98 in ATE ADVANCED **Review,** p. 99 GENERAL **Quiz,** p. 99 in ATE GENERAL **Alternative Assessment,** p. 99 in ATE GENERAL

END-OF-CHAPTER REVIEW AND ASSESSMENT

Chapter Review in Study Guide
Vocabulary and Notes in Study Guide
Chapter Tests with Performance-Based Assessment, Chapter 4 Test
Chapter Tests with Performance-Based Assessment, Performance-Based Assessment 4
Concept Mapping Transparency 4

internetconnect

Holt, Rinehart and Winston On-line Resources
go.hrw.com

For worksheets and other teaching aids related to this chapter, visit the HRW Web site and type in the keyword: **HSTRCK**

National Science Teachers Association
www.scilinks.org

Encourage students to use the sciLINKS numbers listed in the internet connect boxes to access information and resources on the **NSTA** Web site.

Chapter 4 • Chapter Organizer

Chapter Resources & Worksheets

Visual Resources

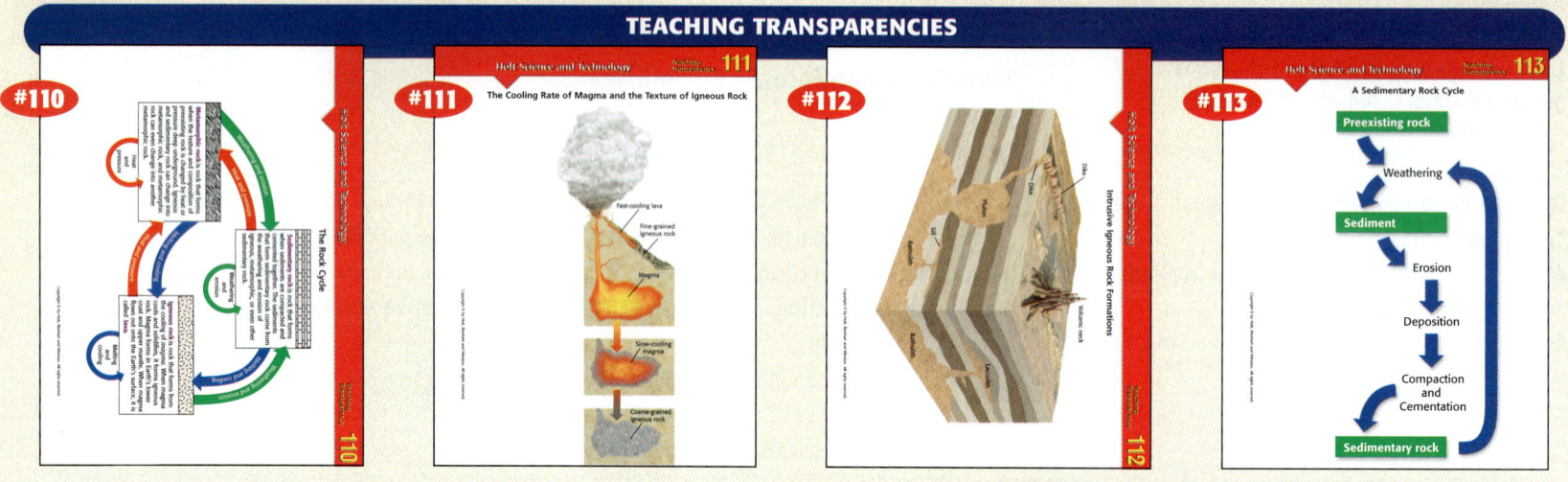

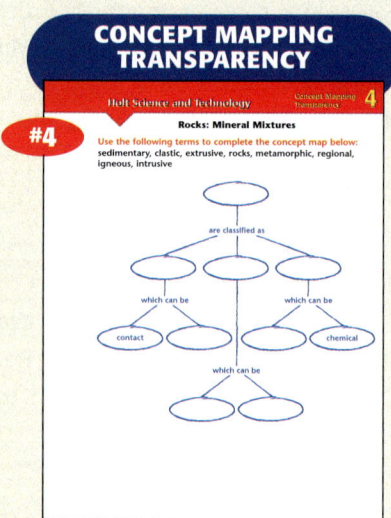

Meeting Individual Needs

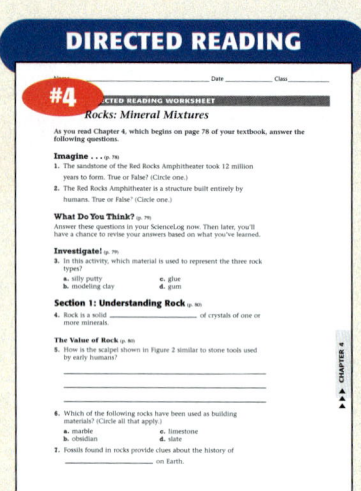

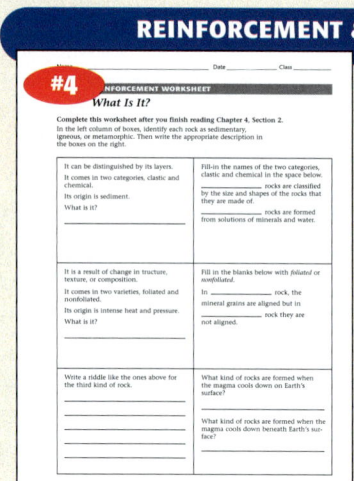

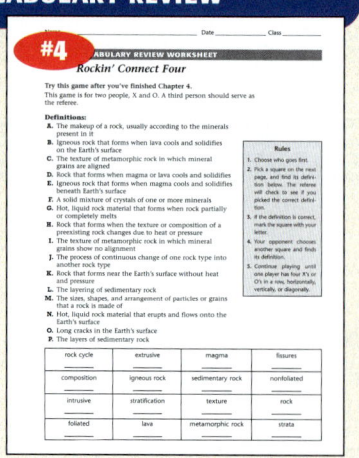

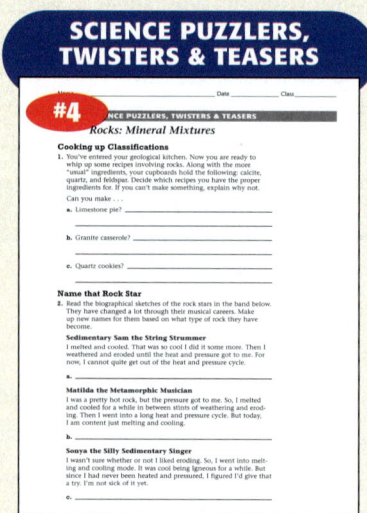

Chapter 4 • Rocks: Mineral Mixtures

Review & Assessment

STUDY GUIDE

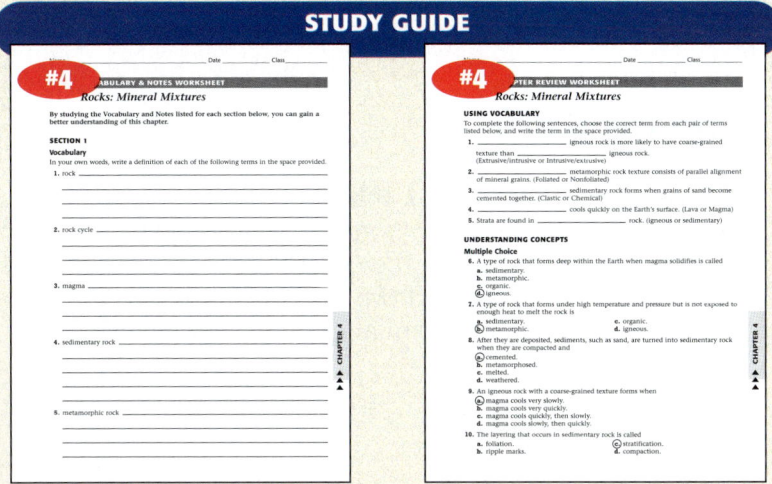

CHAPTER TESTS WITH PERFORMANCE-BASED ASSESSMENT

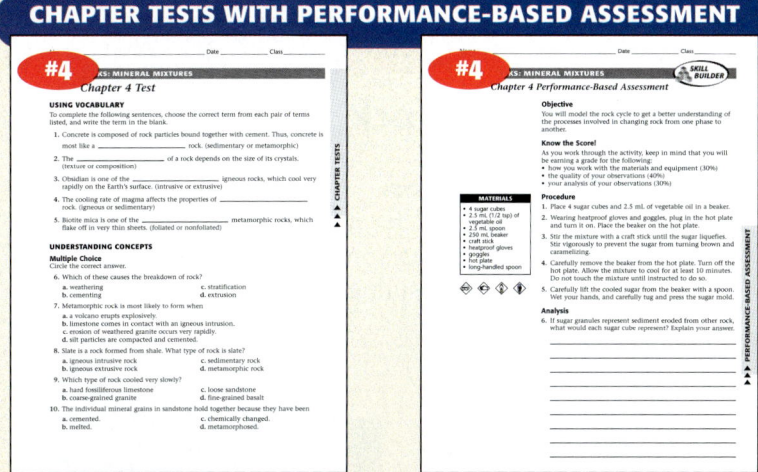

Lab Worksheets

LABS YOU CAN EAT

WHIZ-BANG DEMONSTRATIONS

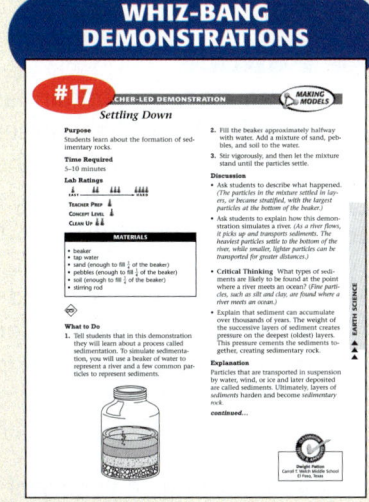

LONG-TERM PROJECTS & RESEARCH IDEAS

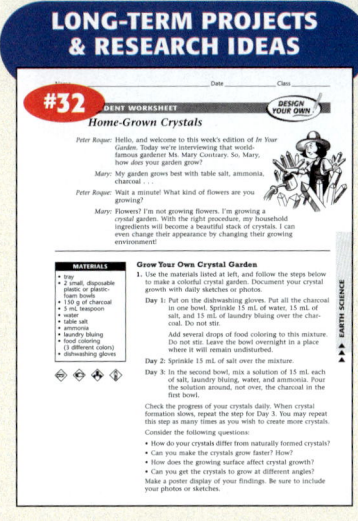

DATASHEETS FOR LABBOOK

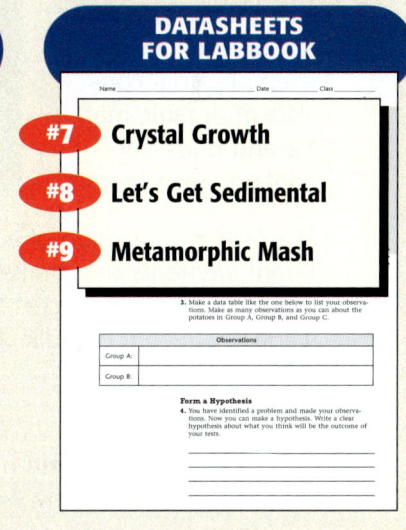

- #7 Crystal Growth
- #8 Let's Get Sedimental
- #9 Metamorphic Mash

Applications & Extensions

CRITICAL THINKING & PROBLEM SOLVING

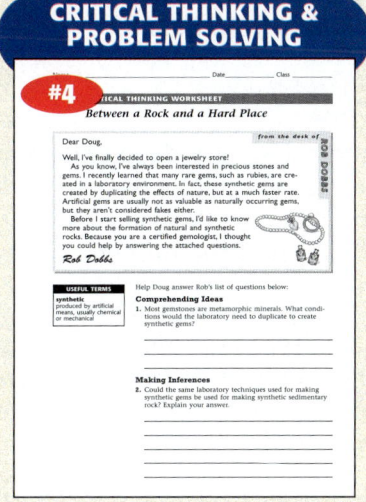

SCIENTISTS IN ACTION

INTERACTIVE EXPLORATIONS

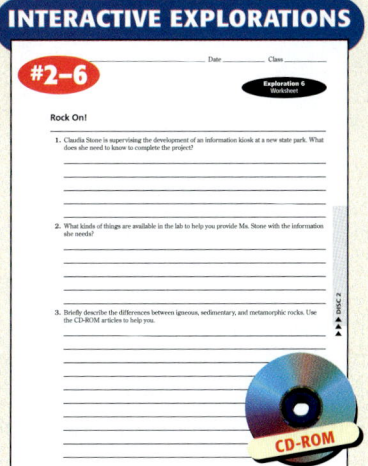

Chapter 4 • Chapter Resources & Worksheets   77D

Chapter Background

SECTION 1

Understanding Rock

▶ **Rock Composition**
This chapter focuses on the mineral composition of rock, not its bulk composition. These are two very different means of measuring rock composition.

- The *mineral composition* of a rock refers to the proportions of the different *minerals* in the rock and is usually expressed in percentages by volume. But not all rocks consist of minerals. For example, coal consists of organic matter and does not contain any minerals.

- The *bulk composition* of a rock is the sum of the different *elements* that make up the rock and is usually expressed in percentages by weight. Mineral composition is affected by bulk composition.

IS THAT A FACT!

- Although rocks contain many elements, the rocks in Earth's crust are nearly 94 percent oxygen by volume.

- Ninety-five percent of the outer 10 km of Earth is igneous and metamorphic rock.

- Although sedimentary rock makes up less than 5 percent of the Earth's crust, it is spread thinly over much of the planet's surface. Sedimentary rock covers 75 percent of the Earth's continental surfaces!

SECTION 2

Igneous Rock

▶ **The Great Dike of Rhodesia**
Dikes can range in width from a few millimeters to thousands of meters. The Great Dike of Rhodesia, in Africa, is the largest known dike on Earth. It has an average width of 10 km and extends for almost 600 km.

IS THAT A FACT!

- A common name for quartz is rock crystal. Its name comes from the Greek word *krystallos,* meaning "ice."

▶ **Pumice**
Some magmas contain dissolved gases such as carbon dioxide. When these gases come out of magma in the form of small bubbles, the magma greatly increases its volume, causing an enormous buildup of pressure. This results in a violent volcanic eruption. The result is a frothy-looking rock called pumice. Pumice is full of small holes called vesicles, where the trapped gases used to be. Depending on how much space is taken up by vesicles, some types of pumice can float in water!

- Pumice has a variety of industrial and household uses. Its abrasive qualities make it perfect for use in scouring and cleaning products. People use chunks of pumice in the bathtub to remove callouses from their feet.

IS THAT A FACT!

- Igneous rocks that form deep underground are called plutonic rocks, after Pluto, the god of the underworld in Roman mythology. Volcanic rocks are named after Vulcan, the Roman god of metalworking and fire.

- Although many people think of lava as a thin and runny liquid, lava flows are often quite viscous. Usually the temperature has cooled enough for crystals to begin forming, which can give lava a consistency similar to that of thick oatmeal.

Chapter 4 • Rocks: Mineral Mixtures

Section 3

Sedimentary Rock

▶ **Working with Clay**
Clay is composed primarily of silicate minerals. Clays are easy to work with when they are wet because the tiny plate-shaped silicate crystals are trapped between water molecules. As the water evaporates, the silicates are cemented into place and the clay becomes brittle and difficult to work with.

IS THAT A FACT!

- Bentonite, a form of clay composed of very fine silicate crystals, has a wide variety of industrial applications. Some forms of bentonite can expand as much as 300 percent when mixed with water. Bentonite is used to make cat litter, to line artificial ponds, to remove impurities from wines and juices, to treat waste water, and in a variety of applications for oil drilling.

- The Mississippi River carries sediment from land as far away as the Appalachians and the Rocky Mountains. The Mississippi Delta, at the Gulf of Mexico, covers about 33,700 km². The delta has been forming for the last 2 million years.

Section 4

Metamorphic Rock

▶ **Foliated Rocks**
Foliated rocks develop during regional metamorphism. In slate, tiny flakes of mica line up into sheets. In some schists, mica forms dark or light layers, and the crystals are large enough to see. Gneiss has a coarse texture, and alternating layers are dominated by different minerals.

▶ **Metamorphosis in a Lab**
How do scientists determine the geologic history of a metamorphic rock? Geologists can estimate the temperature and pressure that metamorphosed a rock by simulating the process in a laboratory. When geologists know the chemical composition of certain minerals within a rock, they can subject a similar compound to a range of temperatures and pressures. By observing the laboratory results, they can make predictions about how similar materials behave in nature. Geologists can determine the temperature at which metamorphosis occurred within 20°C and the pressure within a fraction of a kilobar.

▶ **Carrara Marble**
In the mountains around Carrara, Italy, a marble prized for its purity has been quarried for at least 2,000 years. Its whiteness is due to the lack of organic materials in the limestone from which it recrystallized. Carrara marble was used in the interior of the Pantheon, in Rome. It is also found in the Leaning Tower of Pisa, in the pavement of Saint Peter's Basilica, in Vatican City, and in the Kennedy Center, in Washington, D.C.

IS THAT A FACT!

- Metamorphic rocks are a challenge to study because they form within a wide range of heat and pressure. Scientists must distinguish between the geologic history of the metamorphic rock and the history of the igneous, sedimentary, or previously metamorphosed rocks it formed from. For the same reason, however, metamorphic rocks offer many important clues about tectonic activity in the Earth's past.

- Metamorphism occurs quickly at high temperatures, but it also occurs at temperatures that are surprisingly low. For example, clay minerals in mudstone and shale can begin to metamorphose at temperatures as low as 50°C! This reaction, however, takes many millions of years to occur.

For background information about teaching strategies and issues, refer to the *Professional Reference for Teachers.*

Chapter 4 • Chapter Background

Rocks: Mineral Mixtures

 Pre-Reading Questions

Students may not know the answers to these questions before reading the chapter, so accept any reasonable response.

Suggested Answers

1. A mineral is an inorganic crystalline solid with a definite chemical composition. A rock is a solid mixture of one or more minerals or organic materials like coal.

2. Answers will vary. Rocks are used as surgical blades and building materials and are studied to learn about the history of Earth and other planets.

3. There are many ways a rock can form: when magma cools and solidifies, when sediments or the remains of organisms are deposited and cemented together, when minerals crystallize out of sea water, or when the composition or texture of a pre-existing rock changes due to heat or pressure.

 Directed Reading Worksheet 4

 Science Puzzlers, Twisters & Teasers Worksheet 4

 Guided Reading Audio CD
English or Spanish, Chapter 4

Rocks: Mineral Mixtures

Sections

1. Understanding Rock . . . 80
   Apply 84
   MathBreak 85
   Internet Connect 86
2. Igneous Rock 87
   Internet Connect 90
3. Sedimentary Rock 91
   Internet Connect 94
4. Metamorphic Rock 95
   QuickLab 96
   Biology Connection . . . 99
   Internet Connect 99

Chapter Review 102
Feature Articles 104, 105
LabBook 642–647

 **Pre-Reading Questions**

1. What is the difference between a rock and a mineral?
2. What are some modern uses of rocks?
3. How does rock form?

---

internet connect

HRW On-line Resources
go.hrw.com
For worksheets and other teaching aids, visit the HRW Web site and type in the keyword: **HSTRCK**

www.scilinks.com
Use the *sci*LINKS numbers at the end of each chapter for additional resources on the **NSTA** Web site.

www.cnnfyi.com
Visit the CNN Web site for current events coverage and classroom resources.

Steps for a Giant?

Irish legend claims that the mythical hero Finn MacCool built the Giant's Causeway, shown here. According to legend, these stepping stones were used to cross the sea in order to invade a neighboring island. Actually, this rock formation is the result of the cooling of huge amounts of molten rock. As the molten rock cooled, it formed tall, hexagonal pillars called *columnar joints*. Columnar joints can be seen in basalt rocks around the world. In this chapter, you will learn more about how rocks form.

START-UP Activity

CLASSIFYING OBJECTS

Scientists use the physical and chemical properties of rocks to classify them. Classifying objects such as rocks requires close attention to many properties. Do this exercise to get some classifying practice.

Procedure

1. Your teacher will give you a **bag containing several objects**. Examine the objects and note features such as size, color, shape, texture, smell, and any unique properties.
2. Invent three different ways to sort these objects. You may have only one group or as many as 14.
3. Create an identification key explaining how you organized the objects into each group.

Analysis

4. What properties did you use to sort the items?
5. Were there any objects that could fit into more than one group? How did you solve this problem?
6. Which properties might you use to classify rocks? Explain your answer.

START-UP Activity

CLASSIFYING OBJECTS

MATERIALS

FOR EACH GROUP:
- bag of objects, such as an apple, a lemon, a green ball, a sugar cube, a pair of sunglasses, a piece of chalk, a paper clip, a plastic spoon, a pencil, a pen, a ruler, a rock, a twig, a tissue, an eraser, a screw, and a nail.

Answers to START-UP Activity

4. Answers will vary. Sample answer: I sorted the objects by color, size, and what they are made of.
5. Answers will vary. Sample answer: Yes, there were objects that could fit into more than one group. I solved this problem by deciding which characteristics were more important and sorting the object into a matching group.
6. Answers will vary. Accept all reasonable responses. Students may mention color, texture, luster, and hardness.

SECTION 1

Focus

Understanding Rock

In this section students learn about the variety of ways rocks are used in human civilization. The section explains the rock cycle and introduces the three types of rock: igneous, sedimentary, and metamorphic. Students learn how each type of rock forms and that rocks are classified by texture and mineral composition.

Bellringer

Ask students to make a list of the ways rock is used in their life. Encourage them to think of imaginative answers.

(People use rock to sharpen knives; make gardens or borders in yards; produce fertilizer; carve statues; create jewelry; and construct buildings, roads, and sidewalks.)
`Sheltered English`

1 Motivate

ACTIVITY

Have students examine samples of various types of rock and take notes on their characteristics, such as texture, color, weight, and composition. Then divide the class into groups of four. Groups should hypothesize about how each rock formed and suggest three different uses for each type of rock.

 Directed Reading Worksheet 4 Section 1

Section 1

Terms to Learn

rock
rock cycle
magma
composition
texture
igneous rock
sedimentary rock
metamorphic rock

What You'll Do

- Describe two ways rocks were used by early humans, and describe two ways they are used today.
- Describe how each type of rock changes into another as it moves through the rock cycle.
- List two characteristics of rock that are used to help classify it.

Understanding Rock

The Earth's crust is made up mostly of rock. But what exactly is rock? **Rock** is simply a solid mixture of crystals of one or more minerals. However, some types of rock, such as coal, are made of organic materials. Rocks come in all sizes—from pebbles to formations thousands of kilometers long!

The Value of Rock

Rock has been an important natural resource as long as humans have existed. Early humans used rocks as hammers to make other tools. They discovered that they could make arrowheads, spear points, knives, and scrapers by carefully hammering flint, chert, and obsidian rocks. See **Figure 1.** These rocks were shaped to form extremely sharp edges and points. Even today, obsidian is used to form special scalpels, as shown in **Figure 2.**

Rock has also been used for centuries to make buildings, roads, and monuments. **Figure 3** shows some inventive uses of rock by both ancient and modern civilizations. Buildings have been made out of marble, granite, sandstone, limestone, and slate. Modern buildings also use concrete, in which rock is an important ingredient. Concrete is one of the most common building materials used today.

Figure 1 This stone tool was made and used more than 5,000 years ago.

Figure 2 This stone tool was made recently. It is an obsidian scalpel used in delicate operations.

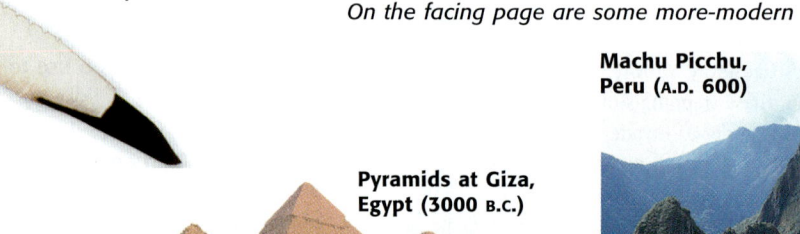

Figure 3 These photos show a few samples of structures built with rock. On this page are structures built by ancient civilizations. On the facing page are some more-modern examples.

Machu Picchu, Peru (A.D. 600)

Pyramids at Giza, Egypt (3000 B.C.)

80

SCIENCE HUMOR

In 1976, Gary Dahl of California began marketing Pet Rocks. They came in a carrying case with a training manual and a pedigree that certified that they came from a California beach. In no time at all, more than 1 ton of the stones were sold. People held Pet Rock beauty contests and bought specialized foods and beds for them. There were even Pet Rock cemeteries!

Humans have a long history with rock. Certain types of rock have helped us to survive and to develop both our ancient and modern civilizations. Rock is also very important to scientists. The study of rocks helps answer questions about the history of the Earth and our solar system. Rocks provide a record of what the Earth and other planets were like before recorded history.

The fossils some rocks contain also provide clues about lifeforms that lived billions of years ago, long before dinosaurs walked the Earth. **Figure 4** shows how rocks can capture evidence of life that became extinct long ago. Without such fossils, scientists would know very little about the history of life on Earth. The answers we get from studying rocks often cause us to ask even more questions!

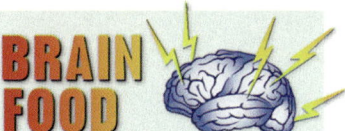

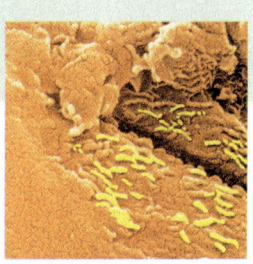

Some meteorites are actually rocks that come from other planets. Below is a microscopic view of a meteorite that came from Mars. The tiny structures may indicate that microscopic life once existed on Mars.

Figure 4 *These fossils were found on a mountaintop. Their presence indicates that what is now a mountaintop was once the bottom of a shallow sea.*

Exeter Cathedral, Exeter, England (A.D. 1120–1520)

LBJ Library, Austin, Texas (1972)

CONNECT TO LIFE SCIENCE

European songbirds and jackdaws break the shells of snails by hammering them against rocks. Egyptian vultures break open ostrich eggs by grasping a pebble in their beak and pounding on the shell until it breaks. Have students research other animals that also use stones as tools, such as sea otters. Students can then demonstrate for the class how these tools are used.

2 Teach

BRAIN FOOD

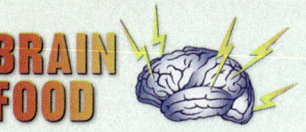

In 1996, scientists analyzed a meteorite from Mars and discovered possible microscopic fossils of primitive bacteria. The scientists also found organic molecules and mineral features that could indicate biological activity. When combined with other indirect evidence, this discovery raises the possibility that life once existed on Mars. But this evidence is hotly debated in the scientific community. Encourage students to learn more about the evidence for and against life on Mars.

MISCONCEPTION ALERT

The terms *rocks* and *rock formations* refer to the same material, but rock formations are large-scale bodies of rock, such as plutons, batholiths, and sedimentary strata, while rocks can be any size.

CROSS-DISCIPLINARY FOCUS

Writing **History** Between A.D. 900 and 1400 the Anasazi Indians of the American Southwest carved small towns in cliff sides. In what is now Cambodia, a vast temple complex called Angkor was carved from brick, sandstone, and laterite in the twelfth century. In the 1300s, African traders built the Great Zimbabwe, an elaborate walled city guarded by huge monoliths. Have students write a report or build a model of one of these ancient sites.

Section 1 • Understanding Rock **81**

2) Teach, continued

USING THE FIGURE

 Ask students to use the information in the rock-cycle illustration to draw a diagram of the rock cycle in their ScienceLog. The first step in the textbook illustration is the formation of sedimentary rock; ask students to begin their rock cycle with a different step. Encourage them to write a descriptive caption for every stage of the rock cycle.

MEETING INDIVIDUAL NEEDS

Learners Having Difficulty
Have students prepare a *Rock Dictionary*. Ask them to list the three types of rock and the processes that occur in the rock cycle. Ask students to record the dictionary definition for each rock type or process and then define it in their own words. Encourage students to make up mnemonic devices, such as jokes or rhymes, to help them remember the meaning of each term.
Sheltered English

MISCONCEPTION ALERT

Rocks rarely undergo the complete process shown in the rock-cycle diagram. Sedimentary rocks can become igneous rocks, and metamorphic rocks can become sedimentary rocks. Some students may not realize the length of time it takes for changes to occur in the rock cycle. The process shown in the diagram can take billions of years.

Teaching Transparency 110
"The Rock Cycle"

The Rock Cycle

The rocks in the Earth's crust are constantly changing. Rock changes its shape and composition in a variety of ways. The way rock forms determines what type of rock it is. The three main types of rock are *igneous*, *sedimentary*, and *metamorphic*. Each type of rock is a part of the *rock cycle*. The **rock cycle** is the process by which one rock type changes into another. Follow this diagram to see one way sand grains can change as they travel through the rock cycle.

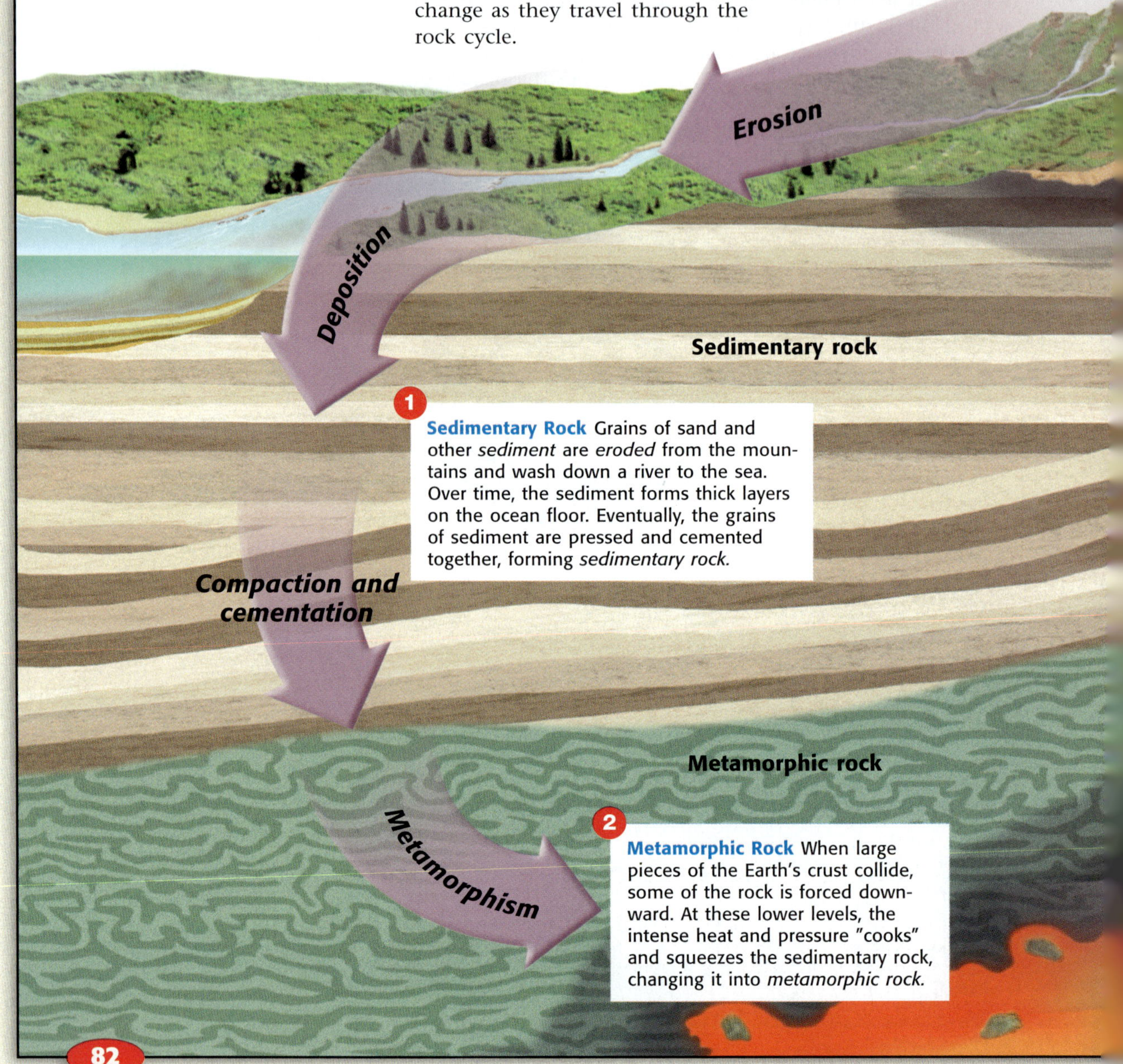

Erosion

Deposition

Sedimentary rock

① Sedimentary Rock Grains of sand and other *sediment* are *eroded* from the mountains and wash down a river to the sea. Over time, the sediment forms thick layers on the ocean floor. Eventually, the grains of sediment are pressed and cemented together, forming *sedimentary rock*.

Compaction and cementation

Metamorphic rock

Metamorphism

② Metamorphic Rock When large pieces of the Earth's crust collide, some of the rock is forced downward. At these lower levels, the intense heat and pressure "cooks" and squeezes the sedimentary rock, changing it into *metamorphic rock*.

Multicultural CONNECTION

The Islamic scholar Avicenna (980–1037) contributed immensely to our knowledge of medicine, astronomy, mathematics, and geology. In the *Book of Minerals* he described how rivers and seas laid down sediment that eventually became rock. Avicenna's theories contributed to the foundations of Western geology. Many of his controversial ideas did not gain acceptance in Europe until the 1600s. Encourage interested students to learn more about the life and work of Avicenna.

82   Chapter 4 • Rocks: Mineral Mixtures

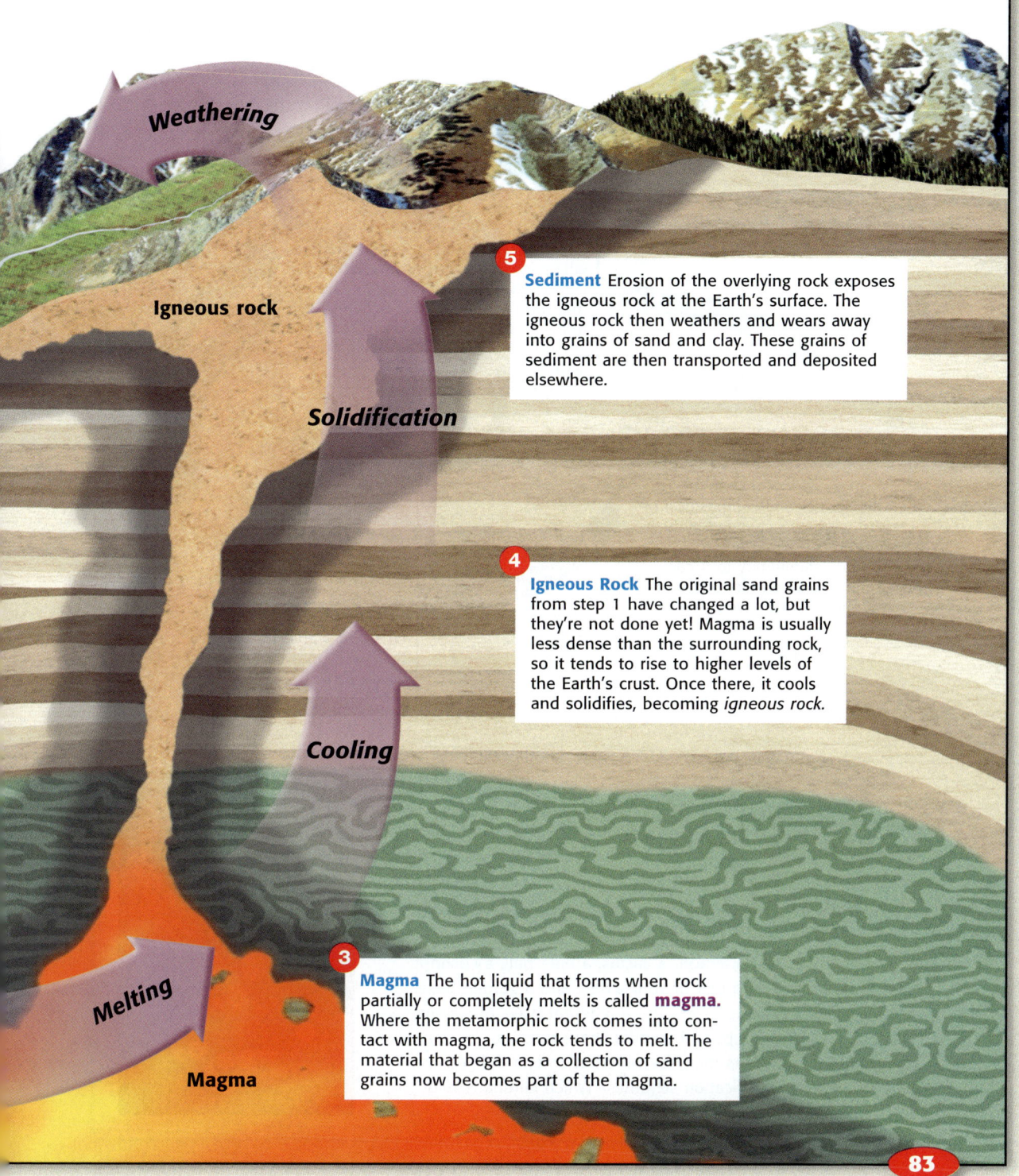

5 Sediment Erosion of the overlying rock exposes the igneous rock at the Earth's surface. The igneous rock then weathers and wears away into grains of sand and clay. These grains of sediment are then transported and deposited elsewhere.

4 Igneous Rock The original sand grains from step 1 have changed a lot, but they're not done yet! Magma is usually less dense than the surrounding rock, so it tends to rise to higher levels of the Earth's crust. Once there, it cools and solidifies, becoming *igneous rock*.

3 Magma The hot liquid that forms when rock partially or completely melts is called **magma**. Where the metamorphic rock comes into contact with magma, the rock tends to melt. The material that began as a collection of sand grains now becomes part of the magma.

CONNECT TO LIFE SCIENCE

Many important substances on Earth follow cycles. Examples include water, nitrogen, sulfur, carbon, and phosphorous. Have students make a poster depicting the rock cycle and one other cycle in nature. Ask them to consider the ways that these cycles interact with each other.

CROSS-DISCIPLINARY FOCUS

Language Arts Ask students to imagine being an ancient grain of sand on a beach. Have them write a letter to a young igneous rock describing their lifetime in the rock cycle. Students can share their letters with the class.

REAL-WORLD CONNECTION

Invite a local rock collector to address the class, and share his or her collection with the class. Tell the students to collect some rocks from their neighborhood for the collector to identify.

MISCONCEPTION ALERT

In some areas of the United States, especially in regions that experience long, cold winters, some people speak of rocks "growing." In the fall, farm fields are cleared of large rocks. The following spring, large rocks are found again in the fields and people say that the rocks have "grown" over the winter. In fact, when the ground freezes, it shifts and heaves, pushing buried rocks toward the surface.

IS THAT A FACT!

The space probes *Viking 1* and *Viking 2* provided detailed images of a gigantic volcano on Mars called Olympus Mons. The volcano is 25 km high, three times as high as Mount Everest. NASA scientists believe Olympus Mons is the largest volcano in the solar system.

Science Bloopers

In the Middle Ages, people believed that some rocks, called *eagle stones*, could reproduce. Scholars reported that the rocks crack like eggs and small stones pour out. Today, scientists call them *atetites*, or *clay-ironstone concretions*. Atetites have a shell of iron-rich clay that encloses smaller clay pebbles.

Section 1 • Understanding Rock

② Teach, continued

GROUP ACTIVITY

Divide the class into small groups. Give each group samples of sandstone, limestone, and conglomerate. Number the samples. Provide a magnifying glass, a small dental pick, and paper towels to capture any pieces of rock that break off during the activity. Write the following instructions on the board:

1. Describe the color and texture of the specimen.
2. Using your unaided eye, examine the particles that make up the rock. Describe what you see.
3. Using the magnifying glass, try to identify the mineral composition of the specimen.
4. Use the dental pick to test the cohesiveness of the rocks, and record what you discover.
5. Try to classify each rock as fine-grained, medium-grained, or coarse-grained.

After groups have analyzed the rocks, discuss their findings.
Sheltered English

TOPIC: Rock Formations
GO TO: www.scilinks.org
sciLINKS NUMBER: HSTE100

Now that you know something about the natural processes that make the three major rock types, you can see that each type of rock can become any other type of rock. This is why it is called a cycle—there is no beginning or end. All rocks are at some stage of the rock cycle and can change into a different rock type. **Figure 5** shows how the three types of rock change form.

Figure 5 The Rock Cycle

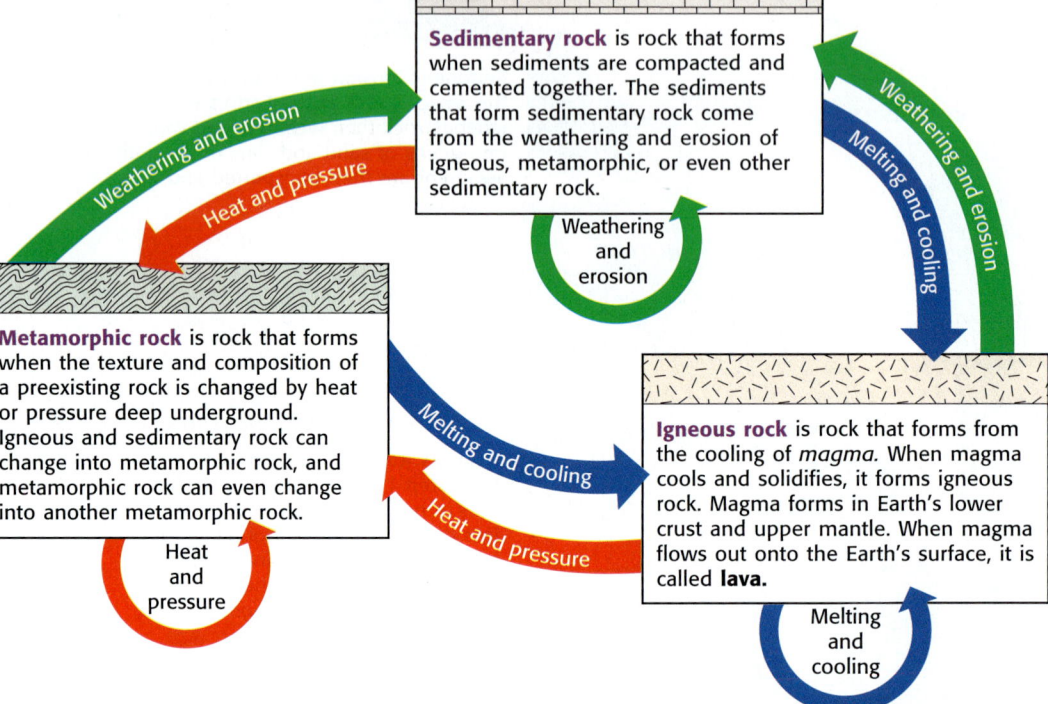

Classifying Objects

Suppose you have an apple, a tomato, a peach, a kiwi fruit, a pineapple, a banana, a lemon, a cactus, a blue ball, a coconut, a brick, a sugar cube, a pair of sunglasses, and a garden hose. Use your imagination to invent three different ways to classify these objects into groups with similar characteristics. You may have only 1 group or as many as 14. What criteria did you use for each of your classification schemes? Which criteria would you use to classify rocks?

84

Answers to APPLY

Answers will vary. (These questions are intended to get the students to anticipate the content in the next two pages.)

Q: What happens to a small stone when it works up its courage?

A: It becomes a little boulder.

84   Chapter 4 • Rocks: Mineral Mixtures

The Nitty-Gritty on Rock Classification

You now know that scientists classify all rock into three main types based on how they formed. But did you know that each type of rock is divided into even smaller groups? These smaller groups are also based on differences in the way rocks form. For example, all igneous rock forms when hot liquid cools and solidifies. But some igneous rocks form when lava cools on the Earth's surface, while others form when magma cools deep beneath the surface. Therefore, igneous rock is divided into two smaller groups, depending on how and where it forms. In the same way, sedimentary and metamorphic rocks are also divided into smaller groups. How do Earth scientists know how to classify different rocks? They study them in detail using two important criteria—*composition* and *texture*.

Composition The minerals a rock is made of determine the **composition** of the rock. For example, a rock that is made up mostly of the mineral quartz will have a composition very similar to quartz. A rock that is made of 50 percent quartz and 50 percent feldspar will have a very different overall composition. Use this idea to compare the examples given in **Figure 6**.

MATH BREAK

What's in It?
Assume that a granite rock you are studying is made of 30 percent quartz, 55 percent feldspar, and the rest biotite mica. What percentage of the rock is biotite mica?

Figure 6 The overall composition of a rock depends on the minerals it contains.

MATH and MORE

A percentage is a ratio that is expressed in terms of hundredths. When analyzing pure substances, percentage composition remains the same at any mass. For example, in terms of atomic mass, the percentage of oxygen atoms in water is 88.8 percent whether you are describing a single raindrop or an entire ocean.

Math Skills Worksheet 20
"Parts of 100: Calculating Percentages"

Answer to MATHBREAK
100 percent of rock − (30 percent quartz + 55 percent feldspar) = 15 percent biotite mica

CONNECT TO LIFE SCIENCE

Some birds swallow stones to help with digestion. The stones settle in a specialized stomach compartment called the gizzard. As seeds, stems, and leaves enter the gizzard, its strong muscles contract, and the stones grind up the tough cellulose fibers into pieces that are small enough to digest. To see how a gizzard functions, have students fill a small cloth bag with different-sized pebbles. Add some breakfast cereal and birdseed to the bag. Knead the bag to see what happens to the food. Tell students that some dinosaurs had gizzards as well.

Homework

Illustration Have students make a poster that illustrates the rock cycle. Encourage them to cut out pictures from magazines of the different types of rock and processes in the rock cycle. For example, marble is a metamorphic rock that could be represented by a picture of a marble statue.
<mark>Sheltered English</mark>

TOPIC: Composition of Rock
GO TO: www.scilinks.org
sciLINKS NUMBER: HSTE090

Teaching Transparency 63
"The Digestive System of a Bird"

Section 1 • Understanding Rock

3) Extend

RESEARCH

Investigate Your Area Students can search the Internet to learn about nearby places that are good for rock hunting. Ask students to report their findings to the class.

4) Close

Quiz

1. Name four processes that change rock from one type to another. (weathering, changes in pressure, melting, and cooling)
2. Explain how making glass is similar to the formation of igneous rock. (Glass is made by melting quartz sand grains.)
3. Explain how mixing concrete and allowing it to harden is similar to the formation of sedimentary rock. (Concrete is a mixture of different compounds and rock particles. After it is poured, it hardens much like sedimentary rock.)
4. Explain how baking bricks in a kiln is similar to the formation of metamorphic rock. (Bricks are made from clay and are baked to make them strong and resistant to weathering. Bricks are "metamorphosed" because they have different properties than dried clay.)

ALTERNATIVE ASSESSMENT

Have students write a skit portraying the rock cycle. Roles can include the minerals that make up rock and the forces that affect them. To represent the forces—heat, pressure, erosion, and weathering—suggest that students create special costumes.

Texture The **texture** of a rock is determined by the sizes, shapes, and positions of the grains of which it is made. Rocks that are made entirely of small grains, such as silt or clay particles, are said to have a *fine-grained* texture. Rocks that are made of large grains, such as pebbles, are said to have a *coarse-grained* texture. Rocks that have a texture between fine- and coarse-grained are said to have a *medium-grained* texture. Examples of these textures are shown in **Figure 7.**

Figure 7 *These three sedimentary rocks are made up of grains of different sizes. Can you see the differences in their textures?*

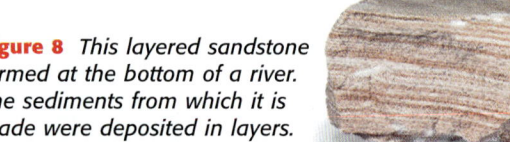

Fine-grained — Siltstone
Medium-grained — Sandstone
Coarse-grained — Conglomerate

Each rock type has a different kind of texture that can provide good clues to how and where the rock formed. For example, the rock shown in **Figure 8** has a texture that reflects how it formed. Both texture and composition are important characteristics that scientists use to understand the origin and history of rocks. Keep these characteristics in mind as you continue reading through this chapter.

Figure 8 *This layered sandstone formed at the bottom of a river. The sediments from which it is made were deposited in layers.*

internetconnect

SCILINKS. NSTA
TOPIC: Composition of Rock
GO TO: www.scilinks.org
sciLinks Number: HSTE090

REVIEW

1. List two ways rock is important to humans today.
2. What are the three major rock types, and how can they change from one type to another type?
3. How is lava different from magma?
4. **Comparing Concepts** Explain the difference between texture and composition.

Answers to Review

1. Answers will vary.
2. Igneous rock forms when magma cools and solidifies. Sedimentary rock forms when sediments are cemented and compacted together or when minerals crystallize out of sea water. Metamorphic rock forms when the texture or mineral composition of a preexisting rock is changed by heat or pressure.
3. Magma is a hot liquid that exists underground. Lava is magma that erupts and flows onto the Earth's surface.
4. The texture of a rock is determined by the sizes, shapes, and positions of the grains that make it up. The composition of a rock is determined by the kinds of minerals the rock is made of.

Igneous Rock

The word *igneous* comes from the Latin word for "fire." Magma cools into various types of igneous rock depending on the composition of the magma and the amount of time it takes the magma to cool and solidify. Like all other rock, igneous rock is classified according to its composition and texture.

Origins of Igneous Rock

Magma and lava solidify in much the same way that water freezes. When magma or lava cools down enough, it solidifies, or "freezes," to form igneous rock. One difference between water freezing and magma freezing is that water freezes at 0°C and magma and lava freeze at between 700°C and 1,250°C.

There are three ways magma can form: when rock is heated, when pressure is released, or when rock changes composition. To see how this can happen, follow along with **Figure 9**.

Figure 9 There are three ways a rock can melt.

Temperature An increase in temperature deep within the Earth's crust can cause the minerals in a rock to melt. Different minerals melt at different temperatures. So depending on how hot a rock gets, some of the minerals can melt while other minerals remain solid.

Pressure The high pressure deep within the Earth forces minerals to stay in the solid state, when otherwise they would melt from the intense heat. When hot rocks rise to shallow depths, the pressure is finally released and the minerals can melt.

Composition Sometimes fluids like water and carbon dioxide enter a rock that is close to its melting point. When these fluids combine with the rock, they can lower the melting point of the rock enough for it to melt and form magma.

WEIRD SCIENCE

Surtsey is a volcanic island south of Iceland that people actually saw being born! In 1963, fishermen far out at sea saw jets of spray, steam, and lava shooting more than 30 m out of the ocean. One month later the volcano broke through the surface to form an island. By the time the eruptions ended, Surtsey covered an area of approximately 2.8 km². Seabirds started visiting, and tough grasses began to sprout. Today scientists think Surtsey may erode completely if the volcano doesn't erupt again.

2) Teach

CONNECT TO LIFE SCIENCE

Until 1977, biologists thought few life-forms lived at ocean depths where sunlight does not reach. When scientists in the submersible *Alvin* explored the bottom of a deep ocean trench called the Galápagos Rift, they discovered structures called black smokers that release dissolved mineral compounds and heat the water. Scientists were amazed to discover an entire ecosystem that did not depend on photosynthesis for energy. This discovery has led many scientists to speculate that life may also have evolved in the outer solar system—particularly in the oceans that may exist under the surface of Europa, one of Jupiter's moons. Have students research the bizarre life-forms that scientists found living around black smokers.

Multicultural CONNECTION

In the Tule Lake region of northern California, volcanic eruptions created a rugged landscape of broken lava beds with glassy, splintery edges, deep trenches, and small lava caves where people can live—and hide.

In 1872, the United States and the Modoc Indians went to war. The Modocs set up a stronghold for 50 people in the jagged lava beds. The terrain was so hard to negotiate that the Modocs held off more than 1,000 federal troops for more than 5 months. Today, this area is part of Lava Beds National Monument.

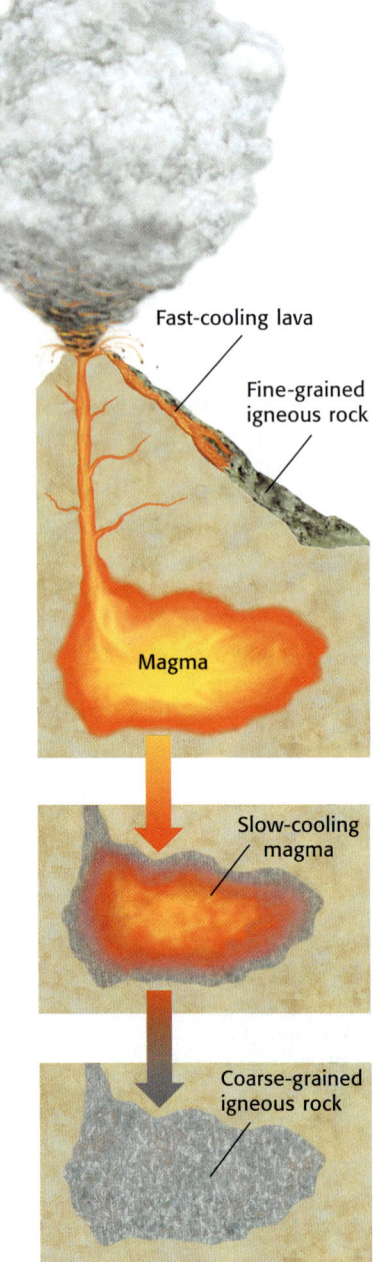

Figure 11 The amount of time it takes for magma or lava to cool determines the texture of igneous rock.

Teaching Transparency 111
"The Cooling Rate of Magma and the Texture of Igneous Rock"

Composition and Texture of Igneous Rock

Look at the rocks in **Figure 10**. All of these are igneous rocks, even though they look very different from one another. These rocks differ from one another in what they are made of and how fast they cooled.

The light-colored rocks are not only lighter in color but also less dense. They are rich in elements such as silicon, aluminum, sodium, and potassium. These lightweight rocks are called *felsic*. The darker rocks are denser than the felsic rocks. These rocks are rich in iron, magnesium, and calcium and are called *mafic*.

Figure 10 Light-colored igneous rock generally has a felsic composition. Dark-colored igneous rock generally has a mafic composition.

	Coarse-grained	Fine-grained
Felsic	Granite	Rhyolite
Mafic	Gabbro	Basalt

Now look at **Figure 11**. This illustration shows what happens to magma when it cools at different rates. The longer it takes for the magma or lava to cool, the more time mineral crystals have to grow. And the more time the crystals have to grow, the coarser the texture of the resulting igneous rock.

✓ Self-Check

Rank the rocks shown in Figure 10 by how fast they cooled. Hint: Pay attention to their texture. *(See page 726 to check your answer.)*

Answers to Self-Check

From fastest-cooled to slowest-cooled, the rocks in **Figure 10** are: basalt, rhyolite, gabbro, and granite.

Igneous Rock Formations

You have probably seen igneous rock formations that were caused by lava cooling on the Earth's surface. But not all magma reaches the surface. Some magma cools and solidifies deep within the Earth's crust.

Intrusive Igneous Rock When magma cools beneath the Earth's surface, the resulting rock is called **intrusive.** Intrusive rock usually has a coarse-grained texture. This is because it is well insulated by the surrounding rock and thus cools very slowly.

Intrusive rock formations are named for their size and the way in which they intrude, or push into, the surrounding rock. *Plutons* are large, balloon-shaped intrusive formations that result when magma cools at great depths. Intrusive rocks are also called *plutonic rocks,* after Pluto, the Roman god of the underworld. **Figure 12** shows an example of an intrusive formation that has been exposed on the Earth's surface. Some common intrusive rock formations are shown in **Figure 13.**

Figure 12 Enchanted Rock, near Llano, Texas, is an exposed pluton made of granite.

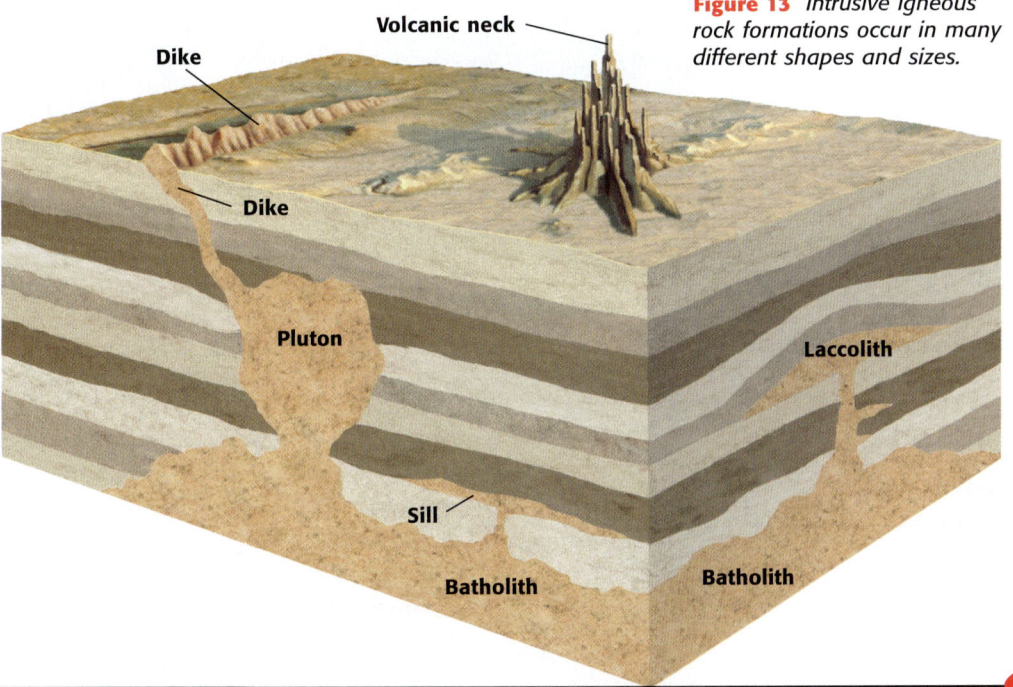

Figure 13 Intrusive igneous rock formations occur in many different shapes and sizes.

Science Bloopers

In the eighteenth century some scholars thought lava formed when underground coal deposits caught fire. They believed that heat from the fires melted the surrounding rock, producing lava. This is impossible, but underground coal fires do exist—one has been burning in Australia for over 2,000 years!

Scientists at Odds

Abraham Gottlob Werner was a geologist in the late eighteenth century who believed that layers of basalt found in sedimentary rock were sedimentary rocks that formed under the ocean. James Hutton opposed him vehemently, arguing that basalt and other igneous rocks formed by the cooling of magma.

Section 2 • Igneous Rock

3 Close

Quiz

1. Describe felsic and mafic rocks, and name three elements that occur in each type. (Felsic rock is lighter in color and weight; it is rich in aluminum, silicon, sodium, and potassium. Mafic rock is darker and heavier; it is rich in iron, magnesium, and calcium.)

2. What is the difference between intrusive and extrusive rock? (Intrusive rock forms from magma that solidifies while still underground, while extrusive rock forms from magma that solidifies after it has reached the surface.)

ALTERNATIVE ASSESSMENT

Have students create a model cross section that shows the formation of both intrusive and extrusive igneous rock. Supply students with several different colors of clay so they can color-code different formations, such as the magma source, dikes, sills, plutons, and the lava that forms extrusive rock. **Sheltered English**

Crystal Growth PG 642

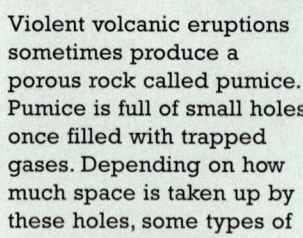

BRAIN FOOD

Violent volcanic eruptions sometimes produce a porous rock called pumice. Pumice is full of small holes once filled with trapped gases. Depending on how much space is taken up by these holes, some types of pumice can even float!

internet connect

SC_INKS_ NSTA
TOPIC: Igneous Rock
GO TO: www.scilinks.org
sciLINKS NUMBER: HSTE093

Extrusive Igneous Rock Igneous rock that forms on the Earth's surface is called **extrusive**. Most volcanic rock is extrusive. Extrusive rock cools quickly on the surface and contains either very small crystals or none at all.

When lava erupts from a volcano, a formation called a *lava flow* is made. You can see an active lava flow in **Figure 14.** But lava does not always come from volcanoes. Sometimes lava erupts from long cracks in the Earth's surface called *fissures*. When a large amount of lava flows out of a fissure, it can cover a vast area, forming a plain called a *lava plateau*. Preexisting landforms are often buried by extrusive igneous rock formations.

Figure 14 *Below is an active lava flow. When exposed to surface conditions, lava quickly cools and solidifies, forming a fine-grained igneous rock.*

REVIEW

1. What two properties are used to classify igneous rock?
2. How does the cooling rate of lava or magma affect the texture of an igneous rock?
3. **Interpreting Illustrations** Use the diagram in Figure 13 to compare a sill with a dike. What makes them different from each other?

Answers to Review

1. texture and color (mineral composition)
2. When magma cools slowly, crystals have a long time to grow, so the igneous rock that forms is coarse-grained. When magma cools quickly, crystals have a short time to grow, so the igneous rock that forms is fine-grained.
3. Both a sill and a dike are sheetlike bodies of igneous rock. A sill intrudes rock parallel to the surrounding rock layers. A dike cuts across the surrounding rock layers.

Section 3

Terms to Learn
strata
stratification

What You'll Do
- Describe how the three types of sedimentary rock form.
- Explain how sedimentary rocks record Earth's history.

Sedimentary Rock

Wind, water, ice, sunlight, and gravity all cause rock to *weather* into fragments. **Figure 15** shows how some sedimentary rocks form. Through the process of erosion, rock fragments, called sediment, are transported from one place to another. Eventually the sediment is deposited in layers. Sedimentary rock then forms as sediments become compacted and cemented together.

Origins of Sedimentary Rock

As new layers of sediment are deposited, the layers eventually become compressed, or compacted. Dissolved minerals separate out of the water to form a natural glue that binds the sediments together into sedimentary rock. Sedimentary rock forms at or near the Earth's surface, without the heat and pressure involved in the formation of igneous and metamorphic rocks. The physical features of sedimentary rock tell part of its history. The most noticeable feature of sedimentary rock is its layers, or **strata**. Road cuts and construction zones are good places to observe sedimentary rock formations, and as you can see in **Figure 16,** canyons carved by rivers provide some spectacular views.

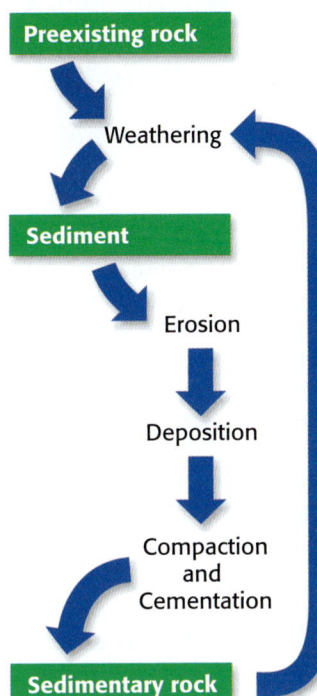

Figure 15 A Sedimentary Rock Cycle

Figure 16 Millions of years of erosion by the Colorado River have revealed the rock strata in the walls of the Grand Canyon.

Q: What did the limestone rock say to the geologist?

A: Don't take me for granite.

Teaching Transparency 113
"A Sedimentary Rock Cycle"

Directed Reading Worksheet 4 Section 3

SECTION 3

Focus

Sedimentary Rock
This section explores how sedimentary rock forms and how it accumulates in layers, or strata. Students distinguish between clastic and chemical sedimentary rock and learn how each forms.

Bellringer
Ask students to write about how layers in sedimentary rock are like the rings in a tree. How are they different? What information can geologists infer by examining sedimentary layers?

1) Motivate

Demonstration

Dissolution of Minerals
Limestone forms when calcium carbonate crystallizes out of ocean water. Students may not believe that water contains the chemical components of dissolved minerals. If you live in an area with hard water, have students observe ice melting in warm water. After the ice melts, there is a layer of fluffy calcium carbonate that forms at the bottom of the glass. If you live in an area with soft water, make hard water by dissolving a little baking soda (sodium bicarbonate) and calcium chloride in water. Then freeze it into ice cubes. Use these ice cubes for the demonstration.

TOPIC: Sedimentary Rock
GO TO: www.scilinks.org
sciLINKS NUMBER: HSTE095

2) Teach

USING THE FIGURE

Point out that **Figure 18** illustrates part of a cyclical process. First rain falls to Earth, drenching the soil. Calcium and carbonate dissolve in the rainwater and are washed out to sea. As some of the sea water evaporates and returns to the atmosphere, the calcium and carbonate accumulate in the ocean. When the concentration of these two substances becomes high enough, the substances combine, forming crystals of calcium carbonate, $CaCO_3$. The calcium carbonate settles on the sea floor, where it begins to accumulate as a limestone deposit. If this limestone deposit is uplifted and becomes part of a continental landmass, the cycle will continue as erosion contributes calcium and carbonate to the ocean again.
Sheltered English

CONNECT TO LIFE SCIENCE

Calcium carbonate is an important compound for many different animals. Many mollusks remove calcium and carbonate from the sea water and combine them in special tissues that then harden to form a calcium carbonate shell. When the mollusk dies, its shell either dissolves back into the water or becomes part of the sediment on the bottom of the ocean. If the shell is part of deposited sediment, it may become a fossil. Have students research the Mazon Creek deposits, in Kansas, to learn more about these kinds of fossil beds.

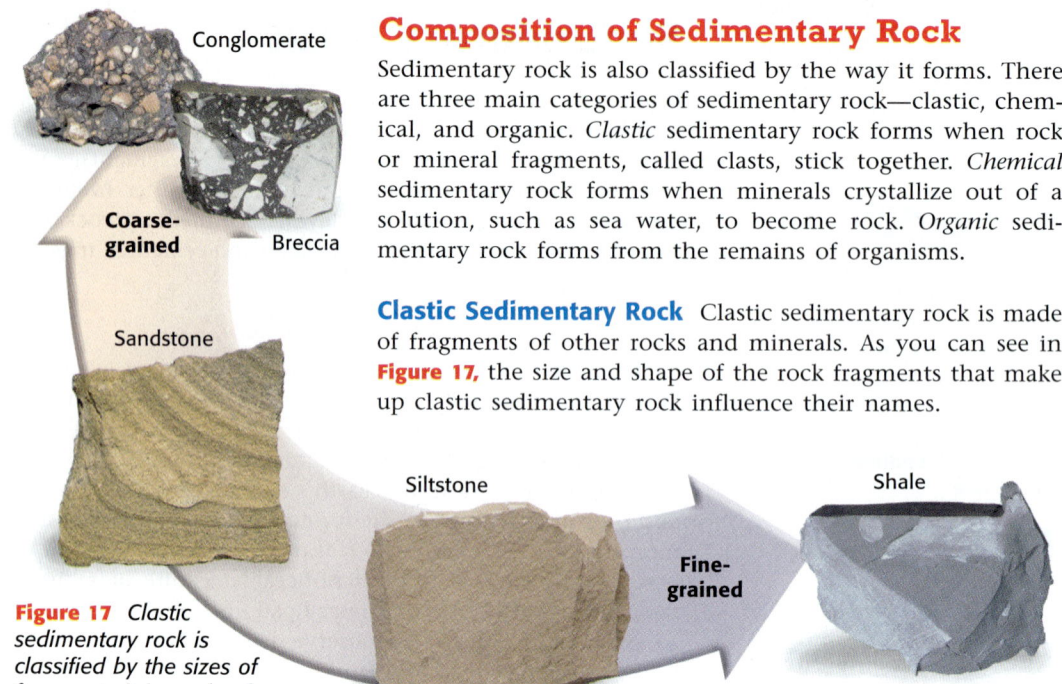

Figure 17 Clastic sedimentary rock is classified by the sizes of fragments it is made of.

Composition of Sedimentary Rock

Sedimentary rock is also classified by the way it forms. There are three main categories of sedimentary rock—clastic, chemical, and organic. *Clastic* sedimentary rock forms when rock or mineral fragments, called clasts, stick together. *Chemical* sedimentary rock forms when minerals crystallize out of a solution, such as sea water, to become rock. *Organic* sedimentary rock forms from the remains of organisms.

Clastic Sedimentary Rock Clastic sedimentary rock is made of fragments of other rocks and minerals. As you can see in **Figure 17,** the size and shape of the rock fragments that make up clastic sedimentary rock influence their names.

Chemical Sedimentary Rock Chemical sedimentary rock forms from *solutions* of minerals and water. As rainwater slowly makes its way to the ocean, it dissolves some of the rock material it passes through. Some of this dissolved material eventually forms the minerals that make up chemical sedimentary rock. One type of chemical sedimentary rock, chemical limestone, is made of calcium carbonate ($CaCO_3$), or the mineral calcite. It forms when calcium and carbonate become so concentrated in the sea water that calcite crystallizes out of the sea water solution, as shown in **Figure 18.**

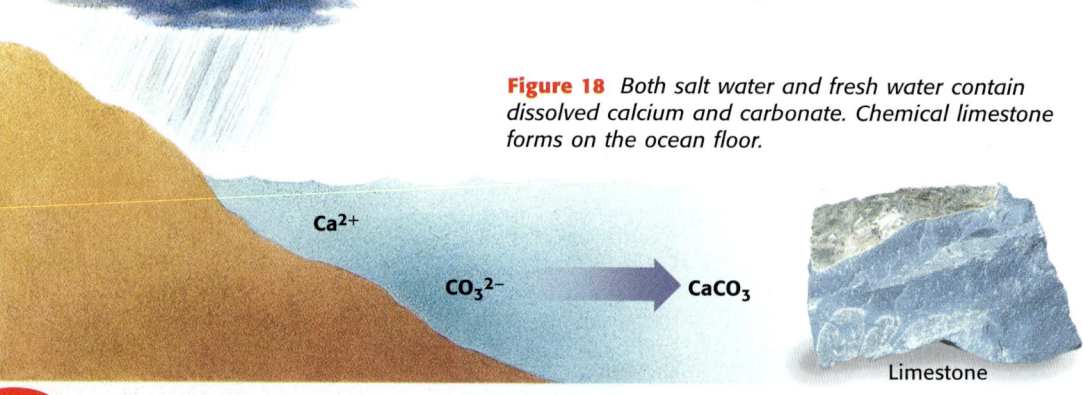

Figure 18 Both salt water and fresh water contain dissolved calcium and carbonate. Chemical limestone forms on the ocean floor.

SCIENTISTS AT ODDS

In the 1700s, the Neptunists and the Plutonists disagreed vehemently about how rocks form. Neptunists believed that all rocks developed from sediment laid down by a vast primordial ocean. The Plutonists believed rock formation was caused by heat from Earth's core. James Hutton's colleague, Sir James Hall, demonstrated the Plutonists' theories by melting rock in a furnace and letting it cool, showing how it changed from one form to another. This demonstration was a major victory for the Plutonists' arguments, but the debate raged for years until Charles Lyell synthesized both arguments in 1830 with *Principles of Geology*.

Organic Sedimentary Rock

Most limestone forms from the remains of animals that once lived in the ocean. This organic material consists of shells or skeletons, which are made of calcium carbonate that the animals get from sea water.

For example, some limestone is made of the skeletons of tiny organisms called coral. Coral are very small, but they live in huge colonies, as shown in **Figure 19.** Over time, the remains of these sea animals accumulate on the ocean floor. These animal remains eventually become cemented together to form *fossiliferous* (FAHS uhl IF uhr uhs) *limestone.*

Fossils are the remains or traces of plants and animals that have been preserved in sedimentary rock. Fossils have given us enormous amounts of information about ancient life-forms and how they lived. Most fossils come from animals that lived in the oceans. Another type of organic limestone, shown in **Figure 20,** forms from organisms that leave their shells in the mud on the ocean floor.

Figure 19 Sea animals called coral create huge deposits of limestone. As they die, their skeletons accumulate on the ocean floor.

Figure 20 Shellfish, such as clams (above right), get the calcium for their shells from sea water. When these organisms die, their shells collect on the ocean floor, eventually becoming rock (below). In time, huge rock formations result (right).

RETEACHING

Now that students have learned about both chemical and clastic sedimentary rock, have them refer back to **Figure 15.** It is a diagram of the clastic sedimentary rock cycle. Have students explain the steps of the cycle and then create a diagram that shows the chemical sedimentary rock cycle.

REAL-WORLD CONNECTION

The most abundant material in toothpaste is water and the second-most abundant is chalk. Chalk is a sedimentary rock which often contains the shells of ancient diatoms, and it is used as an abrasive to clean teeth.

DISCUSSION

Chemical sedimentary rock can be divided into two categories: chemical and biochemical. Some rare forms of limestone are purely the result of a chemical process by which calcium carbonate precipitates out of sea water. But most limestones are biochemical because they form from the skeletons of marine organisms that extracted calcium and carbonate from sea water. Coal is also a biochemical sedimentary rock.

CROSS-DISCIPLINARY FOCUS

Fine Arts One type of printing used to reproduce fine art is called lithography. Lithography uses a flat piece of fine-grained, porous limestone. Interestingly, many important fossil beds were discovered while people quarried for lithographic limestone. The same qualities that make some limestone good for lithography also allow the preservation of extremely detailed fossils. Ask students to find out more about lithography and lithographic limestone beds around the world.

IS THAT A FACT!

The Great Barrier Reef, a long coral reef that lies off the northeastern coast of Australia, is the most massive structure ever built by living creatures. It is more than 2,000 km long and covers an area of 207,000 km².

WEIRD SCIENCE

The Bonneville Salt Flats, in Utah, are the remnants of a vast lake. After the last ice age, most of the lake drained quickly, but the remaining water slowly evaporated, leaving behind the salt flats. The Great Salt Lake is the largest of the few lakes left after Lake Bonneville evaporated.

Section 3 • Sedimentary Rock

3) Extend

GROUP ACTIVITY

Divide students into two groups to investigate sandstone, shale, and limestone. The first group should work together to learn how the rocks form. The second group should investigate how the rocks are used in industry, architecture, or the arts. Both could investigate rock formations that have become tourist attractions. Members of each group should prepare exhibits, posters, or models to demonstrate what they have learned.

4) Close

Quiz

1. How does chemical limestone form? (It forms when calcium carbonate crystallizes out of sea water.)
2. What is stratification, and why is it important to Earth scientists? (Stratification is the layering of rock. It is important because it records many events in Earth's history as well as erosion and deposition rates.)

ALTERNATIVE ASSESSMENT

To review sedimentary rock formation, have students draw a picture of an environment that shows the source of sediments and where they are deposited. A second drawing should show what the environment will look like millions of years later after sedimentary rock has formed.

Sedimentary Rock Structures

Many sedimentary rock features can tell you about the way the rock formed. The most characteristic feature of sedimentary rock is **stratification,** or layering. Strata differ from one another depending on the kind, size, and color of their sediment. The rate of deposition can also affect the thickness of the layers. Sedimentary rocks sometimes record the motion of wind and water waves on lakes, seas, rivers, and sand dunes. Some of these features are shown in **Figures 21** and **22.**

Figure 21 Wind caused these slanted deposits, called cross-beds, but water can also cause them.

Figure 22 These ripple marks were made by flowing water and were preserved when the sediments became sedimentary rock. Ripple marks can also form from the action of wind.

TOPIC: Sedimentary Rock
GO TO: www.scilinks.org
***sci*LINKS NUMBER:** HSTE095

REVIEW

1. Describe the process by which clastic sedimentary rock forms.
2. List three sedimentary rock structures, and explain how they record geologic processes.
3. **Analyzing Relationships** Both clastic and chemical sedimentary rocks are classified according to texture and composition. Which property is more important for each sedimentary rock type? Explain.

▼ **Answers to Review**

1. Clastic sedimentary rock forms when sediments become compacted and cemented together.
2. Three sedimentary structures are strata, ripple patterns, and fossils. Strata form when layers of sediment are deposited on top of each other. Ripple patterns form when sediments are shaped by flowing air or water before the sediments turn into rock. Fossils form from the remains of organisms in sedimentary rock.
3. Texture is more important in classifying clastic sedimentary rock because clastic sedimentary rock is made of different sizes of sediments. Composition is more important in classifying chemical sedimentary rock because chemical sedimentary rock forms from different materials that crystallize out of solution.

Metamorphic Rock

Terms to Learn
foliated
nonfoliated

What You'll Do
- Describe two ways a rock can undergo metamorphism.
- Explain how the mineral composition of rocks changes as they undergo metamorphism.
- Describe the difference between foliated and nonfoliated metamorphic rock.

The word *metamorphic* comes from *meta,* meaning "changed," and *morphos,* meaning "shape." Remember, metamorphic rocks are those in which the structure, texture, or composition of the rock has changed. Rock can undergo metamorphism by heat or pressure acting alone or by a combination of the two. All three types of rock—igneous, sedimentary, and even metamorphic—can change into metamorphic rock.

Origins of Metamorphic Rock

The texture or mineral composition of a rock can change when its surroundings change. If the temperature or pressure of the new environment is different from the one the rock formed in, the rock will undergo metamorphism.

Most metamorphic change is caused by increased pressure that takes place at depths greater than 2 km. At depths greater than 16 km, the pressure can be more than 4,000 times the pressure of the atmosphere! Look at **Figure 23.** This rock, called garnet schist, formed at a depth of about 30 km. At this depth, some of the crystals the rock is made of change as a result of the extreme pressure. Other types of schist form at much shallower depths.

The temperature at which metamorphism occurs ranges from 50°C to 1,000°C. At temperatures higher than 1,000°C, most rocks will melt. Metamorphism does not melt rock—when rock melts, it becomes magma and then igneous rock. In **Figure 24** you can see that this rock was deformed by intense pressure.

Figure 23 *At top is a metamorphic rock called garnet schist. At bottom is a microscopic view of a thin slice of a garnet schist.*

Figure 24 *In this outcrop, you can see an example of how sedimentary rock was deformed as it underwent metamorphism.*

This rock in **Figure 23** is called garnet schist because it includes the mineral garnet. In the microscopic view, the brightly colored shapes are crystals of the mineral biotite mica, the black and white crystals are quartz, and the speckled grain in the upper right part of the circle is garnet. Have students compare the garnet schist with siltstone and shale, discussed in the sedimentary rock section. What is different? (Under high temperature and pressure conditions, both of these sedimentary rocks can become garnet schist.)

2 Teach

QuickLab

MATERIALS
- paper
- black-ink pen
- plastic play putty

Answer to QuickLab

3. The "crystals" became stretched and deformed. The "granite" changed its shape because of the force applied to it.

CROSS-DISCIPLINARY FOCUS

Art Invite a potter to talk to the class about the processes involved in firing clay. Then have the class explore the different types of clay products that potters create (earthenware, stoneware, and ceramics) and the composition of the clays and glazes potters use.

GUIDED PRACTICE

As you discuss **Figure 25,** be sure students understand that a metamorphic rock's composition and the heat and pressure it receives determine how much it deforms. Students should understand that the bulk composition of rock does not change during metamorphism unless fluids are introduced to the rock. However, the mineral composition of the rock may change as heat and pressure change. Ask students to think of some analogies for contact metamorphism (for example, an egg frying in a skillet). Have students draw rocks undergoing contact metamorphism. Have the class think of some analogies for regional metamorphism (for example, making toast). Then have students draw rocks undergoing regional metamorphism.

QuickLab

Stretching Out

1. Draw your version of a granite rock on a **piece of paper** with a **black-ink pen.** Be sure to include the outline of the rock, and fill it in with different crystal shapes.
2. Mash some **plastic play putty** over the "granite," and slowly peel it off.
3. After making sure that the outline of your "granite" has been transferred to the putty, push and pull on the putty. What happened to the "crystals"? What happened to the "granite"?

TRY at HOME

Contact Metamorphism One way rock can undergo metamorphism is by coming into contact with magma. When magma moves through the crust, it heats the surrounding rock and "cooks" it. As a result, the magma changes some of the minerals in the surrounding rock into other minerals. The greatest change takes place where magma comes into direct contact with the surrounding rock. The effect of heat gradually lessens with distance from the magma. As you can see in **Figure 25,** contact metamorphism only happens next to igneous intrusions.

Regional Metamorphism When enormous pressure builds up in rock that is deeply buried under other rock formations, or when large pieces of the Earth's crust collide with each other, regional metamorphism occurs. The pressure and increased temperature that exist under these conditions cause rock to become deformed and chemically changed. This kind of metamorphic rock is underneath most continental rock formations.

Self-Check

How could a rock undergo both contact and regional metamorphism? *(See page 726 to check your answer.)*

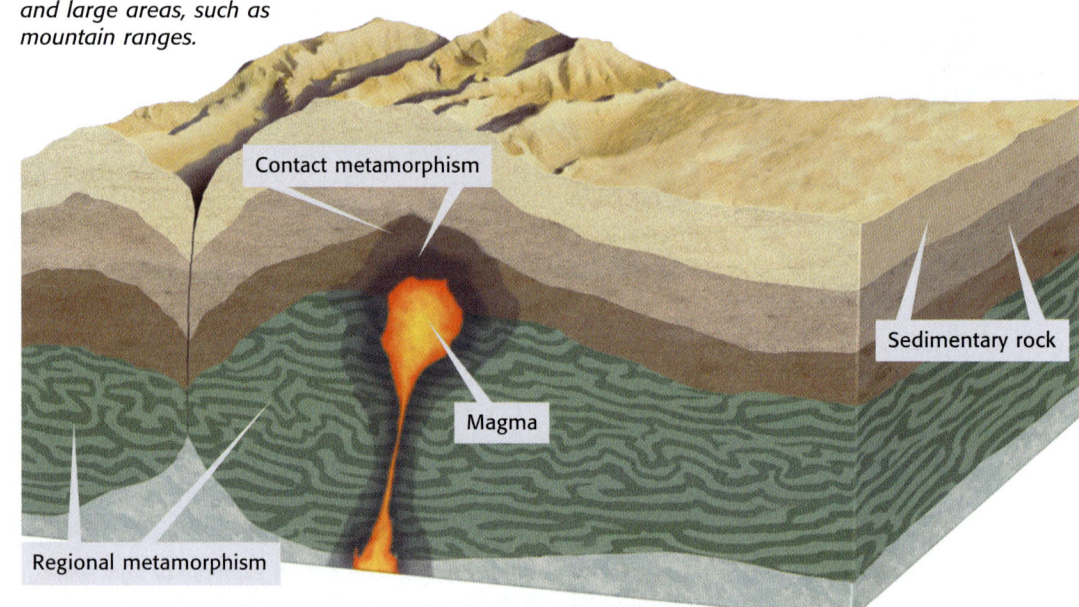

Figure 25 Metamorphism occurs over small areas, such as next to bodies of magma, and large areas, such as mountain ranges.

Answer to Self-Check

Answers will vary. A rock can come into contact with magma and also be subjected to pressure underground.

IS THAT A FACT!

The largest expanse of exposed metamorphic rock in the world is the Canadian Shield, a huge horseshoe-shaped region encircling Hudson Bay. Covering about half of Canada, it is about 4,586,900 km² and is the source of more than 70 percent of the minerals mined in Canada.

96 Chapter 4 • Rocks: Mineral Mixtures

Composition of Metamorphic Rock

When conditions within the Earth's crust change because of collisions between continents or the intrusion of magma, the temperature and pressure of the existing rock change. Minerals that were present in the rock when it formed may no longer be stable in the new environment. The original minerals change into minerals that are more stable in the new temperature and pressure conditions. Look at **Figure 26** to see an example of how this happens.

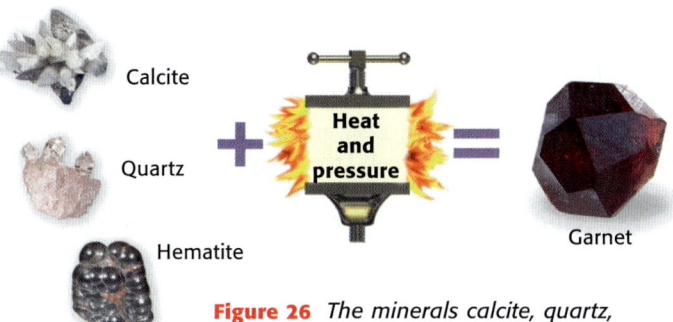

Figure 26 *The minerals calcite, quartz, and hematite combine and recrystallize to form the metamorphic mineral garnet.*

Activity

Did you know that you have a birthstone? Birthstones are gemstones, or mineral crystals. For each month of the year, there are one or two different birthstones. Find out which birthstone or birthstones you have by doing research in your school library or on the Internet. The names of birthstones are not usually the same as their actual mineral names. In what kind of rock would you likely find your birthstone? Why?

Many of these new minerals occur only in metamorphic rock. As shown in **Figure 27,** some metamorphic minerals form only within a specific range of temperature and pressure conditions. When scientists observe these metamorphic minerals in a rock, they can estimate the temperature and depth (pressure) at which recently exposed rock underwent metamorphism.

Figure 27 *Scientists can understand a metamorphic rock's history by observing the minerals it contains. For example, metamorphic rock containing garnet formed at a greater depth than one that contains only chlorite.*

Chlorite
400°C
4–32 km

Muscovite mica
700°C
5–34 km

Garnet
700–1,200°C
25–60 km

3) Extend

DISCUSSION

Display metamorphic rocks in groups of foliated rocks (slate, schist, phyllite, gneiss) and non-foliated rocks (quartzite, marble, hornfels, soapstone). Have students compare the rocks according to color, appearance, and composition. Explain that regional metamorphism tends to produce *foliated rocks*, while contact metamorphism tends to produce *nonfoliated rocks*. Ask students to predict what the terms mean then read this page to see if they were correct.

MATH and MORE

Metamorphic rock usually forms at depths greater than 16 km. To convert kilometers to miles, multiply the number of kilometers by 0.6. For example, 16 km multiplied by 0.6 is equal to 9.6 mi. Tell students that the continental crust can be up to 100 km thick. How many miles is that? **(60 mi)**

The crust under the ocean is about 5 km thick. How many miles is that? **(3 mi)**

Students might be interested in comparing these distances with the distance to a nearby town or landmark.

 Math Skills Worksheet 31 "The Unit Factor and Dimensional Analysis"

Metamorphic Mash

 **Reinforcement Worksheet 4** "What Is It?"

Textures of Metamorphic Rock

As you know, texture helps to classify igneous and sedimentary rock. The same is true of metamorphic rock. All metamorphic rock has one of two textures—*foliated* or *nonfoliated*. **Foliated** metamorphic rock consists of minerals that are aligned and look almost like pages in a book. **Nonfoliated** metamorphic rock does not appear to have any regular pattern. Let's take a closer look at each of these types of metamorphic rock to find out how they form.

Foliated Metamorphic Rock Foliated metamorphic rock contains mineral grains that are aligned by pressure. Strongly foliated rocks usually contain flat minerals, like biotite mica. Look at **Figure 28**. Shale consists of layers of clay minerals. When subjected to slight heat and pressure, the clay minerals change into mica minerals and the shale becomes a fine-grained, foliated metamorphic rock called slate.

Metamorphic rocks can become other metamorphic rocks if the environment changes again. With additional heat and pressure, slate can change into phyllite, another metamorphic rock. When phyllite is exposed to additional heat and pressure, it can change into a metamorphic rock called schist.

As the degree of metamorphism increases, the arrangement of minerals in the rock changes. With additional heat and pressure, coarse-grained minerals separate into bands in a metamorphic rock called *gneiss* (pronounced "nice").

Figure 28 *The effects of metamorphism depend on the heat and pressure applied to the rock. Here you can see what happens to shale when it is exposed to more and more heat and pressure.*

Wouldn't it be "gneiss" to make your own foliated rock? Turn to page 647 in your LabBook to find out how.

Homework

Investigate Your Area Have students look at stone buildings and houses around their town. Ask students to identify the rock used in construction as igneous, sedimentary, or metamorphic. Which rock type was most commonly used? Which was used least? Encourage students to find out the origin of rock used in buildings in your community.

WEIRD SCIENCE

When rocks metamorphose under high temperature and pressure, they become plastic and can be easily deformed. It is not unusual for spherical pebbles in a conglomerate to be stretched into ellipses more than 30 times their original diameter!

Nonfoliated Metamorphic Rock Nonfoliated metamorphic rocks are shown in **Figure 29.** Do you notice anything missing? The lack of aligned mineral grains makes them nonfoliated. They are rocks commonly made of only one, or just a few, minerals.

Sandstone is a sedimentary rock made of distinct quartz sand grains. But when sandstone is subjected to the heat and pressure of metamorphism, the spaces between the sand grains disappear as they recrystallize, forming quartzite. Quartzite has a shiny, glittery appearance. It is still made of quartz, but the mineral grains are larger. When limestone undergoes metamorphism, the same process happens to the mineral calcite, and the limestone becomes marble. Marble has larger calcite crystals than limestone. You have probably seen marble in buildings and statues.

Marble

Quartzite

Biology CONNECTION

The term *metamorphosis* means "change in form." When certain animals undergo a dramatic change in the shape of their body, they are said to have undergone a metamorphosis. As part of their natural life cycle, moths and butterflies go through four stages of life. After they hatch from an egg, they are in the larval stage in the form of a caterpillar. In the next stage they build a cocoon or become a chrysalis. This is called the pupal stage. They finally emerge into the adult stage of their life, complete with wings, antennae, and legs!

Figure 29 *Marble and quartzite are nonfoliated metamorphic rocks. As you can see in the microscopic views, none of the mineral crystals are aligned.*

REVIEW

1. What environmental factors cause rock to undergo metamorphism?
2. What is the difference between foliated and nonfoliated metamorphic rock?
3. **Making Inferences** If you had two metamorphic rocks, one with garnet crystals and the other with chlorite crystals, which one would have formed at a deeper level in the Earth's crust? Explain.

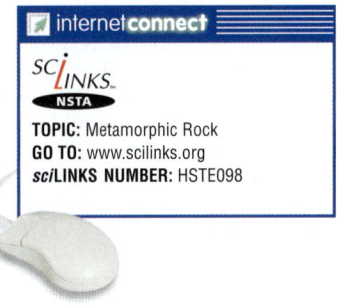
internet connect
sciLINKS NSTA
TOPIC: Metamorphic Rock
GO TO: www.scilinks.org
sciLINKS NUMBER: HSTE098

GOING FURTHER
Several types of minerals found in metamorphic rock, such as garnet, tourmaline, and serpentine, are used in sculpture and in jewelry making. Encourage students to choose one of these minerals, research it, and create a poster illustrating how it forms and what its uses are.

4) Close

Quiz

1. Explain what a regionally metamorphosed rock is. (A regionally metamorphosed rock has been changed by intense pressure and heat across great regions of the crust rather than by direct contact with magma.)
2. What does the composition of a metamorphic rock tell you about the rock's origin and formation? (Different metamorphic minerals indicate different temperature and pressure conditions that existed when they formed.)

ALTERNATIVE ASSESSMENT
Have students prepare a lesson about this chapter to present to a second-grade class. They will need to prepare vocabulary lists, illustrations, and worksheets to help the younger students understand the types of rock, their uses, and how they form.

Critical Thinking Worksheet 4 "Between a Rock and a Hard Place"

Interactive Explorations CD-ROM "Rock On!"

▼ Answers to Review

1. Increased pressure and increased temperature can cause metamorphism.
2. The two types of rock differ in texture. Foliated metamorphic rock consists of minerals that are aligned and look like pages in a book. Nonfoliated metamorphic rock does not appear to have any regular patterns.
3. The rock with garnet crystals would have formed deeper in the Earth because the mineral garnet forms at a higher temperature and a higher pressure than the mineral chlorite.

Chapter Highlights

VOCABULARY DEFINITIONS

SECTION 1

rock a solid mixture of crystals of one or more minerals or other materials

rock cycle the process by which one rock type changes into another rock type

magma the hot liquid that forms when rock partially or completely melts; may include mineral crystals

sedimentary rock rock that forms when sediments are compacted and cemented together

metamorphic rock rock that forms when the texture and composition of preexisting rock changes due to heat or pressure

igneous rock rock that forms from the cooling of magma

composition the makeup of a rock; describes either the minerals or elements present in it

texture the sizes, shapes, and positions of the grains that a rock is made of

SECTION 2

intrusive the type of igneous rock that forms when magma cools and solidifies beneath Earth's surface

extrusive the type of igneous rock that forms when lava or pyroclastic material cools and solidifies on the Earth's surface

Chapter Highlights

SECTION 1

Vocabulary
- rock (p. 80)
- rock cycle (p. 82)
- magma (p. 83)
- sedimentary rock (p. 84)
- metamorphic rock (p. 84)
- igneous rock (p. 84)
- composition (p. 85)
- texture (p. 86)

Section Notes
- Rocks have been used by humans for thousands of years, and they are just as valuable today.
- Rocks are classified into three main types—igneous, sedimentary, and metamorphic—depending on how they formed.
- The rock cycle describes the process by which a rock can change from one rock type to another.
- Scientists further classify rocks according to two criteria—composition and texture.
- Molten igneous material creates rock formations both below and above ground.

SECTION 2

Vocabulary
- intrusive (p. 89)
- extrusive (p. 90)

Section Notes
- The texture of igneous rock is determined by the rate at which it cools. The slower magma cools, the larger the crystals are.
- Felsic igneous rock is light-colored and lightweight, while mafic igneous rock is dark-colored and heavy.
- Igneous material that solidifies at the Earth's surface is called extrusive, while igneous material that solidifies within the crust is called intrusive.

Lab
Crystal Growth (p. 642)

✓ Skills Check

Math Concepts

MINERAL COMPOSITION Rocks are classified not only by the minerals they contain but also by the amounts of those minerals. Suppose a particular kind of granite is made of feldspar, biotite mica, and quartz. If you know that feldspar makes up 55 percent of the rock and biotite mica makes up 15 percent of the rock, the remaining 30 percent must be made of quartz.

```
  55% feldspar              100% of granite
+ 15% biotite mica    or  −  55% feldspar
+ 30% quartz              −  15% biotite mica
= 100% of granite         =  30% quartz
```

Visual Understanding

PIE CHARTS The pie charts on page 85 help you visualize the relative amounts of minerals in different types of rock. The circle represents the whole rock, or 100 percent. Each part, or "slice," of the circle represents a fraction of the rock.

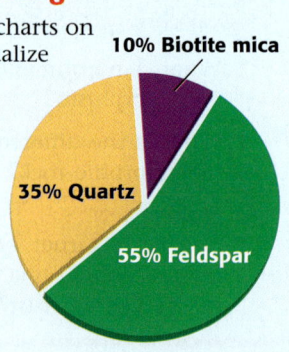

Lab and Activity Highlights

Crystal Growth **PG 642**

Let's Get Sedimental **PG 645**

Metamorphic Mash **PG 647**

 Datasheets for LabBook (blackline masters for these labs)

100 Chapter 4 • Rocks: Mineral Mixtures

SECTION 3

Vocabulary
strata *(p. 91)*
stratification *(p. 94)*

Section Notes
- Clastic sedimentary rock is made of rock and mineral fragments that are compacted and cemented together. Chemical sedimentary rock forms when minerals crystallize out of a solution such as sea water. Organic sedimentary rock forms from the remains of organisms.
- Sedimentary rocks record the history of their formation in their features. Some common features are strata, ripple marks, and fossils.

Lab
Let's Get Sedimental *(p. 645)*

SECTION 4

Vocabulary
foliated *(p. 98)*
nonfoliated *(p. 98)*

Section Notes
- One kind of metamorphism is the result of magma heating small areas of surrounding rock, changing its texture and composition.
- Most metamorphism is the product of heat and pressure acting on large regions of the Earth's crust.
- The mineral composition of a rock changes when the minerals it is made of recrystallize to form new minerals. These new minerals are more stable under increased temperature and pressure.
- Metamorphic rock that contains aligned mineral grains is called foliated, and metamorphic rock that does not contain aligned mineral grains is called nonfoliated.

Lab
Metamorphic Mash *(p. 647)*

VOCABULARY DEFINITIONS, continued

SECTION 3

strata layers of sedimentary rock that form from the deposition of sediment

stratification the layering of sedimentary rock

SECTION 4

foliated the texture of metamorphic rock in which the mineral grains are aligned like the pages of a book

nonfoliated the texture of metamorphic rock in which mineral grains show no alignment

 Vocabulary Review Worksheet 4

 Blackline masters of these Chapter Highlights can be found in the **Study Guide.**

---

internet connect

 **GO TO:** go.hrw.com

Visit the **HRW** Web site for a variety of learning tools related to this chapter. Just type in the keyword:

KEYWORD: HSTRCK

 **GO TO:** www.scilinks.org

Visit the **National Science Teachers Association** on-line Web site for Internet resources related to this chapter. Just type in the *sci*LINKS number for more information about the topic:

TOPIC:	sciLINKS NUMBER:
Composition of Rock	HSTE090
Igneous Rock	HSTE093
Sedimentary Rock	HSTE095
Metamorphic Rock	HSTE098
Rock Formations	HSTE100

101

Lab and Activity Highlights

LabBank

 Labs You Can Eat, Famous Rock Groups, Lab 11

Whiz-Bang Demonstrations, Settling Down, Demo 17

Long-Term Projects & Research Ideas, Home-Grown Crystals, Project 32

Interactive Explorations CD-ROM

 CD 2, Exploration 6, "Rock On!"

Chapter Review Answers

USING VOCABULARY

1. Intrusive/extrusive
2. Foliated
3. Clastic
4. Lava
5. sedimentary

UNDERSTANDING CONCEPTS

Multiple Choice

6. d
7. b
8. a
9. a
10. c
11. b
12. c
13. b
14. c
15. b

Short Answer

16. Answers will vary. In the rock cycle, igneous, sedimentary, and metamorphic rock can change into other rock types through a variety of natural processes. Although rock material changes form, it still remains a part of the rock cycle.
17. Sandstone has a coarser-grained texture than siltstone. Both sandstone and siltstone are clastic sedimentary rocks.

Concept Mapping Transparency 4

Blackline masters of this Chapter Review can be found in the **Study Guide.**

Chapter Review

USING VOCABULARY

To complete the following sentences, choose the correct term from each pair of terms listed below:

1. __?__ igneous rock is more likely to have coarse-grained texture than __?__ igneous rock. (*Extrusive/intrusive* or *Intrusive/extrusive*)
2. __?__ metamorphic rock texture consists of parallel alignment of mineral grains. (*Foliated* or *Nonfoliated*)
3. __?__ sedimentary rock forms when grains of sand become cemented together. (*Clastic* or *Chemical*)
4. __?__ cools quickly on the Earth's surface. (*Lava* or *Magma*)
5. Strata are found in __?__ rock. (*igneous* or *sedimentary*)

UNDERSTANDING CONCEPTS

Multiple Choice

6. A type of rock that forms deep within the Earth when magma solidifies is called
   a. sedimentary.   c. organic.
   b. metamorphic.   d. igneous.

7. A type of rock that forms under high temperature and pressure but is not exposed to enough heat to melt the rock is
   a. sedimentary.   c. organic.
   b. metamorphic.   d. igneous.

8. After they are deposited, sediments, such as sand, are turned into sedimentary rock when they are compacted and
   a. cemented.
   b. metamorphosed.
   c. melted.
   d. weathered.

9. An igneous rock with a coarse-grained texture forms when
   a. magma cools very slowly.
   b. magma cools very quickly.
   c. magma cools quickly, then slowly.
   d. magma cools slowly, then quickly.

10. The layering that occurs in sedimentary rock is called
    a. foliation.   c. stratification.
    b. ripple marks.   d. compaction.

11. An example of a clastic sedimentary rock is
    a. obsidian.   c. gneiss.
    b. sandstone.   d. marble.

12. A common sedimentary rock structure is
    a. a sill.   c. cross-bedding.
    b. a pluton.   d. a lava flow.

13. An example of mafic igneous rock is
    a. granite.   c. quartzite.
    b. basalt.   d. pumice.

14. Chemical sedimentary rock forms when
    a. magma cools and solidifies.
    b. minerals are twisted into a new arrangement.
    c. minerals crystallize from a solution.
    d. sand grains are cemented together.

15. Which of the following is a foliated metamorphic rock?
    a. sandstone   c. shale
    b. gneiss   d. basalt

Short Answer

16. In no more than three sentences, explain the rock cycle.

17. How are sandstone and siltstone different from one another? How are they the same?

102 Chapter 4 • Rocks: Mineral Mixtures

18. In one or two sentences, explain how the cooling rate of magma affects the texture of the igneous rock that forms.

Concept Mapping

19. Use the following terms to create a concept map: rocks, clastic, metamorphic, nonfoliated, igneous, intrusive, chemical, foliated, organic, extrusive, sedimentary.

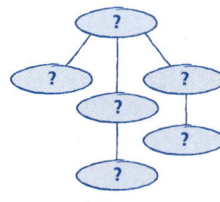

CRITICAL THINKING AND PROBLEM SOLVING

Write one or two sentences to answer the following questions:

20. The sedimentary rock coquina is made up of pieces of seashells. Which of the three kinds of sedimentary rock could it be? Explain.

21. If you were looking for fossils in the rocks around your home and the rock type that was closest to your home was metamorphic, would you find many fossils? Why or why not?

22. Suppose you are writing a book about another planet. In your book, you mention that the planet has no atmosphere or weather. Which type of rock will you not find on the planet? Explain.

23. Imagine that you want to quarry or mine granite. You have all of the equipment, but you need a place to quarry. You have two pieces of land to choose from. One piece is described as having a granite batholith under it, and the other has a granite sill. If both plutonic bodies were at the same depth, which one would be a better buy for you? Explain your answer.

MATH IN SCIENCE

24. If a 60 kg granite boulder were broken down into sand grains and if quartz made up 35 percent of the boulder's mass, how many kilograms of the resulting sand would be quartz grains?

INTERPRETING GRAPHICS

The red curve on the graph below shows how the melting point of a particular rock changes with increasing temperature and pressure. Use the graph to answer the questions below.

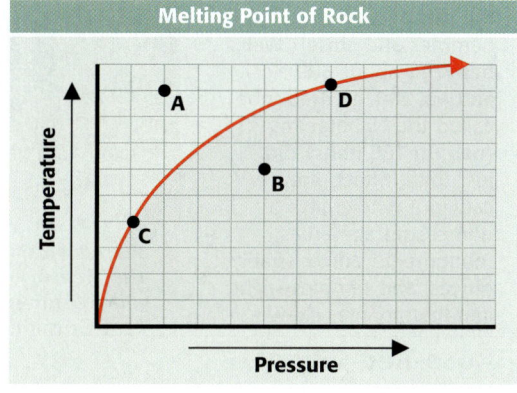

25. What type of material, liquid or solid, would you find at point A? Why?

26. What would you find at point B?

27. Points C and D represent different temperature and pressure conditions for a single, solid rock. Why does this rock have a higher melting temperature at point D than it does at point C?

Take a minute to review your answers to the Pre-Reading Questions found at the bottom of page 78. Have your answers changed? If necessary, revise your answers based on what you have learned since you began this chapter.

18. When magma cools slowly, crystals have a long time to grow, so they grow to a much larger size than they do when magma cools quickly.

Concept Mapping
19. An answer to this exercise can be found at the end of this book.

CRITICAL THINKING AND PROBLEM SOLVING

20. The seashells that make up coquina are made by shellfish, so coquina is an organic sedimentary rock. (Coquina could also be considered a clastic sedimentary rock because the shell fragments are clasts that have been deposited.)

21. You would not find many fossils where you lived because fossils are found in sedimentary rock, not metamorphic rock. (Occasionally, fossils are preserved in metamorphic rock that was once sedimentary rock.)

22. You will not find sedimentary rock because no weathering of rock can occur because there is no atmosphere.

23. The property with the batholith would be a better buy because batholiths are much bigger than sills.

MATH IN SCIENCE

24. 35% of 60 kg = 60 × 0.35 = 21 kg

INTERPRETING GRAPHICS

25. The material at point A is magma. It is magma because everything above the curve on the graph is liquid.
26. solid rock
27. Although at point D the rock is at a higher temperature, it has much more pressure on it, which keeps it solid.

Chapter 4 • Chapter Review **103**

SCIENCE, TECHNOLOGY, AND SOCIETY
Rock City

Background

Just north of Petra is another huge temple, the magnificent El-Deir. This temple was carved from the mountainside, and it sits 1,200 m above the valley floor. Its facade is 50 m wide and 45 m tall, and its huge doorway is 8 m high.

Science, Technology, and Society
Rock City

Today when we dig into a mountainside to build a highway or make room for a building, we use heavy machinery and explosives. Can you imagine doing the same job with just a hammer and chisel? Well, between about 300 B.C. and A.D. 200, an Arab tribe called the Nabataeans (nab uh TEE uhns) did just that. In fact, they carved a whole city—homes, storage areas, monuments, administrative offices, and temples—right into the mountainsides!

▲ Petra's most famous building, the Treasury, was shown in the movie *Indiana Jones and the Last Crusade.*

Rose-Red City

This amazing city in southern Jordan is Petra (named by the Roman emperor Hadrian Petra during a visit in A.D. 131). A poet once described Petra as "the rose-red city" because all the buildings and monuments were carved from the pink sandstone mountains surrounding Petra.

Using this reddish stone, the Nabataeans lined the main street in the center of the city with tall stone columns. The street ends at what was once the foot of a mountain but is now known as the Great Temple—a two-story stone religious complex larger than a football field!

The High Place of Sacrifice, another site near the center of the city, was a mountaintop. The Nabataeans leveled the top and created a place of worship more than 1,000 m above the valley floor. Today visitors climb stairs to the top. Along the way, they pass dozens of tombs carved into the pink rock walls.

Tombs and More Tombs

There are more than 800 other tombs dug into the mountainsides in and around Petra. One of them, the Treasury (created for a Nabataean ruler), stands more than 40 m high! It is a magnificent building with an elaborate facade. Behind the massive stone front, the Nabataeans carved one large room and two smaller rooms deeper into the mountain.

Petra Declines

The Nabataeans once ruled an area extending from Petra to Damascus. They grew wealthy and powerful by controlling important trade routes near Petra. But their wealth attracted the Roman Empire, and in A.D. 106, Petra became a Roman province. Though the city prospered under Roman rule for almost another century, a gradual decline in Nabataean power began. The trade routes by land that the Nabataeans controlled for hundreds of years were abandoned in favor of a route by the Red Sea. People moved and the city faded. By the seventh century, nothing was left of Petra but empty stone structures.

Think About It!

▶ Petra is sometimes referred to as a city "from the rock as if by magic grown." Why might such a city seem "magic" to us today? What might have encouraged the Nabataeans to create this city? Share your thoughts with a classmate.

Answer to Think About It!
Answers will vary. (Students can do research to find out more about Nabataean culture.)

Glass Scalpels

Would you want your surgeon to use a scalpel that was thousands of years old? Probably not, unless it was a razor-sharp knife blade made of obsidian, a natural volcanic glass. Such blades and arrowheads were used for nearly 18,000 years by our ancestors. Recently, physicians have found a new use for these Stone Age tools. Obsidian blades, once used to hunt woolly mammoths, are now being used as scalpels in the operating room!

Obsidian or Stainless Steel?

Traditionally, physicians have used inexpensive stainless-steel scalpel blades for surgical procedures. Steel scalpels cost about $2 each, and surgeons use them just once and throw them away. Obsidian scalpels are more expensive—about $20 each—but they can be used many times before they lose their keen edge. And obsidian scalpel blades can be 100 times sharper than traditional scalpel blades!

During surgery, steel scalpels actually tear the skin apart. Obsidian scalpels divide the skin and cause much less damage. Some plastic surgeons use obsidian blades to make extremely fine incisions that leave almost no scarring. An obsidian-scalpel incision heals more quickly because the blade causes less damage to the skin and other tissues.

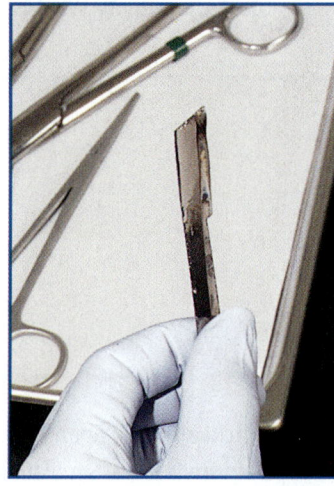

▲ *An obsidian scalpel can have an edge as fine as a single molecule.*

Many patients have allergic reactions to mineral components in steel blades. These patients often do not have an allergic reaction when obsidian scalpels are used. Given all of these advantages, it is not surprising that some physicians have made the change to obsidian scalpels.

A Long Tradition

Early Native Americans were among the first people to recognize that chipped obsidian has extremely sharp edges. Native Americans made obsidian arrowheads and knife blades by flaking away chips of rock by hand. Today obsidian scalpels are fashioned in much the same way by a *knapper,* a person who makes stone tools by hand. Knappers use the same basic technique that people have used for thousands of years to make obsidian blades and other stone tools.

Find Out for Yourself!

▶ Making obsidian blades and other stone tools requires a great deal of skill. Find out about the steps a knapper follows to create a stone tool. Find a piece of rock, and see if you can follow the steps to create a stone tool of your own. Be careful not to hit your fingers, and wear safety goggles.

HEALTH WATCH
Glass Scalpels

Background

Medical professionals use a variety of tools and treatments that rely on rocks and minerals. As students have learned in this chapter, every rock has unique properties that vary depending on its composition, its crystalline structure, and the conditions in which it formed. For example, obsidian's most prominent characteristic is the lack of a crystalline structure.

Students will know that diamonds are valuable gemstones, but they may be surprised that diamonds are frequently used in medicine. For example, dentists use drill bits coated with synthetic diamonds. Synthetic diamonds are used because they are much less expensive than their natural counterparts and are disposable. Diamonds are four times harder than the next hardest natural mineral.

Chapter Organizer

CHAPTER ORGANIZATION	TIME MINUTES	OBJECTIVES	LABS, INVESTIGATIONS, AND DEMONSTRATIONS
Chapter Opener pp. 106–107	45	National Standards: SAI 1, ST 2, SPSP 5	**Start-Up Activity** What Is the Sun's Favorite Color? p. 107
Section 1 Natural Resources	90	▶ Determine how humans use natural resources. ▶ Contrast renewable resources with nonrenewable resources. ▶ Explain how humans can conserve natural resources. SAI 1, SPSP 2, 4	
Section 2 Fossil Fuels	135	▶ Classify the different forms of fossil fuels. ▶ Explain how fossil fuels are obtained. ▶ Identify problems with fossil fuels. ▶ List ways to deal with fossil-fuel problems. SAI 1, SPSP 1, 2, 4, 5, ES 1k, 3d	**QuickLab,** Rock Sponge, p. 113 GENERAL **Demonstration,** Simulating Reservoirs, p. 113 in ATE GENERAL
Section 3 Alternative Resources	90	▶ Describe alternatives to the use of fossil fuels. ▶ List advantages and disadvantages of using alternative energy resources. UCP 5, ST 2, SPSP 2, 4, 5, ES 3d; LabBook UCP 2, 3, SAI 1, ST 1	**Interactive Explorations CD-ROM,** The Generation Gap GENERAL A **Worksheet** is also available in the **Interactive Explorations Teacher's Edition.** **Skill Builder,** Make a Water Wheel, p. 648 BASIC **Datasheets for LabBook,** Make a Water Wheel, Datasheet 10 BASIC **Discovery Lab,** Power of the Sun, p. 650 BASIC **Datasheets for LabBook,** Power of the Sun, Datasheet 11 BASIC **Long-Term Projects & Research Ideas,** Project 33 ADVANCED

*See page **T20** for a complete correlation of this book with the*

NATIONAL SCIENCE EDUCATION STANDARDS.

TECHNOLOGY RESOURCES

 Guided Reading Audio CD English or Spanish, Chapter 5

 One-Stop Planner CD-ROM with Test Generator

 Interactive Explorations CD-ROM CD 1, Exploration 6, The Generation Gap

CNN. Scientists in Action, Forming the Future of Energy Efficiency, Segment 7

Science, Technology & Society, BioDiesel, Segment 6

Wind Power, Segment 14

Multicultural Connections, China's Solar Nomads, Segment 10

Chapter 5 • Energy Resources

CLASSROOM WORKSHEETS, TRANSPARENCIES, AND RESOURCES	SCIENCE INTEGRATION AND CONNECTIONS	REVIEW AND ASSESSMENT
Science Puzzlers, Twisters & Teasers, Worksheet 5 `ADVANCED` **Directed Reading Worksheet 5** `BASIC`	**Connect to Geography,** p. 107 in ATE `GENERAL`	
Directed Reading Worksheet 5, Section 1 `BASIC` **Transparency 77,** Practicing Conservation **Reinforcement Worksheet 5,** What Are My Resources? `GENERAL`	**Connect to Environmental Science,** p. 108 in ATE **Real-World Connection,** p. 109 in ATE **Connect to Life Science,** p. 109 in ATE **Apply,** p. 110 `GENERAL` **Eye on the Environment:** Sitting on Your Trash, p. 130 `ADVANCED`	**Review,** p. 110 `GENERAL` **Quiz,** p. 110 in ATE `GENERAL` **Alternative Assessment,** p. 110 in ATE `GENERAL`
Directed Reading Worksheet 5, Section 2 `BASIC` **Transparency 115,** Porous Rocks Are Reservoirs for Fossil Fuels **Math Skills for Science Worksheet 20,** Parts of 100: Calculating Percentages `GENERAL` **Transparency 116,** Formation of Coal **Reinforcement Worksheet 5,** If It's a Fossil, How Is It a Fuel? `BASIC`	**Chemistry Connection,** p. 112 **Multicultural Connection,** p. 112 in ATE **Cross-Disciplinary Focus,** p. 112 in ATE `ADVANCED` **Real-World Connection,** p. 114 in ATE `ADVANCED` **Math and More,** Percent Carbon, p. 115 in ATE `BASIC` **Eureka!** Oil Rush! p. 131 `GENERAL`	**Review,** p. 114 `GENERAL` **Homework,** p. 115 in ATE `ADVANCED` **Review,** p. 117 `GENERAL` **Quiz,** p. 117 in ATE `GENERAL` **Alternative Assessment,** p. 117 in ATE `GENERAL`
Directed Reading Worksheet 5, Section 3 `BASIC` **Math Skills for Science Worksheet 36,** Radioactive Decay and the Half-life `GENERAL` **Transparency 117,** Generating Energy with Fission **Critical Thinking Worksheet 5,** Nature's Gold `ADVANCED`	**Cross-Disciplinary Focus,** p. 119 in ATE **Biology Connection,** p. 120 **Connect to Astronomy,** p. 120 in ATE `ADVANCED` **Real-World Connection,** p. 121 in ATE **Cross-Disciplinary Focus,** p. 122 in ATE **Connect to Physical Science,** p. 123 in ATE **Multicultural Connection,** p. 123 in ATE `ADVANCED` **MathBreak,** Miles per Acre, p. 124 `GENERAL` **Multicultural Connection,** p. 124 in ATE	**Review,** p. 122 `GENERAL` **Self-Check,** p. 123 **Homework,** p. 123 in ATE `GENERAL` **Review,** p. 125 `GENERAL` **Quiz,** p. 125 in ATE `GENERAL` **Alternative Assessment,** p. 125 in ATE `BASIC`

END-OF-CHAPTER REVIEW AND ASSESSMENT

Chapter Review in Study Guide
Vocabulary and Notes in Study Guide
Chapter Tests with Performance-Based Assessment, Chapter 5 Test
Chapter Tests with Performance-Based Assessment, Performance-Based Assessment 5
Concept Mapping Transparency 5

---

internetconnect

 Holt, Rinehart and Winston On-line Resources
go.hrw.com
For worksheets and other teaching aids related to this chapter, visit the HRW Web site and type in the keyword: **HSTENR**

 **National Science Teachers Association**
www.scilinks.org
Encourage students to use the *sci*LINKS numbers listed in the internet connect boxes to access information and resources on the **NSTA** Web Site.

Chapter 5 • Chapter Organizer **105B**

Chapter Resources & Worksheets

Visual Resources

TEACHING TRANSPARENCIES

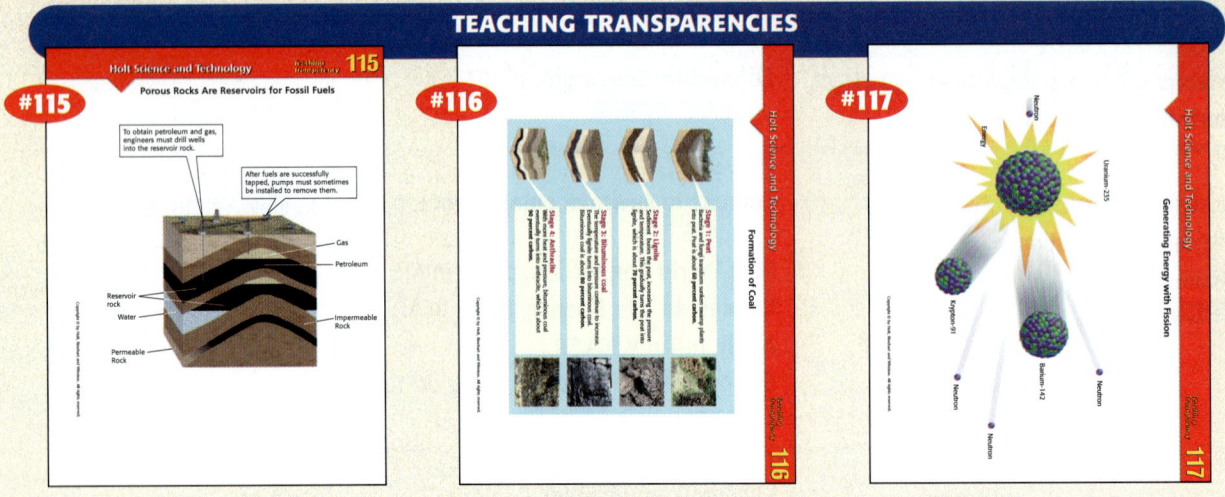

TEACHING TRANSPARENCIES

CONCEPT MAPPING TRANSPARENCY

Meeting Individual Needs

DIRECTED READING

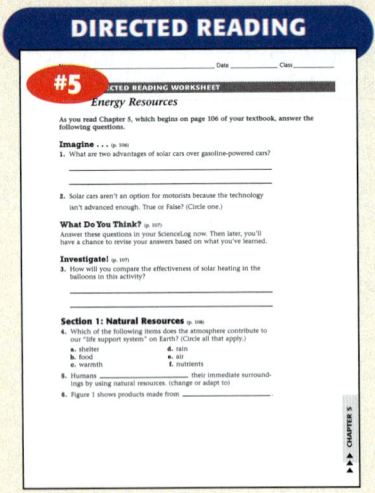

REINFORCEMENT & VOCABULARY REVIEW

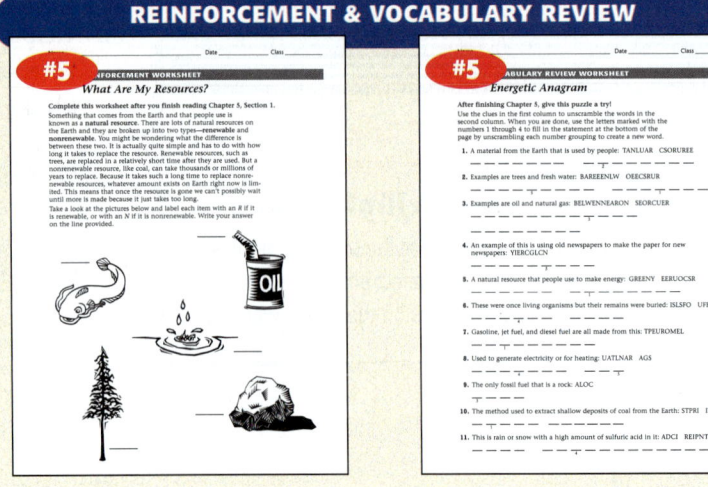

SCIENCE PUZZLERS, TWISTERS & TEASERS

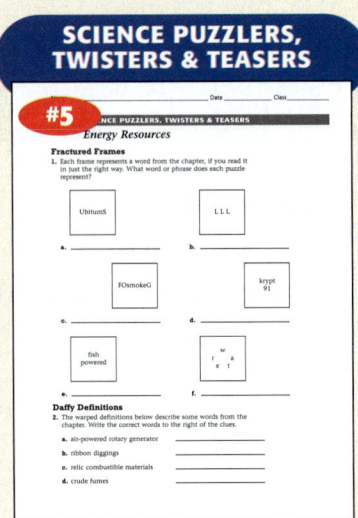

Chapter 5 • Energy Resources

Chapter 5 • Energy Resources

Review & Assessment

STUDY GUIDE

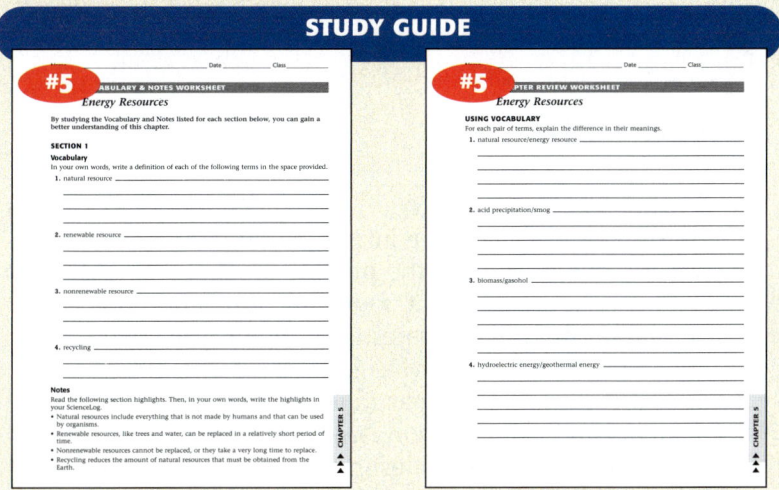

CHAPTER TESTS WITH PERFORMANCE-BASED ASSESSMENT

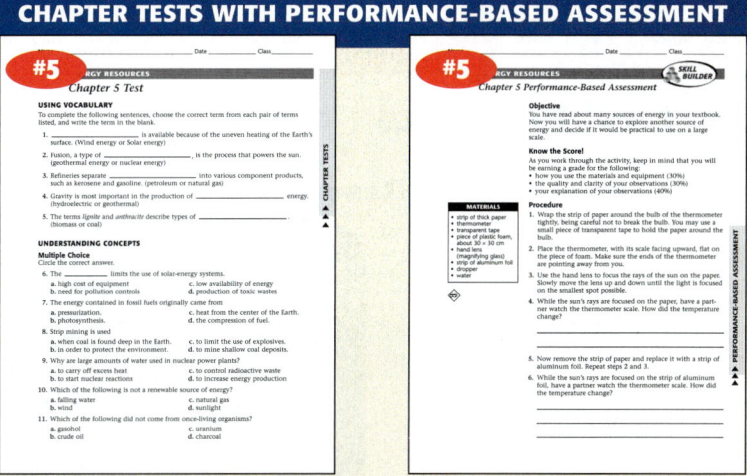

Lab Worksheets

LONG-TERM PROJECTS & RESEARCH IDEAS

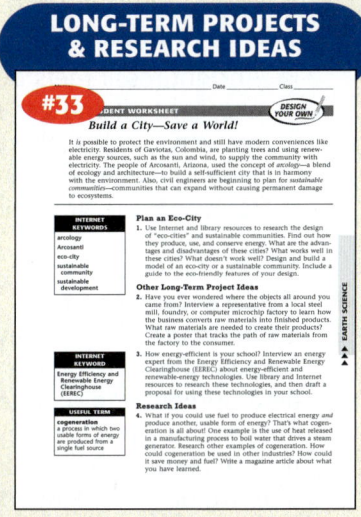

DATASHEETS FOR LABBOOK

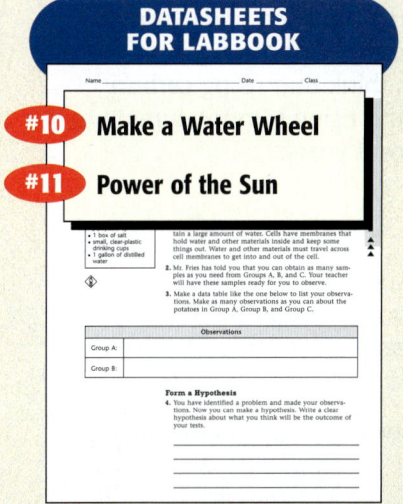

Applications & Extensions

CRITICAL THINKING & PROBLEM SOLVING

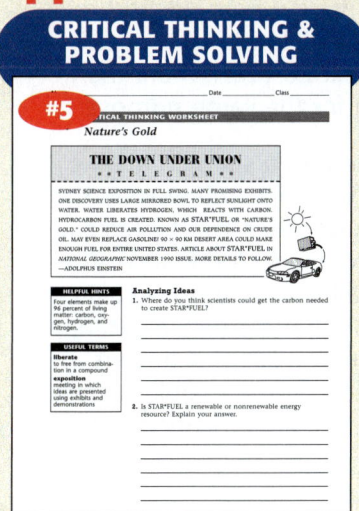

MULTICULTURAL CONNECTIONS

SCIENCE TECHNOLOGY

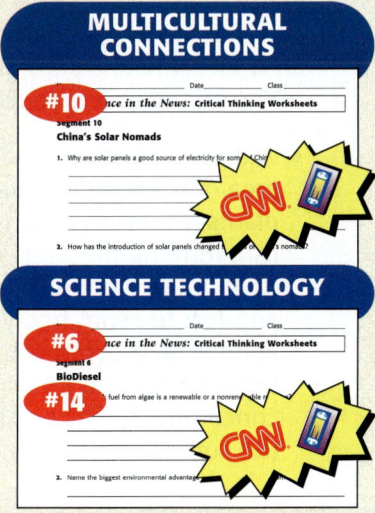

SCIENTISTS IN ACTION

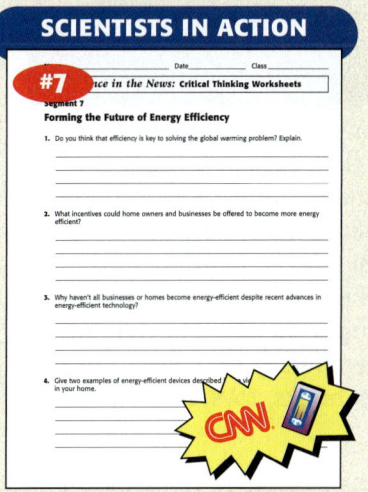

INTERACTIVE EXPLORATIONS

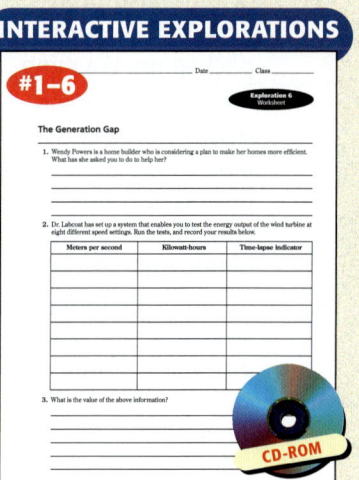

Chapter 5 • Chapter Resources & Worksheets   105D

Chapter Background

SECTION 1
Natural Resources

▶ **Interconnected Resources**

The Earth's resources are intricately linked. For example, clearing trees affects the water quality downstream from a forest. We should pay attention not only to the rate at which we use natural resources but also to how our use affects other resources. The use of fossil fuels offers another example; fossil-fuel combustion adds enormous quantities of carbon dioxide, a greenhouse gas, to the atmosphere. Many scientists think that rising carbon dioxide levels are linked to the rising temperatures the Earth has experienced in recent years.

▶ **The Three Rs**

Over the past three decades, environmentalists have encouraged consumers to consider the three Rs—reduce, recycle, and reuse—to conserve Earth's natural resources.

- When buying new items, consumers who want to save money and conserve resources should buy in bulk or purchase products with minimal packaging. Washing and reusing plastic bags is another way to conserve petroleum-based natural resources. Use of cloth rags and napkins instead of paper towels and paper napkins is one way to reduce paper consumption. Glass and ceramic plates and cups and metal cutlery are more environmentally responsible than paper plates and plastic cups and utensils. Donating used items to charities and friends and family members is one way to recycle clothes, shoes, appliances, books, toys, and other such items.

SECTION 2
Fossil Fuels

▶ **Light Up Your Life**

Before automobiles were invented and before electricity was discovered, one of the primary functions of fossil fuels was to provide light. Kerosene lamps became popular in the United States after the first oil well was drilled in 1859 in Pennsylvania. At the same time, use of coal gas and natural gas in lamps was increasing. Coal gas had been used in lamps as early as 1784. By the early 1800s, most cities in the United States and Europe had coal-gas street lights. Electric lamps did not replace the gaslights until the early 1900s.

IS THAT A FACT!

▶ Ancient fossil reefs buried underground make excellent oil and gas reservoirs because the reefs are very porous. The productivity of the oil fields in Alberta, Canada, is due to the presence of Devonian reefs that are 408 million to 360 million years old.

▶ **"Rigs-to-Reefs"**

Environmentalists usually consider offshore oil rigs to be detrimental to marine ecosystems because they disturb animal life and pose a risk of oil spills. Since 1979, however, obsolete oil rigs have become, many people believe, a welcome addition to these areas. In 1979, the Rigs-to-Reefs program was initiated when a rig was moved from offshore Louisiana to a designated site off Florida to become an artificial reef. During the next 20 years, more than 500 platforms were relocated for the same purpose.

- Within 6 months of placement in a suitable marine area, a platform is covered with invertebrates and plants. These organisms attract other invertebrates and fish, forming the basis of a complex food chain. The open framework of the rig allows water to circulate and fish to swim freely through the structure. Marine animals and commercial and recreational anglers benefit from the artificial reefs. Some people remain concerned, however, about residual pollution from the submerged rigs.

Chapter 5 • Energy Resources

SECTION 3

Alternative Resources

▶ Chernobyl
The radioactive fallout from the 1986 Chernobyl nuclear accident affected people, livestock, and crops.

- Although only 31 people died from direct exposure, about 600,000 people were "significantly exposed" to the fallout. At least 50,000 people received 50 rads of radiation. About 10,000 people were exposed to at least 100 rads and suffered from radiation sickness. For comparison, a person undergoing a chest X ray is exposed to a maximum of 1 rad.

- Livestock also suffered from the fallout. At least 86,000 head of cattle were evacuated from the area immediately after the accident. The sale of milk, meat, and many fruits and vegetables was banned in 1986 and 1987 in cities near Chernobyl. Many countries across Europe lost crops and other kinds of vegetation due to radioactive contamination.

▶ Concentrating Solar Power Systems
Concentrating solar power systems harness solar energy by focusing reflected sunlight onto a receiver. The receiver absorbs the light and converts it into thermal energy, which is then used to generate electricity.

- **Solar trough systems** consist of parabolic, mirrored troughs that focus sunlight onto oil-filled tubes at the troughs' focal points. The sunlight heats the oil, which then heats water. Steam from the heated water turns turbines in a generator to produce electricity.

- **Solar power towers** use thousands of mirrors to reflect sunlight onto a receiver that is mounted on a tall tower. The receiver contains salt that stores the solar energy as thermal energy. The salt heats water, creating steam that turns turbines to produce electricity.

- **Solar dish systems** use circular mirrors arranged into the shape of a dish to concentrate solar energy onto a receiver. The receiver transfers the energy to an engine that generates electricity.

▶ Geothermal Energy
Geothermal energy is tapped from places on Earth that are heated by their proximity to volcanic activity. It is currently used in Japan, parts of Russia, Iceland, Italy, New Zealand, and on the western coast of the United States.

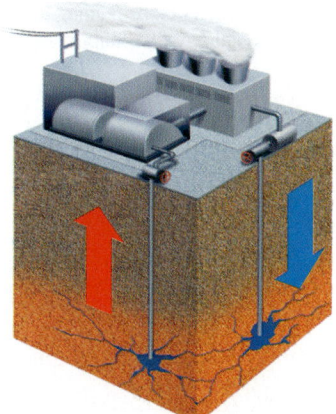

- Iceland is the world leader in using geothermal energy for space heating. Over 85 percent of Icelanders use geothermal energy to warm their homes! The cost is only about one-third of what it would cost if they burned oil to power electric heaters. Industries in Iceland use geothermal energy because it is inexpensive, widely available, and very reliable.

IS THAT A FACT!
- Traditional fuels, such as wood and animal dung, are used to meet one-quarter of India's energy needs.

For background information about teaching strategies and issues, refer to the *Professional Reference for Teachers.*

Energy Resources

 Pre-Reading Questions

Students may not know the answers to these questions before reading the chapter, so accept any reasonable response.

Suggested Answers

1. Answers will vary. Sample answer: coal, petroleum, iron ore, diamonds
2. fossil fuels
3. A solar cell is an individual cell that converts light into electrical energy, while a solar panel is a panel composed of many solar cells wired together.

 Directed Reading Worksheet 5

 Science Puzzlers, Twisters & Teasers Worksheet 5

 Guided Reading Audio CD English or Spanish, Chapter 5

Energy Resources

Sections

1. Natural Resources.... 108
   Apply 110
   Internet Connect..... 110
2. Fossil Fuels......... 111
   Chemistry
     Connection 112
   QuickLab 113
   Internet Connect..... 117
3. Alternative
   Resources.......... 118
   Biology Connection .. 120
   Internet Connect 122
   MathBreak 124

Chapter Review 128
Feature Article 130, 131
LabBook 648–651

1. List four nonrenewable resources.
2. On which energy resources do humans currently depend the most?
3. What is the difference between a solar cell and a solar panel?

106

Living Inside Your Trash?

Would you believe that this house is made from empty soda cans and old tires? Well, it is! Not only does this house use recycled materials, but it also saves Earth's energy resources. This house gets all its energy from the sun and uses rainwater for household activities. In this chapter, you will learn about what Earth's energy resources are and how we can conserve them.

Architect Mike Reynolds designed The Castle in Taos, New Mexico.

internet connect

 **HRW On-line Resources**
go.hrw.com
For worksheets and other teaching aids, visit the HRW Web site and type in the keyword: **HSTENR**

www.scilinks.com
Use the sciLINKS numbers at the end of each chapter for additional resources on the **NSTA** Web site.

www.cnnfyi.com
Visit the CNN Web site for current events coverage and classroom resources.

106 Chapter 5 • Energy Resources

WHAT IS THE SUN'S FAVORITE COLOR?

Are some colors better than others at absorbing the sun's energy? If so, how might this relate to collecting solar energy? Try the following activity to answer these questions.

Procedure

1. Obtain **at least five balloons** that are the same size and shape. One of the balloons should be white, and one should be black.
2. Place **one large ice cube or several small cubes** in each balloon. Each balloon should contain the same amount of ice.
3. Line the balloons up on a flat, uniformly colored surface that receives direct sunlight. Make sure that all the balloons receive the same amount of sunlight and that the openings in the balloons are not facing directly toward the sun.
4. Keep track of how much time it takes for the ice to melt completely in each of the balloons. You can tell how much ice has melted in each balloon by pinching the balloon's opening and then gently squeezing the balloon.

Analysis

5. In which balloon did the ice melt first? Why?
6. What color would you paint a device used to collect solar energy?

WHAT IS THE SUN'S FAVORITE COLOR?

MATERIALS

FOR EACH GROUP:
- 5 different-colored, round balloons
- scissors
- ice cubes
- watch or clock with a second hand

Teacher's Notes

Balloons must be identical except for color. Also, note that one balloon in each group must be black and one must be white.

A single, large ice cube or several small cubes are enough for each balloon. Stress to students that they should not use too much ice or it will take too long to get results. You might have students mark their balloons with permanent markers before they add the ice so that each group is able to identify its balloons.

Answers to START-UP Activity

5. The ice in the black balloon melted first; the darker an object is, the more light energy it will absorb.
6. black

SECTION 1

Focus

Natural Resources

In this section, students learn the difference between renewable and nonrenewable resources. They also learn why conservation and recycling are important.

🔔 Bellringer

Display the following items:

a plastic sandwich bag, a piece of paper, a pencil, a glass of water, 1 qt of motor oil, an empty soda can, a wooden match, a salt shaker, and some aquarium charcoal

Challenge students to determine what all of these items have in common. Lead students to conclude that all these items have their origin in natural resources. Have students help you make a list of which resources are renewable and which are nonrenewable.
`Sheltered English`

1) Motivate

DISCUSSION

Kinds of Energy Have students brainstorm to form a list of different kinds of energy, including light energy, chemical energy, potential energy, kinetic energy, and thermal energy. Review the meaning of each term, if necessary. Now is also a good time to review the law of conservation of energy, which states that energy is never created or destroyed—it can only be changed from one form to another.

Directed Reading Worksheet 5 Section 1

108   Chapter 5 • Energy Resources

Section 1

Terms to Learn
natural resource
renewable resource
nonrenewable resource
recycling

What You'll Do
- Determine how humans use natural resources.
- Contrast renewable resources with nonrenewable resources.
- Explain how humans can conserve natural resources.

Natural Resources

Think of the Earth as a giant life-support system for all of humanity. The Earth's atmosphere, waters, and solid crust provide almost everything we need to survive. The atmosphere provides the air we need to breathe, maintains air temperatures, and produces rain. The oceans and other waters of the Earth provide food and needed fluids. The solid part of the Earth provides nutrients and minerals.

Interactions between the Earth's systems can cause changes in the Earth's environments. Organisms must adapt to these changes if they are to survive. Humans have found ways to survive by using natural resources to change their immediate surroundings. A **natural resource** is any natural substance, organism, or energy form that living things use. Few of the Earth's natural resources are used in their unaltered state. Most resources are made into products that make people's lives more comfortable and convenient, as shown in **Figure 1**.

Figure 1 Lumber, gasoline, and electricity are all products that come from natural resources.

This pile of lumber is made of wood, which comes from trees.

The gasoline in this can is made from oil pumped from the Earth's crust.

Electricity generated by these wind turbines ultimately comes from the sun's energy.

CONNECT TO ENVIRONMENTAL SCIENCE

There are numerous opportunities for students to become involved in volunteer efforts to conserve and recycle natural resources. As a class, find out what opportunities there are in your area. Students may be interested in a beach or river cleanup, tree planting, or a resource conservation public outreach program. Suggest that students volunteer two weekends as they study this chapter. At the end of the chapter, students can share their volunteer experiences with the class and present opportunities for their classmates to become involved.

Renewable Resources

Some natural resources are renewable. A **renewable resource** is a natural resource that can be used and replaced over a relatively short time. **Figure 2** shows two examples of renewable resources. Although many resources are renewable, humans often use them more quickly than they can be replaced. Trees, for example, are renewable, but humans are currently cutting trees down more quickly than other trees can grow to replace them.

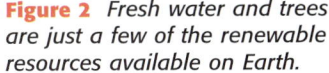

Figure 2 Fresh water and trees are just a few of the renewable resources available on Earth.

Nonrenewable Resources

Not all of Earth's natural resources are renewable. A **nonrenewable resource** is a natural resource that cannot be replaced or that can be replaced only over thousands or millions of years. Examples of nonrenewable resources are shown in **Figure 3**. The amounts of nonrenewable resources on Earth are fixed with respect to their availability for human use. Once nonrenewable resources are used up, they are no longer available. Oil and natural gas, for example, exist in limited quantities. When these resources become scarce, humans will have to find other resources to replace them.

Figure 3 Nonrenewable resources, such as coal and natural gas, can be replaced only over thousands or millions of years once they are used up.

CONNECT TO LIFE SCIENCE

Round out your discussion of nonrenewable resources by introducing students to the three Rs of conservation. Use Teaching Transparency 77 as a guide to help students list as many examples as possible of reducing, reusing, and recycling.

Teaching Transparency 77 "Practicing Conservation"

2 Teach

REAL-WORLD CONNECTION

Aluminum is refined from the ore bauxite, which is deposited in a thin layer at the Earth's surface. Worldwide, bauxite strip mines cover more of the Earth's surface than any other type of metal ore mine. Aluminum production uses so much electrical power that the metal has been referred to as "congealed electricity." To produce six aluminum cans, it takes the energy equivalent of 1 L of gasoline. For this reason, aluminum smelters are located close to sources of cheap, reliable power, such as the hydroelectric dams in the Pacific Northwest, Quebec, and the Amazon. When the environmental damage caused by producing new aluminum is considered, the importance of recycling becomes clear. Recycling one aluminum can saves enough energy to run a television set for 4 hours! Currently, the United States obtains about 20 percent of its aluminum from recycling. Have students write a persuasive letter explaining why that percentage should increase.

MEETING INDIVIDUAL NEEDS

Learners Having Difficulty Have students help you define renewable and nonrenewable resources. Provide students with two pieces of poster board, scissors, glue, and magazines. Have them attach pictures of products made from renewable resources to one poster board and pictures of products made from nonrenewable resources to the other. Beside each type of resource, have them describe where it is from, how it is obtained, the environmental effects of extracting and using the resource, and have them suggest ways it can be conserved or recycled.

Section 1 • Natural Resources

Answers to APPLY

Answers to the first three questions will vary. Answers to the fourth question might include reusing, recycling, and minimizing the use of products made from renewable and nonrenewable resources.

3) Close

Quiz

1. Explain why sunlight is our most valuable natural resource. (Light from the sun is an energy source that plants use to create food and that we can harness to do work. Students may also note that the energy in fossil fuels has its origin in sunlight.)

2. Explain the difference between conserving a resource and recycling it. (Conserving a resource means using it sparingly and not wasting it. Recycling refers to the reuse of natural resources to make new products.)

ALTERNATIVE ASSESSMENT

Concept Mapping Have students use the following terms to construct a concept map:

use, disposal, recycling, nonrenewable resource, reuse, production, renewable resource

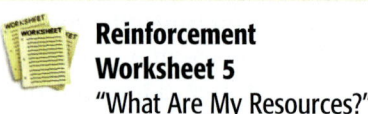
Reinforcement Worksheet 5
"What Are My Resources?"

TOPIC: Natural Resources
GO TO: www.scilinks.org
*sci*LINKS NUMBER: HSTE105

Renewable or Nonrenewable?

Find five products in your home that were made from natural resources. List the resource or resources from which each product was made. Label each resource as renewable or nonrenewable.

Are the products made from mostly renewable or nonrenewable resources? Are those renewable resources plentiful on Earth? Do humans use those renewable resources more quickly than the resources can be replaced? What can you do to help conserve nonrenewable resources and renewable resources that are becoming more scarce?

Figure 4 You can recycle many household items to help conserve natural resources.

Conserving Natural Resources

Whether the natural resources we use are renewable or nonrenewable, we should be careful how we use them. To conserve natural resources, we should try to use them only when necessary. For example, leaving the faucet running while brushing your teeth wastes clean water. Turning the faucet on only to rinse your brush saves a lot of water that you or others need for other uses.

Another way to conserve natural resources is to recycle, as shown in **Figure 4**. **Recycling** is the process by which used or discarded materials are treated for reuse. Recycling allows manufacturers to reuse natural resources when making new products. This in turn reduces the amount of natural resources that must be obtained from the Earth. For example, recycling aluminum cans reduces the amount of aluminum that must be mined from the Earth's crust to make new cans.

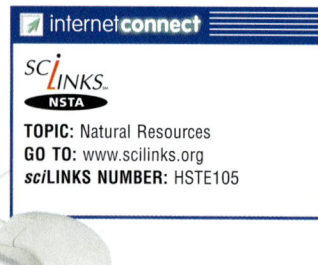
TOPIC: Natural Resources
GO TO: www.scilinks.org
*sci*LINKS NUMBER: HSTE105

REVIEW

1. How do humans use most natural resources?
2. What is the difference between renewable and nonrenewable resources?
3. Name two ways to conserve natural resources.
4. **Applying Concepts** List three renewable resources not mentioned in this section.

Answers to Review

1. Humans consume most natural resources by using products made from the resources.
2. Renewable resources can be replaced over a relatively short time, while nonrenewable resources cannot be replaced or can be replaced only over thousands or millions of years.
3. We can conserve natural resources by using them only when necessary and by recycling them.
4. Answers will vary.

Section 2

Fossil Fuels

Terms to Learn
energy resource, coal, fossil fuel, strip mining, petroleum, acid precipitation, natural gas, smog

What You'll Do
- Classify the different forms of fossil fuels.
- Explain how fossil fuels are obtained.
- Identify problems with fossil fuels.
- List ways to deal with fossil-fuel problems.

Energy resources are natural resources that humans use to produce energy. There are many types of renewable and nonrenewable energy resources, and all of the energy released from these resources ultimately comes from the sun. The energy resources on which humans currently depend the most are fossil fuels. **Fossil fuels** are nonrenewable energy resources that form in the Earth's crust over millions of years from the buried remains of once-living organisms. Energy is released from fossil fuels when they are burned. There are many types of fossil fuels, which exist as liquids, gases, and solids, and humans use a variety of methods to obtain and process them. These methods depend on the type of fossil fuel, where the fossil fuel is located, and how the fossil fuel formed. Unfortunately, the methods of obtaining and using fossil fuels can have negative effects on the environment. Read on to learn about fossil fuels and the role they play in our lives.

Liquid Fossil Fuels—Petroleum

Petroleum, or crude oil, is an oily mixture of flammable organic compounds from which liquid fossil fuels and other products, such as asphalt, are separated. Petroleum is separated into several types of fossil fuels and other products in refineries, such as the one shown in **Figure 5**. Among the types of fossil fuels separated from petroleum are gasoline, jet fuel, kerosene, diesel fuel, and fuel oil.

Figure 5 Fossil fuels and other products are separated from petroleum in a process called fractionation. *In this process, petroleum is gradually heated in a tower so that different components boil and vaporize at different temperatures.*

Science Bloopers
On January 10, 1901, oil from the famous Spindletop well near Beaumont, Texas, began to flow. In fact, the crude oil spewed higher than 90 m into the air! Caught off guard by the tremendous volume of petroleum, 100,000 barrels per day, drillers took 9 days to cap the well.

Is That A Fact!
During the early 1900s, petroleum was so plentiful in Texas that it sold for about 3¢ per barrel. At about the same time, water—a renewable resource—sold for about $6 per barrel!

SECTION 2

Focus
Fossil Fuels
In this section, students will learn how fossil fuels, such as petroleum, natural gas, and coal, form and where deposits of these fuels are found in the United States. Students will also learn about some of the ways we obtain fossil fuels and about the environmental problems associated with obtaining and using fossil fuels.

Bellringer
Pose this question on the board or an overhead projector:

What does the term *fossil fuels* imply about the source of these fuels? (The term *fossil fuels* implies that these fuels are derived from the remains of ancient life.)

1) Motivate

DISCUSSION

Fossil Fuel Use Lead students in a discussion about why fossil fuels, such as coal and gasoline, are so widely used as energy resources. (Answers may include their cost, availability, and ease of use.)

Challenge students to think about what qualities a good fuel should have. (It should be abundant, affordable, easy to obtain, have a high ratio of energy to weight, be easy to transport, and produce little waste.)

Give students 10 minutes to write about how the disadvantages of fossil fuel use affect them.

 Directed Reading Worksheet 5 Section 2

Section 2 • Fossil Fuels   111

2 Teach

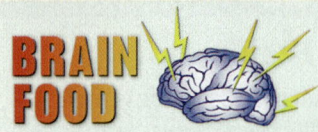

BRAIN FOOD

One characteristic all fossil fuels share is that they are formed from the remains of organisms that lived long ago. Over millions of years, these remains are buried by sediment and rock. Rising pressure and temperature cause slow chemical changes that result in coal, petroleum, or natural gas. When hydrocarbons burn, or combine rapidly with oxygen, they release energy. The energy that originally formed the carbon-hydrogen bonds was captured by plants and incorporated in their tissues by photosynthesis.

DISCUSSION

Tell students that combustion of natural gas creates very little soot, carbon monoxide, or nitrogen oxides—it burns "cleaner" than other fossil fuels. Then ask students why industrialized societies have developed a reliance on solid and liquid fossil fuels rather than on gaseous fossil fuels. Provide a hint by asking whether it is easier to design a leak-proof container for 1 L of milk or 1 L of oxygen.

Multicultural CONNECTION

Natural gas seeps were first discovered in ancient Persia (now Iran) between 6000 and 2000 B.C. Records from China indicate use of natural gas by 900 B.C. The Chinese drilled the first known natural gas well using bamboo poles and primitive drill bits. The well was 140 m deep. In Europe, natural gas was first discovered in England in 1659.

Chemistry CONNECTION

Petroleum and natural gas are both made of compounds called hydrocarbons. A *hydrocarbon* is an organic compound containing only carbon and hydrogen.

Gaseous Fossil Fuels—Natural Gas

Gaseous fossil fuels are classified as **natural gas.** Most natural gas is used for heating and for generating electricity. The stove in your kitchen may be powered by natural gas. Many motor vehicles, such as the van in **Figure 6,** are fueled by liquefied natural gas. Vehicles like these produce less air pollution than vehicles powered by gasoline.

Methane is the main component of natural gas. But other natural-gas components, such as butane and propane, can be separated and used by humans. Butane is often used as fuel for camp stoves. Propane is used as a heating fuel and as a cooking fuel, especially for outdoor grills.

Figure 6 Vehicles powered by liquefied natural gas are becoming more common.

Solid Fossil Fuels—Coal

The solid fossil fuel that humans use most is coal. **Coal** is a solid fossil fuel formed underground from buried, decomposed plant material. Coal, the only fossil fuel that is a rock, was once the leading source of energy in the United States. People burned coal for heating and transportation. Many trains in the 1800s and early 1900s were powered by coal-burning steam locomotives.

People began to use coal less because burning coal often produces large amounts of air pollution and because better energy resources were discovered. Coal is no longer used much as a fuel for heating or transportation in the United States. However, many power plants, like the one shown in **Figure 7,** burn coal to produce electricity.

Figure 7 This coal is being gathered so that it may be burned in the power plant shown in the background.

CROSS-DISCIPLINARY FOCUS

Language Arts Petroleum is more than a fuel source; it is refined to make plastics and other petrochemical products we use every day. Petrochemicals are used to create medicines, inks, solvents, clothing, fertilizers, and many other products. Have students make a list of 20 products made from petroleum. Then have students write a short story that is based in a world with no petroleum products. They can set their stories in the nineteenth century, when petrochemical products did not exist, or in a world of the future when petroleum reserves have been exhausted.

How Do Fossil Fuels Form?

All fossil fuels form from the buried remains of ancient organisms. But different types of fossil fuels form in different ways and from different types of organisms. Petroleum and natural gas form mainly from the remains of microscopic sea life. When these organisms die, their remains settle on the ocean floor, where they decay and become part of the ocean sediment. Over time, the sediment slowly becomes rock, trapping the decayed remains. Through physical and chemical changes over millions of years, the remains become petroleum and gas. Gradually, more rocks form above the rocks that contain the fossil fuels. Under the pressure of overlying rocks and sediments, the fossil fuels are squeezed out of their source rocks and into permeable rocks. As shown in **Figure 8,** these permeable rocks become reservoirs for petroleum and natural gas. The formation of petroleum and natural gas is an ongoing process. Part of the remains of today's sea life will probably become petroleum and natural gas millions of years from now.

Rock Sponge

1. Place samples of **sandstone, limestone,** and **shale** in separate **Petri dishes.**
2. Place 5 drops of light **machine oil** on each rock sample.
3. Observe and record the time required for the oil to be absorbed by each of the rock samples.
4. Which rock sample absorbed the oil fastest? Why?
5. Based on your findings, describe a property that allows for easy removal of fossil fuels from reservoir rock.

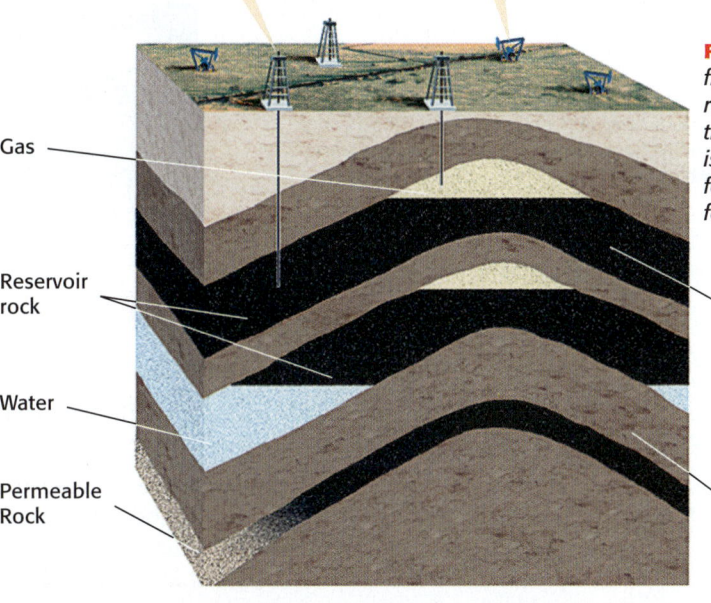

To obtain petroleum and gas, engineers must drill wells into the reservoir rock.

After fuels are successfully tapped, pumps must sometimes be installed to remove them.

Figure 8 *Petroleum and gas rise from source rock into reservoir rock. Sometimes the fuels are trapped by overlying rock that is impermeable. Rocks that are folded upward are excellent fossil-fuel traps.*

Gas
Reservoir rock
Water
Permeable Rock
Petroleum
Impermeable Rock

TOPIC: Fossil Fuels
GO TO: www.scilinks.org
sciLINKS NUMBER: HSTE120

Teaching Transparency 115
"Porous Rocks Are Reservoirs for Fossil Fuels"

QuickLab

MATERIALS

FOR EACH STUDENT:
- samples of sandstone, limestone, and shale
- Petri dishes
- light machine oil
- eyedropper

Answers to QuickLab

4. Answers will vary. The rock sample with the highest percentage of interconnected pore space should soak up the oil the fastest. Most reservoir rock is limestone that has many connected pores.
5. Oil and gas move easily through reservoir rock that has a high percentage of interconnected pore space. This allows for easy removal of liquid fossil fuels.

DEMONSTRATION

MATERIALS

- clean, empty glass jar
- 100 mL each of rubbing alcohol, water, and vegetable oil
- red and blue food coloring

Simulating Reservoirs Petroleum does not fill all the available pore space in a subsurface reservoir. Natural gas often accumulates above an oil deposit, as shown in **Figure 8.** When it is located on top of an oil deposit, natural gas can be obtained through shallow drilling.

Tell students that the alcohol represents natural gas and that the cooking oil represents petroleum. Add a few drops of blue food coloring to the water and a few drops of red food coloring to the alcohol. Ask students to help you determine the correct order to add the liquids to the jar to match the layers in **Figure 8.**
Sheltered English

Section 2 • Fossil Fuels

2 Teach, continued

USING THE FIGURE
Have students answer the questions below.

- What kinds of organisms play an important role in coal production? (bacteria, plants, and fungi)
- In a given area, which would be older: peat or lignite deposits? (Lignite; peat is an earlier stage of coal formation.)

REAL-WORLD CONNECTION
Have students find out what fuel sources are used to produce electricity in their community. If fossil fuels are used, have students identify the fuel's source and explain how the fuel is transported to the power plant. As an extension, have students create a list of 15 ways electricity consumption in your community can be reduced. Students could create sign-up sheets and see how many people they can find to pledge to follow their 15-step energy conservation plan.

INDEPENDENT PRACTICE
Concept Mapping Have students construct concept maps that show the different methods of extraction used for various fossil fuels. Their maps should include the formation of the fuel, the location, and the extraction system. One type of fuel may have two or more locations and extraction methods. Encourage students to do additional research to complete their maps.

Teaching Transparency 116 "Formation of Coal"

114 Chapter 5 • Energy Resources

Coal Formation Coal forms differently from petroleum and natural gas. Coal forms underground over millions of years from decayed swamp plants. When swamp plants die, they sink to the bottom of the swamps. This begins the process of coal formation, which is illustrated below. Notice that the percentage of carbon increases with each stage. The higher the carbon content, the cleaner the material burns. However, all grades of coal will pollute the air when burned.

The Process of Coal Formation

Stage 1: Peat
Bacteria and fungi transform sunken swamp plants into peat. Peat is about **60 percent carbon**.

Stage 2: Lignite
Sediment buries the peat, increasing the pressure and temperature. This gradually turns the peat into lignite, which is about **70 percent carbon**.

Stage 3: Bituminous coal
The temperature and pressure continue to increase. Eventually lignite turns into bituminous coal. Bituminous coal is about **80 percent carbon**.

Stage 4: Anthracite
With more heat and pressure, bituminous coal eventually turns into anthracite, which is about **90 percent carbon**.

REVIEW

1. Name a solid, liquid, and gaseous fossil fuel.
2. What component of coal-forming organic material increases with each step in coal formation?
3. **Comparing Concepts** What is the difference between the organic material from which coal forms and the organic material from which petroleum and natural gas mainly form?

Answers to Review

1. Answers will vary. The solid fossil fuel mentioned in this section is coal. Liquid fossil fuels mentioned in this section include gasoline, jet fuel, kerosene, diesel fuel, and fuel oil (petroleum is an acceptable answer). Gaseous fossil fuels mentioned in this section include methane, butane, and propane (natural gas is an acceptable answer).

2. carbon

3. Coal forms from buried, decayed swamp plants, while oil and natural gas form mainly from buried, decayed sea life.

Where Are Fossil Fuels Found?

Fossil fuels are found in many parts of the world, both on land and beneath the ocean. As shown in **Figure 9,** the United States has large reserves of petroleum, natural gas, and coal. In spite of all our petroleum reserves, we import about one-half of our petroleum and petroleum products from the Middle East, South America, and Africa.

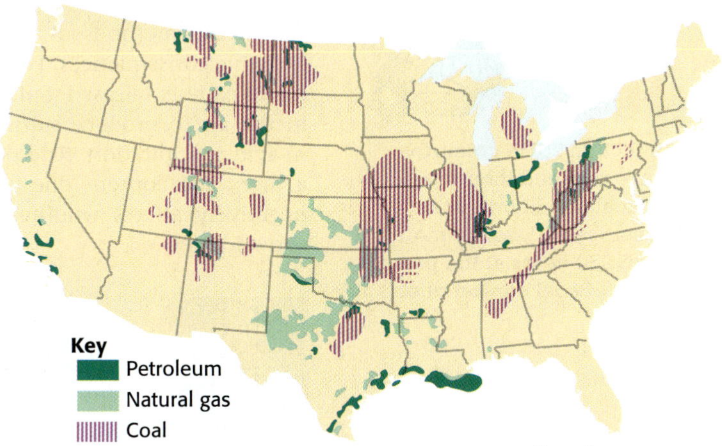

Figure 9 Most oil and gas produced in the continental United States comes from California, Louisiana, and Texas.

Key
- Petroleum
- Natural gas
- Coal

How Do Humans Obtain Fossil Fuels?

Humans use different methods to remove fossil fuels from the Earth's crust. These methods depend on the type of fuel being obtained and its location. Petroleum and natural gas are removed from the Earth by drilling wells into rock that contains these resources. Oil wells exist both on land and in the ocean. For offshore drilling, engineers mount drills on platforms that are secured to the ocean floor or float at the ocean's surface. **Figure 10** shows an offshore oil rig.

Coal is obtained either by mining deep beneath the Earth's surface or by strip mining. **Strip mining** is a process in which rock and soil are stripped from the Earth's surface to expose the underlying materials to be mined. Strip mining is used to mine shallow coal deposits. **Figure 11** shows a coal strip mine.

Figure 10 Large oil rigs, some more than 300 m tall, operate offshore in many places, such as the Gulf of Mexico and the North Sea.

Figure 11 Strip miners use explosives to blast away rock and soil and to expose the material to be mined.

3) Extend

DEBATE

Drilling in a Wildlife Refuge
The U.S. Fish and Wildlife Service, which administers Alaska's Arctic National Wildlife Refuge, states that its primary mandate is "to protect the wildlife and habitats of this area for the benefit of people now and in the future." The refuge's coastal plain is the calving ground for the Porcupine caribou herd, the most important land-based denning area for the entire Beaufort Sea polar bear population, home for 350 reintroduced musk oxen, and an important habitat for more than 180 bird species. Environmentalists claim that oil drilling on the refuge would bring pollution and disrupt the lives of the animals that use the coastal plain. Oil-industry executives say that they would drill on only 8 percent of the refuge (the 1.5-million-acre coastal plain); that oil revenues would benefit the state and federal governments, that more than 250,000 jobs would be created, and that importing foreign oil is too expensive.

Have students learn more about the issue and debate whether or not oil drilling should be allowed in Arctic National Wildlife Refuge.

internet connect
TOPIC: Nonrenewable Resources
GO TO: www.scilinks.org
sciLINKS NUMBER: HSTE115

BRAIN FOOD
Although some countries have reduced their use of coal, the known coal reserves will last no more than 250 years at the present rates of coal consumption.

Problems with Fossil Fuels

Although fossil fuels provide energy for our technological world, the methods of obtaining and using them can have negative consequences. For example, when coal is burned, sulfur dioxide is released. Sulfur dioxide combines with moisture in the air to produce sulfuric acid, which is one of the acids in acid precipitation. **Acid precipitation** is rain or snow that has a high acid content due to air pollutants. Acid precipitation negatively affects wildlife, plants, buildings, and statues, as shown in **Figure 12.**

Figure 12 *Acid precipitation can dissolve parts of statues.*

Coal Mining The mining of coal can also create environmental problems. Strip mining removes soil, which plants need for growth and some animals need for shelter. If land is not properly repaired afterward, strip mining can destroy wildlife habitats. Coal mines that are deep underground, such as the one shown in **Figure 13,** can be hazardous to the men and women working in them. Coal mining can also lower local water tables, pollute water supplies, and cause the overlying earth to collapse.

Petroleum Problems Obtaining petroleum can also cause environmental problems. In 1989, the supertanker *Exxon Valdez* spilled about 257,000 barrels of crude oil into the water when it ran aground off the coast of Alaska. The oil killed hundreds of thousands of animals and damaged the local fishing industry.

Figure 13 *Coal dust can damage the human respiratory system. And because coal dust is flammable, it increases the danger of fire and explosion in coal mines.*

SCIENTISTS AT ODDS

One of the products of burning fossil fuels is carbon dioxide. Scientists recognize carbon dioxide as a greenhouse gas—a gas that traps thermal energy and increases the temperature of the Earth's atmosphere. Most scientists agree that both carbon dioxide levels and global temperatures are increasing.

However, they have different opinions about the many possible ways rising carbon dioxide levels may be affecting the Earth's climate. Have students find newspaper and magazine articles about this issue and write a balanced essay presenting both sides of the debate.

Smog Burning petroleum products causes a big environmental problem called smog. **Smog** is a photochemical fog produced by the reaction of sunlight and air pollutants. Smog is particularly serious in places such as Denver and Los Angeles. In these cities, the sun shines most of the time, there are millions of automobiles, and surrounding mountains prevent the wind from blowing pollutants away. Smog levels in some cities, including Denver and Los Angeles, have begun to decrease in recent years.

Dealing with Fossil-Fuel Problems

So what can be done to solve fossil-fuel problems? Obviously we can't stop using fossil fuels any time soon—we are too dependent on them. But there are things we can do to minimize the negative effects of fossil fuels. By traveling in automobiles only when absolutely necessary, people can cut down on car exhaust in the air. Carpooling, riding a bike, walking, and using mass-transit systems also help by reducing the number of cars on the road. These measures help reduce the negative effects of using fossil fuels, but they do not eliminate the problems. Only by using certain alternative energy resources, which you will learn about in the next section, can we eliminate them.

Figure 14 *Using mass transit, walking, or riding your bike can help reduce air pollution due to burning fossil fuels.*

REVIEW

1. Name a state with petroleum, natural-gas, and coal reserves.
2. How do we obtain petroleum and natural gas? How do we obtain coal?
3. Name three problems with fossil fuels. Name three ways to minimize the negative effects of fossil fuels.
4. **Making Inferences** Why does the United States import petroleum from other regions even though the United States has its own petroleum reserves?

internetconnect

SC**LINKS.**
NSTA

TOPIC: Fossil Fuels
GO TO: www.scilinks.org
*sci*LINKS NUMBER: HSTE120

4) Close

Quiz

1. What is the relationship between petroleum and liquid fossil fuels? (Petroleum is the mixture of compounds from which liquid fossil fuels are separated.)
2. Explain why we use different methods to extract fossil fuels from the Earth's crust. (We use different methods because fossil fuels differ in their location and composition.)
3. When an oil and gas reservoir is drilled, which substance is generally encountered first—oil or natural gas? Why? (natural gas; because it is less dense than oil and it migrates to the top of the reservoir)
4. Coal beds have been found in Antarctica. Explain how this could be. (Answers will vary. Antarctica had a warmer climate in the past, and the warmer temperatures allowed plants to grow. These plants were buried and eventually became coal formations.)

ALTERNATIVE ASSESSMENT

Have each student find out about the fossil fuel resources of a particular continent. Ask them to create a map showing where the petroleum, coal, and natural gas deposits are found in the continent. Students can supplement their maps with information and illustrations showing how these resources are extracted, how they are used, and the environmental problems associated with them.

Reinforcement Worksheet 5
"If It's a Fossil, How Is It a Fuel?"

Answers to Review

1. Answers will vary. Use **Figure 9** to check students' answers.
2. We obtain petroleum and natural gas by drilling wells into rock formations that contain these resources. We obtain coal by mining.
3. Answers will vary. Problems include oil spills, loss of soil from strip mining coal, and the production of smog due to burning fossil fuels. Ways of minimizing negative effects include carpooling, riding a bike, walking, using public transportation, and recycling products made from petroleum.
4. America imports petroleum because it is cheaper in other regions and because those regions have enacted fewer environmental regulations on petroleum production and transport.

Section 2 • Fossil Fuels

SECTION 3

Focus

Alternative Resources

In this section, students will learn about some of the alternatives to fossil fuels. The section also includes a discussion of the pros and cons of alternative energy sources.

Show students a picture of a wind farm, a solar energy facility, and a hydroelectric dam. Ask them which, if any, of these alternative energy facilities might be well suited to their community. Explain that the energy resources used in these facilities are just some of the alternatives to fossil fuels available.

1 Motivate

DISCUSSION

Have each student make a list of 10 ways in which he or she uses electricity every day. Compile a master list on the board, and discuss alternatives to each activity. (Letting one's hair dry on its own, for example, is an alternative to using a hair dryer.) Have each student try two of these suggestions at home and report back to class.

Directed Reading Worksheet 5 Section 3

Teaching Transparency 117 "Generating Energy with Fission"

Section 3

Terms to Learn
nuclear energy   biomass
solar energy   gasohol
wind energy   geothermal
hydroelectric   energy
 energy

What You'll Do
- Describe alternatives to the use of fossil fuels.
- List advantages and disadvantages of using alternative energy resources.

Alternative Resources

The energy needs of industry, transportation, and housing are increasingly met by electricity. However, most electricity is currently produced from fossil fuels, which are nonrenewable and cause pollution when burned. For people to continue their present lifestyles, new sources of energy must become available.

Splitting the Atom

Nuclear energy is an alternative source of energy that comes from the nuclei of atoms. Most often it is produced by a process called *fission*. Fission is a process in which the nuclei of radioactive atoms are split and energy is released, as shown in **Figure 15.** Nuclear power plants use radioactive atoms as fuel. When fission takes place, a large amount of energy is released. The energy is used to produce steam to run electric generators in the power plant.

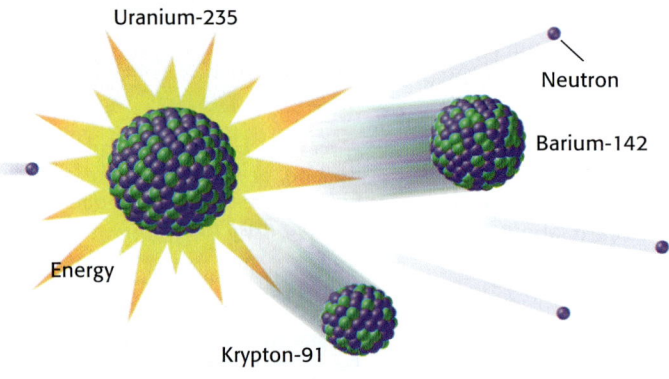

Figure 15 The process of fission generates a tremendous amount of energy.

Pros and Cons Nuclear power plants provide alternative sources of energy without the problems that come with fossil fuels. So why don't we use nuclear energy instead of fossil fuels? Nuclear power plants produce dangerous wastes. The wastes are unsafe because they are radioactive. Radioactive wastes must be removed from the plant and stored until they lose their radioactivity. But nuclear wastes can remain dangerously radioactive for thousands of years. A safe place must be found to store these wastes so that radiation cannot escape into the environment.

Figure 16 Areas or objects marked with this symbol should be approached only after taking proper precautions.

MISCONCEPTION ALERT

Nuclear energy is the energy that exists in the bonds that hold together atomic nuclei. The breaking of these bonds, or nuclear fission, occurs at an uncontrolled rate in an atomic bomb. By contrast, the rate of fission in a nuclear power plant is carefully controlled. As long as nuclear power plants are designed and operated properly, they release safe amounts of radiation and no particulate pollution. It is incredibly efficient: 500 g of uranium-235 has nearly 3 million times the energy-producing potential of the same amount of coal. The greatest problem with nuclear power is locating a safe place to store the waste products generated during fission.

Because nuclear power plants generate a lot of energy, large amounts of water are used in cooling towers, like the ones shown in **Figure 17,** to cool the plants. If a plant's cooling system were to stop working, the plant would overheat, and its reactor could possibly melt. Then a large amount of radiation could escape into the environment, as it did at Chernobyl, Ukraine, in 1986.

Combining Atoms

Another type of nuclear energy is produced by *fusion.* Fusion is the joining of nuclei of small atoms to form larger atoms. This is the same process that is thought to produce energy in the sun.

The main advantage of fusion is that it produces few dangerous wastes. The main disadvantage of fusion is that very high temperatures are required for the reaction to take place. No known material can withstand temperatures that high, so the reaction must occur within a special environment, such as a magnetic field. So far, fusion reactions have been limited to laboratory experiments.

Figure 17 *Cooling towers are one of many safety mechanisms used in nuclear power plants. Their purpose is to prevent the plant from overheating.*

Sitting in the Sun

When sunlight falls on your skin, the warmth you feel is part of solar energy. **Solar energy** is energy from the sun. Every day, the Earth receives more than enough solar energy to meet all of our energy needs. And because the Earth continuously receives solar energy, the energy is a renewable resource.

There are two common ways that we use solar energy. Sunlight can be changed into electricity by the use of solar cells. You may have used a calculator, like the one shown in **Figure 18,** that was powered by solar cells.

Figure 18 *This solar calculator receives all the energy it needs through the four solar cells located above its screen.*

2 Teach

READING STRATEGY

Mnemonics The following mnemonic device will help students remember the difference between fission and fusion. "Atomic nuclei sp**li**t during f**i**ssion and **u**nite during f**u**sion."

DISCUSSION

Nuclear Energy Use the following questions to stimulate discussion about nuclear energy.

- What is nuclear fission? How does it generate electricity?
- Where is nuclear energy currently being used?
- What are the advantages and disadvantages of nuclear fission?
- Where should nuclear reactors and storage sites be located?

CROSS-DISCIPLINARY FOCUS

History Since the age of nuclear energy began in the early 1960s, public and scientific support for nuclear power has shifted many times. By the mid-1970s, however, it was clear that nuclear power was not the panacea promised by its proponents. The construction of new reactors had become so costly that the electricity generated by nuclear plants was more expensive than that generated by coal-fired power plants. Public concern over safety and waste disposal grew, and in addition, the demand for electricity increased less than expected. Since 1977, no orders have been placed for nuclear plants in the United States. Encourage students to research the history of nuclear power in the United States and other countries.

SCIENTISTS AT ODDS

Fortunately, only a few serious accidents have occurred since the world began using nuclear energy. In 1991, the International Atomic Energy Agency issued a report on the Chernobyl accident that concluded that "future increases over the natural incidence of cancers or heredity effects would be difficult to discern." In 1996, however, some cancer rates were 100 to 200 times higher than normal in areas contaminated by the fallout from the accident. Encourage students to find out the current status of the area around the Chernobyl reactor and report back to class.

Section 3 • Alternative Resources

2) Teach, continued

READING STRATEGY

Activity Before they read the information on solar cells and solar collectors, have students deduce whether each of the statements below is true or false. When students have finished reading these two pages, have them correct any wrong answers and rewrite the false statements to make them true. Students can use this activity as a basis for creating an alternative energy misconception fact sheet.

- A solar cell produces only a very small amount of electricity. (true)
- Solar cells are not commonly used because they cause a great deal of pollution. (false)
- The expense of a solar power system does not pay off to consumers over time. (false)
- Solar water heaters are most efficient in the far northern parts of the United States. (false)

MISCONCEPTION ALERT

Solar energy is for all practical purposes an inexhaustible source of energy. However, it is important to note that the sun doesn't shine 24 hours a day in most areas nor is it always directly overhead. Using solar energy efficiently depends on the time of day, local weather conditions, the time of year, and an area's latitude. To solve some of these problems, solar power systems use batteries to store the electricity they generate.

Biology CONNECTION

Did you know that the energy from petroleum, coal, and natural gas is really a form of stored solar energy? All organisms ultimately get their energy from sunlight and store it in their cells. When ancient organisms died and became trapped in sediment, some of their energy was stored in the fossil fuel that formed in the sediment. So the gasoline that powers today's cars contains energy from sunlight that fell on the Earth millions of years ago!

Solar Cells A single solar cell produces only a tiny amount of electricity. For small electronic devices, such as calculators, this is not a problem because enough energy can be obtained with only a few cells. But in order to provide enough electricity for larger objects, such as a house, thousands of cells are needed. Many homes and businesses use solar panels mounted on their roof to provide much of their needed electricity. Solar panels are large panels made up of many solar cells wired together. **Figure 19** shows a building with solar panels.

Figure 19 *Although they are expensive to install, solar panels are good investments in the long run.*

Counting the Cost Solar cells are reliable and quiet, have no moving parts, and can last for years with little maintenance. They produce no pollution during use, and pollution created by their manufacturing process is very low.

So why doesn't everyone use solar cells? The answer is cost. While solar energy itself is free, solar cells are relatively expensive to make. The cost of a solar-power system could account for one-third of the cost of an entire house. But in remote areas where it is difficult and costly to run electric wires, solar-power systems can be a realistic option. In the United States today, tens of thousands of homes use solar panels to produce electricity. Can you think of other places that you have seen solar panels? Take a look at **Figure 20.**

Figure 20 *Perhaps you have seen solar panels used in this manner in your town.*

CONNECT TO ASTRONOMY

In space, conserving natural resources is very important. Many of the innovations in alternative energy research began in the space program. For example, NASA scientists must create solar panels that use solar energy as efficiently as possible and design materials that insulate space probes from the temperature extremes of space. Students may be interested in researching the recent NASA development dubbed "aerogel," the lightest solid on Earth. Aerogel, a nearly transparent substance, is only three times as dense as air and has 20 times the insulating power of window glass. Suggest that students share their findings in class.

Solar Heating Another use of solar energy is direct heating through solar collectors. Solar collectors are dark-colored boxes with glass or plastic tops. A common use of solar collectors is heating water, as shown in **Figure 21.** Over 1 million solar water heaters have been installed in the United States. They are especially common in Florida, California, and some southwestern states.

As with solar cells, the problem with solar collectors is cost. But solar collectors quickly pay for themselves—heating water is one of the major uses of electricity in American homes. Also, solar collectors can be used to generate electricity.

Large-Scale Solar Power Experimental solar-power facilities, such as the one shown in **Figure 22,** have shown that it is possible to generate electricity for an entire city. Facilities like this one are designed to use mirrors to focus sunlight onto coated steel pipes filled with synthetic oil. The oil is heated by the sunlight and is then used to heat water. The heated liquid water turns to steam, which is used to drive electric generators.

An alternative design for solar-power facilities is one that uses mirrors to reflect sunlight onto a receiver on a central tower. The receiver captures the sunlight's energy and stores it in tanks of molten salt. The stored energy is then used to create steam, which drives a turbine in an electric generator. *Solar Two,* a solar-power facility designed in this manner, was capable of generating enough energy to power 10,000 homes in southern California.

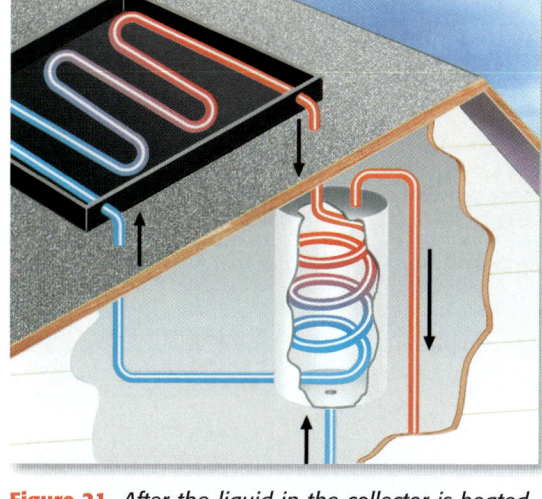

Figure 21 *After the liquid in the collector is heated by the sun, it is pumped through tubes that run through a water heater, causing the temperature of the water to rise.*

Turn to page 650 to calculate the power of the sun.

Figure 22 *This solar-power facility in the Mojave Desert used sun-tracking mirrors called heliostats.*

IS THAT A FACT!

In 1980, the production cost of generating electricity from solar energy averaged 60¢ per kilowatt hour. By 1990, costs were reduced to an average of 16¢ per kilowatt hour. Solar energy systems in the United States have a combined capacity of 354 MW!

 **PG 650**

Power of the Sun

GUIDED PRACTICE

Put the statements below on an overhead transparency in the order shown. Ask students to sequence the statements to explain how the solar power facility in the Mojave Desert works.

- The oil is heated and in turn heats water. (3)
- Computer-guided mirrors collect solar energy. (1)
- The heated water turns into steam, which is used to turn generators that produce electricity. (4)
- Mirrors focus sunlight onto pipes that are filled with oil. (2)

GROUP ACTIVITY

Building a Solar Cooker Solar cookers have been used successfully in many developing countries where deforestation is a problem. There are many different designs for solar cookers available on the Internet. Have groups of students research, build, and test their own solar cookers. Consider organizing a contest to see which group can build the most efficient solar cooker.

Safety Caution: Warn students not to stare at reflected sunlight for long periods of time.

REAL-WORLD CONNECTION

Invite an expert in the field of alternative energy to speak with the class. If this is not possible, have students write a short report about an alternative energy invention of their choice.

Section 3 • Alternative Resources

Capture the Wind

Wind is created indirectly by solar energy through the uneven heating of air. There is a tremendous amount of energy in wind, called **wind energy**. You can see the effects of this energy unleashed in a hurricane or tornado. Wind energy can also be used productively by humans. Wind energy can turn a windmill that pumps water or produces electricity.

Wind Turbines Today, fields of modern wind turbines—technological updates of the old windmills—generate significant amounts of electricity. Clusters of these turbines are often called wind farms. Wind farms are located in areas where winds are strong and steady. Most of the wind farms in the United States are in California. The amount of energy produced by California wind farms could power all of the homes in San Francisco.

Steady Breezes There are many benefits of using wind energy. Wind energy is renewable. Wind farms can be built in only 3–6 months. Wind turbines produce no carbon dioxide or other air pollutants during operation. The land used for wind farms can also be used for other purposes, such as cattle grazing, as shown in **Figure 23**. However, the wind blows strongly and steadily enough to produce electricity on a large scale only in certain places. Currently, wind energy accounts for only a small percentage of the energy used in the United States.

Figure 23 *Wind turbines take up only a small part of the ground's surface. This allows the land on wind farms to be used for more than one purpose.*

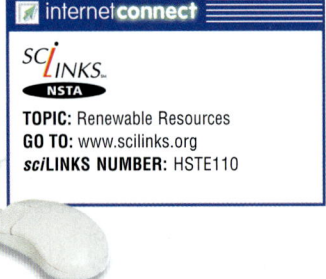

TOPIC: Renewable Resources
GO TO: www.scilinks.org
sciLINKS NUMBER: HSTE110

REVIEW

1. Briefly describe two ways of using solar energy.
2. In addition to multiple turbines, what is needed to produce electricity from wind energy on a large scale?
3. **Analyzing Methods** Nuclear power plants are rarely found in the middle of deserts or other extremely dry areas. If you were going to build a nuclear plant, why would you not build it in the middle of a desert?

Hydroelectric Energy

The energy of falling water has been used by humans for thousands of years. Water wheels, such as the one shown in **Figure 24,** have been around since ancient times. In the early years of the Industrial Revolution, water wheels provided energy for many factories. More recently, the energy of falling water has been used to generate electricity. Electricity produced by falling water is called **hydroelectric energy.**

Harnessing the Water Cycle Hydroelectric energy is inexpensive and produces little pollution, and it is renewable because water constantly cycles from the ocean to the air, to the land, and back to the ocean. But like wind energy, hydroelectric energy is not available everywhere. Hydroelectric energy can be produced only where large volumes of falling water can be harnessed. Huge dams, like the one in **Figure 25,** must be built on major rivers to capture enough water to generate significant amounts of electricity.

Figure 24 *Falling water turns water wheels, which turn giant millstones used to grind grain into flour.*

Figure 25 *Falling water turns huge turbines inside hydroelectric dams, generating electricity for millions of people.*

Turn to page 648 to make your own water wheel.

At What Price? Increased use of hydroelectric energy could reduce the demand for fossil fuels, but there are trade-offs. Construction of the large dams necessary for hydroelectric power plants often destroys other resources, such as forests and wildlife habitats. For example, hydroelectric dams on the Lower Snake and Columbia Rivers in Washington disrupt the migratory paths of local populations of salmon and steelhead. Large numbers of these fish die each year because their life cycle is disrupted. Dams can also decrease water quality and create erosion problems.

✓ Self-Check
How are ancient water wheels like modern hydroelectric dams? *(See page 726 to check your answer.)*

2) Teach, continued

Multicultural CONNECTION

With 70 percent of people in developing countries burning wood and charcoal for heating and cooking fuel, the use of alternative biomass fuels is crucial to slowing rates of deforestation. In the Bolivian highlands of South America, the llama is a traditional beast of burden, but its dung is even more important as a source of biomass fuel. In India, cow dung is used in many rural areas for heating and cooking fuel. In the deserts of Arabia, the nomadic Bedouin use camel dung as fuel, and many people in Tibet and Nepal use yak dung as fuel. Dried yak dung is the main fuel available on the treeless Tibetan plateaus. In China and other countries, methane produced from composting pig manure is used to generate electricity.

MEETING INDIVIDUAL NEEDS

Advanced Learners Have students research and prepare reports on biomass fuels. Students might choose to research the use of lumber industry wastes, agricultural wastes, organic municipal wastes, food processing wastes, aquatic plants and algae, and municipal sewage.

Answers to MATHBREAK
2.5 acres

Critical Thinking Worksheet 5 "Nature's Gold"

Interactive Explorations CD-ROM "The Generation Gap"

Powerful Plants

Plants are similar to solar collectors, absorbing energy from the sun and storing it for later use. Leaves, wood, and other parts of plants contain the stored energy. Even the dung of plant-grazing animals is high in stored energy. These sources of energy are called biomass. **Biomass** is organic matter that contains stored energy.

Burning Biomass Biomass energy can be released in several ways. The most common is the burning of biomass. Approximately 70 percent of people living in developing countries heat their homes and cook their food by burning wood or charcoal. In the United States this number is about 5 percent. Scientists estimate that the burning of wood and animal dung accounts for approximately 14 percent of the world's total energy use.

Figure 26 *In many parts of the world where firewood is scarce, people burn animal dung for energy. This woman is preparing cow dung that will be dried and used as fuel.*

MATH BREAK

Miles per Acre
Imagine that you own a car that runs on alcohol made from corn that you grow. You drive your car about 15,000 miles in a year, and you get 240 gallons of alcohol from each acre of corn that you process. If your car gets 25 mi/gal, how many acres of corn would you have to grow to fuel your car for a year?

Gasohol Plant material can also be changed into liquid fuel. Plants containing sugar or starch, for example, can be made into alcohol. The alcohol is burned as a fuel or mixed with gasoline to make a fuel mixture called **gasohol.** An acre of corn can produce more than 1,000 L of alcohol. But in the United States we use a lot of fuel for our cars. It would take about 40 percent of the entire United States corn harvest to produce enough alcohol to make just 10 percent of the fuel we use in our cars! Biomass is obviously a renewable source of energy, but producing biomass requires land that could be used for growing food.

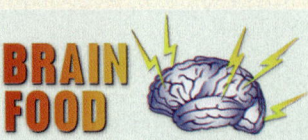
BRAIN FOOD

Water at the ocean's surface can be 25°C warmer than water 1,000 m below. Ocean Thermal Energy Conversion (OTEC) uses this temperature difference to produce electricity. Some systems use an ammonia-filled pipe that runs in a closed loop deep into the ocean. In deep, cold water, the fluid is liquid, but as it rises through the warm surface water, it becomes a gas. This expansion drives a turbine that generates electricity. The gas condenses, and the cycle repeats. Open-cycle OTEC plants, which can generate as much as 210 kW, use sea water as the condensing fluid and produce desalinized water as a byproduct.

Deep Heat

Imagine being able to tap into the energy of the Earth. In a few places this is possible. This type of energy is called geothermal energy. **Geothermal energy** is energy from within the Earth.

Geothermal Energy In some locations, rainwater penetrates porous rock near a source of magma. The heat from the magma heats the water, often turning it to steam. The steam and hot water escape through natural vents called geysers, or through wells drilled into the rock. The steam and water contain geothermal energy. Some geothermal power plants use primarily steam to generate electricity. This process is illustrated in **Figure 27**. In recent years, geothermal power plants that use primarily hot water instead of steam have become more common.

Geothermal energy can also be used as a direct source of heat. In this process, hot water and steam are used to heat a fluid that is pumped through a building in order to heat the building. Buildings in Iceland are heated in this way from the country's many geothermal sites.

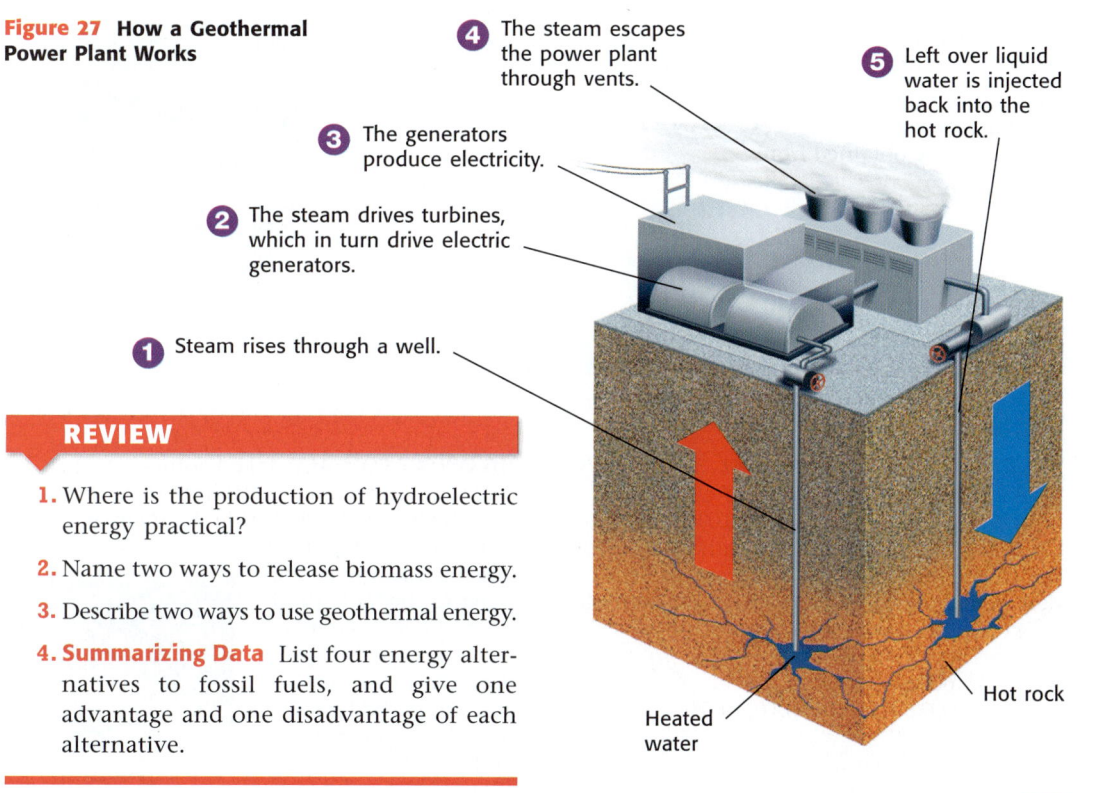

Figure 27 How a Geothermal Power Plant Works

1. Steam rises through a well.
2. The steam drives turbines, which in turn drive electric generators.
3. The generators produce electricity.
4. The steam escapes the power plant through vents.
5. Left over liquid water is injected back into the hot rock.

Heated water · Hot rock

REVIEW

1. Where is the production of hydroelectric energy practical?
2. Name two ways to release biomass energy.
3. Describe two ways to use geothermal energy.
4. **Summarizing Data** List four energy alternatives to fossil fuels, and give one advantage and one disadvantage of each alternative.

---

3) Extend

GOING FURTHER

Encourage students to find out more about an alternative energy source of their choice. Then challenge them to create an accurate model showing how the energy source is used and present it to the class.

4) Close

Quiz

1. Compare and contrast fission and fusion. (Both are nuclear reactions that generate vast amounts of energy. Fission, which is presently used to generate energy, is the splitting of an atomic nucleus. Fusion is the joining of atomic nuclei.)
2. How are plants used to produce energy? (Burning wood, crops, and alcohol made from plants are some ways plants are used to produce energy.)
3. Where in the United States is geothermal energy a good alternative? (California, Hawaii, and the Yellowstone National Park area)

ALTERNATIVE ASSESSMENT

Have students compile a table that lists each fuel mentioned in this chapter and compares the advantages and disadvantages of each. As an alternative, have students apply what they have learned in this chapter to compile a list of suggestions for making their home, school, or classroom less wasteful of natural resources.

▼ Answers to Review

1. Hydroelecticity is practical in areas where there are large volumes of moving water.
2. Answers may vary. Methods given in text are: burning biomass and converting plant material to alcohol that can be burned.
3. Steam and hot water heated by geothermal energy can be used to generate electricity. Steam and water heated by geothermal energy can also be used as a direct heat source.
4. Answers will vary. Any four of the six alternative energy resources featured in this section are acceptable, as are reasonable alternatives not mentioned in this section.

Section 3 • Alternative Resources

Chapter Highlights

Vocabulary Definitions

SECTION 1

natural resource any natural substance, organism, or energy form that living things use

renewable resource a natural resource that can be used and replaced over a relatively short time

nonrenewable resource a natural resource that cannot be replaced or that can be replaced only over thousands or millions of years

recycling the process by which used or discarded materials are treated for reuse

SECTION 2

energy resource a natural resource that humans use to produce energy

fossil fuel a nonrenewable energy resource that forms in the Earth's crust over millions of years from the buried remains of once-living organisms

petroleum an oily mixture of flammable organic compounds from which liquid fossil fuels and other products are separated; crude oil

natural gas a gaseous fossil fuel

coal a solid fossil fuel formed underground from buried, decomposed plant material

strip mining a process in which rock and soil are stripped from the Earth's surface to expose the underlying materials to be mined

acid precipitation precipitation that contains acids due to air pollution

smog a photochemical fog produced by the reaction of sunlight and air pollutants

Chapter Highlights

SECTION 1

Vocabulary
natural resource (p. 108)
renewable resource (p. 109)
nonrenewable resource (p. 109)
recycling (p. 110)

Section Notes
- Natural resources include everything that is not made by humans and that can be used by organisms.
- Renewable resources, like trees and water, can be replaced in a relatively short period of time.
- Nonrenewable resources cannot be replaced, or they take a very long time to replace.
- Recycling reduces the amount of natural resources that must be obtained from the Earth.

SECTION 2

Vocabulary
energy resource (p. 111)
fossil fuel (p. 111)
petroleum (p. 111)
natural gas (p. 112)
coal (p. 112)
strip mining (p. 115)
acid precipitation (p. 116)
smog (p. 117)

Section Notes
- Fossil fuels, including petroleum, natural gas, and coal, form from the buried remains of once-living organisms.
- Petroleum and natural gas form mainly from the remains of microscopic sea life.
- Coal forms from decayed swamp plants and varies in quality based on its percentage of carbon.
- Petroleum and natural gas are obtained through drilling, while coal is obtained through mining.
- Obtaining and using fossil fuels can cause many environmental problems, including acid precipitation, water pollution, and smog.

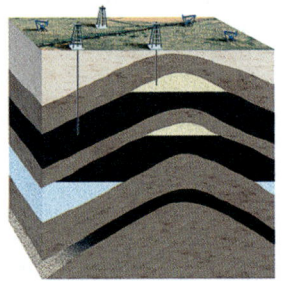

✓ Skills Check

Math Concepts

THE CARBON CONTENT OF COAL Turn back to page 114 to study the process of coal formation. Notice that at each stage, 10% more of the organic material becomes carbon. To calculate the percentage of carbon present at the next stage, just add 10%, or 0.10. For example:

peat → lignite
60% → 70%
0.60 + 0.10 = 0.70, or 70%

Visual Understanding

NO DIRECT CONTACT Take another look at Figure 21 on page 121. It is important to realize that the heated liquid inside the solar collector's tubes never comes in direct contact with the water in the tank. Cold water enters the tank, receives energy from the hot, coiled tube, and leaves the tank when someone turns on the hot-water tap.

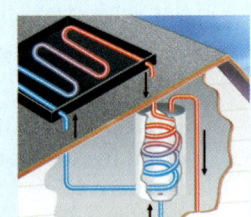

Lab and Activity Highlights

Make a Water Wheel `PG 648`

Power of the Sun `PG 650`

Datasheets for LabBook
(blackline masters for these labs)

126 Chapter 5 • Energy Resources

SECTION 3

Vocabulary
- nuclear energy (p. 118)
- solar energy (p. 119)
- wind energy (p. 122)
- hydroelectric energy (p. 123)
- biomass (p. 124)
- gasohol (p. 124)
- geothermal energy (p. 125)

Section Notes
- Nuclear energy is most often produced by fission.
- Radioactive wastes and the threat of overheating in nuclear power plants are among the major problems associated with using nuclear energy.
- Solar energy can be converted to electricity by using solar cells.
- Solar energy can be used for direct heating by using solar collectors.
- Solar energy can be converted to electricity on both a small and large scale.
- Although harnessing wind energy is practical only in certain areas, the process produces no air pollutants, and land on wind farms can be used for more than one purpose.
- Hydroelectric energy is inexpensive, renewable, and produces little pollution. However, hydroelectric dams can damage wildlife habitats, create erosion problems, and decrease water quality.
- Plant material and animal dung that contains plant material can be burned to release energy.
- Some plant material can be converted to alcohol. This alcohol can be mixed with gasoline to make a fuel mixture called gasohol.
- Geothermal energy can be harnessed from hot, liquid water and steam that escape through natural vents or through wells drilled into the Earth's crust. This energy can be used for direct heating or can be converted to electricity.

Labs
Make a Water Wheel (p. 648)
Power of the Sun (p. 650)

VOCABULARY DEFINITIONS, continued

SECTION 3

nuclear energy the form of energy associated with changes in the nucleus of an atom; an alternative energy resource

solar energy energy from the sun

wind energy energy in wind

hydroelectric energy electricity produced by falling water

biomass organic matter, such as plants, wood, and waste, that contains stored energy

gasohol a mixture of gasoline and alcohol that is burned as a fuel

geothermal energy energy from within the Earth

Vocabulary Review Worksheet 5

Blackline masters of these Chapter Highlights can be found in the **Study Guide**.

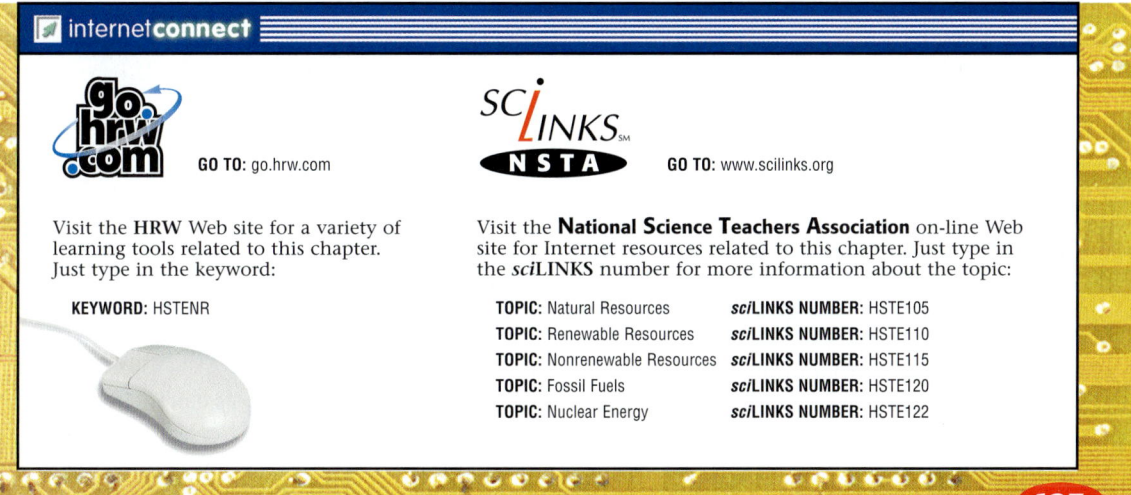

internet connect

GO TO: go.hrw.com

Visit the **HRW** Web site for a variety of learning tools related to this chapter. Just type in the keyword:

KEYWORD: HSTENR

GO TO: www.scilinks.org

Visit the **National Science Teachers Association** on-line Web site for Internet resources related to this chapter. Just type in the *sci*LINKS number for more information about the topic:

TOPIC	*sci*LINKS NUMBER
Natural Resources	HSTE105
Renewable Resources	HSTE110
Nonrenewable Resources	HSTE115
Fossil Fuels	HSTE120
Nuclear Energy	HSTE122

Lab and Activity Highlights

LabBank

Long-Term Projects & Research Ideas, Build a City–Save a World! Project 33

Interactive Explorations CD-ROM

CD 1, Exploration 6, "The Generation Gap"

Chapter Review

USING VOCABULARY

For each pair of terms, explain the difference in their meanings.

1. natural resource/energy resource
2. acid precipitation/smog
3. biomass/gasohol
4. hydroelectric energy/geothermal energy

UNDERSTANDING CONCEPTS

Multiple Choice

5. Of the following, the one that is a renewable resource is
   a. coal.
   b. trees.
   c. oil.
   d. natural gas.

6. All of the following are separated from petroleum except
   a. jet fuel.
   b. lignite.
   c. kerosene.
   d. fuel oil.

7. Which of the following is a component of natural gas?
   a. gasohol
   b. methane
   c. kerosene
   d. gasoline

8. Peat, lignite, and anthracite are all stages in the formation of
   a. petroleum.
   b. natural gas.
   c. coal.
   d. gasohol.

9. Which of the following factors contribute to smog problems?
   a. high numbers of automobiles
   b. lots of sunlight
   c. mountains surrounding urban areas
   d. all of the above

10. Which of the following resources produces the least pollution?
    a. solar energy
    b. natural gas
    c. nuclear energy
    d. petroleum

11. Nuclear power plants use a process called ___?___ to produce energy.
    a. fission
    b. fusion
    c. fractionation
    d. None of the above

12. A solar-powered calculator uses
    a. solar collectors.
    b. solar panels.
    c. solar mirrors.
    d. solar cells.

13. Which of the following is a problem with using wind energy?
    a. air pollution
    b. amount of land required for wind turbines
    c. limited locations for wind farms
    d. none of the above

14. Dung is a type of
    a. geothermal energy.
    b. gasohol.
    c. biomass.
    d. None of the above

Short Answer

15. Because renewable resources can be replaced, why do we need to conserve them?

16. How does acid precipitation form?

17. If sunlight is free, why is electricity from solar cells expensive?

128

Concept Mapping

18. Use the following terms to create a concept map: fossil fuels, wind energy, energy resources, biomass, renewable resources, solar energy, nonrenewable resources, natural gas, gasohol, coal, oil.

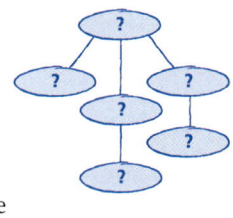

CRITICAL THINKING AND PROBLEM SOLVING

Write one or two sentences to answer the following questions:

19. How would your life be different if all fossil fuels suddenly disappeared?

20. Are fossil fuels really nonrenewable? Explain.

21. What solutions are there for the problems associated with nuclear waste?

22. How could the problems associated with the dams in Washington and local fish populations be solved?

23. What limits might there be on the productivity of a geothermal power plant?

MATH IN SCIENCE

24. Imagine that you are designing a solar car. If you mount solar cells on the underside of the car as well as on the top in direct sunlight, and it takes five times as many cells underneath to generate the same amount of electricity generated by the cells on top, what percentage of the sunlight is reflected back off the pavement?

INTERPRETING GRAPHICS

The chart below shows how various energy resources meet the world's energy needs. Use the chart to answer the following questions:

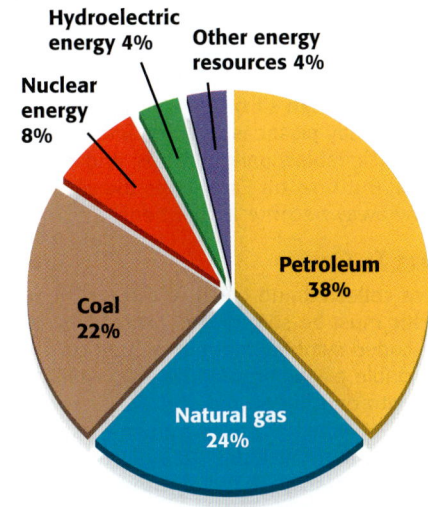

25. What percentage of the world's total energy needs is met by coal? by natural gas? by hydroelectric energy?

26. What percentage of the world's total energy needs is met by fossil fuels?

27. How much more of the world's total energy needs is met by petroleum than by natural gas?

 Take a minute to review your answers to the Pre-Reading Questions found at the bottom of page 106. Have your answers changed? If necessary, revise your answers based on what you have learned since you began this chapter.

Concept Mapping

18.  An answer to this exercise can be found at the end of this book.

CRITICAL THINKING AND PROBLEM SOLVING

19. Answers will vary. Answers should discuss using alternative energy resources.
20. Answers will vary. We label certain resources as nonrenewable because it takes a long time for them to be replenished. Fossil fuels (and many other nonrenewable resources) are renewable in the sense that they will probably be renewed in the future. But they cannot be renewed in time for us to count on them as energy resources.
21. Answers will vary. Answers may discuss storing nuclear waste in safe areas or minimizing or eliminating the use of nuclear energy to avoid producing more radioactive waste.
22. Answers will vary. Answers may discuss modifying the dams to allow fish populations to migrate, decreasing erosion, and improving water quality. Students may even suggest moving the dams to an area where migratory fish populations would not be affected. Encourage students to research these problems at a library or on the Internet.
23. Answers will vary. Students may discuss the amount of geothermal energy available or the number of vents the plant uses.

MATH IN SCIENCE

24. 20%

INTERPRETING GRAPHICS

25. 22%; 24%; 4%
26. 84%
27. 14%

 Concept Mapping Transparency 5

Blackline masters of this Chapter Review can be found in the **Study Guide.**

Chapter 5 • Chapter Review   129

EYE ON THE ENVIRONMENT

Sitting on Your Trash

Did you know that the average person creates about 2 kg of waste every day? About 7 percent of this waste is composed of plastic products that can be recycled. Instead of adding to the landfill problem, why not recycle your plastic trash so you can sit on it? Well you can, you know! Today plastic is recycled into products like picnic tables, park benches, and even highchairs! But how on Earth does the plastic you throw away become a park bench?

Sort It Out

Once collected and taken to a recycling center, plastic must be sorted. This process involves the coded symbols that are printed on every recyclable plastic product we use. Each product falls into one of two types of plastic—*polyethylene* or *polymer.* The plastic mainly used to make furniture includes the polyethylene plastics called *high density polyethylene,* or HDPE, and *low density polyethylene,* or LDPE. These are items such as milk jugs, detergent bottles, plastic bags, and grocery bags.

Grind It and Wash It

The recycling processes for HDPE and LDPE are fairly simple. Once it reaches the processing facility, HDPE plastic is ground into small flakes about 1 cm in diameter. In the case of LDPE plastic, which are thin films, a special grinder is used to break it down. From that point on, the recycling process is pretty much the same for LDPE and HDPE. The pieces are then washed with hot water and detergent. In this step, dirt and things like labels are removed. After the wash, the flakes are dried with blasts of hot air.

Recycle It!

Some recycling plants sell the recycled flakes. But others may reheat the flakes, change the color by adding a pigment, and then put the material in a *pelletizer.* The little pellets that result are then purchased by a company that molds the pellets into pieces of plastic lumber. This plastic lumber is used to create flowerpots, trash cans, pipes, picnic tables, park benches, toys, mats, and many other products!

From waste...

to plastic lumber...

to a park bench!

Can You Recycle It?

▶ The coded symbol on a plastic container tells you what type of plastic the item is made from, but it doesn't mean that you can recycle it in your area. Find out which plastics can be recycled in your state.

130

Answer to Can You Recycle It?
Answers will vary.

Eureka!
Oil Rush!

You may have heard of the great California gold rush. In 1849, thousands of people moved to the West hoping to strike gold. But you may not have heard about another rush that followed 10 years later. What lured people to northwestern Pennsylvania in 1859? The thrill of striking oil!

Demand for Petroleum
People began using oil as early as 3000 B.C., and oil has been a valuable substance ever since. In Mesopotamia, people used oil to waterproof their ships. The Egyptians and Chinese used oil as a medicine. It was not until the late 1700s and early 1800s that people began to use oil as a fuel. Oil was used to light homes and factories.

Petroleum Collection
But what about the oil in northwestern Pennsylvania? Did people use the oil in Pennsylvania before the rush of 1859? Native Americans were the first to dig pits to collect oil near Titusville, Pennsylvania. Early settlers used the oil as a medicine and as a fuel to light their homes. But their methods for collecting the oil were very inefficient.

The First Oil Well
In 1859, "Colonel" Edwin L. Drake came up with a better method of collecting oil from the ground. Drilling for oil! Drake hired salt-well drillers to burrow to the bedrock where oil deposits lay. But each effort was unsuccessful because water seeped into the wells, causing them to cave in. Then Drake came up with a unique idea that would make him a very wealthy man. Drake suggested that the drillers drive an iron pipe down to the bedrock 21.2 m below the surface. Then they could drill through the inner diameter of the pipe. The morning after the iron pipe was drilled, Drake woke to find that the pipe had filled with oil!

Oil City
Within 3 months, nearly 10,000 people rushed to Oil City, Pennsylvania, in search of the wealth that oil promised. Within 2 years, the small village became a bustling oil town of 50,000 people! In 1861, the first gusher well was drilled nearby, and some 3,000 barrels of oil spouted out daily. Four years later, the first oil pipeline carried crude oil a distance of 8 km.

▲ *Edwin Drake (right) and his friend Peter Wilson (left) in front of Drake Oil Well, near Titusville, Pennsylvania*

Find Out for Yourself!
▶ Drake's oil well was the first well used to collect oil from the ground. Research the oil wells today. How are they similar to Drake's well?

Answer to Find Out for Yourself!
Today's oil wells are somewhat similar to Drake's oil well in that they also use a metal pipe. First a hole, or *well bore,* is drilled into the ground. The equivalent of Drake's metal pipe is a metal casing that is inserted into the well bore. Cement is pumped into the hole and fills the narrow space between the well bore and the casing. Once the cement dries, the casing is bonded to the well bore and prevents the contamination of oil, gas, and water resources that otherwise might flow through the oil well.

Eureka!
Oil Rush!

Background
Until 1880, people in the United States relied on vegetable and animal oils to light their homes. The production of oil products from these sources was time intensive and costly. Whales, in particular, became rare because they were hunted for their oils during the nineteenth century.

Drake's well ushered in the modern era of the petroleum industry. His drilling methods allowed oil to be collected quickly and inexpensively. By 1900, nearly 64 million barrels of oil had been collected in the United States. Many of Drake's original techniques have been adapted and are still being used today.

In 1896, the first offshore oil drilling operations were started off the coast of California. The operations opened new and potentially lucrative opportunities to oil speculators. By 1938, the first oil platform had been built off the Louisiana coast.

Some experts wonder whether we will face an oil shortage in the near future. Fewer and fewer oil reserves are being discovered. Some people wonder if the recently discovered oil deposits in the Caspian Sea may be the site of the last great oil rush.

Encourage students to consider alternative sources of energy. For example, they may want to investigate the use of solar energy to power cars and heat homes.

Chapter Organizer

CHAPTER ORGANIZATION	TIME MINUTES	OBJECTIVES	LABS, INVESTIGATIONS, AND DEMONSTRATIONS
Chapter Opener pp. 132–133	45	National Standards: SAI 1, HNS 1, 2, ES 2b	**Start-Up Activity** Making Fossils, p. 133
Section 1 Earth's Story and Those Who First Listened	45	▶ Identify the role of uniformitarianism in Earth science. ▶ Contrast uniformitarianism with catastrophism. ▶ Describe how the role of catastrophism in Earth science has changed. UCP 2, 4, SAI 1, HNS 1–3, ES 2a	**Inquiry Labs,** A Penny for Your Thoughts, Lab 10 GENERAL
Section 2 Relative Dating: Which Came First?	90	▶ Explain how relative dating is used in geology. ▶ Explain the principle of superposition. ▶ Demonstrate an understanding of the geologic column. ▶ Identify two events and two features that disrupt rock sequences. ▶ Explain how physical features are used to determine relative ages. UCP 1–4, SAI 1, 2, ES 2b; LabBook UCP 1, 2, SAI 1	**Demonstration,** p. 137 in ATE GENERAL **Discovery Lab,** How DO You Stack Up? p. 652 ADVANCED **Datasheets for LabBook,** How DO You Stack Up? Datasheet 12 ADVANCED **Labs You Can Eat,** Geopancakes, Lab 12 BASIC
Section 3 Absolute Dating: A Measure of Time	90	▶ Explain how radioactive decay occurs. ▶ Explain how radioactive decay relates to radiometric dating. ▶ List three types of radiometric dating. ▶ Determine the best type of radiometric dating to use to date an object. UCP 1, 3, SAI 1	**Long-Term Projects and Research Ideas,** Project 34 ADVANCED
Section 4 Looking at Fossils	90	▶ Describe how different types of fossils are formed. ▶ List the types of fossils that are not part of organisms. ▶ Demonstrate how fossils can be used to determine changes in environments and in the organisms the fossils came from. ▶ Describe index fossils, and explain how they are used. UCP 3, ST 2, SPSP 5, ES 1k, ES 2b	
Section 5 Time Marches On	90	▶ Demonstrate an understanding of the geologic time scale. ▶ Identify important dates on the geologic time scale. ▶ Identify the eon we know the most about, and explain why we know more about it than other eons. UCP 1–4, SAI 1, ES 2b	**EcoLabs And Field Activities,** Rock of Ages, Field Activity 10 ADVANCED **QuickLab,** Make a Time Scale, p. 155 GENERAL

See page **T20** for a complete correlation of this book with the

NATIONAL SCIENCE EDUCATION STANDARDS.

TECHNOLOGY RESOURCES

 Guided Reading Audio CD English or Spanish, Chapter 6

 One-Stop Planner CD-ROM with Test Generator

 CNN. Scientists in Action, Dinosaur Egg Discovery, Segment 9, Creating Digital Dinos, Segment 12

Multicultural Connections, A Thailand Fossil Discovery, Segment 4 Protecting New Mexico's Petroglyphs, Segment 6

Chapter 6 • The Rock and Fossil Record

CLASSROOM WORKSHEETS, TRANSPARENCIES, AND RESOURCES	SCIENCE INTEGRATION AND CONNECTIONS	REVIEW AND ASSESSMENT
Directed Reading Worksheet 6 BASIC **Science Puzzlers, Twisters & Teasers,** Worksheet 6 ADVANCED	**Career: Paleontologist,** p. 161 GENERAL	
Directed Reading Worksheet 6, Section 1 BASIC **Transparency 118,** Hutton and the Principle of Uniformitarianism	**Multicultural Connection,** p. 134 in ATE **Biology Connection,** p. 135 **Apply,** p. 135 GENERAL **Cross-Disciplinary Focus,** p. 136 in ATE GENERAL	**Review,** p. 136 GENERAL **Quiz,** p. 136 in ATE GENERAL **Alternative Assessment,** p. 136 in ATE GENERAL
Directed Reading Worksheet 6, Section 2 BASIC **Transparency 119,** Constructing the Geologic Column **Transparency 120,** Formation of Unconformities **Reinforcement Worksheet 6,** A Geologic Column Sandwich GENERAL	**Real-World Connection,** p. 140 in ATE	**Homework,** p. 140 in ATE GENERAL **Review,** p. 141 GENERAL **Quiz,** p. 141 in ATE GENERAL **Alternative Assessment,** p. 141 in ATE GENERAL
Directed Reading Worksheet 6, Section 3 BASIC **Transparency 263,** Radioactive Decay and Half-life	**MathBreak, Get a Half-Life!** p. 143 GENERAL **Math and More,** p. 143 in ATE GENERAL **Connect to Physical Science,** p. 143 in ATE **Cross-Disciplinary Focus,** p. 144 in ATE ADVANCED **Connect to Life Science,** p. 145 in ATE	**Review,** p. 145 GENERAL **Quiz,** p. 145 in ATE GENERAL **Alternative Assessment,** p. 145 in ATE GENERAL
Directed Reading Worksheet 6, Section 4 BASIC **Critical Thinking Worksheet 6,** Adiós Alamosaurus ADVANCED	**Science, Technology, and Society:** CAT Scanning Fossils, p. 160 GENERAL	**Self-Check,** p. 148 **Homework,** p. 150 in ATE GENERAL **Review,** p. 150 GENERAL **Quiz,** p. 150 in ATE GENERAL **Alternative Assessment,** p. 150 in ATE ADVANCED
Directed Reading Worksheet 6, Section 5 BASIC **Transparency 121,** The Geologic Time Scale	**Biology Connection,** p. 151 **Connect to Life Science,** p. 152 in ATE **Math and More,** p. 153 in ATE GENERAL **Cross-Disciplinary Focus,** p. 153 in ATE	**Homework,** pp. 152, 154 in ATE ADVANCED **Review,** p. 155 GENERAL **Quiz,** p. 155 in ATE GENERAL **Alternative Assessment,** p. 155 in ATE GENERAL

internetconnect

 **Holt, Rinehart and Winston On-line Resources**
go.hrw.com
For worksheets and other teaching aids related to this chapter, visit the HRW Web site and type in the keyword: **HSTFOS**

 **National Science Teachers Association**
www.scilinks.org
Encourage students to use the *sci*LINKS numbers listed in the internet connect boxes to access information and resources on the **NSTA** Web site.

END-OF-CHAPTER REVIEW AND ASSESSMENT

Chapter Review in Study Guide
Vocabulary and Notes in Study Guide
Chapter Tests with Performance-Based Assessment, Chapter 6 Test, Performance-Based Assessment 6
Concept Mapping Transparency 6

Chapter 6 • Chapter Organizer **131B**

Chapter Resources & Worksheets

Visual Resources

TEACHING TRANSPARENCIES

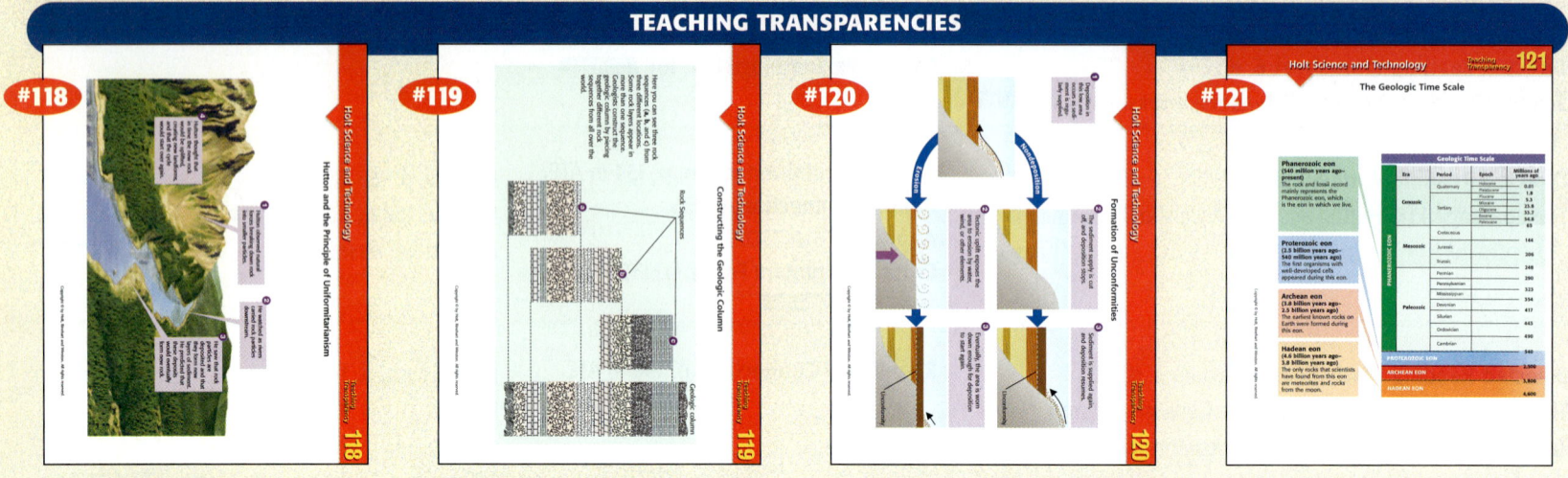

#118 Hutton and the Principle of Uniformitarianism
#119 Constructing the Geologic Column
#120 Formation of Unconformities
#121 The Geologic Time Scale

TEACHING TRANSPARENCIES

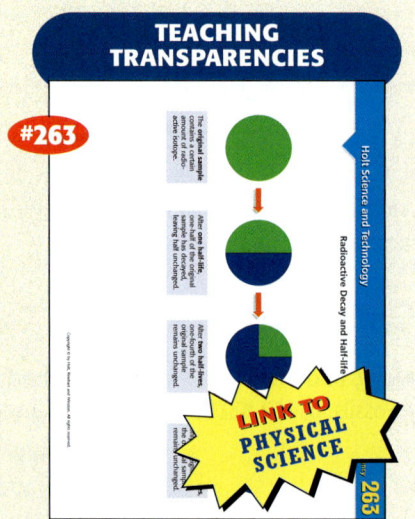

#263 Radioactive Decay and Half-life — LINK TO PHYSICAL SCIENCE

CONCEPT MAPPING TRANSPARENCY

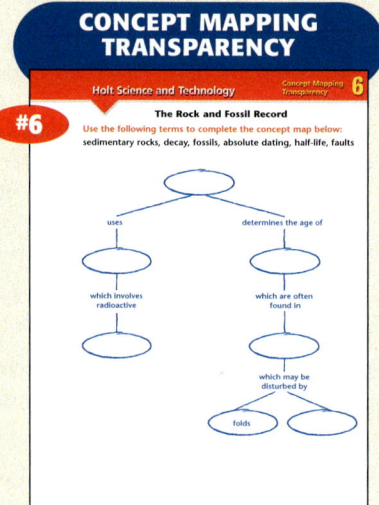

#6 The Rock and Fossil Record

Meeting Individual Needs

DIRECTED READING

#6 The Rock and Fossil Record

REINFORCEMENT & VOCABULARY REVIEW

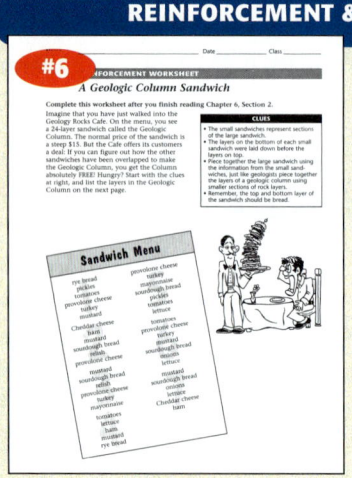

#6 A Geologic Column Sandwich
#6 Vocabulary Unconformity

SCIENCE PUZZLERS, TWISTERS & TEASERS

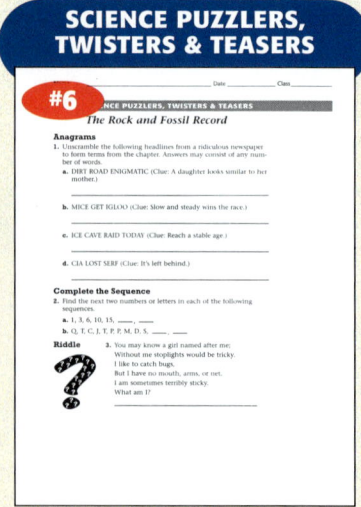

#6 The Rock and Fossil Record

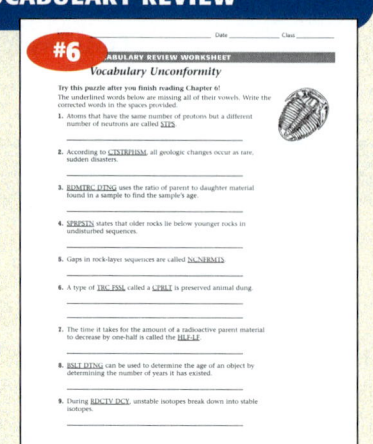

131C Chapter 6 • The Rock and Fossil Record

Chapter 6 • The Rock and Fossil Record

Review & Assessment

STUDY GUIDE
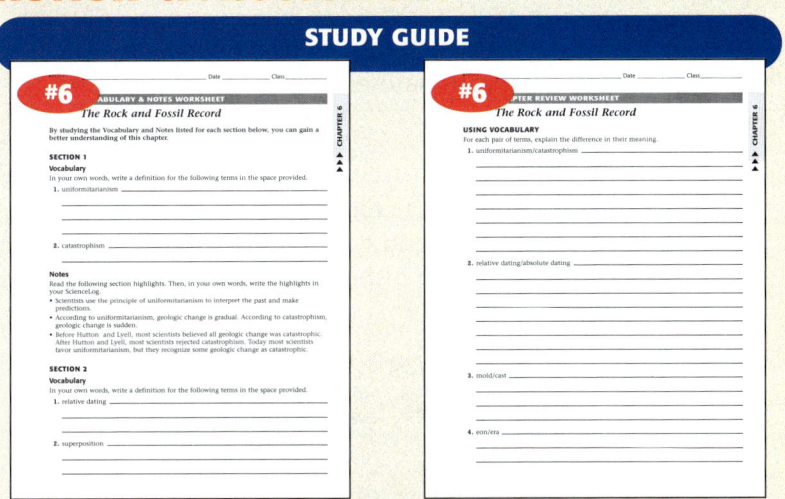

CHAPTER TESTS WITH PERFORMANCE-BASED ASSESSMENT
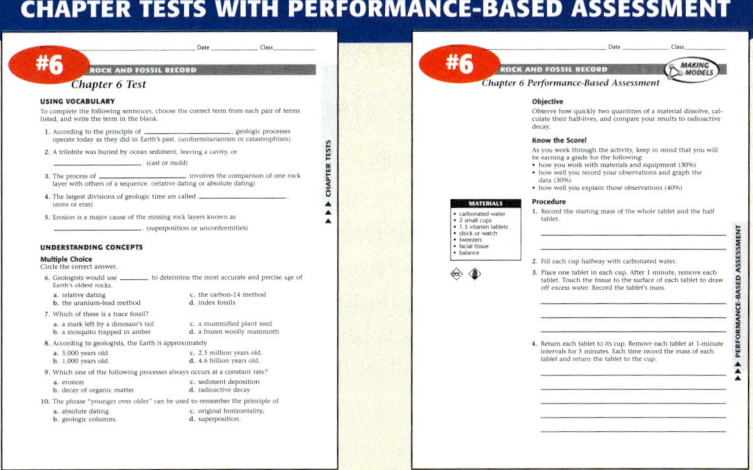

Lab Worksheets

INQUIRY LABS
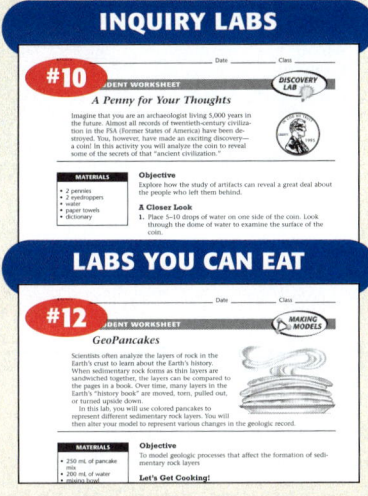

ECOLABS & FIELD ACTIVITIES
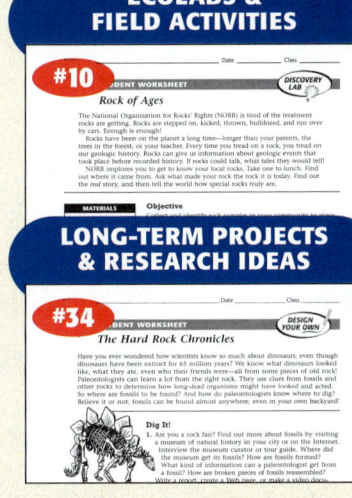

DATASHEETS FOR LABBOOK
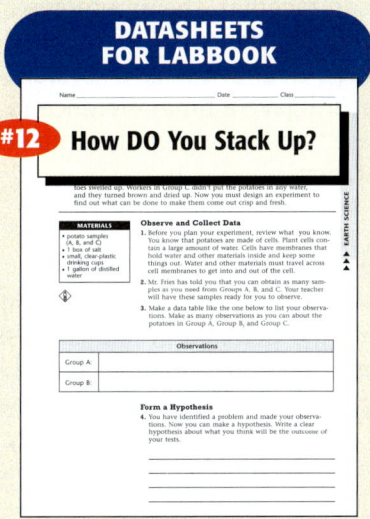

LABS YOU CAN EAT
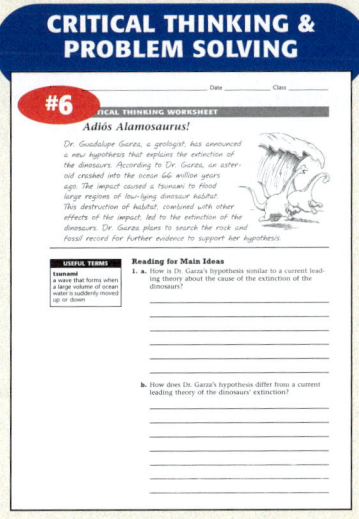

LONG-TERM PROJECTS & RESEARCH IDEAS
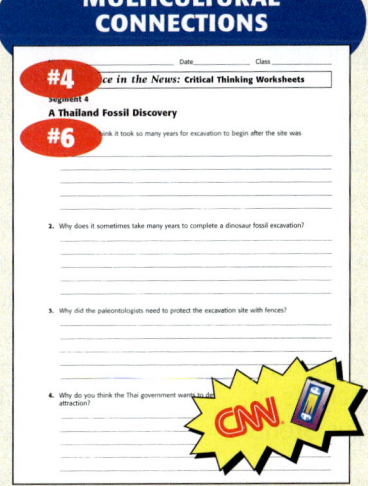

Applications & Extensions

CRITICAL THINKING & PROBLEM SOLVING

MULTICULTURAL CONNECTIONS
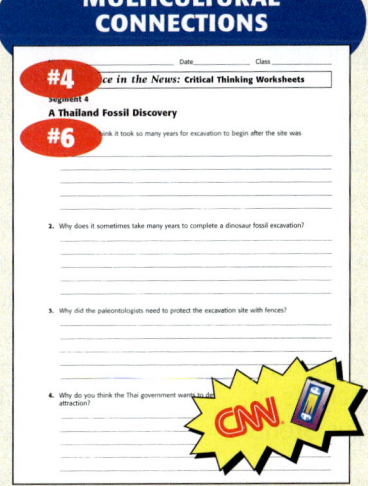

SCIENTISTS IN ACTION
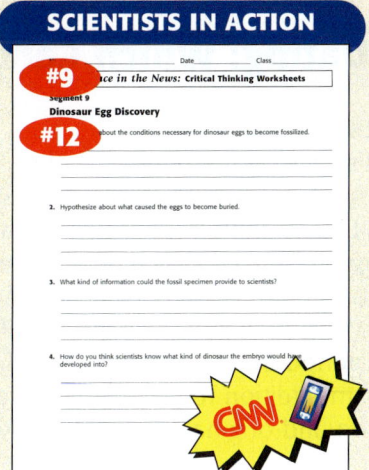

Chapter 6 • Chapter Resources & Worksheets

Chapter Background

SECTION 1

Earth's Story and Those Who First Listened

▶ **Baron Georges Cuvier**
Baron Georges Cuvier, a French naturalist and pioneer in comparative anatomy, was the leading proponent of catastrophism. He used his skills as an anatomist to figure out what extinct animals looked like from just a few fossil bones.

▶ **Evolution and Uniformitarianism**
The development of geology and the theory of evolution are closely tied together. The arguments of both fields lent support and evidence for each other. The fossil record provided clear evidence of evolution, and the biological record gave a time reference to geology. The union of these two fields gave rise to paleontology and historical geology.

▶ **Actualism**
Although James Hutton was the first to introduce the principles of uniformitarianism, he is considered an actualist, not a strict uniformitarianist. He recognized that while many geologic processes happen slowly, some occur more abruptly. Contemporary geologists accept actualism as a more logical explanation of Earth's history.

SECTION 2

Relative Dating: Which Came First?

▶ **Nicolaus Steno**
Credit for discovering the principles of superposition and original horizontality is given to Niels Stensen (also known as Nicolaus Steno), born in Denmark on January 10, 1638. Though originally trained in anatomy and medicine, Steno became interested in geology while serving as the house physician to Grand Duke Ferdinand II of Tuscany. It was during this period that Steno made significant geologic discoveries. In addition to establishing the principles of superposition and original horizontality, Nicolaus Steno was one of the first Western scientists to argue that fossils were organic in nature.

IS THAT A FACT!

🔺 Despite his numerous contributions to medicine and geology, Nicolaus Steno gave up his scientific career in 1677 to become a bishop. He died 9 years later on December 6, 1686.

SECTION 3

Absolute Dating: A Measure of Time

▶ **Marie and Pierre Curie**
The Curies met in spring 1894 while Marie was studying mathematics and physics at the Sorbonne, in Paris. They married in 1895 and worked together in Pierre's laboratory. Marie began work on her doctoral thesis shortly after 1896, the year Henri Becquerel discovered that a strange radiation was emitted by uranium. Marie continued Becquerel's work, obtained her doctorate on radioactive substances in 1903, and won the Nobel Prize for physics with her husband and Becquerel.

• In 1906, Pierre was killed in a wagon accident in Paris. Marie, grief-stricken, dedicated the rest of her life to the work she and her husband had begun. She headed his laboratory at the Sorbonne and became the first woman lecturer at the university. In 1911, Marie Curie received her second Nobel Prize, this time in chemistry for isolating pure radium. She died on July 4, 1934, of leukemia, no doubt caused by her prolonged exposure to radiation.

131E Chapter 6 • The Rock and Fossil Record

Chapter 6 • The Rock and Fossil Record

▶ **Radiometric Age-Dating**
The work of Becquerel and the Curies eventually changed the fields of archaelogy, geology, and paleontology. Before their work, geologists were restricted to using relative methods of dating when trying to determine the age of rocks and minerals. However, after it was discovered that radioactive elements decay at a constant rate, the American chemist Willard Libby developed radiocarbon dating in the late 1940s.

▶ **Clock Numerals and Cancer**
The carcinogenic effects of radium were discovered by accident in the 1930s. A paste of radium salts and zinc sulfide was used to paint numbers on watch faces to make them glow. Radium was discontinued after it was discovered that many of the radium painters developed mouth and throat cancer. To form a precise brush point, the painters, mostly women, used their mouth to moisten the brush tip between strokes. The element promethium, which emits less-hazardous radiation, soon replaced radium.

SECTION 4
Looking at Fossils

▶ **Prehistoric Weevil DNA**
In 1993, research in the field of fossil DNA took a tremendous leap forward when Dr. George Poinar, of the University of California at Berkeley, successfully extracted fragmented DNA from the tissue of a 125-million-year-old weevil encased in amber found in Lebanon. The weevil was so well preserved in the amber that even its muscle tissue was intact.

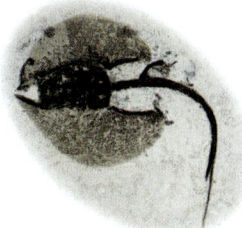

▶ **Coelacanths: Living Fossils**
Coelacanths are large, carnivorous, lobe-finned fish. Their fossil record dates back to over 350 million years ago and, until recently, they were believed to have become extinct about 65 million years ago. In 1938, Marjorie Courtenay-Latimer, a museum curator in a small port village near Cape Town, South Africa, noticed an unusual blue-finned fish among the day's catch at the local docks—it was a coelacanth! A second coelacanth was recovered in 1952 by anglers, again off the African coast. It is believed that only a few hundred of the fish still survive and, in 1995, researchers declared the animal in danger of extinction.

- In 1998, Dr. Mark Erdmann confirmed at least two coelacanth specimens from North Sulawesi, Indonesia, 10,000 km from the African coast. The coelacanths were discovered living in volcanic caves below sea level. It is hoped that coelacanths live in many of the unexplored sea caves of the Indonesian archipelago.

IS THAT A FACT!

▶ The largest coprolite ever found is a 65-million-year-old mound of feces probably left by a *Tyrannosaurus rex.* It is 43 cm across and 15 cm high.

SECTION 5
Time Marches On

▶ **Life in the Precambrian Era**
The period of time spanning from the formation of Earth 4.6 billion years ago to 540 million years ago is called the Precambrian era. It encompasses more than 80 percent of the geologic time scale. Until the discovery of soft-bodied organisms in Australia in 1947, paleontologists believed that only single-celled microorganisms and blue-green algae lived during this period. Now scientists know that a wide variety of animals resembling jellyfish, annelids, and even echinoderms evolved in Precambrian seas between 590 and 700 million years ago. These are so far the oldest known multicellular organisms.

For background information about teaching strategies and issues, refer to the *Professional Reference for Teachers.*

CHAPTER 6

The Rock and Fossil Record

 Pre-Reading Questions

Students may not know the answers to these questions before reading the chapter, so accept any reasonable response.

Suggested Answers

1. Students might mention both absolute and relative dating methods.
2. No; trace fossils are preserved evidence of animal activity and do not contain any animal parts.
3. Answers will vary. Students should note that scientists analyze the rock and fossil record and observe processes occurring today in order to form theories about the Earth's history.

 Directed Reading Worksheet 6

 Science Puzzlers, Twisters & Teasers Worksheet 6

 Guided Reading Audio CD English or Spanish, Chapter 6

CHAPTER 6

The Rock and Fossil Record

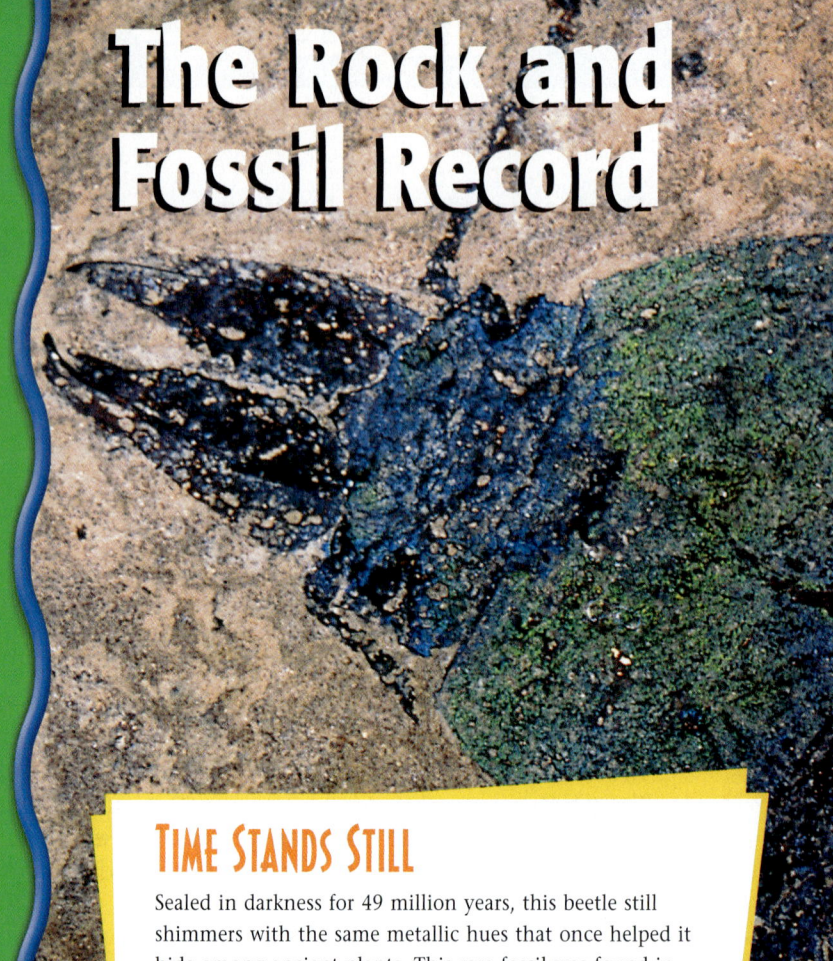

Sections

1. Earth's Story and Those Who First Listened 134
   - Apply 135
   - Biology Connection .. 135
   - Internet Connect 136
2. Relative Dating: Which Came First? 137
3. Absolute Dating: A Measure of Time ... 142
   - MathBreak 143
   - Internet Connect 145
4. Looking at Fossils 146
   - Internet Connect 150
5. Time Marches On 151
   - Biology Connection .. 151
   - QuickLab 155
   - Internet Connect 155

Chapter Review 158
Feature Articles 160, 161
LabBook 652–655

 **Pre-Reading Questions**

1. How can you determine if some rocks and fossils are older than others?
2. Are fossils always made up of parts of plants or animals?
3. How do scientists study the Earth's history?

TIME STANDS STILL

Sealed in darkness for 49 million years, this beetle still shimmers with the same metallic hues that once helped it hide among ancient plants. This rare fossil was found in Messel, Germany. In the same rock formation, scientists have found fossilized crocodiles, bats, birds, and frogs. A living stag beetle *(below)* has a similar form and color. Do you think that these two beetles would live in similar environments? What do you think Messel, Germany, was like 49 million years ago? In this chapter, you will learn how scientists answer questions like these.

---

internetconnect

 **HRW On-line Resources**
go.hrw.com
For worksheets and other teaching aids, visit the HRW Web site and type in the keyword: **HSTFOS**

 **www.scilinks.com**
Use the *sci*LINKS numbers at the end of each chapter for additional resources on the **NSTA** Web site.

www.cnnfyi.com
Visit the CNN Web site for current events coverage and classroom resources.

START-UP Activity

MAKING FOSSILS

How do scientists learn from fossils? In this activity, you will study "fossils" and identify the object that made each.

Procedure

1. You and three or four of your classmates will be given several pieces of **modeling clay** and a paper sack containing a few **small objects.**
2. Press each object firmly into a piece of clay. Try to leave a fossil imprint showing as much detail as possible.
3. After you have made an imprint of each object, exchange your model fossils with another group.
4. In your ScienceLog, describe the fossils you have received. List as many details as possible. What patterns and textures do you observe?
5. Work as a group to identify each fossil and check your results. Were you right?

Analysis

6. What kinds of details were important in identifying your fossils? What kinds of details were not preserved in the imprints? For example, can you tell the color of the objects?
7. Explain how Earth scientists follow similar methods when studying fossils.

START-UP Activity

MAKING FOSSILS

MATERIALS

FOR EACH GROUP:
- several pieces of modeling clay
- a paper sack containing several small objects, such as coins, paper clips, buttons, army men, or any other objects with recognizable textures or shapes.

Answers to START-UP Activity

6. Sample answer: Textures and distinctive shapes were useful in identifying the model fossils. Small details, colors, and the internal structures of the objects were not preserved.

7. Sample answer: Earth scientists carefully observe fossil remains to determine what organism left them.

SECTION 1

Focus

Earth's Story and Those Who First Listened

In this section, students explore the beginnings of modern geology by comparing and contrasting uniformitarianism and catastrophism—two early theories regarding geologic processes. Students learn that the forces that shaped the Earth around them are still at work today and that modern geology is a synthesis of both theories.

🔔 Bellringer

On the board write "The Present is the Key to the Past." Tell students that this phrase was the cornerstone of the uniformitarianist theory developed by geologist James Hutton in the late 1700s. Have students write a few sentences about how studying the present could reveal the story of Earth's history. Have students illustrate their comments with a few sketches of processes they can see today that also occurred millions of years ago.

1 Motivate

ACTIVITY

 Have students design a poster announcing an upcoming debate between a catastrophist and a uniformitarian. Encourage students to use attention-catching phrases and illustrations that would attract supporters from both sides. Have them summarize the major points of both sides, and display the finished posters in the classroom. **Sheltered English**

Section 1

Terms to Learn
uniformitarianism
catastrophism

What You'll Do
- Identify the role of uniformitarianism in Earth science.
- Contrast uniformitarianism with catastrophism.
- Describe how the role of catastrophism in Earth science has changed.

Earth's Story and Those Who First Listened

Humans have wondered about Earth's history for thousands of years. But the branch of Earth science called *geology,* which involves the study of Earth's history, got a late start. The main concept of modern geology was not outlined until the late eighteenth century. Within a few decades, this concept replaced a more traditional concept of Earth's history. Today, both concepts are an essential part of Earth science.

The Principle of Uniformitarianism

In 1795, a philosopher and scientist named James Hutton published *Theory of the Earth*, in which he wrote that Earth's landforms are constantly changing. As shown in **Figure 1,** Hutton assumed that these changes result from geologic processes—such as the breakdown of rock and the transport of sediment—that remain uniform, or do not change, over time. This assumption is now called uniformitarianism. **Uniformitarianism** is a principle that states that the same geologic processes shaping the Earth today have been at work throughout Earth's history. "The present is the key to the past" is a phrase that best summarizes uniformitarianism.

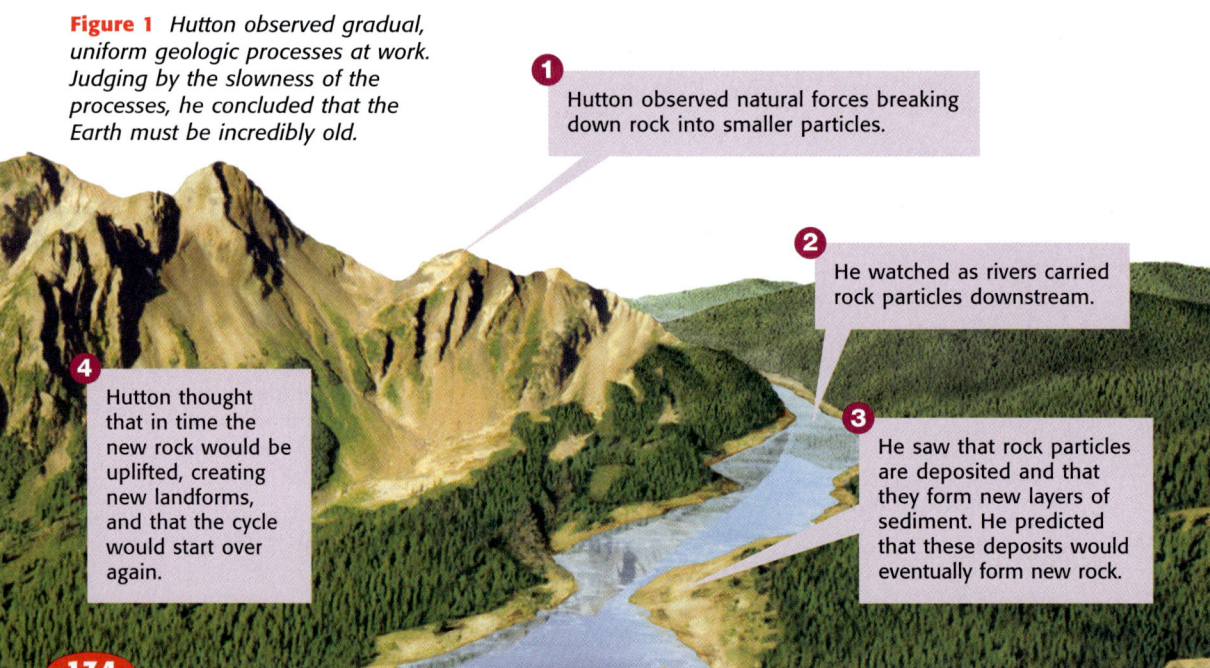

Figure 1 Hutton observed gradual, uniform geologic processes at work. Judging by the slowness of the processes, he concluded that the Earth must be incredibly old.

① Hutton observed natural forces breaking down rock into smaller particles.

② He watched as rivers carried rock particles downstream.

③ He saw that rock particles are deposited and that they form new layers of sediment. He predicted that these deposits would eventually form new rock.

④ Hutton thought that in time the new rock would be uplifted, creating new landforms, and that the cycle would start over again.

🌎 Multicultural CONNECTION

Many of the ideas that form the basis of modern geology came from Scottish scientists. Among the famous Scottish geologists are James Hutton, Charles Lyell, Sir James Hall, Roderick Murchison, and John Playfair. Have students research these or other Scottish geologists to discover the contributions they made to modern geology.

IS THAT A FACT!

James Hutton's colleague, Sir James Hall, dramatically demonstrated Hutton's theories by melting rock in a furnace and letting it cool, showing how it changed from one form to another. This demonstration struck a major blow against the catastrophists.

134 Chapter 6 • The Rock and Fossil Record

Making Assumptions

Examine the photographs at right. List the letters of the photos in the order you think the photos were taken. Now think of all the assumptions that you made to infer that order. Write down as many of these assumptions as you can. Compare notes with your classmates. Did you get the same sequence? Were your assumptions similar?

In science, assumptions must also be made. For example, you assume that the sun will rise each day. Briefly explain the importance of being able to count on certain things always being the same. How does this apply to uniformitarianism?

Uniformitarianism Versus Catastrophism In Hutton's time most people thought that the Earth had existed for only thousands of years. This was not nearly enough time for the gradual geologic processes that Hutton described to have shaped our planet. But uniformitarianism was not immediately accepted. Instead, most scientists believed in catastrophism. **Catastrophism** is a principle that states that all geologic change occurs suddenly. Supporters of catastrophism claimed that the formation of all Earth's features, such as its mountains, canyons, and seas, could be explained by rare, sudden events called *catastrophes*. These unpredictable catastrophes caused rapid geologic changes over large areas—sometimes even globally.

Uniformitarianism Wins! Despite Hutton's observations, catastrophism remained geology's guiding principle for decades. It took the work of Charles Lyell, another scientist, for people to seriously consider uniformitarianism.

From 1830 to 1833, Lyell published three volumes collectively titled *Principles of Geology*, in which he reintroduced uniformitarianism. Armed with Hutton's notes and new evidence of his own, Lyell successfully challenged the principle of catastrophism. Lyell saw no reason to doubt that major geologic change happened the same way in the past as it does in the present—gradually.

Biology CONNECTION

As a friend of Charles Lyell, Charles Darwin was greatly influenced by Lyell's uniformitarian ideas. Lyell's influence became clear when Darwin published *On the Origin of Species by Natural Selection* in 1859. Similar to uniformitarianism, Darwin's theory of evolution proposes that changes in species occur gradually over long periods of time.

2 Teach

Answers to APPLY
Answers will vary. Accept all reasonable responses.

REAL-WORLD CONNECTION

Use the following example to discuss uniformitarianism and catastrophism. Tell students to suppose they have a cousin. They see their cousin when she is born, again when she is 3 years old and again when she is 7 and 14. Students will notice a dramatic difference each time they see her. Ask students why they know those changes took place gradually instead of suddenly.

Sheltered English

DEBATE

Uniformitarianism Vs. Catastrophism Ask students to engage in a debate that might have taken place between James Hutton and the catastrophists. Emphasize to students representing the catastrophists that their argument had a strong theological base and was the accepted geologic theory of the time. Help students imagine the opposition James Hutton must have faced when he introduced his ideas. Students can advertise their debates with the posters they made in the Motivate activity.

TOPIC: Earth's Story
GO TO: www.scilinks.org
*sci*LINKS NUMBER: HSTE130

When Mr. Hutton studied Earth's tiers,
He proposed what was rejected for years:
That to form rocks of lime,
It takes EONS of time,
Not an evening, as proposed by his peers.

 Directed Reading Worksheet 6 Section 1

 Teaching Transparency 118 "Hutton and the Principle of Uniformitarianism"

Section 1 • Earth's Story and Those Who First Listened

3 Close

CROSS-DISCIPLINARY FOCUS

Language Arts Although Charles Darwin and Charles Lyell were avid correspondents and good friends, they did not agree on everything. Darwin was quick to accept the principle of uniformitarianism (he read Lyell's *Principles of Geology* before his famous 1831 HMS *Beagle* voyage), but Lyell did not readily embrace Darwin's theories of natural selection. It was not until much later in life that Charles Lyell became a vigorous supporter of Darwin's ideas. Invite students to write a script for a conversation that the two scientists might have had. Have them imagine that Darwin has just returned from his *Beagle* journey. What questions might Darwin and Lyell have exchanged? Students can present the conversations as short skits.

Quiz

1. What is catastrophism?
   (the idea that geologic change occured suddenly as a result of infrequent disastrous events)
2. Describe uniformitarianism.
   (the view that the Earth is shaped by gradual changes that are still occurring today)

ALTERNATIVE ASSESSMENT

Writing Have students write a letter to Charles Lyell or James Hutton. The letter should explain why the student agrees or disagrees with the scientist's theories. Suggest that students end the letter with at least two questions that they would like to ask the scientist. Have students exchange letters and answer each other's questions.

BRAIN FOOD
Did you know that the first dinosaur bones were not identified until 1841? Hutton and Lyell developed their ideas without knowledge of these giants of prehistory.

Modern Geology—A Happy Medium

Today scientists realize that neither uniformitarianism nor catastrophism accounts for all of Earth's history. Although most geologic change is gradual and uniform, catastrophes do occur occasionally. For example, huge craters have been found where asteroids and comets are thought to have struck Earth in the past. Some of these strikes indeed may have been catastrophic. Some scientists think one such asteroid strike led to the extinction of the dinosaurs, as explained in **Figure 2**. The impact of an asteroid is thought to have spread debris into the atmosphere around the entire planet, blocking the sun's rays and causing major changes in the global climate.

Figure 2 Today scientists think that sudden events are responsible for some changes in Earth's past. An asteroid hitting Earth, for example, may have led to the extinction of the dinosaurs 65 million years ago.

internetconnect
SCLINKS NSTA
TOPIC: Earth's Story
GO TO: www.scilinks.org
sciLINKS NUMBER: HSTE130

REVIEW

1. Why do Earth scientists need the principle of uniformitarianism in order to make predictions?
2. What is the difference between uniformitarianism and catastrophism?
3. **Summarizing Data** How has the role of catastrophism in Earth science changed?

Answers to Review

1. Scientists make predictions based on the past as well as the present. To make predictions, they must assume that geologic processes will be similar in the future.
2. Catastrophism states that the geologic history of the Earth was dominated by sudden, drastic changes that built features such as mountains, valleys, and oceans. Uniformitarianism argues that the Earth is shaped by slow, gradual processes that can still be observed today.
3. Geologists now agree that sudden catastrophic events such as asteroid impacts or volcanic eruptions can also cause geologic change.

Section 2

Terms to Learn

relative dating
superposition
geologic column
unconformity

What You'll Do

- Explain how relative dating is used in geology.
- Explain the principle of superposition.
- Demonstrate an understanding of the geologic column.
- Identify two events and two features that disrupt rock sequences.
- Explain how physical features are used to determine relative ages.

Relative Dating: Which Came First?

Imagine that you are a detective investigating a crime scene. What is the first thing you would do? You might begin by dusting the scene for fingerprints or by searching for witnesses. As a detective, your goal is to figure out the sequence of events that took place before you arrived at the scene.

Geologists have a similar goal when investigating the Earth. They try to determine the order of events that led to how the Earth looks today. But instead of fingerprints and witnesses, geologists rely on rocks and fossils. Determining whether an object or event is older or younger than other objects or events is called **relative dating.**

The Principle of Superposition

Suppose you have an older brother who takes a lot of photographs of your family but never puts them into an album. He just piles them in a box. Over the years, he keeps adding new pictures to the top of the stack. Think about the family history recorded in those pictures. Where are the oldest pictures—the ones taken when you were a baby? Where are the most recent pictures—those taken last week?

Rock layers, such as the ones shown in **Figure 3,** are like stacked pictures. The oldest layers are at the bottom. As you move from bottom to top, the layers get more recent, or younger. Scientists call this superposition. **Superposition** is a principle that states that younger rocks lie above older rocks in undisturbed sequences. "Younger over older" is a phrase you can use to remember this principle.

Figure 3 *Rock layers are like photos stacked over time—the younger ones lie above the older ones.*

MISCONCEPTION ALERT

Students may ask about the vertical lines perpendicular to the rock layers in **Figure 3.** Explain that the lines are not geologic features. They are cores that were drilled into the rock for explosive charges when the road was cut. The younger layers of rock are just below the trees, and the older layers are just above the road.

Directed Reading Worksheet 6 Section 2

SECTION 2

Focus

Relative Dating: Which Came First?

In this section, students learn how the principle of superposition is used to interpret Earth's history. They will practice relative dating techniques and learn how the geologic column is used to understand the sequence of Earth's rock formations. The section concludes with a discussion of three types of unconformities that occur in rock layers.

Bellringer

Ask students to arrange the following sentences in a logical order to make a short story:

> I stood in the checkout line.
> I selected two apples.
> I walked home from the store.
> I gave the cashier money.
> I went to the store.
> The cashier gave me change.
> I was hungry.

Sheltered English

1 Motivate

DEMONSTRATION

Stack several books on your desk. Tell students that the books represent layers of rock that were deposited at different times. Ask students: Which layer would be the oldest? (the one on the bottom)

Which rock layer is the youngest? (the one on top)

Ask students to discuss how they arrived at these answers, and tell them that they have just applied a basic geologic concept—the principle of superposition.

Section 2 • Relative Dating: Which Came First?   **137**

2) Teach

Answer to Activity

4. The book contains all of the chapters in the correct order. Similarly, the geologic column is a sequence of all the known rock layers and fossils. By using the geologic column, geologists can put rock layers in the correct order even if some layers are missing.

INDEPENDENT PRACTICE

The geologic column is an easy concept for students to understand if they get some hands-on practice. Before the lesson, you may wish to make photocopies of the exercise at the bottom of this page. Cut out the columns, and have students work independently to correctly align them.
Sheltered English

MISCONCEPTION ALERT

Emphasize to students that no single locality in the world has a continuous sequence of all the rocks formed throughout geologic history. The geologic column is an idealized sequence of rock layers that have accumulated around the world since the Earth formed. The geologic column was first pieced together in the mid-nineteenth century, and it is continually revised as geologists map more of the Earth.

Teaching Transparency 119 "Constructing the Geologic Column"

Activity

1. Write the titles of 10 chapters of this book on 10 note cards (one title on each note card).
2. Shuffle the cards and exchange them with a partner. Try to put your partner's titles in the correct order without using your book.
3. Compare your order with the order in the book.
4. Your work would have been easier if you had been allowed to use your book. How does this relate to geologists using the geologic column to put rock layers in order?

Disturbing Forces Some rock-layer sequences, however, are disturbed by forces from within the Earth. These forces can push other rocks into a sequence, tilt or fold rock layers, and break sequences into movable parts. Sometimes these forces even put older layers above younger layers, which goes against superposition. The disruptions of rock sequences caused by these forces pose a great challenge to geologists trying to determine the relative ages of rocks. Fortunately, geologists can get help from a very valuable tool—the geologic column.

The Geologic Column

To make their job easier, geologists combine data from all the known undisturbed rock sequences around the world. From this information, geologists create the *geologic column*. The **geologic column** is an ideal sequence of rock layers that contains all the known fossils and rock formations on Earth arranged from oldest to youngest.

Geologists rely on the geologic column to interpret rock sequences. For example, when geologists are not sure about the age of a rock sequence they are studying, they gather information about the sequence and compare it to the geologic column. Geologists also use the geologic column to identify the layers in puzzling rock sequences, such as sequences that have been folded over.

Constructing the Geologic Column

Here you can see three rock sequences (**a, b,** and **c**) from three different locations. Some rock layers appear in more than one sequence. Geologists construct the geologic column by piecing together different rock sequences from all over the world.

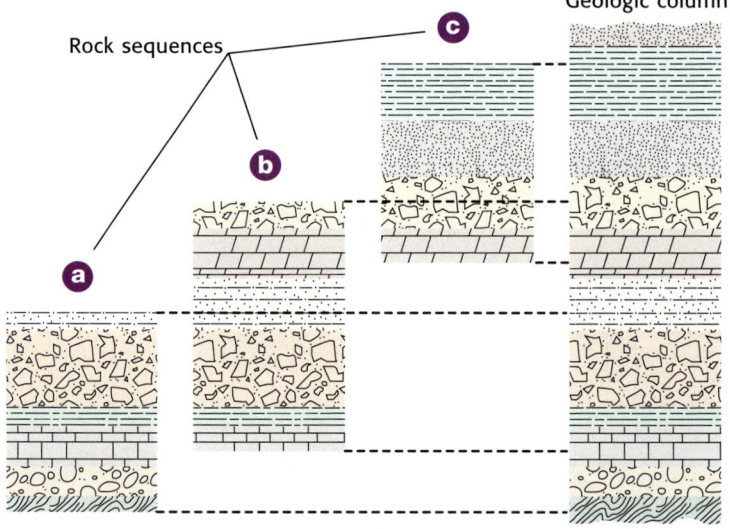

internetconnect
TOPIC: Relative Dating
GO TO: www.scilinks.org
sciLINKS NUMBER: HSTE135

Chapter 6 • The Rock and Fossil Record

Disturbed Rock Layers

Geologists often find features that cut through existing rock layers. Geologists use the relationships between rock layers and the features that cut across them to assign relative ages to the features and the layers. They know that those features are younger than the rock layers because the rock layers had to be present before the features could cut across them.

Faults and intrusions are examples of features that cut across rock layers. A *fault* is a break in the Earth's crust along which blocks of the crust slide relative to one another. Another cross-cutting feature is an intrusion. An *intrusion* is molten rock from the Earth's interior that squeezes into existing rock and cools. **Figure 4** illustrates both of these features.

Turn to page 652 in the LabBook to learn how geologists construct the geologic column.

Figure 4 A fault (left) and an intrusion (right) are always younger than the layers they cut across.

Geologists assume that the way sediment is deposited to form rock layers—in horizontal layers—has not changed over time. According to this principle, if rock layers are not horizontal, something must have disturbed them after they formed. This principle allows geologists to determine the relative ages of rock layers and the events that disturbed them.

Folding and tilting are two additional types of events that disturb rock layers. *Folding* occurs when rock layers bend and buckle from Earth's internal forces. *Tilting* occurs when internal forces in the Earth slant rock layers without folding them. **Figure 5** illustrates the results of folding and tilting.

Figure 5 Folding (left) and tilting (right) are events that are always younger than the rock layers they affect.

3) Extend

GROUP ACTIVITY

Try to arrange a field trip to a local area with exposed rock strata. If possible, contact a geologist from a local university or a museum to accompany the group. In small groups of three or four, have students try to find at least two unconformities and explain their origins. Encourage students to make drawings of the rock formations that they observe, labeling the features that are described in this chapter.

REAL-WORLD CONNECTION

Road cuts are excellent places to study the geology of your area. Tell students that the next time they are in a car and pass a road cut, they should try to spot unconformities. One unconformity is at the point where soil meets the bedrock. If students want to explore a road cut by foot, remind them to exercise caution around unstable rocks and passing cars.

GOING FURTHER

Have students study **Figure 6** and then work independently to create a comic strip that continues the sequence of images in the figure. Students can illustrate events such as intrusions, tilting, folding, faulting, or volcanic deposition as well as unconformities. Have students share their illustrations with the class and explain the geologic history of their comic strip.

Teaching Transparency 120
"Formation of Unconformities"

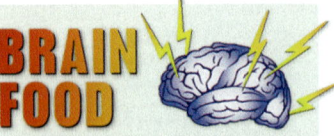

Many high-rise apartment and office buildings exhibit something similar to an unconformity—they do not have a 13th floor. Instead, the floors skip from 12 to 14.

Gaps in the Record—Unconformities

Faults, intrusions, and the effects of folding and tilting can make dating rock layers a challenge. But sometimes layers of rock are missing altogether, creating a gap in the geologic record. To think of this another way, let's say that you stack your newspapers every day after reading them. Now let's suppose you want to look at a paper you read 10 days ago. You know that the paper you want should be 10 papers deep in the stack. But when you look, the paper is not there. What happened? Perhaps you forgot to put the paper in the stack. Now instead of a missing newspaper, imagine a missing rock layer.

Missing Evidence Missing rock layers create gaps in rock-layer sequences called unconformities. An **unconformity** is a surface that represents a missing part of the geologic column. Unconformities also represent missing time—time that was not recorded in layers of rock. When geologists find unconformities, they must question whether the "missing layers" were actually present or whether they were somehow removed. **Figure 6** shows how *nondeposition* and *erosion* create unconformities.

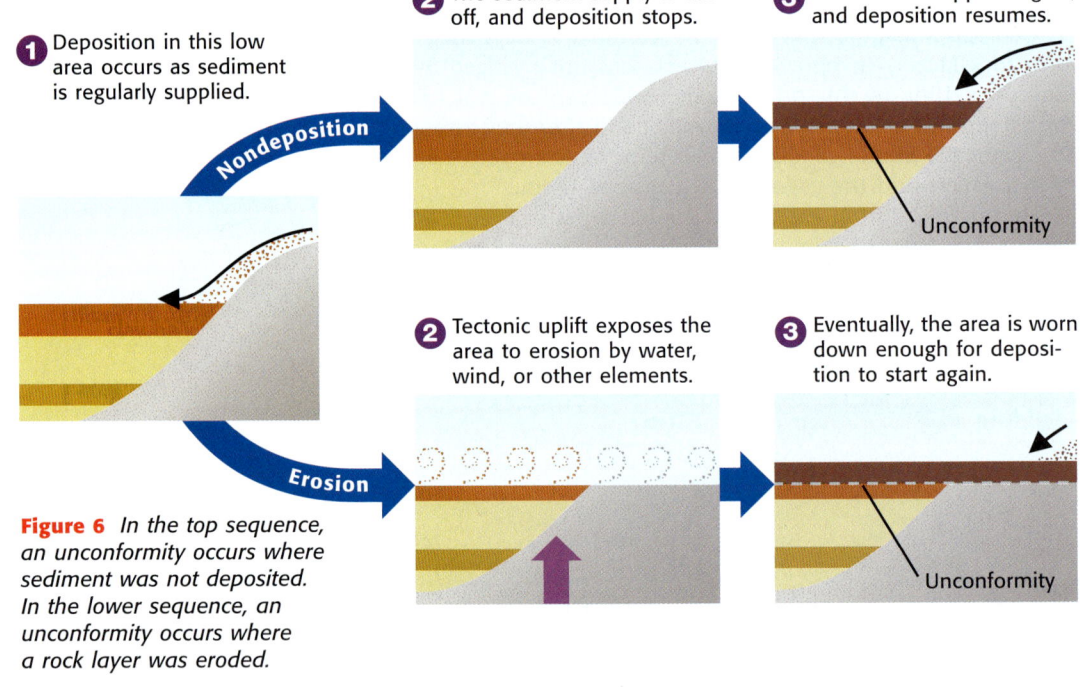

① Deposition in this low area occurs as sediment is regularly supplied.

② The sediment supply is cut off, and deposition stops.

③ Sediment is supplied again, and deposition resumes.

Nondeposition

② Tectonic uplift exposes the area to erosion by water, wind, or other elements.

③ Eventually, the area is worn down enough for deposition to start again.

Erosion

Figure 6 In the top sequence, an unconformity occurs where sediment was not deposited. In the lower sequence, an unconformity occurs where a rock layer was eroded.

Homework

Making Models Have students draw and label disconformities, nonconformities, and angular unconformities in their ScienceLog. Ask them to identify the youngest and the oldest rocks and include examples of intrusions, folds, and faults.

IS THAT A FACT!

Unconformities can represent a short gap in the geologic record or a very long one. The time gap can be as little as a few hundred years or as much as several billion years. Geologists must analyze many different variables to determine how much time an unconformity represents.

140 Chapter 6 • The Rock and Fossil Record

Types of Unconformities

Most unconformities form by both erosion and nondeposition. But other factors can complicate matters. To simplify the study of unconformities, geologists put them in three major categories—disconformities, nonconformities, and angular unconformities. The three diagrams at right illustrate these three categories.

Rock-Layer Puzzles

Geologists often find rock-layer sequences that have been affected by more than one of the events and features mentioned in this section. For example, an intrusion may squeeze into rock layers that contain an unconformity and that have been cut across by a fault. Determining the order of events that led to such a sequence is like piecing together a jigsaw puzzle.

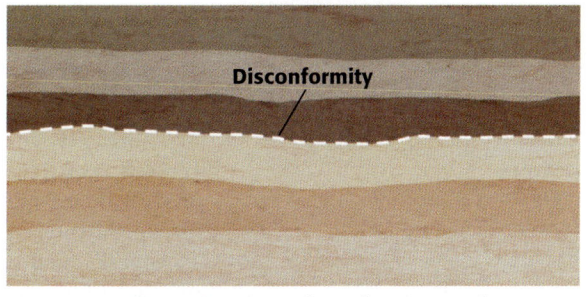

Figure 7 A **disconformity** exists where part of a sequence of parallel rock layers is missing. While often hard to see, a disconformity is the most common type of unconformity.

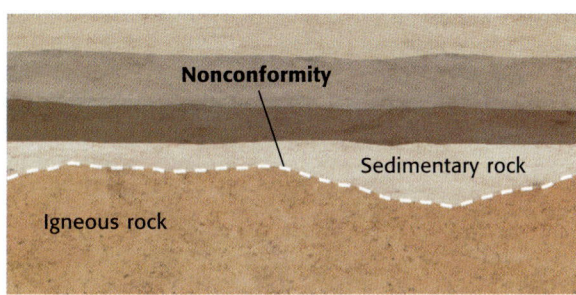

Figure 8 A **nonconformity** exists where sedimentary rock layers lie on top of an eroded surface of non-layered igneous or metamorphic rock.

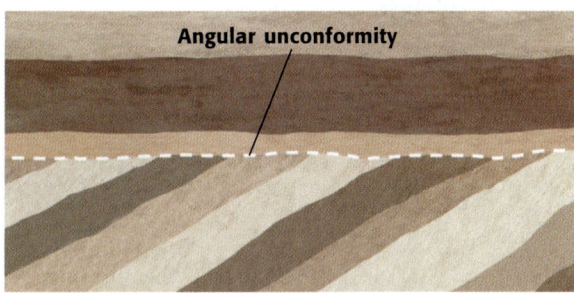

Figure 9 An **angular unconformity** exists between horizontal rock layers and rock layers that are tilted or folded. The tilted or folded layers were eroded before horizontal layers formed above them.

REVIEW

1. In a rock-layer sequence that hasn't been disturbed, are older layers found on top of younger layers? What rule do you use to answer this question?
2. List five events or features that can disturb rock-layer sequences.
3. Consider a fault that cuts through all the layers of a rock-layer sequence. Is the fault older or younger than the layers? Explain.
4. **Analyzing Methods** Unlike other types of unconformities, disconformities are hard to recognize because all the layers are horizontal. How does a geologist know when he or she is looking at a disconformity?

4) Close

Quiz

1. Explain what an unconformity is. Give an example. (Unconformities are gaps in an area's geologic column. Examples include disconformities, nonconformities, and angular unconformities.)
2. How do uniformitarianism and the theory of evolution support each other? (Answers will vary. Students should note that both theories suggested that the Earth is much older than previously thought. In addition, they both state that change occurs gradually over time.)

ALTERNATIVE ASSESSMENT

On the board or overhead projector, use different colors to create a rock formation consisting of five rock layers, an angular unconformity, a nonconformity, and two different fossils located in different layers. Ask students:

- Where is the angular unconformity and the nonconformity? How are they different? (An angular unconformity exists where layers were tilted and covered by new rock layers. The nonconformity is where non-layered rock has eroded and sedimentary rock is deposited on its surface.)
- Partially erase the top layer of rock; then add two more layers of "deposition." Ask students to name this type of unconformity. (disconformity)

Reinforcement Worksheet 6 "A Geologic Column Sandwich"

Answers to Review

1. No; the younger layers are found on top. the principle of superposition
2. Answers will vary but should include a fault, an intrusion, a disconformity, a nonconformity, and an angular unconformity.
3. The fault is younger than the layers. The layers had to be present for the fault to cut across them.
4. Disconformities represent a gap in the geologic column. If part of the column is missing from the layers, then the geologist has observed a disconformity.

SECTION 3

Focus

Absolute Dating: A Measure of Time

This section explains how absolute dating can determine the actual age of a fossil or a rock. Students will be able to explain the nature of radioactive decay and describe how radiometric dating measures the radioactive decay of different isotopes to calculate the age of the parent material.

🔔 Bellringer

Have students assess whether these statements describe relative or absolute age:

"She is my younger sister." (relative age)

"He is 12 years old." (absolute age)

Ask students to write a short paragraph explaining why geologists use both absolute and relative dating to interpret the past.

1 Motivate

ACTIVITY

Ask two students to be the geologists in this activity. The rest of the class will be radioactive isotopes in a newly formed rock sample. Tell the isotopes to stand up and that they have a half-life of 1 minute. Have the geologists go outside the classroom and wait. After 1 minute has elapsed, tell half of the isotopes to sit down. After another minute, ask half of the students left standing to sit down. Continue this pattern until one student remains standing. Ask the geologists to determine the age of the sample based on the number of original isotopes and the length of a half-life.

Section 3

Terms to Learn
absolute dating
isotopes
radioactive decay
radiometric dating
half-life

What You'll Do
- Explain how radioactive decay occurs.
- Explain how radioactive decay relates to radiometric dating.
- List three types of radiometric dating.
- Determine the best type of radiometric dating to use to date an object.

MISCONCEPTION ALERT

Students may associate atomic decay with other types of organic decay they know about. Explain that some elements have forms called isotopes. Some isotopes have unstable atomic nuclei that tend to change, or decay. The chance that an atom will decay at any given moment is very small, but that chance is constant. Unstable atoms do not "wear out" or "grow old." From the moment they form to the moment they decay, they always have the same probability of decaying. For example, every potassium-40 atom in a sample has a 50:50 chance of decaying during the course of 1.3 billion years. After 1.3 billion years, half the P-40 atoms will have decayed. Every unstable isotope has a characteristic half-life. Some half-lives last only a ten-thousandth of a second!

Absolute Dating: A Measure of Time

By using relative dating, scientists can determine the relative ages of rock layers. To determine the actual age of a layer of rock or a fossil, however, scientists must rely on absolute dating. **Absolute dating** is a process of establishing the age of an object, such as a fossil or rock layer, by determining the number of years it has existed. In this section, we will concentrate on radiometric dating, which is the most common method of absolute dating.

Radioactive Decay

To determine the absolute ages of fossils and rocks, scientists most often analyze radioactive isotopes. **Isotopes** are atoms of the same element that have the same number of protons but have different numbers of neutrons. Most isotopes are stable, meaning that they stay in their original form. But some isotopes are unstable. Scientists call unstable isotopes *radioactive*. Radioactive isotopes tend to break down into stable isotopes of other elements in a process called **radioactive decay**. **Figure 10** shows how one type of radioactive decay occurs. Because radioactive decay occurs at a steady pace, scientists can use the relative amounts of stable and unstable isotopes present in an object to determine the object's age.

Unstable isotope
6 protons, 8 neutrons

Figure 10 During radioactive decay, an unstable parent isotope breaks down into a stable daughter isotope.

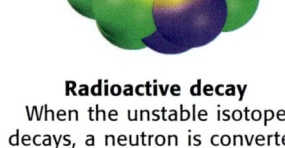

Radioactive decay
When the unstable isotope decays, a neutron is converted into a proton. In the process, an electron is released.

Stable isotope
7 protons, 7 neutrons

Dating Rocks—How Does It Work? Consider a stream of molten lava flowing out of a volcano. As long as the lava is in liquid form, the daughter material that is already present and the parent material are free to mix and move around. But eventually the lava cools and becomes solid igneous rock. When this happens, the parent and daughter materials often end up in different minerals. Scientists know that any daughter material found in the same mineral as the parent material most likely formed after the lava became solid rock. Scientists compare the amount of new daughter material with the amount of parent material that remains. The more new daughter material there is, the older the rock is.

Radiometric Dating

If you know the rate of decay for an element in a rock, you can figure out the age of the rock. Determining the absolute age of a sample based on the ratio of parent material to daughter material is called **radiometric dating.** For example, let's say that it takes 10,000 years for half the parent material in a rock sample to decay into daughter material. You analyze the sample and find equal amounts of parent material and daughter material. This means that half the original radioactive isotope has decayed and that the sample must be about 10,000 years old.

What if one-fourth of your sample is parent material and three-fourths is daughter material? You would know that it took 10,000 years for half the original sample to decay and another 10,000 years for half of what remained to decay. The age of your sample would be 2 × 10,000, or 20,000, years. **Figure 11** shows how this steady decay works. The time it takes for one-half of a radioactive sample to decay is called a **half-life.**

MATHBREAK

Get a Half-Life!
After observing the process illustrated in Figure 11, complete the chart below in your ScienceLog.

Parent left	Half-life in years	Age in years
1/8	?	30,000
?	1.3 billion	3.9 billion
1/4	10,000	?

Figure 11 After every half-life, the amount of parent material decreases by one-half.

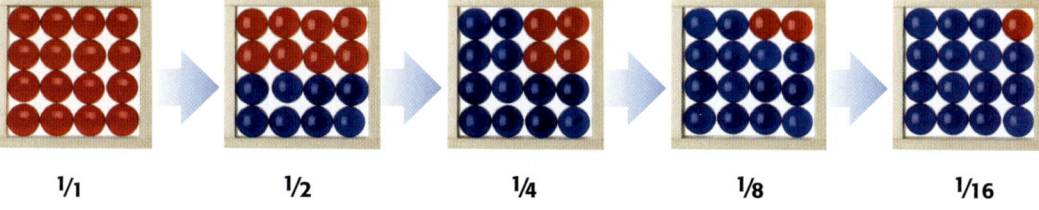

1/1   1/2   1/4   1/8   1/16

Science Bloopers

Before the hazards of radiation were discovered, X-ray machines were sometimes used in shoe stores. Salespeople would take X rays of a person's foot inside a new shoe to check for proper fit. This practice was discontinued as the detrimental effects of radiation were discovered.

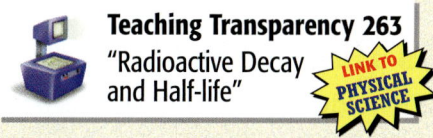
Teaching Transparency 263
"Radioactive Decay and Half-life"
LINK TO PHYSICAL SCIENCE

Directed Reading
Worksheet 6 Section 3

3) Extend

CROSS-DISCIPLINARY FOCUS

History Have students work together in small groups to research Effigy Mounds National Monument. Each group of students could create a display with photographs, articles, and interesting information about the artifacts found there. Encourage students to find out more about how absolute dating is used at other archaeological sites.

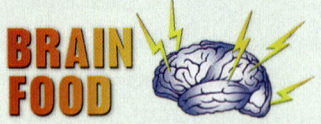

The carbon-14 dating method reports the age of a substance as the number of years before present (abbreviated B.P.). The term *before present* uses the year 1950 as a reference point. Ask students why scientists chose one year as a reference. (If scientists used the current year as a reference, the age of a specimen would change every year.)

TOPIC: Absolute Dating
GO TO: www.scilinks.org
sciLINKS NUMBER: HSTE140

Types of Radiometric Dating

Imagine traveling back through the centuries to a time long before Columbus arrived in America. You are standing along the bluffs of what will one day be called the Mississippi River. You see dozens of people building large mounds. Who are these people, and what are they building?

The people you saw in your time travel were American Indians, and the structures they were building were burial mounds. The area you imagined is now an archaeological site called Effigy Mounds National Monument. **Figure 12** shows one of these mounds.

According to archaeologists, people lived at Effigy Mounds from 2,500 years ago to 600 years ago. How do archaeologists know these dates? They have dated bones and other objects in the mounds using radiometric dating. Scientists use different radiometric dating techniques based on the estimated age of an object. As you read on, think about how the half-life of an isotope relates to the age of the object being dated. Which technique would you use to date the burial mounds?

BRAIN FOOD
Did you know that scientists have radiometrically dated moon rocks? The ages they have determined suggest that the moon formed when the Earth was still molten.

Figure 12 *This burial mound at Effigy Mounds resembles a snake.*

Uranium-Lead Method Uranium-238 is a radioactive isotope that eventually decays to lead-206. The half-life of uranium-238 is 4.5 billion years. The older the rock is, the more daughter material (lead-206) there will be in the rock. Uranium-lead dating can be used for rocks more than 10 million years old. Younger rocks do not contain enough daughter material to be accurately measured by this method.

IS THAT A FACT!
The oldest rock sample on record is a metamorphic gneiss from northern Canada, dated at 3.9 billion years old. Zircon crystals from Australia were found to be 4.2 billion years old, but they are part of much younger rock.

Q: What is the first thing you have to do before you date a dinosaur?

A: Ask it out.

Chapter 6 • The Rock and Fossil Record

Potassium-Argon Method Another isotope used for radiometric dating is potassium-40. Potassium-40 has a half-life of 1.3 billion years, and it eventually decays to argon and calcium. Geologists measure argon as the daughter material for radiometric dating. This method is mainly used to date rocks older than 100,000 years.

Carbon-14 Method The carbon-14 method works differently from the two methods already mentioned. The element carbon is normally found in three forms, the stable isotopes carbon-12 and carbon-13 and the radioactive isotope carbon-14. These carbon isotopes combine with oxygen to form the gas carbon dioxide, which is taken in by plants during photosynthesis. As long as a plant is alive, new carbon dioxide with a constant carbon-14 to carbon-12 ratio is continually taken in. Animals that eat plants contain the same ratio of carbon isotopes.

Once a plant or animal dies, however, no new carbon is taken in. The amount of carbon-14 begins to decrease as the plant or animal decays, and the ratio of carbon-14 to carbon-12 decreases. This decrease can be measured in a laboratory, such as the one shown in **Figure 13**. Because the half-life of carbon-14 is only 5,730 years, this dating method is mainly used for dating things that lived within the last 50,000 years.

Figure 13 Some samples containing carbon must be cleaned and burned before their age can be determined.

REVIEW

1. Explain how radioactive decay occurs.
2. How does radioactive decay relate to radiometric dating?
3. List three types of radiometric dating.
4. **Applying Concepts** Which radiometric-dating method would be most appropriate for dating artifacts found at Effigy Mounds? Explain.

internet connect

SC*i*LINKS NSTA

TOPIC: Absolute Dating
GO TO: www.scilinks.org
***sci*LINKS NUMBER:** HSTE140

4) Close

Quiz

1. When using the carbon-14 dating method, which sample would be older, a sample with a ratio of carbon-14 to carbon-12 of 2 to 1 or a sample with a ratio of 3 to 1? (the sample with a 2 to 1 ratio)
2. What is a half-life? (the time it takes for one-half of a radioactive isotope to decay)

ALTERNATIVE ASSESSMENT

Display three different "fossils" for students. Tell students that the first sample is about 30,000 years old, the second is about 1 million years old, and the last came from the Paleozoic era, around 400 million years ago. Ask students to state which dating method they would use to determine the absolute age of each fossil.

CONNECT TO
LIFE SCIENCE

Carbon-14 is constantly created in the atmosphere by cosmic radiation. There is one atom of radioactive carbon-14 for every trillion atoms of carbon-12 in the atmosphere. Plants absorb carbon-14 directly through their leaves as carbon dioxide. Animals take in carbon-14 indirectly when they eat plants. Although carbon-14 disintegrates at a constant rate, it is continuously renewed as long as an organism remains alive. When an organism dies, it stops absorbing new carbon-14 and its radiocarbon "clock" is set.

Answers to Review

1. Radioactive decay occurs as a radioactive isotope breaks down into a stable isotope. This happens as the isotope loses an electron and a neutron becomes a proton.
2. Radioactive decay occurs at a constant rate. By determining the ratio between the parent material and the daughter material in an object, scientists can determine how old the object is.
3. uranium-lead, carbon-14, and potassium-argon
4. Carbon-14 would be the best method to date artifacts from Effigy Mounds. This is because carbon-14 has a relatively short half-life of 5,730 years.

Section 3 • Absolute Dating: A Measure of Time

SECTION 4

Focus

Looking at Fossils
This section describes different types of fossils and how they are formed. Students learn how fossils provide information about the organisms that left them behind as well as the environment they inhabited. Students will also discover how index fossils are used to determine the relative age of rock layers.

🔔 Bellringer
Tell students that a fossil is any naturally preserved evidence of life. Ask them to write a few sentences to describe the fossil record of their own lives that might be found 65 million years from now. Stress to students that fossils must be naturally preserved. Have students share their ideas with the class.
Sheltered English

1) Motivate

GROUP ACTIVITY
Carbon impressions of plants can form when leaves are buried in sediment. As the plant decays, a thin film of carbon is left behind. Have students work in groups to make carbon "fossil" imprints. To each group, distribute a leaf, two sheets of white paper, and a piece of carbon paper. Instruct the groups to place their leaf on a sheet of white paper and cover it with the carbon paper, carbon side up. Next, cover the carbon paper with another sheet of white paper. Now have groups rub over the leaf using the side of a ruler. Ask them to describe which features were preserved and which were lost.

Section 4

Terms to Learn
fossil
permineralization
petrification
trace fossil
coprolite
mold
cast
index fossil

What You'll Do
◆ Describe how different types of fossils are formed.
◆ List the types of fossils that are not part of organisms.
◆ Demonstrate how fossils can be used to determine changes in environments and in the organisms the fossils came from.
◆ Describe index fossils, and explain how they are used.

Looking at Fossils

Imagine you and your classmates are on a cross-country science field trip to Coralville, a town in east-central Iowa. Your teacher takes your class to a nearby stone quarry and points to a large rock wall that looks just like a coral reef. "This is how Coralville got its name," your teacher explains. "There used to be a living coral reef right here. What you see today is a fossilized coral reef." But you know that coral reefs are found in warm tropical oceans and that Iowa is more than 1,000 km away from any ocean! How did this huge coral reef end up in the middle of Iowa? To answer this question, you need to learn about fossils.

Fossilized Organisms

A **fossil** is any naturally preserved evidence of life. Fossils exist in many forms. The most easily recognizable fossils are preserved organisms, such as the stingray shown at right, or parts of organisms. Usually these fossils occur in rock. But as you will see, other materials can also preserve evidence of life.

Fossils in Rocks When organisms die, the soft, fleshy parts of their bodies decompose, leaving only the hard parts. Occasionally, these hard parts get buried quickly in sediment and are preserved while the sediment turns to rock.

It takes more time for hard body parts such as bones, shells, and wood to decompose. For this reason, organisms with hard body parts are more likely to become fossils than those with only soft parts.

Mineral Replacement Organisms can also be preserved by **permineralization**, a process in which minerals fill in pore spaces of an organism's tissues. Minerals can also replace the original tissues of organisms. **Petrification** of an organism, shown in **Figure 14**, occurs when the organism's tissues are completely replaced by minerals.

Figure 14 *These pieces of petrified wood are made of stone.*

SCIENTISTS AT ODDS
The discovery of dinosaur fossils in the American northwest during the later half of the nineteenth century led to a frenzy of amateur paleontology known as the Bone Rush. Paleontologists trying to make a name for themselves would stop at nothing to discover a new species of dinosaur. In the 1870s, two American paleontologists, Edward Drinker Cope and Othniel Charles Marsh, were bitter rivals. In 1878, Marsh and Cope were both excavating fossils near Como Bluff, Wyoming. They had separate excavations and did not want to share findings. Both groups found more fossils than they could carry. To prevent the other group from taking their finds, they smashed all the fossils they couldn't carry!

Fossils in Amber Imagine a fly or a mosquito landing in a drop of tree sap and getting stuck. Suppose that the insect gets covered by more sap. When the sap hardens, the insect will be preserved inside. Hardened tree sap is called *amber*. Some of our best insect fossils are found in amber, as shown in **Figure 15.**

Mummification When organisms die in dry places, such as deserts, they can sometimes dry out so fast that there isn't enough time for even their soft parts to decay. This process is called *mummification*. Mummified organisms don't decay because the bacteria that feed on dead organisms can't live without water. Some food, like dried fruit and beef jerky, is preserved in a similar way.

Figure 15 *This insect is perfectly preserved in amber.*

Frozen Fossils Imagine a huge animal that looks like an elephant with long hair walking along a glacier 12,000 years ago. It's a woolly mammoth. Suddenly, the beast slips and falls between two huge pieces of ice into a deep crack. With no way out, the animal freezes and is preserved until the glacier thaws thousands of years later. Scientists find fossils of woolly mammoths and many other organisms when glaciers thaw. These frozen specimens are some of the best fossils.

Fossils in Tar There are places where tar occurs naturally in thick, sticky pools. One such place is the La Brea tar pits, in Los Angeles County, California. These pits of thick oil and tar were present when saber-toothed cats roamed the Earth 40,000 years ago, as shown in **Figure 16.**

Much of what we know about these extinct cats comes from fossils found in the La Brea tar pits. But saber-toothed cats are not the only organisms found in the pits. Scientists have found fossils of many other mammals as well as plants, snails, birds, salamanders, and insects.

Figure 16 *Many animals, including saber-toothed cats, became fossils after sinking in tar pits.*

2) Teach

READING STRATEGY

Writing Activity Ask students to write short paragraphs exploring possible scenarios for each type of fossilization described in this section. Encourage students to illustrate each scenario and to include details of the paleo-environment at the time of fossilization. Sheltered English

ACTIVITY

Making Fossils Distribute the following materials to groups of students:

several leaves or small shells, a small amount of petroleum jelly, plaster of Paris, water, waxed paper, a square of heavy cardboard, and a milk carton

Have each group fill the container halfway with plaster. Add some water, and combine the mixture to form a smooth, thick paste. Pour the plaster mixture onto the cardboard square covered by waxed paper. The plaster should be 5 mm thick. Coat the leaves or the shells with petroleum jelly, and place them jelly side down into the plaster. Allow the plaster to dry for 24 hours before removing the leaves or the shells. Groups may wish to create a fossil record of a mystery environment and exchange it for another group to interpret.

MISCONCEPTION ALERT

Many people assume that when they see dinosaur bones in a museum, they are looking at the actual bones that made up the dinosaur. It is important to point out that paleontologists rarely display the actual fossilized dinosaur bones, instead they make casts of the bones. Using the casts, they make fiberglass reproductions of the bones. The fiberglass bones are much lighter than the originals and can stand on their own.

Directed Reading Worksheet 6 Section 4

TOPIC: Looking at Fossils
GO TO: www.scilinks.org
sciLINKS NUMBER: HSTE145

Section 4 • Looking at Fossils

2 Teach, continued

DEBATE

Have students debate the pros and cons of amateur fossil collecting. They should understand that amateur fossil collectors have made some amazing discoveries and have advanced paleontology. On the other hand, amateur fossil collectors have lost important information by improperly removing fossils or not recording data about locations or associated fossils. Have them conclude the debate by writing a handbook for amateur fossil collectors.

Answer to Self-Check

Coprolites and tracks are trace fossils because they are evidence of animal activity rather than fossilized organisms.

BRAIN FOOD

In 1997, the most complete skeleton of a *Tyrannosaurus rex* ever found was auctioned. The dinosaur, named Sue, was purchased for $8.36 million by the Field Museum of Natural History in Chicago. Scientists were relieved because they feared that a private collector would buy the fossil skeleton and that scientists and the public would not be able to view it. Have students find out more about the bitter custody battle involving Sue, the U.S. government, the Cheyenne Indians, a private rancher, and a commercial paleontology company. Ask students how they feel about people owning and controlling fossils. At what point is it okay to own a fossil, and at what point should scientists be in control of a fossil?

Other Types of Fossils

What happens when scientists cannot find any remains of plants or animals? Is there anything else that might indicate an organism's former presence?

Trace Fossils Any naturally preserved evidence of an animal's activity is called a **trace fossil**. An easily recognizable type of trace fossil is a *track*. Just like animals today, the animals in the past left tracks. These ancient tracks became fossils when they filled with sediment that eventually turned to rock.

Imagine that the tracks shown here were made by a ferocious *Tyrannosaurus rex*. While the animal that made them is long gone, the fossil tracks remain as evidence that it once prowled the Earth.

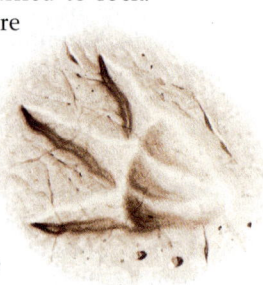

Burrows are another type of trace fossil. Burrows are shelters made by animals that dig into the ground. Like tracks, burrows are preserved when they are filled in with sediment and buried quickly.

Coprolites are a third type of trace fossil. The word *coprolite* (KAHP roh LIET) is from the Greek words meaning "dung stone." **Coprolites** are preserved feces, or dung, from animals. Coprolites can provide valuable information about the habits and diets of the animals that left them. **Figure 17** shows a coprolite that is more than 5 million years old.

Figure 17 This coprolite came from a prehistoric mammal.

✓ Self-Check

Why are tracks and coprolites considered trace fossils? *(See page 726 to check your answer.)*

Molds and Casts A **mold** is a cavity in the ground or rock where a plant or animal was buried. Often the cavity has been filled in, leaving a cast of the original organism. A **cast** is an object created when sediment fills a mold and becomes rock. A cast shows what the outside of the organism looked like. **Figure 18** shows a mold and cast from the same organism.

Figure 18 The ammonite cast on the left formed when sediment filled the ammonite mold on the right and became rock.

Science Bloopers

How *Brontosaurus* lost its name is a story full of science bloopers. In 1877, Othniel Marsh hastily described a new species of dinosaur based on a few vertebrae and part of a pelvis. He named this dinosaur *Apatosaurus*. In 1879, Marsh went on to announce the discovery of another new dinosaur, the *Brontosaurus*, which was also based on incomplete remains. Not until 1903 was it discovered that the new dinosaurs were actually members of the same species! It was decided that the dinosaur should be called *Apatosaurus* instead of *Brontosaurus*. Controversy continued when, in the 1970s, scientists found that Marsh had put the wrong skull on *Apatosaurus*.

Using Fossils to Interpret the Past

By examining fossils, scientists can find out what was happening in the environment when the sediments surrounding the fossils were deposited. Scientists can also interpret how plants and animals have changed over time by studying fossils from different parts of the geologic column.

Changes in Environments

Fossils can reveal changes that have occurred in parts of the Earth. By studying the coral-reef fossils and applying the principle of uniformitarianism, for example, scientists have determined that Iowa was once covered by a shallow sea. This is hard to believe when you look at Iowa's landscape today!

Iowa is just one example of where inconsistent fossils have been found. Who would have expected fossils of coral to be found in the landlocked state of Iowa? Likewise, who would have expected fossils of marine organisms on the top of a mountain? But that is exactly what scientists found on mountaintops in Canada, as shown in **Figure 19**. The presence of these fossils means that these rocks were once below the surface of an ocean.

Figure 19 *Scientists often find rocks that contain marine fossils on mountaintops. These rocks were pushed up from below sea level millions of years ago.*

Changes in Life Older rock layers contain organisms different from those found in younger rock layers. The record stored in the rocks shows a change in life-forms over the years. For example, rock layers that contain fish fossils are found beneath the oldest rock layers that contain fossils of amphibians. Amphibians, such as frogs and salamanders, are animals with characteristics that allow them to live both on land and in water. On top of these rock layers are the oldest layers that contain fossils of reptiles, most of which lived only on land. Using the principle of superposition, we know that fish existed before amphibians because fish were found in a lower layer of rock. In the same way, we know that amphibians existed before reptiles.

149

4 Close

Quiz

1. Would a shark tooth make a good index fossil? Why or why not? (A shark tooth would not make a good index fossil because sharks have existed for more than 200 million years; index fossils are useful because they existed for a short period of time.)

2. Why do the frigid temperatures of Siberia and the sticky tar of the La Brea Tar Pits preserve fossils so well? (Both environments retard the decay of an organism and help preserve it.)

Alternative Assessment

 Have students prepare a "how-to" guide for the fossilization processes described in this section. Students should imagine that they are instructing an untrained person in how to preserve an organism using sedimentation, amber, mummification, tar, ice, and permineralization. Emphasize that this assignment should read like a recipe; details are important.

Homework

Modern Index Fossils Which organisms would make good index fossils for marking the end of the twentieth century? Have students research species that have become extinct during the last 100 years and illustrate what their fossils might look like.

 **Critical Thinking Worksheet 6** "Adiós Alamosaurus!"

Using Fossils to Date Rocks

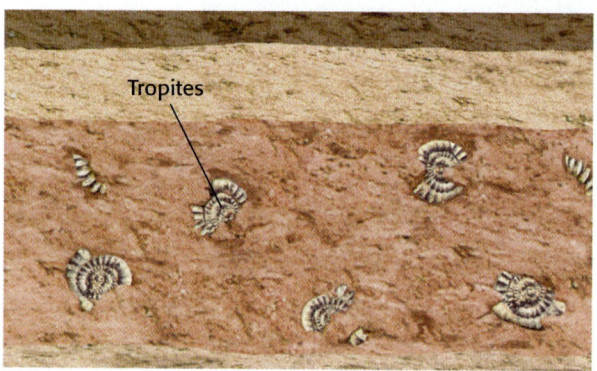

Geologists sometimes use *index fossils* to date rocks while in the field. **Index fossils** are fossils of organisms that lived during a relatively short, well-defined time span. Whenever geologists find an index fossil in a rock layer, they know where in the geologic column the rock layer fits. This enables them to give the layer a date without directly using radiometric dating. Good index fossils also have a wide distribution around the world.

An example of an index fossil is a genus of trilobites called *Phacops*, shown above. Trilobites are extinct, but they looked like a cross between a modern horseshoe crab and a pill bug. *Phacops* lived in shallow oceans about 400 million years ago. Where geologists find a fossil of this trilobite, they can assume that the surrounding rock is about 400 million years old.

Another good index fossil is a genus of ammonites called *Tropites*, shown in **Figure 20**. Ammonites were marine animals that looked a lot like modern squids, but they lived in coiled shells with complex inner walls. *Tropites* lived between 230 million and 208 million years ago. Where geologists find them in a rock layer, they know that the rock layer is between 208 million and 230 million years old.

Figure 20 Tropites, *a genus of ammonites, existed for only about 20 million years, which makes it a good index fossil.*

internetconnect

SC*i*LINKS NSTA
TOPIC: Looking at Fossils
GO TO: www.scilinks.org
*sci*LINKS NUMBER: HSTE145

REVIEW

1. Describe two ways that fossils can form.
2. List two types of fossils that are not part of an organism.
3. What are index fossils? How do scientists use them to date rocks?
4. **Making Inferences** If you find rock layers containing fish fossils in a desert, what can you infer about that area of the desert?

Answers to Review

1. Answers will vary. Fossils can form as organisms are deposited in layers of sediment. If the sediment becomes rock, the organism may be preserved as a fossil. Permineralization is another way fossils can form. In this process, minerals form in the pore spaces between an organism's tissues. Petrification occurs if the tissues are completely replaced by minerals.

2. Answers will vary. Students may mention animal burrows, coprolites, or animal tracks.

3. Index fossils are fossils of organisms that lived during a relatively short, defined period of time. Index fossils help scientists date a rock layer without directly using radiometric dating.

4. Answers will vary. The desert was once an ocean, stream, or lake.

Section 5

Terms to Learn
geologic time scale
eon
era
period
epoch

What You'll Do
- Demonstrate an understanding of the geologic time scale.
- Identify important dates on the geologic time scale.
- Identify the eon we know the most about, and explain why we know more about it than about other eons.

Time Marches On

Remember the stack of family pictures mentioned in Section 2? The oldest pictures were on the bottom, and the newest ones were on the top. By looking through the pictures in order, you could see the sequence of events and changes that occurred in your family's history. In studying the history of the Earth, scientists follow a similar process. But instead of looking at pictures, they analyze rock layers and the fossils they contain.

Rock Layers and Geologic Time

One of the best places in North America to see the Earth's history recorded in rock layers is in Grand Canyon National Park, shown in **Figure 21**. The Colorado River has cut the canyon nearly 2 km deep in some places. During this process, countless layers of rock have been eroded by the river. These layers represent nearly 2 billion years of geologic time!

Figure 21 The rock layers in the Grand Canyon correspond to a very large section of the geologic column.

Biology CONNECTION

The Grand Canyon is so wide and deep that organisms on either side of the canyon took different evolutionary paths. As the Colorado River formed the canyon, groups of individuals from the same species became separated and could no longer interact. Over millions of years, these groups developed differently and became different species.

BRAIN FOOD

The Grand Canyon may be big, but Valles Marineris, on Mars, is much bigger. The Valles Marineris is a system of canyons 4,000 km long. The canyons have a maximum depth of 7–10 km. If Valles Marineris were on Earth, it would stretch across the United States from New York to Los Angeles. Ask students to hypothesize how such a vast system of canyons formed on Mars. (The canyons may have formed from tectonic activity. The flow of water on the surface of Mars may have eroded the canyon further.)

SECTION 5

Focus

Time Marches On

In this section, students are introduced to the geologic time scale. The section discusses the important biological and geological events of each eon and era. The section concludes with a QuickLab in which students construct their own geologic time scale to help them understand the length of each eon.

🔔 Bellringer

Post the following question for students:

If the history of Earth was the length of one calendar year, what do you think is the date of the arrival of modern humans? (7:40 P.M., December 31)

1) Motivate

DISCUSSION

After students study the photograph of the Grand Canyon in **Figure 21**, ask them how they can identify different rock layers. (Each layer has a different thickness and color.)

Where are the oldest layers? (near the base of the canyon)

Why is the Grand Canyon such an important place to study the geologic history of western North America? (The Colorado River has cut through nearly 2 billion years of geologic history.)

If the Earth is 4.6 billion years old, how much of Earth's history do the layers of the Grand Canyon represent? (less than half)

 Directed Reading Worksheet 6 Section 5

2) Teach

READING STRATEGY

Mnemonics Help students devise mnemonic sentences to learn and remember the eons of geologic history. For example, "**H**appy **A**ardvarks **Pr**ance for **Ph**otographers" could be used to recall the **H**adean, **A**rchean, **Pr**oterozoic, and **Ph**anerozoic eons. Other mnemonic sentences will help students learn the eras, periods, and epochs.
Sheltered English

CONNECT TO LIFE SCIENCE

The study of Earth's history has given rise to highly specific subdivisions of Earth science. Paleobotany, for example, studies the history of the plant kingdom. Have interested students find out how plant and pollen fossils can provide clues about past environments and how they have changed over time.

MEETING INDIVIDUAL NEEDS

Learners Having Difficulty As you begin to discuss the geologic time scale, write the names of the four eons on the board. Ask students to use the text to help you list the characteristics of each eon. Have students find the dates of each eon, the biological events that define it, and other facts. Have students copy the information in their ScienceLog for future study and review.
Sheltered English

Teaching Transparency 121
"The Geologic Time Scale"

The Geologic Time Scale

While the rock layers in the Grand Canyon represent the time that passed as they formed, the geologic column represents the billions of years that have passed since the first rocks formed on Earth. Geologists must grapple with the time represented by the geologic column as well as the time between Earth's formation and the formation of Earth's oldest known rocks. Altogether, geologists study 4.6 billion years of Earth's history! To make their job easier, geologists have created the geologic time scale. The **geologic time scale**, which is shown in **Figure 22**, is a scale that divides Earth's 4.6-billion-year history into distinct intervals of time.

Figure 22 The geologic time scale accounts for Earth's entire history. It is divided into four major parts called eons.

Phanerozoic eon
(540 million years ago–present)
The rock and fossil record mainly represents the Phanerozoic eon, which is the eon in which we live.

Proterozoic eon
(2.5 billion years ago–540 million years ago)
The first organisms with well-developed cells appeared during this eon.

Archean eon
(3.8 billion years ago–2.5 billion years ago)
The earliest known rocks on Earth formed during this eon.

Hadean eon
(4.6 billion years ago–3.8 billion years ago)
The only rocks that scientists have found from this eon are meteorites and rocks from the moon.

Geologic Time Scale

	Era	Period	Epoch	Millions of years ago
PHANEROZOIC EON	Cenozoic	Quaternary	Holocene	0.01
			Pleistocene	1.8
		Tertiary	Pliocene	5.3
			Miocene	23.8
			Oligocene	33.7
			Eocene	54.8
			Paleocene	65
	Mesozoic	Cretaceous		144
		Jurassic		206
		Triassic		248
	Paleozoic	Permian		290
		Pennsylvanian		323
		Mississippian		354
		Devonian		417
		Silurian		443
		Ordovician		490
		Cambrian		540
PROTEROZOIC EON				2,500
ARCHEAN EON				3,800
HADEAN EON				4,600

Homework

Research Before the theory of plate tectonics and the invention of radiometric dating, scientists developed many elaborate experiments to determine the age of the Earth. In the mid-1700s, a French scientist estimated the age of Earth to be 75,000 years old. He based his estimate on the cooling rate of iron cannonballs. By the 1930s, the estimated age of Earth reached 1 billion years, but it was not until the middle of this century that we determined the current estimate at 4.6 billion. Have interested students research the different methods that were used in the past to estimate the age of Earth.

Divisions of Time Geologists have divided Earth's history into sections of time, as shown on the geologic time scale in Figure 22. The largest divisions of geologic time are **eons.** The four eons in turn are divided into **eras,** which are the second-largest divisions of geologic time. Eras are divided into **periods,** which are the third-largest divisions of geologic time. Some periods are divided into **epochs** (EP uhks), which are the fourth-largest division of geologic time. Look again at Figure 22. Can you figure out what epoch we live in?

The boundaries between geologic time intervals represent major changes on Earth. These changes include the appearance or disappearance of life-forms, changes in the global climate, and changes in rock types. For example, each of the three eras of the Phanerozoic eon are characterized by unique life-forms.

The Paleozoic Era *Paleozoic* means "old life." The Paleozoic era lasted from about 540 to 248 million years ago. It is the first era that is well represented by fossils.

At the beginning of the Paleozoic era, there were no land organisms. Imagine how empty the landscape must have looked! By the middle of the era, plants started appearing on land. By the end of the era, amphibians were living partially on the land, and insects were abundant. **Figure 23** shows what the land might have looked like late in the Paleozoic era. The Paleozoic era came to an end with a mass extinction—nearly 90 percent of all species perished.

Living in the Past
How do scientists know what life was like in prehistoric times? Turn to page 161 to learn how one paleontologist finds out.

Figure 23 *Jungles were present during the Paleozoic era, but there were no birds singing in the trees and no monkeys swinging from the branches. Birds and mammals didn't evolve until much later.*

3 Extend

DEBATE

The Ancestry of Dinosaurs
Have students research and debate the ancestry of dinosaurs. Are they related more closely to reptiles or to birds? One side can gather evidence to support the theory that dinosaurs were cold-blooded and were more closely related to today's reptiles. The other side can use evidence to show that dinosaurs were more likely warmblooded and related to present-day birds.

MISCONCEPTION ALERT

Illustrations of dinosaurs and ancient environments are based on artists' conceptions. For example, scientists are sure about the skeletal structure of most dinosaurs, but skin type and skin color are open to interpretation. *Tyrannosaurus rex* might not have had lips, and *Triceratops* might not have had cheeks. Artists have drawn these types of features on dinosaurs because these make the dinosaurs look familiar. The actual fossils do not suggest these types of features at all. In addition, most if not all movies about prehistoric life are abundant with paleontological inaccuracies. A classic example is the depiction of prehistoric humans and dinosaurs coexisting at the same time period. Show parts of these films to see how many inaccuracies students can point out.

The Mesozoic Era *Mesozoic* means "middle life." The Mesozoic era lasted from about 248 million years ago until about 65 million years ago. This era is also known as the Age of Reptiles. Dinosaurs, such as the ones shown in **Figure 24**, inhabited the land and the water.

Although reptiles dominated the Mesozoic era, birds and small mammals began to evolve late in the era. Most scientists think that birds evolved directly from a type of dinosaur. By the end of the Mesozoic era, about 50 percent of all species on Earth, including the dinosaurs, became extinct.

Figure 24 Imagine walking in the desert and bumping into these fierce creatures! It's a good thing humans didn't evolve in the Mesozoic era, which was dominated by dinosaurs.

The Cenozoic Era *Cenozoic* means "recent life." The Cenozoic era began about 65 million years ago and continues to the present. We live in the Cenozoic era.

Whereas the Mesozoic era is called the Age of Reptiles, the Cenozoic era is called the Age of Mammals. After the mass extinction at the end of the Mesozoic era, mammals became abundant on Earth, as shown in **Figure 25**. Many types of mammals that lived earlier in the Cenozoic era are now extinct, including woolly mammoths, saber-toothed cats, and giant sloths.

Figure 25 Thousands of species of mammals evolved during the Cenozoic era. This scene shows species from the early Cenozoic era that are now extinct.

Homework

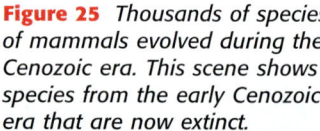

Prehistoric Animals Ask each student to choose a favorite prehistoric animal. Then have students find information about that animal and the time period it lived in. University Web sites are an excellent place to look for this information. Students can present their information as an oral presentation or as a poster.

IS THAT A FACT!

How long and heavy were the heaviest dinosaurs? Some dinosaurs were almost as large as blue whales, and the average elephant weighs less than the tongue of a blue whale.

154 Chapter 6 • The Rock and Fossil Record

Can You Imagine 4.6 Billion Years?

It's hard to picture 4.6 billion of anything, especially years. As humans, we do quite well to live to be 100 years old. Given this perspective, it is very difficult to think of Earth as being billions of years old. One way to do this is to organize the geologic time scale into the frame of 12 hours, with the first moment of Earth's history being noon and the present moment being midnight. This has been done on the Earth-history clock shown in **Figure 26**. On the Earth-history clock, the millions of years of evolution that you just read about occurred within the last hour. Human civilizations appeared within the last second! Perhaps you now have a better understanding of just how old the Earth is and just how brief humans' existence has been.

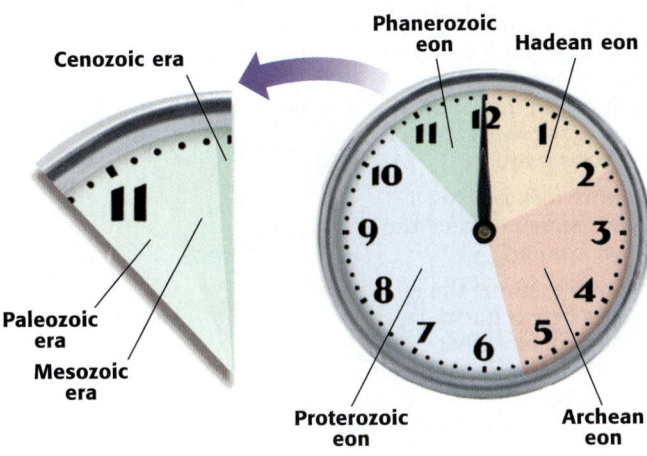

Figure 26 On the Earth-history clock, which organizes Earth's history into the frame of 12 hours, 1 hour equals 383 million years, 1 minute equals 6.4 million years, and 1 second equals 106,000 years.

QuickLab

Make a Time Scale

1. Using a pair of **scissors**, cut a length of **adding-machine tape** 46 cm long.
2. Starting at one end of the tape, use a **ruler** and a **black marker** to draw a line across the width of the tape at the following measurements: 5.4 cm, 25 cm, and 38 cm.
3. Using **colored markers**, color the sections of tape as follows:
   0 cm–5.4 cm = green
   5.4 cm–25 cm = blue
   25 cm–38 cm = red
   38 cm–46 cm = yellow
4. Your tape represents the geologic time scale, and the present moment is at 46 cm. What is the name of each time interval on your scale?

REVIEW

1. How many eras are in the Phanerozoic eon? List them.
2. In this section, extinctions at the end of two geologic time intervals are mentioned. What are these two intervals, and when did each interval end?
3. Which eon do we know the most about? Why?
4. **Making Predictions** What future event might mark the end of the Cenozoic era?

internetconnect

SC**LINKS**
NSTA

TOPIC: Geologic Time
GO TO: www.scilinks.org
***sci*LINKS NUMBER:** HSTE150

Section 5 • Time Marches On **155**

Chapter Highlights

VOCABULARY DEFINITIONS

SECTION 1

uniformitarianism a principle that states that the same geologic processes shaping the Earth today have been at work throughout Earth's history

catastrophism a principle that states that all geologic change occurs suddenly

SECTION 2

relative dating determining whether an object or event is older or younger than other objects or events

superposition a principle that states that younger rocks lie above older rocks in undisturbed sequences

geologic column an ideal sequence of rock layers that contains all the known fossils and rock formations on Earth arranged from oldest to youngest

unconformity a surface that represents a missing part of the geologic column

SECTION 3

absolute dating the process of establishing the age of an object, such as a fossil or rock layer, by determining the number of years it has existed

isotopes atoms of the same element that have the same number of protons but have different numbers of neutrons

radioactive decay a process in which radioactive isotopes tend to break down into stable isotopes of other elements

radiometric dating determining the absolute age of a sample based on the ratio of parent material to daughter material

half-life for a particular radioactive sample, the time it takes for one-half of the sample to decay

Chapter Highlights

SECTION 1

Vocabulary
uniformitarianism (p. 134)
catastrophism (p. 135)

Section Notes
- Scientists use the principle of uniformitarianism to interpret the past and make predictions.
- According to uniformitarianism, geologic change is gradual. According to catastrophism, geologic change is sudden.
- Before Hutton and Lyell, most scientists believed all geologic change was catastrophic. After Hutton and Lyell, most scientists rejected catastrophism. Today most scientists favor uniformitarianism, but they recognize some geologic change as catastrophic.

SECTION 2

Vocabulary
relative dating (p. 137)
superposition (p. 137)
geologic column (p. 138)
unconformity (p. 140)

Section Notes
- Geologists use relative dating to determine the relative age of objects.
- Geologists assume that younger layers lie above older layers in undisturbed rock-layer sequences. This is called superposition.
- The entire rock and fossil record is represented by the geologic column.
- Geologists examine the relationships between rock layers and the structures that cut across them in order to determine relative ages.
- Geologists also determine relative ages by assuming that all rock layers were originally horizontal.
- Unconformities form where rock layers are missing, and they represent time that is not recorded in the rock record.

Labs
How DO You Stack Up? (p. 652)

✓ Skills Check

Math Concepts

HALF-LIVES Remember from Figure 11 on page 143 that the ratio of parent material to daughter material decreases by one-half with each half-life. An easy way to think of this is to multiply the ratio by $1/2$ for each half-life. This is shown below.

$$\frac{1}{1} \times \frac{1}{2} = \frac{1}{2};\ \frac{1}{2} \times \frac{1}{2} = \frac{1}{4};$$
$$\frac{1}{4} \times \frac{1}{2} = \frac{1}{8};\ \text{and}\ \frac{1}{8} \times \frac{1}{2} = \frac{1}{16}$$

Visual Understanding

FAULTS AND UNCONFORMITIES It is important to realize that faults and unconformities are not bodies of rock. They are types of surfaces where bodies of rock contact each other.

Lab and Activity Highlights

How DO You Stack Up?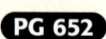

 Datasheets for LabBooks
(blackline masters for these labs)

156 Chapter 6 • The Rock and Fossil Record

SECTION 3

Vocabulary

absolute dating (p. 142)
isotopes (p. 142)
radioactive decay (p. 142)
radiometric dating (p. 143)
half-life (p. 143)

Section Notes

- During radioactive decay, an unstable parent isotope of one element decays at a constant rate into a stable daughter isotope of a different element.
- The absolute age of samples of some rocks and fossils can be determined by the ratio of unstable isotopes to stable isotopes in the samples. This is called radiometric dating.
- The radiometric-dating method scientists use depends on the estimated age of the object they are dating.

SECTION 4

Vocabulary

fossil (p. 146)
permineralization (p. 146)
petrification (p. 146)
trace fossil (p. 148)
coprolite (p. 148)
mold (p. 148)
cast (p. 148)
index fossil (p. 150)

Section Notes

- Any naturally preserved evidence of life is considered a fossil.
- There are many ways fossils can form, such as mineral replacement, mummification, and freezing.
- Fossils can be used to show how environments and organisms have changed over time.
- Fossils, especially index fossils, can be used to date rocks.

SECTION 5

Vocabulary

geologic time scale (p. 152)
eon (p. 153)
era (p. 153)
period (p. 153)
epoch (p. 153)

Section Notes

- The history of the Earth is recorded in rock layers.
- The 4.6 billion years of Earth's history is represented on the geologic time scale, including the intervals not represented in the rock and fossil record.
- There are several different time intervals on the geologic time scale.
- Scientists know very little about the Earth's early history. This is because the rock and fossil record primarily represents the last eon of Earth's history.

VOCABULARY DEFINITIONS, continued

SECTION 4

fossil any naturally preserved evidence of life

permineralization a process in which minerals fill in pore spaces of an organism's tissues

petrification a process in which an organism's tissues are completely replaced by minerals

trace fossil any naturally preserved evidence of an animal's activity

coprolites preserved feces, or dung, from animals

mold a cavity in the ground or rock where a plant or animal was buried

cast an object created when sediment fills a mold and becomes rock

index fossil a fossil of an organism that lived during a relatively short, well-defined time span; a fossil that is used to date the rock layers in which it is found

SECTION 5

geologic time scale a scale that divides Earth's 4.6-billion-year history into distinct intervals of time

eon the largest division of geologic time

era the second-largest division of geologic time

period the third-largest division of geologic time

epoch the fourth-largest division of geologic time

---

internet connect

GO TO: go.hrw.com

Visit the **HRW** Web site for a variety of learning tools related to this chapter. Just type in the keyword:

KEYWORD: HSTFOS

GO TO: www.scilinks.org

Visit the **National Science Teachers Association** on-line Web site for Internet resources related to this chapter. Just type in the sciLINKS number for more information about the topic:

TOPIC	sciLINKS NUMBER
TOPIC: Earth's Story	sciLINKS NUMBER: HSTE130
TOPIC: Relative Dating	sciLINKS NUMBER: HSTE135
TOPIC: Absolute Dating	sciLINKS NUMBER: HSTE140
TOPIC: Looking at Fossils	sciLINKS NUMBER: HSTE145
TOPIC: Geologic Time	sciLINKS NUMBER: HSTE150

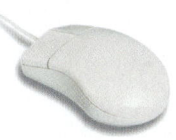

157

Lab and Activity Highlights

LabBank

Inquiry Labs,
A Penny for Your Thoughts, Lab 10

EcoLabs & Field Activities,
Rock of Ages, Field Activity 10

Labs You Can Eat,
Geopancakes, Lab 12

Long-Term Projects & Research Ideas,
The Hard Rock Chronicles, Project 34

Vocabulary Review Worksheet 6

Blackline masters of these Chapter Highlights can be found in the **Study Guide**.

Chapter Review

USING VOCABULARY

For each pair of terms, explain the difference in their meaning.

1. uniformitarianism/catastrophism
2. relative dating/absolute dating
3. mold/cast
4. eon/era
5. geologic time scale/geologic column

UNDERSTANDING CONCEPTS

Multiple Choice

6. Which of the following words does not describe catastrophic geologic change?
   a. sudden
   b. widespread
   c. gradual
   d. rare

7. Scientists assign relative ages by using
   a. potassium-argon dating.
   b. the principle of superposition.
   c. radioactive half-lives.
   d. the ratios of isotopes.

8. Rock layers cut by a fault formed
   a. after the fault.
   b. before the fault.
   c. at the same time as the fault.
   d. Cannot be determined

9. If the half-life of an unstable element is 5,000 years, what percentage of the parent material will be left after 10,000 years?
   a. 100   c. 50
   b. 75   d. 25

10. Of the following unstable isotopes, which has the longest half-life?
    a. uranium-238
    b. potassium-40
    c. carbon-14

11. Fossils can be
    a. petrified.
    b. dried out.
    c. frozen.
    d. All of the above

12. Of the following geologic time intervals, which is the shortest?
    a. an eon
    b. a period
    c. an era
    d. an epoch

13. If Earth's history is put on a scale of 12 hours, human civilizations would have been around for
    a. hours.
    b. minutes.
    c. less than 1 second.

Short Answer

14. What is the principle of superposition? How is it used by geologists?

15. Describe how plant and animal remains become petrified.

16. Explain how a fossil cast forms.

158

Concept Mapping

17. Use the following terms to create a concept map: age, absolute dating, half-life, radioactive decay, radiometric dating, relative dating, superposition, geologic column, isotopes.

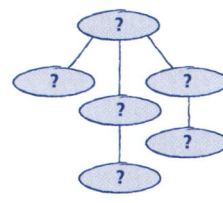

CRITICAL THINKING AND PROBLEM SOLVING

Write one or two sentences to answer the following questions:

18. You may have heard the term *petrified wood*. Why doesn't a "petrified" tree contain any wood?
19. How do tracks and burrows end up in the rock and fossil record?
20. How do you know that an intrusion is younger than its surrounding rock layers?

MATH IN SCIENCE

21. Copy the graph below onto a separate sheet of paper. Place a dot on the *y*-axis at 100 percent. Then place a dot on the graph at each half-life to show how much of the parent material is left. Connect the points with a curved line. Will the percentage of parent material ever reach zero? Explain.

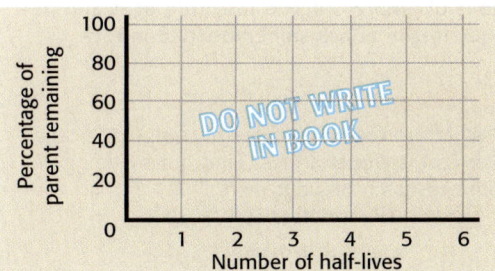

INTERPRETING GRAPHICS

Examine the drawing below, and answer the following questions.

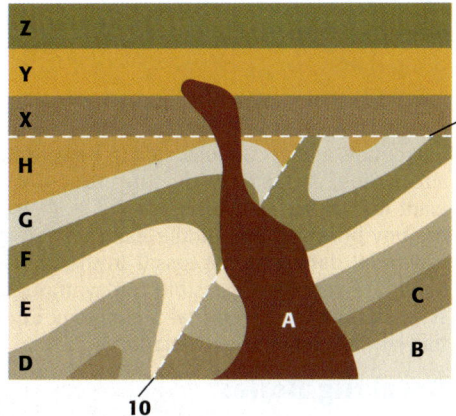

22. Is intrusion A younger or older than layer X?
23. What kind of unconformity is marked by 5?
24. Is intrusion A younger or older than fault 10? Why?
25. Other than the intrusion and faulting, what event occurred in layers B, C, D, E, F, G, and H? Number this event, the intrusion, and the faulting in the order they occurred.

 Take a minute to review your answers to the Pre-Reading Questions found at the bottom of page 132. Have your answers changed? If necessary, revise your answers based on what you have learned since you began this chapter.

159

Concept Mapping

17. 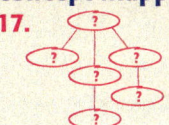 An answer to this exercise can be found at the end of this book.

CRITICAL THINKING AND PROBLEM SOLVING

18. The petrified tree does not contain any wood because the wood tissue in the tree was completely replaced by minerals.
19. Animals leave tracks and create burrows in soil. Sediment fills in these features and buries them quickly. Over time, the sediment becomes rock and preserves these trace fossils.
20. The intrusion is always younger because the rock layers had to be present before the intrusion could disturb them.

MATH IN SCIENCE

21.

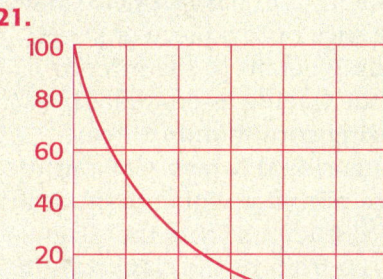

Mathematically, the percentage of parent material will never reach zero. In a real sample, however, all of the parent material will eventually decay.

INTERPRETING GRAPHICS

22. younger
23. an angular unconformity
24. Intrusion A is younger than fault 10 because the intrusion is not disturbed by the fault.
25. Erosion; the fault occurred first, then layers eroded, and finally the intrusion occurred.

 Concept Mapping Transparency 6

 Blackline masters of this Chapter Review can be found in the **Study Guide**.

SCIENCE, TECHNOLOGY, AND SOCIETY

CAT Scanning Fossils

Teaching Strategy
You may want to devote class time to illustrate how a three-dimensional CAT scan is derived from hundreds of two-dimensional X rays. If students have trouble visualizing this, you can use a three-dimensional model.

Obtain a sliced loaf of bread. After numbering each slice in order with either a marker or with flagged toothpicks, randomly distribute a slice to each student, and have students trace the slice onto a piece of paper, adding details to the interior of the tracing as desired. This tracing corresponds to two-dimensional X rays. Call out the slice numbers sequentially, and have students bring the slices to the front of the classroom in order. As each slice is received, place the slice in a stack so students can see the three-dimensional shape emerge. The three-dimensional shape corresponds to the three-dimensional image of a fossil after all of the X rays have been "stacked" by a computer.

Science, Technology, and Society

CAT Scanning Fossils

Imagine that you've just found the fossilized skull of a small prehistoric mammal. You examine it very carefully, taking note of its size, shape, and external features. But you also want to look at features inside the skull, like the tiny bones of the middle ear. Can you do it without damaging the fossil? In the past it would have been impossible. Today, though, scientists are using medical technology to do this kind of detailed examination.

Breaking Bones
Paleontologists want to learn all they can about the fossils they study. They want to know about internal structures as well as external ones. Paleontologists usually grind a fossil away layer by layer, recording their observations as they go. Unfortunately, by the time they finish analyzing all the internal structures, the fossil is destroyed! This is a real problem if you want to show someone else your discovery.

Scientists with X-ray Vision
Now paleontologists have another choice. *Computerized axial tomography* (CAT scanning) is quickly replacing the more destructive method of studying internal structures. Originally designed as medical technology to examine the inside of the human skull, CAT scans provide interior views of a fossil without even touching its surface.

To understand how a CAT scan works, imagine a dolphin jumping through a hoop. As the dolphin passes through the hoop a CAT scan machine takes an X-ray picture of it from *every point around the hoop.* In effect, the machine takes a series of cross-section X-ray pictures of the dolphin. A computer then assembles these "slices" to create a three-dimensional picture of the dolphin. Every part of the dolphin's insides can then be studied without dissecting the dolphin.

When a paleontologist needs to reconstruct an entire skull, a series of two-dimensional "slice" shots is taken and the "slices" are combined through computer imaging to produce a three-dimensional image of the skull—inside and out!

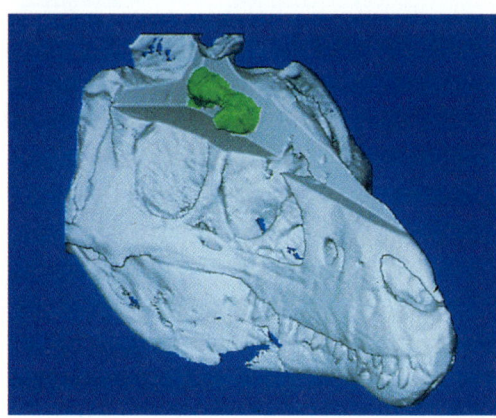

▲ *This CAT scan shows the size and location of the dinosaur* Nanotyrannosaurus rex's *brain.*

What's Hidden Inside?
Using CAT scans, scientists have learned much more about the internal structures of fossils. They have used CAT scans to look at the skeletons of embryos inside fossilized eggs and to study fragile bones still embedded in rock.

On Your Own
▶ What are the advantages of using CAT scans over conventional X rays? Find out by doing some research on your own.

Sample Answer to On Your Own
A conventional X ray gives an image of all layers of the skull at one time, superimposed on each other, making it difficult to see details behind opaque layers of rock or fossilized bone. CAT scans can produce virtual "sections" through an object, making it possible to see all of the internal features clearly.

CAREERS

PALEONTOLOGIST

Jack Horner found his first fossil bones at age 7 or 8 while collecting rocks at his father's quarry. From then on, he was hooked on dinosaurs. "I became a paleontologist because I like to dig in the dirt, discover things, and piece together puzzles," Horner says. As one of the world's leading experts on dinosaurs, Horner is curator of paleontology at the Museum of the Rockies, in Bozeman, Montana.

A mother nuzzles her babies in a nest. Nearby, another mother lets out a worried yelp; one of her babies has crawled out of its nest and is scampering away. The mother quickly captures her baby and returns it to safety. Puppies? Birds? No—dinosaurs! Or so Jack Horner believes.

Horner has come to this conclusion by comparing dinosaur fossils with modern alligators and birds. "I am studying how dinosaur bones developed, and I'm comparing them with the development of bones of alligators and birds so that we can learn more about dinosaur growth and nesting behaviors," Horner says. "I think that birds probably evolved from dinosaurs. If I find fossils of several nests close to each other, that tells me that the dinosaurs that built those nests may have lived together in a group."

Meeting the Challenge

As a child, Horner had difficulties in school because he had a learning disability called dyslexia. But no learning disability could dampen Horner's enthusiasm for science, especially the study of dinosaurs. "I like dinosaurs and figuring out what the world looked like at different times in the past. I've always liked the detective work that's involved in paleontology. You can't study a living dinosaur, so you have to figure out everything using clues from the past."

Boning Up on the Latest . . .

One of Horner's current projects is analyzing whether *Tyrannosaurus rex* was a vicious predator, as is often pictured, or a scavenger, eating other animals' kills. The more he studies fossil clues, the more Horner leans toward accepting the scavenger hypothesis. "Predatory animals require certain characteristics in order to be efficient killers. They need to be able to run fast, and they need to be able to maneuver and leap," Horner explains. "*T. rex* couldn't run fast, wasn't agile, and couldn't jump around or even fall down without doing serious damage to itself or even dying."

Decide for Yourself

▶ Observe the behavior of birds in your area. Focus on one or two species. Note their eating habits, the sounds they make, and their interactions with other birds. Do you think birds might have evolved from dinosaurs? Use your observations to support your theory.

▲ A model of a Maisasaura hatching.

CAREERS
Paleontologist— Jack Horner

Background

As Jack Horner compared the behavior of modern birds with the fossil evidence of dinosaurs, he began to think that dinosaurs behaved more like birds than lizards. Further evidence led him to hypothesize that birds evolved from dinosaurs. For example, evidence suggests that some dinosaurs guarded their eggs and took care of their young, much like birds do.

Other scientists disagree with the "birds from dinosaurs" theory, and the relationship between dinosaurs and modern birds remains a hotly debated topic among scientists.

Answer to Decide for Yourself
Answers will vary.

UNIT 3

TIMELINE
The Restless Earth

In this unit, you will learn about the Earth's internal structure. Many mysteries remain because we cannot see very far inside the Earth. The deepest holes we can dig barely scratch the planet's surface. If the Earth were an orange, our attempts to dig into it would not even break through the peel. One way scientists can learn about the Earth's interior is by studying earthquakes and volcanoes. This timeline shows some of the events that have occurred as scientists have tried to understand our dynamic Earth.

1864
Jules Verne's *A Journey to the Center of the Earth* is published. In this fictional story, the heroes enter and exit the Earth through volcanoes.

1883
Krakatau erupts, killing 36,000 people.

1966
A worldwide network of seismographs is established.

1979
Volcanoes are discovered on Io, one of Jupiter's moons.

1980
Mount St. Helens erupts.

1896
Henry Ford builds his first car.

1906
San Francisco burns in the aftermath of an earthquake.

1935
Charles Richter devises a system of measuring the strength of earthquakes.

1912
Alfred Wegener proposes his continental-drift theory.

1951
Color television is introduced in the United States.

1994
An eight-legged robot named *Dante II* descends into the crater of an active volcano in Alaska.

1997
The population of the Caribbean island of Montserrat dwindles to less than half its original size as frequent eruptions of the Soufriere Hills volcano force evacuations.

1982
Compact discs (CDs) and compact-disc players are made available to the public.

The Restless Earth

Chapter Organizer

CHAPTER ORGANIZATION	TIME MINUTES	OBJECTIVES	LABS, INVESTIGATIONS, AND DEMONSTRATIONS
Chapter Opener pp. 164–165	45	National Standards: SAI 1, SPSP 5, ES 1b, 2a	**Start-Up Activity** Continental Collisions, p. 165
Section 1 Inside the Earth	90	▶ Identify and describe the layers of the Earth by what they are made of. ▶ Identify and describe the layers of the Earth by their physical properties. ▶ Define *tectonic plate*. ▶ Explain how scientists know about the structure of Earth's interior. UCP 2, SAI 1, SPSP 5, ES 1a	**QuickLab**, Floating Mountains, p. 171 GENERAL **Labs You Can Eat**, Rescue Near the Center of the Earth, Lab 13 GENERAL **Whiz-Bang Demonstrations**, Thar She Blows! Demo 18 GENERAL
Section 2 Restless Continents	90	▶ Describe Wegener's theory of continental drift, and explain why it was not accepted at first. ▶ Explain how sea-floor spreading provides a way for continents to move. ▶ Describe how new oceanic crust forms at mid-ocean ridges. ▶ Explain how magnetic reversals provide evidence for sea-floor spreading. UCP 2, HNS 1, ES 2a	**Labs You Can Eat**, Cracks in the Hard-Boiled Earth, Lab 14 BASIC
Section 3 The Theory of Plate Tectonics	90	▶ Describe the three forces thought to move tectonic plates. ▶ Describe the three types of tectonic plate boundaries. ▶ Explain how scientists measure the rate at which tectonic plates move. UCP 2, SPSP 4, 5, HNS 1, 3, ES 1b; LabBook SAI 1, ST 1	**Making Models**, Convection Connection, p. 656 GENERAL **Datasheets for LabBook**, Convection Connection, Datasheet 13 GENERAL **Labs You Can Eat**, Dough Fault of Your Own, Lab 15 ADVANCED
Section 4 Deforming the Earth's Crust	90	▶ Describe major types of folds. ▶ Explain how the three major types of faults differ. ▶ Name and describe the most common types of mountains. ▶ Explain how various types of mountains form. SAI 1, ES 1b, 1c, 2a; LabBook UCP 2, SAI 1	**Demonstration**, p. 181 in ATE GENERAL **Making Models**, Oh, the Pressure! p. 657 GENERAL **Datasheets for LabBook**, Oh, the Pressure! Datasheet 14 GENERAL **Long-Term Projects & Research Ideas**, Project 35 ADVANCED

*See page **T20** for a complete correlation of this book with the* **NATIONAL SCIENCE EDUCATION STANDARDS.**

TECHNOLOGY RESOURCES

 Guided Reading Audio CD English or Spanish, Chapter 7

 One-Stop Planner CD-ROM with Test Generator

 CNN Scientists in Action, Studying Sea Floor Tectonics, Segment 10

Chapter 7 • Plate Tectonics

CLASSROOM WORKSHEETS, TRANSPARENCIES, AND RESOURCES	SCIENCE INTEGRATION AND CONNECTIONS	REVIEW AND ASSESSMENT
Directed Reading Worksheet 7 BASIC **Science Puzzlers, Twisters & Teasers,** Worksheet 7 ADVANCED		
Directed Reading Worksheet 7, Section 1 BASIC **Transparency 122,** The Composition of the Earth **Transparency 123,** The Earth's Crust, Lithosphere, and Asthenosphere **Transparency 124,** The Earth's Mesosphere, Outer Core, and Inner Core **Transparency 125,** The Tectonic Plates **Reinforcement Worksheet 7,** The Layered Earth GENERAL **Critical Thinking Worksheet 7,** Planet of Waves ADVANCED	**Math and More,** p. 167 in ATE BASIC **Connect to Physical Science,** p. 167 in ATE **MathBreak,** Using Models, p. 168 GENERAL **Connect to Physical Science,** p. 168 in ATE **Biology Connection,** p. 169 **Cross-Disciplinary Focus,** p. 170 in ATE ADVANCED **Multicultural Connection,** p. 171 in ATE	**Review,** p. 172 GENERAL **Quiz,** p. 172 in ATE GENERAL **Alternative Assessment,** p. 172 in ATE GENERAL
Directed Reading Worksheet 7, Section 2 BASIC **Transparency 28,** Evolution of the Galápagos Finches **Transparency 126,** The Breakup of Pangaea	**Connect to Life Science,** p. 174 in ATE **Connect to Physical Science,** p. 175 in ATE **Physics Connection,** p. 176	**Review,** p. 176 GENERAL **Quiz,** p. 176 in ATE GENERAL **Alternative Assessment,** p. 176 in ATE ADVANCED
Directed Reading Worksheet 7, Section 3 BASIC **Teaching Transparencies 127–129** **Math Skills for Science Worksheet 4,** A Shortcut for Multiplying Large Numbers GENERAL **Reinforcement Worksheet 7,** A Moving Jigsaw Puzzle BASIC	**Cross-Disciplinary Focus,** p. 178 in ATE GENERAL **Math and More,** p. 179 in ATE BASIC **Science, Technology, and Society:** Living on the Mid-Atlantic Ridge, p. 192 GENERAL **Scientific Debate:** Continental Drift, p. 193 GENERAL	**Homework,** p. 179 in ATE ADVANCED **Review,** p. 180 GENERAL **Quiz,** p. 180 in ATE GENERAL **Alternative Assessment,** p. 180 in ATE GENERAL
Directed Reading Worksheet 7, Section 4 BASIC	**Cross-Disciplinary Focus,** p. 182 in ATE **Connect to Life Science,** p. 183 in ATE **Apply,** p. 184 GENERAL **Multicultural Connection,** pp. 185, 187 in ATE **Connect to Astronomy,** p. 185 in ATE	**Homework,** p. 182 in ATE GENERAL **Self-Check,** p. 183 **Review,** p. 187 GENERAL **Quiz,** p. 187 in ATE GENERAL **Alternative Assessment,** p. 187 in ATE ADVANCED

 Holt, Rinehart and Winston On-line Resources
go.hrw.com
For worksheets and other teaching aids related to this chapter, visit the HRW Web site and type in the keyword: **HSTTEC**

 **National Science Teachers Association**
www.scilinks.org
Encourage students to use the sciLINKS numbers listed in the internet connect boxes to access information and resources on the **NSTA** Web site.

END-OF-CHAPTER REVIEW AND ASSESSMENT

Chapter Review in Study Guide
Vocabulary and Notes in Study Guide
Chapter Tests with Performance-Based Assessment, Chapter 7 Test, Performance-Based Assessment 7
Concept Mapping Transparency 7

Chapter 7 • Chapter Organizer   **163B**

Chapter Resources & Worksheets

Visual Resources

TEACHING TRANSPARENCIES

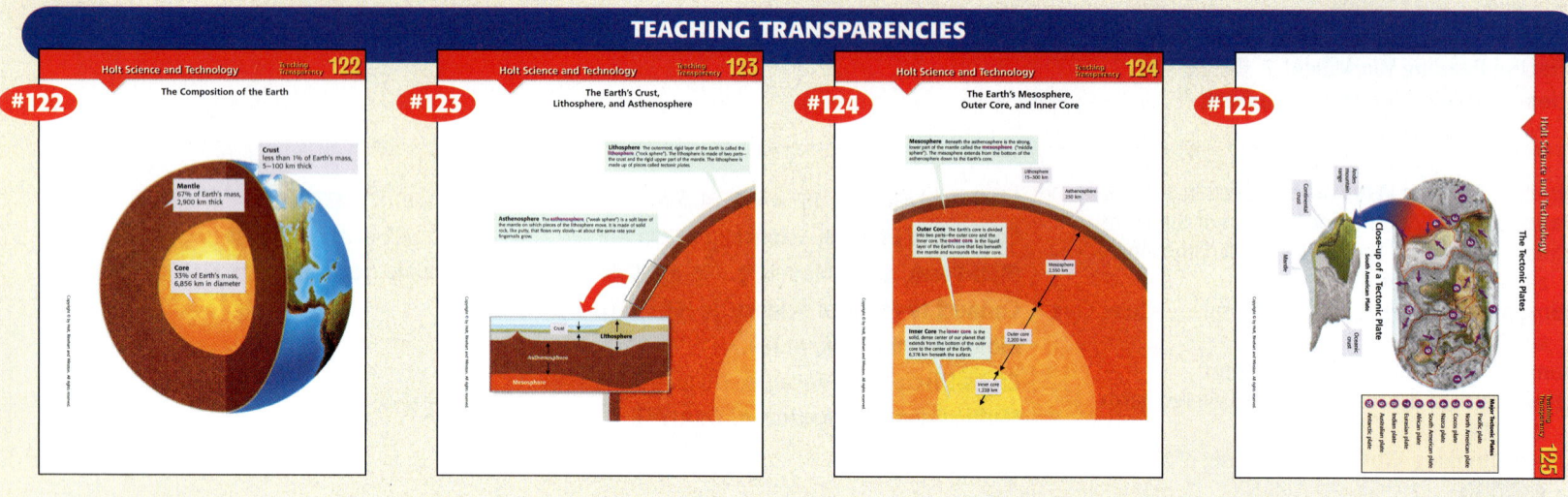

TEACHING TRANSPARENCIES

CONCEPT MAPPING TRANSPARENCY

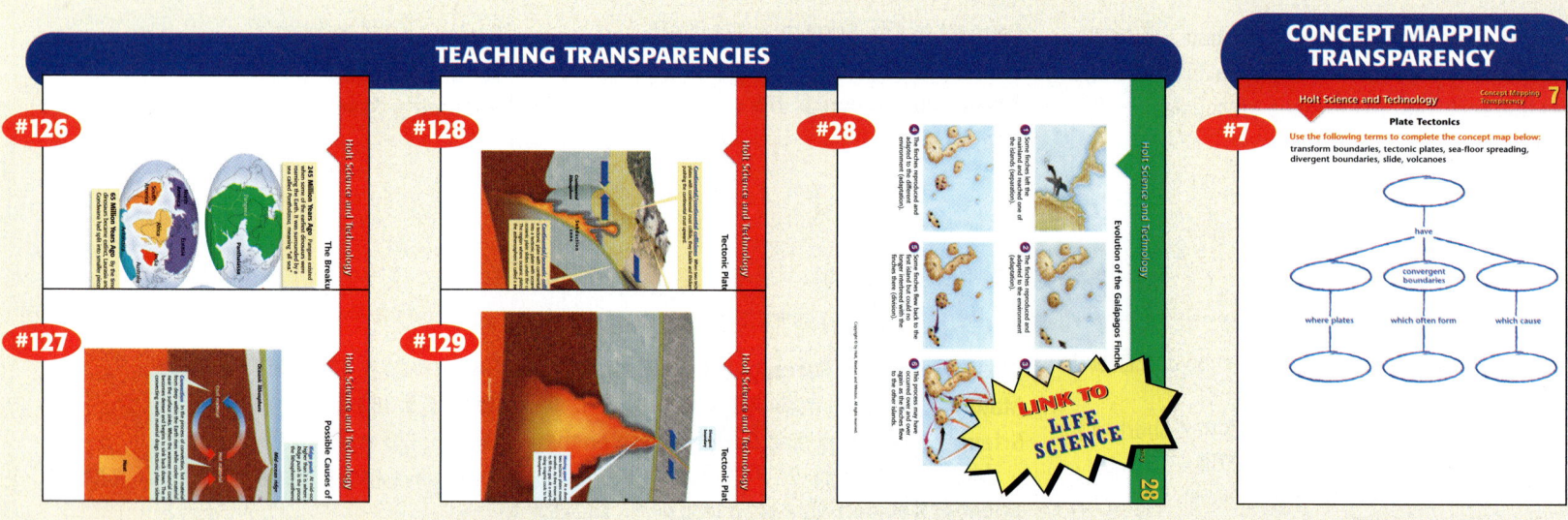

Meeting Individual Needs

DIRECTED READING

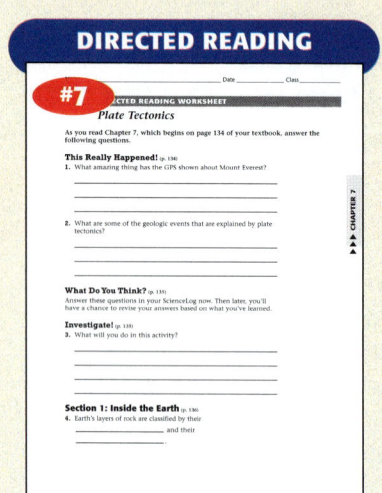

REINFORCEMENT & VOCABULARY REVIEW

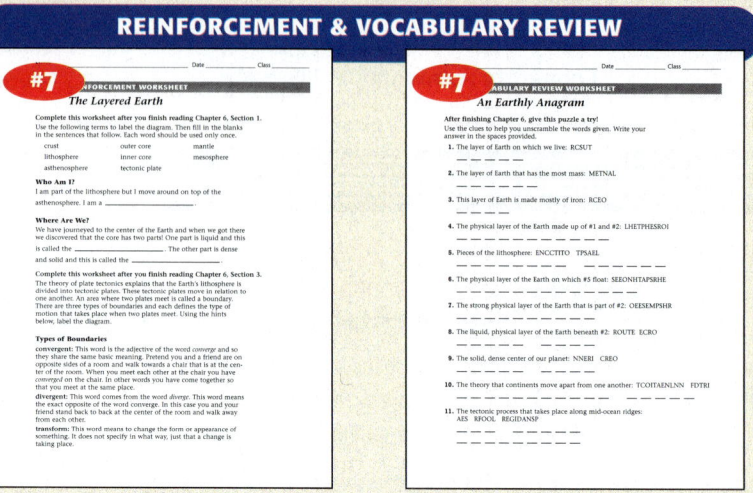

SCIENCE PUZZLERS, TWISTERS & TEASERS

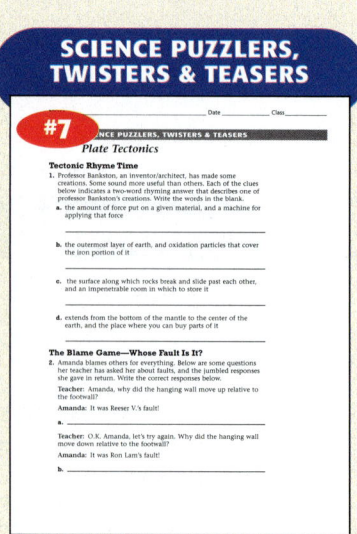

Chapter 7 • Plate Tectonics

Chapter 7 • Plate Tectonics

Review & Assessment

STUDY GUIDE
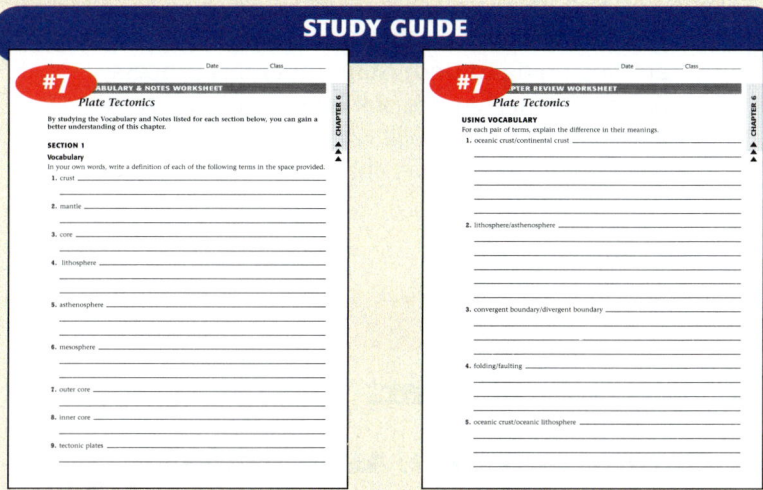

CHAPTER TESTS WITH PERFORMANCE-BASED ASSESSMENT
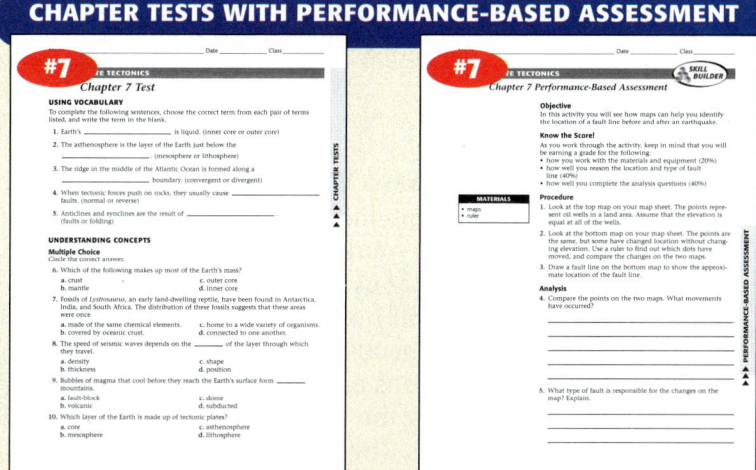

Lab Worksheets

LABS YOU CAN EAT
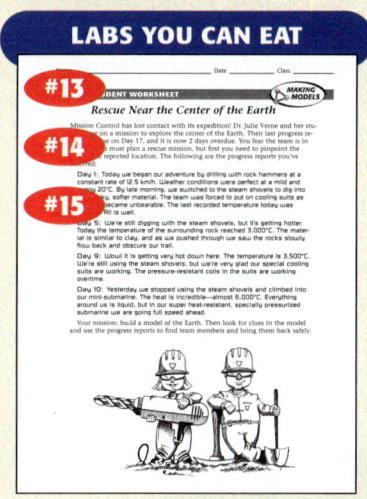

WHIZ-BANG DEMONSTRATIONS

LONG-TERM PROJECTS & RESEARCH IDEAS
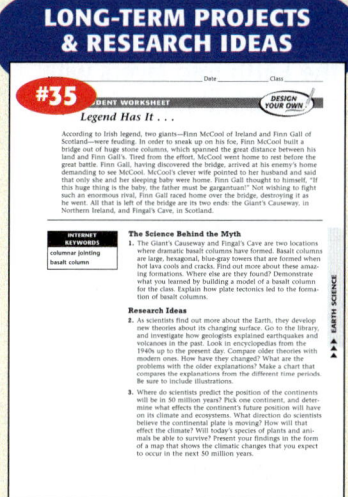

DATASHEETS FOR LABBOOK
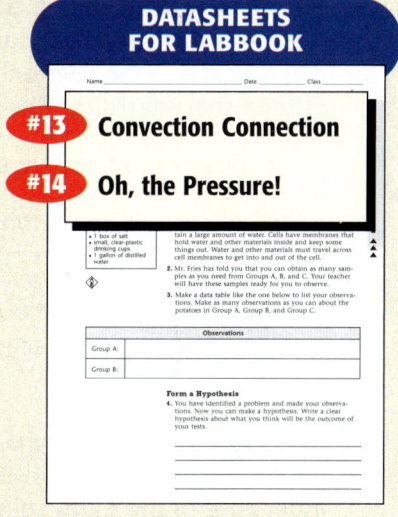

Applications & Extensions

CRITICAL THINKING & PROBLEM SOLVING
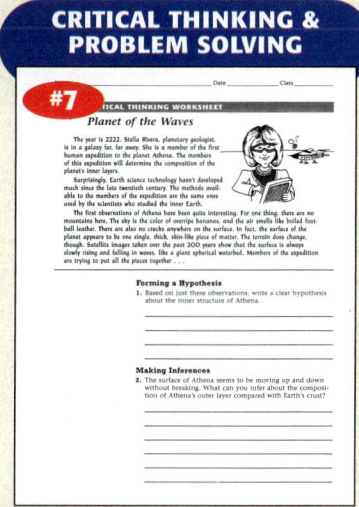

SCIENTISTS IN ACTION
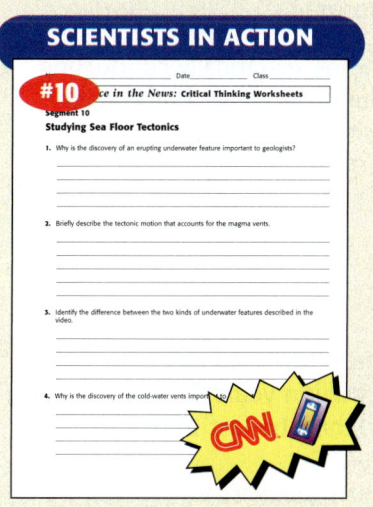

Chapter 7 • Chapter Resources & Worksheets

Chapter Background

SECTION 1
Inside the Earth

▶ **Continents and the Earth's Crust**
Continents are large, continuous landmasses composed of crust that is generally much older than the surrounding oceanic crust. The core of a continent, called a craton, is generally composed of ancient, crystalline igneous and metamorphic rock. Cratons are relatively thick and make up the most stable part of continents. They range from 200 million to 3.9 billion years of age.

▶ **Heat Within the Earth**
The Earth's internal heat contributes to the process of differentiation—the division of the Earth into layers with distinct characteristics. This heat has three main sources:

- the decay of radioactive elements
- the collapse of iron into Earth's core during its formation
- leftover energy from the accretion and compression of particles that coalesced to form Earth

▶ **Earth's Inner Core**
Research conducted in 1996 suggests that the solid inner core of the Earth spins faster than the rest of the planet. This 2,456 km wide ball of hot iron moves at a speed that would allow it to lap Earth's surface once every 400 years. This information may give scientists clues about how the Earth formed.

- The Earth's outer core is a hot, electrically conducting liquid thought to be continuously moved by convection. This layer's conductivity combines with the differential spin of the Earth's inner core to create powerful electric currents that, in turn, generate the Earth's magnetic field.

IS THAT A FACT!

◆ Earth's magnetic poles have reversed more than 177 times in the last 85 million years. The most recent switch occurred within the last 2 million years. With complex computer models, scientists are beginning to understand how this process happens, but they are still unable to predict the next time the poles will reverse or how life on Earth will be affected by this change.

SECTION 2
Restless Continents

▶ **Continental Drift: An Old Idea**
The idea that the continents were once joined together was not a new idea in Alfred Wegener's time. In 1620, Francis Bacon noted that the continents seemed to fit together like a jigsaw puzzle, but no one could understand how they moved. In 1858, a French scientist named Antonio Snider-Pellegrini cited fossil evidence that suggested the continents had been joined. Wegener's studies in 1915 were the first exhaustive research on the topic, combining evidence from many disciplines. In 1958, an American geologist named Frank Taylor pointed out geologic similarities between South America and Africa. But neither scientist could explain how the continents had separated, and their observations were dismissed. It was not until the discovery of sea-floor spreading that the continental drift hypothesis was accepted.

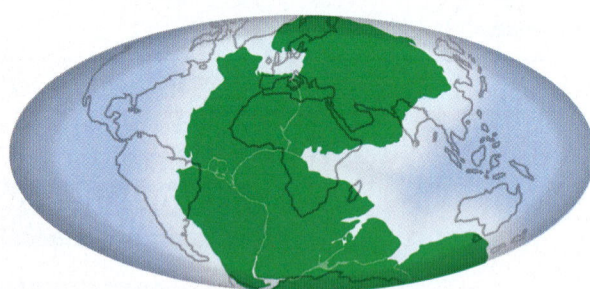

▶ **Testing the Continental Drift Hypothesis**
After sea-floor spreading was discovered in the 1960s, research groups tested Wegener's hypothesis using as many methods as possible:

- The edges of continental slopes were mapped with sonar and shown to fit together even better than the coastlines did.

Chapter 7 • Plate Tectonics

- New radiometric dating methods showed that rocks in corresponding parts of Africa and South America formed at the same time.

- The dating of igneous rocks around mid-ocean ridges showed a symmetrical pattern, with older rocks located farther away from the rifts. Few rocks older than 180 million years were discovered on the ocean floor. This indicates that the oceanic lithosphere is continuously recycled.

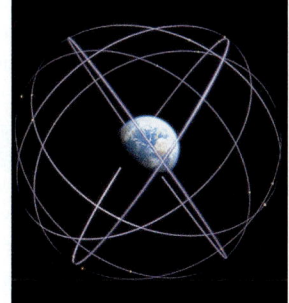

- Scientists found that zones of magnetic reversals also followed a symmetrical pattern on either side of mid-ocean ridges, matching the pattern revealed by the ages of those rocks.

- The horizontal magnetic reversals recorded in the ocean floor matched those recorded in vertical sequences of lava flows on continents.

▶ Harry Hammond Hess (1906–1969)

Henry Hess was an American geologist who proposed the idea of sea-floor spreading in 1960, thus playing a key role in developing the theory of plate tectonics. Hess suggested that convection within the Earth was continuously creating new ocean floor at the mid-ocean ridges. He also theorized that rocks would be older at increasing distances from these ridges, an expectation confirmed by research beginning in 1963. Hess also correctly explained the subduction of oceanic crust beneath less dense continental crust.

SECTION 3

The Theory of Plate Tectonics

▶ Trenches

Where an oceanic plate subducts under another tectonic plate, a long, steep-sided trench forms on the sea floor. On average, subduction trenches are 2,000–4,000 m lower than the rest of the ocean floor. Nevertheless, some animals, including species of sea cucumbers, sea anemones, and marine worms, are capable of living in the cold, pressurized depths of ocean trenches.

IS THAT A FACT!

▶ The Mariana Trench, which is 2,500 km long and 11,033 m below sea level at its deepest, is the deepest known point on Earth. This trench is located where the Pacific plate is subducted beneath the Philippine plate.

SECTION 4

Deforming the Earth's Crust

▶ Fault Versus Fold

Tectonic activity exerts a tremendous amount of pressure on crustal rocks; whether they bend or break depends on several factors:

- type of stress—If stress is applied gradually, rocks often fold; if stress is applied suddenly, rocks tend to fault.

- composition of rock—Brittle rocks, such as sandstone, tend to break; ductile (easily bent) rocks, such as shale, tend to fold.

- temperature—As the temperature at the point of stress increases, rocks are more likely to fold rather than fault.

For background information about teaching strategies and issues, refer to the *Professional Reference for Teachers*.

Plate Tectonics

Pre-Reading Questions

Students may not know the answers to these questions before reading the chapter, so accept any reasonable response.

Suggested Answers

1. Mountain ranges move because they are part of tectonic plates, which move around on top of the asthenosphere.
2. Mountains can form in three main ways: when rock layers are folded as tectonic plates collide; when the crust is stretched due to tension, forming a large number of normal faults; and when volcanoes are formed as molten rock erupts onto the Earth's surface.

Directed Reading Worksheet 7

Science Puzzlers, Twisters & Teasers Worksheet 7

Guided Reading Audio CD
English or Spanish, Chapter 7

CHAPTER 7

Plate Tectonics

Sections

1. **Inside the Earth** 166
   MathBreak 168
   Biology Connection .. 169
   QuickLab 171
   Internet Connect 172
2. **Restless Continents** ... 173
   Physics Connection .. 176
3. **The Theory of Plate Tectonics** 177
   Internet Connect 180
4. **Deforming the Earth's Crust** 181
   Apply 184
   Internet Connect 187

Chapter Review 190
Feature Articles 192, 193
LabBook 656–659

Pre-Reading Questions

1. Why do entire mountain ranges move?
2. How do mountains form?

164

When Continents Collide

The Himalayas are the highest mountains on Earth. They are located between India and Asia in a region where two continents are slowly crashing into each other. This photo shows the highest mountain of all—Mount Everest. At an elevation of 8,848 m, the air at the top of Mount Everest is so thin that climbers must bring their own oxygen! In this chapter you will learn about how and where different types of mountains form. You will also learn about how scientists came up with *plate tectonics*, the theory that revolutionized geology.

Mountain climbers must brave extreme conditions when climbing mountains such as Mount Everest.

---

internet connect

HRW On-line Resources
go.hrw.com
For worksheets and other teaching aids, visit the HRW Web site and type in the keyword: **HSTTEC**

www.scilinks.com
Use the *sci*LINKS numbers at the end of each chapter for additional resources on the **NSTA** Web site.

www.cnnfyi.com
Visit the CNN Web site for current events coverage and classroom resources.

164 Chapter 7 • Plate Tectonics

START-UP Activity

CONTINENTAL COLLISIONS

As you can see, continents not only move, but they can also crash into each other. In this activity, you will model the collision of two continents.

Procedure

1. Obtain **two stacks of paper,** each about 1 cm thick.
2. Place the two stacks of paper on a **flat surface,** such as a desk.
3. Very slowly, push the stacks of paper together so that they collide. Continue to push the stacks until the paper in one of the stacks folds over.
4. Repeat step 3, but this time push the two stacks together at a different angle. For example, if you pushed the flat edges together in step 3, try pushing the corners of the paper together this time.

Analysis

5. What happens to the stacks of paper when they collide with each other?
6. Do all of the pieces of paper get pushed upward? If not, what happens to those pieces that do not get pushed upward?
7. What type of landform does this model predict as the result of a continental collision?

START-UP Activity

CONTINENTAL COLLISIONS

MATERIALS

FOR EACH STUDENT:
- two stacks of paper
- flat surface

Answers to START-UP Activity

5. The stacks of paper buckle and fold over. One stack of paper slid under the other.
6. No, some pieces of paper slid under the opposite stack, while others slid into the other stack.
7. Continental collisions form large mountain ranges like the Himalayas.

SECTION 1

Focus

Inside the Earth

This section describes the classification of the Earth according to composition (crust, mantle, and core) and according to physical structure (lithosphere, asthenosphere, mesosphere, outer core, and inner core). Students then learn about *tectonic plates*. The section concludes with a discussion of how scientists study seismic waves to map the Earth's interior.

🔔 Bellringer

On the board or an overhead projector, pose the following question to your students at the beginning of class:

If you journeyed to the center of the Earth, what do you think you would see along the way?

Have students draw an illustration of their journey in their ScienceLog. **Sheltered English**

1) Motivate

COOPERATIVE LEARNING

Pose the following situation to small groups of students for discussion: Measurements show that the land west of the San Andreas Fault, in California, is moving toward the northwest at a rate of 5 cm per year relative to the land east of the fault. What forces do you think cause this movement? Where do these forces come from? When groups agree on a hypothesis, have them create illustrations or a model they can use to explain their theory to the class.

Section 1

Terms to Learn

crust
mantle
core
lithosphere
asthenosphere
mesosphere
outer core
inner core
tectonic plate

What You'll Do

- Identify and describe the layers of the Earth by what they are made of.
- Identify and describe the layers of the Earth by their physical properties.
- Define *tectonic plate*.
- Explain how scientists know about the structure of Earth's interior.

Inside the Earth

The Earth is not just a ball of solid rock. It is made of several layers with different physical properties and compositions. As you will discover, scientists think about the Earth's layers in two ways—by their *composition* and by their *physical properties*.

Earth's layers are made of different mixtures of elements. This is what is meant by differences in composition. Many of the Earth's layers also have different physical properties. Physical properties include temperature, density, and ability to flow. Let's first take a look at the composition of the Earth.

The Composition of the Earth

The Earth is divided into three layers—the *crust, mantle,* and *core*—based on what each one is made of. The lightest materials make up the outermost layer, and the densest materials make up the inner layers. This is because lighter materials tend to float up, while heavier materials sink.

The Crust The **crust** is the outermost layer of the Earth. Ranging from 5 to 100 km thick, it is also the thinnest layer of the Earth. And because it is the layer we live on, we know more about this layer than we know about the other two.

There are two types of crust—continental and oceanic. *Continental crust* has a composition similar to granite. It has an average thickness of 30 km. *Oceanic crust* has a composition similar to basalt. It is generally between 5 and 8 km thick. Because basalt is denser than granite, oceanic crust is denser than continental crust.

Figure 1 Oceanic crust is thinner but denser than continental crust.

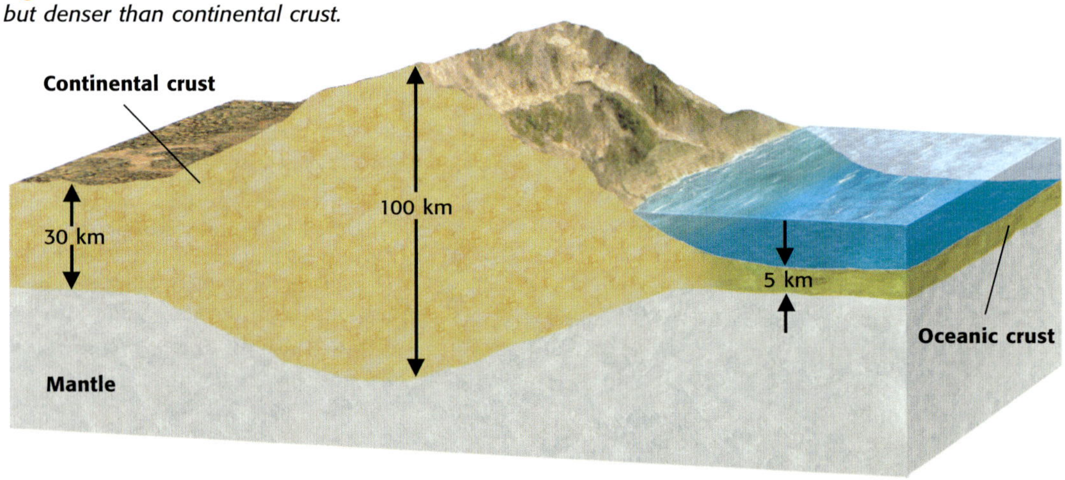

Directed Reading Worksheet 7 Section 1

IS THAT A FACT!

Two lines of evidence indicate that Earth's core is a mixture of iron and nickel. The core's density, which is similar to a mixture of iron and nickel, was determined by studying the way seismic waves travel through it. The Earth's magnetic field also suggests this composition.

166 Chapter 7 • Plate Tectonics

The Mantle The **mantle** is the layer of the Earth between the crust and the core. Compared with the crust, the mantle is extremely thick and contains most of the Earth's mass.

No one has ever seen what the mantle really looks like. It is just too far down to drill for a sample. Scientists must infer what the composition and other characteristics of the mantle are from observations they make on the Earth's surface. In some places mantle rock has been pushed up to the surface by tectonic forces, allowing scientists to observe the rock directly.

As you can see in **Figure 2,** another place scientists look is on the ocean floor, where molten rock from the mantle flows out of active volcanoes. These underwater volcanoes are like windows through the crust into the mantle. The "windows" have given us strong clues about the composition of the mantle. Scientists have learned that the mantle's composition is similar to that of the mineral olivine, which has large amounts of iron and magnesium compared with other common minerals.

The Core By studying the different layers that make up the Earth, geologists can get an idea of which elements each is made of. They think that the Earth's *core* is made mostly of iron, with smaller amounts of nickel and possibly some sulfur and oxygen. The **core** extends from the bottom of the mantle to the center of the Earth. As you can see in **Figure 3,** the diameter of the planet Mars is slightly smaller than that of the Earth's core.

Figure 2 Volcanic vents on the ocean floor, such as this one off the coast of Hawaii, allow magma to escape from the mantle beneath oceanic crust.

Crust less than 1% of Earth's mass, 5–100 km thick

Mantle 67% of Earth's mass, 2,900 km thick

Core 33% of Earth's mass, 6,856 km in diameter

Mars 11% the mass of Earth, 6,787 km in diameter

Figure 3 The Earth is made up of three layers, as shown here.

2) Teach

USING THE FIGURE

Discuss scale models with students, and point out that the illustrations showing cross sections of the Earth in Sections 1 and 2 are drawn to scale. These include **Figures 1, 3, 6, 12,** and **13.** Have students identify illustrations in the text that are not drawn to scale and practice making scale drawings of the Earth's structure.

MATH and MORE

Tell students to assume that the average thickness for the crust is 50 km, and have them calculate how much thicker the mantle is than the crust. Invite volunteers to write their calculations on the board. (2,900 km ÷ 50 km = 58; The mantle is 58 times thicker than the crust.)

CONNECT TO PHYSICAL SCIENCE

Use **Figure 3** to discuss the relationship between mass, volume, and density. Point out that although the core is 33 percent of Earth's mass, it is only 10 percent of Earth's volume. The Earth's core is composed mostly of iron, which is much denser than the mantle and crustal rocks that make up the rest of the Earth. Ask students to draw conclusions about the density of Mars compared to the density of the Earth's core.

Teaching Transparency 122 "The Composition of the Earth"

MISCONCEPTION ALERT

Explain the differences between radius, diameter, and thickness. In **Figure 3,** the crust and mantle are shells measured by their thickness. The core is a sphere, so it is measured by its diameter or radius.

2 Teach, continued

Answers to MATHBREAK

$\frac{150 \text{ km}}{6,378 \text{ km}} = 0.0235 = 2.35\%$

$2.35\% \times 1.00 \text{ m} = 0.0235 \text{ m}$, or 2.35 cm

READING STRATEGY

Prediction Guide Before students read this page, ask them the following question: If you could burrow to the center of the Earth, what would you expect to happen to the pressure, the temperature, and the solidity of matter? Each successive layer will:

a. become hotter, have higher pressure, and become more liquid

b. become cooler, have higher pressure, and become harder

c. become hotter, have lower pressure, and become more liquid

d. become hotter and have higher pressure; the solidity of layers will depend on temperature and pressure

(answer: d)

CONNECT TO PHYSICAL SCIENCE

The composition of the core is probably similar throughout. Why, then, is part of the core liquid and the rest solid? You would think that if the outer core were hot enough to be in a liquid state, the inner core would be at least as hot, if not hotter. The difference in physical states is due not to differences in temperature but to differences in pressure. Even though the inner core is extremely hot, the high pressure keeps the material in a solid state. The outer core, on the other hand, has less pressure. The pressure in the outer core is just low enough that the hot iron can stay in a liquid state.

168 Chapter 7 • Plate Tectonics

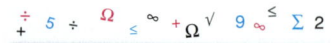

MATH BREAK

Using Models
Imagine that you are building a model of the Earth that is going to have a radius of 1 m. You find out that the average radius of the Earth is 6,378 km and that the thickness of the lithosphere is about 150 km. What percentage of the Earth's radius is the lithosphere? How thick (in centimeters) would you make the lithosphere in your model?

 Teaching Transparency 123 "The Earth's Crust, Lithosphere, and Asthenosphere"

The Structure of the Earth

So far we have talked about the composition of the Earth. Another way to look at how the Earth is made is to examine the physical properties of its layers. The Earth is divided into five main physical layers—the *lithosphere, asthenosphere, mesosphere, outer core,* and *inner core*. As shown below, each layer has its own set of physical properties.

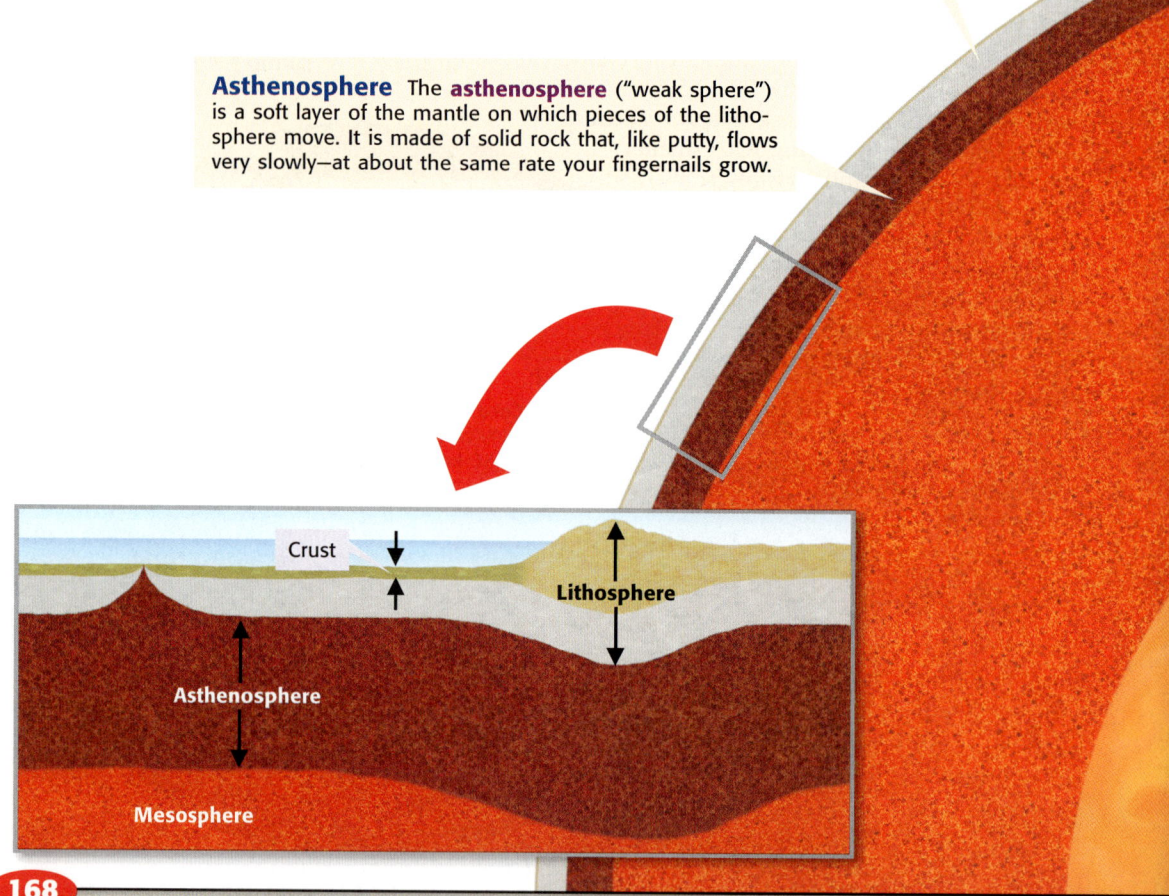

Lithosphere The outermost, rigid layer of the Earth is called the **lithosphere** ("rock sphere"). The lithosphere is made of two parts—the crust and the rigid upper part of the mantle. The lithosphere is divided into pieces called *tectonic plates*.

Asthenosphere The **asthenosphere** ("weak sphere") is a soft layer of the mantle on which pieces of the lithosphere move. It is made of solid rock that, like putty, flows very slowly—at about the same rate your fingernails grow.

MISCONCEPTION ALERT

Be sure students understand that the two systems of naming Earth's layers describe different properties. *Crust, mantle,* and *core* describe differences in chemical makeup; *lithosphere, asthenosphere,* and *mesosphere* describe differences in the response of the material to stress caused by differences in temperature and pressure.

Mesosphere Beneath the asthenosphere is the strong, lower part of the mantle called the **mesosphere** ("middle sphere"). The mesosphere extends from the bottom of the asthenosphere down to the Earth's core.

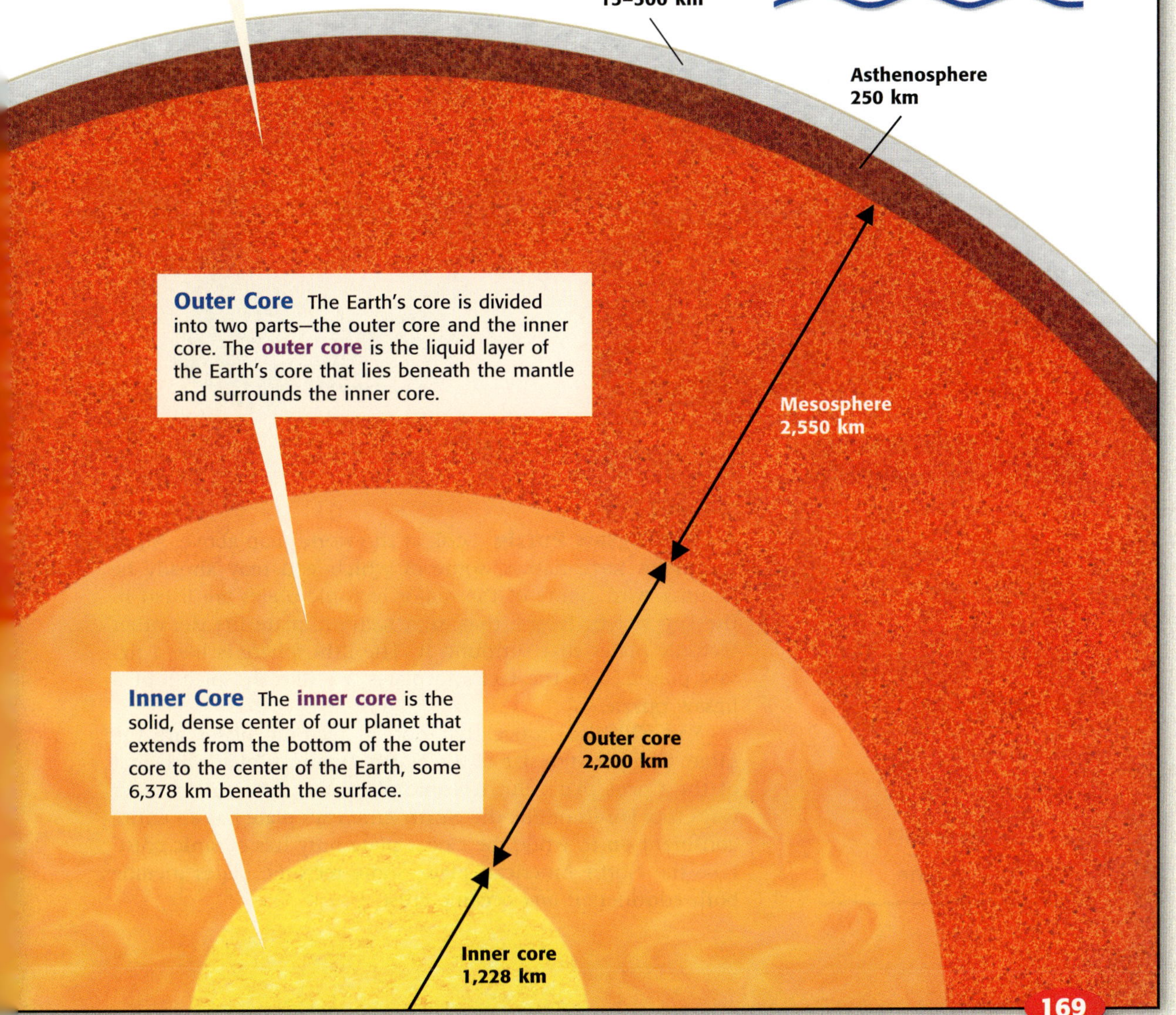

Outer Core The Earth's core is divided into two parts—the outer core and the inner core. The **outer core** is the liquid layer of the Earth's core that lies beneath the mantle and surrounds the inner core.

Inner Core The **inner core** is the solid, dense center of our planet that extends from the bottom of the outer core to the center of the Earth, some 6,378 km beneath the surface.

Biology CONNECTION

Scientists call the part of the Earth where life is possible the *biosphere*. The biosphere is the layer of the Earth above the crust and below the uppermost part of the atmosphere. It includes the oceans, the land surface, and the lower part of the atmosphere.

Lithosphere 15–300 km
Asthenosphere 250 km
Mesosphere 2,550 km
Outer core 2,200 km
Inner core 1,228 km

READING STRATEGY

Mnemonics Encourage students to look up and learn the meanings of the following prefixes:

litho-, meaning "rock" (The lithosphere is the Earth's solid, rocky crust.)

astheno-, meaning "weak" (The asthenosphere is a layer of slowly flowing rock beneath the lithosphere.)

meso-, meaning "middle" (The mesosphere lies between the asthenosphere and the outer core.)

By associating the prefix with the meaning, students may find it easier to remember the physical characteristics and locations of the Earth's layers. <mark>Sheltered English</mark>

USING THE FIGURE

Define the term *viscous,* and have students read about each layer in the illustration on these two pages. Ask students to sketch a simple model of the layers on scratch paper and label each layer "Solid," "Liquid," or "Viscous." As students work from the outside in, what pattern do they notice? (solid, viscous, solid, liquid, solid)

Ask students to explain why the inner core is not liquid. (Although the inner core is very hot, it is solid because of the pressure exerted on it.)

IS THAT A FACT!

The center of the Earth's core is hotter than the surface of the sun! The temperature of Earth's inner core reaches 6,000°C. The photosphere of the sun, which we see as its surface, has a temperature of 5,500°C. The sun's core temperature, however, is 15,000,000°C.

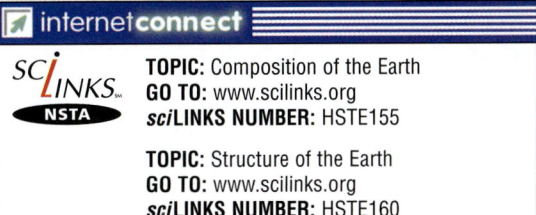

internetconnect

TOPIC: Composition of the Earth
GO TO: www.scilinks.org
*sci*LINKS NUMBER: HSTE155

TOPIC: Structure of the Earth
GO TO: www.scilinks.org
*sci*LINKS NUMBER: HSTE160

 Teaching Transparency 124 "The Earth's Mesosphere, Outer Core, and Inner Core"

Section 1 • Inside the Earth

2 Teach, continued

CROSS-DISCIPLINARY FOCUS

Language Arts *Tectonic* comes from the Greek word *tektonikos,* meaning "of a builder." Ask students to consider how this meaning is appropriate for tectonic plates. In what ways are tectonic plates responsible for building features on the Earth's surface? Have students write a poem that describes how the movement of tectonic plates slowly shapes the landscape around us.

BRAIN FOOD

The deepest hole ever drilled into the continental crust was in the Kola Peninsula, in Russia, in 1984. It was 12,226 m deep! It is very difficult to drill much deeper than that because the deeper you go, the hotter it gets. If you drill too deep, the hot rock flows around the drill bit, filling the hole faster than it can be drilled.

Have students calculate the depth, in kilometers, of the deepest human-made hole. Did it extend to the asthenosphere? (12.2 km; no)

Teaching Transparency 125
"The Tectonic Plates"
"Close-up of a Tectonic Plate"

Tectonic Plates

Tectonic plates are pieces of the lithosphere that move around on top of the asthenosphere. But what exactly does a tectonic plate look like? How big are tectonic plates? How and why do they move around? To answer these questions, start by thinking of the lithosphere as a giant jigsaw puzzle.

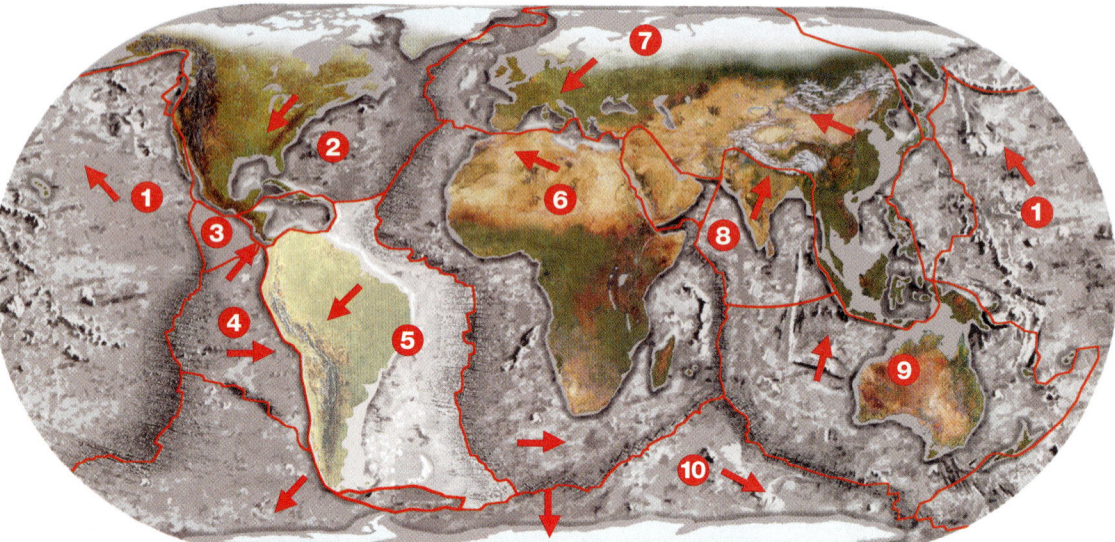

Figure 4 Tectonic plates fit together like the pieces of a jigsaw puzzle. On this map, the relative motions of some of the major tectonic plates are shown with arrows.

Major Tectonic Plates
1. Pacific plate
2. North American plate
3. Cocos plate
4. Nazca plate
5. South American plate
6. African plate
7. Eurasian plate
8. Indian plate
9. Australian plate
10. Antarctic plate

A Giant Jigsaw Puzzle Look at the world map above. All of the plates have names, some of which you may already be familiar with. Some of the major tectonic plates are listed in the key at left. Notice that each tectonic plate fits the other tectonic plates that surround it. The lithosphere is like a jigsaw puzzle, and the tectonic plates are like the pieces of a jigsaw puzzle.

You will also notice that not all tectonic plates are the same. Compare the size of the North American plate with that of the Cocos plate. But tectonic plates are different in other ways too. For example, the North American plate has an entire continent on it, while the Cocos plate only has oceanic crust. Like the North American plate, some tectonic plates include both continental *and* oceanic crust.

MISCONCEPTION ALERT

Be sure students realize that tectonic plates are not always neatly divided along continental lines. For example, the North American plate includes the North American continent, Greenland, half of Iceland, and part of Eurasia. All six of the Earth's large continental plates contain a continent and a large section of oceanic lithosphere. Some of the smaller tectonic plates contain only oceanic crust.

170   Chapter 7 • Plate Tectonics

A Tectonic Plate Close-up What would a tectonic plate look like if you could lift it out of its place? **Figure 5** shows what the South American plate might look like if you could. Notice that this tectonic plate consists of both oceanic and continental crust, just like the North American plate.

The thickest part of this tectonic plate is on the South American continent, under the Andes mountain range. The thinnest part of the South American plate is at the Mid-Atlantic Ridge.

Figure 5 *The South American plate is one of the many pieces of the spherical "jigsaw puzzle" we call the lithosphere.*

Tip of the Iceberg If you could look at a tectonic plate from the side, you would see that mountain ranges are like the tips of icebergs—there is much more material below the surface than above. Mountain ranges that occur in continental crust have very deep roots relative to their height. For example, the Rocky Mountains rise less than 5 km above sea level, but their roots go down to about 60 km *below* sea level.

But if continental crust is so much thicker than oceanic crust, why doesn't it sink down below the oceanic crust? Think back to the difference between continental and oceanic crust. Continental crust stands much higher than oceanic crust because it is both thicker and less dense. Both kinds of crust are less dense than the mantle and "float" on top of the asthenosphere, similar to the way ice floats on top of water.

QuickLab

Floating Mountains

1. Take a large **block** of wood and place it in a clear plastic **container**. The block of wood represents the mantle part of the lithosphere.

2. Fill the container with **water** at least 10 cm deep. The water represents the asthenosphere. Use a ruler to measure how far the top of the wood block sits above the surface of the water.

3. Now try loading the block of wood with several different **wooden objects**, each with a different weight. These objects represent different amounts of crustal material loaded onto the lithosphere during mountain building. Measure how far the block sinks under each different weight.

4. What can you conclude about how the tectonic plate reacts to increasing weight of crustal material?

5. What happens to a tectonic plate when the crustal material is removed?

TRY at HOME

3 Extend

QuickLab

MATERIALS
- block of wood
- plastic container
- water
- wooden objects

Teacher Notes: In step 3, the wooden objects should each weigh less than the original wooden block. Explain to students that removing the wooden objects is analogous to large-scale erosion of crustal materials.

Answers to QuickLab

4. As a tectonic plate is weighed down with crustal material, it sinks lower into the asthenosphere.

5. When the weight is removed, the tectonic plate rises back up to its former level.

GROUP ACTIVITY

Pair students and have them plan and build a three-dimensional model of a tectonic plate on the asthenosphere. Students might use materials such as cardboard, wood, and clay. Remind students to label the continental crust, oceanic crust, and lithosphere, as well as any surface topographical features, such as mountain ranges. When models are complete, have students display them and give a brief presentation to the class. Students can use their models later in this chapter to simulate convergent, divergent, and transform motion. **Sheltered English**

Reinforcement Worksheet 7 "The Layered Earth"

Multicultural CONNECTION

The contact between the crust and the mantle is called the Mohorovičić discontinuity, or the Moho. The discontinuity is caused by a density difference between the crust and the mantle. It was discovered by a Croatian geologist named Andrija Mohorovičić. While investigating a 1909 earthquake in Croatia, he noticed there had been two sets of seismic waves. He theorized that the existence of these two sets was caused by a density difference between the crust and the mantle. Further studies indicated that the discontinuity is found worldwide. Have interested students find out more about the Moho and Gutenberg discontinuities.

Section 1 • Inside the Earth

4) Close

USING THE FIGURE

The key for **Figure 6** shows the speeds of only one type of seismic wave—the compression, or P wave. P waves can travel through both liquids and solids and thus can travel through the liquid outer core, unlike other seismic waves. Have students describe what happens when the speed of seismic waves changes. (They also change direction.)

Quiz

1. The crust is the Earth's only solid layer. (false)
2. The inner core of the Earth is solid and made primarily of iron. (true)
3. Temperature and pressure increase toward the center of the Earth. (true)
4. The asthenosphere is the thinnest layer. (false)

ALTERNATIVE ASSESSMENT

 Have students write a story describing their own "journey to the center of the Earth," or they may choose to write a travel guide that describes the experience of traveling through Earth's different layers. Have students draw and color-code a model of Earth to include with their project. Emphasize that this model must show layers defined by chemical composition (crust, mantle, and core) and by physical traits (lithosphere, asthenosphere, mesosphere, outer core, and inner core.)

 Critical Thinking Worksheet 7 "Planet of Waves"

172 Chapter 7 • Plate Tectonics

Mapping the Earth's Interior

How do we know all these things about the deepest parts of the Earth, where no one has ever been? Scientists have never even drilled through the crust, which is only a thin skin on the surface of the Earth. So how do we know so much about the mantle and the core?

Would you be surprised to know that the answers come from earthquakes? When an earthquake occurs, vibrations called seismic waves are produced. *Seismic waves* are vibrations that travel through the Earth. Depending on the density and strength of material they pass through, seismic waves travel at different speeds. For example, a seismic wave traveling through solid rock will go faster than a seismic wave traveling through a liquid.

When an earthquake occurs, *seismographs* measure the difference in the arrival times of seismic waves and record them. Seismologists can then use these measurements to calculate the density and thickness of each physical layer of the Earth. **Figure 6** shows how one kind of seismic wave travels through the Earth.

- **Lithosphere** 7–8 km/second
- **Asthenosphere** 7–11 km/second
- **Mesosphere** 11–13 km/second
- **Outer core** 7–10 km/second
- **Inner core** 11–12 km/second

Figure 6 *The speed of seismic waves depends on the density of the material they travel through. The denser the material, the faster seismic waves move.*

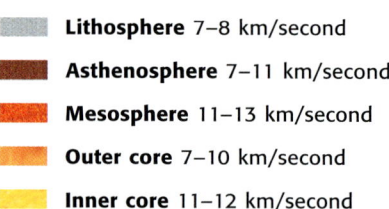

TOPIC: Composition of the Earth, Structure of the Earth
GO TO: www.scilinks.org
sciLINKS NUMBER: HSTE155, HSTE160

REVIEW

1. What is the difference between continental and oceanic crust?
2. How is the lithosphere different from the asthenosphere?
3. How do scientists know about the structure of the Earth's interior? Explain.
4. **Analyzing Relationships** Explain the difference between the crust and the lithosphere.

Answers to Review

1. Oceanic crust is thin and dense compared with continental crust. Continental crust and granite have a similar composition, and oceanic crust and basalt have a similar composition.
2. The lithosphere is rigid and is divided into tectonic plates. The asthenosphere is a layer of soft mantle material that flows very slowly.
3. Scientists measure the different speeds at which seismic waves travel through different parts of the Earth. This indicates the density and thickness of each layer the waves pass through.
4. The crust and the lithosphere are the outermost layers of the Earth, but the lithosphere includes the crust and the rigid, uppermost part of the mantle.

Section 2

Terms to Learn
continental drift
sea-floor spreading

What You'll Do
- Describe Wegener's theory of continental drift, and explain why it was not accepted at first.
- Explain how sea-floor spreading provides a way for continents to move.
- Describe how new oceanic crust forms at mid-ocean ridges.
- Explain how magnetic reversals provide evidence for sea-floor spreading.

Restless Continents

Take a look at **Figure 7.** It shows how continents would fit together if you removed the Atlantic Ocean and moved the land together. Is it just coincidence that the coastlines fit together so well? Is it possible that the continents were actually together sometime in the past?

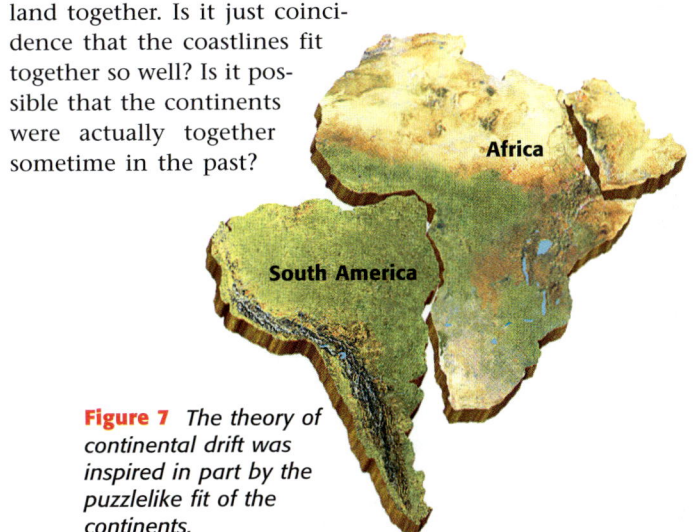

Figure 7 The theory of continental drift was inspired in part by the puzzlelike fit of the continents.

Wegener's Theory of Continental Drift

One scientist who looked at the pieces of this puzzle was Alfred Wegener (VEG e nuhr). In the early 1900s he wrote about his theory of *continental drift*. **Continental drift** is the theory that continents can drift apart from one another and have done so in the past. This theory seemed to explain a lot of puzzling observations, including the very good fit of some of the continents.

Continental drift also explained why fossils of the same plant and animal species are found on both sides of the Atlantic Ocean. Many of these ancient species could not have made it across the Atlantic Ocean. As you can see in **Figure 8,** without continental drift, this pattern of fossil findings would be hard to explain. In addition to fossils, similar types of rock and evidence of the same ancient climatic conditions were found on several continents.

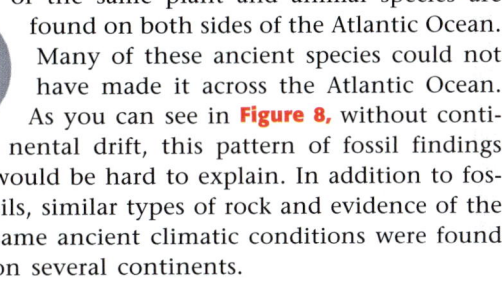

Mesosaurus

Glossopteris

Figure 8 Fossils of *Mesosaurus*, a small, aquatic reptile, and *Glossopteris*, an ancient plant species, have been found on several continents.

IS THAT A FACT!
By the time Alfred Wegener was 32, he had set a world record for balloon flight, earned a doctorate in astronomy, made two meteorological expeditions to Greenland, and written the paper that was the main catalyst for the greatest geologic insight of the twentieth century.

WEIRD SCIENCE
In **Figure 7,** the southern tips of South America and Africa do not touch, while **Figure 8** indicates that they did touch in the past. According to one interpretation, the southern tip of South America was wrapped around the southern tip of Africa when the two continents were together.

2) Teach

GUIDED PRACTICE

Have students work in small groups to create a model of Pangaea. Provide each group with two world maps. With pencils, students can mark hypothetical glacial grooves extending from the poles of both maps. Have them cut the continents out of one map and treat them as puzzle pieces, seeing how they best fit together. Refer to both the complete and the altered maps, and help students explain and demonstrate how each continent moved from its original position. **Sheltered English**

CONNECT TO LIFE SCIENCE

Before Pangaea broke up, dinosaurs roamed the entire continent. The populations were very widespread. As Pangaea began to break up, the populations of dinosaurs were fragmented and isolated on the new continents. The fossil record indicates that dinosaurs began to evolve divergently as a result. By the time dinosaurs became extinct, about 65 million years ago, there was great diversity among the different dinosaurs. Use the Teaching Transparencies listed below to discuss natural selection and the breakup of Pangaea. Have groups of students research different dinosaurs that lived after the breakup of Pangaea and speculate why these dinosaurs evolved the way they did.

Teaching Transparency 28
"Evolution of the Galápagos Finches" *LINK TO LIFE SCIENCE*

Teaching Transparency 126
"The Breakup of Pangaea"

174 Chapter 7 • Plate Tectonics

Continental drift also explained puzzling evidence left by ancient glaciers. Glaciers cut grooves in the ground that indicate the direction they traveled. When you look at the placement of today's continents, these glacial activities do not seem to be related. But when you bring all of these continental pieces back to their original arrangement, the glacial grooves match! Along with fossil evidence, glacial grooves supported Wegener's idea of continental drift.

The Breakup of Pangaea

Wegener studied many observations before establishing his theory of continental drift. He thought that all the separate continents of today were once joined in a single landmass that he called *Pangaea,* which is Greek for "all earth." As shown in **Figure 9,** almost all of Earth's landmasses were joined together in one huge continent 245 million years ago.

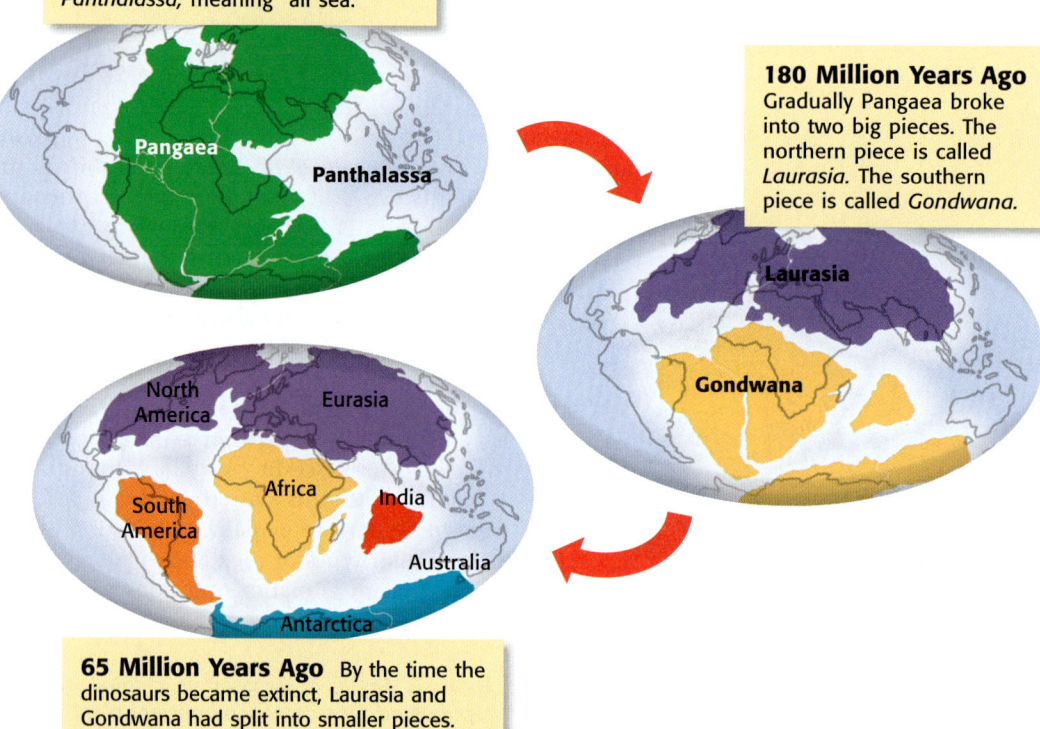

Figure 9 Over time, Earth's continents have changed shape and traveled great distances.

245 Million Years Ago Pangaea existed when some of the earliest dinosaurs were roaming the Earth. It was surrounded by a sea called *Panthalassa,* meaning "all sea."

180 Million Years Ago Gradually Pangaea broke into two big pieces. The northern piece is called *Laurasia.* The southern piece is called *Gondwana.*

65 Million Years Ago By the time the dinosaurs became extinct, Laurasia and Gondwana had split into smaller pieces.

MISCONCEPTION ALERT

Pangaea was not the only supercontinent that existed. Some 500 million years before Pangaea began to form, another supercontinent dominated the globe—Rodinia. Some scientists speculate that the formation of supercontinents occurs as a cycle of accretion and breakup. If this is true, there may have been as many as 10 different supercontinents in the last 3 billion years and there may be more in the future!

Sea-Floor Spreading

When Wegener put forth his theory of continental drift, many scientists would not accept his theory. What force of nature, they wondered, could move entire continents? In Wegener's day, no one could answer that question. It wasn't until many years later that new evidence provided some clues.

In **Figure 10** you will notice that there is a chain of submerged mountains running through the center of the Atlantic Ocean. The chain is called the Mid-Atlantic Ridge, part of a worldwide system of ocean ridges. Mid-ocean ridges are underwater mountain chains that run through Earth's ocean basins.

Mid-ocean ridges are places where sea-floor spreading takes place. **Sea-floor spreading** is the process by which new oceanic lithosphere is created as older materials are pulled away. As tectonic plates move away from each other, the sea floor spreads apart and magma rises to fill in the gap. Notice in **Figure 11** that the crust increases in age the farther it is from the mid-ocean ridge. This is because new crust continually forms from molten material at the ridge. The oldest crust in the Atlantic Ocean is found along the edges of the continents. It dates back to the time of the dinosaurs. The newest crust is in the center of the ocean. This crust has just formed!

Figure 10 The Mid-Atlantic Ridge is part of the longest mountain chain in the world.

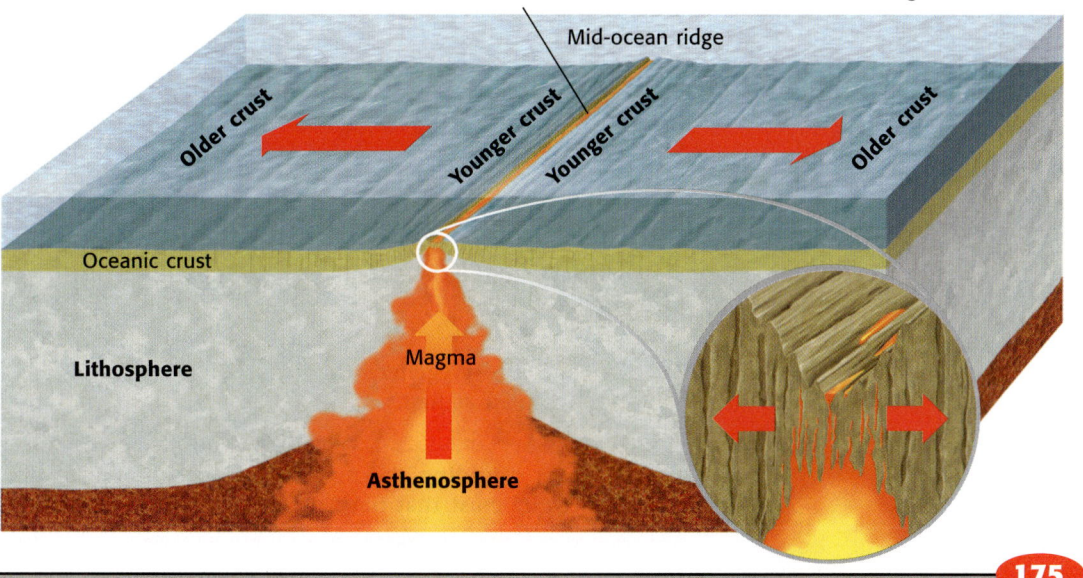

Figure 11 Sea-floor spreading creates new oceanic lithosphere at mid-ocean ridges.

3) Extend

USING THE FIGURE

Have students use **Figure 11** to explain the forces that pull rocks outward from mid-ocean ridges. Guide their explanations by asking the following questions:

- Why does molten rock from the mantle come to the surface at the ridges?
- Why does the ocean floor spread apart at the ridges?
- Why is rock formed at the ridges called *new* rock?

Stress that mid-ocean ridges are not always in the middle of an ocean. Have students compare the locations of mid-ocean ridges in **Figure 4**.

CONNECT TO PHYSICAL SCIENCE

Explain that researchers used sonar to discover that the ocean floor is not flat. In the 1950s, scientists broadcast sound waves toward the sea floor and measured how long it took the waves to return. The echoes revealed the existence of oceanic valleys and mountains. In short, the ocean floors turned out to be as varied as the continents! Scientists were most amazed to find a chain of undersea mountains snaking thousands of kilometers around the globe—the mid-ocean ridges.

Science Bloopers

Before the discovery of the Mid-Atlantic Ridge, many scientists thought that a land bridge had once connected South America and Africa. Despite the fact that there was no evidence to support it, the popular land-bridge theory was used to explain why the fossil record was similar on both continents.

SCIENTISTS AT ODDS

Many geologists ridiculed Wegener's theories because they had been taught that continents and ocean basins were fixed in their positions. These scientists knew of no force that could move an entire continent, and they discounted the overwhelming evidence that continental drift had occurred.

4 Close

BRAIN FOOD

Why is the south pole of the bar magnet in **Figure 12** located at the Earth's north pole during "normal polarity"? Explain to students that magnetic attraction occurs between the opposite poles of magnets. The north-seeking pole of a compass needle actually points to the south pole of Earth's magnetic field. Thus, during periods of "normal polarity" what we call the Earth's magnetic north pole is actually the south pole of Earth's magnetic field. This concept can be easily demonstrated by placing the south pole of a bar magnet next to a compass. The compass needle will point toward the south pole of the bar magnet in the same way it tends to point toward the south pole of Earth's magnetic field, what we call magnetic north.

Quiz

1. If the Earth's crust is growing at mid-ocean ridges, why doesn't the Earth itself grow larger? (because the Earth's crust is part of the rock cycle)

2. What was Pangaea? (the large landmass that later broke up to form two supercontinents and then fragmented further to form the six continents of today)

ALTERNATIVE ASSESSMENT

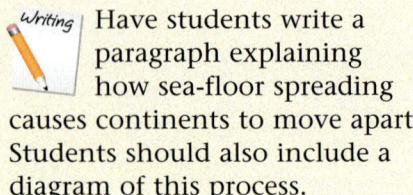 Have students write a paragraph explaining how sea-floor spreading causes continents to move apart. Students should also include a diagram of this process.

176 Chapter 7 • Plate Tectonics

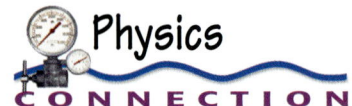

All matter has the property of magnetism, though in most cases it is very weak compared with that of magnets. This explains why researchers have been able to levitate a frog—by creating a very strong magnetic field beneath it!

Magnetic Reversals

Some of the most important evidence of sea-floor spreading comes from magnetic reversals recorded in the ocean floor. Throughout Earth's history, the north and south magnetic poles have changed places many times. When Earth's magnetic poles change place, this is called a *magnetic reversal*.

The molten rock at the mid-ocean ridges contains tiny grains of magnetic minerals. These mineral grains act like compasses. They align with the magnetic field of the Earth. Once the molten rock cools, the record of these tiny compasses is literally set in stone. This record is then carried slowly away from the spreading center as sea-floor spreading occurs. As you can see in **Figure 12,** when the Earth's magnetic field reverses, a new band is started, and this time the magnetic mineral grains point in the opposite direction. The new rock records the direction of the Earth's magnetic field. This record of magnetic reversals was the final proof that sea-floor spreading does occur.

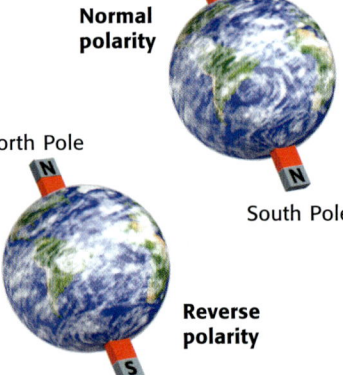
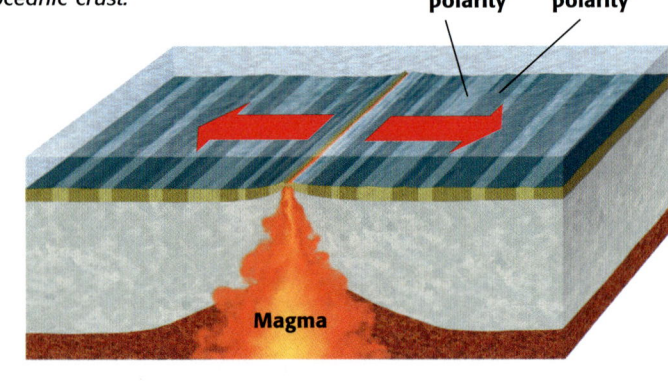

Figure 12 *Magnetic reversals in oceanic crust are shown here as bands of light and dark blue oceanic crust.*

REVIEW

1. List three puzzling occurrences that the theory of continental drift helped to explain, and describe how it explained them.

2. Explain why Wegener's theory of continental drift was not accepted at first.

3. **Identifying Relationships** Explain how the processes of sea-floor spreading and magnetic reversal produce bands of oceanic crust that have different magnetic polarities.

▼ Answers to Review

1. Occurrences include the puzzlelike fit of the continents, the match of glacial grooves, the occurrence of fossils of the same species on different continents, and the distribution of rock types and ancient climatic zones. Continental drift explained that these coincidences exist because at one time, all the continents were joined together in one large landmass.

2. Wegener's theory of continental drift described the movement of continents but did not explain the force that moved them.

3. During sea-floor spreading, new oceanic crust forms on either side of the mid-ocean ridge. The changing polarity of the Earth's magnetic poles causes the new oceanic crust to have alternating bands of normal and reverse polarity.

Section 3

The Theory of Plate Tectonics

Terms to Learn
- plate tectonics
- convergent boundary
- subduction zone
- divergent boundary
- transform boundary

What You'll Do
- Describe the three forces thought to move tectonic plates.
- Describe the three types of tectonic plate boundaries.
- Explain how scientists measure the rate at which tectonic plates move.

The proof of sea-floor spreading supported Wegener's original idea that the continents move. But because both oceanic and continental crust appear to move, a new theory was devised to explain both continental drift and sea-floor spreading—the theory of *plate tectonics*. **Plate tectonics** is the theory that the Earth's lithosphere is divided into tectonic plates that move around on top of the asthenosphere.

Possible Causes of Tectonic Plate Motion

An incredible amount of energy is needed to move something as massive as a tectonic plate! We still don't know exactly why tectonic plates move as they do, but recently scientists have come up with some possible answers, as shown in **Figure 13**. Notice how all three are affected by heat and gravity.

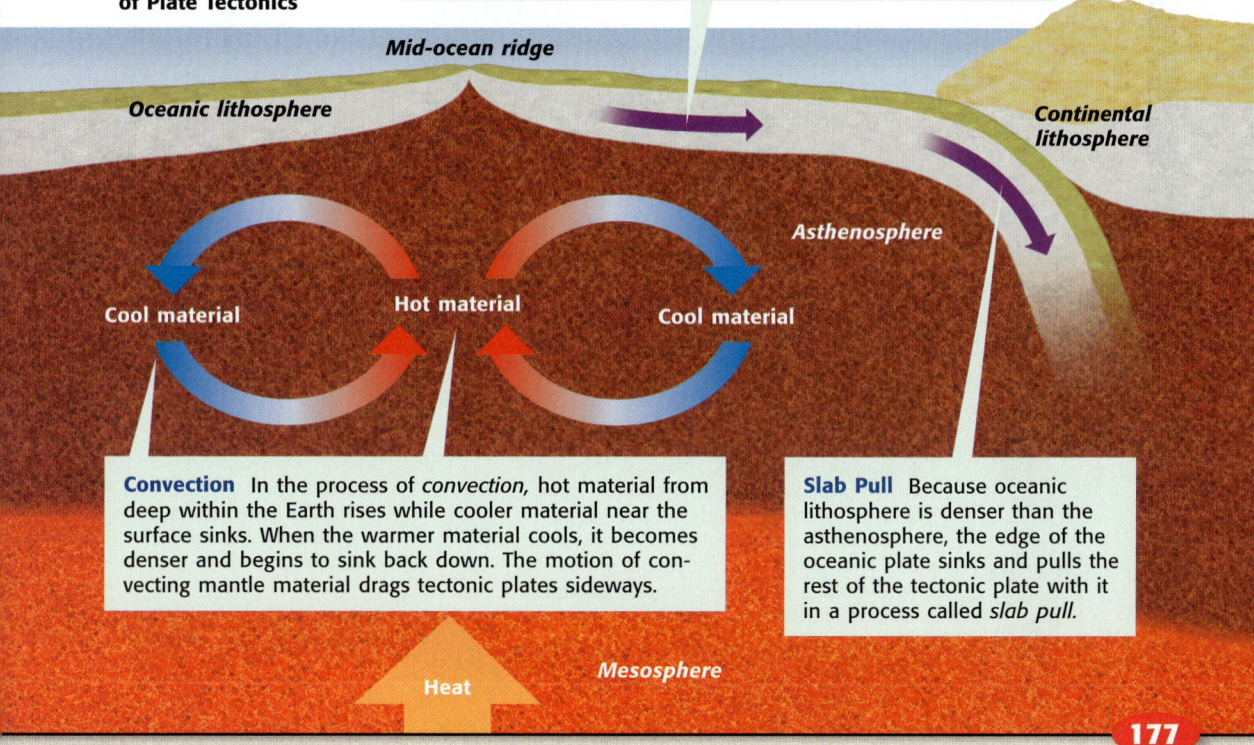

Figure 13 Three Possible Driving Forces of Plate Tectonics

Ridge Push At mid-ocean ridges, the oceanic lithosphere is higher than it is where it sinks beneath continental lithosphere. *Ridge push* is the process by which an oceanic plate slides down the lithosphere-asthenosphere boundary.

Convection In the process of *convection*, hot material from deep within the Earth rises while cooler material near the surface sinks. When the warmer material cools, it becomes denser and begins to sink back down. The motion of convecting mantle material drags tectonic plates sideways.

Slab Pull Because oceanic lithosphere is denser than the asthenosphere, the edge of the oceanic plate sinks and pulls the rest of the tectonic plate with it in a process called *slab pull*.

IS THAT A FACT!

Convection currents circulate material deep inside the Earth in a long, slow movement. The material cools near the surface and then sinks again into the depths. A single particle can take hundreds of millions of years to make a complete circle.

 **Teaching Transparency 127** "Possible Causes of Tectonic Plate Motion"

 Directed Reading Worksheet 7 Section 3

SECTION 3

Focus

The Theory of Plate Tectonics

This section discusses the plate tectonic model of Earth's crustal movements. Students learn about possible causes of some plate movements: convection within the mantle, ridge push at mid-ocean ridges, and slab pull at subduction zones. It also describes the types of plate boundaries and how scientists use GPS satellites to track plate motion.

Bellringer

Have students calculate the number of years that it took New York and the west coast of Africa to reach their current locations, 676,000,000 cm apart, if the sea floor is spreading an average of 4 cm a year. (Students will calculate that the Atlantic Ocean has been spreading apart for about 169 million years. Point out that this is fairly close to the estimate of when the breakup of Pangaea began 180 million years ago.)

1) Motivate

DISCUSSION

Discuss **Figure 13** with students, and point out how the movement of tectonic plates is driven by differences in temperature and density. In *slab pull* and *ridge push*, gravity pulls the oceanic plate downward because it is more dense than the continental lithosphere. In *convection*, hot material rises because it is less dense than cooler material, which sinks.

Section 3 • The Theory of Plate Tectonics

2 Teach

MEETING INDIVIDUAL NEEDS

Advanced Learners Challenge students to explain why continental/oceanic and oceanic/oceanic convergent boundaries result in subduction, whereas continental/continental convergent boundaries do not. Then have them:

- create an illustrated chart showing the five types of boundary movements
- write captions explaining both how the boundaries move and the forces responsible for their movement

DISCUSSION

Ask students to imagine trying to push a heavy crate along a concrete sidewalk. When you start to push, the box doesn't move. But as you push harder, the box finally slips a little and then stops again. Tectonic plates tend to move in similar jerks and jolts. When they move with a sudden jerk, an earthquake occurs. **Sheltered English**

INDEPENDENT PRACTICE

Have students refer back to **Figure 4** to locate examples of different types of tectonic plate boundaries given in **Figure 14**. (Teaching Transparencies 128 and 129 reproduce **Figure 14** for classroom use.) Test students' understanding of tectonic plate boundaries by asking them to identify which kind of boundary each red line in **Figure 4** represents.

Convection Connection

Tectonic Plate Boundaries

All tectonic plates have boundaries with other tectonic plates. These boundaries are divided into three main types depending on how the tectonic plates move relative to one another. Tectonic plates can collide, separate, or slide past each other. **Figure 14** shows some examples of tectonic plate boundaries.

Convergent Boundaries When two tectonic plates push into one another, the boundary where they meet is called a **convergent boundary**. What happens at a convergent boundary depends on what kind of crust—continental or oceanic—the leading edge of each tectonic plate has. As you can see below, there are three types of convergent boundaries—continental/continental, continental/oceanic, and oceanic/oceanic.

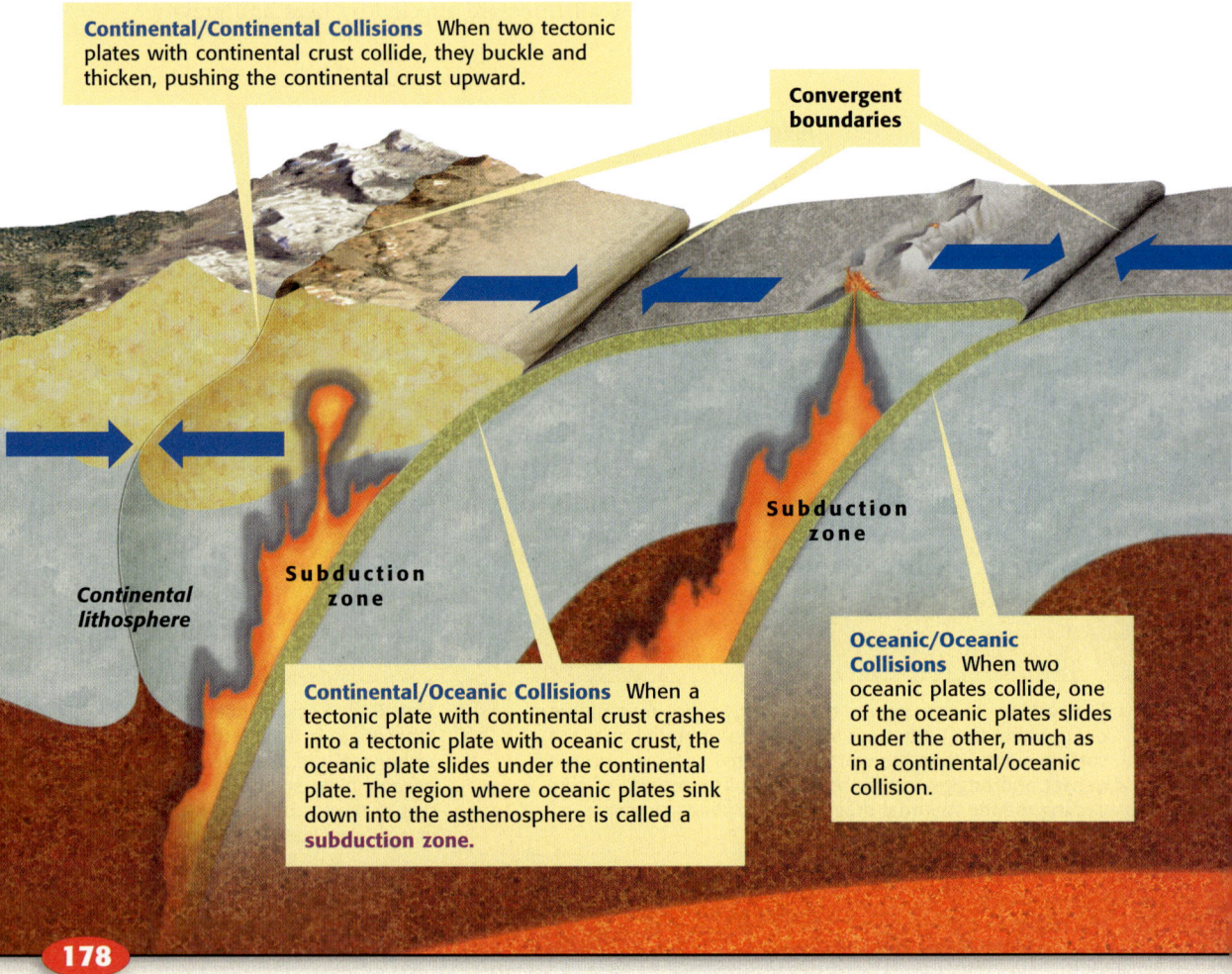

Figure 14 This diagram shows five tectonic plate boundaries. Notice that there are three types of convergent boundaries.

Continental/Continental Collisions When two tectonic plates with continental crust collide, they buckle and thicken, pushing the continental crust upward.

Continental/Oceanic Collisions When a tectonic plate with continental crust crashes into a tectonic plate with oceanic crust, the oceanic plate slides under the continental plate. The region where oceanic plates sink down into the asthenosphere is called a **subduction zone**.

Oceanic/Oceanic Collisions When two oceanic plates collide, one of the oceanic plates slides under the other, much as in a continental/oceanic collision.

Teaching Transparency 128 "Tectonic Plate Boundaries: A"

Teaching Transparency 129 "Tectonic Plate Boundaries: B"

CROSS-DISCIPLINARY FOCUS

 **Language Arts** Have students write a short story about a rock, from its formation from magma at an oceanic ridge to its subduction at a tectonic plate boundary.

Divergent Boundaries When two tectonic plates move away from one another, the boundary between them is called a **divergent boundary.** Remember sea-floor spreading? Divergent boundaries are where new oceanic lithosphere forms. The mid-ocean ridges that mark the spreading centers are the most common type of divergent boundary. However, divergent boundaries can also be found on continents.

Transform Boundaries When two tectonic plates slide past each other horizontally, the boundary between them is called a **transform boundary.** The San Andreas Fault, in California, is a good example of a transform boundary. This fault marks the place where the Pacific plate and the North American plate slide past each other.

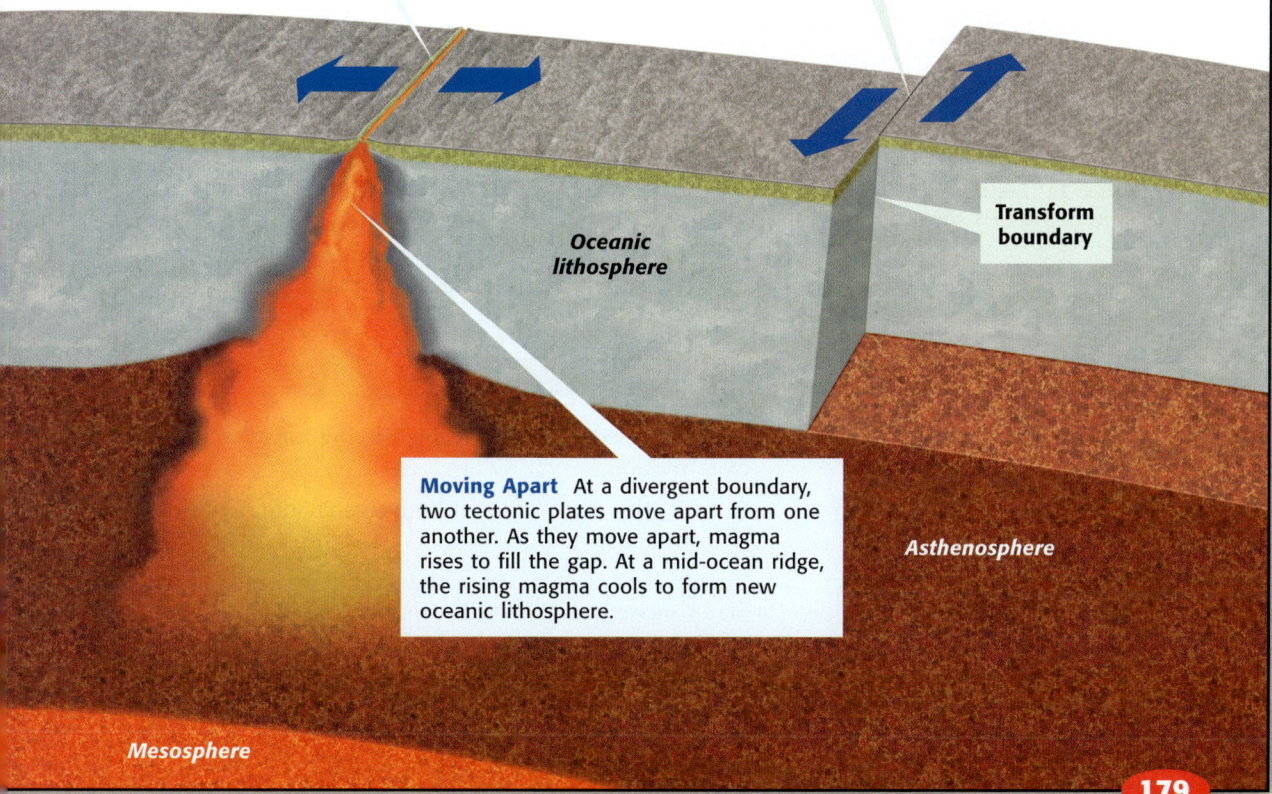

Sliding Past At a transform boundary, two tectonic plates slide past one another. Because tectonic plates are not smooth, they grind and jerk as they slide, producing earthquakes!

Moving Apart At a divergent boundary, two tectonic plates move apart from one another. As they move apart, magma rises to fill the gap. At a mid-ocean ridge, the rising magma cools to form new oceanic lithosphere.

Homework

 **Writing Assignment** Alfred Wegener wrote, "If it turns out that sense and meaning are now becoming evident in the whole history of the Earth's development, why should we hesitate to toss the old views overboard?"

Ask students to think about why the acceptance of new ideas in science is a slow process. Ask students to explain why continental drift and another controversial theory took a long time to be accepted.

3) Extend

GROUP ACTIVITY

Challenge students to model the types of movement at each type of plate boundary. Have them work in pairs with materials they have chosen. Possible materials include sheets of foam padding, cardboard, modeling clay, or phone books.

As students demonstrate plate movements, they should be prepared to explain the composition of each plate and the differences between the forces at work. Sheltered English

INDEPENDENT PRACTICE

Writing Tell students to hypothesize about what kinds of geologic features occur at different types of plate boundaries. Then have them compare a topographic world map with the tectonic plate map in **Figure 4.** Encourage them to do library and Internet research to find out if their hypotheses were correct. Suggest that they summarize their findings in a brief report.

MATH and MORE

The distance between New York and Paris increases every year. Currently, the two cities are moving apart by about 2 cm per year. This may not sound like much, but have students calculate the increase in distance in 1 million years. (20 km)

How much will the distance increase in 100 million years? (2,000 km)

 Math Skills Worksheet 4 "A Shortcut for Multiplying Large Numbers"

Section 3 • The Theory of Plate Tectonics

4 Close

Quiz

1. Why are there several categories of convergent plate boundaries? (Plates that are pushed together behave differently, depending on their composition and density.)

2. Tell where you would expect to see the following features:
   a. tall, wrinkled mountains in the middle of a continent (convergent continental/continental boundary)
   b. a long parallel ridge on the ocean floor surrounded by parallel zones of magnetic reversal (divergent boundary)

3. Explain the process of subduction. (A denser oceanic plate is forced beneath a less-dense oceanic or continental plate at a convergent boundary. Gravity pulls the oceanic plate into the asthenosphere, where it begins to melt.)

ALTERNATIVE ASSESSMENT

Have students work in groups or with a partner to make models of different kinds of tectonic plate boundaries using modeling clay. Have students label their models, add appropriate surface features, and explain the processes responsible for the features.
Sheltered English

Reinforcement Worksheet 7
"A Moving Jigsaw Puzzle"

Tracking Tectonic Plate Motion

Just how fast do tectonic plates move? The answer to this question depends on many factors, such as the type of tectonic plate, the shape of the tectonic plate, and the way it interacts with the tectonic plates that surround it. Tectonic movements are generally so slow and gradual that you can't see or feel them—they are measured in centimeters per year.

One exception to this rule is the San Andreas Fault, in California. The Pacific plate and the North American plate do not slide past each other smoothly nor continuously. Instead, this movement happens in jerks and jolts. Sections of the fault remain stationary for years and then suddenly shift several meters, causing an earthquake. Large shifts that occur at the San Andreas fault can be measured right on the surface. Unfortunately for scientists, however, most movements of tectonic plates are very difficult to measure. So how do they do it?

The Global Positioning System Scientists use a network of satellites called the *Global Positioning System* (GPS), shown in **Figure 15,** to measure the rate of tectonic plate movement. Radio signals are continuously beamed from satellites to GPS ground stations, which record the exact distance between the satellites and the ground station. Over time, these distances change slightly. By recording the time it takes for the GPS ground stations to move a given distance, scientists can measure the rate of motion of each tectonic plate.

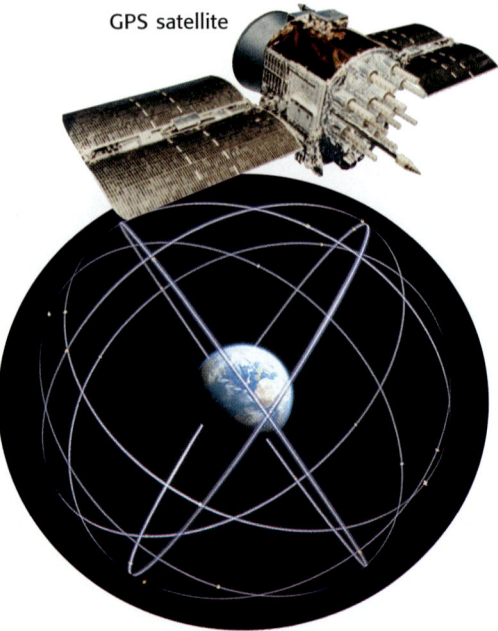

Figure 15 *The image above shows the orbits of the GPS satellites.*

TOPIC: Tectonic Plates
GO TO: www.scilinks.org
*sci*LINKS NUMBER: HSTE165

REVIEW

1. List and describe three possible driving forces of tectonic plate motion.
2. How do the three types of convergent boundaries differ from one another?
3. Explain how scientists measure the rate at which tectonic plates move.
4. **Identifying Relationships** When convection takes place in the mantle, why does cooler material sink, while warmer material rises?

Answers to Review

1. Ridge push occurs when an oceanic plate slides down the tilted slope of the lithosphere/asthenosphere boundary. Slab pull occurs when the sinking edge of an oceanic plate pulls the rest of the plate down with it into the subduction zone. Convection occurs when hot mantle material in the asthenosphere convects, dragging the tectonic plate sideways.

2. Convergent boundaries can occur between two oceanic plates, two continental plates, or between an oceanic and a continental plate.

3. They measure tectonic plate movement by using a network of satellites to track the movement of GPS ground stations over long periods of time.

4. Cooler material sinks because it is denser than warmer material.

Section 4

Deforming the Earth's Crust

Terms to Learn
stress
compression
tension
folding
fault
normal fault
reverse fault
strike-slip fault

What You'll Do
- Describe major types of folds.
- Explain how the three major types of faults differ.
- Name and describe the most common types of mountains.
- Explain how various types of mountains form.

Have you ever tried to bend something, only to have it break? Try this: take a long, uncooked piece of spaghetti, and bend it very slowly, and only a little. Now bend it again, but this time much farther and faster. What happened to it the second time? How can the same material bend at one time and break at another? The answer is that the *stress* you put on it was different. **Stress** is the amount of force per unit area that is put on a given material. The same principle works on the rocks in the Earth's crust. The conditions under which a rock is stressed determine its behavior.

Rocks Get Stressed

When rock changes its shape due to stress, this reaction is called *deformation*. In the example above, you saw the spaghetti deform in two different ways—by bending and by breaking. **Figure 16** illustrates this concept. The same thing happens in rock layers. Rock layers can bend when stress is placed on them. But when more stress is placed on them, they can break. Rocks can deform due to the forces of plate tectonics.

The type of stress that occurs when an object is squeezed, as when two tectonic plates collide, is called **compression.** Compression can have some spectacular results. The Rocky Mountains and the Cascade Range are two examples of compression at a convergent plate boundary.

Another form of stress is *tension*. **Tension** is stress that occurs when forces act to stretch an object. As you might guess, tension occurs at divergent plate boundaries, when two tectonic plates pull away from each other. In the following pages you will learn how these two tectonic forces—compression and tension—bend and break rock to form some of the common landforms you already know.

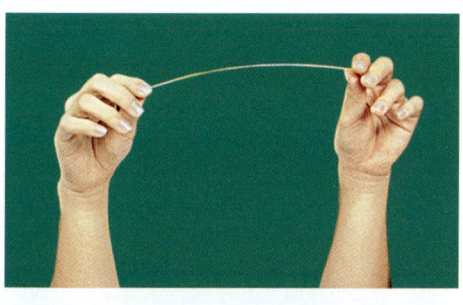
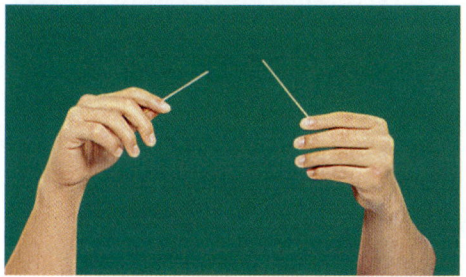

Figure 16 *With a small amount of stress, uncooked spaghetti bends. Additional stress causes it to break.*

Science Bloopers

In the 1800s, some scientists believed mountains formed as the result of Earth's shrinking. The theory proposed that Earth had once been a ball of semimolten rock; as it cooled, it shrank and wrinkles formed on the surface, much as an apple skin wrinkles as the fruit dries. This popular theory was not discarded until the structure and age of the Earth were better understood in the twentieth century.

2) Teach

READING STRATEGY

Activity As students read this section, have them sketch the following examples in their ScienceLog:
- folds that illustrate anticlines and synclines
- a fold that illustrates a monocline
- a normal fault
- a reverse fault
- a strike-slip fault

Have students label each sketch clearly, provide a caption, and draw arrows showing the direction of the forces causing the deformation. **Sheltered English**

CROSS-DISCIPLINARY FOCUS

Geography Plate tectonics play an important role in the formation of most mountain ranges. Mountain ranges in turn influence the weather around them. Because mountains are high, they influence the flow of air in a region, causing a rain shadow effect. Have interested students select a mountain range and learn more about how it affects the weather in its area. Tell students they should find out what rain shadows are and give a few geographic examples of them. Students should also explore how a certain mountain range supports a variety of ecosystems.

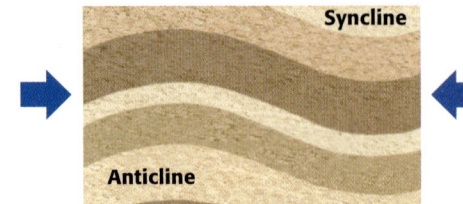
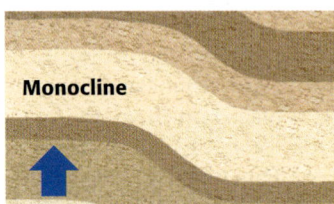

Figure 17 When tectonic forces put stress on rock layers, they can cause the layers to bend and fold. *Anticlines* and *synclines* form when horizontal stress acts on rock. *Monoclines* form when vertical stress acts on rock.

Folding

Folding occurs when rock layers bend due to stress in the Earth's crust. We assume that all sedimentary rock layers started out as horizontal layers. So when you see a fold, you know that deformation has taken place. Depending on how the rock layers deform, different types of folds are made. **Figure 17** shows the two most common types—*anticlines* and *synclines*.

Another type of fold is a *monocline*. In a monocline, rock layers are folded so that both ends of the fold are still horizontal. Imagine taking a stack of paper and laying it on a table top. Think of all the sheets of paper as different rock layers. Now put a book under one end of the stack. You can see that both ends of the sheets are still horizontal, but all the sheets are bent in the middle.

Folds can be large or small. Take a look at **Figure 18.** The largest folds are measured in kilometers. They can make up the entire side of a mountain. Other folds are still obvious but much smaller. Note the size of the pocket knife in the smaller photo. Now look at the smallest folds. You would measure these folds in centimeters.

Figure 18 The larger photo at right shows mountain-sized folds in the Rocky Mountains. The smaller photo shows a rock with much smaller folds.

Homework

Making Models Have students select a topographic feature in your state that resulted from the deformation of the Earth's crust and find out about how it formed. Tell them to choose appropriate materials and create a model of the formation. Point out that they may need to create a cutaway view to show layers within the formation. Finally, ask students to write labels explaining the formation's features and the tectonic forces that caused them.

Faulting

While some rock layers bend and fold when stress is applied, other rock layers break. The surface along which rocks break and slide past each other is called a **fault.** The blocks of crust on each side of the fault are called *fault blocks*.

If a fault is not vertical, it is useful to distinguish between its two sides—the *hanging wall* and the *footwall*. **Figure 19** shows the difference between a hanging wall and a footwall. Depending on how the hanging wall and footwall move relative to each other, one of two main types of faults can form.

Figure 19 *The position of a fault block determines whether it is a hanging wall or a footwall.*

Normal Faults A *normal fault* is shown in **Figure 20.** The movement of a **normal fault** causes the hanging wall to move down relative to the footwall. Normal faults usually occur when tectonic forces cause tension that pulls rocks apart.

Figure 20 *When rocks are pulled apart due to tension, normal faults often result.*

Reverse Faults A *reverse fault* is shown in **Figure 21.** The movement of a **reverse fault** causes the hanging wall to move up relative to the footwall—the "reverse" of a normal fault. Reverse faults usually happen when tectonic forces cause compression that pushes rocks together.

Figure 21 *When rocks are pushed together by compression, reverse faults often result.*

Self-Check

How is folding different from faulting? *(See page 726 to check your answer.)*

Is That A Fact!

Thrust faults are large-scale, low-angle reverse faults caused by the collision of tectonic plates. They are an example of what can happen when stress (compression) is applied to the crust. Large-scale folding can also result from compression.

Answers to Self-Check

When folding occurs, sedimentary rock strata bend but do not break. When faulting occurs, sedimentary rock strata break along a fault and the fault blocks on either side move relative to each other.

Reteaching

Have students refer to **Figure 19** while you give this explanation of hanging walls and footwalls: When a fault occurs at an angle, the hanging wall is the block on top of the fault surface while the footwall is the block beneath it. Have students identify both the hanging walls and the footwalls in **Figures 20** and **21.**

Discussion

Refer to **Figure 20,** and point out that in a normal fault the hanging wall moves downward. Ask students to describe the tectonic force that causes this type of fault movement. (tension or stretching from plate movements pulling rocks apart)

Invite a volunteer to use **Figure 21** to discuss the forces that cause reverse faults. (When plate movements squeeze rocks together, compression forces the hanging wall up and the footwall down.) Sheltered English

CONNECT TO LIFE SCIENCE

Point out that living at high altitudes places stress on organisms. This stress has led to the evolution of various adaptations. For example, because there is less oxygen at high altitudes, some animals that live on mountains produce more red blood cells. This makes the blood more efficient at delivering oxygen to body tissues. Have students find out about the adaptations of other organisms (including humans) that live in high-altitude environments.

Section 4 • Deforming the Earth's Crust

2) Teach, continued

ACTIVITY

Making Models Have students use two blocks of wood to model the three types of fault movements. Tell students to sand one side of each block until it is smooth and to score another side until it is rough.

Inform students that the San Andreas Fault is a strike-slip fault. As they demonstrate the strike-slip movement, have them:
- slide smooth wood surfaces together
- slide rough wood surfaces together
- compare the amounts of resistance
- explain why movement at a strike-slip fault causes earthquakes

It is important that students understand the relationship between strike-slip faults and the transform boundaries where tectonic plates meet. Some transform boundaries are actually systems of hundreds or thousands of strike-slip faults. The San Andreas Fault is an example of a particularly large strike-slip fault located between the Pacific and North American plates. In addition to the San Andreas Fault, a number of other strike-slip faults make up this transform boundary. Such large-scale strike-slip faults are often called transform faults. Strike-slip faults are not always associated with tectonic plate boundaries, however.

Figure 22 *The photo at left is a normal fault. The photo at right is a reverse fault.*

Telling the Difference It's easy to tell the difference between a normal fault and a reverse fault in diagrams with arrows. But what about the faults in **Figure 22?** You can certainly see the faults, but which one is a normal fault, and which one is a reverse fault? In the top left photo, one side has obviously moved relative to the other. You can tell this is a normal fault by looking at the sequence of sedimentary rock layers. You can see by the relative positions of the two dark layers that the hanging wall has moved down relative to the footwall.

Strike-slip Faults A third major type of fault is called a *strike-slip fault*. **Strike-slip faults** occur when opposing forces cause rock to break and move horizontally. If you were standing on one side of a strike-slip fault looking across the fault when it moved, the ground on the other side would appear to move to your left or right.

Tectonics and Natural Gas

Natural gas is used in many homes and factories as a source of energy. Some companies explore for sources of natural gas just as other companies explore for oil and coal. Like oil, natural gas travels upward through rock layers until it hits a layer through which it cannot travel and becomes trapped. Imagine that you are searching for pockets of trapped natural gas. Would you expect to find these pockets associated with anticlines, synclines, or faults? Explain your answer in your ScienceLog. Include drawings to help in your explanation.

Answers to APPLY
Pockets of natural gas would tend to get trapped in anticlines and faults because impermeable layers in these structures can seal off upward movement of the gas. In a syncline, the natural gas will still travel upward along the bottom of an impermeable layer.

184   Chapter 7 • Plate Tectonics

Plate Tectonics and Mountain Building

You have just learned about several ways the Earth's crust changes due to the forces of plate tectonics. When tectonic plates collide, land features that start out as small folds and faults can eventually become great mountain ranges. The reason mountains exist is that tectonic plates are continually moving around and bumping into one another. As you can see in **Figure 23,** most major mountain ranges form at the edges of tectonic plates.

When tectonic plates undergo compression or tension, they can form mountains in several different ways. Let's take a look at three of the most common types of mountains—*folded mountains, fault-block mountains,* and *volcanic mountains.*

Folded Mountains *Folded mountains* form when rock layers are squeezed together and pushed upward. If you take a pile of paper on a table top and push on opposite edges of the pile, you will see how a folded mountain forms. You saw how these layers crunched together in Figure 17. **Figure 24** shows an example of a folded mountain range that formed at a convergent boundary.

Figure 23 Most of the world's major mountain ranges form at tectonic plate boundaries. Notice that the Appalachian Mountains, however, are located in the middle of the North American plate.

Figure 24 Once as mighty as the Himalayas, the Appalachians have been worn down by hundreds of millions of years of weathering and erosion.

BRAIN FOOD

Did you know that plate tectonics is responsible for creating not only mountains but some of the lowest places on Earth as well? It's true. When one tectonic plate is subducted beneath another, a deep valley called a *trench* forms at the boundary. The Mariana Trench is the deepest point in the oceans—11,033 m below sea level!

IS THAT A FACT!

The Sierra Nevada, in California, and the Teton Range, in Wyoming, are examples of fault-block mountains. The Appalachian Mountains, in eastern North America, are an example of folded mountains.

BRAIN FOOD

Ask students to write a one page paper explaining their thoughts about the following quote:

"What we have been pleased to call 'solid Earth' is not as solid as we thought. It is energetic, dynamic, and fundamentally restless."

—Jonathan Weiner, *Planet Earth*

Multicultural CONNECTION

By the twelfth century, Chinese scientists recognized the fact that some mountains had been elevated from the ocean floor and that fossils were the remains of organisms that lived in the distant past. Chinese scientists discovered these facts more than 700 years before European scientists. Have interested students research some of the other early advances of Chinese geologists.

CONNECT TO ASTRONOMY

Earth is not the only place with mountains. Astronomers give extraterrestrial mountains the name *mons*, while extraterrestrial mountain ranges are called either *montes* or *highlands*. Encourage students to find out more about the formation of mountains on Mercury, Mars, Earth's moon, or one of the moons of Jupiter or Saturn. Have students compare the mountains they study with mountains on Earth.

3) Extend

RETEACHING

After students have read this section, invite volunteers to sketch examples of each type of mountain on the board. Ask other students to explain how each mountain type forms. Have them refer to the diagram and add labels and arrows to show the direction of forces at work. **Sheltered English**

ACTIVITY

Tell students to locate photographs of mountains in magazines, books, or on the Internet. Have them cut out, copy, or print these images and mount them on paper. Then have them write the type of mountain and a description of how it formed on a card and tape the card to the back of the photo.

Number and post the photos around the room so that students can view the "gallery" and write their own guesses about each mountain. Have students check their guesses against the cards.

internetconnect

TOPIC: Faults
GO TO: www.scilinks.org
sciLINKS NUMBER: HSTE170

TOPIC: Mountain Building
GO TO: www.scilinks.org
sciLINKS NUMBER: HSTE175

Formation of the Appalachian Mountains

Look back at Figure 23. The Appalachians are in the middle of the North American plate. How can this be? Shouldn't they be at the edge of a tectonic plate? Follow along in this diagram to find the answer.

① About 500 million years ago, the landmasses that would become North America and Africa were on a collision course.

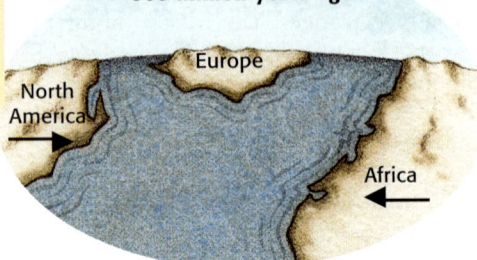
500 million years ago

390 million years ago
Appalachian Mountains

② About 390 million years ago, these tectonic plates collided, and the crust between them buckled and folded, forming the Appalachian Mountains.

③ About 208 million years ago, North America and Africa began to break apart, and a mid-ocean ridge formed between them. By 65 million years ago, a huge amount of new oceanic lithosphere had formed between the two tectonic plates. Because of this, the Appalachian Mountains were no longer at a tectonic plate boundary at all.

65 million years ago

Figure 25 When the crust is subjected to tension, the rock can break along a series of normal faults, resulting in fault-block mountains.

Fault-block Mountains Where tectonic forces put enough tension on the Earth's crust, a large number of normal faults can result. *Fault-block mountains* form when this faulting causes large blocks of the Earth's crust to drop down relative to other blocks. **Figure 25** shows one way this can happen.

IS THAT A FACT!

When the Appalachian Mountains formed, they were probably very similar to the Himalayas. The Appalachians were of a comparable height and must have been characterized by frequent seismic activity. The Appalachians are about 350 million years older than the Himalayas, however, and have been worn down steadily by weathering and erosion over hundreds of millions of years.

Chapter 7 • Plate Tectonics

When sedimentary rock layers are tilted up by faulting, they can produce mountains with sharp, jagged peaks. As you can see in **Figure 26**, the Tetons, in western Wyoming, are a spectacular example of this type of mountain.

Figure 26 The Tetons formed as a result of tectonic forces that stretched the Earth's crust, causing it to break in a series of normal faults. Compare this photo with the illustration in Figure 25.

Volcanic Mountains Most of the world's major volcanic mountains are located at convergent boundaries. *Volcanic mountains* form when molten rock erupts onto the Earth's surface. Unlike folded and fault-block mountains, volcanic mountains form from new material being added to the Earth's surface. Most volcanic mountains tend to form over the type of convergent boundaries that include subduction zones. There are so many volcanic mountains around the rim of the Pacific Ocean that early explorers named it the *Ring of Fire*.

REVIEW

1. What is the difference between an anticline and a syncline?
2. What is the difference between a normal fault and a reverse fault?
3. Name and describe the type of tectonic stress that forms folded mountains.
4. Name and describe the type of tectonic stress that forms fault-block mountains.
5. **Making Predictions** If a fault occurs in an area where rock layers have been folded, which type of fault is it likely to be? Why?

internet connect

SC/INKS NSTA

TOPIC: Faults, Mountain Building
GO TO: www.scilinks.org
sciLINKS NUMBER: HSTE170, HSTE175

4) Close

Quiz

1. What three features form when rock layers bend? (anticlines, synclines, and monoclines)
2. Why are the Appalachian Mountains now located in the middle of the North American plate? (The Appalachians formed when North America and Africa collided. In time, the plates separated and so much new crust was created that the mountains were no longer at the plate boundary.)

ALTERNATIVE ASSESSMENT

Have students choose a mountain range to research. Then ask students to identify in writing the relationship between the mountain range and the forces that created it. Students can summarize their findings in a letter informing scientists living in the 1700s how mountains form and what causes earthquakes.

Multicultural CONNECTION

Although cultures living in mountainous regions are some of the world's most impoverished populations, they inhabit remarkably diverse ecosystems and have developed innovative technologies to live at high altitudes, where resources may be scarce. Encourage students to learn about a culture living in the Andes, the Himalayas, the Alps, or the Appalachians. Students should give a presentation about the culture they studied and conclude with a round-table discussion of the problems and opportunities mountain cultures face.

▼ Answers to Review

1. An anticline is shaped like an upside-down bowl, while a syncline resembles a bowl that is right side up.
2. In a normal fault, the hanging wall moves down relative to the footwall. In a reverse fault, the hanging wall moves up relative to the footwall.
3. Folded mountains form when compression acts on rock strata (such as when two continental plates collide) so that the layers of rock are pushed up into huge folds.
4. Fault-block mountains form when tension pulls rock apart, causing a large number of normal faults to form. When some of these fault blocks drop down relative to others, fault-block mountains form.
5. A reverse fault is likely to form because both reverse faults and folding occur in areas where compression takes place.

Section 4 • Deforming the Earth's Crust

Chapter Highlights

VOCABULARY DEFINITIONS

SECTION 1

crust the thin, outermost layer of the Earth, or the uppermost part of the lithosphere

mantle the layer of the Earth between the crust and the core

core the central, spherical part of the Earth below the mantle

lithosphere the outermost, rigid layer of the Earth that consists of the crust and the rigid upper part of the mantle

asthenosphere the soft layer of the mantle on which pieces of the lithosphere move

mesosphere literally, the "middle sphere"—the strong, lower part of the mantle between the asthenosphere and the outer core

outer core the liquid layer of the Earth's core that lies beneath the mantle and surrounds the inner core

inner core the solid, dense center of the Earth

tectonic plate a piece of the lithosphere that moves around on top of the asthenosphere

SECTION 2

continental drift the theory that continents can drift apart from one another and have done so in the past

sea-floor spreading the process by which new oceanic lithosphere is created at mid-ocean ridges as older materials are pulled away from the ridge

Vocabulary Review Worksheet 7

Chapter Highlights

SECTION 1

Vocabulary
- crust (p. 166)
- mantle (p. 167)
- core (p. 167)
- lithosphere (p. 168)
- asthenosphere (p. 168)
- mesosphere (p. 169)
- outer core (p. 169)
- inner core (p. 169)
- tectonic plate (p. 170)

Section Notes
- The Earth is made of three basic compositional layers—the crust, the mantle, and the core.
- The Earth is made of five main structural layers—lithosphere, asthenosphere, mesosphere, outer core, and inner core.
- Tectonic plates are large pieces of the lithosphere that move around on the Earth's surface.
- Knowledge about the structure of the Earth comes from the study of seismic waves caused by earthquakes.

SECTION 2

Vocabulary
- continental drift (p. 173)
- sea-floor spreading (p. 175)

Section Notes
- Wegener's theory of continental drift explained many puzzling facts, including the fit of the Atlantic coastlines of South America and Africa.
- Today's continents were originally joined together in the ancient continent Pangaea.
- Some of the most important evidence for sea-floor spreading comes from magnetic reversals recorded in the ocean floor.

Skills Check

Math Concepts

MAKING MODELS Suppose you built a model of the Earth that had a radius of 100 cm (diameter of 200 cm). The radius of the real Earth is 6,378 km, and the thickness of its outer core is 2,200 km. What percentage of the Earth's radius is the outer core? How thick would the outer core be in your model?

$$\frac{2{,}200 \text{ km}}{6{,}378 \text{ km}} = 0.34 = 34\%$$

$$34\% \text{ of } 100 \text{ cm} = 0.34 \times 100 \text{ cm} = 34 \text{ cm}$$

Visual Understanding

SEA-FLOOR SPREADING This close-up view of a mid-ocean ridge shows how new oceanic lithosphere forms. As the two tectonic plates pull away from each other, magma fills in the cracks that open between them. When this magma solidifies, it becomes the newest part of the oceanic plate.

Lab and Activity Highlights

Convection Connection PG 656

Oh, the Pressure! PG 657

Datasheets for LabBook (blackline masters for these labs)

SECTION 3

Vocabulary

plate tectonics *(p. 177)*
convergent boundary *(p. 178)*
subduction zone *(p. 178)*
divergent boundary *(p. 179)*
transform boundary *(p. 179)*

Section Notes

- The processes of ridge push, convection, and slab pull provide some possible driving forces for plate tectonics.
- Tectonic plate boundaries are classified as convergent, divergent, or transform.
- Data from satellite tracking indicate that some tectonic plates move an average of 3 cm a year.

Labs

Convection Connection *(p. 656)*

SECTION 4

Vocabulary

stress *(p. 181)*
compression *(p. 181)*
tension *(p. 181)*
folding *(p. 182)*
fault *(p. 183)*
normal fault *(p. 183)*
reverse fault *(p. 183)*
strike-slip fault *(p. 184)*

Section Notes

- As tectonic plates move next to and into each other, a great amount of stress is placed on the rocks at the boundary.
- Folding occurs when rock layers bend due to stress.
- Faulting occurs when rock layers break due to stress and then move on either side of the break.
- Mountains are classified as either folded, fault-block, or volcanic, depending on how they form.
- Mountain building is caused by the movement of tectonic plates. Different types of movement cause different types of mountains.

Labs

Oh, the Pressure! *(p. 657)*

VOCABULARY DEFINITIONS, continued

SECTION 3

plate tectonics the theory that the Earth's lithosphere is divided into tectonic plates that move around on top of the asthenosphere

convergent boundary the boundary between two colliding tectonic plates

subduction zone the region where an oceanic plate sinks down into the asthenosphere at a convergent boundary, usually between continental and oceanic plates

divergent boundary the boundary between two tectonic plates that are moving away from each other

transform boundary the boundary between two tectonic plates that are sliding past each other horizontally

SECTION 4

stress the amount of force per unit area that is put on a given material

compression the type of stress that occurs when an object is squeezed

tension the type of stress that occurs when forces act to stretch an object

folding the bending of rock layers due to stress in the Earth's crust

fault a break in the Earth's crust along which two blocks of the crust slide relative to one another

normal fault a fault in which the hanging wall moves down relative to the footwall

reverse fault a fault in which the hanging wall moves up relative to the footwall

strike-slip fault a fault in which the two fault blocks move past each other horizontally

---

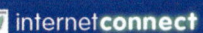

internetconnect

 **GO TO:** go.hrw.com

Visit the **HRW** Web site for a variety of learning tools related to this chapter. Just type in the keyword:

KEYWORD: HSTTEC

 **GO TO:** www.scilinks.org

Visit the **National Science Teachers Association** on-line Web site for Internet resources related to this chapter. Just type in the *sci*LINKS number for more information about the topic:

TOPIC	*sci*LINKS NUMBER
Composition of the Earth	HSTE155
Structure of the Earth	HSTE160
Tectonic Plates	HSTE165
Faults	HSTE170
Mountain Building	HSTE175

189

Lab and Activity Highlights

LabBank

 Whiz-Bang Demonstrations, Thar She Blows! Demo 18

Labs You Can Eat
- Rescue Near the Center of the Earth, Lab 13
- Cracks in the Hard-Boiled Earth, Lab 14
- Dough Fault of Your Own, Lab 15

 Long-Term Projects & Research Ideas, Legend Has It, Project 35

 Blackline masters of these Chapter Highlights can be found in the **Study Guide.**

Chapter 7 • Chapter Highlights   **189**

Chapter Review

USING VOCABULARY

For each pair of terms, explain the difference in their meanings.

1. oceanic crust/continental crust
2. lithosphere/asthenosphere
3. convergent boundary/divergent boundary
4. folding/faulting
5. oceanic crust/oceanic lithosphere
6. normal fault/reverse fault

UNDERSTANDING CONCEPTS

Multiple Choice

7. The part of the Earth that is a liquid is the
   a. crust.
   b. mantle.
   c. outer core.
   d. inner core.

8. The part of the Earth on which the tectonic plates are able to move is the
   a. lithosphere.
   b. asthenosphere.
   c. mesosphere.
   d. subduction zone.

9. The ancient continent that contained all the landmasses is called
   a. Pangaea.
   b. Gondwana.
   c. Laurasia.
   d. Panthalassa.

10. The type of tectonic plate boundary involving a collision between two tectonic plates is
    a. divergent.
    b. transform.
    c. convergent.
    d. normal.

11. The type of tectonic plate boundary that sometimes has a subduction zone is
    a. divergent.
    b. transform.
    c. convergent.
    d. normal.

12. The San Andreas fault is an example of a
    a. divergent boundary.
    b. transform boundary.
    c. convergent boundary.
    d. normal boundary.

13. When a fold is shaped like an arch, with the fold in an upward direction, it is called a(n)
    a. monocline.
    b. anticline.
    c. syncline.
    d. decline.

14. The type of fault in which the hanging wall moves down relative to the footwall is called
    a. strike-slip.
    b. reverse.
    c. normal.
    d. fault-block.

15. The type of mountain involving huge sections of the Earth's crust being pushed up into anticlines and synclines is the
    a. folded mountain.
    b. fault-block mountain.
    c. volcanic mountain.
    d. strike-slip mountain.

16. Continental mountain ranges are usually associated with
    a. divergent boundaries.
    b. transform boundaries.
    c. convergent boundaries.
    d. normal boundaries.

17. Mid-ocean ridges are associated with
    a. divergent boundaries.
    b. transform boundaries.
    c. convergent boundaries.
    d. normal boundaries.

Short Answer

18. A tectonic plate is a large piece of the lithosphere that moves around on top of the asthenosphere.
19. Wegener's theory did not explain the driving force responsible for continental drift.
20. Stress occurs in the Earth's crust because the crust is a part of all tectonic plates, and tectonic plates are constantly colliding, pulling apart, and sliding past each other.

Short Answer

18. What is a tectonic plate?
19. What was the major problem with Wegener's theory of continental drift?
20. Why is there stress on the Earth's crust?

Concept Mapping

21. Use the following terms to create a concept map: sea-floor spreading, convergent boundary, divergent boundary, subduction zone, transform boundary, tectonic plates.

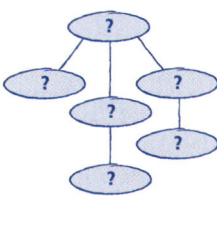

CRITICAL THINKING AND PROBLEM SOLVING

Write one or two sentences to answer each of the following questions:

22. Why is it necessary to think about the different layers of the Earth in terms of both their composition and their physical properties?
23. Folded mountains usually form at the edge of a tectonic plate. How can you explain old folded mountain ranges located in the middle of a tectonic plate?
24. New tectonic plate material continually forms at divergent boundaries. Tectonic plate material is also continually destroyed in subduction zones at convergent boundaries. Do you think the total amount of lithosphere formed on Earth is about equal to the amount destroyed? Why?

MATH IN SCIENCE

25. Assume that a very small oceanic plate is between a mid-ocean ridge to the west and a subduction zone to the east. At the ridge, the oceanic plate is growing at a rate of 5 km every million years. At the subduction zone, the oceanic plate is being destroyed at a rate of 10 km every million years. If the oceanic plate is 100 km across, in how many million years will the oceanic plate disappear?

INTERPRETING GRAPHICS

Imagine that you could travel to the center of the Earth. Use the diagram below to answer the questions that follow.

Composition	Structure
Crust (50 km)	Lithosphere (150 km)
Mantle (2,900 km)	Asthenosphere (250 km)
	Mesosphere (2,550 km)
Core (3,428 km)	Outer core (2,200 km)
	Inner core (1,228 km)

26. How far beneath Earth's surface would you have to go to find the liquid material in the Earth's core?
27. At what range of depth would you find mantle material but still be within the lithosphere?

 Take a minute to review your answers to the Pre-Reading Questions found at the bottom of page 164. Have your answers changed? If necessary, revise your answers based on what you have learned since you began this chapter.

Concept Mapping

21.  An answer to this exercise can be found at the end of this book.

CRITICAL THINKING AND PROBLEM SOLVING

22. Some layers of the Earth (such as the inner and outer cores) have the same composition but different physical properties.
23. At the time they formed, the folded mountains must have been on the edge of a tectonic plate. New material was later added to the tectonic plate, causing the folded mountains to be located closer to the center of the plate.
24. Answers will vary. The amount of crust formed is roughly equal to the amount of crust destroyed globally. If this were not true, the Earth would be either expanding or shrinking.

MATH IN SCIENCE

25. In 1 million years, the tectonic plate grows 5 km on one side but shrinks by 10 km on the other side. Every 1 million years, the tectonic plate shrinks by 5 km. In 20 million years, the tectonic plate will disappear entirely.

Rate of tectonic plate destruction:
5 km/y − 10 km/y = −5 km/y

The tectonic plate will completely disappear in:

$$\frac{100 \text{ km}}{5 \text{ km/y}} = 20 \text{ million years}$$

INTERPRETING GRAPHICS

26. 150 km + 250 km + 2,550 km = 2,950 km
27. between 50 and 150 km

Concept Mapping Transparency 7

 Blackline masters of this Chapter Review can be found in the **Study Guide**.

Science, Technology, and Society

Living on the Mid-Atlantic Ridge

Imagine living hundreds of kilometers from other people on an icy outcrop of volcanic rock surrounded by the cold North Atlantic Ocean. How would you stay warm? For the people of Iceland, this is an important question that affects their daily lives. Iceland is a volcanic island situated on the Mid-Atlantic Ridge, just south of the Arctic Circle. Sea-floor spreading produces active volcanoes, earthquakes, hot springs, and geysers that make life on this island seem a little unstable. However, the same volcanic force that threatens civilization provides the heat necessary for daily life. Icelanders use the geothermal energy supplied by their surroundings in ways that might surprise you.

▲ The Blue Lagoon in Iceland is the result of producing energy from water power.

Let's Go Geothermal!

Geothermal literally means "earth heat," *geo-* meaning "earth" and *therme* meaning "heat." Around the ninth century A.D., Iceland's earliest settlers took advantage of the Earth's heat by planting crops in naturally heated ground. This encouraged rapid plant growth and an early harvest of food. In 1928, Iceland built its first public geothermal utility project—a hole drilled into the Earth in order to pump water from a hot spring. After the oil crisis of the 1970s, geothermal-energy projects were built on a grand scale in Iceland. Today 85 percent of all houses in Iceland are heated by geothermal energy. Hot water from underground pools is pumped directly to houses, where it is routed through radiators to provide heating.

Geothermal water is also pumped to homes to provide hot tap water. This natural source meets all the hot-water needs for the city of Reykjavik, with a population of about 150,000 people!

There are still other uses for this hot water. For example, it is used to heat 120 public swimming pools. Picture yourself swimming outside in naturally hot water during the dead of winter! Greenhouses, where fruits and vegetables are grown, are also warmed by this water. Even fish farming on Iceland's exposed coastline wouldn't be possible without geothermal energy to adjust the water temperature. In other industries, geothermal energy is used to dry timber, wool, and seaweed.

Power Production

Although hydropower (producing energy from water power) is the principal source of electricity in Iceland, geothermal energy is also used. Water ranging in temperature from 300–700°C is pumped into a reservoir, where the water turns into steam that forces turbines to turn. The spinning motion of these turbines generates electricity. Power generation from geothermal sources is only about 5–15 percent efficient and results in a very large amount of water runoff. At the Svartsengi power plant, this water runoff has created a beautiful pool that swimmers call the Blue Lagoon.

Going Further

▶ Can you think of other abundant clean-energy resources? How could we harness such sources?

SCIENTIFIC DEBATE

Continental Drift

When Alfred Wegener proposed his theory of continental drift in the early 1900s, many scientists laughed at the idea of continents plowing across the ocean. In fact, many people found his theory so ridiculous that Wegener, a university professor, had difficulty getting a job! Wegener's theory jolted the very foundation of geology.

Alfred Wegener (1880–1930)

Wegener's Theory

Wegener used geologic, fossil, and glacial evidence gathered on opposite sides of the Atlantic Ocean to support his theory of continental drift. For example, Wegener recognized geologic similarities between the Appalachian Mountains, in eastern North America, and the Scottish Highlands, as well as similarities between rock strata in South Africa and Brazil. He believed that these striking similarities could be explained only if these geologic features were once part of the same continent.

Wegener proposed that because they are less dense, continents float on top of the denser rock of the ocean floor. Although continental drift explained many of Wegener's observations, he could not find scientific evidence to develop a complete explanation of how continents move.

The Critics

Most scientists were skeptical of Wegener's theory and dismissed it as foolishness. Some critics held fast to old theories that giant land bridges could explain similarities among fossils in South America and Africa. Others argued that Wegener's theory could not account for the tremendous forces that would have been required to move continents such great distances. Wegener, however, believed that these forces could be the same forces responsible for earthquakes and volcanic eruptions.

The Evidence

During the 1950s and 1960s, discoveries of sea-floor spreading and magnetic reversal provided the evidence that Wegener's theory needed and led to the theory of plate tectonics. The theory of plate tectonics describes how the continents move. Today geologists recognize that continents are actually parts of moving tectonic plates that float on the asthenosphere, a layer of partially molten rock.

Like the accomplishments of so many scientists, Wegener's accomplishments went unrecognized until years after his death. The next time you hear a scientific theory that sounds far out, don't underestimate it. It may be proven true!

Also an Astronomer and Meteorologist

Wegener had a very diverse background in the sciences. He earned a Ph.D. in astronomy from the University of Berlin. But he was always very interested in geophysics and meteorology. His interest in geophysics led to his theory on continental drift. His interest in meteorology eventually led to his death. He froze to death in Greenland while returning from a rescue mission to bring food to meteorologists camped on a glacier.

On Your Own

▶ Photocopy a world map. Carefully cut out the continents from the map. Be sure to cut along the line where the land meets the water. Slide the continents together like a jigsaw puzzle. How does this relate to the tectonic plates and continental drift?

Chapter Organizer

CHAPTER ORGANIZATION	TIME MINUTES	OBJECTIVES	LABS, INVESTIGATIONS, AND DEMONSTRATIONS
Chapter Opener pp. 194–195	45	National Standards: SAI 1, ST 1, SPSP 3, 4	**Start-Up Activity** Bend, Break, or Shake, p. 195
Section 1 What Are Earthquakes?	90	▶ Determine where earthquakes come from and what causes them. ▶ Identify different types of earthquakes. ▶ Describe how earthquakes travel through the Earth. UCP 2, SAI 1, HNS 1, ES 1b	**Demonstration,** Faults and Earthquakes, p. 197 in ATE **BASIC** **QuickLab,** Modeling Seismic Waves, p. 201 **GENERAL**
Section 2 Earthquake Measurement	120	▶ Explain how earthquakes are detected. ▶ Demonstrate how to locate earthquakes. ▶ Describe how the strength of an earthquake is measured. UCP 3, SAI 1, 2, SPSP 3, 4, HNS 1, 3; LabBook UCP 3, SAI 1	**Skill Builder,** Earthquake Waves, p. 662 **ADVANCED** **Datasheets for LabBook,** Earthquake Waves, Datasheet 16 **ADVANCED**
Section 3 Earthquakes and Society	120	▶ Explain earthquake hazard. ▶ Compare methods of earthquake forecasting. ▶ List ways to safeguard buildings against earthquakes. ▶ Outline earthquake safety procedures. UCP 2, 3, SAI 1, SPSP 1, 3–5; LabBook UCP 2, 5, SAI 1, ST 1, SPSP 5	**Design Your Own,** Quake Challenge, p. 660 **GENERAL** **Datasheets for LabBook,** Quake Challenge, Datasheet 15 **GENERAL** **Whiz-Bang Demonstrations,** When Buildings Boogie, Demo 19 **GENERAL**
Section 4 Earthquake Discoveries Near and Far	90	▶ Describe how seismic studies reveal Earth's interior. ▶ Summarize seismic discoveries on other cosmic bodies. HNS 2, ES 1a	**Demonstration,** Mapping with Seismic Waves, p. 212 in ATE **GENERAL** **Long-Term Projects & Research Ideas,** Project 36 **ADVANCED**

*See page **T20** for a complete correlation of this book with the*

NATIONAL SCIENCE EDUCATION STANDARDS.

TECHNOLOGY RESOURCES

 Guided Reading Audio CD English or Spanish, Chapter 8

 One-Stop Planner CD-ROM with Test Generator

 CNN. Scientists in Action, Earthquake Architect, Segment 11

Chapter 8 • Earthquakes

Chapter 8 • Earthquakes

CLASSROOM WORKSHEETS, TRANSPARENCIES, AND RESOURCES	SCIENCE INTEGRATION AND CONNECTIONS	REVIEW AND ASSESSMENT
Directed Reading Worksheet 8 BASIC **Science Puzzlers, Twisters & Teasers,** Worksheet 8 ADVANCED		
Directed Reading Worksheet 8, Section 1 BASIC **Transparency 130,** Elastic Rebound **Transparency 280,** Transverse and Longitudinal Waves **Transparency 131,** Primary Wave **Transparency 131,** Secondary Wave **Transparency 131,** Surface Wave	**Cross-Disciplinary Focus,** p. 196 in ATE **Multicultural Connection,** p. 197 in ATE **Cross-Disciplinary Focus,** p. 199 in ATE **Multicultural Connection,** p. 199 in ATE **Physics Connection,** p. 200 **Connect to Physical Science,** p. 200 in ATE ADVANCED	**Homework,** p. 197 in ATE ADVANCED **Homework,** p. 198 in ATE GENERAL **Self-Check,** p. 199 **Review,** p. 201 GENERAL **Quiz,** p. 201 in ATE GENERAL **Alternative Assessment,** p. 201 in ATE GENERAL
Transparency 132, Finding an Earthquake's Epicenter **Directed Reading Worksheet 8,** Section 2 BASIC **Reinforcement Worksheet 8,** Complete a Seismic Story BASIC **Math Skills for Science Worksheet 43,** Earthquake Power! GENERAL	**Multicultural Connection,** p. 202 in ATE **MathBreak,** Moving Up the Scale, p. 204 GENERAL	**Review,** p. 204 GENERAL **Quiz,** p. 204 in ATE GENERAL **Alternative Assessment,** p. 204 in ATE GENERAL
Directed Reading Worksheet 8, Section 3 BASIC **Math Skills for Science Worksheet 5,** Dividing Whole Numbers with Long Division GENERAL	**Cross-Disciplinary Focus,** p. 206 in ATE **Math and More,** p. 206 in ATE GENERAL **Connect to Life Science,** p. 207 in ATE **Apply,** p. 210 GENERAL **Weird Science:** Can Animals Predict Earthquakes? p. 218 ADVANCED **Eye on the Environment:** What Causes Such Destruction? p. 219 GENERAL	**Self-Check,** p. 206 **Homework,** pp. 208, 209 in ATE GENERAL **Review,** p. 210 GENERAL **Quiz,** p. 210 in ATE GENERAL **Alternative Assessment,** p. 210 in ATE GENERAL
Transparency 133, Discoveries in the Earth's Interior **Directed Reading Worksheet 8,** Section 4 BASIC **Critical Thinking Worksheet 8,** Nearthlings Unite! ADVANCED		**Homework,** p. 212 in ATE ADVANCED **Review,** p. 213 GENERAL **Quiz,** p. 213 in ATE GENERAL **Alternative Assessment,** p. 213 in ATE GENERAL

END-OF-CHAPTER REVIEW AND ASSESSMENT

Chapter Review in Study Guide
Vocabulary and Notes in Study Guide
Chapter Tests with Performance-Based Assessment, Chapter 8 Test
Chapter Tests with Performance-Based Assessment, Performance-Based Assessment 8
Concept Mapping Transparency 8

---

internet connect

 Holt, Rinehart and Winston On-line Resources
go.hrw.com

For worksheets and other teaching aids related to this chapter, visit the HRW Web site and type in the keyword: **HSTEQK**

 **National Science Teachers Association**
www.scilinks.org

Encourage students to use the sciLINKS numbers listed in the internet connect boxes to access information and resources on the **NSTA** Web site.

Chapter 8 • Chapter Organizer   **193B**

Chapter Resources & Worksheets

Visual Resources

TEACHING TRANSPARENCIES

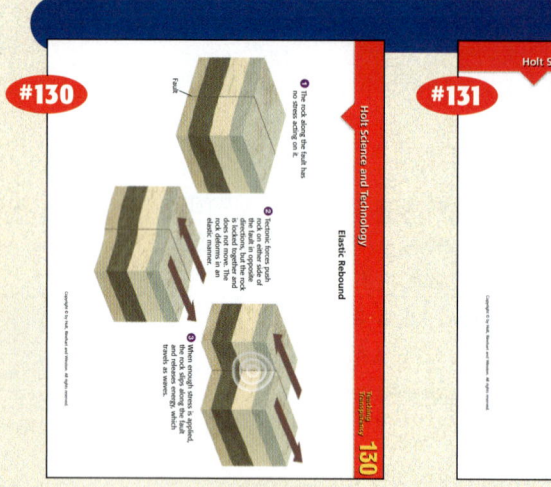
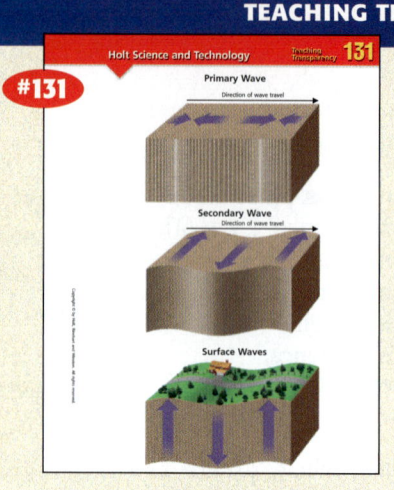

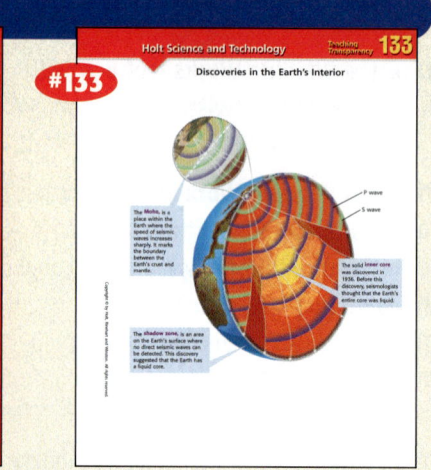

TEACHING TRANSPARENCIES

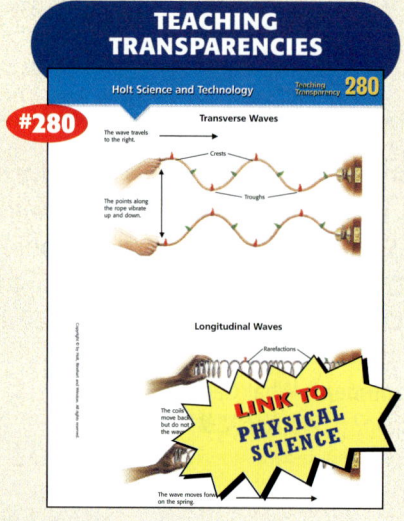

CONCEPT MAPPING TRANSPARENCY

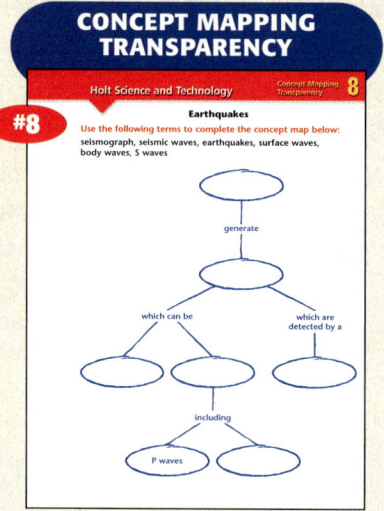

Meeting Individual Needs

DIRECTED READING

REINFORCEMENT & VOCABULARY REVIEW

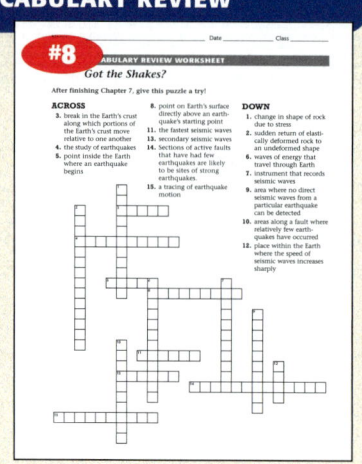

SCIENCE PUZZLERS, TWISTERS & TEASERS

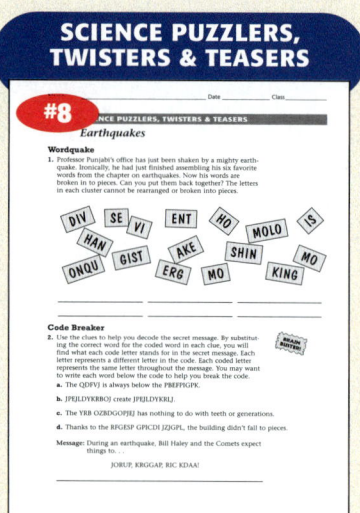

Chapter 8 • Earthquakes

Chapter 8 • Earthquakes

Review & Assessment

STUDY GUIDE

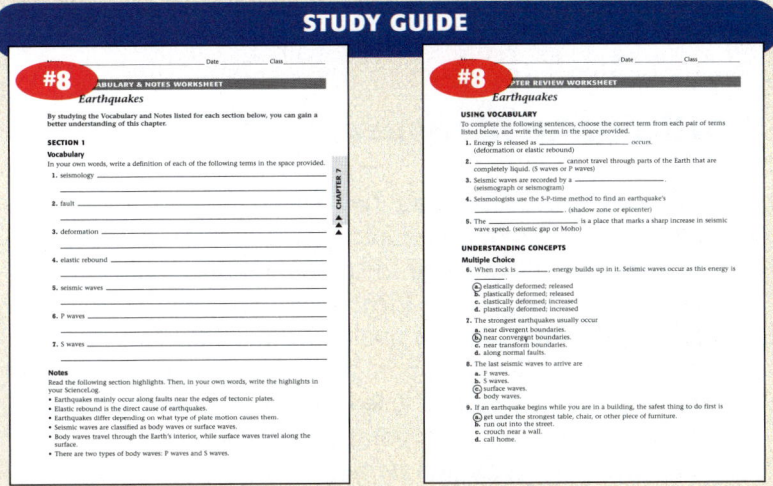

CHAPTER TESTS WITH PERFORMANCE-BASED ASSESSMENT

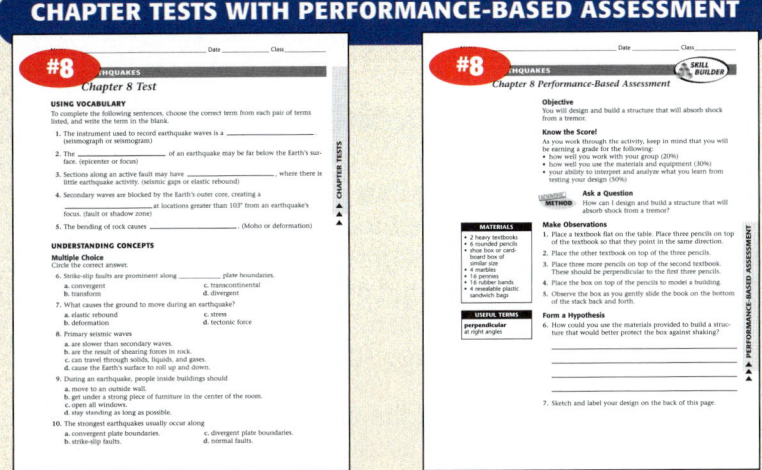

Lab Worksheets

WHIZ-BANG DEMONSTRATIONS

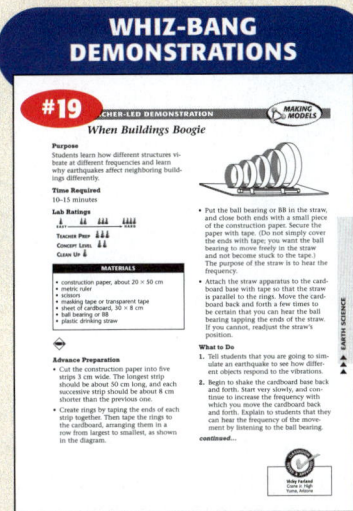

LONG-TERM PROJECTS & RESEARCH IDEAS

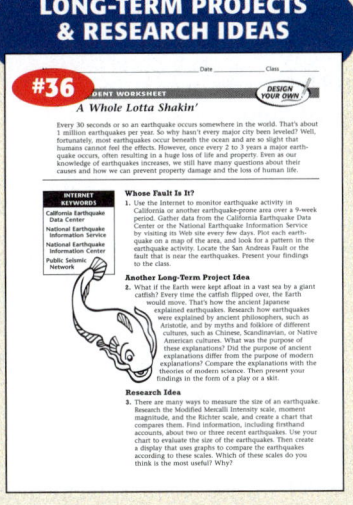

DATASHEETS FOR LABBOOK

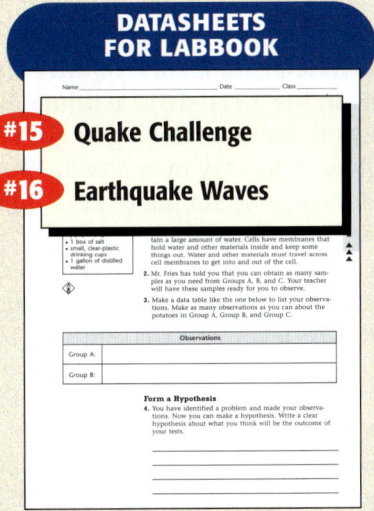

Applications & Extensions

CRITICAL THINKING & PROBLEM SOLVING

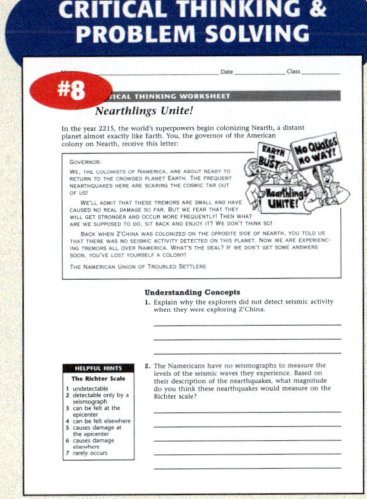

SCIENTISTS IN ACTION

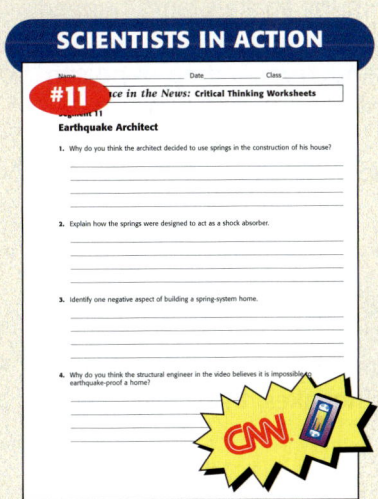

Chapter 8 • Chapter Resources & Worksheets

Chapter Background

SECTION 1

What Are Earthquakes?

▶ **Earthquake Origins**
Shallow earthquakes are those that originate within about 60 km of Earth's surface. Intermediate-depth earthquakes are those that originate between depths of about 60 km and 300 km. Deep earthquakes are those that originate below 300 km.

- Tectonic activity is not the only source of earthquakes. Earthquakes can also be caused by volcanic eruptions and by the impacts of cosmic bodies. These earthquakes, however, are less common than those occurring along faults.

▶ **The New Madrid Earthquakes**
Eyewitnesses to the 1811–1812 earthquakes in New Madrid, Missouri, reported seeing bright flashes of light and a dull glow in the sky over a wide area. Reeking sulfurous odors also accompanied the quakes. Many survivors were convinced that the quakes were a heavenly sign meant to frighten the local citizens back to church. As a result, church attendance in the area skyrocketed between 1811 and 1812!

▶ **The Punishment of Loki**
In Scandinavian mythology, earthquakes are believed to be caused by the clever prankster Loki. The gods decided to punish Loki when they discovered that he killed Balder, the god of light and joy. Loki was chained in a deep cave, and a huge, poisonous snake was hung above him. As the poison from the snake's fangs dripped down, Loki's sister tried to protect him by catching the poison in a cup. Sometimes, however, a drop of poison would splash Loki, causing him unbearable pain. At those times he would pull so violently on his chains that the ground above would tremble.

IS THAT A FACT!

▶ In 1755, in Lisbon, Portugal, an earthquake occurred that killed an estimated 60,000 people. It was this tragedy that resulted in an analytic and systematic approach to studying earthquakes, the basis of seismology.

SECTION 2

Earthquake Measurement

▶ **Magnitude Versus Intensity**
Earthquakes can be measured by magnitude or intensity. An earthquake's magnitude is a quantitative measurement of its strength. The Richter scale is used to measure magnitude. Intensity is a qualitative measurement of an earthquake's effect in a particular area. The Modified Mercalli Intensity scale is used to assess an earthquake's intensity. This scale incorporates observations of the earthquake's effects at a particular location. Although an earthquake may have different intensities at different locations, it has only one magnitude.

▶ **Seismic Rock**
In 1992, a British rock group caused some miniature earthquakes at one of their concerts! Scientists were at first mystified by the seismic events they recorded. Upon investigating the tremors, however, researchers at the Global Seismology Research Group, in Scotland, discovered that the energy patterns of the tremors matched those of certain hit songs and were generated by the foot stomping of the more than 30,000 fans at a nearby stadium!

IS THAT A FACT!

▶ One of the best structures for resisting damage from earthquakes is a wood-framed building. Wood-framed buildings are not very rigid and can therefore flex quite a bit without collapsing.

▶ The strongest earthquake recorded to date occurred in Chile in 1960. It measured 9.5 on the Richter scale. This is equivalent to detonating more than 1 billion tons of TNT!

Chapter 8 • Earthquakes

SECTION 3

Earthquakes and Society

▶ **Magnetometers**
Magnetometers are devices that measure changes in the Earth's magnetic field, which can be indicative of an upcoming quake. Elastic strain can cause slight magnetic variations in the rock. Detecting these variations can help seismologists predict earthquakes.

▶ **Survival of Structures**
The ability of a structure to withstand a quake depends on a variety of factors, including the composition of the ground on which the structure stands. Structures built on waterlogged or unconsolidated sediment, such as sand, are more likely to suffer intense damage than structures built on bedrock.

IS THAT A FACT!

- Sand boils are common during earthquakes that occur in areas with unconsolidated sediments. Loose, sandy sediments behave like a fluid as the ground moves. This condition can create a miniature "geyser" that spews buried debris from beneath the Earth's surface.

SECTION 4

Earthquake Discoveries Near and Far

▶ **Sunquakes**

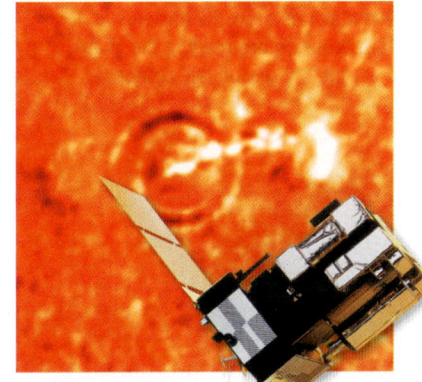

The waves generated by "sunquakes" resemble those produced when an object is dropped into a standing body of water. Unlike water ripples, however, in which a series of waves travels at constant velocity, a single series of solar seismic waves may vary in velocity from 35,400 km/h to 402,300 km/h. "Sunquakes" release enormous amounts of energy. Scientists estimate that a "sunquake" observed in 1996 released an incredible amount of energy—equivalent to covering Earth's land masses with a meter-deep pile of dynamite and detonating it all at once!

▶ **The Passive Seismic Experiment**
The passive seismic experiment, conducted via the *Apollo 11–16* space missions, produced some significant information about the moon. The experiment suggested that the moon has three distinct layers—a crust, a mantle, and a small, dense core. The studies also suggest that most significant "moonquakes" originate within the moon's mantle; few start in the crust. On Earth, most significant quakes originate in the crust.

IS THAT A FACT!

- The average "moonquake" is about one-millionth as strong as the average earthquake.

For background information about teaching strategies and issues, refer to the *Professional Reference for Teachers*.

CHAPTER 8

Earthquakes

 Pre-Reading Questions

Students may not know the answers to these questions before reading the chapter, so accept any reasonable response.

Suggested Answers

1. Elastic rebound along active faults is the direct cause of most earthquakes. Answers that attribute earthquakes to tectonic-plate movement or the movement of rock along faults are acceptable. Less appropriate answers may attribute earthquakes to volcanic eruptions or explosions.

2. Earthquake strength varies according to the type of tectonic-plate motion that causes them. Also, some earthquakes are stronger than others because more elastic deformation builds up along certain faults or parts of faults than along others.

3. It depends on how they are built. Some buildings are reinforced to withstand earthquakes better than other buildings.

 Directed Reading Worksheet 8

 Science Puzzlers, Twisters & Teasers Worksheet 8

 Guided Reading Audio CD English or Spanish, Chapter 8

CHAPTER 8

Earthquakes

Sections

1. What Are Earthquakes? 196
   - Physics Connection ... 200
   - QuickLab 201
   - Internet Connect 201
2. Earthquake Measurement 202
   - MathBreak 204
   - Internet Connect 204
3. Earthquakes and Society 205
   - Apply 210
   - Internet Connect 210
4. Earthquake Discoveries Near and Far 211
   - Internet Connect 213

Chapter Review 216
Feature Articles 218, 219
LabBook 660–663

 **Pre-Reading Questions**

1. What causes earthquakes?
2. Why are some earthquakes stronger than others?
3. Why do some buildings remain standing during earthquakes while others fall down?

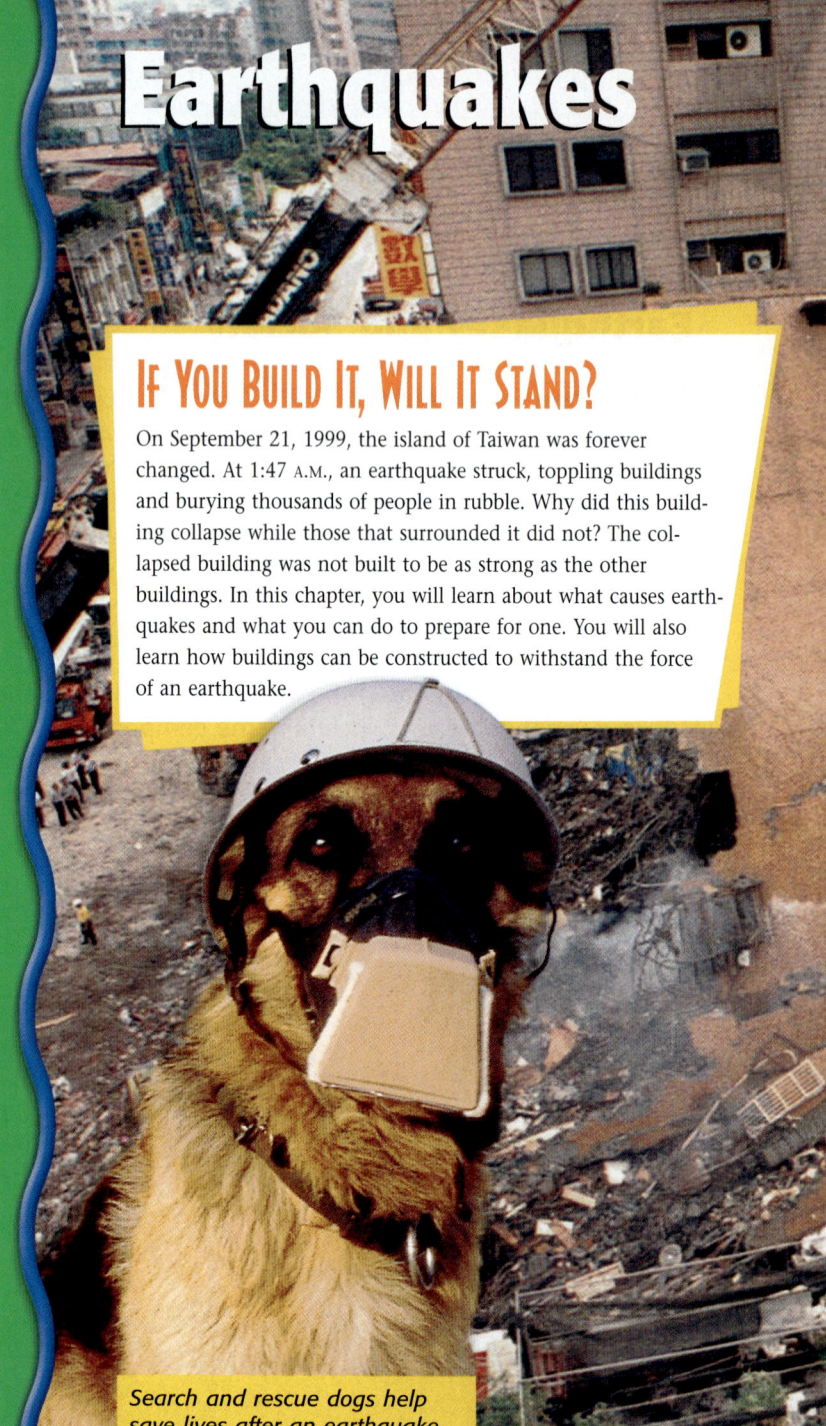

If You Build It, Will It Stand?

On September 21, 1999, the island of Taiwan was forever changed. At 1:47 A.M., an earthquake struck, toppling buildings and burying thousands of people in rubble. Why did this building collapse while those that surrounded it did not? The collapsed building was not built to be as strong as the other buildings. In this chapter, you will learn about what causes earthquakes and what you can do to prepare for one. You will also learn how buildings can be constructed to withstand the force of an earthquake.

Search and rescue dogs help save lives after an earthquake.

internet connect

 **HRW On-line Resources**
go.hrw.com
For worksheets and other teaching aids, visit the HRW Web site and type in the keyword: **HSTEQK**

 **sciLINKS NSTA**
www.scilinks.com
Use the sciLINKS numbers at the end of each chapter for additional resources on the **NSTA** Web site.

 **CNNfyi.com**
www.cnnfyi.com
Visit the CNN Web site for current events coverage and classroom resources.

BEND, BREAK, OR SHAKE

If you were in a building during an earthquake, what would you want the building to be made of? To answer this question, you need to know how building materials react to stress.

Procedure

1. Gather a **small wooden stick,** a **wire clothes hanger,** and a **plastic clothes hanger.**

2. Draw a straight line on a **sheet of paper.** Use a **protractor** to measure and draw the following angles from the line: 20°, 45°, and 90°.

3. Put on your safety goggles. Using the angles that you drew as a guide, try bending each item 20° and then releasing it. What happens? Does it break? If it bends, does it return to its original shape? Write your observations in your ScienceLog.

4. Repeat step 3, but bend each item 45°. Repeat the test again, but bend each item 90°.

Analysis

5. How do the materials' responses to bending compare?

6. Where earthquakes happen, engineers use building materials that are flexible but do not break or stay bent. Which materials from this experiment would you want building materials to behave like? Explain your answer.

START-UP Activity

BEND, BREAK, OR SHAKE

MATERIALS

FOR EACH GROUP:
- small wooden stick flexible enough to bend
- wire clothes hanger
- plastic clothes hanger
- sheet of paper *(1 per student)*
- protractor *(1 per student)*

Safety Caution

Remind students to review all safety cautions and icons before beginning this lab activity.

Teacher's Notes

Assist students who have difficulty manipulating the protractor or provide them with paper on which the angles have already been drawn.

Answers to START-UP Activity

5. Answers will vary depending on the materials used and on the strength of the materials.

6. Desirable building materials would behave like the materials that did not bend permanently or break.

Chapter 8 • Earthquakes

SECTION 1

Focus

What Are Earthquakes?

This section discusses the seismic events known as earthquakes. Students learn where earthquakes most commonly occur and what causes them. The section also covers different kinds of earthquakes and discusses how earthquakes travel as waves of energy through the Earth.

Bellringer

Ask students to write a few sentences in their ScienceLog describing what they think an earthquake is. Ask volunteers to read their descriptions. Students can review what they wrote after completing this section.
Sheltered English

1) Motivate

DISCUSSION

Explain to students that *seismos* is a Greek word meaning "to shake." Have students make a list of all the words that contain the root *seis-*. (These include *seismology, seismologists, seismic, seismographs, Seismosaurus,* and *seismograms.*) Have students copy the words onto a sheet of paper and consult a dictionary to divide each word into its proper parts. Then have students define each word part and write a definition of each complete term using the meanings of its parts.
Sheltered English

Directed Reading Worksheet 8 Section 1

Section 1

Terms to Learn
seismology   seismic waves
fault   P waves
deformation   S waves
elastic rebound

What You'll Do
- Determine where earthquakes come from and what causes them.
- Identify different types of earthquakes.
- Describe how earthquakes travel through the Earth.

What Are Earthquakes?

The word *earthquake* defines itself fairly well. But there is more to an earthquake than just ground shaking. In fact, there is a branch of Earth science devoted to earthquakes called seismology (siez MAHL uh jee). **Seismology** is the study of earthquakes. Earthquakes are complex, and they present many questions for *seismologists*, the scientists who study earthquakes.

Where Do Earthquakes Occur?

Most earthquakes take place near the edges of tectonic plates. *Tectonic plates* are giant masses of solid rock that make up the outermost part of the Earth. **Figure 1** shows the Earth's tectonic plates and the locations of recent major earthquakes recorded by scientists.

Tectonic plates move in different directions and at different speeds. Two plates can push toward each other or pull away from each other. They can also slip past each other like slow-moving trains traveling in opposite directions.

As a result of these movements, numerous features called faults exist in the Earth's crust. A **fault** is a break in the Earth's crust along which blocks of the crust slide relative to one another. Earthquakes occur along faults due to this sliding.

Faults occur in many places, but they are especially common near the edges of tectonic plates where they form the boundaries along which the plates move. This is why earthquakes are so common near tectonic plate boundaries.

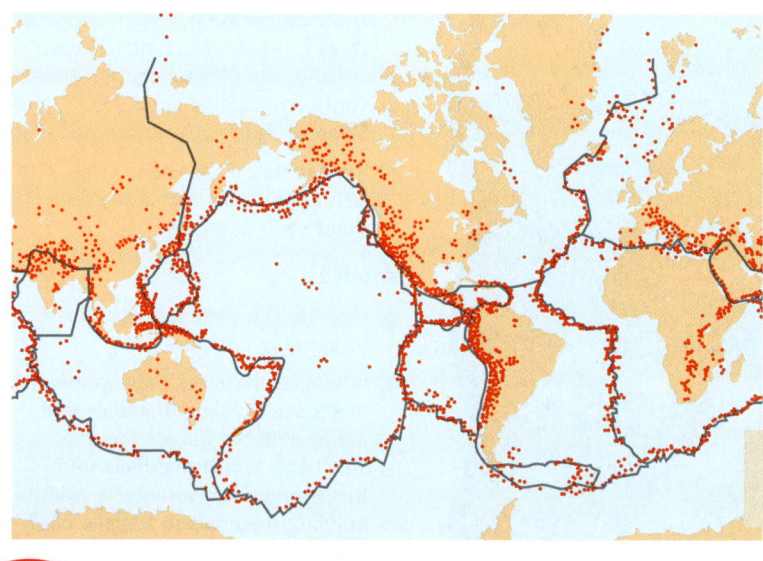

Figure 1 The largest and most active earthquake zone lies along the plate boundaries surrounding the Pacific Ocean.

— Plate boundary
• Recorded earthquake

CROSS-DISCIPLINARY FOCUS

History Aristotle was one of the first to attribute earthquakes to Earth processes. He hypothesized that earthquakes were caused by strong winds blowing through a myriad of caverns deep in the Earth's interior. Until the seventeenth century, many people believed that earthquakes were caused by large, restless creatures beneath the Earth's surface. It wasn't until the late 1700s that scientists began a systematic study of earthquakes. But as recently as the late 1800s, scientists did not know the true cause of earthquakes. Students can make a timeline illustrating the development of seismology from the ancient Greeks to the present.

What Causes Earthquakes?

As tectonic plates push, pull, or scrape against each other, stress builds up along faults near the plates' edges. In response to this stress, rock in the plates deforms. **Deformation** is the change in the shape of rock in response to stress. Rock along a fault deforms in mainly two ways—in a plastic manner, like a piece of molded clay, or in an elastic manner, like a rubber band. *Plastic deformation*, which is shown in **Figure 2,** does not lead to earthquakes.

Elastic deformation, however, does lead to earthquakes. While rock can stretch farther than steel without breaking, it will break at some point. Think of elastically deformed rock as a stretched rubber band. You can stretch a rubber band only so far before it breaks. When the rubber band breaks, it releases energy, and the broken pieces return to their unstretched shape.

Like the return of the broken rubber-band pieces to their unstretched shape, **elastic rebound** is the sudden return of elastically deformed rock to its original shape. Elastic rebound occurs when more stress is applied to rock than the rock can withstand. During elastic rebound, rock releases energy that causes an earthquake, as shown in **Figure 3.**

Figure 2 This photograph, taken in Hollister, California, shows how plastic deformation along the Calaveras Fault permanently bent a wall.

Figure 3 Elastic Rebound and Earthquakes

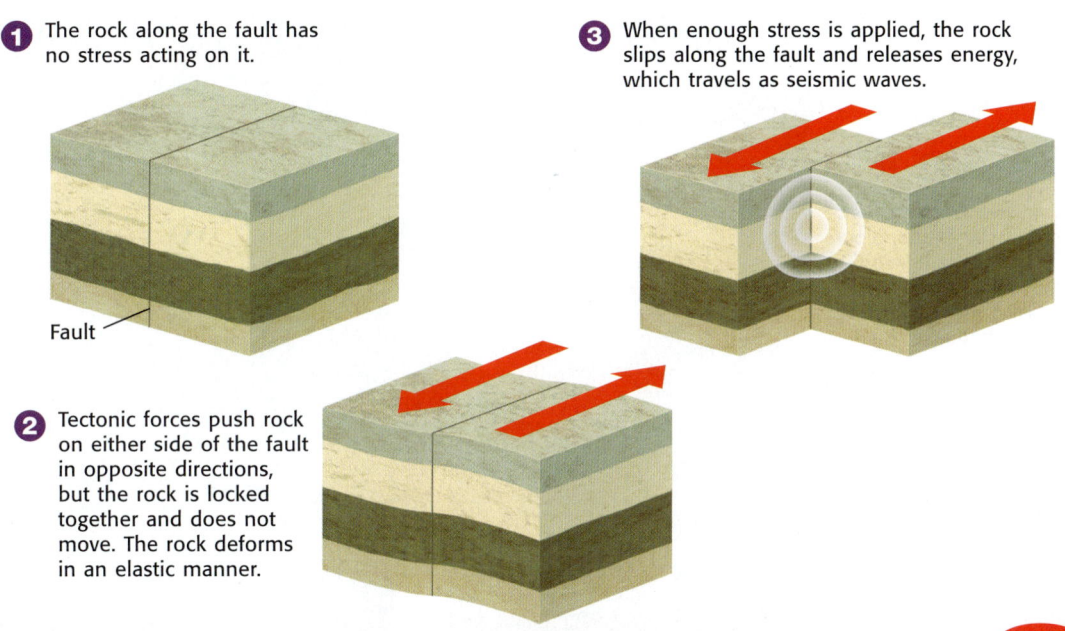

① The rock along the fault has no stress acting on it.

② Tectonic forces push rock on either side of the fault in opposite directions, but the rock is locked together and does not move. The rock deforms in an elastic manner.

③ When enough stress is applied, the rock slips along the fault and releases energy, which travels as seismic waves.

Fault

2) Teach, continued

USING THE FIGURE

Each circle in the illustration is a magnified view of a fault at the edge of a tectonic plate. In fact, large systems of multiple faults define the boundaries between plates. The sliding of crust along these faults and the overall movement of crust along plate boundaries are similar. For example, the block of crust to the right of the reverse fault moves down relative to the block to the left of the fault. Similarly, the plate to the right of the convergent plate boundary moves down relative to the plate to the left of the boundary.

GROUP ACTIVITY

Forces and Faults For each pair of students, obtain a pair of wooden blocks cut at an angle. Ask students to demonstrate normal-fault movement by sliding the top block down relative to the bottom block. To show a reverse fault, students should slide the top block up relative to the bottom block. Have them slide the blocks horizontally to demonstrate a strike-slip fault. Make sure students see how divergent, convergent, and transform motion cause the different types of fault movement.

READING STRATEGY

Mnemonics A footwall is the rock beneath an inclined fault. Using these mnemonic devices, students can remember the difference between a normal fault and a reverse fault by noting the movement of the footwall.
- **FUN** **F**ootwall **U**p is **N**ormal
- **FDR** **F**ootwall **D**own is **R**everse

Are All Earthquakes the Same?

Earthquakes differ in strength and in the depth at which they begin. These differences depend on the type of tectonic plate motion that produces the earthquake. Examine the chart and the diagram below to learn how earthquakes differ.

Plate motion	Prominent fault type	Earthquake characteristics
Transform	strike-slip fault	moderate, shallow
Convergent	reverse fault	strong, deep
Divergent	normal fault	weak, shallow

Transform motion occurs where two plates slip past each other.

Transform motion creates **strike-slip faults.** Blocks of crust slide horizontally past each other, causing moderate, shallow earthquakes.

198

Homework

Ask students to draw the three types of faults illustrated on these pages. Students should label each fault, state the type of plate motion that creates each fault, and write a brief description of the earthquakes associated with each type of fault. Encourage students to locate an example of each type of tectonic plate boundary on a map.

(An example of a transform plate boundary is the San Andreas Fault, in California; an example of a convergent plate boundary is off the west coast of South America—convergent motion created the Andes; an example of a divergent plate boundary is the Mid-Atlantic Ridge, on the bottom of the Atlantic Ocean.)
Sheltered English

Self-Check

Name two differences between the results of convergent motion and the results of divergent motion. *(See page 726 to check your answer.)*

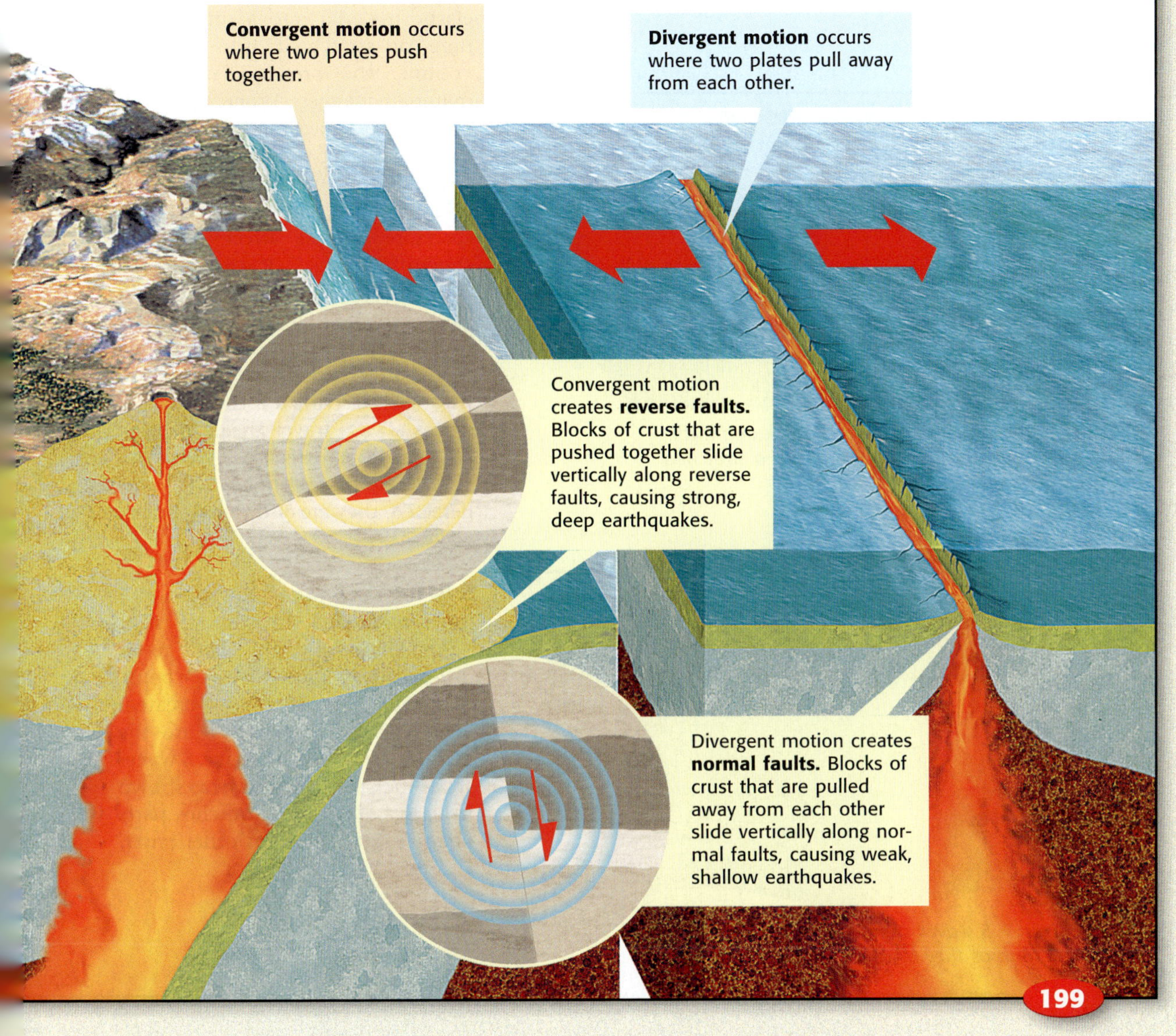

Convergent motion occurs where two plates push together.

Divergent motion occurs where two plates pull away from each other.

Convergent motion creates **reverse faults.** Blocks of crust that are pushed together slide vertically along reverse faults, causing strong, deep earthquakes.

Divergent motion creates **normal faults.** Blocks of crust that are pulled away from each other slide vertically along normal faults, causing weak, shallow earthquakes.

Answers to Self-Check

Convergent motion creates reverse faults, while divergent motion creates normal faults. Convergent motion produces deep, strong earthquakes, while divergent motion produces shallow, weak earthquakes.

CROSS-DISCIPLINARY FOCUS

Language Arts John James Audubon was in Kentucky during the New Madrid earthquakes. He wrote that "the ground rose and fell in successive furrows like the ruffled waters of a lake. The earth waved like a field of corn before a breeze." After sharing this quote with the class, ask students to use similes and metaphors to write their own description of an earthquake.

American Indian legends refer to the unstable crust in the New Madrid, Missouri area. One story describes how Chief Reelfoot of the Chickasaw tribe kidnapped a bride from the Choctaw tribe. Just as the Chief and his bride were about to be married, a great earthquake caused the ground under them to collapse. The entire wedding party was drowned as a river flooded the area, forming Reelfoot Lake, in Tennessee. Geologists now know that the lake was indeed formed by the New Madrid earthquakes.

WEIRD SCIENCE

Many people assume that major earthquakes in the United States occur only on the West Coast. However, major quakes have occurred in South Carolina and Missouri—far from any active plate boundaries. The four major tremors of the 1811–1812 earthquakes in New Madrid, Missouri, were so intense that, according to reports, they altered the flow of the Mississippi River and rang church bells in Boston! The cause of these quakes baffled scientists until the late 1970s, when they found a series of faults deep beneath sediment deposited by the Mississippi River. The area is still seismically active, and large quakes may still occur.

Section 1 • What Are Earthquakes? **199**

3 Extend

MEETING INDIVIDUAL NEEDS

Learners Having Difficulty
Tell students that the *P* in *P waves* and the *S* in *S waves* stand for two descriptive words each. The letters describe how each type of wave affects rock; *P* stands for *pressure,* and *S* stands for *shear.* *P* also stands for *primary,* while *S* stands for *secondary.* This scheme describes the arrival times of each type of wave—P waves always arrive first, and S waves always arrive second.
Sheltered English

CONNECT TO PHYSICAL SCIENCE

Use Transparency 280 to discuss the differences between P waves (longitudinal) and S waves (transverse). Have students create a labeled poster of S waves and identify the trough, crest, wave period, wavelength, and wave height. Then have students make a list of the differences between P waves and S waves. Lists should include but are not limited to the following:

- P waves travel faster than S waves.
- P waves travel through solids, liquids, and gases; S waves cannot travel through materials that are completely liquid.
- P waves move rock back and forth between a squeezed and stretched position, while S waves shear rock back and forth.

 **Teaching Transparency 280**
"Transverse and Longitudinal Waves"

All types of waves share basic features. Understanding one type, such as seismic waves, can help you understand many other types. Other types of waves include light waves, sound waves, and water waves.

How Do Earthquakes Travel?

Remember that rock releases energy when it springs back after being deformed. This energy travels in the form of seismic waves. **Seismic waves** are waves of energy that travel through the Earth. Seismic waves that travel through the Earth's interior are called *body waves.* There are two types of body waves: P waves and S waves. Seismic waves that travel along the Earth's surface are called *surface waves.* Different types of seismic waves travel at different speeds and move the materials that they travel through differently.

P Is for Primary If you squeeze an elastic material into a smaller volume or stretch it into a larger volume, the pressure inside the material changes. When you suddenly stop squeezing or stretching the material, it springs briefly back and forth before returning to its original shape. This is how P waves (pressure waves) affect rock, as shown in **Figure 4. P waves,** which travel through solids, liquids, and gases, are the fastest seismic waves. Because they are the fastest seismic waves and because they can move through all parts of the Earth, P waves always travel ahead of other seismic waves. Because P waves are always the first seismic waves to be detected, they are also called *primary* waves.

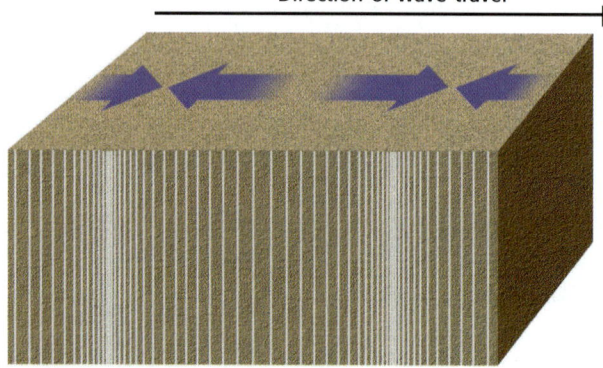

Figure 4 *P waves move rock back and forth between a squeezed position and a stretched position as they travel through it.*

S Is for Secondary Rock can also be deformed from side to side. When the rock springs back to its original position after being deformed, S waves are created. **S waves,** or shear waves, are the second-fastest seismic wave. S waves shear rock back and forth, as shown in **Figure 5.** *Shearing* stretches parts of rock sideways from other parts.

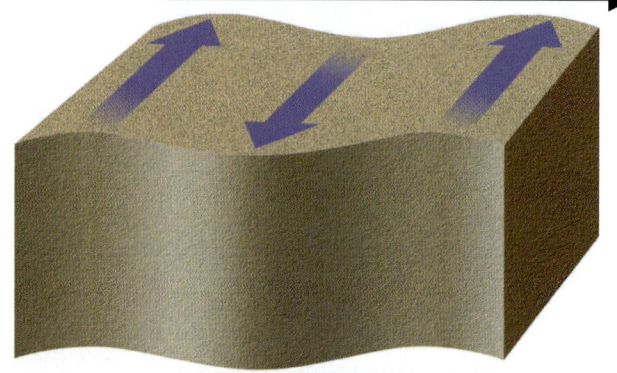

Figure 5 *S waves shear rock back and forth as they travel through it.*

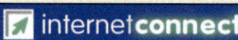
 **TOPIC:** What Is an Earthquake?
GO TO: www.scilinks.org
*sci*LINKS NUMBER: HSTE180

Unlike P waves, S waves cannot travel through parts of the Earth that are completely liquid. Also, S waves are slower than P waves and always arrive second; thus, they are also called *secondary* waves.

Surface Waves Surface waves move the ground up and down in circles as the waves travel along the surface. This is shown in **Figure 6**. Many people have reported feeling like they were on a roller coaster during an earthquake. This feeling comes from surface waves passing along the Earth's surface. Surface waves travel more slowly than body waves but are more destructive. Most damage during an earthquake comes from surface waves, which can literally shake the ground out from under a building.

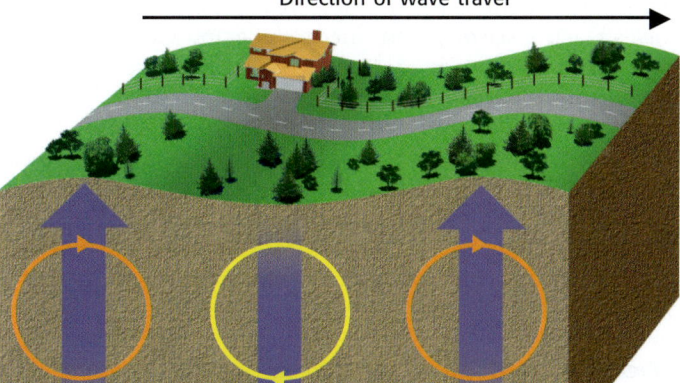

Figure 6 *Surface waves move the ground much like ocean waves move water particles.*

QuickLab

Modeling Seismic Waves

1. Stretch a **spring toy** lengthwise on a **table**.
2. Hold one end of the spring while a partner holds the other end. Push your end toward your partner's end, and observe what happens.
3. Repeat step 2, but this time shake the spring from side to side.
4. Which type of seismic wave is represented in step 2? in step 3?

TRY at HOME

REVIEW

1. Where do earthquakes occur?
2. What directly causes earthquakes?
3. Arrange the types of earthquakes caused by the three plate-motion types from weakest to strongest.
4. **Analyzing Relationships** Why are surface waves more destructive to buildings than P waves or S waves?

---

internet connect

SC_{LINKS} NSTA

TOPIC: What Is an Earthquake?
GO TO: www.scilinks.org
sciLINKS NUMBER: HSTE180

201

Answers to Review

1. Answers may vary. Most earthquakes take place near the edges of tectonic plates.
2. Answers may vary. Most earthquakes occur when rock releases energy during elastic rebound.
3. Earthquakes caused by divergent motion are weakest; earthquakes caused by transform motion are moderate; and earthquakes caused by convergent motion are strongest.
4. As surface waves travel across the surface, they move the ground up and down in circles. Surface waves are more destructive because they cause the ground to move more than P waves and S waves.

QuickLab

MATERIALS

FOR EACH PAIR:
• small metal or plastic spring toys

Answer to QuickLab

4. P waves are represented in step 2, and S waves are represented in step 3.

4) Close

Quiz

1. What is a fault? (A fault is a break in the Earth's crust along which blocks of the crust slide relative to one another.)
2. Name two ways in which rock along a fault deforms in response to stress. (Rock deforms in a plastic manner, like a piece of molded clay, or in an elastic manner, like a rubber band.)

ALTERNATIVE ASSESSMENT

Concept Mapping Have students create a concept map explaining the relationship between tectonic plate motion, earthquake characteristics, and fault types.

Teaching Transparency 131
"Primary Wave"
"Secondary Wave"
"Surface Wave"

Section 1 • What Are Earthquakes?

SECTION 2

Focus

Earthquake Measurement
In this section students learn how seismographs are used to detect and locate earthquakes. This section explains the difference between an earthquake's focus and its epicenter. Students will also learn how the Richter scale is used to measure the strength of earthquakes.

Bellringer
Ask students to create a qualitative scale for gauging earthquake intensity. Students should use brief phrases to describe the effects of very minor to extreme earthquakes. Discuss the advantages and disadvantages of their finished scale. Tell them that they will learn about a quantitative scale for earthquake measurement in this chapter.

1 Motivate

ACTIVITY
Ask students to close their eyes. Tell them that you will move to some part of the room and snap your fingers. When they hear you snap, have them point to where they think you are standing. Have students keep their eyes closed while you return to the front of the room. Ask the class to locate where you were standing, and have a helper stand in that spot. Ask students how they were able to pinpoint your location. Explain that when an earthquake occurs, it is noted at seismic stations around the world. By comparing the time it took the tremors to reach each station, the earthquake's origin can be pinpointed.

Section 2

Terms to Learn
seismograph   epicenter
seismogram   focus

What You'll Do
- Explain how earthquakes are detected.
- Demonstrate how to locate earthquakes.
- Describe how the strength of an earthquake is measured.

Figure 7 The line in a seismogram traces the movement of the ground as it shakes. The more the ground moves, the farther back and forth the line traces.

Multicultural CONNECTION
A Chinese man named Chang Heng designed the first known earthquake detector around A.D. 132. It was a bronze urn decorated with six dragons' heads. Each head held a bronze ball in its mouth. A pendulum was suspended inside the urn. During a tremor, the urn would strike the pendulum, causing one of the balls to drop into the open mouth of a bronze toad below. The ball would make a loud noise, signaling the occurrence of an earthquake. By noting which ball fell, people could determine the direction of the earthquake's epicenter. Have students design their own earthquake detector and share it with the class.

Earthquake Measurement

After an earthquake occurs, seismologists try to find out when and where it started. Earthquake-sensing devices enable seismologists to record and measure seismic waves. These measurements show how far the seismic waves traveled. The measurements also show how much the ground moved. Seismologists use this information to pinpoint where the earthquake started and to find out how strong the earthquake was.

Locating Earthquakes
How do seismologists know when and where earthquakes begin? They depend on earthquake-sensing instruments called seismographs. **Seismographs** are instruments located at or near the surface of the Earth that record seismic waves. When the waves reach a seismograph, the seismograph creates a seismogram, such as the one in **Figure 7**. A **seismogram** is a tracing of earthquake motion created by a seismograph.

When Did It Happen? Seismologists use seismograms to calculate when an earthquake started. An earthquake starts when rock slips suddenly enough along a fault to create seismic waves. Seismologists find an earthquake's start time by comparing seismograms and noting the difference in arrival times of P waves and S waves.

Where Did It Happen? Seismologists also use seismograms to find an earthquake's epicenter. An **epicenter** is the point on the Earth's surface directly above an earthquake's starting point. A **focus** is the point inside the Earth where an earthquake begins. **Figure 8** shows the relationship between an earthquake's epicenter and its focus.

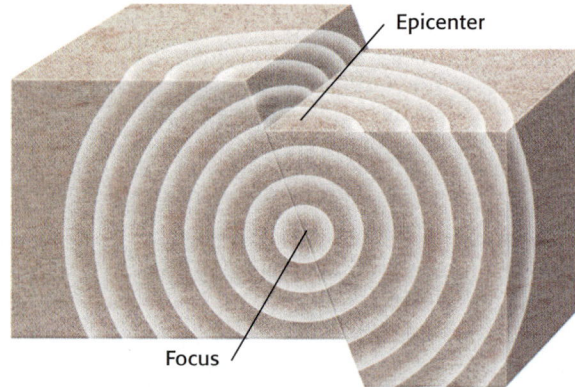

Figure 8 An earthquake's epicenter is on the Earth's surface directly above the earthquake's focus.

202   Chapter 8 • Earthquakes

Putting It All Together Perhaps the most common method by which seismologists find an earthquake's epicenter is the *S-P-time method*. When using the S-P-time method, seismologists begin by collecting several seismograms of the same earthquake from different locations. Seismologists then place the seismograms on a time-distance graph so the first P waves line up with the P-wave curve and the first S waves line up with the S-wave curve. This is shown in **Figure 9.**

After the seismograms are placed on the graph, seismologists can see how far away from each station the earthquake was by reading the distance axis. After seismologists find out the distances, they can find the earthquake's epicenter as shown below.

Figure 9 Seismologists subtract a wave's travel time (read from the vertical axis) from the time that the wave was recorded. This indicates when the earthquake started. The distance of the stations from the epicenter is read from the horizontal axis.

Finding an Earthquake's Epicenter

① A circle is drawn around a seismograph station. The radius of the circle equals the distance from the seismograph to the epicenter. (This distance is taken from the time-distance graph.)

② When a second circle is drawn around another seismograph station, it overlaps the first circle in two spots. One of these spots is the earthquake's epicenter.

③ When a third circle is drawn around a third seismograph station, all three circles intersect in only one spot. This spot is the earthquake's epicenter.

SCIENTISTS AT ODDS

When Charles Richter was a 27-year-old graduate student, he was working on a catalog of earthquakes in southern California. He wanted to find an objective way to compare earthquakes. Up to that point, geologists used the Mercalli scale to classify earthquakes. Giuseppe Mercalli developed the scale in 1902 to describe the intensity of earthquakes. The Mercalli scale was based on the observations of people who witnessed an earthquake and on the damage it caused. Richter wanted to devise a more objective, quantitative measure of earthquake strength. This desire led him to develop the Richter scale in 1935, which is based on measurements from seismographs.

Answers to MATHBREAK

The energy released by an earthquake with a magnitude of 3.0 is about 31.7n. The energy released by an earthquake with a magnitude of 4.0 is about 1,005n. The energy released by an earthquake with a magnitude of 5.0 is about 31,855n. The energy released by an earthquake with a magnitude of 6.0 is about 1,009,804n.

3) Close

Quiz

1. How is an earthquake's epicenter related to its focus? (The epicenter is the point on the Earth's surface directly above the focus, which is where the earthquake originates.)

2. As seismic waves travel farther, what happens to the difference in arrival times of P and S waves? (It increases.)

ALTERNATIVE ASSESSMENT

Have students identify 10 recent earthquakes with a magnitude greater than 5.0 on the Richter scale. Students can compile their findings in a table that includes the epicenter and the magnitude of the quake, the damage it caused, and any other interesting information about the quake. Challenge students to find trends in the data.

 Math Skills Worksheet 43 "Earthquake Power!"

 Reinforcement Worksheet 8 "Complete a Seismic Story"

MATH BREAK

Moving Up the Scale

If the amount of energy released by an earthquake with a magnitude of 2.0 on the Richter scale is n, what are the amounts of energy released by earthquakes with the following magnitudes in terms of n: 3.0, 4.0, 5.0, and 6.0? (Hint: The energy released by an earthquake with a magnitude of 3.0 is 31.7n.)

TOPIC: Earthquake Measurement
GO TO: www.scilinks.org
sciLINKS NUMBER: HSTE185

Measuring Earthquake Strength

"How strong was the earthquake?" is a common question asked of seismologists. This is not an easy question to answer. But it is an important question for public officials, safety organizations, and businesses as well as seismologists. Fortunately, seismograms can be used not only to determine an earthquake's epicenter and its start time but also to find out an earthquake's strength.

The Richter Scale The *Richter scale* is commonly used to measure earthquake strength. It is named after Charles Richter, an American seismologist who developed the scale in the 1930s. A modified version of the Richter scale is shown below.

Modified Richter Scale	
Magnitude	**Estimated effects**
2.0	can be detected only by seismograph
3.0	can be felt at epicenter
4.0	felt by most in area
5.0	causes damage at epicenter
6.0	causes widespread damage
7.0	causes great, widespread damage

Earthquake Energy There is a pattern in the Richter scale relating an earthquake's magnitude and the amount of energy released by the earthquake. Each time the magnitude increases by 1 unit, the amount of energy released becomes 31.7 times larger. For example, an earthquake with a magnitude of 5.0 on the Richter scale will release 31.7 times as much energy as an earthquake with a magnitude of 4.0 on the Richter scale.

REVIEW

1. What is the difference between a seismogram and a seismograph?

2. How many seismograph stations are needed to use the S-P-time method? Why?

3. **Doing Calculations** If the amount of energy released by an earthquake with a magnitude of 7.0 on the Richter scale is x, what is the amount of energy released by an earthquake with a magnitude of 6.0 in terms of x?

Answers to Review

1. A seismograph is an instrument that records seismic waves. A seismogram, which is created by a seismograph, is a tracing of the ground's motion during an earthquake.

2. Three; two seismograph stations can narrow the location of the earthquake to two possible locations. Adding a third enables scientists to determine which of the two locations is correct.

3. $\frac{x}{31.7}$

Section 3

Earthquakes and Society

Terms to Learn
gap hypothesis
seismic gap

What You'll Do
- Explain earthquake hazard.
- Compare methods of earthquake forecasting.
- List ways to safeguard buildings against earthquakes.
- Outline earthquake safety procedures.

Earthquakes are a fascinating part of Earth science, but they are very dangerous. Seismologists have had some success in predicting earthquakes, but simply being aware of earthquakes is not enough. It is important for people in earthquake-prone areas to be prepared.

Earthquake Hazard

Earthquake hazard measures how prone an area is to experiencing earthquakes in the future. An area's earthquake-hazard level is determined by past and present seismic activity. Look carefully at the map in **Figure 10.** As you can see, some areas of the United States have a higher earthquake-hazard level than others. This is because some areas have more seismic activity than others. The West Coast, for example, has a very high earthquake-hazard level because it has a lot of seismic activity. Areas such as the Gulf Coast or the Midwest have much lower earthquake-hazard levels because they do not have as much seismic activity.

Can you find the area where you live on the map? What level or levels of earthquake hazard are shown for your area? Look at the hazard levels in nearby areas. How do their hazard levels compare with your area's hazard level? What could explain the earthquake-hazard levels in your area and nearby areas?

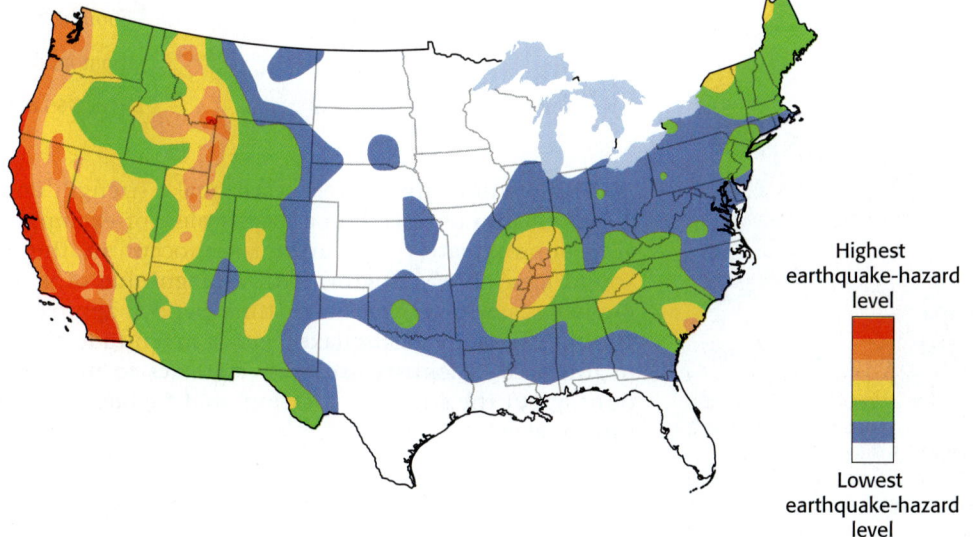

Figure 10 *This is an earthquake-hazard map of the continental United States. It shows various levels of earthquake hazard for different areas of the country.*

Highest earthquake-hazard level

Lowest earthquake-hazard level

IS THAT A FACT!

On March 27, 1964, an earthquake with a magnitude of 9.1 occurred in southern Alaska. The earthquake, which is the strongest recorded earthquake in North America, lasted for about 4 minutes. When it was over, about 215,000 km² of land had been either raised or lowered. The port on Montague Island was raised 10 m, stranding ships that had been docked in the port. After the earthquake, four tsunamis swept the coastline, adding to the destruction.

Section 3

Focus

Earthquakes and Society
In this section students learn how earthquake hazard is determined. The section explores the methods seismologists use to predict when and where earthquakes will occur. Students learn about the technologies used to reinforce buildings against earthquakes. The section concludes with a discussion of earthquake safety procedures.

🔔 Bellringer

If any of your students have experienced an earthquake, have them write a short paragraph in their ScienceLog describing how they felt and what they did to protect themselves during the quake. Have students who have not experienced a quake write a paragraph describing what they *think* they would do during a moderate earthquake.

1) Motivate

DISCUSSION

Have students examine **Figure 10.** Challenge them to explain why the West Coast has such high levels of earthquake hazard. If they need a hint, have them look again at **Figure 1,** in Section 1. (The correct explanation is that there is a tectonic plate boundary along the western coast of the United States.)

Directed Reading Worksheet 8 Section 3

Section 3 • Earthquakes and Society

2) Teach

Answer to Self-Check

120

READING STRATEGY

Prediction Guide Have students determine whether the following statements are true or false before they read the rest of this section:

- Hundreds of thousands of earthquakes that occur each year are not felt by people. (true)
- During an earthquake, rigid pipelines for natural gas and water are more resistant to damage than flexible pipelines are. (false)
- Because earthquakes are unpredictable, people cannot prepare for them. (false)

CROSS-DISCIPLINARY FOCUS

Art Have students find out what has been done to protect sculptures from earthquake damage at the J. Paul Getty Museum, in Pacific Palisades, California, or at another museum in an earthquake-prone area.

MATH and MORE

Have students use **Figure 11** to convert the average number of minor earthquakes that occur each year to the number that occur each day. (49,000 quakes a year ÷ 365 days a year = 134 quakes a day)

 Math Skills Worksheet 5 "Dividing Whole Numbers with Long Division"

Self-Check

According to the chart below, about how many earthquakes with a magnitude between 6.0 and 6.9 occur annually? *(See page 726 to check your answer.)*

Earthquake Forecasting

Predicting when and where earthquakes will occur and how strong they will be is a difficult task. However, by closely monitoring active faults and other areas of seismic activity, seismologists have discovered some patterns in earthquakes that allow them to make some broad predictions.

Strength and Frequency As you learned earlier, earthquakes vary in strength. And you can probably guess that earthquakes don't occur on a set schedule. But what you may not know is that the strength of earthquakes is related to how often they occur. The chart in **Figure 11** provides more detail on this relationship.

Figure 11 *Generally, with each step down in earthquake magnitude, the number of earthquakes per year is about 10 times greater.*

Worldwide Earthquake Frequency (Based on Observations Since 1900)		
Descriptor	**Magnitude**	**Average occurring annually**
Great	8.0 and higher	1
Major	7.0–7.9	18
Strong	6.0–6.9	120
Moderate	5.0–5.9	800
Light	4.0–4.9	about 6,200
Minor	3.0–3.9	about 49,000
Very minor	2.0–2.9	about 365,000

This relationship between earthquake strength and frequency is also observed on a local scale. For example, each year approximately 10 earthquakes occur in the Puget Sound area of Washington with a magnitude of 4 on the Richter scale. Over this same time period, approximately 10 times as many earthquakes with a magnitude of 3 occur in this area. Scientists use these statistics to make predictions about the strength, location, and frequency of future earthquakes.

Can animals predict earthquakes? To decide for yourself, turn to page 218 to read about links between animal behavior and earthquakes.

Science Bloopers

In 1989, Iben Browning, a self-taught climatologist, predicted that a large earthquake would occur near New Madrid, Missouri. He based his prediction on the fact that the gravitational pull of the sun and the moon on the area would be very strong on December 3, 1990. Seismologists dismissed his prediction, but after the story made the news, public interest increased. As the date approached, schools in New Madrid were dismissed and emergency personnel were prepared. Some residents left town, while other people flocked to New Madrid to experience a major earthquake. The much-awaited day passed without the slightest tremor.

Chapter 8 • Earthquakes

The Gap Hypothesis Another method of predicting an earthquake's strength, location, and frequency is based on the gap hypothesis. The **gap hypothesis** states that sections of active faults that have had relatively few earthquakes are likely to be the sites of strong earthquakes in the future. The areas along a fault where relatively few earthquakes have occurred are called **seismic gaps**. **Figure 12** below shows an example of a seismic gap.

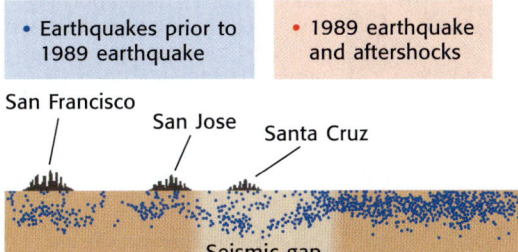
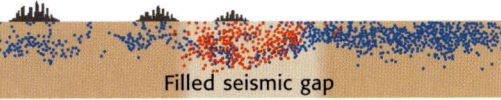

Figure 12 *This diagram shows a cross section of the San Andreas Fault. Note how the seismic gap was filled by the 1989 earthquake and its* aftershocks, *which are weaker earthquakes that follow a stronger earthquake.*

The gap hypothesis helped seismologists forecast the approximate time, strength, and location of the 1989 Loma Prieta earthquake in the San Francisco Bay area. The seismic gap that they identified is illustrated in Figure 12. In 1988, seismologists predicted that over the next 30 years there was a 30 percent chance that an earthquake with a magnitude of at least 6.5 would fill this seismic gap. Were they correct? The Loma Prieta earthquake, which filled in the seismic gap in 1989, measured 7.1 on the Richter scale. That's very close, considering how complicated the forecasting of earthquakes is.

Figure 13 *An earthquake shook the ground floor out from under the second story of this apartment building, which then collapsed.*

Earthquakes and Buildings

Much like a judo master knocks the feet out from under his or her opponent, earthquakes shake the ground out from under buildings and bridges. Once the center of gravity of a structure has been displaced far enough off the structure's supporting base, most structures simply collapse.

Figure 13 shows what can happen to buildings during an earthquake. These buildings were not designed or constructed to withstand the forces of an earthquake.

Science Bloopers

In 1976, scientists forecasted a major quake for the Kwangtung province, in China. Thousands of people evacuated their homes for more than 2 months. Finally, people were allowed to return. Shortly after people returned to their homes, two earthquakes and many aftershocks occurred in the region.

SCIENCE HUMOR

Q: What do you get when a cow is caught in an earthquake?

A: a milkshake

3 Extend

Answers to Activity
Accept all reasonable responses.

USING THE FIGURE

Have students answer the following questions using the illustrations on this page:

- How are the mass damper system and the active tendon system alike? (In both systems, motion sensors detect movement and send this information to a computer. The computer signals devices that counteract the movement of the structure.)
- What is a base isolator? (a shock absorber that prevents seismic waves from traveling through a structure)
- What advantage do flexible pipes have over rigid metal pipes during an earthquake? (Flexible pipes twist and bend more readily than metal pipes, which tend to snap when subjected to significant seismic tremors.)

DEBATE

Nuclear Waste: Is Any Area Seismically Stable? Scientists must consider the geologic stability of potential sites for nuclear waste facilities. Have students research and debate the issue of nuclear waste disposal. Have them consider that there are few viable options for the disposal of the world's nuclear waste. Remind them that no one can be sure that an area will be stable over the thousands of years it takes for nuclear waste to decay.

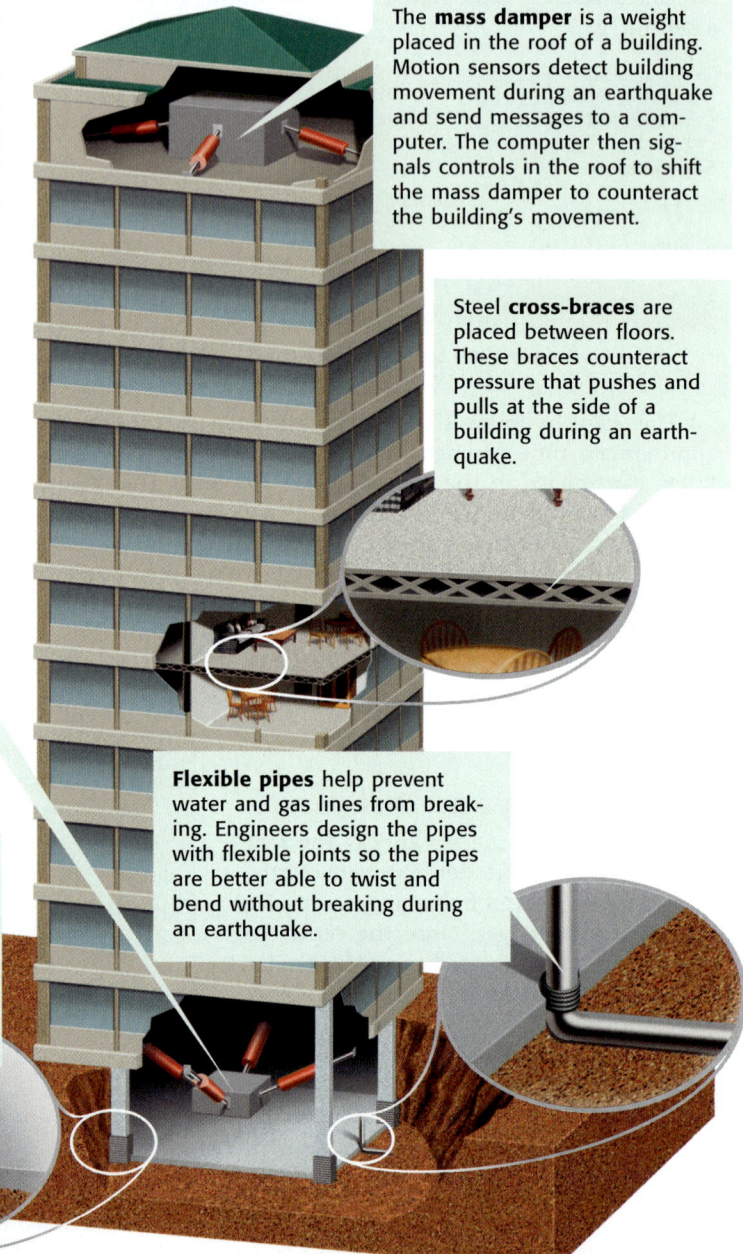

Activity

Research a tall building to find out how its structure is reinforced. Would any of the building's reinforcements safeguard it against earthquakes? Has an earthquake occurred in the building's area since the building was constructed? If so, how well did the building withstand the shaking?

TRY at HOME

Earthquake Resistant Buildings People have learned a lot from building failure during earthquakes. Architects and engineers use the newest technology to design and construct buildings and bridges to better withstand earthquakes. Study this diagram carefully to learn about some of this modern technology.

The **mass damper** is a weight placed in the roof of a building. Motion sensors detect building movement during an earthquake and send messages to a computer. The computer then signals controls in the roof to shift the mass damper to counteract the building's movement.

Steel **cross-braces** are placed between floors. These braces counteract pressure that pushes and pulls at the side of a building during an earthquake.

The **active tendon system** works much like the mass damper system in the roof. Sensors notify a computer that the building is moving. Then the computer activates devices to shift a large weight to counteract the movement.

Flexible pipes help prevent water and gas lines from breaking. Engineers design the pipes with flexible joints so the pipes are better able to twist and bend without breaking during an earthquake.

Base isolators act as shock absorbers during an earthquake. They are made of layers of rubber and steel wrapped around a lead core. Base isolators absorb seismic waves, preventing them from traveling through the building.

208

Homework

Investigate Your Area Have students conduct a survey of their home and make a list of at least five things that should be altered to ensure minimal damage in the event of an earthquake. Changes might include reinforcing the foundation, adding steel support bars to unsupported areas of the building, bolting refrigerators and tall bookshelves to the walls, reinforcing old walls with plywood, securing water heaters, and replacing rigid pipes with flexible pipes. Suggest that students also include a floor plan that shows safe and unsafe places and possible escape routes.

208   Chapter 8 • Earthquakes

Are You Prepared for an Earthquake?

If you live in an earthquake-prone area or ever plan to visit one, there are many things you can do to protect yourself and your property from earthquakes. Plan ahead so you will know what to do before, during, and after an earthquake. Stick to your plan as closely as possible.

Before the Shaking Starts The first thing you should do is safeguard your house against earthquakes. For example, put heavier objects on lower shelves so they do not fall on anyone during the earthquake. You can also talk to adults about having your home reinforced. Make a plan with others (your family, neighbors, or friends) to meet somewhere after the earthquake is over. This way someone will know you are safe. During the earthquake, waterlines, power lines, and roadways may be damaged. Therefore, you should store nonperishable food, water, a fire extinguisher, a flashlight with batteries, and a first-aid kit in a place you can access after the earthquake.

Figure 14 *Simple precautions can greatly reduce the chance of injury during an earthquake.*

When the Shaking Starts The best thing to do if you are indoors is to crouch or lie face down under a table or desk in the center of a room, as shown in **Figure 15.** If you are outside, lie face down away from buildings, power lines, and trees, and cover your head with your hands. If you are in a car on an open road, you should stop the car and remain inside.

Figure 15 *These students are participating in an earthquake drill.*

Turn to page 660 to build your own earthquake-safe building.

WEIRD SCIENCE

Engineers have devised giant shock absorbers for buildings. The shock absorbers contain a ferrofluid solution that becomes rigid in a magnetic field. When an earthquake occurs, a computer controls electromagnets in the shock absorbers to damp the vibrations!

TOPIC: Earthquakes and Society
GO TO: www.scilinks.org
sciLINKS NUMBER: HSTE190

ACTIVITY

Earthquake Kit Collect the following items: bottled water, nonperishable foods, a flashlight, batteries, a bucket, rubber gloves, safety goggles, a first-aid kit, money, an electric can opener, a few perishable food items, a small TV (not battery-operated), a battery-operated radio, clean rags, tissues and toilet paper, a deck of playing cards, and a blanket. Have students take turns deciding which items would be useful should a severe earthquake occur in your area. Use questions to help students realize that electricity and fresh water may not be available for some time after the quake.
Sheltered English

GOING FURTHER

People on the highest floors of tall buildings often feel minor tremors that go unnoticed by people on the ground. This is because tall buildings exaggerate minor tremors. Demonstrate this concept by holding a meterstick upright by the end and shaking it back and forth. Tell students to observe the difference in movement between the top and the bottom of the meterstick.

Quake Challenge

Homework

Presentation Have students create a poster to promote earthquake safety. Posters should focus on one of the following: preparing for an earthquake, what to do during an earthquake, or what to do after an earthquake. Students can create a display to educate the school about earthquake safety.

4 Close

Quiz

1. What is the gap hypothesis? (The gap hypothesis states that sections of active faults that have had relatively few earthquakes are likely to be the sites of strong earthquakes in the future.)

2. Why should you lie under a table or desk during an earthquake? (The table or desk might prevent falling objects from hitting you and causing injury.)

3. What are aftershocks? (They are weaker earthquakes that follow stronger earthquakes.)

ALTERNATIVE ASSESSMENT

Ask students to write a description of the hazards they might face if an earthquake occurred when they were in each of the following situations:

- asleep in bed (collapsing building)
- at the beach (tsunamis)
- snow skiing (avalanche)

GROUP ACTIVITY

Have small groups research how to make a building earthquake-proof. They should consider the site for the building and brainstorm about ways to protect the building. They can illustrate their best ideas and use descriptive labels to show how their building works. Have groups present their ideas to the class.

Answer to APPLY

Answers will vary but should reflect some precautions and procedures mentioned in this section.

---

internet connect

SCI LINKS NSTA
TOPIC: Earthquakes and Society
GO TO: www.scilinks.org
sciLINKS NUMBER: HSTE190

After the Shaking Stops Being in an earthquake is a startling experience. Afterward, you should not be surprised to find yourself and others puzzled about what happened. You should try to calm down, get your bearings, and remove yourself from immediate danger, such as downed power lines, broken glass, and fire hazards. Be aware that there may be aftershocks. Recall your earthquake plan, and follow it through.

REVIEW

1. How is an area's earthquake hazard determined?
2. Which earthquake forecast predicts a more precise location—a forecast based on the relationship between strength and frequency or a forecast based on the gap hypothesis?
3. Describe two ways that buildings are reinforced against earthquakes.
4. Name four items that you should store in case of an earthquake.
5. **Using Graphics** Would the street shown in the photo at left be a safe place during an earthquake? Why or why not?

Earthquake Safety Plan

You are at home reading the evening news. On the front page you read a report from the local seismology station. Scientists predict an earthquake in your area sometime in the near future. You realize that you are not prepared.

Make a detailed outline of how you would prepare yourself and your home for an earthquake. Then write a list of safety procedures to follow during an earthquake. When you are done, exchange your work with a classmate. How do your plans differ from your classmate's? How might you work together to improve your earthquake safety plans?

210

Answers to Review

1. It is determined by past and present seismic activity.
2. A forecast based on the gap hypothesis would predict a more precise location.
3. Describing any two features from this section (mass damper, cross braces, active tendon system, flexible pipes, and base isolators) is acceptable. Students may also describe features they learn about through additional research.
4. Answers will vary. Students may list some items not mentioned in the textbook. Items mentioned in this section include nonperishable food, water, a fire extinguisher, a flashlight with batteries, and a first-aid kit.
5. No; you would be very close to tall buildings that could collapse during the earthquake.

Section 4

Earthquake Discoveries Near and Far

Terms to Learn
Moho
shadow zone

What You'll Do
- Describe how seismic studies reveal Earth's interior.
- Summarize seismic discoveries on other cosmic bodies.

The study of earthquakes has led to many important discoveries about the Earth's interior. Seismologists learn about the Earth's interior by observing how seismic waves travel through the Earth. Likewise, seismic waves on other cosmic bodies allow seismologists to study the interiors of those bodies.

Discoveries in Earth's Interior

Have you ever noticed how light bends in water? If you poke part of a pencil into water and look at it from a certain angle, the pencil looks bent. This is because the light waves that bounce off the pencil bend as they pass through the water's surface toward your eye. Seismic waves bend in much the same way as they travel through rock. Seismologists have learned a lot about the Earth's interior by studying how seismic waves bend.

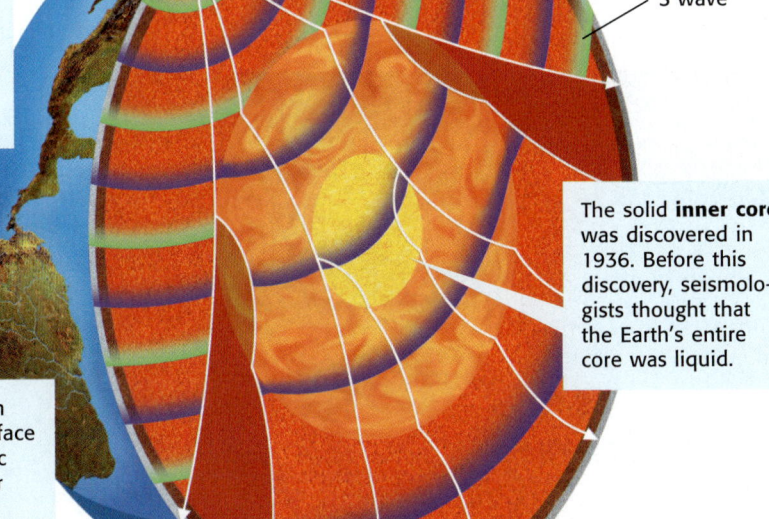

The **Moho** is a place within the Earth where the speed of seismic waves increases sharply. It marks the boundary between the Earth's crust and mantle.

The solid **inner core** was discovered in 1936. Before this discovery, seismologists thought that the Earth's entire core was liquid.

The **shadow zone** is an area on the Earth's surface where no direct seismic waves from a particular earthquake can be detected. This discovery suggested that the Earth has a liquid core.

P wave
S wave

SCIENTISTS AT ODDS

Until Inge Lehmann published her paper titled "P¹" in 1936, most seismologists thought that the Earth's core was entirely liquid. Lehmann's work proved that the Earth's core had two parts—an outer, liquid part and an inner, solid part. She came up with her idea partly by calculating the time it took waves to pass through the Earth's core. Her discovery was based on observations of the reflection and refraction of seismic waves generated by deep-focus earthquakes.

2) Teach

DEMONSTRATION

Mapping with Seismic Waves
Place a clear, shallow glass pan containing 3 to 5 cm of water on an overhead projector. Turn on the projector, and produce waves by touching the surface of the water with your finger. Students will see the waves radiate from the point where you touched the water. Tell students that these waves simulate those that radiate out from an earthquake's epicenter. Next place a solid object, such as a coffee cup, in the pan. Repeat the demonstration, and ask students to describe what happens to the waves when they encounter the object. **(Students should see that the solid object deflects the waves.)**

Explain that this is similar to what happens to seismic waves as they pass through the Earth. As seismic waves encounter different zones of Earth's interior, their paths change.

3) Extend

RESEARCH

 The seismic experiments on the moon helped scientists learn a great deal about the moon's structure and formation. Have students find out about different hypotheses regarding the origin of the moon. Have students make written evaluations of the strengths and weaknesses of these hypotheses. Tell them to base their evaluations on their understanding of the scientific method.

BRAIN FOOD

Many scientists think part of the moon was once part of the Earth. It is thought that when the Earth was almost entirely molten, a Mars-sized object collided with the Earth, knocking off part of Earth's mantle. The mantle material and material from the impacting body then began orbiting the Earth. Eventually, the orbiting material joined to form the moon.

Quakes and Shakes on Other Cosmic Bodies

Seismologists have taken what they have learned from earthquakes and applied it to studies of other cosmic bodies, such as planets, moons, and stars. They have been able to learn about the interiors of these cosmic bodies by studying how seismic waves behave within them. The first and perhaps most successful seismic test on another cosmic body was on Earth's moon.

The Moon In July 1969, humans set foot on the moon for the first time. They brought with them a seismograph. Not knowing if the moon was seismically active, they left nothing to chance—they purposely crashed their landing vehicle back into the moon's surface after they left to create artificial seismic waves. What happened after that left seismologists astonished.

If the lander had crashed into the Earth, the equivalent seismograms would have lasted 20–30 seconds at most. The surface of the moon, however, vibrated for more than an hour and a half! At first scientists thought the equipment was not working properly. But the seismograph recorded similar signals produced by meteoroid impacts and "moonquakes" long after the astronauts had left the moon. **Figure 16** shows the nature of these seismic events, which were observed remotely from Earth.

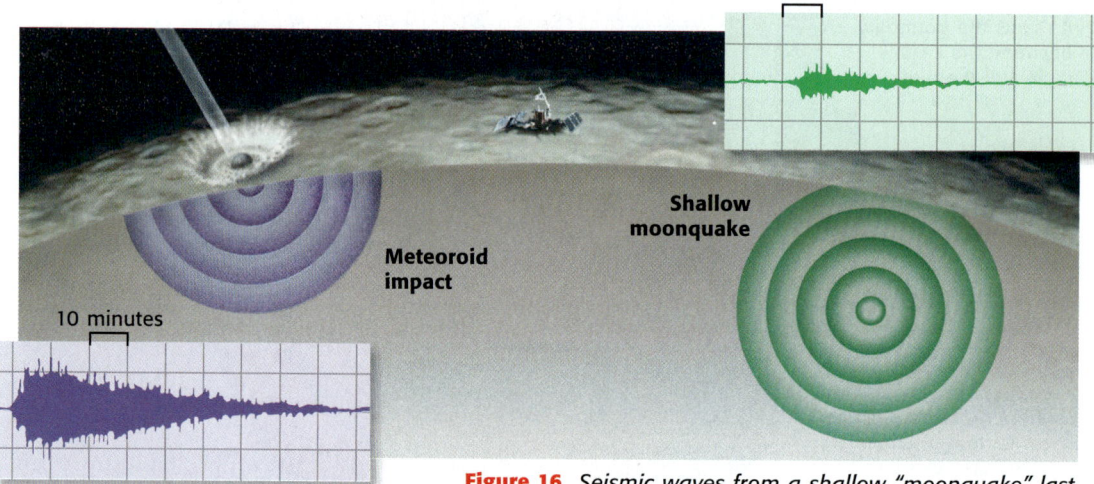

Figure 16 Seismic waves from a shallow "moonquake" last 50 minutes. Seismic waves from a meteoroid impact last an hour and a half. Similar disturbances on Earth last less than a minute.

Homework

Research Have students find out more about "moonquakes" and the research conducted by the Apollo space missions, such as the passive seismic experiment. Students could learn more about other cosmic bodies to find out if there are new discoveries about their seismic activity.

IS THAT A FACT!

"Moonquakes" fall into three categories: deep quakes, which might result from the gravitational pull of Earth; shallow quakes, which may be caused by the heating and cooling of the moon's surface; and quakes caused by the collision of objects with the moon's surface.

Mars In 1976, a space probe called *Viking 1* allowed seismologists to learn about seismic activity on Mars. The probe, which was controlled remotely from Earth, landed on Mars and conducted several experiments. A seismograph was placed on top of the spacecraft to measure seismic waves on Mars. However, as soon as the craft landed, *Viking 1*'s seismograph began to shake. Scientists immediately discovered that Mars is a very windy planet and that the seismograph was working mainly as a wind gauge!

Although the wind on Mars interfered with the seismograph, the seismograph recorded seismograms for months. During that time, only one possible "marsquake" shook the seismograph harder than the wind did.

The Sun Seismologists have also studied seismic waves on the sun. Because humans cannot directly access the sun, scientists study it remotely by using a satellite called *SOHO*. Information gathered by *SOHO* has shown that solar flares produce seismic waves. *Solar flares* are powerful magnetic disturbances in the sun. The seismic waves that result cause "sunquakes," which are similar to earthquakes but are generally much stronger. For example, a moderate sunquake, shown in **Figure 17** beneath an image of *SOHO*, released more than 1 million times as much energy as the Great Hanshin earthquake mentioned at the beginning of this chapter!

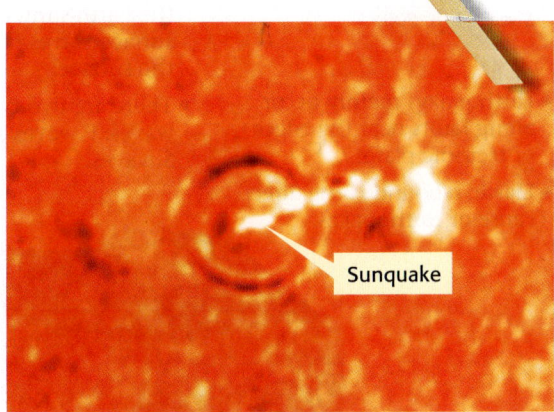

Figure 17 SOHO *detects "sunquakes" that dwarf the greatest earthquakes in history.*

REVIEW

1. What observation of seismic-wave travel led to the discovery of the Moho?
2. Briefly describe one discovery seismologists have made about each of the following cosmic bodies: the moon, Mars, and the sun.
3. **Interpreting Graphics** Take another look at the figure on the first page of Section 4. Why don't S waves enter the Earth's outer core?

internetconnect

sciLINKS
NSTA

TOPIC: Earthquake Discoveries Near and Far
GO TO: www.scilinks.org
sciLINKS NUMBER: HSTE195

4) Close

Quiz

1. Name three features in the Earth's interior that were discovered by studying seismic waves. (the Moho, the inner core, and the shadow zone)
2. What is the shadow zone? What does it tell scientists about Earth's interior? (The shadow zone is an area on the Earth's surface that does not receive seismic waves from a particular earthquake. It tells scientists that at least part of the Earth's core is liquid.)
3. How do "sunquakes" compare with earthquakes? ("Sunquakes" are much stronger than earthquakes.)

ALTERNATIVE ASSESSMENT

Writing Have students read sections of Jules Verne's *A Journey to the Center of the Earth*. Ask them to write short stories about traveling through the Earth's interior based on what they now know about the Earth's structure.

Critical Thinking Worksheet 8 "Nearthlings Unite!"

Answers to Review

1. Seismologists found a sharp increase in the speed of seismic waves and the bending of seismic waves at the Moho boundary.
2. Answers will vary. Possible answers include:
   - Seismic waves last a lot longer on the moon than they do on Earth.
   - Mars is not very seismically active.
   - "Sunquakes" are generally a lot stronger than earthquakes.
3. S waves do not enter the outer core because they cannot travel through parts of the Earth that are completely liquid.

Section 4 • Earthquake Discoveries Near and Far

Chapter Highlights

VOCABULARY DEFINITIONS

SECTION 1

seismology the study of earthquakes

fault a break in the Earth's crust along which blocks of the crust slide relative to one another due to tectonic forces

deformation the change in the shape of rock in response to stress

elastic rebound the sudden return of elastically deformed rock to its undeformed shape

seismic waves waves of energy that travel through the Earth

P waves the fastest type of seismic wave; can travel through solids, liquids, and gases; also known as pressure waves and primary waves

S waves the second-fastest type of seismic wave; cannot travel through materials that are completely liquid; also known as shear waves and secondary waves

SECTION 2

seismograph an instrument located at or near the surface of the Earth that records seismic waves

seismogram a tracing of earthquake motion created by a seismograph

epicenter the point on the Earth's surface directly above an earthquake's starting point

focus the point inside the Earth where an earthquake begins

Chapter Highlights

SECTION 1

Vocabulary
- **seismology** (p. 196)
- **fault** (p. 196)
- **deformation** (p. 197)
- **elastic rebound** (p. 197)
- **seismic waves** (p. 200)
- **P waves** (p. 200)
- **S waves** (p. 200)

Section Notes
- Earthquakes mainly occur along faults near the edges of tectonic plates.
- Elastic rebound is the direct cause of earthquakes.
- Earthquakes differ depending on what type of plate motion causes them.
- Seismic waves are classified as body waves or surface waves.
- Body waves travel through the Earth's interior, while surface waves travel along the surface.
- There are two types of body waves: P waves and S waves.

SECTION 2

Vocabulary
- **seismograph** (p. 202)
- **seismogram** (p. 202)
- **epicenter** (p. 202)
- **focus** (p. 202)

Section Notes
- Seismographs detect seismic waves and record them as seismograms.
- An earthquake's focus is the underground location where seismic waves begin. The earthquake's epicenter is on the surface directly above the focus.
- Seismologists use the S-P-time method to find an earthquake's epicenter.
- Seismologists use the Richter scale to measure an earthquake's strength.

Labs
Earthquake Waves (p. 662)

✓ Skills Check

Math Concepts

EARTHQUAKE STRENGTH The energy released by an earthquake increases by a factor of 31.7 with each increase in magnitude. The energy released decreases by a factor of 31.7 with each decrease in magnitude. All you have to do is multiply or divide.

If magnitude 4 releases energy y, then:
- magnitude 5 releases energy $31.7y$
- magnitude 3 releases energy $\frac{y}{31.7}$

Visual Understanding

TIME-DISTANCE GRAPH Note on the time-distance graph in Figure 9 that the difference in arrival times between P waves and S waves increases with distance from the epicenter.

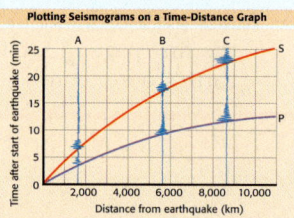

Lab and Activity Highlights

Earthquake Waves PG 662

Quake Challenge PG 660

Datasheets for LabBook
(blackline masters for these labs)

SECTION 3

Vocabulary
gap hypothesis (p. 207)
seismic gap (p. 207)

Section Notes
- Earthquake hazard measures how prone an area is to experiencing earthquakes in the future.
- Some earthquake predictions are based on the relationship between earthquake strength and earthquake frequency. As earthquake frequency decreases, earthquake strength increases.

- Predictions based on the gap hypothesis target seismically inactive areas along faults for strong earthquakes in the future.
- An earthquake usually collapses a structure by displacing the structure's center of gravity off the structure's supporting base.
- Buildings and bridges can be reinforced to minimize earthquake damage.
- People in earthquake-prone areas should plan ahead for earthquakes.

Labs
Quake Challenge (p. 660)

SECTION 4

Vocabulary
Moho (p. 211)
shadow zone (p. 211)

Section Notes
- The Moho, shadow zone, and inner core are features discovered on and inside Earth by observing seismic waves.
- Seismology has been used to study other cosmic bodies.
- Seismic waves last much longer on the moon than they do on Earth.
- Based on early seismic studies, Mars appears much less active seismically than the Earth.
- "Sunquakes" produce energy far greater than any earthquakes we know of.

VOCABULARY DEFINITIONS, continued

SECTION 3

gap hypothesis states that sections of active faults that have had relatively few earthquakes are likely to be the sites of strong earthquakes in the future

seismic gap an area along a fault where relatively few earthquakes have occurred

SECTION 4

Moho a place within the Earth where the speed of seismic waves increases sharply; marks the boundary between the Earth's crust and mantle

shadow zone an area on the Earth's surface where no direct seismic waves from a particular earthquake can be detected

 Vocabulary Review Worksheet 8

 Blackline masters of these Chapter Highlights can be found in the **Study Guide.**

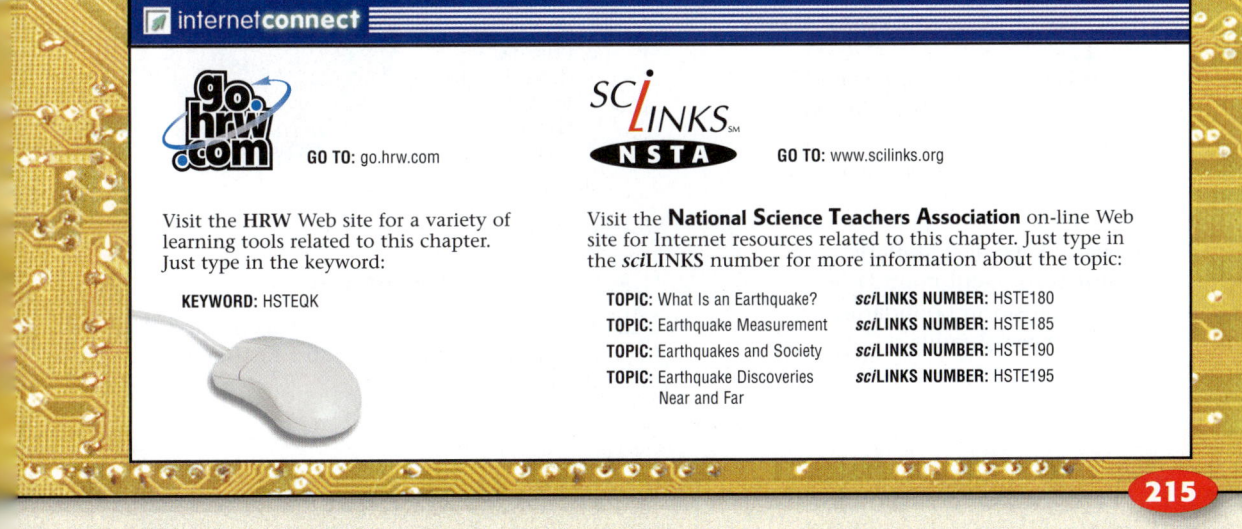

internet connect

GO TO: go.hrw.com

Visit the **HRW** Web site for a variety of learning tools related to this chapter. Just type in the keyword:

KEYWORD: HSTEQK

GO TO: www.scilinks.org

Visit the **National Science Teachers Association** on-line Web site for Internet resources related to this chapter. Just type in the sciLINKS number for more information about the topic:

TOPIC	sciLINKS NUMBER
TOPIC: What Is an Earthquake?	sciLINKS NUMBER: HSTE180
TOPIC: Earthquake Measurement	sciLINKS NUMBER: HSTE185
TOPIC: Earthquakes and Society	sciLINKS NUMBER: HSTE190
TOPIC: Earthquake Discoveries Near and Far	sciLINKS NUMBER: HSTE195

Lab and Activity Highlights

LabBank

 Whiz-Bang Demonstrations, When Buildings Boogie, Demo 19

Long-Term Projects & Research Ideas, Whole Lotta Shakin', Project 36

Chapter Review

USING VOCABULARY

To complete the following sentences, choose the correct term from each pair of terms listed below:

1. Energy is released as __?__ occurs. (*deformation* or *elastic rebound*)

2. __?__ cannot travel through parts of the Earth that are completely liquid. (*S waves* or *P waves*)

3. Seismic waves are recorded by a __?__. (*seismograph* or *seismogram*)

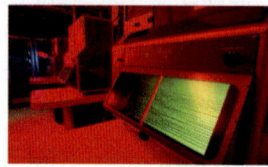

4. Seismologists use the S-P-time method to find an earthquake's __?__. (*shadow zone* or *epicenter*)

5. The __?__ is a place that marks a sharp increase in seismic wave speed. (*seismic gap* or *Moho*)

UNDERSTANDING CONCEPTS

Multiple Choice

6. When rock is __?__, energy builds up in it. Seismic waves occur as this energy is __?__.
   a. elastically deformed; released
   b. plastically deformed; released
   c. elastically deformed; increased
   d. plastically deformed; increased

7. The strongest earthquakes usually occur
   a. near divergent boundaries.
   b. near convergent boundaries.
   c. near transform boundaries.
   d. along normal faults.

8. The last seismic waves to arrive are
   a. P waves.
   b. S waves.
   c. surface waves.
   d. body waves.

9. If an earthquake begins while you are in a building, the safest thing to do first is
   a. get under the strongest table, chair, or other piece of furniture.
   b. run out into the street.
   c. crouch near a wall.
   d. call home.

10. Studying earthquake waves currently allows seismologists to do all of the following *except*
    a. determine when an earthquake started.
    b. learn about the Earth's interior.
    c. decrease an earthquake's strength.
    d. determine where an earthquake started.

11. If a planet has a liquid core, then S waves
    a. speed up as they travel through the core.
    b. maintain their speed as they travel through the core.
    c. change direction as they travel through the core.
    d. cannot pass through the core.

Short Answer

12. What is the relationship between the strength of earthquakes and earthquake frequency?

13. You learned earlier that if you are in a car during an earthquake and are out in the open, it is best to stay in the car. Briefly describe a situation in which you might want to leave a car during an earthquake.

14. How did seismologists determine that the outer core of the Earth is liquid?

Concept Mapping

15. Use the following terms to create a concept map: focus, epicenter, earthquake start time, seismic waves, P waves, S waves.

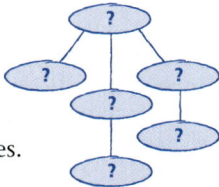

CRITICAL THINKING AND PROBLEM SOLVING

Write one or two sentences to answer the following questions:

16. How might the wall in Figure 2 appear if it had deformed elastically instead of plastically?

17. Why do strong earthquakes occur where there have not been many recent earthquakes? (Hint: Think about what gradually happens to rock before an earthquake occurs.)

18. What could be done to solve the wind problem with the seismograph on Mars? Explain how you would set up the seismograph.

MATH IN SCIENCE

19. Based on the relationship between earthquake magnitude and frequency, if 150 earthquakes with a magnitude of 2 occur in your area this year, about how many earthquakes with a magnitude of 4 should occur in your area this year?

INTERPRETING GRAPHICS

The graph below illustrates the relationship between earthquake magnitude and the height of the tracings on a seismogram. Charles Richter initially formed his magnitude scale by comparing the heights of seismogram readings for different earthquakes. Study the graph, and then answer the questions that follow.

Seismogram Height Vs. Earthquake Magnitude

20. What would the magnitude of an earthquake be if the height of its seismogram readings were 10 mm?

21. Look at the shape of the curve on the graph. What does this tell you about the relationship between seismogram heights and earthquake magnitudes? Explain.

Reading Check-up
Take a minute to review your answers to the Pre-Reading Questions found at the bottom of page 194. Have your answers changed? If necessary, revise your answers based on what you have learned since you began this chapter.

Concept Mapping

15. An answer to this exercise can be found at the end of this book.

CRITICAL THINKING AND PROBLEM SOLVING

16. If the wall in Figure 2 had deformed elastically instead of plastically, it might appear broken or cracked.

17. Strong earthquakes occur where there have not been many recent earthquakes because a lot of elastic deformation builds up along active faults where rock has not moved for awhile. The more deformation that builds up, the more energy the rock releases when it finally slips along the fault.

18. Answers will vary. One solution might be to place the seismograph in a hole or depression that is shielded from wind.

MATH IN SCIENCE

19. one or two

INTERPRETING GRAPHICS

20. 4
21. Answers will vary slightly. The relationship is logarithmic, not linear. Students should recognize that seismogram heights increase at a larger rate with each increase in earthquake magnitude.

Concept Mapping Transparency 8

Blackline masters of this Chapter Review can be found in the **Study Guide.**

Weird Science
Can Animals Predict Earthquakes?

Background
There have been many studies on the different types of animal responses to the geophysical environment. Most of these studies illustrated that the behavior of living organisms is affected by electromagnetic fields. Studies have been performed on how migrating birds find their way and how fish navigate. Fish such as catfish and sharks utilize electroreceptors to detect objects around them and to communicate. Even earthworms respond to changes in Earth's magnetic field.

An American geologist named Jim Berkland has been a strong proponent of using animals to predict earthquakes. It is likely that students pursuing further research in this area will encounter his name often. Berkland has successfully predicted a few earthquakes by observing animal behavior. However, he does not always correctly predict the magnitude of the earthquakes.

CAN ANIMALS PREDICT EARTHQUAKES?

It Could Happen to You!
One day you come home from visiting a friend for the weekend and learn that your dog Pepper is hiding under your bed. Your father explains that he has been trying to get Pepper out from under the bed for the last 6 hours. Just then your mother enters the room and says that she has found two snakes in the backyard—and that makes a total of five in 2 days! This is very odd because you usually don't find more than one each year.

All the animals seem to be acting very strange. Your goldfish is even hiding behind a rock. You wonder if there is some explanation.

What's Going On?
So what's your guess? What do you think is happening? Did you guess that an earthquake is about to occur? Well, if you did, you are probably right!

Publications from as far back as 1784 record unusual animal behavior prior to earthquakes. Some examples included zoo animals refusing to go into their shelters at night and domestic cattle seeking high ground. Other animals, like lizards, snakes, and small mammals, evacuate their underground burrows, and wild birds leave their usual habitats. All of these events occurred a few days, several hours, or a few minutes before the earthquakes happened.

Animals on Call?
Today the majority of scientists look to physical instruments in order to help them predict earthquakes. Yet the fact remains that none of the geophysical instruments we have allow scientists to predict exactly when an earthquake will occur. Could animals know the answer?

▼ *Goldfish or earthquake sensor?*

There are changes in the Earth's crust that occur prior to an earthquake, such as magnetic field changes, subsidence (sinking), tilting, and bulging of the surface. These things can be monitored by modern instruments. Many studies have shown that electromagnetic fields affect the behavior of living organisms. Is it possible that animals close to the epicenter of an earthquake are able to sense changes in their environment? Should we pay attention?

You Decide
▶ Currently, the United States government does not fund research that investigates whether animals can predict earthquakes. Have a debate with your classmates about whether the government should fund such research.

Answer to You Decide
Encourage students to understand both sides of this debate. Because government funding is limited, using these funds for one area of study could result in a reduction in the funding for other areas. Would students be willing to fund a study about animals predicting earthquakes if it meant decreasing the funding toward protecting the environment? Would it be better to require states in seismically active areas to fund this research themselves, either publicly or privately? Ask students to come up with solutions.

EYE ON THE ENVIRONMENT

What Causes Such Destruction?

At 5:04 P.M. on October 14, 1989, life in California's San Francisco Bay Area seemed as normal as ever. The third game of the World Series was underway in Candlestick Park, now called 3Com Park. While 62,000 fans filled the park, other people were rushing home from a day's work. By 5:05 P.M., however, things had changed drastically. The fact sheet of destruction looks like this:

Injuries:	3,757
Deaths:	68
Damaged homes:	23,408
Destroyed homes:	1,018
Damaged businesses:	3,530
Destroyed businesses:	366
Financial loss:	over $6 billion

The Culprit

The cause of such destruction was a 7.1 magnitude earthquake that lasted for 20 seconds. Its epicenter was 97 km south of San Francisco in an area called Loma Prieta. The earthquake was so strong that people in San Diego and western Nevada (740 km away) felt it too. Considering the earthquake's high magnitude and the fact that it occurred during rush hour, it is amazing that more people did not die. However, the damage to buildings was widespread—it covered an area of 7,770 km². And by October 1, 1990, there had been more than 7,000 aftershocks of this quake.

Take Heed

Engineers and seismologists had expected a major earthquake, so the amount of damage they saw from this earthquake was no surprise. But experts agree that if the earthquake were of a higher magnitude or centered closer to Oakland, San Jose, or San Francisco, the damage would have been much worse. They are concerned that people who live in these areas aren't paying attention to the warning this earthquake represents.

Many people have a false sense of security because their buildings withstood the quake with little or no damage. But engineers and seismologists agree that the only reason the buildings survived was because the ground motion in those areas was fairly low.

Tomorrow May Be Too Late

Many buildings that withstood this earthquake were poorly constructed and would not withstand another earthquake. Experts say there is a 50 percent chance that one or more 7.0 magnitude earthquakes will occur in the San Francisco Bay Area in the next 30 years. And the results of the next quake could be much more devastating if people don't reinforce their buildings before it's too late.

▲ *Notice the different levels of destruction for various buildings on the same street.*

On Your Own

▶ Research the engineering innovations for constructing bridges and buildings in areas with seismic activity. Share your information with the class.

Chapter Organizer

CHAPTER ORGANIZATION	TIME MINUTES	OBJECTIVES	LABS, INVESTIGATIONS, AND DEMONSTRATIONS
Chapter Opener pp. 220–221	45	National Standards: SAI 1, ST 1, SPSP 3, 4	**Start-Up Activity** Anticipation, p. 221
Section 1 Volcanic Eruptions	90	▶ Distinguish between nonexplosive and explosive volcanic eruptions. ▶ Explain how the composition of magma determines the type of volcanic eruption that will occur. ▶ Classify the main types of lava and volcanic debris. SAI 1, HNS 2, ES 1c	**QuickLab,** Bubble, Bubble, Toil and Trouble, p. 224 GENERAL
Section 2 Volcanoes' Effects on Earth	90	▶ Describe the effects that volcanoes have on Earth. ▶ Compare the different types of volcanoes. ST 2, SPSP 3–5, HNS 1, 3, ES 1c; LabBook SAI 1	**Discovery Lab,** Some Go "Pop," Some Do Not, p. 664 GENERAL **Datasheets for LabBook,** Some Go "Pop," Some Do Not, Datasheet 17 GENERAL **Whiz-Bang Demonstrations,** How's Your Lava Life? Demo 21 GENERAL
Section 3 What Causes Volcanoes?	135	▶ Describe the formation and movement of magma. ▶ Explain the relationship between volcanoes and plate tectonics. ▶ Summarize the methods scientists use to predict volcanic eruptions. UCP 3, SAI 1, ST 2, SPSP 5, ES 1b, 1c; LabBook SAI 1, ST 2	**QuickLab,** Reaction to Stress, p. 230 GENERAL **Interactive Explorations CD-ROM,** What's the Matter? ADVANCED A **Worksheet** is also available in the **Interactive Explorations Teacher's Edition.** **Skill Builder,** Volcano Verdict, p. 666 GENERAL **Datasheets for LabBook,** Volcano Verdict, Datasheet 18 GENERAL **Labs You Can Eat,** Hot Spots, Lab 16 GENERAL **Whiz-Bang Demonstrations,** What Makes a Vent Event? Demo 20 GENERAL **Long-Term Projects & Research Ideas,** Project 37 ADVANCED

*See page **T20** for a complete correlation of this book with the* **NATIONAL SCIENCE EDUCATION STANDARDS.**

TECHNOLOGY RESOURCES

 Guided Reading Audio CD English or Spanish, Chapter 9

 One-Stop Planner CD-ROM with Test Generator

 CNN Scientists in Action, Volcano Hunters, Segment 13

 Interactive Explorations CD-ROM CD 1, Exploration 4, What's the Matter?

Chapter 9 • Volcanoes

Chapter 9 • Volcanoes

CLASSROOM WORKSHEETS, TRANSPARENCIES, AND RESOURCES	SCIENCE INTEGRATION AND CONNECTIONS	REVIEW AND ASSESSMENT
Directed Reading Worksheet 9 BASIC **Science Puzzlers, Twisters & Teasers,** Worksheet 9 ADVANCED	**Cross-Disciplinary Focus,** p. 221 in ATE	
Directed Reading Worksheet 9, Section 1 BASIC **Transparency 208,** Summarizing the Changes of State	**Connect to Life Science,** p. 223 in ATE **Multicultural Connection,** p. 223 in ATE **Connect to Physical Science,** p. 224 in ATE ADVANCED **Biology Connection,** p. 226 **Across the Sciences:** Europa: Life on a Moon? p. 241 GENERAL	**Review,** p. 226 GENERAL **Quiz,** p. 226 in ATE GENERAL **Alternative Assessment,** p. 226 in ATE GENERAL
Directed Reading Worksheet 9, Section 2 BASIC **Transparency 134,** Three Types of Volcanoes **Problem Solving Worksheet 9,** Eruption Disruption ADVANCED **Transparency 135,** The Formation of a Caldera **Reinforcement Worksheet 9,** A Variety of Volcanoes BASIC	**Connect to Astronomy,** p. 227 in ATE **Cross-Disciplinary Focus,** p. 228 in ATE **Science, Technology, and Society:** Robot in the Hot Seat, p. 240 ADVANCED	**Review,** p. 229 GENERAL **Quiz,** p. 229 in ATE GENERAL **Alternative Assessment,** p. 229 in ATE GENERAL
Transparency 136, The Formation of Magma **Directed Reading Worksheet 9,** Section 3 BASIC **Math Skills for Science Worksheet 35,** Using Temperature Scales GENERAL **Transparency 137,** How a Hot Spot Forms Volcanoes **Reinforcement Worksheet 9,** Tectonic Plate Movement BASIC	**Cross-Disciplinary Focus,** p. 231 in ATE **MathBreak,** How Hot Is Hot? p. 232 GENERAL **Real-World Connection,** p. 232 in ATE **Apply,** p. 235 GENERAL	**Self-Check,** p. 231 **Homework,** pp. 232, 234 in ATE GENERAL **Review,** p. 235 GENERAL **Quiz,** p. 235 in ATE GENERAL **Alternative Assessment,** p. 235 in ATE ADVANCED

internetconnect

Holt, Rinehart and Winston On-line Resources
go.hrw.com
For worksheets and other teaching aids related to this chapter, visit the HRW Web site and type in the keyword: **HSTVOL**

National Science Teachers Association
www.scilinks.org
Encourage students to use the *sci*LINKS numbers listed in the internet connect boxes to access information and resources on the **NSTA** Web site.

END-OF-CHAPTER REVIEW AND ASSESSMENT

Chapter Review in Study Guide
Vocabulary and Notes in Study Guide
Chapter Tests with Performance-Based Assessment, Chapter 9 Test
Chapter Tests with Performance-Based Assessment, Performance-Based Assessment 9
Concept Mapping Transparency 9

Chapter Resources & Worksheets

Visual Resources

TEACHING TRANSPARENCIES

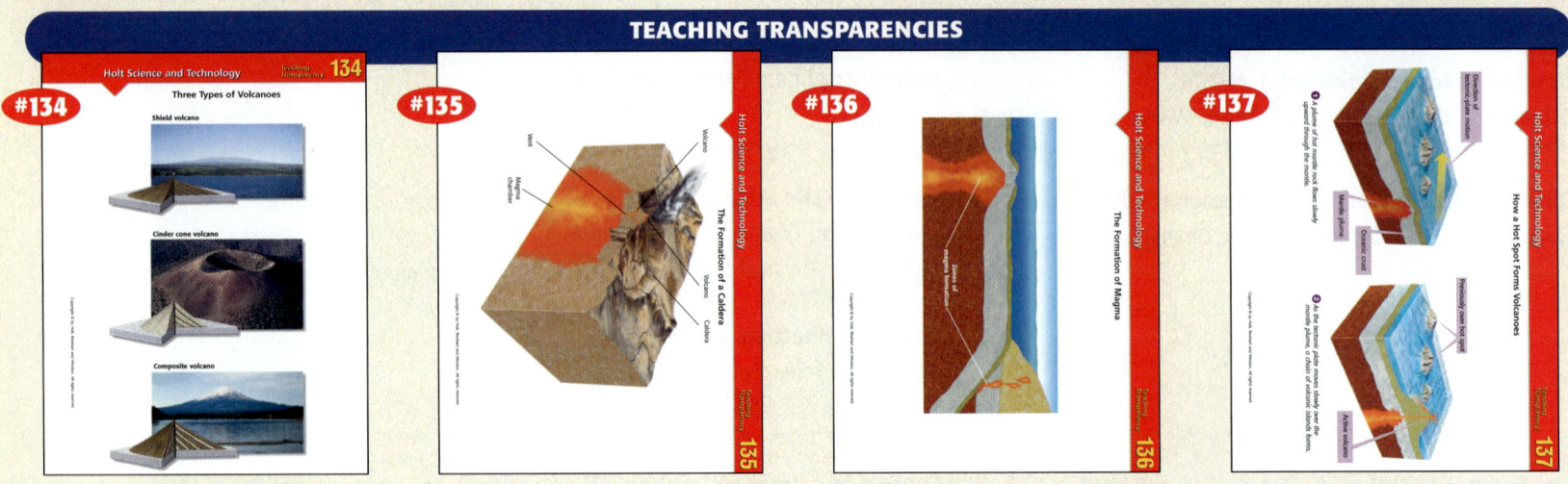

TEACHING TRANSPARENCIES

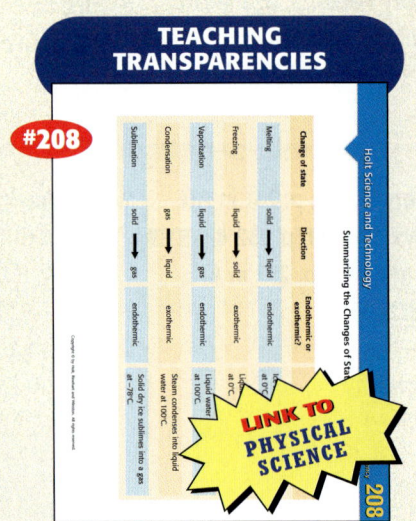

CONCEPT MAPPING TRANSPARENCY

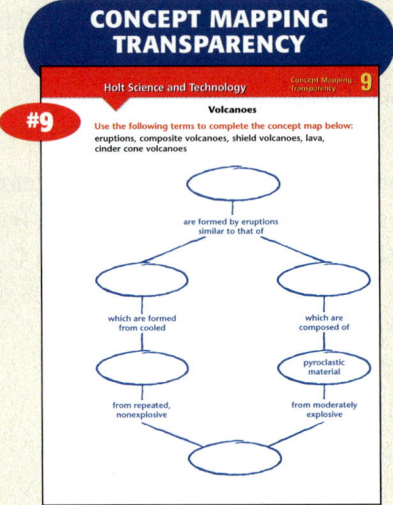

Meeting Individual Needs

DIRECTED READING

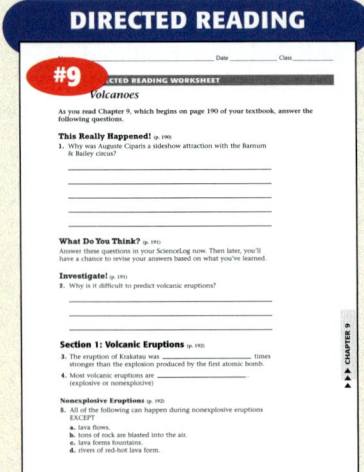

REINFORCEMENT & VOCABULARY REVIEW

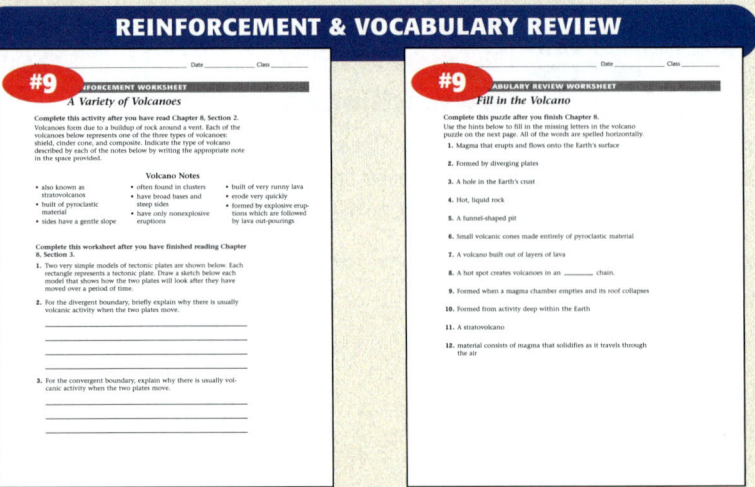

SCIENCE PUZZLERS, TWISTERS & TEASERS

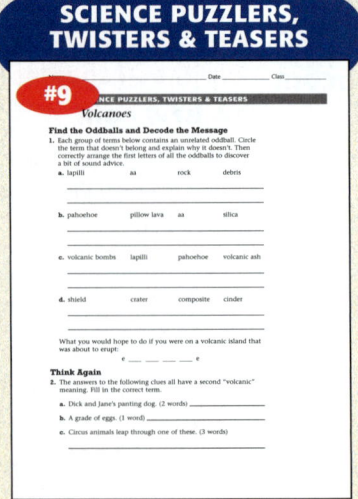

Chapter 9 • Volcanoes

Chapter 9 • Volcanoes

Review & Assessment

STUDY GUIDE
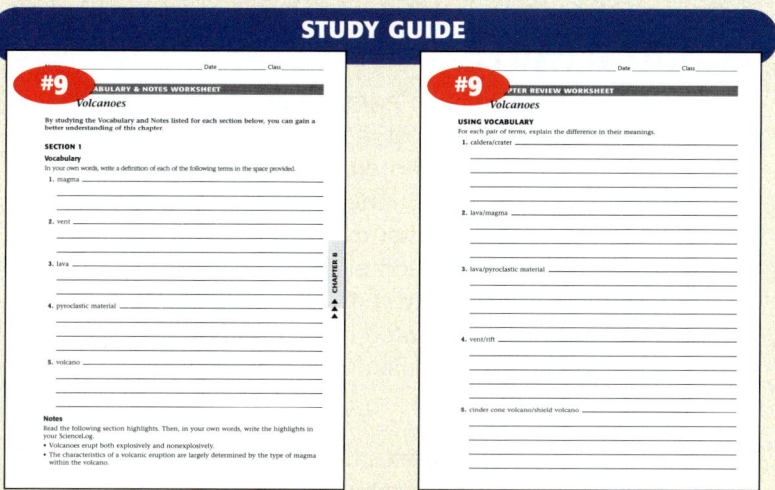

CHAPTER TESTS WITH PERFORMANCE-BASED ASSESSMENT
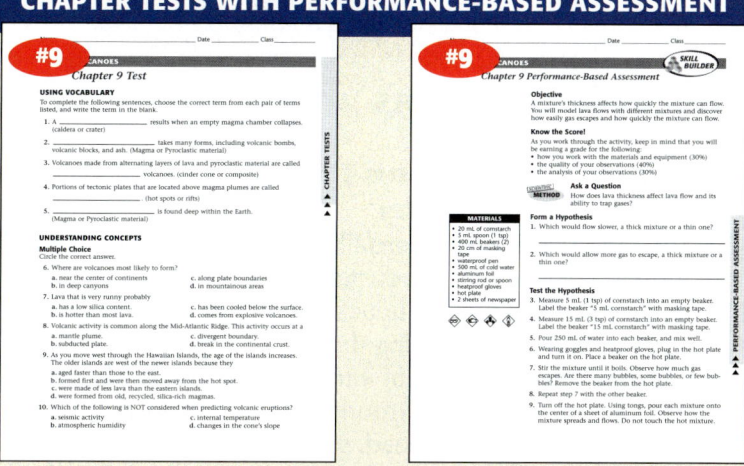

Lab Worksheets

LABS YOU CAN EAT
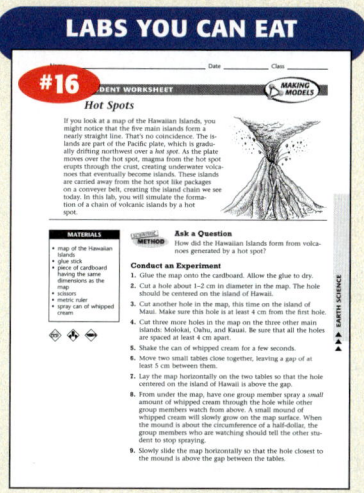

WHIZ-BANG DEMONSTRATIONS
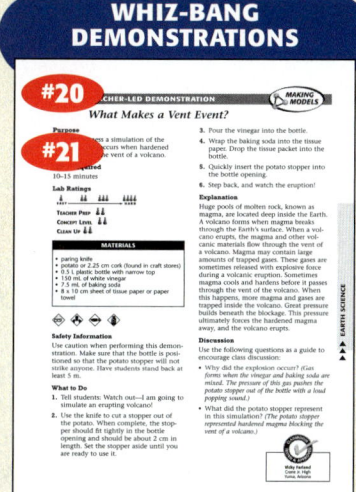

LONG-TERM PROJECTS & RESEARCH IDEAS
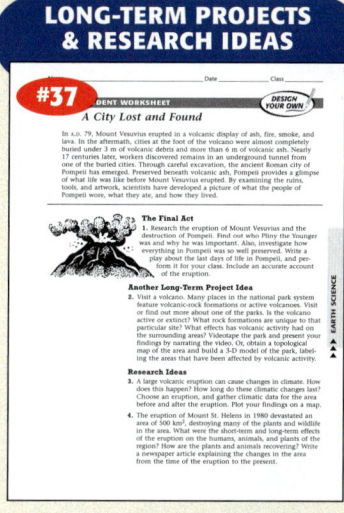

DATASHEETS FOR LABBOOK
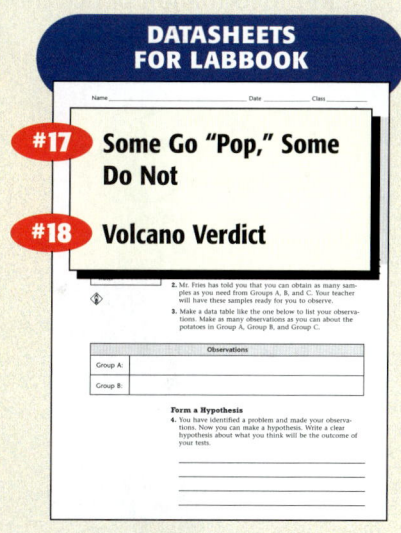

Applications & Extensions

CRITICAL THINKING & PROBLEM SOLVING
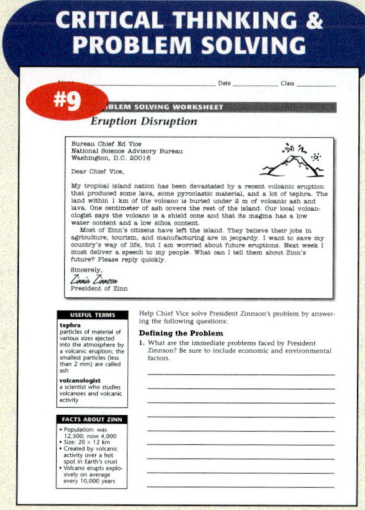

SCIENTISTS IN ACTION
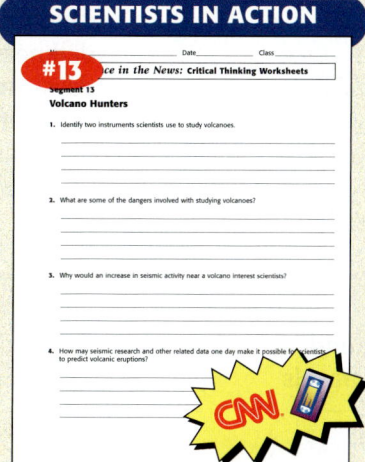

INTERACTIVE EXPLORATIONS
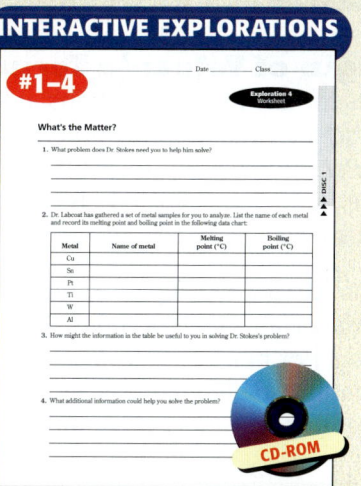

Chapter 9 • Chapter Resources & Worksheets **219D**

Chapter Background

SECTION 1

Volcanic Eruptions

▶ **Mineral Formation in Subduction Zones**
The formation of commercially valuable minerals is common in areas where subduction creates volcanoes. As magma formed from subducted crust rises, it heats the surrounding rocks, causing the fluids they contain to circulate near the point of intrusion. The hot fluids react with the magma and surrounding rocks, dissolving some metals (including iron, lead, silver, and gold). As the fluid rises through the Earth's crust, mineral precipitation occurs at points where it cools. This process can result in the formation of rich mineral veins.

▶ **The Origin of Volcanic Terms**
Many terms for nonviolent eruptions are Hawaiian. Drops of liquid lava that blow into fine spiky strands are called *Pele's hair,* after the Hawaiian goddess of fire. *Limu o Pele,* or "Pele's seaweed," is the term for delicate, translucent sheets of spatter filled with tiny glass bubbles.

- The terms for violent eruptions, however, are generally not Hawaiian. *Nuée ardente,* French for "burning cloud," is a hot mass of volcanic gases, ash, and debris that is expelled explosively and then travels at hurricane speeds down a mountainside.

IS THAT A FACT!

- The Tambora volcano eruption in Indonesia is the largest in the last 200 years. The volcano erupted on April 10 and 11, 1815. The eruption and the resulting tsunamis killed more than 10,000 people. Ash covered so much land that farmland was devastated; disease and famine killed 82,000 more.

- During the Tambora eruption, so much ash was thrown into the atmosphere that weather patterns were affected worldwide. Scholars believe the eruption caused the "Year Without a Summer" in 1816, when snow fell in New England in July.

SECTION 2

Volcanoes' Effects on Earth

▶ **The Krakatau Explosion**
When the island of Krakatau, in Indonesia, exploded in 1883, it caused a shockwave that sped around the world seven times. The volcano ejected about 18 km³ of volcanic material into the air. One ash cloud reached 80 km high, and the explosion was heard on islands in the Indian Ocean nearly 4,600 km away. The ash clouds blocked out the sun and everything within 80 km of the volcano was plunged into complete darkness for more than two days. The volcano collapsed and the island lost 21 km² of land. All that was left was a caldera lying as deep as 275 m beneath the ocean!

- In 1927, a cloud of sulfur and ash rose from the water above the volcano—Krakatau's magma chamber was not gone. It was the beginning of Anak Krakatau, or "Child of Krakatau," which rose from the original volcano's crater. By 1990, Anak Krakatau was 300 m high, and it continues to grow.

Chapter 9 • Volcanoes

▶ **Fighting Lava with Water**
Most attempts to divert lava away from homes and towns have failed. However, when lava flows in Iceland threatened to engulf a seaport and its harbor, the townspeople decided on a unique approach. Using ocean-going firefighting boats, they pumped icy water from the bay onto the oncoming lava. The water cooled the lava fast enough to divert the flow. Hawaiians have tried to divert lava flows this way but with little success.

IS THAT A FACT!

- When lava flows in a defined channel, a crust forms on the surface. If the crust remains stationary while the lava below is still flowing, a lava tube or a lava cave several kilometers long can result.

SECTION 3

What Causes Volcanoes?

▶ **Merapi, "Mountain of Fire"**
There are more active volcanoes in Indonesia than anywhere else on Earth—130! Perhaps the most dangerous volcano is called Merapi, or "Mountain of Fire," on the island of Java. Since 1548, Merapi has erupted violently 68 times. In 1998, it became active again, and people began to evacuate the area. Scientists are worried about the city of Yogyakarta, which lies just 70 km north of the volcano and is home to about 500,000 people. A large eruption could completely destroy the city.

Ring of Fire

▶ **Predicting the Mount Pinatubo Eruptions**
Perhaps the most successful prediction of a volcanic eruption was on Mount Pinatubo, in the Philippine Islands. When Pinatubo became active in March and April 1991, scientists rushed to the area and quickly established monitoring systems. Groups of scientists from the Philippines and the United States distributed  a five-level alert system to civil defense and local officials. Evacuations began when an eruption appeared imminent (Level 4 alert); ultimately, more than 100,000 people evacuated the area. There were enormous losses of land, housing, and crops, but because of the preparations and warnings, there were only 700 deaths.

- Pinatubo was what geologists call a well-behaved volcano. It behaved as the geologists predicted, becoming increasingly active and then exploding. Most volcanoes are not so well behaved. For example, the same monitoring methods have been much less successful on Montserrat, in the Caribbean.

IS THAT A FACT!

- The youngest Hawaiian "island," Loihi, is 3,500 m above the ocean floor, but it must grow almost 1 km before coming out of the ocean. That, scientists say, could take more than 20,000 years.

- Native Hawaiians believed that Pele, the fire goddess, was responsible for volcanic activity on the islands. According to their tradition, Pele lives in the active crater of Kilauea. When angered, she stamps her feet, causing earthquakes and sending forth lava. Legend maintains that she appears as an old woman just before an eruption.

For background information about teaching strategies and issues, refer to the *Professional Reference for Teachers*.

Volcanoes

Pre-Reading Questions

Students may not know the answers to these questions before reading the chapter, so accept any reasonable response.

Suggested Answers

1. A volcanic eruption is caused when pressure forces magma to rise toward the Earth's surface. If there is a vent or opening for the magma to escape through, it is extruded as lava in a volcanic eruption.

2. Lava is magma that has been extruded on the Earth's surface. Magma forms when rock melts due to changes in the composition of the rock, a decrease in pressure, or an increase in temperature.

Directed Reading Worksheet 9

Science Puzzlers, Twisters & Teasers Worksheet 9

Guided Reading Audio CD
English or Spanish, Chapter 9

Sections

1. **Volcanic Eruptions** 222
   QuickLab 224
   Biology Connection .. 226
   Internet Connect 226

2. **Volcanoes' Effects on Earth** 227
   Internet Connect ... 229

3. **What Causes Volcanoes?** 230
   QuickLab 230
   MathBreak 232
   Internet Connect ... 235
   Apply 235

Chapter Review 238
Feature Articles 240, 241
LabBook 664–667

Volcanoes

HOT LAVA, QUIET ERUPTION

Volcanic eruptions come in all sizes. In places like Hawaii, most eruptions are nonviolent. Lava flows in Hawaii are made of rock called basalt, which flows easily. Basaltic lava flows travel slowly but can reach a temperature of nearly 1,200°C! The lava flow shown here is slowly creeping across a road. As you can see, calm eruptions of lava can threaten property more than human life. In this chapter you will learn about nonexplosive eruptions, explosive eruptions, the formation of magma, and the ways that scientists are trying to predict volcanic eruptions.

This type of eruption is called a lava fountain.

Pre-Reading Questions

1. What causes a volcanic eruption?
2. What is lava, and how does it form?

internet connect

HRW On-line Resources
go.hrw.com
For worksheets and other teaching aids, visit the HRW Web site and type in the keyword: **HSTVOL**

SCiLINKS NSTA
www.scilinks.com
Use the *sci*LINKS numbers at the end of each chapter for additional resources on the **NSTA** Web site.

CNNfyi.com
www.cnnfyi.com
Visit the CNN Web site for current events coverage and classroom resources.

START-UP Activity

ANTICIPATION

As you will see in this activity, volcanic eruptions are very difficult to predict.

Procedure

1. Place **10 mL of baking soda** in the center of a sheet of **bathroom tissue.** Fold the corners over the baking soda and crease the edges so that they stay in place. Place the tissue packet in the middle of a **large pan.**

2. Put **modeling clay** around the top edge of a **funnel.** Turn the funnel upside down over the tissue packet. Press down to make a tight seal.

3. Put your safety goggles on and add **50 mL of vinegar** and **several drops of liquid dish soap** to a 200 mL **beaker,** and stir.

4. Predict how much time will elapse before your volcano erupts.

5. Pour the liquid into the upturned funnel. Using a **stopwatch,** record the time you began to pour and the time your volcano erupts. How close was your prediction?

Analysis

6. How does your model represent the natural world?

7. What are some limitations of your model?

8. Based on the predictions of the entire class, what can you conclude about the accuracy of predicting volcanic eruptions?

START-UP Activity

ANTICIPATION

MATERIALS

FOR EACH GROUP:
- 10 mL baking soda
- bathroom tissue
- large pan
- modeling clay
- funnel
- 50 mL vinegar
- liquid dishwashing soap
- 200 mL beaker
- stopwatch

Safety Caution

Students should wear safety goggles during this activity.

Answers to START-UP Activity

6. The model simulates the buildup of pressure below the surface that causes an eruption. Magma and the vinegar/soap mixture are both liquids. The sides of a volcano and the funnel and modeling clay are solids.

7. The materials used for the model are different. Also the temperature and pressure in a real volcano are much higher than those produced in the model.

8. Eruptions are very difficult to predict. As in the experiment, you can know that an eruption will occur in the near future, but it may be impossible to predict the exact moment of eruption.

Chapter 9 • Volcanoes

SECTION 1

Focus

Volcanic Eruptions

In this section, students learn about explosive and nonexplosive eruptions and about how the composition of magma affects these eruptions. Students learn to identify the internal structure of a volcano and the types of lava and pyroclastic material produced in an eruption.

Bellringer

Ask students to create a labeled drawing in their ScienceLog that illustrates what happens when a volcano erupts. Then have students describe the photographs shown on this page. Ask them to think about what causes lava to have such different characteristics. Have students share their ideas with the class. **Sheltered English**

1) Motivate

ACTIVITY

 *Writing* Have students write a letter to a friend from a fictional survivor of the St. Pierre eruption described at the beginning of this chapter. Have students describe what the volcano was like hours before the eruption, the eruption itself, and the aftermath. Students can then exchange letters.

Directed Reading Worksheet 9 Section 1

Section 1

Terms to Learn
volcano
lava
pyroclastic material

What You'll Do
- Distinguish between nonexplosive and explosive volcanic eruptions.
- Explain how the composition of magma determines the type of volcanic eruption that will occur.
- Classify the main types of lava and volcanic debris.

Volcanic Eruptions

Think about the force of the explosion produced by the first atomic bomb used in World War II. Now imagine an explosion 10,000 times stronger, and you get an idea of how powerful a volcanic eruption can be. As you may know, volcanic eruptions give rise to volcanoes. A **volcano** is a mountain that forms when molten rock, called *magma*, is forced to the Earth's surface.

Fortunately, few volcanoes give rise to explosive eruptions like that of Mount Pelée. Most eruptions are of a nonexplosive variety. You can compare these two types of eruptions by looking at the photographs on this and the next page.

Nonexplosive Eruptions

When people think of volcanic eruptions, they often imagine rivers of red-hot lava, called *lava flows*. Lava flows come from nonexplosive eruptions. **Lava** is magma that flows onto the Earth's surface. Relatively calm outpourings of lava, like the ones shown below, can release a huge amount of molten rock. Some of the largest mountains on Earth grew from repeated lava flows over hundreds of thousands of years.

▲ Sometimes nonexplosive eruptions can spray lava into the air. Lava fountains, such as this one, rarely exceed a few hundred meters in height.

▶ In this nonexplosive eruption, a continuous stream of lava pours quietly from the crater of Kilauea, in Hawaii.

◀ Lava can flow many kilometers before it finally cools and hardens. As you can see in this photograph, lava flows often pose a greater threat to property than to human life.

222

MISCONCEPTION ALERT

Although explosive volcanoes get the most attention, nonexplosive extrusions play a much more significant role in shaping our world. For instance, much of the ocean floor is covered by basaltic pillow lava, and nonexplosive volcanoes formed many of the Pacific islands.

IS THAT A FACT!

The volcano Mauna Kea is the tallest mountain in the world. It rises 4 km above sea level, and its slopes descend 5 km below the ocean. Hawaii's mass depresses the ocean floor another 8 km. This makes the volcano 17 km tall, almost twice the height of Mount Everest!

Explosive Eruptions

Take a look at **Figure 1**. In an explosive volcanic eruption, clouds of hot debris and gases shoot out from the volcano, often at supersonic speeds. Instead of producing lava flows, molten rock is blown into millions of pieces that harden in the air. The dust-sized particles can circle the globe for years in the upper atmosphere, while larger pieces of debris fall closer to the volcano.

In addition to shooting molten rock into the air, an explosive eruption can blast millions of tons of solid rock from a volcano. In a matter of minutes, an explosive eruption can demolish rock formations that took thousands of years to accumulate. Thus, as shown in **Figure 2**, a volcano may actually shrink in size rather than grow from repeated eruptions.

Figure 1 In what resembles a nuclear explosion, volcanic debris rockets skyward during an eruption of Mount Redoubt, in Alaska.

Figure 2 Within minutes, the 1980 eruption of Mount St. Helens, in Washington, blasted away a whole side of the mountain, flattening and scorching 600 km² of forest.

Multicultural CONNECTION

The Klickitat tribe of the Pacific Northwest had two names for Mount St. Helens. The first name was Loo-Wit, which referred to a lovely maiden who changed into a beautiful white mountain. Their other name was Tah-one-lat-clah, or "fire mountain," indicating their knowledge that the volcano was prone to eruptions. Ask students why they think the tribe had two very different names for Mount St. Helens. Have students research other American Indian names and legends for volcanic peaks in North America.

2) Teach

CONNECT TO LIFE SCIENCE

Nonexplosive volcanoes, like Kilauea, on the island of Hawaii, may produce several different lava flows during an eruption. If these flows surround an area of forest, they create an island in a sea of lava. Hawaiians call such areas *kipukas*, or "islands of survival." Over the last 20 years, biologists have studied populations of animals isolated in kipukas and have found interesting evidence for evolution. Picture-wing drosophila flies have exhibited changes that ultimately could produce new species. Suggest that students research how the volcanic origin of the Hawaiian Islands contributes to the diversity of life found there.

COOPERATIVE LEARNING

Have groups prepare and present a mock radio program about a volcanic eruption of one of the following volcanoes:

Mount St. Helens, Vesuvius, Mount Pinatubo, or Nevada del Ruiz

Group members will research the event together. Two will write the script. One student could produce sound effects. One student will be the moderator, and two will be on-the-spot reporters. The remaining students will play people directly affected by the eruption (teachers, students, store owners, and rescue personnel). Make sure students describe the event from the first signs of volcanic activity to the aftermath. **Sheltered English**

Section 1 • Volcanic Eruptions   **223**

2 Teach, continued

QuickLab

MATERIALS
- 2 small drinking cups
- water
- honey
- 2 straws

Answers to QuickLab

3. Answers will vary.
4. The honey is thicker, so the air bubbles move much more slowly than in water.
5. Because the honey is thicker than water, it traps more air bubbles. Magma that is thicker will trap more gases, which creates a buildup of pressure. The more pressure that builds up, the more violent the volcanic eruption will be.

CONNECT TO PHYSICAL SCIENCE

Use Teaching Transparency 208 to discuss changes of state in magma. When water or carbon dioxide are part of minerals in a rock, they are in the solid state. When rock melts to form magma, it changes to liquid. When this happens, the water and carbon dioxide dissolved in the magma are also liquid. When temperature and pressure conditions allow, water and carbon dioxide in the magma solution exsolve, or vaporize, changing from liquid to gas. This greatly increases the volume of the magma and often results in violent eruptions. When the magma erupts on the surface, it cools and solidifies, changing from a liquid to a solid state.

 **Teaching Transparency 208** "Summarizing the Changes of State" **LINK TO PHYSICAL SCIENCE**

224   Chapter 9 • Volcanoes

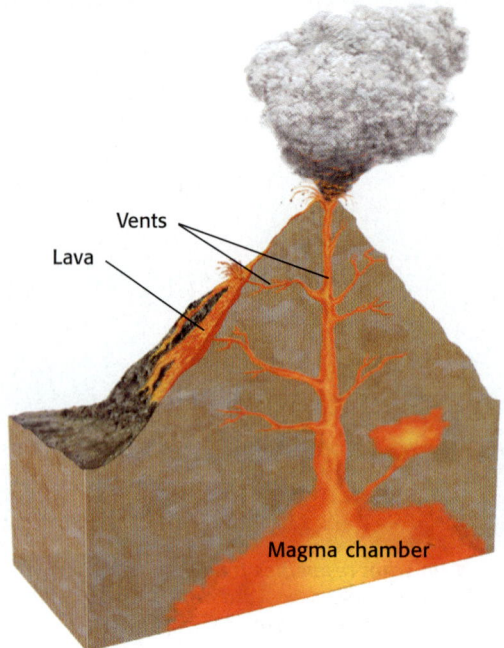

Figure 3 Volcanoes form around vents that release magma onto the Earth's surface.

Cross Section of a Volcano

Whether they produce explosive or nonexplosive eruptions, all volcanoes share the same basic features. **Figure 3** shows some of the features that you might see if you could look inside an erupting volcano. Deep underground, the driving force that creates volcanoes is hot liquid material known as magma. Magma rises through holes in the Earth's crust called *vents*. Vents can channel magma all the way up to the Earth's surface during an eruption.

Magma

By comparing the composition of magma from different types of eruptions, scientists have made an important discovery—the composition of the magma determines whether a volcanic eruption is nonexplosive, explosive, or somewhere in between.

Water A volcano is more likely to erupt explosively if its magma has a high water content. The effect water has on magma is similar to the effect carbon dioxide gas has in a can of soda. When you shake the can up, the carbon dioxide that was dissolved in the soda is released, and because gases need much more room than liquids, a great amount of pressure builds up. When you open the can, soda comes shooting out. The same phenomenon occurs with explosive volcanic eruptions.

Silica Explosive eruptions are also caused by magma that contains a large percentage of silica (a basic building block of most minerals). Silica-rich magma has a thick, stiff consistency. It flows slowly and tends to harden in the volcano's vent. This plugs the vent, resulting in a buildup of pressure as magma pushes up from below. If enough pressure builds up, an explosive eruption results. Thick magma also prevents water vapor and other gases from easily escaping. Magma that contains a smaller percentage of silica has a thinner, runnier consistency. Gases escape this type of magma more easily, making it less likely that explosive pressure will build up.

QuickLab

Bubble, Bubble, Toil and Trouble

With a few simple items, you can easily discover how the consistency of a liquid affects the flow of gases.

1. Fill a **drinking cup** halfway with **water** and another cup halfway with **honey.**
2. Using a **straw,** blow into the water and observe the bubbles.
3. Take another straw and blow into the honey. What happens?
4. How does the honey behave differently from the water?
5. How do you think this difference relates to volcanic eruptions?

TRY at HOME

224

It may seem illogical that water makes magma more likely to explode. Explain that magma contains water and that the water is dissolved in the magma. When the water changes from a liquid to a gas, its volume increases dramatically. This change causes a pressure increase that can generate a great deal of explosive force. Discuss what would happen if students boiled water in a pot with a tight lid. Then have them think of other examples where water can be an explosive force, such as in a car's radiator or in popcorn.

What Erupts from a Volcano?

Depending on how explosive a volcanic eruption is, magma erupts as either *lava* or *pyroclastic material*. **Pyroclastic material** consists of the rock fragments created by explosive volcanic eruptions. Nonexplosive eruptions produce mostly lava. Explosive eruptions produce mostly pyroclastic material. Over many years, a volcano may alternate between eruptions of lava and eruptions of pyroclastic material. Eruptions of lava and pyroclastic material may also occur as separate stages of a single eruption event.

Fire and ice! A phrase to describe volcanoes? That depends on where they are. Turn to page 241 to find out more.

Lava Like magma, lava ranges in consistency from thick to thin. *Blocky lava* is so thick in consistency that it barely creeps along the ground. Other types of lava, such as *pahoehoe* (pah HOY hoy), *aa* (AH ah), and *pillow lava*, are thinner in consistency and produce faster lava flows. These types of lava are shown in the photographs below.

▶ **Blocky lava** is cool, stiff lava that cannot travel far from the erupting vent. Blocky lava usually oozes from a volcano, forming jumbled heaps of sharp-edged chunks.

▲ **Pahoehoe** lava flows slowly, like wax dripping from a candle, forming a glassy surface with rounded wrinkles.

▲ **Aa** is a Hawaiian word that refers to a type of lava that has a jagged surface. This slightly stiffer lava pours out quickly and forms a brittle crust. The crust is torn into jagged pieces as the molten lava underneath continues to move.

▲ **Pillow lava** forms when lava erupts underwater. As you can see here, it forms rounded lumps that are the size and shape of pillows.

225

WEIRD SCIENCE

Lava cools very slowly not only because it is very hot to start with but also because it is a good insulator. When a Mexican lava flow in 1952 stopped, it was 10 m thick. In 1956, four years later, the lava still steamed when it rained.

READING STRATEGY

Mnemonics The word *pyroclastic* has two parts: *pyro*, Greek for "fire," and *clastic*, Greek for "broken." Other words that include *pyro-* are *pyrotechnics*, which describes "fire art," or fireworks, and *pyrometer*, a thermometer that measures temperatures too high for a mercury thermometer. Have students invent other words that include the prefix *pyro-*. Sheltered English

DISCUSSION

Discuss with students the differences between a *direct relationship* and an *inverse relationship*. Explain that when they push a swing, it goes higher and faster. This is a direct relationship. To illustrate an inverse relationship, explain that when they push down on one end of a seesaw, the other end rises. Then ask students to think about the role of water and silica in magma. Discuss them in terms of how they have a *direct relationship* with an explosion: as the amount of water or silica increases, the possibility of explosion also increases. Then discuss the way that silica affects lava's speed and consistency in terms of their *inverse relationship*: as the amount of silica increases, the speed of the lava decreases, and vice versa. Sheltered English

GROUP ACTIVITY

Introduce the concept of viscosity by having students describe the observable differences in flow rate as you pour molasses or honey, water, and vegetable oil down a gently sloping cookie sheet. (They should observe that the molasses or honey flows slowest, oil flows somewhat faster, and water flows very fast.)

Explain to students that viscosity is a liquid's resistance to flow. Honey has a high viscosity, so it flows very slowly. Water has a low viscosity, so it flows easily. Ask the students how magma's composition affects its viscosity. (The more silica that is present in magma, the greater its viscosity.)

TOPIC: Volcanic Eruptions
GO TO: www.scilinks.org
sciLINKS NUMBER: HSTE205

Section 1 • Volcanic Eruptions   **225**

3) Extend

GOING FURTHER

Writing *Lahar* is an Indonesian term for a particularly deadly kind of volcanic mudflow. A lahar is a flow of water-saturated volcanic debris that races down the slope of a volcano with the consistency of wet cement. Lahars generally occur when a volcano's snowcap is suddenly melted by an eruption. When Nevada del Ruiz erupted in Colombia, its lahar killed more than 25,000 people. Have students research and report on lahars from two eruptions.

4) Close

Quiz

1. Describe the lava flow from a nonexplosive eruption. (a calm stream that can flow for hundreds of kilometers)

2. Describe an explosive eruption. (Ash, hot debris, gases, and chunks of rock spew from a volcano.)

3. Define *blocky* lava, *pahoehoe* lava, and *aa* lava. (*blocky* lava: cool, stiff lava that doesn't travel very fast; *pahoehoe* lava: flows quickly and forms a wrinkled surface, looks like coiled rope; *aa* lava: flows slowly and forms a brittle, jagged crust.)

ALTERNATIVE ASSESSMENT

Provide cornstarch, salt, and water to make a paste. Then have students experiment with the ingredients to create representations of the types of lava discussed in this section. Have students work independently to describe the eruptions that would produce each lava type.

226 Chapter 9 • Volcanoes

Pyroclastic Material Pyroclastic material is produced when magma explodes from a volcano and solidifies in the air. It is also produced when existing rock is shattered by powerful eruptions. It comes in a variety of sizes, from boulders the size of houses to particles so small they can remain suspended in the atmosphere for years. The photographs on this page show four major kinds of pyroclastic material: volcanic bombs, volcanic blocks, lapilli (luh PILL ee), and volcanic ash.

Volcanic blocks *are the largest pieces of pyroclastic material. They consist of solid rock blasted out of the volcano.*

Biology CONNECTION

Volcanoes provide some of the most productive farmland in the world. It can take thousands of years for volcanic rock to break down into usable soil nutrients. On the other hand, the ash from a single explosive eruption can greatly increase the fertility of soil in only a few years and can keep the soil fertile for centuries.

Volcanic bombs *are large blobs of magma that harden in the air. The shape of the bomb shown here resulted from the magma's spinning through the air as it cooled.*

Lapilli, *which means "little stones" in Italian, are pebble-like bits of magma that became solid before they hit the ground.*

Volcanic ash *forms when the gases in stiff magma expand rapidly and the walls of the gas bubbles explode into tiny glasslike slivers.*

internet connect

sciLINKS NSTA
TOPIC: Volcanic Eruptions
GO TO: www.scilinks.org
sciLINKS NUMBER: HSTE205

REVIEW

1. Is a nonexplosive volcanic eruption more likely to produce lava or pyroclastic material? Explain.

2. If a volcano contained magma with small proportions of water and silica, would you predict a nonexplosive eruption or an explosive one? Why?

3. **Making Inferences** Pyroclastic material is classified primarily by the size of the particles. What is the basis for classifying lava?

226

Answers to Review

1. A nonexplosive eruption is more likely to produce lava than pyroclastic material because lava is thin and runny compared with pyroclastic material.

2. A nonexplosive eruption should result. Water turns to steam, which builds up a great amount of pressure, leading to explosive eruptions. Silica-rich magma is thick, allowing it to trap volcanic gases, such as steam, causing explosive eruptions.

3. Lava is classified according to how it flows. Blocky lava is thickest and flows very slowly because it is mostly solidified. *Aa* lava is still thick but is made of smaller blocks and thus flows faster than blocky lava. *Pahoehoe* lava is thin and runny, and it flows quickly, forming a ropy texture. Pillow lava forms under water.

Section 2

Terms to Learn
shield volcano
cinder cone volcano
composite volcano
crater
caldera

What You'll Do
- Describe the effects that volcanoes have on Earth.
- Compare the different types of volcanoes.

Volcanoes' Effects on Earth

The effects of volcanic eruptions can be seen both on land and in the air. Heavier pyroclastic materials fall to the ground, causing great destruction, while ash and escaping gases affect global climatic patterns. Volcanoes also build mountains and plateaus that become lasting additions to the landscape.

An Explosive Impact

Because it is thrown high into the air, ash ejected during explosive volcanic eruptions can have widespread effects. The ash can block out the sun for days over thousands of square kilometers. Volcanic ash can blow down trees and buildings and can blanket nearby towns with a fine powder.

Flows and Fallout As shown in **Figure 4**, clouds of hot ash can flow rapidly downhill like an avalanche, choking and searing every living thing in their path. Sometimes large deposits of ash mix with rainwater or the water from melted glaciers during an eruption. With the consistency of wet cement, the mixture flows downhill, picking up boulders, trees, and buildings along the way. As volcanic ash falls to the ground, the effects can be devastating. Buildings may collapse under the weight of so much ash. Ash can also dam up river valleys, resulting in massive floods. And although ash is an effective plant fertilizer, too much ash can smother crops, causing food shortages and loss of livestock.

Figure 4 During the 1991 eruption of Mount Pinatubo, in the Philippines, clouds of volcanic gases and ash sped downhill at up to 250 km/h.

Climatic Changes In large-scale eruptions, volcanic ash, along with sulfur-rich gases, can reach the upper atmosphere. As the ash and gases spread around the globe, they can block out enough sunlight to cause the average global surface temperature to drop noticeably. The eruption of Mount Pinatubo in 1991 caused average global temperatures to drop by as much as 0.5°C. Although this may not seem like a large change in temperature, such a shift can disrupt climates all over the world. The lower average temperatures may last for several years, bringing wetter, milder summers and longer, harsher winters.

SCIENTISTS AT ODDS

Today most scientists think that dinosaurs became extinct 65 million years ago when a large asteroid struck Earth. But a small group of volcanologists have a controversial hypothesis that the gases and ash released from a series of large volcanic eruptions may have caused the extinction. Encourage students to find out more about these theories.

CONNECT TO ASTRONOMY

Early astronomers thought that the dark patches on the moon were lunar seas, but today we know that they are basins filled with solidified lava that erupted after the moon's formation. Have students research volcanism on another planet or moon in our solar system.

2 Teach

Some Go "Pop," Some Do Not   PG 664

Meeting Individual Needs

Learners Having Difficulty Have students copy descriptive phrases about the three types of volcanoes in their ScienceLog. Beside the entries, have them draw a cross section of each type of volcano. Students should find an example of each volcano type and write three paragraphs about it. The paragraphs should describe how the volcano fits its category, detail its last eruption, and explain how the volcano's shape is linked to the way it erupted. **Sheltered English**

Meeting Individual Needs

Advanced Learners In 1943, Dominic Pulido, a farmer in central Mexico, was working in his cornfield when the ground began to tremble and a noise like thunder filled the air. Pulido discovered a fissure in the field about 0.5 m deep. The ground began to swell and formed a mound 2.5 m high! A volcano named Paricutín was being born. In one year, the cinder cone volcano grew to 334 m high! Encourage students to read *Hill of Fire,* by Thomas P. Lewis, and write a book report about it.

Teaching Transparency 134
"Three Types of Volcanoes"

Problem Solving Worksheet 9
"Eruption Disruption"

To find out more about the types of volcanoes, turn to page 664 in the LabBook.

Different Types of Volcanoes

The lava and pyroclastic material that erupt from volcanoes create a variety of landforms. Perhaps the best known of all volcanic landforms are the volcanoes themselves. Volcanoes result from the buildup of rock around a vent. Three basic types of volcanoes are illustrated in **Figure 5.**

Figure 5 Three Types of Volcanoes

Shield volcano

Cinder cone volcano

Composite volcano

Shield volcanoes are built out of layers of lava from repeated nonexplosive eruptions. Because the lava is very runny, it spreads out over a wide area. Over time, the layers of lava create a volcano with gently sloping sides. Although their sides are not very steep, shield volcanoes can be enormous. Hawaii's Mauna Kea, the shield volcano shown here, is the largest mountain on Earth. Measured from its base on the sea floor, Mauna Kea is taller than Mount Everest, the tallest mountain on land.

Cinder cone volcanoes are small volcanic cones made entirely of pyroclastic material from moderately explosive eruptions. The pyroclastic material forms steeper slopes with a narrower base than the lava flows of shield volcanoes, as you can see in this photo of the volcano Paricutín, in Mexico. Cinder cone volcanoes usually erupt for only a short time and often occur in clusters, commonly on the sides of shield and composite volcanoes. They erode quickly because the pyroclastic particles are not cemented together by lava.

Composite volcanoes, sometimes referred to as *stratovolcanoes,* are one of the most common types of volcanoes. They form by explosive eruptions of pyroclastic material followed by quieter outpourings of lava. The combination of both types of eruptions forms alternating layers of pyroclastic material and lava. Composite volcanoes, such as Japan's Mount Fuji, shown here, have broad bases and sides that get steeper toward the summit.

Cross-Disciplinary Focus

History One of World War II's fiercest battles was fought on the volcanic island of Iwo Jima. More than 6,000 Allied soldiers and 20,000 Japanese soldiers died fighting for an island about 8 km long and 4 km wide. Have students research the battle of Iwo Jima and prepare a map to show why this volcanic island was difficult to capture.

Is That a Fact!

The fastest lava flow recorded moved at a speed of 60 km/h—about the same speed as a champion thoroughbred racehorse.

Craters and Calderas

At the top of the central vent in most volcanoes is a funnel-shaped pit called a **crater**. (Craters are also the circular pits made by meteorite impacts.) The photograph of the cinder cone on the previous page shows a well-defined crater. A crater's funnel shape results from explosions of material out of the vent as well as the collapse of material from the crater's rim back into the vent. A **caldera** forms when a magma chamber that supplies material to a volcano empties and its roof collapses. This causes the ground to sink, leaving a large, circular depression, as shown in **Figure 6**.

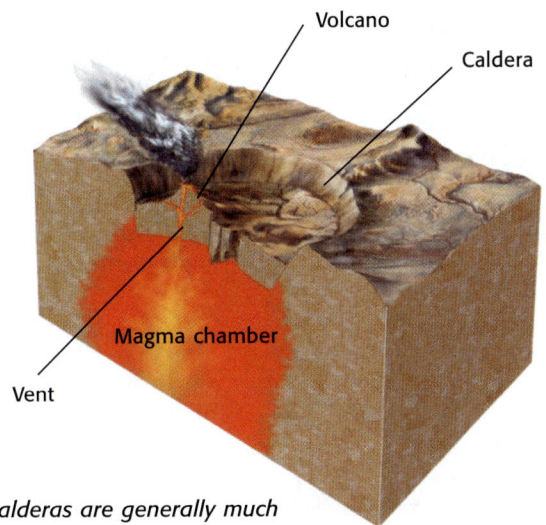

Figure 6 *Calderas are generally much larger than volcanic craters.*

Lava Plateaus

The most massive outpourings of lava do not come from individual volcanoes. Most of the lava on Earth's continents erupts from long cracks, or *fissures,* in the crust. In this non-explosive type of eruption, runny lava pours from a series of fissures and may spread evenly over thousands of square kilometers. The resulting landform is known as a *lava plateau.* The Columbia River Plateau, a lava plateau that formed about 15 million years ago, can be found in the northwestern United States.

REVIEW

1. Briefly explain why the ash from a volcanic eruption can be hazardous.
2. Why do cinder cone volcanoes have narrower bases and steeper sides than shield volcanoes?
3. **Comparing Concepts** Briefly describe the difference between a crater and a caldera.

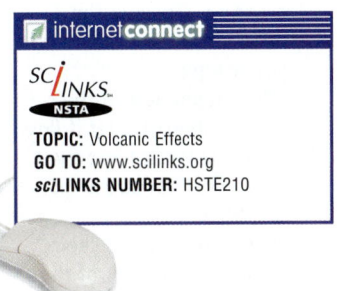

TOPIC: Volcanic Effects
GO TO: www.scilinks.org
*sci*LINKS NUMBER: HSTE210

RESEARCH

Have students form pairs and search books, magazines, or Internet sites for pictures of craters, calderas, and lava plateaus. Have pairs use their findings to make a model of one of these features. **Sheltered English**

3) Close

Quiz

1. Describe the shapes of shield, cinder cone, and composite volcanoes. (shield volcano: broad area with gentle shallow slopes; cinder cone volcano: generally smaller, steeper, more angled sides; composite volcano: high, covers less area than shield volcanoes, has sides that become steeper as they near the crater)

2. What causes a caldera? (A volcano's magma chamber empties, causing the ground above it to collapse.)

3. What is a lava plateau? (a layered formation caused when lava erupts from long cracks, or fissures, and covers a wide area)

ALTERNATIVE ASSESSMENT

 Have students draw a poster of an explosive volcano. Have them illustrate flows, fallout, and a crater or caldera. Students must label and write a caption for all the volcano's parts.

 Teaching Transparency 135 "The Formation of a Caldera"

 Reinforcement Worksheet 9 "A Variety of Volcanoes"

Answers to Review

1. Answers will vary. Volcanic ash is hazardous when it dams rivers, causing floods, and when it smothers crops, resulting in food shortages.
2. Shield volcanoes are made of lava flows, which are thin and runny, and spread out over large areas. Cinder cone volcanoes are made of pyroclastic material, which is thick and piles up around the volcano.
3. A crater forms when the rock around the main vent of a volcano is blasted out in an explosive eruption, forming an inverted cone-shaped depression. Most volcanoes have craters at their summits. A caldera forms when the magma chamber that feeds a volcano empties. When this happens, the roof of the magma chamber collapses, forming a circular depression. Calderas are usually much larger than craters.

SECTION 3

Focus

What Causes Volcanoes?

In this section, students learn how magma forms and how pressure and heat affect the temperature at which rocks melt. The section draws a connection between volcanic activity and tectonic movement and concludes with a discussion of the challenges involved in predicting eruptions.

🔔 Bellringer

Ask students to imagine they live on a volcanic island. Have them list in their ScienceLog the signals that would tell them the volcano was about to erupt.

1) Motivate

DISCUSSION

Have students brainstorm about measures a community could take to protect citizens from a volcanic eruption and then write their ideas in their ScienceLog. Have them compare their suggestions with the information they learn in the chapter.

 **Teaching Transparency 135** "The Formation of Magma"

 Directed Reading Worksheet 9 Section 3

Section 3

Terms to Learn
rift   hot spot

What You'll Do
- Describe the formation and movement of magma.
- Explain the relationship between volcanoes and plate tectonics.
- Summarize the methods scientists use to predict volcanic eruptions.

QuickLab

Reaction to Stress

1. Make a pliable "rock" by pouring 60 mL (1/4 cup) of **water** into a **plastic cup** and adding 150 mL of **cornstarch,** 15 mL (1 tbsp) at a time. Stir well after each addition.
2. Pour half of the cornstarch mixture into a **clear bowl.** Carefully observe how the "rock" flows. Be patient—this is a slow process!
3. Scrape the rest of the "rock" out of the cup with a **spoon.** Observe the behavior of the "rock" as you scrape.
4. What happened to the "rock" when you let it flow by itself? What happened when you put stress on the "rock"?
5. How is this pliable "rock" similar to the rock of the upper part of the mantle?

 TRY at HOME

230

QuickLab

MATERIALS
- water
- plastic cup
- cornstarch
- stirring stick
- clear bowl
- spoon

What Causes Volcanoes?

Scientists have learned a great deal over the years about what happens when a volcano erupts. Many of the results are dramatic and immediately visible. Unfortunately, understanding what causes a volcano to erupt in the first place is much more difficult. Scientists must rely on models based on rock samples and other data that provide insight into volcanic processes. Because it is so difficult to "see" what is going on deep inside the Earth, there are many uncertainties about why volcanoes form.

The Formation of Magma

You learned in the previous section that volcanoes form by the eruption of lava and pyroclastic material onto the Earth's surface. But the key to understanding why volcanoes erupt is understanding how magma forms. As you can see in **Figure 7,** volcanoes begin when magma collects in the deeper regions of the Earth's crust and in the uppermost layers of the mantle, the zone of intensely hot and pliable rock beneath the Earth's crust.

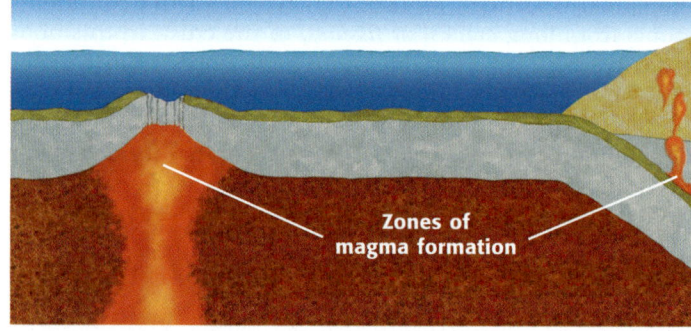

Figure 7 *Magma forms below the Earth's surface in a region that includes the lower crust and part of the upper mantle.*

Pressure and Temperature Although hot and pliable, the rock of the mantle is considered a solid. But the temperature of the mantle is high enough to melt almost any rock, so why doesn't it melt? The answer has to do with pressure. The weight of the rock above the mantle exerts a tremendous amount of pressure. This pressure keeps the atoms of mantle rock tightly packed, preventing the rock from changing into a liquid state. An increase in pressure raises the melting point of most materials.

Answers to QuickLab

4. When left alone, the "rock" flowed like a liquid but very slowly. When pressure was applied by the spoon, the "rock" broke, acting like a solid.
5. Because of the high pressure, the mantle is a solid. But over long periods of time, the mantle flows, acting more like a liquid.

As you can see in **Figure 8,** rock melts and forms magma when the temperature of the rock increases or when the pressure on the rock decreases. Because the temperature of the mantle is relatively constant, a decrease in pressure is usually what causes magma to form.

Density Once formed, the magma rises toward the surface of the Earth because it is less dense than the surrounding rock. Magma is commonly a mixture of liquid and solid mineral crystals and is therefore normally less dense than the completely solid rock that surrounds it. Like air bubbles that form on the bottom of a pan of boiling water, magma will rise toward the surface.

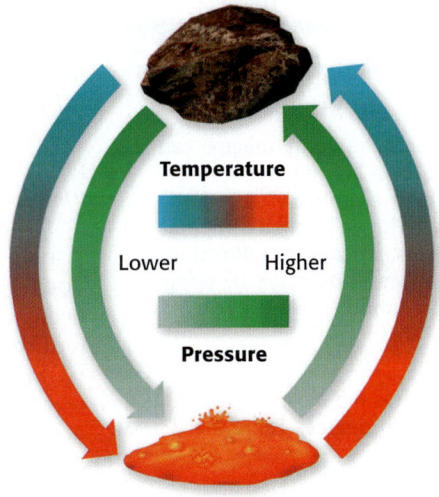

 **Self-Check**

What two factors may cause solid rock to become magma? *(See page 726 to check your answer.)*

Figure 8 *This diagram shows how both pressure and temperature affect the formation of magma within the mantle.*

Where Volcanoes Form

The locations of volcanoes around the globe provide clues to how volcanoes form. The world map in **Figure 9** shows the location of the world's active volcanoes on land. It also shows tectonic plate boundaries. As you can see, a large number of the volcanoes lie directly on tectonic plate boundaries. In fact, the plate boundaries surrounding the Pacific Ocean have so many volcanoes that these boundaries together are called the *Ring of Fire.*

Why are most volcanoes on tectonic plate boundaries? These boundaries are where the plates either collide with one another or separate from one another. At these boundaries, it is easier for magma to travel upward through the crust. In other words, the boundaries are where the action is!

Figure 9 *Tectonic plate boundaries are likely places for volcanoes to form. The Ring of Fire contains nearly 75 percent of the world's active volcanoes on land.*

IS THAT A FACT!

Kilauea, in Hawaii, is one of the most studied volcanoes in the world. It has been erupting regularly since 1983. Every day, enough lava to pave a two-lane road 32 km long pours from the volcano.

Answers to Self-Check

Solid rock may become magma when pressure is released, when the temperature rises above its melting point, or when its composition changes.

2) Teach

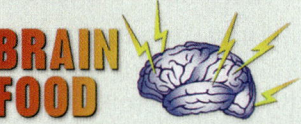

Igneous rocks form when either magma or lava cools and solidifies. If they are from the same source, often the only difference between the two is the rate at which they cool. Because magma is underground, it cools much more slowly than lava. A molten rock that cools slowly generally has larger crystals than one that cools faster.

How could scientists use this information to study an igneous outcrop? (By studying mineral crystal size and type, scientists can determine the origin of igneous rock.)

CROSS-DISCIPLINARY FOCUS

Geography Point out to students that most volcanic activity takes place on the ocean floor, where vast amounts of lava rise through rifts or volcanoes at diverging plate boundaries. Ask students to identify a spot where plates are diverging. (Sample answer: the Mid-Atlantic Ridge)

What plates are diverging along the Mid-Atlantic Ridge? (the North American and Eurasian plates)

What landmass formed by volcanic activity along this diverging plate boundary? (the island of Iceland)

Then point out to students that Iceland is merely a visible part of the Mid-Atlantic Ridge. Also explain that volcanic eruptions along diverging tectonic plates are generally much less violent than volcanoes typical of convergent boundaries.

Section 3 • What Causes Volcanoes?

2) Teach, continued

REAL-WORLD CONNECTION

 Earthquake tremors are often a warning signal that a volcano is about to erupt. In the months before the explosive eruption of Mount St. Helens, small earthquakes, which grew in number and intensity, shook the area. On March 27, 1980, the volcano began venting steam and ash. Geologists had set up seismometers to record the frequency, location, and magnitude of the quakes. Electronic surveying equipment employed laser beams to measure ground swelling as the lava dome rose. Tiltmeters measured changes in the mountain's slope. Steam gauges recorded water temperatures, pH levels, and amounts of suspended minerals in the waters around the volcano. Gas sensors on the ground and in aircraft monitored hydrogen, carbon dioxide, and sulfur dioxide levels that might signal the movement of magma toward the surface. Have students write a report about the prediction of the Mount St. Helens eruption and the eruption itself.

Answer to MATHBREAK

$°F = \frac{9}{5} \times 1{,}400°C + 32 = 2{,}552°F$

Math Skills Worksheet 35
"Using Temperature Scales"

TOPIC: What Causes Volcanoes?
GO TO: www.scilinks.org
sciLINKS NUMBER: HSTE215

TOPIC: The Ring of Fire
GO TO: www.scilinks.org
sciLINKS NUMBER: HSTE220

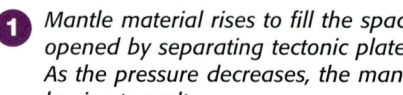

MATHBREAK

How Hot Is Hot?
Inside the Earth, magma can reach a burning-hot 1,400°C! You are probably more familiar with Fahrenheit temperatures, so convert 1,400°C to degrees Fahrenheit by using the formula below.

$$°F = \frac{9}{5}°C + 32$$

What is the magma's temperature in degrees Fahrenheit?

When Tectonic Plates Separate When two tectonic plates separate and move away from each other, a *divergent boundary* forms. As the tectonic plates separate, a deep crack, or **rift**, forms between the plates. Mantle material then rises to fill in the gap. Because the mantle material is now closer to the surface, the pressure on it decreases. This decrease in pressure causes the mantle rock to partially melt and become magma.

Because magma is less dense than the surrounding rock, it rises up through the rift. As the magma rises, it cools down, and the pressure on it decreases. So even though it becomes cooler as it rises, it remains molten because of the reduced pressure.

Magma continuously rises up through the rift between the separating plates and creates new crust. Although a few divergent boundaries exist on land, most are located on the ocean floor. There they produce long mountain chains called mid-ocean spreading centers, or *mid-ocean ridges*. **Figure 10** shows the process of forming such an underwater mountain range at a divergent boundary.

Figure 10 How Magma Forms at a Divergent Boundary

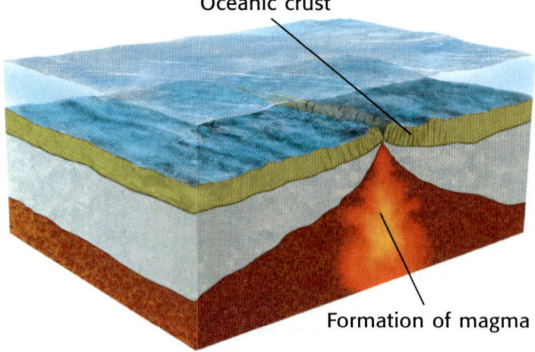

① Mantle material rises to fill the space opened by separating tectonic plates. As the pressure decreases, the mantle begins to melt.

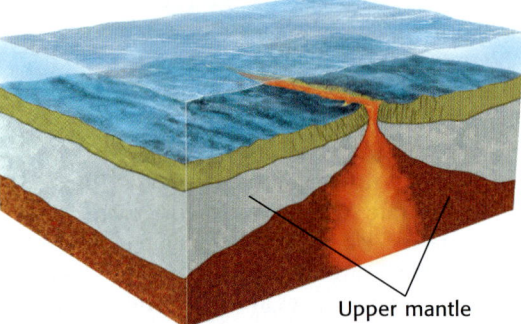

② Because magma is less dense than the surrounding rock, it rises toward the surface, where it forms new crust on the ocean floor.

232

Homework

Debate How reliable are volcano warnings? An estimated 500 million people around the world live either on or near a volcano, and each year more than 100 volcanoes erupt on Earth. The potential for an eruption to affect a large number of people is great. Scientists are using tools such as seismographs, laser range finders, and satellites to learn more about volcanoes and volcanic eruptions, but they are still not able to accurately predict volcanic eruptions. Encourage students to research the recent advances in volcano-eruption prediction and debate whether scientists will ever be able to make accurate predictions, and what kinds of technology would make this possible.

When Tectonic Plates Collide

If you slide two pieces of notebook paper into one another on a flat desktop, the papers will either buckle upward or one piece of paper will move under the other. This gives you an idea of what happens when tectonic plates collide. The place where two tectonic plates collide is called a *convergent boundary*.

Convergent boundaries are commonly located where oceanic plates collide with continental plates. The oceanic crust is denser and thinner and therefore moves underneath the continental crust. The movement of one tectonic plate under another is called *subduction*, shown in **Figure 11**.

As the descending oceanic crust scrapes past the continental crust, it sinks deeper into the mantle, getting hotter. As it does so, the pressure on the oceanic crust increases as well. The combination of increased heat and pressure causes the water contained in the oceanic crust to be released. The water then mixes with the mantle rock, which lowers the rock's melting point, causing it to melt.

Figure 11 How Magma Forms at a Convergent Boundary

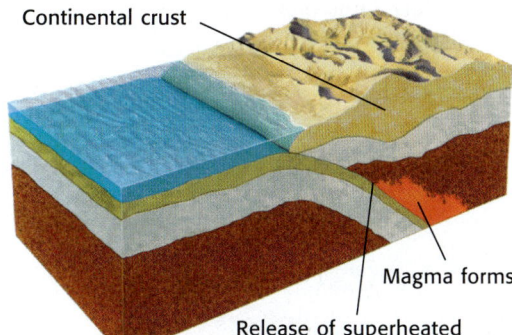

1. As the oceanic plate moves downward, some of the rock melts and forms magma.

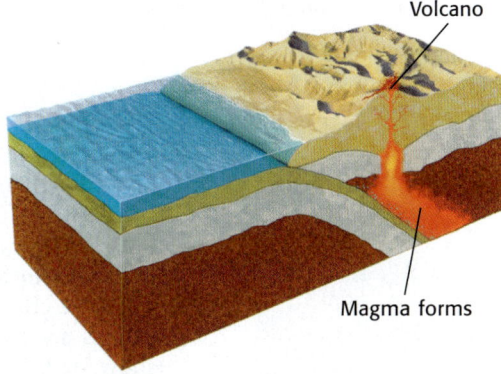

2. When magma is less dense than the surrounding rock, it rises toward the surface.

Hot Spots

Not all magma develops along tectonic plate boundaries. For example, the Hawaiian Islands, some of the most well-known volcanoes on Earth, are nowhere near a plate boundary. The volcanoes of Hawaii and several other places on Earth are known as *hot spots*. **Hot spots** are places on the Earth's surface that are directly above columns of rising magma, called *mantle plumes*. Mantle plumes begin deep in the Earth, possibly at the boundary between the mantle and the core. Scientists are not sure what causes these plumes, but some think that a combination of heat conducted upward from the core and heat from radioactive elements keeps the plumes rising.

IS THAT A FACT!

In the Caribbean, a submarine volcano named Kick'em Jenny is gaining a very bad reputation. As one sailboat captain said, "Kick'em Jenny . . . has a reputation of kicking up a nasty sea." Between 1986 and 1996, the volcano grew over 50 m; its top is now only 200 m below sea level. It's close enough to the surface that eruptions can cause waves and turbulence in the sea. Volcanologists are concerned that a large eruption could cause devastating tsunamis throughout the Caribbean.

3) Extend

COOPERATIVE LEARNING

More than 30 earthquakes a year are caused by the movement of magma beneath Mount Rainier, in Washington State. It is the second most seismically active volcano in the Cascade Range, after Mount St. Helens. Because the area around Mount Rainier is so heavily populated, an eruption would endanger thousands of people and destroy property worth millions of dollars. Many groups of people are studying Mount Rainier and preparing for a possible eruption.

Divide the class into groups and give the following assignments:

- **Research Group** Members investigate the volcano's history to determine why it has been ranked as a "decade volcano."

- **Early-Warning Group** Members research how the volcano's activity is being monitored with scientific equipment and other methods.

- **Washington State Emergency Management Agency (WaSEMA) Group** Members find out how this state organization plans to help people in case of an eruption.

- **Schools, Police, and Fire Group** This group investigates how local agencies would design a plan for warning and a plan for the aftermath of an eruption.

After the groups research their areas, have them make presentations using posters, models, maps, and graphs.

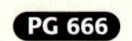
Volcano Verdict — PG 666

A hot spot often produces a long chain of volcanoes. This is because the mantle plume stays in the same spot, while the tectonic plate above moves over it. The Hawaiian Islands, for example, are riding on the Pacific plate, which is moving slowly to the northwest. **Figure 12** shows how a hot spot can form a chain of volcanic islands.

Figure 12 How a Hot Spot Forms Volcanoes

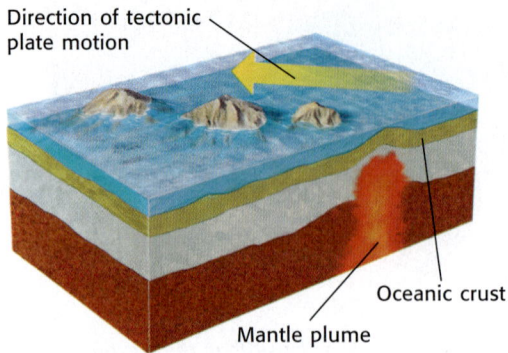
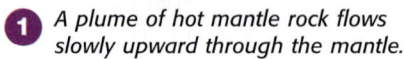
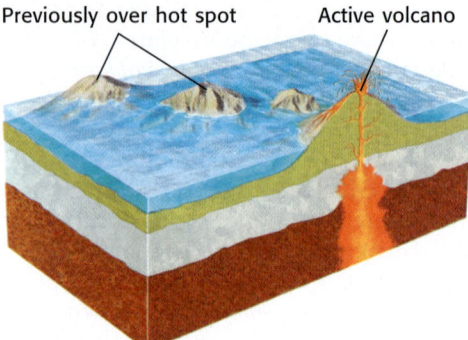

① A plume of hot mantle rock flows slowly upward through the mantle.

② As the tectonic plate moves slowly over the mantle plume, a chain of volcanic islands forms.

Predicting Volcanic Eruptions

To help predict volcanic eruptions, scientists classify volcanoes based on their eruption histories and on how likely it is that they will erupt again. *Extinct* volcanoes are those that have not erupted in recorded history and probably never will again. *Dormant* volcanoes are those that are not currently erupting but have erupted at some time in recorded history. *Active* volcanoes are those that are in the process of erupting or that show signs of erupting in the very near future.

Measuring Small Quakes Most active volcanoes produce small earthquakes as the magma within them moves upward and causes the surrounding rock to shift. Just before an eruption, the number and intensity of the small earthquakes increase, and the occurrence of quakes may be continuous. These earthquakes are measured with a *seismograph*, as shown in **Figure 13**.

Figure 13 Seismographs help scientists determine when magma is moving beneath a volcano.

Measuring Slope Measurements of a volcano's slope also give scientists clues with which to predict eruptions. For example, bulges in the volcano's slope may form as magma pushes against the inside of the volcano. By attaching an instrument called a *tiltmeter* to the surface of the volcano, scientists can detect small changes in the angle of the slope.

Teaching Transparency 137 "How a Hot Spot Forms Volcanoes"

Reinforcement Worksheet 9 "Tectonic Plate Movement"

Homework

There are volcanic hot spots in Yellowstone Park, Easter Island, Baja California, Hawaii, the Marquesas, the Canary Islands, Cameroon, Iceland, the Galápagos Islands, and the Samoan Islands. Have each student prepare a report on a hot spot, using maps, models, and details of the hot spot's history.

234 Chapter 9 • Volcanoes

Measuring Volcanic Gases The outflow of volcanic gases from a volcano can also help scientists predict eruptions. Some scientists think that the ratio of certain gases, especially that of sulfur dioxide (SO_2) to carbon dioxide (CO_2), is important in predicting eruptions. They know that when this ratio changes, it is an indication that things are changing in the magma chamber down below! As you can see in **Figure 14,** collecting this type of data is often dangerous.

Measuring Temperature from Orbit Some of the newest methods scientists are using to predict volcanic eruptions rely on satellite images. Many of these images record infrared radiation, which allows scientists to measure changes in temperature over time. They are taken from satellites orbiting more than 700 km above the Earth. By analyzing images taken at different times, scientists can determine if the site is getting hotter as magma pushes closer to the surface.

Figure 14 *As if getting this close to an active volcano is not dangerous enough, the gases that are being collected here are extremely poisonous.*

REVIEW

1. How does pressure determine whether the mantle is solid or liquid?
2. Describe a technology scientists use to predict volcanic eruptions.
3. **Interpreting Illustrations** Figure 9, shown earlier in this chapter, shows the locations of active volcanoes on land. Describe where on the map you would plot the location of underwater volcanoes and why. (Do not write in this book.)

TOPIC: What Causes Volcanoes?
GO TO: www.scilinks.org
sciLINKS NUMBER: HSTE215

Calling an Evacuation?

Although scientists have learned a lot about volcanoes, they cannot predict eruptions with total accuracy. Sometimes there are warning signs before an eruption, but often there are none. Imagine that you are the mayor of a town near a large volcano, and a geologist warns you that an eruption is probable. You realize that ordering an evacuation of your town could be an expensive embarrassment if the volcano doesn't erupt. But if you decide to keep quiet, people could be in serious danger if the volcano does erupt. Considering the social and economic consequences of your decision, your job is perhaps even more difficult. What would you do?

Answers to Review

1. Where there is enough pressure on the mantle, the atoms in the rock are forced to stay close together, keeping it solid. Where this pressure is released, mantle rock melts.
2. Answers will vary but should include a discussion of one of the following: measuring changes in the frequency of small earthquakes near the volcano; measuring changes in the slope of the volcano; measuring changes in the ratios of different volcanic gases over time; and measuring changes in how much thermal energy escapes a volcano by using infrared satellite images.
3. Underwater volcanoes should appear along the margins of all tectonic plates. Most volcanic activity happens at tectonic plate boundaries.

RESEARCH

The International Association of Volcanology and Chemistry of the Earth's Interior (IAVCEI) has declared 15 volcanoes to be "decade volcanoes," or volcanoes that pose enough danger that they warrant focused scientific attention. Have students prepare reports on the decade-volcano program. They may research IAVCEI's criteria, the designated volcanoes, a particular volcano's history, and monitoring and research of the volcano.

4) Close

Quiz

1. What conditions make magma rise? *(when magma is less dense than the surrounding rock and when it has a conduit to move up through)*
2. Define a rift. *(a series of deep cracks that occur where tectonic plates separate)*

ALTERNATIVE ASSESSMENT

Post a map of the world on the bulletin board that shows the location of tectonic plates. Have volunteers use pins and string to outline the plates on the map. Have other students use flagged pins to mark the location of the volcanoes they learned about in this chapter. Then pair students, and have partners explain how tectonic plate boundaries and volcanoes are related. Each partner should evaluate the other's understanding by assessing their descriptions of rifts, converging tectonic plates, diverging tectonic plates, subduction, hot spots, and magma formation.

Section 3 • What Causes Volcanoes?

Chapter Highlights

Vocabulary Definitions

Section 1

volcano a mountain that forms when molten rock, called magma, is forced to the Earth's surface

lava magma that flows onto the Earth's surface

pyroclastic material fragments of rock that are created by explosive volcanic eruptions

Section 2

shield volcano a large, gently sloped volcano that forms from repeated, nonexplosive eruptions of lava

cinder cone volcano a small, steeply sloped volcano that forms from moderately explosive eruptions of pyroclastic material

composite volcano a volcano made of alternating layers of lava and pyroclastic material; also called *stratovolcano*

crater a funnel-shaped pit around the central vent of a volcano

caldera a circular depression that forms when a magma chamber empties and causes the ground above to sink

Chapter Highlights

SECTION 1

Vocabulary
volcano *(p. 222)*
lava *(p. 222)*
pyroclastic material *(p. 225)*

Section Notes
- Volcanoes erupt both explosively and nonexplosively.
- The characteristics of a volcanic eruption are largely determined by the type of magma within the volcano.
- The amount of silica in magma determines whether it is thin and fluid or thick and stiff.
- Lava hardens into characteristic features that range from smooth to jagged, depending on how thick the lava is and how quickly it flows.
- Pyroclastic material, or volcanic debris, consists of solid pieces of the volcano as well as magma that solidifies as it travels through the air.

SECTION 2

Vocabulary
shield volcano *(p. 228)*
cinder cone volcano *(p. 228)*
composite volcano *(p. 228)*
crater *(p. 229)*
caldera *(p. 229)*

Section Notes
- The effects of volcanic eruptions are felt both locally and around the world.
- Volcanic mountains can be classified according to their composition and overall shape.
- Craters are funnel-shaped pits that form around the central vent of a volcano. Calderas are large bowl-shaped depressions formed by a collapsed magma chamber.

✓ Skills Check

Math Concepts

CONVERTING TEMPERATURE SCALES So-called low-temperature magmas can be 1,100°C. Just how hot is such a magma? If you are used to measuring temperature in degrees Fahrenheit, you can use a simple formula to find out.

$$°F = \tfrac{9}{5}°C + 32$$

$$°F = \tfrac{9}{5}(1{,}100) + 32$$

$$°F = 1{,}980 + 32 = 2{,}012$$

$$2{,}012°F = 1{,}100°C$$

Visual Understanding

CALDERAS Calderas are caused by the release of massive amounts of magma from beneath the Earth's surface. When the volume of magma decreases, it no longer exerts pressure to hold the ground up. As a result, the ground sinks, forming a caldera.

Lab and Activity Highlights

Some Go "Pop," Some Do Not PG 664

Volcano Verdict PG 666

 Datasheets for LabBook
(blackline masters for these labs)

236 Chapter 9 • Volcanoes

SECTION 2

- In the largest type of volcanic eruption, lava simply pours from long fissures in the Earth's crust to form lava plateaus.

Labs
Some Go "Pop," Some Do Not (p. 664)

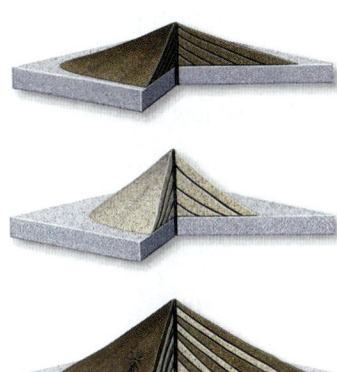

SECTION 3

Vocabulary
rift (p. 232)
hot spot (p. 233)

Section Notes

- Volcanoes result from magma formed in the mantle.
- When pressure is reduced, some of the solid rock of the already hot mantle melts to form magma.
- Because it is less dense than the surrounding rock, magma rises to the Earth's surface. It either erupts as lava or solidifies in the crust.
- Most volcanic activity takes place along tectonic plate boundaries, where plates either separate or collide.

- Volcanoes also occur at hot spots. Chains of volcanic islands can form when tectonic plates move relative to the hot spot.
- Volcanic eruptions cannot be predicted with complete accuracy. But scientists now have several methods of forecasting future eruptions.

Labs
Volcano Verdict (p. 666)

VOCABULARY DEFINITIONS, continued

SECTION 3

rift a deep crack that forms between tectonic plates as they separate

hot spot a place on Earth's surface that is directly above a column of rising magma called a mantle plume

Vocabulary Review Worksheet 9

Blackline masters of these Chapter Highlights can be found in the **Study Guide**.

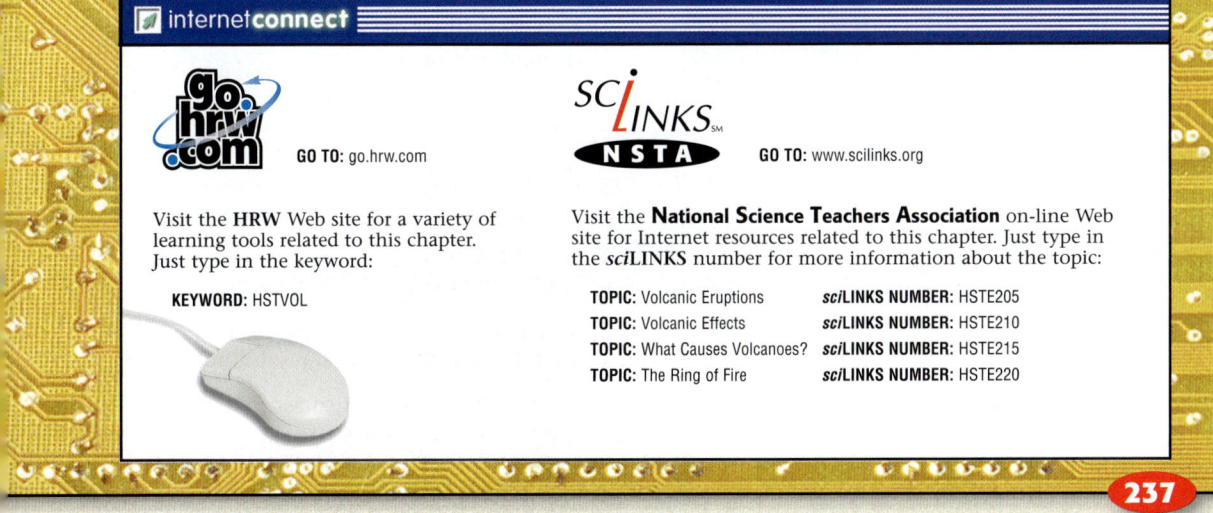

internetconnect

GO TO: go.hrw.com

Visit the **HRW** Web site for a variety of learning tools related to this chapter. Just type in the keyword:

KEYWORD: HSTVOL

GO TO: www.scilinks.org

Visit the **National Science Teachers Association** on-line Web site for Internet resources related to this chapter. Just type in the *sci*LINKS number for more information about the topic:

TOPIC: Volcanic Eruptions — *sci*LINKS NUMBER: HSTE205
TOPIC: Volcanic Effects — *sci*LINKS NUMBER: HSTE210
TOPIC: What Causes Volcanoes? — *sci*LINKS NUMBER: HSTE215
TOPIC: The Ring of Fire — *sci*LINKS NUMBER: HSTE220

Lab and Activity Highlights

LabBank

Whiz-Bang Demonstrations
- How's Your Lava Life? Demo 21
- What Makes a Vent Event? Demo 20

Labs You Can Eat, Hot Spots, Lab 16

Long-Term Projects & Research Ideas, A City Lost and Found, Project 37

Interactive Explorations CD-ROM

CD 1, Exploration 4, "What's the Matter?"

Chapter Review

USING VOCABULARY

For each pair of terms listed below, explain the difference in their meanings.

1. caldera/crater
2. lava/magma
3. lava/pyroclastic material
4. vent/rift
5. cinder cone volcano/shield volcano

UNDERSTANDING CONCEPTS

Multiple Choice

6. The type of magma that often produces a violent eruption can be described as
   a. thin due to high silica content.
   b. thick due to high silica content.
   c. thin due to low silica content.
   d. thick due to low silica content.

7. When lava hardens quickly to form ropy formations, it is called
   a. aa lava.
   b. pahoehoe lava.
   c. pillow lava.
   d. blocky lava.

8. Volcanic dust and ash can remain in the atmosphere for months or years, causing
   a. decreased solar reflection and higher temperatures.
   b. increased solar reflection and lower temperatures.
   c. decreased solar reflection and lower temperatures.
   d. increased solar reflection and higher temperatures.

9. Mount St. Helens, in Washington, covered the city of Spokane with tons of ash. Its eruption would most likely be described as
   a. nonexplosive, producing lava.
   b. explosive, producing lava.
   c. nonexplosive, producing pyroclastic material.
   d. explosive, producing pyroclastic material.

10. Magma forms within the mantle most often as a result of
    a. high temperature and high pressure.
    b. high temperature and low pressure.
    c. low temperature and high pressure.
    d. low temperature and low pressure.

11. At divergent plate boundaries,
    a. heat from the Earth's core produces mantle plumes.
    b. oceanic plates sink, causing magma to form.
    c. tectonic plates move apart.
    d. hot spots produce volcanoes.

12. A theory that helps to explain the causes of both earthquakes and volcanoes is the theory of
    a. pyroclastics.
    b. plate tectonics.
    c. climatic fluctuation.
    d. mantle plumes.

Short Answer

13. Briefly describe two methods that scientists use to predict volcanic eruptions.

14. Describe how differences in magma affect volcanic eruptions.

15. Along what types of tectonic plate boundaries are volcanoes generally found? Why?

16. Describe the characteristics of the three types of volcanic mountains.

Concept Mapping

17. Use any of the terms from the vocabulary lists in Chapter Highlights to construct a concept map that illustrates the relationship between types of magma, the eruptions they produce, and the shapes of the volcanoes that result.

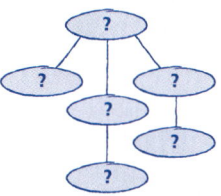

CRITICAL THINKING AND PROBLEM SOLVING

Write one or two sentences to answer the following questions:

18. Imagine that you are exploring a volcano that has been dormant for some time. You begin to keep notes on the types of volcanic debris you encounter as you walk. Your first notes describe volcanic ash, and later your notes describe lapilli. In what direction would you most likely be traveling—toward or away from the crater? Explain.

19. Loihi is a future Hawaiian island in the process of forming on the ocean floor. Considering how this island chain formed, tell where you think the new volcanic island will be located and why.

20. What do you think would happen to the Earth's climate if volcanic activity increased to 10 times its current level?

MATH IN SCIENCE

21. Midway Island is 1,935 km northwest of Hawaii. If the Pacific plate is moving to the northwest at 9 cm/yr, how long ago was Midway Island located over the hot spot that formed it?

INTERPRETING GRAPHICS

The following graph illustrates the average change in temperature above or below normal for a community over several years.

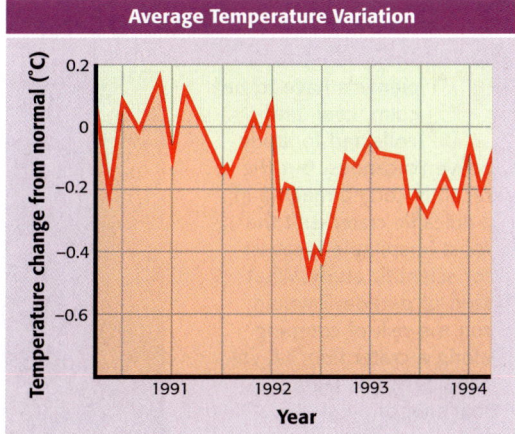

22. If the variation in temperature over the years was influenced by a major volcanic eruption, when did the eruption most likely take place? Explain.

23. If the temperature were plotted only in yearly intervals rather than several times per year, how might your interpretation be different?

 **Reading Check-up** Take a minute to review your answers to the Pre-Reading Questions found at the bottom of page 220. Have your answers changed? If necessary, revise your answers based on what you have learned since you began this chapter.

239

Concept Mapping Transparency 9

Blackline masters of this Chapter Review can be found in the **Study Guide**.

---

lava and pyroclastic material. Composite volcanoes have large, gently sloping bases and steep sides.

Concept Mapping

17. An answer to this exercise can be found at the end of this book.

CRITICAL THINKING AND PROBLEM SOLVING

18. You would be traveling toward the volcano because the larger the pyroclastic material is, the closer it will be to the vent. It takes more energy to move larger particles than it does to move smaller particles.

19. The new island will be located southeast of Hawaii because the Pacific plate is moving toward the northwest.

20. The overall surface temperature of the Earth would decrease because the volcanic ash in the atmosphere would block out much of the sun's energy. (Students may also note that volcanic eruptions release large amounts of CO_2, which could cause longer-term global warming.)

MATH IN SCIENCE

21. 1 km = 1,000 m = 100,000 cm
1,935 km = 193,500,000 cm
193,500,000/9 cm per year = **21,500,000 years**

INTERPRETING GRAPHICS

22. The eruption probably happened in 1992 because that year had the lowest temperature below normal. The volcanic ash that was erupted into the atmosphere blocked the sunlight and lowered the temperature.

23. If the temperature was measured once a year, the graph would indicate that 1991 had the lowest temperature. This would indicate that the eruptions happened in 1991 instead of 1992.

Chapter 9 • Chapter Review   **239**

Science, Technology, and Society

Robot in the Hot Seat

Scientists have to be calm, cool, and collected to study active volcanoes. But the recently cooled magma in a volcanic crater isn't the most hospitable location for scientific study. What kind of daredevil would run the risk of creeping along a crater floor? A volcanologist like *Dante II*, that's who!

Hot Stuff

A volcano crater may seem empty after a volcano erupts, but it is in no way devoid of volcanic information. Gases hissing up through the crater floor give scientists clues about the molten rock underneath, which may help them understand how and why volcanoes erupt repeatedly. But these gases may be poisonous or scalding hot, and the crater's floor can crack or shift at any time. Over the years, dozens of scientists have been seriously injured or killed while trying to explore volcano craters. Obviously, volcanologists needed some help studying the steamy abyss.

Getting a Robot to Take the Heat

Enter *Dante II*, an eight-legged robot with cameras for eyes and computers for a brain. In 1994, led by a team of scientists from NASA, Carnegie Mellon University, and the Alaskan Volcano Observatory, *Dante II* embarked on its first mission. It climbed into a breach called Crater Peak on the side of Mount Spurr, an active volcano in Alaska. Anchored at the crater's rim by a strong cable, *Dante II* was controlled partly by internal computers and partly by a team of scientists. The team communicated with the robot through a satellite link and Internet connections. *Dante II* moved very slowly, taking pictures and collecting scientific data. It was equipped with gas sensors that provided continuous readings of the crater gases. It performed the tasks human scientists could not, letting the humans keep their cool.

▲ *Dante II*

Mission Accomplished?

During its expedition, *Dante II* encountered large rocks, some of which were as big as the robot itself. In addition, while climbing out of the volcano, *Dante II* slipped and fell, damaging one of its legs. Eventually *Dante II* had to be rescued by helicopter because its support cable broke. Despite these obstacles, *Dante II* was able to gather valuable data from the volcano's crater.

Dante II's mission also met one of NASA's objectives: to prove that robots could be used successfully to explore extreme terrain, such as that found on planetary surfaces. *Dante II* paved the way for later robotic projects, such as the exploration of the surface of Mars by the *Sojourner* rover in 1997.

Write About It

▶ Write a proposal for a project in which a robot is used to explore a dangerous place. Don't forget to include what types of data the robot would be collecting.

ACROSS THE SCIENCES

EARTH SCIENCE • LIFE SCIENCE

Europa: Life on a Moon?

Smooth and brownish white, one of Jupiter's moons, Europa, has fascinated scientists and science-fiction writers for decades. More recently, scientists were excited by tantalizing images from the Galileo Europa Mission. Could it be that life is lurking (or sloshing) beneath Europa's surface?

An Active History

Slightly smaller than Earth's moon, Europa is the fourth largest of Jupiter's moons. It is unusual among other bodies in the solar system because of its extraordinarily smooth surface. The ridges and brownish channels that crisscross Europa's smooth surface may tell a unique story—the surface appears to be a slushy combination of ice and water. Some scientists think that the icy ridges and channels are ice floes left over from ancient volcanoes that erupted water! The water flowed over Europa's surface and froze, like lava flows and cools on Earth's surface.

A Slushy Situation

Scientists speculate that Europa's surface consists of thin tectonic plates of ice floating on a layer of slush or water. These plates, which would look like icy rafts floating in an ocean of slush, have been compared to giant glaciers floating in polar regions on Earth.

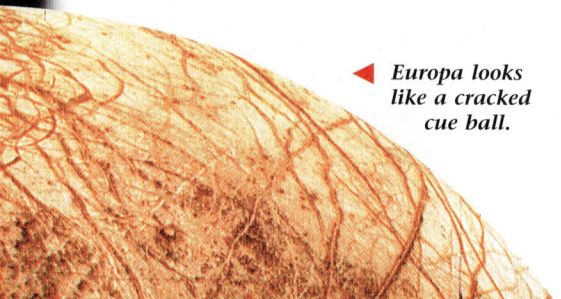

◀ Europa looks like a cracked cue ball.

Where plates push together, the material of the plates may crumple, forming an icy ridge. Where plates pull apart, warmer liquid mixed with darker silicates may erupt toward the surface and freeze, forming the brownish icy channels that create Europa's cracked cue-ball appearance.

Life on Europa?

These discoveries have led scientists to consider an exciting possibility: Does Europa have an environment that could support primitive life-forms? In general, at least three things are necessary for life as we know it to develop—water, organic compounds (substances that contain carbon), and heat. Europa has water, and organic compounds are fairly common in the solar system. But is it hot enough? Europa's slushy nature suggests a warm interior. One theory is that the warmth is the result of Jupiter's strong gravitational pull on Europa. Another theory is that warmth is brought to Europa's surface by convection heating.

So does Europa truly satisfy the three requirements for life? The answer is still unknown, but the sloshing beneath Europa's surface has sure heightened some scientists' curiosity!

If You Were in Charge . . .

▶ If you were in charge of NASA's space-exploration program, would you send a spacecraft to look for life on Europa? (Remember that this would cost millions of dollars and would mean sacrificing other important projects!) Explain your answer.

ACROSS THE SCIENCES
Europa: Life on a Moon?

Teaching Strategy

The latest information about Europa can be found at the NASA Web site. You could ask students to compare Europa with Callisto or Ganymede, which some scientists believe could also support life.

Answers to If You Were in Charge . . .

Accept all reasonable answers. Factors that students should consider are the tremendous costs associated with sending astronauts on long-term space travel. Even if the spaceship did not carry astronauts, the cost of sending a probe would be more than a hundred million dollars. To pay for a project of that nature, taxes would have to be raised or money would have to be taken from other government programs, such as health care, defense spending, environmental protection, or law enforcement.

UNIT 4

TIMELINE
Reshaping the Land

In this unit, you will learn about the way the surface of the Earth changes. There is a constant struggle between the forces that build up Earth's land features and those that break them down. The mountains built by Earth's internal forces are torn down by the actions of weathering and erosion. This timeline shows some of the events that have occurred in this struggle as natural changes in the Earth's features continue to take place.

320 Million years ago
Vast swamps along the western edge of the Appalachian Mountains are buried by sediment and form the largest coal fields in the world.

280 Million years ago
The shallow inland sea that covered much of what is now the midwestern United States fills with sediment and disappears.

1880
Cleopatra's Needle, a granite obelisk, is moved from Egypt to New York City. Within the next 100 years, the weather and pollution severely damage the 3,000-year-old monument.

1930
Carlsbad Caverns National Park is established. It features the nation's deepest limestone cave and one of the largest underground chambers in the world.

1941
Mount Rushmore is completed—an example of purposeful human erosion.

140 Million years ago
The mouth of the Mississippi River is near present-day Cairo, Illinois.

65 Million years ago
Dinosaurs become extinct.

6 Million years ago
The Colorado River begins to carve the Grand Canyon, which today is roughly 2 km deep.

12,000 Years ago
The Great Lakes form at the end of the last ice age.

1775
The Battle of Bunker Hill, a victory for the Colonials, takes place on a drumlin, a tear-shaped mound of sediment that was formed by an ice-age glacier 10,000 years earlier.

1987
An iceberg twice the size of Rhode Island breaks off the edge of Antarctica's continental glacier.

1998
Hong Kong opens a new airport on an artificial island. Almost 150 million metric tons of rock and soil were deposited in the South China Sea to form the 3,000-acre island.

Reshaping the Land 243

Chapter Organizer

CHAPTER ORGANIZATION	TIME MINUTES	OBJECTIVES	LABS, INVESTIGATIONS, AND DEMONSTRATIONS
Chapter Opener pp. 244–245	45	National Standards: UCP 2, SAI 1, SPSP 5, ES 2a	**Start-Up Activity** What's the Difference?, p. 245
Section 1 Weathering	45	▶ Describe how ice, rivers, tree roots, and animals cause mechanical weathering. ▶ Describe how water, acids, and air cause chemical weathering of rocks. SAI 1, ES 1c, 1k; LabBook UCP 2, SAI 1	**Making Models,** Rockin' Through Time, p. 669 **BASIC** **Datasheets for LabBook,** Rockin' Through Time, Datasheet 20 **BASIC** **Discovery Lab,** Great Ice Escape, p. 668 **GENERAL** **Datasheets for LabBook,** Great Ice Escape, Datasheet 19 **GENERAL** **QuickLab,** Acids React! p. 250 **GENERAL** **Whiz-Bang Demonstrations,** When It Rains, It Fizzes, Demo 22 **GENERAL**
Section 2 Rates of Weathering	90	▶ Explain how the composition of rock affects the rate of weathering. ▶ Describe how a rock's total surface area affects the rate at which it weathers. ▶ Describe how mechanical and chemical weathering work together to break down rocks and minerals. ▶ Describe how differences in elevation and climate affect the rate of weathering. SAI 1, ES 1c	**EcoLabs and Field Activities,** Whether It Weathers (or Not), EcoLab 11 **GENERAL**
Section 3 From Bedrock to Soil	90	▶ Define *soil*. ▶ Explain the difference between residual and transported soils. ▶ Describe the three soil horizons. ▶ Describe how various climates affect soil. ES 1e, 1k	
Section 4 Soil Conservation	90	▶ Describe three important benefits that soil provides. ▶ Describe three methods of preventing soil erosion. SPSP 2, 4, 5	**Long-Term Projects and Research Ideas,** Project 38 **ADVANCED**

*See page **T20** for a complete correlation of this book with the* **NATIONAL SCIENCE EDUCATION STANDARDS.**

TECHNOLOGY RESOURCES

 Guided Reading Audio CD English or Spanish, Chapter 10

 One-Stop Planner CD-ROM with Test Generator

 CNN. Eye on the Environment, Prairie Restoration, Segment 16

Science, Technology & Society, Homemade Dirt, Segment 16

Chapter 10 • Weathering and Soil Formation

Chapter 10 • Weathering and Soil Formation

CLASSROOM WORKSHEETS, TRANSPARENCIES, AND RESOURCES	SCIENCE INTEGRATION AND CONNECTIONS	REVIEW AND ASSESSMENT
Directed Reading Worksheet 10 `BASIC` **Science Puzzlers, Twisters & Teasers,** Worksheet 10 `ADVANCED`		
Directed Reading Worksheet 10, Section 1 `BASIC` **Transparency 259,** pH Values of Common Materials **Transparency 138,** Chemical Weathering **Reinforcement Worksheet 10,** Autobiography of a Rock `BASIC`	**Chemistry Connection,** p. 246 **Multicultural Connection,** p. 246 in ATE **Connect to Physical Science,** p. 247 in ATE `ADVANCED` **Connect to Life Science,** p. 248 in ATE **Connect to Physical Science,** p. 249 in ATE	**Self-Check,** p. 248 **Homework,** p. 248 in ATE `GENERAL` **Review,** p. 251 `GENERAL` **Quiz,** p. 251 in ATE `GENERAL` **Alternative Assessment,** p. 251 in ATE `GENERAL`
Directed Reading Worksheet 10, Section 2 `BASIC` **Transparency 139,** Weathering and Surface Area	**Connect to Physical Science,** p. 252 in ATE **MathBreak,** The Power of 2, p. 253 `GENERAL`	**Review,** p. 254 `GENERAL` **Quiz,** p. 254 in ATE `GENERAL` **Alternative Assessment,** p. 254 in ATE `GENERAL`
Directed Reading Worksheet 10, Section 3 `BASIC` **Transparency 140,** Soil Horizons	**Connect to Life Science,** p. 256 in ATE **Multicultural Connection,** p. 257 in ATE **Connect to Environmental Science,** p. 257 in ATE `BASIC` **Across the Sciences:** Worms of the Earth, p. 266 `ADVANCED`	**Homework,** p. 255 in ATE `GENERAL` **Review,** p. 258 `GENERAL` **Quiz,** p. 258 in ATE `GENERAL` **Alternative Assessment,** p. 258 in ATE `GENERAL`
Directed Reading Worksheet 10, Section 4 `BASIC` **Reinforcement Worksheet 10,** Where the Tall Corn Grows `BASIC` **Critical Thinking Worksheet 10,** Buying the Farm `ADVANCED`	**Connect to Life Science,** p. 259 in ATE **Multicultural Connection,** p. 260 in ATE **Math and More,** p. 261 in ATE `GENERAL` **Eye on the Environment:** Losing Ground, p. 267	**Homework,** p. 260 in ATE `ADVANCED` **Review,** p. 261 `GENERAL` **Quiz,** p. 261 in ATE `GENERAL` **Alternative Assessment,** p. 261 in ATE `GENERAL`

END-OF-CHAPTER REVIEW AND ASSESSMENT

Chapter Review in Study Guide
Vocabulary and Notes in Study Guide
Chapter Tests with Performance-Based Assessment, Chapter 10 Test
Chapter Tests with Performance-Based Assessment, Performance-Based Assessment 10
Concept Mapping Transparency 10

internetconnect

Holt, Rinehart and Winston On-line Resources
go.hrw.com
For worksheets and other teaching aids related to this chapter, visit the HRW Web site and type in the keyword: **HSTWSF**

National Science Teachers Association
www.scilinks.org
Encourage students to use the sciLINKS numbers listed in the internet connect boxes to access information and resources on the **NSTA** Web site.

Chapter Resources & Worksheets

Visual Resources

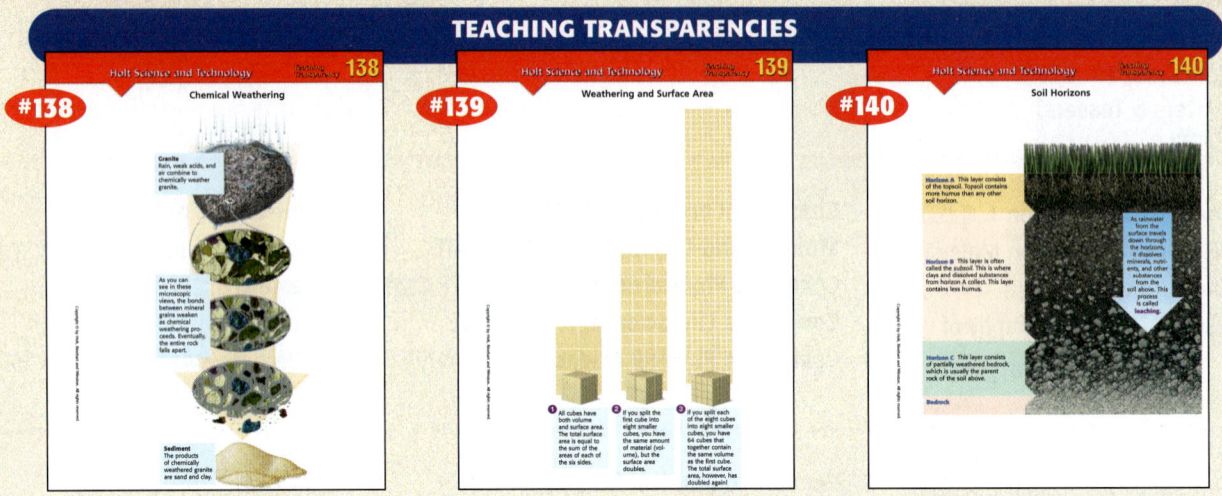

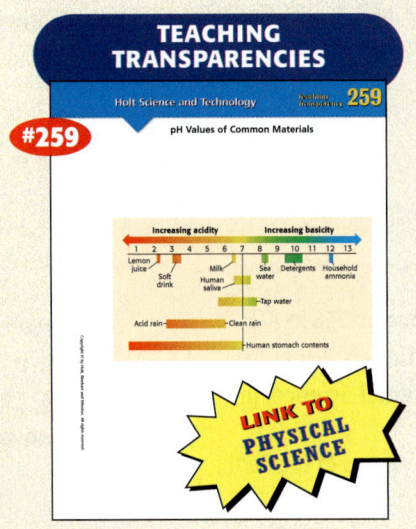

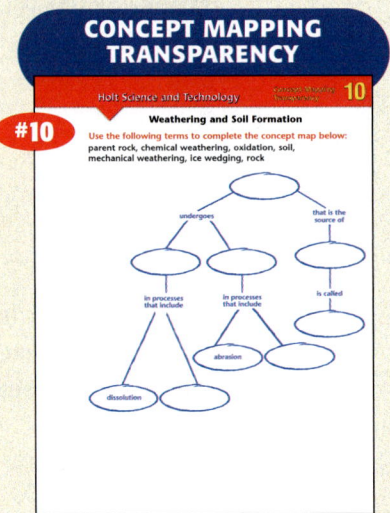

Meeting Individual Needs

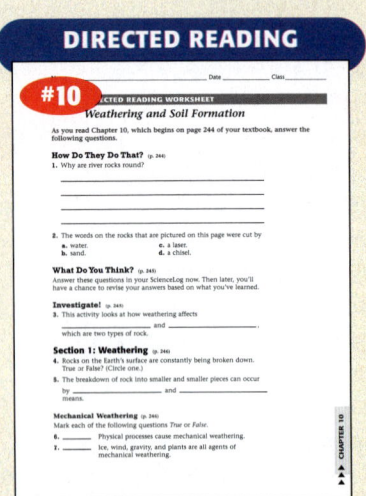

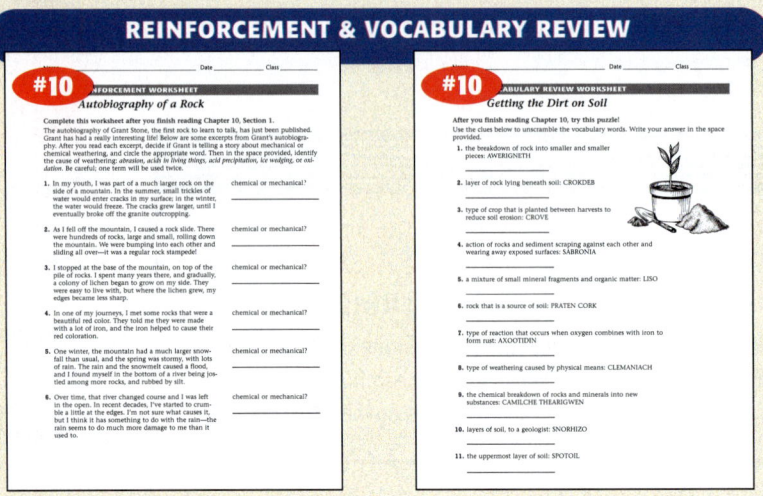

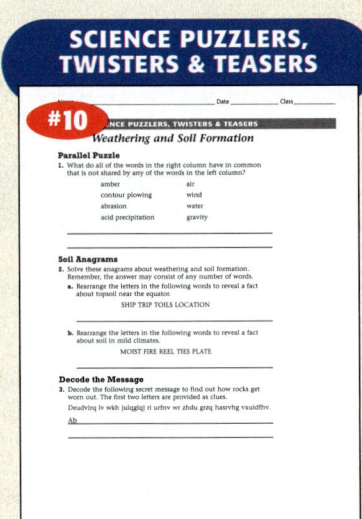

Chapter 10 • Weathering and Soil Formation

Chapter 10 • Weathering and Soil Formation

Review & Assessment

STUDY GUIDE

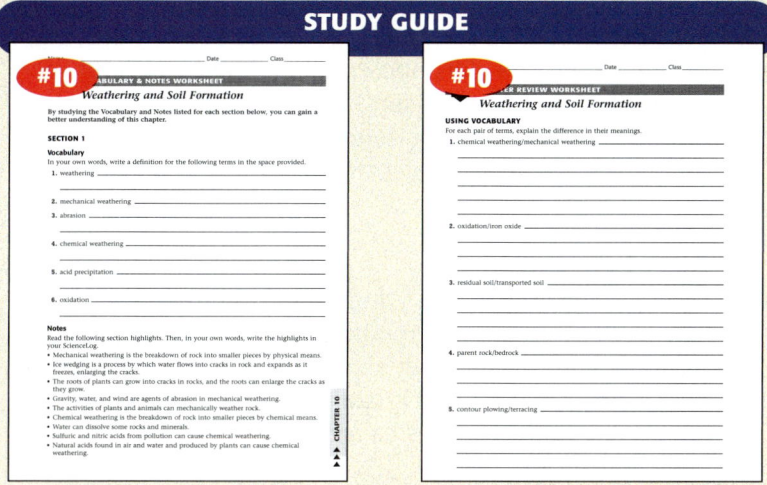

CHAPTER TESTS WITH PERFORMANCE-BASED ASSESSMENT

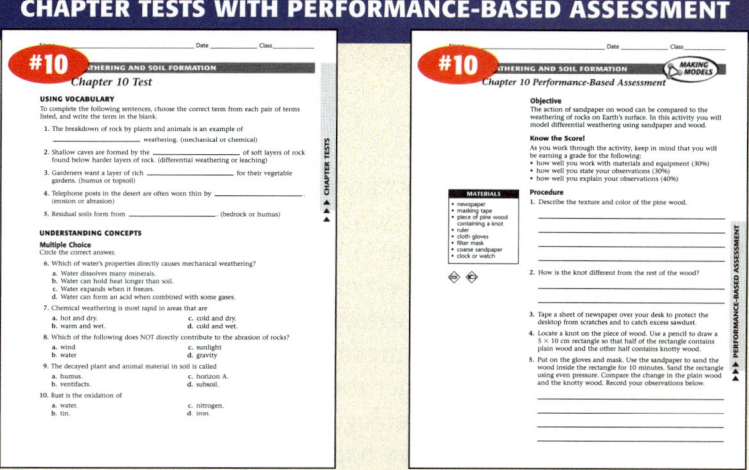

Lab Worksheets

WHIZ-BANG DEMONSTRATIONS

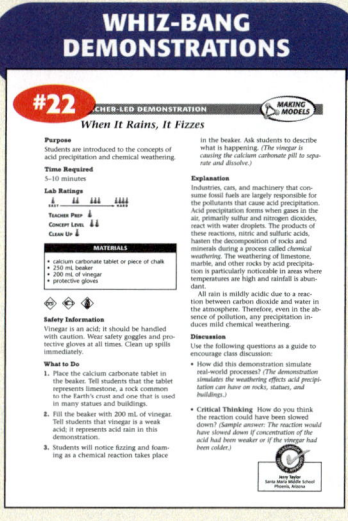

ECOLABS & FIELD ACTIVITIES

LONG-TERM PROJECTS & RESEARCH IDEAS

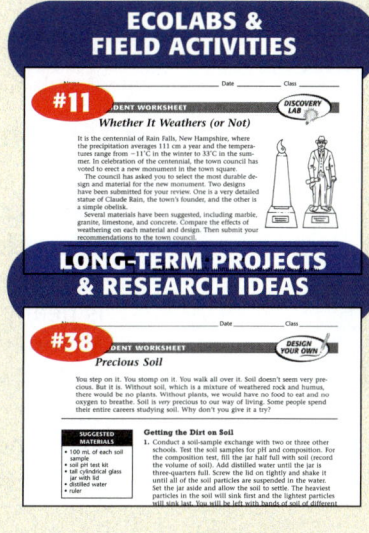

DATASHEETS FOR LABBOOK

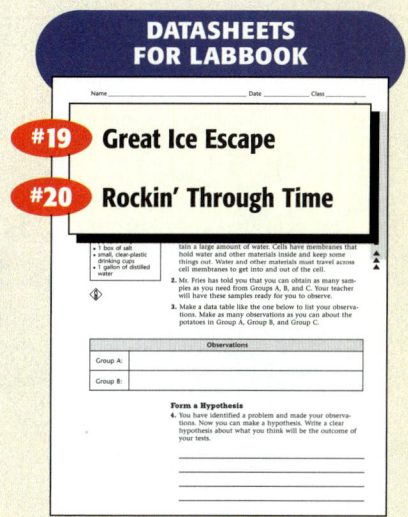

Applications & Extensions

CRITICAL THINKING & PROBLEM SOLVING

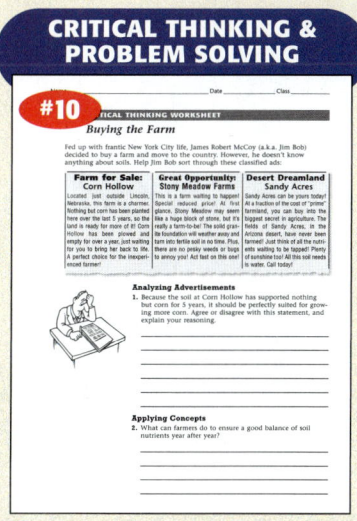

EYE ON THE ENVIRONMENT

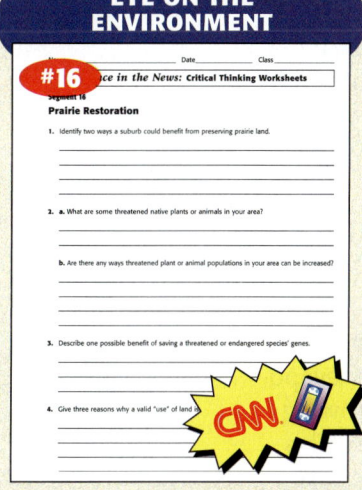

SCIENCE TECHNOLOGY

Chapter Background

SECTION 1

Weathering

▶ **Thermal Contraction and Expansion**
There is much scientific debate over whether the daily and seasonal heating and cooling of rocks causes widescale weathering. In desert environments, where temperature ranges can be extreme, small rocks can shatter from expansion and contraction. But does this type of weathering occur in larger rocks and in climates that are more temperate? Geologists attempting to replicate this process in a lab have had little success. In one experiment granite samples were repeatedly heated and cooled by more than 100°C, and no fracturing was observed. This suggests that if thermal expansion and contraction weathers rock, it may do so over the course of hundreds of thousands of years.

IS THAT A FACT!

◾ Before the invention of power drills and saws, stonemasons sometimes filled existing joints and cracks in rocks with water and waited for ice wedging to split the rocks. Obviously, this method was effective only in areas where temperatures dropped to freezing or below.

▶ **Salt Cracking**
In places where ground water contains dissolved salts, salt water seeps into bedrock. When the water evaporates, the dissolved salts crystallize, and the growing crystals can exert enough force to fracture rock. This process, known as salt cracking, can be seen at the ocean, where sea cliffs become pitted and cracked from salt deposits. In desert regions salt cracking erodes the base of some sandstone formations, leaving an unweathered rock balancing on an eroded pedestal.

▶ **Sandstorms**
During a sandstorm, the wind may blow more than 160 km/h. The friction created by moving sand grains not only abrades rock but also generates static electricity. Some people caught in sandstorms have experienced painful headaches caused by the buildup of static electricity.

SECTION 2

Rates of Weathering

▶ **Mineral Composition and Weathering Rates**
The order in which minerals crystallize from magma is nearly the same as the order in which they weather. Minerals that form quickly and at high temperatures and pressures within Earth tend to be unstable at the surface, and they are less resistant to chemical weathering. Minerals that form slowly and at lower temperatures are much more resistant to the effects of weathering.

Chapter 10 • Weathering and Soil Formation

SECTION 3

From Bedrock to Soil

▶ **Types of Soils in the United States**
The soils of the mainland United States can be divided into two major types—*pedocal* and *pedalfer*. Pedocal is a calcium-rich soil that covers most of the western United States. Pedocal gets its name from the Latin *ped*, meaning "soil," joined with *cal*, representing calcium. Pedalfer is an iron- and aluminum-rich soil that covers most of the eastern half of the country. The *al* in pedalfer stands for aluminum; the *fer* stands for ferrum (iron).

▶ **Salinization**
All ground water contains small concentrations of salts. If arid or semiarid soils are intensively irrigated, the soil can accumulate so much salt that it cannot support plant life. This process, called salinization, can ruin croplands. Some historical scholars argue that salinization contributed to the decline and fall of many ancient societies, including the Babylonian civilization.

IS THAT A FACT!

- *Regolith* is a term that describes all of the weathered material that lies over the bedrock. *Soil* refers to the upper layers of the regolith that can support plant life.

- The term *regolith* is derived from the Greek word *rhegos,* meaning "blanket," and the Old English *lithos* meaning "rock." This derivation is important because it denotes the protective qualities of soil. Like a blanket, the soil protects the rock below from weathering. In mountain regions where soil is easily eroded, bedrock weathers much more quickly.

SECTION 4

Soil Conservation

▶ **Farming in the Imperial Valley**
Although desert soils are low in organic matter, they are not necessarily poor soils. Desert soil such as that of the Imperial Valley in California is actually quite rich with the minerals needed for plant growth. Water diverted from the Colorado River is used to irrigate the valley, and it is now one of the nation's major farming regions, growing such crops as alfalfa, cotton, and sugar beets. While the Imperial Valley is incredibly productive, agriculture in the region relies heavily on the use of fertilizers. There is also much debate over whether the Imperial Valley diverts too much water from the Colorado River. In addition, people are concerned because irrigation has concentrated salts in the soil and polluted the nearby Salton Sea.

▶ **Federal Soil Conservation Service**
In response to the devastating windstorms that swept across the Great Plains, the U.S. Department of Agriculture formed the Soil Conservation Service in 1935. Working with ranchers and farmers, conservationists instituted such strategies as contour plowing and terracing, planting trees as windbreaks, allowing land to lie fallow, and planting drought-resistant crops.

IS THAT A FACT!

- In some places across the United States, soil conservation researchers have implemented an innovative approach to roadside erosion control. Organic wastes, which otherwise would be dumped in landfills, are spread along the sides of highways. The nutrient-rich wastes help grasses grow, and the grass roots anchor soil in place.

For background information about teaching strategies and issues, refer to the *Professional Reference for Teachers.*

Weathering and Soil Formation

 Pre-Reading Questions

Students may not know the answers to these questions before reading the chapter, so accept any reasonable response.

Suggested Answers

1. Answers will vary. Both wind and water cause the abrasion of rock surfaces. Students may also mention ice wedging or chemical weathering.
2. Answers will vary. Soil supports plant life and plants are the base of the food chain.
3. Answers will vary. Weathering breaks down rocks, contributing to the formation of soil.

 Directed Reading Worksheet 10

 Science Puzzlers, Twisters & Teasers Worksheet 10

 Guided Reading Audio CD English or Spanish, Chapter 10

Weathering and Soil Formation

Sections

1. Weathering 246
   Chemistry
   Connection 246
   QuickLab 250
   Internet Connect 251
2. Rates of Weathering .. 252
   MathBreak 253
   Internet Connect 254
3. From Bedrock
   to Soil 255
   Internet Connect 258
4. Soil Conservation 259
   Internet Connect 261

Chapter Review 264
Feature Articles 266, 267
LabBook 668–669

 **Pre-Reading Questions**

1. How do water and air cause rocks to crumble?
2. Why is soil one of our most important resources?
3. How are weathering and soil formation related?

NICE AND COZY

Badgers live throughout North America, Africa, Europe, Asia, and the Middle East. Although badgers are sometimes considered to be pests, they play an important ecological role. Badgers are known for their burrowing ability. They dig in the soil for food and build underground homes. As the badgers dig through the soil, they expose rock and soil to air and water. In this chapter, you will learn how animals like the badger and other natural processes contribute to weathering and soil formation.

---

internet connect

 **HRW On-line Resources**
go.hrw.com
For worksheets and other teaching aids, visit the HRW Web site and type in the keyword: **HSTWSF**

 **sciLINKS NSTA**
www.scilinks.com
Use the sciLINKS numbers at the end of each chapter for additional resources on the **NSTA** Web site.

 **CNNfyi.com**
www.cnnfyi.com
Visit the CNN Web site for current events coverage and classroom resources.

WHAT'S THE DIFFERENCE?

In this chapter, you will learn about the processes and rates of weathering. Do this activity to learn about how the size and surface area of a material affect how quickly the substance breaks down.

Procedure

1. Fill **two small containers** about half full with **water**.
2. Add **one sugar cube** to one container.
3. Add 1 tsp of **granulated sugar** to the other container.
4. Using **two different spoons,** stir the water and sugar in each container at the same rate.
5. Using a **stopwatch,** measure how long it takes for the sugar to dissolve in each container.

Analysis

6. Did the sugar dissolve at the same rate in both containers? Explain why or why not.
7. Which do you think would wear away faster—a large rock or a small rock? Explain your answer.

START-UP Activity

WHAT'S THE DIFFERENCE?

MATERIALS
For Each Group: • 2 small containers   • water   • sugar cube   • 1 tsp. granulated sugar   • 2 different spoons   • stopwatch or timepiece with second hand

Answers to START-UP Activity

6. The granulated sugar dissolved faster than the sugar cube because the grains of sugar had more surface area than the sugar cube. Therefore, more of the granulated sugar dissolved in a shorter period of time.

7. A small rock would wear away faster because it has more surface area for weathering to affect.

SECTION 1

Focus

Weathering

In this section, students will learn how mechanical processes such as ice wedging, abrasion, and plant and animal activities contribute to the weathering of rock. Students will also learn how water, acid precipitation, oxidation, and the growth of lichens cause chemical weathering of rock.

Bellringer

Ask students to think about how potholes form in paved roads. Have them write a few sentences in their ScienceLog that describe how water contributes to the formation of potholes. Students should illustrate how cycles of freezing and thawing cause potholes to grow. **Sheltered English**

1 Motivate

GROUP ACTIVITY

Have groups of students find photographs in magazines that illustrate weathering. Examples might include rusted cars, mailboxes or bikes; sidewalks or walls that have been cracked by plant roots; potholes; and weathered statues and buildings. Then have groups try to find photographs of rock formations that depict similar kinds of weathering. Ask the class to help you group the photographs into examples of physical weathering and chemical weathering.

 Directed Reading Worksheet 10 Section 1

Section 1

Terms to Learn

weathering
mechanical weathering
abrasion
chemical weathering
acid precipitation
oxidation

What You'll Do

◆ Describe how ice, rivers, tree roots, and animals cause mechanical weathering.
◆ Describe how water, acids, and air cause chemical weathering of rocks.

Chemistry CONNECTION

Almost all liquids contract when they freeze to form a solid—their volume decreases and their density increases. When these substances freeze, the frozen solid sinks. Just the opposite occurs to water when it freezes. Water expands and becomes less dense, which is why ice floats in water.

246

Multicultural CONNECTION

In the second century B.C., Buddhist monks began carving an intricate system of caves in a massive basalt flow in central India. The Ajanta caves comprised a complex of monasteries, temples, and living quarters. The caves were adorned with beautiful frescoes and carvings and then mysteriously abandoned in the seventh century. They were rediscovered by British game hunters less than 200 years ago. The Ajanta caves are notable not only for their artwork but also for the manner in which they were carved. The monks first cut channels in the rock and then jammed dry logs in the crevices. They poured water on top of the logs and waited for the expanding wood to shatter the rock. In this way, they carved 30 caves out of solid rock.

Weathering

Weathering is the breakdown of rock into smaller and smaller pieces. Rocks on Earth's surface are undergoing weathering all the time, either by mechanical means or by chemical means. You will learn the difference as you read on. You will also learn how these processes shape the surface of our planet.

Mechanical Weathering

If you were to crush one rock with another rock, you would be demonstrating one type of mechanical weathering. **Mechanical weathering** is simply the breakdown of rock into smaller pieces by physical means. Agents of mechanical weathering include ice, wind, water, gravity, plants, and even animals.

Ice As you know, water has the unusual property of expanding when it freezes. (This is just the opposite of most substances.) When water seeps into a crack in a rock during warm weather and then freezes during cold weather, it expands. And when it expands, it pushes against the sides of the crack, forcing it to open wider. This process is called *ice wedging*. **Figure 1** shows how ice wedging occurs over time.

Figure 1 The granite at right has been broken down by repeated ice wedging, as shown in the illustration below.

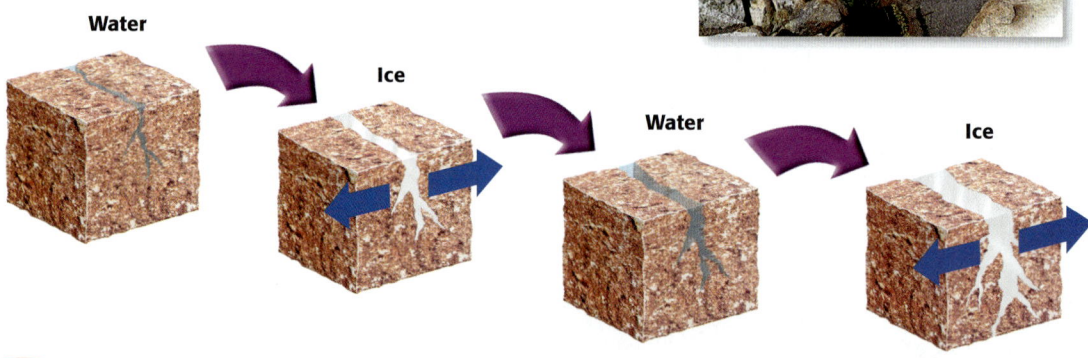

246 Chapter 10 • Weathering and Soil Formation

Wind, Water, and Gravity When you write on a chalkboard, a process called *abrasion* takes place. As you scrape the piece of chalk against the chalkboard, some of the chalk rubs off to make a line on the board. As particles of chalk are worn off, the piece of chalk wears down and becomes more rounded at the tip. The same thing happens to rocks. In nature, **abrasion** is the action of rocks and sediment grinding against each other and wearing away exposed surfaces.

Abrasion can happen in many ways. For example, when rocks and pebbles roll along the bottom of swiftly flowing rivers, they bump into and scrape against each other. They eventually become river rocks, as shown in **Figure 2**.

Wind also causes abrasion. For example, when wind blows sand against exposed rock, the sand eventually wears away the rock's surface. **Figure 3** shows what this kind of sandblasting can do.

Abrasion also occurs when rocks fall on one another. **Figure 4** shows a rock slide. You can imagine the forces rocks exert on each other as they tumble down a mountainside. In fact, any time one rock hits another, abrasion takes place.

You can make your own "river rocks" in just a few shakes. See page 669 in your LabBook.

Figure 2 *These river rocks are rounded because they have been tumbled in the riverbed by fast-moving water for many years.*

Figure 3 *This rock has been shaped by blowing sand. Such rocks are called* ventifacts.

Figure 4 *Rocks grind against each other in a rock slide, creating smaller and smaller rock fragments.*

2 Teach

LabBook PG 669
Rockin' Through Time

READING STRATEGY

Prediction Guide After students read the definition of *weathering* in the first paragraph of this section, have them decide whether the following statements are true or false:

- Very hard rocks do not weather. (false)
- Water can weather rock. (true)
- A snowflake can be acidic enough to weather rock. (true)
- Plants play an important role in weathering rock. (true)

CONNECT TO PHYSICAL SCIENCE

Another process of mechanical weathering is called *exfoliation*. Rocks generally form under great pressure. As the material overlying a rock formation is removed by erosion and tectonic activity, the pressure on the formation is reduced. As the pressure is reduced, the rock expands in volume, and long, curved cracks develop parallel to the rock's surface. In this way, an outcrop "sheds" layers of rock. Exfoliation can often be observed in granite outcrops. Ask students to describe why granite formations are prone to exfoliation. (Granite forms underground, so it forms under a great deal of pressure from the rock above. A granite pluton 15 km underground forms at 5,000 times the pressure at Earth's surface. As the granite is pushed toward the surface, and the overlying rock is weathered away, the pressure on the rock is reduced, and the granite exfoliates.)

IS THAT A FACT!

Mount Fuji is a dormant volcano that is a source of national pride among the Japanese. Unfortunately, the forces of mechanical weathering threaten to change the volcano's conical shape and near-perfect symmetry. To preserve the mountain's shape, the Japanese government has built a 17 m long concrete brace over a widening crevice near the mountain's summit. Before action was taken, as much as 300,000 tons of rock and soil had fallen down the mountainside every year.

Section 1 • Weathering

2 Teach, continued

LabBook PG 668
The Great Ice Escape

MISCONCEPTION ALERT

Students may be surprised to learn that animals such as earthworms, coyotes, and rabbits play significant roles in weathering rock. Point out that human activity also contributes to the weathering of rock and to the formation of soil. People move large amounts of soil and rock whenever they farm, build, or drive off-road vehicles. In addition, people blast through rock to make tunnels, roads, mines, and quarries. If you also consider the effect of air pollution on the weathering of rock, the effects of human activity become even more significant.

CONNECT TO LIFE SCIENCE

As ground-dwelling termites construct their homes, they excavate an enormous amount of soil and rock fragments. In some parts of the world, termites must burrow to great depths to mine the wet clay they need to build their mounds. Occasionally, the termites strike it rich. Geochemical prospectors have learned from indigenous cultures in Africa, Asia, Australia, and South America to analyze termite mounds for ore deposits such as tin, silver, gold, diamonds, and uranium. In some parts of Africa, gold concentrations in termite mounds are rich enough that people earn money by panning gold from them.

Figure 5 *Although they grow slowly, tree roots are strong enough to break solid rock.*

Plants You may not think of plants as being strong, but some plants can easily break rocks. Have you ever seen how tree roots can crack sidewalks and streets? Roots aren't fast, but they certainly are powerful! Plants often send their roots into existing cracks in rocks. As the plant gets bigger, the force of the expanding root becomes so strong that the crack is made larger. Eventually, the entire rock can split apart, as you can see in **Figure 5**.

Animals Believe it or not, earthworms cause a lot of weathering! They burrow through the soil and move soil particles around. This exposes fresh surfaces to continued weathering. Would you believe that some kinds of tropical worms move an estimated 100 metric tons of soil per acre every year? Almost any animal that burrows causes mechanical weathering. Ants, mice, coyotes, and rabbits all make their contribution. **Figure 6** shows some of these animals in action. The mixing and digging that animals do often contribute to another type of weathering, called *chemical weathering*. You will learn about this next.

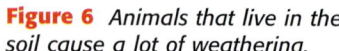

Self-Check

Describe the property of water that causes ice wedging. *(See page 726 to check your answer.)*

Figure 6 *Animals that live in the soil cause a lot of weathering.*

Answer to Self-Check
Water expands as it freezes. This expansion exerts a force great enough to crack rock.

Homework

Making Observations Ask students to keep a journal in which they note processes of weathering and soil formation in your area. Ask them to pay particular attention to plant and animal activity. Encourage students to write a short entry each day detailing their observations.

Chemical Weathering

If you place a drop of strong acid on a rock, it will probably "eat away" a small part of the rock. This is an example of chemical weathering. **Chemical weathering** is the chemical breakdown of rocks and minerals into new substances. The most common agents of chemical weathering are water, weak acids, air, and soil. **Figure 7** shows the chemical weathering of granite.

Water If you drop a sugar cube into a glass of water, it will dissolve after a few minutes. If you drop a piece of chalk into a glass of water, it will also dissolve, only much slower than a sugar cube. Both cases are examples of chemical weathering. Even hard rock, like granite, is broken down by water; it just may take a few thousand years.

Acid Precipitation A car battery contains sulfuric acid, a very dangerous acid that should never touch your skin. A weaker form of sulfuric acid can be found in nature. In fact, precipitation such as rain and snow is naturally acidic and contains carbonic acid. Small amounts of sulfuric and nitric acids from natural sources, such as volcanoes, can make precipitation even more acidic. These acids can slowly break down rocks and other matter.

Precipitation that contains acids due to air pollution is called **acid precipitation.** Acid precipitation contains more acid than normal precipitation, so it can cause very rapid weathering of rock. Even the bronze statue shown in **Figure 8** is being chemically weathered by acid precipitation.

Figure 8 *This statue is being damaged by acid precipitation.*

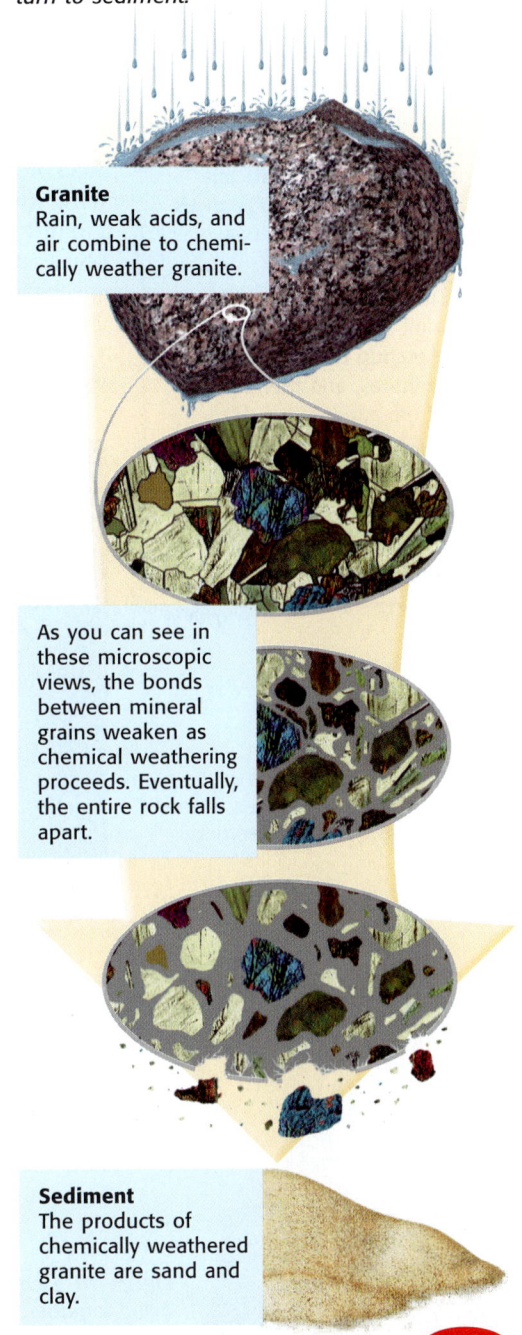

Figure 7 *After thousands of years of chemical weathering, even hard rock, like granite, can turn to sediment.*

Granite
Rain, weak acids, and air combine to chemically weather granite.

As you can see in these microscopic views, the bonds between mineral grains weaken as chemical weathering proceeds. Eventually, the entire rock falls apart.

Sediment
The products of chemically weathered granite are sand and clay.

IS THAT A FACT!

When carbon dioxide dissolves in water, it forms carbonic acid, making rainwater naturally acidic. When water is in equilibrium with atmospheric carbon dioxide, it has a pH of about 5.6. Rain, snow, sleet, or hail with a pH of less than 5.6 is considered acid precipitation.

Teaching Transparency 138
"Chemical Weathering"

Reinforcement Worksheet 10
"Autobiography of a Rock"

COOPERATIVE LEARNING

Have student groups focus on different aspects of acid precipitation, and have the class organize a task force presentation for your school or community.

- The **monitoring group** can test the pH of precipitation in your area by using a pH test kit. Students can also test the pH of tap water, surface runoff, rivers, and lakes. Have students contact the local weather service to find records of the pH of precipitation in your area over several decades. The monitoring group can present its findings in graphs and other visual displays.

- The **research group** can prepare a presentation on the causes and effects of acid precipitation. They should also focus on legislation and other solutions for the air pollution problems that contribute to acid precipitation.

CONNECT TO PHYSICAL SCIENCE

Students are often confused by the pH scale. The term *pH* is French and translates as "power of hydrogen." It refers to the concentration of hydronium ions in a solution. In a measurement of the pH of an acid, a decrease of one number on the pH scale represents an increase in the concentration of hydronium ions by a power of ten. Thus an acid with a pH of 2 is one hundred times as concentrated as an acid with a pH of 4. Remind students that acidic solutions have a pH less than 7, and that basic solutions have a pH greater than 7.

Teaching Transparency 259
"pH Values of Common Materials"

Section 1 • Weathering

3) Extend

QuickLab

Safety Caution: Students with allergies to tomatoes should use a cotton swab to apply the ketchup.

Answers to QuickLab

2. Answers will vary. Students might note that the grime reacted chemically with the acid in the ketchup and dissolved.

3. Answers will vary. Students should note that rocks react with acids in the same way that the grime reacted with the ketchup.

RETEACHING

To reinforce the difference between chemical and mechanical weathering, show students two matches. To demonstrate mechanical weathering, break one of the matches. To show chemical weathering, light the other match and let it burn. Next, have students decide whether each of the following phenomena is an example of mechanical or chemical weathering.

- a rockfall on a mountainside (mechanical)
- a rusty bridge (chemical)
- lichens and mosses growing on a boulder (chemical)
- an alpine glacier advancing down a valley (mechanical)
- a mole burrowing in the ground (mechanical)

Sheltered English

COOPERATIVE LEARNING

Have groups work together to write a five-question quiz about the material in Section 1. Have the groups exchange quizzes and work together to answer the questions.

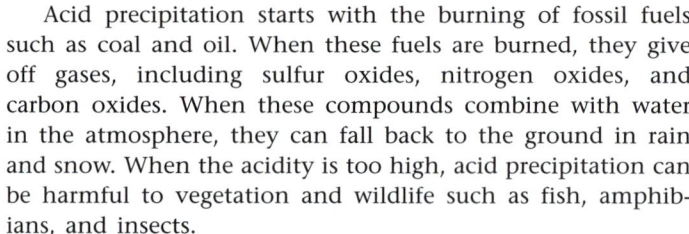

QuickLab

Acids React!

Have you ever heard someone refer to a certain food as being "acidic"? You consume acids in your food every day. For example, ketchup contains weak acids that can react with certain substances in a rather dramatic way. Try this:

1. Take a **penny** that has a dull appearance, rub **ketchup** on it for several minutes, and then rinse it off.
2. Where did all the grime go?
3. How is this similar to what happens to a rock when it is exposed to natural acids during weathering?

TRY at HOME

Figure 9 At right is one of the many rooms of Mammoth Cave, a limestone cave system in Kentucky.

Acid precipitation starts with the burning of fossil fuels such as coal and oil. When these fuels are burned, they give off gases, including sulfur oxides, nitrogen oxides, and carbon oxides. When these compounds combine with water in the atmosphere, they can fall back to the ground in rain and snow. When the acidity is too high, acid precipitation can be harmful to vegetation and wildlife such as fish, amphibians, and insects.

Acid in Ground Water In certain places ground water contains weak acids, such as carbonic or sulfuric acid. When this ground water comes in contact with limestone, the limestone breaks down. Over a long period of time, this can have some spectacular results. Enormous caverns, like the one shown in **Figure 9,** can form as the limestone is eaten away. Limestone, you may remember, is made of calcite, which reacts strongly with acid.

Acids in Living Things Another source of acids for weathering might surprise you. Take a look at **Figure 10.** Lichens produce organic acids that can slowly break down rock. If you have ever taken a walk in a park or forest, you have probably seen lichens growing on the sides of trees or rocks. Lichens can also grow in places where some of the hardiest plants cannot. Lichens can be found in deserts, in arctic areas, and in areas high above timberline, where even trees don't grow.

Figure 10 Lichens, which consist of fungi and algae living together, contribute to chemical weathering.

---

internetconnect

SCLINKS
NSTA

TOPIC: Weathering
GO TO: www.scilinks.org
sciLINKS NUMBER: HSTE230

Air The car shown in **Figure 11** is undergoing chemical weathering due to the air. The oxygen in the air is reacting with the iron in the car, causing the car to rust. Water speeds up the process, but the iron would rust even if no water were present. This process also happens in certain types of rocks, particularly those containing iron, as you can see in **Figure 12**. Scientists call this process *oxidation*.

Oxidation is a chemical reaction in which an element, such as iron, combines with oxygen to form an oxide. (The chemical name for rust is *iron oxide*.) Oxidation is a common type of chemical weathering, and rust is probably the most familiar result of oxidation.

Activity

Imagine that you are a tin can—shiny, new, and clean. But something happens, and you don't make it to a recycling bin. Instead, you are left outside at the mercy of the elements. In light of what you have learned about physical and chemical weathering, write a story about what happens to you over a long period of time. What is your ultimate fate?

TRY at HOME

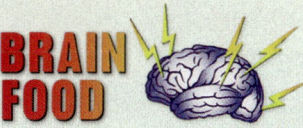

BRAIN FOOD

Studying rock strata for signs of the oxidation of ferric minerals is like reading the rings of a tree: geologists can determine the concentration of oxygen in Earth's atmosphere throughout geologic time. Until about 3 billion years ago, the concentration of oxygen in Earth's atmosphere was not significant enough to oxidize iron. After that time, sedimentary deposits show layers of oxidized and unoxidized iron, indicating that oxygen concentrations fluctuated. Rocks formed after 1.8 billion years ago are uniformly oxidized. What does this suggest? (that oxygen concentrations have not changed significantly since that time)

Figure 12 The red color of the rock at Capitol Reef National Park is due to the oxidation of iron.

Figure 11 Rust is a result of chemical weathering.

REVIEW

1. Describe three ways abrasion occurs in nature.
2. Describe the similarity between the ways tree roots and ice mechanically weather rock.
3. **Making Generalizations** Why does acid precipitation weather rocks faster than normal precipitation does?

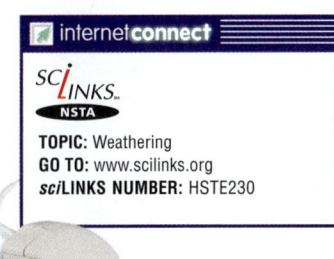

internet connect

SCILINKS
NSTA

TOPIC: Weathering
GO TO: www.scilinks.org
*sci*LINKS NUMBER: HSTE230

4) Close

Quiz

1. How do earthworms aid in weathering? (When earthworms burrow, they move soil particles around. This exposes fresh surfaces to weathering.)
2. What human activities can increase the acidity of precipitation? (any activities that burn fossil fuels, such as driving cars, heating homes, and producing electricity)

ALTERNATIVE ASSESSMENT

Have groups do research to come up with five multiple-choice trivia cards for a game that tests the player's knowledge of weathering. Students can use the cards in a class trivia challenge.

▼ **Answers to Review**

1. Answers will vary. Sample answer: Abrasion can occur when rocks scrape against each other in a landslide, when rocks are tumbled by the water in a river, or when rocks are "sandblasted" by small particles carried in the wind.
2. Both tree roots and ice enter cracks in rock and expand, making the cracks wider and shattering the rock.
3. Acid rain is more acidic than regular rain, so it reacts faster with the minerals in rocks.

Section 1 • Weathering

SECTION 2

Focus

Rates of Weathering

This section explores why different types of rock weather at different rates, and how the surface area of rock affects the rate at which it weathers. In addition, students learn why elevation and climate are important factors affecting weathering rates.

Bellringer

Ask students to imagine that they are in a sand-castle-building competition at the beach. Ask them to come up with a variety of ways to protect their castle against the weathering effects of the wind and waves. Students can illustrate their ideas and share them with the class.

1 Motivate

GROUP ACTIVITY

Supply each group with one clear glass containing a calcium antacid tablet and a second containing a tablet cut into quarters. Tell students that antacid tablets and limestone both contain calcium carbonate, which dissolves in acidic solutions. Ask students to pour enough vinegar into the glasses to cover the tablets. As students observe the reactions, ask them which of the tablets "weathers" more rapidly. Students can repeat the experiment with a crushed tablet. Lead students to conclude that surface area affects the rate at which things weather. Ask students if the crushed tablet released more gas than the whole tablet. **(No, the surface-area-to-volume ratio only affects the rate at which the reaction occurs.)**

Section 2

Terms to Learn
differential weathering

What You'll Do

- Explain how the composition of rock affects the rate of weathering.
- Describe how a rock's total surface area affects the rate at which it weathers.
- Describe how mechanical and chemical weathering work together to break down rocks and minerals.
- Describe how differences in elevation and climate affect the rate of weathering.

Rates of Weathering

Different types of rock weather at different rates. Some types of rock weather quickly, while other types weather slowly. The rate at which a rock weathers depends on many factors—climate, elevation, and, most important, what the rock is made of.

Differential Weathering

Hard rocks, such as granite, weather more slowly than softer rocks, such as limestone. This is because granite is made of minerals that are generally harder and more chemically stable than the minerals in limestone. **Differential weathering** is a process by which softer, less weather-resistant rocks wear away, leaving harder, more weather-resistant rocks behind.

Figure 13 shows a spectacular landform that has been shaped by differential weathering. Devils Tower, the core of an ancient volcano, was once a mass of molten rock deep within an active volcano. When the molten rock solidified, it was protected from weathering by the softer rock of the volcano. After thousands of years of weathering, the soft outer parts of the volcano have worn away, leaving the harder, more resistant rock of Devils Tower behind. Of course, not all landforms are this spectacular. But if you look closely, you can see the effects of differential weathering in almost any landscape.

Figure 13 *Devils Tower is a landform known as a* volcanic neck. *The illustration is an artist's conception of how the original volcano may have looked. The photo inset shows Devils Tower as it appears today.*

CONNECT TO PHYSICAL SCIENCE

Why is the intrusive volcanic rock that makes up Devils Tower more resistant to weathering than the extrusive volcanic rock of the former volcano? Both rock types had the same composition. The difference is their *cohesiveness*. The intrusive rock cooled more slowly than the extrusive rock. As the rock slowly cooled, it formed large crystals that interlocked like a 3-D jigsaw puzzle. This made the volcanic neck more resistant to weathering. In contrast, the rock that made up the outside of the volcano cooled quickly. It was made of much smaller crystals and *groundmass* material—material that cooled so fast it didn't form crystals. Have students draw a series of time-lapse illustrations to show the formation of the volcanic neck in **Figure 13**.

252   Chapter 10 • Weathering and Soil Formation

The Shape of Weathering

As you know, weathering takes place on the outside surface of rocks. So the more surface area that is exposed to weathering, the faster the rock will be worn down. A large rock has a large surface area, but it also has a large volume. Because of this, it will take a long time for a large rock to wear down.

If a big rock is broken into smaller rocks, weathering occurs much more quickly. This is because a smaller rock has more surface area relative to its volume. This means that more of a small rock is exposed to the weathering process. The cubes in **Figure 14** show how this principle works.

Figure 14 *As surface area increases, total volume stays the same. Each square in the background represents the face of a cube.*

① All cubes have both volume and surface area. The total surface area is equal to the sum of the areas of each of the six sides.

② If you split the first cube into eight smaller cubes, you have the same amount of material (volume), but the surface area doubles.

③ If you split each of the eight cubes into eight smaller cubes, you have 64 cubes that together contain the same volume as the first cube. The total surface area, however, has doubled again!

MATH BREAK

The Power of 2

You can calculate the surface area of a square or rectangle by multiplying its width times its length ($w \times l$). For example, one side of a cube that measures 5 cm by 5 cm has a surface area of 25 cm². Now you try:

What is the surface area of one side of a cube that is 8 cm wide and 8 cm long? What is the surface area of the entire cube? (Hint: A cube has six equal sides.)

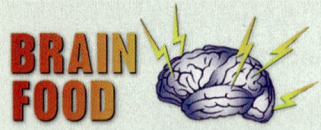

BRAIN FOOD

In 1881, Egypt gave the United States a granite obelisk known as Cleopatra's Needle. It was placed in New York City's Central Park. For almost 3,500 years, the obelisk had stood in the dry, hot climate of Egypt and showed few signs of weathering. After only 75 years in the humid, polluted air and temperature extremes of its new home, the hieroglyphics carved into the windward side of the obelisk were nearly weathered away.

3) Close

Quiz

1. Different types of rock weather at different rates, true or false? (true)
2. Chemical weathering has no effect on the rate of mechanical weathering, true or false? (false)
3. What factors contribute to accelerated weathering rates at high elevations? (wind, precipitation, and gravity)

ALTERNATIVE ASSESSMENT

Investigate Your Area A cemetery is a great place to observe the effects of differential weathering because several different kinds of rock are used to make headstones, and most of the headstones are dated. Schedule a field trip to a cemetery, or encourage interested students to visit a cemetery on their own. Have them compare the dates and types of stone used to determine which kinds of stone are most susceptible to weathering.

Weathering and Climate

Imagine that two people have the same kind of bicycle. The frames of both bikes are made of steel. One person lives in a hot, dry desert in New Mexico, and the other lives on the warm, humid coastline of Florida, as shown in **Figure 15.** Both bicycles are outside all the time. Which bike do you think will have more problems with rust?

If you think the Florida bike will have more rust problems, you are right! Rust is iron oxide, and oxidation occurs more quickly in warm, humid climates. This is true for bikes, rocks, or anything else that is affected by chemical weathering.

Figure 15 The climate in which this bike is located affects the rate at which it weathers, or rusts.

Weathering and Elevation

When a new mountain range forms, the rock is exposed to air and water. As a result, the mountain range gets slowly weathered down. Weathering occurs in the same way on mountains as it does everywhere else, but rocks at high elevations are exposed to more wind, rain, and ice than rocks at lower elevations.

Gravity also takes its toll. The steepness of mountain slopes strengthens the effects of mechanical and chemical weathering. Rainwater quickly runs off the sides of mountains, carrying sediment with it. This continual removal of sediment exposes fresh rock surfaces to the effects of weathering. When rocks fall away from the sides of mountains, new surfaces are exposed to weathering. As you have learned, the greater the surface area is, the faster weathering occurs. If new mountain ranges didn't keep forming, eventually there would be no mountains at all!

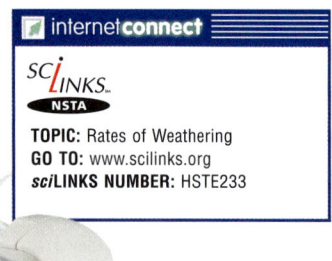

internetconnect

sciLINKS NSTA
TOPIC: Rates of Weathering
GO TO: www.scilinks.org
sciLINKS NUMBER: HSTE233

REVIEW

1. How does surface area affect the rate of weathering?
2. How does climate affect the rate of weathering?
3. **Making Inferences** Does the rate at which a rock undergoes chemical weathering increase or stay the same when the rock becomes more mechanically weathered? Why?

▼ Answers to Review

1. Increasing the surface area of a rock increases the rate at which it weathers.
2. Answers will vary. In hot, dry climates, weathering happens more slowly than in hot, humid climates. This is because the presence of water increases the rate of weathering. Temperature extremes also accelerate weathering rates.
3. Mechanical weathering breaks down rock into smaller pieces, which increases its surface area. This exposes more surface area to the effects of chemical weathering.

From Bedrock to Soil

Terms to Learn
soil
bedrock
parent rock
humus
topsoil
leaching

What You'll Do
- Define *soil*.
- Explain the difference between residual and transported soils.
- Describe the three soil horizons.
- Describe how various climates affect soil.

What is soil? The answer depends on who you ask. A farmer may have a different answer than an engineer. To a scientist, **soil** is a loose mixture of small mineral fragments and organic material. The layer of rock beneath soil is called **bedrock**.

Sources of Soil

Not all soils are the same. In fact, soils differ from one another in many ways. Because soils are made from weathered rock fragments, the type of soil that forms depends on the type of rock that weathers. For example, the soil that forms from granite will be different from the soil that forms from limestone. The rock that is the source of soil is called **parent rock**.

Figure 16 shows a layer of soil over bedrock. In this case, the bedrock is the parent rock because the soil above it formed from the bedrock below. Soil that remains above the bedrock from which it formed is called *residual soil*. Notice the trees growing in this soil. Plants and other organisms, plus chemical weathering from water, help break down the parent rock into soil.

After soil forms, it can be blown or washed away from its parent rock. Once the soil is deposited, it is called *transported soil*. **Figure 17** shows one way that soil is transported from one place to another. The movement of glaciers is also responsible for deposits of transported soil.

Living Things Also Add to Soil In addition to bits of rock, soils also contain very small particles of decayed plant and animal material called **humus** (HYU muhs). In other words, humus is the organic part of the soil. Humus contains nutrients necessary for plant growth. In general, soil that contains as much as 20–30 percent humus is considered to be very healthy soil for growing plants.

Figure 16 *Residual soil is soil that rests on top of its parent rock.*

Figure 17 *Transported soil may be moved long distances from its parent rock by rivers such as this one.*

2) Teach

GROUP ACTIVITY

MATERIALS

FOR EACH GROUP:
- soil samples (including potting soil)
- resealable plastic bags
- sterile spatula and tongs
- several pieces of bread (without preservatives)

Along with bacteria, fungi are the major decomposers of organic material in soil. Soil fungi excrete enzymes that break down organic matter into simpler substances that they can absorb. This process plays a crucial role in the circulation of nutrients at Earth's surface.

Have groups bring in several varieties of soil, such as clay, loam, and silt. To prevent contamination, emphasize that all materials should be handled with sterilized instruments. Have students put 20–30 drops of distilled water on each of the bread slices. Using the spatula, students should then sprinkle a small portion of each soil sample onto a piece of bread, one sample per piece of bread. Next, students should use the tongs to place each piece of bread in a separate, labeled plastic bag. One piece of bread with no soil should be used as a control. Place the bags in a dark box or drawer. After 5–7 days, students can use a stereomicroscope or a compound microscope to analyze the mold grown from each sample. Have students sketch what they observe and draw conclusions about the concentrations of organic materials and fungi in each sample.

Teaching Transparency 140
"Soil Horizons"

Soil Layers

As you've already learned, much of the material in residual soil comes from the bedrock that lies below it. Because of the way it forms, soil often ends up in a series of layers, with humus-rich soil on top, sediment below that, and bedrock on the bottom. Geologists call these layers *horizons*. The word *horizon* tells you that the layers are horizontal. **Figure 18** shows what these horizons can look like. You can see these layers in some road cuts.

The top layer of soil is often called the **topsoil**. Topsoil contains more humus than the layers below it, so it is rich in the nutrients plants need in order to be healthy. This is why good topsoil is necessary for farming. Topsoil is in limited supply because it can take hundreds and even thousands of years to form.

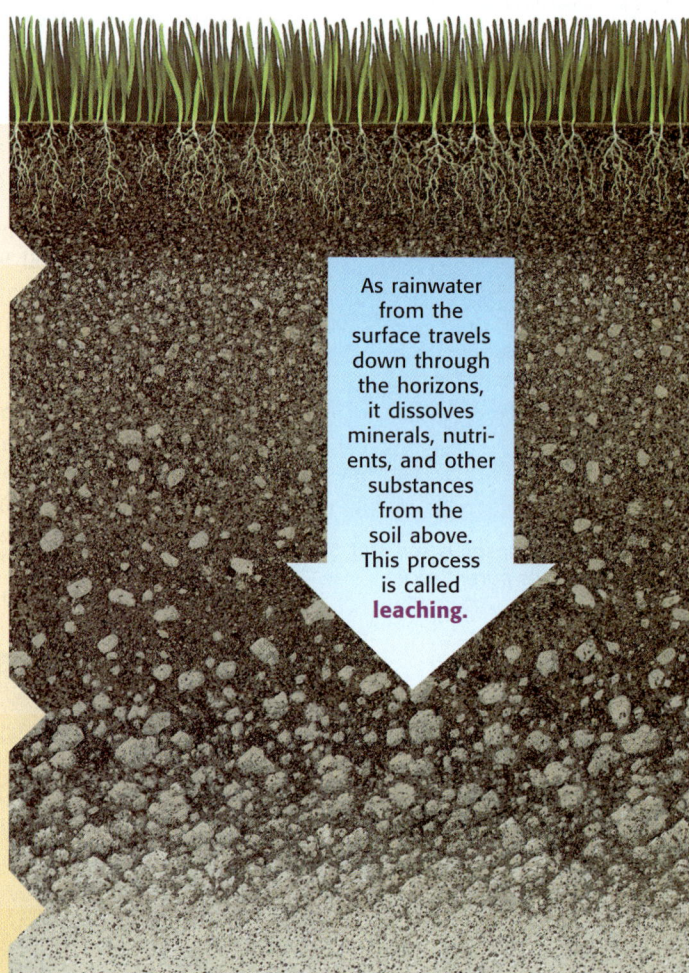

Figure 18 This is what the layers of soil might look like if you dug a hole down to bedrock.

Horizon A This layer consists of the topsoil. Topsoil contains more humus than any other soil horizon.

Horizon B This layer is often called the *subsoil*. This is where clays and dissolved substances from horizon A collect. This layer contains less humus.

Horizon C This layer consists of partially weathered bedrock, which is usually the parent rock of the soil above.

Bedrock

As rainwater from the surface travels down through the horizons, it dissolves minerals, nutrients, and other substances from the soil above. This process is called **leaching**.

CONNECT TO LIFE SCIENCE

Students may be surprised to learn that soil is a thriving ecosystem. In 1 m³ of soil, there may be 10 million roundworms and 50,000 small insects and mites. In a single gram of fertile soil, there may be 50,000 algae, 400,000 fungi, and 2.5 million bacteria. Have students construct a Berlese funnel to collect small organisms from soil.

IS THAT A FACT!

Where do soda cans and airplanes come from? The soil of course! The process of soil leaching produces concentrated bauxite deposits in a thin layer at Earth's surface. Bauxite is the ore that is refined to produce aluminum.

Soil and Climate

Soil types vary from place to place. As you know, this is partly due to differences in parent rocks. But it is also due to differences in climate. As you read on, you will see that climate can make big differences in the types of soil that develop around the world.

Tropical Climates Take a look at **Figure 19.** In tropical climates the air is very humid and the land receives a large amount of rain. You might think that a lot of rain always leads to good soil for growing plants. But remember that as water moves through the soil, it leaches material from the topsoil downward. Heavy rains cause this downward movement to occur quickly and constantly. The result is that tropical topsoil is very thin.

The vegetation growing in the topsoil keeps heavy rains from eroding it away. The vegetation, in turn, depends on the thin topsoil because the subsoil will not support lush plant growth. Agricultural and mining practices that disrupt this fragile balance can expose the topsoil to erosion. Once the topsoil is gone, the original plants will not return, and the production of topsoil will stop.

Figure 19 The soil in tropical rain forests supports some of the lushest vegetation on Earth. However, tropical topsoil is extremely thin.

Desert Climates While tropical climates get lots of rain, deserts get very little. Because of the lack of rain, deserts have very low rates of chemical weathering. When ground water trickles in from surrounding areas, some of it seeps upward. But as soon as the water gets close to the surface, it evaporates. This means that any materials that were dissolved in the water get left behind in the soil.

Often the chemicals left behind are various types of salts. The salts can sometimes get so concentrated that the soil becomes toxic, even to desert plants! This is one of the reasons for Death Valley's name. **Figure 20** shows the floor of Death Valley, in California.

Figure 20 Very few plants can survive the harsh conditions of desert soils.

BRAIN FOOD

In some desert areas, a special type of soil called cryptogamic soil is actually alive! This soil is composed of different species of mosses, lichens, fungi, and algae. Cryptogamic soil is sometimes known as "brown sugar soil" because it is dark brown and crusty. The spongy soil absorbs moisture readily, and when disturbed by freezing, it uplifts and cracks. The cracks are important to desert ecosystems because plant seeds get lodged in the cracks, and the moisture allows them to germinate. Cryptogamic soils are continually disrupted by cycles of freezing and thawing, but they can be severely damaged if they are walked on. Ask students to find out why walking on cryptogamic soil could damage it.

Multicultural CONNECTION

The Lacandon Maya of Mexico have developed sustainable farming methods that do not destroy the fragile soil of the tropical rain forest. On a small piece of land they grow both food crops and tree crops, a practice known as agroforestry. After a few years, they let the farmland recover by allowing it to become a forest again. The Lacandon Maya's approach to farming is recognized for its ecological soundness and has been replicated in many countries. This approach only works when a population has a lot of land area to spare so that some can lie fallow. Have students research sustainable farming techniques and create a model or poster to share with the class.

CONNECT TO ENVIRONMENTAL SCIENCE

Some windswept deserts have very little surface soil because wind has carried off most of the smaller particles. This leaves an exposed layer of pebbles and gravel too heavy to be moved by the wind. This layer, called desert pavement, may take hundreds of years to form, but once established, it protects the desert from further erosion. Desert pavement is easily destroyed by off-road vehicles. Ask students to write a persuasive essay arguing that such sensitive desert areas should or should not be off limits to vehicles.

3) Extend

GOING FURTHER

Have student groups collect two soil samples from the same area, one from the surface and one from 16–20 cm down. Groups should fill two test tubes about one-quarter full with each soil sample and add water until the tubes are three-quarters full. Have students gently shake the covered tubes for several minutes. Place the test tubes in a rack and leave them overnight. Students should be able to observe the different compositions of layers that formed in the two test tubes. Soil components will settle according to weight; humus will be on top. The surface soil will probably contain noticeably more humus than the below-surface soil. Students might also notice a separation by grain size, with larger grains on the bottom.

4) Close

Quiz

1. The source of mineral fragments in soil is called the (parent rock).
2. The organic part of soil is called (humus).
3. What practices threaten the topsoil in tropical biomes? (agriculture and mining)

ALTERNATIVE ASSESSMENT

 Have students imagine that they are on a world trip during which they travel to every climate mentioned in the section. Tell them to write a series of postcards in which they describe what the soil is like in each climate. The picture on each card should be a magazine photograph that illustrates the soil in that climate.

Figure 21 *The rich soils in areas with a temperate climate support a vast farming industry.*

Figure 22 *Arctic soils, such as the soil along Denali Highway, in Alaska, cannot support lush growth.*

Temperate Climates Much of the continental United States has a temperate climate. An abundance of both mechanical and chemical weathering occurs in temperate climates. Temperate areas get enough rain to cause a high level of chemical weathering, but not so much that the nutrients are leached out. As a result, thick, fertile soils develop, as you can see in **Figure 21**.

Temperate soils are some of the most productive soils in the world. In fact, the midwestern part of the United States has earned the nickname "breadbasket" for the many crops the region's soil supports.

Arctic Climates You might not think that cold arctic climates are at all like desert climates. But many arctic areas have so little precipitation that they are actually cold deserts. As in the hot deserts, chemical weathering occurs very slowly, which means that soil formation also occurs slowly. This is why soil in arctic areas tends to be thin and is unable to support many plants, as shown in **Figure 22**.

internet connect

SC_iLINKS NSTA
TOPIC: Soil and Climate
GO TO: www.scilinks.org
*sci*LINKS NUMBER: HSTE235

REVIEW

1. What is the difference between residual and transported soils?
2. Which layer of soil is the most important for growing crops? Explain.
3. **Identifying Relationships** In which type of climate would leaching be more common—tropical or desert? Explain.

▼ Answers to Review

1. Residual soils form from the weathering of the parent rock beneath them; transported soils form in one place and are carried by wind or water to another place.
2. The topsoil (horizon A) is most important for growing crops because it contains the organic materials that crops need to grow.
3. Leaching would be more common in a tropical climate because more water passes through the soil.

Section 4

Terms to Learn

soil conservation
erosion

What You'll Do

◆ Describe three important benefits that soil provides.
◆ Describe three methods of preventing soil erosion.

Soil Conservation

If we do not take care of our soils, we can ruin them or even lose them altogether. Many people assume that if you simply plow a field and bury some seeds, plants will grow. They also assume that if you grew a crop last year, you can grow it again next year. These ideas might seem reasonable at first, but farmers and others involved with agriculture know better. Soil is a resource that must be conserved. **Soil conservation** consists of the various methods by which humans take care of the soil. Let's take a look at why soil is so important and worth conserving.

The Importance of Soil

Consider some of the benefits of soil. Soil provides minerals and other nutrients for plants. If the soil loses these nutrients, then plants will not be able to grow. Take a look at the plants shown in **Figure 23.** The plants on the bottom look unhealthy because they are not getting enough nutrients. Even though there is enough soil to support their roots, the soil is not providing them with the food they need. The plants on the top are healthy because the soil they live in is rich in nutrients.

Poor agricultural practices often cause rich soils to lose their nutrients. It is important to have healthy soil in order to have healthy plants. All animals get their energy from plants, either directly or indirectly.

Housing Soil also provides a place for animals to live. Earthworms, grubs, spiders, moles, and prairie dogs all live in soil. If the soil disappears, so do the homes of these animals. These animals are also important to the soil and to plant growth because they help break down plant and animal matter to make humus.

Figure 23 Both photos above show the same crop. But the soil in the bottom photo is depleted of its nutrients.

CONNECT TO LIFE SCIENCE

Loam refers to a type of soil that, depending on the amount of humus, is best for plant growth. Because loam contains an ideal balance of different-size particles (sand, silt, and clay), the soil can retain the air and water essential for plant growth. Soils that are sandy have poor water-retention properties because the soil particles have too much space between them. Claylike soils lack air spaces and may be impervious to water. Have students research and report on some of the ways that plants have adapted to live in inhospitable soils.

SECTION 4

Focus

Soil Conservation

This section discusses the fundamental importance of soil to all forms of life. Students learn that soil provides nutrients for plants to grow and stores ground water. They then explore some methods to prevent nutrient loss and erosion in topsoil.

🔔 Bellringer

Tell students that soil has been called "the bridge between life and the inanimate world." Then share Franklin D. Roosevelt's quote: "The nation that destroys its soil destroys itself." Have students write a ScienceLog entry that explores the meaning of both quotes.

1) Motivate

DISCUSSION

Students may think that all soils are merely dirt. Soils have different characteristics, depending on their composition. Engineers study soil types when planning roads and buildings. Different types of soils require different engineering considerations. For example, soils high in clay swell with rainfall and contract when they dry. The expanding and contracting can cause shifting and cracking in roadbeds and building foundations. If possible, arrange for a county extension agent, a soil conservationist, a geologist, or an engineer to speak with the class about the importance of understanding soil types.

 **Directed Reading Worksheet 10** Section 4

Section 4 • Soil Conservation   **259**

② Teach

ACTIVITY

Obtain three 4-in. flowerpots. Fill one with gravel, one with clay, and one with potting soil. Place them on a plank of wood over a sink. Have three students slowly pour 500 mL of water into each pot simultaneously. Ask students to note which pot retains the most water. Explain that the gravel started to leak first because the spaces between gravel are too large to hold the water. The potting soil has much smaller spaces, where water can be stored. The clay has very small spaces and will not allow water to pass through. Have students then explain in writing which material they would choose for the following activities:

- lining the foundation of a house so it drains quickly (gravel)
- sowing grass seed (potting soil)
- lining the bottom of an artificial pond so that it doesn't leak (clay)

Multicultural CONNECTION

By the early twentieth century, a century of cotton cultivation in the southern United States had so depleted the soil of nutrients that the area faced an agricultural crisis. An African-American scientist named George Washington Carver convinced farmers to plant peanuts and soybeans instead of cotton. Carver knew that these crops would restore a key nutrient—nitrogen—to the soil. The soil recovered, and Carver's work helped revitalize the agricultural economy of the South. Encourage students to learn more about the life and contributions of this remarkable scientist.

Figure 24 When it rains, soil helps to store water that can later be used by plants and animals. When soil is removed or covered over, rainwater drains away.

Storage Another benefit of soil is that it holds water, as shown in **Figure 24.** You might think of reservoirs, lakes, or even large tanks as places where water is stored. But soil is also extremely important in storing water. When water cannot sink into the ground, it quickly flows off somewhere else. Now that we have looked at the importance of soil, let's look at some ways we can maintain soil.

Figure 25 Some of the topsoil that was once in this field has eroded, and the subsoil that remains is less able to support plant growth.

Preventing Soil Erosion

Erosion is the process by which wind and water transport soil and sediment from one location to another. When soil is left unprotected, it is subject to erosion. **Figure 25** shows a field that has been stripped of part of its topsoil because no plants were growing in it. So while plants need soil to grow, plants are needed to keep topsoil from being eroded by wind and water. Soil conservation practices, like those discussed on the next page, help ensure that the soil is preserved for generations to come.

Homework

Indigenous Agriculture The ancient Maya of Central America used specialized agricultural techniques to maximize their corn crops. Because the Maya lived in a tropical area with karst topography, most of the soil naturally eroded into sinkholes or depressions. The Maya intensively planted in these locations. The soil above a sinkhole is ideal because it has the richest topsoil, and all surface water drains into the depressions. Have interested students find out more about the agricultural innovations of other indigenous cultures. Students may be surprised to learn that some of these techniques are still being used today.

Cover Crops Farmers can plant cover crops to prevent soil erosion. A *cover crop* is a crop that is planted between harvests to reduce soil erosion and to replace certain nutrients in the soil. Soybeans and clover are common cover crops.

Crop Rotation Fertile soil is soil that is rich in the nutrients that come from humus. If you grow the same crop year after year in the same field, certain nutrients become depleted. To slow this process down, crops can be changed from year to year. This practice, called *crop rotation*, is a common way to keep soils nutrient-rich.

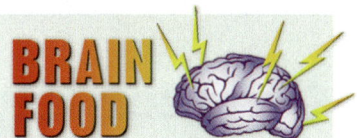

BRAIN FOOD

Nearly 4 billion metric tons of soil are washed or blown away from the United States every year. Worldwide, more than 70 billion metric tons of soil are lost each year to soil erosion!

Contour Plowing and Terracing How would you decide which direction to plow the rows in a field? If farmers plowed rows so that they ran up and down hills, what might happen during the first heavy rain? Hundreds of little river valleys would channel the rainwater down the hill, eroding the soil.

Take a look at the left-hand photo in **Figure 26**. Notice how the farmer has plowed across the slope of the hills instead of up and down the hills. This is called *contour plowing,* and it makes the rows act like a series of little dams instead of a series of little rivers. What if the hills are really steep? Farmers can use *terracing*, shown in the right-hand photo, to change one steep field into a series of smaller flat fields.

Figure 26 *Contour plowing and terracing are effective methods of preventing soil erosion.*

REVIEW

1. Describe three essential benefits that soil provides.
2. How does crop rotation benefit soil?
3. List three methods of soil conservation, and describe how each helps to prevent the loss of soil.
4. **Applying Concepts** Why do all animals, even meat eaters, depend on soil to survive?

internetconnect

SC_{LINKS} NSTA
TOPIC: Soil Conservation
GO TO: www.scilinks.org
sciLINKS NUMBER: HSTE240

Chapter Highlights

VOCABULARY DEFINITIONS

SECTION 1

weathering the breakdown of rock into smaller and smaller pieces by mechanical or chemical means

mechanical weathering the breakdown of rock into smaller pieces by physical means

abrasion the grinding and wearing down of rock surfaces by other rock or sand particles

chemical weathering the chemical breakdown of rocks and minerals into new substances

acid precipitation precipitation that contains acids due to air pollution

oxidation a chemical reaction in which an element combines with oxygen to form an oxide

Chapter Highlights

SECTION 1

Vocabulary
- weathering (p. 246)
- mechanical weathering (p. 246)
- abrasion (p. 247)
- chemical weathering (p. 249)
- acid precipitation (p. 249)
- oxidation (p. 251)

Section Notes
- Mechanical weathering is the breakdown of rock into smaller pieces by physical means.
- Ice wedging is a process by which water flows into cracks in rock and expands as it freezes, enlarging the cracks.
- The roots of plants can grow into cracks in rocks, and the roots can enlarge the cracks as they grow.
- Gravity, water, and wind are agents of abrasion in mechanical weathering.
- The activities of plants and animals can mechanically weather rock.
- Chemical weathering is the breakdown of rock into smaller pieces by chemical means.
- Water can dissolve some rocks and minerals.
- Sulfuric and nitric acids from pollution can cause chemical weathering.
- Natural acids found in air and water and produced by plants can cause chemical weathering.
- Oxidation can cause chemical weathering when oxygen combines with iron and other metallic elements.

Labs
Great Ice Escape (p. 668)
Rockin' Through Time (p. 669)

✓ Skills Check

Math Concepts

A CUBE'S TOTAL SURFACE AREA A cube has six sides—each is an identical square. To find the total surface area of a cube, first find the area of one of its sides. Then multiply the area of the square by 6 to find the total surface area of the cube. What is the total surface area of a cube that is 10 cm wide and 10 cm tall?

Area of a square = $l \times w$
Area of a cube = $6\,(l \times w)$

10 cm $\times$ 10 cm = 100 cm^2
6 $\times$ 100 cm^2 = 600 cm^2

Visual Understanding

DIFFERENTIAL WEATHERING When a volcano becomes extinct, molten rock solidifies beneath the surface, forming harder, more weather-resistant rock than the sides of the volcano are made of. Shown in Figure 13, Devils Tower is a dramatic example of differential weathering at work.

Lab and Activity Highlights

Great Ice Escape PG 668

Rockin' Through Time PG 669

 Datasheets for LabBook
(blackline masters for these labs)

262   Chapter 10 • Weathering and Soil Formation

SECTION 2

Vocabulary
differential weathering (p. 252)

Section Notes
- The rate at which weathering occurs depends partly on the composition of the rock being weathered.
- The greater the surface area of a rock is, the faster the rate of weathering.
- Different climates promote different rates of weathering.
- Weathering usually occurs at a faster rate at higher elevations.

SECTION 3

Vocabulary
soil (p. 255)
bedrock (p. 255)
parent rock (p. 255)
humus (p. 255)
topsoil (p. 256)
leaching (p. 256)

Section Notes
- Soil is made up of loose, weathered material that can include organic material called humus.
- Residual soils rest on top of their parent rock, and transported soils collect in areas far from their parent rock.
- Soil usually consists of horizons, layers that are different from one another.
- Soil types vary, depending on the climate in which they form.

SECTION 4

Vocabulary
soil conservation (p. 259)
erosion (p. 260)

Section Notes
- Soils are important because they provide nutrients for plants, homes for animals, and storage for water.
- Soils need to be protected from nutrient depletion and erosion through the use of soil conservation methods.

VOCABULARY DEFINITIONS, continued

SECTION 2

differential weathering the process by which softer, less weather-resistant rocks wear away, leaving harder, more weather-resistant rocks

SECTION 3

soil a loose mixture of small mineral fragments and organic material

bedrock the layer of rock beneath soil

parent rock rock that is the source of soil

humus very small particles of decayed plant and animal material in soil

topsoil the top layer of soil that generally contains humus

leaching the process by which rainwater dissolves and carries away the minerals and nutrients in topsoil

SECTION 4

soil conservation the various methods by which humans take care of the soil

erosion the removal and transport of material by wind, water, or ice

 Blackline masters of these Chapter Highlights can be found in the **Study Guide.**

internet connect

 **GO TO:** go.hrw.com

Visit the **HRW** Web site for a variety of learning tools related to this chapter. Just type in the keyword:

KEYWORD: HSTWSF

 **GO TO:** www.scilinks.org

Visit the **National Science Teachers Association** on-line Web site for Internet resources related to this chapter. Just type in the sciLINKS number for more information about the topic:

TOPIC: Weathering   sciLINKS NUMBER: HSTE230
TOPIC: Rates of Weathering   sciLINKS NUMBER: HSTE233
TOPIC: Soil and Climate   sciLINKS NUMBER: HSTE235
TOPIC: Soil Conservation   sciLINKS NUMBER: HSTE240
TOPIC: Soil Types   sciLINKS NUMBER: HSTE245

263

Lab and Activity Highlights

LabBank

 Whiz-Bang Demonstrations
When It Rains, It Fizzes, Demo 22

 Long-Term Projects & Research Ideas,
Precious Soil, Project 38

EcoLabs and Field Activities,
Whether It Weathers (or Not), EcoLab 11

Chapter Review Answers

USING VOCABULARY

1. The chemical breakdown of rocks and minerals into new substances is called chemical weathering. Mechanical weathering is the physical breakdown of rocks and minerals; it does not result in new substances.
2. Oxidation is a chemical reaction that occurs when an element combines with oxygen. Rust, or iron oxide, is the result of one type of oxidation.
3. Residual soil is the soil that remains directly above the parent rock it came from. When the residual soil is carried by wind, water, or ice and deposited in another place, it is called transported soil.
4. Any rock layer directly beneath the soil is called bedrock. The rock that is the source of the soil is called the parent rock.
5. Contour plowing is a soil conservation technique in which a farmer plows across the slope of a hill rather than up and down it. Terracing is a technique in which the slope of a steep hill is divided into smaller flat fields that resemble stair steps.

UNDERSTANDING CONCEPTS

Multiple Choice

6. b   11. c
7. c   12. c
8. a   13. b
9. d   14. c
10. a   15. c

Short Answer

16. Mechanical weathering is the physical process of breaking down rock and minerals into smaller and smaller pieces. Chemical weathering is a chemical reaction that breaks down rock and minerals by changing them into different substances.
17. Caves usually form in limestone. This is because limestone reacts with the acid found in ground water.

264 Chapter 10 • Weathering and Soil Formation

Chapter Review

USING VOCABULARY

For each pair of terms, explain the difference in their meanings.

1. chemical weathering/mechanical weathering
2. oxidation/iron oxide
3. residual soil/transported soil
4. parent rock/bedrock
5. contour plowing/terracing

UNDERSTANDING CONCEPTS

Multiple Choice

6. Weathering by abrasion is usually caused by
   a. animals, plants, and wind.
   b. wind, water, and gravity.
   c. ice wedging, animals, and water.
   d. plants, gravity, and ice wedging.

7. Two acids found in acid precipitation are
   a. hydrochloric acid and sulfuric acid.
   b. nitric acid and hydrochloric acid.
   c. sulfuric acid and nitric acid.

8. Rust is produced by the oxidation of
   a. iron.   c. aluminum.
   b. tin.   d. manganese.

9. An acid normally involved in the formation of caves is
   a. nitric acid.
   b. hydrofluoric acid.
   c. hydrochloric acid.
   d. carbonic acid.

10. The soil horizon that contains humus is
    a. horizon A.   c. horizon C.
    b. horizon B.

11. The soil horizon that is made up of partially broken bedrock is
    a. horizon A.   c. horizon C.
    b. horizon B.

12. Tropical soils have the
    a. thickest horizon B.
    b. thickest horizon A.
    c. thinnest horizon A.
    d. thinnest horizon B.

13. The humus found in soils comes from
    a. parent rock. c. bedrock.
    b. plants and animals. d. horizon B.

14. Contour plowing means plowing
    a. up and down the slope of a hill.
    b. in steps along a hill.
    c. across the slope of a hill.
    d. in circles.

15. The main reason farmers use crop rotation is to slow down the process of
    a. soil removal by wind.
    b. soil removal by water.
    c. nutrient depletion.
    d. soil compaction.

Short Answer

16. Describe the two major types of weathering.
17. In what type of rock do caves usually form?

264

Concept Mapping Transparency 10

Blackline masters of this Chapter Review can be found in the **Study Guide.**

18. Why is Devils Tower higher than the surrounding area?
19. What can happen to soil when soil conservation is not practiced?

Concept Mapping

20. Use the following terms to create a concept map: weathering, chemical weathering, mechanical weathering, abrasion, ice wedging, oxidation, soil.

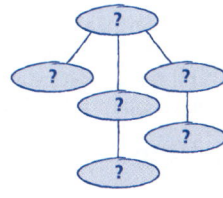

CRITICAL THINKING AND PROBLEM SOLVING

Write one or two sentences to answer the following questions:

21. Heat generally speeds up chemical reactions. But weathering, including chemical weathering, is usually slowest in hot, dry climates. Why is this?
22. How can too much rain deplete soil of its nutrients?
23. How does mechanical weathering speed up the effects of chemical weathering?

MATH IN SCIENCE

24. Imagine you are a geologist working in your natural laboratory—a mountainside. You are trying to find out the speed at which ice wedging occurs. You measure several cycles of freezing and thawing in a crack in a boulder. You discover that the crack gets deeper by about 1 mm per year. The boulder is 25 cm tall. Given this rate, how long will it take for ice wedging to split this boulder in half?

INTERPRETING GRAPHICS

The graph below shows how the density of water changes when temperature changes. The denser a substance is, the less volume it occupies. In other words, as most substances get colder, they contract and become more dense. But water is unlike most other substances—when it freezes, it expands and becomes less dense.

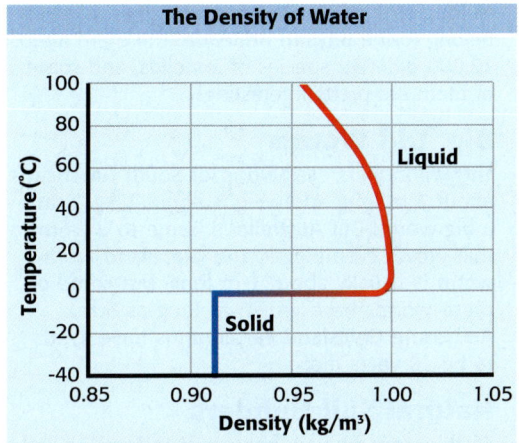

25. Which will have the greater density, water at 40°C or water at −20°C?
26. How would the line in the graph look different if water behaved like most other liquids?
27. Which substance would be a more effective agent of mechanical weathering, water or some other liquid? Why?

Take a minute to review your answers to the Pre-Reading Questions found at the bottom of page 244. Have your answers changed? If necessary, revise your answers based on what you have learned since you began this chapter.

---

18. The rock that makes up Devils Tower is more resistant to weathering than the surrounding rock.
19. If soil conservation is not practiced, soil can be depleted of nutrients or eroded and transported away.

Concept Mapping

20. 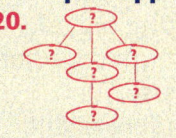 An answer to this exercise can be found at the end of this book.

CRITICAL THINKING AND PROBLEM SOLVING

21. Hot, dry climates generally have less precipitation than more temperate climates. Moisture enables chemical weathering to occur more quickly. The lack of moisture inhibits all processes of mechanical weathering except abrasion.
22. As water passes through soil, it carries the soil's nutrients with it. This process is called leaching.
23. Mechanical weathering increases the surface area of rock, thus exposing more of the rock to the effects of chemical weathering.

MATH IN SCIENCE

24. 1 cm = 10 mm
    25 cm = 250 mm
    250 mm/1 mm per year = 250 years

INTERPRETING GRAPHICS

25. water at 40°C
26. The line would slope downward from left to right.
27. Water is more effective than other liquids because it expands when it freezes.

ACROSS THE SCIENCES
Worms of the Earth

Background
Students may be interested in researching the use of earthworms for composting organic wastes. Earthworms will consume yard and garden waste, food waste, and even cardboard and paper. Their castings can be harvested and used to provide organic fertilizer for yards or gardens. There are numerous Internet sites with detailed information on this topic.

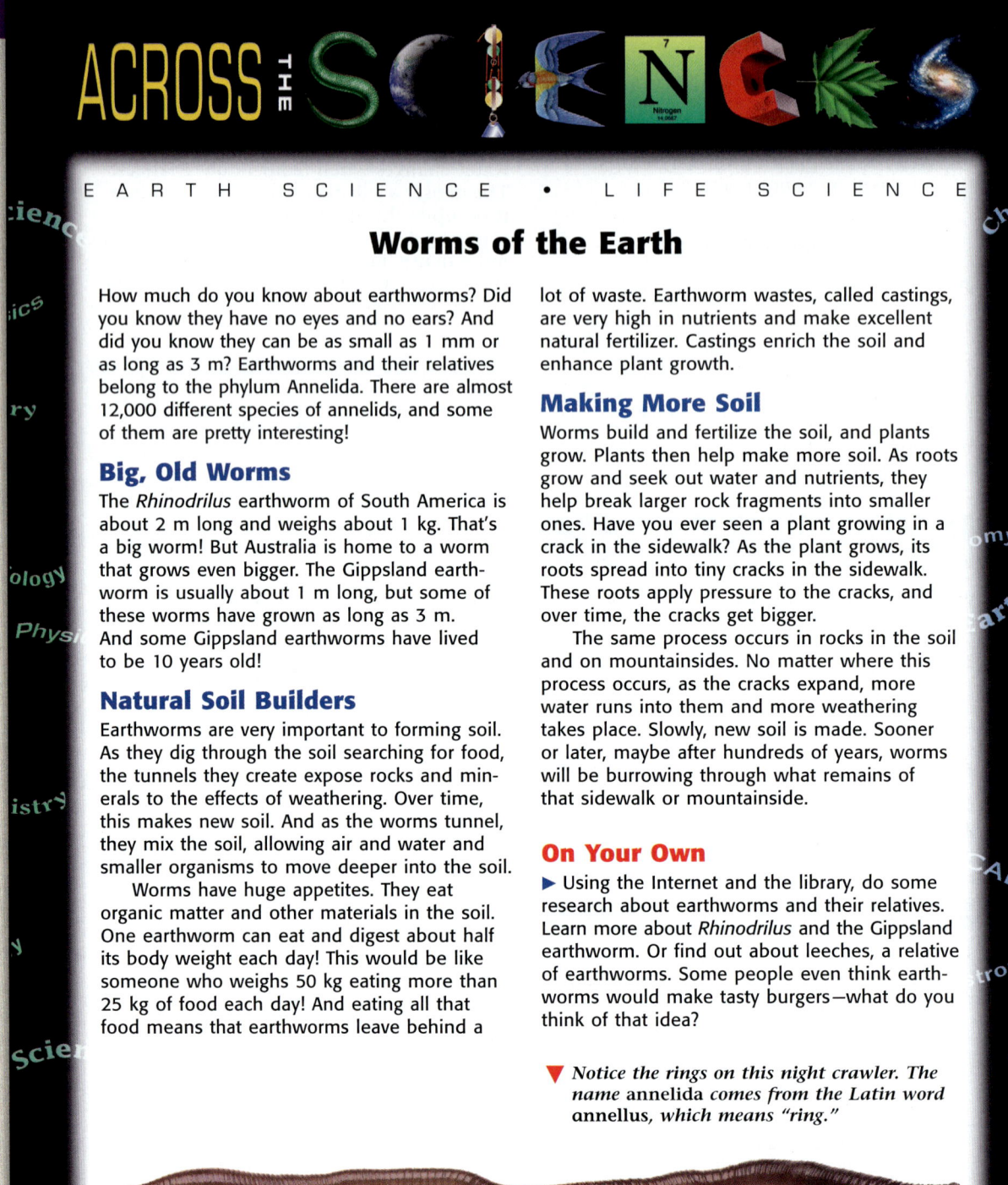

EARTH SCIENCE • LIFE SCIENCE

Worms of the Earth

How much do you know about earthworms? Did you know they have no eyes and no ears? And did you know they can be as small as 1 mm or as long as 3 m? Earthworms and their relatives belong to the phylum Annelida. There are almost 12,000 different species of annelids, and some of them are pretty interesting!

Big, Old Worms
The *Rhinodrilus* earthworm of South America is about 2 m long and weighs about 1 kg. That's a big worm! But Australia is home to a worm that grows even bigger. The Gippsland earthworm is usually about 1 m long, but some of these worms have grown as long as 3 m. And some Gippsland earthworms have lived to be 10 years old!

Natural Soil Builders
Earthworms are very important to forming soil. As they dig through the soil searching for food, the tunnels they create expose rocks and minerals to the effects of weathering. Over time, this makes new soil. And as the worms tunnel, they mix the soil, allowing air and water and smaller organisms to move deeper into the soil.

Worms have huge appetites. They eat organic matter and other materials in the soil. One earthworm can eat and digest about half its body weight each day! This would be like someone who weighs 50 kg eating more than 25 kg of food each day! And eating all that food means that earthworms leave behind a lot of waste. Earthworm wastes, called castings, are very high in nutrients and make excellent natural fertilizer. Castings enrich the soil and enhance plant growth.

Making More Soil
Worms build and fertilize the soil, and plants grow. Plants then help make more soil. As roots grow and seek out water and nutrients, they help break larger rock fragments into smaller ones. Have you ever seen a plant growing in a crack in the sidewalk? As the plant grows, its roots spread into tiny cracks in the sidewalk. These roots apply pressure to the cracks, and over time, the cracks get bigger.

The same process occurs in rocks in the soil and on mountainsides. No matter where this process occurs, as the cracks expand, more water runs into them and more weathering takes place. Slowly, new soil is made. Sooner or later, maybe after hundreds of years, worms will be burrowing through what remains of that sidewalk or mountainside.

On Your Own
▶ Using the Internet and the library, do some research about earthworms and their relatives. Learn more about *Rhinodrilus* and the Gippsland earthworm. Or find out about leeches, a relative of earthworms. Some people even think earthworms would make tasty burgers—what do you think of that idea?

▼ *Notice the rings on this night crawler. The name* annelida *comes from the Latin word* annellus, *which means "ring."*

Answer to On Your Own
Gippsland earthworms are found in southeastern Australia. They live in clay soils found near rivers. People claim that a gurgling sound can be heard as the worms move down in their tunnels. *Rhinodrilus* is the largest land-dwelling segmented worm in the world. This South American earthworm is 2.5 cm thick, nearly 2 m long, and can weigh 1 kg. Parasitic leeches, which are related to earthworms, consume the blood of mammals and other vertebrates. Most land-dwelling parasitic leeches position themselves on low-growing plants and wait for suitable hosts to pass by. Some leeches sense body heat to find their prey. Other leeches climb trees to seek out mammals and birds. One South African species feeds on sea snails. These leeches not only kill the snails but liquefy them and suck up their flesh. Most leeches are compassionate parasites: leech saliva contains an antiseptic and a local anesthetic.

EYE ON THE ENVIRONMENT

Losing Ground

▲ *In this example of sustainable farming, a new crop of soybeans grows up through the decaying remains of a corn crop.*

In the 1930s, massive dust storms in Oklahoma, Texas, Colorado, and New Mexico blew away the precious topsoil of many farms. Overplowing and a lack of rain caused this catastrophe—the Dust Bowl—that wreaked havoc on people's lives for 6 years. In the last 40 years, almost one-third of the world's topsoil has been lost to erosion. At the same time, the world's population has grown by 250,000 people per day. With more people to feed and less land to farm, some people are worried about having enough food to feed everyone.

Adding to the Problem

The topsoil on farmland is exposed to the full force of the weather. There are no trees to protect the loosely packed topsoil in a recently plowed field. Because of wind and water erosion, one hectare of farmland can lose more than 100,000 kg of soil in a year. Compare this loss to the mere 10–50 kg of soil lost in an average year by a forest densely packed with trees.

Tipping the Scales

In a healthy ecosystem, topsoil lost through erosion is replaced by other natural processes. These include the decomposition of organic matter by microorganisms and the breakdown of rocks by weathering. When a balance exists between the soil that is lost and the new soil that forms, the rate of topsoil loss is called sustainable. Currently, about 90 percent of the cropland in the United States is losing topsoil at a faster rate than is sustainable.

Sustainable Farming

The good news is that by changing their farming practices, many farmers have reduced the amount of soil lost from their fields. The critical step is to leave some plants growing in the ground. This protects the soil from the direct effects of wind and rain.

Many farmers have already switched to methods of sustainable farming. As the world's population continues to increase, more food will be needed. Because of this, preserving the topsoil that we have left will become more and more important.

On Your Own

▶ Find out what is meant by the term *desertification*. How does it relate to topsoil erosion?

EYE ON THE ENVIRONMENT

Losing Ground

Background

The Sahel region of northern Africa offers an excellent example of desertification. In the past, people in the drier part of the Sahel grazed animals, while those in the wetter part planted crops. The grazing animals were herded from place to place to find fresh grass and leaves. The cropland was planted only 4 or 5 years at a time, and then was allowed to lie fallow for several years. These methods allowed the land to support the people.

Today, population growth has led to overuse of the land. Several crops a year may be planted on the same land, and fallow periods are shortened or eliminated, causing the soil to lose its fertility. More and more animals are put out to graze. Trees and shrubs are cut for use as fuel or animal feed until few plants are left to hold the soil in place or to trap any rain that falls. The topsoil in the Sahel is carried away by wind and rain, and the land is becoming a desert.

Answer to On Your Own

The official definition for desertification (established at the 1992 Earth Summit) is "the land degradation in arid, semi-arid, and dry semi-humid areas resulting from various factors, including climate variations and human activities." One of the primary causes of desertification is overgrazing by animals. Today, fences prevent not only domestic animals but also wild animals from migrating to find food. Other causes of desertification are agricultural cultivation on marginal lands, the destruction of vegetation in semi-arid land, and poor irrigation practices. Desertification accelerates topsoil erosion because the land loses plant cover, exposing more soil to erosion.

Chapter Organizer

CHAPTER ORGANIZATION	TIME MINUTES	OBJECTIVES	LABS, INVESTIGATIONS, AND DEMONSTRATIONS
Chapter Opener pp. 268–269	45	National Standards: SAI 1	**Start-Up Activity** Stream Weavers, p. 269
Section 1 The Active River	90	▶ Illustrate the water cycle. ▶ Describe a drainage basin. ▶ Explain the major factors that affect the rate of stream erosion. ▶ Identify the stages of river development. UCP 1, 5, SAI 1, ES 1c, 1f, 1g, 2a; LabBook UCP 2, SAI 1, ES 1f	**Demonstration,** p. 271 in ATE **GENERAL** **Making Models,** Water Cycle–What Goes Up . . . , p. 546 **GENERAL** **Datasheets for LabBook,** Water Cycle–What Goes Up . . . , Datasheet 21 **GENERAL**
Section 2 Stream and River Deposits	90	▶ Describe the different types of stream deposits. ▶ Explain the relationship between rich agricultural regions and river flood plains. SPSP 3, 4, ES 1c	**Demonstration,** Modeling Deposition, p. 277 in ATE **BASIC**
Section 3 Water Underground	90	▶ Identify and describe the location of a water table. ▶ Describe the characteristics of an aquifer. ▶ Explain how caves and sinkholes form as a result of erosion and deposition. SAI 1, SPSP 2, ES 1c, 1f, 1g	**Demonstration,** p. 280 in ATE **GENERAL** **QuickLab,** Degree of Permeability, p. 281 **GENERAL**
Section 4 Using Water Wisely	90	▶ Describe the stages of treatment for water at a sewage treatment plant. ▶ Compare a septic system with a sewage treatment plant. ▶ Explain how ground water can be both a renewable and a nonrenewable resource. SAI 1, SPSP 1, 2, 5, ES 1c; LabBook UCP 2, 3, ST 2, SAI 1, SPSP 5	**Interactive Explorations CD-ROM,** Flood Bank **GENERAL** A **Worksheet** is also available in the **Interactive Explorations Teacher's Edition.** **Discovery Lab,** Clean Up Your Act, p. 672 **GENERAL** **Datasheets for LabBook,** Clean Up Your Act, Datasheet 22 **GENERAL** **EcoLabs & Field Activities,** The Frogs Are Off Course, Field Activity 12 **ADVANCED** **Long-Term Projects & Research Ideas,** Project 39 **ADVANCED**

See page T20 for a complete correlation of this book with the **NATIONAL SCIENCE EDUCATION STANDARDS.**

TECHNOLOGY RESOURCES

 Guided Reading Audio CD English or Spanish, Chapter 11

 One-Stop Planner CD-ROM with Test Generator

 Interactive Explorations CD-ROM CD 1, Exploration 8, Flood Bank

 CNN Science, Technology & Society, Tapping into Yellowstone's Hot Springs, Segment 1
Eye on the Environment, Watch for Flooding, Segment 9
China's Superdam, Segment 10

Chapter 11 • The Flow of Fresh Water

CLASSROOM WORKSHEETS, TRANSPARENCIES, AND RESOURCES	SCIENCE INTEGRATION AND CONNECTIONS	REVIEW AND ASSESSMENT
Directed Reading Worksheet 11 `BASIC` **Science Puzzlers, Twisters & Teasers,** Worksheet 11 `ADVANCED`		**Homework,** p. 269 in ATE
Math Skills for Science Worksheet 6, Checking Division with Multiplication `GENERAL` **Transparency 141,** The Water Cycle **Directed Reading Worksheet 11,** Section 1 `BASIC` **Transparency 75,** River Features	**Real-World Connection,** p. 272 in ATE **MathBreak,** Calculating a Stream's Gradient, p. 273 `GENERAL` **Connect to Physical Science,** p. 273 in ATE `BASIC` **Cross-Disciplinary Focus,** p. 275 in ATE `ADVANCED`	**Self-Check,** p. 274 **Homework,** p. 274 in ATE `GENERAL` **Review,** p. 276 `GENERAL` **Quiz,** p. 276 in ATE `GENERAL` **Alternative Assessment,** p. 276 in ATE `GENERAL`
Directed Reading Worksheet 11, Section 2 `BASIC` **Reinforcement Worksheet 11,** Fresh Water in the United States `BASIC`	**Astronomy Connection,** p. 278	**Self-Check,** p. 278 **Homework,** p. 278 in ATE `ADVANCED` **Review,** p. 279 `GENERAL` **Quiz,** p. 279 in ATE `GENERAL` **Alternative Assessment,** p. 279 in ATE `GENERAL`
Transparency 142, The Water Table **Directed Reading Worksheet 11,** Section 3 `BASIC` **Transparency 143,** Artesian Formation **Transparency 143,** The Water Table and Wells **Reinforcement Worksheet 11,** Dig It! `GENERAL` **Problem Solving Worksheet 11,** Water Crisis at Happy Acres `ADVANCED`	**Multicultural Connection,** p. 280 in ATE **Real-World Connection,** p. 281 in ATE `ADVANCED` **Connect to Life Science,** p. 282 in ATE **Environment Connection,** p. 283 **Weird Science:** Bubble, Boil, & Squirt, p. 294 `GENERAL`	**Self-Check,** p. 282 **Review,** p. 284 `GENERAL` **Quiz,** p. 284 in ATE `GENERAL` **Alternative Assessment,** p. 284 in ATE `GENERAL`
Directed Reading Worksheet 11, Section 4 `BASIC` **Math Skills for Science Worksheet 3,** Multiplying Whole Numbers `GENERAL`	**Multicultural Connection,** p. 286 in ATE **Math and More,** p. 287 in ATE `BASIC` **Connect to Environmental Science** p. 288 in ATE **Apply,** p. 288 `GENERAL` **Eye on the Environment:** Disaster Along the Delta, p. 295 `GENERAL`	**Homework,** p. 286 in ATE `ADVANCED` **Review,** p. 289 `GENERAL` **Quiz,** p. 289 in ATE `GENERAL` **Alternative Assessment,** p. 289 in ATE `GENERAL`

END-OF-CHAPTER REVIEW AND ASSESSMENT

Chapter Review in Study Guide
Vocabulary and Notes in Study Guide
Chapter Tests with Performance-Based Assessment, Chapter 11 Test
Chapter Tests with Performance-Based Assessment, Performance-Based Assessment 11
Concept Mapping Transparency 11

internet connect

Holt, Rinehart and Winston On-line Resources
go.hrw.com
For worksheets and other teaching aids related to this chapter, visit the HRW Web site and type in the keyword: **HSTDEP**

National Science Teachers Association
www.scilinks.org
Encourage students to use the sciLINKS numbers listed in the internet connect boxes to access information and resources on the **NSTA** Web site.

Chapter 11 • Chapter Organizer **267B**

Chapter Resources & Worksheets

Visual Resources

TEACHING TRANSPARENCIES

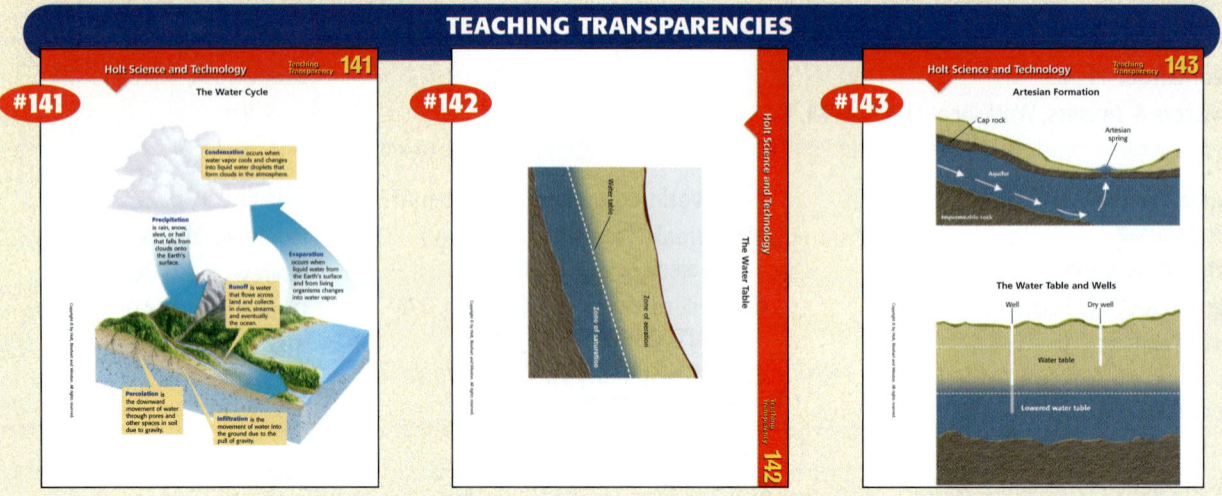

TEACHING TRANSPARENCIES | **CONCEPT MAPPING TRANSPARENCY**

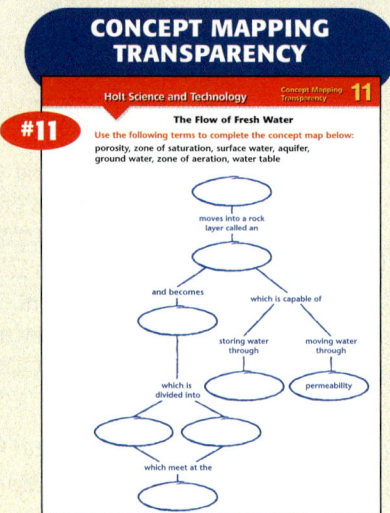

Meeting Individual Needs

DIRECTED READING | **REINFORCEMENT & VOCABULARY REVIEW** | **SCIENCE PUZZLERS, TWISTERS & TEASERS**

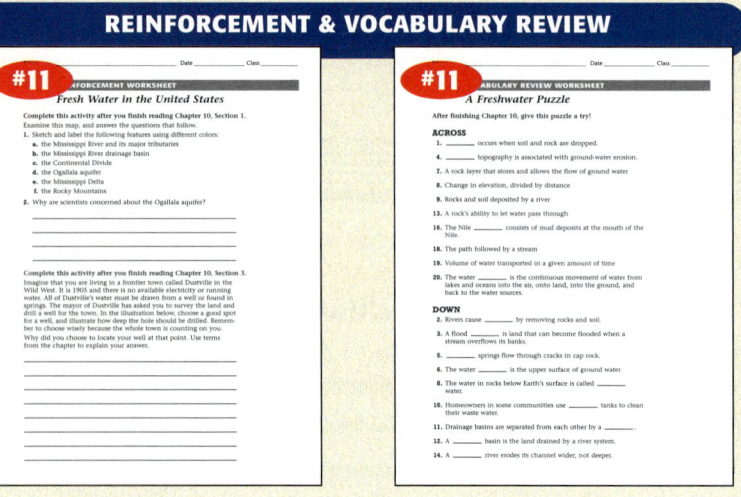
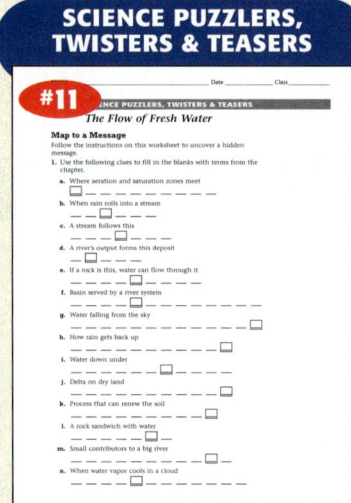

267C Chapter 11 • The Flow of Fresh Water

Chapter 11 • The Flow of Fresh Water

Review & Assessment

STUDY GUIDE

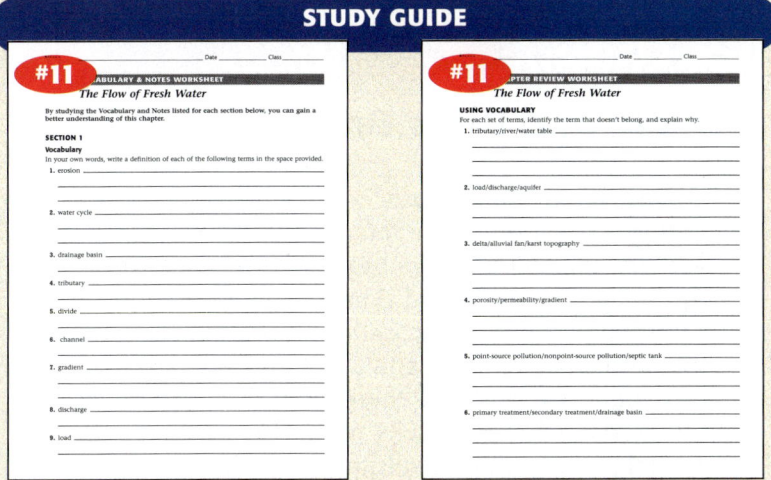

CHAPTER TESTS WITH PERFORMANCE-BASED ASSESSMENT

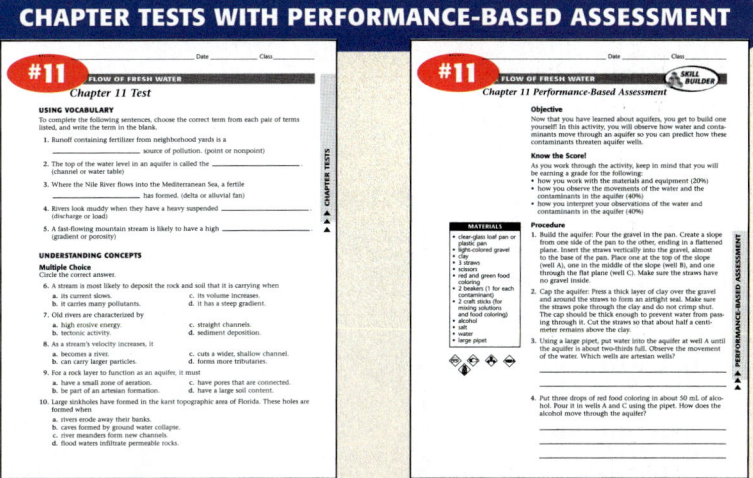

Lab Worksheets

ECOLABS & FIELD ACTIVITIES

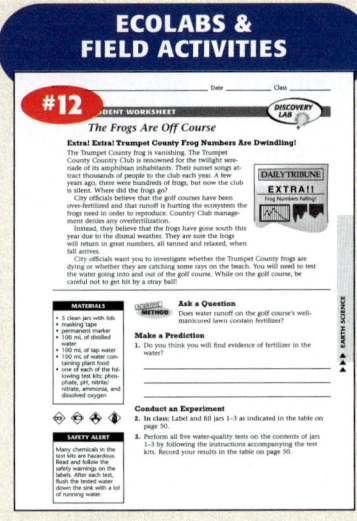

LONG-TERM PROJECTS & RESEARCH IDEAS

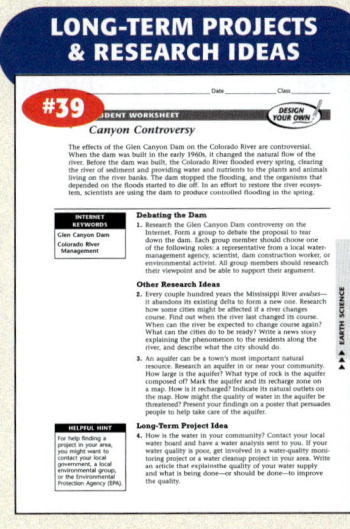

DATASHEETS FOR LABBOOK

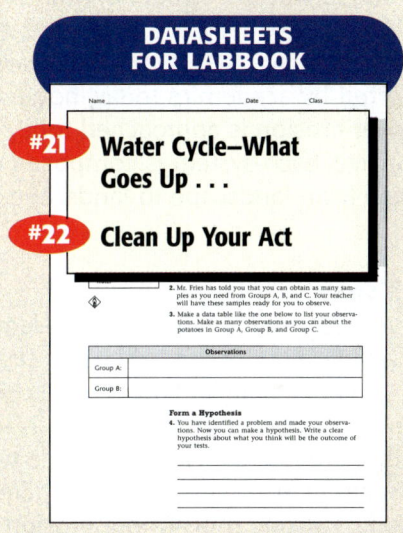

Applications & Extensions

CRITICAL THINKING & PROBLEM SOLVING

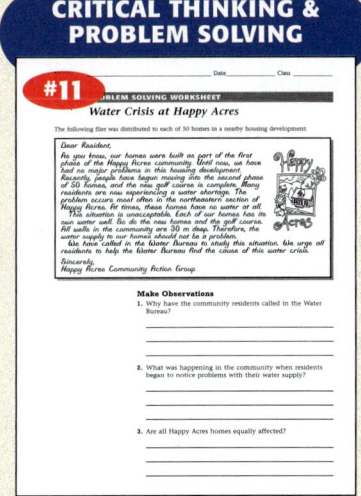

SCIENCE TECHNOLOGY

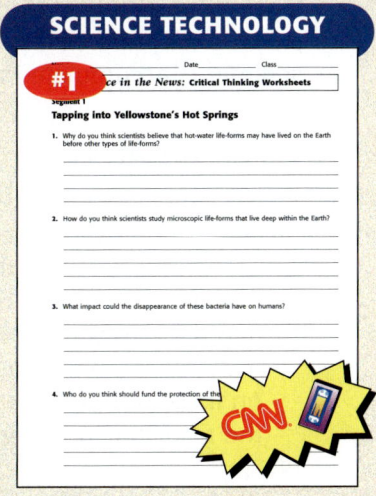

EYE ON THE ENVIRONMENT

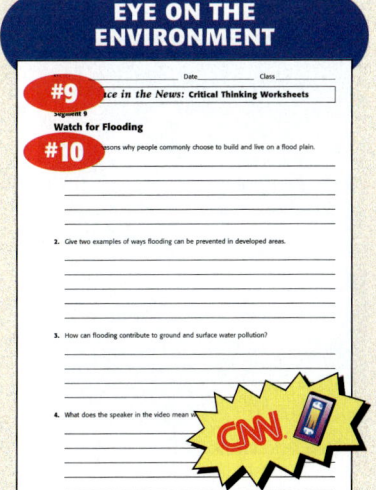

INTERACTIVE EXPLORATIONS

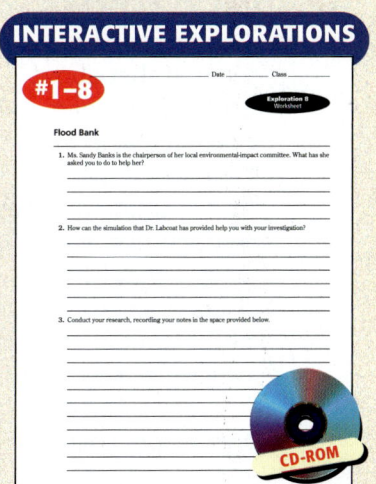

Chapter 11 • Chapter Resources & Worksheets

Chapter Background

SECTION 1
The Active River

▶ **William Morris Davis**

William Morris Davis (1850–1934) was a famous American geographer who was the first to propose the erosion cycle. Davis theorized that landscapes are initially uplifted. Streams flow rapidly from the uplifted land, cutting into the landscape. Gradually, the landscape's slope is reduced. Eventually, the landscape changes into an old erosional surface that is fairly flat. Davis's theory is not supported by academics today, however. The process of river erosion is approached today from a systems perspective. Each system is composed of different parts that vary from landscape to landscape.

▶ **Stream Flow**

Streams have two general types of flow—laminar and turbulent. Laminar flow occurs when the stream load moves in a generally parallel flow. This occurs where the water moves slowly and the channel is smooth. Streams with a greater velocity experience turbulent flow. The stream load generally is rolled, lifted, and bounced along, causing much more erosion in the stream channel.

IS THAT A FACT!

▪ Geologists have learned that about 300 million years ago, massive rivers may have run down the Appalachian Mountains through river valleys 32 km wide! These rivers drained much of the continent, emptying into the ocean at today's Alabama-Mississippi coastline.

SECTION 2
Stream and River Deposits

▶ **Drainage Patterns**

A drainage pattern is the arrangement of river channels in a drainage basin. A drainage pattern is determined by an area's geology and climate. One of the most common patterns, called *dendritic,* is a treelike pattern that forms where rocks and sediments are flat. A *parallel* pattern occurs where there are valleys and ridges. And a *radial* pattern results when streams flow from a central peak, such as a volcanic mountain.

▶ **Deltas**

The word *delta* was first used by the Greek historian Herodotus to describe the mouth of a river. In the fifth century B.C., Herodotus was traveling in Egypt when he saw the triangular mouth of the Nile River and named the shape after the Greek letter ∆, delta.

▶ **Paleoecology at Work**

Paleoecologists study the rock and fossil record to understand what ancient environments were like. For example, paleoecologists learned that a great inland sea once covered the Plains states by studying thick layers of sedimentary rock in the area, such as sandstone, shale, and chalk. Such rocks form only when sediments accumulate in calm waters.

IS THAT A FACT!

▪ Over the last 6,000 years, the Mississippi River delta has shifted from east to west several times. Today the river empties to the east, but scientists think that if left alone the river would change its course and head toward a swampy region called the Atchafalaya. Only massive dams keep the Mississippi on its present course. If the river channel changes, the river may no longer pass through New Orleans.

Chapter 11 • The Flow of Fresh Water

SECTION 3

Water Underground

▶ Caves as Shelters

The flow of fresh water underground created caves that were just as important to the development of human civilizations as fertile flood plains. Humans have used caves as shelters for hundreds of thousands of years. Evidence suggests that use of caves for shelter coincides with the first controlled use of fire. Hearths that may be 750,000 years old have been found in the cave of l'Escale, in southeastern France.

- In China, excavations in a cave called Chou-k'ou-tien have yielded 400,000-year-old fossilized remains of *Homo erectus.* Evidence of charred animal bones suggests that the inhabitants may have cooked their food.

IS THAT A FACT!

- The largest cave chamber in the world is the Sarawak chamber, in Malaysia. The chamber is 600 m long and has an average width of 450 m.

SECTION 4

Using Water Wisely

▶ Aquifers

There are two types of aquifers. The first occurs in *consolidated formations,* those formed from solid rock overlaid with permeable rock that is saturated with water. The second kind of aquifer forms in *unconsolidated formations*—loose sand, soil, and gravel. The amount of water contained in an unconsolidated aquifer depends on how tightly the materials are packed. Because of this, sand and gravel, which are coarse-grained, are usually high-yield aquifers, while formations that are finer-grained tend to hold less water.

▶ Acequias in New Mexico

New Mexico gets only an average of 32.5 cm of rain per year, so water conservation is critical. Because wide irrigation ditches lose a great deal of water to evaporation, New Mexicans have relied for centuries on shallow earthen ditches fed by local rivers to supply growing plants with water. Each ditch, called an *acequia,* provides water to a small area. Acequias allow for water to seep into the ground, minimizing evaporation and allowing water to reach plant roots. Water that isn't absorbed by the soil returns to the river, providing water to people downstream to irrigate their fields.

IS THAT A FACT!

- When ground water is depleted so quickly that the system cannot recharge, there can be dramatic consequences. At Edwards Air Force Base, in California, the aquifer has shrunk so quickly that ground settling has led to sinks and fissures. One of the fissures is about 625 m long!

- A comprehensive 1998 study conducted by the Nature Conservancy warns that continued pollution of the nation's 2,100 rivers and streams threatens approximately 40 percent of fresh-water fish species and two-thirds of mussel species with extinction. In addition, the degradation of our fresh-water sources poses a threat to human health and threatens the country's $16 billion sport-fishing industry.

For background information about teaching strategies and issues, refer to the *Professional Reference for Teachers.*

The Flow of Fresh Water

 Pre-Reading Questions

Students may not know the answers to these questions before reading the chapter, so accept any reasonable response.

Suggested Answers

1. Answers will vary. Accept all reasonable responses. Sample answer: Running water erodes the landscape, redistributing sediment.
2. Erosion is the removal and transport of sediment. Deposition is the dropping off of sediment.

 Directed Reading Worksheet 11

 Science Puzzlers, Twisters & Teasers Worksheet 11

 Guided Reading Audio CD English or Spanish, Chapter 11

The Flow of Fresh Water

Sections

1. The Active River 270
   MathBreak 273
   Internet Connect 276
2. Stream and River Deposits 277
   Astronomy Connection 278
   Internet Connect ... 279
3. Water Underground .. 280
   QuickLab 281
   Environment Connection 283
   Internet Connect ... 284
4. Using Water Wisely... 285
   Apply 288
   Internet Connect 289

Chapter Review 292
Feature Articles 294, 295
LabBooks........... 670–675

 **Pre-Reading Questions**

1. What role does water play in shaping the surface of the Earth?
2. What is the difference between erosion and deposition?

The Sound Is Deafening

You can hear the thundering roar of Iguaçu (EE gwah SOO) Falls for miles. The Iguaçu River travels more than 500 km across Brazil before it tumbles off the edge of a volcanic plateau in a series of 275 individual waterfalls separated by forested islands. Over the past 20,000 years, erosion has caused the falls to move 28 km upstream. Where will they be 20,000 years from now? In this chapter, you will learn how flowing water shapes Earth's surface.

---

internet connect

  **HRW On-line Resources**

go.hrw.com
For worksheets and other teaching aids, visit the HRW Web site and type in the keyword: **HSTDEP**

www.scilinks.com
Use the sciLINKS numbers at the end of each chapter for additional resources on the **NSTA** Web site.

www.cnnfyi.com
Visit the CNN Web site for current events coverage and classroom resources.

STREAM WEAVERS

How do streams and river systems develop? Do the following activity to find out.

Procedure

1. Begin with a **bucket of sand** and enough **gravel** to fill the bottom of a **rectangular plastic washtub**.

2. Spread the gravel in a layer at the bottom of the washtub. Place 4–6 cm of sand on top of the gravel. Add more sand to one end of the washtub to form a slope.

3. Make a small hole in the bottom of a **paper cup**. Attach the cup to the inside of the tub with a **clothespin**. The cup should be placed at the end that has more sand. Fill the cup with water, and observe the **water** as it moves over the sand. Use a **magnifying lens** to observe features of the stream more closely.

4. Record your observations in your ScienceLog.

Analysis

5. At the start of your experiment, how did the moving water affect the sand?

6. As time passed, how did the moving water affect the sand?

7. Explain how this activity modeled the development of streams. In what ways was it accurate? How was it inaccurate?

STREAM WEAVERS

MATERIALS
For Each Group: • bucket of sand • gravel • rectangular plastic washtub • paper cup • clothespin • water • magnifying lens

Teacher's Notes

Students can tilt the tub by placing a block of wood or a book under one end.

Answers to START-UP Activity

5. The moving water cut into the sand, forming a small groove.

6. As time passed, the moving water cut deeper into the sand, creating a wider groove.

7. Accept all reasonable responses. Sample answer: Runoff (water) moves over the land, cutting a gully into the dirt. At first the gully is shallow and narrow, but over time the gully widens and becomes deeper. If there is enough water, the gully eventually becomes a river. Students should note that the model is accurate in that moving water does produce similar landforms. The model is inaccurate for several reasons, including its scale and the fact that the rivers flow over varied terrain, not just uniform sand deposits.

Chapter 11 • The Flow of Fresh Water

SECTION 1

Focus

The Active River

This section introduces the water cycle and discusses the role that rivers play in the movement of fresh water. Students will learn that rivers are changing, dynamic systems that continually shape the land. The section discusses the factors that contribute to rates of stream erosion and concludes with a discussion of the life cycle of rivers.

🔔 Bellringer

Have students write a paragraph about an imaginary canoe trip down a river. They could choose the river described in the chapter opener or another river of their choice. Ask students to describe the river's features and hypothesize how those features formed.
Sheltered English

1 Motivate

ACTIVITY

Discuss the photograph of the Grand Canyon shown in **Figure 1**. Help students compare the size of the canyon with the size of the Empire State Building, which is 381 m tall. Ask students to calculate how many Empire State Buildings it would take to create a stack as deep as the Grand Canyon. (1.6 km deep = 1,600 m; 1,600 ÷ 381 = 4.2)

The Grand Canyon is 29 km wide at its widest point. How many Empire State Buildings laid end-to-end would fit in the canyon's widest point?
(29 km = 29,000 m; 29,000 ÷ 381 = 76)

Section 1

Terms to Learn

erosion
water cycle
tributary
drainage basin
divide
channel
load

What You'll Do

- Illustrate the water cycle.
- Describe a drainage basin.
- Explain the major factors that affect the rate of stream erosion.
- Identify the stages of river development.

The Active River

You are probably familiar with the Grand Canyon, shown in **Figure 1.** But did you know that about 6 million years ago, the area now known as the Grand Canyon was nearly as flat as a pancake? The Colorado River cut down into the rock and formed the Grand Canyon over millions of years by washing billions of tons of soil and rock from its riverbed. This process is a type of *erosion*. **Erosion** is the removal and transport of surface material, such as rock and soil. Rivers are not the only agents of erosion. Wind, rain, ice, and snow can cause erosion as well.

Because of erosion caused by water, the Grand Canyon is now about 1.6 km deep and 446 km long. In this section, you will learn about stream development, river systems, and the different factors that affect the rate of stream erosion.

Figure 1 The Grand Canyon is located in northwestern Arizona. It formed over millions of years as running water eroded rock and soil. In some places the canyon is 29 km wide.

Water, Water Everywhere

Have you ever wondered how rivers keep flowing and where rivers get their water? The water cycle answers these and other questions. The **water cycle,** shown on the next page, is the continuous movement of water from water sources, such as lakes or oceans, into the air, onto land, into the ground, and back to the water sources.

 Math Skills Worksheet 6 "Checking Division with Multiplication"

 **internetconnect**

TOPIC: The Grand Canyon
GO TO: www.scilinks.org
sciLINKS NUMBER: HSTE255

270   Chapter 11 • The Flow of Fresh Water

The Water Cycle

Condensation occurs when water vapor cools and changes into liquid water droplets that form clouds in the atmosphere.

Precipitation is rain, snow, sleet, or hail that falls from clouds onto the Earth's surface.

Runoff is water that flows across land and collects in rivers, streams, and eventually the ocean.

Evaporation occurs when liquid water from the Earth's surface and from living organisms changes into water vapor.

Infiltration is the movement of water into the ground due to the pull of gravity.

Percolation is the downward movement of water through pores and other spaces in soil due to gravity.

IS THAT A FACT!

Under average conditions, the Mississippi River carries about 17,000 m³ of water every second. A small carry-on suitcase is about 0.03 m³, so watching the river go by on an average day is equivalent to watching about 566,666 suitcases pass by you every second!

Be sure students realize that water evaporates from the soil and vegetation as well as from rivers and other bodies of water.

2) Teach

 **PG 670**
Water Cycle—What Goes Up . . .

DEMONSTRATION

Add a teaspoon of brightly colored tempera paint to about half a cup of soil. Place the soil in a funnel lined with filter paper, and place the funnel over a large jar. Tell students that the tempera paint represents nutrients in the soil. Ask students to predict what will happen to the nutrients in the soil when it rains. Demonstrate by slowly pouring water into the funnel. Discuss the important role that rivers play in distributing soil nutrients.

MEETING INDIVIDUAL NEEDS

Learners Having Difficulty
Have students make a field guide for rivers. Suggest that they include photographs of streams and rivers and write captions to describe each photo. The captions should incorporate terms such as *gradient*, *erosion*, *load*, *channel*, and *meanders*. Finally, have them hypothesize about the river's speed, load, and erosional capacity. **Sheltered English**

 Teaching Transparency 141
"The Water Cycle"

 Directed Reading Worksheet 11 Section 1

Section 1 • The Active River

2 Teach, continued

Answers to Activity
Tributaries: Musselshell, Yellowstone, Badlands, Heart, Grand, Moreau, Cheyenne, White, Niobrara, Elkhorn, Loup, Platte, Kansas, Ohio, Arkansas, Red

Cities: Bismarck, Omaha, Kansas City, Saint Louis, Memphis, Baton Rouge, New Orleans

Distance: approximately 3,900 km

Hint: Measure the distance with a string, then find the actual distance traveled by using the map's scale.

GROUP ACTIVITY
Have pairs of students use a map or atlas to create a poster that illustrates the river systems and drainage basins of North America. Encourage them to use arrows to indicate the direction of flow in major rivers and draw the divides that separate each drainage basin. Working independently, students could make a map that shows the river systems of your county or state.

REAL-WORLD CONNECTION
Meteorologists recognize the power of moving water, and they issue special warnings when there is a danger of floods. Ask students to guess how much moving water it takes to knock an adult off his or her feet:

15 cm, 30 cm, or 1 m. (15 cm)

Ask them how deep the water would have to be to sweep away a car:

more than 2 m, at least 1.5 m, or less than 1 m. (less than 1 m)

Demonstrate these water depths using a meterstick, and caution students to be careful around flowing water.

Activity

Imagine that you are planning a rafting trip down the Missouri River to the Mississippi River. On a map of the United States, trace the route of your trip from the Rocky Mountains in Montana to the mouth of the Mississippi River, in Louisiana. What major tributaries would you travel past? What cities would you pass through? Mark them on the map. How many kilometers would you travel on this trip?

TRY at HOME

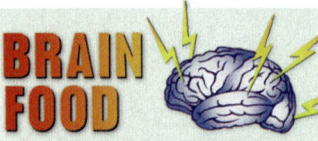

BRAIN FOOD

The Amazon River basin, in South America, is the world's largest drainage basin. It has an area of about 6 million square kilometers. That's almost twice as big as the United States' largest drainage basin, the Mississippi River basin!

River Systems

Look at the pattern of lines on the palm of your hand. Notice how some of the smaller lines join together to form larger lines. Now imagine those lines are rivers and streams. The smaller lines would be the streams and tributaries and the larger lines would be rivers. **Tributaries** are smaller streams or rivers that flow into larger ones. Like the network of lines on the palm of your hand, streams and rivers make up a network on land. This network of streams and rivers is called a river system and it drains an area of its runoff.

Drainage Basins River systems are divided into regions known as drainage basins. A **drainage basin,** or *watershed,* is the land drained by a river system, which includes the main river and all of its tributaries. The largest drainage basin in the United States is the Mississippi River basin. It has hundreds of tributaries that extend from the Rocky Mountains, in the West, to the Appalachian Mountains, in the East.

The map in **Figure 2** shows that the Mississippi River drainage basin covers more than one-third of the United States. Other major drainage basins in the United States are the Columbia, Rio Grande, and Colorado River basins.

Divides Drainage basins are separated from each other by an area called a **divide.** A divide is generally an area of higher ground than the basins it separates. On the map below, you can see that the Continental Divide is a major divide in the United States. On which side do you live?

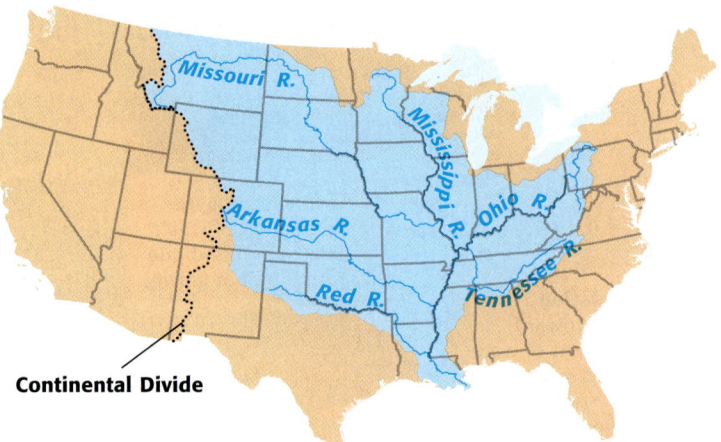

Figure 2 The Continental Divide runs through the Rocky Mountains. It separates the drainage basins that flow into the Atlantic Ocean and the Gulf of Mexico from those that flow into the Pacific Ocean.

Science Bloopers

In 1935, a dam was constructed in California to prevent sediment from filling Gibraltar Reservoir. This dam created Mono Reservoir. The watershed above Mono Reservoir was burned by forest fires, and people worried that sediment would fill Gibraltar Reservoir before plants had a chance to regrow and hold the soil. Unfortunately, the next 2 years saw record rainfall. Sediment completely filled Mono Reservoir and half-filled Gibraltar Reservoir.

Stream Erosion

As a stream forms, it erodes soil and rock to create a channel. A **channel** is the path that a stream follows. At first, stream channels are small and steep. As more rock and soil are transported downstream, the channels become wider and deeper. When streams become longer, they are referred to as rivers. Have you ever wondered why some streams flow faster than others?

Gradient The stream shown in **Figure 3** is flowing down a steep mountain side. This stream has a high gradient. *Gradient* is the measure of the change in elevation over a certain distance. A high gradient gives a stream or river more energy to erode rock and soil. A river or stream with a low gradient, such as the one in **Figure 4,** has less energy for erosion.

Discharge The amount of water a stream or river carries in a given amount of time is called *discharge*. The discharge of a stream increases when a major storm occurs or when warm weather rapidly melts snow. As the stream's discharge increases, its erosive energy, speed, and load increase.

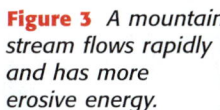

MATH BREAK
Calculating a Stream's Gradient

If a river starts at an elevation of 4,900 m and travels 450 km downstream to a lake that is at an elevation of 400 m, what is the stream's gradient?

Figure 3 A mountain stream flows rapidly and has more erosive energy.

Figure 4 A river on a flat plain flows slowly and has less erosive energy.

IS THAT A FACT!

Most river water comes from rainfall and melted snow that flows down from mountains. Why do some rivers continue to flow during a severe drought? These rivers are probably lower than the water table, so their flow is maintained by seepage from ground water.

WEIRD SCIENCE

Stream piracy occurs when one river "steals" another. If the land dividing two streams is eroded, one stream can "capture" the headwaters of the other. The eroding stream eventually pirates all of the other stream's water.

Answer to MATHBREAK

4,900 m − 400 m = 4,500 m

$\frac{4,500 \text{ m}}{450 \text{ km}} = 10$ m/km

DISCUSSION

Have students think about watering a garden using a hose. Ask whether they would spray the water at full blast or gently. Would they lay the hose on the ground or hold it at waist level? Refer to this example as you work through the concepts of erosion, gradient, and discharge. **Sheltered English**

CONNECT TO PHYSICAL SCIENCE

Water flowing downstream can be compared to a rock tumbling down a mountainside. Water's potential energy is constantly being converted into kinetic energy. The reservoir of a hydroelectric dam has tremendous potential energy; when the gates are open, that potential energy is converted into kinetic energy that spins a turbine. The turbine then generates electrical energy. Ask students to come up with other devices that use the potential energy of water. **(Examples include a flush toilet and a water tank.)**

MISCONCEPTION ALERT

When water flows down a river channel, it does not flow straight down the channel. Water flowing in a river or stream channel moves in a helical or corkscrew motion. This motion causes erosion on the bank where the water is rising and causes deposition on the bank where the water is falling. The helical flow of water helps explain the formation of bends or meanders in the channel.

Section 1 • The Active River

2 Teach, continued

GROUP ACTIVITY

Assign each group of students one of the world's major rivers. Have each group prepare a poster on the river indicating its headwaters and mouth. The poster should also include major tributaries. Have students indicate a change in the river's gradient by shading the area with colored pencils. Encourage students to discover interesting facts about their river, such as the ecosystem the river supports and the river's effects on human populations living near it.

COOPERATIVE LEARNING

Stream Load To help students learn the differences between the types of loads that streams carry, engage groups of four in this activity. Have groups fill a plastic jar three-quarters full of water. Provide a few small pebbles, a quarter cup of soil, and 3 tbsp of salt for each group. Have students choose which material best represents a stream's bed load (the pebbles), its suspended load (the soil), and its dissolved load (the salt).

Have students add all three materials to the jar and then shake it carefully to simulate a stream's load. After the contents have been thoroughly mixed, ask students to hypothesize how they could remove each material from the jar. (The pebbles settle to the bottom and can be picked out easily. If the water remains still long enough, the sediment will settle to the bottom of the jar. The salt can be removed through evaporation.)

Answer to Self-Check

If a river slowed down, the suspended load would be deposited.

Load The materials carried in a stream's water are collectively called the stream's **load**. The size of the particles in the stream's load is affected by the stream's speed. Fast-moving streams can carry large particles. The load also affects the stream's rate of erosion. Rocks and pebbles bounce and scrape along the bottom and sides of the stream bed. The illustration below shows the three ways a stream can carry its load.

① A stream can bounce large materials, such as pebbles and boulders, along the stream bed. These rocks are called the **bed load**.

② A stream can carry small rocks and soil in suspension. These materials, called the **suspended load**, make the river look muddy.

③ Some material is carried in solution, meaning that the material is dissolved in the water. The **dissolved load** consists of dissolved materials, such as sodium and calcium.

Self-Check

What would happen to a suspended load if the river slowed down? (See page 726 to check your answer.)

Homework

Writing Have students prepare an *Encyclopedia of Rivers* with a full definition of each new term in the section and at least one illustration for each term.

SCIENCE HUMOR

Q: What is a flood?

A: a river that's too big for its bridges

274 Chapter 11 • The Flow of Fresh Water

The Stages of a River

In the early 1900s, William Morris Davis developed a model that identified the stages of river development. According to this model, rivers evolve from a youthful stage to an old-age stage. Davis believed that all rivers erode in the same way and at the same rate. Today, however, scientists support a different model that considers the effects of a river's environment on stream development. For example, because different material erodes at different rates, one river may develop more quickly than another river. Many factors, including climate, gradient, and load, influence the development of a river. Although scientists no longer use Davis's model to explain river development, they still use many of his terms to describe a river. Remember, these terms do not tell the actual age of a river. Instead, they are used to describe the general characteristics of the river.

Figure 5 *This youthful river is located in Yellowstone National Park in Wyoming. The rapids and falls are located where the river flows over hard, resistant rock.*

Youthful Rivers A youthful river, like the one shown in **Figure 5,** erodes its channel deeper rather than wider. The river flows quickly because of its steep gradient. Its sides and channel are steep and straight. The river tumbles over rocks in rapids and waterfalls. Youthful rivers have few tributaries.

Mature Rivers A mature river, as shown in **Figure 6,** erodes its channel wider rather than deeper. The gradient of a mature river is not as steep as that of a youthful river, and there are fewer falls and rapids. A mature river is fed by many tributaries, and because of its good drainage, it has more discharge than a younger river.

Figure 6 *A mature river, such as this one in Peru, begins to curve back and forth. The bends in the river's channel are called* meanders.

275

3) Extend

READING STRATEGY

Prediction Guide Write "Young," "Mature," "Old," and "Rejuvenated" on the board. Have students brainstorm about concepts, words, or images related to these terms, and write their suggestions below the terms. Next add the dictionary definitions of the terms. Then discuss how the terms might describe a river. Have students write their ideas in their ScienceLog and then compare their ideas with the descriptions in the text.
Sheltered English

INDEPENDENT PRACTICE

Illustrating River Stages As students read the section on the stages of a river, have them illustrate the stages in their ScienceLog. Encourage students to draw a cross section of the river channel and valley. Students should label the parts of their diagrams and write a brief description of each stage of river development.

CROSS-DISCIPLINARY FOCUS

Writing — History In the eighteenth and nineteenth centuries, the Mississippi River served as an important trade route for the Midwest. Riverboats carried people and goods up and down the Mississippi River. The riverboats carried resources such as grains, meat, and animal skins down the river. Have interested students research how the Mississippi River influenced the history of the Midwest or write a short essay on the history of a city built on a Midwestern river, such as Saint Louis, New Orleans, or Kansas City. They should concentrate on how the river was important to the city's growth and development. Students should also find out how the Mississippi River is used today.

Section 1 • The Active River **275**

4 Close

Quiz

1. How does rainfall or snowmelt affect a river's discharge and its ability to cause erosion? (Rainfall and snowmelt increase a river's discharge and the amount of erosion it can cause.)

2. Explain the three types of materials carried by a river. (bed load: large materials that roll or bounce along a riverbed; suspended load: materials that float suspended in a river; dissolved load: materials dissolved in a river)

ALTERNATIVE ASSESSMENT

Display the Teaching Transparency listed below, and discuss the features labeled. Then divide students into groups, and have them use modeling clay to make a model of a river, incorporating the concepts they have learned in this chapter. Students can use pins with attached labels to indicate river features.

Teaching Transparency 75 "River Features"

TOPIC: Rivers and Streams
GO TO: www.scilinks.org
sciLINKS NUMBER: HSTE260

Figure 7 *This old river is located in New Zealand.*

Figure 8 *This rejuvenated river is located in Canyonlands National Park, Utah.*

Old Rivers An old river has a low gradient and extremely low erosive power. Instead of widening and deepening its banks, the river deposits sediment in its channel and along its banks. Old rivers, like the one in **Figure 7,** are characterized by wide, flat *flood plains,* or valleys, and more meanders. Also, an older river has fewer tributaries than a mature river because the smaller tributaries have merged.

Rejuvenated Rivers Rejuvenated rivers occur where the land is raised by the Earth's tectonic forces. When land rises, the river's gradient becomes steeper. The increased gradient of a rejuvenated river allows the river to cut more deeply into the valley floor, as shown in **Figure 8.** Steplike *terraces* often form on both sides of a stream valley as a result of rejuvenation. Terraces are nearly flat portions of the landscape that end at a steep cliff.

internetconnect

TOPIC: Rivers and Streams
GO TO: www.scilinks.org
sciLINKS NUMBER: HSTE260

REVIEW

1. How does the water cycle help to develop river systems?
2. Describe a drainage basin.
3. What are three factors that affect the rate of stream erosion?
4. **Summarizing Data** How do youthful, mature, and old rivers differ?

Answers to Review

1. Answers will vary. Accept all reasonable responses.
2. A drainage basin is the land drained by a river system, including the main river and all of its tributaries.
3. Three factors that affect the rate of stream erosion are a stream's gradient, its discharge, and its load.
4. Youthful rivers are steep and straight, with fewer tributaries. Mature rivers have more curves, tributaries, and discharge than youthful rivers, as well as a lower gradient. Old rivers have less erosive power than mature rivers do.

Section 2

Terms to Learn

deposition
alluvium
delta
alluvial fan
flood plain

What You'll Do

- Describe the different types of stream deposits.
- Explain the relationship between rich agricultural regions and river flood plains.

Stream and River Deposits

You have learned that flowing rivers can pick up and move soil and rock. Sooner or later, this material must be deposited somewhere. **Deposition** is the process by which material is dropped, or settles. Imagine a mud puddle after a rainy day. If the water is not disturbed, the soil particles will eventually settle and the muddy water will become clear again. Deposition also forms and renews some of the world's most productive soils. People who live in the lower Mississippi River valley, for example, depend on the river to bring them new, fertile soil.

Deposition in Water

After rivers erode rock and soil, they deposit the rock and soil downstream. Rock and soil deposited by streams is called **alluvium.** Alluvium is dropped at places in a river where the speed of the current decreases. Take a look at **Figure 9** to see how this type of deposition occurs.

Figure 9 *This model illustrates erosion and deposition at a bend, or meander, of a river.*

a. Erosion occurs on the outside bank where the water flows faster.

b. Deposition occurs along the inside bank where the water flows slower.

WEIRD SCIENCE

The Okavango River, in Africa, flows approximately 1,600 km through Angola, Namibia, and Botswana before it empties into the middle of the Kalahari Desert, where it evaporates! The river's alluvial fan provides a haven for the desert's plants and animals.

TOPIC: Stream Deposits
GO TO: www.scilinks.org
***sci*LINKS NUMBER:** HSTE263

Section 2 • Stream and River Deposits   **277**

2) Teach

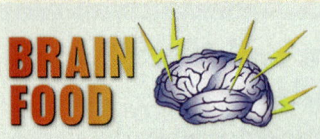

Ask students to examine a map of the United States and to note that rivers often serve as state borders. For instance, the Ohio River is the border between Indiana and Kentucky. But meanders can sometimes shift the course of the river. Does the state border then change? To prevent feuding between states, the courts have declared that state boundaries do not change when a river shifts.

COOPERATIVE LEARNING

Gold Rush Between 1870 and 1898, many prospectors discovered gold in Canada's Yukon Territory. Dreams of getting rich overnight lured people to the Klondike River area in vast numbers.

Have students research the Yukon gold rush. Divide the class into three groups. Have Group 1 prepare a presentation on how the gold deposits formed. Have Group 2 prepare a presentation on how the gold ore became placer deposits in the Klondike River. Have Group 3 prepare a presentation on the geography of the Yukon's river systems.

Students can also find out about life in the gold fields and present their findings using models or posters.

Reinforcement Worksheet 11
"Fresh Water in the United States"

Figure 10 Miners rushed to California in the 1850s to find gold. They often found it in the bends of rivers in placer deposits.

 **Astronomy CONNECTION**

The remains of an ancient riverbed have been discovered on Mars. Satellite images show the deposits of stream channels, which indicate that liquid water once existed on the surface of this now dry and frozen planet.

278

Answer to Self-Check
Answers will vary. A river might slow where there is a bend, when the gradient decreases, or where the river empties into a large body of water.

Heavy minerals are sometimes deposited at places in a river where the current slows down. This kind of alluvium is called a *placer deposit*. Some placer deposits contain gold, as **Figure 10** shows. During the California gold rush, which began in 1849, many miners panned for gold in the placer deposits of rivers.

Designing a Delta The current also slows when a river empties into a large body of water, such as a lake or an ocean. Much of the river's load may be deposited where the river reaches the large body of water, forming a fan-shaped deposit called a **delta**. In **Figure 11** you can see an astronaut's view of the Nile Delta. A delta usually forms on a flat surface and consists mostly of mud. These mud deposits form new land, causing the coastline to grow.

Figure 11 Alluvium is dropped at the mouth of the Nile River, forming a delta.

If you look back at the map of the Mississippi River drainage basin in Figure 2, you can see where the Mississippi River flows into the Gulf of Mexico. This is where the Mississippi Delta has formed. Each of the fine mud particles in the delta began its journey far upstream. Parts of Louisiana are made up of particles that were transported from as far away as Montana, Minnesota, Ohio, and Illinois.

 **Self-Check**

What is one factor that causes the current of a river to slow? *(See page 726 to check your answer.)*

Homework

Investigate Your Area Have students find out how your city or county is working to control flooding and erosion along area streams and rivers. Have them write a brief report on a watershed project in their area. You may consider inviting a watershed engineer to speak to the class.

Deposition on Land

When a fast-moving mountain stream flows onto a flat plain, the stream slows down. As the stream slows down, it deposits alluvium where the mountain meets the flat plain, forming an alluvial fan, such as the one shown in **Figure 12.** **Alluvial fans** are fan-shaped deposits that form on dry land.

During periods of high rainfall or rapid snowmelt, a sudden increase in the volume of water flowing into a stream can cause the stream to overflow its banks, flooding the surrounding land. This land is called a **flood plain.** When a stream floods, a layer of alluvium is deposited across the flood plain. Each flood adds another layer of alluvium.

Fatal Flooding Flood plains are very rich farming areas because periodic flooding brings new soil to the land. However, flooding can cause extensive property damage. Much farming activity takes place in the Mississippi River valley, a large flood plain with very rich soil. When the Mississippi River flooded in 1993, however, farms were abandoned and whole towns had to be evacuated. The flood was so huge that it caused damage in nine Midwestern states. **Figure 13** shows an area that was flooded just north of St. Louis, Missouri.

Figure 12 An alluvial fan, such as this one from the Sierra Nevada, in California, forms when an eroding stream changes rapidly into a depositing stream.

Figure 13 The normal flow of the Mississippi River and Missouri River is shown in black. The area that was flooded when both rivers spilled over their banks in 1993 is shaded red.

REVIEW

1. What happens to a river's flow that causes alluvium to be deposited?
2. How are alluvial fans and deltas similar? How are they different?
3. Explain why flood plains are good farming areas.
4. **Identifying Relationships** What factors increase the likelihood that alluvium will be deposited?

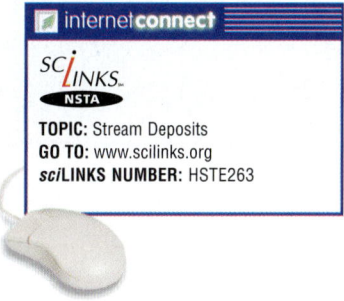

internetconnect

SC_**LINKS**_ **NSTA**
TOPIC: Stream Deposits
GO TO: www.scilinks.org
sciLINKS NUMBER: HSTE263

SECTION 3

Focus

Water Underground

In this section, students will learn what ground water is and where it is found. The section discusses the formation of aquifers and their importance to agriculture and human populations. Students will learn how wells and springs bring water from aquifers to the surface. The section concludes with a discussion of how the movement of ground water forms caves and sinkholes.

Bellringer

Pose the following scenario to students on the board or overhead projector:

A family lives 50 km from the nearest stream or lake and gets water from a well. Where does the water in the well come from? (It comes from water stored underground.)

1 Motivate

DEMONSTRATION

Layer an aquarium with gravel, sand, and potting soil until it is three-quarters full. Pack the material firmly. Add water until you can clearly see areas of aeration and saturation. Ask students to compare this model to **Figure 14.** Using a marker, draw a line for the water table on the glass. Introduce the terms *zone of saturation* and *zone of aeration*, and discuss the difference between the two. Sheltered English

Teaching Transparency 142
"The Water Table"

Section 3

Terms to Learn

ground water
water table
aquifer
porosity
permeability
recharge zone
artesian spring

What You'll Do

- Identify and describe the location of a water table.
- Describe the characteristics of an aquifer.
- Explain how caves and sinkholes form as a result of erosion and deposition.

Water Underground

Although we can see surface water in streams and lakes, there is a lot of water flowing underground that we cannot see. The water located within the rocks below the Earth's surface is called **ground water.** Ground water not only is an important resource but also plays an important role in erosion and deposition.

Location of Ground Water

Surface water seeps underground into the soil and rock. Earth scientists divide this underground area into two zones. The upper zone, called the *zone of aeration,* usually is not completely filled with water. The rock and soil that make up this zone are filled with water only immediately after a rain. Farther down, the water accumulates in an area called the *zone of saturation.* Here the spaces between the rock particles are filled with water.

These two zones meet at an underground boundary known as the **water table,** as shown in **Figure 14.** The water table rises during wet seasons and drops during dry seasons. In wet regions the water table can be just beneath the soil's surface or at the surface. But in deserts the water table may be hundreds of meters underground.

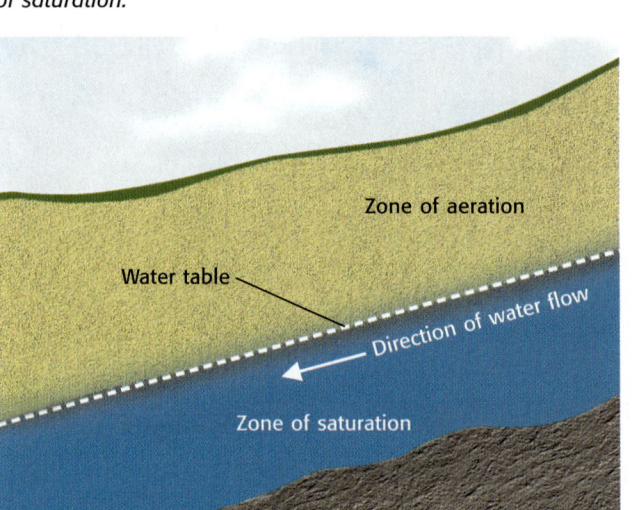

Figure 14 The water table is the upper surface of the zone of saturation.

Aquifers

Some types of rock can hold large quantities of water, while other types can hold little or no water. A rock layer that stores and allows the flow of ground water is called an **aquifer.**

To qualify as an aquifer, a rock layer must be *porous,* or contain open spaces. A rock's **porosity** is the amount of open space between individual rock particles. The rock layer must also allow water to pass freely through it, from one pore to another. If the pores are connected, ground water can flow through the rock layer. A rock's ability to let water pass through it is called **permeability.** A rock that tends to stop the flow of water is impermeable.

Multicultural CONNECTION

The Maya, one of the early civilizations of the Americas, believed that rain clouds formed in caves and then rose to the sky. Elaborate ceremonies were performed in caves for the rain god. Have interested students find out more about how caves and rituals were important to early Mesoamerican civilizations.

IS THAT A FACT!

Geologists estimate that aquifers hold 50 million cubic kilometers of water worldwide. There is about 20 times more water underground than in all the rivers, lakes, and the atmosphere.

Aquifer Geology and Geography The best aquifers are usually formed of sandstone, limestone, or layers of sand and gravel. Some aquifers cover large underground areas and are an important source of water for cities and agriculture. The map in **Figure 15** shows the location of aquifers in the United States.

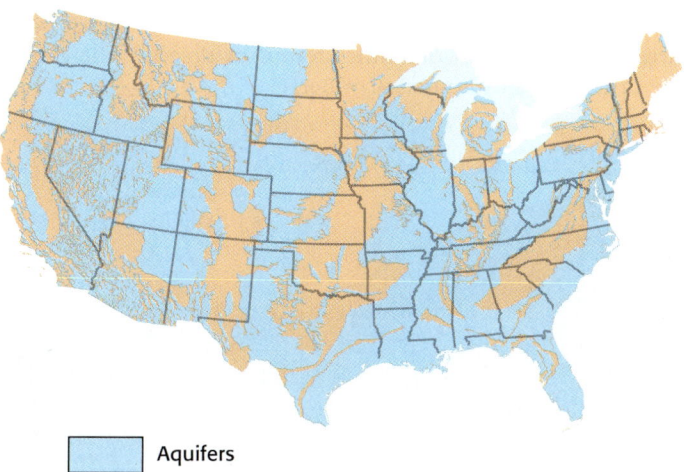

Figure 15 Aquifers in the Continental United States

Recharge Zones Like rivers, aquifers are dependent on the water cycle to maintain a constant flow of water. The ground surface where water enters an aquifer is called the **recharge zone**. The size of the recharge zone varies depending on how permeable rock is at the surface. In an area that contains a permeable rock layer, the water can seep down into the aquifer. In areas where the aquifer is confined on top by an impermeable rock layer, the recharge zone is restricted to areas where there is a permeable rock layer.

Springs and Wells

Ground-water movement is determined by the slope of the water table. Just like surface water, ground water tends to move downslope, toward lower elevations. If the water table reaches the Earth's surface, water will flow out from the ground, forming a *spring*. Springs are an important source of drinking water. Lakes form in low areas, where the water table is higher than the Earth's surface.

QuickLab

Degree of Permeability

1. Obtain five **plastic-foam cups.**
2. Fill one cup halfway with **soil**, such as garden soil. Pack the soil.
3. Fill a second cup halfway with **sand**. Pack the sand.
4. Poke 5 to 7 holes in the bottom of each cup with a sharpened **pencil**.
5. Fill a third cup with **water**. Hold one of the remaining empty cups under the cup filled with soil. Pour the water into the top cup.
6. Allow the cup to drain for 45 seconds, and then put the cup aside (even if it is still draining). Put the cup filled with water aside.
7. Repeat steps 5 and 6 with the cup of sand. Compare the volumes of the two cups of water. The cup that allowed the most water to pass holds the more permeable sediment.

TRY at HOME

A mud pie the size of a house—where would you see something like that? Turn to page 294 to find out.

2 Teach

QuickLab

MATERIALS
- 5 plastic-foam cups
- soil
- sand
- pencil
- water

Teacher Notes: There are no safety precautions required for this experiment. Cover the work area with plastic, and have students wear lab aprons and plastic gloves.

REAL-WORLD CONNECTION

Investigate Your Area Ground water is a drinking water source for about 60 percent of the population of the United States. Encourage students to find out where their drinking water comes from. Students can do research in local newspapers to learn about issues affecting the quality of their drinking water and prepare a poster illustrating the path that local ground water follows from a rain cloud to a faucet. If there is time, arrange for a tour of a local water treatment plant.

MISCONCEPTION ALERT

Students may think that ground water creates vast underground lakes or rivers. This happens only rarely. Most ground water moves through spaces in rock and soil similar to the way water is stored in a sponge.

Directed Reading Worksheet 11 Section 3

WEIRD SCIENCE

Only recently have scientists discovered how much fresh water flows into the oceans from ground water. When the tide comes in, sea water seeps into the sediments of coastal land, mixing with the ground water. When the tide recedes, the water mixture is drawn out to sea; the ground water is recharged and the cycle repeats. In addition, many fresh-water aquifers drain directly into the ocean. These findings are significant because pollution in ground water can seriously threaten the oceans.

Section 3 • Water Underground

2) Teach, continued

USING THE FIGURE

Guide students through **Figures 16** and **17**. List the labels on the board. Help students define each term and explain that artesian springs are driven by hydraulic pressure. Artesian springs occur in areas where the water table is above the outlet for the spring. If students have ever siphoned a liquid, they have applied the principle that causes artesian springs to flow. Challenge students to demonstrate an artesian spring using a water-filled container and a length of tubing.
Sheltered English

Much of Australia's ground water is stored in artesian formations, such as those fed by a vast underground rock formation called the Great Artesian Basin. Unfortunately, most of the water is too salty for people to drink or use for irrigation. Have students find out how this water could be processed in a desalination plant.

Answer to Self-Check

The impermeable rock layer in the aquifer traps the water in the permeable layer below. This creates the pressure needed to form an artesian spring.

 Teaching Transparency 143
"Artesian Formation"
"The Water Table and Wells"

Artesian Springs A sloping layer of permeable rock sandwiched between two layers of impermeable rock is called an *artesian formation*. The permeable rock is an aquifer, and the top layer of the impermeable rock is called a *cap rock*, as shown in **Figure 16**. Artesian formations are the source of water for **artesian springs**. Artesian springs are springs that form where cracks occur naturally in the cap rock and the pressurized water in the aquifer flows through the cracks to the surface. Artesian springs are sometimes found in deserts, where they are often the only source of water.

Figure 16 *Artesian springs form when water from an aquifer flows through cracks in the cap rock of an artesian formation.*

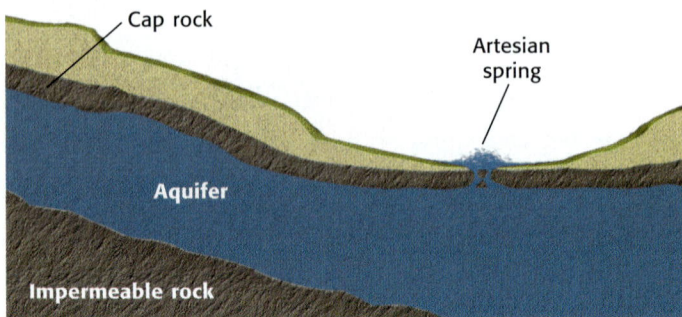

Wells A *well* is a human-made hole that is deeper than the level of the water table; therefore, wells fill with ground water, as shown in **Figure 17**. If a well is not deep enough, it will dry up when the water table falls below the bottom of the well. Also, if too many wells in an area remove ground water too rapidly, the water table will drop and all the wells will run dry.

Figure 17 *A good well is drilled deep enough so that when the water table drops, the well still contains water.*

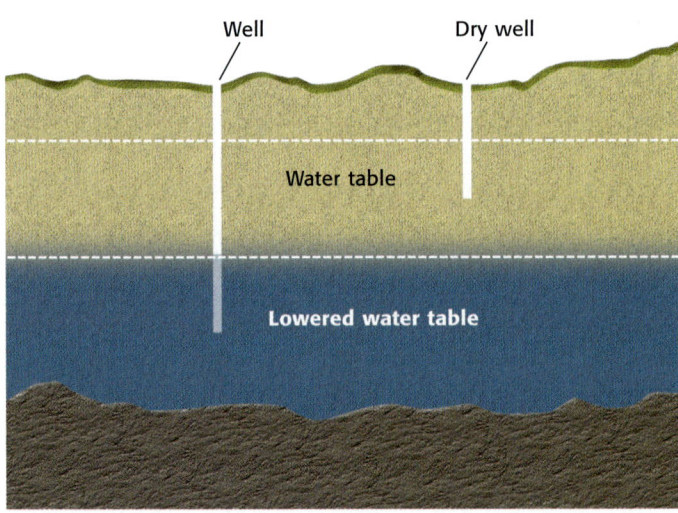

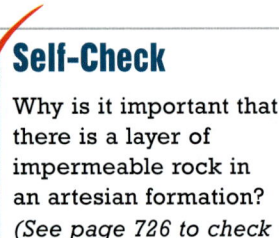

Self-Check

Why is it important that there is a layer of impermeable rock in an artesian formation? *(See page 726 to check your answer.)*

CONNECT TO LIFE SCIENCE

Elephants that live in the desert of Namibia may travel 4 days to find a water hole. Once there, they might have to dig almost a meter into the sand to reach clear water. Antelopes, such as springbok and eland, and other desert-dwelling animals depend on the elephants to penetrate the water table. Have students research ways in which desert plants and animals have adapted to regions with little surface water.

Underground Erosion and Deposition

Unlike a river, which erodes its banks when water moves over rock and soil, ground water erodes certain types of rock by dissolving the rock. Most of the world's caves formed over thousands of years as ground water dissolved limestone. Limestone, which is made of calcium carbonate, dissolves easily in water. As a result, caves form. Some caves reach spectacular proportions, such as the one in **Figure 18**.

Figure 18 At Carlsbad Caverns, in New Mexico, underground passages and enormous "rooms" have been eroded below the surface of the Earth.

Cave Formations While caves are formed by erosion, they also show signs of deposition. Water that drips from a crack in a cave's ceiling leaves behind deposits of calcium carbonate. These deposits of calcium carbonate are a type of limestone called *dripstone*. Water and dissolved limestone can drip downward into sharp, icicle-shaped dripstone features known as a stalactites. At the same time, water drops that fall to the cave's floor add to cone-shaped dripstone features known as stalagmites. If water drips long enough, the stalactites and stalagmites can reach each other and join, forming a dripstone column.

Environment CONNECTION

Most bat species live in caves. These night-flying mammals navigate by sound and can reach speeds of 95 km/h. Today scientists know that bats play an extremely important role in the environment. Bats are great consumers of insects, and many bat species pollinate plants and distribute seeds.

IS THAT A FACT!

Mount Shasta is a dormant volcano in the Shasta River basin, in California. During snowmelts, the Shasta River doesn't receive much runoff, however. The snowmelt is absorbed by the porous volcanic slopes and reemerges through springs at the bottom of the river valley.

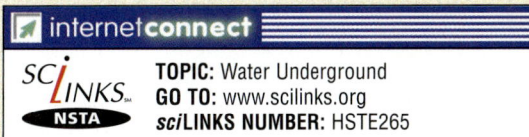

TOPIC: Water Underground
GO TO: www.scilinks.org
***sci*LINKS NUMBER:** HSTE265

3 Extend

GROUP ACTIVITY

MATERIALS

FOR EACH GROUP:
- 2 jars
- washing soda (sodium carbonate)
- spoon
- dish
- paper clips
- yarn

Tell students to fill the jars with very warm water and stir a few spoonfuls of washing soda into each jar. Students should stop when the soda no longer dissolves. Set the dish between the jars. Clip paper clips to the ends of the yarn, and lower each end into a different jar. After 2 or 3 days, some of the soda-water mixture will have moved through the yarn by capillary action, and the solution will have dripped onto the plate, forming a stalactite and stalagmite by evaporation.

GOING FURTHER

Have students research Mammoth Cave, in Kentucky, to learn more about the unique formations there. Then help them construct a "virtual cave." Have students work in groups to create models of the cave's formations using modeling clay. Different groups can model different sections of the cave. Students can also make an audio tape tour of the cave that tells visitors about the structures, including how they formed.

Sinkholes When the water table is lower than the level of a cave, the cave is no longer supported by the water underneath. The roof of the cave can then collapse, leaving a circular depression called a *sinkhole*. Surface streams can "disappear" into sinkholes and then flow through underground caves. Sinkholes often form lakes in areas where the water table is high. Central Florida is covered with hundreds of round sinkhole lakes. **Figure 19** shows how underground caves can affect a landscape.

Figure 19 This city block shows the effects of a sinkhole in Winter Park, Florida.

TOPIC: Water Underground
GO TO: www.scilinks.org
sciLINKS NUMBER: HSTE265

REVIEW

1. What is the water table?
2. What is an aquifer?
3. What are some of the features formed by underground erosion and deposition?
4. **Analyzing Relationships** What is the relationship between the zone of aeration, the zone of saturation, and the water table?

284

4) Close

Quiz

1. Define *porosity* and *permeability*. (Porosity is the amount of open space between rock particles. Permeability is the ability of rock to allow water to flow through it.)
2. Describe the formation that produces an artesian spring. (A cap rock seals off a permeable layer of rock that is filled with water. If the water table is above the cap rock, water under pressure can escape through an opening in the cap rock.)
3. What is a spring? What is a well? (A spring forms where the water table reaches the surface and water flows out. A well is a human construction that extends below the water table. Water flows into the well's opening and is pumped to the surface.)

ALTERNATIVE ASSESSMENT

Concept Mapping Have students use the following terms to make a concept map:

ground water, water table, aquifer, porosity, permeability, artesian spring, sinkhole, spring, well, cave, dripstone

Sheltered English

Reinforcement Worksheet 11 "Dig It!"

Problem Solving Worksheet 11 "Water Crisis at Happy Acres"

Answers to Review

1. Answers will vary. The water table is the level to which the ground is saturated by water.
2. An aquifer is a rock layer that stores and allows the flow of ground water.
3. Caves and sinkholes form by groundwater erosion. Stalagmites, stalactites, and dripstone columns form by underground deposition.
4. The water table is the underground boundary where the zone of aeration and the zone of saturation meet.

Section 4: Using Water Wisely

Terms to Learn
point-source pollution
nonpoint-source pollution
sewage treatment plant
septic tank

What You'll Do
- Describe the stages of treatment for water at a sewage treatment plant.
- Compare a septic system with a sewage treatment plant.
- Explain how ground water can be both a renewable and a nonrenewable resource.

All living things need water to survive. But there is a limited amount of fresh water available on Earth. Only 3 percent of Earth's water is drinkable. And of the 3 percent that is drinkable, 75 percent is frozen in the polar icecaps. That's more than 100 times the volume of water found in the Earth's lakes and streams! This frozen water is not readily available for our use. Therefore, it is important that we use our water resources wisely.

Water Pollution

Surface water, such as rivers and lakes, and ground water are often polluted by waste from cities, factories, and farms. One type of pollution is called **point-source pollution** because it comes from one particular point, such as a sewer pipe or a factory drain. Fortunately, laws prohibit much of this type of pollution.

There is growing concern, however, about another type of pollution, called **nonpoint-source pollution.** This type of pollution, as shown in **Figure 20,** is much more difficult to control because it does not come from a single source. Most nonpoint-source pollution contaminates rivers and lakes by runoff. The main sources of nonpoint-source pollution are street gutters, fertilizers, eroded soils and silt from farming and logging, drainage from mines, and salts from irrigation.

As you know, ground water is an important source of fresh water. In fact, more than half of all household water in the United States comes from ground water. Farms use ground water for irrigation. Because ground water is supplied by water from the Earth's surface, ground water can become contaminated when surface water is polluted. And once polluted, ground water is very difficult to clean up.

Figure 20 The runoff from this irrigation system could collect pesticides and other pollutants. The result would be nonpoint-source pollution.

IS THAT A FACT!

According to a 1998 U.S. Geological Survey report, water use in the United States has decreased 2 percent since 1990 and almost 10 percent since 1980, despite an increase in population. The report attributes this to public awareness and community conservation efforts.

2) Teach

Multicultural CONNECTION

Writing Encourage students to use library or Internet resources to investigate traditional American Indian beliefs about the Earth, including its rivers. Students may also be interested to find out about controversies involving American Indian tribes and the use of water resources, such as fisheries. Ask them to write a brief report summarizing their findings.

COOPERATIVE LEARNING

Divide the class into small groups, and challenge each group to create a board game. Tell them that the object of the game is to be the first player to successfully travel through a sewage treatment plant. Provide each group with poster board, plain index cards, and markers. Direct them to create a game board that leads players through the plant and incorporates the concepts they have learned about in this section. Have them use the index cards to write clues and questions directing players' movements through the sewage treatment process. For example, they might write, "If you can define primary treatment, advance to the aeration tank." Have students create written rules, and allow time for the game to be played.

Each year more than 2.5 million people die from waterborne diseases, such as cholera and typhoid. With better sewage treatment, many of these lives could be saved.

Cleaning Polluted Water

When you flush the toilet or watch water go down the shower drain, do you ever wonder where this water goes? If you live in a city or large town, the water flows through sewer pipes to a sewage treatment plant. **Sewage treatment plants** are factories that clean the waste materials out of water that comes from the sewer or drains. These plants help protect the environment from water pollution. They also protect us from diseases that are easily transmitted through dirty water.

Primary Treatment When water reaches a sewage treatment plant, it is cleaned in two different ways. First it goes through a series of steps known as *primary treatment*. In primary treatment, dirty water is passed through a large screen to catch solid objects, such as paper, rags, and bottle caps. The water is then placed in a large tank, where smaller particles can sink and be filtered out. These particles include things such as food, coffee grounds, and soil. Any floating oils and scum are skimmed off the surface.

Secondary Treatment At this point, the water is ready for *secondary treatment*. In secondary treatment, the water is sent to an aeration tank, where it is mixed with oxygen and bacteria. The bacteria feed on the wastes and use the oxygen. The water is then sent to another settling tank, where chlorine is added to disinfect the water. The water is finally released into a water source—a stream, a lake, or the ocean. **Figure 21** shows the major components of a sewage treatment plant.

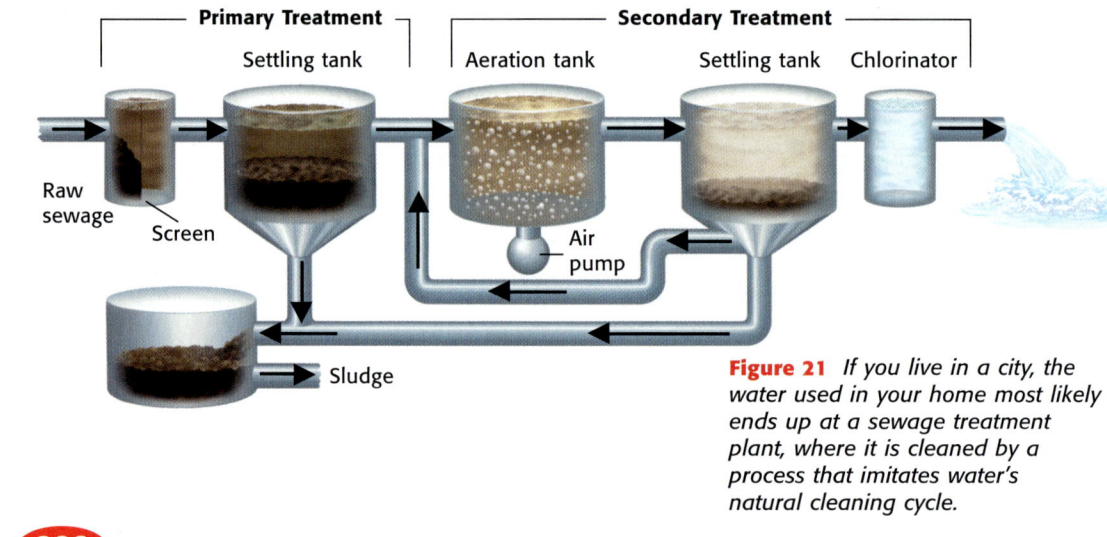

Figure 21 *If you live in a city, the water used in your home most likely ends up at a sewage treatment plant, where it is cleaned by a process that imitates water's natural cleaning cycle.*

Homework

Presentation Have students research sources of nonpoint-source pollution. Ask them to make posters for a community action campaign to reduce nonpoint-source pollution. Display students' posters in the classroom or around school.

MISCONCEPTION ALERT

Students may think that they cannot do anything to conserve water and prevent pollution. Point out to students that there are many things they can do to contribute to conservation. Tell students that by changing a few habits, they can greatly reduce their water consumption and reduce water pollution.

Another Way to Clean Waste Water If you live in an area without a sewage treatment plant, your house probably has a septic tank, such as the one shown in **Figure 22.** A **septic tank** is a large underground tank that collects and cleans waste water from a household. Waste water flows from the house into the tank, where the solids sink to the bottom. Bacteria consume these wastes on the bottom of the tank. The water flows from the tank into a group of buried pipes. The buried pipes distribute the water, enabling it to soak into the ground. This group of pipes is called a *drain field.*

Get your hands dirty and learn about some of the methods used to clean up water. Check out page 672 of the LabBook.

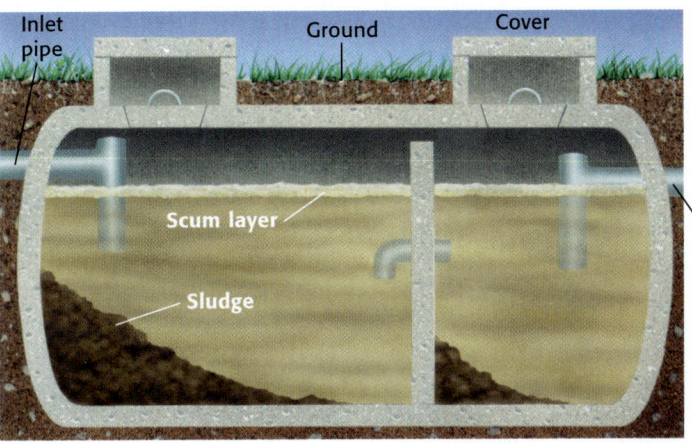

Figure 22 Most septic tanks must be cleaned out every few years in order to work properly.

Where the Water Goes

The chart in **Figure 23** shows how an average household in the United States uses water. Notice that less than 8 percent of the water we use in our homes is used for drinking. The rest is used for flushing toilets, doing laundry, bathing, and watering lawns and plants.

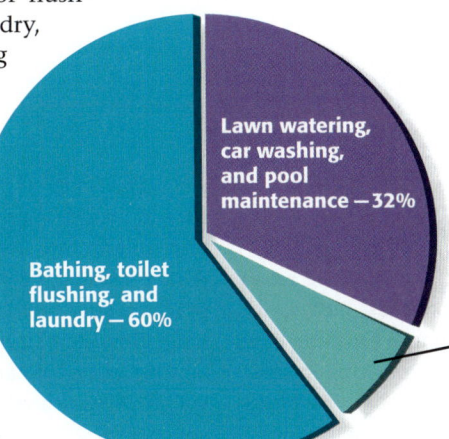

Figure 23 The average household in the United States uses about 100 gal of water per day. This pie chart shows some common uses of this 100 gal.

Lawn watering, car washing, and pool maintenance — 32%

Bathing, toilet flushing, and laundry — 60%

Drinking, cooking, washing dishes, running a garbage disposal — 8%

Activity

Study the chart at left and determine where the majority of water is used. Think of some ways that you can decrease the amount of water that you use in your home. Share your suggestions with your class.

Clean Up Your Act

MATH and MORE

Low-flush toilets use about 6 L of water per flush. Standard toilets use 19 L of water per flush. How much water is saved in a week by replacing a standard toilet with a low-flush toilet? Assume the toilet is flushed 10 times a day. **(910 L)**

How much water would be saved in a year? **(47,450 L)**

Math Skills Worksheet 3 "Multiplying Whole Numbers"

DEBATE

Should Water Conservation Be Enforced? Point out to students that many communities are enacting mandatory water conservation measures. For example, Albuquerque, New Mexico, has adopted a water-conservation policy in an effort to reduce per capita water use by 30 percent. However, some people are opposed to government regulation of water use. Divide the class into two groups, and assign each group a position in the debate. Have students use library or Internet resources to research their position.

IS THAT A FACT!

Mining can be a major source of water pollution. Although coal and mineral ores are part of Earth's rock formations and soil, some can be dangerous if they are concentrated in ground water and rivers and streams. Four major river basins in Pennsylvania are being polluted by runoff from thousands of abandoned coal mines. As a result, more than 4,800 km of stream water and ground water have been contaminated with acidic runoff containing toxic metals. The impact has been enormous; many of the streams are now devoid of fish.

Answers to Activity

Sample answers: I will make sure the dishwasher is completely full when it is being used. If I'm washing dishes in the sink, I won't let the water run continuously. I'll turn the shower off when lathering up. And I won't do several small loads of laundry if I can do fewer large loads instead.

3 Extend

CONNECT TO ENVIRONMENTAL SCIENCE

Settlement of the American West followed the conquest of its rivers. Damming and controlling rivers created usable farmland, allowed settlement in flood plains, and powered industry. Beginning in the 1930s, massive hydroelectric dams were built across many western rivers. Following this example, many countries have begun to dam their rivers to provide water for irrigation and drinking, to control flooding, and to produce electricity. While dams provide many benefits, large dam projects face increasing criticism for numerous social, environmental, economic, and safety concerns. Around the world, as many as 60 million people have been displaced by dams. Even more have suffered from the effects of dams downstream: farmland deprived of flood sediments and water for irrigation becomes unusable, fisheries become less productive, and epidemics of waterborne disease often follow large dam projects. Although hydropower is hailed as a cheap, nonpolluting source of energy, the true cost and impact of hydropower is often great. Should projects such as China's Three Gorges Dam be stopped? After America has benefitted so much from dam projects, can we ask developing countries not to exploit their water resources? Encourage students to find out more and debate these issues in class.

Answer to Apply

Answers will vary. Accept all reasonable responses.

Water in Industry The chart on the previous page shows how fresh water is used in homes. Even more water is required for industry, as shown in **Figure 24.** Water is used to cool power stations, to clean industrial products, to extract minerals, and to create power for factories. Many industries are trying to conserve water by reusing it in their production processes. In the United States, most of the water used in factories is recycled at least once. At least 90 percent of this water can be treated and returned to surface water.

Ground-water supplies also need to be monitored. Although ground water is considered to be a *renewable resource,* a resource that can be replenished, recycling ground water can be a lengthy process. When overused, ground water can sometimes be categorized as a *nonrenewable resource,* a substance that cannot be replaced once it is used. Ground water collects and moves slowly, and water taken from some aquifers might not be replenished for many years.

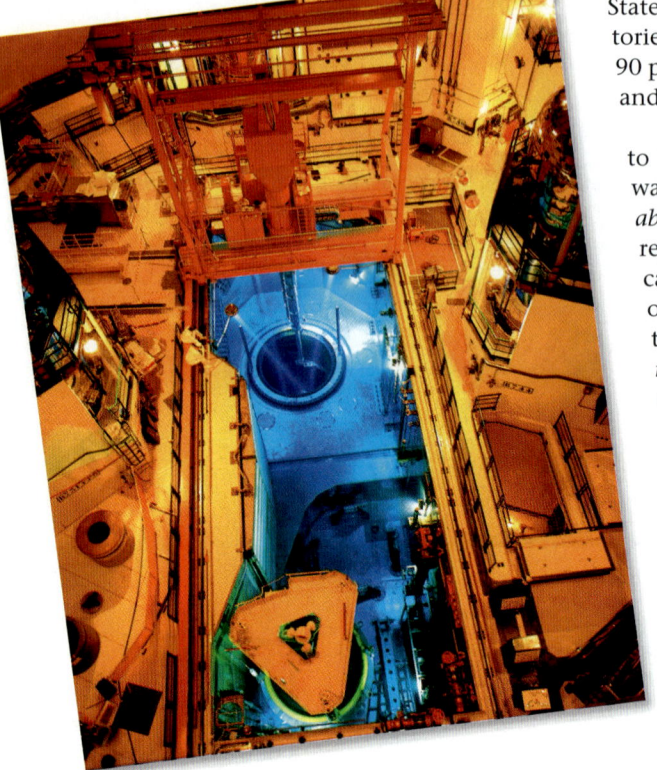

Figure 24 *The core of a nuclear reactor is cooled by water.*

Wasting Water?

How much water do you use when you brush your teeth? Picture yourself at home brushing your teeth. Time how long it takes you to go through the procedure. In your ScienceLog, write down the steps you take, making sure to include how many times you turn on and turn off the faucet. During what percentage of the time spent brushing your teeth is the water running? How do you think you might be wasting water? What are some ways that you could conserve water while brushing your teeth?

TOPIC: Water Pollution and Conservation
GO TO: www.scilinks.org
sciLINKS NUMBER: HSTE270

Water in Agriculture The Ogallala aquifer is the largest known aquifer in North America. The map in **Figure 25** shows that the Ogallala aquifer runs beneath the ground through eight states, from South Dakota to Texas. For the last 100 years, the aquifer has been used heavily for farming. The Ogallala aquifer provides water for approximately one-fifth of the cropland in the United States. Recently, the water table in the aquifer has dropped so low that some scientists say that it would take at least 1,000 years to replenish the aquifer if it were no longer used.

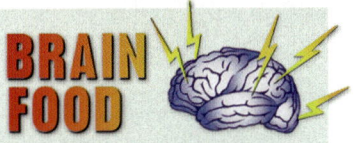

The Ogallala aquifer can hold enough water to fill Lake Huron. At this time, however, the aquifer is being used 25 times as fast as it is being replenished.

Figure 25 Because the Ogallala aquifer has been such a good source of ground water, it has become overused. The water table has dropped more than 30 m in some areas.

Water resources are different from other resources. Because water is necessary for life, there is no alternative resource. Aquifers are often overused and therefore do not have time to replenish themselves. Like surface water, ground water must be conserved.

REVIEW

1. What is the difference between nonpoint-source and point-source pollution?
2. Summarize the process of water treatment in a sewage treatment plant.
3. What is the difference between a renewable resource and a nonrenewable resource?
4. **Summarizing Data** How does a septic tank work?

internet connect

SC*LINKS*
NSTA

TOPIC: Water Pollution and Conservation
GO TO: www.scilinks.org
sciLINKS NUMBER: HSTE270

4 Close

Quiz

1. What are two sources of nonpoint-source pollution? (Sample answers: street gutters, fertilizers, eroded soils and silt from farming and logging, drainage from mines, and salts from irrigation)

2. How do sewage treatment plants protect the environment? (They clean polluted water before it is returned to a water source.)

ALTERNATIVE ASSESSMENT

Provide students with poster board and markers. Direct them to create posters illustrating how nonpoint-source pollution can cause contamination of both surface water and ground water. Their diagrams should reflect the understanding that pollution of surface water can spread to ground water. **Sheltered English**

COOPERATIVE LEARNING

Divide the class into small groups. Challenge each group to write a public-service announcement to educate the public about the need to conserve water and to avoid polluting ground water. The announcements should include definitions of nonrenewable and renewable resources and outline practical steps that everyone can take to protect water resources. **Sheltered English**

Interactive Explorations CD-ROM "Flood Bank"

Answers to Review

1. Point-source pollution comes from a single, identifiable source, whereas nonpoint-source pollution does not.
2. When water enters a sewage plant, it goes through two treatments. In primary treatment, most of the solid material is settled out. In secondary treatment, the water is cleaned by bacteria that feed on the waste and chlorine that kills the bacteria.
3. A renewable resource can be replaced or recycled. Once a nonrenewable resource is used up, it cannot be replaced.
4. Used water from a home flows into an underground tank, where bacteria feed on the solid waste. The rest of the water flows through underground pipes, which distribute it into the surrounding soil.

Section 4 • Using Water Wisely   **289**

Chapter Highlights

Vocabulary Definitions

SECTION 1

erosion the removal and transport of material by wind, water, or ice

water cycle the continuous movement of water from water sources into the air, onto land, into and over the ground, and back to the water sources; a cycle that links all of the Earth's solid, liquid, and gaseous water together

tributary a smaller stream or river that flows into a larger one

drainage basin the land drained by a river system, which includes the main river and all of its tributaries

divide an area of higher ground that separates drainage basins

channel the path a stream follows

load the materials carried in a stream's water

SECTION 2

deposition the process by which material is dropped or settles

alluvium rock and soil deposited by streams

delta a fan-shaped deposit of alluvium at the mouth of a stream, where the stream empties into a large body of water

alluvial fan fan-shaped deposits of alluvium that form on dry land

flood plain an area along a river formed from sediments deposited by floods

Chapter Highlights

SECTION 1

Vocabulary
- erosion (p. 270)
- water cycle (p. 270)
- tributary (p. 272)
- drainage basin (p. 272)
- divide (p. 272)
- channel (p. 273)
- load (p. 274)

Section Notes
- Erosion is the removal and transport of soil and rock.
- The water cycle is the continuous movement of water from water sources into the air, onto land, and back into water sources.
- A drainage basin, or watershed, includes a main river and all of its tributaries.
- The rate of stream erosion is affected by many factors, including the stream's gradient, discharge, speed, and load.
- Gradient is the change in elevation over distance.
- Discharge is the volume of water moved by a stream in a given amount of time.
- A stream's load is the material a stream can carry.
- Rivers can be described as youthful, mature, old, or rejuvenated.

Labs
Water Cycle—What Goes Up . . . (p. 670)

SECTION 2

Vocabulary
- deposition (p. 277)
- alluvium (p. 277)
- delta (p. 278)
- alluvial fan (p. 279)
- flood plain (p. 279)

Section Notes
- Deposition occurs when eroded soil and rock are dropped.
- Alluvium is the material deposited by rivers and streams.
- Deltas are deposits of alluvium at a river's mouth.
- Alluvial fans are deposits of alluvium at the base of a mountain.
- Flood plains are rich farming areas because flooding brings new soils to the area.

✓ Skills Check

Math Concepts

A STREAM'S GRADIENT One factor that can affect the speed of a river is its gradient. The gradient is a measure of the change in elevation over a certain distance. You can use the following equation to calculate a stream's gradient:

$$\text{gradient} = \frac{\text{change in elevation}}{\text{distance}}$$

For example, consider a river that starts at an elevation of 5,500 m and travels 350 km downstream to a lake, which is at an elevation of 2,000 m. By using the formula above, you would find the stream's gradient to be 10 m/km.

$$10 \text{ m/km} = \frac{(5,500 \text{ m} - 2,000 \text{ m})}{350 \text{ km}}$$

Visual Understanding

A STREAM'S LOAD Look back at the diagram on page 274 to review the different types of loads a stream can carry.

A SEWAGE TREATMENT PLANT Study Figure 21 on page 286 to review the two processes used to clean water in a sewage treatment plant.

Lab and Activity Highlights

Water Cycle—
What Goes Up . . .   PG 670

Clean Up Your Act   PG 672

 Datasheets for LabBook
(blackline masters for these labs)

290 Chapter 11 • The Flow of Fresh Water

SECTION 3

Vocabulary
- ground water (p. 280)
- water table (p. 280)
- aquifer (p. 280)
- porosity (p. 280)
- permeability (p. 280)
- recharge zone (p. 281)
- artesian spring (p. 282)

Section Notes
- Ground water is located below the Earth's surface.
- Ground water can dissolve rock, especially limestone.
- The zone of aeration and the zone of saturation meet at a boundary called the water table.
- An aquifer is a porous and permeable rock layer through which ground water flows.
- A sinkhole forms when the water table is lower than the roof of an underground cave.

SECTION 4

Vocabulary
- point-source pollution (p. 285)
- nonpoint-source pollution (p. 285)
- sewage treatment plant (p. 286)
- septic tank (p. 287)

Section Notes
- Sewage is treated in sewage treatment plants and in septic tanks.
- In a sewage treatment plant, water is cleaned in two different ways—primary treatment and secondary treatment.
- While water is generally considered to be a renewable resource, when overused it can sometimes be categorized as a nonrenewable resource.

Labs
Clean Up Your Act (p. 672)

VOCABULARY DEFINITIONS, continued

SECTION 3

ground water water that is located within rocks below the Earth's surface

water table an underground boundary where the zone of aeration and the zone of saturation meet

aquifer a rock layer that stores and allows the flow of ground water

porosity amount of open space between individual rock particles

permeability a rock's ability to let water pass through it

recharge zone the ground surface where water enters an aquifer

artesian spring a spring that forms where cracks occur naturally in the cap rock and the pressurized water in the aquifer flows through the cracks to the surface

SECTION 4

point-source pollution pollution that comes from one particular source area

nonpoint-source pollution pollution that comes from many sources and that cannot be traced to specific sites

sewage treatment plant a factory that cleans waste materials out of water that comes from sewers or drains

septic tank a large, underground tank that collects and cleans waste water from a household

---

internet connect

GO TO: go.hrw.com

Visit the **HRW** Web site for a variety of learning tools related to this chapter. Just type in the keyword:

KEYWORD: HSTDEP

GO TO: www.scilinks.org

Visit the **National Science Teachers Association** on-line Web site for Internet resources related to this chapter. Just type in the *sci*LINKS number for more information about the topic:

TOPIC	sciLINKS NUMBER
The Grand Canyon	HSTE255
Rivers and Streams	HSTE260
Stream Deposits	HSTE263
Water Underground	HSTE265
Water Pollution and Conservation	HSTE270

Lab and Activity Highlights

LabBank

EcoLabs & Field Activities, The Frogs Are Off Course, Field Activity 12

Long-Term Projects & Research Ideas, Canyon Controversy, Project 39

Interactive Explorations CD-ROM

CD 1, Exploration 8, "Flood Bank"

Vocabulary Review Worksheet 11

Blackline masters of these Chapter Highlights can be found in the **Study Guide.**

Chapter 11 • Chapter Highlights

Chapter Review Answers

USING VOCABULARY

1. A tributary flows into a river. A water table is the boundary between the zone of aeration and the zone of saturation.
2. An aquifer is a rock layer that stores and allows the flow of ground water. The recharge zone is an area on the Earth's surface where water enters an aquifer. Load refers to the materials carried by a stream.
3. Deltas and alluvial fans are both fan-shaped alluvial deposits. A divide is an area of high ground between drainage basins.
4. Porosity and permeability are the two characteristics that a rock layer must have to qualify as an aquifer. Deposition is the process by which a stream drops part of its load.
5. Point-source and nonpoint-source pollution are two types of pollution that contaminate surface and ground water. A septic tank is used to collect and treat polluted water.
6. Primary and secondary treatments are the two different ways that a sewage treatment plant cleans water. A drainage basin is the area that encompasses a river and all of its tributaries.

UNDERSTANDING CONCEPTS

Multiple Choice

7. d
8. c
9. c
10. a
11. d
12. d
13. d
14. c
15. c

Chapter Review

USING VOCABULARY

For each set of terms, identify the term that doesn't belong, and explain why.

1. tributary/river/water table
2. load/recharge zone/aquifer
3. delta/alluvial fan/divide
4. porosity/permeability/deposition
5. point-source pollution/nonpoint-source pollution/septic tank
6. primary treatment/secondary treatment/drainage basin

UNDERSTANDING CONCEPTS

Multiple Choice

7. Which of the following processes is not part of the water cycle?
   a. evaporation
   b. infiltration
   c. condensation
   d. deposition

8. Which type of stream load makes a river look muddy?
   a. bed load
   b. dissolved load
   c. suspended load
   d. gravelly load

9. What features are common in youthful river channels?
   a. meanders
   b. flood plains
   c. rapids
   d. sandbars

10. Which depositional feature is found at the coast?
    a. delta
    b. flood plain
    c. alluvial fan
    d. placer deposit

11. Caves are mainly a product of
    a. erosion by rivers.
    b. river deposition.
    c. water pollution.
    d. erosion by ground water.

12. The largest drainage basin in the United States is the
    a. Amazon.
    b. Columbia.
    c. Colorado.
    d. Mississippi.

13. An aquifer must be
    a. nonporous and nonpermeable.
    b. nonporous and permeable.
    c. porous and nonpermeable.
    d. porous and permeable.

14. Which of the following is a point source of water pollution?
    a. fertilizer from a farming area
    b. runoff from city streets
    c. a wastewater pipe
    d. leaking septic tanks

15. During primary treatment at a sewage treatment plant,
    a. water is sent to an aeration tank.
    b. water is mixed with bacteria and oxygen.
    c. dirty water is passed through a large screen.
    d. water is sent to a settling tank where chlorine is added.

Short Answer

16. What is the relationship between tributaries and rivers?
17. How are aquifers replenished?
18. Why are caves usually found in limestone-rich regions?

Short Answer

16. Tributaries flow into rivers and supply them with water.
17. Aquifers are replenished in the recharge zone. This is an area where a permeable rock layer allows water to percolate down into the aquifer.
18. Limestone is made of calcium carbonate, which dissolves easily in water. Ground water dissolves the limestone, producing caves.

Concept Mapping

19. Use the following terms to create a concept map: zone of aeration, zone of saturation, water table, gravity, porosity, permeability.

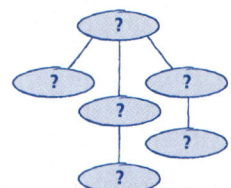

CRITICAL THINKING AND PROBLEM SOLVING

Write one or two sentences to answer the following questions:

20. What role does water play in erosion and deposition?
21. What are the features of a river channel that has a steep gradient?
22. Why is ground water hard to clean up?
23. Imagine you are hiking beside a mature stream. What would the stream be like?
24. How can water be considered both a renewable and a nonrenewable resource? Give an example of each case.

MATH IN SCIENCE

25. A sinkhole has formed in a town with a population of 5,000. The town is declared a disaster area, and $2 million is given to the town by the federal government. The local government uses 60 percent of the money for repairs to city property, and the rest is given to the townspeople.
    a. How much would each person receive?
    b. If there are 2,000 families in the town, how much would each family receive?
    c. Would each family receive enough money to help them rebuild a home? If not, how could the money be distributed more fairly?

INTERPRETING GRAPHICS

The hydrograph below illustrates river flow over a period of 1 year. The discharge readings are from the Yakima River, in Washington. The Yakima River flows eastward from the Cascade Mountains to the Columbia River.

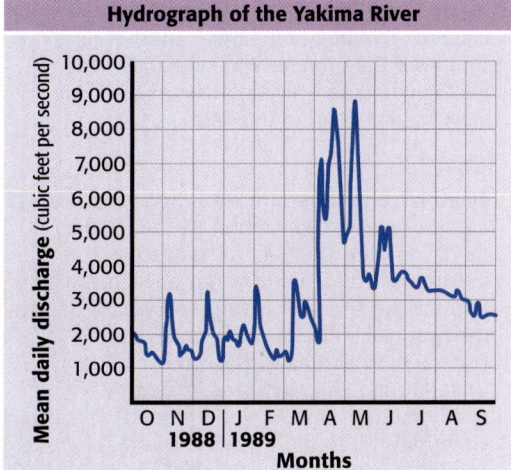

26. In which months is there the highest river discharge?
27. Why is there such a high river discharge during these months?
28. What might cause the peaks in river discharge between November and March?

 Take a minute to review your answers to the Pre-Reading Questions found at the bottom of page 268. Have your answers changed? If necessary, revise your answers based on what you have learned since you began this chapter.

Concept Mapping

19. 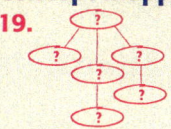 An answer to this exercise can be found at the end of this book.

CRITICAL THINKING AND PROBLEM SOLVING

20. Water flows across a landscape, eroding, transporting, and depositing material. Water is an agent of erosion and deposition.
21. A river channel that has a steep gradient is straight and narrow with rapids, waterfalls, and V-shaped valleys.
22. Once ground water becomes polluted, it is hard to clean up because it is not at the surface, where cleanup is done. Also, it moves very slowly and will therefore take a long time to clean up.
23. Answers will vary. A mature stream is wide with meanders. A mature stream can have a lot of discharge due to the size of its drainage basin.
24. Water is a renewable resource when it can be replaced or recycled. Rain is a renewable resource. Water is nonrenewable when it is consumed faster than it can be replenished. An example is the Ogallala aquifer.

MATH IN SCIENCE

25. a. $160
    b. $400
    c. Accept all reasonable responses. Sample answer: No; more money should be distributed to the families whose houses were directly affected by the sinkhole.

INTERPRETING GRAPHICS

26. April and May
27. Accept all reasonable responses. (spring snowmelt from the mountains, high rainfall)
28. winter storms or thaws

Concept Mapping Transparency 11

Blackline masters of this Chapter Review can be found in the **Study Guide**.

Chapter 11 • Chapter Review

WEIRD SCIENCE
Bubble, Boil, & Squirt

Background
Yellowstone National Park, located in northwestern Wyoming and southern Montana, includes more than 10,000 geothermal features. All of these features are the product of Yellowstone's unique geographic position. About half of Yellowstone Park lies on top of three major calderas that formed between 0.6 million and 2 million years ago. A caldera is a circular depression formed when the roof of a magma chamber collapses as a result of a volcanic eruption. The heat from the most recent caldera accounts for the large number of geothermal features in the park.

Fumaroles are the vents that emit the volcanic gas responsible for forming mud pots.

BUBBLE, BOIL, & SQUIRT

In parts of Yellowstone National Park boiling water blasts into the sky, lakes of strange-colored mud boil and gurgle, and hot gases hiss from the ground. What are these strange geologic features? What causes them? The story begins deep in the Earth.

Old Geysers
One of Yellowstone's main tourist attractions is a *geyser* called Old Faithful. Erupting every 60 to 70 minutes, Old Faithful sends a plume of steam and scalding-hot water as high as 60 m into the air. A geyser is formed when a narrow vent connects one or more underground chambers to Earth's surface. These underground chambers are heated by nearly molten rock. As underground water flows into the vent and chambers, it is heated above 100°C. The superheated water quickly turns to steam and explodes first toward the surface and then into the air. And Old Faithful erupts right on schedule!

Nature's Hot Tub
A *hot spring* is a geyser without pressure. Its vents are wider than a geyser's, and they let the underground water cool a little and flow to the surface rather than erupt in a big fountain. To be called a hot spring, the water must be at least as warm as human body temperature (37°C). Some underground springs are several hundred degrees Celsius.

Flying Mud Pies
Mud pots form when steam or hot underground water trickles to the surface and chemically weathers and dissolves surface features, such as rocks. The mixture of dissolved rock and water creates a boiling, bubbling pool of sticky liquid clay. But don't get too close! Occasionally, the steam will rise quickly and forcefully enough to make the mud pot behave like a volcano. When it does, a mud pot can toss car-sized gobs of mud high into the air!

Some mud pots become *paint pots* when microorganisms or brightly colored minerals are mixed in. For instance, if there is a lot of iron in the mud, the paint pot will turn reddish brown or yellowish brown. Other minerals and bacteria can make the mud white or bluish in color. Some paint pots may even gurgle up blobs in several different colors.

▲ *Mud Pot in Yellowstone National Park*

What Do You Think?
▶ Some people believe that tapping geothermal energy sources such as geysers could harm the delicate ecology of those sources. Find out about the benefits and risks of using geothermal energy. What is your opinion?

Sample Answer to What Do You Think?
The main advantage of geothermal energy is that, unlike fossil fuels, it doesn't produce pollution and is a renewable resource. Also, geothermal energy plants require less space than normal power plants. However, some scientists believe that using geothermal energy from geysers could disrupt the natural flow of hot springs and possibly disrupt ground-water sources. Some geysers recently used to make electricity have stopped producing steam. Other possible consequences of the disruption of geothermal areas are as follows: the extinction of microorganisms that thrive in hot waters, collapsing calderas, and more-frequent volcanic eruptions.

EYE ON THE ENVIRONMENT

Disaster Along the Delta

As the sun rises over the delta wetlands of the Mississippi River, fishermen test their skills. Long-legged birds step lightly through the marsh, hunting fish or frogs for breakfast. And hundreds of species of plants and animals start another day in this fragile ecosystem. But the delta ecosystem is in danger of being destroyed.

The threat comes from efforts to make the Mississippi more useful. Large portions of the river bottom were dredged to make the river deeper for ship traffic. Underwater channels were built to control flooding. What no one realized was that sediments that were once deposited to form new land now pass through the deep channels and flow out into the ocean.

Those river sediments replaced the land that was lost every year to erosion. Without the sediments, the river can't replace the land lost to erosion. And so the Mississippi River delta is disappearing. By 1995, more than half the wetlands were already gone, swept out to sea by waves along the Louisiana coast.

Sedimental Journey

The Mississippi River journeys 3,766 km to empty 232 million metric tons of sediment into the Gulf of Mexico each year. The end of the Mississippi River delta forms the largest area of wetlands in North America. A *delta* forms when sediments settle at the mouth of a river. At the Mississippi River delta, the sediments build up and form new land along the Louisiana coastline. The area around the delta is called *wetlands*. It has fertile soil, which produces many crops, and a variety of habitats—marsh, freshwater, and saltwater—that support many species of plants and animals.

Taking Action to Preserve the Delta

Since the mid-1980s, local, state, and federal governments, along with Louisiana citizens and businesses, have been working together to monitor and restore the Mississippi River delta. Some projects to protect the delta include filling in canals that divert the sediments and even using old Christmas trees as fences to trap the sediments! With the continued efforts of scientists, government leaders, and concerned citizens, the Mississippi River delta stands a good chance of recovering.

Explore the Delta

▶ Find out more about the industries and organisms that depend on the Mississippi River delta for survival. What will happen to them if we don't take care of the ecosystem?

▲ *The Mississippi River flows from Minnesota through the Midwest to the Gulf of Mexico in the southern United States.*

EYE ON THE ENVIRONMENT

Disaster Along the Delta

Background

The word *Mississippi* comes from a Native American word that means "big river." The Mississippi River flows for 3,766 km from its source, in Minnesota, to its mouth, in the Gulf of Mexico. More than 2,897 km of the river can be navigated by ships and boats for commercial, transportational, and recreational uses.

The Mississippi River forms part of the boundaries of 10 different states. As it travels to the Gulf of Mexico, other rivers—such as the Ohio and the Missouri—flow into it and increase the volume of water in the Mississippi River.

The Mississippi River delta covers about 33,700 km². It continuously nourishes the coastal wetlands that provide a habitat for diverse populations of plants and animals.

The erosion and sinking of land near the Mississippi River delta has seriously disrupted local economies. For instance, the coastal commercial and recreational fishing industries contribute about $2 billion to Louisiana's economy every year and provide about 50,000 to 70,000 jobs for the people of Louisiana. Also, the coastal wetlands provide coastal residents with protection from hurricanes and other storms. Currently, the erosion in this area accounts for 80 percent of the nation's loss of coastal wetlands per year.

Answers to Explore the Delta

The coastal wetlands at the Mississippi River delta provide a habitat for diverse communities of plants and animals, such as fish, shellfish, and birds. The wetlands are the nursery and feeding area for millions of waterfowl. These species and the industries that rely on them, such as fishing and tourism, will suffer greatly if the wetland ecosystems are not protected. If erosion is severe enough, buildings, highways, phone lines, and pipelines will need to be relocated.

Chapter Organizer

CHAPTER ORGANIZATION	TIME MINUTES	OBJECTIVES	LABS, INVESTIGATIONS, AND DEMONSTRATIONS
Chapter Opener pp. 296–297	45	National Standards: SAI 1, ES 2a	**Start-Up Activity** Making Waves, p. 297
Section 1 Shoreline Erosion and Deposition	90	▶ Explain the connection between storms and wave erosion. ▶ Explain how waves break in shallow water. ▶ Describe how beaches form. ▶ Describe types of coastal landforms created by wave action. UCP 3, SAI 1, SPSP 2, 3, ES 1c	**Whiz-Bang Demonstrations,** Between a Rock and a Hard Place, Demo 23 `BASIC` **Whiz-Bang Demonstrations,** Rising Mountains, Demo 24 `GENERAL`
Section 2 Wind Erosion and Deposition	90	▶ Explain why areas with fine materials are more vulnerable to wind erosion. ▶ Describe how wind moves sand and finer materials. ▶ Describe the effects of wind erosion. ▶ Describe the difference between dunes and loess. SAI 1, ST 2, SPSP 2, HNS 1–3, ES 1c, 2a; LabBook UCP 2, 3, SAI 1	**QuickLab,** Making Desert Pavement, p. 305 `GENERAL` **Making Models,** Dune Movement, p. 676 `BASIC` **Datasheets for LabBook,** Dune Movement, Datasheet 23 `BASIC`
Section 3 Erosion and Deposition by Ice	90	▶ Summarize why glaciers are important agents of erosion and deposition. ▶ Explain how ice in a glacier flows. ▶ Describe some of the landforms eroded by glaciers. ▶ Describe some of the landforms deposited by glaciers. UCP 3, SAI 1, SPSP 3, ES 1c, 2a; LabBook UCP 2, SAI 1, ES 1c	**Making Models,** Gliding Glaciers, p. 677 `GENERAL` **Datasheets for LabBook,** Gliding Glaciers, Datasheet 24 `GENERAL` **Discovery Lab,** Creating a Kettle, p. 679 `BASIC` **Datasheets for LabBook,** Creating a Kettle, Datasheet 25 `BASIC`
Section 4 Gravity's Effect on Erosion and Deposition	90	▶ Explain how slope is related to mass movement. ▶ State how gravity affects mass movement. ▶ Describe different types of mass movement. SAI 1, SPSP 3, 4, ES 1c	**QuickLab,** Angle of Repose, p. 316 `GENERAL` **Long-Term Projects & Research Ideas,** Project 40 `ADVANCED`

See page T20 for a complete correlation of this book with the **NATIONAL SCIENCE EDUCATION STANDARDS.**

TECHNOLOGY RESOURCES

 Guided Reading Audio CD English or Spanish, Chapter 12

 One-Stop Planner CD-ROM with Test Generator

 CNN. Science, Technology & Society, Battling over the Oregon Inlet, Segment 17

Eye on the Environment, Shrinking Wetlands, Segment 8

Chapter 12 • Agents of Erosion and Deposition

CLASSROOM WORKSHEETS, TRANSPARENCIES, AND RESOURCES	SCIENCE INTEGRATION AND CONNECTIONS	REVIEW AND ASSESSMENT
Directed Reading Worksheet 12 BASIC **Science Puzzlers, Twisters & Teasers,** Worksheet 12 ADVANCED		
Math Skills for Science Worksheet 31, The Unit Factor and Dimensional Analysis GENERAL **Directed Reading Worksheet 12,** Section 1 BASIC **Science Skills Worksheet 2,** Using Your Senses GENERAL **Teaching Transparency 144,** Coastal Landforms Created by Wave Erosion: A **Teaching Transparency 145,** Coastal Landforms Created by Wave Erosion: B	**MathBreak,** Counting Waves, p. 299 GENERAL **Connect to Physical Science,** p. 299 in ATE **Math and More,** p. 299 in ATE BASIC **Multicultural Connection,** p. 300 in ATE ADVANCED **Connect to Life Science,** p. 301 in ATE ADVANCED **Eye on the Environment:** Beach Today, Gone Tomorrow, p. 325 GENERAL	**Self-Check,** p. 299 **Review,** p. 303 GENERAL **Quiz,** p. 303 in ATE GENERAL **Alternative Assessment,** p. 303 in ATE GENERAL
Transparency 146, Saltation **Directed Reading Worksheet 12,** Section 2 BASIC **Transparency 147,** Migration of Sand Dunes **Critical Thinking Worksheet 12,** A Future in Sand ADVANCED	**Connect to Life Science,** pp. 304, 305, 307 in ATE **Apply,** p. 306 GENERAL **Multicultural Connection,** p. 306 in ATE GENERAL **Cross-Disciplinary Focus,** p. 307 in ATE **Biology Connection,** p. 308 **Science, Technology, and Society:** Boulder Boogie, p. 324 GENERAL	**Self-Check,** p. 305 **Homework,** p. 307 in ATE GENERAL **Review,** p. 308 GENERAL **Quiz,** p. 308 in ATE GENERAL **Alternative Assessment,** p. 308 in ATE GENERAL
Directed Reading Worksheet 12, Section 3 BASIC **Math Skills for Science Worksheet 17,** Using Proportions and Cross-Multiplication GENERAL **Transparency 148,** Landscape Features Carved by Alpine Glaciers **Reinforcement Worksheet 12,** An Alpine Vacation BASIC	**MathBreak,** Speed of a Glacier, p. 311 GENERAL **Connect to Physical Science,** p. 311 in ATE GENERAL **Cross-Disciplinary Focus,** p. 312 in ATE **Cross-Disciplinary Focus,** p. 313 in ATE ADVANCED **Real-World Connection,** p. 314 in ATE **Cross-Disciplinary Focus,** p. 314 in ATE	**Self-Check,** p. 311 **Homework,** p. 312 in ATE ADVANCED **Homework,** p. 313 in ATE BASIC **Review,** p. 315 GENERAL **Quiz,** p. 315 in ATE GENERAL **Alternative Assessment,** p. 315 in ATE GENERAL
Transparency 220, The Law of Universal Gravitation **Directed Reading Worksheet 12,** Section 4 BASIC	**Physics Connection,** p. 317 **Connect to Physical Science,** p. 317 in ATE GENERAL **Real-World Connection,** p. 318 in ATE **Connect to Life Science,** pp. 318, 319 in ATE	**Homework,** p. 317 in ATE ADVANCED **Review,** p. 319 GENERAL **Quiz,** p. 319 in ATE GENERAL **Alternative Assessment,** p. 319 in ATE GENERAL

END-OF-CHAPTER REVIEW AND ASSESSMENT

Chapter Review in Study Guide
Vocabulary and Notes in Study Guide
Chapter Tests with Performance-Based Assessment, Chapter 12 Test
Chapter Tests with Performance-Based Assessment, Performance-Based Assessment 12
Concept Mapping Transparency 12

internetconnect

Holt, Rinehart and Winston On-line Resources
go.hrw.com
For worksheets and other teaching aids related to this chapter, visit the HRW Web site and type in the keyword: **HSTICE**

National Science Teachers Association
www.scilinks.org
Encourage students to use the *sci*LINKS numbers listed in the internet connect boxes to access information and resources on the **NSTA** Web site.

Chapter Resources & Worksheets

Visual Resources

TEACHING TRANSPARENCIES

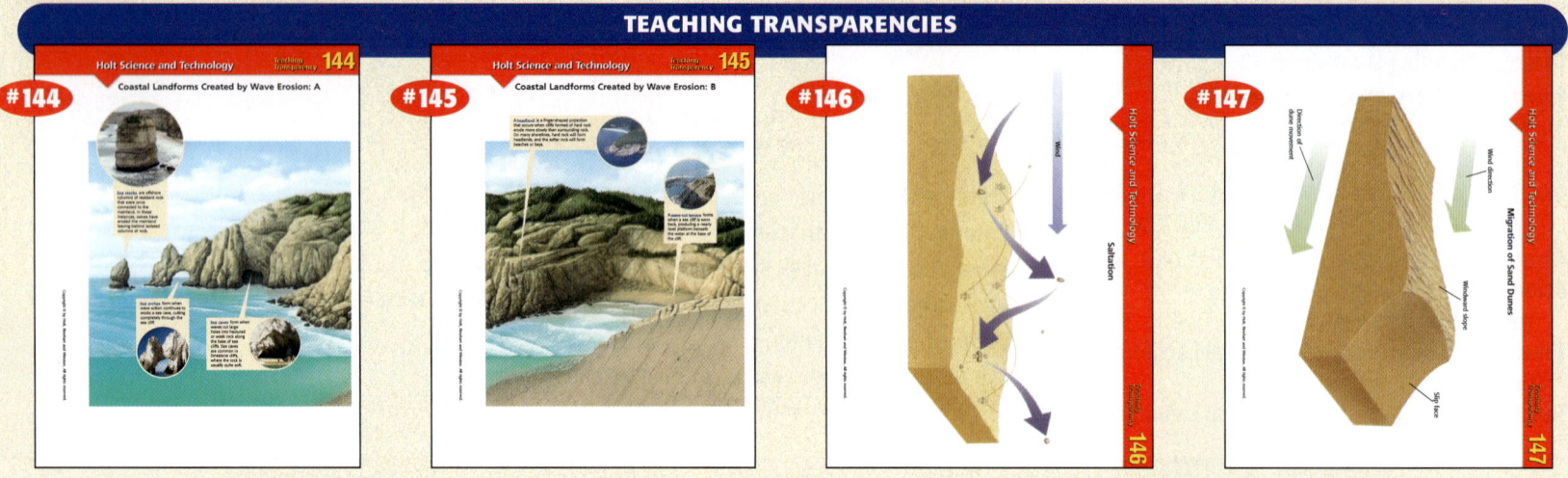

TEACHING TRANSPARENCIES

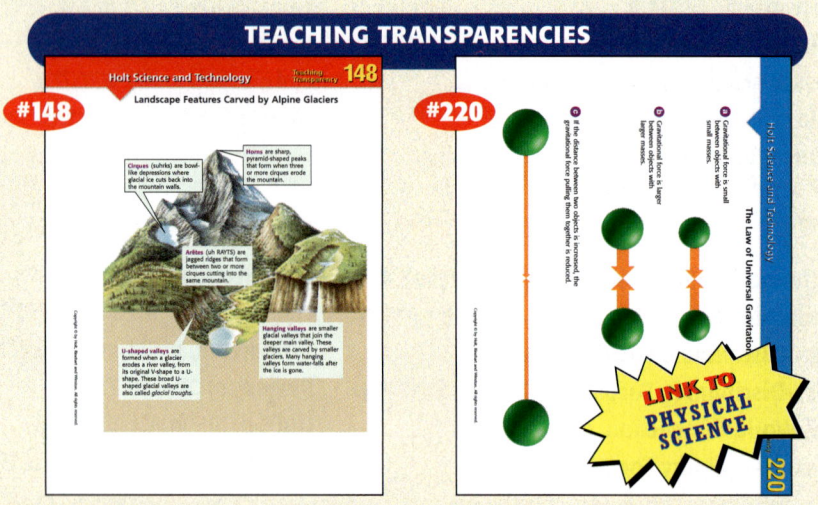

CONCEPT MAPPING TRANSPARENCY

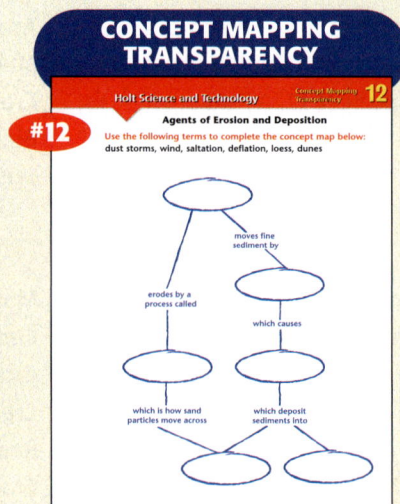

Meeting Individual Needs

DIRECTED READING

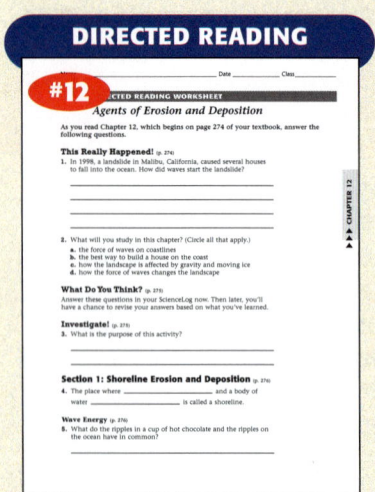

REINFORCEMENT & VOCABULARY REVIEW

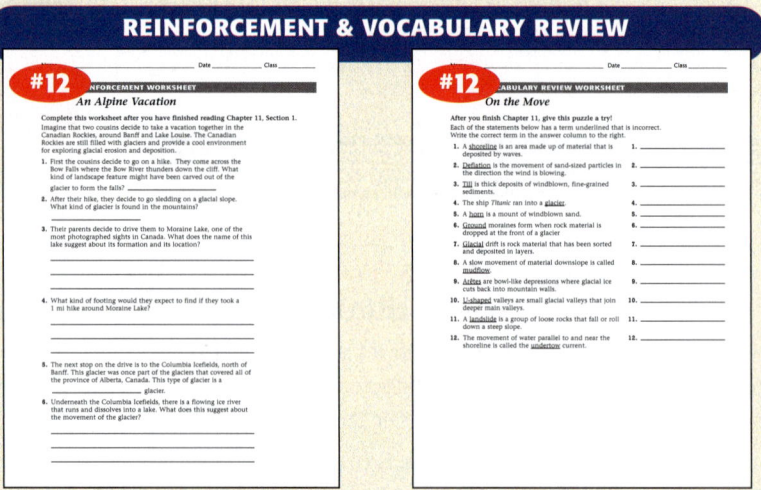

SCIENCE PUZZLERS, TWISTERS & TEASERS

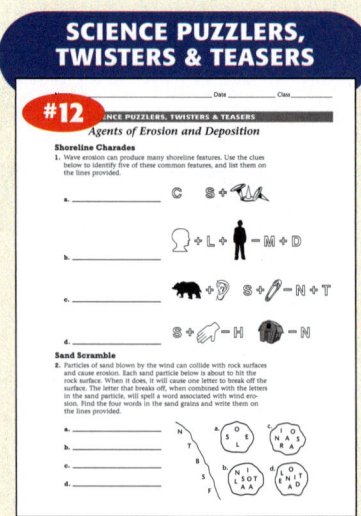

Chapter 12 • Agents of Erosion and Deposition

Chapter 12 • Agents of Erosion and Deposition

Review & Assessment

STUDY GUIDE

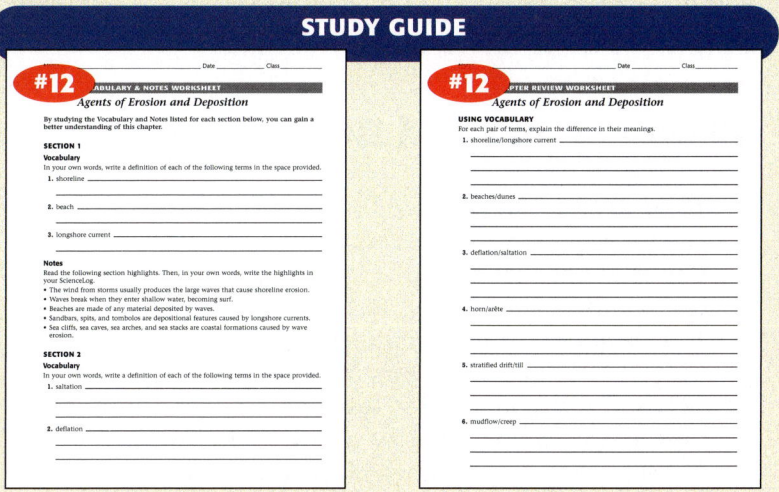

CHAPTER TESTS WITH PERFORMANCE-BASED ASSESSMENT

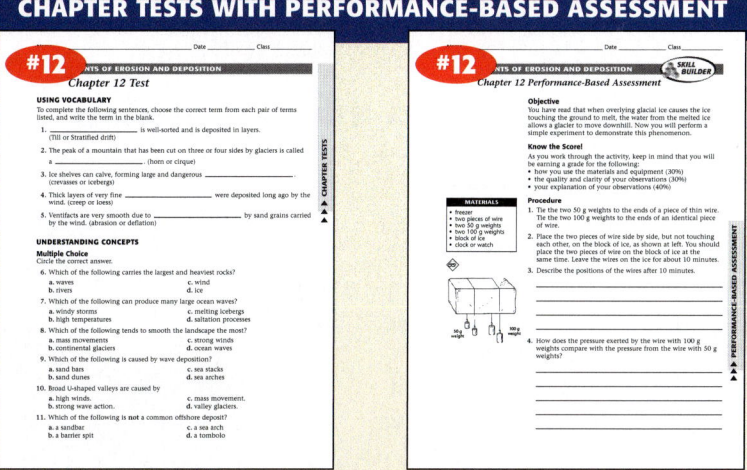

Lab Worksheets

WHIZ-BANG DEMONSTRATIONS

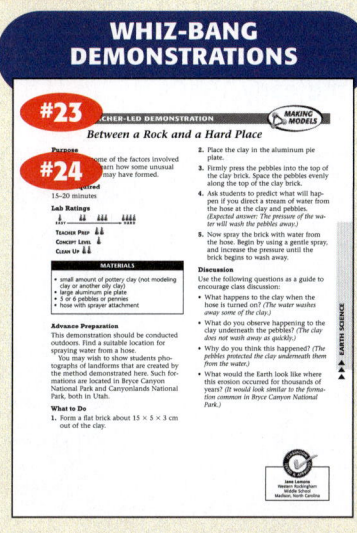

LONG-TERM PROJECTS & RESEARCH IDEAS

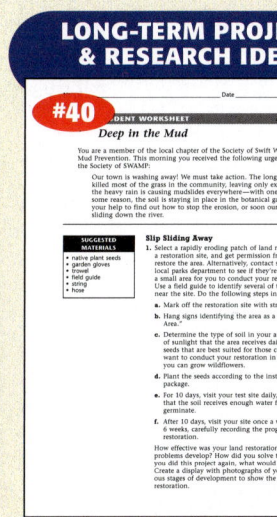

DATASHEETS FOR LABBOOK

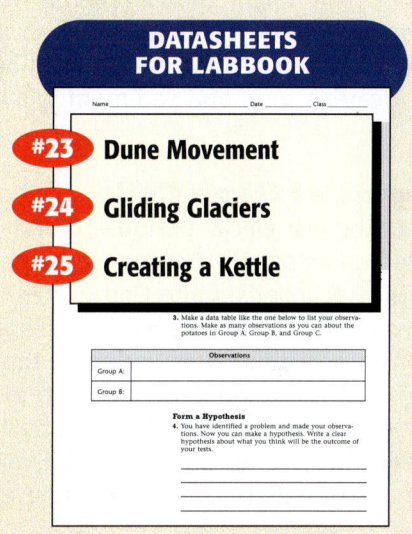

Applications & Extensions

CRITICAL THINKING & PROBLEM SOLVING

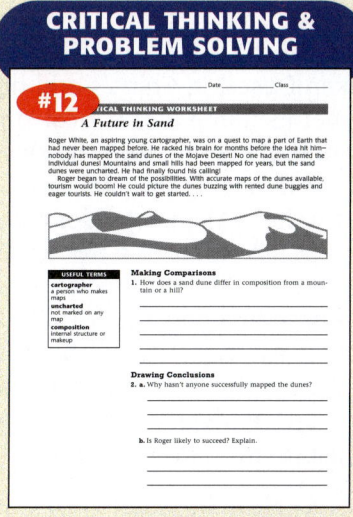

SCIENCE TECHNOLOGY

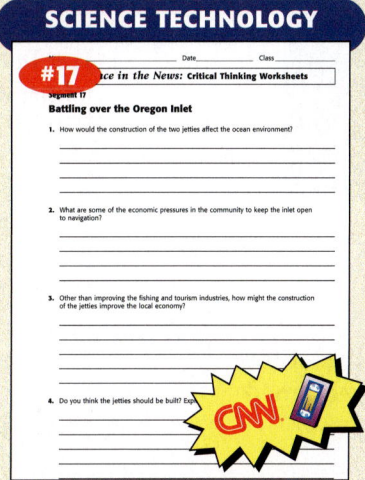

EYE ON THE ENVIRONMENT

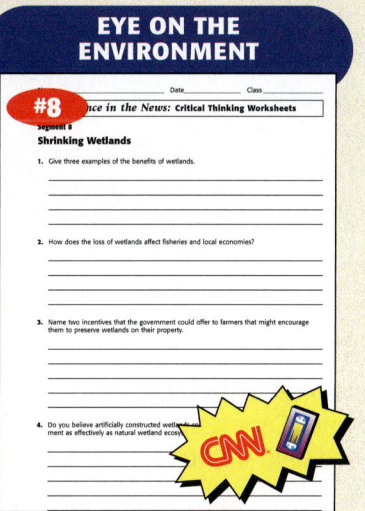

Chapter 12 • Chapter Resources & Worksheets   **295D**

Chapter Background

SECTION 1

Shoreline Erosion and Deposition

▶ **Acrobatic Waves**

To understand shoreline erosion, it's helpful to understand the forces acting in a breaking wave. Breaking waves can be thought of as somersaulting water. As waves move toward shallow coastal waters, the wavelengths shorten, crests crowd together, and wave height grows. When a wave becomes too top-heavy, it somersaults over itself, rushing onto the shore. As the water flows back into the ocean, it carries sand and sediment with it.

▶ **The Origins of Cape Cod**

At the end of the last glacial period—10,000 years ago—glaciers receding across North America helped form Cape Cod, Massachusetts. Cape Cod was initially mounds of outwash debris left behind by the glaciers. These mounds were then surrounded by the rising sea. Over time, currents eroded land and filled in depressions between the islands. Sandbars connected the islands to each other and the mainland. Since that time, Cape Cod has lost 3.2 km of coastline to ocean erosion.

IS THAT A FACT!

◆ Scientists predict that if the erosion continues at the current rate, Cape Cod will be completely reclaimed by the ocean in 4,000–5,000 years.

SECTION 2

Wind Erosion and Deposition

▶ **The Dust Bowl**

The Dust Bowl was a section of the Great Plains of the United States that extended from southeastern Colorado and southwestern Kansas to the panhandles of Texas and Oklahoma and to northeastern New Mexico. In the early 1930s, following years of overcultivation in the 1920s, the region suffered a severe drought. Exposed topsoil was carried away by strong spring winds. Windblown soil sometimes blocked out the sun, and the dirt piled up in drifts like snow. Occasionally, huge dust storms blew across the country and reached the East Coast. The wind erosion was gradually halted when the federal government planted windbreaks and large areas of grasslands were restored. The area had mostly recovered by the early 1940s.

▶ **Lost Cities of the Takla Makan Desert**

The Takla Makan Desert in China's arid northwest is so inhospitable that its name in the local language means "Go in, and you don't come out." The desert is covered with treacherous dunes of fine, dry sand. Buried under those dunes are the remains of cities that prospered along the ancient Silk Road. The Silk Road was a trade route that connected China to civilizations in the West. NASA's Spaceborne Imaging Radar (SIR-C), which flew on space shuttles twice in 1994, is being used to examine the desert. The radar-imaging technology has already helped archaeologists locate some cities and promises to help them find other ruins.

Chapter 12 • Agents of Erosion and Deposition

SECTION 3

Erosion and Deposition by Ice

▶ **Glaciers and Drinking Water**

About 10 percent of Earth's surface is covered with glaciers. The water frozen in glaciers makes up almost 75 percent of the world's freshwater supply. Arapaho Glacier, a small glacier in Colorado, provides water to more than 75,000 people living in the city of Boulder.  Many countries have explored the possibility of obtaining drinking water from glaciers, even by towing icebergs to a nearby harbor!

IS THAT A FACT!

- Glaciers flow at different rates. Most glaciers flow at a rate of 1 m per day or less, but some flow much faster. In 1936, the Black Rapids Glacier, in Alaska, was measured flowing at a rate of 30 m per day.

- If all of Earth's glaciers simultaneously melted, sea level would rise more than 65 m, submerging coastal cities all over the world.

▶ **Battles on Siachen Glacier**

At 70 km, the Siachen Glacier is one of the world's longest. It's in the Karakoram Range, on the India–Pakistan border. It is also the site of the world's highest battles. Indian and Pakistani soldiers have fought over the disputed territory of Kashmir on peaks as high as 6,400 m (21,000 ft).

▶ **The Great Lakes**

The Great Lakes were formed by the movement of ice sheets during the Pleistocene epoch. These glaciers advanced over the land, gouging out a series of deep basins. As the glaciers melted, the basins filled with meltwater, and the five Great Lakes were formed.

SECTION 4

Gravity's Effect on Erosion and Deposition

▶ **Scree**

Mountain stones and boulders loosened by weathering and carried downward by gravity may be deposited in long, loose heaps called scree at the base of a mountain.

IS THAT A FACT!

- When an earthquake measuring 5 on the Richter scale occurred near Mount St. Helens on May 18, 1980, it triggered a landslide of more than 2 km³ of rock and ice. Immediately afterward, an eruption began, and an explosion of steam and volcanic gases produced a lahar that raced down the mountain at speeds of up to 250 km/h.

For background information about teaching strategies and issues, refer to the *Professional Reference for Teachers*.

Agents of Erosion and Deposition

Pre-Reading Questions

Students may not know the answers to these questions before reading the chapter, so accept any reasonable response.

Suggested Answers

1. Answers may vary. Waves and wind both erode and deposit sediment. Students may also note that wind causes waves.
2. Answers may vary.

Directed Reading Worksheet 12

Science Puzzlers, Twisters & Teasers Worksheet 12

Guided Reading Audio CD
English or Spanish, Chapter 12

CHAPTER 12

Agents of Erosion and Deposition

Sections

1. **Shoreline Erosion and Deposition** 298
   MathBreak 299
2. **Wind Erosion and Deposition** 304
   QuickLab 305
   Apply 306
   Biology Connection... 308
   Internet Connect 308
3. **Erosion and Deposition by Ice** 309
   MathBreak 311
   Internet Connect 315
4. **Gravity's Effect on Erosion and Deposition** 316
   QuickLab 316
   Physics Connection... 317
   Internet Connect 319

Chapter Review 322
Feature Articles 324, 325
LabBook............ 676–679

Pre-Reading Questions

1. What do waves and wind have in common?
2. How do waves, wind, and ice erode and deposit rock materials?

The Crashing Surf

On February 8, 1998, unusually large waves crashed against the cliffs along Broad Beach Road in Malibu, California. Eventually, the ocean-eroded cliffs buckled, causing a landslide. One house collapsed into the ocean, while two more dangled on the edge of the cliff. What made these waves stronger than usual? How can water cause this much damage? In this chapter, you will study how waves shape beaches and coastlines. You will also learn how wind, moving ice, and gravity sculpt the surface of our planet.

---

internet connect

HRW On-line Resources
go.hrw.com
For worksheets and other teaching aids, visit the HRW Web site and type in the keyword: **HSTICE**

sciLINKS NSTA
www.scilinks.com
Use the *sci*LINKS numbers at the end of each chapter for additional resources on the **NSTA** Web site.

CNNfyi.com
www.cnnfyi.com
Visit the CNN Web site for current events coverage and classroom resources.

296 Chapter 12 • Agents of Erosion and Deposition

START-UP Activity

MAKING WAVES

Did you know that beaches and shorelines are shaped by crashing waves? See for yourself by creating some waves of your own.

Procedure

1. Make a beach by adding **sand** to one end of a **washtub**.
2. Fill the washtub with **water** to a depth of 5 cm.
3. In your ScienceLog, sketch the beach profile (side view), and label it "A."
4. Place a **block** at the end of the washtub opposite the beach. Move the block up and down very slowly to create small waves for 2 minutes. Sketch the new beach profile and label it "B."
5. Again place a block at the end of the washtub opposite the beach. Move the block up and down more rapidly to create large waves for 2 minutes. Sketch the new beach profile and label it "C."

Analysis

6. Compare the three beach profiles. What is happening to the beach?
7. How do small waves and large waves erode the beach differently?
8. What other factors might contribute to beach erosion?

START-UP Activity

MAKING WAVES

MATERIALS

FOR EACH GROUP:
- sand
- washtub
- tap water
- wooden or plastic block

Answers to START-UP Activity

6. The beach is slowly receding, or eroding.
7. Small waves erode less shoreline than large waves. Therefore, large waves have a greater impact on the shoreline.
8. Accept all reasonable responses. Sample answers: Lack of vegetation increases beach erosion. Wind and storms contribute to beach erosion.

Chapter 12 • Agents of Erosion and Deposition

SECTION 1

Focus

Shoreline Erosion and Deposition

This section explores how wave action sculpts and builds shorelines. Students first focus on the formation of beaches and offshore landforms by deposition and then learn how waves erode the shoreline. Students explore the formation of sea cliffs, sea stacks, sea arches, and sea caves, and learn how waves work to erode cliffs, creating headlands and wave-cut terraces.

🔔 Bellringer

 Ask students to think about where sand comes from. Have them write a short poem in their ScienceLog about how ocean waves create sand from rock.

1 Motivate

ACTIVITY

Explain to students that shorelines are dynamic, changing environments because ocean waves and currents continually erode and redeposit sand. Have each student draw a "filmstrip" illustrating the changes that could occur in the history of a beach.

Encourage students to illustrate the processes that cause these changes and to write a caption that explains each frame and the time interval that elapses between scenes. Students can present their filmstrips to the class. **Sheltered English**

Section 1

Shoreline Erosion and Deposition

Terms to Learn
shoreline
beach
longshore current

What You'll Do
- Explain the connection between storms and wave erosion.
- Explain how waves break in shallow water.
- Describe how beaches form.
- Describe types of coastal landforms created by wave action.

What images pop into your head when you hear the word *beach*? You probably picture sand, blue ocean as far as the eye can see, balmy breezes, and waves. In this section you will learn how all those things relate to erosion and deposition along the shoreline. A **shoreline** is where land and a body of water meet. *Erosion*, as you may recall, is the breakdown and movement of materials. *Deposition* takes place when these materials are dropped. Waves can be powerful agents of erosion and deposition, as you will soon learn.

Wave Energy

Have you ever noticed the tiny ripples created by your breath when you blow on a cup of hot chocolate to cool it? Similarly, the wind moves over the ocean surface, producing ripples called *waves*. The size of a wave depends on how hard the wind is blowing and the length of time the wind blows. The harder and longer the wind blows, the bigger the wave is. Try it the next time you drink cocoa.

The wind that comes from severe winter storms and summer hurricanes generally produces the large waves that cause shoreline erosion. Waves may travel hundreds or even thousands of kilometers from a storm before reaching the shoreline. Some of the largest waves to reach the California coast are produced by storms as far away as Alaska and Australia. Thus, the California surfer in **Figure 1** can ride a wave produced by a storm on the other side of the Pacific Ocean.

Figure 1 Waves produced by storms on the other side of the Pacific Ocean propel this surfer toward a California shore.

⚠️ MISCONCEPTION ALERT

It is a popular misconception that a wave is a moving wall of water. Water actually moves up and down rather than forward as wave energy travels through it. When waves break, however, as shown in **Figure 1**, they do carry water with them.

298   Chapter 12 • Agents of Erosion and Deposition

Wave Trains On your imaginary visit to the beach, do you remember seeing just one wave? Of course not; waves don't move alone. They travel in groups called *wave trains*, as shown in **Figure 2**. As wave trains move away from their source, they travel through the ocean water without interruption. When they reach shallow water, they change form and begin to break. The ocean floor crowds the lower part of the wave, shortening the wave length and increasing the wave height. This results in taller, more closely spaced waves.

When the top of the wave becomes so tall that it cannot support itself, it begins to curl and break. These breaking waves are known as *surf*. Now you know how surfers got their name. The *wave period* is the time interval between breaking waves. Wave periods are usually 10 to 20 seconds long.

Figure 2 Because waves travel in wave trains, they break at regular intervals.

The Pounding Surf A tremendous amount of energy is released when waves break, as shown in **Figure 3**. A crashing wave can break solid rock or throw broken rocks back against the shore. The rushing water in breaking waves can easily wash into cracks in rock, helping to break off large boulders or fine grains of sand. The loose sand picked up by the waves polishes and wears down coastal rocks. Waves can also move sand and small rocks and deposit them in other locations, forming beaches.

Figure 3 *Breaking waves crash against the rocky shore, releasing their energy.*

MATH BREAK

Counting Waves

How many waves do you think reach a shoreline in a day if the wave period is 10 seconds?
(Hint: Calculate how many waves occur in a minute, in an hour, and in a day.)

Self-Check

Would a large wave or a small wave have more erosive energy? Why? *(See page 726 to check your answer.)*

2) Teach

CONNECT TO PHYSICAL SCIENCE

The waves in lakes and oceans are a form of energy traveling through a medium—water. Other energy waves, such as sound waves, also require a medium through which to travel. Some waves, however, such as light and radio waves, can travel through a vacuum.

MATH and MORE

Have students calculate how many waves would reach a shoreline in 24 hours with periods of 15 and 20 seconds.

(With a 15-second period, 5,760 waves would reach the shore. With a 20-second period, 4,320 waves would reach the shore.)

Math Skills Worksheet 31 "The Unit Factor and Dimensional Analysis"

Answer to MATHBREAK

In 1 minute, six waves occur. In 1 hour, 360 waves occur. In 1 day, 8,640 waves occur.

$$60 \div 10 = 6 \text{ waves}$$
$$6 \times 60 = 360 \text{ waves}$$
$$360 \times 24 = 8,640 \text{ waves}$$

Directed Reading Worksheet 12 Section 1

Answer to Self-Check

A large wave has more erosive energy than a small wave because a large wave releases more energy when it breaks.

2 Teach, continued

USING THE FIGURE

Draw students' attention to **Figure 5.** Point out that when water strikes the shoreline at an angle and then retreats in a direction perpendicular to the shore, material is moved along the beach in a zigzag pattern. Inform students that this is known as *beach* or *longshore drift*.

Encourage students to use the Internet or reference texts in their school library to learn more about longshore drift. Ask students to prepare labeled diagrams in their ScienceLog illustrating the phenomenon.
Sheltered English

Multicultural CONNECTION

The Polynesians are considered some of the greatest navigators of the ancient world. Polynesians visited and inhabited more than 10,000 islands throughout the South Pacific. They navigated not by using maps but by carefully observing stars, winds, and waves. On cloudy nights, they listened to the way the waves rocked and slapped against their dugout canoes. The Polynesians understood how wave patterns could indicate the direction of land or the presence of dangerous reefs or sandbars. Encourage students to discover more about Polynesian cultures in the past and present.

Figure 4 Beaches are made of different types of material deposited by waves.

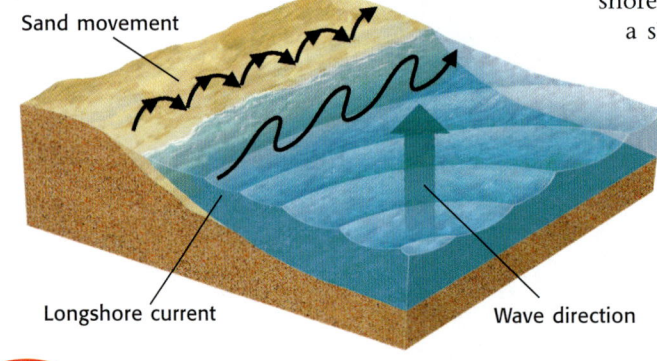

Figure 5 When waves strike the shoreline at an angle, sand migrates along the beach in a zigzag path.

Wave Deposits

Waves carry an assortment of materials, including sand, rock fragments, and shells. Often this material is deposited on the shore. But as you will learn, this is not always the case.

Beaches You would probably recognize a beach if you saw one. But technically, a **beach** is any area of the shoreline made up of material deposited by waves. Some beach material arrives on the shoreline by way of rivers. Other beach material is eroded from areas located near the shoreline.

Not all beaches are the same. Compare the beaches shown in **Figure 4.** Notice that the colors and textures vary. This is because the type of material found on a beach depends on its source. Light-colored sand is the most common beach material. Much of this sand comes from the quartz in continental rock. But not all beaches are made of light-colored sand. For instance, on many tropical islands, beaches are made of fine white coral material, and some Florida beaches are made of tiny pieces of broken seashells. In Hawaii, there are black sand beaches made of eroded volcanic lava. In areas where stormy seas are common, beaches are made of pebbles and larger rocks.

Wave Angle Makes a Difference The movement of sand along a beach depends on the angle at which the waves strike the shore. Most waves approach the beach at a slight angle and retreat in a direction more perpendicular to the shore. This moves the sand in a zigzag pattern along the beach, as you can see in **Figure 5.**

Science Skills Worksheet 2
"Using Your Senses"

Q: Why does the beach think the ocean is friendly?

A: because it waves all the time

300 Chapter 12 • Agents of Erosion and Deposition

Offshore Deposits Waves moving at an angle to the shoreline push water along the shore, creating longshore currents. A **longshore current** is a movement of water near and parallel to the shoreline. Sometimes waves erode material from the shoreline, and a longshore current transports and deposits it offshore, creating landforms in open water. Some of these landforms are shown in **Figure 6.**

Figure 6 Sandbars and barrier spits are types of offshore deposits.

A **sandbar** is an underwater or exposed ridge of sand, gravel, or shell material.

A **barrier spit,** like Cape Cod, Massachusetts, occurs when an exposed sandbar is connected to the shoreline.

Wave Erosion

Wave erosion produces a variety of features along a shoreline. *Sea cliffs,* like the ones in **Figure 7,** are formed when waves erode and undercut rock, producing steep slopes. Waves strike the base of the cliff, wearing away the soil and rock and making the cliff steeper. The rate at which the sea cliffs erode depends on the hardness of the rock and the energy delivered by the waves. Sea cliffs made of hard rock, such as granite, erode very slowly. Other sea cliffs, such as those made of soft sedimentary rock, erode rapidly, especially during storms.

Figure 7 Ocean-view homes built on sedimentary rock are often threatened as cliffs erode.

CONNECT TO LIFE SCIENCE

Beaches and intertidal zones can be a challenging place for organisms to live. Beaches offer little protection from predators, and the intertidal zone is periodically pounded by waves and exposed to the sun. Most of the organisms that live in these areas have special adaptations for survival. Have students research how different organisms are adapted for living in these environments. Suggest that students use their research to create a diorama that illustrates an intertidal zone.

BRAIN FOOD

Despite the numerous changes wrought by the sea, people still live and vacation as close to the water as possible. Inevitably, property is damaged. Government loan subsidies to these property owners cost taxpayers millions of dollars a year. Encourage students to consider the costs and benefits of erosion prevention. What solutions to the problem would they propose? How would they finance their plans? Allow time for them to share their ideas with the class.

IS THAT A FACT!

During storms and at high tide, waves deposit sand at the back of a sloping beach, forming a feature called a *berm*. Berms mark the highest point that waves reached during the last storm or high tide. Although berms may obstruct beachfront views, leveling them is not a good idea: they prevent the erosion of inland soil.

3 Extend

GROUP ACTIVITY
Coastal Features Board Game
To reinforce section concepts, divide the class into small groups, and challenge each to create a board game. Tell students that the object of the game is for players to visit as many coastal landforms as they can. Provide each group with poster board, plain index cards, and markers. Direct them to create a game board that leads players along a coastline, encountering the features they have learned about. Have students use the index cards to write questions and clues to direct players' movements along the "coast." For example, they might write, "If you can describe how the sea arch formed, you may move ahead to the sea stack. If not, you lose a turn." Have groups create written game rules, exchange games, and play their games. **Sheltered English**

GOING FURTHER
Have students research and model different methods that have been used to control shoreline erosion. Encourage students to discover which methods have been effective and which have failed. Students can also develop their own plans for minimizing erosion and present them to the class.

Teaching Transparency 144
"Coastal Landforms Created by Wave Erosion: A"

TOPIC: Wave Erosion
GO TO: www.scilinks.org
sciLINKS NUMBER: HSTE280

Shaping a Shoreline Much of the erosion responsible for landforms you might see along the shoreline takes place during storms. Large waves generated by storms release far more energy on the shoreline than do normal waves. This energy is so powerful that it is capable of removing huge chunks of rock. The following illustrations show some of the major landscape features that result from wave erosion.

Coastal Landforms Created by Wave Erosion

Sea stacks are offshore columns of resistant rock that were once connected to the mainland. In these instances, waves have eroded the mainland, leaving behind isolated columns of rock.

Sea arches form when wave action continues to erode a sea cave, cutting completely through the rock.

Sea caves form when waves cut large holes into fractured or weak rock along the base of sea cliffs. Sea caves are common in limestone cliffs, where the rock is usually quite soft.

 SCIENCE

Sometimes, even when the weather is clear and calm, huge waves, called *rogue waves,* unexpectedly appear. These waves are responsible for damaging or sinking several ships a year. Rogue waves are a poorly understood phenomenon of the high seas. One reason so little is known about them is that their random nature makes them hard to study.

302 Chapter 12 • Agents of Erosion and Deposition

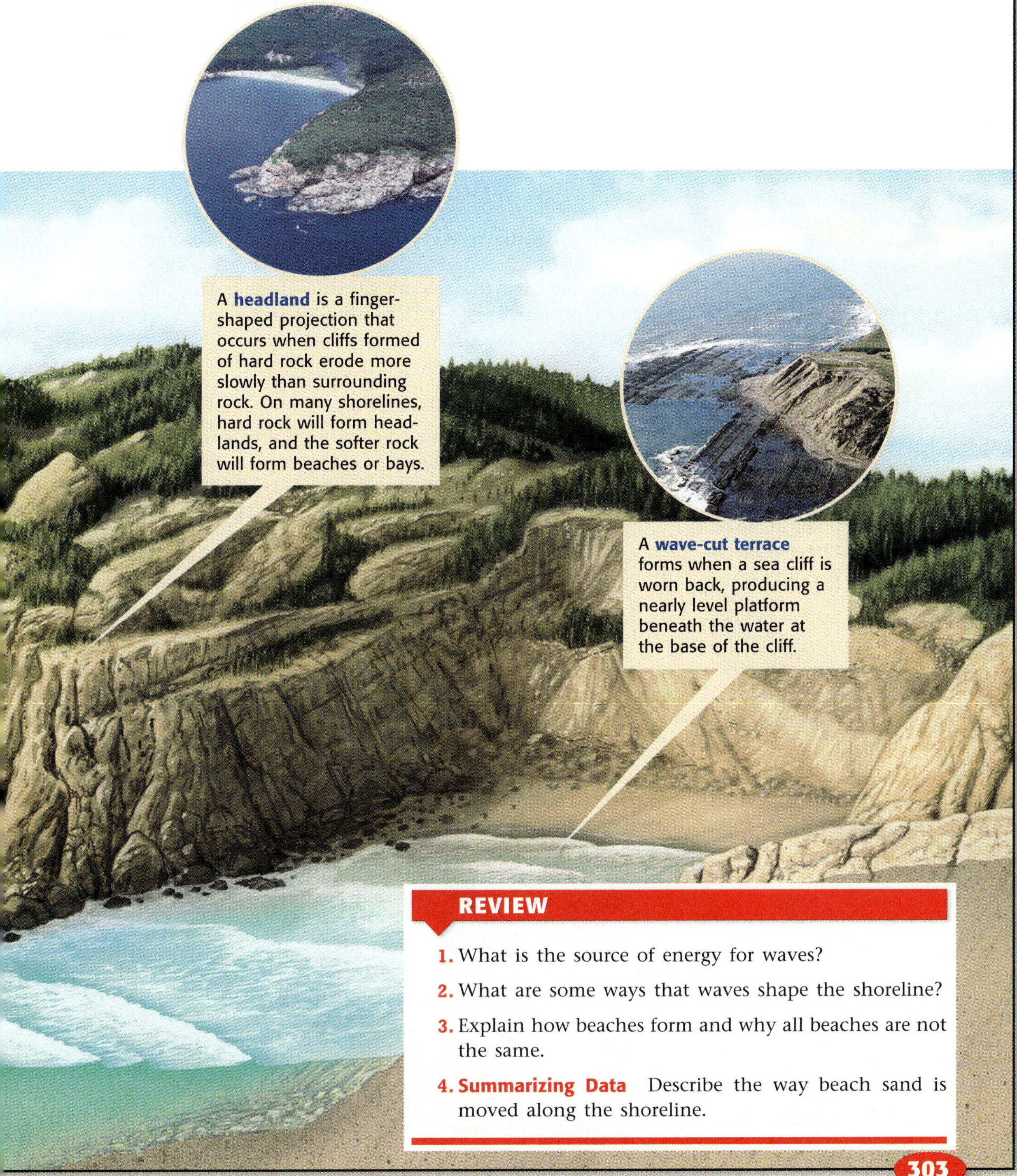

A **headland** is a finger-shaped projection that occurs when cliffs formed of hard rock erode more slowly than surrounding rock. On many shorelines, hard rock will form headlands, and the softer rock will form beaches or bays.

A **wave-cut terrace** forms when a sea cliff is worn back, producing a nearly level platform beneath the water at the base of the cliff.

REVIEW

1. What is the source of energy for waves?
2. What are some ways that waves shape the shoreline?
3. Explain how beaches form and why all beaches are not the same.
4. **Summarizing Data** Describe the way beach sand is moved along the shoreline.

4) Close

Quiz

1. What is a wave period? (It is the time it takes for two waves to pass a fixed point.)
2. What determines the way sand moves on a beach? (the direction in which waves strike the shore)
3. Describe how sea stacks, sea caves, and headlands are formed. (Sea stacks are columns of resistant rock left behind when a headland erodes. Sea caves form when waves erode large holes in fractured or weak rock at the base of sea cliffs. A headland forms when cliffs made of hard rock erode more slowly than the surrounding rock; this results in a finger-shaped projection.)

ALTERNATIVE ASSESSMENT

Have students work independently to make a model of several land features created by waves. Ask them to present their models to the class and explain how the water strikes the shore to create the landforms. Have them brainstorm about what organisms, if any, would live on the landforms they modeled.

Teaching Transparency 145 "Coastal Landforms Created by Wave Erosion: B"

Answers to Review

1. Wind is the source of wave energy.
2. Sample answer: Waves erode rock, creating headlands and undercutting sea cliffs, sea caves, stacks, and sea arches. Waves also deposit material, forming landforms such as beaches, spits, and sandbars.
3. Beaches are usually made of geologic material eroded from areas of higher elevation. Rivers deposit this material in oceans. Waves and currents then redeposit the material along the shoreline to form beaches. All beaches are not the same because source materials vary.
4. Beach sand is moved by waves and by longshore currents. If the waves arrive at the shore at an angle, and retreat perpendicular to the shoreline, sand is deposited in a zigzag pattern. Longshore currents move sand in the direction they flow, parallel to the shore.

Section 1 • Shoreline Erosion and Deposition

SECTION 2

Focus

Wind Erosion and Deposition

In this section, students learn about the effects of wind erosion. They will explore the three major processes of wind erosion: saltation, deflation, and abrasion. Section 2 explains how the wind deposits materials, such as sand and loess. Students also learn about the migration of sand dunes.

🔔 Bellringer

Ask students to answer the following question in their ScienceLog:

What causes wind? (Students should understand that wind is caused by energy from the sun. The sun heats the Earth unevenly; the unequal energy distribution causes pressure differences which, in turn, cause air to move.)

1) Motivate

DISCUSSION

Wind Erosion Engage students in a discussion about the ways wind shapes the Earth's surface. Encourage them to compare the wind with waves. (They should recognize that both change the Earth's shape by erosion and deposition.)

Ask students to think of examples of the wind's effects on landscapes they have observed. (Answers might include the formation of sand dunes, wind-weathered surfaces, and so on.)

Point out that this section will explore the ways in which wind acts to erode and deposit materials on Earth.

Section 2

Terms to Learn

saltation   dune
deflation   loess
abrasion

What You'll Do

- Explain why areas with fine materials are more vulnerable to wind erosion.
- Describe how wind moves sand and finer materials.
- Describe the effects of wind erosion.
- Describe the difference between dunes and loess deposits.

Have you ever tried to track a moving rock? Sounds silly, but in California some rocks keep sneaking around. To find out more, turn to page 324.

Wind Erosion and Deposition

Most of us at one time or another have been frustrated by a gusty wind that blew an important stack of papers all over the place. Remember how fast and far the papers traveled, and how it took forever to pick them up because every time you caught up with them they were on the move again? If you are familiar with this scene, then you already know how wind erosion works. Certain locations are more vulnerable to wind erosion than others. Areas with fine, loose rock material that have little protective plant cover can be significantly affected by the wind. Plant roots anchor sand and soil in place, reducing the amount of wind erosion. The landscapes most commonly shaped by wind processes are deserts and coastlines.

Process of Wind Erosion

Wind moves material in different ways. In areas where strong winds occur, material is moved by saltation. **Saltation** is the movement of sand-sized particles by a skipping and bouncing action in the direction the wind is blowing. As you can see in **Figure 8**, the wind causes the particles to bounce. When bouncing sand particles knock into one another, some particles bounce up in the air and fall forward, striking other sand particles. The impact may in turn cause these particles to roll forward or bounce up in the air.

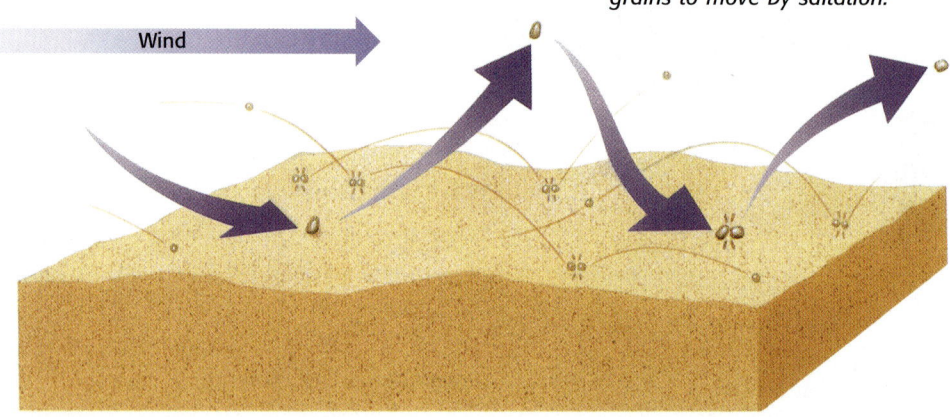

Figure 8 The wind causes sand grains to move by saltation.

CONNECT TO LIFE SCIENCE

Point out to students that many desert animals have special adaptations to protect themselves from windblown sand. For example, some lizards have transparent eyelids that shield their eyes from blowing sand while still allowing them to see.

Encourage students to use their school library to learn more about animal adaptations that protect against blowing sand. Have them prepare brief oral reports to share their findings with the class.

Deflation The lifting and removal of fine sediment by wind is called **deflation.** During deflation, wind removes the top layer of fine sediment or soil, leaving behind rock fragments that are too heavy to be lifted by the wind. This hard, rocky surface, consisting of pebbles and small broken rocks, is known as *desert pavement.* An example is shown in **Figure 9.**

Figure 9 *Desert pavement, like that found in the Painted Desert, in Arizona, forms when wind removes all the fine materials.*

Have you ever blown on a layer of dust while cleaning off a dresser? If you have, you might have noticed that in addition to your face getting dirty, a little scooped-out depression formed in the dust. Similarly, where there is little vegetation, wind may scoop out depressions in the sand. These depressions, like the one shown in **Figure 10,** are known as *deflation hollows.*

Figure 10 *Wind erosion can cause deflation hollows to become hundreds of meters wide.*

QuickLab

Making Desert Pavement

1. Spread a mixture of **dust, sand,** and **gravel** on an outdoor **table.**
2. Place an **electric fan** at one end of the table.
3. Put on **safety goggles** and a **filter mask.** Aim the fan across the sediment. Start the fan on its lowest speed. Record your observations in your ScienceLog.
4. Turn the fan to a medium speed and then to a high speed to imitate a desert wind storm. Record your observations at each speed.
5. What is the relationship between the wind speed and the sediment size that is moved?
6. Does the remaining sediment fit the definition of desert pavement?

Self-Check

Why do deflation hollows form in areas where there is little vegetation? *(See page 726 to check your answer.)*

CONNECT TO LIFE SCIENCE

Each year, equatorial trade winds carry millions of tons of reddish-brown dust from the Sahara Desert to Florida. Sahara dust causes hazy skies in Florida and travels as far as South America, providing nutrients for organisms that live in the rain-forest canopies. Traveling over the Pacific Ocean, yellow dust from Mongolia's Gobi Desert reaches Hawaii, fertilizing iron-deficient regions of the Pacific Ocean. Where the dust settles, plankton populations increase, enriching the food chain. One researcher has linked this phenomenon to global climate change. According to this theory, desertification increases during glacial periods, so more sediment is deposited in the oceans. This deposition encourages plankton growth, which removes CO_2 from the atmosphere, further cooling the planet.

2 Teach, continued

Answer to APPLY

Answers will vary. Deflation caused the Dust Bowl.

Multicultural CONNECTION

The term *hammada* refers to areas of desert pavement. The term is Arabic in origin, as are many of the words used to describe desert features. This is because many of Earth's deserts are located in Arabic-speaking countries. Challenge students to use the Internet or reference texts to compile a list of terms that describe desert features. **(Terms with Arabic origins include *erg*, which describes sandy desert; *reg*, which are loose stones; *barchan*, which are crescent-shaped dunes; and *seif*, which are sword-shaped dunes.)**

 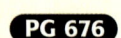

Dune Movement

MEETING INDIVIDUAL NEEDS

Learners Having Difficulty
Students may have difficulty visualizing how rock can be abraded by sand. Demonstrate the abrasiveness of sand by briskly rubbing quartz sandpaper on a softer rock specimen, and allow students to observe the changes. Remind them that sandblasting is used in many industrial applications to "erode" hard surfaces. **Sheltered English**

Describing the Dust Bowl

When a long period without rain, known as a *drought*, occurs, areas that are farmed or overgrazed can suffer extensive soil loss and dense dust storms. The removal of plants exposes the soil, making it more vulnerable to wind erosion.

During the 1930s, a section of the Great Plains suffered severe wind erosion and dust storms. This area became known as the *Dust Bowl*. The dust darkened the skies so much that street lights were left on during the day in Midwestern cities.

In areas where the conditions were even worse, people had to string ropes from their houses to their barns so they wouldn't get lost in the dense dust. The dust was so bad that people slept with damp cloths over their face to keep from choking. Describe the major erosional process that caused the Dust Bowl.

Turn on a hair dryer—no, not to style your hair, but to find out how dunes migrate. Check out page 676 of the LabBook.

Abrasion The grinding and wearing down of rock surfaces by other rock or sand particles is called **abrasion**. Abrasion commonly occurs in areas where there are strong winds, loose sand, and soft rocks. The blowing of millions of sharp sand grains creates a sandblasting effect that helps to erode, smooth, and polish rocks.

Wind-Deposited Materials

Like a stack of papers blowing in the wind, all the material carried by the wind is eventually deposited downwind. The amount and size of particles the wind can carry depend on wind speed. The faster the wind blows, the more material and the heavier the particles it can carry. As wind speed slows, heavier particles are deposited first.

Dunes When the wind hits an obstacle, such as a plant or a rock, it slows down. As the wind slows, it deposits, or drops, the heavier material. As the material collects, it creates an additional obstacle. This obstacle causes even more material to be deposited, forming a mound. Eventually even the original obstacle becomes buried. The mounds of wind-deposited sand are called **dunes**. Dunes are common in deserts and along the shores of lakes and oceans.

IS THAT A FACT!

The Yellow River flows across China to the Yellow Sea. The river and sea get their names from the yellow loess that washes off the Gobi Desert and colors the water.

How Dunes Move Dunes tend to move in the direction of strong prevailing winds. Different wind conditions produce dunes in various shapes and sizes. A dune usually has a gently sloped side and a steeply sloped side, or *slip face,* as shown in **Figure 11.** In most cases, the gently sloped side faces the wind. The wind is constantly transporting material up this side of the dune. As sand moves over the crest, or peak, of the dune, it slides down the slip face, creating a steep slope.

Figure 11 Dunes migrate in the direction of the wind.

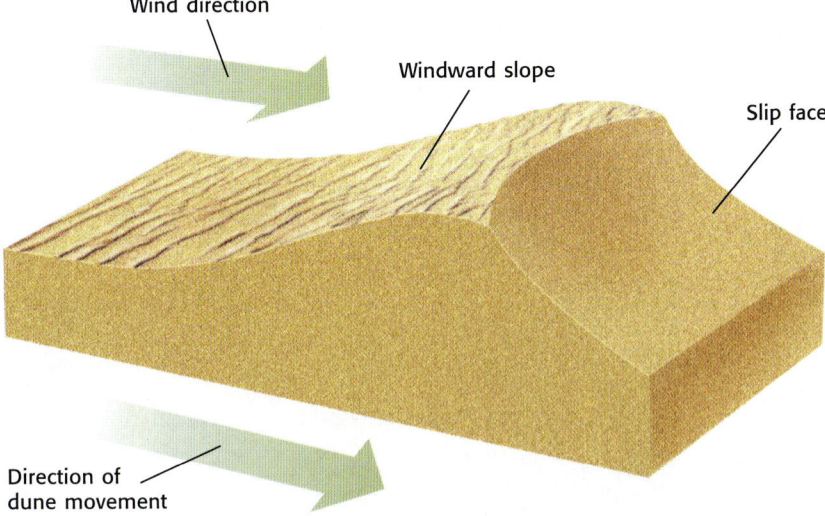

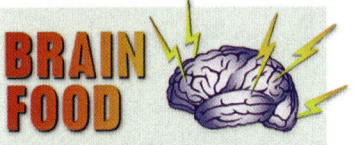

The largest sand dunes ever recorded were found in east-central Algeria in the Sahara. These dunes measured about 4.8 km long and 430 m high.

Disappearing Dunes and the Desert Tortoise

Dunes provide homes for hundreds of plant and animal species, including the desert tortoise. This tortoise, found in the Mojave and Sonoran Deserts of the southwestern United States, is able to live where ground temperatures are very hot. It escapes the heat by digging burrows in the sand dunes. The desert tortoise has a problem, though. Dune buggies and other motorized vehicles are destroying the dunes. Dunes are easily disturbed and are vulnerable to erosion. Motorized off-road vehicles break down dunes, destroying habitat of the tortoise as well as many other animal and plant species. For this reason, state and federal wildlife and land-management agencies have taken an active role in helping protect the habitat of the desert tortoise and other sensitive desert species by making some areas off-limits to off-road vehicles.

3 Extend

GOING FURTHER

Encourage students to learn about the many different kinds of dunes that can form when windblown sand meets obstacles. Have them make posters illustrating the types of dunes and indicating the wind patterns that create them. Ask students to explore the differences between beach dunes and desert dunes. Display the posters in the classroom.

CONNECT TO LIFE SCIENCE

Writing Encourage interested students to use library or Internet resources to investigate the living organisms that make sand dunes their home. Have them select one plant or animal and write a brief report describing its habitat, its predators and/or prey, and the adaptations it has made to live in the sand-dune environment. **Sheltered English**

CROSS-DISCIPLINARY FOCUS

Language Arts Remind students that drought and dust storms plagued the Great Plains in the 1930s. Encourage them to read about the effects of the Dust Bowl in selections from John Steinbeck's *The Grapes of Wrath.* Have them prepare book reports describing how the Joad family was affected economically and psychologically by this event.

Teaching Transparency 147 "Migration of Sand Dunes"

Homework

Create a Diagram Challenge students to make diagrams similar to **Figure 11** illustrating why the gently sloping side of a dune usually faces windward. Have them clearly indicate the direction in which the wind and the sand are moving, and have them write a caption summarizing the phenomenon. (The diagrams should indicate that when moving sand meets an obstacle, it falls to the ground and forms a dune. The wind, however, continues to move forward, causing the sand to form a slope against the obstacle. Wind continues to blow sand up the slope to its apex, whereupon the sand falls, creating a sharper slope on the other side.)

Section 2 • Wind Erosion and Deposition

4 Close

Quiz

1. Why is sand more likely to move by saltation than silt? (Sand is heavier than dust and silt, so as it moves, it tends to bounce along the ground. Silt is light enough to be carried by the wind.)

2. How does the process of deflation form desert pavement? (Deflation lifts and carries away lighter materials, while the heavier stones remain as desert pavement.)

3. Describe how dunes form. (When wind encounters an obstacle, it slows down, depositing some of the heavier material it is carrying. Gradually, this material grows to become a mound and then a dune.)

ALTERNATIVE ASSESSMENT

Concept Mapping Have students use section vocabulary to construct a concept map that explores the ways wind can shape the Earth's surface.

Critical Thinking Worksheet 12 "A Future in Sand"

TOPIC: Wind Erosion
GO TO: www.scilinks.org
sciLINKS NUMBER: HSTE285

The sidewinder adder is a poisonous snake that lives in the dunes of the Namib Desert, in southwestern Africa. It is called a sidewinder because of the way it rolls its body to one side as it moves across the sand. This motion allows the snake to move above loose, sliding sand. Its close cousin, the sidewinder rattlesnake, found in the deserts of the southwestern United States, uses a similar motion to move.

TOPIC: Wind Erosion
GO TO: www.scilinks.org
sciLINKS NUMBER: HSTE285

Loess Wind can deposit material much finer than sand. Thick deposits of this windblown, fine-grained sediment are known as **loess** (LOH es). Loess feels much like the talcum powder you use after a shower.

Because wind carries fine-grained material much higher and farther than it carries sand, loess deposits are sometimes found far away from their source. Many loess deposits came from glacial sources during the last ice age.

Loess is present in much of the midwestern United States, along the eastern edge of the Mississippi Valley, and in eastern Oregon and Washington. Huge bluffs of loess are found in Mississippi, as shown in **Figure 12**.

Loess deposits can easily be prepared for growing crops and are responsible for the success of many of the grain-growing areas of the world.

Figure 12 *The thick loess deposits found in Mississippi contribute to the state's fertile soil.*

REVIEW

1. What areas have the greatest amount of wind erosion and deposition? Why?
2. Explain the process of saltation.
3. What is the difference between a dune and a loess deposit?
4. **Analyzing Relationships** Explain the relationship between deflation and dune movement.

Answers to Review

1. Deserts and coastlines experience the greatest amount of wind erosion and deposition because they are composed of fine, loose material and have little vegetation to anchor the sediment in place.

2. Saltation is the movement of sand-sized particles by bouncing and skipping in the direction that the wind is blowing. The wind lifts sand particles into the air. When the particles land, they hit other particles, causing them to bounce forward.

3. Dunes are made of sand. Loess is made of finer materials that are the size of dust particles. Loess can be carried much higher and farther by wind than can sand.

4. Deflation removes dune sediment. The material is then carried by the wind and redeposited elsewhere, creating another dune.

Chapter 12 • Agents of Erosion and Deposition

Section 3

Terms to Learn
glacier, glacial drift, iceberg, stratified drift, crevasse, till

What You'll Do
- Summarize why glaciers are important agents of erosion and deposition.
- Explain how ice in a glacier flows.
- Describe some of the landforms eroded by glaciers.
- Describe some of the landforms deposited by glaciers.

Erosion and Deposition by Ice

Can you imagine an ice cube the size of a football stadium? Well, glaciers can be even bigger than that. A **glacier** is an enormous mass of moving ice. Because glaciers are very heavy and have the ability to move across the Earth's surface, they are capable of eroding, moving, and depositing large amounts of rock materials. And while you will never see a glacier chilling a punch bowl, you might one day visit some of the spectacular landscapes carved by glacial activity.

Glaciers—Rivers of Ice

Glaciers form in areas so cold that snow stays on the ground year-round. Areas like these, where you can chill a can of juice by simply carrying it outside, are found at high elevations and in polar regions. Because the average temperature is freezing or near freezing, snow piles up year after year. Eventually, the weight of the snow on top causes the deep-packed snow to become ice crystals, forming a giant ice mass. These ice packs then become slow-moving "rivers of ice" as they are set in motion by the pull of gravity on their extraordinary mass.

Alpine Glaciers There are two main types of glaciers, *alpine* and *continental*. **Figure 13** shows an alpine glacier. As you can see, this type of glacier forms in mountainous areas. One common type of alpine glacier is a *valley glacier*. Valley glaciers form in valleys originally created by stream erosion. These glaciers flow slowly downhill, widening and straightening the valleys into broad U-shapes as they travel.

Figure 13 Alpine glaciers start as snowfields in mountainous areas.

Glaciers can be very noisy. As they move and stretch, they howl, shriek, pop, groan, and make explosive noises. These sounds can be so loud that they have kept high-altitude mountaineers awake at night!

Directed Reading Worksheet 12 Section 3

SECTION 3

Focus
Erosion and Deposition by Ice

This section examines how glaciers form and how they shape the Earth's surface. Students will learn to identify different types of glaciers and understand how they move. Finally, students will focus on the changes to the Earth's landscape caused by ice erosion and deposition.

Bellringer
Tell students that 14,000 years ago, much of North America was covered in a thick layer of ice called a *continental glacier*, which moved as far as southern Illinois. Humans were living in North America at the time. Have students imagine they encounter this glacier as an early human, and write a paragraph in their ScienceLog about the experience.

1) Motivate

GROUP ACTIVITY
Glacier Game Give groups of students a world map, two dice, and string to explore the causes and effects of glacial movement. Have each group brainstorm six causes and six effects of glacial movement; these will become 12 possible moves in a glacier game. With each roll of the dice, the group's glacier (represented by a line of string on the map) will either advance or recede. For example, a roll of 5 might mean, "Volcanic eruption triggers global cooling, glacier advances 100 km." The winning group will be the first to have their glacier advance to your hometown.

2) Teach

Answers to Activity
Sample Answer: The iceberg that struck the *Titanic* traveled approximately 2,000 km from Greenland to Newfoundland. Accept all reasonable responses for the mapping exercise.

GUIDED PRACTICE
Have students compare in writing the process of making a snowball with that of forming glacial ice. Students should understand that snowflakes are compressed together when both snowballs and glaciers are formed. When a snowball is made, thermal energy from a person's hands partially melts the snow. As the snowball is squeezed, the snowball becomes denser and harder. Alpine glaciers form in a similar way, but pressure comes from the snow pack above. A cycle of freezing and thawing causes the snow to gradually become glacial ice. Because temperatures always remain below freezing in Antarctica, ice sheets form as lower layers of snow are compressed by the weight of overlying layers. **Sheltered English**

Activity
How far do you think the iceberg that struck the *Titanic* drifted before the two met that fateful night in 1912? Plot on a map of the North Atlantic Ocean the route of the *Titanic* from Southampton, England, to New York. Then plot a possible route of the drifting iceberg from Greenland to where the ship sank, just south of the Canadian island province of Newfoundland.

Continental Glaciers Not all glaciers are true "rivers of ice." In fact, some glaciers continue to get larger, spreading across entire continents. These glaciers, called continental glaciers, are huge continuous masses of ice. **Figure 14** shows the largest type of this glacier, a *continental ice sheet*. Ice sheets can cover millions of square kilometers with ice. The continent of Antarctica is almost completely covered by one of the largest ice sheets in the world, as you can see below. This ice sheet is approximately one and a half times the size of the United States. It is so thick—more than 4,000 m in places—that it buries everything but the highest mountain peaks.

Figure 14 Antarctica contains approximately 91 percent of all the glacial ice on the planet.

Ice Shelves An area where the ice is attached to the ice sheet but is resting on open water is called an *ice shelf*. The largest ice shelf is the Ross Ice Shelf, shown in **Figure 15**, which is attached to the ice sheet that covers Antarctica. This ice shelf covers an area of ocean about the size of Texas.

Figure 15 Icebergs break off the Ross Ice Shelf into the Ross Sea.

Icebergs Large pieces of ice that break off an ice shelf and drift into the ocean are called **icebergs.** The process by which an iceberg forms is called *calving*. Because most of an iceberg is below the surface of the water, it can be a hazard for ships that cannot see how far the iceberg extends. In the North Atlantic Ocean near Newfoundland, the *Titanic* struck an iceberg that calved off the Greenland ice sheet.

IS THAT A FACT!
How do snowflakes become massive blocks of glacial ice? As the snow melts and is compacted, the grains become more dense. As snow packs to a greater density, the air spaces among ice crystals are pressed out. Eventually, the ice recrystallizes to a stage between flakes and ice called *firn*. Over time, with more pressure from overlying layers of snow, the firn will recrystallize again to become glacial ice.

Glaciers on the Move When enough ice builds up on a slope, the ice begins to move downhill. The thickness of the ice and the steepness of the slope determine how fast a glacier will move. Thick glaciers move faster than thin glaciers, and the steeper the slope is, the faster the glacier will move. Glaciers move by two different methods. They move when the weight of the ice causes the ice at the bottom to melt. The water from the melted ice allows the glacier to move forward, like a partially melted ice cube moving across your kitchen counter. Glaciers also move when solid ice crystals within the glacier slip over each other, causing a slow forward motion. This process is similar to placing a deck of cards on a table and then tilting the table. The top cards will slide farther than the lower cards. Like the cards, the upper part, or surface, of the glacier flows faster than the glacier's base.

Crevasses As a glacier flows forward, sometimes crevasses occur. A **crevasse** (kruh VAS), as shown in **Figure 16,** is a large crack that forms where the glacier picks up speed or flows over a high point. Crevasses form because the ice cannot stretch quickly, and it cracks. They can be dangerous for people who are traveling across glaciers because a bridge layer of snow can hide them from view.

Self-Check

How are ice crevasses related to glacier flow?
(See page 726 to check your answer.)

Brain Food

Many icebergs now being calved by Alaskan glaciers are made of millions of snowflakes that fell at about the time Columbus arrived in the Americas.

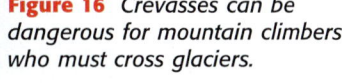

MATH BREAK

Speed of a Glacier
An alpine glacier is estimated to be moving forward at 5 m per day. Calculate how long it will take for the ice to reach a road and campground located 0.5 km from the front of the advancing glacier.

1 km = 1,000 m

Figure 16 *Crevasses can be dangerous for mountain climbers who must cross glaciers.*

IS THAT A FACT!

When metal pipes are drilled through a glacier's layers, they eventually bend in the direction of flow, demonstrating that glacial layers tend to move at different speeds. One cause of this is friction—layers in closest contact with Earth are often slowed by friction.

 **SCIENCE**

In September 1991, a melting glacier deposited an unusual load in Italy near its border with Austria: the frozen body of a 5,300-year-old man!

CONNECT TO
PHYSICAL SCIENCE

Point out to students that while most glaciers move only a few meters a year, certain conditions can cause *glacial surge*. When glaciers surge, or flow rapidly, they may travel 30 m in a day. Encourage students to use the Internet or library resources to investigate glacial surges. Have them explain in writing why this phenomenon occurs. (Students should understand that friction between the glacier and land is reduced, allowing gravity to pull the ice downhill faster. Before and during a glacial surge, meltwater does not drain away from the glacier; instead it builds up beneath the ice. The water decreases the friction between the glacier and the land below, permitting the glacier to flow more rapidly.)

RETEACHING

You may wish to demonstrate for students the comparison made on this page between a sliding deck of cards and one type of glacial flow. This process is called *internal plastic flow*.

Answer to MATHBREAK

(0.5 km × 1,000 m/km) ÷ 5 m = 100 days

Answer to Self-Check

When a moving glacier picks up speed or flows over a high point, a crevasse may form. This occurs because the ice cannot stretch quickly while it is moving and therefore cracks.

 Math Skills Worksheet 17
"Using Proportions and Cross-Multiplication"

Section 3 • Erosion and Deposition by Ice

2 Teach, continued

GROUP ACTIVITY

Making Models Divide the class into pairs, and ask each pair to select a landscape feature created by glaciers. Provide modeling clay for students to make a model of the feature. Have each pair present its model to the class and demonstrate how the feature was formed using another color of clay to represent the glacier. Sheltered English

Homework

Investigate Your Area If you live in an area that has been affected by glaciers, ask the class to find evidence of glacial erosion and deposition in your area. If not, ask each student to select a landform created by glacial activity and use atlases or other resources to learn where these features are found. For example, the Matterhorn, in Switzerland, is an example of a *horn*. Have students locate their feature on a classroom map and present a short report on what they learned.

CROSS-DISCIPLINARY FOCUS

Language Arts Students will enjoy reading about the adventures of high altitude mountaineers and polar explorers. Have them read selections from the accounts of Antarctic explorers such as Robert Falcon Scott, Ernest Shackleton, or Richard Byrd. Students may also enjoy reading about mountaineers such as Reinhold Messner, Sir Edmund Hillary, or Dr. Johan Reinhard. Students should prepare a presentation for the class about the person they studied, and discuss the explorer's description of glaciers.

Landforms Carved by Glaciers

Alpine glaciers and continental glaciers produce landscapes that are very different from one another. Alpine glaciers carve out rugged features in the mountain rocks through which they flow. Continental glaciers smooth the landscape by scraping and removing features that existed before the ice appeared, flattening even some of the highest mountains. **Figure 17** and **Figure 18** show the very different landscapes that each glacial type produces.

Figure 17
Continental glaciers smooth and flatten the landscape.

Figure 18
The hard ice of alpine glaciers carved out this rugged landscape.

IS THAT A FACT!

During the last glacial period, the northern part of North America was covered by as much as 4,000 m of ice. The weight of the ice pushed the North American continent down by almost 400 m. Since the ice sheet melted about 10,000 years ago, the continent has risen over 300 m. Parts of the continent are still rising. For example, Maine is rising at a rate of 2mm per year. Parts of Canada are rising even faster. This process is known as isostatic rebound.

Alpine glaciers carve out large amounts of rock material, creating spectacular landforms. These glaciers are responsible for landscapes such as the Rocky Mountains and the Alps. **Figure 19** shows the kind of landscape that is sculpted by alpine glacial erosion and revealed after the ice melts back.

Figure 19 Landscape Features Carved by Alpine Glaciers

Horns are sharp, pyramid-shaped peaks that form when three or more cirque glaciers erode the mountain.

Cirques (suhrks) are bowl-like depressions where glacial ice cuts back into the mountain walls.

Arêtes (uh RAYTS) are jagged ridges that form between two or more cirques cutting into the same mountain.

U-shaped valleys are formed when a glacier erodes a river valley from its original V-shape to a U-shape. These broad U-shaped glacial valleys are also called *glacial troughs*.

Hanging valleys are smaller glacial valleys that join the deeper main valley. These valleys are carved by smaller glaciers. Many hanging valleys form waterfalls after the ice is gone.

READING STRATEGY

Activity Draw students' attention to **Figure 19**. Challenge them to write new captions to describe each landscape feature carved by glaciers. Sheltered English

CROSS-DISCIPLINARY FOCUS

History Encourage students to research Camp Century, a city built by the United States government inside the Greenland ice sheet. Ask them to research the purpose of the project, the discoveries scientists made, the obstacles faced by the engineers, and the problems that eventually led to the abandonment of the project. Have them write brief reports about their findings. (Students will find that the purpose of Camp Century was twofold: to learn about glaciers and life in the extreme Arctic environment and to protect the United States from attack—missiles were concealed in ice tunnels. The biggest problem the engineers encountered was the need to continually dig their way into the camp because new snow kept accumulating and the glacial layers shifted. Each year, the camp was pressed about a half-meter farther into the glacial ice by new snow.)

Teaching Transparency 148
"Landscape Features Carved by Alpine Glaciers"

SCIENCE HUMOR

As glaciers travel downward, forming U-shaped valleys, outcrops of hard rock may remain on the valley floor. These smooth rocks are called *roches moutonnees*. This French term meaning "sheep rocks" comically describes the rounded outcroppings, which look like sheep grazing in the valley.

Homework

Preparing Tables Have students work independently to create tables summarizing the characteristics and formation of the following landforms: arêtes, horns, hanging valleys, U-shaped valleys, and cirques. Have them keep the tables to use as study guides for the Chapter Review.

3) Extend

REAL-WORLD CONNECTION

Glaciers throughout the world provide fresh water that helps regulate the flow of large rivers and recharge aquifers. Scientists are concerned, however, that a permanent increase in global temperatures would alter this naturally controlled process. If the 13,800,000 km^2 Antarctic ice sheet melted, sea level could rise 60 m, with devastating effects. Coastal towns and cities would be flooded, and some islands would disappear. Have students draw a map of what the coastline of the United States would look like if the sea level rose 60 m.

COOPERATIVE LEARNING

 Divide the class into small groups, and ask them to imagine an Earth untouched by glaciers. Have them work together to make a poster showing such a planet. Encourage them to consider not only Earth's landscape but also the living things inhabiting it. Ask students to share their posters with the class.

Gliding Glaciers

TOPIC: Glaciers
GO TO: www.scilinks.org
sciLINKS NUMBER: HSTE290

Figure 20 Striations, such as these seen in Central Park, in New York City, are evidence of glacial erosion.

How did this glacier get into my classroom? To find out more about glaciers and erosion, turn to page 677 of the LabBook.

Striations While many of the erosional features created by glaciers are unique to alpine glaciers, alpine and continental glaciers share some common features. For example, when a glacier erodes the landscape, the glacier picks up rock material and carries it away. This debris is transported on the glacier's surface as well as beneath and within the glacier. Many times, rock material is frozen into the glacier's bottom. As the glacier moves, the rock pieces scrape and polish the surface rock. Larger rocks embedded in the glacier gouge out grooves in the surface rock. As you can see in **Figure 20,** these grooves, called *striations,* help scientists determine the direction of ice flow.

Types of Glacial Deposits

When a glacier melts, all the material it has been carrying is dropped. **Glacial drift** is the general term used to describe all material carried and deposited by glaciers. Glacial drift is divided into two main types, based on whether the material is sorted or unsorted.

Stratified Drift Rock material that has been sorted and deposited in layers by water flowing from the melted ice is called **stratified drift.** Many streams are created by the meltwater from the glacier. These streams carry an abundance of sorted material, which is deposited in front of the glacier in a broad area called an *outwash plain.* Sometimes a block of ice is left in the outwash plain when the glacier retreats. During the time it takes for the ice to melt, sediment builds up around the block of ice. After the ice has melted, a depression called a *kettle* is left. Kettles commonly fill with water, forming a lake or pond, as shown in **Figure 21.**

Figure 21 Stratified drift is deposited on outwash plains in which kettle lakes are often found.

CROSS-DISCIPLINARY FOCUS

Geography The spectacular fjords of Norway are underwater valleys carved by glaciers. During the Pleistocene epoch, glaciers traveled beyond the coastline, digging trenches in the ocean floor. When they retreated to the coast, sea water flooded the valleys that the glaciers had formed. Have groups make a map showing the position of glaciers during different eras of geologic time.

Till Deposits The second type of glacial drift, **till,** is unsorted rock material that is deposited directly by the ice when it melts. *Unsorted* means that the till is made up of different sizes of rock material, ranging from large boulders to fine glacial silt. As a glacier flows, it carries different sizes of rock fragments. When the glacier melts, the unsorted material is deposited on the ground surface.

The most common till deposits are *moraines.* Moraines generally form ridges along the edges of glaciers. They are produced when glaciers carry material to the front of the ice and along the sides of the ice. As the ice melts, the sediment and rock it is carrying are dropped, forming the different types of moraines. The various types of moraines are shown in **Figure 22.**

Medial moraines form when two different valley glaciers with lateral moraines meet.

Lateral moraines form along each side of a glacier.

Ground moraines are the unsorted material left beneath a glacier.

Terminal moraines form when eroded rock material is dropped at the front of the glacier.

Figure 22 *Moraines provide clues to where glaciers once were located.*

REVIEW

1. How does glaciation change the appearance of mountains?
2. Explain why continental glaciers smooth the landscape and alpine glaciers create a rugged landscape.
3. What do moraines indicate?
4. **Applying Concepts** How can a glacier deposit both sorted and unsorted material?

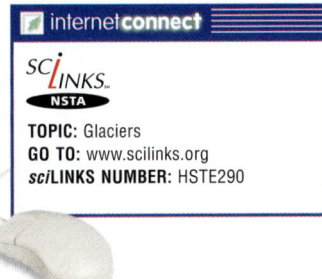
TOPIC: Glaciers
GO TO: www.scilinks.org
sciLINKS NUMBER: HSTE290

Answers to Review

1. Glaciers create unique mountain features, such as horns, cirques, arêtes, hanging valleys, and broad U-shaped valleys.
2. Continental glaciers smooth the landscape because they cover it entirely and scrape away older surface features. Alpine glaciers create rugged landscapes because they cover only portions of mountains. Moving downhill, they cut into the mountains, creating dramatic features that were not there before.
3. Moraines indicate that a glacier once flowed through an area and dropped its sediment load.
4. Meltwater streams flowing through a glacier carry sorted material. Unsorted material is deposited when a glacier melts entirely.

Creating a Kettle

4) Close

Quiz

1. What are the differences between continental ice sheets and alpine glaciers? (Continental ice sheets are large and tend to expand across entire continents. Alpine glaciers are smaller and form in mountainous areas.)
2. What is the difference between icebergs and ice shelves? (Ice shelves are attached on one side to an ice sheet but rest on open water; icebergs are large pieces of ice that break off ice shelves into the ocean.)
3. Why is the study of glaciers important? (Answers will vary. Students may note that many of Earth's landforms were created by glacial movement, that glaciers contain much of Earth's fresh water, and that melting glaciers can cause sea levels to rise.)

ALTERNATIVE ASSESSMENT

Have students work independently to create a small glacier handbook that includes illustrations and descriptions of 10 terms used in this section. Their books should include examples of stratified drift, outwash plains, kettles, till, and moraines.

Reinforcement Worksheet 12
"An Alpine Vacation"

Section 3 • Erosion and Deposition by Ice

SECTION 4

Focus

Gravity's Effect on Erosion and Deposition

This section introduces gravity as an agent of erosion and deposition. Students learn that mass movements caused by gravity are affected by the material's size, weight, shape, and moisture content and by the slope on which the material rests. Students then learn about landslides, mudslides, and volcanic lahars. The section also examines the effect of slow mass movements, such as creep.

🔔 Bellringer

Write the following sentence on the board or overhead projector:

   Watch for falling rocks!

Ask students to describe in their ScienceLog places where a warning sign like this would be necessary. Ask students to consider what factors contribute to make a rockfall zone.

1) Motivate

DISCUSSION

Ask students to review the three processes of erosion and deposition that they have learned about so far: shoreline erosion, wind erosion, and glacial erosion. Then ask students how rocks move from mountaintops to valleys. Tell them that gravity is an important force influencing erosion and deposition. Explain that although events like rockfalls and mudslides occur rapidly, most erosion and deposition occurs very slowly as gravity pulls material downward.

Section 4

Terms to Learn
mass movement
rock fall
landslide
mudflow
creep

What You'll Do
- Explain how slope is related to mass movement.
- State how gravity affects mass movement.
- Describe different types of mass movement.

QuickLab

Angle of Repose

1. Pour a **container** of **dry sand** onto a lab table.
2. With a **protractor**, measure the slope of the sand, or the *angle of repose*.
3. Pour another beaker of sand on top of the first pile.
4. Measure the angle of repose again for the new pile.
5. Which pile is more likely to collapse? Why?

QuickLab

MATERIALS
- beaker
- dry sand
- protractor

Gravity's Effect on Erosion and Deposition

Waves, wind, and ice are all agents of erosion and deposition that you can see. And though you can't see it and might not be aware of it, gravity is also an agent of erosion and deposition constantly at work on the Earth's surface. Gravity not only influences the movement of water, such as waves, streams, and ice, but also causes rocks and soil to move downslope. **Mass movement** is the movement of any material, such as rock, soil, or snow, downslope. Mass movement is controlled by the force of gravity and can occur rapidly or slowly.

Angle of Repose

If dry sand is piled up, it will move downhill until the slope becomes stable. The *angle of repose* is the steepest angle, or slope, at which loose material will not slide downslope. This is demonstrated in **Figure 23.** The angle of repose is different for each type of surface material. Characteristics of the surface material, such as its size, weight, shape, and moisture level, determine at what angle the material will move downslope.

Figure 23 *If the slope on which material rests is less than the angle of repose, the material will stay in place. If the slope is greater than the angle of repose, the material will move downslope.*

Answer to QuickLab

5. The second pile is more likely to collapse because it has a steeper slope, which was created by the addition of sediment. The steeper the slope, the more likely mass movement will occur.

Rapid Mass Movement

The most destructive mass movements occur suddenly and rapidly. Rapid mass movement occurs when material, such as rock and soil, moves down-slope quickly. A rapid mass movement can be very dangerous, destroying everything in its path.

Rock Falls While driving along a mountain road, you might have noticed signs that warn of falling rock. A **rock fall** happens when a group of loose rocks falls down a steep slope, as seen in **Figure 24**. Steep slopes are sometimes created to make room for a road in mountainous areas. Loosened and exposed rocks above the road tend to fall as a result of gravity. The rocks in a rock fall can range in size from small fragments to large boulders.

Landslides Another type of rapid mass movement is a *landslide*. A **landslide** is the sudden and rapid movement of a large amount of material downslope. A *slump* is an example of one kind of landslide. Slumping occurs when a block of material moves downslope over a curved surface, as seen in **Figure 25**.

Physics CONNECTION

Gravity is the force of attraction between objects. It is one of the major forces that cause rocks and soil to move from one place to another. The more mass an object has, the more attraction there is between it and other objects.

Figure 24 If enough rock falls from a mountain, a pile forms at the base of the slope. This pile of rock debris is called a talus slope.

Figure 25 A slump is a type of landslide that occurs when a small block of land becomes detached and slides downhill.

SCIENTISTS AT ODDS

Long run-out landslides have been the focus of much scientific debate because they appear to defy the laws of physics. Long run-out slides occur when massive amounts of rock, sometimes half a mountainside, suddenly give way. Moving at tremendous speeds (more than 160 km/h), they behave more like liquid than rock. These landslides can travel 20 times the height that they fall—in 1903, a long run-out landslide in Frank, Canada, traveled 1 km uphill! Some geologists think that these landslides travel on top of a layer of vibrating rocks which act like a conveyer belt, moving materials incredible distances.

Section 4 • Gravity's Effect on Erosion and Deposition

3) Extend

ACTIVITY

Making Models Provide students with poster board and markers. Have them each create a diagram of one form of mass movement, such as a landslide, mudslide, or creep. Direct them to label relevant parts of their diagrams and to write captions that explain the phenomenon illustrated.

MEETING INDIVIDUAL NEEDS

Learners Having Difficulty
Ask students to prepare a demonstration that compares mass movements of different materials on varying slopes. Provide a cookie sheet, dry sand, small pebbles, and gravel. Have them raise one end of the cookie sheet about 2 cm. Ask students to use a protractor to measure the angle of repose for each material. Have students repeat the procedure after moistening the materials, and ask them to make conclusions about the effect of water saturation on mass movement.
`Sheltered English`

REAL-WORLD CONNECTION

Lack of vegetative cover contributes to the frequency and severity of mudslides. Tree roots stabilize the soil and absorb ground water. Deforestation accelerates erosion of slopes. In 1995, there were 260 landslides in British Columbia's Clayquot Sound region during the rainy season. Only 33 were in unlogged areas. As a class, find out more about the connections between large-scale logging operations and recent mudslides. Students may wish to investigate the relationship between deforestation in Central America and the devastating mudslides that followed Hurricane Mitch in 1998.

Mudflows A **mudflow** is a rapid movement of a large mass of mud. Mudflows, which are like giant moving mud pies, occur when a large amount of water mixes with soil and rock. The water causes the slippery mass of mud to flow rapidly downslope. Mudflows most commonly occur in mountainous regions when a long dry season is followed by heavy rains. As you can see in **Figure 26,** a mudflow can carry trees, houses, cars, and other objects that lie in its path.

Figure 26 *This photo shows one of the many mudflows that have occurred in California during rainy winters.*

Lahars The most dangerous mudflows occur as a result of volcanic eruptions. Mudflows of volcanic origin are called *lahars*. Lahars can move at speeds of more than 80 km/h and are as thick as concrete. In mountains with snowy peaks, a volcanic eruption can suddenly melt a great amount of ice, causing a massive and rapid lahar, as shown in **Figure 27**. The water from the ice liquefies the soil and volcanic ash, sending a hot mudflow downslope. Other lahars are caused by heavy rains on volcanic ash.

Figure 27 *This lahar overtook the city of Kyushu, in Japan.*

CONNECT TO LIFE SCIENCE

In 1980, six successive storms caused devastating mudslides in California. The storms dropped 33 cm of rain, transforming the soil into a sea of oozing mud. Soil on slopes oozed out from under the foundations of houses, sending them crashing into canyons and valleys. Twenty-four people were killed, and millions of dollars in damage was done. Many believe that the mudslides were so massive because the area was recently logged.

Slow Mass Movement

Sometimes you don't even notice mass movement occurring. While rapid mass movements are visible and dramatic, slow mass movements happen a little at a time. However, because slow mass movements occur more frequently, more material is moved collectively over time.

Creep Although most slopes appear to be stable, they are actually undergoing slow mass movement, as shown in **Figure 28.** The extremely slow movement of material downslope is called **creep.** Many factors contribute to creep. Water breaks up rock particles, allowing them to move freely. The roots of growing plants act as a wedge, forcing rocks and soil particles apart. Burrowing animals, such as gophers and groundhogs, loosen rock and soil particles.

Figure 28 Tilted fence posts and bent tree trunks are evidence that creep is occurring.

REVIEW

1. In your own words, explain why slump occurs.
2. What factors increase the potential for mass movement?
3. How do slope and gravity affect mass movement?
4. **Analyzing Relationships** Some types of mass movement are considered dangerous to humans. Which types are most dangerous? Why?

internet connect

SCILINKS NSTA

TOPIC: Mass Movement
GO TO: www.scilinks.org
sciLINKS NUMBER: HSTE295

CONNECT TO LIFE SCIENCE

Because trees need light to grow, they usually grow straight upward, toward the sun. However, if the soil on a slope is creeping downhill, the trees will develop bent trunks, as shown in **Figure 28.** The trunks bend because the trees continue to grow upward even as their roots travel downhill.

4) Close

Quiz

1. What is the relationship between the angle of repose and the slope required for mass movement to occur? (Mass movement will occur only if the angle of the material is steeper than the angle of repose.)
2. What is creep? (Creep is the slow movement of surface material downslope.)
3. Does slow mass movement or rapid mass movement move more material down a slope? Why? (Slow mass movement, such as creep, occurs more frequently than rapid mass movement, so it moves more material over time.)

ALTERNATIVE ASSESSMENT

Divide the class into small groups, and challenge each group to write a public-service announcement designed to educate the public about the dangers of one form of mass movement. Instruct them to focus on the causes and consequences of these phenomena. Allow time for each group to perform its announcement for the class.

▼ **Answers to Review**

1. Slump occurs when a block of material moves downslope over a curved surface.
2. Steep slopes, heavy rainfall or snowfall, volcanic eruptions, and alternating freezing and thawing temperatures increase the chances that mass movement will occur.
3. Mass movement occurs on slopes as a result of gravitational pull. The effect of gravity depends on the characteristics of the surface material. The steeper the slope, the more likely it is that mass movement will occur.
4. Answers may vary. Accept all reasonable responses. Rapid mass movements are the most dangerous type of mass movement because a large amount of material moves rapidly and without warning.

Chapter Highlights

VOCABULARY DEFINITIONS

SECTION 1

shoreline the boundary between land and a body of water

beach an area of the shoreline made up of material deposited by waves

longshore current the movement of water near and parallel to the shoreline

SECTION 2

saltation the movement of sand-sized particles by a skipping and bouncing action in the direction the wind is blowing

deflation the lifting and removal of fine sediment by wind

abrasion the grinding and wearing down of rock surfaces by other rock or sand particles

dune a mound of wind-deposited sand

loess thick deposits of windblown, fine-grained sediments

 Vocabulary Review Worksheet 12

 Blackline masters of these Chapter Highlights can be found in the **Study Guide**.

Chapter Highlights

SECTION 1

Vocabulary
shoreline (p. 298)
beach (p. 300)
longshore current (p. 301)

Section Notes
- The wind from storms usually produces the large waves that cause shoreline erosion.
- Waves break when they enter shallow water, becoming surf.
- Beaches are made of any material deposited by waves.
- Sandbars and spits are depositional features caused by longshore currents.
- Sea cliffs, sea caves, sea arches, and sea stacks are coastal formations caused by wave erosion.

SECTION 2

Vocabulary
saltation (p. 304)
deflation (p. 305)
abrasion (p. 306)
dune (p. 306)
loess (p. 308)

Section Notes
- Wind is an important agent of erosion and deposition in deserts and along coastlines.
- Saltation is the process of the wind bouncing sand grains downwind along the ground.
- Deflation is the removal of materials by wind. If deflation removes all fine rock materials, a barren surface called desert pavement is formed.
- Abrasion is the grinding and wearing down of rock surfaces by other rock or sand particles.
- Dunes are formations caused by wind-deposited sand.
- Loess is wind-deposited silt, and it forms soil material good for farming.

Labs
Dune Movement (p. 676)

✓ Skills Check

Math Concepts

WAVE PERIOD Waves travel in intervals that are usually between 10 and 20 seconds apart. Use the following equation to calculate how many waves reach the shore in 1 minute:

$$\text{number of waves per minute} = \frac{60 \text{ seconds}}{\text{waves period (seconds)}}$$

After you find out how many waves reach the shore in 1 minute, you can figure out how many waves occur in an hour or even a day. For example, consider a wave period of 15 seconds. Using the formula above, you find that 4 waves occur in 1 minute. To find out how many waves occur in 1 hour, multiply 4 by 60. To find out how many waves occur in 1 day, multiply 240 by 24.

$$\text{number of waves per day} = \frac{60}{15} \times 60 \times 24 = 5{,}760$$

Visual Understanding

U-SHAPED VALLEYS AND MORE Look back at the illustration on page 313 to review the different types of landscape features carved by alpine glaciers.

Lab and Activity Highlights

Dune Movement PG 676

Gliding Glaciers PG 677

Creating a Kettle PG 679

 **Datasheets for LabBook** (blackline masters for these labs)

SECTION 3

Vocabulary
- **glacier** *(p. 309)*
- **iceberg** *(p. 310)*
- **crevasse** *(p. 311)*
- **glacial drift** *(p. 314)*
- **stratified drift** *(p. 314)*
- **till** *(p. 315)*

Section Notes
- Masses of moving ice are called glaciers.
- There are two main types of glaciers—alpine glaciers and continental glaciers.
- Glaciers move when the ice that comes into contact with the ground melts and when ice crystals slip over one another.
- Alpine glaciers produce rugged landscape features, such as cirques, arêtes, and horns.
- Continental glaciers smooth the landscape.
- There are two main types of glacial deposits—stratified drift and till.
- Some of the landforms deposited by glaciers include outwash plains and moraines.

Labs
- Gliding Glaciers *(p. 677)*
- Creating a Kettle *(p. 679)*

SECTION 4

Vocabulary
- **mass movement** *(p. 316)*
- **rock fall** *(p. 317)*
- **landslide** *(p. 317)*
- **mudflow** *(p. 318)*
- **creep** *(p. 319)*

Section Notes
- Mass movement is the movement of material downhill due to the force of gravity.
- The angle of repose is the steepest slope at which loose material will remain at rest.
- Rock falls, landslides, and mudflows are all types of rapid mass movement.
- Creep is a type of slow mass movement.

VOCABULARY DEFINITIONS, continued

SECTION 3

glacier an enormous mass of moving ice

iceberg a large piece of ice that breaks off an ice shelf and drifts into the ocean

crevasse a large crack that forms where a glacier picks up speed or flows over a high point

glacial drift all material carried and deposited by glaciers

stratified drift rock material that has been sorted and deposited in layers by water flowing from the melted ice of a glacier

till unsorted rock material that is deposited directly by glacial ice when it melts

SECTION 4

mass movement the movement of any material downslope

rock fall a group of loose rocks that fall down a steep slope

landslide a sudden and rapid movement of a large amount of material downslope

mudflow the rapid movement of a large mass of mud/rock and soil mixed with a large amount of water that flows downhill

creep the extremely slow movement of material downslope

---

internet connect

GO TO: go.hrw.com

Visit the **HRW** Web site for a variety of learning tools related to this chapter. Just type in the keyword:

KEYWORD: HSTICE

GO TO: www.scilinks.org

Visit the **National Science Teachers Association** on-line Web site for Internet resources related to this chapter. Just type in the sciLINKS number for more information about the topic:

TOPIC: Wave Erosion	sciLINKS NUMBER: HSTE280
TOPIC: Wind Erosion	sciLINKS NUMBER: HSTE285
TOPIC: Glaciers	sciLINKS NUMBER: HSTE290
TOPIC: Mass Movement	sciLINKS NUMBER: HSTE295
TOPIC: Wetlands	sciLINKS NUMBER: HSTE300

Lab and Activity Highlights

LabBank

Whiz-Bang Demonstrations
- Between a Rock and a Hard Place, Demo 23
- Rising Mountains, Demo 24

Long-Term Projects & Research Ideas,
Deep in the Mud, Project 40

Chapter Review

USING VOCABULARY

Explain the difference between the words in the following pairs:

1. shoreline/longshore current
2. beaches/dunes
3. deflation/saltation
4. glacier/loess
5. stratified drift/till
6. mudflow/creep

UNDERSTANDING CONCEPTS

Multiple Choice

7. *Surf* refers to
   a. large storm waves in the open ocean.
   b. giant waves produced by hurricanes.
   c. breaking waves.
   d. small waves on a calm sea.

8. When waves cut completely through a headland, a ___?___ is formed.
   a. sea cave   c. sea stack
   b. sea cliff   d. sea arch

9. A narrow strip of sand that is formed by wave deposition and is connected to the shore is called a ___?___
   a. marine terrace. c. spit.
   b. sandbar.   d. headland.

10. A wind-eroded depression is called a
    a. dune.   c. deflation hollow.
    b. desert pavement. d. dust bowl.

11. Where is the world's largest ice sheet located?
    a. Greenland
    b. Canada
    c. Alaska
    d. Antarctica

12. The process of calving forms ___?___
    a. continental ice sheets.
    b. icebergs.
    c. U-shaped valleys.
    d. moraines.

13. What term describes all types of glacial deposits?
    a. drift   c. till
    b. loess   d. outwash

14. Which of the following is not a landform created by an alpine glacier?
    a. cirque   c. horn
    b. deflation hollow d. arête

15. What is the term for a mass movement of volcanic origin?
    a. lahar   c. creep
    b. slump   d. rock fall

16. Which of the following is a slow mass movement?
    a. mudflow   c. creep
    b. landslide d. rock fall

Short Answer

17. Why do waves break when they get near the shore?

18. What role do storms play in coastal erosion?

19. How do humans increase the erosion caused by dust storms?

322 Chapter 12 • Agents of Erosion and Deposition

20. In what direction do sand dunes move?
21. Why are glaciers such effective agents of erosion and deposition?
22. List some evidence for creep.

Concept Mapping

23. Use the following terms to create a concept map: deflation, dust storm, saltation, dune, loess.

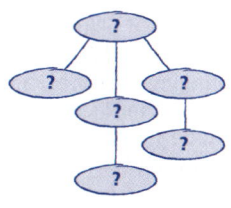

CRITICAL THINKING AND PROBLEM SOLVING

Write one or two sentences to answer the following questions:

24. What role does wind play in the processes of erosion and deposition?
25. What are the main differences between alpine glaciers and continental glaciers?
26. Describe the different types of moraines.
27. What kind of mass movement occurs continuously, day after day? Why can't you see it?

MATH IN SCIENCE

28. While standing on a beach, you can estimate a wave's speed in kilometers per hour. This is done by counting the seconds between each arriving wave crest to determine the wave period and then multiplying the wave period by 3.5. Calculate the speed of a wave with a 10-second period.

INTERPRETING GRAPHICS

The following graph illustrates coastal erosion and deposition occurring at an imaginary beach over a period of 8 years.

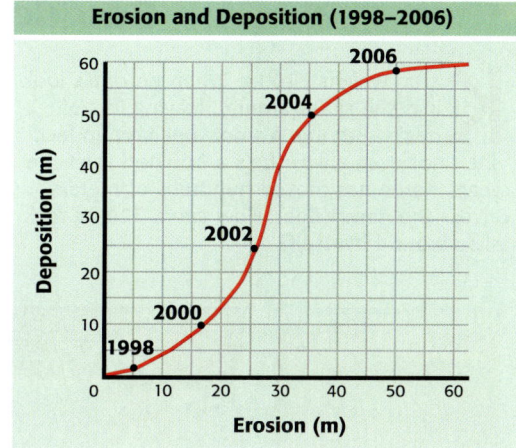

29. What is happening to the beach over time?
30. In what year does the amount of erosion that has occurred along the shoreline equal the amount of deposition?
31. Based on the erosion and deposition data for 2000, what might happen to the beach in the years to follow?

 Take a minute to review your answers to the Pre-Reading Questions found at the bottom of page 296. Have your answers changed? If necessary, revise your answers based on what you have learned since you began this chapter.

Concept Mapping

23.  An answer to this exercise can be found at the end of this book.

CRITICAL THINKING AND PROBLEM SOLVING

24. Wind removes sediment through saltation and deflation and deposits it in a different area. Wind also erodes the surface of materials, such as rocks, through abrasion.
25. Alpine glaciers are generally smaller than continental glaciers. Alpine glaciers carve out rugged landscapes, while continental glaciers smooth the landscape. Alpine glaciers form in the mountains, and continental glaciers spread across a continent.
26. Lateral moraines are the till that is deposited on the side of a glacier. Medial moraines form when the lateral moraines of two glaciers are pushed together. Terminal moraines are the till that is deposited at the front of a glacier. Ground moraines are the material left beneath a glacier.
27. Creep happens every day. You can't see it happening because it is a slow mass movement.

MATH IN SCIENCE

28. $10 \times 3.5 = 35$ km/h

INTERPRETING GRAPHICS

29. At first, more soil is being eroded than deposited. The area is losing beach. After 2002, more soil is being deposited than eroded. The beach is getting larger.
30. 2002
31. In 2000, more sand is being eroded than deposited; the coastline is losing land. This would lead you to believe that the coastline would continue shrinking. But by 2002, the coastline stops losing land and begins growing. The most recent data indicates that the coastline will continue growing.

SCIENCE, TECHNOLOGY, AND SOCIETY
Boulder Boogie

Background
Scientists who first studied the Death Valley boulders suggested that the rocks moved because they were embedded in a rigid ice sheet. The trails of two of the rocks, named Jacki and Julie, showed remarkable congruence when Messina measured the distance between them as they moved. Although their movement across the Racetrack appeared to be a type of synchronized ballet, Messina found that the rocks converged as they twirled around. If the rocks were stuck in ice, they would remain the same distance apart; if the ice sheet shattered, the rocks would diverge. This data allowed Messina to rule out the rigid-ice-sheet theory.

Teaching Strategy
Point out that rain makes the surface of the lake bed slippery, allowing the rocks to be moved more easily. To demonstrate this, you may wish to have students experiment with wet and dry clay to compare the friction between the two surfaces.

Science, Technology, and Society

Boulder Boogie

Karen weighs 320 kg. When no one's looking, she slides around, leaving lots of tracks. But Karen's not a person. In fact, she's not even alive—she's a boulder! Over the years, Karen has moved hundreds of meters across the desert floor. How can a 320 kg rock slide around by itself?

▲ A mystery in Death Valley: What moved this rock across the desert floor?

▲ New technology is helping Paula Messina study the paths of the "dancing rocks."

Slipping and Sliding
Karen is one of the mysterious dancing rocks of Death Valley. These rocks slide around—sometimes together, sometimes alone. There are nearly 200 of them, and they range in size from small to very large. No one has seen them move, but their trails show where they've been.

The rocks are scattered across a dry lake bed, called the Racetrack, in Death Valley, California. The Racetrack is very flat and has almost no plants or wildlife. Several times a year, powerful storms rip across the lake bed, bringing plenty of rain, wind, and sometimes snow. The Racetrack's clay surface becomes slippery, and that's apparently when the rocks dance.

Puzzles and Clues
What could push a 320 kg boulder hundreds of yards across the mud? With the help of technology, scientists like Paula Messina are finally getting some answers. Messina uses a global positioning system (GPS) receiver and a geographic information system (GIS) to study the rocks. Using GPS satellites, Messina is able to map the movements of the rocks. Her measurements are more accurate than ever before. This new device measures the locations within centimeters! A computer equipped with GIS software constructs maps that allow her to study how the rock movement relates to the terrain. Messina's investigations with this equipment have led her to conclude that wind is probably pushing the rocks.

But how does the wind push such massive rocks? Messina thinks the gaps in the mountains at one end of the valley funnel high-speed winds down onto the slippery clay surface, pushing the rocks along. And why do some rocks move while others nearby do not? This mystery will keep Messina returning to Death Valley for years.

Search and Find
▶ Go to the library or the Internet, and research the many uses for GPS devices. Make a list in your ScienceLog of all the uses for GPS devices you find.

Answers to Search and Find
Students' answers will vary but might include one of the following: for marine navigation, for aviation, to find ancient trails, or to find water.

EYE ON THE ENVIRONMENT

Beach Today, Gone Tomorrow

Beaches are fun, right? But what if you went to the coast and found that the road along the beach had washed away? It could happen. In fact, erosion is stripping away beaches from islands and coastlines around the world.

An Island's Beaches

The beaches of Anguilla, a small Caribbean island, are important to the social, economic, and environmental well-being of the island and its inhabitants. Anguilla's sandy shores protect coastal areas from wave action and provide habitats for coastal plants and animals. The shores also provide important recreational areas for tourists and local residents. When Hurricane Luis hit Anguilla in 1995, Barney Bay was completely stripped of sand. But Anguilla's erosion problems started long before Luis hit the island. Normal ocean wave action had already washed away some beaches.

Back in the United States

Louisiana provides a good example of coastal problems in the United States. Louisiana has 40 percent of the nation's coastal wetlands. As important as these wetlands are, parts of the Louisiana coast are disappearing at a rate of 65 to 90 km^2 per year. That's a football field every 15 minutes! At that rate of erosion, Louisiana's new coastline would be 48 km inland by the year 2040!

Save the Sand

The people of Louisiana and Anguilla have acted to stop the loss of their coastlines. But many of their solutions are only temporary. Waves, storms, and human activity continue to erode coastlines. What can be done about beach erosion?

Scientists know that beaches and wetlands come and go to a certain extent. Erosion is part of a natural cycle. Scientists must first determine how much erosion is normal for a particular area and how much is the result of human activities or some unusual process. The next step is to preserve or stabilize existing sand dunes, preserve coastal vegetation, and plant more shrubs, vines, grasses, and trees. The people of Louisiana and Anguilla have learned a lot from their problems and are taking many of these steps to slow further erosion. If steps are taken to protect valuable coastal areas, beaches will be there when you go on vacation.

Before

After

▲ This is what Barney Bay looked like in 1995 before and after Hurricane Luis.

Extending Your Knowledge

▶ What are barrier islands? How are they related to coastal erosion? On your own, find out more about barrier islands and why it is important to preserve them.

EYE ON THE ENVIRONMENT

Beach Today, Gone Tomorrow

Background

State and federal agencies, as well as concerned Louisiana citizens and businesses, have been taking steps in the right direction to preserve the Louisiana coast. A joint effort is being made to rebuild and restore the wetlands. Rebuilding methods include using sediments from near-shore sandbars to create wetlands and refilling canals, which were previously sending loose sediment directly to the ocean.

TOPIC: Wetlands
GO TO: www.scilinks.org
sciLINKS NUMBER: HSTE300

Answer to Extending Your Knowledge

Barrier islands are long, narrow islands formed by the deposition of sediment. Louisiana's barrier islands formed when the Mississippi River changed course. As one delta was abandoned, a new one formed, and a series of islands developed at the end of the old delta. These islands protect the coast from devastating winds and waves created by offshore storms. If the barrier islands were to completely disappear, Louisiana could lose an additional 48 km of shoreline. Experts suggest that the most effective means to preserve Louisiana's barrier islands would be to nourish them. Beach nourishment involves the transport of sand from other areas in order to replenish the area lost to erosion.

UNIT 5

TIMELINE
Oceanography

In this unit, you will learn about the Earth's oceans and the vast landscapes they cover. Together, the oceans form the largest single feature on the planet. In fact, they cover approximately 70 percent of the Earth's surface. Now that's a lot of water! Not only do the oceans serve as home for countless living organisms, but they also affect life on land. You will learn more about the oceans in this unit as well as in the timeline presented here. Take a deep breath, and dive in!

1872
The HMS *Challenger* begins its four-year voyage. Its discoveries lay the foundation for the science of oceanography.

1851
Herman Melville's novel *Moby-Dick* is published.

1977
Thermal vent communities of creatures that exist without sunlight are discovered on the ocean floor.

1978
Louise Brown, the first "test-tube baby," is born in England.

1986
Commercial whaling is officially banned by the International Whaling Commission, but some whaling continues.

1927
Charles Lindbergh completes the first nonstop solo airplane flight over the Atlantic Ocean.

1914
The Panama Canal is completed, linking the Atlantic Ocean with the Pacific Ocean.

1938
A coelacanth is discovered in the Indian Ocean near South Africa. Called a fossil fish, the coelacanth was thought to have been extinct for 60 million years.

1960
Jacques Piccard and Don Walsh dive to a record 10,910 m below sea level in their bathyscaph *Trieste*.

1943
Jacques Cousteau and Émile Gagnon invent the Aqualung, a breathing device that allows divers to freely explore the silent world of the oceans.

1990
The tunnel under the English Channel is completed, making train and auto travel between Great Britain and France possible.

1998
Ben Lecomte of Austin, Texas, successfully swims across the Atlantic Ocean from Massachusetts to France, a distance of 6,015 km. His record-breaking feat took 74 days.

Oceanography

Chapter Organizer

CHAPTER ORGANIZATION	TIME MINUTES	OBJECTIVES	LABS, INVESTIGATIONS, AND DEMONSTRATIONS
Chapter Opener pp. 328–329	45	National Standards: SAI 1, ST 1, 2, SPSP 5	**Start-Up Activity** Exit Only? p. 329
Section 1 Earth's Oceans	135	▶ Name the major divisions of the global ocean. ▶ Describe the history of Earth's oceans. ▶ Summarize the properties and other aspects of ocean water. ▶ Summarize the interaction between the ocean and the atmosphere. ES 1b, 1d, 1f, 1g, 1h, 1j, 2a	
Section 2 The Ocean Floor	90	▶ Identify the two major regions of the ocean floor. ▶ Classify subdivisions and features of the two major regions of the ocean floor. ▶ Describe technologies for studying the ocean floor. UCP 2, 3, SAI 1, ST 2, SPSP 5, HNS 1, 3, ES 1b, 1c; LabBook UCP 2, 3, SAI 1, ST 1, HNS 3	**Making Models,** Probing the Depths, p. 680 GENERAL **Datasheets for LabBook,** Probing the Depths, Datasheet 26 GENERAL
Section 3 Life in the Ocean	90	▶ Identify and describe the three groups of marine organisms. ▶ Identify and describe the benthic and pelagic environments. ▶ Classify the zones of the benthic and pelagic environments.	**Interactive Explorations CD-ROM,** Sea Sick GENERAL A **Worksheet** is also available in the **Interactive Explorations Teacher's Edition.**
Section 4 Resources from the Ocean	90	▶ List two methods of harvesting the ocean's living resources. ▶ List nonliving resources in the ocean. ▶ Describe the ocean's energy resources. SAI 1, ST 2, SPSP 2, 4, 5	**QuickLab,** How Much Fresh Water Is There? p. 349 GENERAL **Inquiry Labs,** Surf's Up! Lab 11 GENERAL
Section 5 Ocean Pollution	90	▶ List different types of ocean pollution. ▶ Explain how to prevent or minimize different types of ocean pollution. ▶ Outline what is being done to control ocean pollution. ST 2, SPSP 2, 4, 5	**Discovery Lab,** Investigating an Oil Spill, p. 682 GENERAL **Datasheets for LabBook,** Datasheet 27 GENERAL **EcoLabs & Field Activities,** EcoLab 13 GENERAL **Whiz-Bang Demonstrations,** Fowl Play, Demo 25 **Long-Term Projects & Research Ideas,** Project 41 ADVANCED

See page **T20** for a complete correlation of this book with the **NATIONAL SCIENCE EDUCATION STANDARDS.**

TECHNOLOGY RESOURCES

 Guided Reading Audio CD English or Spanish, Chapter 13

 One-Stop Planner CD-ROM with Test Generator

 CNN. Multicultural Connections, Segment 9

Scientists in Action, Segment 17 and 18

 Interactive Explorations CD-ROM CD 2, Exploration 2, Sea Sick

Chapter 13 • Exploring the Oceans

Chapter 13 • Exploring the Oceans

CLASSROOM WORKSHEETS, TRANSPARENCIES, AND RESOURCES	SCIENCE INTEGRATION AND CONNECTIONS	REVIEW AND ASSESSMENT
Science Puzzlers, Twisters & Teasers, Worksheet 13 `ADVANCED` **Directed Reading Worksheet 13** `BASIC`		
Transparency 149, Divisions of the Global Oceans **Directed Reading Worksheet 13,** Section 1 `BASIC` **Transparency 150,** Ocean Salinity **Transparency 151,** The Ocean and the Water Cycle	**Connect to Physical Science,** p. 331 in ATE `BASIC` **Connect to Physical Science,** p. 333 in ATE **Cross-Disciplinary Focus,** p. 334 in ATE `GENERAL` **Multicultural Connection,** p. 335 in ATE `GENERAL`	**Self-Check,** p. 331 **Review,** p. 334 `GENERAL` **Review,** p. 336 `GENERAL` **Quiz,** p. 336 in ATE `GENERAL` **Alternative Assessment,** p. 336 in ATE `ADVANCED`
Directed Reading Worksheet 13, Section 2 `BASIC` **Transparencies 152–153,** Revealing the Ocean Floor, A and B **Math Skills for Science Worksheet 3,** Multiplying Whole Numbers; **Worksheet 15,** Multiplying and Dividing Fractions `GENERAL` **Transparency 154,** How Sonar Works	**Connect to Physical Science,** p. 338 in ATE `GENERAL` **Math and More,** p. 338 in ATE `GENERAL` **Cross-Disciplinary Focus,** pp. 339, 340 in ATE **MathBreak,** Depths of the Deep, p. 340 **Across the Sciences:** Exploring Ocean Life, p. 360 `GENERAL`	**Self-Check,** p. 339 **Homework,** p. 339 in ATE `GENERAL` **Review,** p. 341 `GENERAL` **Quiz,** p. 341 in ATE `GENERAL` **Alternative Assessment,** p. 341 in ATE `GENERAL`
Transparency 155, The Three Groups of Marine Life **Directed Reading Worksheet 13,** Section 3 `BASIC` **Transparency 27,** Natural Selection in Four Steps **Reinforcement Worksheet 13,** The Ocean's Environment `BASIC`	**Biology Connection,** p. 343 **Multicultural Connection,** p. 343 in ATE `ADVANCED` **Connect to Life Science,** p. 344 in ATE **Connect to Life Science,** p. 345 in ATE	**Homework,** p. 343 in ATE `GENERAL` **Review,** p. 345 `GENERAL` **Quiz,** p. 345 in ATE `GENERAL` **Alternative Assessment,** p. 345 in ATE `GENERAL`
Directed Reading Worksheet 13, Section 4 `BASIC` **Reinforcement Worksheet 13,** The Oceans and Us `BASIC` **Critical Thinking Worksheet 13,** Chain Reaction `ADVANCED`	**Connect to Environmental Science,** p. 346 in ATE `ADVANCED` **Real-World Connection,** pp. 347, 348 in ATE **Connect to Physical Science,** p. 349 in ATE **Eye on the Environment,** p. 361 `ADVANCED`	**Homework,** pp. 348, 349 in ATE `GENERAL` **Review,** p. 350 `GENERAL` **Quiz,** p. 350 in ATE `GENERAL` **Alternative Assessment,** p. 350 in ATE `GENERAL`
Directed Reading Worksheet 13, Section 5 `BASIC`	**Environment Connection,** p. 352 **Math and More,** p. 353 in ATE `ADVANCED` **Connect to Environmental Science,** p. 353 in ATE **Apply,** p. 354 `ADVANCED`	**Homework,** p. 352 in ATE `ADVANCED` **Review,** p. 355 `GENERAL` **Quiz,** p. 355 in ATE `GENERAL` **Alternative Assessment,** p. 355 in ATE `GENERAL`

internet connect

 Holt, Rinehart and Winston On-line Resources
go.hrw.com
For worksheets and other teaching aids related to this chapter, visit the HRW Web site and type in the keyword: **HSTOCE**

 **National Science Teachers Association**
www.scilinks.org
Encourage students to use the *sci*LINKS numbers listed in the internet connect boxes to access information and resources on the **NSTA** Web site.

END-OF-CHAPTER REVIEW AND ASSESSMENT

Chapter Review in Study Guide
Vocabulary and Notes in Study Guide
Chapter Tests with Performance-Based Assessment, Chapter 13 Test, Performance-Based Assessment 13
Concept Mapping Transparency 13

Chapter 13 • Chapter Organizer **327B**

Chapter Resources & Worksheets

Visual Resources

TEACHING TRANSPARENCIES

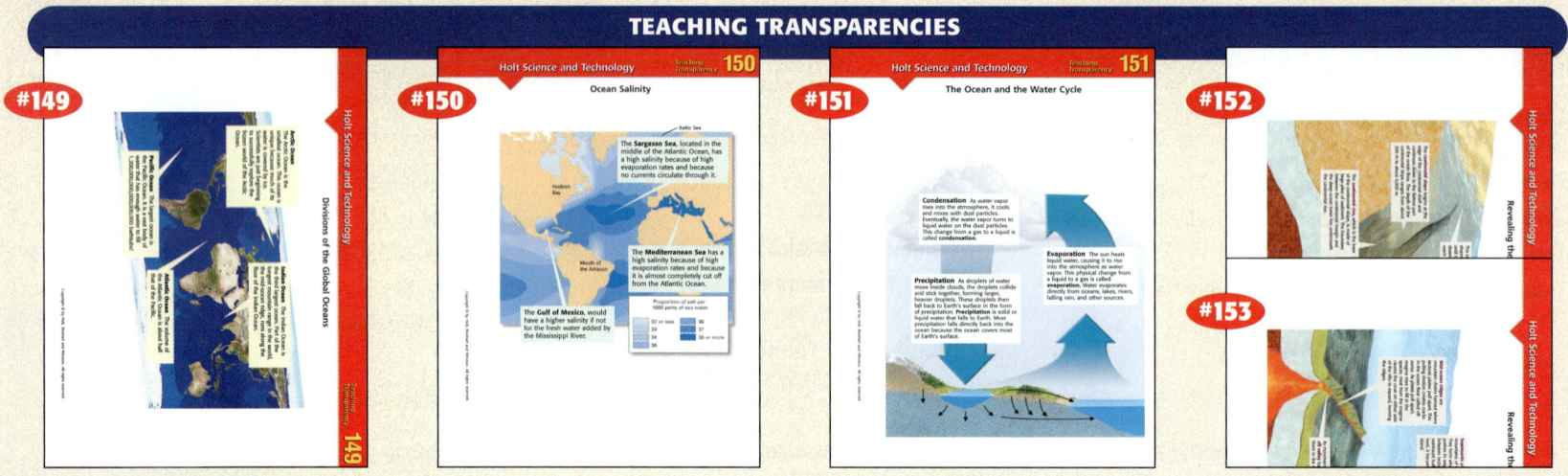

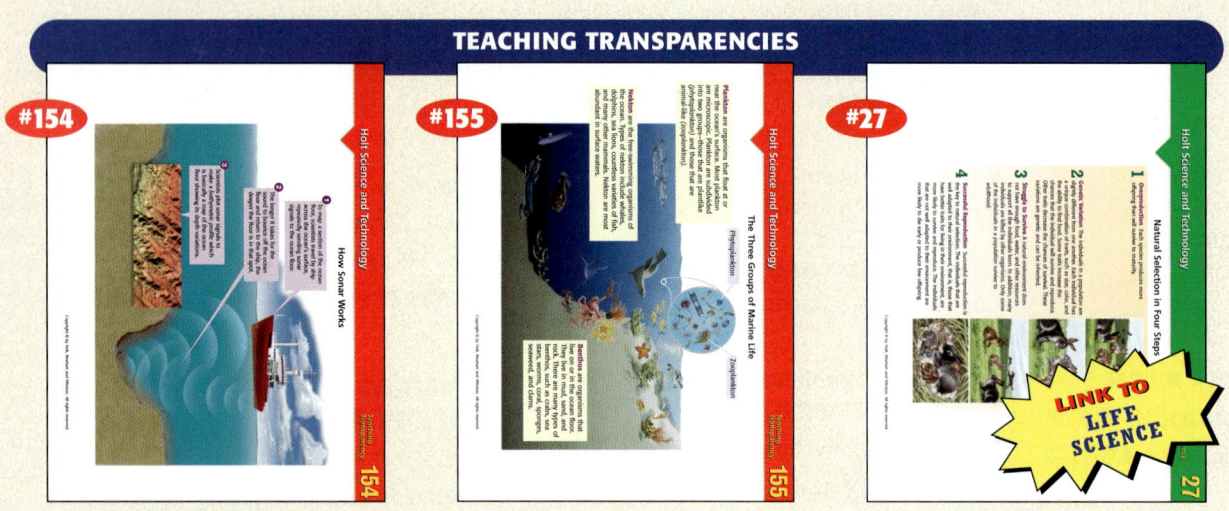

CONCEPT MAPPING TRANSPARENCY

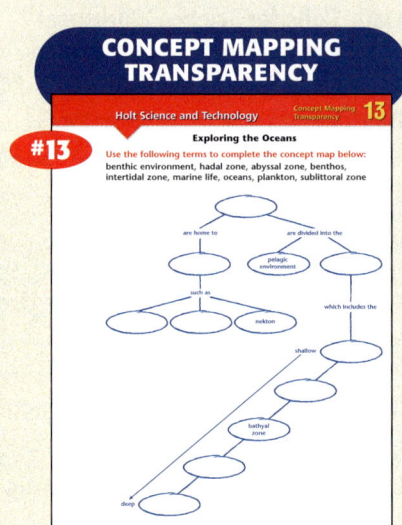

Meeting Individual Needs

DIRECTED READING

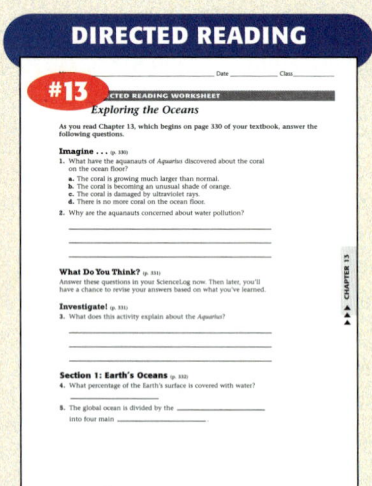

REINFORCEMENT & VOCABULARY REVIEW

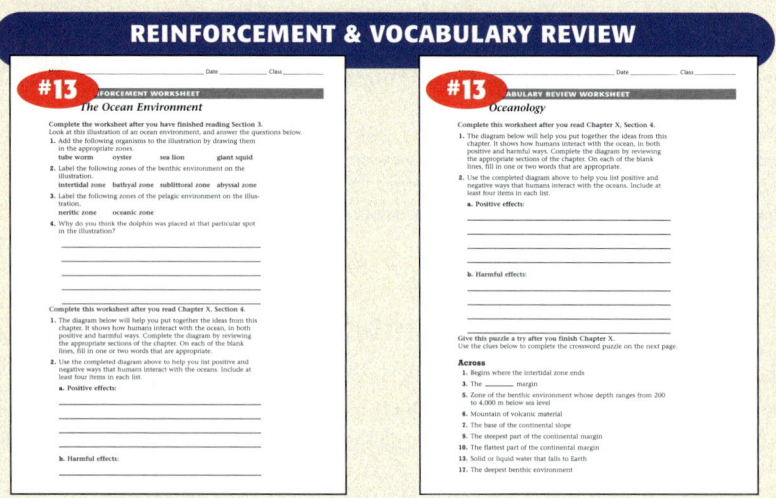

SCIENCE PUZZLERS, TWISTERS & TEASERS

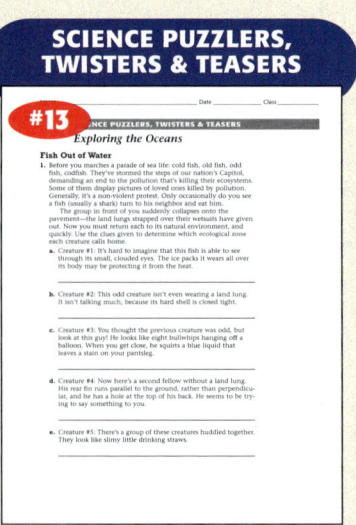

Chapter 13 • Exploring the Oceans

Chapter 13 • Exploring the Oceans

Review & Assessment

STUDY GUIDE
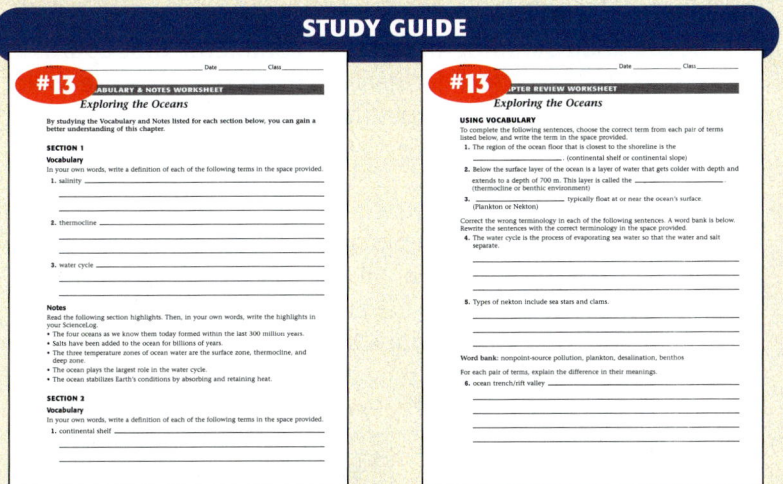

CHAPTER TESTS WITH PERFORMANCE-BASED ASSESSMENT
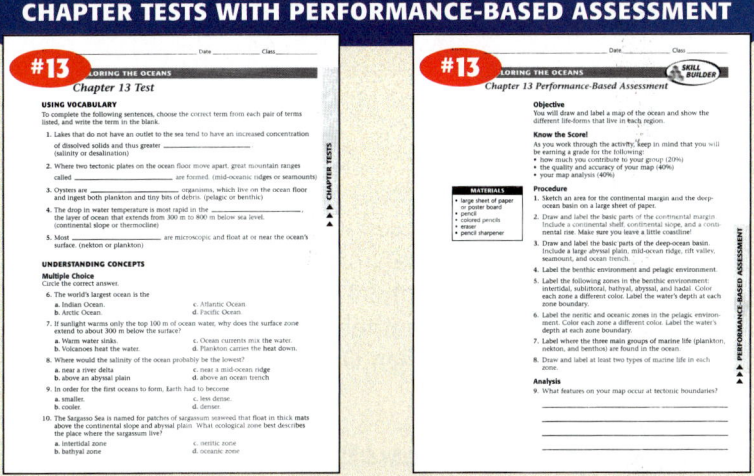

Lab Worksheets

INQUIRY LABS
LONG-TERM PROJECTS & RESEARCH IDEAS
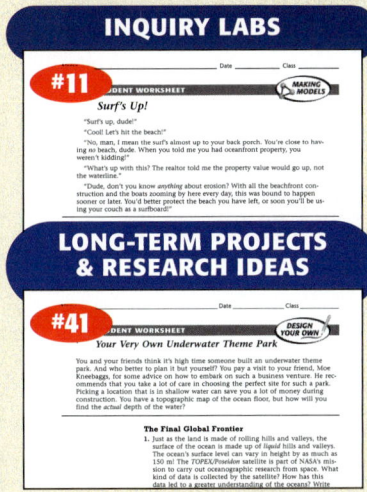

ECOLABS & FIELD ACTIVITIES
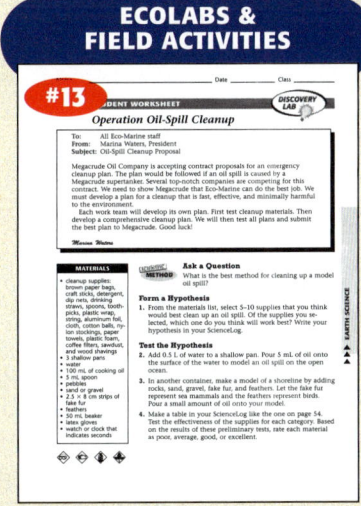

WHIZ-BANG DEMONSTRATIONS
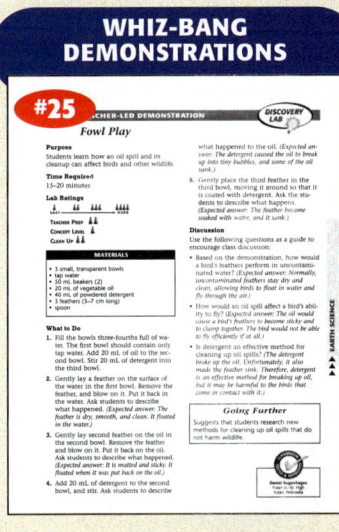

DATASHEETS FOR LABBOOK
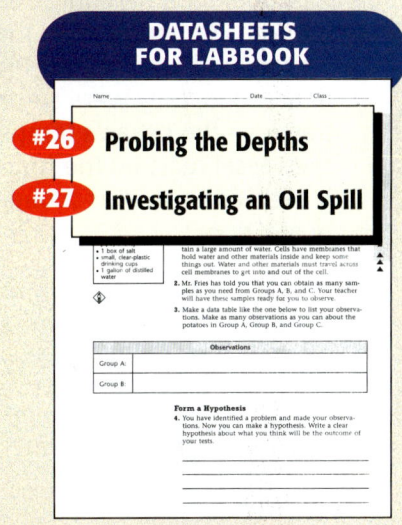

Applications & Extensions

CRITICAL THINKING & PROBLEM SOLVING
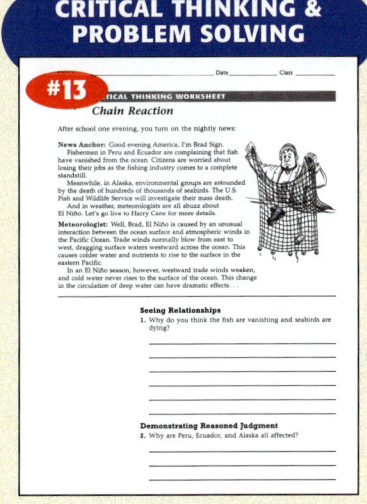

MULTICULTURAL CONNECTIONS
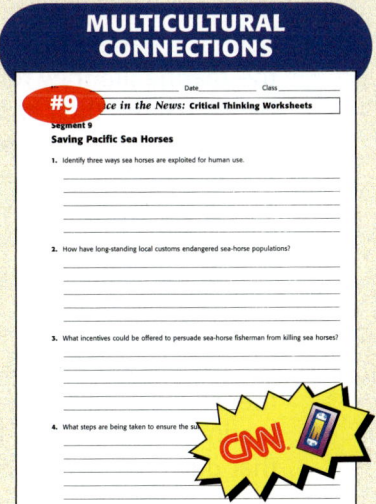

SCIENTISTS IN ACTION
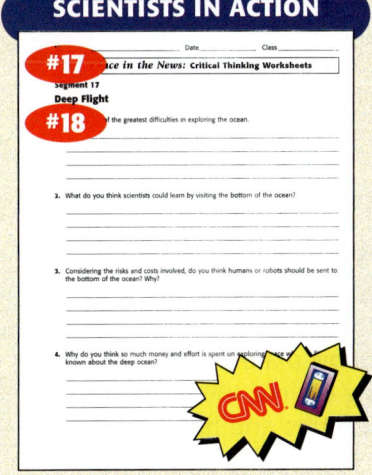

INTERACTIVE EXPLORATIONS
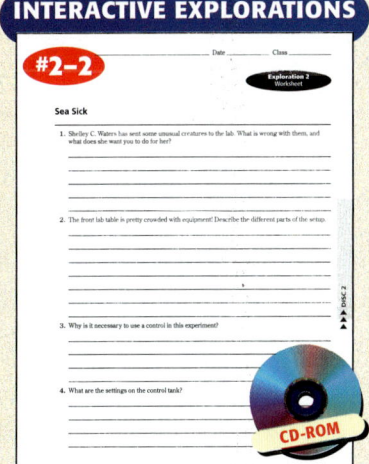

Chapter 13 • Chapter Resources & Worksheets **327D**

Chapter Background

SECTION 1

Earth's Oceans

▶ **The Global Ocean**
Historically, the global ocean was divided into five oceans: the Atlantic, Pacific, Indian, Arctic, and Antarctic Oceans. Today, most oceanographers agree that the Antarctic Ocean is actually the southernmost section of the Atlantic, Pacific, and Indian Oceans.

▶ **The Mariana Trench**
In 1960, the *Trieste,* a small submersible designed to explore the ocean to great depths, set out on a voyage that until then had only been imagined: it descended into the Mariana Trench, the deepest known place on the Earth. As Jacques Piccard and a companion descended, they were surprised to feel abrupt changes between the ocean's temperature layers. Every time the vessel reached the boundary between two layers, it seemed to stop as though it had reached the ocean floor.

IS THAT A FACT!

- The average depth of each ocean is as follows:
  Arctic: 1,038 m
  Atlantic: 3,735 m
  Indian: 3,872 m
  Pacific: 4,188 m

- The average depth for all the oceans is about 3,800 m.

SECTION 2

The Ocean Floor

▶ **The Renewal of a Planet**
Submersible missions such as *Alvin*'s have enabled oceanographers to witness the creation of oceanic crust and the forces that drive tectonic plate movement. By observing molten rock welling up into the ocean, they have seen how new seafloor forms and have gained a better understanding of how the continents drift apart. Trained to "read" rock formations, these scientists use their observations to reconstruct the Earth's history.

IS THAT A FACT!

- The oceans' deep-water sound channels carry sound waves for hundreds of kilometers. Whales and other marine animals take advantage of these properties for long-range communication and to search for food. Whales communicate with clicks, whistles, squeaks, and songs that convey information. Scientists aren't sure what these songs mean, but they do know that whales can communicate at distances as great as 1,600 km!

SECTION 3

Life in the Ocean

▶ **A World of Its Own**
In 1977, scientists aboard *Alvin* witnessed an astonishing new world around deep-sea vents. Exploring hydrothermal vents 320 km off the Galápagos Islands, these explorers saw an amazing multitude of unusual marine populations—giant clams and worms, fish, and crabs—gathered in an abyssal oasis.

- Using a special claw attachment, scientists harvested samples of the marine life they found. When they analyzed their specimens, they were in for a surprise—the water smelled like rotten eggs! This smell came from hydrogen sulfide dissolved in the water around the vents.

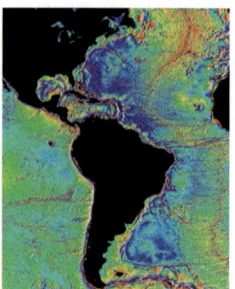

- The scientists discovered that certain marine bacteria thrive on the hydrogen sulfide released by vents in the ocean floor. These bacteria are food for the other marine creatures, and they are part of a food chain that does not rely on photosynthesis for energy.

Chapter 13 • Exploring the Oceans

▶ Creatures of the Dark

The most imaginative science-fiction author would be hard pressed to conceive of creatures as bizarre as the organisms inhabiting the deep sea. Living in perpetual darkness, some—such as the cookie-cutter shark—are bioluminescent. Others lack any organs or structures for vision or photosensitivity. Many benthic (ocean bottom) animals look more like plants than animals. Some exhibit such unique methods of feeding, reproduction, and movement that they are difficult to classify under our current system.

IS THAT A FACT!

- The word *plankton* comes from the Greek *planktos*, meaning "wandering." Because plankton float at or near the ocean's surface, they "wander" with the ocean currents. Interestingly, tiny plankton are the sole sustenance of two of the largest marine animals—the blue whale and the basking shark. The word *planets* is also derived from the same root and refers to the observation that the planets appear to wander among the stars.

SECTION 4

Resources from the Ocean

▶ Food for Thought

Fish are an invaluable ocean resource, providing a significant percentage of the world's protein needs every year. About 75 million tons of fish are harvested from the ocean each year. But many fish populations have been depleted by overfishing.

- Concerned that too few fish will remain to breed, scientists determine the maximum sustainable yield, or the amount of fish that can be harvested each year without jeopardizing future catches. Using the scientists' guidelines, governments sometimes impose fishing restrictions to manage fish populations. Many people are working to ensure that the world can continue to count on fish for food.

▶ Sea Thermal Plants

Harnessing tidal and wave energy is not the only way to get electrical power from the ocean. Since 1979, the United States government has operated an Ocean Thermal Energy Conversion (OTEC) plant off the coast of Hawaii, where the temperature differential between surface and deeper water layers is converted into electrical energy.

SECTION 5

Ocean Pollution

▶ Thermal Pollution

Pesticides, oil, sludge, and trash are not the only harmful pollutants released into our oceans. Power plants can cause thermal pollution by releasing heated water into the sea. Thermal pollution may result in only a 1- or 2-degree temperature difference in the area near the heat source, but that can have profound effects on the ecology. Fish populations may migrate away from the affected area, and overgrowth of other organisms, or "algal blooms," may occur.

▶ Close Quarters

Closed-in seas are particularly vulnerable to damage from ocean pollution. The shores and adjacent waters of the Mediterranean, Baltic, and Adriatic Seas have been fouled with city sewage, factory waste, and fertilizer and pesticide runoff from farms. Their open waters have been affected by dumping and oil spills.

For background information about teaching strategies and issues, refer to the *Professional Reference for Teachers*.

Chapter 13
Exploring the Oceans

Pre-Reading Questions

Students may not know the answers to these questions before reading the chapter, so accept any reasonable response.

Suggested Answers

1. The oceans have changed in size, shape, and salinity over time. Other changes that are not covered in this chapter include changes in marine life, water chemistry, and sea level.

2. Technologies that scientists use to study the ocean without going under water include sonar, satellites, seismic technology, and dredging.

3. Answers will vary. Some resources mentioned in this chapter include fish, oil, natural gas, fresh water, minerals, tidal energy, and wave energy.

Directed Reading Worksheet 13

Science Puzzlers, Twisters & Teasers Worksheet 13

Guided Reading Audio CD
English or Spanish, Chapter 13

Chapter 13
Exploring the Oceans

Sections

1. **Earth's Oceans** 330
   Internet Connect 334
2. **The Ocean Floor** 337
   Internet Connect 339
   MathBreak 340
3. **Life in the Ocean** 342
   Biology Connection .. 343
   Internet Connect 345
4. **Resources from the Ocean** 346
   QuickLab 349
   Internet Connect 350
5. **Ocean Pollution** 351
   Environment Connection 352
   Apply 354
   Internet Connect 355

Chapter Review 358
Feature Articles 360, 361
LabBook 680–683

Pre-Reading Questions

1. How have Earth's oceans changed over time?
2. Name two ways to study the ocean without going under water.
3. Name two valuable resources that are taken from the ocean.

---

internet connect

HRW On-line Resources
go.hrw.com
For worksheets and other teaching aids, visit the HRW Web site and type in the keyword: **HSTOCE**

SCLINKS NSTA
www.scilinks.com
Use the sciLINKS numbers at the end of each chapter for additional resources on the **NSTA** Web site.

www.cnnfyi.com
Visit the CNN Web site for current events coverage and classroom resources.

A New World Under Water

Seventy-one percent of the Earth's surface is covered by ocean water. However, large portions of the oceans, especially the deepest parts and the parts nearest the poles, remain completely unexplored. In the past several decades, new technologies have made underwater exploration possible, allowing scientists to gather important information about the Earth's greatest resource. In this chapter, you'll learn about the fascinating world under the water and the important part the oceans play in making our planet livable.

START-UP Activity

EXIT ONLY?

To study what life under water would be like, scientists sometimes live in underwater laboratories. How do these scientists enter and leave these labs? Believe it or not, the simplest way is through a hole in the lab's floor. You might think water would come in through the hole, but it doesn't. People inside the lab can breathe freely and can come and go through the hole at any time. How is this possible? Do the following activity to find out.

Procedure

1. Fill a **large bowl** about two-thirds full of **water.**
2. Turn a **clear plastic cup** upside down.
3. Slowly guide the cup straight down into the water. Be careful not to tip the cup.
4. Record your observations in your ScienceLog.

Analysis

5. How does the air inside the cup affect the water below the cup?
6. How do your findings relate to the hole in the bottom of the underwater research lab?

START-UP Activity

EXIT ONLY?

MATERIALS
For Each Group: • large bowl • small, clear plastic cup

Teacher's Notes

A cylindrical cup (one that does not taper) is best for this activity.

Answers to START-UP Activity

5. Sample answer: The air inside the cup prevented the water below it from filling the space inside the cup.
6. Answers will vary. Sample answer: Just as the air in the cup keeps the water from filling the cup, the air in the underwater research lab keeps water from coming through the hole in the bottom of the lab.

SECTION 1

Focus

Earth's Oceans

In this section students learn how the global ocean is divided as well as how the oceans formed. They explore the properties of ocean water, including factors that affect salinity, temperature zones, and surface temperature changes. Finally, they learn how the ocean interacts with the atmosphere and the land via the water cycle.

Bellringer

Show students a photo of Earth from outer space, and ask them to list some of the planet's most obvious features. Have them predict the percentage of land and water on Earth. Tell students that water covers 71 percent of Earth's surface and that liquid water is very rare in our solar system. Discuss the significance of Earth's abundant water resources.

1 Motivate

ACTIVITY

Discuss the divisions of the global ocean shown on this page, noting that the volume of the Pacific Ocean is 724 million cubic kilometers. The volume of the Atlantic Ocean is about 322 million cubic kilometers, the volume of the Indian Ocean is about 292 million cubic kilometers, and the volume of the Arctic Ocean is about 12 million cubic kilometers. Have students use graduated cylinders filled with water to demonstrate these ratios. (The Pacific Ocean would be 724 mL, the Atlantic Ocean would be 322 mL, the Indian Ocean would be 292 mL, and the Arctic Ocean would be 12 mL.)

Section 1

Terms to Learn
salinity
thermocline
water cycle

What You'll Do
- Name the major divisions of the global ocean.
- Describe the history of Earth's oceans.
- Summarize the properties and other aspects of ocean water.
- Summarize the interaction between the ocean and the atmosphere.

Earth's Oceans

Earth stands out from the other planets in our solar system primarily for one reason—71 percent of the Earth's surface is covered with water. Most of Earth's water is found in the global ocean, which is divided by the continents into four main oceans. This is shown in the figure below. The ocean is a unique body of water that plays many roles in regulating Earth's environment. Read on to learn more about one of our most important resources—the ocean.

Divisions of the Global Ocean

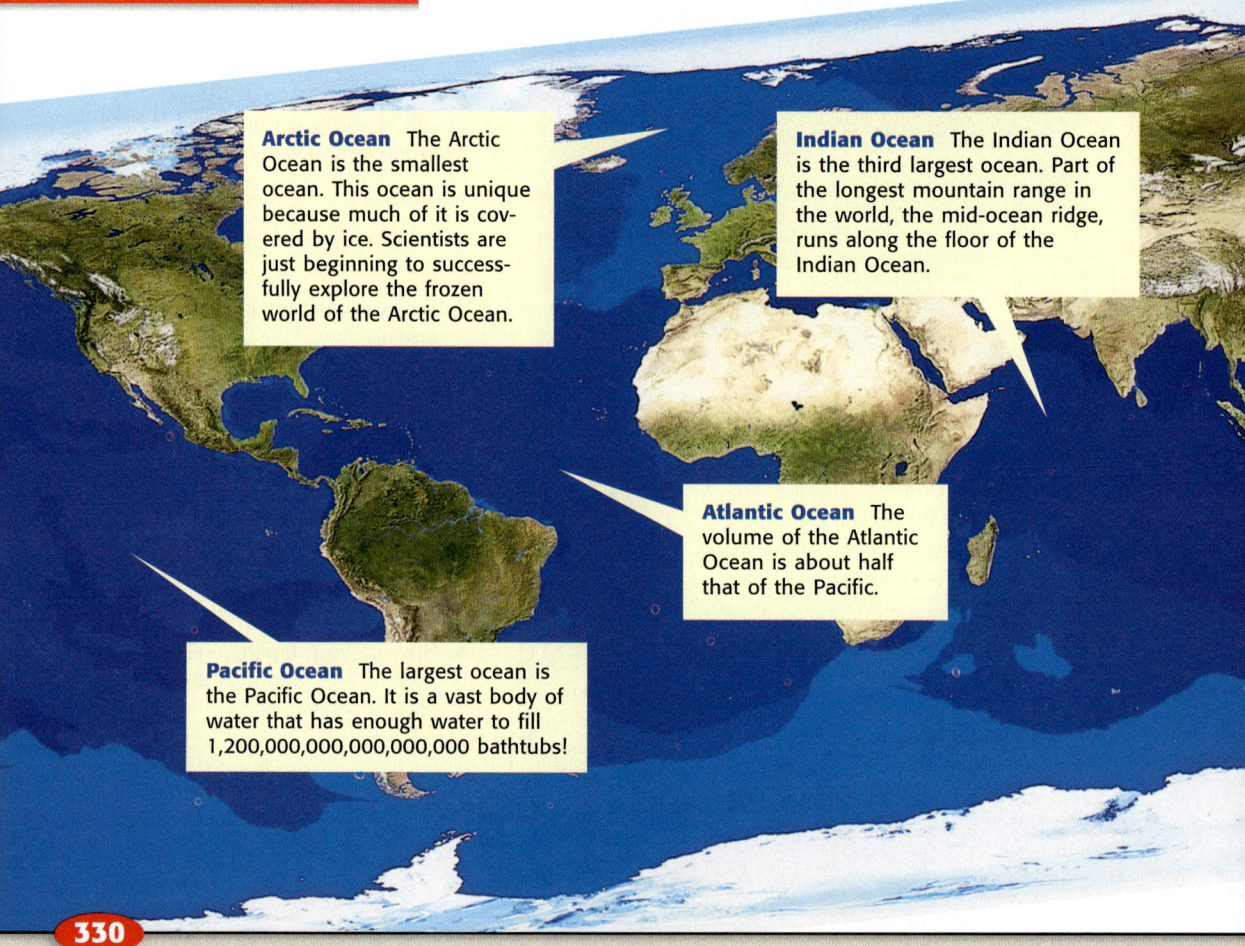

Arctic Ocean The Arctic Ocean is the smallest ocean. This ocean is unique because much of it is covered by ice. Scientists are just beginning to successfully explore the frozen world of the Arctic Ocean.

Indian Ocean The Indian Ocean is the third largest ocean. Part of the longest mountain range in the world, the mid-ocean ridge, runs along the floor of the Indian Ocean.

Atlantic Ocean The volume of the Atlantic Ocean is about half that of the Pacific.

Pacific Ocean The largest ocean is the Pacific Ocean. It is a vast body of water that has enough water to fill 1,200,000,000,000,000,000 bathtubs!

Teaching Transparency 149 "Divisions of the Global Oceans"

Directed Reading Worksheet 13 Section 1

IS THAT A FACT!

The global ocean covers nearly 376 million square kilometers. The entire North American continent, by comparison, covers only a little more than 24 million square kilometers.

How Did the Oceans Form?

About four and a half billion years ago, the Earth was a very different place. There were no oceans. Volcanoes spewed lava, ash, and gases all over the planet, which was much hotter than it is today. The volcanic gases, including water vapor, began to form Earth's atmosphere. While the atmosphere developed, the Earth was cooling. Sometime before 4 billion years ago, the Earth cooled enough for water vapor to condense and fall as rain. The rain began filling the lower levels of Earth's surface, and the first oceans began to form.

Earth's oceans have changed a lot throughout history. Scientists who study oceans have learned much about the oceans' history, as shown in the diagram below.

Self-Check

Examine the diagram below. If North America and South America continue to drift westward and Asia continues to drift eastward, what will eventually happen? *(See page 726 to check your answer.)*

The Recent History of Earth's Oceans

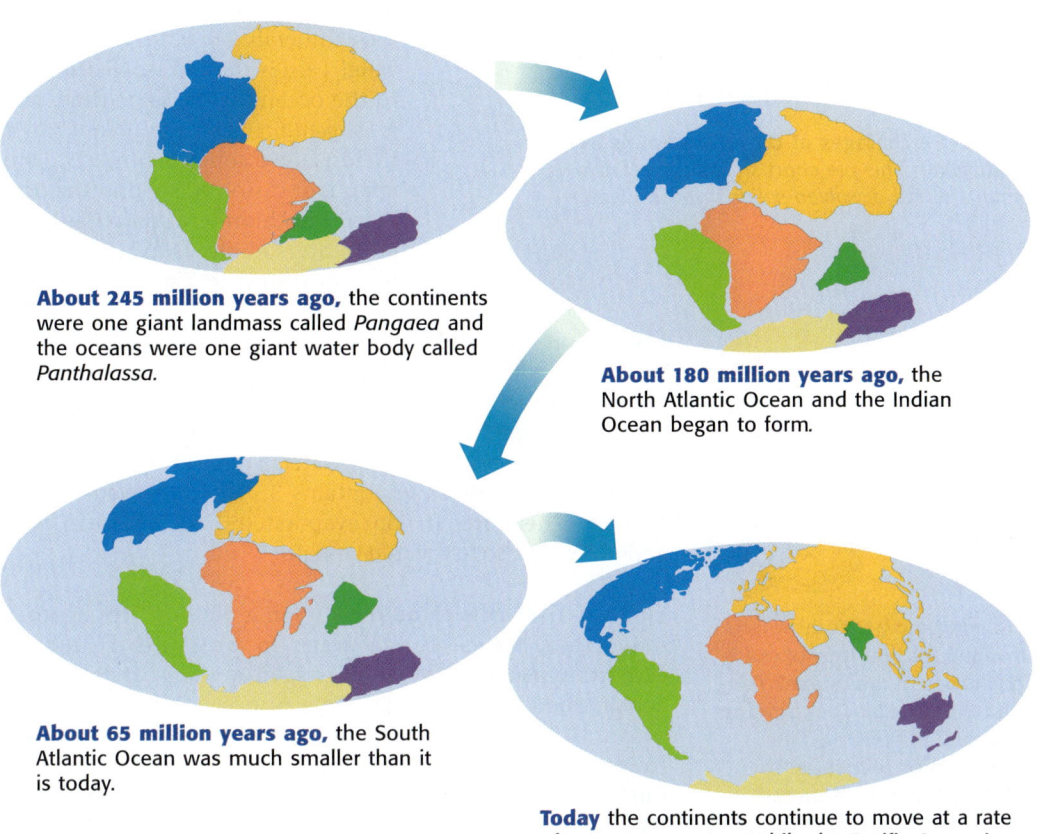

About 245 million years ago, the continents were one giant landmass called *Pangaea* and the oceans were one giant water body called *Panthalassa*.

About 180 million years ago, the North Atlantic Ocean and the Indian Ocean began to form.

About 65 million years ago, the South Atlantic Ocean was much smaller than it is today.

Today the continents continue to move at a rate of 1–10 cm per year. While the Pacific Ocean is getting smaller, the other oceans are expanding.

2 Teach, continued

MISCONCEPTION ALERT

In **Figure 1,** students may notice that the percentages of some of the elements dissolved in ocean water are particularly low. This does not necessarily mean these elements are not abundant in the ocean. Organisms, such as diatoms and coral, remove dissolved minerals containing some of these elements and use them to make hard body parts. Ask students to note the two elements that are most abundant. (sodium and chloride) Ask them what these elements form when they are combined. (sodium chloride or salt)

BRAIN FOOD

To help students conceptualize the concentration of gold in sea water, point out that 1 billion metric tons of ocean water contains about 4 kg of gold. Have students think of strategies to remove gold from sea water. On land, some mining companies use a bacteria called *Thiobacillus ferrooxidans* to extract gold and copper from mine wastes. Have students find out more about this process and whether it could be used to recover gold from the oceans.

Characteristics of Ocean Water

You know that ocean water is different from the water that flows from the faucet of your kitchen sink. For one thing, ocean water is not safe to drink. But there are other characteristics that make ocean water special.

Ocean Water Is Salty Have you ever swallowed a mouthful of water while swimming in the ocean? It sure had a nasty taste, didn't it? Most of the salt in the ocean is the same kind of salt that we sprinkle on our food. Scientists call this salt *sodium chloride*.

The ocean is so salty because salt has been added to it for billions of years. As rivers and streams flow toward the oceans, they dissolve various minerals on land. The running water carries these dissolved minerals to the ocean. At the same time, water is *evaporating* from the ocean, leaving the dissolved solids behind. The most abundant dissolved solid in the ocean is sodium chloride, a compound of the elements sodium (Na) and chlorine (Cl), as shown in **Figure 1.**

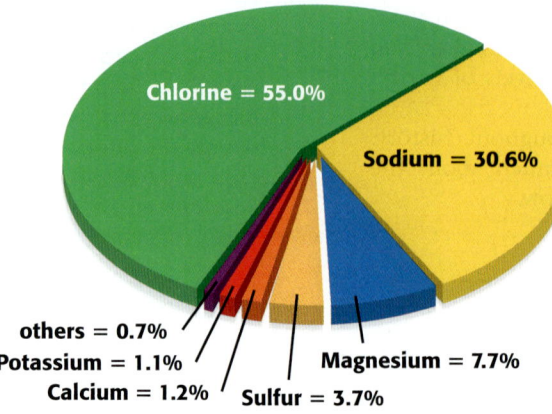

Figure 1 Percentages of Dissolved Solids in Ocean Water *This pie chart shows the relative amounts of the dissolved solids in ocean water.*

Chlorine = 55.0%
Sodium = 30.6%
others = 0.7%
Potassium = 1.1%
Calcium = 1.2%
Sulfur = 3.7%
Magnesium = 7.7%

Chock-full of Solids If more water evaporates than enters the ocean, the ocean's salinity increases. **Salinity** is a measure of the amount of dissolved salts and other solids in a given amount of liquid. Salinity is usually measured as grams of dissolved solids per kilogram of water. Think of it this way: 1 kg (1,000 g) of ocean water contains 35 g of dissolved solids on average. Therefore, if you evaporated 1 kg of ocean water, about 35 g of solids would remain.

BRAIN FOOD

Did you know that there are about 9 million tons of gold dissolved in the ocean? Too bad the gold's concentration is only 0.000004 mg per kilogram of sea water. Mining the gold from the water would be difficult, and the cost of removing it would be greater than the gold's value.

Factors That Affect Salinity Some areas of the ocean are saltier than others. Coastal water in areas with hotter, drier climates typically have a higher salinity than coastal water in cooler, more humid areas. This is because less fresh water runs into the ocean in drier areas and because heat increases the evaporation rate. Evaporation removes water but leaves salts and other dissolved solids behind. Also, coastal areas where major rivers run into the ocean have a relatively low salinity. In these areas, the rivers add to the ocean large volumes of fresh water, which contains fewer dissolved solids than sea water.

Q: Why is the ocean salty?

A: because fish don't like pepper

Another factor that affects ocean salinity is water movement. Surface water in some areas of the ocean, such as bays, gulfs, and seas, circulates less than surface water in other parts. Areas in the open ocean that have no currents running through them can also be slow moving. **Figure 2** shows how salinity variations relate to many factors.

Temperature Zones The temperature of ocean water decreases as the depth of the water increases. However, this does not occur gradually from the ocean's surface to its bottom. Water in the ocean can be divided into three layers according to temperature. As you can see in the graph below, the water at the top is much warmer than the average temperature of the ocean.

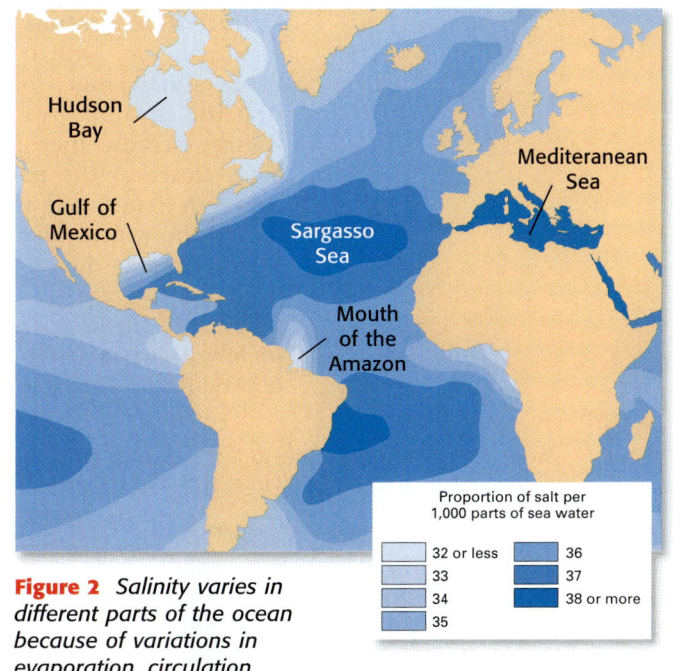

Figure 2 Salinity varies in different parts of the ocean because of variations in evaporation, circulation, and freshwater inflow.

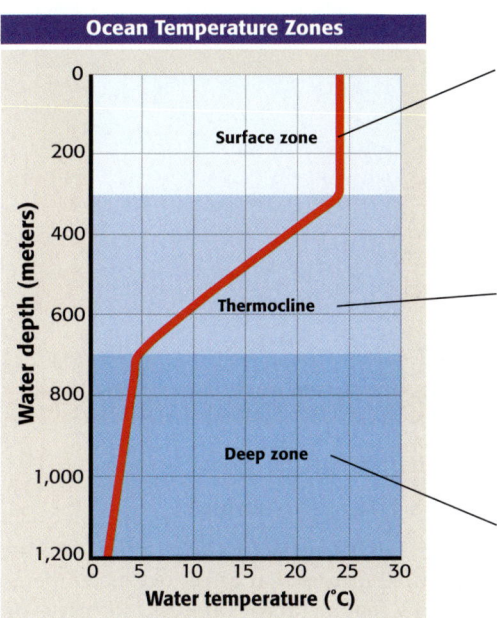

Surface zone
The surface zone is the warm, top layer of ocean water that extends to 300 m below sea level. Sunlight heats the top 100 m of the surface zone. Surface currents mix the heated water with cooler water below.

Thermocline
The **thermocline** is a layer of water extending from 300 m below sea level to about 700 m below sea level. In this zone, water temperature drops with increased depth faster than it does in the other two zones.

Deep zone
This bottom layer extends from the base of the thermocline to the bottom of the ocean. The temperature in this zone averages a chilling 2°C.

IS THAT A FACT!

The deepest water in the ocean is colder than 0°C, but it remains liquid because of its salinity and the increased pressures at that depth.

WEIRD SCIENCE

The Amazon River feeds so much fresh water into the Atlantic Ocean that the ocean water has different salinity and color almost 160 km from shore!

MEETING INDIVIDUAL NEEDS

Learners Having Difficulty To help students visualize the temperature zones of the ocean, ask them to make cross-section diagrams of the ocean, labeling the surface zone, thermocline, and deep zone. Have them write captions for their drawings that explain the relationship between temperature and depth. **Sheltered English**

CONNECT TO PHYSICAL SCIENCE

Sound waves travel faster in warm water than in cold water. A technique called acoustic thermometry of ocean climate (ATOC) measures the time it takes for sound to travel a known distance through the ocean. Using this method, oceanographers can determine the average temperature of the ocean water with great accuracy.

MISCONCEPTION ALERT

Although the graph of ocean temperature zones only extends to a depth of 1,200 m, the ocean is much deeper than 1,200 m in most places, and the deep zone extends all the way to the bottom of the ocean. The rate at which temperature decreases with depth is constant throughout the deep zone. Students should also realize that the depth of each ocean zone varies according to the depth of the ocean floor.

Teaching Transparency 150 "Ocean Salinity"

Section 1 • Earth's Oceans

2) Teach, continued

GROUP ACTIVITY

Making Models Using balloons and permanent markers, students can model how latitude affects ocean surface temperatures. Have them clearly label the poles and equator on their balloons and indicate surface water temperatures between the two. Have them use colored pens to draw bands around their balloons. They should construct a key for their colors, correlating warmer temperatures with the colors closest to the equator. After they color in the shapes of the continents, students can present their models to the class.

CROSS-DISCIPLINARY FOCUS

Geography Encourage students to use atlases or globes to locate the four main oceans. Suggest that students draw a map of the oceans that indicates modern or ancient trade routes and illustrate it with drawings of animals that are unique to each ocean. Students might also make a chart in which they compare all of the oceans by size, average temperature, depth, and other characteristics.

TOPIC: Exploring Earth's Oceans
GO TO: www.scilinks.org
sciLINKS NUMBER: HSTE305

Surface Temperature Changes Temperatures in the surface zone vary with latitude and the time of year. Surface temperatures range from 1°C near the poles to about 24°C near the equator. Areas of the ocean along the equator are warmer because they receive more sunlight per year than areas closer to the poles. However, the sun's rays in the Northern Hemisphere are more direct during the summer than during the winter. Therefore, the surface zone absorbs more thermal energy during the summer.

If you live near the coast, you may know firsthand how different a dip in the ocean feels in December than it feels in July. **Figure 3** shows how surface-zone temperatures vary depending on the time of year.

Figure 3 *These satellite images show that the surface temperatures in the northern Pacific Ocean change with the seasons.*

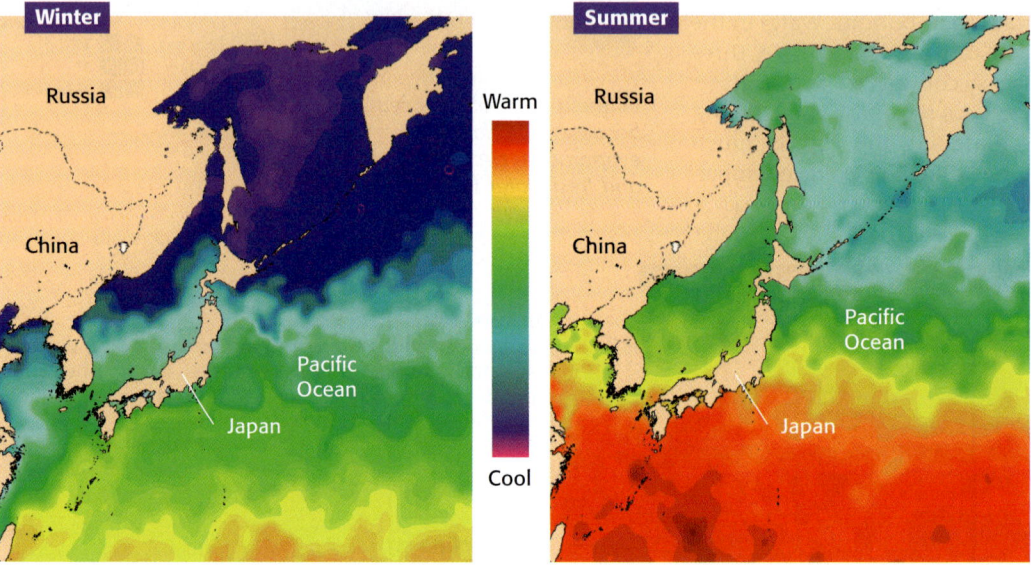

REVIEW

1. Name the major divisions of the global ocean.
2. Explain how Earth's first oceans formed.
3. **Summarizing Data** List three factors that affect salinity in the ocean and three factors that affect ocean temperatures. Explain how each factor affects salinity or temperature.

Answers to Review

1. The major divisions of the global ocean are the Pacific Ocean, the Atlantic Ocean, the Indian Ocean, and the Arctic Ocean.
2. Sometime before 4 billion years ago, the Earth cooled enough for water vapor in the atmosphere to condense and fall as rain. The rain began filling the lower levels of Earth's surface, and the first oceans began to form.
3. The factors affecting salinity are the type of climate, the addition or removal of fresh water, and water movement; the factors affecting temperature are water depth, latitude, and the time of year. Explanations will vary.

The Ocean and the Water Cycle

If you could sit on the moon and look down at Earth, what would you see? You would notice that Earth's surface is made up of three basic components—water, land, and air. All three are involved in an ongoing process called the water cycle, as shown below. The **water cycle** is a cycle that links all of Earth's solid, liquid, and gaseous water together. The ocean is an important part of the water cycle because nearly all of Earth's water is found in the ocean.

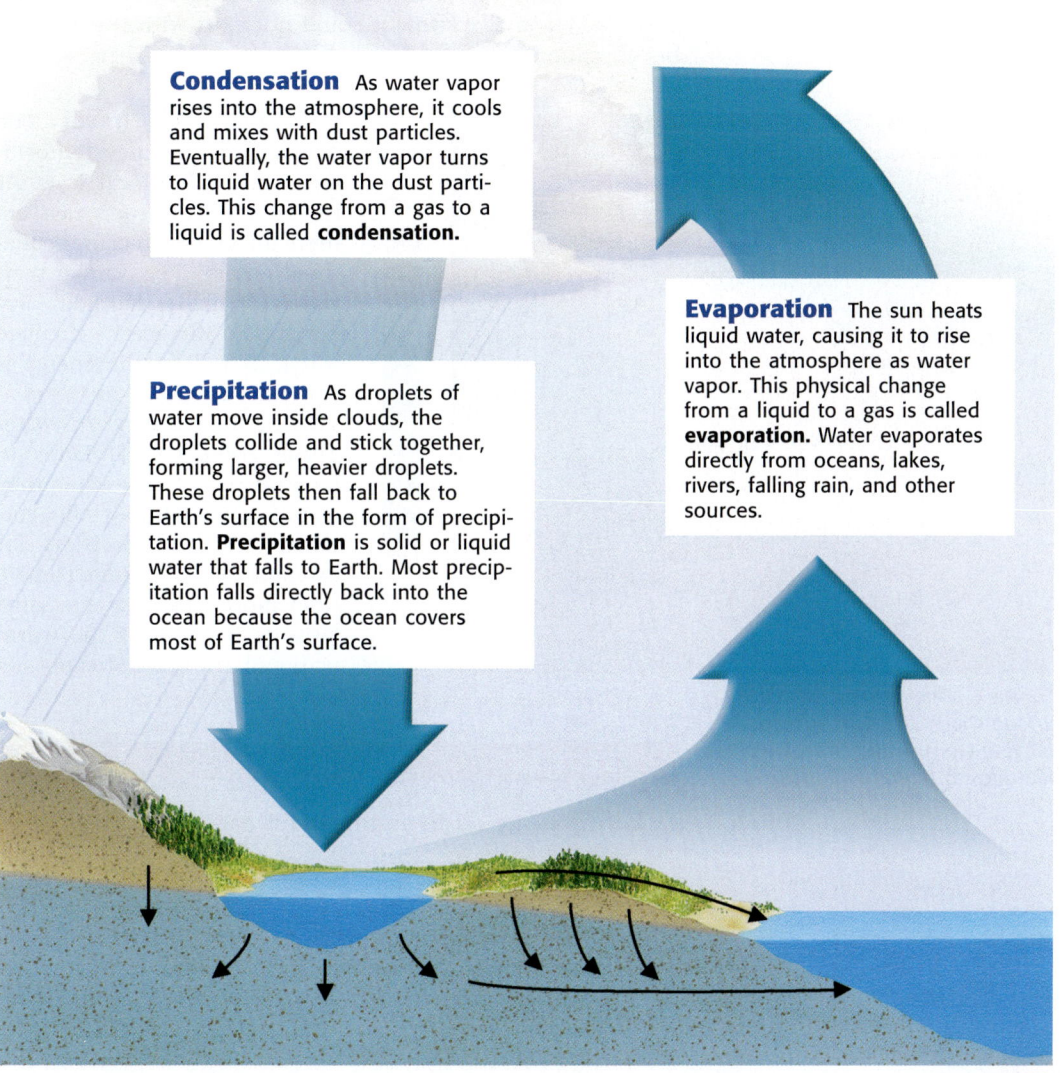

Condensation As water vapor rises into the atmosphere, it cools and mixes with dust particles. Eventually, the water vapor turns to liquid water on the dust particles. This change from a gas to a liquid is called **condensation**.

Precipitation As droplets of water move inside clouds, the droplets collide and stick together, forming larger, heavier droplets. These droplets then fall back to Earth's surface in the form of precipitation. **Precipitation** is solid or liquid water that falls to Earth. Most precipitation falls directly back into the ocean because the ocean covers most of Earth's surface.

Evaporation The sun heats liquid water, causing it to rise into the atmosphere as water vapor. This physical change from a liquid to a gas is called **evaporation**. Water evaporates directly from oceans, lakes, rivers, falling rain, and other sources.

IS THAT A FACT!
Eighteen thousand years ago much of Earth's water was frozen in glaciers and icecaps, and the Atlantic coast was miles farther out than it is today. Modern-day divers exploring the Chesapeake Bay found a mound of oyster shells—the remains of a long-ago picnic—40 m below sea level!

 **Teaching Transparency 151** "The Ocean and the Water Cycle"

3) Extend

MEETING INDIVIDUAL NEEDS
Advanced Learners Divide the class into small groups, and provide each with a small dish or bowl, a plastic bag with twist-tie, and water. Challenge them to create a model demonstrating the water cycle. (Students might place the dish, filled with water, into the bag and seal it. As water evaporates from the dish, it will condense on the inner surface of the bag, eventually falling as "rain." Allow time for each group to explain its model to the class.)

GOING FURTHER
Challenge students to explain why the oceans are a crucial influence on the world's weather. (The oceans receive and absorb a large portion of the sun's energy. This energy raises the temperature of the oceans, which influences the atmosphere. Winds create currents, which carry warm water to colder areas, and vice versa, affecting local climates. Finally, solar energy evaporates an enormous amount of sea water, which eventually returns to Earth as precipitation.)

Multicultural CONNECTION
About 3,000 years ago, Greek maps of the world had the Mediterranean Sea in the center of a flat world. Oceans surrounded the lands around the Mediterranean Sea. Ask students: Why do you think the Greeks drew the Mediterranean Sea at the center of their maps? (Their known world centered around it.)

In what ways were their maps considered accurate? (The Greek maps had fairly accurate details of local coastlines and topography.)

Section 1 • Earth's Oceans

4) Close

Quiz

1. How is the global ocean divided, and what are the divisions? (It is divided by the continents into four main oceans, the Pacific, the Atlantic, the Indian, and the Arctic.)
2. How do scientists think the oceans are likely to change in the future? (They predict that the oceans will change in size and shape as the continents change position.)

ALTERNATIVE ASSESSMENT

 Encourage students to examine the illustration on page 331. Have them prepare a timeline detailing the history of Earth's oceans. Challenge students to predict how the oceans will change during the next 150 million years. Students can illustrate their timelines with drawings of each stage of Earth's history.

MISCONCEPTION ALERT

Sea level is not the same worldwide for several reasons. Tides alter the ocean's depth constantly and so do winds. Pacific Ocean trade winds blow westward, causing the ocean level to be about a half meter higher on the western side of the Pacific. Sea level is also higher at the equator than at the poles because the warm equatorial waters expand and the centrifugal force of Earth's rotation causes the middle of the planet to bulge.

A Global Thermostat

The ocean plays a vital role in maintaining conditions favorable for life on Earth. Perhaps the most important function of the ocean is to absorb and hold energy from sunlight. This function regulates temperatures in the atmosphere.

A Hot Exchange The ocean absorbs and releases thermal energy much more slowly than dry land does. If it were not for this function of the ocean, the average air temperature on Earth would vary from above 100°C during the day to below –100°C at night. This rapid exchange of energy between the atmosphere and the Earth's surface would cause violent weather patterns. Life as we know it could not exist with these unstable conditions.

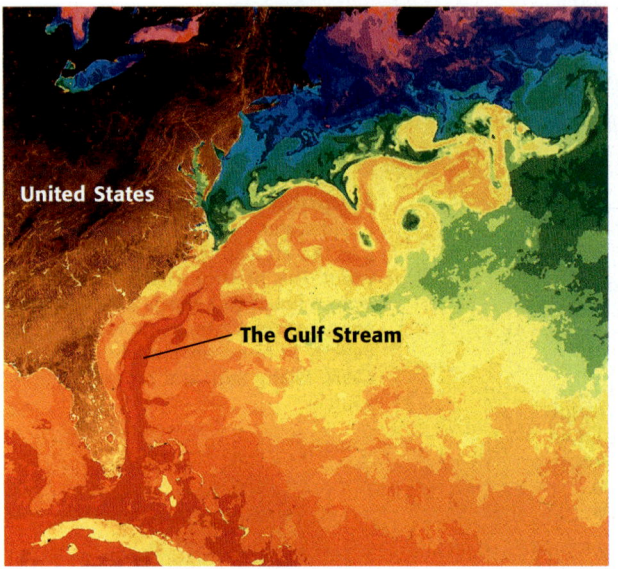

Have Heat, Will Travel The ocean also regulates temperatures on a more local scale. At the equator, the sun's rays are more direct, which causes equatorial waters to be warmer than waters at higher latitudes. But currents in the oceans circulate water, as well as the energy it contains, as shown in **Figure 4**. This circulation of warm water causes some coastal lands to have warmer climates than they would have without the currents. The British Isles, for example, have a warmer climate than most regions at the same latitude because of the warm water of the Gulf Stream.

Figure 4 This infrared satellite image shows the Gulf Stream moving warm water from lower latitudes to higher latitudes.

REVIEW

1. Why is the ocean an important part of the water cycle?
2. Between which two steps of the water cycle does the ocean fit?
3. **Making Inferences** Explain why St. Louis, Missouri, has colder winters and warmer summers than San Francisco, California, even though the two cities are at about the same latitude.

▼ **Answers to Review**

1. The ocean is an important part of the water cycle because nearly all of Earth's water is found in the ocean. In addition, students might note that the ocean absorbs the majority of the solar radiation that reaches the Earth.
2. The ocean fits between precipitation and evaporation in the water cycle.
3. San Francisco is on the coast of the Pacific Ocean. Because the coastal waters absorb and slowly release energy from sunlight, San Francisco has less severe temperature fluctuations. Although St. Louis is at about the same latitude as San Francisco, there is no ocean nearby to regulate temperatures. Thus St. Louis has warmer summers and colder winters than San Francisco.

Section 2

The Ocean Floor

Terms to Learn

continental shelf   mid-ocean ridge
continental slope   rift valley
continental rise   seamount
abyssal plain   ocean trench

What You'll Do

- Identify the two major regions of the ocean floor.
- Classify subdivisions and features of the two major regions of the ocean floor.
- Describe technologies for studying the ocean floor.

Science CONNECTION

Turn to page 360 to meet the most famous underwater explorer who ever lived.

What lies at the bottom of the ocean? How deep is the ocean? These are questions that were once unanswerable. But humans have learned a lot about the ocean floor, especially in the last few decades. Using state-of-the-art technology, scientists have discovered a wide variety of landforms on the ocean floor. Scientists have also determined accurate depths for almost the entire ocean floor.

Exploring the Ocean Floor

Some parts of the ocean are so deep that humans must use special underwater vessels to travel there. Perhaps the most familiar underwater vessel used by scientists to study the ocean floor is the minisub called *Alvin*. Scientists have used *Alvin* for many underwater missions, including searches for sunken ships, the recovery of a lost hydrogen bomb, and explorations of landforms on the sea floor.

Although the use of *Alvin* has enabled scientists to make some amazing discoveries, scientists are developing new vessels for ocean exploration, such as an underwater airplane called *Deep Flight*. This vessel, shown in **Figure 5,** moves through the water much like an airplane moves through the air. Future models of *Deep Flight* will be designed to transport pilots to the deepest part of the ocean.

Figure 5 Like the Wright brothers' first successful airplane, Deep Flight sets the stage for a bright future—this time in underwater "flight."

IS THAT A FACT!

The same explorer who led the first voyage around the world also attempted to determine the depth of the ocean. In 1520, Ferdinand Magellan weighted a 370 m rope with lead, and lowered it into the ocean. Unfortunately, his rope was not long enough to reach the ocean floor. It was not until 1773 that a successful measurement was made. Using Magellan's techniques, explorers found that the depth of the ocean near Norway is about 1,250 m.

SECTION 2

Focus

The Ocean Floor

In this section, students learn about the regional divisions of the ocean floor and the geographic features of each division. They learn how technology has facilitated exploration of the ocean floor, and they learn about the methods used to survey the ocean floor, including sonar and satellites.

🔔 Bellringer

Before students read this section, have them explore their ideas about the ocean floor by telling them to pretend they have walked off the edge of North America and into the depths of the Atlantic Ocean. As they walk along the ocean floor toward Europe, what would they see? Have each student make a drawing of the ocean floor that he or she would see along the way. **Sheltered English**

1) Motivate

DISCUSSION

It has been said that scientists know more about the surface of the moon than about the ocean floor. Most of what scientists know about the ocean floor comes from sonar readings and sample dredging. Ask students to think about why the ocean is so difficult to study and what kinds of technology would help scientists learn more about the deep-ocean floor.

 Directed Reading Worksheet 13 Section 2

Section 2 • The Ocean Floor   337

2 Teach

 PG 680
Probing the Depths

MATH and MORE

Water pressure increases with depth. For every 10 m of depth, the pressure increases by 1 atmosphere (atm). For example, at a depth of 10 m, the pressure is 2 atm, or twice the pressure of the atmosphere at sea level. Ask students:

What is the pressure at 20 m? **(3 atm)**

50 m? **(6 atm)**

100 m? **(11 atm)**

What is the pressure at the bottom of the Mariana Trench? **(greater than 1200 atm)**

 Math Skills Worksheet 3 "Multiplying Whole Numbers"

CONNECT TO PHYSICAL SCIENCE

To show how water pressure changes with depth, take a milk carton and punch three holes in its side: one near the top, one halfway down the side, and one near the bottom. Put one piece of tape over all three holes, and fill the carton with water. Remove the tape quickly. Have students observe the streams of water and explain what they saw. **(The water stream at the bottom of the carton shot out the farthest, with the greatest force. This is because the water above exerted pressure on the water at the bottom of the carton.)**

Want to survey the ocean floor? Turn to page 680 in the LabBook to bring the ocean floor to your desktop.

Figure 6 *The continental margin is subdivided into three depth zones, and the deep-ocean basin consists of one depth zone with several features.*

Revealing the Ocean Floor

What if you were an explorer assigned to map uncharted areas on the planet? You might think there were not many uncharted areas left because most of the land had already been explored. But what about the bottom of the ocean? If you could travel to the bottom of the ocean in *Deep Flight,* you would see the world's largest mountain chain and canyons deeper than the Grand Canyon. And because it is under water, much of this area is unexplored.

As you began your descent into the underwater realm, you would notice two major regions—the *continental margin,* which is made of continental crust, and the *deep-ocean basin,* which is made of oceanic crust. It may help to imagine the ocean as a giant swimming pool; the continental margin is the shallow end and slope of the pool, and the deep-ocean basin is the deep end of the pool. **Figure 6** shows how these two regions are subdivided.

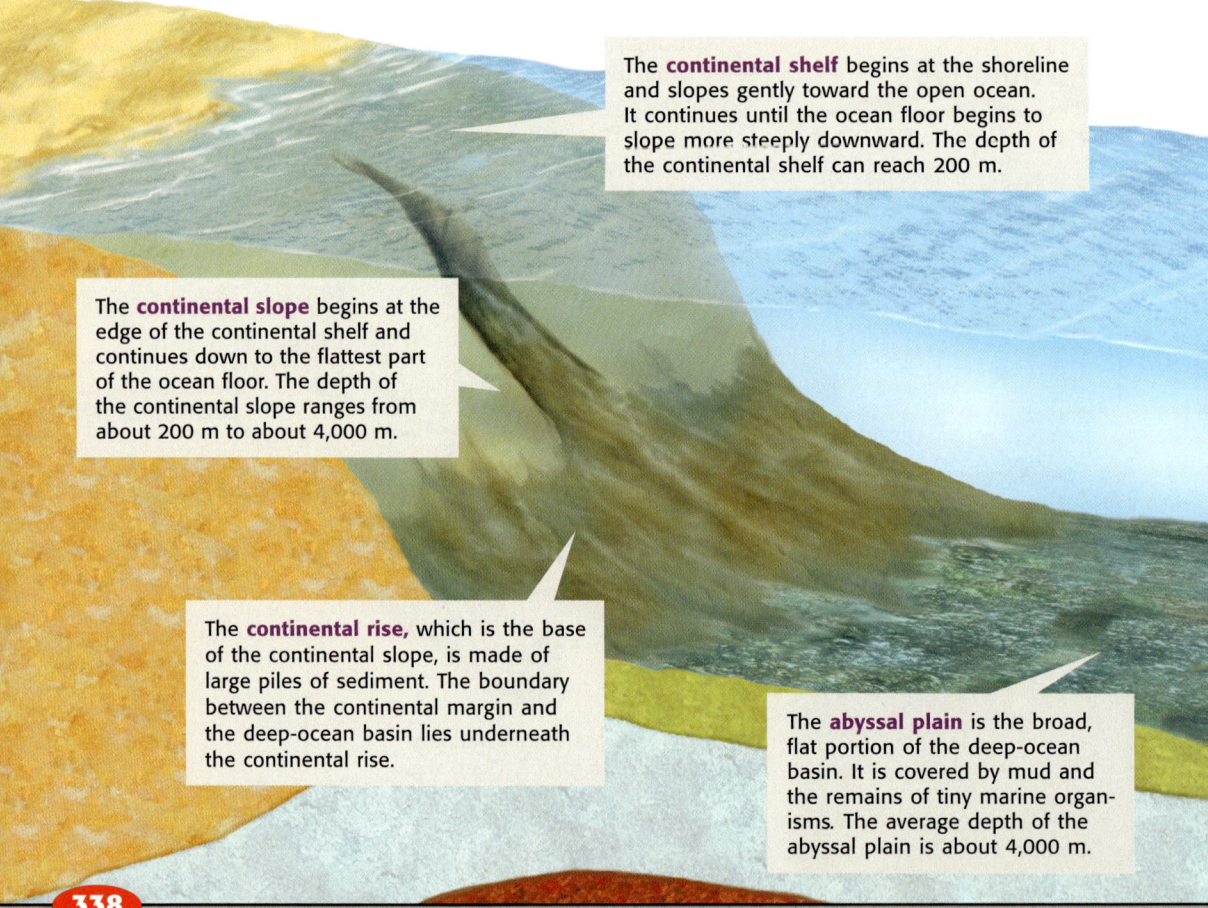

The **continental shelf** begins at the shoreline and slopes gently toward the open ocean. It continues until the ocean floor begins to slope more steeply downward. The depth of the continental shelf can reach 200 m.

The **continental slope** begins at the edge of the continental shelf and continues down to the flattest part of the ocean floor. The depth of the continental slope ranges from about 200 m to about 4,000 m.

The **continental rise,** which is the base of the continental slope, is made of large piles of sediment. The boundary between the continental margin and the deep-ocean basin lies underneath the continental rise.

The **abyssal plain** is the broad, flat portion of the deep-ocean basin. It is covered by mud and the remains of tiny marine organisms. The average depth of the abyssal plain is about 4,000 m.

 **Teaching Transparency 152** "Revealing the Ocean Floor: A"

 **Teaching Transparency 153** "Revealing the Ocean Floor: B"

Q: What lies on the bottom of the ocean and trembles?

A: a nervous wreck

338 Chapter 13 • Exploring the Oceans

Underwater Real Estate As you can see, the continental margin is subdivided into the continental shelf, the continental slope, and the continental rise based on depth and changes in slope. The deep-ocean basin consists of the abyssal plain, with features such as mid-ocean ridges, rift valleys, and ocean trenches that form near the boundaries of Earth's *tectonic plates.* On parts of the abyssal plain that are not near plate boundaries, thousands of seamounts are found on the ocean floor.

✓ Self-Check

How do the locations of rift valleys and ocean trenches differ? *(See page 726 to check your answer.)*

Activity

To get an idea of how deep parts of the ocean are, use an encyclopedia to find out how deep the Grand Canyon is. Compare this depth with that of the Mariana Trench, which is more than 11,000 m deep! Make a model of this difference using clay, or draw a graph of this difference to scale.

TRY at HOME

internet connect

SC*i*LINKS
NSTA

TOPIC: The Ocean Floor
GO TO: www.scilinks.com
*sci*LINKS NUMBER: HSTE310

Mid-ocean ridges are mountain chains formed where *tectonic plates* pull apart. This pulling motion creates cracks in the ocean floor called *rift zones.* As plates pull apart, magma rises to fill in the spaces. Heat from the magma causes the crust on either side of the rifts to expand, forming the ridges.

As mountains build up, a **rift valley** forms between them in the rift zone.

Seamounts are individual mountains of volcanic material. They form where magma pushes its way through or between tectonic plates. If a seamount builds up above sea level, it becomes a volcanic island.

Ocean trenches are seemingly bottomless cracks in the deep-ocean basin. Ocean trenches form where one oceanic plate is forced underneath a continental plate or another oceanic plate.

Homework

Concept Mapping Remind students that volcanic seamounts that rise above the ocean surface become volcanic islands. The Hawaiian Islands formed this way. Have them research other ways islands form. Have students prepare a concept map of the different ways that islands form. They should find that some islands are formed by the growth of coral; some are formed by deposition (barrier islands); and some are continental islands (Great Britain, Madagascar).

CROSS-DISCIPLINARY FOCUS

Art Draw students' attention to **Figure 6,** and have them draw, label, and color their own picture of the depth zones of the ocean floor. Point out the canyon in the continental slope. This is a *submarine canyon.* Most of the sediment that makes up the continental rise travels down from the continental shelf through submarine canyons. Be sure that students have divided the continental margin into the continental shelf, continental slope, and continental rise. They should identify the features of the deep-ocean basin as mid-ocean ridges, seamounts, rift valleys, and ocean trenches. In addition, students can indicate the temperature of the ocean water at each depth by using different colors. **Sheltered English**

USING THE FIGURE

Draw students' attention to the mid-ocean ridges in **Figure 6.** Below the rift zones that characterize mid-ocean ridges, magma rises from below the crust. As the magma erupts as lava, it cools when it enters the water, forming new oceanic crust. Point out that ocean trenches formed by the subduction of plates are some of the deepest places on Earth and often support a diversity of benthic life.

Answer to Self-Check

Rift valleys form where tectonic plates pull apart, and ocean trenches form where one oceanic plate is forced underneath a continental plate or another oceanic plate.

TOPIC: The Ocean Floor
GO TO: www.scilinks.org
*sci*LINKS NUMBER: HSTE310

Section 2 • The Ocean Floor   **339**

3) Extend

RETEACHING

Have students review **Figure 6**, which shows zones and features of the ocean floor. Ask students to choose any two zones or features and describe them in their own words. If describing features, students should include how the features form. Students should also tell why they like each feature or zone. **Sheltered English**

CROSS-DISCIPLINARY FOCUS

Language Arts Tell students that the 1870 publication of *Twenty Thousand Leagues Under the Sea,* by Jules Verne, revived an interest in undersea exploration. Have students read sections of Verne's book aloud in class. Point out that the story inspired engineers to solve the problems plaguing submarines, enabling scientists to reach greater depths in their exploration of the sea.

Answers to MATHBREAK

1. $D = 1{,}500$ m
2. $D = 10{,}500$ m
3. $D = 3{,}975$ m

Explain why the constant $\frac{1}{2}$ is in the equation in the MATHBREAK. The time represented by *t* is the two-way travel time of sound waves. Without using the constant $\frac{1}{2}$, the equation would give the distance to the ocean floor and back to the ship instead of the distance to the floor only.

Math Skills Worksheet 15
"Multiplying and Dividing Fractions"

MATH BREAK

Depths of the Deep

The depths in a bathymetric profile are calculated using the following simple formula:

$$D = \tfrac{1}{2} t \times v$$

D is the depth of the ocean floor, *t* is the time it takes for the sound to reach the bottom and return to the surface, and *v* equals the speed of sound in water (1,500 m/s). Calculate *D* for the following three parts of the ocean floor:

1. a mid-ocean ridge (*t* = 2 s)
2. an ocean trench (*t* = 14 s)
3. an abyssal plain (*t* = 5.3 s)

Viewing the Ocean Floor from Above

In spite of the great success of underwater exploration, sending scientists into deep water is still risky. Fortunately, there are ways to survey the underwater realm from the surface and from high above in space. Read on to learn about two technologies—sonar and satellites—that enable scientists to study the ocean floor without going below the surface.

Seeing by Sonar *Sonar,* which stands for "sound navigation and ranging," is a technology based on the echo-ranging behavior of bats. Scientists use sonar to determine the ocean's depth by sending high-frequency sound pulses from a ship down into the ocean. The sound travels through the water, bounces off the ocean floor, and returns to the ship. The deeper the water is, the longer the round trip takes. Scientists then calculate the depth by multiplying half the travel time by the speed of sound in water (about 1,500 m/s). This process is shown in the illustration below.

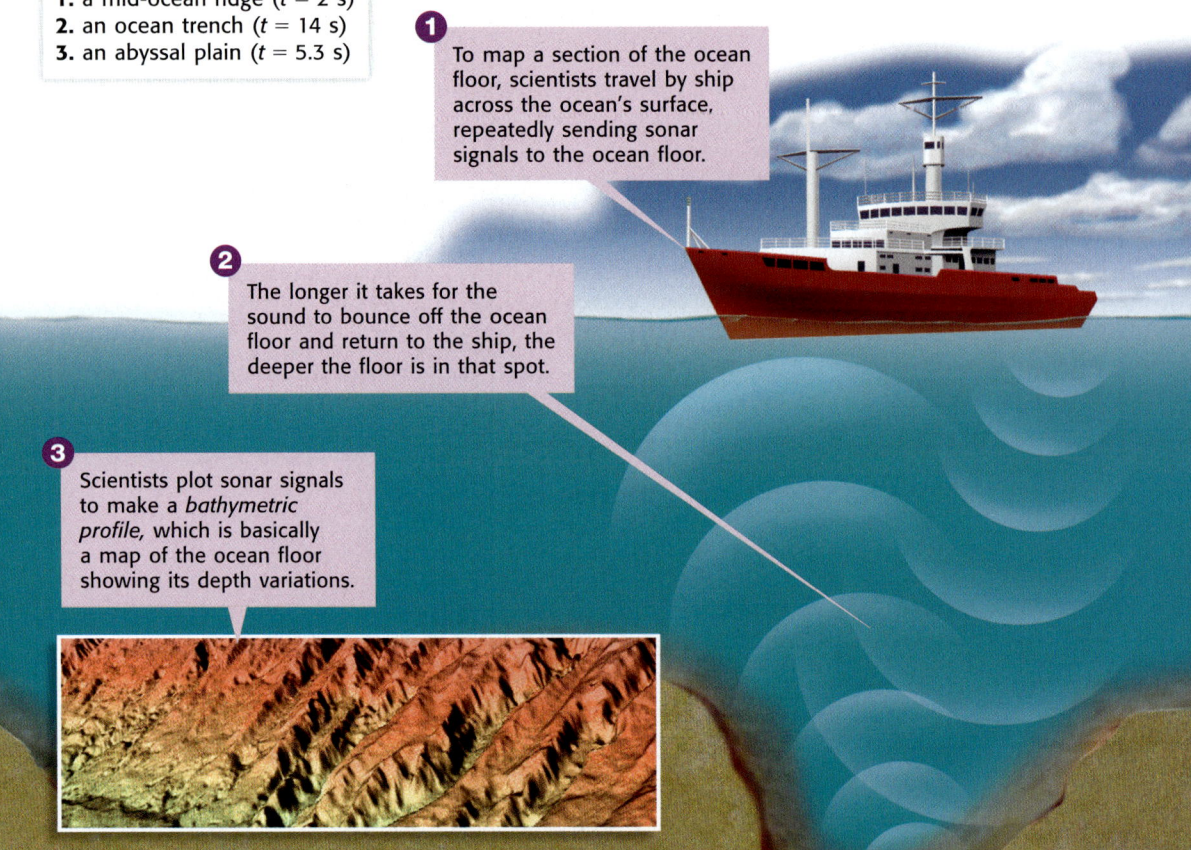

① To map a section of the ocean floor, scientists travel by ship across the ocean's surface, repeatedly sending sonar signals to the ocean floor.

② The longer it takes for the sound to bounce off the ocean floor and return to the ship, the deeper the floor is in that spot.

③ Scientists plot sonar signals to make a *bathymetric profile,* which is basically a map of the ocean floor showing its depth variations.

Teaching Transparency 154
"How Sonar Works"

WEIRD SCIENCE

Though many people know that whales and dolphins communicate by sound, few are aware that shrimp do the same thing. In order to locate food sources and other shrimp, they emit a sound similar to that of bacon frying!

340 Chapter 13 • Exploring the Oceans

Oceanography via Satellite In the 1970s, scientists began studying Earth from satellites in orbit around the Earth. In 1978, scientists launched the satellite *Seasat*. This satellite focused on the ocean, sending images back to Earth that allowed scientists to measure the direction and speed of ocean currents.

Geosat, once a top-secret military satellite, has been used to measure slight changes in the height of the ocean's surface. Different underwater features, such as mountains and trenches, affect the height of the water above them, thus reflecting the underwater topography of the ocean floor. Scientists measure the different heights of the ocean surface and use the measurements to make highly detailed maps of the ocean floor. As illustrated in **Figure 7,** oceanographers can make maps that cover a lot more territory by using satellites than by using ship-based sonar readings.

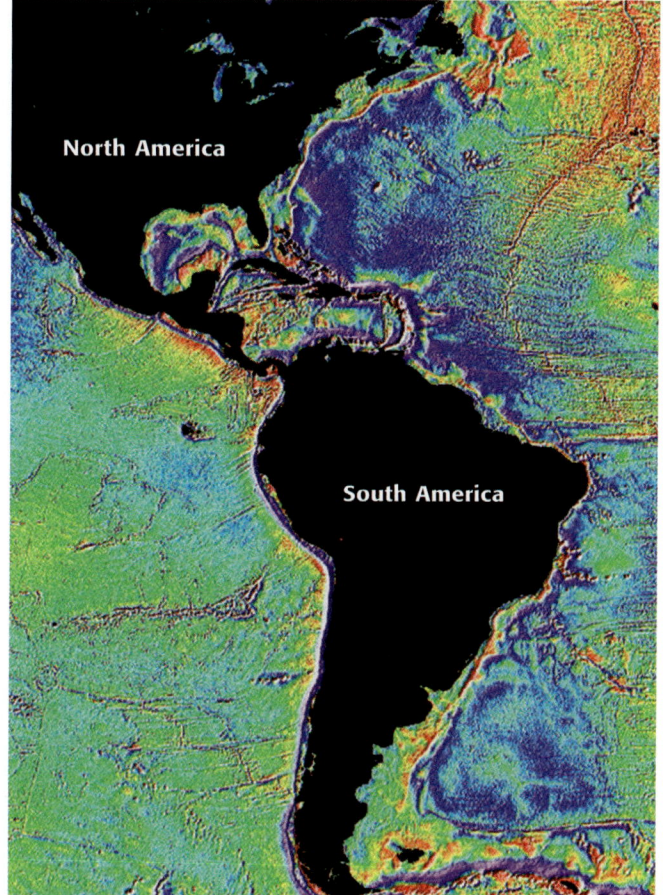

Figure 7 *The map above was generated by satellite measurements of different heights of the ocean surface.*

REVIEW

1. Name the two major regions of the ocean floor.
2. List the subdivisions of the continental margin.
3. List three technologies for studying the ocean floor, and explain how they are used.
4. **Interpreting Graphics** What part of the ocean floor would the bathymetric profile at right represent?

Bathymetric Profile

SECTION 3

Focus

Life in the Ocean

This section introduces a system for classifying marine organisms based on where they live and how they move. Students also learn to describe ecological zones of the ocean and give examples of organisms inhabiting each zone.

Bellringer

Before they read this section, have students imagine they are marine biologists who must classify marine life into three groups. Challenge them to identify the criteria they would use in their classification systems.

1 Motivate

GROUP ACTIVITY

Classifying Divide the class into small groups. Ask them to classify as many items in the classroom as they can based on the following categories:

- height at which the items are located
- what the items are used for

Teaching Transparency 155
"The Three Groups of Marine Life"

Directed Reading Worksheet 13 Section 3

Section 3

Terms to Learn
plankton benthic environment
nekton   pelagic environment
benthos

What You'll Do
- Identify and describe the three groups of marine organisms.
- Identify and describe the benthic and pelagic environments.
- Classify the zones of the benthic and pelagic environments.

Life in the Ocean

The ocean contains a wide variety of life-forms, many of which we know little about. Trying to study them can be quite a challenge for scientists. To make things easier, scientists classify marine organisms into three main groups. Scientists also divide the ocean into two main environments based on the types of organisms that live in them. These two main environments are further subdivided into ecological zones based on locations of different organisms.

The Three Groups of Marine Life

The three main groups of marine life are plankton, nekton, and benthos. Marine organisms are placed into one of these three groups according to where they live and how they move. Carefully examine the figure below to understand the differences between these groups.

Plankton are organisms that float at or near the ocean's surface. Most plankton are microscopic. Plankton are subdivided into two groups—those that are plantlike *(phytoplankton)* and those that are animal-like *(zooplankton)*.

Nekton are the free-swimming organisms of the ocean. Types of nekton include mammals, such as whales, dolphins, and sea lions, as well as many varieties of fish. Nekton are most abundant in surface waters.

Benthos are organisms that live on or in the ocean floor. They live in mud, sand, and rock. There are many types of benthos, such as crabs, sea stars, worms, coral, sponges, seaweed, and clams.

SCIENTISTS AT ODDS

Before the late 1870s, scientists widely believed the "azoic theory" of James Forbes and Alexander Agassiz. This theory argued that no life existed below shallow depths in the oceans. Sir Wyville Thomson disputed this theory, and in 1872, he embarked on a three-and-a-half year voyage to prove his point. The HMS *Challenger* voyage, which established oceanography as a modern science, collected ocean-floor samples from deeper than 8,000 m. Thomson's evidence disproved the azoic theory and greatly expanded our knowledge of the world's oceans. He published his results in *The Depths of the Sea*, the first general textbook on oceanography.

The Benthic Environment

In addition to being divided into zones based on depth, the ocean floor is divided into ecological zones based on where different types of benthos live. These zones are grouped into one major marine environment—the benthic environment. The **benthic environment,** or bottom environment, is the ocean floor and all the organisms that live on or in it.

Intertidal Zone The shallowest benthic zone, the *intertidal zone,* is located between the low-tide and high-tide limits. Twice a day, the intertidal zone transforms. As the tide flows in, the zone is covered with ocean water, and as the tide retreats, the intertidal zone is exposed to the air and sun.

Intertidal organisms must be able to live both underwater and on exposed land. Some organisms attach themselves to rocks and reefs to avoid being washed out to sea during low tide, as shown in **Figure 8.** Clams, oysters, barnacles, and crabs have tough shells that give them protection against strong waves during high tide and against harsh sunlight during low tide. Some animals can burrow in sand or between rocks. Plants such as seaweed have strong *holdfasts* (rootlike structures) that allow them to grow in this zone.

Biology CONNECTION

Coral reefs, found in shallow marine waters, have the largest concentration of life in the ocean. Layers of skeletons from animals called *corals* form the reefs, which are the largest animal structures on Earth. Many other organisms live on, around, and even in coral reefs.

Figure 8 Organisms such as sea anemones and starfish attach themselves to rocks and reefs. These organisms must be able to survive wet and dry conditions.

Sublittoral Zone The *sublittoral zone* begins where the intertidal zones ends, at the low-tide limit, and extends to the edge of the continental shelf. This benthic zone is more stable than the intertidal zone; the temperature, water pressure, and amount of sunlight remain fairly constant. Consequently, sublittoral organisms, such as corals, shown in **Figure 9,** do not have to cope with as much change as intertidal organisms. Although the sublittoral zone extends down 200 m below sea level, plants and most animals stay in the upper 100 m, where sunlight reaches the ocean floor.

Figure 9 Corals, like many other types of organisms, can live in both the sublittoral zone and the intertidal zone. However, they are more common in the sublittoral zone.

Multicultural CONNECTION

Stories of mermaids and sea monsters abound in many different cultures. In some legends, mermaids were good and helped shipwrecked sailors. In others, mermaids lured ships and sailors into dangerous waters. Sea monsters, on the other hand, were always bad, sinking ships and killing sailors. Discuss with students why they think these legends were told. Have them research a legend and write one of their own.

2) Teach

READING STRATEGY

Mnemonics Ask students to create a mnemonic device that will remind them of the zones of the benthic environment. For example, they might write **I**sabel **S**ent **B**art **A**way from **H**ome to remind them that the zones are **I**ntertidal, **S**ublittoral, **B**athyal, **A**byssal, and **H**adal. Ask them to share their mnemonic devices with the class. **Sheltered English**

MISCONCEPTION ALERT

Many people think that rain forests produce most of Earth's oxygen. Actually, ocean phytoplankton are the most productive photosynthesizers on the planet. Because phytoplankton consume the greenhouse gas CO_2 during photosynthesis, many scientists think that phytoplankton populations play a significant role in global climate patterns.

Homework

Have students draw five imaginary organisms, each inhabiting a different benthic zone. Students should describe each plant or animal and explain its particular adaptations for living in that zone. Their drawings and descriptions should include the following:

- how they obtain food
- how they avoid predation
- how they withstand the water pressure and temperature at the depth where they live

Encourage students to share their drawings and explanations with the class. **Sheltered English**

Section 3 • Life in the Ocean

3) Extend

COOPERATIVE LEARNING

Divide the class into groups of five, and provide each group with poster board and markers. Ask them to draw a cross-sectional illustration of the ocean and label the following features:

benthic environment, intertidal zone, sublittoral zone, bathyal zone, abyssal zone, hadal zone

Have each group member illustrate the organisms found in one of the five zones. (Each group should illustrate all of the five zones.) Instruct each group to elect a spokesperson to present the poster to the class.

RESEARCH

 Have students select one of the benthic zones to investigate further. Ask them to focus on the adaptations that organisms living there have developed that enable them to exist in that zone. Students can present their findings in a concept map, poster, or comic book. **Sheltered English**

CONNECT TO LIFE SCIENCE

Because food is so scarce in the deeper parts of the ocean, its inhabitants have special adaptations to ensure their survival. Some gulper eels, for example, have huge jaws and elastic stomachs that allow them to eat fish larger than themselves. Show students photographs of some of these organisms, and use Teaching Transparency 27 to discuss the process of natural selection.

 **Teaching Transparency 27** "Natural Selection in Four Steps" LINK TO LIFE SCIENCE

Figure 10 Octopuses are one of the animals common to the bathyal zone.

Figure 11 Tube worms can tolerate higher temperatures than most other organisms. These animals survive in water as hot as 81°C.

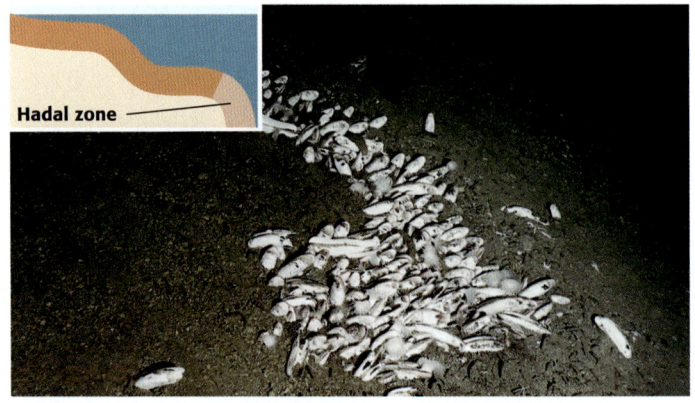

Figure 12 These clams are one of the few types of organisms known to live in the hadal zone.

344

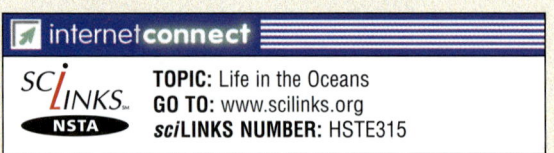
internet connect
TOPIC: Life in the Oceans
GO TO: www.scilinks.org
sciLINKS NUMBER: HSTE315

Bathyal Zone The *bathyal zone* extends from the edge of the continental shelf to the abyssal plain. The depth of this zone ranges from 200 m to 4,000 m below sea level. Because of the lack of sunlight at these depths, plant life is scarce in this part of the benthic environment. Animals in this zone include sponges, *brachiopods,* sea stars, *echinoids,* and octopuses, such as the one shown in **Figure 10**.

Abyssal Zone No plants and very few animals live in the *abyssal zone,* which is on the abyssal plain. Among the abyssal animal types are crabs, sponges, worms, and sea cucumbers. Many of these organisms, such as the tube worms shown in **Figure 11**, live around hot-water vents called *black smokers*. The abyssal zone can reach 6,000 m in depth. Scientists know very little about this benthic zone because it is so deep and dark.

Hadal Zone The deepest benthic zone is the *hadal zone*. This zone consists of the floor of the ocean trenches and any organisms found there. Scientists know even less about the hadal zone than they do about the abyssal zone. So far, scientists have discovered a type of sponge, a few species of worms, and a type of clam, which is shown in **Figure 12**.

SCIENCE HUMOR

Q: What's the best way to catch a fish?

A: Have someone throw it to you.

The Pelagic Environment

The **pelagic environment** is the entire volume of water in the ocean and the marine organisms that live above the ocean floor. There are two major zones in the pelagic environment—the *neritic zone* and the *oceanic zone*.

Neritic Zone The neritic zone includes the volume of water that covers the continental shelf. This warm, shallow zone contains the largest concentration of marine life. This is due to an abundance of sunlight and to the many benthos below the neritic zone that serve as a food supply. Fish, plankton, and marine mammals, such as the one in **Figure 13,** are just a few of the animal groups found here.

Figure 13 Many marine mammals, such as this dolphin, live in the neritic zone.

Oceanic Zone The oceanic zone includes the volume of water that covers the entire sea floor except for the continental shelf. In the deeper parts of the oceanic zone, the water temperature is colder and the pressure is much greater than in the neritic zone. Also, organisms are more spread out in the oceanic zone than in the neritic zone. While many of the same organisms that live in the neritic zone are found throughout the upper regions, some strange animals lurk in the darker depths, as shown in **Figure 14.** Other animals in the deeper parts of this zone include giant squids and some whale species.

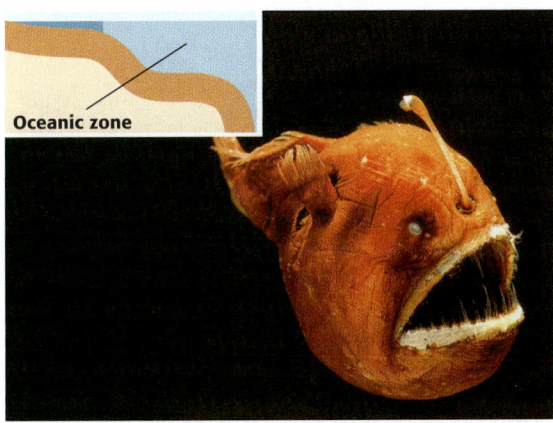

Figure 14 The anglerfish is a tricky predator that uses a natural lure attached to its head to attract prey.

REVIEW

1. List and briefly describe the three main groups of marine organisms.
2. Name the two ocean environments. List the zones of each environment.
3. **Making Predictions** How would the ocean's ecological zones change if sea level dropped 300 m?

internetconnect

TOPIC: Life in Oceans
GO TO: www.scilinks.org
sciLINKS NUMBER: HSTE315

SECTION 4

Focus

Resources from the Ocean

This section discusses the ocean's living and nonliving resources, focusing on the methods used to obtain them. Students are asked to consider the importance of the ocean's resources and explore ways of managing and conserving them.

Bellringer

Before they read this section, write the following sentences on the board and challenge students to identify four items or activities that involve resources that can be obtained from the sea.

"Tabitha drove her car to the market to buy a tuna steak for dinner. When she got home, she poured herself a glass of water, then fired up her gas grill, and cooked the tuna."

1 Motivate

GROUP ACTIVITY

Divide the class into small groups. Have them imagine a world with no ocean resources. Ask them to brainstorm to come up with a list of activities that would no longer be possible. Examples might include eating certain types of seafood, shipping goods by sea, or deep-sea diving. Have each group share its list with the class and discuss the importance of ocean resources.

Directed Reading Worksheet 13 Section 4

Section 4

Terms to Learn

desalination

What You'll Do

- List two methods of harvesting the ocean's living resources.
- List nonliving resources in the ocean.
- Describe the ocean's energy resources.

Resources from the Ocean

The ocean offers a seemingly endless supply of resources. Food, raw materials, energy, and drinkable water are all harvested from the ocean. And there are probably undiscovered resources in unexplored regions of the ocean. As human populations have grown, however, the demand for these resources has increased while the availability has decreased.

Living Resources

People have been harvesting marine plants and animals for food for thousands of years. Many civilizations formed in coastal regions that were rich enough in marine life to support growing human populations. Read on to learn how humans harvest marine life today.

Fishing the Ocean Harvesting food from the ocean is a multi-billion-dollar industry. Of all the seafood taken from the ocean, fish are the most abundant. Almost 75 million tons of fish are harvested each year. With improved technology, such as sonar and drift nets, fishermen have become better at locating and taking fish from the ocean. **Figure 15** illustrates how drift nets are used. In recent years, many people have become concerned that we are overfishing the ocean—taking more fish than can be naturally replaced. Also, a few years ago, the public became aware that animals other than fish, especially dolphins and turtles, were accidentally being caught in drift nets. Today the fishing industry is making efforts to prevent overfishing and damage to other wildlife from drift nets.

Figure 15 Drift nets are fishing nets that cover kilometers of ocean. Fishermen can harvest entire schools of fish in one drift net.

CONNECT TO ENVIRONMENTAL SCIENCE

Factory trawlers are enormous boats that pull nets as large as four football fields and can harvest 400 tons of fish in a single haul. They can stay at sea for months catching, processing, freezing, and packaging fish. Because of their incredible cost (as much as $40 million), they must catch vast quantities of fish to remain operational. Factory trawlers threaten marine ecosystems because they can deplete an entire local fish population and quickly move on. They are also criticized for netting large quantities of *bycatch,* unwanted fish and sea-life that are caught and thrown overboard, often dead or dying. Have students find out more about these ships and the environmental controversies that surround them.

Farming the Ocean As overfishing reduces fish populations and laws regulating fishing become stricter, it is becoming more difficult to supply our demand for fish. To compensate for this, many ocean fish, such as salmon and turbot, are being captively bred in fish farms. Fish farming requires several holding ponds, each containing fish at a certain level of development. **Figure 16** shows a holding pond in a fish farm. When the fish are old enough, they are harvested and packaged for shipping.

Figure 16 *Consuming fish raised in a fish farm helps reduce the number of fish harvested from the ocean.*

Savory Seaweed Fish are not the only seafood harvested in a farmlike setting. Shrimp, oysters, crabs, and mussels are raised in enclosed areas near the shore. Mussels and oysters are grown attached to ropes, as shown in **Figure 17.** Huge nets line the nursery area, preventing the animals from being eaten by their natural predators.

Many species of algae, commonly known as seaweed, are also harvested from the ocean. For example, kelp, a seaweed that grows as much as 33 cm a day, is harvested and used as a thickener in jellies, ice cream, and similar products. The next time you enjoy your favorite ice cream, remember that without seaweed, it would be a runny mess! Seaweed is rich in protein, and several species of seaweed are staples of the Japanese diet. For example, the rolled varieties of sushi, a Japanese dish, are wrapped in seaweed.

Figure 17 *In addition to fish, there are many other types of seafood, such as these mussels, that are raised in farms.*

2) Teach

READING STRATEGY

Prediction Guide Before students read the passage about living ocean resources, ask them to write an answer for the following question:

What are two problems you think might be associated with fishing the oceans? (Sample answers: overfishing, pollution, accidentally catching other animals in drift nets)

DEBATE

Fishing the Ocean Lead students in a debate about the costs and benefits of fishing the oceans. Fish are an important source of protein, but overfishing threatens entire ecosystems. Also, fishing is a major source of employment in the world, but many scientists agree that strong restrictions limiting fishing are important. Help students research and debate these issues, and discuss alternatives to traditional fishing, such as fish farming.

REAL-WORLD CONNECTION

Writing In the United States, more than 50 percent of the population lives and works within 80 km of the sea, even though coastal areas account for only 11 percent of the nation's land area. Have students write a short story that accurately describes the route that a fish takes from the ocean to the dinner table. Encourage them to focus on the human characters in their story. Ask students to consider how this ocean resource benefits the people who catch, process, ship, sell, and eat it.

Science Bloopers

Because starfish eat oysters, oyster fishermen have always battled starfish. In this war, when fishermen pulled up a starfish with a clump of oysters, they cut up the starfish and tossed it overboard. Then scientists pointed out that starfish can regenerate from their parts and that by cutting them up, the fishermen were actually making more starfish!

Section 4 • Resources from the Ocean

2) Teach, continued

REAL-WORLD CONNECTION

Have students make a list of all their daily activities that rely on petroleum. Answers might include taking a hot shower, using a hair dryer, cooking breakfast, driving to school, turning on lights, or washing and drying clothes. Allow time for students to share their lists with classmates, then encourage them to brainstorm about ways they might reduce their reliance on fossil fuels.

GROUP ACTIVITY

 Writing Divide the class into small groups, and encourage each to select a different ocean resource. Have them work together to write a public service announcement designed to convince the public of the resource's value to people. Have them include ways people can help conserve the resource. Ask students to present their announcements to the class.

CROSS-DISCIPLINARY FOCUS

Language Arts Read selections from Samuel Taylor Coleridge's "The Rime of the Ancient Mariner" in class. Discuss the lines:

> "Water, water, everywhere,
> Nor any drop to drink."

Ask students:

- Where does most drinking water come from? (lakes, rivers, underground)
- How can ocean water be made drinkable? (by desalination)

You may wish to revisit this poem as you discuss ocean pollution in the next section.

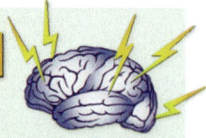

BRAIN FOOD
Did you know that the United States imports more oil than any other nation? Because oil is a nonrenewable resource, scientists continue to research alternatives to fossil fuels, such as solar energy and wind-generated electricity.

Nonliving Resources

Humans harvest many types of nonliving resources from the ocean. These resources provide raw materials, drinkable water, and energy for our expanding population. Some resources are easily obtained, while others are rare or difficult to harvest.

Oil and Natural Gas Modern civilization continues to be very dependent on oil and natural gas as major sources of energy. Oil and natural gas are *nonrenewable resources,* which means that they are used up faster than they can be replenished naturally. Both oil and natural gas are found under layers of impermeable rock. Petroleum engineers must drill through this rock in order to reach the resources.

Searching for Oil How do petroleum engineers know where to drill for oil and natural gas? Ships with seismic equipment are used for this purpose. Special devices send powerful pulses of sound to the ocean floor. The pulses travel through the water and penetrate the rocks below. The pulses are then reflected back toward the ship, where they are recorded by electronic equipment and analyzed by a computer. The computer readings, such as the one in **Figure 18**, indicate how rock layers are arranged below the ocean floor. Petroleum geologists use these readings to locate a promising area to drill.

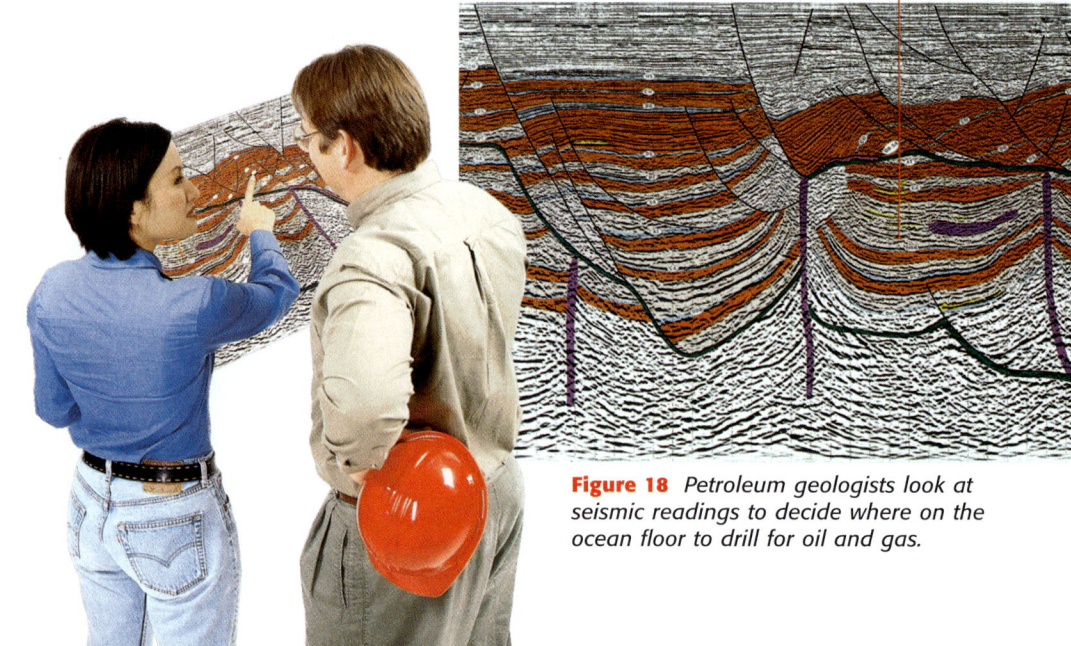

Figure 18 Petroleum geologists look at seismic readings to decide where on the ocean floor to drill for oil and gas.

Homework

 Research Help students research the dangers and drawbacks of petroleum drilling and petroleum use. They should look for information about how heavily the world economy depends on petroleum products and why people should be finding cheap, reliable alternative fuels.

IS THAT A FACT!

Much of the world's petroleum deposits formed millions of years ago when dead organisms accumulated on the ocean floor. Crushed and buried deep beneath the surface by the overlying sediment, this organic matter eventually turned into oil or natural gas.

Fresh Water and Desalination In some areas of the world where fresh water is limited, people desalinate ocean water. **Desalination** is the process of evaporating sea water so that the water and the salt separate. As the water cools and condenses, it is collected and processed for human use. But desalination is not as simple as it sounds, and it is very costly. Countries with an adequate amount of annual rainfall rely on the fresh water provided by precipitation and therefore do not need costly desalination plants. Some countries located in arid regions of the world must build desalination plants to provide an adequate supply of fresh water. Saudi Arabia, located in the desert region of the Middle East, has one of the largest desalination plants in the world.

Sea-Floor Minerals Mining companies are very interested in mineral nodules that are lying on the ocean floor. These nodules are made mostly of manganese, which can be used to make certain types of steel. They also contain iron, copper, nickel, and cobalt. Other nodules are made of phosphates, which are used in making fertilizer.

Nodules are formed from dissolved substances in sea water that stick to solid objects, such as pebbles. As more substances stick to the coated pebble, a nodule begins to grow. Manganese nodules range from the size of a marble to the size of a soccer ball. The photograph in **Figure 19** shows a number of nodules scattered across the ocean floor. It is believed that 15 percent of the ocean floor is covered with these nodules. However, they are located in the deeper parts of the ocean, and mining them is costly and difficult.

QuickLab

How Much Fresh Water Is There?

1. Fill a large **beaker** with 1,000 mL of **water**. This represents all the water on Earth.
2. Carefully pour 970 mL from the beaker into a **graduated cylinder**. This represents the amount of water in the ocean.
3. Pour another 20 mL from the beaker into a **second graduated cylinder**. This represents the amount of water frozen in icecaps and glaciers.
4. Pour another 5 mL into a **third graduated cylinder**. This represents nonconsumable water on land.
5. Take a look at the leftover water. This represents Earth's supply of fresh water.

Put freshwater problems on ice! Turn to page 361 to find out how.

Figure 19 These manganese nodules could make you wealthy if you knew an affordable way to mine them.

3 Extend

QuickLab

MATERIALS

For Each Student:
- large beaker
- 3 graduated cylinders

CONNECT TO PHYSICAL SCIENCE

Explain that the mineral nodules shown in **Figure 19** form much like pearls or rock candy—a solid precipitates out of a chemical solution and adheres to a particle. This particle could be nearly anything—a small pebble or even a piece of shell. The nodules grow larger in a process called accretion as more solids precipitate out of the solution. Students could model accretion by making rock candy with a supersaturated sugar solution and a piece of string.

Homework

Graphing Help students use references to find out how much of the world's energy needs are met by the following:

   oil, natural gas, coal, tidal energy, geothermal energy, wave energy, hydroelectric energy, solar energy, and wind energy

Have students prepare pie charts or bar graphs of their findings.

 Reinforcement Worksheet 13 "The Oceans and Us"

WEIRD SCIENCE

Buried in sea floor sediments at depths greater than 500 m below sea level, an ice called *methane hydrate* may be twice as abundant as all other fossil fuels combined. Methane hydrate has also been discovered in the permafrost of Siberia and Alaska. Clean burning and abundant, methane hydrate could be the fuel of the future, but engineers have not yet discovered an efficient way to mine it. Have students find out about some of the interesting proposals to mine this resource and also about the role decomposing methane hydrates may play in global warming.

4 Close

Quiz

1. Explain some of the ecological risks of using drift nets. (Using drift nets can lead to overfishing, which depletes fish populations. Drift nets also accidentally trap other marine animals such as dolphins and turtles.)

2. What are nonrenewable resources? Give two examples. (Nonrenewable resources are resources that are used up faster than they can be replenished naturally. Natural gas and oil are nonrenewable resources.)

3. What is desalination, and why is it done? (Desalination is the process of evaporating sea water so that the water and the salt separate. Desalination provides fresh water for human use.)

ALTERNATIVE ASSESSMENT

Challenge students to make drawings that demonstrate how tidal energy is harnessed. Encourage them to explain the process to the class, using their drawings as visual aids. Their drawings and explanations should reflect the understanding that water must rush through a narrow channel and move turbines to generate electricity.

Critical Thinking Worksheet 13 "Chain Reaction"

TOPIC: Ocean Resources
GO TO: www.scilinks.org
sciLINKS NUMBER: HSTE320

Figure 20 Using Tides to Generate Electricity

As the tide rises, water enters a bay behind a dam. The gate then closes at high tide.

The gate remains closed as the tide lowers.

At low tide, the gate opens, and the water rushes through the dam, moving the turbines, which in turn create electricity.

TOPIC: Ocean Resources
GO TO: www.scilinks.org
sciLINKS NUMBER: HSTE320

Tidal Energy The ocean creates several types of energy resources simply because of its constant movement. The gravitational pull of the sun and moon causes the ocean to rise and fall as tides. *Tidal energy,* energy generated from the movement of tides, is an excellent alternative source of energy. If the water during high tide can be rushed through a narrow coastal passageway, the water's force can be powerful enough to generate electricity. **Figure 20** shows how this works. Tidal energy is a clean, inexpensive, and renewable resource once the dam is built. A *renewable resource* can be replenished, in time, after being used. Unfortunately, tidal energy is practical only in a few areas of the world, where the coastline has shallow, narrow channels. For example, the coastline at Cook Inlet, in Alaska, is perfect for generating tidal power.

Wave Energy Have you ever stood on the beach and watched as waves crashed onto the shore? This constant motion is an energy resource. Wave energy, like tidal energy, is a clean, renewable resource.

Recently, computer programs have been developed to analyze the energy of waves. Researchers have located certain areas of the world where wave energy can generate enough electricity to make it worthwhile to build power plants. Wave energy in the North Sea is strong enough to produce power for parts of Scotland and England.

REVIEW

1. List two methods of harvesting the ocean's living resources.

2. Name four nonliving resources in the ocean.

3. **Interpreting Graphics** Take another look at Figure 20. As the tide is rising, will the gate be open or closed? How might this affect the turbines?

Answers to Review

1. Answers will vary. Two methods of harvesting the ocean's resources are fishing and farming the ocean.

2. Any four of the following nonliving resources are acceptable: oil, natural gas, fresh water, minerals, tidal energy, and wave energy.

3. As the tide is rising, the gate will be open. The turbines may turn while the water passes through the dam from the open ocean.

Section 5

Ocean Pollution

Terms to Learn

nonpoint-source pollution

What You'll Do

- List different types of ocean pollution.
- Explain how to prevent or minimize different types of ocean pollution.
- Outline what is being done to control ocean pollution.

Humans have used the ocean for waste disposal for hundreds, if not thousands, of years. This has harmed the organisms that live in the oceans as well as animals that depend on marine organisms. People are also affected by polluted oceans. Fortunately, we are becoming more aware of ocean pollution, and we are learning from our mistakes.

Sources of Ocean Pollution

There are many sources of ocean pollution. Some of these sources are easily identified, but others are more difficult to pinpoint. Read on to find out where different types of ocean pollution come from and how they affect the ocean.

Trash Dumping People dump trash in many places, including the ocean. In the 1980s, scientists became alarmed by the kind of trash that was washing up on beaches. Bandages, vials of blood, and syringes (needles) were found among the waste. Some of the blood in the vials even contained the AIDS virus. The Environmental Protection Agency (EPA) began an investigation and discovered that hospitals in the United States produce an average of 3 million tons of medical waste each year. And where does some of this trash end up? You guessed it—in the ocean. Because of stricter laws, much of this medical waste is now buried in sanitary landfills. However, dumping trash in the deeper part of the ocean is still a common practice in many countries.

Figure 21 This barge is headed out to the open ocean, where it will dump the trash it carries.

Huntsville, Alabama hairdresser Phil McCrory has patented a way to use discarded human hair to clean up oil spills. He tested the idea in his son's wading pool using a pair of pantyhose filled with hair. The idea works so well that McCrory has attracted the attention of NASA!

TOPIC: Ocean Pollution
GO TO: www.scilinks.org
sciLINKS NUMBER: HSTE323

Directed Reading Worksheet 13 Section 5

2 Teach

MEETING INDIVIDUAL NEEDS

Learners Having Difficulty
Draw students' attention to the photographs of nonpoint-source pollutants in **Figure 22**. Ask them to think about their daily lives and to list ways they might be contributing to nonpoint-source pollution. Ask them to help you list ways that they could reduce their contribution to nonpoint-source pollution. **Sheltered English**

GROUP ACTIVITY

Have student groups report on the current status of the communities and ecosystems of Prince William Sound in the wake of the *Exxon Valdez* oil spill. Do fishing communities feel that they have been compensated?

Homework

Investigate Your Area Inform students that many companies are creating products that are marketed to be less harmful to the environment. These claims have varying degrees of truth. Have groups choose a product and investigate the environmental statements that are used to market it. For example, a group could visit the detergent aisle of a grocery store to compare products. Have them prepare a list of products claiming to be environmentally friendly and their primary ingredients. Encourage students to use Internet or library resources to determine whether the ingredients listed could be harmful to the environment. Another group could compare the percentage of post-consumer waste in recycled paper products. Have groups present their findings to the class.

Environment CONNECTION

In Austin, Texas, sludge is used to make a compost called *Dillo Dirt*. (*Dillo* refers to *armadillo*, a small aardvark-like mammal common in Texas.) Instead of polluting the Gulf of Mexico, Austinites are using sludge to grow beautiful and beneficial gardens.

Sludge Dumping By 1990, the United States alone had discharged 38 trillion liters of treated sludge into the waters along its coasts. What is sludge, and why is it so bad? To answer this question, we need to define *raw sewage*.

Raw sewage is all the liquid and solid wastes that are flushed down toilets and poured down drains. After collecting in sewer drains, raw sewage is sent through a treatment plant, where it undergoes a cleaning process that removes the solid waste. The solid waste is called *sludge*. In many areas, people dump sludge into the ocean several kilometers offshore, intending for it to settle to and stay on the ocean floor. Unfortunately, currents sometimes stir the sludge up and move it closer to shore. This can pollute beaches and kill marine life. Many countries have banned sludge dumping, but it continues to occur in many areas of the world.

Nonpoint-Source Pollution We usually think of water pollution as coming from large factories, but you may be surprised to know that most of the pollution comes from everyday citizens doing everyday things. This type of pollution, which is shown in **Figure 22,** is called **nonpoint-source pollution** because you cannot pinpoint its exact source. How does this pollution get into the ocean? All waste water and runoff eventually enter a body of water, usually a stream. Every stream leads to a river, and every river leads to the ocean.

Figure 22 Nonpoint-source pollution contributes significantly to ocean pollution. What can you do to cut down on nonpoint-source pollution?

IS THAT A FACT!

The world's first major oil spill occurred on March 18, 1967. The tanker *Torrey Canyon* ran aground off the coast near Cornwall, England. The ship spilled about 870,000 barrels of oil, more than three times the oil spilled by the *Exxon Valdez*.

Oil Spills Because oil is in such high demand across the world, large tankers must transport billions of barrels of it across the oceans. If not handled properly, these transports can quickly turn disastrous. In 1989, the supertanker *Exxon Valdez* struck a reef and spilled more than 260,000 barrels of crude oil. The effect of this accident on wildlife was catastrophic. Many animals died. Alaskans who made their living from fishing lost their businesses. Although many animals were saved, as shown in **Figure 23,** and the Exxon Oil Company spent $2.5 billion to try to clean up the mess, Alaska's wildlife and economy will continue to suffer for decades.

Today many oil companies are using new technology to safeguard against oil spills. Tankers are now being built with two hulls instead of one. This prevents oil from spilling into the ocean if the outside hull of the ship is damaged. **Figure 24** illustrates the design of a double-hulled tanker.

Figure 23 Many oil-covered animals were rescued and cleaned after the *Exxon Valdez* spill.

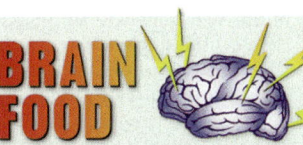

Within the first few weeks of the *Exxon Valdez* oil spill, more than half a million birds, including 109 endangered bald eagles, were covered with oil and drowned. Almost half the sea otters in the area also died either from drowning or from being poisoned by the oil.

Figure 24 If the outside hull of a double-hulled tanker is punctured, the oil will still be contained within the inside hull.

CONNECT TO ENVIRONMENTAL SCIENCE

The Oil Pollution Act of 1990 was a direct response to the *Exxon Valdez* oil spill. The controversial bill had been debated for 14 years; it passed swiftly in the aftermath of the disaster. Under the law, all oil tankers operating in United States waters must be double-hulled by 2015. Compliance has been slow, however; many oil companies have been reluctant to replace the aging boats in their fleets with hundred-million-dollar double-hulled ships. As of 1999, of the 3,294 oil tankers operating worldwide, only 876 were double-hulled.

3) Extend

Investigating an Oil Spill

ACTIVITY

Divide the class into small groups. Provide each group with poster board and markers. Direct each group to work together to create a poster designed to educate the public about the need for clean water. Ask them to focus on ways people can minimize the pollution of our oceans. Consider displaying the posters around the school to educate students and teachers. As an extension, have students draft a letter to a United States Congress member that outlines each group's ideas. **Sheltered English**

RESEARCH

Help students find information to investigate the environmental impact of one of the following:

  developing areas where salt marshes once were, draining mangrove swamps for development, the pollution of ocean waters with agricultural run-off, damming rivers and streams that flow into the ocean, using dynamite to catch fish (common in the Pacific and particularly harmful to coral reefs), or destroying coral reefs to obtain construction materials

Encourage students to focus on the effects of these human behaviors on other organisms, and challenge them to suggest alternatives

Saving Our Ocean Resources

Although humans have done much to harm the ocean's resources, we have also begun to do more to save them. From international treaties to volunteer cleanups, efforts to conserve the ocean's resources are making an impact around the world.

Nations Take Notice When ocean pollution reached an all-time high, many countries recognized the need to work together to solve the problem. In 1989, 64 countries ratified a treaty that prohibits the dumping of mercury, cadmium compounds, certain plastics, oil, and high-level radioactive wastes into the ocean. Many other international agreements restricting ocean pollution have been made, but enforcing them is often difficult.

In spite of efforts to protect the ocean, waste dumping and oil spills still occur, and contaminated organisms continue to wash ashore. Why are the laws not working as well as they should? Enforcing these laws takes money and human resources, and many agencies are lacking in both.

Action in the United States The United States, like many other countries, has taken additional measures to control local pollution. In 1972, Congress passed the Clean Water Act, which put the EPA in charge of issuing permits for any dumping of trash into the ocean. Later that year, a stricter law was passed. The U.S. Marine Protection, Research, and Sanctuaries Act prohibits the dumping of any material that would affect human health or welfare, the marine environment or ecosystems, or businesses that depend on the ocean.

Why worry about a few drops of oil? You might be surprised that a little goes a long way. Turn to page 682 in the LabBook to learn more.

Ocean Treaty

Get together with your classmates and divide yourselves into three groups: Nation A, Nation B, and Nation C. All three nations are located near the ocean, and all three nations share borders. Nation A has a very rich supply of oil, which it transports around the world. Nation B currently depends on nuclear energy and has many nuclear power plants near its shores. Nation B has no place on land to store radioactive waste from its nuclear power plants. Nation C sells nuclear technology to Nation B, buys oil from Nation A, and has the world's most diverse coastal ecosystem. The three nations must form a treaty to safeguard against ocean pollution without seriously harming any of their economies. Can you do it?

Answers to APPLY

Although there are no specific answers, students should consider the following factors:

1. Nation A and Nation C must keep each other satisfied because they depend on the sale of oil from Nation A to Nation C.

2. Nation B and Nation C must keep each other satisfied because Nation B buys nuclear technology from Nation C.

3. Nation C must protect its coastal ecosystem, but Nation C also depends on Nation A's transport of oil and Nation B's use of nuclear energy, both of which can potentially threaten the coastal ecosystem.

Figure 25 The Adopt-a-Beach program in Texas has been a huge success.

Citizens Take Charge Citizens of many countries have demanded that their governments do more to solve the growing problem of ocean pollution. Because of public outcry, the United States now spends more than $130 million each year monitoring the oceans. United States citizens have also begun to take the matter into their own hands. In the early 1980s, citizens began organizing beach cleanups. One of the largest cleanups is the semiannual Adopt-a-Beach program, shown in **Figure 25,** that originated with the Texas Coastal Cleanup campaign. Millions of tons of trash have been gathered from the beaches, and people are being educated about the hazards of ocean dumping.

Though governments pass laws against ocean dumping, keeping the oceans clean is everyone's responsibility. The next time you and your family visit the beach, make sure the only items you leave behind on the sand are hermit crabs, shells, and maybe a few sand dollars.

REVIEW

1. List three types of ocean pollution. How can each of these types be prevented or minimized?
2. Which type of ocean pollution is most common?
3. **Summarizing Data** List and describe three measures that governments have taken to control ocean pollution.

internet connect

SC/INKS
NSTA
TOPIC: Ocean Pollution
GO TO: www.scilinks.org
sciLINKS NUMBER: HSTE323

Chapter Highlights

VOCABULARY DEFINITIONS

SECTION 1

salinity a measure of the amount of dissolved salts and other solids in a given amount of liquid

thermocline a layer of ocean water extending from 300 m below sea level to about 700 m below sea level in which water temperature drops with increased depth faster than in other layers of the ocean

water cycle the continuous movement of water from water sources into the air, onto land, into and over the ground, and back to the water sources; a cycle that links all of the Earth's solid, liquid, and gaseous water together

SECTION 2

continental shelf the flattest part of the continental margin

continental slope the steepest part of the continental margin

continental rise the base of the continental slope

abyssal plain the broad, flat portion of the deep-ocean basin

mid-ocean ridge a long mountain chain that forms on the ocean floor where tectonic plates pull apart; usually extends along the center of ocean basins

rift valley a valley that forms in a rift zone between diverging tectonic plates

seamount an individual mountain of volcanic material on the abyssal plain

ocean trench a seemingly bottomless crevice in the deep-ocean basin that forms where one oceanic plate is forced underneath a continental plate or another oceanic plate

Chapter Highlights

SECTION 1

Vocabulary
- salinity (p. 332)
- thermocline (p. 333)
- water cycle (p. 335)

Section Notes
- The four oceans as we know them today formed within the last 300 million years.
- Salts have been added to the ocean for billions of years.
- The three temperature zones of ocean water are the surface zone, thermocline, and deep zone.
- The ocean plays the largest role in the water cycle.
- The ocean stabilizes Earth's conditions by absorbing and retaining thermal energy.

SECTION 2

Vocabulary
- continental shelf (p. 338)
- continental slope (p. 338)
- continental rise (p. 338)
- abyssal plain (p. 338)
- mid-ocean ridge (p. 339)
- rift valley (p. 339)
- seamount (p. 339)
- ocean trench (p. 339)

Section Notes
- The ocean floor is divided into zones based on depth and slope.
- The continental margin consists of the continental shelf, the continental slope, and the continental rise.
- The deep-ocean basin consists of the abyssal plain, with features such as mid-ocean ridges, rift valleys, seamounts, and ocean trenches.
- In addition to directly studying the ocean floor, scientists indirectly study the ocean floor using sonar and satellites.

Labs
Probing the Depths (p. 680)

✓ Skills Check

Math Concepts

PERCENTAGES Percentages are a way of describing the parts within a whole. Percentages are expressed in hundredths. Take another look at Figure 1 on page 332. The pie chart shows the percentages of dissolved solids in ocean water. The amount of chlorine (Cl) dissolved in the ocean is 55 percent. This means that 55 of every 100 parts of dissolved solids in the ocean are chlorine.

Visual Understanding

TEMPERATURE ZONES Look back at the line graph on page 333 to review why the temperature of the ocean decreases with increasing depth.

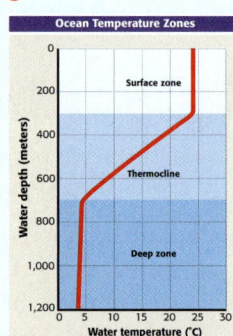

Lab and Activity Highlights

Probing the Depths PG 680

Investigating an Oil Spill PG 682

 **Datasheets for LabBook** (blackline masters for these labs)

356 Chapter 13 • Exploring the Oceans

VOCABULARY DEFINITIONS, continued

SECTION 3

plankton microscopic organisms that float at or near the ocean's surface

nekton free-swimming organisms of the ocean

benthos organisms that live on or in the ocean floor

benthic environment the ocean floor and all the organisms that live on or in it; also known as the bottom environment

pelagic environment the entire volume of water in the ocean and the marine organisms that live above the ocean floor; also known as the water environment

SECTION 4

desalination the process of evaporating sea water so that the water and the salt separate

SECTION 5

nonpoint-source pollution pollution that comes from many sources and that cannot be traced to specific sites

SECTION 3

Vocabulary
- plankton (p. 342)
- nekton (p. 342)
- benthos (p. 342)
- benthic environment (p. 343)
- pelagic environment (p. 345)

Section Notes
- There are three main groups of marine life—plankton, nekton, and benthos.
- The two main ocean environments—the benthic and pelagic environments—are divided into ecological zones based on the locations of organisms that live in the environments.

SECTION 4

Vocabulary
- desalination (p. 349)

Section Notes
- Humans depend on the ocean for living and nonliving resources.
- Ocean farms raise fish and other marine life to help feed growing human populations.
- Nonliving ocean resources include oil and natural gas, fresh water, minerals, and tidal and wave energy.

SECTION 5

Vocabulary
- nonpoint-source pollution (p. 352)

Section Notes
- Types of ocean pollution include trash dumping, sludge dumping, nonpoint-source pollution, and oil spills.
- Nonpoint-source pollution cannot be traced to specific points of origin.
- Efforts to save ocean resources include international treaties and volunteer cleanups.

Labs
- Investigating an Oil Spill (p. 682)

 Vocabulary Review Worksheet 13

 Blackline masters of these Chapter Highlights can be found in the **Study Guide**.

internet connect

 **GO TO:** go.hrw.com

Visit the **HRW** Web site for a variety of learning tools related to this chapter. Just type in the keyword:

KEYWORD: HSTOCE

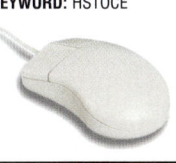 **GO TO:** www.scilinks.org

Visit the **National Science Teachers Association** on-line Web site for Internet resources related to this chapter. Just type in the sciLINKS number for more information about the topic:

TOPIC: Exploring Earth's Oceans	sciLINKS NUMBER: HSTE305
TOPIC: The Ocean Floor	sciLINKS NUMBER: HSTE310
TOPIC: Life in the Oceans	sciLINKS NUMBER: HSTE315
TOPIC: Ocean Resources	sciLINKS NUMBER: HSTE320
TOPIC: Ocean Pollution	sciLINKS NUMBER: HSTE323

357

Lab and Activity Highlights

LabBank

 Inquiry Labs, Surf's Up! Lab 11

Whiz-Bang Demonstrations, Fowl Play, Demo 25

EcoLabs & Field Activities, Operation Oil-Spill Cleanup, EcoLab 13

 Long-Term Projects & Research Ideas, Your Very Own Underwater Theme Park, Project 41

Interactive Explorations CD-ROM

 CD 2, Exploration 2, "Sea Sick"

Chapter 13 • Chapter Highlights **357**

Chapter Review

Chapter Review Answers

USING VOCABULARY

1. continental shelf
2. thermocline
3. Plankton
4. *Desalination* is the process of evaporating sea water so that the water and salt separate.
5. Types of *benthos* include sea stars and clams.
6. An ocean trench forms where one oceanic plate is forced underneath a continental plate or another oceanic plate, while a rift valley forms in a rift zone, where tectonic plates pull apart.
7. Salinity is a measure of the amount of dissolved solids in a given amount of liquid, while desalination is the process of evaporating sea water so that the water and the salt separate.
8. Nekton are free-swimming marine organisms, while benthos are marine organisms that live on or in the ocean floor.
9. The pelagic environment is made up of the water in the ocean and all the organisms that live in the water, while the benthic environment is made up of the ocean floor and all the organisms that live on or in the ocean floor.

UNDERSTANDING CONCEPTS

Multiple Choice
10. b
11. c
12. d
13. c
14. a
15. a

Chapter Review

USING VOCABULARY

To complete the following sentences, choose the correct term from each pair of terms listed below:

1. The region of the ocean floor that is closest to the shoreline is the __?__. (*continental shelf* or *continental slope*)

2. Below the surface layer of the ocean is a layer of water that gets colder with depth and extends to a depth of 700 m. This layer is called the __?__. (*thermocline* or *benthic environment*)

3. __?__ typically float at or near the ocean's surface. (*Plankton* or *Nekton*)

Correct the wrong terminology in each of the following sentences. A word bank is provided.

4. The water cycle is the process of evaporating sea water so that the water and salt separate.

5. Types of nekton include sea stars and clams.

Word bank:
nonpoint-source pollution, plankton, desalination, benthos

Explain the difference between the words in each of the following pairs:

6. ocean trench/rift valley
7. salinity/desalination
8. nekton/benthos
9. pelagic environment/benthic environment

UNDERSTANDING CONCEPTS

Multiple Choice

10. The largest ocean is the
    a. Indian Ocean.
    b. Pacific Ocean.
    c. Atlantic Ocean.
    d. Arctic Ocean.

11. One of the most abundant elements in the ocean is
    a. potassium.
    b. calcium.
    c. chlorine.
    d. magnesium.

12. Which of the following affects the ocean's salinity?
    a. fresh water added by rivers
    b. currents
    c. evaporation
    d. all of the above

13. Most precipitation falls
    a. on land.
    b. into lakes and rivers.
    c. into the ocean.
    d. in rain forests.

14. Which benthic zone has a depth range between 200 m and 4,000 m?
    a. bathyal zone
    b. abyssal zone
    c. hadal zone
    d. sublittoral zone

15. The ocean floor and all the organisms that live on it or in it is the
    a. benthic environment.
    b. pelagic environment.
    c. neritic zone.
    d. oceanic zone.

Short Answer

16. Why does coastal water in areas with hotter, drier climates typically have a higher salinity than coastal water in cooler, more humid areas?
17. What is the difference between the abyssal plain and the abyssal zone?
18. How do the continental shelf, the continental slope, the continental rise, and the continental margin relate to each other?

Concept Mapping

19. Use the following term to create a concept map: marine life, plankton, nekton, benthos, benthic environment, pelagic environment.

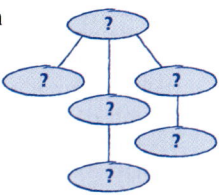

CRITICAL THINKING AND PROBLEM SOLVING

Write one or two sentences to answer the following questions:

20. Other than obtaining fresh water, what benefit comes from desalination?
21. Explain the difference between a bathymetric profile and a seismic reading.

MATH IN SCIENCE

22. Imagine that you are in the kelp-farming business and that your kelp grows 33 cm per day. You begin harvesting when your plants are 50 cm tall. During the first seven days of harvest, you cut 10 cm off the top of your kelp plants each day. How tall would your kelp plants be after the seventh day of harvesting?

INTERPRETING GRAPHICS

Examine the image below, and answer the questions that follow:

Ecological Zones of the Ocean

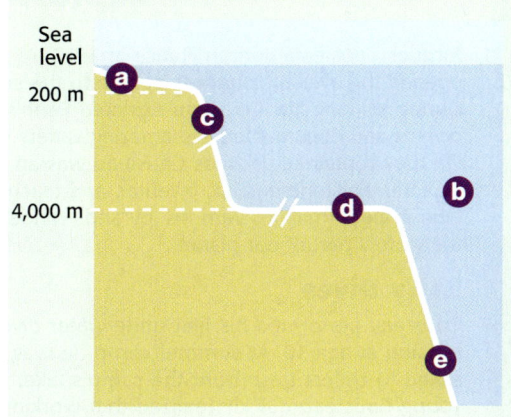

23. At which point (a, b, c, d, or e) would you most likely find an anglerfish?
24. At which point would you most likely find tube worms?
25. Which ecological zone is at point *c*? Which depth zone is at point *c*?
26. Name a type of organism you might find at point *e*.

 **Reading Check-up** Take a minute to review your answers to the Pre-Reading Questions found at the bottom of page 328. Have your answers changed? If necessary, revise your answers based on what you have learned since you began this chapter.

Short Answer
16. because less fresh water runs into the ocean in drier areas and because heat increases the evaporation rate
17. The abyssal plain is the flattest and deepest part of the ocean floor. The abyssal zone is an ecological zone that consists of the abyssal plain and all the organisms that live on or in it.
18. The continental shelf, the continental slope, and the continental rise are sections of the continental margin. Also, the continental rise is part of the continental slope.

Concept Mapping
19. An answer to this exercise can be found at the end of this book.

CRITICAL THINKING AND PROBLEM SOLVING

20. Salt is left behind. Salt can be used for many things.
21. A bathymetric profile shows what the contour of the ocean floor looks like, while a seismic reading shows what rocks beneath the ocean floor look like. (Seismic readings can show the contour of the ocean floor too.)

MATH IN SCIENCE

22. 50 cm + 7(33 cm − 10 cm) = 211 cm

INTERPRETING GRAPHICS

23. *b*
24. *d*
25. ecological zone = bathyal zone, depth zone = continental slope
26. Accept any one of the following: clams, sponges, or worms.

 **Concept Mapping Transparency 13**

 Blackline masters of this Chapter Review can be found in the **Study Guide**.

ACROSS THE SCIENCES
Exploring Ocean Life

Teaching Strategy
In addition to being an inventor and an explorer, Jacques Cousteau was a commentator on the twentieth century and its environmental problems. He was criticized as being a populist because he brought information to the public in common language instead of in academic terms. Help the class find information about his condemnation of French nuclear testing or his controversial opinions on overpopulation and animal testing.

You may want to show your students some of Cousteau's inspired documentaries. Some of his full-length features include *The Silent World, World Without Sun,* and *Voyage to the Edge of the World.* Tapes of his many television series *(The Undersea World of Jacques Cousteau, Cousteau Odyssey,* and *Cousteau Amazon)* may also be available at a public library.

ACROSS THE SCIENCES

EARTH SCIENCE • LIFE SCIENCE

Exploring Ocean Life

Jacques Cousteau, born in France in 1910, opened the eyes of countless people to the sea. During his long life, Cousteau explored Earth's oceans and documented the amazing variety of life they contained. Jacques Cousteau was an explorer, environmentalist, inventor, and teacher who inspired millions with his joy and wonder at the watery part of our planet.

Early Dives
Cousteau performed his first underwater diving mission at age 10. At summer camp he was asked to collect trash from the camp's lake. The young Cousteau quickly realized that working underwater without goggles or breathing equipment was a tremendous challenge.

Cousteau had another early underwater experience when he visited Southeast Asia. He saw people diving into the water to catch fish with their bare hands. This fascinated Cousteau. Even at a young age, he was thinking about how to make equipment that would let a person breathe underwater.

Underwater Flight
As a young man, Cousteau and some friends developed the aqualung, a self-contained breathing system for underwater exploration. As someone who had often dreamed of flying, Cousteau was thrilled with his invention. After one of his first dives, Cousteau explained, "I experimented with all possible maneuvers—loops, somersaults, and barrel rolls. . . . Delivered from gravity and buoyancy, I flew around in space."

Using the aqualung and other underwater equipment he developed, Cousteau began making underwater films. In 1950, he bought a boat named *Calypso,* which became his home and floating laboratory. For the next 40 years, through his films and television series, Cousteau brought what he called "the silent world" of the oceans and seas to living rooms everywhere.

A Protector of Life
Cousteau was long an outspoken defender of the environment. "When I saw all this beauty under the sea, I fell in love with it. And finally, when I realized to what extent the oceans were threatened, I decided to campaign as vigorously as I could against everything that threatened what I loved."

Jacques Cousteau died in 1997 at age 87. Before his death, he dedicated the *Calypso II,* a new research vessel, to the children of the world.

Write About It
▶ Ocean pollution and overfishing are subjects of intense debate. Think about these issues, and discuss them with your classmates. Then write an essay in which you try to convince readers of your point of view.

▲ *Cousteau in front of the* Calypso II

360

Answer to Write About It
Students should be able to find a great deal of information about ocean pollution and overfishing. Many articles have been published in various science magazines, and there is a large number of government and nonprofit Web sites that deal with these issues.

EYE ON THE ENVIRONMENT

Putting Freshwater Problems on Ice

Imagine how different your life would be if you couldn't get fresh water. What would you drink? How would you clean things? The Earth has enough fresh water to supply 100 billion liters to each person, yet water shortages affect millions of people every day. So what's the problem?

The Ice-Water Planet

Three-quarters of Earth's fresh water is frozen in polar icecaps. Plenty of fresh water is there, but people can't use water that is frozen and thousands of kilometers away.

The ice sheet that covers Antarctica is thousands of meters thick and is almost twice the size of the United States. Hundreds of huge chunks break off its edges every year. These icebergs, which are made up entirely of frozen fresh water, float away into the sea and eventually melt. Water from 1 year's worth of these icebergs would be enough to supply all of southern California for more than a century. So why not use it?

Obvious but Not Easy

Transporting icebergs to areas that need fresh water is harder than it sounds. For one thing, many of the icebergs are huge. The largest ever recorded was about the size of Connecticut. Even small icebergs may be 2 km long and 1 km wide.

Researchers have considered many methods of transporting icebergs. Most of the ideas involve pushing or towing icebergs through the water. A few ideas involve attaching engines and propellers directly to the icebergs.

However, because icebergs are so large, it takes a long time to move them. And when an iceberg finally does get somewhere, a considerable amount of it has melted. To prevent melting, insulating materials could be wrapped around an iceberg.

▲ Icebergs such as this one might provide water in the future.

A Worthy Investment

Lakes and ground water still provide the cheapest fresh water in most areas. However, if there is no lake, river, or well water available, icebergs may then be a reasonable option to consider. Even though transporting icebergs is difficult, it may still be worthwhile to try. Irrigating 100 km^2 of desert with water from icebergs might cost as much as $1 million, but purifying enough sea water to irrigate that amount of desert could cost over $1 billion.

People in arid regions have spent considerable time on iceberg research. So far, no one has set up a program for harvesting icebergs. But someday water from icebergs may flow from our household faucets.

An Icy Investigation

▶ Float an ice cube in a bowl of cold water, and record the time it takes the cube to melt. Then try to insulate other ice cubes with different materials, such as cloth, plastic wrap, and aluminum foil. Which material works best? How could this material be used on real icebergs?

EYE ON THE ENVIRONMENT

Putting Freshwater Problems on Ice

Background

Icebergs form in both the Northern and Southern Hemispheres, but they are typically very different in size and appearance. Icebergs in the Northern Hemisphere, such as those that break off from the ice sheet covering Greenland, tend to be spiky and irregularly shaped. Icebergs in the Southern Hemisphere are much larger and usually have a fairly flat top.

People first considered the possibility of using icebergs as a water source many years ago. Just after 1900, Antarctic icebergs were towed by steamships to Callao, Peru. In addition to using icebergs for fresh water, people have proposed using them for air conditioning, as a source of gourmet ice cubes, and even as giant aircraft carriers.

Answers to An Icy Investigation

Answers will vary. Students may find that some materials prevent the ice cubes from melting as quickly as they would if they were unprotected. Students should propose realistic ways of using their materials on icebergs.

Chapter Organizer

CHAPTER ORGANIZATION	TIME MINUTES	OBJECTIVES	LABS, INVESTIGATIONS, AND DEMONSTRATIONS
Chapter Opener pp. 362–363	45	National Standards: SAI 1, SPSP 3, 4, HNS 1, ES 1b	**Start-Up Activity** When *Whirls* Collide, p. 363
Section 1 Currents	90	▶ Describe surface currents, and list the three factors that control them. ▶ Describe deep currents. ▶ Illustrate the factors involved in deep-current movement. ▶ Explain how currents affect climate. SAI 1, HNS 1, 3, ES 1j, 3d; LabBook UCP 2, SAI 1	**Demonstration,** The Coriolis Effect, p. 366 **GENERAL** **Interactive Explorations CD-ROM,** Latitude Attitude **GENERAL** A *Worksheet* is also available in the **Interactive Explorations Teacher's Edition.** **Skill Builder,** Up from the Depths, p. 684 **GENERAL** **Datasheets for LabBook,** Up from the Depths, Datasheet 28 **GENERAL** **Whiz-Bang Demonstrations,** Spin Cycle, Demo 26 **ADVANCED**
Section 2 Waves	90	▶ Identify wave components, and explain how they relate to wave movement. ▶ Describe how ocean waves form and how they move. ▶ Classify types of waves. ▶ Analyze types of dangerous waves. UCP 3, SAI 1, SPSP 3, 4, ES 1b	**QuickLab,** Do the Wave, p. 376 **GENERAL**
Section 3 Tides	90	▶ Explain tides and their relationship with the Earth, the sun, and the moon. ▶ Classify different types of tides. ▶ Analyze the relationship between tides and coastal land. UCP 1, 2, HNS 1, 3, ES 3c; LabBook UCP 2, SAI 1, ST 1, ES 3c	**Making Models,** Turning the Tides, p. 686 **GENERAL** **Datasheets for LabBook,** Turning the Tides, Datasheet 29 **GENERAL** **Long-Term Projects & Research Ideas,** Project 42 **ADVANCED**

*See page **T20** for a complete correlation of this book with the*

NATIONAL SCIENCE EDUCATION STANDARDS.

TECHNOLOGY RESOURCES

 Guided Reading Audio CD English or Spanish, Chapter 14

 One-Stop Planner CD-ROM with Test Generator

 Scientists in Action, Mapping El Niño Erosion, Segment 20

 Interactive Explorations CD-ROM CD 3, Exploration 4, Latitude Attitude

Chapter 14 • The Movement of Ocean Water

Chapter 14 • The Movement of Ocean Water

CLASSROOM WORKSHEETS, TRANSPARENCIES, AND RESOURCES	SCIENCE INTEGRATION AND CONNECTIONS	REVIEW AND ASSESSMENT
Directed Reading Worksheet 14 BASIC **Science Puzzlers, Twisters & Teasers,** Worksheet 14 ADVANCED	**Careers:** Seismologist, p. 386 GENERAL	
Directed Reading Worksheet 14, Section 1 BASIC **Transparency 156,** Earth's Surface Currents **Transparency 156,** The Coriolis Effect **Math Skills for Science Worksheet 25,** What Is Scientific Notation? GENERAL **Transparency 157,** How Deep Currents Form **Transparency 158,** Circulation of Deep and Surface Currents	**Real-World Connection,** p. 364 in ATE GENERAL **Connect to Life Science,** p. 365 in ATE **Real-World Connection,** p. 366 in ATE **Physics Connection,** p. 367 **Math and More,** p. 368 in ATE GENERAL **Connect to Life Science,** p. 369 in ATE ADVANCED **Cross-Disciplinary Focus,** p. 370 in ATE **Real-World Connection,** p. 371 in ATE	**Self-Check,** p. 365 **Review,** p. 367 GENERAL **Homework,** p. 367 in ATE ADVANCED **Homework,** p. 369 in ATE GENERAL **Review,** p. 371 GENERAL **Quiz,** p. 371 in ATE GENERAL **Alternative Assessment,** p. 371 in ATE GENERAL
Transparency 159, Wave Period **Directed Reading Worksheet 14,** Section 2 BASIC **Transparency 160,** Deep-Water Waves Become Shallow-Water Waves **Math Skills for Science Worksheet 11,** What Is a Fraction? GENERAL **Transparency 282,** Wave Speed, Wavelength, and Frequency **Reinforcement Worksheet 14,** Waves to Your Pen Pal BASIC	**MathBreak,** Wave Speed, p. 373 GENERAL **Math and More,** p. 373 in ATE BASIC **Real-World Connection,** p. 374 in ATE **Math and More,** p. 375 in ATE GENERAL **Connect to Environmental Science,** p. 375 in ATE **Connect to Meteorology,** p. 376 in ATE **Apply,** p. 377 ADVANCED	**Homework,** p. 375 in ATE ADVANCED **Review,** p. 377 GENERAL **Quiz,** p. 377 in ATE GENERAL **Alternative Assessment,** p. 377 in ATE GENERAL
Directed Reading Worksheet 14, Section 3 BASIC **Critical Thinking Worksheet 14,** Tides of Trouble ADVANCED **Transparency 161,** Tidal Variations **Reinforcement Worksheet 14,** But What About the Tides? BASIC	**Connect to Environmental Science,** p. 381 in ATE ADVANCED **Health Watch:** Red Tides, p. 387 GENERAL	**Homework,** p. 380 in ATE GENERAL **Review,** p. 381 GENERAL **Quiz,** p. 381 in ATE GENERAL **Alternative Assessment,** p. 381 in ATE GENERAL

internet connect

Holt, Rinehart and Winston On-line Resources
go.hrw.com

For worksheets and other teaching aids related to this chapter, visit the HRW Web site and type in the keyword: **HSTH2O**

National Science Teachers Association
www.scilinks.org

Encourage students to use the sciLINKS numbers listed in the internet connect boxes to access information and resources on the **NSTA** Web site.

END-OF-CHAPTER REVIEW AND ASSESSMENT

Chapter Review in Study Guide
Vocabulary and Notes in Study Guide
Chapter Tests with Performance-Based Assessment, Chapter 14 Test
Chapter Tests with Performance-Based Assessment, Performance-Based Assessment 14
Concept Mapping Transparency 14

Chapter Resources & Worksheets

Visual Resources

TEACHING TRANSPARENCIES

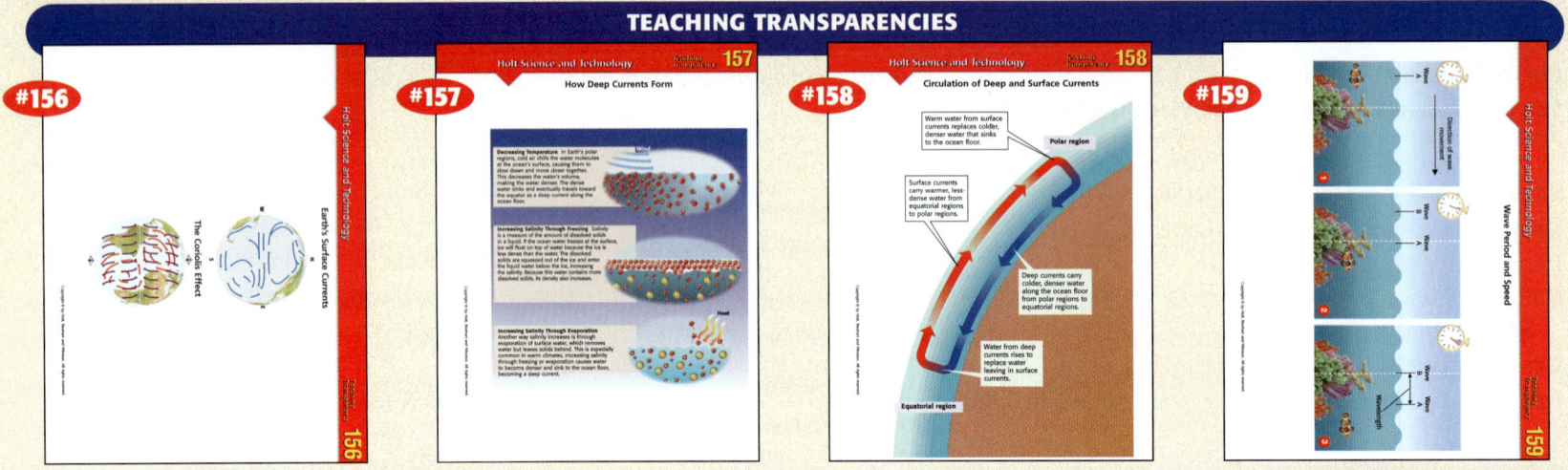

TEACHING TRANSPARENCIES

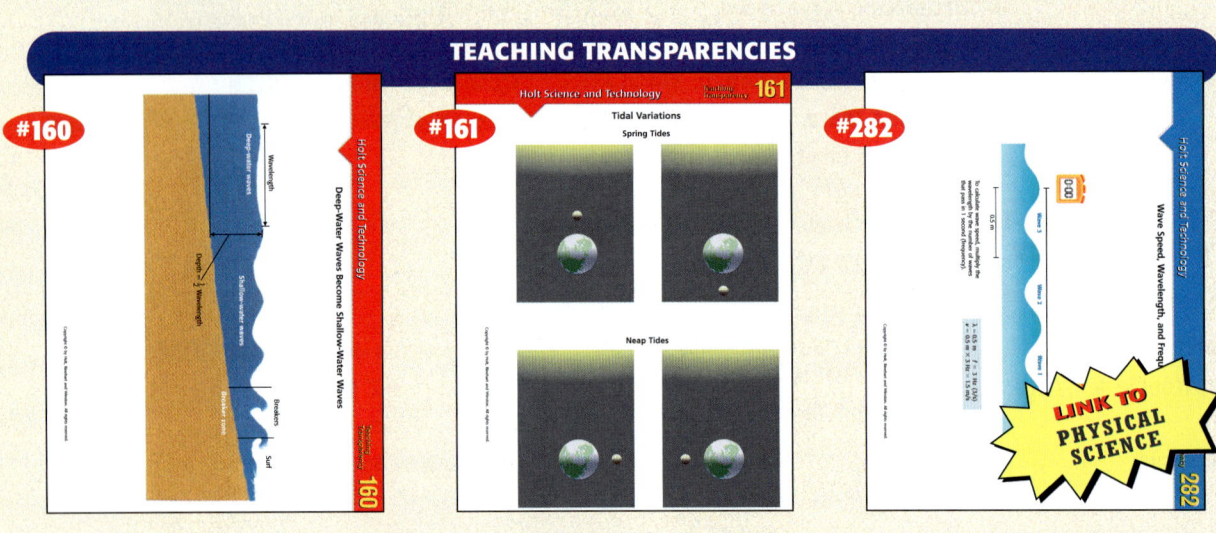

CONCEPT MAPPING TRANSPARENCY

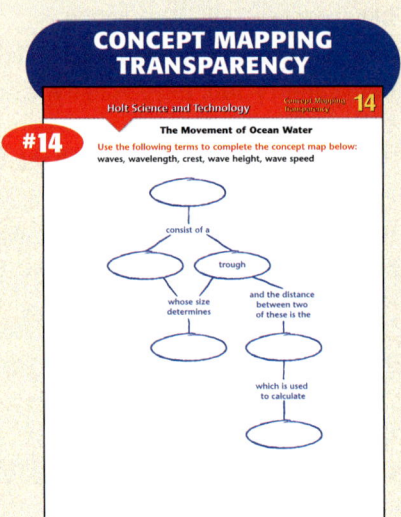

Meeting Individual Needs

DIRECTED READING

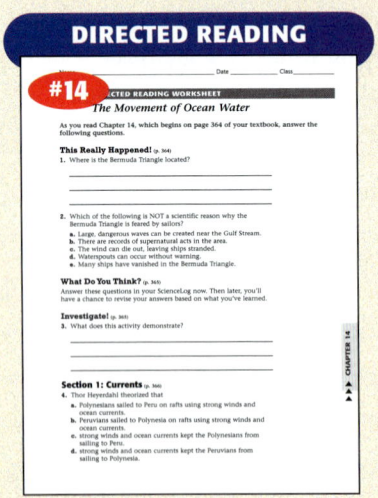

REINFORCEMENT & VOCABULARY REVIEW

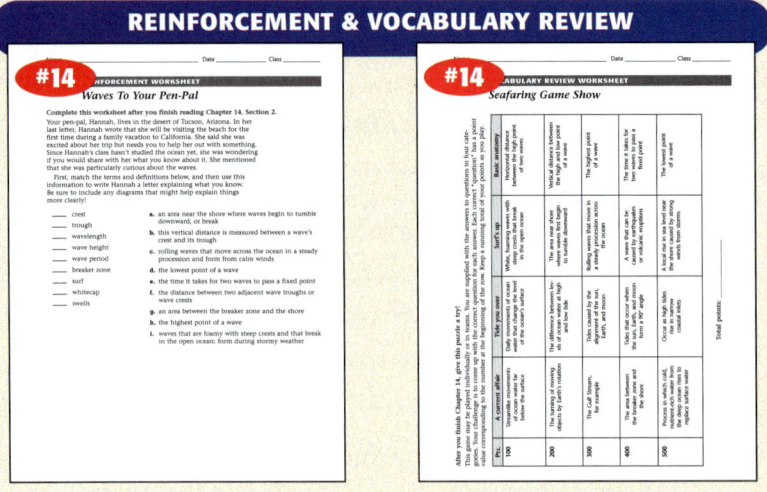

SCIENCE PUZZLERS, TWISTERS & TEASERS

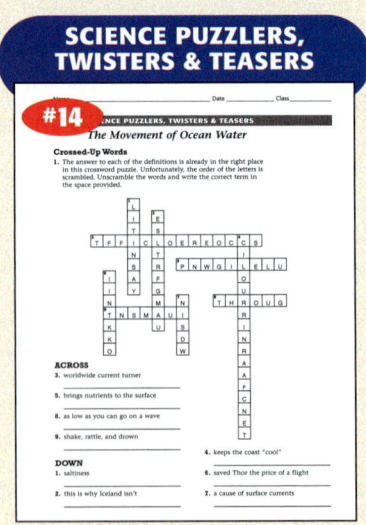

361C Chapter 14 • The Movement of Ocean Water

Chapter 14 • The Movement of Ocean Water

Review & Assessment

STUDY GUIDE
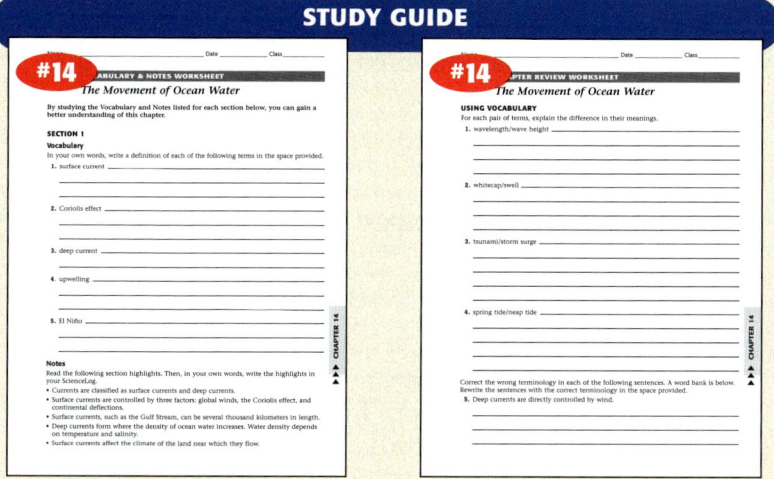

CHAPTER TESTS WITH PERFORMANCE-BASED ASSESSMENT
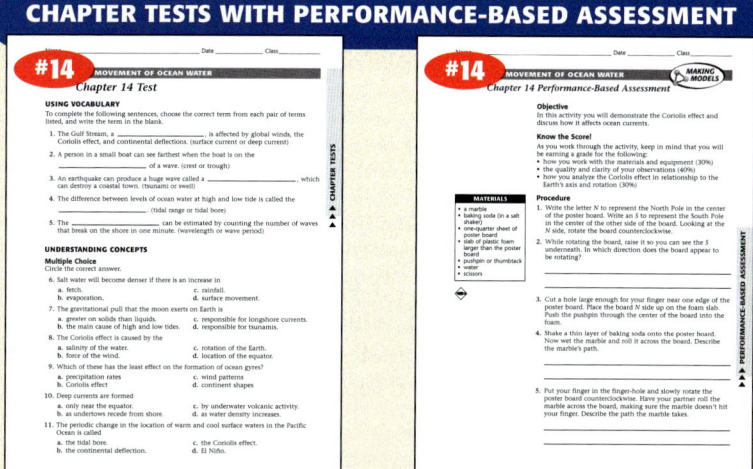

Lab Worksheets

WHIZ-BANG DEMONSTRATIONS
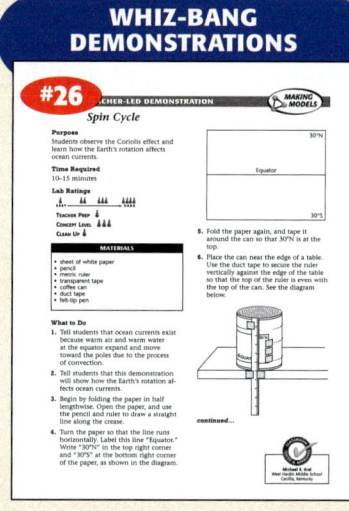

LONG-TERM PROJECTS & RESEARCH IDEAS
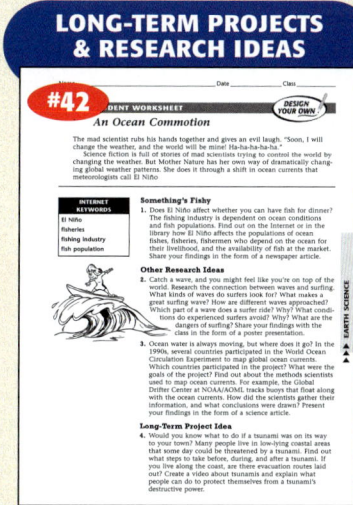

DATASHEETS FOR LABBOOK
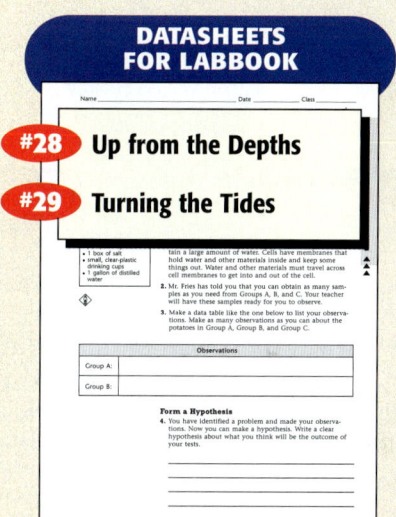

Applications & Extensions

CRITICAL THINKING & PROBLEM SOLVING
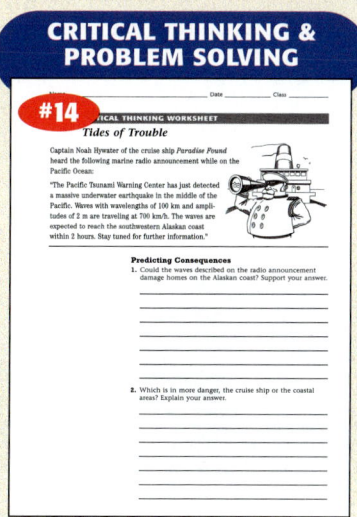

SCIENTISTS IN ACTION
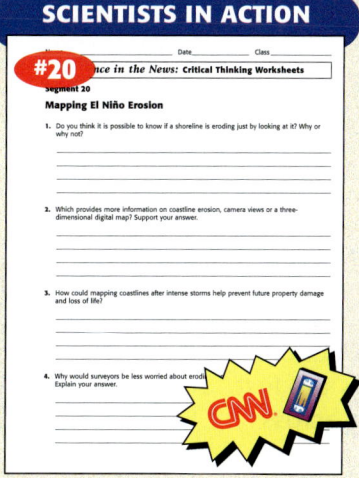

INTERACTIVE EXPLORATIONS
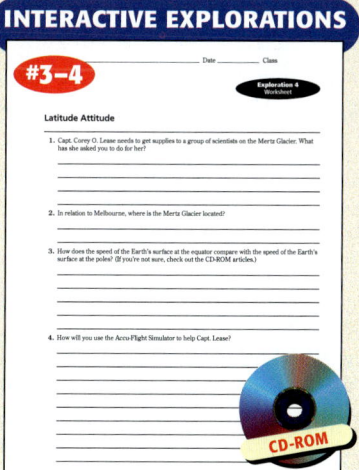

Chapter 14 • Chapter Resources & Worksheets   **361D**

Chapter Background

SECTION 1

Currents

▶ **Solar Radiation**
One of the fundamental energy sources for all ocean currents is solar radiation. Uneven heating of the Earth by the sun creates differences in air pressure. These differences create wind, which drives surface currents. The sun's energy also creates temperature differences in ocean water, driving deep currents.

▶ **The *Ra II* Expedition**
On May 17, 1970, Thor Heyerdahl's *Ra II* expedition attempted to demonstrate that mariners from ancient Egypt could have reached the New World. The eight-man expedition successfully reached its destination in the Barbados on July 12, 1970.

▶ **Gaspard Coriolis**
The Coriolis effect was named after Gaspard Coriolis (1792–1843), a French engineer. Coriolis was the first to attribute the deflection of surface currents across the surface of Earth to a hypothetical force. It was not until later that the force was identified as Earth's rotation.

IS THAT A FACT!

- The strongest and largest ocean current is the Antarctic Circumpolar Current, which is estimated to flow at a rate of 125 million cubic meters per second.

- One of the fastest ocean currents is the Somali Current, in the western Indian Ocean, which flows at a speed of 14.5 km/h.

- The Weddell Sea, where the Antarctic Bottom Water is thought to originate, has the clearest water of any sea. Its clarity has been recorded to a depth of nearly 80 m. In other words, water collected from the upper 80 m of the Weddell Sea is as clear as you would find in a glass of distilled water.

SECTION 2

Waves

▶ **Swells**
Swells are generated in the open ocean by wind and can travel thousands of kilometers to shore. These long-wavelength waves have periods of 10 to 30 seconds. When swells reach shallower water, their height increases, causing them to fall forward. When this occurs, the waves are called breakers.

Chapter 14 • The Movement of Ocean Water

▶ Tsunamis

Tsunami is a Japanese word that means "harbor wave." Japan has experienced many devastating tsunamis throughout history. The subduction of tectonic plates generates the seismic energy necessary to cause tsunamis. Because the Japanese islands are on the edge of deep water and the coastline is rugged, with many small harbors, tsunamis have been particularly destructive. The deep water close to the Japanese islands keeps tsunami wave heights short until the waves are very close to shore; when the waves enter shallow water, they suddenly grow taller. The narrow shape of many Japanese harbors causes tsunamis to grow even taller.

- Tsunamis have the potential to be the most destructive of ocean waves. Their speed averages 500 km/h, and their period ranges from 5 to 60 minutes. Because the wave height of a tsunami is usually less than 2 m in the open ocean, they often pass unnoticed beneath ships.

- The earthquakes that produce destructive tsunamis are generally greater than 6.5 on the Richter scale. Most occur in the Pacific Ocean, where there is a high level of seismic activity near plate boundaries.

SECTION 3
Tides

▶ Perigean Spring Tides

On March 7, 1993, a full moon appeared on the same day that the moon was closest to Earth in its orbit (or its perigee). This event produced extraordinarily high and low tides, called *perigean spring tides*. During perigean spring tides, high tides rise higher than normal onto beaches, while low tides expose parts of the ocean floor that are normally submerged.

IS THAT A FACT!

- The sun exerts only about half the tidal force on Earth that the moon does. This is because the distance between Earth and the sun is much greater than the distance between Earth and the moon.

- High tide that occurs on the side of Earth that faces the moon is called a *direct high tide*. High tide that occurs on the side of Earth opposite the moon is called an *indirect high tide*.

- The Great Lakes also experience tides. Although the tidal range is small compared with that of the oceans, the size and depth of the five lakes make small fluctuations in water level noticeable.

For background information about teaching strategies and issues, refer to the *Professional Reference for Teachers*.

The Movement of Ocean Water

Pre-Reading Questions

Students may not know the answers to these questions before reading the chapter, so accept any reasonable response.

Suggested Answers

1. Factors that control ocean currents include wind, the Earth's rotation, water density, water salinity, water temperature, and continental deflections.

2. Gravitational forces from the sun and moon and the motion of the Earth and the moon around each other cause the ocean tides.

Directed Reading Worksheet 14

Science Puzzlers, Twisters & Teasers Worksheet 14

Guided Reading Audio CD
English or Spanish, Chapter 14

The Movement of Ocean Water

Sections

1. Currents 364
   Physics Connection .. 367
   Internet Connect... 367, 371
2. Waves 372
   MathBreak 373
   QuickLab 376
   Apply 377
   Internet Connect 377
3. Tides 378
   Internet Connect 381

Chapter Review 384
Feature Articles 386, 387
LabBook 684–687

1. What factors control ocean currents?
2. What causes the ocean tides?

362

An Ocean Stream

The Gulf Stream current carries warm tropical water from the Caribbean Sea all the way to the North Atlantic Ocean. The climate in the British Isles, where the current ends, is controlled by the current's warm waters, which make the isles much warmer than other countries nearby. In this chapter, you will learn how currents like the Gulf Stream are formed. You also will learn about the other ways that ocean water moves and how these movements affect our lives.

 **HRW On-line Resources**
go.hrw.com
For worksheets and other teaching aids, visit the HRW Web site and type in the keyword: **HSTH2O**

www.scilinks.com
Use the *sci*LINKS numbers at the end of each chapter for additional resources on the **NSTA** Web site.

www.cnnfyi.com
Visit the CNN Web site for current events coverage and classroom resources.

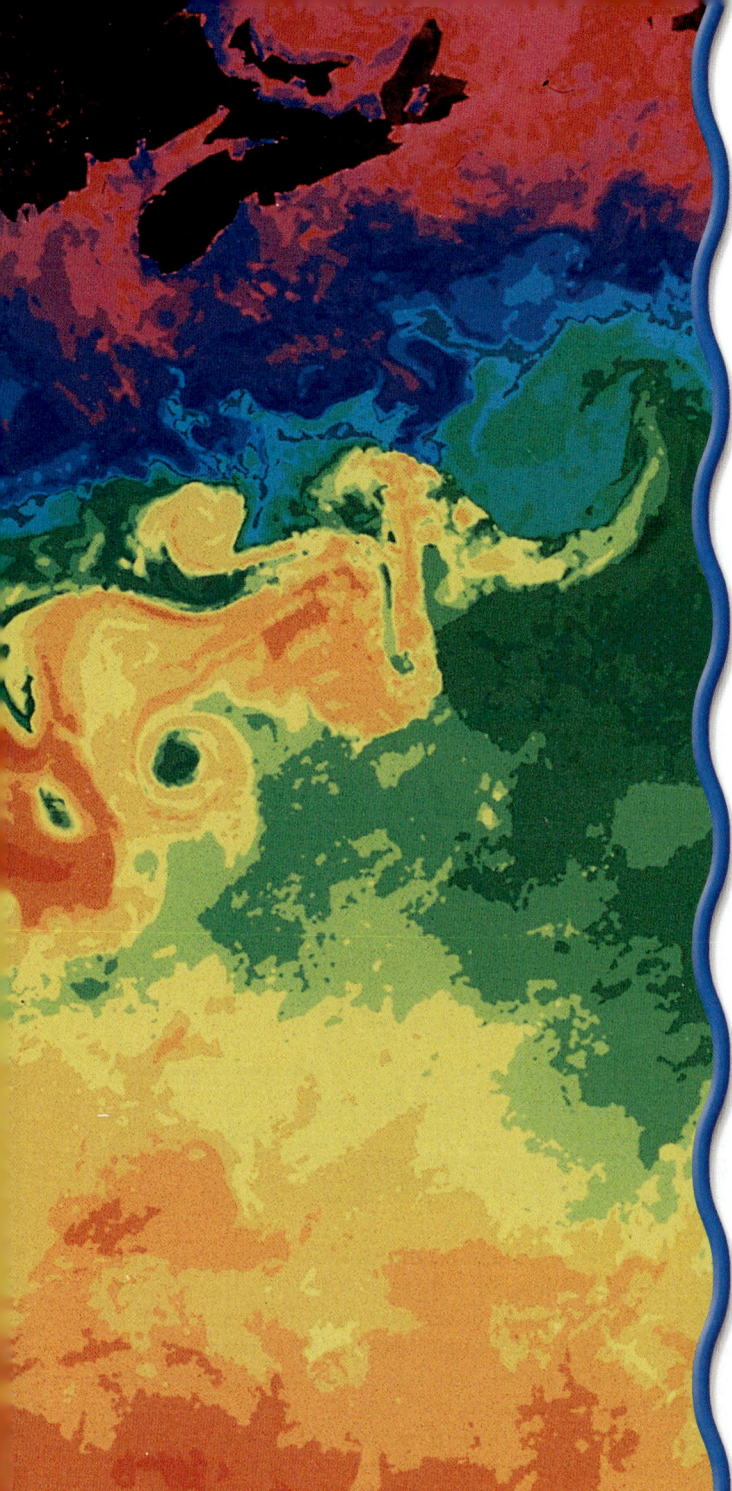

START-UP Activity

WHEN *WHIRLS* COLLIDE

Ocean currents in the Northern Hemisphere flow in a clockwise direction, while currents in the Southern Hemisphere flow in a counterclockwise direction. Sometimes, southern currents flow across the equator into the Northern Hemisphere and begin flowing clockwise. Do this activity to find out how currents flowing in opposite directions affect one another.

Procedure

1. Fill a large **tub** with **water** 5 cm deep.
2. Add **10 drops of red food coloring** to the water on one end of the tub.
3. Add **10 drops of blue food coloring** to the water at the other end of the tub.
4. Using a **pencil**, quickly stir the water at one end of the tub in a clockwise direction while your partner stirs the water at the other end in a counterclockwise direction. Stir both ends for about 5 seconds.
5. In your ScienceLog, draw what you see happening in the tub immediately after you stop stirring. (Both ends should still be swirling.)

Analysis

6. How did the blue water and the red water interact?
7. How does this activity relate to the ocean currents in the Northern and Southern Hemispheres?

START-UP Activity

WHEN *WHIRLS* COLLIDE

MATERIALS
FOR EACH PAIR OF STUDENTS: • large tub • water • red food coloring • blue food coloring • 2 pencils

Teacher's Notes

To avoid moving the tub after it is filled with water, put the tub in position before the water is added. Although food coloring is nontoxic and washes out of clothing, students should be careful not to spill the food coloring on their skin or clothes.

A cake pan similar in size to the tub can be used for this activity. Water depth should be about 5 cm. Advise students to observe the experiment closely—the desired result happens quickly and lasts only a few seconds.

Explore what happens with different types of tubs. Does the depth of the tub change the results?

Answers to START-UP Activity

6. When the blue water left the current it was circulating in, it crossed the middle of the tub, joined the red water, and began circling in the opposite direction. The red water followed the same pattern.

7. Answers will vary. Currents in the Northern Hemisphere circulate in the opposite direction as do currents in the Southern Hemisphere. When a current crosses the equator, it joins other currents and eventually circulates in the direction they are moving.

SECTION 1

Focus

Currents

This section discusses the causes and characteristics of surface and deep currents in the ocean. Students will learn about the different factors related to ocean currents and explore the ways currents and climate are related.

Bellringer

Read excerpts from Thor Heyerdahl's *Kon-Tiki* (1950) or *The Ra Expeditions* (1971) to students. Display a large map of the world that shows the different ocean currents. After showing students the origination and destination points for Heyerdahl's voyages, discuss which currents he would have used to reach his destinations. Point out that DNA testing later showed that Polynesians did not originate in Peru. Have students discuss how a scientific model might be successful, but not accurate. **Sheltered English**

1 Motivate

REAL-WORLD CONNECTION

Have students discuss the characteristics of rivers. Ask students to compare rivers to surface currents. Lead students to the understanding that rivers and surface currents are very different but share some important similarities. For example, both are long, moving bodies of water. However, rivers flow due to the pull of gravity and are usually confined between banks. Surface currents are driven by the wind and the rotation of the Earth.

Section 1

Terms to Learn
surface current upwelling
Coriolis effect El Niño
deep current

What You'll Do
- Describe surface currents, and list the three factors that control them.
- Describe deep currents.
- Illustrate the factors involved in deep-current movement.
- Explain how currents affect climate.

Currents

Imagine that you are stranded on a desert island. You stuff a distress message into a bottle and throw it into the ocean, hoping it will find its way to someone who will send help. Is there any way to predict where your bottle may land?

One Way to Explore Currents

In the 1940s, a Norwegian explorer named Thor Heyerdahl tried to answer similar questions that involved human migration across the ocean. Heyerdahl theorized that the inhabitants of Polynesia originally sailed from Peru on rafts powered only by the wind and ocean currents. Unable to convince scientists of his theory, he decided to prove it. In 1947, Heyerdahl and a crew of five people set sail from Peru on a raft, as shown in **Figure 1**.

Figure 1 The handcrafted Kon-Tiki was made mainly from materials that would have been available to ancient Peruvians.

On the 97th day of their expedition, Heyerdahl and his crew landed on an island in Polynesia. Currents had carried the raft westward more than 6,000 km across the South Pacific. This supported Heyerdahl's theory that ocean currents carried the ancient Peruvians across the Pacific to Polynesia. Now let's take a closer look at currents. For example, what determines the direction in which a current moves? What forces create a current? Read on to learn the answers to these and other questions about currents.

IS THAT A FACT!

No metal was used in the construction of the *Kon-Tiki*. The wood raft was made of thick Peruvian balsa logs and featured a bamboo cabin set in the center, a large steering oar at the stern, and five centerboards. Two masts were used to support the rectangular sail. Although it crashed into a reef when it finally reached Polynesia, the *Kon-Tiki* was restored and is currently on display at a museum in Oslo, Norway.

364 Chapter 14 • The Movement of Ocean Water

Surface Currents

Streamlike movements of water that occur at or near the surface of the ocean are called **surface currents.** Some surface currents are several thousand kilometers in length, traveling across entire oceans. The Gulf Stream, which is one of the longest surface currents, transports 25 times more water than all the rivers in the world. Surface currents are controlled by three factors: global winds, the Coriolis effect, and continental deflections. These three factors keep surface currents flowing in distinct patterns around the Earth.

Global Winds Have you ever blown gently on a cup of hot chocolate? You may have noticed ripples moving across the surface. These ripples are caused by a tiny surface current created by your breath. In much the same way, winds blowing across the Earth's surface create surface currents in the ocean. Surface currents can reach depths of several hundred meters and lengths of several thousand kilometers.

Different winds cause currents to flow in different directions. Near the equator, the winds blow ocean water east to west, but closer to the poles, ocean water is blown west to east, as shown in **Figure 2.** Merchant ships often use these currents to travel more quickly back and forth across the oceans.

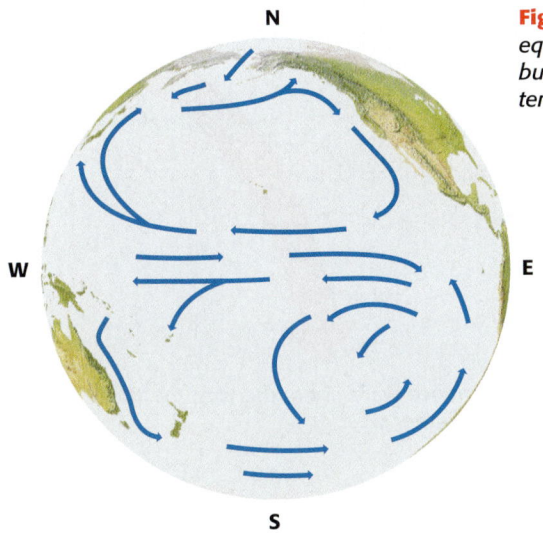

Figure 2 Surface currents near the equator generally flow from east to west, but surface currents closer to the poles tend to flow from west to east.

Self-Check

Take another look at Figure 2. As Heyerdahl made his journey in 1947, from what direction would he have noticed the wind blowing? (See page 726 to check your answer.)

2) Teach, continued

RETEACHING

The Coriolis Effect For students having difficulty understanding the Coriolis effect, use a turntable to demonstrate the concept.

1. Cover the surface of the turntable with a circle of paper cut to fit.
2. Spin the turntable platter and explain that it represents the rotating Earth.
3. Instruct a student to attempt to draw a straight line from the center of the turntable to the edge. A curved line will be formed. The curved line represents the curved path of surface currents due to Earth's rotation.

Sheltered English

REAL-WORLD CONNECTION

Surface currents move in large, slow circles called *gyres*. In 1990, a Korean ship carrying a load of athletic shoes was bound for the United States. During a storm, 80,000 shoes were washed overboard. Six months later, the shoes began to wash up on North American shores from Oregon to British Columbia. This accident turned out to be a big bonus to oceanographers. They created a computer model to predict where the gyres would carry the shoes next. True to the model, the shoes began to wash up in Hawaii three years later. With the help of dedicated beachcombers, this accident has enabled oceanographers to create a detailed map of surface currents in the Pacific Ocean. Have students look at a map of global ocean currents and identify the currents that carried the shoes. Students may also enjoy visiting Web sites that track the movements of other cargo spills.

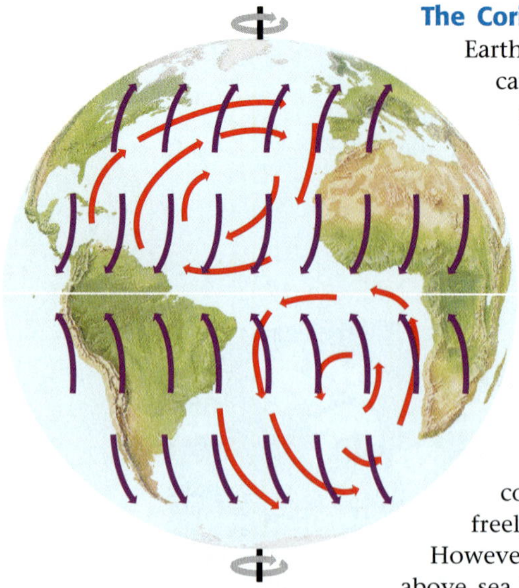

The Coriolis Effect Have you ever thought about how the Earth's rotation affects its surface? The Earth's rotation causes surface currents to move in curved paths rather than in straight lines. The curving of moving objects from a straight path due to the Earth's rotation is called the **Coriolis effect**. To understand the Coriolis effect, imagine trying to roll a ball straight across a turning merry-go-round. Because the merry-go-round is spinning, the path of the ball will curve before it reaches the other side. **Figure 3** shows that ocean currents in the Northern Hemisphere turn clockwise, while ocean currents in the Southern Hemisphere turn counterclockwise.

Continental Deflections If the Earth's surface were covered only with water, surface currents would travel freely across the globe in a very uniform pattern. However, we know that this is not the case—continents rise above sea level over roughly one-third of the Earth's surface. When surface currents meet continents, they *deflect*, or change direction. Notice in **Figure 4** how the Brazil Current deflects southward as it meets the east coast of South America.

Figure 3 The rotation of the Earth causes ocean currents (red arrows) and global winds (purple arrows) to move in opposite directions on either side of the equator.

Activity

Some people think the Coriolis effect can be seen in sinks; that is, water draining from sinks turns clockwise in the Northern Hemisphere and counterclockwise in the Southern Hemisphere. Is this true? Research this question at the library, on the Internet, and in your sinks and tubs at home.

TRY at HOME

Figure 4 If South America were not in the way, the Brazil Current would probably flow farther west.

MISCONCEPTION ALERT

It is a common misconception that the direction in which water drains (clockwise versus counterclockwise) is determined by the Coriolis effect. Allow students to discover this themselves by directing them to do the Activity on this page.

IS THAT A FACT!

The Earth's rotation affects ocean currents directly by causing currents to circle in opposite directions on either side of the equator. Earth's rotation also affects the wind patterns, which in turn drive surface currents.

Taking Temperatures All three factors—global winds, the Coriolis effect, and continental deflections—work together to form a pattern of surface currents on Earth. But currents are also affected by the temperature of the water in which they arise. Warm-water currents begin near the equator and carry warm water to other parts of the ocean. Cold-water currents begin closer to the poles and carry cool water to other parts of the ocean. As you can see on the map in **Figure 5,** all the oceans are connected, and both warm-water and cold-water currents travel from one ocean to another.

Physics CONNECTION

While winds are responsible for ocean currents, the sun is the initial energy source of the currents. Because the sun heats the Earth more in some places than in others, convection currents are formed, which cause winds to blow.

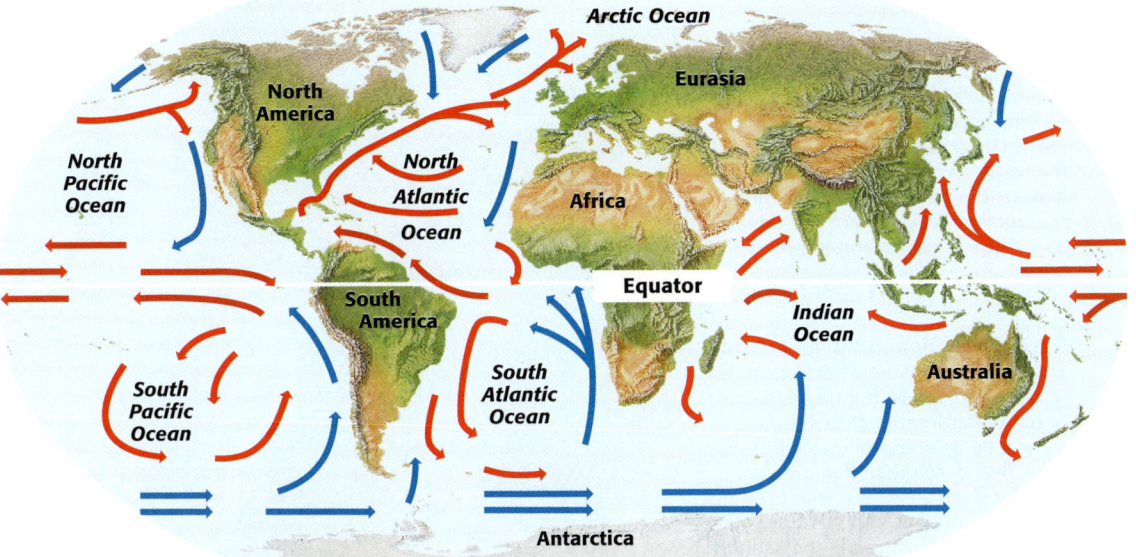

Figure 5 This map shows Earth's surface currents. Warm-water currents are shown as red arrows, and cold-water currents are shown as blue arrows.

REVIEW

1. List the three factors that control surface currents.
2. Explain how the Earth's rotation affects the patterns of surface currents.
3. **Inferring Conclusions** If there were no land on Earth's surface, what would the pattern of surface currents look like? Explain.

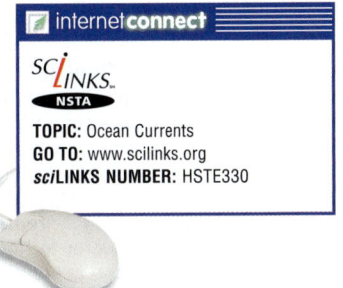

internetconnect

SC LINKS
NSTA

TOPIC: Ocean Currents
GO TO: www.scilinks.org
*sci*LINKS NUMBER: HSTE330

MEETING INDIVIDUAL NEEDS

Learners Having Difficulty
Refer to **Figure 5** to point out that the currents in the Southern Hemisphere turn counterclockwise and the currents in the Northern Hemisphere turn clockwise. Using a globe, show the direction of ocean currents in various areas around the world. Note for students that a current in the South Atlantic Ocean crosses the equator and joins the clockwise-turning currents. Discuss how this process was modeled in the Investigate activity at the beginning of this chapter. **Sheltered English**

Homework

Research Have students choose four coastal cities that are separated by oceans. Ask students to describe in their ScienceLog the currents they would use to sail from one city to the next. Students should use **Figure 5** as a reference for determining which currents they would use. Students can use an atlas or another reference tool to find the names of their currents. They can write their entries in the form of a ship's log.

Teaching Transparency 156
"Earth's Surface Currents"
"The Coriolis Effect"

▼ Answers to Review

1. The three factors that control surface currents are global winds, the Coriolis effect, and continental deflections.
2. The Earth's rotation causes the Coriolis effect. The Coriolis effect is seen in the pattern of the ocean's surface currents—surface currents in the Northern Hemisphere turn clockwise, and surface currents in the Southern Hemisphere turn counterclockwise.
3. Answers will vary. Sample answer: If there were no land on Earth's surface, surface currents would not deflect sharply, as they do when they approach continents.

Section 1 • Currents

2) Teach, continued

Up from the Depths PG 684

READING STRATEGY

Prediction Guide Before students read the section on deep currents, ask them to respond to the following questions:

Do global winds directly cause deep currents? (no)

Can ocean currents be caused by differences in water temperature? (yes)

Can ocean currents be caused by differences in salinity? (yes)

MATH and MORE

Review scientific notation with students. Tell them there are approximately 1.7×10^{19} water molecules in one drop of sea water and 1×10^{44} water molecules in the Mediterranean Sea. Have students help you write these two numbers to show how large they are. For reference, tell students that there are 17 times as many molecules in a drop of water than there are insects on Earth.

Math Skills Worksheet 25 "What Is Scientific Notation?"

Teaching Transparency 157 "How Deep Currents Form"

Turn to page 684 in the LabBook to demonstrate how temperature and salinity affect ocean water.

Deep Currents

Deep currents are streamlike movements of ocean water far below the surface. Unlike surface currents, deep currents are not directly controlled by wind or the Coriolis effect. Instead, they form in parts of the ocean where water density increases. *Density* is the ratio of the mass of a substance to its volume. Two main factors—temperature and salinity—combine to affect the density of ocean water, as shown below. As you can see, both decreasing the temperature of ocean water and increasing the water's salinity increase the water's density.

How Deep Currents Form

Decreasing Temperature In Earth's polar regions, cold air chills the water molecules at the ocean's surface, causing them to slow down and move closer together. This decreases the water's volume, making the water denser. The dense water sinks and eventually travels toward the equator as a deep current along the ocean floor.

Increasing Salinity Through Freezing *Salinity* is a measure of the amount of dissolved solids in a liquid. If the ocean water freezes at the surface, ice will float on top of water because ice is less dense than liquid water. The dissolved solids are squeezed out of the ice and enter the liquid water below the ice, increasing the salinity. Because this water contains more dissolved solids, its density also increases.

Increasing Salinity Through Evaporation Another way salinity increases is through evaporation of surface water, which removes water but leaves solids behind. This is especially common in warm climates. Increasing salinity through freezing or evaporation causes water to become denser and sink to the ocean floor, becoming a deep current.

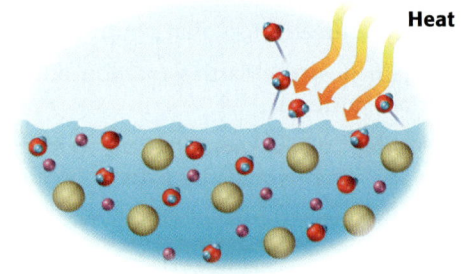

MISCONCEPTION ALERT

Remind students that molecules aren't made of little colored balls—the balls in the illustration on this page are models that represent molecules. The red and blue balls that are attached to one another represent water molecules, and the other balls represent dissolved solids.

Chapter 14 • The Movement of Ocean Water

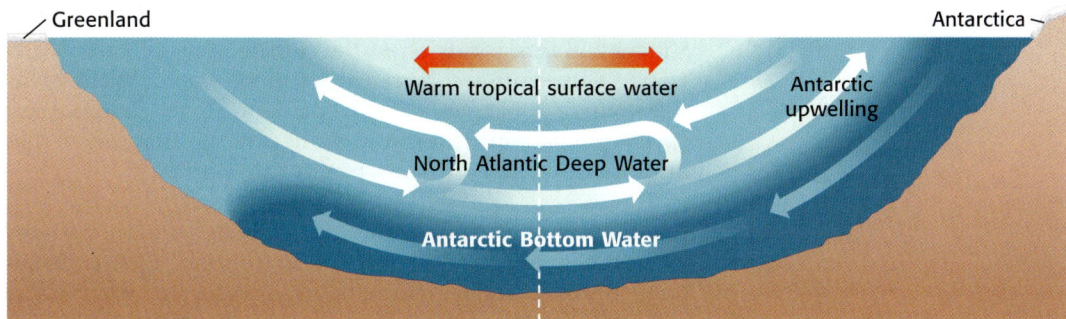

Movement of Deep Currents The movement of deep currents as they travel along the ocean floor is very complex. Differences in temperature and salinity, and therefore in density, cause variations in deep currents. For example, the deepest current, the Antarctic Bottom Water, is denser than the North Atlantic Deep Water. Both currents spread out across the ocean floor as they flow toward the same equatorial region. But when the currents meet, the North Atlantic Deep Water actually flows on top of the denser Antarctic Bottom Water, as shown in **Figure 6.** The Antarctic Bottom Water is so dense that it moves incredibly slowly—it takes 750 years for water in this current to make it from Antarctica's coastal waters to the equator!

Currents Trading Places Now that you understand how deep currents form and how they move along the ocean floor, you can learn how they trade places with surface currents. To see how this works, study **Figure 7.**

Figure 6 Less-dense water always flows on top of denser water, as shown in this cross section.

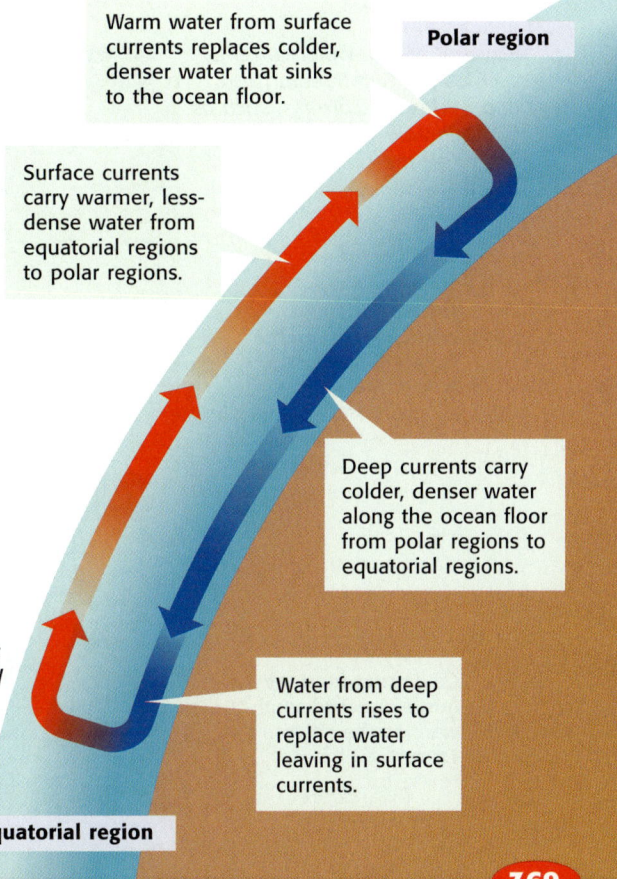

Figure 7 This cross section shows the movement of warm water and cold water between polar and equatorial regions.

USING THE FIGURE

Figure 6 and **Figure 7** may appear to contradict one another. Explain to students that **Figure 6** is a detailed diagram showing the interaction of specific currents, while **Figure 7** is a generalized description of a cycle involving deep currents and surface currents. Make sure students realize that colder water becomes warmer near the equator and that warmer water becomes colder near the poles.

CONNECT TO LIFE SCIENCE

Along some coastlines surface currents diverge, carrying water away from the shore. These flow patterns cause upwelling, the rise of colder deep water that contains many nutrients required by phytoplankton. Where the nutrients reach the surface waters, phytoplankton growth flourishes. Phytoplankton are food for many species of commercial fish. Upwelling is common near the equator and in many coastal zones, usually on the western margins of continents. Populations in these coastal areas depend on the fishing industry as a major source of income and food. Encourage interested students to find out about different species of commercial fish harvested off the western coasts of North and South America and how El Niño affects upwelling.

Homework

Graphing Have students select two pairs of cities on opposite sides of a continent. All the cities should be at approximately the same latitude. One city from each pair should be located on the coast, and the other for each pair should be less than 300 km inland. For example, they could choose San Francisco and Fresno, California, and Norfolk and Roanoke, Virginia. Have students find the average high and low temperatures for each city. Next, have students find the average ocean temperature at the coastal cities. Have students plot the temperatures on a bar graph. Ask students to explain how ocean temperature affects the climate of the coastal cities.

Teaching Transparency 158
"Circulation of Deep and Surface Currents"

Section 1 • Currents

3) Extend

CROSS-DISCIPLINARY FOCUS

History Early in American history, Benjamin Franklin noticed that mail ships took much longer to travel from England to America than from America to England. He then discovered that ships from England were sailing against the Gulf Stream. Franklin revolutionized ocean navigation by designing charts that helped sailors avoid sailing against major surface currents.

BRAIN FOOD

Hurricanes are large tropical storms that originate over large bodies of warm water, such as the Atlantic Ocean or the Caribbean Sea. Hurricanes are created when warm water builds storm clouds, resulting in a massive low-pressure cell. In North America, hurricanes generally make landfall on the East Coast of the United States or the Gulf of Mexico, and they have reached as far north as Maine. On the West Coast, a hurricane has never made landfall in California. Ask students:

Why does the California Current, shown in **Figure 8,** protect California from hurricanes? *(Because it is a cold-water current; the water off the coast of California is not warm enough to generate storm clouds or a low-pressure cell.)*

Surface Currents and Climate

Surface currents greatly affect the climate in many parts of the world. Some surface currents warm or cool coastal areas year-round. Other surface currents sometimes change their circulation pattern. This causes changes in the atmosphere that disrupt the climate in many parts of the world.

Currents That Stabilize Climate Although surface currents are generally much warmer than deep currents, their temperatures do vary. Surface currents are classified as warm-water currents or cold-water currents. Look back at Figure 5 to see where each type is located. Because they are warm or cold, surface currents affect the climate of the land near the area where they flow. For example, warm-water currents create warmer climates in coastal areas that would otherwise be much cooler. Likewise, cold-water currents create cooler climates in coastal areas that would otherwise be much warmer. **Figure 8** shows how a warm-water current and a cold-water current affect coastal climates.

Figure 8 Warm-water currents, such as the Gulf Stream (top), and cold-water currents, such as the California Current (bottom), can affect the climate of coastal regions.

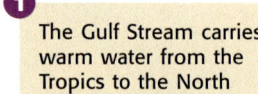

① The Gulf Stream carries warm water from the Tropics to the North Atlantic Ocean.

② The Gulf Stream flows to the British Isles. This creates a relatively mild climate for land at such a high latitude.

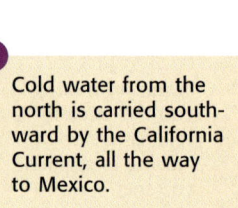
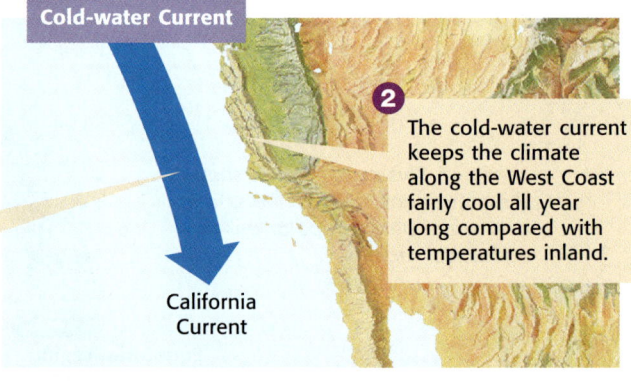

① Cold water from the north is carried southward by the California Current, all the way to Mexico.

② The cold-water current keeps the climate along the West Coast fairly cool all year long compared with temperatures inland.

MISCONCEPTION ALERT

El Niño is not a storm or any kind of weather pattern. It is a periodic change in the location of warm and cool surface waters in the Pacific Ocean. However, El Niño does ultimately cause local weather conditions to differ from typical conditions.

TOPIC: El Niño
GO TO: www.scilinks.org
*sci*LINKS NUMBER: HSTE335

Current Variations—El Niño The surface currents in the tropical region of the Pacific Ocean usually travel with the trade winds from east to west. This builds up warm water in the western Pacific and causes upwelling in the eastern Pacific. **Upwelling** is a process in which cold, nutrient-rich water from the deep ocean rises to the surface and replaces warm surface water. The warm water is blown out to sea by prevailing winds. But every 2 to 12 years, the South Pacific trade winds move less warm water to the western Pacific. As a result, surface water temperatures along the coast of South America rise. Gradually, this warming spreads westward. This periodic change in the location of warm and cool surface waters in the Pacific Ocean is called **El Niño.** El Niño not only affects surface waters but also changes the interaction between the ocean and the atmosphere, resulting in changes in global weather patterns.

BRAIN FOOD

El Niño means "The Child" in Spanish. The term originally referred to a warm current that arrived each year during the Christmas season off the coast of Ecuador and Peru.

Effects of El Niño El Niño alters weather patterns enough to cause disasters, such as flash floods and mudslides in areas of the world that normally receive little rain. **Figure 9** shows homes destroyed by a mudslide in Southern California. While some regions flood, regions that usually get a lot of rain may experience droughts, which can lead to crop failures.

Figure 9 *This damage in Southern California was the result of excessive rain caused by El Niño in 1997.*

REVIEW

1. How do temperature and salinity relate to deep-current movement?
2. Why is the climate in Scotland relatively mild even though the country is located at a high latitude?
3. **Applying Concepts** Many marine organisms depend on upwelling to bring nutrients to the surface. How might an El Niño affect Peruvians' way of life?

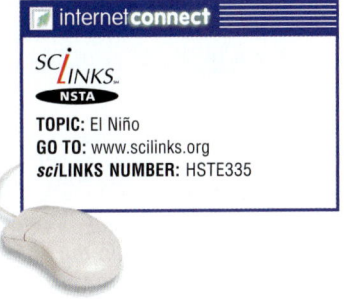

TOPIC: El Niño
GO TO: www.scilinks.org
*sci*LINKS NUMBER: HSTE335

SECTION 2

Focus

Waves

This section describes the characteristics of waves. Students will explore wave formation and movement. They will also learn how to identify different types of waves and measure different wave features. Finally, the section discusses dangerous movements of ocean water.

🔔 Bellringer

Illustrate the following scenario on the board or overhead projector:

You are floating in the ocean 1 km from shore, which is north of you. There is a surface current flowing east. Are you more likely to travel north with the waves toward the shore or east with the surface current? (east, because wave energy travels through the water but the water doesn't travel with the waves)

Tell students that Section 2 will help explain this answer.

1) Motivate

ACTIVITY

Arrange chairs in a long row, and have students sit in the chairs. Then have them stand and sit in succession to form a "human wave." Ask them to discuss and then demonstrate how the shape and motion of the wave could be changed. (Examples include standing and sitting more quickly to decrease the wave period or stretching their arms over their heads as they stand and bringing them down to their sides as they sit to increase the wave height.) **Sheltered English**

Section 2

Terms to Learn

crest
trough
wavelength
wave height
wave period
breaker
surf
whitecap
swells
tsunami
storm surge

What You'll Do

- Identify wave components, and explain how they relate to wave movement.
- Describe how ocean waves form and how they move.
- Classify types of waves.
- Analyze types of dangerous waves.

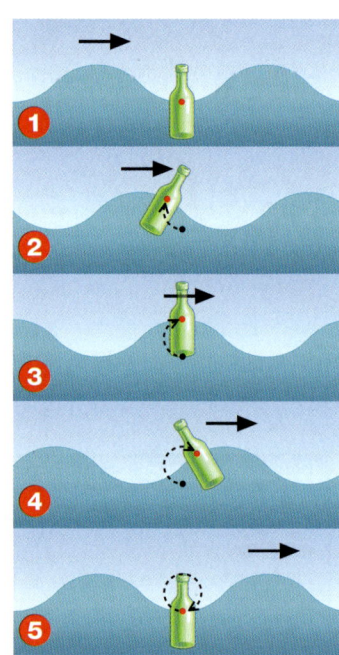

Figure 10 Like the bottle in this figure, water remains in the same place as waves travel through it.

Waves

We all know what ocean waves look like. Even if you've never been to the seashore, you've most likely seen waves on television. But what are ocean waves? How do they form and move? Are all waves the same? And what do they do besides drop shells and sand dollars on the beach? Let us examine ocean waves so that we can answer these questions.

Anatomy of a Wave

Waves are made up of two main components—crests and troughs. A **crest** is the highest point of a wave, and a **trough** is the lowest point. Imagine a thrilling roller coaster designed with many rises and dips. The top of a rise on a roller-coaster track is similar to the crest of a wave, and the bottom of a dip in the track resembles the trough of a wave. The distance between two adjacent wave crests or wave troughs is a **wavelength**. The vertical distance between a wave's crest and its trough is a **wave height**.

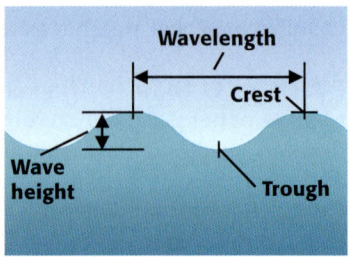

Wave Formation and Movement

If you have watched ocean waves before, you may have noticed that water appears to move across the ocean's surface. However, this movement is only an illusion. Most waves form as wind blows across the water's surface, transferring energy to the water. As the energy moves through the water, so do the waves. But the water itself stays behind, rising and falling in circular movements. Notice in **Figure 10** that the floating bottle remains in the same spot as the waves travel from left to right. The circle of moving water that the bottle moves with has a diameter that is equal to the height of the waves that created it. Underneath this circle are smaller circles of moving water. The diameters of these circles get smaller with depth because wave energy decreases with depth. Wave energy only reaches to a certain depth. Below that depth, the water is not affected by wave energy.

Draw this diagram to show students how the circular motion of water in waves decreases in size as depth increases.

Water below a depth equal to ½ the wavelength is not greatly affected by waves.

The diameter of this circle is equal to the wave height.

372   Chapter 14 • The Movement of Ocean Water

Specifics of Wave Movement

Waves not only come in different sizes but also travel at different speeds. To calculate wave speed, scientists must know the wavelength and the wave period. **Wave period** is the time between the passage of two wave crests (or troughs) at a fixed point, as shown in **Figure 11**. Dividing wavelength by wave period gives you wave speed, as shown below.

$$\frac{\text{wavelength (m)}}{\text{wave period (s)}} = \text{wave speed (m/s)}$$

For any given wavelength, an increase in the wave period will decrease the wave speed, and a decrease in the wave period will increase the wave speed.

MATH BREAK

Wave Speed

Imagine you are in a rowboat on the open ocean. You count 2 waves traveling right under your boat in 10 seconds. You estimate the wavelength to be 3 m. What is the wave speed?

Figure 11 *The illustration below shows how the wave period is determined.*

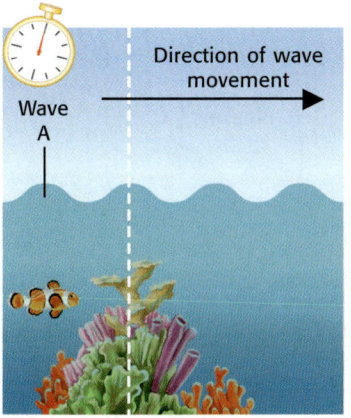
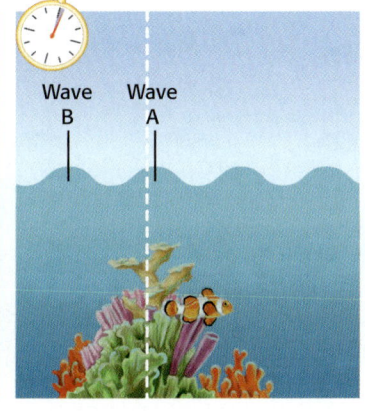
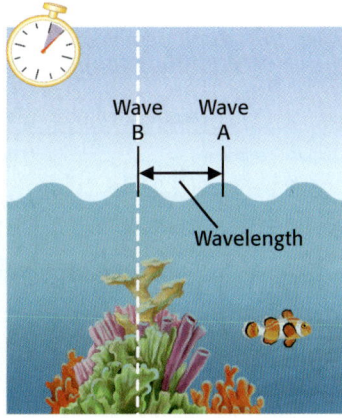

① Notice that the waves are moving from left to right.

② The clock begins running as Wave A passes the reef's peak.

③ The clock stops as Wave B passes the reef's peak. The time shown on the clock (5 seconds) represents the wave period.

Types of Waves

As you learned earlier in this section, wind forms most ocean waves. However, waves can form by other mechanisms. Underwater earthquakes and landslides as well as impacts by cosmic bodies can form different types of waves. The sizes of the different types of waves can vary, but most move the same way. Depending on their size and the angle at which they hit the shore, waves can generate a variety of near-shore events, some of which can be dangerous to humans.

internet connect

TOPIC: Ocean Waves
GO TO: www.scilinks.org
sciLINKS NUMBER: HSTE340

TOPIC: Tsunamis
GO TO: www.scilinks.org
sciLINKS NUMBER: HSTE345

2) Teach, continued

READING STRATEGY

Activity Have students reproduce **Figures 12** and **13** in their ScienceLog. As you read the section, pause at each term, and have them label the terms in their diagram. Make sure students understand each new term before proceeding.

`Sheltered English`

Ask the class why sighting a line of offshore breakers might cause sailors to consider turning their boats around. (As water becomes shallower, the wave height increases and the waves may break. Breaking waves could signal a submerged sandbar or reef; a ship could run aground if it encounters such an obstacle.)

REAL-WORLD CONNECTION

Discuss with students what they should do if they are ever caught in an undertow. Explain that instead of trying to swim against the current, they should signal for help and swim parallel to the shore. This will get them out of the undertow. They can then swim to shore. Diagram this scenario for students, and have them show you the proper direction to swim.

 **Teaching Transparency 160** "Deep-Water Waves Become Shallow-Water Waves"

Deep-Water Waves and Shallow-Water Waves Have you ever wondered why waves increase in height as they approach the shore? The answer has to do with the depth of the water. *Deep-water waves* are waves that move in water that is deeper than one-half of their wavelength. When the waves reach water that is shallower than one-half of their wavelength, they begin to interact with the ocean floor. These waves are called *shallow-water waves*. **Figure 12** shows how deep-water waves become shallow-water waves as they move toward the shore.

As deep-water waves become shallow-water waves, the water particles slow down and build up. This forces more water between wave crests and increases wave height. Gravity eventually pulls the high wave crests down, causing them to crash into the ocean floor as **breakers.** The area where waves first begin to tumble downward, or break, is called the *breaker zone*. Waves continue to break as they move from the breaker zone to the shore. The area between the breaker zone and the shore is called the **surf.**

Figure 12 Deep-water waves become shallow-water waves when they reach depths of less than half of their wavelength.

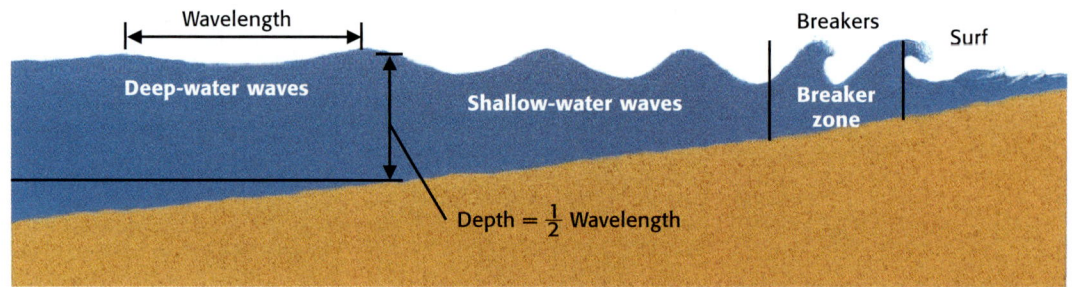

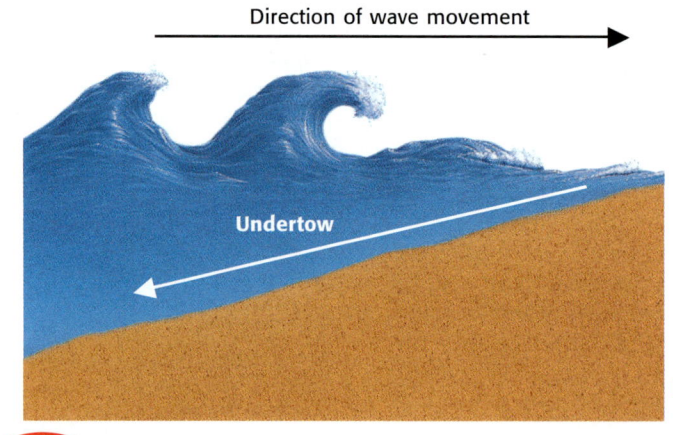

When waves crash on the beach head-on, the water they moved through flows back to the ocean underneath new incoming waves. This movement of water, which carries sand, rock particles, and plankton away from the shore, is called an *undertow*. **Figure 13** illustrates the back-and-forth movement of water at the shore.

Figure 13 Head-on waves create an undertow.

Q: What do two oceans say when they meet?

A: long time no sea

374   Chapter 14 • The Movement of Ocean Water

When waves hit the shore at an angle, they cause water to move along the shore in a current called a *longshore current*. This process is shown in **Figure 14.** Longshore currents are responsible for most sediment transport in beach environments. This movement of sand and other sediment both tears down and builds up the coastline. Unfortunately, longshore currents also carry trash and other types of ocean pollution, spreading it along the shore.

Open-Ocean Waves Sometimes waves called whitecaps form in the open ocean. **Whitecaps** are white, foaming waves with very steep crests that break in the open ocean before the waves get close to the shore. These waves usually form during stormy weather, and they are usually short-lived. Calmer winds form waves called swells. **Swells** are rolling waves that move in a steady procession across the ocean. Swells have longer wavelengths than whitecaps and can travel for thousands of kilometers. **Figure 15** shows how whitecaps and swells differ.

Figure 14 *Longshore currents form where waves approach beaches at an angle.*

Figure 15 *Whitecaps, shown in the photo at left, break in the open ocean, while swells, shown in the photo at right, roll gently in the open ocean.*

MATH and MORE

Whitecaps are usually caused by strong winds. When the wind blows more than 13 km/h, wave height increases faster than wavelength. When wave height is more than one-seventh of the wavelength, whitecaps form. If the wavelength is 3 m, what is the minimum wave height for whitecaps to form? **(about 43 cm)**

If the wavelength is 10 m, what is the minimum wave height for whitecaps to form? **(about 1.43 m)**

If whitecaps begin to form when the wave height reaches 4 m, what is the wavelength? **(about 28 m)**

Math Skills Worksheet 11 "What Is a Fraction?"

Homework

Writing Surfing originated in the South Seas about 2,500 years ago. Polynesian sailors who couldn't get their boats through the rough waves near the shore would surf to land. It is now a recreational sport practiced all over the world.

Have students write a report about the history of surfing. Their report should include an explanation of the characteristics that make specific locations around the world ideal for the sport.

CONNECT TO ENVIRONMENTAL SCIENCE

Beach nourishment involves dredging enormous amounts of sand from the ocean floor and pumping it back onto the shoreline, rebuilding beaches that have been eroded by long-shore currents. It is a common, but controversial, practice along the Atlantic Coast. Some people think the natural erosion of beaches should not be disrupted. Beach erosion is influenced by other human activities, however. For example, artificial dams prevent sediment from reaching protective barrier islands and the dredging of ship channels disrupts the natural movement of sediment along the coast. Encourage students to investigate this issue and form their own opinions.

③ Extend

CONNECT TO METEOROLOGY

The sciences of oceanography and meteorology are combined in the duties of the National Oceanic and Atmospheric Administration (NOAA). Founded in 1970, this federal agency forecasts weather and monitors potentially destructive natural events, such as hurricanes, floods, and tsunamis. Interested students can write to NOAA or visit their Web site for more information.

GOING FURTHER

 Writing Have students research a tsunami that occurred in recent history and write a brief newspaper-style article about it. The articles should explain the cause and effects of the tsunami. Students could learn about the tsunami that struck the Pacific coast of Nicaragua in 1992 or the one that devastated Papua New Guinea in 1998. Encourage students to read their articles to the class.

Answers to QuickLab

4. Answers will vary. As wave energy passed through the rope, the ribbon moved up and down, but it did not move closer to the doorknob. Similarly, wave energy passes through water, moving it up and down, but it does not transport water.

6. Answers will vary. The wave height increased, but wavelength decreased; more waves occurred along the same length of rope.

Do the Wave

1. Tie one end of a thin piece of **rope** to a doorknob.
2. Tie a **ribbon** around the rope halfway between the doorknob and the other end of the rope.
3. Holding the rope at the untied end, quickly move the rope up and down, and observe the ribbon.
4. How does the movement of the rope and ribbon relate to the movement of water and deep-water waves?
5. Repeat step 3, but move the rope higher and lower this time.
6. How does this affect the waves in the rope?

TRY at HOME

Tsunamis Professional surfers often travel to Hawaii to catch some of the highest waves in the world. But even the best surfers would not be able to handle a tsunami. **Tsunamis** are waves that form when a large volume of ocean water is suddenly moved up or down. This movement can be caused by underwater earthquakes, volcanic eruptions, landslides, underwater explosions, or the impact of a meteorite or comet. The majority of tsunamis occur in the Pacific Ocean because of the greater number of earthquakes in that region. **Figure 16** shows how an earthquake can generate a tsunami.

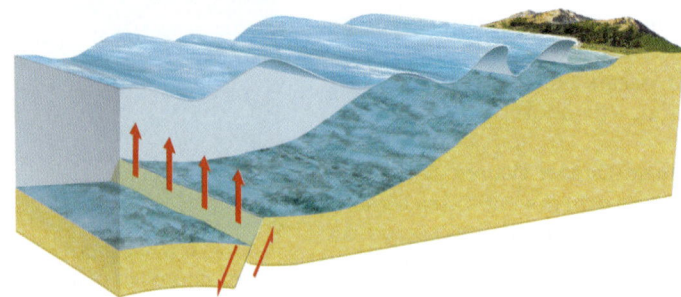

Figure 16 An upward shift in the ocean floor creates an earthquake. The energy released by the earthquake pushes a large volume of water upward, creating a series of tsunamis.

When tsunamis near continents, they slow down and their wavelengths shorten as they interact with the ocean floor. As tsunamis get closer together, their wave height increases. Tsunamis can reach more than 30 m in height as they slam into the coast, destroying just about everything in their path. The powerful undertow created by a tsunami can be as destructive as the tsunami itself. **Figure 17** shows a coastal community devastated by a tsunami.

Figure 17 Imagine the strength of the tsunami that carried this boat so far inland!

WEIRD SCIENCE

In 1946, the crew of a freighter anchored offshore near Hilo, Hawaii, were astounded to witness an enormous tsunami crash on the shore, crushing buildings, felling trees, and carrying boats, piers, and rocks ashore. Moments before, the wave had passed beneath the freighter unnoticed!

IS THAT A FACT!

The highest recorded tsunami was 64 m (210 ft) high; it struck Kamchatka, Siberia, in 1737.

Timing a Tsunami

On May 22, 1960, an earthquake off the coast of South America generated a tsunami that completely crossed the Pacific Ocean. Ten thousand kilometers away from the origin of the earthquake, the tsunami hit the city of Hilo on the coast of Hawaii, causing extensive damage.

If the tsunami traveled at a speed of 188 m/s, how long after the earthquake occurred did the tsunami reach Hilo? If the residents of Hilo heard about the earthquake as soon as it happened, do you think they had enough warning time? What might be done to ensure that this amount of time would be sufficient warning for a tsunami?

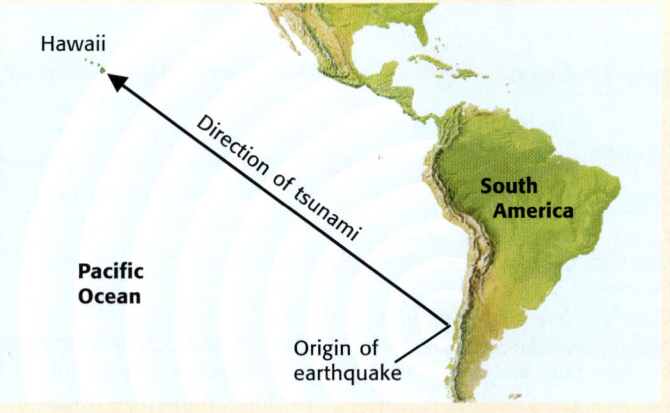

Storm Surges

A **storm surge** is a local rise in sea level near the shore that is caused by strong winds from a storm, such as a hurricane. Winds form a storm surge by blowing water into a big pile under the storm. As the storm moves onto shore, so does the giant mass of water beneath it. Storm surges often disappear as quickly as they form, making them difficult to study. Storm surges contain a lot of energy and can reach about 8 m in height. This often makes them the most destructive part of hurricanes.

REVIEW

1. Explain how water moves as waves travel through it.
2. Where do deep-water waves become shallow-water waves?
3. Name five events that can cause a tsunami.
4. **Doing Calculations** Look again at Figure 11. If the wave speed is 0.8 m/s, what is the wavelength?

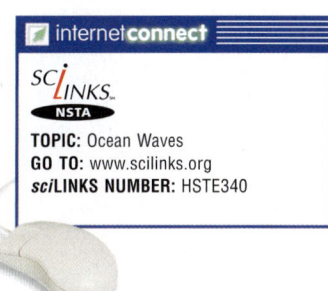

TOPIC: Ocean Waves
GO TO: www.scilinks.org
*sci*LINKS NUMBER: HSTE340

SECTION 3

Focus

Tides

The gravitational attraction of the moon and the sun creates tides on Earth. Students will learn how the position of Earth in relation to the moon and the sun creates different kinds of tides. They will also learn about the effects of coastal topography on tidewaters.

🔔 Bellringer

Measure 0.75 m toward the ceiling from a spot in the center of a wall, and mark this point with a piece of tape. Beside the measurement, write "average high tide." Then measure 0.75 m below the center spot, and label it "average low tide." Ask students, "What do you think is the greatest tidal range in the world?"

After students have guessed, tell them that the world's greatest tidal range occurs in the Bay of Fundy, between Nova Scotia and Maine. There, the tidal range can be more than 15 m. Be prepared to show students how high 15 m (or 10 times the example on the wall) is.

1 Motivate

ACTIVITY

If possible, plan a visit to a coastal area. Beforehand, have the class research intertidal zones and the organisms that inhabit these areas. If a visit to the coast is not possible, have students research intertidal organisms and their survival strategies and share their findings with the class.

Section 3

Terms to Learn

tides
tidal range
spring tides
neap tides

What You'll Do

◆ Explain tides and their relationship with the Earth, the sun, and the moon.
◆ Classify different types of tides.
◆ Analyze the relationship between tides and coastal land.

Tides

You haved learned how winds and earthquakes can move ocean water. But there are less-obvious forces that continually move ocean water in regular patterns called tides. **Tides** are daily movements of ocean water that change the level of the ocean's surface. Tides are influenced by the sun and the moon, and they occur in a variety of cycles.

The Lure of the Moon

The phases of the moon and their relationship to the tides were first discovered more than 2,000 years ago by a Greek explorer named Pytheas. But Pytheas and other early investigators could not explain the relationship. A scientific explanation was not given until 1687, when Sir Isaac Newton's theories on the principle of gravitational pull were published. The gravity of the moon pulls on every particle of the Earth, but the pull is much more noticeable in liquids than in solids. This is because liquids move more easily. Even the liquid in an open soft drink is slightly pulled by the moon's gravity.

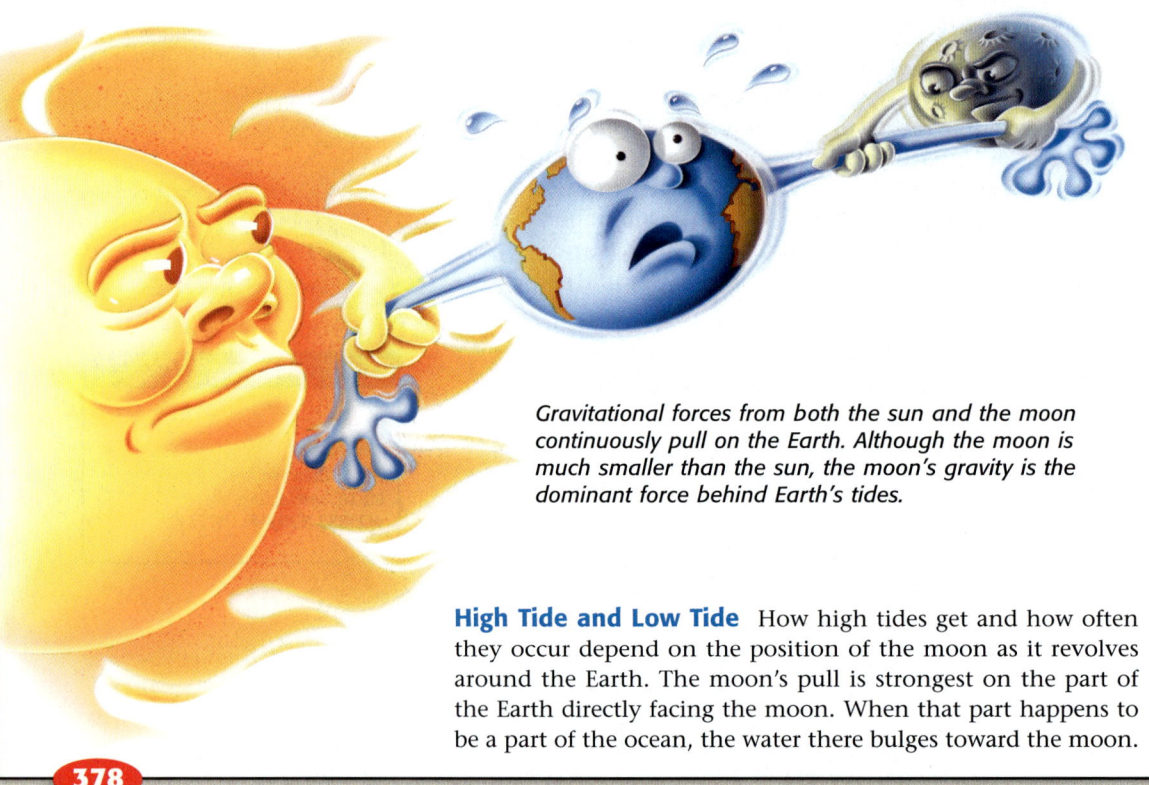

Gravitational forces from both the sun and the moon continuously pull on the Earth. Although the moon is much smaller than the sun, the moon's gravity is the dominant force behind Earth's tides.

High Tide and Low Tide How high tides get and how often they occur depend on the position of the moon as it revolves around the Earth. The moon's pull is strongest on the part of the Earth directly facing the moon. When that part happens to be a part of the ocean, the water there bulges toward the moon.

MISCONCEPTION ALERT

Students may think that water flows horizontally toward or away from the shore due to tides. As students read this section, make sure they understand that low tide occurs in an area because the water is actually pulled away from the area. This decreases the volume of water in that location and causes the water level to lower and the shoreline to move seaward.

378   Chapter 14 • The Movement of Ocean Water

At the same time, water on the opposite side of the Earth bulges due to the motion of the Earth and the moon around each other. These bulges are called *high tides*. Notice in **Figure 18** how the position of the moon causes the water to bulge. Also notice that when high tides occur, water is drawn away from the area between the high tides, causing *low tides* to form.

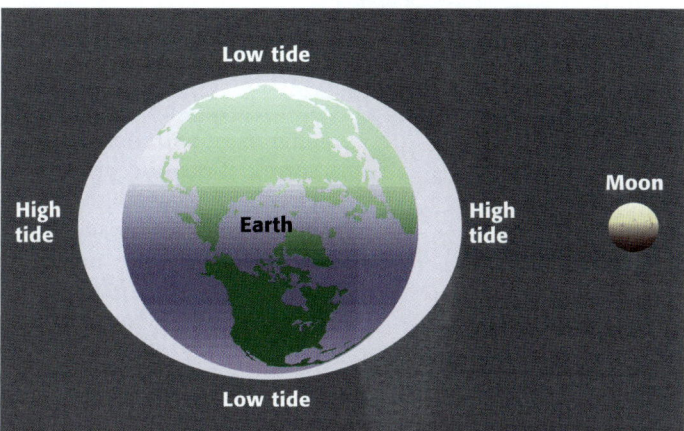

Figure 18 *High tide occurs on the part of Earth that is closest to the moon. At the same time, high tide also occurs on the opposite side of Earth.*

Timing the Tides The rotation of the Earth and the moon's revolution around the Earth determine when tides occur. If the Earth rotated at the same speed that the moon revolves around the Earth, tides would continuously occur at the same spots on Earth. But the moon revolves around the Earth much more slowly than the Earth rotates. **Figure 19** shows that it takes 24 hours and 50 minutes for a spot on Earth that is facing the moon to rotate so that it is facing the moon again.

 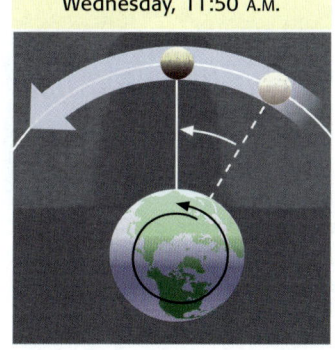

Figure 19 *Tides occur at different spots on Earth because the Earth rotates more quickly than the moon revolves around the Earth.*

Puzzled about why high tide also occurs on the side of the Earth opposite the moon? Turn to page 686 to see how you can find out for yourself.

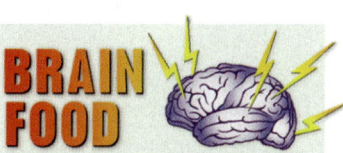

Even dry land has tides. For example, the land in Oklahoma moves up and down several centimeters throughout the day, corresponding with the tides. Tides on the solid part of Earth's surface are usually about one-third the size of ocean tides.

SCIENTISTS AT ODDS

The cause of tides was a hotly debated topic in the sixteenth and seventeenth centuries. Galileo suggested that there was a connection between tides and the Earth's motion. To Galileo, tides proved beyond all doubt that Earth was moving. He argued that because Earth's waters are moving, Earth must be moving too. Johannes Kepler, another prominent scientist of the time, argued that the tides were linked to the moon's phases. Galileo made such a convincing argument that Kepler's ideas were dismissed. It was not until after Newton that scientists accepted that the gravitational forces exerted by the moon and the sun as well as the Earth's rotation are responsible for the tides.

3) Extend

MEETING INDIVIDUAL NEEDS

Learners Having Difficulty Use this demonstration to show how tides are caused.

1. Use a small ball to represent the moon, a globe to represent Earth, and a large ball to represent the sun.
2. Ask a volunteer to help you show how the moon and Earth revolve around the sun.
3. Remind students that the moon and the sun are both "pulling" on Earth.
4. Point out that the moon's "pull" is greater than the sun's. Regions on Earth that are in a straight line from the moon experience high tides.
5. Point out that regions on Earth that face 90° away from the moon experience low tides.

Have students repeat the demonstration for each other to strengthen their understanding. Then ask students to read the text that explains spring tides and neap tides. Challenge students to use the globe and balls to demonstrate how spring tides and neap tides are caused.

Sheltered English

Homework

Graphing Help students look in the newspaper or on the Internet to find daily tidal information for a certain area for 1 month. Record the high- and low-tide measurements on a large chart that can be displayed in the classroom. At the end of the month, determine when spring tide and neap tide occurred. Compare these dates with the full, new, and quarter moon dates on a calendar, and have students graph this data to explain why the dates correspond.

Tidal Variations

The sun also affects tides. The sun is much larger than the moon, but it is also much farther away. As a result, the sun's influence on tides is less powerful than the moon's influence. The combined forces of the sun and the moon on the Earth result in tidal ranges that vary based on the positions of all three bodies. A **tidal range** is the difference between levels of ocean water at high tide and low tide.

Spring Tides When the sun, Earth, and moon are in alignment with one another, spring tides occur. **Spring tides** are tides with maximum daily tidal range that occur during the new and full moons. Spring tides occur every 14 days. The first time spring tides occur is when the moon is between the sun and Earth. The second time spring tides occur is when the moon and the sun are on opposite sides of the Earth. **Figure 20** shows the positions of the sun and moon during spring tides.

Figure 20 During spring tides, the gravitational forces of the sun and moon pull on the Earth either from the same direction (left) or from opposite directions (right).

Neap Tides When the sun, Earth, and moon form a 90° angle, neap tides occur. **Neap tides** are tides with minimum daily tidal range that occur during the first and third quarters of the moon. Neap tides occur halfway between the occurrence of spring tides. When neap tides occur, the gravitational forces on the Earth by the sun and the moon work against each other. **Figure 21** shows the positions of the sun and moon during neap tides.

Figure 21 During neap tides, the sun and moon are at right angles with respect to the Earth. This arrangement minimizes their gravitational effect on the Earth.

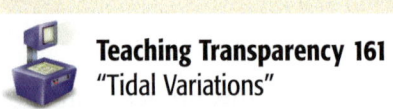

Teaching Transparency 161 "Tidal Variations"

TOPIC: The Tides
GO TO: www.scilinks.org
sciLINKS NUMBER: HSTE350

The moon also creates tides in our atmosphere called lunar winds. Lunar winds move eastward in the morning and westward in the evening. Although these tides travel only 0.08 km/h, they can be detected by studying slight fluctuations in weather patterns.

Tides and Topography

Tides can be accurately predicted once the tidal range has been measured at a certain point over a period of time. This information can be useful for people who live near or visit the coast, as illustrated in **Figure 22.**

Figure 22 *It's a good thing the people on the beach (left) knew when high tide occurred (right). These photos show the Bay of Fundy, in New Brunswick, Canada. The Bay of Fundy has the greatest tidal range on Earth.*

In some coastal areas with narrow inlets, movements of water called tidal bores occur. A *tidal bore* is a body of water that rushes up through a narrow bay, estuary, or river channel during the rise of high tide, causing a very sudden tidal rise. Sometimes tidal bores form waves that rush up the inlets. Tidal bores occur in coastal areas of China, the British Isles, France, and Canada.

REVIEW

1. How does the position of the moon relate to the position of high tides?
2. Which tides have minimum tidal range? Which tides have maximum tidal range?
3. What causes tidal bores?
4. **Applying Concepts** How many days pass between minimum and maximum tidal range in any given area? Explain.

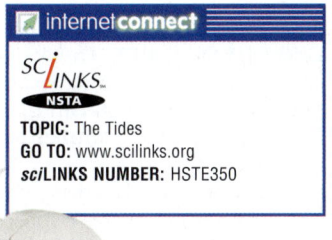

TOPIC: The Tides
GO TO: www.scilinks.org
sciLINKS NUMBER: HSTE350

Chapter Highlights

VOCABULARY DEFINITIONS

SECTION 1

surface current a streamlike movement of water that occurs at or near the surface of the ocean

Coriolis effect the curving of moving objects from a straight path due to the Earth's rotation

deep current a streamlike movement of ocean water far below the surface

upwelling a process in which cold, nutrient-rich water from the deep ocean rises to the surface and replaces warm surface water

El Niño periodic change in the location of warm and cool surface waters in the Pacific Ocean

SECTION 2

crest the highest point of a wave

trough the lowest point of a wave

wavelength the distance between two adjacent wave crests or wave troughs

wave height the vertical distance between a wave's crest and its trough

wave period the time it takes for two wave crests (or troughs) to pass a fixed point

breaker a heightened water wave that begins to tumble downward, or break, upon nearing the shore

Chapter Highlights

SECTION 1

Vocabulary
- surface current (p. 365)
- Coriolis effect (p. 366)
- deep current (p. 368)
- upwelling (p. 371)
- El Niño (p. 371)

Section Notes
- Currents are classified as surface currents and deep currents.
- Surface currents are controlled by three factors: global winds, the Coriolis effect, and continental deflections.
- Surface currents, such as the Gulf Stream, can be several thousand kilometers in length.
- Deep currents form where the density of ocean water increases. Water density depends on temperature and salinity.
- Surface currents affect the climate of the land near which they flow.

Labs
Up from the Depths (p. 684)

SECTION 2

Vocabulary
- crest (p. 372)
- trough (p. 372)
- wavelength (p. 372)
- wave height (p. 372)
- wave period (p. 373)
- breaker (p. 374)
- surf (p. 374)
- whitecap (p. 375)
- swells (p. 375)
- tsunami (p. 376)
- storm surge (p. 377)

Section Notes
- Waves are made up of two main components—crests and troughs.
- Waves are usually created by the transfer of the wind's energy across the surface of the ocean.

✓ Skills Check

Math Concepts

TWO OUT OF THREE The wave equation on page 373 has three variables. If you know two of these variables, you can figure out the third. Take a look at the examples below.

1. wave speed = 0.6 m/s, wave period = 10 s
   wavelength = wave speed × wave period
   = 6 m

2. wave speed = 0.6 m/s, wavelength = 6 m
   wave period = $\dfrac{\text{wavelength}}{\text{wave speed}}$ = 10 s

Visual Understanding

BREAKING WAVES Before shallow-water waves break, their wave height increases and their wavelength decreases. Look at Figure 12 on page 374 again. Notice that the waves are taller and that their crests are closer together near the breaker zone.

Lab and Activity Highlights

Up from the Depths `PG 684`

Turning the Tides `PG 686`

 **Datasheets for LabBook** (blackline masters for these labs)

SECTION 2

- Waves travel through water near the water's surface, while the water itself rises and falls in circular movements.
- Waves travel in the direction the wind blows. If the wind blows over a long distance, the wavelength becomes very large and the waves travel quickly.
- Wind-generated waves are classified as deep-water and shallow-water waves.
- Tsunamis are dangerous waves that can be very destructive to coastal communities.

SECTION 3

Vocabulary
tides (p. 378)
tidal range (p. 380)
spring tides (p. 380)
neap tides (p. 380)

Section Notes
- Tides are caused by the gravitational forces of the moon and sun tugging on the Earth.
- The moon's gravity is the main force behind tides.

- The relative positions of the sun and moon with respect to Earth cause different tidal ranges.
- Maximum tidal range occurs during spring tides.
- Minimum tidal range occurs during neap tides.
- Tidal bores occur as high tide rises in narrow coastal inlets.

Labs
Turning the Tides (p. 686)

VOCABULARY DEFINITIONS, continued

surf the area between the breaker zone and the shore

whitecap a white, foaming wave with a very steep crest that breaks in the open ocean before the wave gets close to the shore

swells rolling waves that move in a steady procession across the ocean

tsunami a wave that forms when a large volume of ocean water is suddenly moved up or down

storm surge a local rise in sea level near the shore that is caused by strong winds from a storm, such as a hurricane

SECTION 3

tides daily movements of ocean water that change the level of the ocean's surface

tidal range the difference between levels of ocean water at high tide and low tide

spring tides tides with maximum daily tidal range that occur during the new and full moons

neap tides tides with minimum daily tidal range that occur during the first and third quarters of the moon

Vocabulary Review Worksheet 14

Blackline masters of these Chapter Highlights can be found in the **Study Guide.**

---

internet connect

GO TO: go.hrw.com

Visit the **HRW** Web site for a variety of learning tools related to this chapter. Just type in the keyword:

KEYWORD: HSTH2O

GO TO: www.scilinks.org

Visit the **National Science Teachers Association** on-line Web site for Internet resources related to this chapter. Just type in the sciLINKS number for more information about the topic:

TOPIC: Ocean Currents	sciLINKS NUMBER: HSTE330
TOPIC: El Niño	sciLINKS NUMBER: HSTE335
TOPIC: Ocean Waves	sciLINKS NUMBER: HSTE340
TOPIC: Tsunamis	sciLINKS NUMBER: HSTE345
TOPIC: The Tides	sciLINKS NUMBER: HSTE350

Lab and Activity Highlights

LabBank

Whiz-Bang Demonstrations, Spin Cycle, Demo 26

Long-Term Projects & Research Ideas, An Ocean Commotion, Project 42

Interactive Explorations CD-ROM

CD 3, Exploration 4, "Latitude Attitude"

Chapter 14 • Chapter Highlights

Chapter Review

USING VOCABULARY

For each pair of terms, explain the difference in their meaning.

1. wavelength/wave height
2. whitecap/swell
3. tsunami/storm surge
4. spring tide/neap tide

Replace the incorrect term in each of the following sentences with the correct term provided in the word bank below:

5. Deep currents are directly controlled by wind.
6. The Coriolis effect reduces upwelling along the coast of South America.
7. Neap tides occur when the moon is between the Earth and the sun.
8. A tidal bore is the difference between levels of ocean water at high tide and low tide.

Word bank: breakers, spring tides, tsunamis, surface currents, tidal range, El Niño.

UNDERSTANDING CONCEPTS

Multiple Choice

9. Surface currents are formed by
   a. the moon's gravity.
   b. the sun's gravity.
   c. wind.
   d. increased water density.

10. Deep currents form when
    a. cold air decreases water density.
    b. warm air increases water density.
    c. the ocean surface freezes and solids from the water underneath are removed.
    d. salinity increases.

11. When waves come near the shore,
    a. they speed up.
    b. they maintain their speed.
    c. their wavelength increases.
    d. their wave height increases.

12. Longshore currents transport sediment
    a. out to the open ocean.
    b. along the shore.
    c. during low tide only.
    d. during high tide only.

13. Whitecaps break
    a. in the surf.
    b. in the breaker zone.
    c. in the open ocean.
    d. as their wavelength increases.

14. Tidal range is greatest during
    a. spring tide.
    b. neap tide.
    c. a tidal bore.
    d. the day only.

384

 Concept Mapping Transparency 14

 Blackline masters of this Chapter Review can be found in the **Study Guide.**

Short Answer

15. Explain the relationship between upwelling and El Niño.

16. Explain what happens when the North Atlantic Deep Water meets the Antarctic Bottom Water.

17. Describe the relative positions of the Earth, the moon, and the sun during neap tide. Where do high tide and low tide occur during this time?

18. Explain the difference between the breaker zone and the surf.

Concept Mapping

19. Use the following terms to create a concept map: wind, deep currents, sun's gravity, types of ocean-water movement, surface currents, tides, increasing water density, waves, moon's gravity.

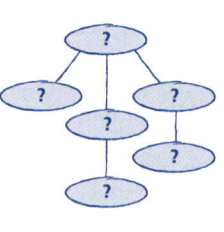

CRITICAL THINKING AND PROBLEM SOLVING

Write one or two sentences to answer the following questions:

20. What would happen to surface currents if the Earth reversed its rotation? Be specific.

21. How would you explain a bottle moving across the water in the same direction the waves are traveling?

22. You and a friend are planning a fishing trip to the ocean. Your friend tells you that the fish bite more in his secret fishing spot during low tide. If low tide occurred at the spot at 7 A.M. today and you are going to fish there in one week, at what time will low tide occur in that spot?

MATH IN SCIENCE

23. If a barrier island that is 1 km wide and 10 km long loses 1.5 m of its width per year to erosion by longshore current, how long will it take for the island to lose one-fourth of its width?

INTERPRETING GRAPHICS

Study the diagram below, and answer the questions that follow.

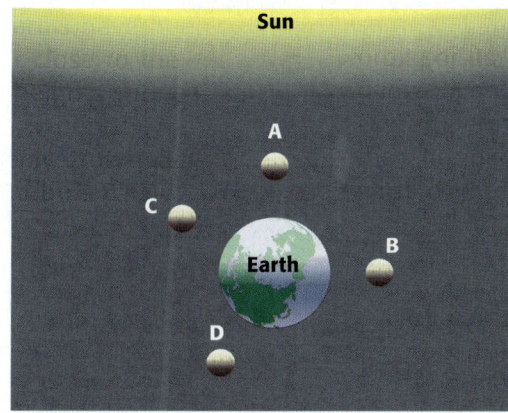

24. At which position (**A, B, C,** or **D**) would the moon be during a neap tide?

25. At which position (**A, B, C,** or **D**) would the moon be during a spring tide?

26. Would tidal range be greater with the moon at position **C** or position **D**? Why?

Take a minute to review your answers to the Pre-Reading Questions found at the bottom of page 362. Have your answers changed? If necessary, revise your answers based on what you have learned since you began this chapter.

Short Answer

15. When El Niño occurs, warm surface water remains along the Pacific coast of South America. This prevents upwelling from occurring along the coast.

16. The North Atlantic Deep Water flows on top of the Antarctic Bottom Water.

17. During neap tide, the sun, the moon, and the Earth form a right angle, with the Earth in the middle. High tide occurs on the side of the Earth facing the moon and on the side opposite the moon. Low tide occurs on the side of the Earth facing the sun and on the side opposite the sun.

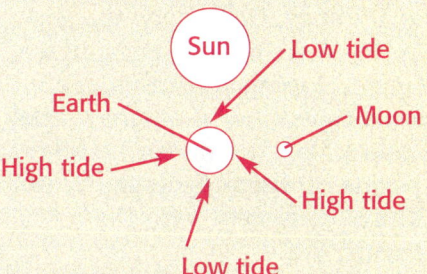

18. The breaker zone is where waves first begin to tumble downward. The surf is the zone between the breaker zone and the shore. In the surf, water moves toward the shore.

Concept Mapping

19. An answer to this exercise can be found at the end of this book.

CRITICAL THINKING AND PROBLEM SOLVING

20. Surface currents in the Northern Hemisphere would rotate counterclockwise, and surface currents in the Southern Hemisphere would rotate clockwise.

21. There would have to be a surface current moving in the same direction as the waves are traveling.

22. 12:50 P.M. (1:15 A.M. is also acceptable.)

MATH IN SCIENCE

23. about 167 years

INTERPRETING GRAPHICS

24. B
25. A
26. D; when the Earth-moon system is viewed from above the Earth's North Pole, the path of the moon around the Earth appears counterclockwise. In this case, the moon would be very near a spring-tide position at position D and very near a neap-tide position at position C.

CAREERS

Seismologist–Hiroo Kanamori

Background

Seismologists study earthquakes. Then why don't we call them earthquake-ologists? Well, the word *seismology* comes from the Greek language, and in Greek, *seismos* means "to shake"!

Dr. Kanamori recently received the Bucher Medal for his outstanding achievements in seismology. He bridged the gap between seismology and physics by developing an earthquake scale called the "moment magnitude scale." It rates earthquakes by the minimum energy released and is consistent with the Richter scale.

CAREERS

SEISMOLOGIST

As a seismologist, **Hiroo Kanamori** studies how earthquakes occur and tries to reduce their impact on our society. He also analyzes the effects of earthquakes on oceans and how earthquakes cause tsunamis (tsoo NAH mes). He has discovered that even weak earthquakes can create tsunamis.

Because most tsunamis are caused by underwater earthquakes, scientists can monitor earthquakes to predict when and where a tsunami will hit land. But the predictions are not always accurate. Very weak earthquakes should not create powerful tsunamis, yet they do. Kanamori calls these special events *tsunami earthquakes,* and he has learned how to predict the size of the resulting tsunamis.

A tsunami can be more dangerous than an earthquake. When people feel the tremors created when the plates slide, they don't always realize that a large tsunami may be on the way. Because of this, people don't expect a tsunami and don't leave the area.

Measuring Tsunami Earthquakes

As tectonic plates grind against each other, they send out seismic waves. These waves travel through the earth's crust and can be recorded by a sensitive machine. But when the plates grind very slowly, only long period seismic waves are recorded. When Kanamori sees a long period wave, he knows that a tsunami will form.

"The speed of the average tsunami is about 800 km/h, which is much slower than the speed of the long period waves at 15,000 km/h. So these special seismic waves arrive at distant recording stations much earlier than a tsunami," explains Kanamori. This important fact lets scientists like Kanamori warn people in the tsunami's path so they can leave the area.

An Interesting Career

Kanamori finds his work very rewarding. "It is always good to see how what we learned in the classroom can solve our real-life problems," he explains. "We can see how physics and mathematics work to explain seemingly complex natural events, such as earthquakes, volcanoes, and tsunamis."

A Challenge

▶ The depth of an ocean influences how fast a tsunami travels. To investigate, fill a 0.5 m long tub with 5 cm of water. Tap the tub. How long does it take for the wave to go back and forth? Add more water, and tap it again. Did the wave move faster or slower?

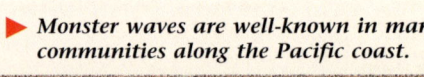

▶ *Monster waves are well-known in many communities along the Pacific coast.*

Answers to A Challenge

The wave moves faster as the water gets deeper. Ask students what happens to the speed of a tsunami wave as it approaches a shoreline. (The tsunami wave slows down as it approaches the shoreline.) Point out that as a tsunami wave slows down, it becomes taller.

Health Watch
Red Tides

Imagine going to the beach only to find that the ocean water has turned red and fish are floating belly up all over the place. This is not an imaginary scene. It really happens. What could cause such widespread damage to the ocean? Single-cell algae, that's what!

Blooming Algae

When certain algae grow rapidly, they clump together on the ocean's surface in an algal bloom that changes the color of the water. People called these algal blooms red tides because the blooms often turned the water red or reddish-brown. They also believed that tidal conditions caused the blooms. Scientists now call these algae explosions harmful algal blooms (HABs) because HABs are not always red, and they are not directly related to tides. The blooms are harmful because certain species of algae produce toxins that can poison fish, shellfish, and people.

Scientists also have learned that the ocean's natural currents may carry HABs hundreds of miles along a coastline. For example, in 1987, the Gulf Stream off the Atlantic coast of Florida carried a toxic bloom up the coast to North Carolina.

▲ *Harmful algal blooms are caused by algae like the one shown above right.*

Troublesome Toxins

Some people who ate tainted shellfish from the North Carolina coast in 1987 suffered from muscular aches, anxiety, sweating, dizziness, diarrhea, vomiting, and abdominal pain. Some algae toxins can even kill people who eat the tainted seafood. Another HAB occurred in 1987 in Nova Scotia, Canada. Four people died from eating contaminated shellfish, and another 150 people suffered from symptoms such as dizziness, headaches, seizures, short-term memory loss, and comas.

In the 1990s, Texas, Maryland, Alaska, and many other coastal states experienced HABs. However, the problem is not confined to North America. Throughout the 1990s, HABs caused health problems in South Africa, Argentina, India, New Zealand, and France.

No Signs to Read

Fish and shellfish are major sources of protein for people all over the world. Unfortunately, there are no outward signs when seafood is contaminated. The toxins don't change the flavor, and cooking the seafood doesn't eliminate the toxins. Sometimes a HAB rides into an area on an ocean current, causing fish to die and people to become ill before authorities are aware of the problem.

Fortunately, scientists all over the world are working on ways to monitor and even predict HABs. As a result, people eventually may be able to eat fish and shellfish without worrying about toxic algae.

Find Out More

▶ Some people think that human activities are causing more HABs than occurred in the past. Other people disagree. Find out more about this issue, and have a class debate about the role humans play in creating HABs.

UNIT 6

TIMELINE
Weather and Climate

In this unit, you will learn more about the ocean of air in which we live. You will learn about the atmosphere and how it affects conditions on the Earth's surface. The constantly changing weather is always a good topic for conversation. It is also the subject of the science of meteorology. Forecasting the weather is not an easy task. Climate, on the other hand, is much more predictable. This timeline shows some of the events that have occurred as scientists have tried to better understand weather and climate.

1281
A sudden typhoon destroys a fleet of Mongolian ships about to reach Japan. This "divine wind," or *kamikaze* in Japanese, saves the country from invasion and conquest.

1656
Saturn's rings are recognized as such. Galileo had seen them in 1612, but his telescope was not strong enough to make them out as rings.

1945
First atmospheric test of an atomic bomb takes place near Alamogordo, New Mexico.

1974

Chlorofluorocarbons (CFCs) are recognized as harmful to the ozone layer.

1982
Weather information becomes available 24 hours a day, 7 days a week on commercial television.

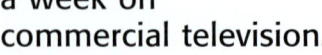

1714
Gabriel Fahrenheit builds the first mercury thermometer.

1749
Benjamin Franklin explains how updrafts of air are caused by the sun's heating of the local atmosphere.

1778
Karl Sheele and Antoine Lavoisier separately conclude that air is mostly made of nitrogen and oxygen.

1838
John James Audubon publishes *The Birds of America*.

1938
The cause of ice ages as a periodic result of the Earth's motion through space is determined by Yugoslav scientist Milutin Milankovitch.

1999
The first nonstop balloon trip around the world is successfully completed when Brian Jones and Bertrand Piccard land in Egypt.

1985
Scientists discover an ozone hole over Antarctica.

1986
The world's worst nuclear accident takes place at Chernobyl, Ukraine, spreading radiation through the atmosphere as far as the western United States.

Weather and Climate

Chapter Organizer

CHAPTER ORGANIZATION	TIME MINUTES	OBJECTIVES	LABS, INVESTIGATIONS, AND DEMONSTRATIONS
Chapter Opener pp. 390–391	45	National Standards: SAI 1	**Start-Up Activity** Air—It's Massive, p. 391
Section 1 Characteristics of the Atmosphere	90	▶ Discuss the composition of the Earth's atmosphere. ▶ Explain why pressure changes with altitude. ▶ Explain how temperature changes with altitude. ▶ Describe the layers of the atmosphere. SPSP 1, 3, 4, ES 1h; LabBook SAI 1, ST 1	**Demonstration,** Air Pressure, p. 392 in ATE GENERAL **Discovery Lab,** Under Pressure! p. 692 GENERAL **Datasheets for LabBook,** Under Pressure! Datasheet 32 GENERAL **Whiz-Bang Demonstrations,** Blue Sky, Demo 27 ADVANCED
Section 2 Heating of the Atmosphere	90	▶ Describe what happens to radiation that reaches the Earth. ▶ Summarize the processes of radiation, conduction, and convection. ▶ Explain how the greenhouse effect could contribute to global warming. UCP 2, SAI 2, SPSP 2–4, ES 1k, 2a; LabBook SAI 1, ST 1	**Demonstration,** p. 399 in ATE ADVANCED **Design Your Own,** Boiling Over! p. 688 GENERAL **Datasheets for LabBook,** Boiling Over! Datasheet 30 GENERAL **EcoLabs & Field Activities,** That Greenhouse Effect! Field Activity 14 GENERAL
Section 3 Atmospheric Pressure and Winds	90	▶ Explain the relationship between air pressure and wind direction. ▶ Describe the global patterns of wind. ▶ Explain the causes of local wind patterns. SAI 1, ES 1j, 3d; LabBook UCP 3, SAI 1, ST 1	**Demonstration,** Air Movement, p. 402 in ATE GENERAL **QuickLab,** Full of "Hot Air," p. 404 GENERAL **Discovery Lab,** Go Fly a Bike! p. 690 BASIC **Datasheets for LabBook,** Go Fly a Bike! Datasheet 31 BASIC
Section 4 The Air We Breathe	90	▶ Describe the major types of air pollution. ▶ Name the major causes of air pollution. ▶ Explain how air pollution can affect human health. ▶ Explain how air pollution can be reduced. SAI 1, SPSP 1–5, ES 1k, 2a	**Demonstration,** p. 411 in ATE GENERAL **Interactive Explorations CD-ROM,** Moose Malady GENERAL A **Worksheet** is also available in the **Interactive Explorations Teacher's Edition.** **Long-Term Projects & Research Ideas,** Project 43 ADVANCED

*See page **T20** for a complete correlation of this book with the*

NATIONAL SCIENCE EDUCATION STANDARDS.

TECHNOLOGY RESOURCES

 Guided Reading Audio CD
English or Spanish, Chapter 15

 One-Stop Planner CD-ROM with Test Generator

 **Interactive Explorations CD-ROM**
CD 2, Exploration 3, Moose Malady

 CNN Eye on the Environment, Global Warming, Segment 13
CO_2 and Arctic Ozone, Segment 14
Multicultural Connections, China Coal, Segment 3
Scientists in Action, Tracking Mercury in the Everglades, Segment 15

Chapter 15 • The Atmosphere

CLASSROOM WORKSHEETS, TRANSPARENCIES, AND RESOURCES	SCIENCE INTEGRATION AND CONNECTIONS	REVIEW AND ASSESSMENT
Directed Reading Worksheet 15 BASIC **Science Puzzlers, Twisters & Teasers,** Worksheet 15 ADVANCED		
Directed Reading Worksheet 15, Section 1 BASIC **Transparency 13,** Photosynthesis and Respiration: What's the Connection? **Transparency 162,** Profile of the Earth's Atmosphere **Reinforcement Worksheet 15,** Earth's Amazing Atmosphere BASIC	**Chemistry Connection,** p. 392 **Connect to Life Science,** p. 393 in ATE **Apply,** p. 395 GENERAL **Connect to Physical Science,** p. 396 in ATE BASIC **Multicultural Connection,** p. 396 in ATE GENERAL	**Self-Check,** p. 394 **Review,** p. 397 GENERAL **Quiz,** p. 397 in ATE GENERAL **Alternative Assessment,** p. 397 in ATE GENERAL
Directed Reading Worksheet 15, Section 2 BASIC **Transparency 163,** Radiation and the Atmosphere **Transparency 164,** Radiation, Convection, and Conduction **Transparency 165,** The Greenhouse Effect	**Connect to Environmental Science,** p. 398 in ATE ADVANCED **Biology Connection,** p. 401 **Connect to Life Science,** p. 401 in ATE	**Homework,** p. 399 in ATE GENERAL **Review,** p. 401 GENERAL **Quiz,** p. 401 in ATE GENERAL **Alternative Assessment,** p. 401 in ATE GENERAL
Directed Reading Worksheet 15, Section 3 BASIC **Transparency 166,** Sea and Land Breezes	**Connect to Physical Science,** p. 402 in ATE **Multicultural Connection,** p. 403 in ATE GENERAL **Environment Connection,** p. 405 **Connect to Life Science,** p. 405 in ATE **Math and More,** p. 406 in ATE ADVANCED **Multicultural Connection,** p. 406 in ATE **MathBreak,** Calculating Groundspeed, p. 407 GENERAL	**Homework,** p. 405 in ATE GENERAL **Review,** p. 407 GENERAL **Quiz,** p. 407 in ATE GENERAL **Alternative Assessment,** p. 407 in ATE BASIC
Directed Reading Worksheet 15, Section 4 BASIC **Transparency 167,** The Formation of Smog **Critical Thinking Worksheet 15,** The Extraordinary GBG5K ADVANCED	**Connect to Physical Science,** p. 410 in ATE **Multicultural Connection,** p. 410 in ATE **Real-World Connection,** p. 410 in ATE **Cross-Disciplinary Focus,** p. 412 in ATE ADVANCED **Health Watch:** Particles in the Air, p. 418 GENERAL **Scientific Debate:** A Cure for Air Pollution? p. 419	**Review,** p. 413 GENERAL **Quiz,** p. 413 in ATE GENERAL **Alternative Assessment,** p. 413 in ATE BASIC

END-OF-CHAPTER REVIEW AND ASSESSMENT

Chapter Review in Study Guide
Vocabulary and Notes in Study Guide
Chapter Tests with Performance-Based Assessment, Chapter 15 Test
Chapter Tests with Performance-Based Assessment, Performance-Based Assessment 15
Concept Mapping Transparency 15

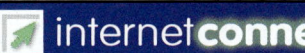

 Holt, Rinehart and Winston On-line Resources
go.hrw.com
For worksheets and other teaching aids related to this chapter, visit the HRW Web site and type in the keyword: **HSTATM**

 **National Science Teachers Association**
www.scilinks.org
Encourage students to use the *sci*LINKS numbers listed in the internet connect boxes to access information and resources on the **NSTA** Web site.

Chapter Resources & Worksheets

Visual Resources

TEACHING TRANSPARENCIES

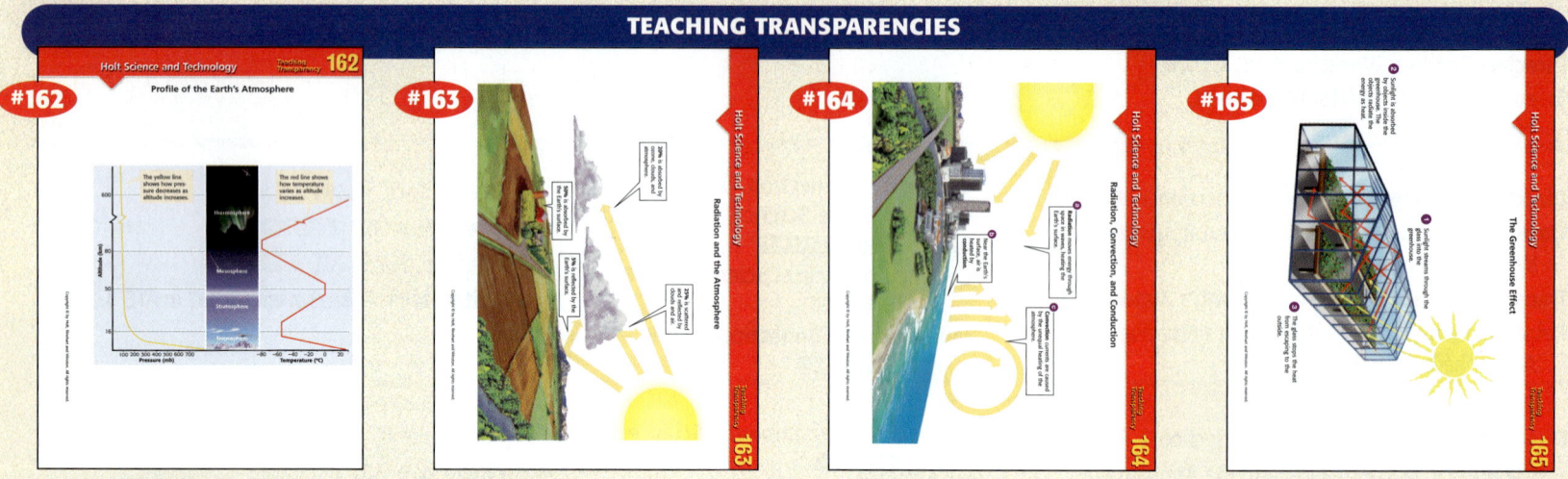

TEACHING TRANSPARENCIES

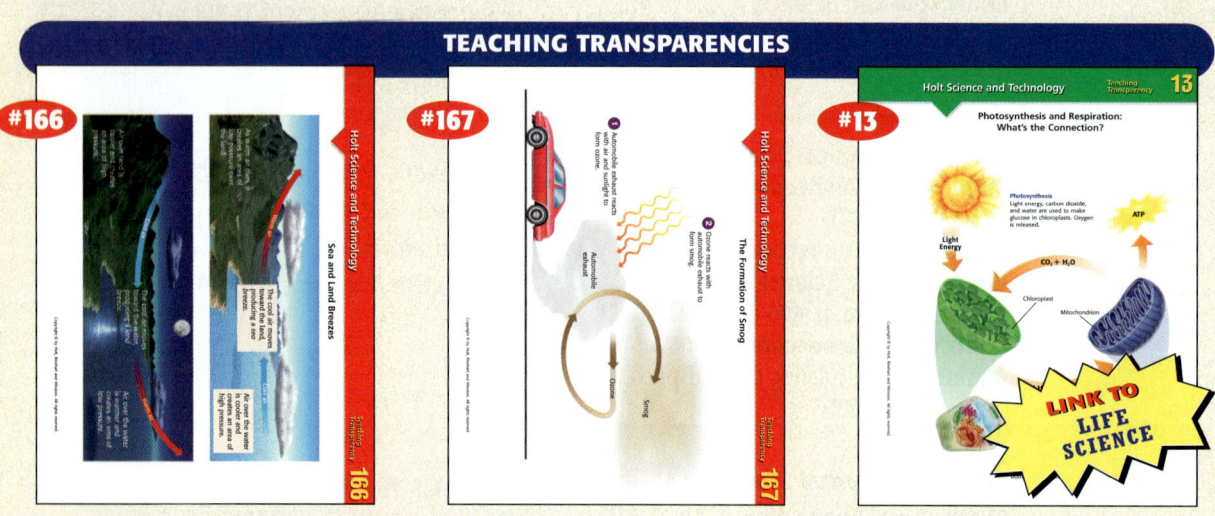

CONCEPT MAPPING TRANSPARENCY

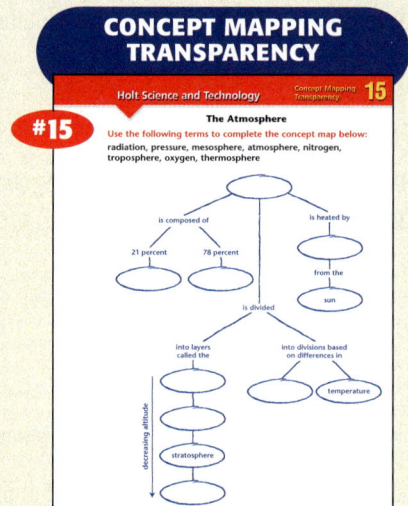

Meeting Individual Needs

DIRECTED READING

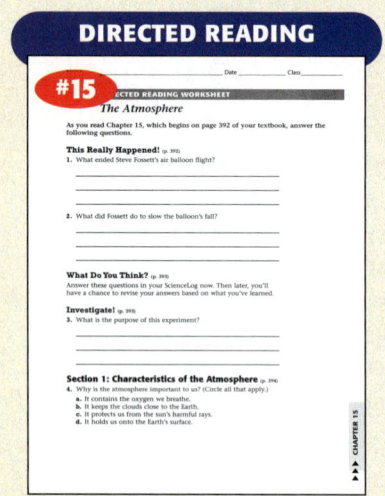

REINFORCEMENT & VOCABULARY REVIEW

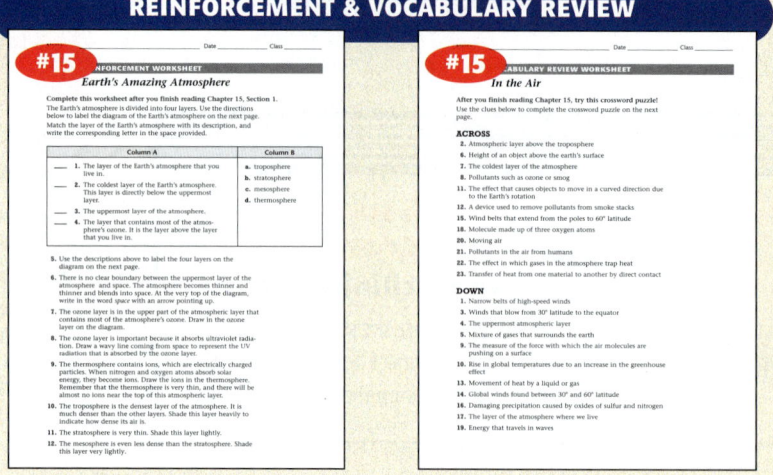

SCIENCE PUZZLERS, TWISTERS & TEASERS

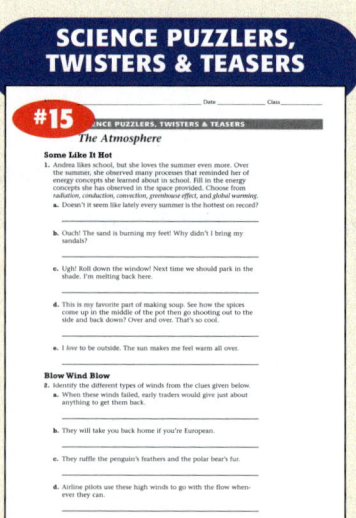

Chapter 15 • The Atmosphere

Chapter 15 • The Atmosphere

Review & Assessment

STUDY GUIDE

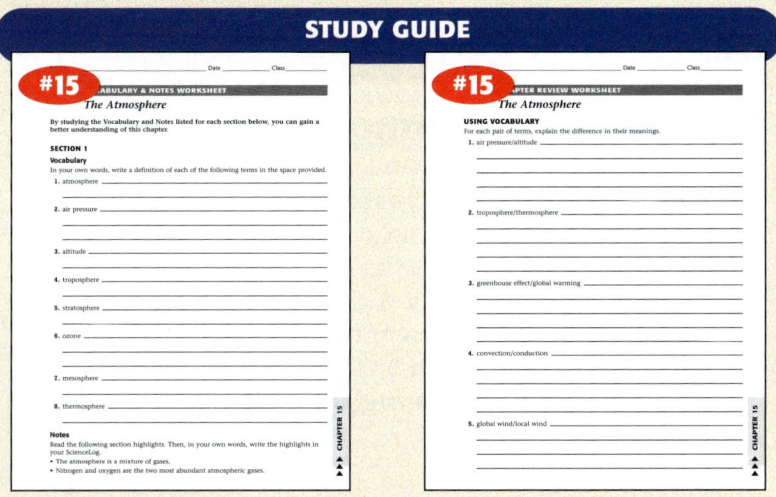

CHAPTER TESTS WITH PERFORMANCE-BASED ASSESSMENT

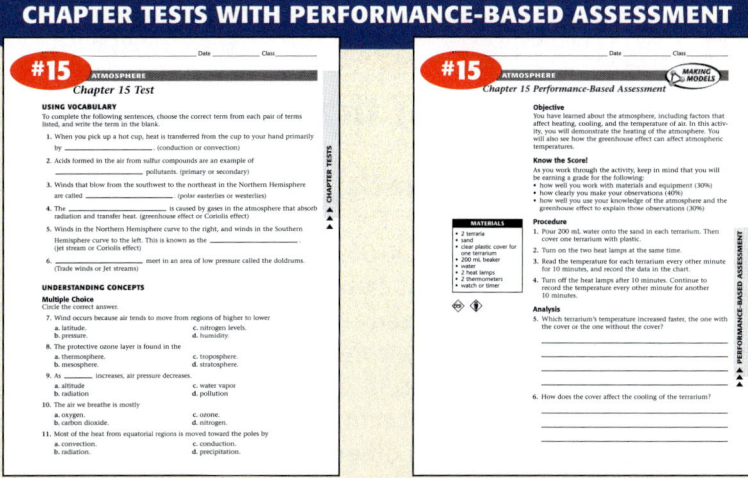

Lab Worksheets

ECOLABS & FIELD ACTIVITIES

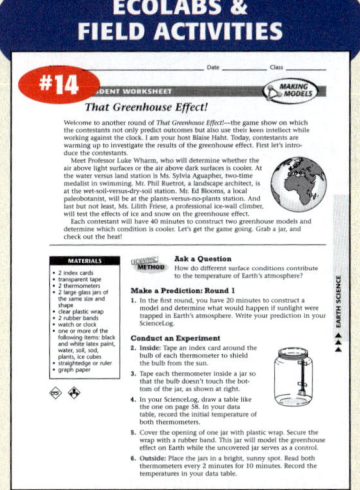

WHIZ-BANG DEMONSTRATIONS

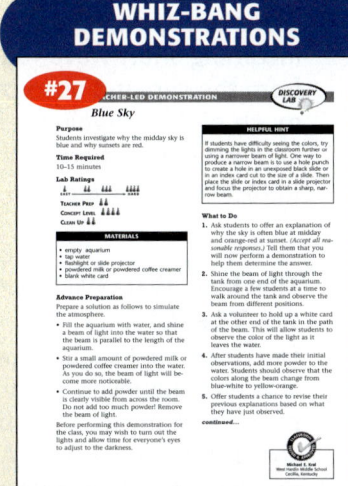

LONG-TERM PROJECTS & RESEARCH IDEAS

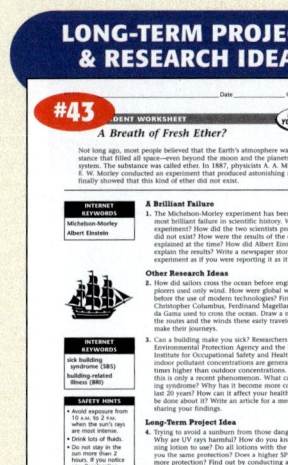

DATASHEETS FOR LABBOOK

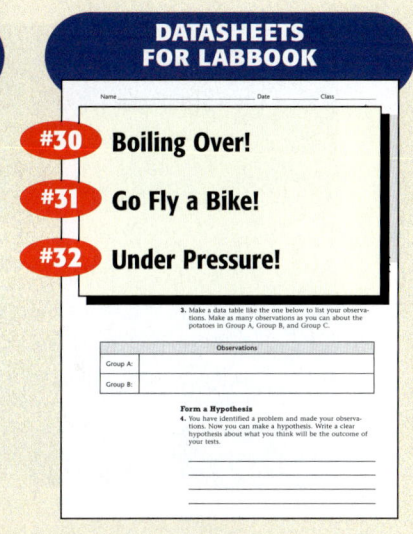

Applications & Extensions

CRITICAL THINKING & PROBLEM SOLVING

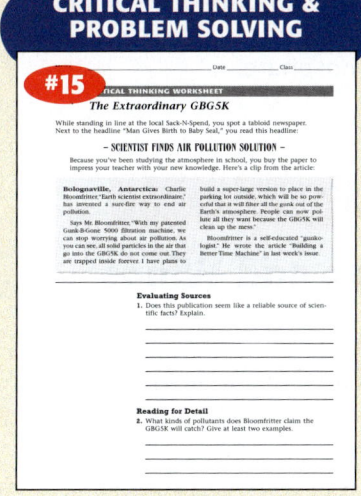

MULTICULTURAL CONNECTIONS

EYE ON THE ENVIRONMENT / SCIENTISTS IN ACTION

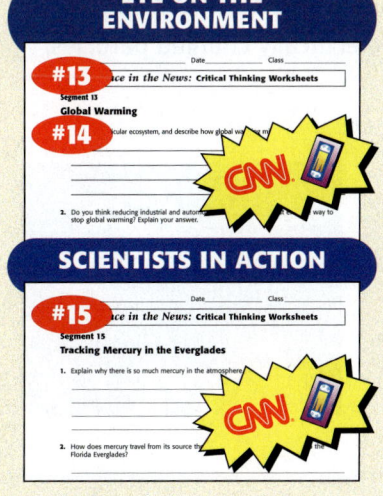

INTERACTIVE EXPLORATIONS

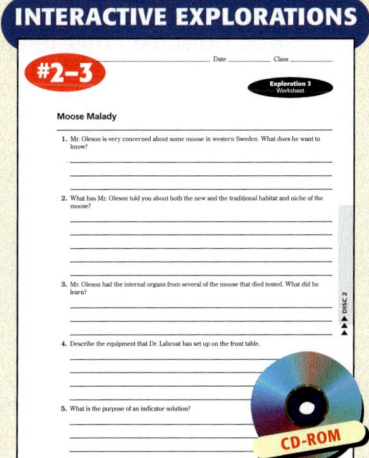

Chapter 15 • Chapter Resources & Worksheets **389D**

Chapter Background

Section 1

Characteristics of the Atmosphere

▶ **Take a Deep Breath!**
Near the Earth's surface, the atmosphere consists of 78.08 percent nitrogen, 20.95 percent oxygen, 0.93 percent argon, 0.03 percent carbon dioxide, and traces of water vapor. Earth's early atmosphere was quite different than it is today, consisting of about 79 percent water vapor, 11–12 percent carbon dioxide, 6 percent sulfur dioxide, 1 percent nitrogen, less than 1 percent hydrogen, and traces of other gases. Scientists theorize that about 95 percent of the oxygen present in today's atmosphere formed as a byproduct of photosynthesis.

▶ **Radio Days**
Fadeouts of radio communications are due to sudden ionospheric disturbances, known as SIDs. These storms can last 15 to 30 minutes and are caused by violent solar outbursts that release electrically charged particles.

IS THAT A FACT!

▶ The Earth's troposphere contains almost 90 percent of the atmosphere's total mass. In the troposphere, temperature decreases at an average rate of 6.4°C/km with increasing altitude.

Section 2

Heating of the Atmosphere

▶ **Cloudy with a Chance of . . .**
Clouds reflect incoming solar radiation very effectively. The amount of solar radiation a cloud can reflect depends on its thickness. A cloud less than 50 m thick can reflect up to 40 percent of incoming solar radiation, while a cloud more than 5,000 m thick can reflect 80 percent or more. The average reflectivity of clouds is about 55 percent.

▶ **Greenhouse Gases**
Water vapor, carbon dioxide, ozone, methane, and chlorofluorocarbons are often called greenhouse gases. These gases transmit incoming short-wave radiation from the sun and absorb much of the outgoing long-wave radiation from the Earth's surface.

▶ **Global Warming—An Idea Before Its Time!**
Since the 1970s, global warming has been a topic of concern. However, a global warming model was proposed as early as 1896 by a Swedish physicist and chemist named Svante Arrhenius. Arrhenius theorized that the carbon dioxide released from burning coal would increase the intensity of Earth's greenhouse effect and lead to global warming. In 1954, it was first suggested that deforestation increases the amount of CO_2 in the atmosphere. Since then, numerous scientific studies have examined the effects of carbon dioxide on the temperature of Earth's atmosphere.

Section 3

Atmospheric Pressure and Winds

▶ **Gustave Coriolis**
Gustave Gaspard Coriolis was a French mathematician and engineer who lived and worked in Paris from

Chapter 15 • The Atmosphere

1792 to 1843. His most well known contribution to science is a paper published in 1835 that introduces the Coriolis effect. In "On the Equations of Relative Motion of Systems of Bodies," Coriolis argued that an internal force (the Coriolis force) acts on a rotating object at a right angle to the objects motion. We now know that the "Coriolis force" is not a force, but an effect. The rotation of the Earth causes matter in motion to be deflected from its path. This deflection is called the Coriolis effect. The Coriolis effect influences the general direction of global winds and open-ocean circulation, as well as the rotational movements of severe weather, such as hurricanes.

IS THAT A FACT!

- When airplanes fly north or south, pilots have to make corrections to counteract the Coriolis effect.

▶ Jet Streaks

Jet streaks are winds within jet streams that flow faster than the adjacent winds. Jet streaks influence storm formation and associated precipitation. Rising jet streaks and the low-pressure area that forms beneath them present favorable conditions for storms to form. Sinking jet streaks inhibit storm formation and precipitation.

IS THAT A FACT!

- The speed of jet streams ranges from about 92 km/h to more than 483 km/h!

SECTION 4

The Air We Breathe

▶ Vog and Laze

Two pollution problems associated with volcanic activity at Earth's surface are vog and laze. Vog is volcanic smog that forms when the sulfur dioxide released during an eruption reacts with sunlight, dust particles, water vapor, and oxygen to form various sulfur compounds, including sulfur dioxide. When Kilauea began to erupt in 1983, it sent about 2,000 tons of sulfur dioxide into the air each day.

- Laze is lava haze, a form of pollution that forms when lava flows react with ocean water. The extreme temperature of the lava causes sea water to vaporize. Physical and chemical interactions create white plumes of hydrochloric acid and concentrated salt water that can threaten the health of people living near volcanoes.

▶ Allowance Trading System

An important part of the EPA's Acid Rain Program is the allowance trading system, which is designed to reduce sulfur-dioxide emissions. In this system, 1 ton of sulfur dioxide (SO_2) emission is equivalent to one allowance. There are a limited number of allowances allocated for each year. Companies can buy, sell or trade allowances freely, but if they exceed their allowances, they must pay a punitive fine. The system allows a company to determine the most cost-effective ways to comply with the Clean Air Act. It can reduce emissions by using technology that conserves energy, by using renewable energy sources, or by updating its pollution-control devices and using low-sulfur fuels.

- Sulfur dioxide allowances are inexpensive and can be bought from the EPA by private citizens, schools, and community and environmental organizations. Purchasing one allowance will reduce a company's allowable SO_2 emissions in a given year by 1 ton.

For background information about teaching strategies and issues, refer to the *Professional Reference for Teachers*.

The Atmosphere

 Pre-Reading Questions

Students may not know the answers to these questions before reading the chapter, so accept any reasonable response.

Suggested Answers
1. Air is made of nitrogen, oxygen, carbon dioxide, water vapor, argon, and other trace gases.
2. The atmosphere is organized in layers based on temperature differences.
3. Wind is the movement of air caused by differences in air pressure. Air moves from areas of high pressure to areas of low pressure.

 Directed Reading Worksheet 15

 Science Puzzlers, Twisters & Teasers Worksheet 15

 Guided Reading Audio CD English or Spanish, Chapter 15

The Atmosphere

Sections

① Characteristics of the Atmosphere 392
   Chemistry Connection 393
   Apply 395
   Internet Connect 397

② Heating of the Atmosphere 398
   Biology Connection .. 401
   Internet Connect 401

③ Atmospheric Pressure and Winds 402
   QuickLab 404
   Environment Connection 405
   MathBreak 407
   Internet Connect 407

④ The Air We Breathe ... 408
   Internet Connect 413

Chapter Review 416
Feature Articles 418, 419
LabBook 688–693

 **Pre-Reading Questions**

1. What is air made of?
2. How is the atmosphere organized?
3. What is wind and how does it move?

FLOATING ON AIR

These skydivers might have checked their parachutes at least a half dozen times before they jumped. They probably also paid particular attention to the day's weather report. Skydivers should know what to expect from the atmosphere. The atmosphere can be unpredictable and dangerous, but it also provides us with the gases needed for our survival on Earth. In this chapter, you will learn about the Earth's atmosphere and how it affects your life.

---

internetconnect

HRW On-line Resources

go.hrw.com
For worksheets and other teaching aids, visit the HRW Web site and type in the keyword: **HSTATM**

www.scilinks.com
Use the *sci*LINKS numbers at the end of each chapter for additional resources on the **NSTA** Web site.

www.cnnfyi.com
Visit the CNN Web site for current events coverage and classroom resources.

START-UP Activity

AIR—IT'S MASSIVE

In this activity, you will find out if air has mass.

Procedure

1. Use a **scale** to find the mass of a **ball,** such as a football or a basketball, with no air in it. Record the mass of the empty ball in your ScienceLog.
2. Pump up the ball with an **air pump.**
3. Use the scale to find the mass of the ball filled with air. Record the mass of the ball filled with air in your ScienceLog.

Analysis

4. Compare the mass of the empty ball with the mass of the ball filled with air. Did the mass of the ball change after you pumped it up?
5. Based on your results, does air have mass? Explain your answer.

START-UP Activity

AIR—IT'S MASSIVE

MATERIALS

FOR EACH GROUP:
- scale
- football or basketball, deflated
- air pump

Answers to START-UP Activity

4. The mass of the empty ball is less than the mass of the ball filled with air. The mass of the ball increased when the ball was pumped up.
5. Air has mass as shown by the increase in mass when the ball is filled with air.

Chapter 15 • The Atmosphere

SECTION 1

Focus

Characteristics of the Atmosphere

This section defines the atmosphere and explains its basic characteristics. It discusses the atmosphere's composition and explains how temperature and pressure are related to altitude. The section concludes with a description of the four layers of the Earth's atmosphere.

 **Bellringer**

Have students list the ways that the atmosphere is different from outer space in their ScienceLog. Tell students that a little more than a century ago, many scientists believed that the Earth's atmosphere blended with a hypothetical substance called *ether* that filled the entire universe. In 1887, the physicist A. A. Michelson demonstrated that the universe is not filled with ether.

1) Motivate

DEMONSTRATION

Air Pressure Fill a paper cup with water, and push a square piece of cardboard firmly against the cup's mouth with one hand. Hold the cardboard in place as you position the cup over a volunteer's hand. Ask the class to predict what will happen when you invert the cup. Quickly invert the cup, being careful to keep the cardboard in place. The cardboard should stay in place, and the water should stay in the cup. Explain that this demonstration illustrates that the atmosphere exerts pressure in all directions.

Note: Practice this demonstration over a sink before doing it in front of the class.

Section 1

Terms to Learn

atmosphere stratosphere
air pressure ozone
altitude mesosphere
troposphere thermosphere

What You'll Do

- Discuss the composition of the Earth's atmosphere.
- Explain why pressure changes with altitude.
- Explain how temperature changes with altitude.
- Describe the layers of the atmosphere.

Characteristics of the Atmosphere

If you were lost in the desert, you could survive for a few days without food and water. But you wouldn't last more than 5 minutes without the *atmosphere*. The **atmosphere** is a mixture of gases that surrounds the Earth. In addition to containing the oxygen we need to breathe, it protects us from the sun's harmful rays. But the atmosphere is always changing. Every breath we take, every tree we plant, and every motor vehicle we ride in affects the composition of our atmosphere. Later you will find out how the atmosphere is changing. But first you need to learn about the atmosphere's composition and structure.

Composition of the Atmosphere

Figure 1 shows the relative amounts of the gases that make up the atmosphere. Besides gases, the atmosphere also contains small amounts of solids and liquids. Tiny solid particles, such as dust, volcanic ash, sea salt, dirt, and smoke, are carried in the air. Next time you turn off the lights at night, shine a flashlight and you will see some of these tiny particles floating in the air. The most common liquid in the atmosphere is water. Liquid water is found as water droplets in clouds. Water vapor, which is also found in the atmosphere, is a gas and is not visible.

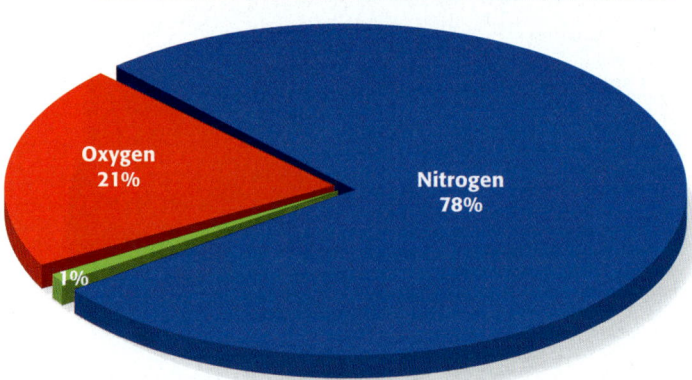

Figure 1 Two gases—nitrogen and oxygen—make up 99 percent of the air we breathe.

Nitrogen is the most abundant gas in the atmosphere. It is released into the atmosphere by volcanic eruptions and when dead plants and dead animals decay.

Oxygen, the second most common gas in the atmosphere, is produced by plant-like protists and plants.

The **remaining 1 percent** of the atmosphere is made up of argon, carbon dioxide, water vapor, and other gases.

Oxygen 21%
Nitrogen 78%
1%

internetconnect

SCILINKS
NSTA

TOPIC: Composition of the Atmosphere
GO TO: www.scilinks.org
sciLINKS NUMBER: HSTE355

Directed Reading Worksheet 15 Section 1

WEIRD SCIENCE

An experiment in 1664 demonstrated the force exerted by the Earth's atmosphere. Most of the air was removed from a hollow sphere whose halves had been sealed together with an airtight gasket. Sixteen horses were needed to pull the metal hemispheres apart!

Atmospheric Pressure and Temperature

Have you ever been in an elevator in a tall building? If you have, you probably remember the "popping" in your ears as you went up or down. As you move up or down in an elevator, the air pressure outside your ears changes, while the air pressure inside your ears stays the same. **Air pressure** is the measure of the force with which the air molecules push on a surface. Your ears pop when the pressure inside and outside of your ears suddenly becomes equal. Air pressure changes throughout the atmosphere. Temperature and the kinds of gases present also change. Why do these changes occur? Read on to find out.

Water is the only substance that exists as a liquid, a solid, and a gas in the Earth's atmosphere.

Pressure Think of air pressure as a human pyramid, as shown in **Figure 2**. The people at the bottom of the pyramid can feel all the weight and pressure of the people on top. The person on top doesn't feel any weight because there isn't anyone above. The atmosphere works in a similar way.

The Earth's atmosphere is held around the planet by gravity. Gravity pulls the gas molecules in the atmosphere toward the Earth's surface, giving them weight. This weight causes the air to push against the Earth's surface. As you move farther away from the Earth's surface, air pressure decreases because fewer gas molecules are pushing on you. **Altitude** is the height of an object above the Earth's surface. As altitude increases, air pressure decreases.

Figure 2 Like the bottom row of the human pyramid, the lower atmosphere experiences greater pressure than the upper atmosphere.

CONNECT TO LIFE SCIENCE

Use Teaching Transparency 13 to show students how photosynthesis and respiration are linked to gas exchange between organisms and the atmosphere. Photosynthesizing plants use carbon dioxide, water, and light energy to produce oxygen. During respiration, plants and animals consume oxygen and release carbon dioxide, water, and energy.

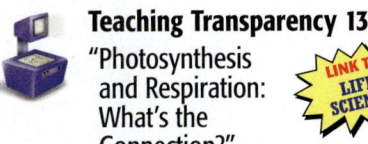

Teaching Transparency 13 "Photosynthesis and Respiration: What's the Connection?" LINK TO LIFE SCIENCE

2) Teach

READING STRATEGY

Prediction Guide After students read this page, ask them the following questions:

- Which gas—oxygen or nitrogen—is the major component of Earth's air? (nitrogen)
- Does air contain anything other than gases? (Yes; it contains solids, such as dust, and liquids, such as water.)

GROUP ACTIVITY

It's a Gas! Have small groups demonstrate how oxygen enters the atmosphere. Suggested materials include a freshwater plant, such as *Elodea*, a small plastic storage beaker, a funnel, a test tube, and water. Tell students to immerse the plant in the water-filled beaker and then cover the plant with the inverted funnel. Have them place a water-filled test tube over the funnel's spout and let the setup sit in a well-lighted area for a few days. After this time, students will observe gas bubbles in the test tube. Inform them that the bubbles they see are made of oxygen gas released during the process of photosynthesis. **Sheltered English**

MISCONCEPTION ALERT

Make sure students realize that water vapor is an invisible gas. The "steam" they observe coming out of a pot of boiling water is composed of water droplets that form as water vapor cools and condenses on particles in the air. Similarly, clouds appear in the sky when the air cools enough for water vapor to condense and form liquid droplets.

Section 1 • Characteristics of the Atmosphere

2 Teach, continued

MEETING INDIVIDUAL NEEDS

Learners Having Difficulty
Students might benefit from using a dictionary to learn the prefixes of the following words:

troposphere, stratosphere, mesosphere, thermosphere

Students will learn that *tropos-* means "change" or "turn," *stratum-* means "layer," *meso-* means "middle," and *thermo-* means "heat." Students should also note that *sphere* means "globe" or "ball." Have students use these meanings to remember the layers of the atmosphere.
Sheltered English

USING THE FIGURE

Have students refer to **Figure 3** to answer these questions:

- Which layer of the atmosphere is closest to Earth? (the troposphere)
- How does temperature change within the stratosphere? (For the first few kilometers, the temperature remains fairly constant. Then the temperature begins rising steeply and levels off again toward the top of the layer.)
- Which atmospheric layer has the greatest range of temperatures? (the thermosphere)
- Approximately how thick is the Earth's atmosphere? (about 600 km)

Students may notice that the iridescent cloud in the thermosphere is an aurora and that the white layer near the top of the stratosphere is the ozone layer.

Teaching Transparency 162
"Profile of the Earth's Atmosphere"

394 Chapter 15 • The Atmosphere

✓ Self-Check
Does air become more or less dense as you climb a mountain? Why? *(See page 726 to check your answer.)*

Answer to Self-Check
As you climb a mountain, the air becomes less dense because there are fewer air molecules. So even though cold air is generally more dense than warm air, it is less dense at higher elevations.

Air Temperature Air temperature also changes as you increase altitude. As you pass through the atmosphere, air temperature changes between warmer and colder conditions. The temperature differences result mainly from the way solar energy is absorbed as it moves downward through the atmosphere. Some parts of the atmosphere are warmer because they contain gases that absorb solar energy. Other parts do not contain these gases and are therefore cooler.

Layers of the Atmosphere

Based on temperature changes, the Earth's atmosphere is divided into four layers—the troposphere, stratosphere, mesosphere, and thermosphere. **Figure 3** illustrates the four atmospheric layers, showing their altitude and temperature. As you can see, each layer has unique characteristics.

Figure 3 Profile of the Earth's Atmosphere

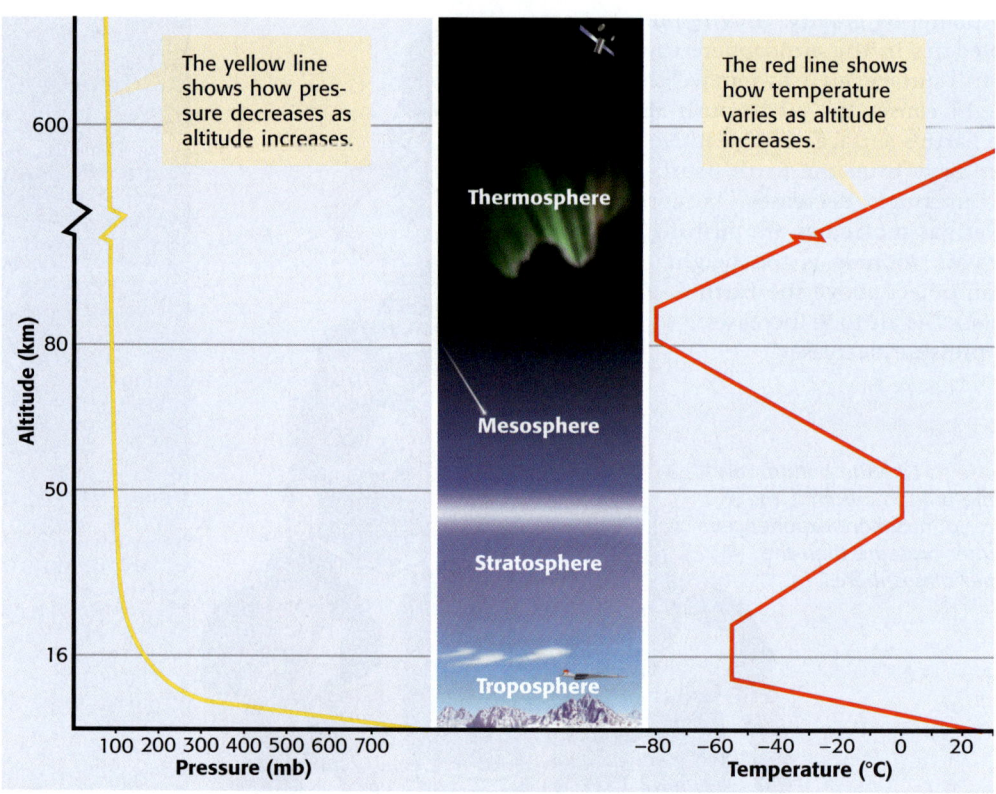

IS THAT A FACT!
The oxygen in the Earth's current atmosphere is produced primarily by phytoplankton (tiny, drifting sea plants) and land plants that release oxygen during photosynthesis.

Troposphere The **troposphere,** which lies next to the Earth's surface, is the lowest layer of the atmosphere. The troposphere is also the densest atmospheric layer, containing almost 90 percent of the atmosphere's total mass. Almost all of Earth's carbon dioxide, water vapor, clouds, air pollution, weather, and life-forms are found in the troposphere. In fact, the troposphere is the layer in which you live. **Figure 4** shows the effects of altitude on temperature in the troposphere.

Stratosphere The atmospheric layer above the troposphere is called the **stratosphere.** In the stratosphere, the air is very thin and contains little moisture. The lower stratosphere is extremely cold, measuring about −60°C. In the stratosphere, the temperature rises with increasing altitude. This occurs because of ozone. **Ozone** is a molecule that is made up of three oxygen atoms, as shown in **Figure 5.** Almost all of the ozone in the atmosphere is contained in the *ozone layer* of the stratosphere. Ozone absorbs solar energy in the form of ultraviolet radiation, warming the air. By absorbing the ultraviolet radiation, the ozone layer also protects life at the Earth's surface.

Figure 4 Snow can remain year-round on a mountain top. That is because as altitude increases, the atmosphere thins, losing its ability to absorb and transfer thermal energy.

Oxygen gas (O_2)   **Ozone (O_3)**

Figure 5 While ozone is made up of three oxygen atoms, the oxygen in the air you breathe is made up of two oxygen atoms.

APPLY

UV and SPFs

People protect themselves from the sun's damaging rays by applying sunblock. Exposure of unprotected skin to the sun's ultraviolet rays over a long period of time can cause skin cancer. The breakdown of the Earth's ozone layer is thinning the layer, which allows some harmful ultraviolet radiation to reach the Earth's surface. Sunblocks contain different ratings of SPFs, or skin protection factors. What do the SPF ratings mean?

3 Extend

GUIDED PRACTICE

On the board, make a table entitled "The Atmosphere." Include the following headings:

Layer, Altitude range, Temperature range, and Other important information

Have volunteers contribute information for each section of the table. **Sheltered English**

CONNECT TO PHYSICAL SCIENCE

Explain that temperature is a measure of the average kinetic energy of randomly vibrating particles and that heat is the transfer of energy between objects of different temperatures. To clarify these concepts, have students imagine a sink full of hot water. Ask them to pretend that they have removed a cup of the hot water from the sink. Students should agree that both volumes of water have the same temperature at this point. Explain that the sink has more thermal energy than the cup because the sink contains more water (and therefore more particles in motion) than the cup.

USING THE FIGURE

Have students use the illustrations in **Figure 6** to compare how energy is transferred in the thermosphere with how it is transferred in the troposphere. How is the thermosphere like a vacuum thermos? (A vacuum thermos surrounds a hot liquid with a partial vacuum. Because there are relatively few air molecules in the vacuum, little energy is transferred from the liquid and it remains hot. Similarly, the thermosphere has few air molecules to transfer energy.)

BRAIN FOOD

Large continent-sized windstorms were detected by the *Upper Atmosphere Research Satellite*. The effect these winds have on weather at the Earth's surface is currently being studied.

Mesosphere Above the stratosphere is the mesosphere. The **mesosphere** is the coldest layer of the atmosphere. As in the troposphere, the temperature drops with increasing altitude. Temperatures can be as low as –93°C at the top of the mesosphere. Scientists have recently discovered large wind storms in the mesosphere with winds reaching speeds of more than 320 km/h.

Thermosphere The uppermost atmospheric layer is the **thermosphere.** Here temperature again increases with altitude because many of the gases are absorbing solar radiation. Temperatures in this layer can reach 1,700°C.

When you think of an area with high temperatures, you probably think of a place that is very hot. While the thermosphere has very high temperatures, it would not feel hot. Temperature and heat are not the same thing. Temperature is a measure of the average energy of particles in motion. A high temperature means that the particles are moving very fast. Heat, on the other hand, is the transfer of energy between objects at different temperatures. But in order to transfer energy, particles must touch one another. **Figure 6** illustrates how the density of particles affects the heating of the atmosphere.

Figure 6 Temperatures in the thermosphere are higher than those in the troposphere, but the air particles are too far apart for energy to be transferred.

The **thermosphere** contains few particles that move fast. The temperature of this layer is high due to the speed of its particles. But because the particles rarely touch one another, the thermosphere does not transfer much energy.

The **troposphere** contains more particles that travel at a slower speed. The temperature of this layer is lower than that of the thermosphere. But because the particles are bumping into one another, the troposphere transfers much more energy.

  Under Pressure!

Different cultures have different explanations for the shimmering lights known as the auroras. Inuit groups thought of the aurora borealis as the torches of spirits that guided souls from Earth to paradise. Have students find out about other myths concerning the auroras.

396 Chapter 15 • The Atmosphere

Ionosphere In the upper mesosphere and the lower thermosphere, nitrogen and oxygen atoms absorb harmful solar energy, such as X rays and gamma rays. This absorption not only contributes to the thermosphere's high temperatures but also causes the gas particles to become electrically charged. Electrically charged particles are called ions; therefore, this part of the thermosphere is referred to as the *ionosphere*. Sometimes these ions radiate energy as light of different colors, as shown in **Figure 7**.

Figure 7 Aurora borealis (northern lights) and aurora australis (southern lights) occur in the ionosphere.

The ionosphere also reflects certain radio waves, such as AM radio waves. If you have ever listened to an AM radio station, you can be sure that the ionosphere had something to do with how clear it sounded. When conditions are right, an AM radio wave can travel around the world after being reflected off the ionosphere. These radio signals bounce off the ionosphere and are sent back to Earth.

REVIEW

1. Explain why pressure decreases but temperature varies as altitude increases.
2. What causes air pressure?
3. How can the thermosphere have high temperatures but not feel hot?
4. **Analyzing Relationships** Identify one characteristic of each layer of the atmosphere, and explain how that characteristic affects life on Earth.

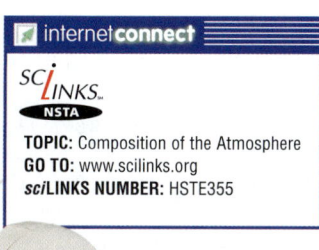

internetconnect

SCLINKS
NSTA

TOPIC: Composition of the Atmosphere
GO TO: www.scilinks.org
*sci*LINKS NUMBER: HSTE355

4) Close

Quiz

1. What are the two main gases in Earth's atmosphere? (nitrogen and oxygen)
2. What is atmospheric pressure? (Atmospheric pressure is the force exerted by molecules of air on a surface.)
3. Name the layers of the atmosphere, starting with the one closest to Earth. (troposphere, stratosphere, mesosphere, thermosphere)
4. What is the ozone layer, and why is it important to Earth? (The ozone layer is a layer of ozone molecules in the stratosphere. The layer filters ultraviolet radiation from the sun and prevents much of this radiation from reaching Earth's surface.)
5. Explain how density affects energy transfer in the air. (The less dense the air is, the less effective it is at transferring energy. Particles that are farther apart, or less densely packed, are less likely to collide with other particles. Particles must collide with one another in order to transfer energy.)

ALTERNATIVE ASSESSMENT

Writing **Poetry** Have each student write a poem that creatively yet accurately describes one layer of Earth's atmosphere. Allow time for volunteers to read their poem aloud or display the poem for others to read on their own.

Reinforcement Worksheet 15 "Earth's Amazing Atmosphere"

▼ Answers to Review

1. Farther away from the Earth's surface, air pressure decreases because there are fewer gas molecules pushing down. Temperature varies due to the way solar energy is absorbed as it moves through the atmosphere.
2. Air pressure is caused as gravity pulls molecules in the atmosphere toward the Earth.
3. In the thermosphere, particles are moving quickly, but because they are few and far apart, they cannot transfer much energy.
4. Sample answer: The gases in the troposphere make life on Earth possible. The stratosphere contains the ozone layer, which absorbs ultraviolet radiation. The mesosphere is the coldest layer of the atmosphere and it may affect weather patterns on Earth. The thermosphere contains the ionosphere, which absorbs harmful solar energy.

Section 1 • Characteristics of the Atmosphere

SECTION 2

Focus

Heating of the Atmosphere

In this section, students learn that the sun is the principal energy source for our planet. They also discover that energy is transferred in one of three ways—by conduction, convection, or radiation. The section concludes with a discussion of the greenhouse effect and global warming.

🔔 Bellringer

Have students suppose that they will be vacationing in two unique spots—the Sahara Desert and the Antarctic ice sheet. Have them decide whether white or black clothing would be best for each location. (Because of its high reflectivity, white would be best for the hot desert. Because of its ability to absorb energy, black clothing would be better for the ice sheet.)

1) Motivate

GROUP ACTIVITY

Refer students to **Figure 8**, noting that on average, 5 percent of incoming solar radiation is reflected from Earth's surface and 50 percent is absorbed. Highly reflective surfaces, such as snow, reflect up to 90 percent of solar radiation, while the oceans reflect only 5 percent. This is noticeable in urban areas—cities with few green spaces and a lot of asphalt can have temperatures 10°C higher than surrounding rural areas. This is called the *heat island effect*. Have groups test an experiment to compare the amount of radiation reflected by asphalt, sidewalk, soil, water, and grass.

398 Chapter 15 • The Atmosphere

Section 2

Terms to Learn
radiation
conduction
convection
greenhouse effect
global warming

What You'll Do
- Describe what happens to radiation that reaches the Earth.
- Summarize the processes of radiation, conduction, and convection.
- Explain how the greenhouse effect could contribute to global warming.

Heating of the Atmosphere

Have you ever walked barefoot across a sidewalk on a sunny day? If so, your foot felt the warmth of the hot pavement. How did the sidewalk become so warm? The sidewalk was heated as it absorbed the sun's energy. The Earth's atmosphere is also heated in several ways by the transfer of energy from the sun. In this section you will find out what happens to the solar energy as it enters the Earth's atmosphere, how the energy is transferred through the atmosphere, and why it seems to be getting hotter every year.

Energy in the Atmosphere

The Earth receives energy from the sun by radiation. **Radiation** is the transfer of energy as electromagnetic waves. Although the sun releases a huge amount of energy, the Earth receives only about two-billionths of this energy. Yet even this small amount of energy has a very large impact on Earth. **Figure 8** shows what happens to all this energy once it enters the atmosphere.

When energy is absorbed by a surface, it heats that surface. For example, when you stand in the sun on a cool day, you can feel the sun's rays warming your body. Your skin

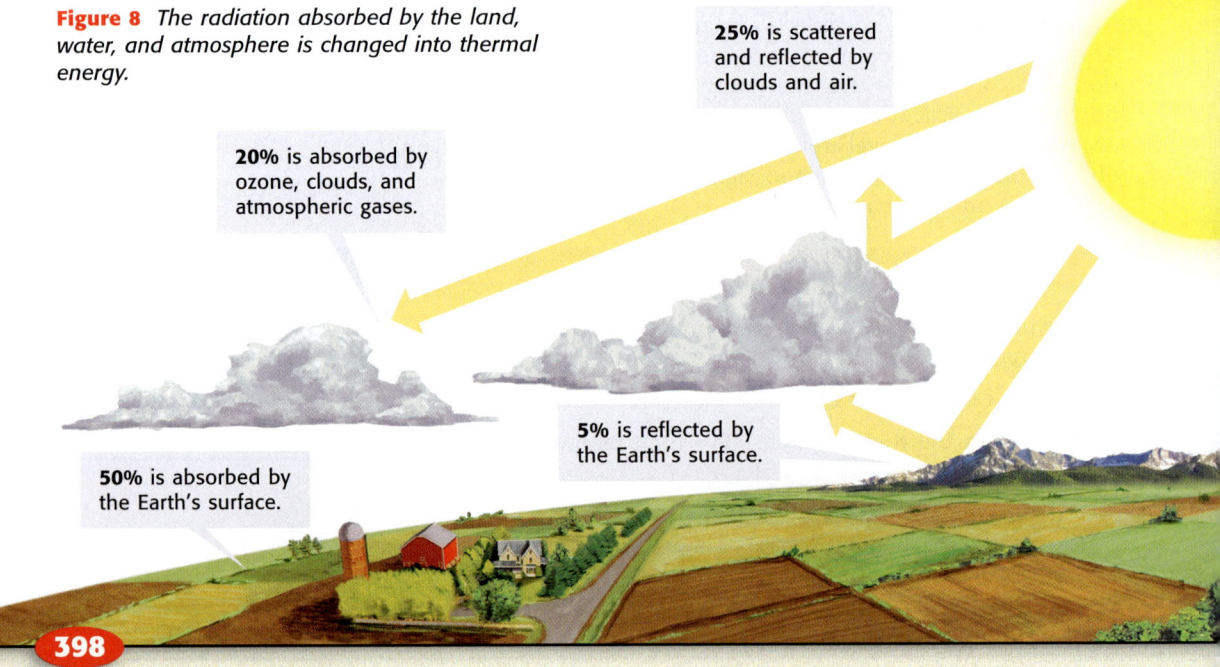

Figure 8 *The radiation absorbed by the land, water, and atmosphere is changed into thermal energy.*

- 25% is scattered and reflected by clouds and air.
- 20% is absorbed by ozone, clouds, and atmospheric gases.
- 5% is reflected by the Earth's surface.
- 50% is absorbed by the Earth's surface.

CONNECT TO ENVIRONMENTAL SCIENCE

The heat island effect occurs because concrete buildings and asphalt absorb solar radiation and reradiate thermal energy, elevating temperatures and increasing the production of smog. The effect is worse in urban areas with little surface water and few trees because the evaporation of water and plant transpiration cools the air. To counteract the heat island effect, cities have begun to preserve green spaces and plant trees. Some cities are beginning to use construction materials with a higher reflectivity, such as white rooftops and concrete streets. Have groups create a model city in a large box or aquarium. Using two light bulbs and a thermometer, they should test strategies to reduce the heat island effect.

absorbs the radiation, causing your skin's molecules to move faster. You feel this as an increase in temperature. The same thing happens when energy is absorbed by the Earth's surface. The energy from the Earth's surface can then be transferred to the atmosphere, which heats it.

Conduction Conduction is the transfer of thermal energy from one material to another by direct contact. Think back to the example about walking barefoot on a hot sidewalk. Conduction occurs when thermal energy is transferred from the sidewalk to your foot. Thermal energy always moves from warm to cold areas. Just as your foot is heated by the sidewalk, the air is heated by land and ocean surfaces. When air molecules come into direct contact with a warm surface, thermal energy is transferred to the atmosphere.

Convection Most thermal energy in the atmosphere moves by *convection*. Convection is the transfer of thermal energy by the circulation or movement of a liquid or gas. For instance, as air is heated, it becomes less dense and rises. Cool air is more dense and sinks. As the cool air sinks, it pushes the warm air up. The cool air is eventually heated by the ground and again begins to rise. This continual process of warm air rising and cool air sinking creates a circular movement of air, called a *convection current,* as shown in **Figure 9**.

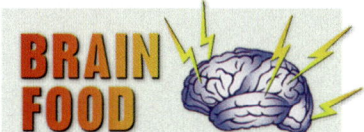

BRAIN FOOD

If the Earth is continually absorbing solar energy and changing it to thermal energy, why doesn't the Earth get hotter and hotter? The reason is that much of this energy is lost to space. This is especially true on cloudless nights.

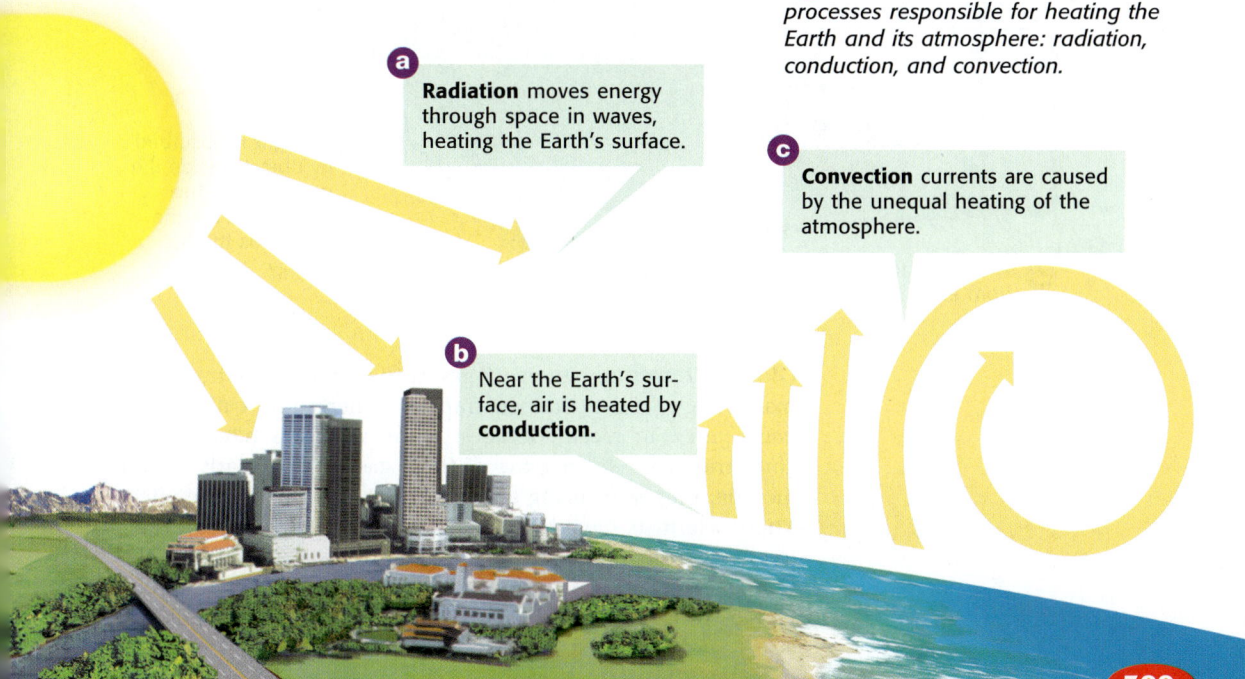

Figure 9 There are three important processes responsible for heating the Earth and its atmosphere: radiation, conduction, and convection.

a **Radiation** moves energy through space in waves, heating the Earth's surface.

b Near the Earth's surface, air is heated by **conduction.**

c **Convection** currents are caused by the unequal heating of the atmosphere.

WEIRD SCIENCE

In New York City in winter, the combined thermal energy released by all vehicles, factories, buildings, and electrical generators is 2.5 times the solar energy that reaches the ground!

Homework

Writing Have students write several paragraphs that compare and contrast various methods used to heat buildings. Suggest that they consider radiators, steam heating systems, heating systems that use furnaces, and solar heating systems. Make sure that students correctly use the terms *radiation, convection,* and *conduction* in their descriptions.

2) Teach

ACTIVITY

Make some popcorn the "old-fashioned" way, using a hot plate or stovetop, oil, and popcorn kernels. As you pop the snack, have volunteers explain how the processes of convection, conduction, and radiation are involved. Point out that a kernel pops when the liquid water stored inside changes to water vapor and expands suddenly. Share the treat with students if time allows. Make sure students with allergies to corn do not eat the popcorn. **Sheltered English**

DEMONSTRATION

Use heat-resistant gloves, a hot plate, a transparent coffee decanter, water, and confetti to demonstrate convection. Fill the decanter about three-fourths full with water. Sprinkle the confetti into the water, and mix it slightly so that it settles to the bottom. Put on the heat-resistant gloves, and hold the decanter so that only one-half of it is on the hot plate. Heat the water. Have students observe the convection currents move the confetti and explain how this demonstration relates to the movement of air in the atmosphere.

 Directed Reading Worksheet 15 Section 2

 **Teaching Transparency 163** "Radiation and the Atmosphere"

 **Teaching Transparency 164** "Radiation, Convection, and Conduction"

Section 2 • Heating of the Atmosphere

3) Extend

GROUP ACTIVITY
Model Greenhouses

MATERIALS

FOR EACH GROUP:
- large jar with lid
- thermometer
- small piece of modeling clay

Have students work in small groups to make model greenhouses by placing the thermometer inside the jar and anchoring it with modeling clay. Next have them seal the jar with the lid.

Have each group put its model in a different sunny spot. Students should observe and record changes in temperature every day for 1 week. Students can compare the temperatures they record with the temperatures in a control jar without a lid. Help students infer that solar energy enters a greenhouse and is converted to thermal energy and that the glass prevents most of the thermal energy from escaping.
Sheltered English

Boiling Over!

Teaching Transparency 165
"The Greenhouse Effect"

internetconnect

SC_iLINKS NSTA

TOPIC: Energy in the Atmosphere
GO TO: www.scilinks.org
*sci*LINKS NUMBER: HSTE360

TOPIC: The Greenhouse Effect
GO TO: www.scilinks.org
*sci*LINKS NUMBER: HSTE365

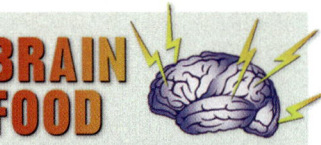

Annual average surface temperatures in the Northern Hemisphere have been higher in the 1990s than at any other time in the past 600 years.

The Greenhouse Effect

As you have already learned, 50 percent of the radiation that enters the Earth's atmosphere is absorbed by the Earth's surface. This energy is then reradiated to the Earth's atmosphere as thermal energy. Gases, such as carbon dioxide and water vapor, can stop this energy from escaping into space by absorbing it and then radiating it back to the Earth. As a result, the Earth's atmosphere stays warm. This is similar to how a blanket keeps you warm at night. The Earth's heating process, in which the gases in the atmosphere trap thermal energy, is known as the **greenhouse effect.** This term is used because the Earth's atmosphere works much like a greenhouse, as shown in **Figure 10.**

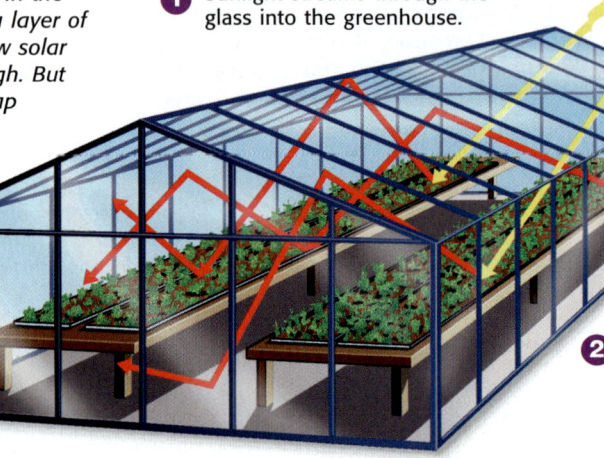

Figure 10 *The gases in the atmosphere act like a layer of glass. The gases allow solar energy to pass through. But some of the gases trap thermal energy.*

① Sunlight streams through the glass into the greenhouse.

② Sunlight is absorbed by objects inside the greenhouse. The objects radiate the energy as thermal energy.

③ The glass stops the thermal energy from escaping to the outside.

Global Warming Not every gas in the atmosphere traps thermal energy. Those that do trap this energy are called *greenhouse gases.* In recent decades, many scientists have become concerned that an increase of these gases, particularly carbon dioxide, may be causing an increase in the greenhouse effect. These scientists have hypothesized that a rise in carbon dioxide as a result of human activity has led to increased global temperatures. A rise in average global temperatures is called **global warming.** If there were an increase in the greenhouse effect, global warming would result.

SCIENTISTS AT ODDS

While there is little argument about the accuracy of the greenhouse-effect model, there is much debate in the scientific community over whether the recent rise in global temperatures is due to global warming or a normal fluctuation in global temperatures. Scientists agree that the use of fossil fuels and CFCs as well as deforestation contribute to global warming in the greenhouse-effect model, but there is debate over which is the predominant cause. Have interested students learn more about global warming and stage a class debate over some of these issues.

The Radiation Balance For the Earth to remain livable, the amount of energy received from the sun and the amount of energy returned to space must be equal. As you saw in Figure 8, about 30 percent of the incoming energy is reflected back into space. Most of the 70 percent that is absorbed by the Earth and its atmosphere is also sent back into space. The balance between incoming energy and outgoing energy is known as the *radiation balance*. If greenhouse gases, such as carbon dioxide, continue to increase in the atmosphere, the radiation balance may be affected. Some of the energy that once escaped into space could be trapped. The Earth's temperatures would continue to rise, causing major changes in plant and animal communities.

Keeping the Earth Livable Some scientists argue that the Earth had warmer periods before humans ever walked the planet, so global warming may be a natural process. Nevertheless, many of the world's nations have signed a treaty to reduce activities that increase greenhouse gases in the atmosphere. Another step that is being taken to reduce high carbon dioxide levels in the atmosphere is the planting of millions of trees by volunteers, as shown in **Figure 11**.

Biology CONNECTION

Did you know that if you lived in Florida, your fingernails and toenails would grow faster than if you lived in Minnesota? Studies by scientists at Oxford University, in England, showed that warm weather helps tissue growth, while cold weather slightly slows it.

Figure 11 Plants take in harmful carbon dioxide and give off oxygen, which we need to breathe.

REVIEW

1. Describe three things that can happen to energy when it reaches the Earth's atmosphere.
2. How is energy transferred through the atmosphere?
3. What is the greenhouse effect?
4. **Inferring Relationships** How does the process of convection rely on conduction?

internet connect

SCILINKS
NSTA
TOPIC: Energy in the Atmosphere
GO TO: www.scilinks.org
sciLINKS NUMBER: HSTE360

CONNECT TO LIFE SCIENCE

The study described in the Biology Connection on this page found that the average fingernail growth in the tropics is 1 mm a day, while in temperate regions, it is 0.8 mm a day. High altitude mountaineers are also familiar with this phenomenon. At altitudes above 6 km (19,600 feet), fingernail and hair growth slows dramatically due to the lack of oxygen. Cuts heal very slowly, and male mountaineers don't need to shave!

4) Close

Quiz

1. What is radiation? (energy transferred as electromagnetic waves)
2. A metal spoon left in a bowl of hot soup feels hot. Which process—radiation, conduction, or convection—is mainly responsible for heating the spoon? (conduction)
3. What is a convection current? (the continual, circular movement of warm and cool particles in a liquid or gas)
4. How does a greenhouse stay warm? (Sunlight goes through the glass. Objects in the structure absorb some of the radiant energy. In turn, the objects radiate thermal energy. The glass prevents the energy from escaping, which warms the greenhouse.)

ALTERNATIVE ASSESSMENT

Writing Have students write a paragraph that compares and contrasts radiation, conduction, and convection. Ask students to explain how each process heats the atmosphere.

▼ **Answers to Review**

1. Answers will vary. Sample answer: Radiation can be absorbed by the Earth's surface. It can be absorbed by ozone, clouds, and the atmosphere or reflected by the Earth's surface and clouds.
2. Answers will vary. Sample answer: Energy is transferred through the atmosphere through radiation, conduction, and convection.
3. The greenhouse effect is the Earth's natural heating process by which gases in the atmosphere trap thermal energy.
4. Answers will vary. Sample answer: The air directly above the Earth's surface is heated by conduction. This warm air is then circulated through the atmosphere by convection currents.

SECTION 3

Atmospheric Pressure and Winds

Terms to Learn
wind
Coriolis effect
trade winds
westerlies
polar easterlies
jet streams

What You'll Do
- Explain the relationship between air pressure and wind direction.
- Describe the global patterns of wind.
- Explain the causes of local wind patterns.

Sometimes it cools you. Other times it scatters tidy piles of newly swept trash. Still other times it uproots trees and flattens buildings, as shown in **Figure 12**. **Wind** is moving air. In this section you will learn about air movement and about the similarities and differences between different kinds of winds.

Figure 12 *In 1998, the winds from Hurricane Mitch reached speeds of 288 km/h, destroying entire towns in Honduras.*

Why Air Moves

Wind is created by differences in air pressure. The greater the pressure difference is, the faster the wind moves. This difference in air pressure is generally caused by the unequal heating of the Earth. For example, the air at the equator is warmer and less dense. This warm, less-dense air rises. As it rises it creates an area of low pressure. At the poles, however, the air is colder and more dense. Colder, more-dense air is heavier and sinks. This cold, sinking air creates areas of high pressure. Pressure differences in the atmosphere at the equator and at the poles cause air to move. Because air moves from areas of high pressure to areas of low pressure, winds generally move from the poles to the equator, as shown in **Figure 13**.

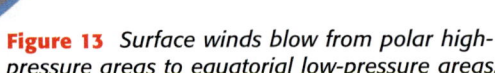

Figure 13 *Surface winds blow from polar high-pressure areas to equatorial low-pressure areas.*

CONNECT TO PHYSICAL SCIENCE

Katabatic wind is the movement of air due to the influence of gravity. This flow can range from a gentle breeze to hurricane-force winds. The world's strongest katabatic winds occur in Antarctica because there is no shortage of cold air and the highest spot is near the center of the continent. Because the continent is roughly cone shaped, winds radiate from the South Pole, accelerating like a car rolling down a hill. Cold, dense air rushes down mountainsides, tumbles across the ice sheets, and spills out over the ocean. The winds can blow for months, and they sometimes reach speeds as great as 320 km/hr! Demonstrate this phenomenon using dry ice and a modeling-clay mountain.

Pressure Belts You may be imagining wind moving in one huge, circular pattern, from the poles to the equator. In fact, the pattern is much more complex. As warm air rises over the equator, it begins to cool. Eventually, it stops rising and moves toward the poles. At about 30° north and 30° south latitude, some of the cool air begins to sink. This cool, sinking air causes a high pressure belt near 30° north and 30° south latitude.

At the poles, cold air sinks. As this air moves away from the poles and along the Earth's surface, it begins to warm. As the air warms, the pressure drops, creating a low-pressure belt around 60° north and 60° south latitude. The circular patterns caused by the rising and sinking of air are called *convection cells*, as shown in **Figure 14.**

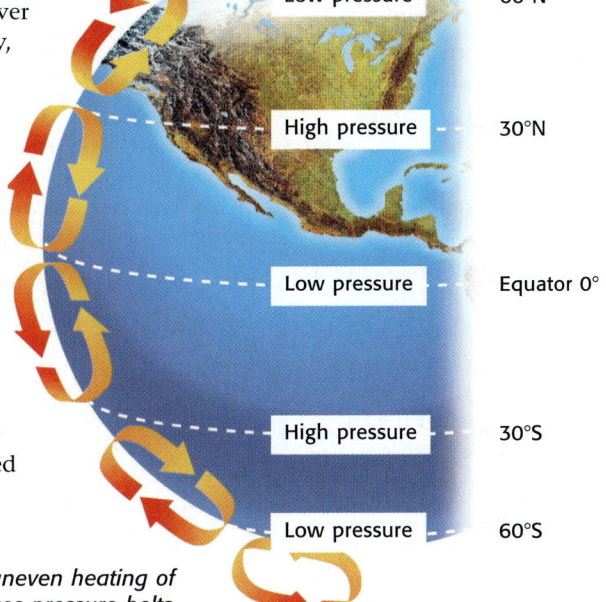

Figure 14 *The uneven heating of the Earth produces pressure belts. These belts occur at about every 30° of latitude.*

Coriolis Effect Winds don't blow directly north or south. The movement of wind is affected by the rotation of the Earth. The Earth's rotation causes wind to travel in a curved path rather than in a straight line. The curving of moving objects, such as wind, by the Earth's rotation is called the **Coriolis effect.** Because of the Coriolis effect, the winds in the Northern Hemisphere curve to the right, and those in the Southern Hemisphere curve to the left.

To better understand how the Coriolis effect works, imagine rolling a marble across a Lazy Susan while it is spinning. What you might observe is shown in **Figure 15.**

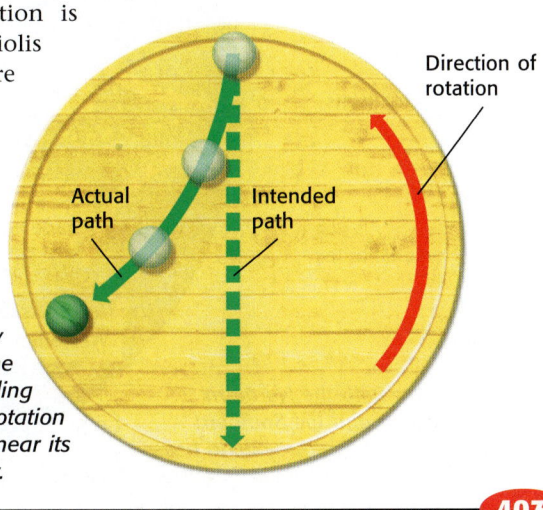

Figure 15 *Because of the Lazy Susan's rotation, the path of the marble curves instead of traveling in a straight line. The Earth's rotation affects objects traveling on or near its surface in much the same way.*

WEIRD SCIENCE

In addition to affecting ocean and atmospheric currents, the Coriolis effect can also be observed in river systems. Rivers in the Northern Hemisphere erode their right banks more than their left banks. Because the Mississippi River and the Yukon River flow roughly north-south in sections, they are good examples of this effect.

2 Teach

Multicultural CONNECTION

Changes in atmospheric pressure are often said to affect fish. Egyptian fishermen notice that mullet move with the wind to prevent getting stuck in muddy water. According to Caribbean lore, a container of shark oil will grow cloudy when a hurricane is imminent. Have students find out about other organisms that might indicate changes in air pressure and other atmospheric phenomena.

MEETING INDIVIDUAL NEEDS

Learners Having Difficulty Try the following activity to help students who have problems understanding the Coriolis effect. You will need a globe, some flour, an eyedropper, red food coloring, and water. Mix a few drops of food coloring with water, and fill the eyedropper with the solution. Dust the globe thoroughly with flour. If the flour doesn't stick, mist the globe lightly with tap water and sprinkle the flour over the globe. Enlist a volunteer to slowly spin the globe counter-clockwise to simulate Earth's rotation. Have another volunteer slowly drop water from the dropper from the top of the globe, at the North Pole. Students will observe that the water is deflected westward in the Northern Hemisphere. Have students demonstrate the Coriolis effect in the Southern Hemisphere by turning the globe upside down and rotating it clockwise.
Sheltered English

Directed Reading Worksheet 15 Section 3

2 Teach, continued

QuickLab

MATERIALS
- large clear-plastic container
- cold water
- packaging string (about 30 cm long)
- small plastic bottle with a narrow neck
- hot water
- red food coloring

Answers to QuickLab

6. The red warm water should rise. This activity models the circulation of air in the atmosphere. If the container were filled with cold water, the colored water would sink.

USING THE FIGURE

Have students use **Figure 16** to answer the following questions:

Where are the trade winds? (the winds that blow from 30° north and south latitudes to the equator)

Describe the motion of the trade winds in the Southern Hemisphere. (They move from the southeast to the northwest.)

How do the westerlies flow in the Northern Hemisphere? (The westerlies flow from the southwest to the northeast.)

What is the name of the windless zone that lies between the trade winds? (the doldrums)

internetconnect
SCILINKS NSTA
TOPIC: Atmospheric Pressure and Winds
GO TO: www.scilinks.org
sciLINKS NUMBER: HSTE370

QuickLab

Full of "Hot Air"

1. Fill a **large clear-plastic container** with **cold water.**
2. Tie the end of a **string** around the neck of a **small bottle.**
3. Fill the small bottle with **hot water,** and add a few drops of **red food coloring** until the water has changed color.
4. Without tipping the small bottle, lower it into the plastic container until it rests on the bottom.
5. Observe what happens.
6. What process does this activity model? What do you think will happen if you fill the small bottle with cold water instead? Try it!

Types of Winds

There are two main types of winds: local winds and global winds. Both types are caused by the uneven heating of the Earth's surface and by pressure differences. *Local winds* generally move short distances and can blow from any direction. *Global winds* are part of a pattern of air circulation that moves across the Earth. These winds travel longer distances than local winds, and they each travel in a specific direction. **Figure 16** shows the location and movement of major global wind systems. First let's review the different types of global winds, and later in this section we will discuss local winds.

Trade Winds In both hemispheres, the winds that blow from 30° latitude to the equator are called **trade winds.** The Coriolis effect causes the trade winds to curve, as shown in Figure 16. Early traders used the trade winds to sail from Europe to the Americas. This is how they became known as "trade winds."

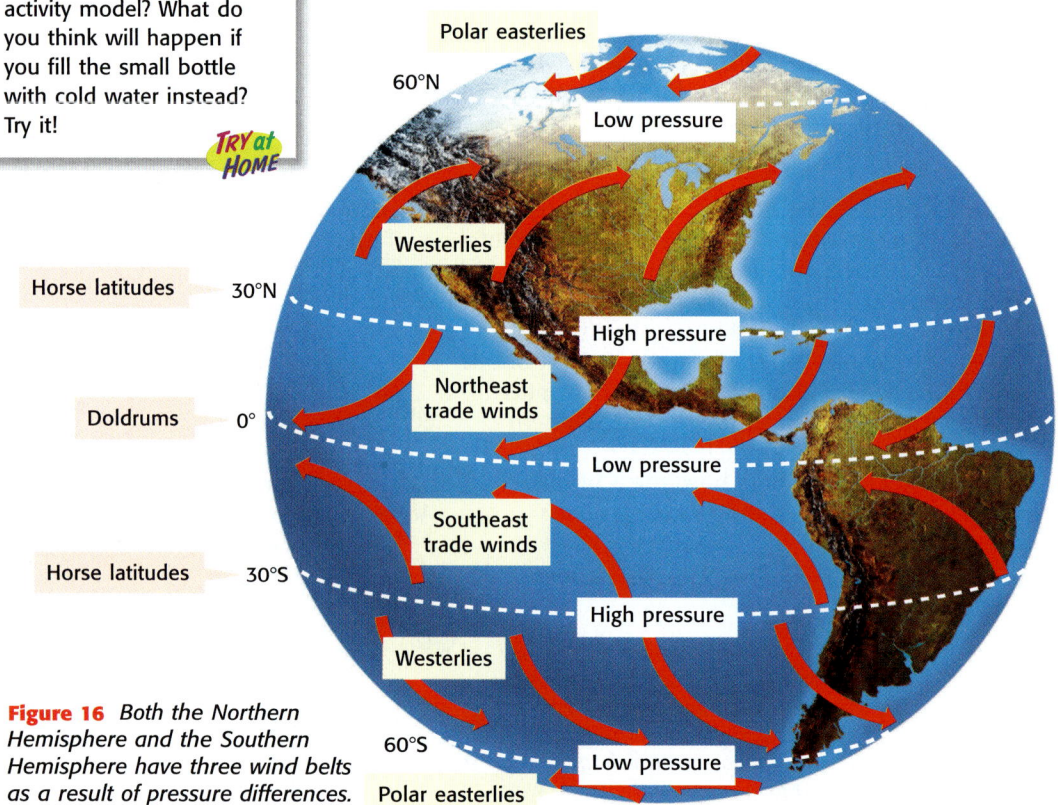

Figure 16 Both the Northern Hemisphere and the Southern Hemisphere have three wind belts as a result of pressure differences.

Science Bloopers

During a World War I naval engagement off the Falkland Islands, British gunners were astonished to see that their artillery shells were landing 100 yd to the left of German ships. The gunners had made corrections for the Coriolis effect at 50° north latitude, not 50° south of the equator. Consequently, their shells fell at a distance from the target equal to twice the Coriolis deflection!

The Doldrums and Horse Latitudes The trade winds of the Northern and Southern Hemispheres meet in an area of low pressure around the equator called the *doldrums*. In the doldrums there is very little wind because of the warm rising air. *Doldrums* comes from an Old English word meaning "foolish." Sailors were considered foolish if they got their ship stuck in these areas of little wind.

At about 30° north and 30° south latitude, sinking air creates an area of high pressure. This area is called the *horse latitudes*. Here the winds are weak. Legend has it that the name horse latitudes was given to these areas when sailing ships carried horses from Europe to the Americas. When the ships were stuck in this area due to lack of wind, horses were sometimes thrown overboard to save drinking water for the sailors.

Westerlies The **westerlies** are wind belts found in both the Northern and Southern Hemispheres between 30° and 60° latitude. The westerlies flow toward the poles in the opposite direction of the trade winds. The westerlies helped early traders return to Europe. Sailing ships, like the one in **Figure 17,** were designed to best use the wind to move the ship forward.

Environment CONNECTION

Humans have been using wind energy for thousands of years. Today wind energy is being tapped to produce electricity at wind farms. Wind farms are made up of hundreds of wind turbines that look like giant airplane propellers attached to towers. Together these wind turbines can produce enough electricity for an entire town.

Figure 17 *This ship is a replica of Columbus's Santa Maria. If it had not sunk, the Santa Maria would have used the westerlies to return to Europe.*

Polar Easterlies The **polar easterlies** are wind belts that extend from the poles to 60° latitude in both hemispheres. The polar easterlies are formed from cold, sinking air moving from the poles toward 60° north and 60° south latitude.

To find out how to build a device that measures wind speed, turn to page 690 of the LabBook.

405

3 Extend

GROUP ACTIVITY

Modeling Sea and Land Breezes Give each group two baking pans—one filled with sand and the other filled with ice. Groups should carefully warm the sand in an oven until it is very warm to the touch. Have the groups place the pans side-by-side. Then they should fold a cardboard windscreen in three places so that it wraps around both pans. As they hold a burning splint or stick of incense at the boundary between the pans, students should see smoke travel toward the hot sand in the same way that the wind blows toward the beach during the daytime. To simulate a land breeze, allow the sand to cool and replace the ice with warm water.

MATH and MORE

A pilot flying 950 km to Chicago is worried about a storm that will hit the city in 2 hours. The plane can fly at 500 km/h. A jet stream flowing in the opposite direction is moving at 250 km/h. If the plane must spend 10 minutes in the jet stream in order to climb above it, can the pilot make it to Chicago before the storm hits?

The pilot can beat the storm:
(500 km/h × $1\frac{5}{6}$ h) + (250 km/h × $\frac{1}{6}$ h) = 958 km in 2 hours

Teaching Transparency 166
"Sea and Land Breezes"

Jet Streams The **jet streams** are narrow belts of high-speed winds that blow in the upper troposphere and lower stratosphere, as shown in **Figure 18**. These winds often change speed and can reach maximum speeds of 500 km/h. Unlike other global winds, the jet streams do not follow regular paths around the Earth.

Knowing the position of the jet stream is important to both meteorologists and airline pilots. Because the jet stream controls the movement of storms, meteorologists can track a storm if they know the location of the jet stream. By flying in the direction of the jet stream, pilots can save time and fuel.

Figure 18 *The jet stream is the white stripe moving diagonally above the Earth.*

Local Winds Local winds are influenced by the geography of an area. An area's geography, such as a shoreline or a mountain, sometimes produces temperature differences that cause local winds like land and sea breezes, as shown in **Figure 19**. During the day, land heats up faster than water. The land heats the air above it. At night, land cools faster than water, cooling the air above the land.

Figure 19 Sea and Land Breezes

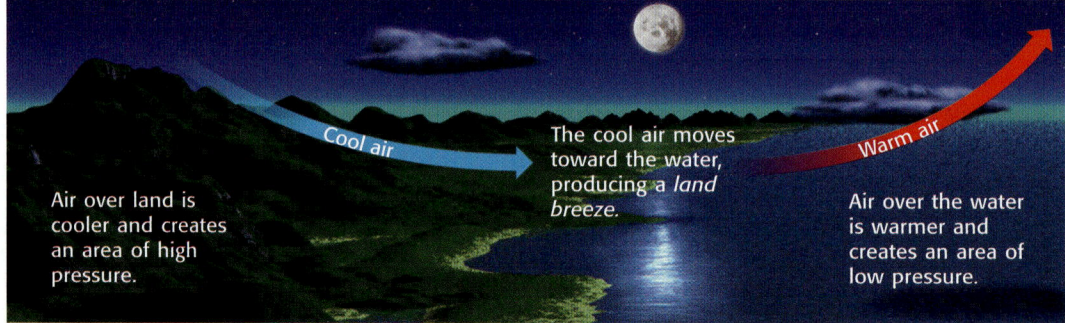

Multicultural CONNECTION

The *chinook,* or "snow eater," is a dry wind that blows down the eastern side of the Rocky Mountains from New Mexico to Canada. Arapaho Indians gave the chinook its name because of its ability to melt large amounts of snow very quickly. Originating as moist air blowing off the Pacific Ocean, it heats up and loses moisture over the Rocky Mountains. When it reaches the Northwest, the chinook is warm and dry enough to melt a half meter of snow in a few hours! Have interested students research other local winds, such as the *sirocco,* the *Santa Ana,* or the *shamal,* that have a profound impact on people's lives.

406 Chapter 15 • The Atmosphere

Mountain and valley breezes are another example of local winds caused by an area's geography. Campers in mountain areas may feel a warm afternoon change into a cold night soon after the sun sets. The illustrations in **Figure 20** show you why.

MATH BREAK

Calculating Groundspeed
An airplane has an airspeed of 500 km/h and is moving into a 150 km/h head wind due to the jet stream. What is the actual groundspeed of the plane? Over a 3-hour flight, how far would the plane actually travel? (Hint: To calculate actual groundspeed, subtract head-wind speed from airspeed.)

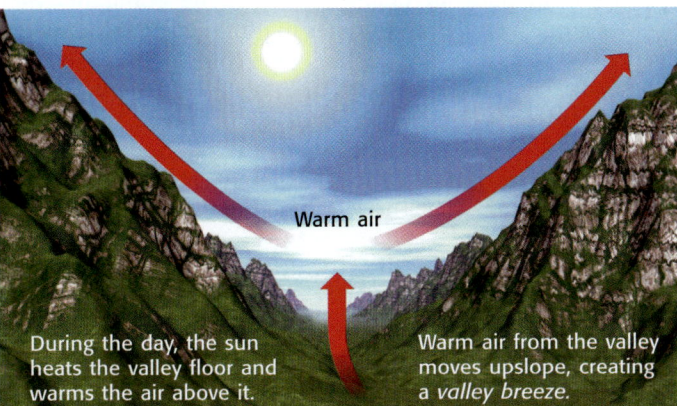

During the day, the sun heats the valley floor and warms the air above it.

Warm air from the valley moves upslope, creating a *valley breeze*.

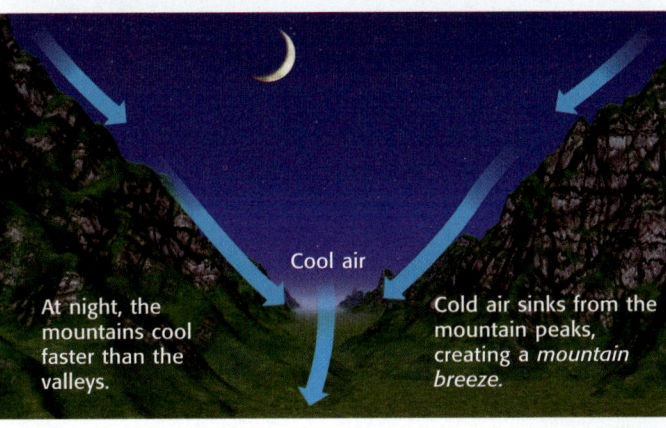

At night, the mountains cool faster than the valleys.

Cold air sinks from the mountain peaks, creating a *mountain breeze*.

Figure 20 *During the day, a gentle breeze blows up the slopes. At night, cold air flows downslope and settles in the valley.*

REVIEW

1. How does the Coriolis effect affect wind movement?
2. What causes winds?
3. Compare and contrast global winds and local winds.
4. **Applying Concepts** Suppose you are vacationing at the beach. It is daytime and you want to go swimming in the ocean. You know the beach is near your hotel, but you don't know what direction it is in. How might the local wind help you find the ocean?

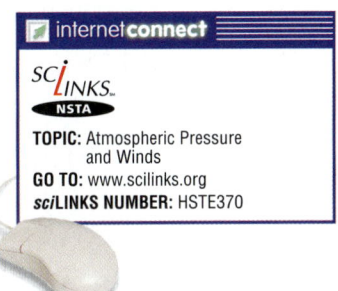

TOPIC: Atmospheric Pressure and Winds
GO TO: www.scilinks.org
sciLINKS NUMBER: HSTE370

Answers to MATHBREAK
500 km/h − 150 km/h = 350 km/h
3 h × 350 km/h = 1,050 km

4) Close

Quiz

1. What is wind? (air that flows between air masses of different pressures and temperatures)
2. How does air temperature over landmasses and adjacent bodies of water change between day and night? (During the day, the air is cooler over water. At night, the air is cooler over land.)
3. What is the Coriolis effect? (the deflection of moving objects due to Earth's rotation)
4. Compare and contrast the trade winds and the westerlies in the Northern Hemisphere. (Both are global wind systems that curve due to the Coriolis effect. Both result from differences in air pressure and temperature. The trade winds that lie between the equator and 30° north latitude blow from the northeast to the southwest. The westerlies lying between 30° and 60° north latitude blow from the southwest to the northeast.)
5. What are two kinds of breezes that result from local topography? (mountain and valley breezes)

Alternative Assessment

Concept Mapping Have students create a concept map using the vocabulary and concepts in this section.

Answers to Review

1. The Coriolis effect prevents winds from blowing directly north or south. Due to the Coriolis effect, trade winds in the Northern Hemisphere curve to the right and trade winds in the Southern Hemisphere curve to the left.
2. Winds are caused by the unequal heating of the Earth's surface and by pressure differences.
3. Local winds travel short distances and can blow from any direction. Global winds travel long distances and travel in specific directions.
4. During the day, a sea breeze is caused by the cooler air over the water moving toward the land. Walking toward the sea breeze would lead you to the ocean.

SECTION 4

Focus

The Air We Breathe

This section defines and discusses air pollution. Students learn the difference between primary and secondary pollutants and explore sources of human-caused air pollution. Students then learn about some broader impacts of air pollution, such as acid precipitation and the ozone hole. Finally, students learn about the health effects of air pollution and what people can do to limit pollution.

Bellringer

Bring a filter mask to class. Have each student make a list of three situations in which one might wear such a mask. For example, surgeons wear such masks to prevent the transfer of disease-causing microbes, and sandblasters wear masks to avoid inhaling dust and paint chips. Tell students that some people living in areas with heavily polluted air wear such masks to protect themselves from impurities in the air they breathe.

1) Motivate

DISCUSSION

Explain that the air inside buildings may be polluted by a variety of sources. Ask students to list possible sources of indoor air pollution. If students have difficulty coming up with examples, tell them that air pollution is often invisible. Chalk dust, cooking oils, carpets, insulation, tobacco smoke, paints, glues, copier machines, space heaters, gas appliances, and fireplaces are just a few sources of indoor air pollution.

408 Chapter 15 • The Atmosphere

Section 4

Terms to Learn
primary pollutants
secondary pollutants
acid precipitation

What You'll Do
- Describe the major types of air pollution.
- Name the major causes of air pollution.
- Explain how air pollution can affect human health.
- Explain how air pollution can be reduced.

The Air We Breathe

Air pollution, as shown in **Figure 21**, is not a new problem. By the middle of the 1700s, many of the world's large cities suffered from poor air quality. Most of the pollutants were released from factories and homes that burned coal for energy. Even 2,000 years ago, the Romans were complaining about the bad air in their cities. At that time the air was thick with the smoke from fires and the smell of open sewers. So you see, cities have always been troubled with air pollution. In this section you will learn about the different types of air pollution, their sources, and what the world is doing to reduce them.

Figure 21 The air pollution in Mexico City is sometimes so dangerous that some people wear surgical masks when they go outside.

Air Quality

Even "clean" air is not perfectly clean. It contains many pollutants from natural sources. These pollutants include dust, sea salt, volcanic gases and ash, smoke from forest fires, pollen, swamp gas, and many other materials. In fact, natural sources produce a greater amount of pollutants than humans do. But we have adapted to many of these natural pollutants.

Most of the air pollution mentioned in the news is a result of human activities. Pollutants caused by human activities can be solids, liquids, or gases. Human-caused air pollution, such as that shown in Figure 21, is most common in cities. As more people move to cities, urban air pollution increases.

 Directed Reading Worksheet 15 Section 4

Q: What did the person say to the polluted air?

A: You take my breath away!

Types of Air Pollution

Air pollutants are generally described as either *primary pollutants* or *secondary pollutants*. **Primary pollutants** are pollutants that are put directly into the air by human or natural activity. **Figure 22** shows some examples of primary air pollutants.

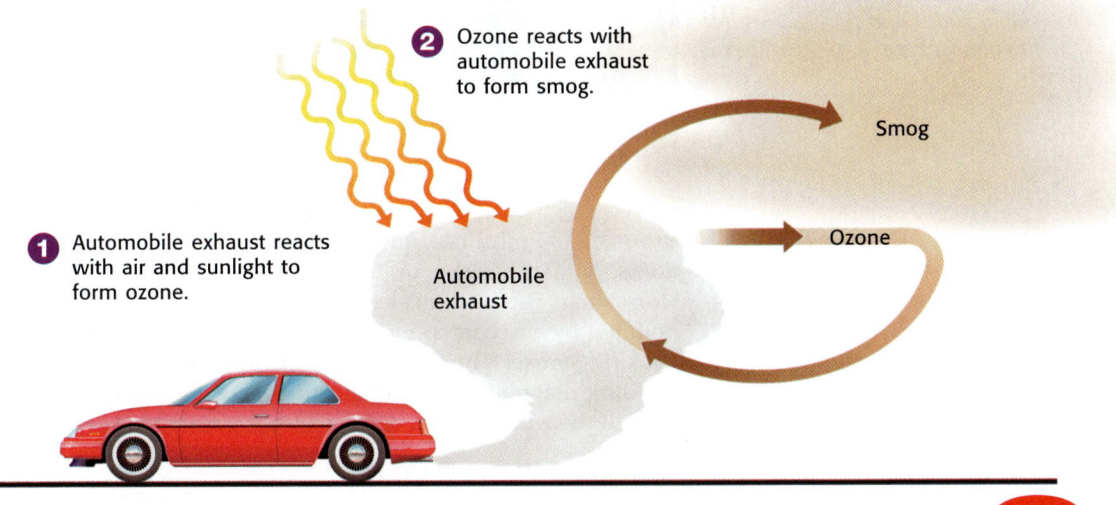

Figure 22 *Exhaust from vehicles, ash from volcanic eruptions, and soot from smoke are all examples of primary pollutants.*

Secondary pollutants are pollutants that form from chemical reactions that occur when primary pollutants come in contact with other primary pollutants or with naturally occurring substances, such as water vapor. Many secondary pollutants are formed when a primary pollutant reacts with sunlight. Ozone and smog are examples of secondary pollutants. As you read at the beginning of this chapter, ozone is a gas in the stratosphere that is helpful and absorbs harmful rays from the sun. Near the ground, however, ozone is a dangerous pollutant that affects the health of all organisms. Ozone and smog are produced when sunlight reacts with automobile exhaust, as illustrated in **Figure 23.**

Figure 23 *Many large cities suffer from smog, especially those with a sunny climate and millions of automobiles.*

① Automobile exhaust reacts with air and sunlight to form ozone.

② Ozone reacts with automobile exhaust to form smog.

IS THAT A FACT!

In addition to forming as a reactant when certain pollutants are exposed to sunlight, ozone also forms during thunderstorms. Lightning provides the energy to change O_2 to O_3. In fact, the distinct smell people notice after an intense thunderstorm is ozone.

2) Teach

GUIDED PRACTICE

List the following pollutants on the board or on an overhead projector:

house dust, pollen, volcanic ash, soot, smog, ground-level ozone, acid rain

Beside the list, make a two-column table with the following column headings:

Primary pollutants, Secondary pollutants

Help students classify each pollutant as either a primary pollutant (house dust, pollen, volcanic ash, and soot) or a secondary pollutant (ground-level ozone, smog, and acid rain). **Sheltered English**

MISCONCEPTION ALERT

Many people believe that polluted air must be visibly smoky or be brown or black in color. Stress that some of the most dangerous air pollutants are those that can't be seen with the naked eye. Challenge students to use the Internet to find out about the various pollutants monitored by the Environmental Protection Agency and other organizations that monitor air quality. Have students compile their results in a table that lists the acceptable amounts allowed in the air, the levels in your community, and the health problems associated with each pollutant.

Teaching Transparency 167 "The Formation of Smog"

Section 4 • The Air We Breathe

2) Teach, continued

CONNECT TO PHYSICAL SCIENCE

Explain to students that much of the human-caused air pollution results from incomplete combustion. *Combustion*, another word for burning, is the process by which substances combine with oxygen rapidly, producing thermal energy. Byproducts are produced when a substance does not burn completely, as in an automobile engine. Many of these byproducts, such as carbon monoxide, are harmful to living organisms.

REAL-WORLD CONNECTION

Air quality varies greatly from place to place. Even in one location, air quality can change greatly from day to day. Have students research the air quality where they live. What are the sources of air pollution where you live? What are the weather conditions that lead to the worst and best air quality in your area?

RESEARCH

Writing Radon is a naturally occurring gas that results from the decay of uranium particularly in igneous rocks, such as granite. Have interested students research the air pollution and health problems associated with radon. Encourage students to assess the potential for significant radon concentrations in your community. Have students write a short informative essay based on their findings.

Sources of Human-Caused Air Pollution

Human-caused air pollution comes from a variety of sources. The major source of air pollution today is transportation, as shown in **Figure 24.** Cars contribute about 60 percent of the human-caused air pollution in the United States. The oxides that come from car exhaust, such as nitrogen oxide, contribute to smog and acid rain. *Oxides* are chemical compounds that contain oxygen and other elements.

Industrial Air Pollution Many industrial plants and electric power plants burn fossil fuels to get their energy. But burning fossil fuels causes large amounts of oxides to be released into the air, as shown in **Figure 25.** In fact, the burning of fossil fuels in industrial and electric power plants is responsible for 96 percent of the sulfur oxides released into the atmosphere.

Some industries also produce chemicals that form poisonous fumes. The chemicals used by oil refineries, chemical manufacturing plants, dry-cleaning businesses, furniture refinishers, and auto-body shops can add poisonous fumes to the air.

Figure 24 *Seventy percent of the carbon monoxide in the United States is produced by fuel-burning vehicles.*

Figure 25 *This power plant burns coal to get its energy and releases sulfur oxides and particulates into the atmosphere.*

Indoor Air Pollution Air pollution is not limited to the outdoors. Sometimes the air inside a home or building is even worse than the air outside. The air inside a building can be polluted by the compounds found in household cleaners and cooking smoke. The compounds in new carpets, paints, and building materials can also add to indoor air pollution, especially if the windows and doors are tightly sealed to keep energy bills low.

Multicultural CONNECTION

Scientists have found high levels of airborne contaminants in the breast milk of Inuit women in Greenland and Arctic Canada. Researchers think the contaminants arrived in these remote areas by a process called global distillation. In this process, contaminants are redistributed around the globe by atmospheric currents. They tend to concentrate in northern areas for the same reason that water vapor condenses on cold glass: gaseous substances tend to condense at colder temperatures.

The Air Pollution Problem

Air pollution is both a local and global concern. As you have already learned, local air pollution, such as smog, generally affects large cities. Air pollution becomes a global concern when local pollution moves away from its source. Winds can move pollutants from one place to another, sometimes reducing the amount of pollution in the source area but increasing it in another place. For example, the prevailing winds carry air pollution created in the midwestern United States hundreds of miles to Canada. One such form of this pollution is acid precipitation.

Figure 26 Acid precipitation can kill living things, such as fish and trees, by making their environment too acidic to live in.

Acid Precipitation Precipitation that contains acids from air pollution is called **acid precipitation.** When fossil fuels are burned, they release oxides of sulfur and nitrogen into the atmosphere. When these oxides combine with water droplets in the atmosphere, they form sulfuric acid and nitric acid, which fall as precipitation. Acid precipitation has many negative effects on the environment, as shown in **Figure 26.**

The Ozone Hole Other global concerns brought about by air pollution include the warming of our planet and the ozone hole in the stratosphere. In the 1970s, scientists determined that some chemicals released into the atmosphere react with ozone in the ozone layer. The reaction results in a breakdown of ozone into oxygen, which does not block the sun's harmful ultraviolet rays. The loss of ozone creates an ozone hole, which allows more ultraviolet rays to reach the Earth's surface. **Figure 27** shows a satellite image of the ozone hole.

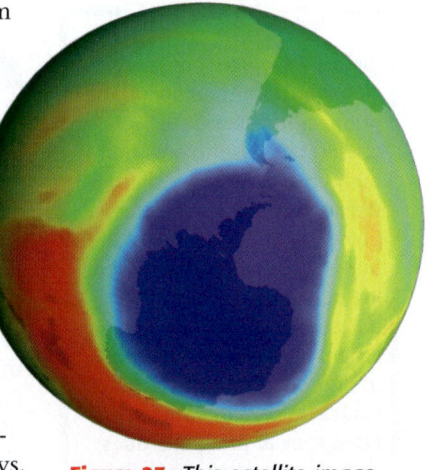

Figure 27 This satellite image, taken in 1998, shows that the ozone hole, the dark blue area, is still growing.

WEIRD SCIENCE

One reason the ozone layer is thinner over Antarctica involves a strange type of cloud. During winter in Antarctica, the stratosphere over the continent receives little light and temperatures can be below –80°C. In these conditions, chemicals in the air freeze and form *polar stratospheric clouds.* When light hits the clouds in spring, it catalyzes ozone-destroying reactions in cloud droplets, drastically reducing ozone concentrations over Antarctica.

GROUP ACTIVITY

Check the air quality near your school by collecting particulate matter. Remove the protective backing from an $8\frac{1}{2} \times 11$ in. sheet of clear contact paper, and place it over a sheet of graph paper. Pin the papers to a piece of cardboard with the sticky side up. Place the cardboard somewhere where it will be undisturbed for 1 day. Students can collect the contact paper and can use the grids on the graph paper and a magnifying glass to count the number of particles they collected. Students should also note particle sizes. As an extension, try this experiment at different times of the year and in different locations in your community.

INDEPENDENT PRACTICE

Writing Have interested students find out how the ozone hole has changed since it was first measured. Have students graph the values on both a yearly and seasonal basis and describe any trends they see. Have them compile their findings into a short report.

DEMONSTRATION

Demonstrate how acid rain affects limestone or marble. Put some limestone or marble chips into a beaker of vinegar. Let the chips sit a few days, and have students note any differences in the surface of the chips and in the acid solution. (Students should observe that the surface of the chips is pitted. The solution will be cloudy.)

3) Extend

RETEACHING

Have students try to answer the questions below without referring to their textbook.

How do primary air pollutants differ from secondary ones? (Primary pollutants enter the atmosphere from human activities and natural events. Secondary pollutants form when primary pollutants react with other primary pollutants or with naturally occurring substances in the air.)

How does smog form? (Smog forms when sunlight reacts with automobile exhaust to create ozone. Ozone then reacts with automobile exhaust to create smog.)

How does acid precipitation form? (Acid precipitation forms when fossil fuels are burned, releasing oxides of nitrogen and sulfur into the air. These oxides combine with moisture in the air to form acids that fall to Earth in rain, snow, sleet, and hail.)

CROSS-DISCIPLINARY FOCUS

Health Have students find out about respiratory diseases that can be aggravated by air pollution, such as asthma. Have students compile their findings into tables that list the diseases, their symptoms, how they are treated, the age groups most commonly afflicted, and the relationship between the diseases and air pollutants.

Answer to Activity

Answers will vary. Accept all reasonable responses.

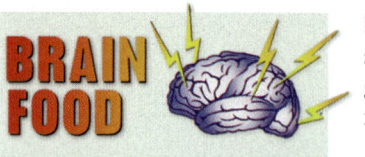

BRAIN FOOD

Nonsmoking city dwellers are three to four times more likely to develop lung cancer than nonsmoking people in rural areas.

Effects on Human Health

You step outside and notice a smoky haze. When you take a deep breath, your throat tingles and you begin to cough. Air pollution like this affects many cities around the world. For example, on March 17, 1992, in Mexico City, all children under the age of 14 were prohibited from going to school because of extremely high levels of air pollution. This is an extreme case, but daily exposure to small amounts of air pollution can cause serious health problems. Children, elderly people, and people with allergies, lung problems, and heart problems are especially vulnerable to the effects of air pollution. **Figure 28** illustrates some of the effects that air pollution has on the human body.

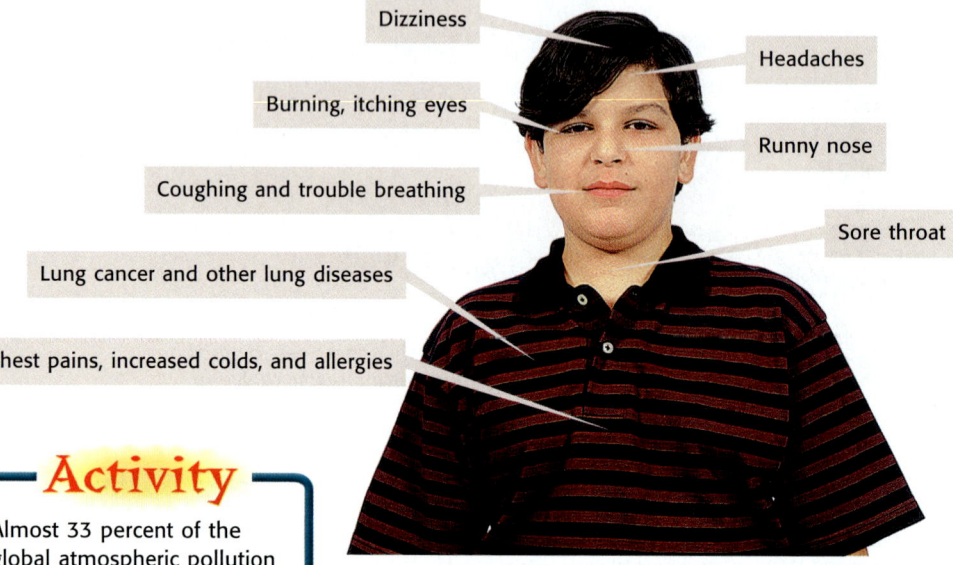

Figure 28 The Environmental Protection Agency blames air pollution for at least 2,000 new cases of cancer each year.

Activity

Almost 33 percent of the global atmospheric pollution from carbon dioxide is caused by power plants that burn coal or other fossil fuels. We rely on these sources of power for a better way of life, but our use of them is polluting our air and worsening our quality of life. Use your school library or the Internet to find out about some other sources of electric power. What special problems does each source of energy bring with it?

TRY at HOME

Cleaning Up Our Act

Is all this talk about bad air making you a little choked up? Don't worry, help is on the way! In the United States, progress has been made in cleaning up the air. One reason for this progress is the Clean Air Act, which was passed by Congress in 1970. The Clean Air Act is a law that gives the Environmental Protection Agency (EPA) the authority to control the amount of air pollutants that can be released from any source, such as cars and factories. The EPA also checks air quality. If air quality worsens, the EPA can set stricter standards. What are car manufacturers and factories doing to improve air quality? Read on to find out.

internetconnect

SCLINKS **TOPIC:** Air Pollution
GO TO: www.scilinks.org
NSTA **sciLINKS NUMBER:** HSTE375

WEIRD SCIENCE

Ice core samples from Greenland show large-scale lead pollution in the atmosphere more than 2,000 years ago. The pollution can be traced to Roman silver mines in southern Spain. When smelting silver ore, large amounts of lead were released into the atmosphere.

Controlling Air Pollution from Vehicles The EPA has required car manufacturers to meet a certain standard for the exhaust that comes out of the tailpipe on cars. New cars now have devices that remove most of the pollutants from the car's exhaust as it exits the tailpipe. Car manufacturers are also making cars that run on fuels other than gasoline. Some of these cars run on hydrogen and natural gas, while others run on batteries powered by solar energy. The car shown in **Figure 29** is electric.

Are electric cars the cure for air pollution? Turn to page 419 and decide for yourself.

Figure 29 Instead of having to refuel at a gas station, an electric car is plugged in to a recharging outlet.

Controlling Air Pollution from Industry The Clean Air Act requires many industries to use scrubbers. A scrubber is a device that attaches to smokestacks to remove some of the more harmful pollutants before they are released into the air. One such scrubber is used in coal-burning power plants in the United States to remove ash and other particles from the smokestacks. Scrubbers prevent 22 million metric tons of ash from being released into the air each year.

Although we have a long way to go, we're taking steps in the right direction to keep the air clean for future generations.

REVIEW

1. How can the air inside a building be more polluted than the air outside?
2. Why might it be difficult to establish a direct link between air pollution and health problems?
3. How has the Clean Air Act helped to reduce air pollution?
4. **Applying Concepts** How is the water cycle affected by air pollution?

internet connect

SC**LINKS**
NSTA

TOPIC: Air Pollution
GO TO: www.scilinks.org
sciLINKS NUMBER: HSTE375

4) Close

Quiz

1. Classify each of the following as either a primary or secondary air pollutant: smog, tobacco smoke, chalk dust, and acid rain. (Tobacco smoke and chalk dust are primary pollutants, while smog and acid rain are secondary pollutants.)
2. What are the three sources of outdoor air pollution? (motor vehicles, industries, electric power plants)
3. What are two health problems that can result from breathing polluted air? (dizziness, headaches, burning, itchy eyes, runny nose, coughing, shortness of breath, sore throat, lung cancer and other respiratory diseases, chest pain, colds, and allergies)

ALTERNATIVE ASSESSMENT

Have students use each of the following terms in a sentence that correctly conveys the meaning of the term:

scrubber, smog, acid precipitation, industrial pollutants, ozone hole, electric car, air quality

Critical Thinking Worksheet 15 "The Extraordinary GBG5K"

Interactive Explorations CD-ROM "Moose Malady"

▼ Answers to Review

1. Answers will vary. Indoor air is polluted by household cleaners, air fresheners, smoke from cooking, as well as industrial compounds found in carpets, paints, building materials, and furniture.
2. Answers will vary. Accept all reasonable responses.
3. The Clean Air Act gives the EPA the authority to control the amount of air pollutants that can be released from any source. The EPA also monitors air quality; if the air quality worsens, the EPA can set stricter standards.
4. Answers will vary. Sample answer: Rainwater can become more acidic as a result of air pollution.

Chapter Highlights

VOCABULARY DEFINITIONS

SECTION 1

atmosphere a mixture of gases that surrounds a planet, such as Earth

air pressure the measure of the force with which air molecules push on a surface

altitude the height of an object above the Earth's surface

troposphere the lowest layer of the atmosphere

stratosphere the atmospheric layer above the troposphere

ozone a gas molecule that is made up of three oxygen atoms and that absorbs ultraviolet radiation from the sun

mesosphere the coldest layer of the atmosphere

thermosphere the uppermost layer of the atmosphere

SECTION 2

radiation the transfer of energy as electromagnetic waves, such as visible light or infrared waves

conduction the transfer of thermal energy from one material to another by direct contact; conduction can also occur within a substance

convection the transfer of thermal energy by the circulation or movement of a liquid or gas

greenhouse effect the natural heating process of a planet, such as the Earth, by which gases in the atmosphere trap thermal energy

global warming a rise in average global temperatures

Chapter Highlights

SECTION 1

Vocabulary
atmosphere (p. 392)
air pressure (p. 393)
altitude (p. 393)
troposphere (p. 395)
stratosphere (p. 395)
ozone (p. 395)
mesosphere (p. 396)
thermosphere (p. 396)

Section Notes
- The atmosphere is a mixture of gases.
- Nitrogen and oxygen are the two most abundant atmospheric gases.
- Throughout the atmosphere, there are changes in air pressure, temperature, and gases.
- Air pressure decreases as altitude increases.
- Temperature differences in the atmosphere are a result of the way solar energy is absorbed as it moves downward through the atmosphere.
- The troposphere is the lowest and densest layer of the atmosphere. All weather occurs in the troposphere.
- The stratosphere contains the ozone layer, which protects us from harmful radiation.
- The mesosphere is the coldest layer of the atmosphere.
- The uppermost atmospheric layer is the thermosphere.

Labs
Under Pressure! (p. 692)

SECTION 2

Vocabulary
radiation (p. 398)
conduction (p. 399)
convection (p. 399)
greenhouse effect (p. 400)
global warming (p. 400)

Section Notes
- The Earth receives energy from the sun by radiation.
- Energy that reaches the Earth's surface is absorbed or reflected.
- Energy is transferred through the atmosphere by conduction and convection.
- The greenhouse effect is caused by gases in the atmosphere that trap thermal energy reflected off and radiated from the Earth's surface.

Labs
Boiling Over! (p. 688)

✓ Skills Check

Math Concepts

FLYING AGAINST THE JET STREAM The groundspeed of an airplane can be affected by the jet stream. The jet stream can push an airplane toward its final destination or slow it down. To find the groundspeed of an airplane, you either add or subtract the wind speed, depending on whether the airplane is moving with or against the jet stream. For example, if an airplane is traveling at an airspeed of 400 km/h and is moving with a 100 km/h jet stream, you would add the jet stream speed to the airspeed of the airplane to calculate the groundspeed.

400 km/h + 100 km/h = 500 km/h

To calculate the groundspeed of an airplane traveling at 400 km/h that is moving into a 100 km/h jet stream, you would subtract the jet-stream speed from the airspeed of the airplane.

400 km/h − 100 km/h = 300 km/h

Visual Understanding

GLOBAL WINDS Study Figure 16 on page 404 to review the global wind belts that result from air pressure differences.

Lab and Activity Highlights

Under Pressure! PG 692

Boiling Over! PG 688

Go Fly a Bike! PG 690

 Datasheets for LabBook
(blackline masters for these labs)

SECTION 3

Vocabulary
- wind (p. 402)
- Coriolis effect (p. 403)
- trade winds (p. 404)
- westerlies (p. 405)
- polar easterlies (p. 405)
- jet streams (p. 406)

Section Notes
- At the Earth's surface, winds blow from areas of high pressure to areas of low pressure.
- Pressure belts exist approximately every 30° of latitude.
- The Coriolis effect makes wind curve as it moves across the Earth's surface.
- Global winds are part of a pattern of air circulation across the Earth and include the trade winds, the westerlies, and the polar easterlies.
- Local winds move short distances, can blow in any direction, and are influenced by geography.

Labs
Go Fly a Bike! (p. 690)

SECTION 4

Vocabulary
- primary pollutants (p. 409)
- secondary pollutants (p. 409)
- acid precipitation (p. 411)

Section Notes
- Air pollutants are generally classified as primary or secondary pollutants.
- Human-caused pollution comes from a variety of sources, including factories, cars, and homes.
- Air pollution can heighten problems associated with allergies, lung problems, and heart problems.
- The Clean Air Act has reduced air pollution by controlling the amount of pollutants that can be released from cars and factories.

VOCABULARY DEFINITIONS, continued

SECTION 3

wind moving air

Coriolis effect the curving of moving objects from a straight path due to the Earth's rotation

trade winds the winds that blow from 30° latitude to the equator

westerlies wind belts found in both the Northern and Southern Hemispheres between 30° and 60° latitude

polar easterlies wind belts that extend from the poles to 60° latitude in both hemispheres

jet streams narrow belts of high-speed winds that blow in the upper troposphere and the lower stratosphere

SECTION 4

primary pollutants pollutants that are put directly into the air by human or natural activity

secondary pollutants pollutants that form from chemical reactions that occur when primary pollutants come in contact with other primary pollutants or with naturally occurring substances, such as water vapor

acid precipitation precipitation that contains acids due to air pollution

---

internetconnect

GO TO: go.hrw.com

Visit the **HRW** Web site for a variety of learning tools related to this chapter. Just type in the keyword:

KEYWORD: HSTATM

GO TO: www.scilinks.org

Visit the **National Science Teachers Association** on-line Web site for Internet resources related to this chapter. Just type in the sciLINKS number for more information about the topic:

TOPIC	sciLINKS NUMBER
Composition of the Atmosphere	HSTE355
Energy in the Atmosphere	HSTE360
The Greenhouse Effect	HSTE365
Atmospheric Pressure and Winds	HSTE370
Air Pollution	HSTE375

Vocabulary Review Worksheet 15

Blackline masters of these Chapter Highlights can be found in the **Study Guide**.

Lab and Activity Highlights

LabBank

Whiz-Bang Demonstrations, Blue Sky, Demo 27

EcoLabs & Field Activities, That Greenhouse Effect! Field Activity 14

Long-Term Projects & Research Ideas, A Breath of Fresh Ether? Project 43

Interactive Explorations CD-ROM

CD 2, Exploration 3, "Moose Malady"

Chapter Review

USING VOCABULARY

Explain the difference between the following sets of words:

1. air pressure/altitude
2. troposphere/thermosphere
3. greenhouse effect/global warming
4. convection/conduction
5. global wind/local wind
6. primary pollutant/secondary pollutant

UNDERSTANDING CONCEPTS

Multiple Choice

7. What is the most abundant gas in the air that we breathe?
   a. oxygen
   b. nitrogen
   c. hydrogen
   d. carbon dioxide

8. The major source of oxygen for the Earth's atmosphere is
   a. sea water.
   b. the sun.
   c. plants.
   d. animals.

9. The bottom layer of the atmosphere, where almost all weather occurs, is the
   a. stratosphere.
   b. troposphere.
   c. thermosphere.
   d. mesosphere.

10. About __?__ percent of the solar energy that reaches the outer atmosphere is absorbed at the Earth's surface.
    a. 20
    b. 30
    c. 50
    d. 70

11. The ozone layer is located in the
    a. stratosphere.
    b. troposphere.
    c. thermosphere.
    d. mesosphere.

12. How does most thermal energy in the atmosphere move?
    a. conduction
    b. convection
    c. advection
    d. radiation

13. The balance between incoming and outgoing energy is called __?__.
    a. convection
    b. conduction
    c. greenhouse effect
    d. radiation balance

14. Most of the United States is located in which prevailing wind belt?
    a. westerlies
    b. northeast trade winds
    c. southeast trade winds
    d. doldrums

15. Which of the following is not a primary pollutant?
    a. car exhaust
    b. acid precipitation
    c. smoke from a factory
    d. fumes from burning plastic

16. The Clean Air Act
    a. controls the amount of air pollutants that can be released from most sources.
    b. requires cars to run on fuels other than gasoline.
    c. requires many industries to use scrubbers.
    d. (a) and (c) only

Short Answer

17. Why does the atmosphere become less dense as altitude increases?
18. Explain why air rises when it is heated.
19. What causes temperature changes in the atmosphere?
20. What are secondary pollutants, and how are they formed? Give an example.

Concept Mapping

21. Use the following terms to create a concept map: altitude, air pressure, temperature, atmosphere.

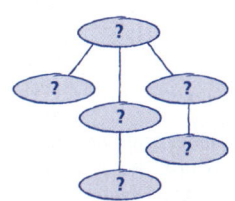

CRITICAL THINKING AND PROBLEM SOLVING

Write one or two sentences to answer the following questions:

22. What is the relationship between the greenhouse effect and global warming?
23. How do you think the Coriolis effect would change if the Earth were to rotate twice as fast? Explain.
24. Without the atmosphere, the Earth's surface would be very different. What are several ways that the atmosphere affects the Earth?

Concept Mapping Transparency 15

Blackline masters of this Chapter Review can be found in the **Study Guide**.

MATH IN SCIENCE

25. Wind speed is measured in miles per hour and in knots. One mile (statute mile or land mile) is 5,280 ft. One nautical mile (or sea mile) is 6,076 ft. Speed in nautical miles is measured in knots. Calculate the wind speed in knots if the wind is blowing at 25 mi/h.

INTERPRETING GRAPHICS

Use the wind-chill chart to answer the questions below.

Wind-Chill Chart					
	Actual thermometer reading (°F)				
Wind Speed	40	30	20	10	0
Knots mph	**Equivalent temperature (°F)**				
Calm	40	30	20	10	0
4 5	37	27	16	6	−5
9 10	28	16	4	−9	−21
13 15	22	9	−5	−18	−36
17 20	18	4	−10	−25	−39
22 25	16	0	−15	−29	−44
26 30	13	−2	−18	−33	−48
30 35	11	−4	−20	−35	−49

26. If the wind speed is 20 mi/h and the temperature is 40°F, how cold will the air seem?
27. If the wind speed is 30 mi/h and the temperature is 20°F, how cold will the air seem?

 Take a minute to review your answers to the Pre-Reading Questions found at the bottom of page 390. Have your answers changed? If necessary, revise your answers based on what you have learned since you began this chapter.

Short Answer

17. As altitude increases, there are fewer gas molecules. Gravity pulls much of the atmosphere's gas molecules close to the Earth's surface.
18. Air rises as it is heated because it becomes less dense.
19. The temperature differences in the atmosphere result mainly from the way solar energy is absorbed as it moves downward through the atmosphere. Some layers are warmer because they contain gases that absorb solar energy.
20. Secondary pollutants form when a primary pollutant reacts with other primary pollutants or with naturally occurring substances. Smog and ozone are examples of secondary pollutants.

Concept Mapping

21. 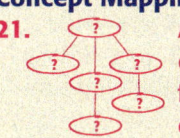 An answer to this exercise can be found at the end of this book.

CRITICAL THINKING AND PROBLEM SOLVING

22. An increase in the greenhouse effect could result in global warming.
23. The Coriolis effect would be more pronounced if the Earth rotated twice as fast. Winds are affected by the rotation of the Earth; if the speed were increased, the curvature would be more pronounced.
24. Answers will vary. Sample answer: The atmosphere protects living organisms from harmful radiation from the sun. Without the atmosphere, more of this radiation would reach the Earth's surface.

MATH IN SCIENCE

25. 22 knots

INTERPRETING GRAPHICS

26. 18°F
27. −18°F

HEALTH WATCH
Particles in the Air

Background

Particulate matter is one of the major forms of air pollution, along with carbon monoxide (a toxic gas), sulfur dioxides (which contribute to acid rain and human respiratory problems), and volatile organic compounds, or VOCs (organic chemicals that vaporize and produce toxic fumes).

Particulates are often formed during mechanical processes that break down materials. These include blasting, drilling, and grinding. Some organic matter, such as certain bacteria, are also considered particulates.

The growing problem of particulate pollution has been addressed by the federal government as well as by many local governments and communities. The Clean Air Act, passed by Congress in 1970, sets maximum emission levels for automobiles and industrial sources of pollution. New filtering technology has also helped industries to reduce the amount of particulates being released into the atmosphere.

- In most cases, the majority of the particulates found indoors in dust are particles of human skin.
- Certain types of asbestos are particularly dangerous as particulates. When inhaled, these asbestos fibers scar the lungs, inhibiting breathing and eventually causing cancer.

Health Watch
Particles in the Air

Take a deep breath. You have probably just inhaled thousands of tiny specks of dust, pollen, and other particles. These particles, called particulates, are harmless under normal conditions. But if concentrations of particulates get too high or if they consist of harmful materials, they are considered to be a type of air pollution.

Because many particulates are very small, our bodies' natural filters, such as nasal hairs and mucous membranes, cannot filter all of them out. When inhaled, particulates can cause irritation in the lungs. Over time, this irritation can lead to diseases such as bronchitis, asthma, and emphysema. The danger increases as the level of particulates in the air increases.

Where There's Smoke . . .

Unfortunately, dust and pollen are not the only forms of particulates. Many of the particulates in the air come from the burning of various materials. For example, when wood is burned, it releases particles of smoke, soot, and ash into the air. Some of these are so small that they can float in the air for days. The burning of fuels such as coal, oil, and gasoline also creates particulates. The particulates from these sources can be very dangerous in high concentrations. That's why particulate concentrations are one measure of air quality. Large concentrations of particulates are visible in the air. Along with other pollutants, particulates are what make polluted air look brown or yellowish brown. But don't be fooled—even air that appears clean can be polluted.

▲ *When the ash from Mount St. Helens settled from the air, it created scenes like this one.*

Eruptions of Particulates

Volcanoes can be the source of incredible amounts of particulates. For example, when Mount St. Helens erupted in 1980, it launched thousands of tons of ash into the surrounding air. The air was so thick with ash that the area became as dark as night. For several hours, the ash completely blocked the light from the sun. When the ash finally settled from the air, it covered the surrounding landscape like a thick blanket of snow. This layer of ash killed plants and livestock for several kilometers around the volcano.

One theory to explain the extinction of dinosaurs is that a gargantuan meteorite hit the Earth with such velocity that the resulting impact created enough dust to block out the sun for years. During this dark period, plants were unable to grow and therefore could not support the normal food chains. Consequently, the dinosaurs died out.

Do Filters Really Filter?

▶ Since the burning of most substances creates particulates, there must be particulates in cigarette smoke. Do some research to find out if the filters on cigarettes are effective at preventing particulates from entering the smoker's body. Your findings may surprise you!

Answers to Do Filters Really Filter?
Answers will vary. Cigarette filters absorb some of the particulates found in cigarette smoke but not all of them.

SCIENTIFIC DEBATE

A Cure for Air Pollution?

Automobile emissions are responsible for at least half of all urban air pollution and a quarter of all carbon dioxide released into the atmosphere. Therefore, the production of a car that emits no polluting gases in its exhaust is a significant accomplishment. The only such vehicle currently available is the electric car. Electric cars are powered by batteries, so they do not produce exhaust gases. Supporters believe that switching to electric cars will reduce air pollution in this country. But critics believe that taxpayers will pay an unfair share for this switch and that the reduction in pollution won't be as great as promised.

▲ Will a switch to electric cars such as this one reduce air pollution?

Electric Cars Will Reduce Air Pollution

Even the cleanest and most modern cars emit pollutants into the air. Supporters of a switch to electric cars believe the switch will reduce pollution in congested cities. But some critics suggest that a switch to electric cars will simply move the source of pollution from a car's tailpipe to the power plant's smokestack. This is because most electricity is generated by burning coal.

In California, electric cars would have the greatest impact. Here most electricity is produced by burning natural gas, which releases less air pollution than burning coal. Nuclear plants and dams release no pollutants in the air when they generate electricity. Solar power and wind power are also emission-free ways to generate electricity. Supporters argue that a switch to electric cars will reduce air pollution immediately and that a further reduction will occur when power plants convert to these cleaner sources of energy.

Electric Cars Won't Solve the Problem

Electric cars are inconvenient because the batteries have to be recharged so often. The batteries also have to be replaced every 2 to 3 years. The nation's landfills are already crowded with conventional car batteries, which contain acid and metals that may pollute ground water. A switch to electric cars would aggravate this pollution problem because the batteries have to be replaced so often.

Also, electric cars will likely replace the cleanest cars on the road, not the dirtiest. A new car may emit only one-tenth of the pollution emitted by an older model. If an older car's pollution-control equipment does not work properly, it may emit 100 times more pollution than a new car. But people who drive older, poorly maintained cars probably won't be able to afford expensive electric cars. Therefore, the worst offenders will stay on the road, continuing to pollute the air.

Analyze the Issue

▶ Do you think electric cars are the best solution to the air pollution problem? Why or why not? What are some alternative solutions for reducing air pollution?

SCIENTIFIC DEBATE
A Cure for Air Pollution?

Background

Electric vehicles have been around for more than 150 years. Their first commercial use was in 1897, when New York City established a fleet of electric taxis. In the years 1899 and 1900 electric vehicles in America outsold all other types of cars. The 1902 Wood's Phaeton had a range of 29 km (18 mi), a top speed of 23 km/h (14 mph), and a price of $2,000.

Much has changed since the time of the Phaeton. Cars powered by hydrogen-oxygen fuel cells are classified as negative-emission vehicles. The cars use oxygen from the air to react with hydrogen in the fuel cell. During the process, harmful particles are removed from the air leaving it cleaner than it was before.

Answers to Analyze the Issue

Answers will vary. Alternative solutions for reducing air pollution might include educating people about the seriousness of air pollution problems and providing incentives for people to use mass transportation. Other ideas might include alternative fuel sources and more-efficient use of the resources we have. Students might also note that slowing the rate of deforestation would help reduce air pollution significantly.

Chapter Organizer

CHAPTER ORGANIZATION	TIME MINUTES	OBJECTIVES	LABS, INVESTIGATIONS, AND DEMONSTRATIONS
Chapter Opener pp. 420–421	45	National Standards: UCP 2, SAI 1, SPSP 3, 4, ES 1i, 1j	**Start-Up Activity** A Meeting of the Masses, p. 421
Section 1 Water in the Air	120	▶ Explain how water moves through the water cycle. ▶ Define *relative humidity*. ▶ Explain what the dew point is and its relation to condensation. ▶ Describe the three major cloud forms. ▶ Describe the four major types of precipitation. UCP 2, 3, SAI 1, SPSP 3, ES 1f, 1i; LabBook UCP 3, SAI 1	**QuickLab,** Out of Thin Air, p. 425 `GENERAL` **Demonstration,** Hail Formation, p. 428 in ATE `BASIC` **Discovery Lab,** Let It Snow! p. 697 `BASIC` **Datasheets for LabBook,** Let It Snow! Datasheet 34 `BASIC` **Whiz-Bang Demonstrations,** It's Raining Again, Demo 29 `GENERAL`
Section 2 Air Masses and Fronts	90	▶ Explain how air masses are characterized. ▶ Describe the four major types of air masses that influence weather in the United States. ▶ Describe the four major types of fronts. ▶ Relate fronts to weather changes. HNS 3, ES 1j	**Demonstration,** p. 430 in ATE `GENERAL` **Whiz-Bang Demonstrations,** When Air Bags Collide, Demo 28 `GENERAL` **Long-Term Projects & Research Ideas,** Project 44 `ADVANCED`
Section 3 Severe Weather	90	▶ Explain what lightning is. ▶ Describe the formation of thunderstorms, tornadoes, and hurricanes. ▶ Describe the characteristics of thunderstorms, tornadoes, and hurricanes. SPSP 3, 4, ES 1i, 1j	**Demonstration,** p. 434 in ATE `GENERAL` **Inquiry Labs,** When Disaster Strikes, Lab 12 `BASIC`
Section 4 Forecasting the Weather	90	▶ Describe the different types of instruments used to take weather measurements. ▶ Explain how to interpret a weather map. ▶ Explain why weather maps are useful. UCP 3, ST 2, SPSP 5, HNS 1; LabBook SAI 1, ST 1	**Demonstration,** p. 440 in ATE `GENERAL` **Skill Builder,** Watching the Weather, p. 694 `BASIC` **Making Models,** Gone with the Wind, p. 698 `GENERAL` **Datasheets for LabBook,** Datasheets 33, 35 `GENERAL` **EcoLabs & Field Activities,** Rain Maker or Rain Faker? Field Activity 15 `ADVANCED`

See page **T20** for a complete correlation of this book with the

NATIONAL SCIENCE EDUCATION STANDARDS.

TECHNOLOGY RESOURCES

 Guided Reading Audio CD English or Spanish, Chapter 16

 One-Stop Planner CD-ROM with Test Generator

 CNN. Eye on the Environment, Hazy Days, Segment 1

Chapter 16 • Understanding Weather

Chapter 16 • Understanding Weather

CLASSROOM WORKSHEETS, TRANSPARENCIES, AND RESOURCES	SCIENCE INTEGRATION AND CONNECTIONS	REVIEW AND ASSESSMENT
Directed Reading Worksheet 16 BASIC **Science Puzzlers, Twisters & Teasers,** Worksheet 16 ADVANCED		**Homework,** p. 421 in ATE GENERAL
Directed Reading Worksheet 16, Section 1 BASIC **Transparency 168,** The Water Cycle **Transparency 169,** Cloud Types Based on Form and Altitude	**Connect to Physical Science,** p. 422 in ATE **MathBreak,** Relating Relative Humidity, p. 423 GENERAL **Connect to Life Science,** p. 423 in ATE ADVANCED **Multicultural Connection,** pp. 424, 425, 428 in ATE **Math and More,** p. 426 in ATE GENERAL **Cross-Disciplinary Focus,** p. 427 in ATE **Connect to Physical Science,** p. 428 in ATE	**Self-Check,** p. 424 **Review,** p. 425 GENERAL **Homework,** p. 426 in ATE BASIC **Homework,** p. 427 in ATE GENERAL **Review,** p. 429 GENERAL **Quiz,** p. 429 in ATE GENERAL **Alternative Assessment,** p. 429 in ATE ADVANCED
Directed Reading Worksheet 16, Section 2 BASIC **Transparency 170,** Air Masses in North America **Transparency 171,** Cold and Warm Fronts **Transparency 172,** Occluded and Stationary Fronts	**Multicultural Connection,** p. 431 in ATE **Connect to Life Science,** p. 431 in ATE **Cross-Disciplinary Focus,** p. 432 in ATE	**Review,** p. 433 GENERAL **Quiz,** p. 433 in ATE GENERAL **Alternative Assessment,** p. 433 in ATE GENERAL
Transparency 268, How Lightning Forms **Directed Reading Worksheet 16,** Section 3 BASIC **Transparency 173,** How a Tornado Forms **Transparency 174,** A Cross Section of a Hurricane **Reinforcement Worksheet 16,** Precipitation Situations BASIC	**Physics Connection,** p. 435 **Math and More,** p. 435 in ATE GENERAL **Real-World Connection,** p. 435 in ATE **Connect to Physical Science,** p. 435 in ATE **Cross-Disciplinary Focus,** p. 437 in ATE **Astronomy Connection,** p. 439 **Holt Anthology of Science Fiction,** *All Summer in a Day* GENERAL	**Homework,** p. 437 in ATE ADVANCED **Review,** p. 439 GENERAL **Quiz,** p. 439 in ATE GENERAL **Alternative Assessment,** p. 439 in ATE GENERAL
Directed Reading Worksheet 16, Section 4 BASIC **Math Skills for Science Worksheet 35,** Using Temperature Scales GENERAL **Critical Thinking Worksheet 16,** Commanding the Sky ADVANCED	**Real-World Connection,** p. 441 in ATE **Connect to Life Science,** p. 441 in ATE **Math and More,** p. 442 in ATE GENERAL **Cross-Disciplinary Focus,** p. 442 in ATE GENERAL **Careers:** Meteorologist—Cristy Mitchell, p. 448 GENERAL	**Review,** p. 443 GENERAL **Quiz,** p. 443 in ATE GENERAL **Alternative Assessment,** p. 443 in ATE ADVANCED

internet connect

 Holt, Rinehart and Winston On-line Resources
go.hrw.com
For worksheets and other teaching aids related to this chapter, visit the HRW Web site and type in the keyword: **HSTWEA**

 **National Science Teachers Association**
www.scilinks.org
Encourage students to use the *sci*LINKS numbers listed in the internet connect boxes to access information and resources on the **NSTA** Web site.

END-OF-CHAPTER REVIEW AND ASSESSMENT

Chapter Review in Study Guide
Vocabulary and Notes in Study Guide
Chapter Tests with Performance-Based Assessment, Chapter 16 Test, Performance-Based Assessment 16
Concept Mapping Transparency 16

Chapter 16 • Chapter Organizer

Chapter Resources & Worksheets

Visual Resources

TEACHING TRANSPARENCIES

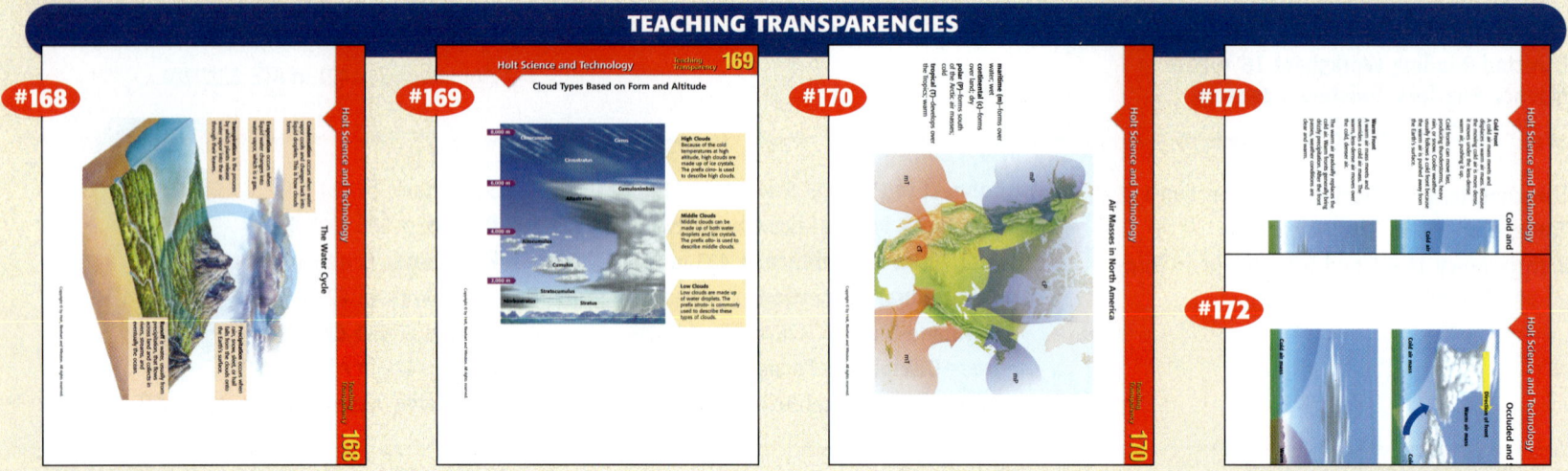

TEACHING TRANSPARENCIES

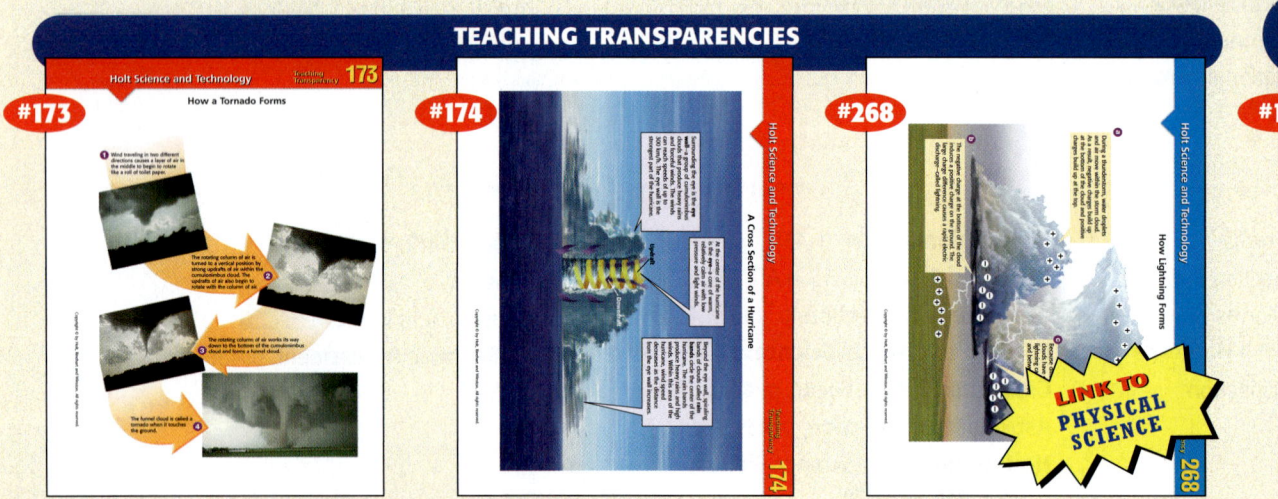

CONCEPT MAPPING TRANSPARENCY

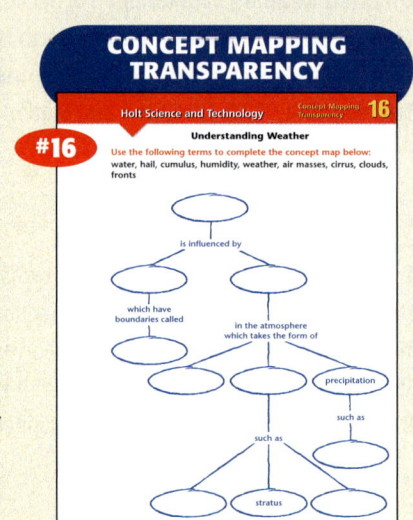

Meeting Individual Needs

DIRECTED READING

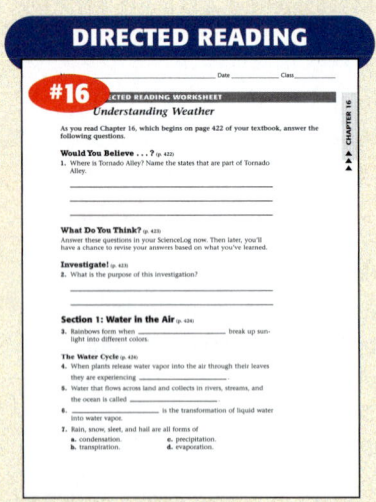

REINFORCEMENT & VOCABULARY REVIEW

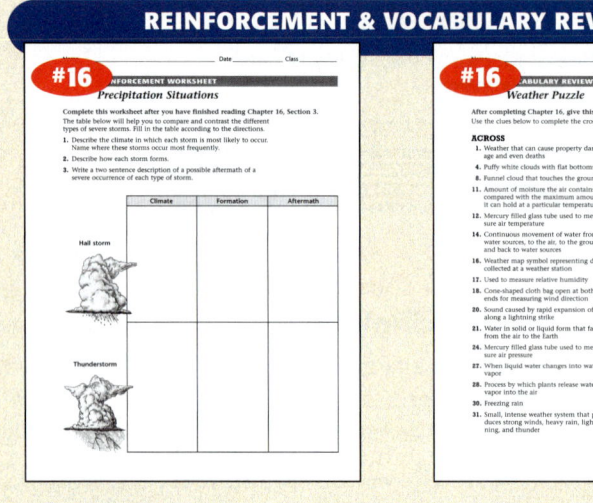

SCIENCE PUZZLERS, TWISTERS & TEASERS

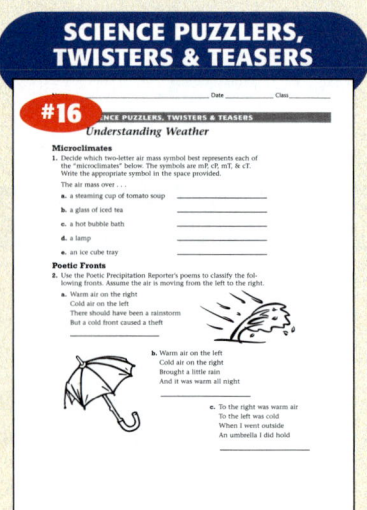

Chapter 16 • Understanding Weather

Chapter 16 • Understanding Weather

Review & Assessment

STUDY GUIDE

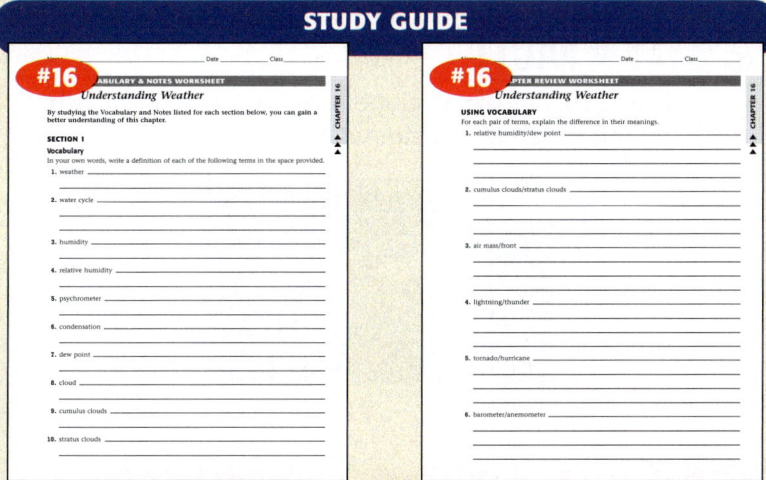

CHAPTER TESTS WITH PERFORMANCE-BASED ASSESSMENT

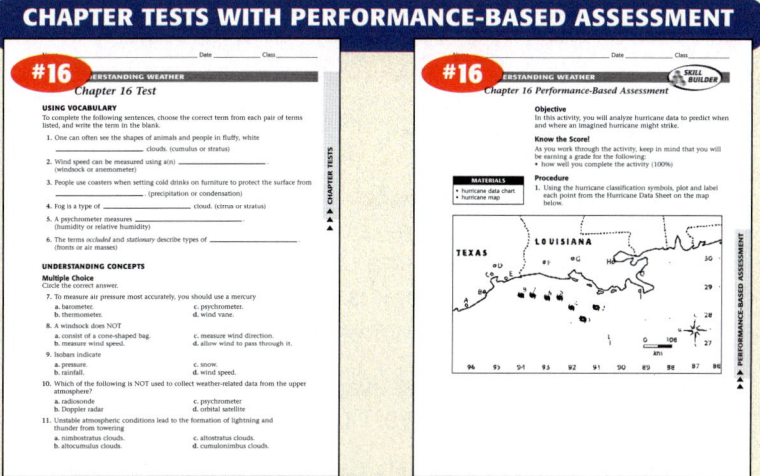

Lab Worksheets

INQUIRY LABS

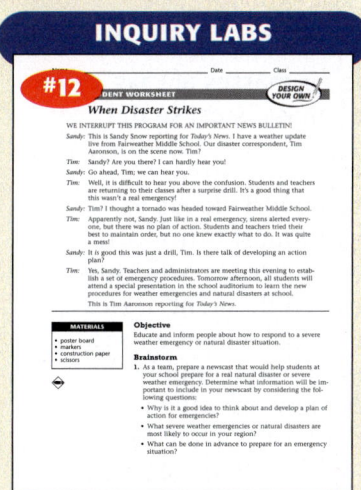

ECOLABS & FIELD ACTIVITIES

LONG-TERM PROJECTS & RESEARCH IDEAS

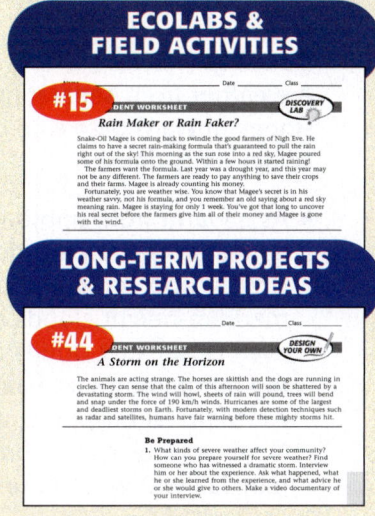

WHIZ-BANG DEMONSTRATIONS

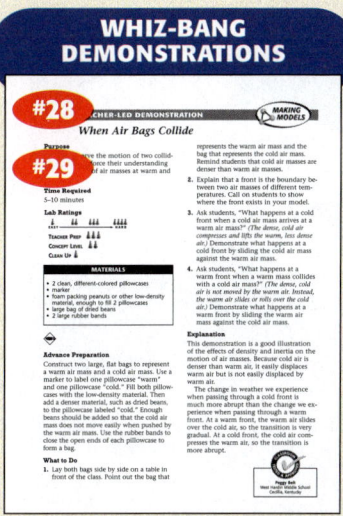

DATASHEETS FOR LABBOOK

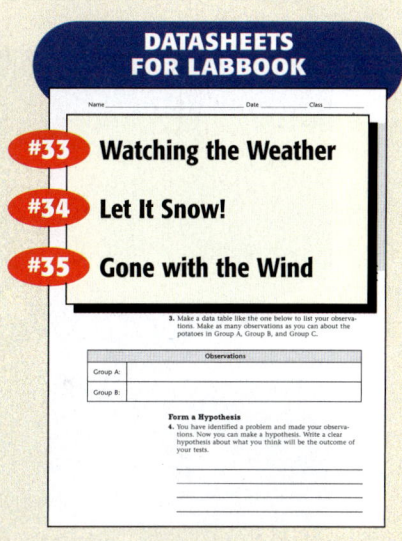

Applications & Extensions

CRITICAL THINKING & PROBLEM SOLVING

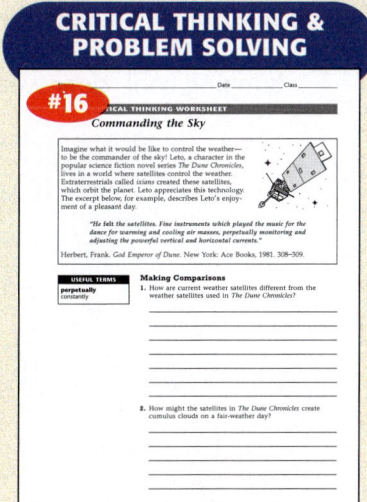

EYE ON THE ENVIRONMENT

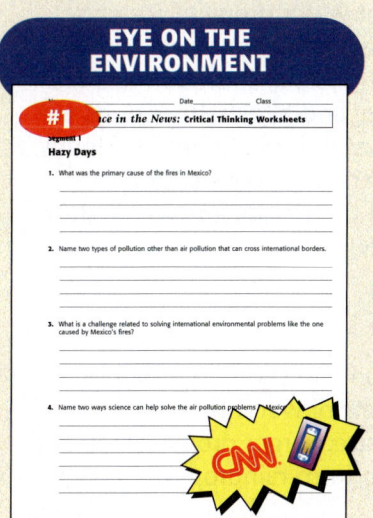

Chapter 16 • Chapter Resources & Worksheets

Chapter Background

SECTION 1

Water in the Air

▶ **Earth's Water Cycle**
Although the atmosphere contains only about 0.001 percent of the total volume of water on the planet (about 1.46×10^9 km³), it is an essential link between land masses and bodies of water on Earth.

- The rate at which water evaporates into Earth's atmosphere is about 5.1×10^{17} L per year.

- About 78 percent of all precipitation falls over Earth's oceans. Of the 22 percent that falls on land, about 65 percent returns to the air by evaporation.

▶ **Clouds**
Clouds may be composed of water droplets, ice crystals, or a combination of the two. For example, cirrus clouds are made of only ice crystals; stratus clouds are made of only water droplets; and altostratus clouds are mixtures of ice and liquid water. Cumulonimbus clouds, which produce snowflakes and hail, consist of water droplets near the bottom of the clouds and ice crystals in the upper parts of the clouds.

▶ **Precipitation**
Because of differences in condensation rates within the cloud, the millions of droplets of water that make up a cloud are not all the same size. Larger drops collide and merge with smaller drops to form raindrops.

IS THAT A FACT!

◆ Hailstones as big as grapefruits have fallen to Earth during some severe storms.

SECTION 2

Air Masses and Fronts

▶ **Fronts**
A weather front separating two air masses always slopes upward over a colder air mass because the colder air is denser.

- As a warm front approaches, the first clouds to appear in the sky are the high clouds: cirrus, cirrostratus, and cirrocumulus. As the front moves closer, medium-height clouds appear. As the front moves even closer, low clouds appear. As the front arrives, the temperature and air pressure drop, and in the Northern Hemisphere, winds blow from the northeast. Nimbostratus clouds bring drizzly precipitation, which may fall within 24 hours of the first cloud sighting.

- When a cold front enters an area, cumulonimbus clouds produce thunderstorms, heavy rain, or snow along the front. After the cold front passes through an area, winds change direction and barometric pressure rises. Behind the front, temperatures usually fall, bringing cool, clear weather to the area.

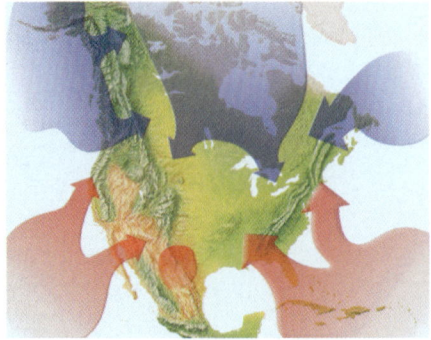

Chapter 16 • Understanding Weather

SECTION 3

Severe Weather

▶ Tornadoes

Meteorologists rate tornado intensity using the Fujita Tornado Intensity Scale. An F0 tornado is a relatively weak storm that may damage chimneys, tree branches, and billboard signs. An F1 tornado is a moderate storm that can peel the surfaces off roofs, overturn mobile homes, and push moving cars off roads. F2 and F3 tornadoes cause considerable to severe damage by tearing roofs off houses, overturning railroad cars, and uprooting mature trees. An F4 tornado is a devastating storm that levels houses and other buildings and tosses cars into the air. The most severe tornado is an F5 storm, which can lift houses off their foundations and carry them great distances. An F5 storm can carry cars over 100 m and strip the bark off trees.

▶ Hurricanes

On the Saffir-Simpson scale, hurricanes fall into five categories. Category 1 hurricanes have sustained winds between 119 and 153 km/h and usually cause relatively minimal damage. Category 2 hurricanes cause moderate damage with winds ranging between 154 and 177 km/h. Category 3 hurricanes cause extensive damage with winds that blow between 178 and 209 km/h. Category 4 hurricanes, like Hurricane Andrew, which struck Florida in 1992, have sustained winds between 210 and 250 km/h. Category 5 hurricanes, classified as catastrophic storms, have sustained winds of more than 250 km/h.

IS THAT A FACT!

▶ A hurricane is called a *willy-willy* in Australia, a *taino* in Haiti, a *baguio* in the Philippines, and a *cordonazo* in western Mexico.

SECTION 4

Forecasting the Weather

▶ Weather-Prediction Methods

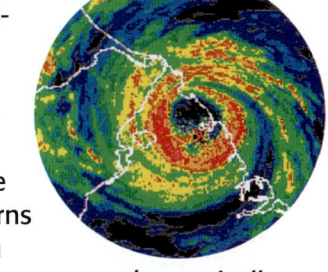

One of the simplest methods for weather prediction, the persistence method, assumes that the atmospheric conditions at the time of a weather forecast will not change in the near future. It is fairly accurate in areas where weather patterns change very slowly, such as in southern California, where summer weather typically changes very little from day to day. Other methods include the following:

- The trends method involves determining high and low pressure areas, gauging the velocity of weather fronts, and locating areas of clouds and precipitation. A forecaster then uses this data to predict where these weather phenomena will be in the future. This method of weather prediction works well only when weather systems maintain constant velocities for a long period of time.

- The climatology method involves averaging weather data that has accumulated over many years to make a forecast. This method is accurate when weather patterns are similar to those expected for a given time of year.

- The numerical weather-prediction (NWP) method uses complex computer programs to generate models of probable air temperature, barometric pressure, wind velocity, and precipitation. A meteorologist then analyzes how he or she thinks the features predicted by the computer will interact to produce the day's weather. One shortcoming of this method is that it requires very accurate, comprehensive data. If initial weather conditions are not known, the prediction of how the system will change might not be accurate. Despite its flaws, the NWP method is one of the most reliable methods available.

For background information about teaching strategies and issues, refer to the *Professional Reference for Teachers*.

CHAPTER 16

Understanding Weather

 Pre-Reading Questions

Students may not know the answers to these questions before reading the chapter, so accept any reasonable response.

Suggested Answers
1. Answers will vary.
2. Weather is caused by the movement and interaction of air masses.

 Directed Reading Worksheet 16

 Science Puzzlers, Twisters & Teasers Worksheet 16

 Guided Reading Audio CD English or Spanish, Chapter 16

CHAPTER 16

Understanding Weather

Sections

1. Water in the Air 422
   - MathBreak 423
   - QuickLab 425
   - Internet Connect 429
2. Air Masses and Fronts 430
   - Internet Connect 433
3. Severe Weather 434
   - Physics Connection ..435
   - Astronomy Connection 439
   - Internet Connect 439
4. Forecasting the Weather 440
   - Internet Connect 443

Chapter Review 446
Feature Articles 448, 449
LabBook 694–699

 **Pre-Reading Questions**

1. Name some different kinds of clouds. How are they different?
2. What causes weather?

Twisting Terror

North America experiences an average of 700 tornadoes per year—more tornadoes than any other continent. Most of these tornadoes hit an area in the central United States called Tornado Alley. Tornado Alley has more tornadoes than any other area because its flatness and location on the Earth's surface make it possible for warm air masses and cold air masses to collide. In this chapter, you will learn about what causes weather and how weather can suddenly turn violent.

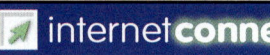

 go.hrw.com
HRW On-line Resources
go.hrw.com
For worksheets and other teaching aids, visit the HRW Web site and type in the keyword: **HSTWEA**

 **SCiLINKS NSTA**
www.scilinks.com
Use the sciLINKS numbers at the end of each chapter for additional resources on the **NSTA** Web site.

 **CNNfyi.com**
www.cnnfyi.com
Visit the CNN Web site for current events coverage and classroom resources.

START-UP Activity

A MEETING OF THE MASSES

In this activity, you will model what happens when two air masses with different temperature characteristics meet.

Procedure

1. Fill a **beaker** with **500 mL of cooking oil.** Fill another **beaker** with **500 mL of water.** The cooking oil represents a less dense warm air mass. The water represents a denser cold air mass.

2. Predict what would happen if you tried to mix the two liquids together. Record your prediction in your ScienceLog.

3. Pour the contents of each beaker into a **clear, plastic rectangular container** at the same time from opposite ends of the container.

4. Observe what happens when the oil and water meet. Record your observations in your ScienceLog.

Analysis

5. What happens when the different liquids meet?

6. Does the prediction you made in step 2 match your results?

7. Based on your results, hypothesize what would happen if a cold air mass met a warm air mass. Record your hypothesis in your ScienceLog.

START-UP Activity

A MEETING OF THE MASSES

MATERIALS

FOR EACH GROUP:
- two 750 mL beakers
- 500 mL cooking oil
- 500 mL water
- clear rectangular container

Answers to START-UP Activity

5. The oil floats on the water.
6. Answers will vary.
7. Answers will vary.

Chapter 16 • Understanding Weather

SECTION 1

Focus

Water in the Air

This section begins with a discussion of the water cycle. It then covers humidity and the process of condensation. Students will learn how to determine relative humidity. Finally, the section discusses cloud types and the forms of precipitation.

🔔 Bellringer

Place two glasses on your desk for students to observe: one filled with ice water and one filled with warm water. Put three drops of food coloring in each glass. Ask students why water droplets form on the outside of the cold container. Does the water seep through the glass? Does it come from the air? Why don't the water beads form on the warm container?

1 Motivate

GROUP ACTIVITY

Divide the class in half: half the students will pretend to be air molecules, and half will be water molecules. Ask the air molecules to stand two shoulder lengths apart in a square grid. Then have the water molecules stand between the air molecules without touching anyone. Tell students that they are modeling a warm air mass. Cool the air mass by moving the air molecules so that they are shoulder length apart. Some of the water molecules will be expelled as "precipitation." Finally, ask the air molecules to stand with their shoulders touching, showing how a cold air mass expels nearly all of the water molecules.

Section 1

Terms to Learn

weather
water cycle
humidity
relative humidity
condensation
dew point
cloud
precipitation

What You'll Do

- Explain how water moves through the water cycle.
- Define *relative humidity*.
- Explain what the dew point is and its relation to condensation.
- Describe the three major cloud forms.
- Describe the four major types of precipitation.

Teaching Transparency 168
"The Water Cycle"

Directed Reading Worksheet 16 Section 1

Water in the Air

There might not be a pot of gold at the end of a rainbow, but rainbows hold another secret that you might not be aware of. Rainbows are evidence that the air contains water. Water droplets break up sunlight into the different colors that you can see in a rainbow. Water can exist in the air as a solid, liquid, or gas. Ice, a solid, is found in clouds as snowflakes. Liquid water exists in clouds as water droplets. And water in gaseous form exists in the air as water vapor. Water in the air affects the weather. **Weather** is the condition of the atmosphere at a particular time and place. In this section you will learn how water affects the weather.

The Water Cycle

Water in liquid, solid, and gaseous states is constantly being recycled through the water cycle. The **water cycle** is the continuous movement of water from water sources, such as lakes and oceans, into the air, onto and over land, into the ground, and back to the water sources. Look at **Figure 1** below to see how water moves through the water cycle.

Figure 1 In the water cycle, water is returned to the Earth's surface through precipitation.

Condensation occurs when water vapor cools and changes back into liquid droplets. This is how clouds form.

Evaporation occurs when liquid water changes into water vapor, which is a gas.

Transpiration is the process by which plants release water vapor into the air through their leaves.

Precipitation occurs when rain, snow, sleet, or hail falls from the clouds onto the Earth's surface.

Runoff is water, usually from precipitation, that flows across land and collects in rivers, streams, and eventually the ocean.

CONNECT TO PHYSICAL SCIENCE

At the Earth's surface and in the atmosphere, energy from the sun moves water through the water cycle. Sunlight provides the energy for evaporation, transpiration, condensation, and precipitation. Have groups work together to create a poster that shows how energy from the sun drives the water cycle.

422 Chapter 16 • Understanding Weather

Humidity

Have you ever spent a long time styling your hair before school and had a bad hair day anyway? You walked outside and—wham—your straight hair became limp, or your curly hair became frizzy. Most bad hair days can be blamed on humidity. **Humidity** is the amount of water vapor or moisture in the air. And it is the moisture in the air that makes your hair go crazy, as shown in **Figure 2**.

As water evaporates, the humidity of the air increases. But air's ability to hold water vapor depends on air temperature. As temperature increases, the air's ability to hold water also increases. **Figure 3** shows the relationship between air temperature and air's ability to hold water.

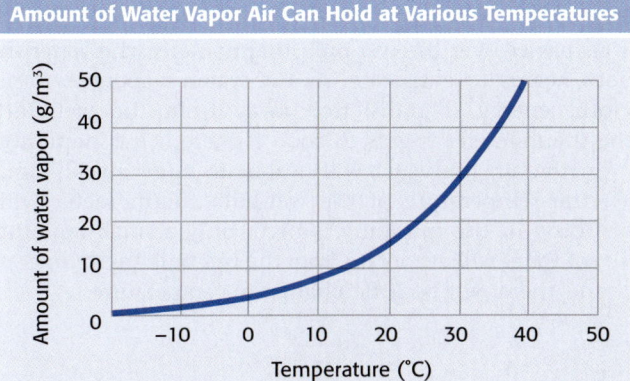

Figure 2 When there is more water in the air, your hair absorbs moisture and becomes longer.

Figure 3 This graph shows that warmer air can hold more water vapor than cooler air.

Relative Humidity

Relative humidity is the amount of moisture the air contains compared with the maximum amount it can hold at a particular temperature. Relative humidity is given as a percentage. When air holds all the water it can at a given temperature, the air is said to be *saturated*. Saturated air has a relative humidity of 100 percent. But how do you find the relative humidity of air that is not saturated? If you know the maximum amount of water vapor air can hold at a particular temperature and you know how much water vapor the air is actually holding, you can calculate the relative humidity.

Suppose that 1 m³ of air at a certain temperature can hold 24 g of water vapor. However, you know that the air actually contains 18 g of water vapor. You can calculate the relative humidity using the following formula:

$$\frac{\text{(present) } 18 \text{ g/m}^3}{\text{(saturated) } 24 \text{ g/m}^3} \times 100 = \text{(relative humidity) } 75\%$$

MATH BREAK

Relating Relative Humidity

Assume that a sample of air 1 m³ at 25°C, contains 11 g of water vapor. Calculate the relative humidity of the air using the value for saturated air shown in Figure 3.

CONNECT TO LIFE SCIENCE

When the air is humid, hair becomes frizzy. Hair is made of a protein called keratin. Each hair fiber has a scaly outer cuticle, which you can feel by running your fingers up and down a single hair. The scales allow moisture to enter the inner part of the hair fiber. When the air is humid, hair absorbs moisture and becomes longer, making it frizzy. Hair dries out and becomes shorter when the air is dry. Because humidity can cause hair length to change by as much as 2.5 percent, a device called a hair hygrometer can very accurately measure changes in humidity. Have students design and build their own hair hygrometers.

2) Teach, continued

Answer to Self-Check
Evaporation occurs when liquid water changes into water vapor and returns to the air. Humidity is the amount of water vapor in the air.

INDEPENDENT PRACTICE
After students have read this page, have them complete the following sentences:

- If the humidity is low, a _____ amount of water will evaporate from a wet-bulb thermometer and the _____ between the wet-bulb reading and the dry-bulb reading of the psychrometer will be high. (large, temperature difference)

- If the dry bulb reads 10°C, and the difference between the thermometers is 8°C, the relative humidity is _____. (15 percent)

MEETING INDIVIDUAL NEEDS
Advanced Learners Have small groups develop an activity to determine the relative humidity at different locations on the same day. Tell them to use the following materials: two identical thermometers, gauze, string, and room-temperature water. Suggest that they create a wet-bulb thermometer by tying a small piece of gauze to the bottom of one thermometer and saturating the covered end with water. Have students record their data in a table. Their data should include information about location, observable weather conditions, time of day, and the duration of the trial.

Self-Check
How does humidity relate to the water cycle? *(Turn to page 726 to check your answer.)*

Water Vapor Versus Temperature If the temperature stays the same, relative humidity changes as water vapor enters or leaves the air. The more water vapor that is in the air at a particular temperature, the higher the relative humidity is. Relative humidity is also affected by changes in temperature. If the amount of water vapor in the air stays the same, the relative humidity decreases as the temperature rises and increases as the temperature drops.

Measuring Relative Humidity A *psychrometer* (sie KRAHM uht uhr) is an instrument used to measure relative humidity. It consists of two thermometers. One thermometer is called a wet-bulb thermometer. The bulb of this thermometer is covered with a damp cloth. The other thermometer is a dry-bulb thermometer. The dry-bulb thermometer measures air temperature.

As air passes over the wet-bulb thermometer, the water in the cloth begins to evaporate. As the water evaporates from the cloth, energy is transferred away from the wet-bulb and the thermometer begins to cool. If there is less humidity in the air, the water will evaporate more quickly and the temperature of the wet-bulb thermometer will drop. If the humidity is high, only a small amount of water will evaporate from the wet-bulb thermometer and there will be little change in temperature.

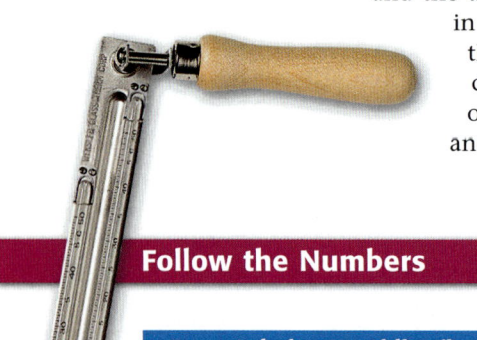

Follow the Numbers

Relative Humidity (in percentage)

Dry-bulb reading (°C)	\multicolumn{8}{c}{Difference between wet-bulb reading and dry-bulb reading (°C)}
	1	2	3	4	5	6	7	8
0	81	64	46	29	13			
2	84	68	52	37	22	7		
4	85	71	57	43	29	16		
6	86	73	60	48	35	24	11	
8	87	75	63	51	40	29	19	8
10	88	77	66	55	44	34	24	15
12	89	78	68	58	48	39	29	21
14	90	79	70	60	51	42	34	26
16	90	81	71	63	54	46	38	30
18	91	82	73	65	57	49	41	34
20	91	83	74	66	59	51	44	37

Relative humidity can be determined using a table such as this one. Locate the column that shows the difference between the wet-bulb and dry-bulb readings. Then locate the row that lists the temperature reading on the dry-bulb thermometer. The value where the column and row intersect is the relative humidity.

Multicultural CONNECTION

Before modern weather instruments were invented, natives on the Chiloé Islands, off the coast of Chile, used shells of the crab *Lithodes antarcticus* to measure relative humidity. A dry shell, normally light gray in color, shows red patches when humidity increases. It will become completely red if the humidity continues to rise, as during the rainy season. Australian Aborigines used dry kelp to predict rain. Some kelps contain magnesium chloride, which absorbs water vapor from the air. The kelp will feel damp long before it actually begins to rain.

The difference in temperature readings between the wet-bulb and dry-bulb thermometers indicates the amount of water vapor in the air. A larger difference between the two readings indicates that there is less water vapor in the air and thus lower humidity.

The Process of Condensation

You have probably seen water droplets form on the outside of a glass of ice water, as shown in **Figure 4.** Did you ever wonder where those water droplets came from? The water came from the surrounding air, and droplets formed because of condensation. **Condensation** is the process by which a gas, such as water vapor, becomes a liquid. Before condensation can occur, the air must be saturated; it must have a relative humidity of 100 percent. Condensation occurs when saturated air cools further.

Figure 4 Condensation occurred when the air next to the glass cooled to below its dew point.

Dew Point Air can become saturated when water vapor is added to the air through evaporation or transpiration. Air can also become saturated, as in the case of the glass of ice water, when it cools to its dew point. The **dew point** is the temperature to which air must cool to be completely saturated. The ice in the glass of water causes the air surrounding the glass to cool to its dew point.

Before it can condense, water vapor must also have a surface to condense on. On the glass of ice water, water vapor condenses on the sides of the glass. Another example you may already be familiar with is water vapor condensing on grass, forming small water droplets called *dew*.

REVIEW

1. What is the difference between humidity and relative humidity?
2. What are two ways that air can become saturated with water vapor?
3. What does a relative humidity of 75 percent mean?
4. How does the water cycle contribute to condensation?
5. **Analyzing Relationships** What happens to relative humidity as the air temperature drops below the dew point?

Out of Thin Air

1. Take a **plastic container**, such as a jar or drinking glass, and fill it almost to the top with room-temperature **water**.
2. Observe the outside of the can or container. Record your observations.
3. Add one or two **ice cubes**, and watch the outside of the container for any changes.
4. What happened to the outside of the container?
5. What is the liquid?
6. Where did the liquid come from? Why?

Answers to Review

1. Humidity is the amount of water vapor in the air. Relative humidity is the amount of water vapor the air contains compared with the maximum amount it can hold at a given temperature.
2. Air can become saturated if water evaporates into the air or if the air temperature drops.
3. The air is holding 75 percent of the amount of water it can hold at a given temperature.
4. Before condensation can occur, the air must be saturated. Evaporation, a part of the water cycle, adds water to the air.
5. As the air temperature drops below the dew point, relative humidity increases to the point that the air becomes saturated with moisture and condensation occurs.

2 Teach, continued

READING STRATEGY

Activity After students read this page, have them arrange the following steps in logical order:

- Water vapor condenses on smoke, dust, salt, and other small particles suspended in air. (4)
- Water vapor is added to the air. (2)
- Warm air rises and cools. (1)
- Air eventually becomes saturated. (3)
- Millions of droplets of liquid water collect to form a cloud. (5)

USING THE FIGURE

Have students carefully study **Figures 5, 6,** and **7.** Challenge them to determine one method of cloud classification based on their observations of the photographs. (In addition to being classified by altitude, as described on the following page, clouds are also classified according to shape.)

MATH and MORE

How heavy is a cloud? The first step in answering this question is to determine the cloud's volume. If an average cumulus cloud is 1,000 m long, 1,000 m wide, and 1,000 m tall, it has a volume of one billion cubic meters. Have students multiply that volume by the weight of water in 1 m³ of a cumulus cloud (0.5 g). (1,000,000,000 m³ × 0.5 g/m³ = 500,000,000 g, or 500,000 kg)

Clouds

Some look like cotton balls, some look like locks of hair, and others look like blankets of gray blocking out the sun. But what *are* clouds and how do they form? And why are there so many different-looking clouds? A **cloud** is a collection of millions of tiny water droplets or ice crystals. Clouds form as warm air rises and cools. As the rising air cools, it becomes saturated. At saturation the water vapor changes to a liquid or a solid depending on the air temperature. At higher temperatures, water vapor condenses on small particles, such as dust, smoke, and salt, suspended in the air as tiny water droplets. At temperatures below freezing, water vapor changes directly to a solid, forming ice crystals.

Figure 5 *Cumulus clouds look like piles of cotton balls.*

Cumulus Clouds Puffy, white clouds that tend to have flat bottoms, as shown in **Figure 5,** are called *cumulus clouds*. Cumulus clouds form when warm air rises. These clouds generally indicate fair weather. However, when these clouds get larger they produce thunderstorms. A cumulus cloud that produces thunderstorms is called a *cumulonimbus cloud*. When *-nimbus* or *nimbo-* is part of a cloud's name, it means that precipitation might fall from the cloud.

Figure 6 *Although stratus clouds are not as tall as cumulus clouds, they cover more area.*

Stratus Clouds Clouds that form in layers, as shown in **Figure 6,** are called *stratus clouds*. Stratus clouds cover large areas of the sky, often blocking out the sun. These clouds are caused by a gentle lifting of a large body of air into the atmosphere. *Nimbostratus clouds* are dark stratus clouds that usually produce light to heavy, continuous rain. When water vapor condenses near the ground, it forms a stratus cloud called *fog*.

Homework

Cloud Models On a poster board, have students use cotton balls to make models of different types of clouds at different altitudes. Students should create labels to describe the clouds and the types of weather they are associated with.

MISCONCEPTION ALERT

What appears to be white smoke from an airplane's engine is not smoke at all. Condensation trails, or *contrails*, form as the combustion of the aircraft's fuel causes water vapor to condense and freeze along the airplane's exhaust tail. A thick contrail that will not dissipate is a sign that a frontal system is approaching.

Cirrus Clouds As you can see in **Figure 7,** *cirrus* (SIR uhs) *clouds* are thin, feathery, white clouds found at high altitudes. Cirrus clouds form when the wind is strong. Cirrus clouds may indicate approaching bad weather if they thicken and lower in altitude.

Clouds are also classified by the altitude at which they form. The illustration in **Figure 8** shows the three altitude groups used to categorize clouds.

Figure 7 *Cirrus clouds are made of ice crystals.*

Figure 8 Cloud Types Based on Form and Altitude

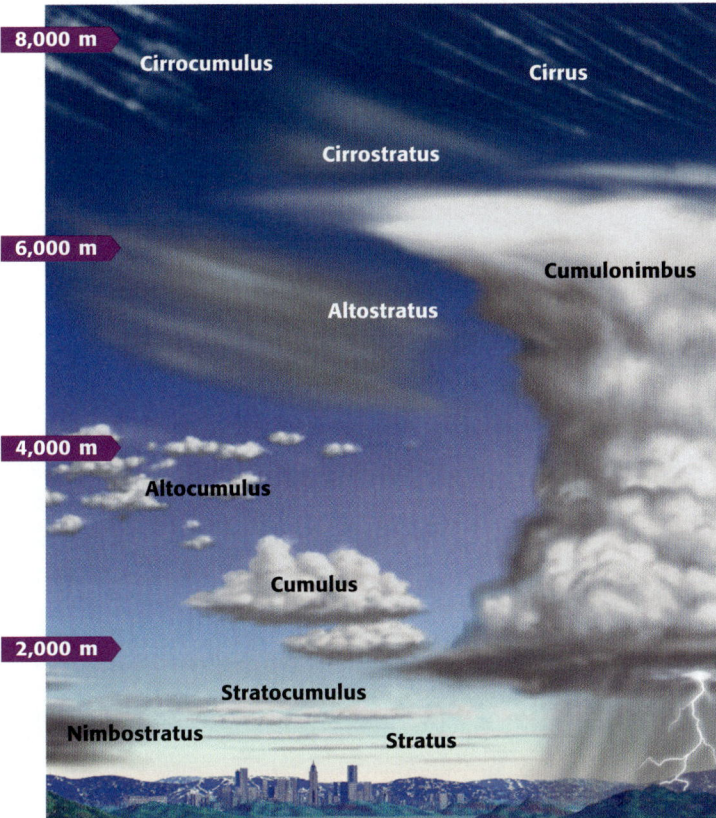

High Clouds
Because of the cold temperatures at high altitude, high clouds are made up of ice crystals. The prefix *cirro-* is used to describe high clouds.

Middle Clouds
Middle clouds can be made up of both water droplets and ice crystals. The prefix *alto-* is used to describe middle clouds.

Low Clouds
Low clouds are made up of water droplets. The prefix *strato-* is commonly used to describe these types of clouds.

CROSS-DISCIPLINARY FOCUS

Language Arts Recording descriptive and useful observations of clouds is an essential skill in amateur meteorology. Show students examples of good and bad cloud descriptions, and discuss the factors that make scientific observations useful. When describing clouds, students should consider these questions: Do they appear close to the ground or high up? Are they white, light gray, or dark gray? Are they flat and sheetlike, rounded and fluffy, or thin and wispy? Are the clouds distinct? Have students make several entries in their weather journal that describe the clouds they observe over the period of a week. Entries should include both descriptions and sketches, and students should write a weather forecast based on the clouds observed each day.

MEETING INDIVIDUAL NEEDS

Learners Having Difficulty Challenge students to use the adjectives and word parts used to classify clouds to generate a list of possible cloud types. Students should describe or illustrate the differences between each type of cloud. Students' lists should include the following names:

cirrus, cirrostratus, cirrocumulus, altocumulus, altostratus, stratus, stratocumulus, nimbostratus, cumulus, cumulonimbus

INDEPENDENT PRACTICE

Concept Mapping Have students construct a concept map using section concepts and terms. Tell them that their map should explain the relative location of clouds in the atmosphere and how they are formed.

Homework

Reporting on Fog Have students research and write a short paper on fog. Tell them that their paper should explain the relationship between fog and clouds. Students will find out about many different types of fog, including radiation fog, ground fog, valley fog, evaporation fog, steam fog, precipitation fog, ice fog, and high fog. It should also discuss where and why fog forms. Challenge students to explain the factors that contribute to the famous fogs of San Francisco or London.

Teaching Transparency 169 "Cloud Types Based on Form and Altitude"

Section 1 • Water in the Air

3) Extend

CONNECT TO PHYSICAL SCIENCE

Explain that a water molecule has a positive end and a negative end. Opposite charges attract, so the positive end of one water molecule attracts the negative end of another. This attraction helps explain why small water droplets that collide are able to form relatively large raindrops. Large raindrops are deformed by air pressure as they fall through the atmosphere. This causes them to be shaped like a hamburger bun with a concave bottom, as shown in **Figure 9**.

DEMONSTRATION

Hail Formation Melt three or four different-colored crayons or candles in separate containers over a hot plate. Dip a thick, weighted string into one color of wax, blow it dry, and repeat with each different color. After you have built up several layers, cut the wax widthwise. Display the concentric ringed formation to the class. Ask students what kind of precipitation forms in a similar manner. (hail)
Sheltered English

GOING FURTHER

Writing Meteorologists sometimes use a technique known as cloud seeding to cause or increase precipitation. Have students research and write a report about this technique. After they have gathered their information, have small groups debate the pros and cons of artificially stimulating precipitation.

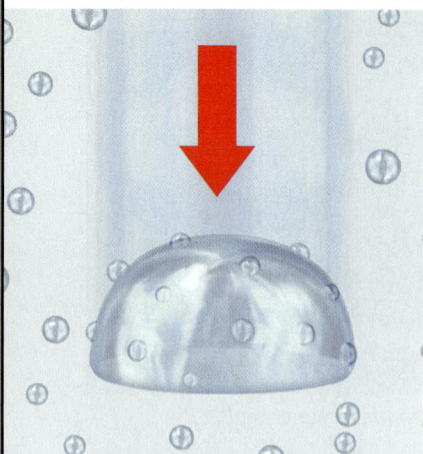

Figure 9 Cloud droplets get larger by colliding and joining with other droplets. When the water droplets become too heavy, they fall as precipitation.

Precipitation

Water vapor that condenses to form clouds can eventually fall to the ground as precipitation. **Precipitation** is water, in solid or liquid form, that falls from the air to the Earth. There are four major forms of precipitation—rain, snow, sleet, and hail.

Rain, the most common form of precipitation, is liquid water that falls from the clouds to Earth. A cloud produces rain when its water droplets become large enough to fall. A cloud droplet begins as a water droplet smaller than the period at the end of this sentence. Before a cloud droplet falls as precipitation, it must increase in size to about 100 times its normal diameter. **Figure 9** illustrates how a water droplet increases in size until it is finally large enough to fall as precipitation.

Snow and Sleet The most common form of solid precipitation is *snow*. Snow forms when temperatures are so cold that water vapor changes directly to a solid. Snow can fall as individual ice crystals or combine to form snowflakes, like the one shown in **Figure 10**.

Sleet, also called freezing rain, forms when rain falls through a layer of freezing air. The rain freezes, producing falling ice. Sometimes rain does not freeze until it hits a surface near the ground. When this happens, the rain changes into a layer of ice called *glaze,* as shown in **Figure 11**.

Figure 10 Snowflakes are six-sided ice crytals that range in size from several millimeters to several centimeters.

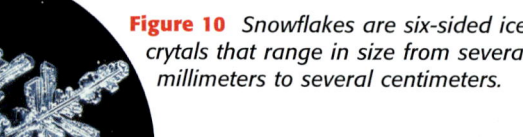

Figure 11 Glaze ice forms as rain freezes on surfaces near the ground.

Multicultural CONNECTION

Have students research the rainmakers in Hopi Indian culture. Students might find out about *Leenangkatsina,* whose flute brings rain; *Qaleetaqa,* who carries lightning and a bull-roarer to bring rain; and *Si'o Sa'lakwmana* or *Pawtiwa,* both of whom bring rain and mist to villages.

 WEIRD SCIENCE

The largest hailstone ever recorded fell on Coffeyville, Kansas, on September 3, 1970. The hailstone was the size of a softball, and weighed 3.7 kg.

428 Chapter 16 • Understanding Weather

Hail Solid precipitation that falls as balls or lumps of ice is called *hail*. Hail usually forms in cumulonimbus clouds. Updrafts of air in the clouds carry raindrops to high altitudes in the cloud, where they freeze. As the frozen raindrops fall, they collide and combine with water droplets. Another updraft of air can send the hail up again high into the cloud. Here the water drops collected by the hail freeze, forming another layer of frozen ice. If the upward movement of air is strong enough, the hail can accumulate many layers of ice. Eventually, the hail becomes too heavy and falls to the Earth's surface, as shown in **Figure 12**. Hail is usually associated with warm weather and most often occurs during the spring and summer months.

Figure 12 *The impact of large hailstones can damage property and crops.*

Measuring Precipitation A *rain gauge* is an instrument used to measure the amount of rainfall. A rain gauge typically consists of a funnel and a cylinder, as shown in **Figure 13**. Rain falls into the funnel and collects in the cylinder. Markings on the cylinder indicate how much rain has fallen.

Snow is measured by both depth and water content. The depth of snow is measured using a measuring stick. The snow's water content is determined by melting the snow and measuring the amount of water.

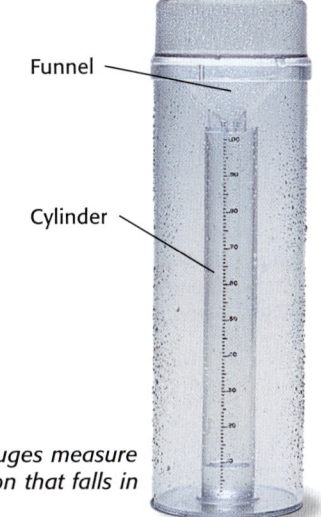

Figure 13 *Rain gauges measure only the precipitation that falls in a particular place.*

REVIEW

1. How do clouds form?
2. Why are some clouds formed from water droplets, while others are made up of ice crystals?
3. Describe how rain forms.
4. **Applying Concepts** How can rain and hail fall from the same cumulonimbus cloud?

4) Close

Quiz

1. Compare and contrast the processes of condensation and evaporation in the water cycle. (Both are processes in Earth's water cycle that involve a change of the state of water. They differ in that condensation occurs when water vapor changes to a liquid, while evaporation occurs when liquid water changes to a gas.)
2. What name would you give a lacy, layered cloud above 6,000 m? (cirrostratus)
3. Compare and contrast snow, sleet, and hail. (All are forms of solid precipitation that fall from clouds. Snow forms when water vapor changes to a solid. Sleet forms when rain falls through a layer of freezing air. Hail forms when raindrops are carried by winds to higher altitudes in a cloud, where they freeze and accumulate layers.)

ALTERNATIVE ASSESSMENT

Have students write an instruction manual on how to form rain, snow, sleet, and hail in the atmosphere. Students should also include information about how to measure these types of precipitation.

Let It Snow! PG 697

Answers to Review

1. Clouds form as warm air rises and cools. As the air cools, it becomes saturated. If there are condensation surfaces available, the water vapor changes physical states to liquid droplets or solid ice crystals, forming a cloud.
2. At higher temperatures, water vapor condenses on surfaces as tiny water droplets. When temperatures are below freezing, water vapor changes directly to ice crystals.
3. Rain forms when a cloud's water droplets become too heavy to remain suspended in the cloud. The droplets grow by colliding and joining with other droplets.
4. Hail forms when raindrops are carried by updrafts of air to higher altitudes in clouds, where the raindrops freeze. Some raindrops may not be caught in the updrafts and will fall to the ground as rain.

Section 1 • Water in the Air

SECTION 2

Focus

Air Masses and Fronts

In this section, students learn what air masses are and how they affect weather in the United States. Students also learn about the boundaries of air masses—known as *fronts*—and the types of weather associated with these boundaries.

🔔 Bellringer

Ask students to write down as many different qualities of air as possible. (Students might note that air can be humid or dry, hot or cold, or have a high pressure or a low pressure.) Tell students that the air they are breathing now was hundreds of miles away yesterday. Ask them to think about what caused that air to move. Explain that air masses tend to flow from areas of high pressure to areas of low pressure, just as the air inside a balloon escapes when the balloon is punctured.

1 Motivate

DEMONSTRATION

Students may have a difficult time understanding how hot and cold air masses stay separated as they move. Tell students that air at different temperatures has different densities. In this respect, air behaves much like water. To demonstrate how temperature can separate liquid masses, fill a large beaker or jar with hot water and a small beaker with cold water. Add several drops of blue food coloring to the cold water to make it visible. Slowly pour the cold water down the side of the jar. Encourage students to describe and explain what they observe.

SECTION 2

Terms to Learn
air mass
front

What You'll Do
- Explain how air masses are characterized.
- Describe the four major types of air masses that influence weather in the United States.
- Describe the four major types of fronts.
- Relate fronts to weather changes.

Air Masses and Fronts

Have you ever wondered how the weather can change so fast? One day the sun is shining and you are wearing shorts, and the next day it is so cold you need a coat. Changes in weather are caused by the movement and interaction of air masses. An *air mass* is a large body of air that has similar temperature and moisture throughout. In this section you will learn about air masses and how their interaction influences the weather.

Air Masses

An air mass gets its moisture and temperature characteristics from the area over which it forms. These areas are called *source regions*. For example, an air mass that develops over the Gulf of Mexico is warm and wet because this area is warm and has a lot of water that evaporates into the air. There are many types of air masses, each associated with a particular source region. The characteristics of these air masses are represented on maps with a two-letter symbol, as shown in **Figure 14**. The first letter indicates the moisture characteristics of the air mass, and the second symbol represents the temperature characteristics of the air mass.

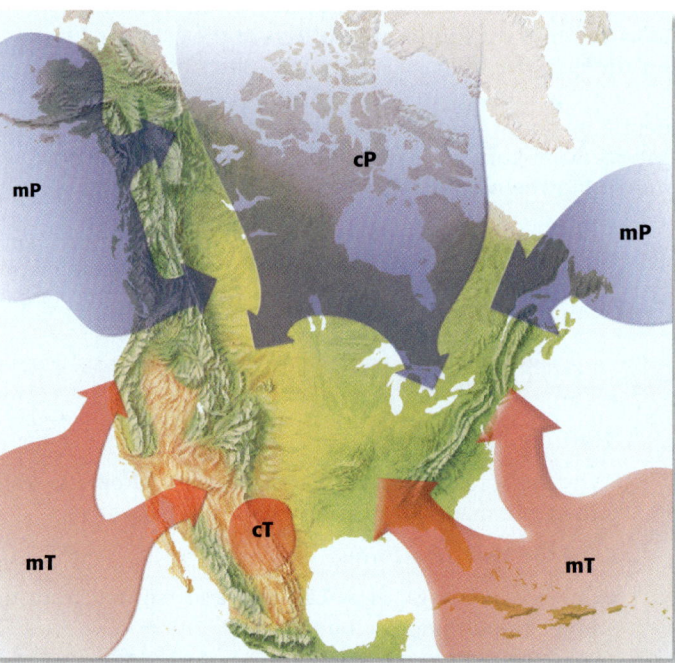

Figure 14 This map shows the source regions for air masses that influence weather in North America.

maritime (m)–forms over water; wet

continental (c)–forms over land; dry

polar (P)–forms over the polar regions; cold

tropical (T)–develops over the Tropics; warm

430

MISCONCEPTION ALERT

People often assume that humid air is heavier than dry air. Actually, humid air rises like a balloon because it is less dense than dry air at the same pressure and temperature. The reason is that water molecules are lighter than N_2 and O_2, the main constituents of air. The more water vapor there is in a mass of air, the more N_2 and O_2 is displaced. In general, when humidity increases, air becomes less dense and rises. As an air mass rises, it cools, the water vapor condenses, and the air mass eventually sinks. If water vapor were heavier than air, clouds would only form at the Earth's surface.

430 Chapter 16 • Understanding Weather

Cold Air Masses Most of the cold winter weather in the United States is influenced by three polar air masses. A continental polar air mass develops over land in northern Canada. In the winter, this air brings extremely cold weather to the United States, as shown in **Figure 15.** In the summer, it generally brings cool, dry weather.

A maritime polar air mass that forms over the North Pacific Ocean mostly affects the Pacific Coast. This air mass is very wet, but not as cold as the air mass that develops over Canada. In the winter, this air mass brings rain and snow to the Pacific Coast. In the summer, it brings cool, foggy weather.

A maritime polar air mass that forms over the North Atlantic Ocean usually affects New England and eastern Canada. In the winter, it produces cold, cloudy weather with precipitation. In the summer, the air mass brings cool weather with fog.

Figure 15 *A cP air mass generally moves southeastward across Canada and into the northern United States.*

Warm Air Masses Four warm air masses influence the weather in the United States. A maritime tropical air mass that develops over warm areas in the North Pacific Ocean is lower in moisture content and weaker than the maritime polar air mass. As a result, southern California receives less precipitation than the rest of California.

Other maritime tropical air masses develop over the warm waters of the Gulf of Mexico and the North Atlantic Ocean. These air masses move north across the East Coast and into the Midwest. In the summer, they bring hot and humid weather, thunderstorms, and hurricanes, as shown in **Figure 16.** In the winter, they bring mild, often cloudy weather.

Figure 16 *People in Texas experience the many thunderstorms brought by mT air masses from the Gulf of Mexico.*

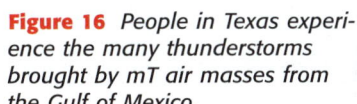

Air masses can extend upward for thousands of meters and can reach the top of the troposphere—an altitude of 10 to 16 km!

CONNECT TO LIFE SCIENCE

Why do people complain of aching joints before a thunderstorm? A study found that nearly 75 percent of arthritis sufferers felt more pain in their joints when air pressure was falling. Although this effect has been thoroughly documented, there is no definitive evidence of why it occurs.

2) Teach

DISCUSSION

Air Masses and You Have students use **Figure 14** to determine which type of air mass is mainly responsible for the weather in your area. Have students describe the general temperatures and humidity typical of your area. Then have students compare their observations with the information in this section.

Multicultural CONNECTION

Local weather patterns are heavily influenced by air masses, which tend to bring predictable weather. All cultures have names for familiar weather patterns. For example, in Tunisia, Africa, weather forecasters often predict "hot and *chili*" conditions. This forecast may not make sense to people elsewhere, but to a Tunisian, *chili* refers to a hot wind blowing from the North African desert. Similarly, in parts of the eastern United States, people refer to the hot, dry, and relatively windless weeks of August as the Indian summer. Have interested students research the names and characteristics of typical weather patterns in other countries.

Directed Reading Worksheet 16 Section 2

Teaching Transparency 170 "Air Masses in North America"

Section 2 • Air Masses and Fronts

2 Teach, continued

READING STRATEGY

Activity As they learn about the different types of fronts, have students draw each front in their ScienceLog. Students should label each diagram with arrows indicating the direction the air masses are moving and write captions describing the type of weather that is associated with the front.

MEETING INDIVIDUAL NEEDS

Learners Having Difficulty Perform the following demonstration to show students how cold and warm fronts form. Obtain a pair of surgical gloves. Use magic markers to color one glove red and the other glove blue. When the gloves are completely dry, put them on. Tell students that the blue glove represents a cold air mass and the red glove represents a warm air mass. To show how a cold front forms, hold your hands in front of you, and move your "blue hand" toward your "red hand." Just before they touch, slide your blue hand under your red hand and push your red hand up. To simulate the formation of a warm front, keep your blue hand stationary, and move your red hand toward your blue hand. As your hands touch, slide your red hand up and over your blue hand. Sheltered English

Teaching Transparency 171 "Cold and Warm Fronts"

internet connect
sciLINKS NSTA
TOPIC: Air Masses and Fronts
GO TO: www.scilinks.org
sciLINKS NUMBER: HSTE385

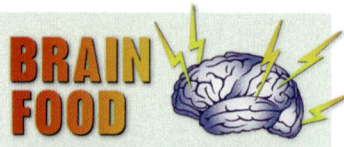

BRAIN FOOD
The term *front* was first used to describe weather systems during World War I in Europe. Meteorologists in Norway thought the boundaries between different air masses were much like the opposing armies on the battle front.

A continental tropical air mass forms over the deserts of northern Mexico and the southwestern United States. This air mass influences weather in the United States only during the summer. It generally moves northeastward, bringing clear, dry, and very hot weather.

Fronts

Air masses with different characteristics, such as temperature and humidity, do not usually mix. So when two different air masses meet, a boundary forms between them. This boundary is called a **front**. Weather at a front is usually cloudy and stormy. The four different types of fronts—cold fronts, warm fronts, occluded fronts, and stationary fronts—are illustrated on these two pages. Fronts are usually associated with weather in the middle latitudes, where there are both cold and warm air masses. Fronts do not occur in the Tropics because only warm air masses exist there.

Cold Front
A cold air mass meets and displaces a warm air mass. Because the moving cold air is more dense, it moves under the less-dense warm air, pushing it up.
  Cold fronts can move fast, producing thunderstorms, heavy rain, or snow. Cooler weather usually follows a cold front because the warm air is pushed away from the Earth's surface.

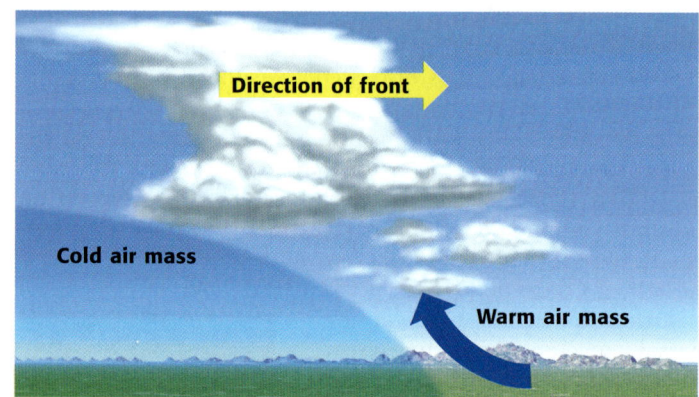

Warm Front
A warm air mass meets and overrides a cold air mass. The warm, less-dense air moves over the cold, denser air. The warm air gradually replaces the cold air.
  Warm fronts generally bring drizzly precipitation. After the front passes, weather conditions are clear and warm.

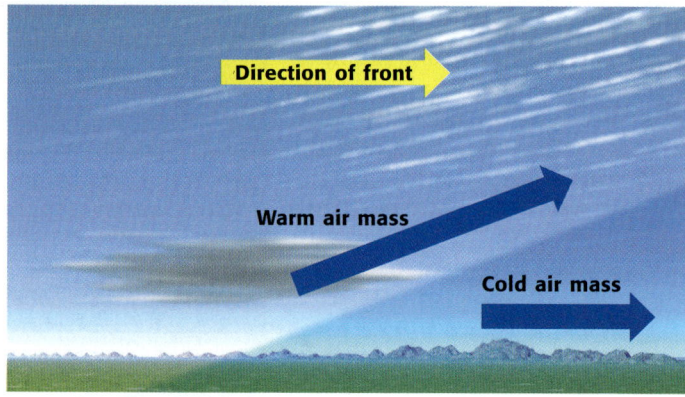

432

CROSS-DISCIPLINARY FOCUS

History During World War I, European nations stopped broadcasting weather reports, fearing that they would be used by advancing enemy troops. This left nonaligned countries such as Norway to develop their own meteorology program. Norwegian meteorologists responded by forming the famous Bergen School, which greatly advanced the field of meteorology. They discovered distinct air masses in the atmosphere and found that these masses traveled with the winds. Influenced by the war, the meteorologists described air masses using military terms. They imagined Europe as a battleground where different air masses fought like armies, each trying to advance on the other. The boundary between the air masses, where the "battle" occurs, was called the front.

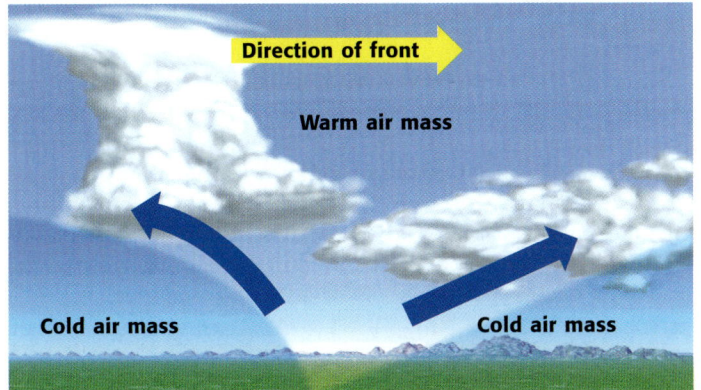

Occluded Front
A faster-moving cold air mass overtakes a slower-moving warm air mass and forces the warm air up. The cold air mass then continues advancing until it meets a cold air mass that is warmer. The cold air mass then forces this air mass to rise.

An occluded front has cool temperatures and large amounts of precipitation.

Stationary Front
A cold air mass meets a warm air mass and little horizontal movement occurs.

The weather associated with a stationary front is similar to that produced by a warm front.

REVIEW

1. What are the characteristics that define air masses?
2. What are the major air masses that influence the weather in the United States?
3. What are fronts, and what causes them?
4. What kind of front forms when a cold air mass displaces a warm air mass?
5. **Analyzing Relationships** Explain why the Pacific Coast has cool, wet winters and warm, dry summers.

internet connect

SCILINKS
NSTA

TOPIC: Air Masses and Fronts
GO TO: www.scilinks.org
sciLINKS NUMBER: HSTE385

433

Answers to Review
1. temperature and moisture
2. maritime tropical, maritime polar, continental tropical, and continental polar
3. Fronts are boundaries that form between two different air masses. Boundaries form because air masses with different moisture and temperature characteristics do not mix easily.
4. a cold front
5. In the winter, the Pacific Coast's climate is governed by a maritime polar air mass that brings wet weather and cool temperatures. In the summer, the Pacific Coast's climate is governed by a maritime tropical air mass that brings warm temperatures and little moisture.

3) Extend

RESEARCH
Have students research and test weather lore to find out if it has a scientific basis. For example, students could research the saying, "Red sky at night, sailor's delight; red sky at morning, sailors take warning."

4) Close

Quiz
1. If a continental polar air mass moves over Ohio in the summer, what will the weather be like? (cool and dry)
2. Why does the continental tropical air mass that forms over northern Mexico bring clear, dry, hot weather? (It forms over the desert, which is hot and contains relatively little moisture.)
3. Explain how a cold front develops. (A cold front develops when a cold air mass moves under a warm air mass, forcing the warmer air upward.)
4. What kind of weather is associated with a stationary front? (It will probably be cloudy and rainy as long as the front lies over an area. After the front passes, the weather will usually clear up.)

ALTERNATIVE ASSESSMENT
Have students list five places in the United States they have visited or would like to visit and the air masses that affect the weather in those places.

 **Teaching Transparency 172** "Occluded and Stationary Fronts"

Section 2 • Air Masses and Fronts

SECTION 3

Focus

Severe Weather

In this section, students learn about the conditions that form thunderstorms, tornadoes, and hurricanes. The discussion of thunderstorms includes an explanation of lightning and thunder, while the discussion of tornadoes and hurricanes includes information on the incredible damage these storms cause.

🔔 Bellringer

Show students a picture of a thunderstorm. Then have them write a one-paragraph description of a thunderstorm in their ScienceLog. Tell them to focus on the characteristics that distinguish thunderstorms from other forms of weather. Ask them to describe the weather conditions immediately before, during, and after a thunderstorm.

1 Motivate

DEMONSTRATION

Perform this demonstration to simulate the forces that cause thunder. Inflate a balloon with air, and tie it closed. Explain that thunder occurs when lightning superheats air, causing the gases to expand rapidly. The air in the balloon is under pressure, so it will also expand rapidly if the pressure is suddenly released. The rapid expansion of air causes vibrations that we hear as sound. Hold up a pin or needle, pause, and pop the balloon with a flourish. Sheltered English

Directed Reading Worksheet 16 Section 3

Section 3

Terms to Learn

thunderstorm   tornado
lightning   hurricane
thunder

What You'll Do

- Explain what lightning is.
- Describe the formation of thunderstorms, tornadoes, and hurricanes.
- Describe the characteristics of thunderstorms, tornadoes, and hurricanes.

Severe Weather

Weather in the mid-latitudes can change from day to day. These changes result from the continual shifting of air masses. Sometimes a series of storms will develop along a front and bring severe weather. *Severe weather* is weather that can cause property damage and even death. Examples of severe weather include thunderstorms, tornadoes, and hurricanes. In this section you will learn about the different types of severe weather and how each type forms.

Thunderstorms

Thunderstorms, as shown in **Figure 17,** are small, intense weather systems that produce strong winds, heavy rain, lightning, and thunder. As you learned in the previous section, thunderstorms can occur along cold fronts. But that's not the only place they develop. There are only two atmospheric conditions required to produce thunderstorms: the air near the Earth's surface must be warm and moist, and the atmosphere must be unstable. The atmosphere is unstable when the surrounding air is colder than the rising air mass. As long as the air surrounding the rising air mass is colder, the air mass will continue to rise.

Thunderstorms occur when warm, moist air rises rapidly in an unstable atmosphere. When the warm air reaches its dew point, the water vapor in the air condenses, forming cumulus clouds. If the atmosphere is extremely unstable, the warm air will continue to rise, causing the cloud to grow into a dark, cumulonimbus cloud. These clouds can reach heights of more than 15 km.

Figure 17 *A typical thunderstorm produces approximately 470 million liters of water and enough electricity to provide power to the entire United States for 20 minutes.*

Trees sometimes explode when struck by lightning. Why? Lightning causes the sap in the tree to vaporize (turn from a liquid to a gas). The steam expands rapidly as it is heated, causing the tree to explode.

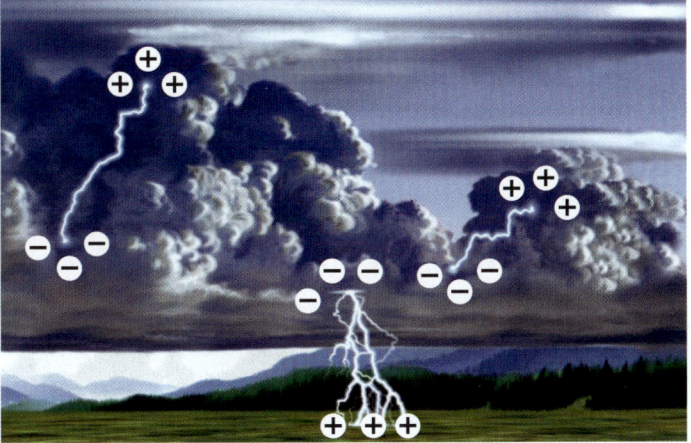

Figure 18 *The upper part of a cloud usually carries a positive electrical charge, while the lower part of the cloud carries mainly negative charges.*

 **Physics CONNECTION**

Have you ever wondered why you don't see lightning and hear thunder at the same time? Well, there's an easy explanation. Light travels faster than sound. The light reaches you almost instantly, but the sound travels only 1 km every 3 seconds. The closer the lightning is to where you are, the sooner you will hear the thunder.

Lightning Thunderstorms are very active electrically. **Lightning** is a large electrical discharge that occurs between two oppositely charged surfaces, as shown in **Figure 18.** Have you ever touched someone after scuffing your feet on the carpet and received a mild shock? If so, you have experienced how lightning forms. While walking around, friction between the floor and your shoes builds up an electrical charge in your body. When you touch someone else, the charge is released.

When lightning strikes, energy is released. This energy is transferred to the air and causes the air to expand rapidly and send out sound waves. **Thunder** is the sound that results from the rapid expansion of air along the lightning strike.

Severe Thunderstorms Severe thunderstorms produce one or more of the following conditions—high winds, hail, flash floods, and tornadoes. Hailstorms damage crops, dent the metal on cars, and break windows. Sudden flash flooding due to heavy rains causes millions of dollars in property damage annually and is the biggest cause of weather-related deaths.

Lightning, which occurs with all thunderstorms, is responsible for thousands of forest fires each year in the United States. Lightning also kills or injures hundreds of people a year in the United States.

Figure 19 *Lightning often strikes the highest object in an area.*

2 Teach

MATH and MORE

To find the distance of a thunderstorm in kilometers, count the number of seconds between a lightning flash and the thunder and divide that number by 3. Ask students: If you see a lightning flash and then hear thunder 21 seconds later, how far away is a storm? (7 km) What if the time difference is 9 seconds? (3 km) 7 seconds? (2.3 km)

REAL-WORLD CONNECTION

Students may be surprised to learn that, on average, lightning kills more people in the United States than tornadoes, floods, or hurricanes do. Discuss lightning safety tips with students, and have them create a poster showing what to do during a thunderstorm.

CONNECT TO PHYSICAL SCIENCE

Lightning can heat the air to 33,000°C, more than five times the temperature of the sun's surface. On average, ten million strokes of lightning strike the Earth every day. Lightning strokes happen because the air currents in a thunderstorm separate charged particles of water and ice. Negatively charged particles tend to accumulate near the bottom of the cloud. When the charge overcomes the electrical resistance of the air, lightning strikes. Use the Teaching Transparency listed below to illustrate how lightning forms.

 Teaching Transparency 268 "How Lightning Forms"

IS THAT A FACT!

The color of lightning can indicate atmospheric conditions.

blue = hail
red = rain
yellow or orange = dust
white = low humidity

 **MISCONCEPTION ALERT**

Inform students that the old saying, "Lightning never strikes twice in the same place," is not true. Lightning has struck the same place, and even the same person, more than once. Ray Sullivan, retired National Park Ranger, has been hit seven times by lightning. Luckily, he has survived the strikes.

Section 3 • Severe Weather

2) Teach, continued

GROUP ACTIVITY

Making Models Have pairs of students work together to model a tornado vortex. Supply each pair with a clean, empty plastic jar with its lid, water, food coloring, a teaspoon of liquid dish soap, and a teaspoon of vinegar. Have students fill the jars about three-quarters full of water. Instruct them to add a few drops of food coloring, the soap, and the vinegar. Instruct them to cap the jar tightly and shake it vigorously. Once the solution is mixed, tell students to give the jars a quick twist with a flick of the wrist. Students will observe that a vortex will form and lengthen. **Sheltered English**

BRAIN FOOD

Most tornadoes develop from thunderstorms at the leading edge of a cold front. Ask students to think about why this is so. (The cool air wedges under the warm air, forcing it to rise rapidly and become unstable. The distinct temperature and pressure differences between the two air masses greatly increase the chance of a tornado forming.)

USING SCIENCE FICTION

Encourage students to read "All Summer in a Day" by Ray Bradbury in the *Holt Anthology of Science Fiction*.

Teaching Transparency 173
"How a Tornado Forms"

Tornadoes

Tornadoes are produced in only 1 percent of all thunderstorms. A **tornado** is a small, rotating column of air that has high wind speeds and low central pressure and that touches the ground. A tornado starts out as a funnel cloud that pokes through the bottom of a cumulonimbus cloud and hangs in the air. It is called a tornado when it makes contact with the Earth's surface. **Figure 20** shows the development of a tornado.

Figure 20 How a Tornado Forms

① Wind traveling in two different directions causes a layer of air in the middle to begin to rotate like a roll of toilet paper.

② The rotating column of air is turned to a vertical position by strong updrafts of air within the cumulonimbus cloud. The updrafts of air also begin to rotate with the column of air.

③ The rotating column of air works its way down to the bottom of the cumulonimbus cloud and forms a funnel cloud.

④ The funnel cloud is called a tornado when it touches the ground.

 **IS THAT A FACT!**

Because of the Coriolis effect, almost all tornadoes in the Northern Hemisphere spin in a counterclockwise direction. Tornadoes in the Southern Hemisphere almost always spin in a clockwise direction.

 **WEIRD SCIENCE**

People have reported seeing "naked" chickens after tornadoes strike rural areas. A likely explanation is that tornadoes cause chickens to shed their feathers, or molt. Chickens often molt when attacked. As the chickens molt, the strong tornado winds blow their feathers off.

Twists of Terror About 75 percent of the world's tornadoes occur in the United States. The majority of these tornadoes happen in the spring and early summer when cold, dry air from Canada collides with warm, moist air from the Tropics. The length of a tornado's path of destruction can vary, but it is usually about 8 km long and 10–60 m wide. Although most tornadoes last only a few minutes, they can cause a lot of damage. This is due to their strong spinning winds. The average tornado has wind speeds between 120 and 180 km/h, but rarer, more violent tornadoes can have spinning winds up to 500 km/h. The winds of tornadoes have been known to uproot trees and destroy buildings, as shown in **Figure 21.** Tornadoes are capable of picking up heavy objects, such as mobile homes and cars, and hurling them through the air.

Figure 21 *The tornado that hit Kissimmee, Florida, in 1998 had wind speeds of up to 416 km/h.*

Hurricanes

A **hurricane,** as shown in **Figure 22,** is a large, rotating tropical weather system with wind speeds of at least 119 km/h. Hurricanes are the most powerful storms on Earth. Hurricanes have different names in other parts of the world. In the western Pacific Ocean, they are called *typhoons.* Hurricanes that form over the Indian Ocean are called *cyclones.*

Hurricanes generally form in the area between 5° and 20° north and south latitude over warm, tropical oceans. At higher latitudes, the water is too cold for hurricanes to form. Hurricanes vary in size from 160 km to 1,500 km in diameter, and they can travel for thousands of miles.

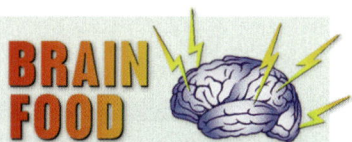

Did you know that fish have been known to fall from the sky? Some scientists think the phenomenon of raining fish is caused by waterspouts. A waterspout is a tornado that occurs over water.

Figure 22 **Hurricane Fran Photographed from Space**

IS THAT A FACT!

Before 1950 hurricanes were named or identified by their latitude and longitude. In the 1950s meteorologists began assigning names to hurricanes. Today, the names are assigned in advance for six-year cycles. The names are submitted by countries potentially in the path of hurricanes and approved by the World Meteorological Organization.

COOPERATIVE LEARNING

Have students work in pairs or small groups to design a poster or other graphic display that compares and contrasts thunderstorms, tornadoes, and hurricanes. Then have the groups display their posters around the class for others to enjoy.

CROSS-DISCIPLINARY FOCUS

History Hurricanes played a significant role in early American history. In 1609, a fleet of ships with settlers from England bound for Virginia was blown off course by a hurricane. Some of the ships landed in Bermuda instead, and the settlers started the first European colony there. Stories of the storm and the shipwreck may have inspired William Shakespeare to write *The Tempest.*

Homework

 **Disaster Plan** Have students find out how to protect themselves during a thunderstorm, tornado, or hurricane. Using their findings, have each student draw up a disaster plan for severe weather. The plan should include general information as well as things that might be specific to their families, such as what to do with the family pet(s), how to assist a person who uses a wheelchair or walker, and so on. Suggest that students review the plan with their family.

TOPIC: Severe Weather
GO TO: www.scilinks.org
sciLINKS NUMBER: HSTE390

3 Extend

RESEARCH

Writing Tell students that creating severe weather takes a lot of energy. Have them research the relationship between energy and storm formation. For example, as a warm air mass rises, energy from water condensation helps fuel hurricanes. The energy released by a typical hurricane in one day is equal to detonating four hundred 20-megaton hydrogen bombs. Challenge students to research these concepts in books, magazines, and the Internet, and compile their findings into a short report.

GROUP ACTIVITY

Have students work in groups to learn about a hurricane of their choosing. Have them find out where the storm formed, its path, the damage it did, and how people recovered from the damage. Ask them to focus on the people involved in the hurricane, from the meteorologists to relief workers. Have each group present the information they gather as a series of simulated newscasts.

GOING FURTHER

Disaster Kit Have groups put together a disaster supply kit that could be used in the event of severe weather. Items that are not easily obtained can be listed on a sheet of paper. Groups can display their kits in class.

Teaching Transparency 174
"A Cross Section of a Hurricane"

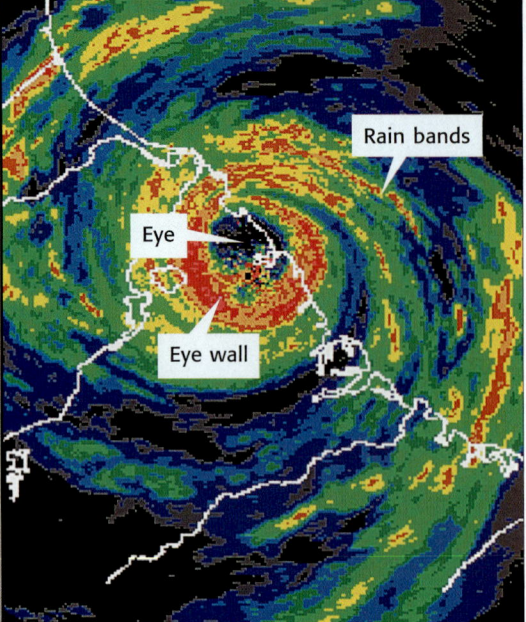

Figure 23 The photo above gives you a bird's-eye view of a hurricane.

Formation of a Hurricane A hurricane begins as a group of thunderstorms moving over tropical ocean waters. Winds traveling in two different directions collide, causing the storm to rotate over an area of low pressure. Because of the Coriolis effect, the storm turns counterclockwise in the Northern Hemisphere and clockwise in the Southern Hemisphere.

Hurricanes get their energy from the condensation of water vapor. Once formed, the hurricane is fueled through contact with the warm ocean water. Moisture is added to the warm air by evaporation from the ocean. As the warm, moist air rises, the water vapor condenses, releasing large amounts of energy. The hurricane continues to grow as long as it is over its source of warm, moist air. When the hurricane moves into colder waters or over land, it begins to die because it has lost its source of energy. **Figure 23** and **Figure 24** show two views of a hurricane.

Figure 24 The view below shows how a hurricane would look if you cut it in half and looked at it from the side. The arrows indicate the flow of air.

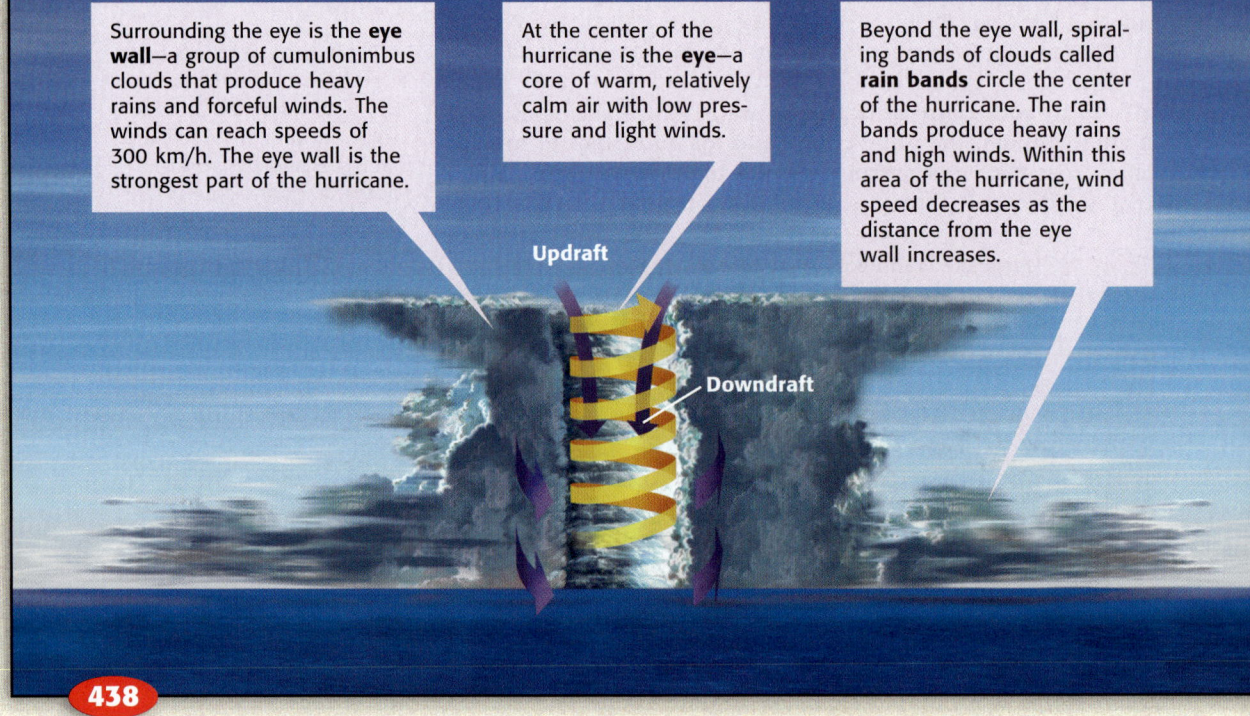

Surrounding the eye is the **eye wall**—a group of cumulonimbus clouds that produce heavy rains and forceful winds. The winds can reach speeds of 300 km/h. The eye wall is the strongest part of the hurricane.

At the center of the hurricane is the **eye**—a core of warm, relatively calm air with low pressure and light winds.

Beyond the eye wall, spiraling bands of clouds called **rain bands** circle the center of the hurricane. The rain bands produce heavy rains and high winds. Within this area of the hurricane, wind speed decreases as the distance from the eye wall increases.

438

Science Bloopers

The Seminole Indians of Florida have used their own observations of nature to successfully predict severe weather. In one instance, their observations of plants and animals indicated that a hurricane was approaching. Though the weather bureau predicted the storm would miss the area, the Seminoles evacuated—and were spared the storm's destruction. In another instance, meteorologists were so sure of their predictions that heavy equipment was moved from the area so that it would be available later to help relief efforts. The Seminoles thought otherwise and remained in the area. The hurricane never reached Florida.

Damage Caused by Hurricanes Hurricanes can cause a lot of damage when they move near or onto land. The speed of the steady winds of most hurricanes ranges from 120 km/h to 150 km/h, and they can reach speeds as high as 300 km/h. Hurricane winds can knock down trees and telephone poles and can damage and destroy buildings and homes.

While high winds cause a great deal of damage, most hurricane damage is caused by flooding associated with heavy rains and storm surges. A *storm surge* is a wall of water that builds up over the ocean due to the heavy winds and low atmospheric pressure. The wall of water gets bigger and bigger as it nears the shore, reaching its greatest height when it crashes onto the shore. Depending on the hurricane's strength, a storm surge can be 1 m to 8 m high and 65 km–160 km long. Flooding causes tremendous damage to property and lives when a storm surge moves onto shore, as shown in **Figure 25.**

Astronomy CONNECTION

The weather on Jupiter is more exciting than that on Earth. Wind speeds reach up to 540 km/h. Storms last for decades, and one—the Great Red Spot of Jupiter—has been swirling around since it was first discovered, in 1664. The Great Red Spot has a diameter of more than one and a half times that of the Earth. It is like a hurricane that has lasted more than 300 years.

Figure 25 In 1998, the flooding associated with Hurricane Mitch devastated Central America. Whole villages were swept away by the flood waters and mudslides. Thousands of people were killed, and damages were estimated to be more than $5 billion.

REVIEW

1. What is lightning?
2. Describe how tornadoes develop. What is the difference between a funnel cloud and a tornado?
3. Why do hurricanes form only over certain areas?
4. **Inferring Relationships** What happens to a hurricane as it moves over land? Why?

internetconnect

SC/**LINKS**
NSTA

TOPIC: Severe Weather
GO TO: www.scilinks.org
***sci*LINKS NUMBER:** HSTE390

4) Close

Quiz

1. What is the relationship between lightning and thunder? (Lightning is an electrical discharge that forms between clouds or between a cloud and the ground. The air around the lightning bolt expands rapidly, producing sound waves that we call thunder.)

2. Explain why tornadoes often destroy buildings in their path. (Buildings are often destroyed by the enormous force exerted by tornado winds and by the strong updrafts that accompany them.)

3. Why don't hurricanes form over land? (A hurricane gets its energy from enormous volumes of warm, moist air, which are not present over landmasses.)

ALTERNATIVE ASSESSMENT

Concept Mapping Have students make a severe-weather concept map. Tell them that their map should illustrate how thunderstorms, tornadoes, and hurricanes form and what their characteristics are.

Reinforcement Worksheet 16 "Precipitation Situations"

Answers to Review

1. Lightning is a large electrical discharge that occurs between two oppositely charged surfaces.

2. A tornado develops when wind traveling in two different directions causes the air in the middle to rotate. The rotating column of air is turned upright by updrafts that begin spinning with it. The rotating air works its way down to the bottom of the cloud and forms a funnel cloud. When the funnel cloud touches the ground, it is called a tornado.

3. Hurricanes form only over warm, tropical oceans because a hurricane requires the energy and moisture from water to fuel it.

4. A hurricane dissipates as it moves over land because it loses its energy source.

SECTION 4

Focus

Forecasting the Weather

In this section, students will learn how we use instruments such as thermometers, barometers, weather balloons, and radar to forecast and report the weather. Students will also learn how meteorologists use weather maps to depict the data they gather.

🔔 Bellringer

Pose this question to students: If you did not have the benefit of the weather forecast on the news, radio, or television, how would you forecast the weather? (Answers will vary. Possible answers include observing the sky and noticing the direction and intensity of the winds.)

1) Motivate

DEMONSTRATION

Air Pressure and Barometers
Students have learned that thunderstorms and hurricanes are low-pressure storm systems. Low pressure usually indicates stormy weather, and high pressure usually indicates clear weather. If possible, show students a barometer, and tell them that barometers are still widely used in weather forecasting. Show students how to read a barometer and how to use the moveable pointer to track whether air pressure is increasing or decreasing.
Sheltered English

Gone with the Wind PG 698

Section 4

Terms to Learn
thermometer   wind vane
barometer   anemometer
windsock   isobars

What You'll Do
♦ Describe the different types of instruments used to take weather measurements.
♦ Explain how to interpret a weather map.
♦ Explain why weather maps are useful.

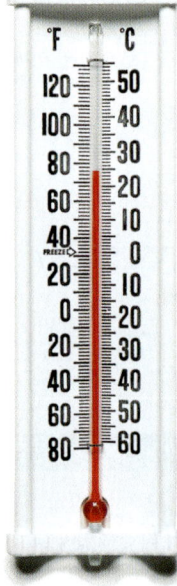

Figure 26 *A liquid thermometer is usually filled with alcohol that is colored red, or mercury, which is silver.*

440

Directed Reading Worksheet 16 Section 4

TOPIC: Forecasting the Weather
GO TO: www.scilinks.org
*sci*LINKS NUMBER: HSTE395

Forecasting the Weather

Have you ever left your house in the morning wearing a short-sleeved shirt, only to need a sweater in the afternoon? At some time in your life, you have been caught off guard by the weather. Weather affects how you dress and your daily plans, so it is important that you get accurate weather forecasts. A *weather forecast* is a prediction of weather conditions over the next 3 to 5 days. Meteorologists observe and collect data on current weather conditions in order to provide reliable predictions. In this section you will learn about some of the methods used to collect weather data and how those data are displayed.

Weather Forecasting Technology

In order for meteorologists to accurately forecast the weather, they need to measure various atmospheric conditions, such as air pressure, humidity, precipitation, temperature, wind speed, and wind direction. Meteorologists use special instruments to collect data on weather conditions both near and far above the Earth's surface. You have already learned about two tools that meteorologists use near the Earth's surface—psychrometers, which are used to measure relative humidity, and rain gauges, which are used to measure precipitation. Read on to learn about other methods meteorologists use to collect data.

Measuring Air Temperature A **thermometer** is a tool used to measure air temperature. A common type of thermometer uses a liquid sealed in a narrow glass tube, as shown in **Figure 26**. When air temperature increases, the liquid expands and moves up the glass tube. As air temperature decreases, the liquid shrinks and moves down the tube.

Air temperature is measured in both degrees Celsius and degrees Fahrenheit. In the United States, television weather forecasters generally report air temperature in degrees Fahrenheit.

MISCONCEPTION ALERT

Students may think that the lowest and highest temperatures occur in the middle of the night and in the middle of the day. Actually, the lowest temperatures usually occur around sunrise because the Earth's surface has radiated thermal energy all night. The highest temperatures usually occur in the late afternoon.

Measuring Air Pressure A **barometer** is an instrument used to measure air pressure. The mercurial barometer provides the most accurate method of measuring air pressure. A mercurial barometer consists of a glass tube sealed at one end that is placed in a container full of mercury. The air pressure pushes on the mercury inside the container, causing the mercury to move up the glass tube. The greater the air pressure is, the higher the mercury will rise.

Measuring Wind Direction Wind direction can be measured using a **windsock** or a **wind vane.** A windsock, as shown in **Figure 27,** is a cone-shaped cloth bag open at both ends. The wind enters through the wide end and leaves through the narrow end. Therefore, the wide end points into the wind.

A wind vane is shaped like an arrow with a large tail and is attached to a pole. The wind pushes the tail of the wind vane, spinning it on the pole until the arrow points into the wind.

Figure 27 *A windsock is a cone-shaped piece of weatherproof material that indicates wind direction.*

Measuring Wind Speed Wind speed is measured by a device called an **anemometer.** An anemometer, as shown in **Figure 28,** consists of three or four cups connected by spokes to a pole. The wind pushes on the hollow sides of the cups, causing them to rotate on the pole. The motion sends a weak electrical current that is measured and displayed on a dial.

Measuring Weather in the Upper Atmosphere You have learned how weather conditions are recorded near the Earth's surface. But in order for meteorologists to better understand weather patterns, they must collect data from higher altitudes. Studying weather at higher altitudes requires the use of more-sophisticated equipment.

Figure 28 *The faster the wind speed is, the faster the cups of the anemometer spin.*

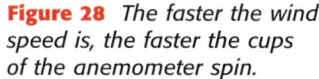
CONNECT TO
LIFE SCIENCE

Middle ear barotrauma is an earache caused by a difference in pressure between the air and a person's middle ear. Although airplane cabins are pressurized, passengers still feel the pressure decrease as the plane climbs and increase as it descends. The trauma occurs when the Eustachian tube, a passageway between the middle ear and the throat, fails to open wide enough to equalize the pressure. Chewing gum, yawning, or simply swallowing often alleviates the condition.

2) Teach

REAL-WORLD CONNECTION
Before sophisticated weather forecasts, people learned to carefully observe the world around them for evidence of changing weather. These clues can be found everywhere. Have students research and test these and other observations.

- Birds fly higher when fair weather is coming. (They fly high to avoid the increased air resistance of a high pressure air mass.)
- Heavy dew condenses early in fair night air. If there is little or no dew, the chance for rain is good.
- Leaves turn over in nonprevailing storm winds.
- Halos form around the sun or moon as light shines through ice particles in the clouds of an advancing rainstorm.
- As a pre-rain low pressure front moves in, odors trapped in objects by high pressure air masses are suddenly released.
- Ants travel in lines when rain is coming and scatter when the weather is clear.
- Robins sing high in fair weather and sing low if rain is approaching.
- Flying insects swarm before a rain; they bite the most when the air is moist.
- Clouds lower as a low pressure system approaches. This signals that a storm is coming.
- Swallows and bats fly lowest when air pressure decreases before a storm. Their sensitive ears are more comfortable when they are flying close to the ground (where air pressure is highest).
- At 15°C, rhododendron leaves stand upright, at 4°C they droop, at –1°C they curl, and at –6°C they turn black.

Section 4 • Forecasting the Weather   **441**

3) Extend

GROUP ACTIVITY

Doppler radar is a type of radar that uses the Doppler effect to determine the direction and speed of weather systems. Radar, an acronym for *radio detection and ranging*, is a device that determines the speed and location of weather systems or moving objects by bouncing radio waves off them. The Doppler effect is the shift in wave frequency detected by an observer due to the motion of the wave source relative to the observer. For example, an ambulance siren may emit sound waves at a uniform rate. But as the ambulance passes you, you may notice that the pitch drops. The reason is that the sound waves seem to be compressed as the ambulance approaches you and seem to spread out as it speeds away. Doppler radar bounces radio waves off weather systems. The reflected waves are used to determine if the system is moving toward or away from the radar source and at what speed it is moving. Challenge students to illustrate the Doppler effect so that the concept makes sense to them, perhaps by making a poster or demonstrating the effect using water waves.

MATH and MORE

Have students use the formulas below to convert 32°F, 72°F, and 5°F into degrees Celsius. Then convert 100°C, 45°C, and 21°C into degrees Fahrenheit.

$C = (F - 32) \times \frac{5}{9}$

$F = (C \times \frac{9}{5}) + 32$

(0°C, 22.2°C, –15°C, 212°F, 113°F, 69.8°F)

 Math Skills Worksheet 35 "Using Temperature Scales"

Figure 29 *Weather balloons carry radio transmitters that send measurements to stations on the ground.*

Activity

Throughout history, people have predicted approaching weather by interpreting natural signs. Animals and plants are usually more sensitive to changes in the atmosphere, such as air pressure, humidity, and temperature, than humans. To find out more about natural signs, research this topic at the library or on the Internet. Try searching using key words and phrases such as "weather and animals" or "weather and plants." Write a short paper on your findings to share with the class.

CROSS-DISCIPLINARY FOCUS

Language Arts Have students find poems about weather and share them with the class. Students could also write their own poem about their favorite and least favorite kinds of weather. The poems should demonstrate some knowledge about the cause of the weather they describe.

Eyes in the Sky Weather balloons carry electronic equipment that can measure weather conditions as high as 30 km above the Earth's surface. Weather balloons, such as the one in **Figure 29,** carry equipment that measures temperature, air pressure, and relative humidity.

Radar is used to find the location, movement, and intensity of precipitation. It can also detect what form of precipitation a weather system is carrying. You might be familiar with a type of radar called Doppler radar. **Figure 30** shows how Doppler radar is used to track precipitation.

Figure 30 *Using Doppler radar, meteorologists can predict a tornado up to 20 minutes before it touches the ground.*

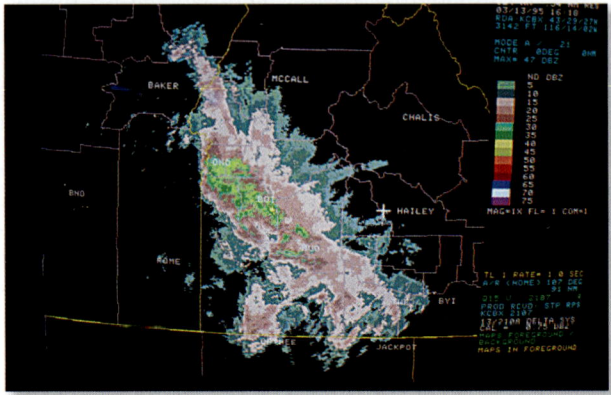

Weather satellites orbiting the Earth provide the images of the swirling clouds you can see on television weather reports. Satellites can measure wind speeds, humidity, and the temperatures at various altitudes.

Weather Maps

As you have learned, meteorologists base their forecasts on information gathered from many sources. In the United States, the National Weather Service (NWS) and the National Oceanic and Atmospheric Administration (NOAA) collect and analyze weather data. The NWS produces weather maps based on information gathered from about 1,000 weather stations across the United States. On these maps, each station is represented by a station model. A *station model,* as shown in **Figure 31,** is a small circle, which shows the location of the weather station, with a set of symbols and numbers surrounding it, which represent the weather data.

IS THAT A FACT!

Bats use the Doppler effect to locate prey and to navigate. Bats emit high-frequency sounds that bounce off objects. If the objects are moving, the wave frequency changes. If the frequency doesn't change, then the bat knows the object is stationary.

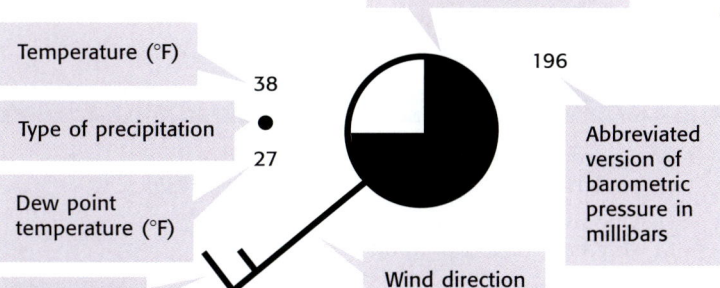

Figure 31 Weather conditions at a station are represented by symbols.

Under Pressure Weather maps also include lines called isobars. Isobars are similar to contour lines on a topographical map, except **isobars** are lines that connect points of equal air pressure rather than equal elevation. Isobar lines that form closed circles represent areas of high or low pressure. These areas are usually marked on a map with a capital *H* or *L*. Fronts are also labeled on weather maps. Weather maps, like the one shown in **Figure 32**, provide useful information for making accurate weather forecasts.

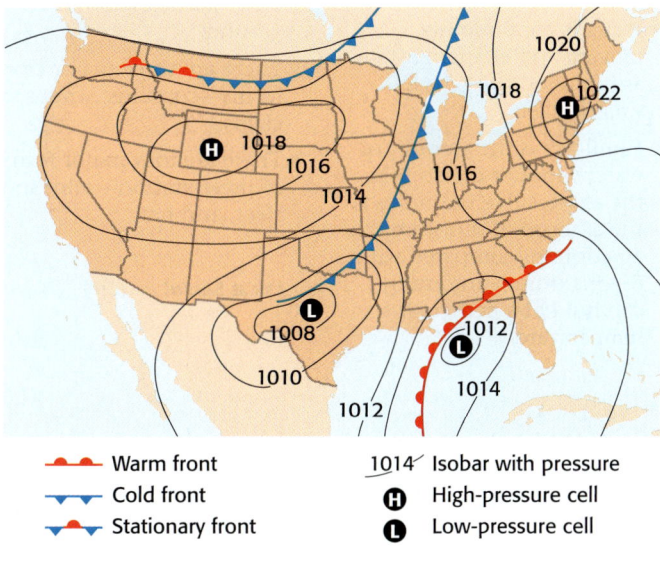

Figure 32 Can you identify the different fronts on the weather map?

REVIEW

1. What are three methods meteorologists use to collect weather data?
2. What are weather maps based on?
3. What does a station model represent?
4. **Inferring Conclusions** Why would a meteorologist compare a new weather map with one 24 hours old?

TOPIC: Forcasting the Weather
GO TO: www.scilinks.org
*sci*LINKS NUMBER: HSTE395

4 Close

Quiz

1. Would water be a useful fluid to use in a thermometer? Explain. (No, water would not be a good thermometer fluid because it expands when it freezes.)
2. What advantage do weather satellites have over ground-based weather stations? (Satellites can gather weather data from much higher altitudes than land-based instruments can.)
3. Why are so many station models used to gather weather data in the United States? (Because the country is so large, and Earth's atmosphere is constantly changing, we need data from many stations to make accurate forecasts.)

ALTERNATIVE ASSESSMENT

Have students use the weather report from their local newspaper over a 1-week period to construct a picture of local weather conditions. Then tell them to analyze their findings by applying what they have learned in this chapter.

Watching the Weather

Critical Thinking Worksheet 16 "Commanding the Sky"

▼ Answers to Review

1. Answers will vary. Sample answer: weather balloons, Doppler radar, and weather satellites
2. Weather maps are based on weather data gathered from weather stations across the United States.
3. A station model represents the location of the weather station and the weather data collected there.
4. Answers may vary. Sample answer: Meteorologists would compare a new weather map with one 24 hours old to see how fast a front is moving.

Chapter Highlights

VOCABULARY DEFINITIONS

SECTION 1

weather the condition of the atmosphere at a particular time and place

water cycle the continuous movement of water from water sources into the air, onto land, into and over the ground, and back to the water sources; a cycle that links all of the Earth's solid, liquid, and gaseous water together

humidity the amount of water vapor or moisture in the air

relative humidity the amount of moisture the air contains compared with the maximum amount it can hold at a particular temperature

condensation the change of state from a gas to a liquid

dew point the temperature to which air must cool to be completely saturated

cloud a collection of millions of tiny water droplets or ice crystals

precipitation solid or liquid water that falls from the air to the Earth

SECTION 2

air mass a large body of air that has similar temperature and moisture throughout

front the boundary that forms between two different air masses

Vocabulary Review Worksheet 16

Chapter Highlights

SECTION 1

Vocabulary
- weather (p. 422)
- water cycle (p. 422)
- humidity (p. 423)
- relative humidity (p. 423)
- condensation (p. 425)
- dew point (p. 425)
- cloud (p. 426)
- precipitation (p. 428)

Section Notes
- Water is continuously moving and changing state as it moves through the water cycle.
- Humidity is the amount of water vapor or moisture in the air. Relative humidity is the amount of moisture the air contains compared with the maximum amount it can hold at a particular temperature.
- Water droplets form because of condensation.
- Dew point is the temperature to which air must cool to be saturated.
- Condensation occurs when the air next to a surface cools to below its dew point.
- Clouds are formed from condensation on dust and other particles above the ground.
- There are three major cloud forms—cumulus, stratus, and cirrus.
- There are four major forms of precipitation—rain, snow, sleet, and hail.

Labs
Let It Snow! (p. 697)

SECTION 2

Vocabulary
- air mass (p. 430)
- front (p. 432)

Section Notes
- Air masses form over source regions. An air mass has similar temperature and moisture content throughout.
- Four major types of air masses influence weather in the United States—maritime polar, maritime tropical, continental polar, continental tropical.
- A front is a boundary between contrasting air masses.
- There are four types of fronts—cold fronts, warm fronts, occluded fronts, and stationary fronts.
- Specific types of weather are associated with each front.

✓ Skills Check

Math Concepts

RELATIVE HUMIDITY Relative humidity is the amount of moisture the air is holding compared with the amount it can hold at a particular temperature. The relative humidity of air that is holding all the water it can at a given temperature is 100 percent, meaning it is saturated. You can calculate relative humidity with the following equation:

$$\frac{\text{(present) g/m}^3}{\text{(saturated) g/m}^3} \times 100 = \text{relative humidity}$$

Visual Understanding

HURRICANE HORSEPOWER Hurricanes are the most powerful storms on Earth. A cross-sectional view helps you identify the different parts of a hurricane. The diagram on page 438 shows a side view of a hurricane.

Lab and Activity Highlights

Watching the Weather **PG 694**

Let It Snow! **PG 697**

Gone with the Wind **PG 698**

Datasheets for LabBook
(blackline masters for these labs)

444 Chapter 16 • Understanding Weather

SECTION 3

Vocabulary
thunderstorm *(p. 434)*
lightning *(p. 435)*
thunder *(p. 435)*
tornado *(p. 436)*
hurricane *(p. 437)*

Section Notes
- Severe weather is weather that can cause property damage and even death.
- Thunderstorms are small, intense storm systems that produce lightning, thunder, strong winds, and heavy rain.
- Lightning is a large electrical discharge that occurs between two oppositely charged surfaces.
- Thunder is the sound that results from the expansion of air along a lightning strike.
- A tornado is a rotating funnel cloud that touches the ground.
- Hurricanes are large, rotating, tropical weather systems that form over the tropical oceans.

SECTION 4

Vocabulary
thermometer *(p. 440)*
barometer *(p. 441)*
windsock *(p. 441)*
wind vane *(p. 441)*
anemometer *(p. 441)*
isobars *(p. 443)*

Section Notes
- Weather balloons, radar, and weather satellites take weather measurements at high altitudes.
- Meteorologists present weather data gathered from stations as station models on weather maps.

Labs
Watching the Weather *(p. 694)*
Gone with the Wind *(p. 698)*

VOCABULARY DEFINITIONS, continued

SECTION 3

thunderstorm a small, intense weather system that produces strong winds, heavy rain, lightning, and thunder

lightning the large electrical discharge that occurs between two oppositely charged surfaces

thunder the sound that results from the rapid expansion of air along a lightning strike

tornado a small, rotating column of air that has high wind speeds and low central pressure and that touches the ground

hurricane a large, rotating tropical weather system with wind speeds of at least 119 km/h

SECTION 4

thermometer a tool used to measure air temperature

barometer an instrument used to measure air pressure

windsock a device used to measure wind direction

wind vane a device used to measure wind direction

anemometer a device used to measure wind speed

isobars lines that connect points of equal air pressure

Blackline masters of these Chapter Highlights can be found in the **Study Guide**.

internet connect

GO TO: go.hrw.com
Visit the **HRW** Web site for a variety of learning tools related to this chapter. Just type in the keyword:
KEYWORD: HSTWEA

GO TO: www.scilinks.org
Visit the **National Science Teachers Association** on-line Web site for Internet resources related to this chapter. Just type in the *sci*LINKS number for more information about the topic:

TOPIC: Collecting Weather Data   *sci*LINKS NUMBER: HSTE380
TOPIC: Air Masses and Fronts   *sci*LINKS NUMBER: HSTE385
TOPIC: Severe Weather   *sci*LINKS NUMBER: HSTE390
TOPIC: Forecasting the Weather   *sci*LINKS NUMBER: HSTE395

Lab and Activity Highlights

LabBank

Whiz-Bang Demonstrations
- It's Raining Again, Demo 29
- When Air Bags Collide, Demo 28

Inquiry Labs, When Disaster Strikes, Lab 12

EcoLabs & Field Activities, Rain Maker or Rain Faker? Field Activity 15

Long-Term Projects & Research Ideas, A Storm on the Horizon, Project 44

Chapter 16 • Chapter Highlights

Chapter Review Answers

USING VOCABULARY

1. Relative humidity is the amount of water vapor the air contains relative to the maximum amount it can hold at a given temperature. Dew point is the temperature to which air must cool to be saturated.
2. Condensation is the process by which a gas changes state to become a liquid. Precipitation is liquid or solid water that falls from the atmosphere to the Earth.
3. An air mass is a large body of air that has the same moisture and temperature throughout. A front is the boundary that forms where two different air masses meet.
4. Lightning is a large electrical discharge that occurs between two oppositely charged surfaces. Thunder is the sound that results from the rapid expansion of air along a lightning strike.
5. A tornado is a small, rotating column of air with high wind speed that touches the ground. A hurricane is a large, rotating tropical weather system with wind speeds equal to or greater than 119 km/h.
6. A barometer measures air pressure. An anemometer measures wind speed.

UNDERSTANDING CONCEPTS

Multiple Choice

7. c
8. d
9. c
10. d
11. b
12. d
13. a
14. c
15. b
16. c

Chapter Review

USING VOCABULARY

Explain the difference between the following sets of words:

1. relative humidity/dew point
2. condensation/precipitation
3. air mass/front
4. lightning/thunder
5. tornado/hurricane
6. barometer/anemometer

UNDERSTANDING CONCEPTS

Multiple Choice

7. The process of liquid water changing to gas is called
   a. precipitation.
   b. condensation.
   c. evaporation.
   d. water vapor.

8. What is the relative humidity of air at its dew-point temperature?
   a. 0 percent
   b. 50 percent
   c. 75 percent
   d. 100 percent

9. Which of the following is not a type of condensation?
   a. fog
   b. cloud
   c. snow
   d. dew

10. High clouds made of ice crystals are called __?__ clouds.
    a. stratus
    b. cumulus
    c. nimbostratus
    d. cirrus

11. Large thunderhead clouds that produce precipitation are called __?__ clouds.
    a. nimbostratus
    b. cumulonimbus
    c. cumulus
    d. stratus

12. Strong updrafts within a thunderhead can produce
    a. snow.
    b. rain.
    c. sleet.
    d. hail.

13. A maritime tropical air mass contains
    a. warm, wet air.
    b. cold, moist air.
    c. warm, dry air.
    d. cold, dry air.

14. A front that forms when a warm air mass is trapped between cold air masses and forced to rise is called a(n)
    a. stationary front.
    b. warm front.
    c. occluded front.
    d. cold front.

15. A severe storm that forms as a rapidly rotating funnel cloud is called a
    a. hurricane.
    b. tornado.
    c. typhoon.
    d. thunderstorm.

16. The lines on a weather map connecting points of equal atmospheric pressure are called
    a. contour lines.
    b. highs.
    c. isobars.
    d. lows.

Short Answer

17. Explain the relationship between condensation and the dew point.

18. Describe the conditions along a stationary front.
19. What are the characteristics of an air mass that forms over the Gulf of Mexico?
20. Explain how a hurricane develops.

Concept Mapping

21. Use the following terms to create a concept map: evaporation, relative humidity, water vapor, dew, psychrometer, clouds, fog.

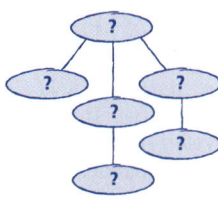

CRITICAL THINKING AND PROBLEM SOLVING

Write one or two sentences to answer the following questions:

22. If both the air temperature and the amount of water vapor in the air change, is it possible for the relative humidity to stay the same? Explain.
23. What can you assume about the amount of water vapor in the air if there is no difference between the wet- and dry-bulb readings of a psychrometer?
24. List the major similarities and differences between hurricanes and tornadoes.

MATH IN SCIENCE

You always see lightning before you hear thunder. That's because light travels at about 300,000,000 m/s, while sound travels only 330 m/s. One way you can determine how close you are to the thunderstorm is by counting how many seconds there are between the lightning and thunder. Usually, it takes thunder about 3 seconds to cover 1 km. Answer the following questions based on this estimate.

25. If you hear thunder 12 seconds after you see the flash of lightning, how far away is the thunderstorm?
26. If you hear thunder 36 seconds after you see the flash of lightning, how far away is the thunderstorm?

INTERPRETING GRAPHICS

Use the weather map below to answer the questions that follow.

- Warm front
- Cold front
- Stationary front

27. Where are thunderstorms most likely to occur? Explain your answer.
28. What are the weather conditions like in Tulsa, Oklahoma? Explain your answer.

 Take a minute to review your answers to the Pre-Reading Questions found at the bottom of page 420. Have your answers changed? If necessary, revise your answers based on what you have learned since you began this chapter.

447

Concept Mapping Transparency 16

Blackline masters of this Chapter Review can be found in the **Study Guide**.

UNDERSTANDING CONCEPTS
Short Answer

17. The air must cool to below its dew point before condensation can occur.
18. Stationary fronts generally bring drizzly precipitation. After the front passes, the weather is generally clear and warm.
19. An air mass that forms over the Gulf of Mexico is warm and wet.
20. A hurricane begins as a group of thunderstorms moving over tropical ocean waters. Winds traveling in two different directions collide, causing the storm to rotate over an area of low pressure. The hurricane is fueled by the condensation of water vapor.

Concept Mapping

21. 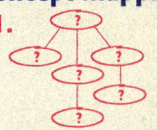 An answer to this exercise can be found at the end of this book.

CRITICAL THINKING AND PROBLEM SOLVING

22. Yes; for example, if both the air temperature and water vapor increased, the relative humidity might remain the same.
23. The air is saturated with water.
24. Answers may vary. Sample answer: Both begin as a result of thunderstorms and are centered around low pressure. Hurricanes occur over water, and tornadoes generally occur over land.

MATH IN SCIENCE

25. (12 s ÷ 3 s) × 1 km = 4 km
26. (36 s ÷ 3 s) × 1 km = 12 km

INTERPRETING GRAPHICS

27. Thunderstorms are most likely to occur in Chicago because a cold front is approaching.
28. Tulsa is experiencing a stationary front. It is probably receiving drizzly precipitation.

Chapter 16 • Chapter Review   **447**

CAREERS

Meteorologist— Cristy Mitchell

Teaching Strategy
Tell students to imagine that they are meteorologists studying another planet in the solar system. Ask:

As a meteorologist, what features would you look for to get information about the climate and the weather? (Students should recognize that climates are strongly influenced by major geographic features. A planet's rotation affects prevailing wind patterns. Other features to look for include mountains, deserts, and large bodies of water.)

Discussion
1. Weather stations operate around the clock, 7 days a week. Do you think you would enjoy the night work and rotating shifts that are part of a meteorologist's job? (Some students may think this is exciting, while others may prefer a 9-to-5 job.)
2. There is an old saying: "You can talk about the weather, but you can't do anything about it." How might this relate to a meteorologist's job? (Although scientists like Cristy Mitchell observe the powerful forces of nature, they cannot do anything to stop them. However, issuing accurate weather warnings can save people's lives.)

CAREERS

METEOROLOGIST

Predicting floods, observing a tornado develop inside a storm, watching the growth of a hurricane, and issuing flood warnings are all in a day's work for **Cristy Mitchell**. As a meteorologist for the National Weather Service, Mitchell spends each working day observing the powerful forces of nature.

When asked what made her job interesting, Mitchell replied, "There's nothing like the adrenaline rush you get when you see a tornado coming! I would say that witnessing the powerful forces of nature is what really makes my job interesting."

Meteorology is the study of natural forces in Earth's atmosphere. Perhaps the most familiar field of meteorology is weather forecasting. However, meteorology is also used in air-pollution control, agricultural planning, and air and sea transportation, and criminal and civil investigations. Meteorologists also study trends in Earth's climate, such as global warming and ozone depletion.

Collecting the Data
Meteorologists collect data on air pressure, temperature, humidity, and wind velocity. By applying what they know about the physical properties of the atmosphere and analyzing the mathematical relationships in the data, they are able to forecast the weather.

Meteorologists use a variety of tools, such as computers and satellites, to collect the data they need to make accurate weather forecasts. Mitchell explained, "The computer is an invaluable tool for me. Through it, I receive maps and detailed information, including temperature, wind speed, air pressure, lightning activity, and general sky conditions for a specific region."

In addition to using computers, Mitchell also uses radar and satellite imagery to show regional and national weather. Meteorologists also use computerized models of the world's atmosphere to help forecast the weather.

Find Out for Yourself
▶ Use the library or the Internet to find information about hurricanes, tornadoes, or thunderstorms. How do meteorologists define these storms? What trends in air pressure, temperature, and humidity do meteorologists use to forecast storms?

▲ *This photograph of Hurricane Elena was taken from the space shuttle Discovery in September 1985.*

Answers to Find Out for Yourself
Students' answers will vary depending upon which topic they choose to research.

Science Fiction

"All Summer in a Day"
by Ray Bradbury

It is raining, just like it has been for 7 long years. That is 2,555 days of nonstop rain. For the men, women, and children who came to build a civilization on Venus, constant rain is a fact of life. But there is one special day—a day when it stops raining and the sun shines gloriously. This day comes about only once every 7 years. And today is that day!

At school the students have been looking forward to this day for weeks. In one class they've read about how the sun is like a lemon, and how hot it is. They've written stories and poems about what it might be like to see the sun.

And now that the day has finally arrived, all of the children in that class are peering through the window, searching for the sun. The children are 9 years old, and all of them but Margot have lived on Venus all their lives. None of them remember the day 7 years ago when the rain stopped. They only recall stories about the sunshine, and now they just can't wait to see it for themselves!

But Margot is different. She longs to see the sun even more than the others. The reason makes the other kids jealous. And jealous kids can be cruel. . . .

What happens to Margot? Find out for yourself by reading Ray Bradbury's "All Summer in a Day" in the *Holt Anthology of Science Fiction*.

Further Reading Students can check out some of Ray Bradbury's other classic stories in the following collections. Or they can visit the library to scan the wide range of Bradbury's publications.

The Veldt, Creative Education, Inc., 1987

The Foghorn, Creative Education, Inc., 1987

S is for Space, Doubleday, 1966

SCIENCE FICTION
"All Summer in a Day"
by Ray Bradbury

Often, a memory can be sustaining; other times, it might be crippling. A priceless experience teaches Margot's classmates a lesson in understanding the power of memory.

Teaching Strategy

Reading Level This is a relatively short story that should not be difficult for the average student to read and comprehend.

Background

About the Author Ray Bradbury is one of the world's most celebrated writers. He was born in the small town of Waukegan, Illinois, in 1920. He moved from place to place as a young boy while his father looked for steady work. Eventually, Bradbury and his family ended up in Los Angeles. There he began a writing career that has spanned over 60 years!

Bradbury has earned top honors in the field of literature, including the World Fantasy Award for lifetime work and the Grand Master Award from Science Fiction Writers of America. An unusual honor came when an astronaut named a crater on the moon Dandelion Crater after Ray Bradbury's novel, *Dandelion Wine*.

Chapter Organizer

CHAPTER ORGANIZATION	TIME MINUTES	OBJECTIVES	LABS, INVESTIGATIONS, AND DEMONSTRATIONS
Chapter Opener pp. 450–451	45	National Standards: SAI 1	**Start-Up Activity** What's Your Angle? p. 451
Section 1 What Is Climate?	90	▶ Explain the difference between weather and climate. ▶ Identify the factors that determine climates. SAI 1, SPSP 1, 3, ES 1j, 3d	**QuickLab,** A Cool Breeze, p. 455 GENERAL **Whiz-Bang Demonstrations,** How Humid Is It? Demo 30 GENERAL
Section 2 Climates of the World	90	▶ Locate and describe the three major climate zones. ▶ Describe the different biomes found in each climate zone. HNS 1, 3; LabBook UCP 2, 3, SAI 1, ST 1	**Demonstration,** Mock Permafrost, p. 465 in ATE GENERAL **Discovery Lab,** For the Birds, p. 701 GENERAL **Datasheets for LabBook,** For the Birds, Datasheet 37 GENERAL **Skill Builder,** Biome Business, p. 704 GENERAL **Datasheets for LabBook,** Biome Business, Datasheet 38 GENERAL
Section 3 Changes in Climate	135	▶ Describe how the Earth's climate has changed over time. ▶ Summarize the different theories that attempt to explain why the Earth's climate has changed. ▶ Explain the greenhouse effect and its role in global warming. UCP 2, 3, SAI 1, 2, ST 2, SPSP 3–5, HNS 1, ES 1k, 2a; LabBook UCP 2, 3, SAI 1	**Demonstration,** The Greenhouse Effect, p. 467 in ATE GENERAL **Skill Builder,** Global Impact, p. 700 GENERAL **Datasheets for LabBook,** Global Impact, Datasheet 36 GENERAL **Long-Term Projects & Research Ideas,** Project 45 ADVANCED

*See page **T20** for a complete correlation of this book with the*

NATIONAL SCIENCE EDUCATION STANDARDS.

TECHNOLOGY RESOURCES

 Guided Reading Audio CD English or Spanish, Chapter 17

 One-Stop Planner CD-ROM with Test Generator

 CNN Eye on the Environment, A Climate Conference, Segment 27

Scientists in Action, Ice Age Discoveries, Segment 23

Chapter 17 • Climate

CLASSROOM WORKSHEETS, TRANSPARENCIES, AND RESOURCES	SCIENCE INTEGRATION AND CONNECTIONS	REVIEW AND ASSESSMENT
Directed Reading Worksheet 17 BASIC **Science Puzzlers, Twisters & Teasers,** Worksheet 17 ADVANCED		
Directed Reading Worksheet 17, Section 1 BASIC **Transparency 175,** Seasons, Latitude, and the Tilt of the Earth **Transparency 176,** Basic Properties of Air **Transparency 177,** An Example of the Rain Shadow Effect	**Multicultural Connection,** p. 452 in ATE **Connect to Geography,** p. 453 in ATE ADVANCED **Math and More,** p. 453 in ATE GENERAL **Multicultural Connection,** p. 455 in ATE **Across the Sciences:** Blame "The Child," p. 476 GENERAL	**Self-Check,** p. 454 **Homework,** p. 455 in ATE ADVANCED **Review,** p. 457 GENERAL **Quiz,** p. 457 in ATE GENERAL **Alternative Assessment,** p. 457 in ATE GENERAL
Transparency 178, Climate Zones of the Earth **Transparency 178,** The Earth's Land Biomes **Directed Reading Worksheet 17,** Section 2 BASIC **Transparency 52,** Transpiration **Math Skills for Science Worksheet 37,** Rain-Forest Math GENERAL **Science Skills Worksheet 18,** Finding Useful Sources GENERAL **Reinforcement Worksheet 17,** A Tale of Three Climates BASIC	**Math and More,** p. 459 in ATE GENERAL **Connect to Environmental Science,** p. 459 in ATE **Biology Connection,** p. 460 **Real-World Connection,** pp. 460, 461 in ATE **Connect to Environmental Science,** pp. 462, 463 in ATE GENERAL **Environment Connection,** p. 465 **Physics Connection,** p. 466	**Self-Check,** p. 460 **Homework,** p. 460 in ATE ADVANCED **Review,** p. 461 GENERAL **Homework,** p. 463 in ATE ADVANCED **Homework,** p. 464 in ATE GENERAL **Review,** p. 466 GENERAL **Quiz,** p. 466 in ATE GENERAL **Alternative Assessment,** p. 466 in ATE GENERAL
Directed Reading Worksheet 17, Section 3 BASIC **Transparency 179,** The Milankovitch Theory of the Causes of the Ice Ages **Critical Thinking Worksheet 17,** Cyberspace Heats Up ADVANCED **Science Skills Worksheet 4,** Understanding Bias GENERAL	**Real-World Connection,** p. 469 in ATE ADVANCED **Cross-Disciplinary Focus,** p. 469 in ATE GENERAL **Multicultural Connection,** p. 469 in ATE **MathBreak,** The Ride to School, p. 470 **Connect to Life Science,** p. 470 in ATE **Apply,** p. 471 GENERAL **Science, Technology, and Society:** Some Say Fire, Some Say Ice..., p. 477 ADVANCED	**Self-Check,** p. 468 **Review,** p. 471 GENERAL **Quiz,** p. 471 in ATE GENERAL **Alternative Assessment,** p. 471 in ATE BASIC

END-OF-CHAPTER REVIEW AND ASSESSMENT

Chapter Review in Study Guide
Vocabulary and Notes in Study Guide
Chapter Tests with Performance-Based Assessment, Chapter 17 Test
Chapter Tests with Performance-Based Assessment, Performance-Based Assessment 17
Concept Mapping Transparency 17

 **internet connect**

 go.hrw.com **Holt, Rinehart and Winston On-line Resources**
go.hrw.com
For worksheets and other teaching aids related to this chapter, visit the HRW Web site and type in the keyword: **HSTCLM**

 SCiLINKS NSTA **National Science Teachers Association**
www.scilinks.org
Encourage students to use the sciLINKS numbers listed in the internet connect boxes to access information and resources on the **NSTA** Web site.

Chapter Resources & Worksheets

Visual Resources

TEACHING TRANSPARENCIES

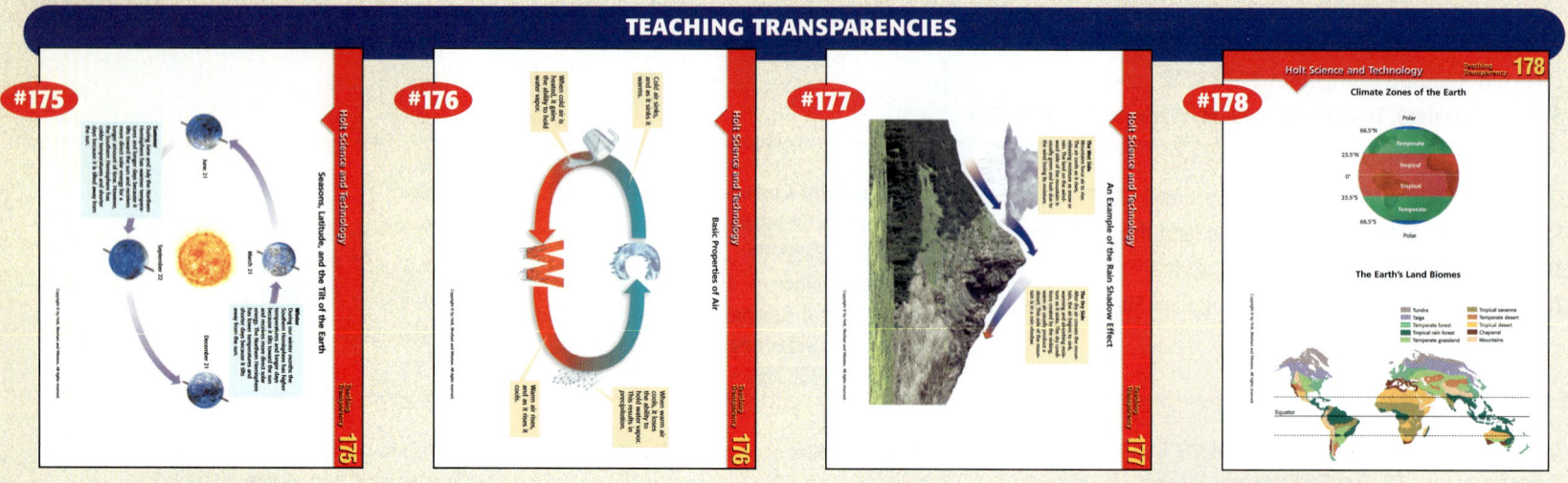

TEACHING TRANSPARENCIES

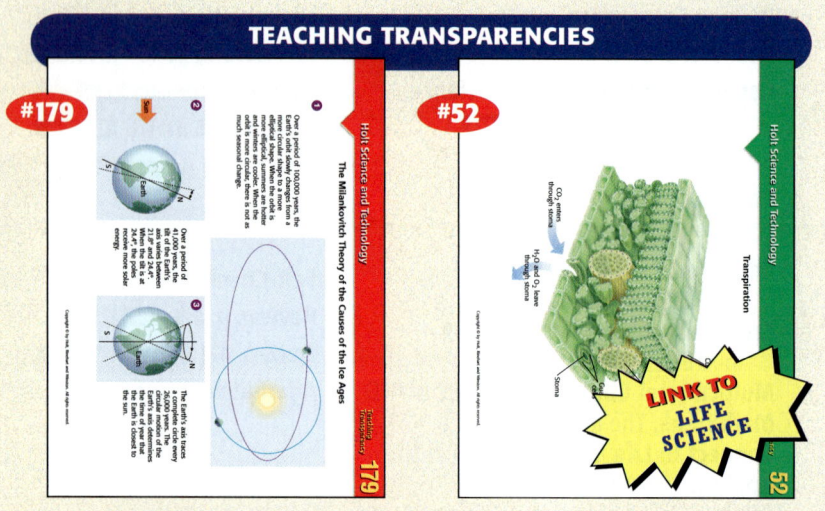

CONCEPT MAPPING TRANSPARENCY

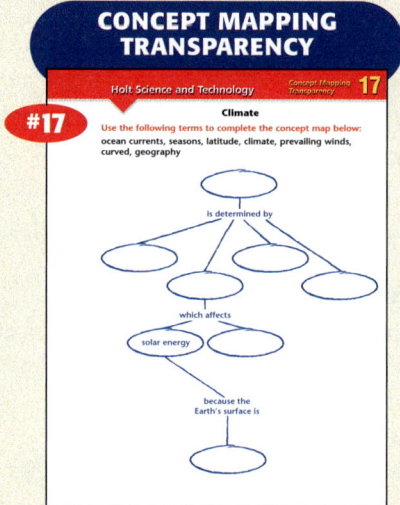

Meeting Individual Needs

DIRECTED READING

REINFORCEMENT & VOCABULARY REVIEW

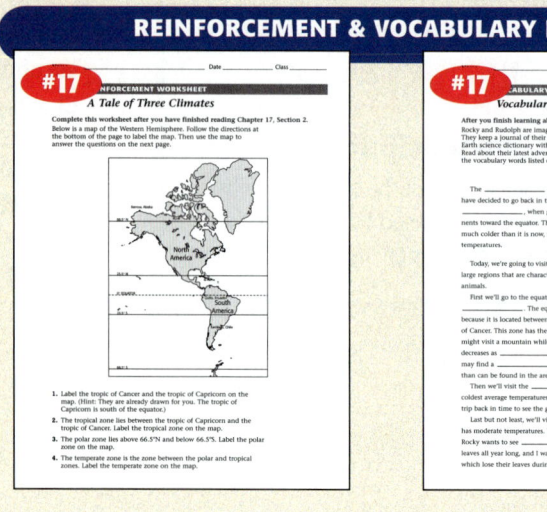

SCIENCE PUZZLERS, TWISTERS & TEASERS

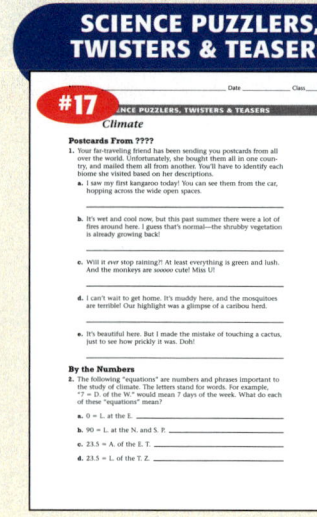

Chapter 17 • Climate

Chapter 17 • Climate

Review & Assessment

STUDY GUIDE

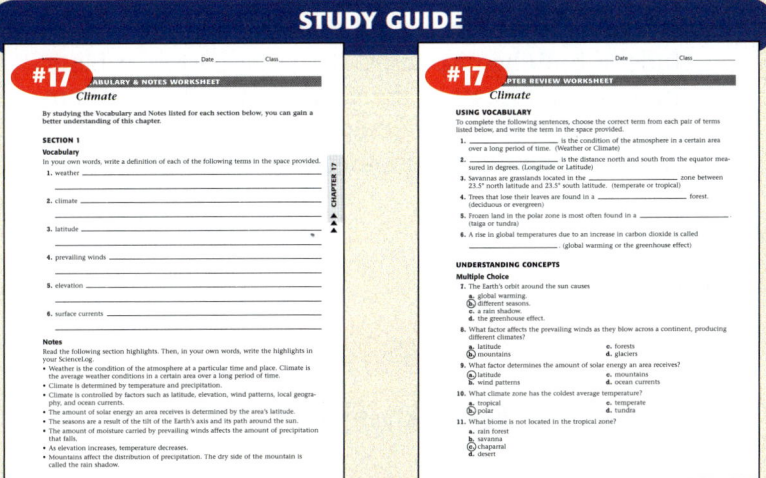

CHAPTER TESTS WITH PERFORMANCE-BASED ASSESSMENT

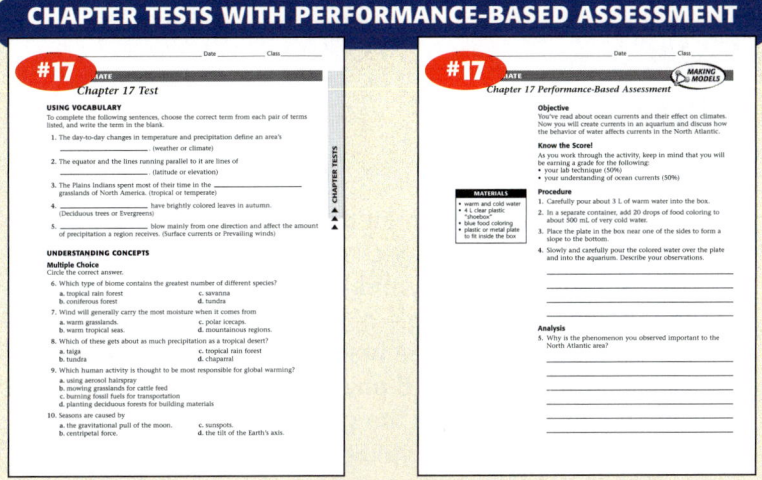

Lab Worksheets

WHIZ-BANG DEMONSTRATIONS

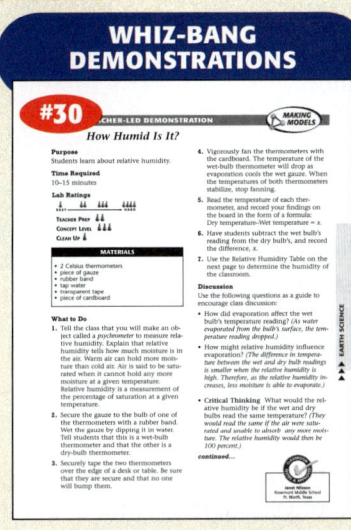

LONG-TERM PROJECTS & RESEARCH IDEAS

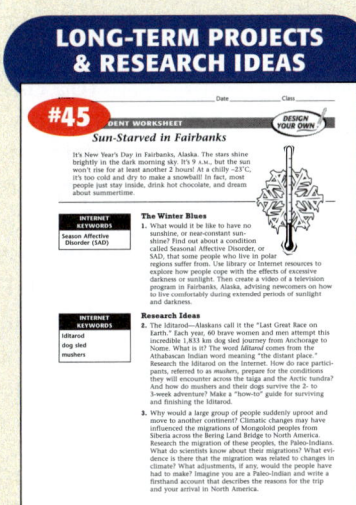

DATASHEETS FOR LABBOOK

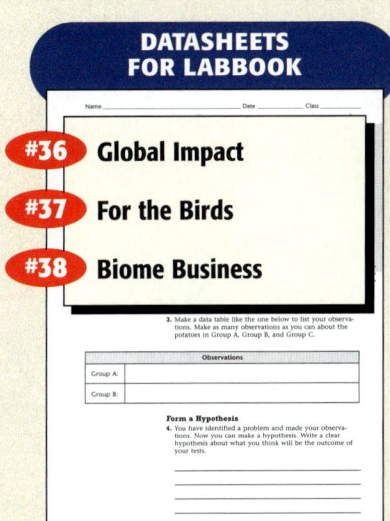

Applications & Extensions

CRITICAL THINKING & PROBLEM SOLVING

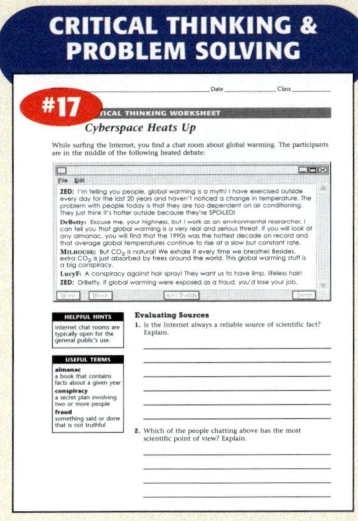

EYE ON THE ENVIRONMENT

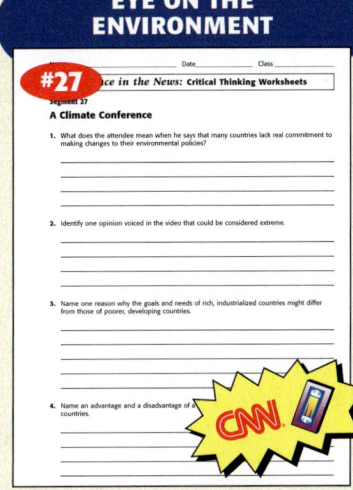

SCIENTISTS IN ACTION

Chapter 17 • Chapter Resources & Worksheets   449D

Chapter Background

SECTION 1

What Is Climate?

▶ **Climatology**
The study of climate can be traced back to Greek scientists of the sixth century B.C. In fact, the word *climate* comes from the Greek word *klíma,* meaning "an inclination," such as the angle of the sun's rays. Climatology can be divided into three branches—global climatology, regional climatology, and physical climatology. Global climatology investigates the general circulation of wind and water currents around Earth. Regional climatology studies the characteristic weather patterns and related phenomena of a particular region. Physical climatology analyzes statistics concerning climatic factors such as temperature, moisture, wind, and air pressure.

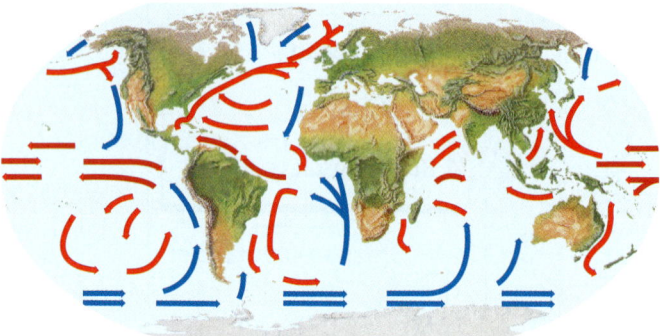

▶ **Global Winds**
Global winds are patterns of air circulation that travel across the Earth. These winds include the trade winds, the prevailing westerlies, and the polar easterlies.

- In both hemispheres, the trade winds blow from 30° latitude to the equator. The Coriolis effect makes the trade winds curve to the right in the Northern Hemisphere, moving northeast to southwest. In the Southern Hemisphere, the trade winds curve to the left and move from southeast to northwest.

- The westerlies are found in both the Northern and Southern Hemispheres between 30° and 60° latitude. In the Northern Hemisphere, the westerlies blow from the southwest to the northeast. In the Southern Hemisphere, they blow from the northwest to the southeast.

- The polar easterlies extend from the poles to 60° latitude in both hemispheres. The polar easterlies blow from the northeast to the southwest in the Northern Hemisphere. In the Southern Hemisphere, these winds blow from the southeast to the northwest.

SECTION 2

Climates of the World

▶ **Climate Classification**
Because climate is a complicated and somewhat abstract concept, more than 100 classification models have been devised, which vary according to the data on which the classifications are based. For instance, there have been attempts to classify climates according to factors such as soil formation, rock weathering, and even effects on human comfort!

- In 1966, Werner Terjung, an American geographer, developed a physiological climate classification. This system categorized climates according to their effects on people's comfort levels. The system focused on four factors that might affect human comfort—temperature, relative humidity, wind speed, and solar radiation.

▶ The Köppen System

The most widely used climate classification system is the Köppen system. This system, named for Wladimir Köppen, the German botanist and climatologist who developed it, uses vegetation regions and average weather statistics to classify local climates. Each vegetation region is characterized by the natural vegetation that is predominant there. Critics have found fault with the Köppen system because it considers only average monthly temperatures and precipitation, ignoring other factors, such as winds, cloud cover, and daily temperature extremes.

SECTION 3

Changes in Climate

▶ Pangaea

In 1620, the British philosopher Francis Bacon noted that Africa and South America looked as if they could fit together like puzzle pieces. But it was not until the early twentieth century that the German meteorologist Alfred Wegener proposed a theory that all the continents were once one landmass. Wegener's hypothesis was supported by the existence of similar plant and animal fossils on different continents. Although his theory was initially ridiculed, Wegener was vindicated after World War II when sea-floor spreading and a mechanism for continental drift were discovered.

IS THAT A FACT!

- *Pangaea,* the name Wegener gave to the supercontinent, is Greek for "all earth."

▶ The Greenhouse Effect

Gases such as carbon dioxide, methane, and chlorofluorocarbons (CFCs) are known as greenhouse gases because they "trap" thermal energy in Earth's atmosphere by absorbing infrared radiation that would otherwise be emitted into space. Normal amounts of greenhouse gases, with the exception of CFCs (which are artificial chemicals), are necessary for life on Earth because they keep Earth's average temperature at 15°C. Without them, Earth would be frozen; the average temperature would be about –18°C.

- CFCs are manufactured chemicals that contain chlorine, fluorine, and carbon. Before 1978, when the United States banned the use of CFCs, they were widely used as propellants in aerosol cans. They are also a component of plastic foam and of a coolant used in air conditioners.

- There is much less methane in the air than carbon dioxide. However, per molecule, methane absorbs 20 times more infrared radiation than carbon dioxide, and its concentration in the atmosphere is increasing. Methane is a natural product of animal digestion. A significant amount of the methane released into the atmosphere is produced by livestock. Methane is also produced as microorganisms decompose organic material.

IS THAT A FACT!

- Burning 1 gal of gasoline produces 9 kg of carbon dioxide.

- Using 1 kWh of electrical energy from a coal-fired power plant produces 5.5 kg of carbon dioxide.

For background information about teaching strategies and issues, refer to the *Professional Reference for Teachers.*

Chapter 17

Climate

Pre-Reading Questions

Students may not know the answers to these questions before reading the chapter, so accept any reasonable response.

Suggested Answers

1. Weather is the condition of the atmosphere at a certain time or place. Climate is the average weather conditions over a long period of time.
2. Answers will vary. The increased use of fossil fuels may cause the climate to become warmer. This is because the carbon dioxide released into the atmosphere traps heat.

 Directed Reading Worksheet 17

 Science Puzzlers, Twisters & Teasers Worksheet 17

 Guided Reading Audio CD English or Spanish, Chapter 17

Chapter 17

Climate

Sections

1. **What Is Climate?** 452
   - QuickLab 455
   - Internet Connect 457
2. **Climates of the World** .. 458
   - Biology Connection .. 460
   - Internet Connect 461
   - Environment Connection 465
   - Physics Connection .. 466
3. **Changes in Climate** 467
   - MathBreak 470
   - Apply 471
   - Internet Connect 471
- Chapter Review 474
- Feature Articles 476, 477
- LabBook 700–705

Pre-Reading Questions

1. What is the difference between weather and climate?
2. List ways in which human influences such as pollution and technology can affect climate.

A Hot New Home

Snow macaques normally live in cold pine forests in the mountains of Japan. However, in 1972, a group of these monkeys was relocated to a ranch in southern Texas. The monkeys were forced to adapt to a radically different climate and environment, which meant learning how to live with higher temperatures, different plants, and different animals. In this chapter, you will learn about the factors that affect climate and about the different environments found in each climate.

---

internet connect

 HRW On-line Resources
go.hrw.com
For worksheets and other teaching aids, visit the HRW Web site and type in the keyword: **HSTCLM**

 **SCLINKS NSTA**
www.scilinks.com
Use the sciLINKS numbers at the end of each chapter for additional resources on the **NSTA** Web site.

 **CNNfyi.com**
www.cnnfyi.com
Visit the CNN Web site for current events coverage and classroom resources.

START-UP Activity

WHAT'S YOUR ANGLE?

Because the Earth is round, the sun's solar rays strike the Earth's surface at different angles. Try this activity to find out how the amount of solar energy received at the equator differs from the amount received at the poles.

Procedure

1. Plug in a **lamp,** and position it 30 cm from a **globe.**
2. Point the lamp so that the light shines directly on the globe's equator.
3. Using **adhesive putty,** attach a **thermometer** to the globe's equator in a vertical position. Attach **another thermometer** to the globe's north pole so that the tip points toward the lamp.
4. Record the temperature reading of each thermometer in your ScienceLog.
5. Turn on the lamp, and let the light shine on the globe for 3 minutes.
6. When the time is up, turn off the lamp, and record the temperature reading of each thermometer again.

Analysis

7. Was there a difference between the final temperature at the globe's north pole and that at the globe's equator? If so, what was it?

START-UP Activity

WHAT'S YOUR ANGLE?

MATERIALS
FOR EACH GROUP: • lamp • globe • adhesive putty • 2 thermometers

Safety Caution

Remind students to review all safety cautions and icons before beginning this lab activity. Students should not touch the lamp's bulb while it is on or immediately after it has been turned off.

Teacher's Notes

If you have time, encourage students to repeat the experiment, positioning one thermometer at the equator and one at the South Pole. Have them compare their results. Students could also attempt to simulate how Earth's orbit affects the seasons.

Answer to START-UP Activity

7. The final temperature at the globe's North Pole was cooler than the final temperature at the globe's equator. This is because the globe's equator received more direct energy from the light bulb than the globe's North Pole received.

Chapter 17 • Climate **451**

SECTION 1

Focus

What Is Climate?
In this section, students learn the difference between weather and climate. They examine how latitude, prevailing winds, geography, and ocean currents affect an area's climate.

 **Bellringer**

Have students imagine they have entered a contest for a free trip to a place with a perfect climate. To win, they need to describe in 25 words or less their idea of a perfect climate.
Sheltered English

1) Motivate

DISCUSSION
Tell students that in the early 1900s, a geographer named Ellsworth Huntington conducted controversial research to see if he could determine the ideal climate for human beings—the type of climate that would result in optimal physical and mental well-being. He concluded that a climate with considerable daily and seasonal weather changes and an average temperature of 18°C was ideal. Ask students whether they agree or disagree with Huntington and why.

 Directed Reading Worksheet 17 Section 1

Section 1

Terms to Learn
weather   prevailing winds
climate   elevation
latitude   surface currents

What You'll Do
- Explain the difference between weather and climate.
- Identify the factors that determine climates.

What Is Climate?

You have just received a call from a friend who is coming to visit you tomorrow. He is wondering what clothing to bring and wants to know about the current weather in your area. You step outside, check to see if there are rain clouds in the sky, and note the temperature. But what if your friend asked you about the climate in your area? What is the difference between weather and climate?

The main difference between weather and climate has to do with time. **Weather** is the condition of the atmosphere at a particular time and place. Weather conditions vary from day to day. **Climate**, on the other hand, is the average weather conditions in an area over a long period of time. Climate is determined by two main factors, temperature and precipitation. Study the map in **Figure 1**, and see if you can describe the climate in northern Africa.

Figure 1 How does the climate in northern Africa differ from the climate where you live?

Multicultural CONNECTION

Weather and climate have inspired a great number of rhymes, greetings, sayings, and other folklore. For example, in the hot, wet climate of Venezuela, indigenous people sometimes greet each other by saying, "How have the mosquitoes used you?" Russia's cold climate inspired the saying, "There's no bad weather, only bad clothing." Invite students to interview friends and relatives or research weather and climate folklore in another country. Have them share their findings with the class.

As you can see in **Figure 2,** if you were to take a trip around the world, or even across the United States, you would experience different climates. For example, if you visited the Texas coast in the summer, you would find it hot and humid. But if you visited interior Alaska during the summer, it would probably be much cooler and less humid. Why are the climates so different? The answer is complicated. It includes factors such as latitude, wind patterns, geography, and ocean currents.

Figure 2 *Summer in Texas is different from summer in Alaska.*

Latitude

Think of the last time you looked at a globe. Do you recall the thin horizontal lines that circle the globe? These horizontal lines are called lines of latitude. **Latitude** is the distance north or south, measured in degrees, from the equator. In general, the temperature of an area depends on its latitude. The higher the latitude is, the colder the climate is. For example, one of the coldest places on Earth, the North Pole, is at 90° north of the equator. On the other hand, the equator, which has a latitude of 0°, is hot.

It's Hot! It's Not! Why are there such temperature differences at different latitudes? The answer has to do with solar energy. Solar energy heats the Earth. Latitude determines the amount of solar energy a particular area receives. You can see how this works in **Figure 3.** Notice that the sun's rays hit the area around the equator directly, at nearly a 90° angle. At this angle, a small area of the Earth's surface receives more direct solar energy, resulting in high temperatures. Near the poles, however, the sun's rays strike the surface at a lesser angle than at the equator. This lesser angle spreads the same amount of solar energy over a larger area, resulting in lower temperatures.

Figure 3 *The sun's rays strike the Earth's surface at different angles because the surface is curved.*

2) Teach

MATH and MORE

Each degree or line of latitude is approximately 111 km, and there are 180 lines of latitude circling the Earth. Have students calculate the circumference of the Earth at the poles. **(111 km/line × 180 = 19,980 km)** Then multiply by 2, because the Earth is a sphere. **(39,960 km)**

CONNECT TO GEOGRAPHY

Monsoons are recurrent global weather patterns that dramatically affect the populations, economies, and environment of South Asia. The wet summer monsoon usually begins mid-June, when temperatures rise sharply in Asia's interior, causing the air above the land to warm and rise. This creates a low pressure area that draws warm, moist air inland from the Indian and Pacific oceans. This moisture-laden air cools as it moves across the continent, and heavy rains, thunderstorms, and flooding occur. The heaviest rains occur where this air mass meets the foothills of the Himalayas. During a winter monsoon, the interior of Asia cools rapidly. This cool, dense air creates an immense high pressure center, forcing cool, dry air to flow outward toward the oceans. As the air mass travels, it warms and becomes even drier. This results in warm, dry winters. Encourage students to write a report about the effect of monsoons on the environment, economy, and people of South Asia.

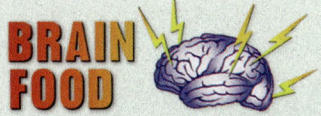

Ask students to find locations on a United States or world map where they have visited or where friends or relatives live. Write the locations and their latitudinal positions on the board. Ask students to help you list some observations about the climate in each area.

TOPIC: What Is Climate?
GO TO: www.scilinks.org
***sci*LINKS NUMBER:** HSTE405

Section 1 • What Is Climate?

2) Teach, continued

COOPERATIVE LEARNING

Ask two volunteers to act as the Earth and the sun. Give the "sun" a flashlight and the "Earth" a globe with a half-meridian mounting. Turn off the lights, and have the volunteers sit on the floor. Ask the "sun" to shine the flashlight on the globe, and ask the "Earth" to slowly spin the globe. Have the class notice which parts of the globe are most exposed to the light. Next, have the "Earth" make a complete revolution slowly around the "sun" while at the same time rotating the globe. Make sure that the volunteer always keeps the axis of the globe oriented in the same direction. Stop the "Earth" at each season so students can observe the flashlight's rays on the two hemispheres. If necessary, repeat this activity with other volunteers.
Sheltered English

MISCONCEPTION ALERT

Students may think that the distance between the Earth and the sun determines the seasons. Actually, the Earth is closer to the sun during the Northern Hemisphere's winter. Remind them that the Earth's tilt as it orbits the sun determines where solar radiation is concentrated and thus determines the seasons.

Answer to Self-Check

Australia has summer during our winter months, December–March.

Teaching Transparency 175
"Seasons, Latitude, and the Tilt of the Earth"

454 Chapter 17 • Climate

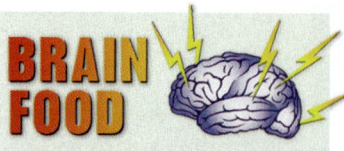
BRAIN FOOD
The polar regions receive almost 24 hours of daylight each day in the summer and almost 24 hours of darkness each day in the winter.

Seasons and Latitude In most places in the United States, the year consists of four seasons. Winter is probably cooler than summer where you live. But there are places in the world that do not have such seasonal changes. For example, areas near the equator have approximately the same temperatures and same amount of daylight year-round. **Figure 4** shows how latitude determines the seasons.

Winter
During our winter months the Southern Hemisphere has higher temperatures and longer days because it tilts toward the sun and receives more direct solar energy. The Northern Hemisphere has lower temperatures and shorter days because it tilts away from the sun.

June 21

December 21

September 22

Summer
During our summer months the Northern Hemisphere has warmer temperatures and longer days because it tilts toward the sun and receives more direct solar energy for a longer amount of time. However, the Southern Hemisphere has colder temperatures and shorter days because it is tilted away from the sun.

Figure 4 The Earth is tilted on its axis at a 23.5° angle. This tilt affects how much solar energy an area receives as the Earth moves around the sun.

 Self-Check

During what months does Australia have summer? (See page 726 to check your answer.)

IS THAT A FACT!

Tutunendo, Colombia, is the rainiest place in the world. It averages almost 12 m of rain per year. Cherrapunji, India, received more than 9 m of rain in 1 month—the most rainfall ever recorded in a month. The hottest day ever recorded occurred in Libya, where it reached 58°C (136°F) in 1922. Antarctica holds the record as the coldest place on Earth, with temperatures reaching –89°C (–128°F).

Prevailing Winds

Prevailing winds are winds that blow mainly from one direction. These winds influence an area's moisture and temperature. Before you learn how the prevailing winds affect climate, take a look at **Figure 5** to learn about some of the basic properties of air.

Figure 5 *Because warm air is less dense, it tends to rise. Cooler, denser air tends to sink.*

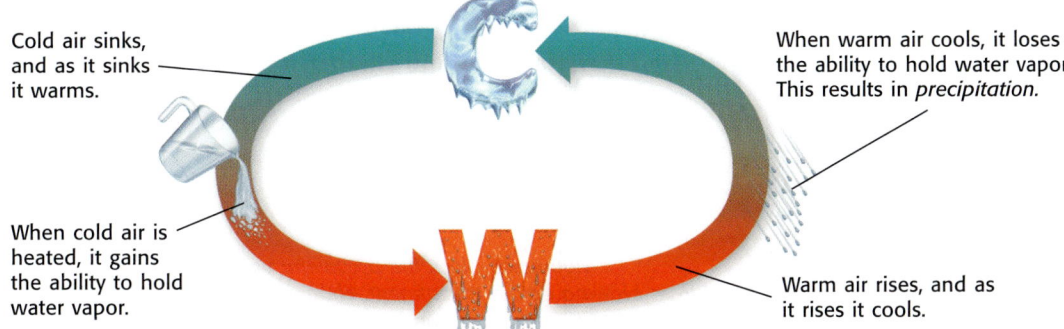

Cold air sinks, and as it sinks it warms.

When cold air is heated, it gains the ability to hold water vapor.

When warm air cools, it loses the ability to hold water vapor. This results in *precipitation*.

Warm air rises, and as it rises it cools.

Prevailing winds affect the amount of precipitation that a region receives. If the prevailing winds form from warm air, they will carry moisture. If the prevailing winds form from cold air, they will probably be dry.

The amount of moisture in prevailing winds is also affected by whether the winds blow across land or across a large body of water. Winds that travel across large bodies of water absorb moisture. Winds that travel across land tend to be dry. Even if a region borders the ocean, the area might be dry if the prevailing winds blow across the land, as shown in **Figure 6**.

Figure 6 *The Sahara Desert, in northern Africa, is extremely dry because of the dry prevailing winds that blow across the continent.*

QuickLab

A Cool Breeze

1. Hold a **thermometer** next to the top edge of a **cup of water** containing **two ice cubes**. Read the temperature next to the cup.
2. Have your lab partner fan the surface of the cup with a **paper fan**. Read the temperature again. Has the temperature changed? Why? Record your answer in your ScienceLog.

Multicultural CONNECTION

Charles Edward Anderson was the first African American to receive a Ph.D. in meteorology. Anderson began his career in meteorology during World War II. He was a captain in the Air Force and served as a weather officer for the Tuskegee Airmen Regiment. He earned his Ph.D. in 1960 from the Massachusetts Institute of Technology. His work focused on cloud physics, the forecasting of severe storms, and weather on other planets.

Homework

Using Maps Have students look at a map and find five cities at about the same latitude in a single continent. They should research the annual rainfall for each city and the direction of the prevailing winds. Students can create a bar graph showing the differences in rainfall for each city and attempt to explain the patterns they notice by identifying physical features on the map. If their data contradicts what they have learned in this section, ask them to suggest explanations.

QuickLab

MATERIALS

FOR EACH PAIR OF STUDENTS:
- thermometer
- cup of water
- 2 ice cubes
- paper fan

Answers to QuickLab

2. The temperature dropped after we fanned the surface of the cup. This is because the air traveling across the cup's surface picked up cold air from the ice, thereby changing the air temperature.

Teaching Transparency 176 "Basic Properties of Air"

Section 1 • What Is Climate?

3 Extend

Answers to Activity
Mountain ranges: the Sierra Nevada, Rocky Mountains, Appalachians. The Sierra Nevada exhibit the biggest variance from one side of the mountain range to the other; there is green vegetation on one side and a desert on the other. The prevailing wind blows from the west.

USING THE FIGURE
Remind students that winds traveling across large bodies of water, such as the ocean, absorb moisture. Have students study **Figure 7,** and then ask them to consider which side of the mountain is likely to be closer to a large body of water. (the left side) The inset photographs in **Figure 7** were taken in California's Sierra Nevada mountain range. Ask students to examine the photographs closely and describe as many details as possible.
Sheltered English

GOING FURTHER
Have students find out which prevailing winds affect climate in the United States and in which direction they blow. Students can compile their findings in a short report that explains how a particular prevailing wind influences climate in a region.

Teaching Transparency 177
"An Example of the Rain Shadow Effect"

Activity
Using a physical map, locate the mountain ranges in the United States. Does climate vary from one side of a mountain range to the other? If so, what does this tell you about the climatic conditions on either side of the mountain? From what direction are the prevailing winds blowing?
TRY at HOME

Geography
Mountains can influence an area's climate by affecting both temperature and precipitation. For example, Kilimanjaro, the tallest mountain in Africa, has snow-covered peaks year-round, even though it is only about 3° (320 km) south of the equator. Temperatures on Kilimanjaro and in other mountainous areas are affected by elevation. **Elevation** is the height of surface landforms above sea level. As the elevation increases, the atmosphere becomes less dense. When the atmosphere is less dense, its ability to absorb and hold thermal energy is reduced and temperatures are therefore lower.

Mountains also affect the climate of nearby areas by influencing the distribution of precipitation. **Figure 7** shows how the climates on two sides of a mountain can be very different.

Figure 7 Mountains block the prevailing winds from blowing across a continent, changing the amount of moisture the wind carries.

The Wet Side
Mountains force air to rise. The air cools as it rises, releasing moisture as snow or rain. The land on the windward side of the mountain is usually green and lush due to the wind losing its moisture.

The Dry Side
After dry air crosses the mountain, the air begins to sink, warming and absorbing moisture as it sinks. The dry conditions created by the sinking, warm air usually produce a desert. This side of the mountain is in a *rain shadow*.

SCIENCE HUMOR
Western and eastern Oregon have very different climates because the Cascade Mountains divide the state. Oregonians living east of the Cascades complain, "It's so dry, the jackrabbits carry canteens." West of the Cascades, people say, "It's so wet, folks don't tan, they rust!"

IS THAT A FACT!
Large lakes, such as the Great Lakes, in the United States and Canada, and Lake Victoria, in east-central Africa, affect local climates. This phenomenon, called *the lake effect,* helps keep the surrounding land cooler in the summer and warmer in the winter.

456 Chapter 17 • Climate

Ocean Currents

Because of water's ability to absorb and release thermal energy, the circulation of ocean surface currents has an enormous effect on an area's climate. **Surface currents,** which can be either warm or cold, are streamlike movements of water that occur at or near the surface of the ocean. **Figure 8** shows the pattern of the major warm and cold ocean surface currents.

Current Events As surface currents move, they carry warm or cool water to different locations. The surface temperature of the water affects the temperature of the air above it. Warm currents heat the surrounding air and cause warmer temperatures, while cool currents cool the surrounding air and cause cooler temperatures. For example, the Gulf Stream current carries warm water northward off the east coast of North America past Iceland, an island country located just below the Arctic Circle. The warm water from the Gulf Stream heats the surrounding air, creating warmer temperatures in southern Iceland. Iceland experiences milder temperatures than Greenland, its neighboring country, where the climate is not influenced by the Gulf Stream.

Science CONNECTION

What is El Niño? Can it affect our health? Turn to page 476 to find out.

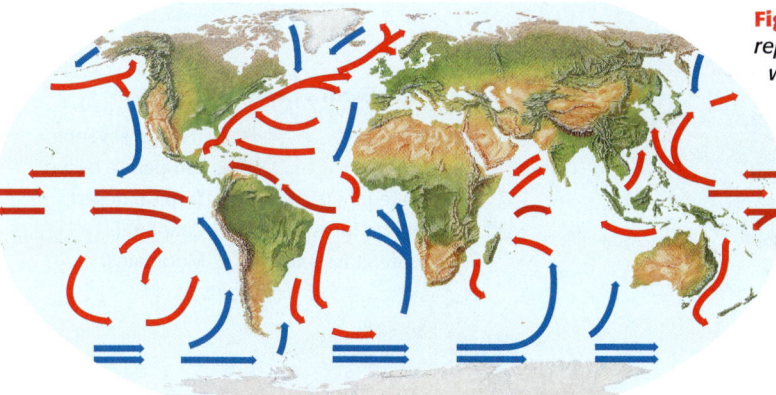

Figure 8 *The red arrows represent the movement of warm surface currents. The blue arrows represent the movement of cold surface currents.*

REVIEW

1. What is the difference between weather and climate?
2. How do mountains affect climate?
3. Describe how air temperature is affected by ocean surface currents.
4. **Analyzing Relationships** How would seasons be different if the Earth did not tilt on its axis?

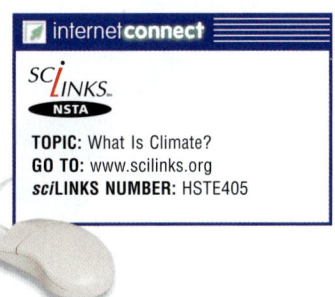

TOPIC: What Is Climate?
GO TO: www.scilinks.org
sciLINKS NUMBER: HSTE405

4) Close

Quiz

1. Why are the poles colder than the equator? (At the poles, the sun's rays strike the Earth's surface at a less direct angle than at the equator; the same amount of solar energy is spread over a larger area.)
2. Is precipitation more likely to occur when the prevailing winds are formed from warm air or when they are formed from cold air? (warm air)
3. Why are temperatures milder in Iceland than in Greenland? (The Gulf Stream brings warm water to the ocean around Iceland. This warm water heats the air, making temperatures milder.)

ALTERNATIVE ASSESSMENT

Climate Game Organize students into several teams to play a simulated popular game show. Have one team act as the game-show host and think of statements that reinforce section concepts, such as, "This determines how much solar energy an area receives." Have the other teams compete to formulate questions that the statements answer. Remind the "contestants" that they must phrase their answers in the form of a question. In the example above, the question could be "What is the Earth's tilt?"

Answers to Review

1. Weather is the condition of the atmosphere at a particular time and place. Climate is the average weather conditions in a certain area over a long period of time.
2. Mountains can influence an area's temperature and precipitation. Temperature is affected by elevation. The windward side of a mountain receives much more precipitation than the rain-shadow side.
3. The surface temperature of water affects the temperature of the air above it. As surface currents move, they carry warm or cool water to different locations. This changes the temperature of the air in the area.
4. If the Earth did not tilt on its axis, there would be no seasons. The same amount of solar radiation would reach both hemispheres year-round.

Section 1 • What Is Climate?

SECTION 2

Focus

Climates of the World

In this section, students learn the location and the characteristics of the three major climate zones and the different types of biomes that are found in each zone.

Ask students to describe in their ScienceLog differences between the plant life where they live and the plant life in an area they have visited. Ask students to think about how climate influences the vegetation in these areas. **Sheltered English**

1 Motivate

ACTIVITY

 Writing Have each student choose a country to focus on for this section. Students should record the area's latitude and geographic characteristics in their ScienceLog. Tell students to imagine they are on a fact-finding mission concerning the area's climate, the people that live there, and the plant and animal life of the region. Have them record evidence about the area's climate as they read the section.

 Teaching Transparency 178
"Climate Zones of the Earth"
"The Earth's Land Biomes"

Directed Reading Worksheet 17 Section 2

Section 2

Climates of the World

Terms to Learn
biome
tropical zone
temperate zone
deciduous
evergreens
polar zone
microclimate

What You'll Do
◆ Locate and describe the three major climate zones.
◆ Describe the different biomes found in each climate zone.

Have you ever wondered why the types of plants and animals in one part of the world are different from those found in another part? One reason involves climate. Plants and animals that have adapted to one climate may not be able to live in another climate. For instance, frogs do not live in Antarctica.

The three major climate zones of Earth—tropical, temperate, and polar—are illustrated in **Figure 9.** Each zone has a temperature range that relates to its latitude. However, in each of these zones there are several types of climates due to differences in the geography and the amount of precipitation. Because of the various climates in each zone, there are different biomes. A **biome** is a large region characterized by a specific type of climate and the plants and animals that live there.

Figure 10 shows the distribution of the Earth's land biomes. In this section we will review each of the three major climate zones and the biomes that are found in each zone.

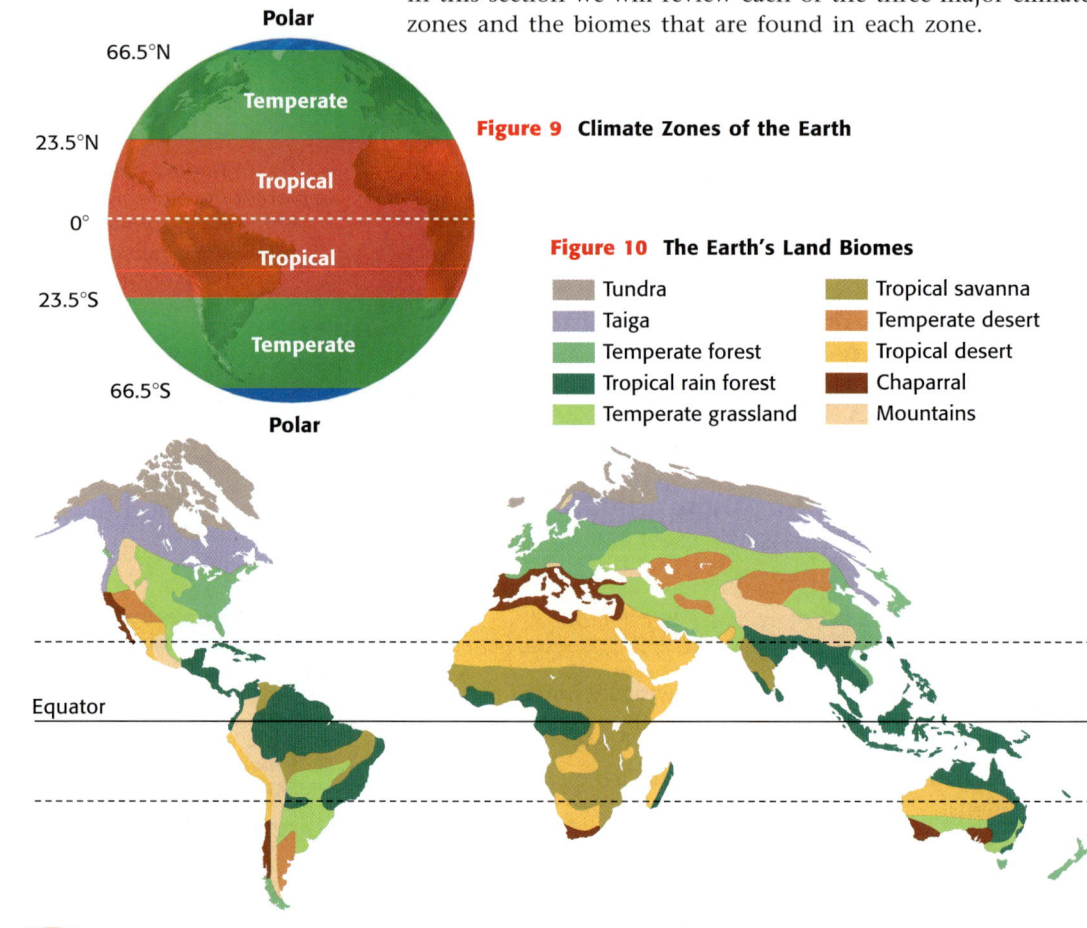

Figure 9 Climate Zones of the Earth

Figure 10 The Earth's Land Biomes
- Tundra
- Taiga
- Temperate forest
- Tropical rain forest
- Temperate grassland
- Tropical savanna
- Temperate desert
- Tropical desert
- Chaparral
- Mountains

458

WEIRD SCIENCE

In addition to having land biomes, Earth also has marine biomes. It is difficult to distinguish biomes in the oceans by latitude, however. Marine biomes are determined by water depth. Some of the animals that inhabit the deeper biomes have very interesting adaptations. For example, the anglerfish, which lives in total darkness, has a clever hunting strategy: a luminescent "lure" trails from the fish's jaw and attracts prey within reach of its enormous, sharp teeth.

458 Chapter 17 • Climate

The Tropical Zone

The **tropical zone**, or the *Tropics*, is the warm zone located around the equator, as shown in **Figure 11**. This zone extends from the tropic of Cancer to the tropic of Capricorn. As you have learned, latitudes in this zone receive the most solar radiation. Temperatures are therefore usually hot, except at high elevations. Within the tropical zone there are three types of biomes—tropical rain forest, tropical desert, and tropical savanna. **Figure 12** shows the distribution of these biomes.

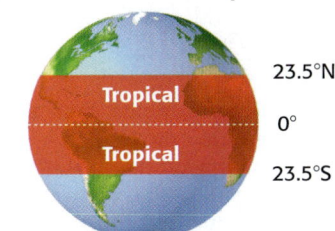

Figure 11 The Earth's Tropical Zone

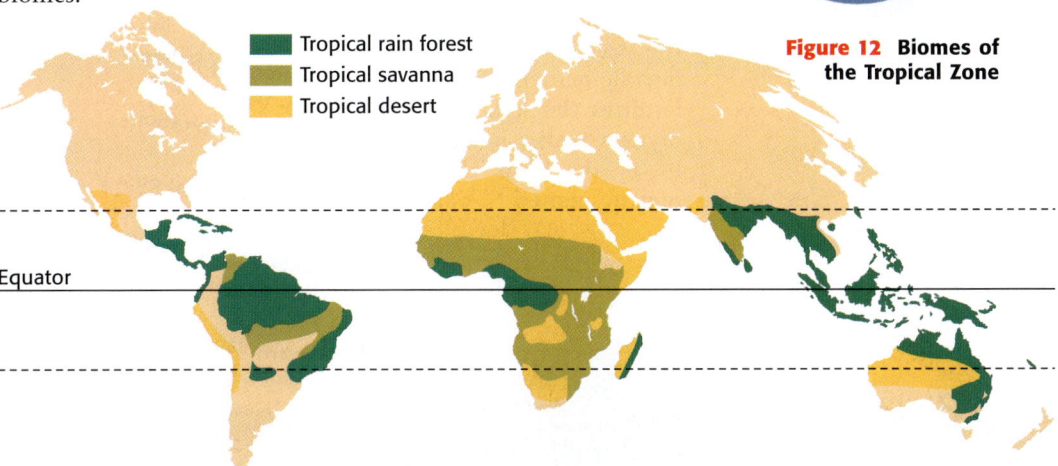

Figure 12 Biomes of the Tropical Zone

Tropical Rain Forest Tropical rain forests are always warm and wet. Because they are located near the equator, they receive strong sunlight year-round, causing little difference between seasons.

Tropical rain forests contain the greatest number of plant and animal species of any biome. But in spite of the lush vegetation, shown in **Figure 13,** the soil in rain forests is poor. The rapid decay of plants and animals returns nutrients to the soil, but these nutrients are quickly absorbed and used by the plants. The nutrients that are not immediately used by the plants are washed away by the heavy rains, leaving soil that is thin and nutrient poor.

Figure 13 In tropical rain forests, many of the trees form aboveground roots that provide extra support for the trees in the thin soil.

Avg. Temperature Range: 25°C–28°C (77°F–82°F)
Avg. Yearly Precipitation: 200 cm or more
Soil Characteristics: thin and nutrient poor
Vegetation: mahogany, ebony, rosewood, and balsa trees; vines, ferns, and bamboo
Animals: monkeys, lemurs, parrots, snakes, tree frogs, bats, pigs, small antelopes, tigers, jaguars, and leopards

MISCONCEPTION ALERT

It's not a jungle out there. The popular image of a tropical rain forest is of dense jungle undergrowth, but this occurs only along rivers or places that humans have cleared. Students may also confuse rain forests with forests in monsoon-climate regions. While rain forests have a fairly steady rate of precipitation, monsoon forests have a rainy season and a dry season. Rainfall during the rainy season may be measured in meters. During the dry season, the monsoon forest may receive little or no rainfall for many months. In fact, many monsoon-forest plants have some of the same adaptations for dry conditions that desert plants have.

2) Teach

READING STRATEGY

Prediction Guide Have students consider the following statements:
- Some deserts are cold. (true)
- The polar zone has below-freezing temperatures year-round. (false)

MATH and MORE

Rain forests actually "recycle" much of their rain. In the Amazon rain forest about three-quarters of all rainfall comes from the evaporation of water and the process of *transpiration* (the release of water vapor through leaf pores, or stomata). Use Transparency 52 to discuss this process. How much rain is "recycled" if an Amazon rain forest gets 650 cm of rain annually? (488 cm)

 Teaching Transparency 52 "Transpiration"

CONNECT TO ENVIRONMENTAL SCIENCE

It is estimated that as much as 130,000 km² of tropical rain forest is currently being deforested each year. At this rate the tropical rain forests will be gone in 30 years. Much of the rain forest is being converted to grassland for grazing or is being logged. The loss of the forest has a great influence on local and global climates.

 Math Skills Worksheet 37 "Rain-Forest Math"

2) Teach, continued

REAL-WORLD CONNECTION

Deserts are expanding at an accelerating rate. In the last 100 years, the estimated area of land occupied by deserts rose from 9.4 percent to 23.3 percent. Many factors have contributed to this, including climatic shifts, overgrazing, and overuse of the land through inefficient agricultural practices. As a class, find out what is being done to stop desertification in Western Africa and other areas of the world.

COOPERATIVE LEARNING

Many people believe that conditions in the desert biomes are so extreme that they are nearly devoid of life. In fact, many different kinds of deserts can support thriving ecological communities. Have students choose a tropical or temperate desert and create a poster display to teach the class about its location, the organisms that inhabit the desert, and other facts about the desert. Students could study the Gobi Desert, the Sahara Desert, the Great Sandy Desert, the Sonoran Desert, the Patagonian Desert, the Namib Desert, or another desert of their choice.

Homework

Research Draw students' attention to an important distinction between the vegetation in Old World and New World tropical deserts. Cactus is a succulent found in the New World. Euphorbia is a succulent found in the Old World. Have students find photographs of these types of plants and share them with the class.

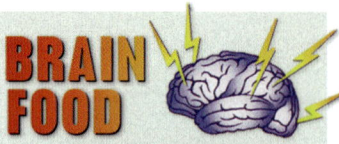

Most desert rodents, such as the kangaroo rat, hide in burrows during the day and are active at night, when the temperatures are cooler.

Biology CONNECTION

Some desert animals, such as the spadefoot toad, survive the scorching summer heat by burying themselves in the ground and sleeping through the dry season.

Tropical Deserts A desert is an area that receives less than 25 cm of rainfall per year. Because of this low yearly rainfall, deserts are the driest places on Earth. Desert plants, shown in **Figure 14,** are adapted to survive in a place with little water.

Deserts can be divided into hot deserts and cold deserts. The majority of hot deserts, such as the Sahara, in Africa, are tropical deserts. Hot deserts are caused by cool sinking air masses. Daily temperatures in tropical deserts vary from very hot daytime temperatures (50°C) to cool nighttime temperatures (20°C). Winters in hot deserts are usually mild. Because of the dryness, the soil is poor in organic matter, which fertilizes the soil. The dryness makes it hard to break down dead organic matter.

Avg. Temperature Range: 16°C–50°C (61°F–120°F)
Avg. Yearly Precipitation: 0–25 cm
Soil Characteristics: poor in organic matter
Vegetation: succulents (cactus and euphorbia), shrubs, thorny trees
Animals: kangaroo rats, lizards, scorpions, snakes, birds, bats, toads

Figure 14 Plants called succulents have adapted to dry conditions by developing fleshy stems and leaves to store water and a waxy coating to prevent water loss. A cactus is a type of succulent.

✓ Self-Check

If desert soil is so nutrient rich, why are deserts not suitable for agriculture? *(See page 726 to check your answer.)*

Answer to Self-Check

Because of its dryness, desert soil is poor in organic matter, which fertilizes the soil. Without this natural fertilizer, crops would not be able to grow.

IS THAT A FACT!

The world's largest desert, the Sahara, covers more than 9 million square kilometers—about the size of the United States. In contrast, the largest desert in the United States, is the Mojave Desert. It covers 38,900 km², which is nearly twice the size of New Jersey.

Tropical Savannas Tropical savannas, sometimes referred to as grasslands, are dominated by tall grasses, with trees scattered here and there. **Figure 15** is a photo of an African savanna. The climate is usually very warm, with a dry season that lasts four to eight months followed by short periods of rain. Savanna soils are generally nutrient poor, but grass fires, which are common during the dry season, leave the soils nutrient enriched.

Many plants have adapted to fire and use it to reproduce. Grasses sprout from their roots after the upper part of the plant is burned. The seeds of some plant species require fire in order to grow. For example, some species need fire to break open the seed's outer skin. Only after this skin is broken can the seed grow. Other species drop their seeds at the end of fire season. The heat from the fire triggers the plants to drop their seeds into the newly enriched soil.

Avg. Temperature Range: 27°C–32°C (80°F–90°F)

Avg. Yearly Precipitation: 100 cm

Soil Characteristics: generally nutrient poor

Vegetation: tall grasses (3–5 m), trees, thorny shrubs

Animals: gazelles, rhinoceroses, giraffes, lions, hyenas, ostriches, crocodiles, elephants

Figure 15 The grass of a tropical savanna is 3–5 m tall, much taller than that of a temperate grassland.

REVIEW

1. What are the soil characteristics of a tropical rain forest?
2. In what way has savanna vegetation adapted to fire?
3. **Summarizing Data** How do each of the tropical biomes differ?

TOPIC: Climates of the World
GO TO: www.scilinks.org
sciLINKS NUMBER: HSTE410

MEETING INDIVIDUAL NEEDS

Learners Having Difficulty
Help students learn the characteristics of each of the nine biomes by having them make a graphic organizer for each climate zone. Have them match the appropriate biomes with each climate zone folder. Each biome should have its own fact sheet complete with information about temperature, precipitation, soil, plants, and animals. Students can also paste photographs taken from magazines that show plants and animals that inhabit each biome. **Sheltered English**

REAL-WORLD CONNECTION

Some of the large mammals of the savanna, such as the elephant, are losing habitat because of the increase in grazing by domestic animals and the effects of hunting. Encourage students to find out more about conservation efforts in parks that are in tropical savannas.

MISCONCEPTION ALERT

Is a biome an ecosystem? Yes; a biome is a large region that is defined by the characteristic plants and animals that inhabit it. But a biome can contain many different ecosystems. An ecosystem can be as small as the community of microorganisms in a human stomach or as large as an entire biome.

Answers to Review

1. The soil in a tropical rain forest is thin and nutrient poor. Nutrients are rapidly returned to the soil, but these nutrients are quickly absorbed and used by the plants. The remaining nutrients are washed away by heavy rains.
2. Many plants require fire to reproduce. The seeds of some plants require fire to break open the seed's outer skin so the plant can grow. The heat from the fire triggers other plants to drop their seeds into the newly enriched soil.
3. Answers will vary. Accept all reasonable responses. The tropical biomes differ in the amount of precipitation they receive and in their average temperature. This in turn affects the vegetation, the soil type, and the animals that live in each biome.

Section 2 • Climates of the World

2 Teach, continued

READING STRATEGY

Prediction Guide If your community is in the continental United States, with the exception of Alaska, point out to students that they live in the temperate climate zone. The temperate climate zone is made up of four biomes: temperate forest, temperate grassland, chaparral, and temperate desert.

Write the following sentence on the board and have students copy it into their ScienceLog:

"I think we live in the _____ biome because _____."

Have them complete the sentence with the name of the biome and some ideas that support their statement.

MISCONCEPTION ALERT

You don't need to travel to the tropics to find a rain forest. Western Washington state is home to the largest temperate rain forest in the world. Moss-covered trees more than 500 years old stand 60 m tall and are 5 m in diameter. The ground is covered by ferns, moss, salmonberries, and the thorny Hercules's club. The growth is not as diverse as the tropical forests, but it is every bit as lush. The forest receives 380 cm of rain a year! Have students find out more about this remarkable ecosystem and the efforts to preserve it.

TOPIC: Climates of the World
GO TO: www.scilinks.org
sciLINKS NUMBER: HSTE410

The Temperate Zone

The **temperate zone,** as shown in **Figure 16,** is the climate zone between the Tropics and the polar zone. Temperatures in the temperate zone tend to be moderate. The continental United States is in the temperate zone, which includes the following four biomes: temperate forest, temperate grassland, chaparral, and temperate desert. **Figure 17** shows the distribution of the biomes found in the temperate zone.

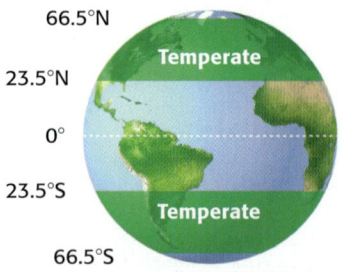

Figure 16 The Earth's Temperate Zones

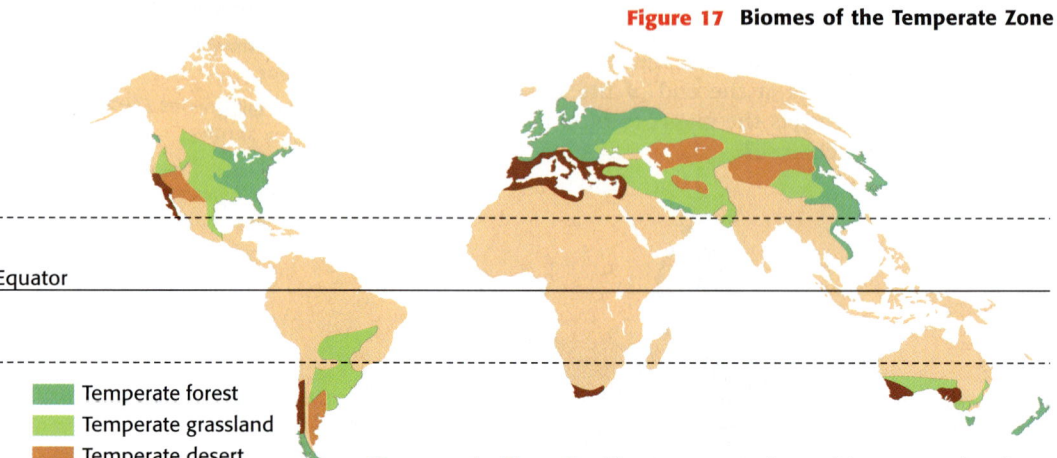

Figure 17 Biomes of the Temperate Zone

- Temperate forest
- Temperate grassland
- Temperate desert
- Chaparral

Temperate Forests The temperate forest biomes tend to have very high amounts of rainfall and seasonal temperature differences. Because of these distinct seasonal changes, summers are usually warm and winters are usually cold. The largest temperate forests are deciduous, such as the one shown in **Figure 18.** **Deciduous** trees are trees that lose their leaves when the weather becomes cold. These trees tend to be broad-leaved. The soils in deciduous forests are usually quite fertile because of the high organic content contributed by decaying leaves that drop every winter.

Figure 18 Deciduous trees have leaves that change color and drop when temperatures become cold.

Avg. Temperature Range: 0°C–28°C (32°F–82°F)
Avg. Yearly Precipitation: 76–250 cm
Soil Characteristics: very fertile, organically rich
Vegetation: deciduous and evergreen trees, shrubs, herbs
Animals: deer, bears, boars, badgers, squirrels, wolves, wild cats, red foxes, owls, and many other birds

Another type of temperate forest is the evergreen forest. **Evergreens** are trees that keep their leaves year-round. Evergreens can be either broad-leaved trees or needle-leaved trees, such as pine trees. Mixed forests of broad-leaved and needle-leaved trees can be found in humid climates, such as Florida, where winter temperatures rarely fall below freezing.

CONNECT TO ENVIRONMENTAL SCIENCE

The settlement of humans in temperate forests around the world has greatly fragmented these areas. Much of the temperate forest has been converted to agricultural land or logged. Fragmentation has a negative impact on many plants and animals that have certain habitat requirements. In fact, fragmentation has led to the extinction of many species. The temperate forest is also vulnerable to air pollution resulting from industrial activity. Acid precipitation and ozone has damaged entire forests, either killing the trees or making them more susceptible to disease. Have students write a persuasive essay explaining the importance of conserving Earth's temperate forests.

Temperate Grasslands Temperate grasslands, such as those shown in **Figure 19,** occur in regions that receive too little rainfall for trees to grow. This biome has warm summers and cold winters. The temperate grasslands are known by many local names—the *prairies* of North America, the *steppes* of Eurasia, the *veldt* of Africa, and the *pampas* of South America. Grasses are the most common type of vegetation found in this biome. Because grasslands have the most fertile soils of all biomes, much of the temperate grassland has been plowed to make room for croplands.

Avg. Temperature Range: −6°C–26°C (21°F–78°F)
Avg. Yearly Precipitation: 38–76 cm
Soil Characteristics: most fertile soils of all biomes
Vegetation: grasses
Animals: large grazing animals, including the bison of North America, the kangaroo of Australia, and the antelope of Africa

Figure 19 *The world's grasslands once covered about 42 percent of Earth's total land surface. Today they occupy only about 12 percent of the Earth's surface.*

Chaparrals Chaparral regions, as shown in **Figure 20,** have cool, wet winters and hot, dry summers. The vegetation is mainly evergreen shrubs, which are short, woody plants with thick, waxy leaves. The waxy leaves are adaptations that help prevent water loss in dry conditions. These shrubs grow in rocky, nutrient-poor soil. Like tropical-savanna vegetation, chaparral vegetation has adapted to fire. In fact, some plants, such as chamise, can grow back from their roots after a fire.

Avg. Temperature Range: 11°C–26°C (51°F–78°F)
Avg. Yearly Precipitation: 48–56 cm
Soil Characteristics: rocky, nutrient-poor soils
Vegetation: evergreen shrubs, scrubby trees, herbs
Animals: ground squirrels, deer, elk, mountain lions, coyotes, wolves

Figure 20 *Some plant species found in chaparral produce substances that help them catch on fire. These species require fire to reproduce.*

IS THAT A FACT!
Some grasses have defensive adaptations against grazing animals. Cordgrass, also known as rip gut, is found in marshy grassland areas and has sharp, hooklike barbs on its leaves that can easily cut an animal's mouth or a person's hands.

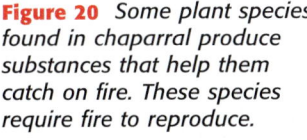 **Science Skills Worksheet 18** "Finding Useful Sources"

2 Teach, continued

BRAIN FOOD

Chile's arid northern desert land is one of the driest places on Earth. It receives so little rainfall that the yearly average is listed as "immeasurable." Surprisingly, people live there. They get drinking water by harvesting the fog. The village of Chungungo has built 75 fog-catching nets that supply 11,000 L of clean water a day. The nets, which look like giant volleyball nets, are positioned in the hills above the town. As the mountain fog passes through the nets, beads of water collect and are channeled to a large pipeline that supplies the village with water. Scientists believe this technology could be used in 30 other countries to supply safe and inexpensive water for drinking and agriculture.

Homework

Graphing Have students construct a bar graph that compares the average yearly precipitation ranges for the nine biomes discussed in the text. Have them use their graph to determine which biomes receive the most rain, which biomes receive the least rain, and which biome has the widest variation in annual precipitation. Suggest that students obtain yearly precipitation records for your region and compare them with the information in their graph.

Temperate Deserts The temperate desert biomes, like the one shown in **Figure 21,** tend to be cold deserts. Like all deserts, cold deserts receive less than 25 cm of rainfall annually. Temperate deserts can be very hot in the daytime, but—unlike hot deserts—they tend to be very cold at night.

Avg. Temperature Range: 1°C–50°C (34°F–120°F)
Avg. Yearly Precipitation: 0–25 cm
Soil Characteristics: poor in organic matter
Vegetation: succulents (cactus), shrubs, thorny trees
Animals: kangaroo rats, lizards, scorpions, snakes, birds, bats, toads

Figure 21 The Great Basin Desert is in the rain shadow of the Sierra Nevada.

The temperatures sometimes drop below freezing. This large change in temperature between day and night is caused by low humidity and cloudless skies. These conditions allow for a large amount of energy to reach, and thus heat, the Earth's surface during the day. However, these same characteristics allow the energy to escape at night, causing temperatures to drop. You probably rarely think of snow and deserts together, but temperate deserts often receive light snow during the winter.

Temperate deserts are dry because they are generally located inland, far away from a moisture source, or are located on the rain-shadow side of a mountain range.

The Polar Zone

The **polar zone** includes the northernmost and southernmost climate zones, as shown in **Figure 22.** Polar climates have the coldest average temperatures. The temperatures in the winter stay below freezing, and the temperatures during the summer months remain chilly. **Figure 23,** on the next page, shows the distribution of the biomes found in the polar zone.

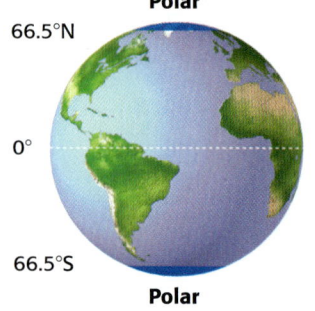

Figure 22 The Earth's Polar Zones

WEIRD SCIENCE

Lichens are primitive organisms that thrive in the polar zone. Some lichens in the Arctic have been determined to be 4,500 years old. To protect themselves from the cold, some lichens live 2 cm inside rocks! Despite their ability to survive in extremely harsh arctic conditions, most lichens have an extremely low tolerance for sulfur dioxide air pollution. As a result, they are usually not found in industrialized areas.

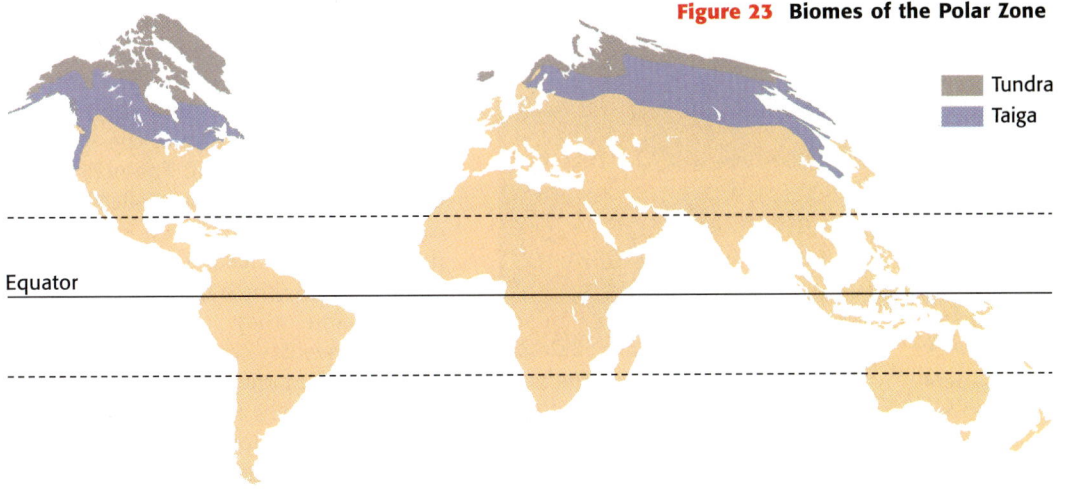

Figure 23 Biomes of the Polar Zone

- Tundra
- Taiga

Equator

Tundra Next to deserts, the tundra, as shown in **Figure 24**, is the driest place on Earth. This biome has long, cold winters with almost 24 hours of night and short, cool summers with almost 24 hours of daylight. In the summer, only the top meter of soil thaws. Underneath the thawed soil lies a permanently frozen layer of soil, called *permafrost*. This frozen layer prevents the water in the thawed soil from draining. Because of the poor drainage, the upper soil layer is muddy and is therefore an excellent breeding ground for insects, such as mosquitoes. Many birds migrate to the tundra during the summer to feed on the insects.

Environment CONNECTION

Subfreezing climates contain almost no decomposing bacteria. The well-preserved body of John Torrington, a member of an expedition that explored the Northwest Passage in Canada in the 1840s, was uncovered in 1984, appearing much as it did when he died, more than 140 years earlier.

Avg. Temperature Range: −27°C–5°C (−17°F–41°F)
Avg. Yearly Precipitation: 0–25 cm
Soil Characteristics: frozen
Vegetation: mosses, lichens, sedges, and dwarf trees
Animals: rabbits, lemmings, reindeer, caribou, musk oxen, wolves, foxes, birds, and polar bears

Figure 24 In the tundra, mosses and lichens cover rocks. Dwarf trees grow close to the ground to protect themselves from strong winds and to absorb energy from the Earth's sunlit surface.

3) Extend

LabBook PG 704
Biome Business

DEMONSTRATION

Mock Permafrost Prepare for the demonstration by punching five holes in the bottom of two coffee cans and filling each can one-third full with potting soil. Slowly add water to one can until it begins to drain through the bottom; the soil should be moist but not saturated. Allow the excess water to drain, and pack the soil firmly. Place that can in a freezer for 6 to 8 hours. Bring the two cans to class, and have students gather at a sink. Hold the can with the unfrozen soil over the sink, and slowly pour a glass of water onto the soil. Repeat with the frozen can. Discuss with students why muddy or "marshy" areas form in the frozen soil and why the soil did not drain.

GROUP ACTIVITY

Have groups write a brochure for a summer camp in the biome of their choice. Suggest that they include information about the environment that will entice people to come and helpful tips about how to prepare for the area's climate.

WEIRD SCIENCE

Conical hills, called pingos, form in the arctic tundra when frozen ground water trapped under the permafrost is forced up due to pressure. As the frozen ground water rises, it pushes the ground over it upward. Pingos can be up to 46 m high and 400 m across.

MISCONCEPTION ALERT

Students may think that the tundra is a relatively small and barren portion of the world. Actually, 1/10 of the Earth's land is tundra, and about 600 species of plants are native to the biome. Ninety-nine percent of those plants are perennials—the growing season is too short for annuals, which need time to produce flowers and seeds.

Section 2 • Climates of the World

4 Close

Quiz

1. What are the three major climate zones? (the tropical zone, the temperate zone, and the polar zone)
2. Can a climate zone contain more than one biome? (A climate zone may contain several different biomes.)
3. What is a microclimate? (a small region with unique climate characteristics)

ALTERNATIVE ASSESSMENT

Concept Mapping Have students create a concept map that shows how each of the nine biomes is influenced by precipitation and temperature.

RESEARCH

Have students research the various microclimates that can be found on either side of Mount Shasta, in California. Have them find out which plants and animals are dominant at different elevations. They may want to present their findings in a color-coded diagram of the mountain with a key that explains the main characteristics of each microclimate.

For the Birds

Reinforcement Worksheet 17 "A Tale of Three Climates"

Avg. Temperature Range: −10°C–15°C (14°F–59°F)
Avg. Yearly Precipitation: 40–61 cm
Soil Characteristics: acidic soil
Vegetation: mosses, lichens, conifers
Animals: birds, rabbits, moose, elk, wolves, lynxes, and bears

Figure 25 The taiga is the major source of wood for paper.

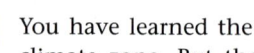
Physics CONNECTION
Roof temperatures can get so hot that you can fry an egg on them! In a study of roofs on a sunny day when the air temperature was 13°C, scientists recorded roof temperatures ranging from 18°C to 61°C depending on color and material of the roof.

To find out more about microclimates, turn to page 701 of the LabBook.

Taiga (Northern Coniferous Forest)

Just south of the tundra lies the taiga biome. The taiga, as shown in **Figure 25**, has long, cold winters and short, warm summers. Like the tundra, the soil during the winter is frozen. The majority of the trees are evergreen needle-leaved trees called *conifers,* such as pine, spruce, and fir trees. The needles and bendable branches allow these trees to shed heavy snow before they can be damaged. Conifer needles contain acidic substances. When the needles die and fall to the soil, they make the soil acidic. Most plants cannot grow in acidic soil, and therefore the forest floor is bare except for some mosses and lichens.

Microclimates

You have learned the types of biomes that are found in each climate zone. But the climate and the biome of a particular place can also be influenced by local conditions. **Microclimates** are small regions with unique climatic characteristics. For example, elevation can affect an area's climate and therefore its biome. Tundra and taiga biomes exist in the Tropics on high mountains. How is this possible? Remember that as the elevation increases, the atmosphere loses its ability to absorb and hold thermal energy. This results in lower temperatures.

Cities are also microclimates. In a city, temperatures can be 1°C to 2°C warmer than the surrounding rural areas. This is because buildings and pavement made of dark materials absorb solar radiation instead of reflecting it. There is also less vegetation to take in the sun's rays. This absorption of the sun's rays by buildings and pavement heats the surrounding air and causes temperatures to rise.

REVIEW

1. Describe how tropical deserts and temperate deserts differ.
2. List and describe the three major climate zones.
3. **Inferring Conclusions** Rank each biome according to how suitable it would be for growing crops. Explain your reasoning.

Answers to Review

1. Answers will vary. Sample answer: Tropical deserts are hot deserts, and temperate deserts are cold deserts. Winters in tropical deserts are usually mild, but temperate deserts often receive light snow during winter.
2. The three climate zones are the tropical zone, the temperate zone, and the polar zone. The tropical zone receives the most direct solar radiation; therefore the temperatures are generally hot. Temperatures in the temperate zone tend to be moderate. The temperate zone experiences seasonal variations, such as warm summers and cold winters. During winter, the temperatures in the polar zone stay below freezing. During the summer, temperatures remain cold but they can be above freezing.
3. Answers will vary.

Section 3

Terms to Learn
ice age
global warming
greenhouse effect

What You'll Do
- Describe how the Earth's climate has changed over time.
- Summarize the different theories that attempt to explain why the Earth's climate has changed.
- Explain the greenhouse effect and its role in global warming.

Changes in Climate

As you know, the weather constantly changes—sometimes several times in one day. Saturday, your morning baseball game was canceled because of rain, but by that afternoon the sun was shining. Now think about the climate where you live. You probably haven't noticed a change in climate, because climates change slowly. What causes climates to change? Until recently, climatic changes were connected only to natural causes. However, studies indicate that human activities may have an influence on climatic change. In this section, you will learn how natural and human factors may influence climatic change.

Ice Ages

The geologic record indicates that the Earth's climate has been much colder than it is today. In fact, much of the Earth was covered by sheets of ice during certain periods. An **ice age** is a period during which ice collects in high latitudes and moves toward lower latitudes. Scientists have found evidence of many major ice ages throughout the Earth's geologic history. The most recent ice age began about 2 million years ago.

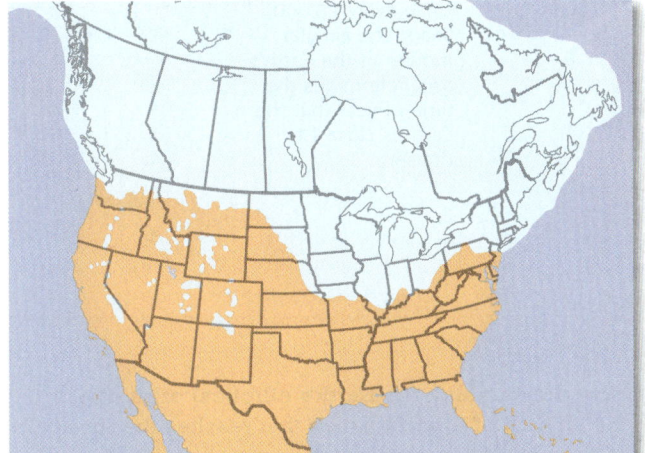

Figure 26 During the last glacial period, which ended 10,000 years ago, the Great Lakes were covered by an enormous block of ice that was 1.5 km high.

Glacial Periods
During an ice age, there are periods of cold and periods of warmth. These periods are called glacial and interglacial periods. During *glacial periods*, the enormous sheets of ice advance, getting bigger and covering a larger area as shown in **Figure 26.** Because a large amount of ocean water is frozen during glacial periods, sea level drops.

MISCONCEPTION ALERT

Students may be confused about the difference between an ice age and a glacial period. An ice age is the gradual cooling of the planet over thousands of years. During this time, glaciers repeatedly spread outward from the Earth's poles toward the equator. Ice ages are characterized by glacial periods (when glaciers spread) and interglacial periods (when glaciers retreat). Glacial periods can happen rather quickly—often in less than 30 years. Ice cores indicate that sudden glaciation periods could be caused by changes in major ocean currents or by volcanic eruptions.

SECTION 3

Focus
Changes in Climate
This section describes significant changes in the Earth's climate. Students learn how different theories attempt to explain the cause of ice ages. Students also learn about the greenhouse effect and how the human production of greenhouse gases may contribute to global warming.

Bellringer
Have students imagine that the climate of the area where they live has changed so that it is now warmer than it used to be. Have students write down five different ways they think the area would be affected by warmer temperatures.

1) Motivate

DEMONSTRATION
The Greenhouse Effect Tell students that the glass windows in a greenhouse are similar to the Earth's atmosphere. The glass allows radiant energy to enter but prevents thermal energy from escaping. Have students place a thermometer in a plastic bag on a sunny windowsill. Place another thermometer next to the plastic bag. After 30 minutes, have a student read the two thermometers and compare the differences in temperature.
Sheltered English

Directed Reading Worksheet 17 Section 3

Section 3 • Changes in Climate 467

2) Teach

MEETING INDIVIDUAL NEEDS

Advanced Learners Have students find out why scientists study the dust concentrations and gas composition of glacial ice in places such as Antarctica and Greenland. Have them explain why these and other data provide evidence about the last glacial period and other ice ages. Suggest that students share their findings with the class by giving an oral presentation.

In the early 1980s, astronomer Carl Sagan and four other scientists proposed a theory that the fallout from a nuclear war could result in disastrous climatic changes. The fallout, consisting of billions of tons of dust and ash ejected into the atmosphere, would act as a shield, blocking out so much of the sun's rays that it would cause periods of darkness and below-freezing temperatures possibly lasting a year or longer. This scenario is described as a "nuclear winter." Discuss with students the similarities between the nuclear-winter theory and the theory that suggests glaciation is caused by catastrophic events such as massive volcanic eruptions.

 **Teaching Transparency 179** "The Milankovitch Theory of the Causes of the Ice Ages"

468 Chapter 17 • Climate

Interglacial Periods Warmer times that occur between glacial periods are called *interglacial periods*. During an interglacial period, the ice begins to melt and the sea level rises again. The last interglacial period began 10,000 years ago and is still occurring. Why do these periods occur? Will the Earth have another glacial period in the future? These questions have been debated by scientists for the past 200 years.

Motions of the Earth There are many theories about the causes of ice ages. Each theory attempts to explain the gradual cooling that leads to the development of enormous ice sheets that periodically cover large areas of the Earth's surface. The *Milankovitch theory* explains why an ice age isn't just one long cold spell but instead alternates between cold and warm periods. Milutin Milankovitch, a Yugoslavian scientist, proposed that changes in the Earth's orbit and in the tilt of the Earth's axis cause ice ages, as illustrated in **Figure 27**.

Figure 27 *According to the Milankovitch theory, the amount of solar radiation the Earth receives varies due to three kinds of changes in the Earth's orbit.*

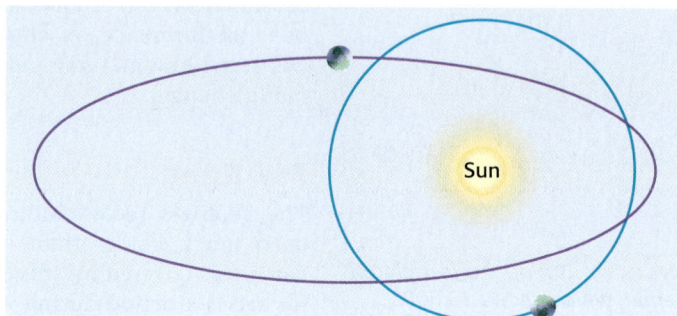

1. Over a period of 100,000 years, the Earth's orbit slowly changes from a more circular shape to a more elliptical shape. When the orbit is more elliptical, the contrast between seasons is greater in one hemisphere and less in the other hemisphere. When the orbit is more circular, there is not as much seasonal change.

2. Over a period of 41,000 years, the tilt of the Earth's axis varies between 21.8° and 24.4°. When the tilt is at 24.4°, the poles receive more solar energy.

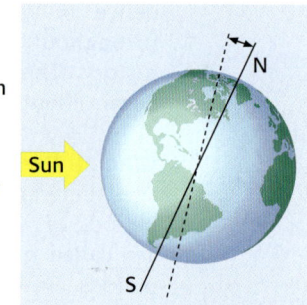

3. The Earth's axis traces a complete circle every 26,000 years. The circular motion of the Earth's axis determines the time of year that the Earth is closest to the sun.

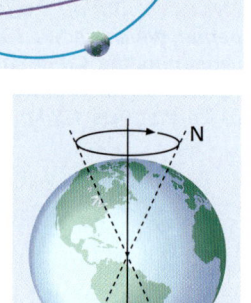

✓ Self-Check

How do you think the Earth's elliptical orbit affects the amount of solar radiation that reaches the surface? (See page 726 to check your answer.)

468

Answer to Self-Check

The Earth's elliptical orbit causes seasonal differences. When the Earth's orbit is more elliptical, summers are hotter because the Earth is closer to the sun and receives more solar radiation. However, the Earth also moves farther from the sun in winter and receives less solar radiation. (Point out that the elliptical orbit of the Earth shown in **Figure 27** is exaggerated for effect. The change in orbits from circular to more elliptical is actually very slight.)

WEIRD SCIENCE

During the last glacial period, animals that live in the northern part of North America, such as the Arctic fox, wolf, grizzly bear, and caribou, were living in Oklahoma, Missouri, and Texas!

Volcanic Eruptions There are many natural factors that can affect global climate. Catastrophic events, such as volcanic eruptions, can influence climate. Volcanic eruptions send large amounts of dust, ash, and smoke into the atmosphere. Once in the atmosphere, the dust, smoke, and ash particles act as a shield, blocking out so much of the sun's rays that the Earth cools. **Figure 28** shows how dust particles from a volcanic eruption block the sun.

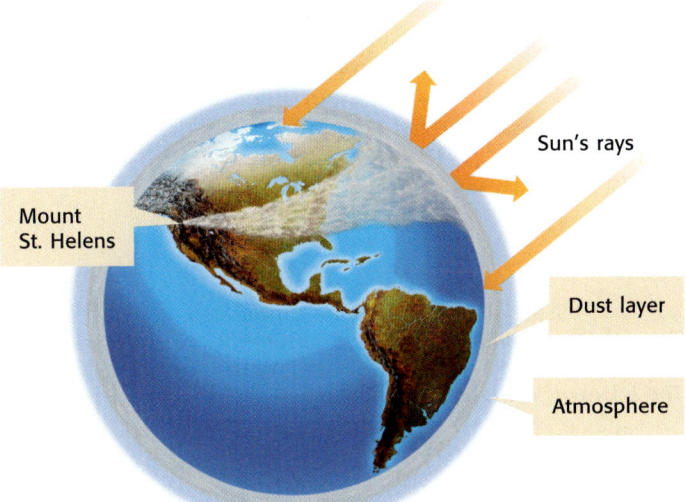

Figure 28 *Volcanic eruptions, such as the one that occurred at Mount St. Helens, shown above, produce dust that reflects sunlight, as shown at left.*

Plate Tectonics The Earth's climate is further influenced by plate tectonics and continental drift. One theory proposes that ice ages occur when the continents are positioned closer to the polar regions. For example, approximately 250 million years ago, all the continents were connected near the South Pole in one giant landmass called Pangaea, as shown in **Figure 29.** During this time, ice covered a large area of the Earth's surface. As Pangaea broke apart, the continents moved toward the equator, and the ice age ended. During the last ice age, many large landmasses were positioned in the polar zones. Antarctica, northern North America, Europe, and Asia all were covered with large sheets of ice.

Figure 29 *Much of Pangaea—the part that is now Africa, South America, India, Antarctica, Australia, and Saudi Arabia—was covered by continental ice sheets.*

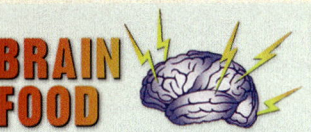

When the climate starts to cool, ice sheets grow and creep over the Earth. Ice sheets act as reflectors, reflecting solar radiation away from the Earth, causing it to cool even more. The more the Earth cools, the larger glaciers grow.

REAL-WORLD CONNECTION

Tell students that washing clothes in cold water instead of hot water can reduce the amount of carbon dioxide released into the atmosphere. This is because fossil fuels are used to heat the water. For example, a household that uses cold water to do two loads of laundry a week releases about 225 kg *less* carbon dioxide into the atmosphere each year. Have students calculate what the annual reduction in released carbon dioxide would be if the family of every student in the class used cold water for laundry.

CROSS-DISCIPLINARY FOCUS

History Archaeological evidence suggests that North America was originally settled by people who walked here from Asia between 15,000 and 25,000 years ago. At that time, sea levels were as much as 150 m lower, exposing the land between Alaska and Siberia. The sea level was lower because the ice sheets that spread across the Northern Hemisphere contained vast amounts of water. Have students write a short report about other human migrations thought to be caused by climate change.

It is difficult for scientists to predict climate changes because weather data has been accurately recorded for less than 200 years. However, the meteorological records of the Chinese date back to 1216 B.C. While these records do not indicate temperature, they do record rainfall, sleet, snow, humidity, and wind direction. There are also comments on unusually warm or cool temperatures. Have interested students research the reasons for collecting the data and find out how it is used today.

Section 3 • Changes in Climate

3 Extend

Answers to MATHBREAK

Answers will vary.

Given: The distance from home to school is 3 mi.

3 mi (1.6 km/mi) = 4.8 km

4.8 km/day (20 day/month) = 96 km/month

96 ÷ 20 = 4.8 gal of gas

4.8 gal (9 kg/gal) = 43.2 kg of carbon dioxide

CONNECT TO LIFE SCIENCE

There are many consequences of global warming. One possibility is the spread of tropical diseases, such as malaria and dengue fever. Both of these diseases are carried by a specific species of mosquito. These mosquitoes have a minimum temperature at which they can survive and breed. Ask students to create a temperature map for the world and identify the areas that are most likely to have a problem with these diseases.

Global Impact

 Critical Thinking Worksheet 17 "Cyberspace Heats Up"

 Science Skills Worksheet 4 "Understanding Bias"

MATH BREAK

The Ride to School

Find out how much carbon dioxide is released into the atmosphere each month from the car or bus that transports you to school.

1. Figure out the distance from your home to school.
2. From this figure, calculate how many kilometers you travel to and from school, in a car or bus, per month.
3. Divide this number by 20. This represents approximately how many gallons of gas are used during your trips to school.
4. If burning 1 gal of gasoline produces 9 kg of carbon dioxide, how much carbon dioxide is released?

internetconnect

TOPIC: Changes in Climate
GO TO: www.scilinks.org
sciLINKS NUMBER: HSTE415

TOPIC: Modeling Earth's Climate
GO TO: www.scilinks.org
sciLINKS NUMBER: HSTE420

Global Warming

Is the Earth really experiencing global warming? **Global warming** is a rise in average global temperatures that can result from an increase in the greenhouse effect. To understand how global warming works, you must first learn about the greenhouse effect.

Greenhouse Effect The **greenhouse effect** is the Earth's natural heating process, in which gases in the atmosphere trap thermal energy. The Earth's atmosphere performs the same function as the glass windows in a car. Think about the car illustrated in **Figure 30**. It's a hot summer day, and you are about to get inside the car. You immediately notice that it feels hotter inside the car than outside. Then you sit down and—ouch!—you burn yourself on the seat.

Figure 30 Sunlight streams into the car through the clear glass windows. The seats absorb the radiant energy and change it into thermal energy. The energy is then trapped in the car.

Window to the World Greenhouse gases allow sunlight to pass through the atmosphere. It is absorbed by the Earth's surface and reradiated as thermal energy. Many scientists hypothesize that the rise in global temperatures is due to an increase of carbon dioxide, a greenhouse gas, as a result of human activity. Most evidence indicates that the increase in carbon dioxide is caused by the burning of fossil fuels that releases carbon dioxide into the atmosphere.

SCIENTISTS AT ODDS

Svante Arrhenius was the first scientist to propose that the global climate was changing as a result of human activities. He put forth his theory in 1905. Other scientists ridiculed his ideas. It was not until much later that scientists took a serious look at the effects of carbon dioxide on the global climate.

Another factor that may add to global warming is deforestation. *Deforestation* is the process of clearing forests, as shown in **Figure 31**. In many countries around the world, forests are being burned to clear land for agriculture. All types of burning release carbon dioxide into the atmosphere, thereby increasing the greenhouse effect. Plants use carbon dioxide to make food. As plants are removed from the Earth, the carbon dioxide that would have been used by the plants builds up in the atmosphere.

Figure 31 *Clearing land by burning leads to increased levels of carbon dioxide in the atmosphere.*

Consequences of Global Warming Many scientists think that if the average global temperature continues to rise, some regions of the world might experience flooding. Warmer temperatures could cause the icecaps to melt, raising the sea level and flooding low-lying areas, such as the coasts.

Areas that receive little rainfall, such as deserts, might receive even less due to increased evaporation. Scientists predict that the Midwest, an agricultural area, could experience warmer, drier conditions. A change in climate such as this could harm crops. But farther north, such as in Canada, weather conditions for farming would improve.

Reducing Pollution

A city just received a warning from the Environmental Protection Agency for exceeding the automobile fuel emissions standards. If you were the city manager, what suggestions would you make to reduce the amount of automobile emissions?

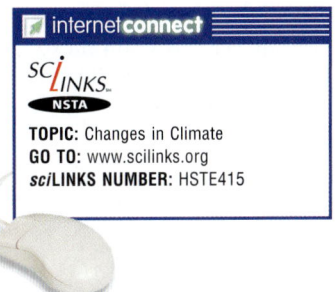

REVIEW

1. How has the Earth's climate changed over time? What might have caused these changes?
2. Explain how the greenhouse effect warms the Earth.
3. What are two ways that humans contribute to the increase in carbon dioxide levels in the atmosphere?
4. **Analyzing Relationships** How will the warming of the Earth affect agriculture in different parts of the world?

internet connect

SC_iLINKS
NSTA

TOPIC: Changes in Climate
GO TO: www.scilinks.org
*sci*LINKS NUMBER: HSTE415

Chapter Highlights

VOCABULARY DEFINITIONS

SECTION 1

weather the condition of the atmosphere at a particular time and place

climate the average weather conditions in an area over a long period of time

latitude the distance north or south from the equator; measured in degrees

prevailing winds winds that blow mainly from one direction

elevation the height of an object above sea level; the height of surface landforms above sea level

surface currents a streamlike movement of water that occurs at or near the surface of the ocean

Chapter Highlights

SECTION 1

Vocabulary
- weather (p. 452)
- climate (p. 452)
- latitude (p. 453)
- prevailing winds (p. 455)
- elevation (p. 456)
- surface currents (p. 457)

Section Notes

- Weather is the condition of the atmosphere at a particular time and place. Climate is the average weather conditions in a certain area over a long period of time.
- Climate is determined by temperature and precipitation.
- Climate is controlled by factors such as latitude, elevation, wind patterns, local geography, and ocean surface currents.

- The amount of solar energy an area receives is determined by the area's latitude.
- The seasons are a result of the tilt of the Earth's axis and its path around the sun.
- The amount of moisture carried by prevailing winds affects the amount of precipitation that falls.
- As elevation increases, temperature decreases.

- Mountains affect the distribution of precipitation. The dry side of the mountain is called the rain shadow.
- As ocean surface currents move across the Earth, they redistribute warm and cool water. The temperature of the surface water affects the air temperature.

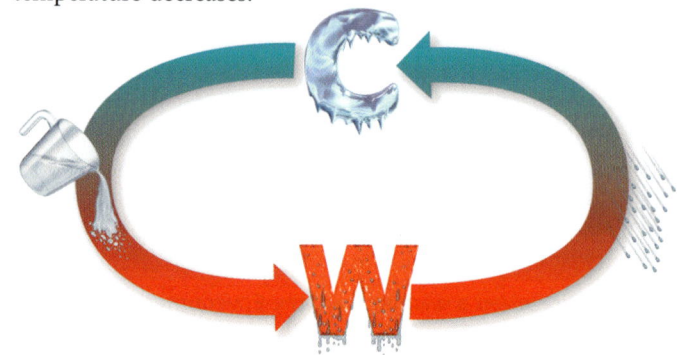

✓ Skills Check

Visual Understanding

THE SEASONS Seasons are determined by latitude. The diagram on page 454 shows how the tilt of the Earth affects how much solar energy an area receives as the Earth moves around the sun.

THE RAIN SHADOW The illustration on page 456 shows how the climates on two sides of a mountain can be very different. A mountain can affect the climate of areas nearby by influencing the amount of precipitation these areas receive.

LAND BIOMES OF THE EARTH Look back at Figure 10 on page 458 to review the distribution of the Earth's Land Biomes.

Lab and Activity Highlights

For the Birds PG 701

Biome Business PG 704

Global Impact PG 700

 Datasheets for LabBook (blackline masters for these labs)

SECTION 2

Vocabulary
- **biome** (p. 458)
- **tropical zone** (p. 459)
- **temperate zone** (p. 462)
- **deciduous** (p. 462)
- **evergreens** (p. 462)
- **polar zone** (p. 464)
- **microclimate** (p. 466)

Section Notes
- The Earth is divided into three climate zones according to latitude—the tropical zone, the temperate zone, and the polar zone.
- The tropical zone is the zone around the equator. The tropical rain forest, tropical desert, and tropical savanna are in this zone.
- The temperate zone is the zone between the tropical zone and the polar zone. The temperate forest, temperate grassland, chaparral, and temperate desert are in this zone.
- The polar zones are the northernmost and southernmost zones. The taiga and tundra are in this zone.

Labs
- For the Birds (p. 701)
- Biome Business (p. 704)

SECTION 3

Vocabulary
- **ice age** (p. 467)
- **global warming** (p. 470)
- **greenhouse effect** (p. 470)

Section Notes
- Explanations for the occurrence of ice ages include changes in the Earth's orbit, volcanic eruptions, and plate tectonics and continental drift.
- Some scientists believe that global warming is occurring as a result of an increase in carbon dioxide from human activity.
- If global warming continues, it could drastically change climates, causing either floods or drought.

Labs
- Global Impact (p. 700)

VOCABULARY DEFINITIONS, continued

SECTION 2

biome a large region characterized by a specific type of climate and the plants and animals that live there

tropical zone the warm zone located around the equator

temperate zone the climate zone between the Tropics and the polar zone

deciduous describes trees that lose their leaves when the weather becomes cold

evergreens trees that keep their leaves year-round

polar zone the northernmost and southernmost climate zones

microclimate a small region with unique climatic characteristics

SECTION 3

ice age a period during which ice collects in high latitudes and moves toward lower latitudes

global warming a rise in average global temperatures

greenhouse effect the natural heating process of a planet, such as the Earth, by which gases in the atmosphere trap thermal energy

 Vocabulary Review Worksheet 17

 Blackline masters of these Chapter Highlights can be found in the **Study Guide**.

internet connect

 **GO TO:** go.hrw.com

Visit the **HRW** Web site for a variety of learning tools related to this chapter. Just type in the keyword:

KEYWORD: HSTCLM

 **GO TO:** www.scilinks.org

Visit the **National Science Teachers Association** on-line Web site for Internet resources related to this chapter. Just type in the *sci*LINKS number for more information about the topic:

TOPIC:	What Is Climate?	*sci*LINKS NUMBER:	HSTE405
TOPIC:	Climates of the World	*sci*LINKS NUMBER:	HSTE410
TOPIC:	Changes in Climate	*sci*LINKS NUMBER:	HSTE415
TOPIC:	Modeling Earth's Climate	*sci*LINKS NUMBER:	HSTE420

Lab and Activity Highlights

LabBank

 Whiz-Bang Demonstrations,
How Humid Is It? Demo 30

Long-Term Projects & Research Ideas,
Sun-Starved in Fairbanks, Project 45

Chapter Review Answers

USING VOCABULARY

1. Climate
2. Latitude
3. tropical
4. deciduous
5. tundra
6. global warming

UNDERSTANDING CONCEPTS

Multiple Choice

7. b	11. c
8. b	12. a
9. a	13. d
10. b	14. b

Short Answer

15. Higher latitudes receive less solar radiation because the sun's rays strike the Earth's surface at a less direct angle. This spreads the same amount of solar energy over a larger area, resulting in lower temperatures.

16. The amount of precipitation an area receives can depend on whether the region's prevailing winds form from a warm air mass or from a cold air mass. If the winds form from a warm air mass, they will probably carry moisture. If the winds form from a cold air mass, they will probably be dry. Precipitation is more likely to occur when the prevailing winds are warm and moist.

17. Answers will vary. Sample answer: Tundra and taiga biomes can be found on tropical mountains. This is because air at higher elevations retains less thermal energy than air at lower elevations.

18. Plants have adapted by developing fleshy leaves to store water and a waxy coating to prevent water loss. Animals are more active at night, when temperatures are cooler, and they burrow during the day.

Chapter Review

USING VOCABULARY

To complete the following sentences, choose the correct term from each pair of terms listed below.

1. __?__ is the condition of the atmosphere in a certain area over a long period of time. (*Weather* or *Climate*)

2. __?__ is the distance north and south from the equator measured in degrees. (*Longitude* or *Latitude*)

3. Savannas are grasslands located in the __?__ zone between 23.5° north latitude and 23.5° south latitude. (*temperate* or *tropical*)

4. Trees that lose their leaves are found in a(n) __?__ forest. (*deciduous* or *evergreen*)

5. Frozen land in the polar zone is most often found in a __?__. (*taiga* or *tundra*)

6. A rise in global temperatures due to an increase in carbon dioxide is called __?__. (*global warming* or *the greenhouse effect*)

UNDERSTANDING CONCEPTS

Multiple Choice

7. The tilt of Earth as it orbits the sun causes
   a. global warming.
   b. different seasons.
   c. a rain shadow.
   d. the greenhouse effect.

8. What factor affects the prevailing winds as they blow across a continent, producing different climates?
   a. latitude   c. forests
   b. mountains   d. glaciers

9. What factor determines the amount of solar energy an area receives?
   a. latitude   c. mountains
   b. wind patterns   d. ocean currents

10. What climate zone has the coldest average temperature?
    a. tropical   c. temperate
    b. polar   d. tundra

11. What biome is not located in the tropical zone?
    a. rain forest   c. chaparral
    b. savanna   d. desert

12. What biome contains the greatest number of plant and animal species?
    a. rain forest   c. grassland
    b. temperate forest d. tundra

13. Which of the following is not a theory for the cause of ice ages?
    a. the Milankovitch theory
    b. volcanic eruptions
    c. plate tectonics
    d. the greenhouse effect

14. Which of the following is thought to contribute to global warming?
    a. wind patterns
    b. deforestation
    c. ocean surface currents
    d. microclimates

19. Both the tundra and desert biomes receive very little precipitation.

Concept Mapping

20. An answer to this exercise can be found at the end of this book.

Short Answer

15. Why do higher latitudes receive less solar radiation than lower latitudes?

16. How does wind influence precipitation patterns?

17. Give an example of a microclimate. What causes the unique temperature and precipitation characteristics of this area?

18. How have desert plants and animals adapted to this biome?

19. How are tundra and deserts similar?

Concept Mapping

20. Use the following terms to create a concept map: climate, global warming, deforestation, greenhouse effect, flooding.

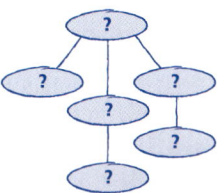

CRITICAL THINKING AND PROBLEM SOLVING

Write one or two sentences to answer the following questions:

21. Explain how ocean surface currents are responsible for milder climates.

22. In your own words, explain how a change in the Earth's orbit can affect the Earth's climates as proposed by Milutin Milankovitch.

23. Explain why the climate differs drastically on each side of the Rocky Mountains.

24. What are some steps you and your family can take to reduce the amount of carbon dioxide that is released into the atmosphere?

MATH IN SCIENCE

25. If the air temperature near the shore of a lake measures 24°C, and if the temperature increases by 0.05°C every 10 m traveled away from the lake, what would the air temperature be 1 km from the lake?

INTERPRETING GRAPHICS

The following illustration shows the Earth's orbit around the sun.

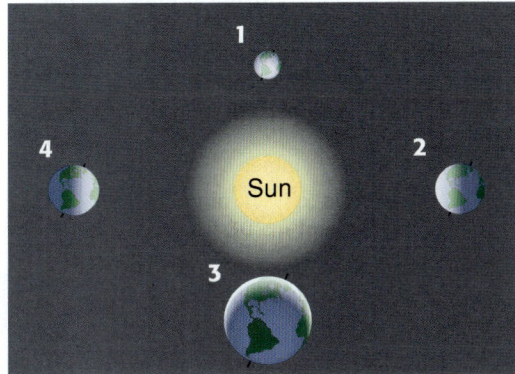

26. At what position, **1, 2, 3,** or **4**, is it spring in the Southern Hemisphere?

27. At what position does the South Pole receive almost 24 hours of daylight?

28. Explain what is happening in each climate zone in both the Northern Hemisphere and Southern Hemisphere at position **4**.

 Take a minute to review your answers to the Pre-Reading Questions found at the bottom of page 450. Have your answers changed? If necessary, revise your answers based on what you have learned since you began this chapter.

CRITICAL THINKING AND PROBLEM SOLVING

21. Warmer surface currents heat the surrounding air, and colder surface currents cool the surrounding air. A warm surface current might bring warmer temperatures to a cold area. A cold surface current might cool an area that is generally hot.

22. Answers will vary. Sample answer: A change in the Earth's orbit can affect the Earth's climates by limiting or increasing the amount of solar radiation the Earth receives.

23. The climate differs on each side of the Rocky Mountains because the mountains affect the distribution of precipitation. The windward side receives more precipitation because as the warm air is forced to rise, it releases precipitation. As the dry air crosses the mountain, it sinks, warming and absorbing the moisture.

24. Answers will vary.

MATH IN SCIENCE

25. 1 km = 1,000 m
1,000 m ÷ 10 m = 100
100 × .05°C = 5°C
24°C + 5°C = 29°C

INTERPRETING GRAPHICS

26. 3
27. 2
28. In the tropical zone temperatures are warm. The temperate zone in the Northern Hemisphere is experiencing summer. The temperate zone in the Southern Hemisphere is experiencing winter. Deciduous trees have shed their leaves. The polar zone in the Northern Hemisphere is experiencing almost 24 hours of daylight. Temperatures are cool, and the top meter of soil is thawing. The polar zone in the Southern Hemisphere is experiencing almost 24 hours of night. Temperatures are extremely cold, and the soil is frozen.

 Blackline masters of this Chapter Review can be found in the **Study Guide.**

ACROSS THE SCIENCES
Blame "The Child"

Background
Another pattern in the global weather system is called the *southern oscillation*. In 1924, the British mathematician Gilbert Walker described a see-saw pattern in tropical Pacific air pressure. He found that when air pressure is low around Australia, it is high to the east, in Tahiti. Conversely, when air pressure is high in Australia, it is low in Tahiti. This see-saw effect is called the southern oscillation.

By the 1970s, scientists realized that El Niño and the southern oscillation are part of a huge oceanic-atmospheric system that affects the weather in many parts of the world.

ACROSS THE SCIENCES

EARTH SCIENCE • LIFE SCIENCE

Blame "The Child"

El Niño, which is Spanish for "the child," is the name of a weather event that occurs in the Pacific Ocean. Every 2 to 12 years, the interaction between the ocean surface and atmospheric winds creates El Niño. This event influences weather patterns in many regions of the world.

Difficult Breathing
For Indonesia and Malaysia, El Niño meant droughts and forest fires in 1998. Thousands of people in these countries suffered from respiratory ailments from breathing the smoke caused by these fires. Heavy rains in San Francisco created extremely high mold-spore counts. These spores cause problems for people with allergies. The spore count in February in San Francisco is usually between 0 and 100. In 1998, the count was often higher than 8,000!

Rodent Invasion
In areas where El Niño creates heavy rains, the result is lush vegetation. This lush vegetation provides even more food and shelter for rodents. As the rodent population increases, so does the threat of the diseases they spread. In states like Arizona, Colorado, and New Mexico, this means there is a greater chance among humans of contracting hantaviral pulmonary syndrome (HPS).

HPS is carried by deer mice and remains in their urine and feces. People are infected when they inhale dust contaminated with mouse feces or urine. Once infected, a person experiences flulike symptoms that can sometimes lead to fatal kidney or lung disease.

More Rodents and Insects
Heavy rains near Los Angeles might encourage a rodent-population explosion in the mountains east of the city. If so, there could be an increase in the number of rodents infected with bubonic plague. More infected rodents means more infected fleas, which carry bubonic plague to humans.

Ticks and mosquitoes could also increase in number. These insects can spread disease too. For example, ticks can carry Lyme disease, ehrlichiosis, babesiosis, and Rocky Mountain spotted fever. Mosquitoes can spread malaria, dengue fever, encephalitis, and Rift Valley fever.

◀ *If this flea carries bubonic plague bacteria, just one bite can infect a person.*

What About Camping?
Because all of these diseases can be fatal to humans, people must take precautions. Camping in the great outdoors increases the risk of infection. Campers should steer clear of rodents and their burrows. Don't forget to dust family pets with flea powder, and don't let them roam free. Try to remember that an ounce of prevention is worth a pound of cure.

Find Out More
▶ How do you think El Niño affects the fish and mammals that live in the ocean? Write your answer in your ScienceLog, and then do some research to see if you are correct.

Answer to Find Out More
Answers will vary. Due to a shortage of phytoplankton, El Niño forces fish to find food in other areas. For example, mako sharks, which normally live in warm tropical waters, were found in the chilly waters of Monterey Bay, California. Birds such as pelicans might end up in areas that are far from their normal habitat. This was the case in Arica, Chile, in August 1997, when the number of local pelicans grew from 200 to 4,000 in just a few weeks. The population surge was believed to be caused by El Niño. If food is not available, El Niño can cause starvation among some species. The Galápagos penguin population, for example, decreased by 50 percent due to weather caused by El Niño and La Niña.

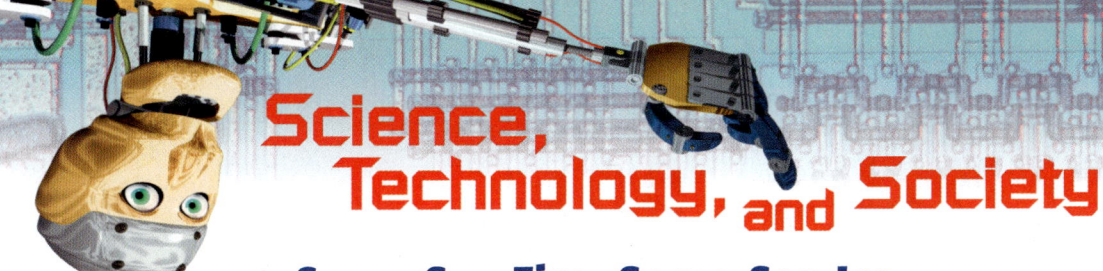

Science, Technology, and Society

Some Say Fire, Some Say Ice . . .

The Earth's climate has undergone many drastic changes. For example, 6,000 years ago in the part of North Africa that is now a desert, hippos, crocodiles, and early Stone Age people shared shallow lakes that covered the area. Grasslands stretched as far as the eye could see.

Scientists have known for many years that Earth's climate has changed. What they didn't know was why. Using supercomputers and complex computer programs, scientists may now be able to explain why North Africa's lakes and grasslands became a desert. And that information may be useful for predicting future heat waves and ice ages.

Climate Models

Scientists who study Earth's atmosphere have developed climate models to try to imitate Earth's climate. A climate model is like a very complicated recipe with thousands of ingredients. These models do not make exact predictions about future climates, but they do estimate what might happen.

What ingredients are included in a climate model? One important ingredient is the level of greenhouse gases (especially carbon dioxide) in the atmosphere. Land and ocean water temperatures from around the globe are other ingredients. So is information about clouds, cloud cover, snow, and ice cover. And in more recent models, scientists have included information about ocean currents.

A Challenge to Scientists

Earth's atmosphere-ocean climate system is extremely complex. One challenge for scientists is to understand all the system's parts. Another is to understand how those parts work together. But understanding Earth's climate system is critical. An accurate climate model should help scientists predict heat waves, floods, and droughts.

Even the best available climate models must be improved. The more information scientists can include in a climate model, the more accurate the results. Today data are available from more locations, and scientists need more-powerful computers to process all the data.

As more-powerful computers are developed to handle all the data in a climate model, scientists' understanding of Earth's climate changes will improve. This knowledge should help scientists better predict the impact human activities have on global climate. And these models could help scientists prevent some of the worst effects of climate change, such as global warming or another ice age.

▲ *This meteorologist is using a high-powered supercomputer to do climate modeling.*

A Challenge for You

▶ Earth's oceans are a major part of the climate model. Find out some of the ways oceans affect climate. Do you think human activities are changing the oceans?

UNIT 7

TIMELINE
Astronomy

In this unit, you will learn about the oldest of the sciences. Long before science was called science, people looked up at the night sky and tried to understand the meaning of the twinkling lights above. Early astronomers charted the stars and built calendars based on the movement of the moon and planets. Now the International Space Station is being built to further our exploration of the heavens. This timeline shows some of the events that have occurred throughout history as scientists have come to understand more about our planet's "neighborhood" in space.

1054
Chinese and Arabic astronomers record the appearance of a supernova—an exploding star. Strangely, no European observations of this event have ever been found.

1582
Ten days are dropped from October as the Julian calendar is replaced by the Gregorian calendar.

1977
Voyager 1 and *Voyager 2* are launched on missions to Jupiter, Saturn, and beyond. Now more than 10 trillion kilometers away from Earth, they are still sending back information about outer space.

1983
Sally Ride becomes the first American woman to travel in space.

1987
The year is shortened by one second to realign it with the Gregorian calendar.

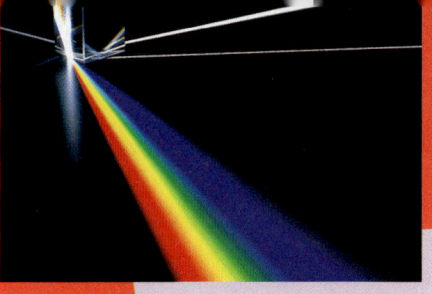

▶ 1665
Using a prism, Isaac Newton discovers that white light is composed of different colors.

▶ 1898
H. G. Wells's book *The War of the Worlds* is published.

◀ 1958
NASA, the National Aeronautics and Space Administration, is established to oversee the exploration of space.

◀ 1970
Apollo 13 is damaged shortly after leaving orbit. The spacecraft's three astronauts navigate around the moon in order to return safely to Earth.

1924
An astronomer named Edwin Hubble confirms the existence of other galaxies.

▶ 1998
John Glenn becomes the oldest human in space. His second trip into space comes 36 years after he became the first American to orbit the Earth.

▶ 1992
Astronomers discover the first planet outside the solar system.

2003
America celebrates the 100th anniversary of the Wright brothers' historic flight at Kitty Hawk, North Carolina.

Astronomy

479

Chapter Organizer

CHAPTER ORGANIZATION	TIME MINUTES	OBJECTIVES	LABS, INVESTIGATIONS, AND DEMONSTRATIONS
Chapter Opener pp. 480–481	45	National Standards: UCP 3, SAI 1, ST 1, 2, SPSP 5	**Start-Up Activity** Indoor Stargazing, p. 481
Section 1 Astronomy— The Original Science	45	▶ Identify the units of a calendar. ▶ Evaluate calendars from different ancient civilizations. ▶ Explain how our modern calendar developed. ▶ Summarize how astronomy began in ancient cultures and developed into a modern science. UCP 2, SAI 2, ST 2, SPSP 5, HNS 1–3, ES 3b, 3c; LabBook SAI 1, ST 1, ES 3b	**Design Your Own,** Create a Calendar, p. 706 GENERAL **Datasheets for LabBook,** Create a Calendar, Datasheet 39 GENERAL
Section 2 Mapping the Stars	90	▶ Describe constellations, and explain how astronomers use them. ▶ Explain how to measure altitude. ▶ Explain right ascension and declination. ▶ Evaluate the scale of the universe. UCP 3, SAI 1, ST 2, SPSP 5, HNS 1, ES 3d; LabBook UCP 2, SAI 1, HNS 1, ES 3b	**QuickLab,** Using a Sky Map, p. 490 GENERAL **Skill Builder,** The Sun's Yearly Trip Through the Zodiac, p. 708 GENERAL **Datasheets for LabBook,** The Sun's Yearly Trip Through the Zodiac, Datasheet 40 GENERAL **Inquiry Labs,** Constellation Prize, Lab 13 ADVANCED
Section 3 Telescopes— Then and Now	90	▶ Compare and contrast refracting telescopes with reflecting telescopes. ▶ Explain why the atmosphere is an obstacle to astronomers and how they overcome the obstacle. ▶ List the types of electromagnetic radiation, other than visible light, that astronomers use to study space. SAI 1, ST 2, SPSP 4, 5, HNS 1, 3; LabBook SAI 1, ST 1	**Demonstration,** Mystery of the Floating Penny, p. 497 in ATE GENERAL **Demonstration,** p. 498 in ATE BASIC **Skill Builder,** Through the Looking Glass, p. 710 GENERAL **Datasheets for LabBook,** Through the Looking Glass, Datasheet 41 GENERAL **Whiz-Bang Demonstrations,** Refraction Action, Demo 31 GENERAL **Long-Term Projects and Research Ideas,** Project 46 ADVANCED

*See page **T20** for a complete correlation of this book with the*

NATIONAL SCIENCE EDUCATION STANDARDS.

TECHNOLOGY RESOURCES

 Guided Reading Audio CD English or Spanish, Chapter 18

 One-Stop Planner CD-ROM with Test Generator

  **Science, Technology & Society,** Taking Earth's Pulse, Segment 21

Scientists in Action, Discovering a New Planet, Segment 24

Chapter 18 • Observing the Sky

Chapter 18 • Observing the Sky

CLASSROOM WORKSHEETS, TRANSPARENCIES, AND RESOURCES	SCIENCE INTEGRATION AND CONNECTIONS	REVIEW AND ASSESSMENT
Directed Reading Worksheet 18 BASIC **Science Puzzlers, Twisters & Teasers,** Worksheet 18 ADVANCED		
Directed Reading Worksheet 18, Section 1 BASIC **Reinforcement Worksheet 18,** Stella Star, Ace Reporter BASIC	**Cross-Disciplinary Focus,** p. 482 in ATE ADVANCED **Multicultural Connection,** pp. 483, 484, 485 in ATE **Real-World Connection,** p. 487 in ATE BASIC	**Homework,** p. 484 in ATE ADVANCED **Homework,** p. 486 in ATE ADVANCED **Self-Check,** p. 487 **Review,** p. 488 GENERAL **Quiz,** p. 488 in ATE GENERAL **Alternative Assessment,** p. 488 in ATE GENERAL
Directed Reading Worksheet 18, Section 2 BASIC **Transparency 180,** Spring Constellations in the Northern Hemisphere **Transparency 181,** Finding Stars in the Night Sky **Transparency 182,** Ascension and Declination Lines **Transparency 183,** Considering Scale in the Universe	**Cross-Disciplinary Focus,** p. 489 in ATE **Real-World Connection,** p. 491 in ATE **Multicultural Connection,** p. 491 in ATE **Physics Connection,** p. 493 **MathBreak,** Understanding Scale, p. 494 **Math and More,** p. 494 in ATE BASIC **Cross-Disciplinary Focus,** p. 494 in ATE **Science, Technology, and Society:** Planet or Star? p. 506 GENERAL	**Self-Check,** p. 490 **Homework,** p. 492 in ATE GENERAL **Review,** p. 495 GENERAL **Quiz,** p. 495 in ATE GENERAL **Alternative Assessment,** p. 495 in ATE GENERAL
Directed Reading Worksheet 18, Section 3 BASIC **Transparency 299,** How Your Eyes Work **Transparency 184,** Refracting Telescope **Transparency 184,** Reflecting Telescope **Critical Thinking Worksheet 18,** Through the Eyes of a Telescope ADVANCED **Transparency 185,** The Electromagnetic Spectrum	**Connect to Physical Science,** p. 496 in ATE **Math and More,** p. 498 in ATE GENERAL **Connect to Life Science,** p. 499 in ATE **Eye on the Environment:** Eyes on the Sky, p. 507 GENERAL	**Homework,** p. 497 in ATE BASIC **Homework,** p. 500 in ATE ADVANCED **Review,** p. 501 GENERAL **Quiz,** p. 501 in ATE GENERAL **Alternative Assessment,** p. 501 in ATE GENERAL

 Holt, Rinehart and Winston On-line Resources
go.hrw.com
For worksheets and other teaching aids related to this chapter, visit the HRW Web site and type in the keyword: **HSTOBS**

 **National Science Teachers Association**
www.scilinks.org
Encourage students to use the *sci*LINKS numbers listed in the internet connect boxes to access information and resources on the **NSTA** Web site.

END-OF-CHAPTER REVIEW AND ASSESSMENT

Chapter Review in Study Guide
Vocabulary and Notes in Study Guide
Chapter Tests with Performance-Based Assessment, Chapter 18 Test
Chapter Tests with Performance-Based Assessment, Performance-Based Assessment 18
Concept Mapping Transparency 18

Chapter 18 • Chapter Organizer 479B

Chapter Resources & Worksheets

Visual Resources

TEACHING TRANSPARENCIES

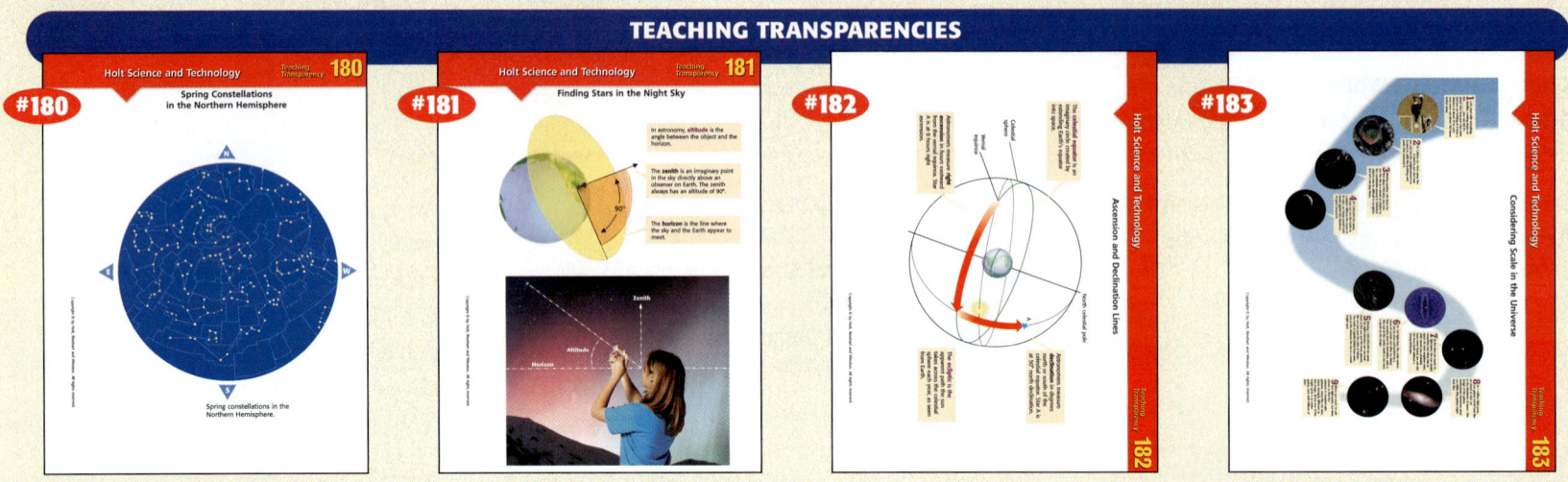

TEACHING TRANSPARENCIES

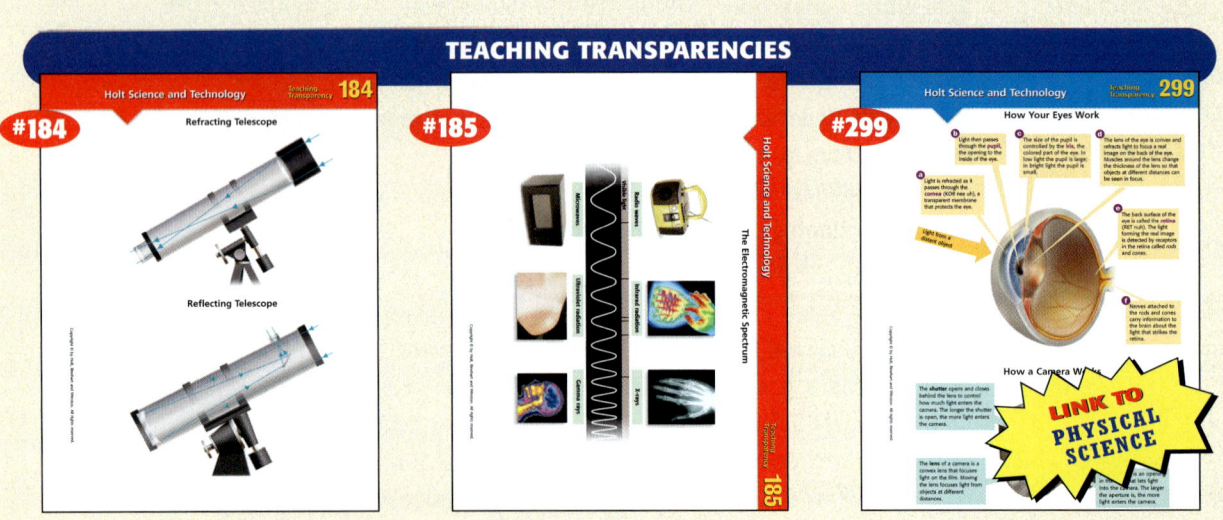

CONCEPT MAPPING TRANSPARENCY

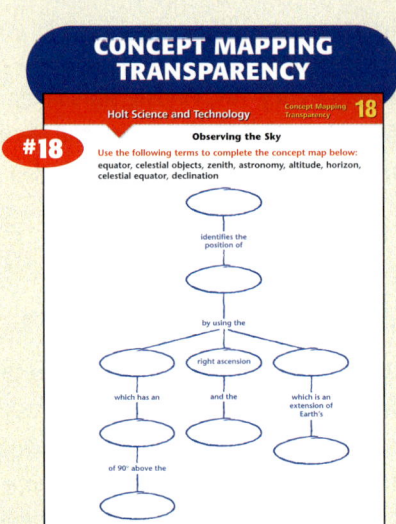

Meeting Individual Needs

DIRECTED READING

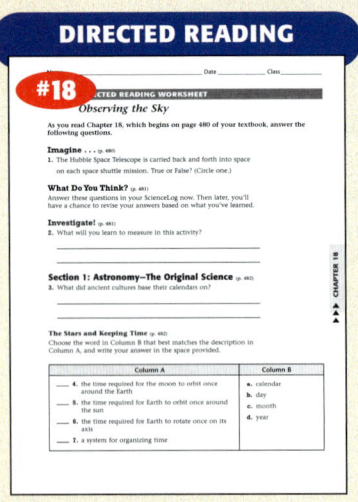

REINFORCEMENT & VOCABULARY REVIEW

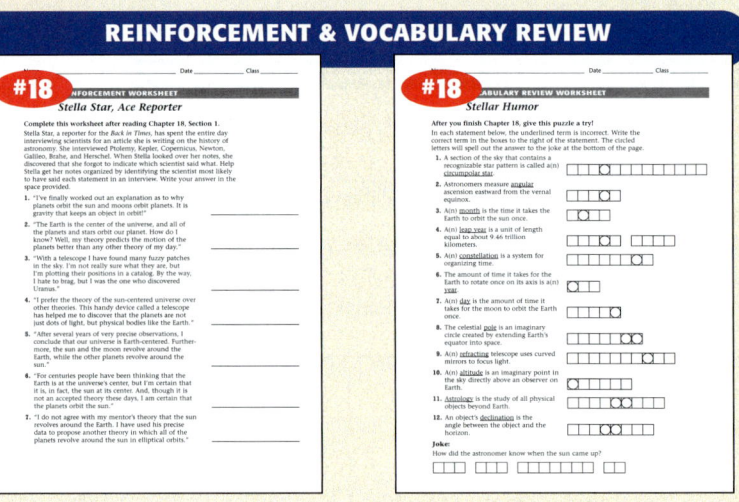

SCIENCE PUZZLERS, TWISTERS & TEASERS

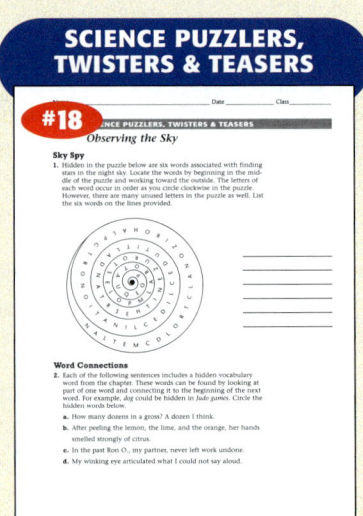

Chapter 18 • Observing the Sky

Chapter 18 • Observing the Sky

Review & Assessment

STUDY GUIDE

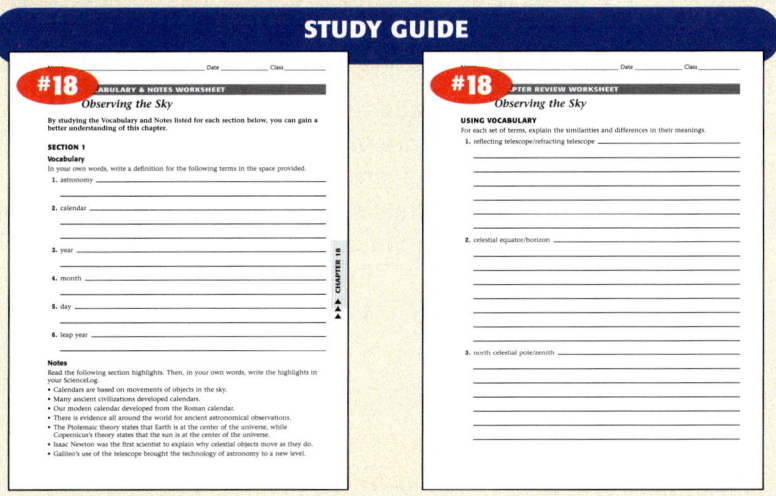

CHAPTER TESTS WITH PERFORMANCE-BASED ASSESSMENT

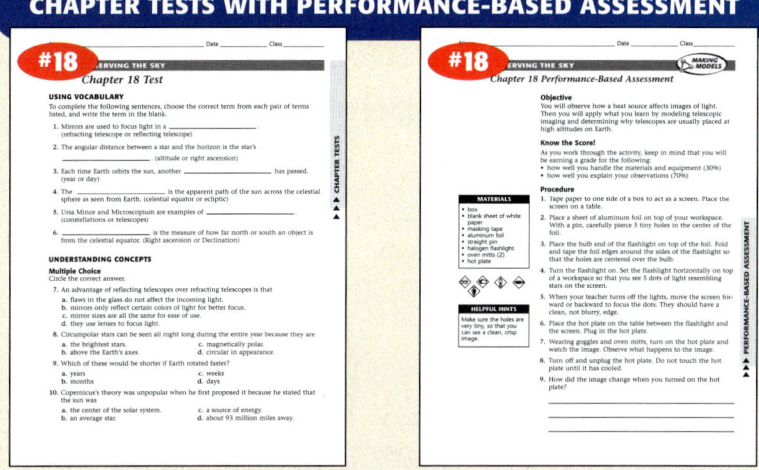

Lab Worksheets

INQUIRY LABS

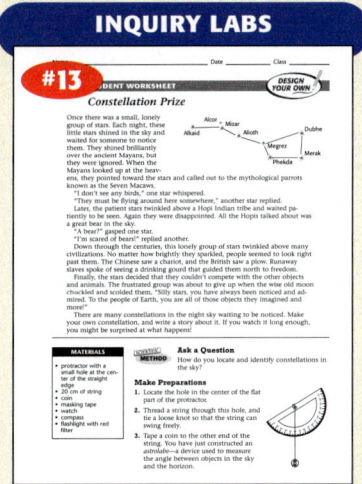

WHIZ-BANG DEMONSTRATIONS

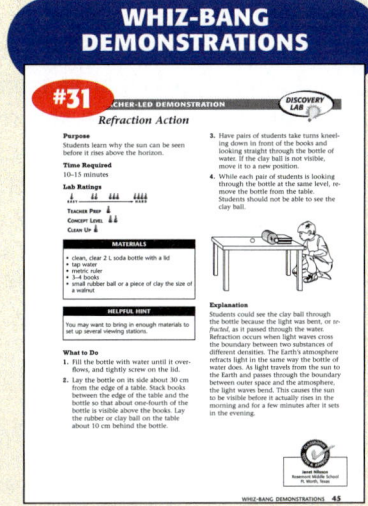

LONG-TERM PROJECTS & RESEARCH IDEAS

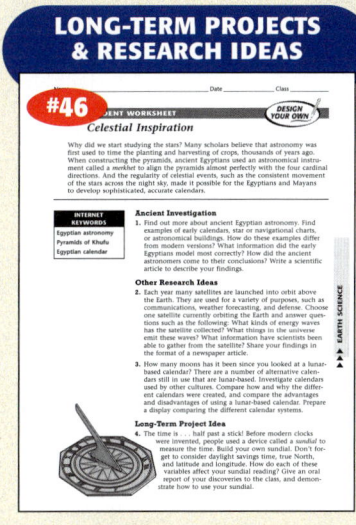

DATASHEETS FOR LABBOOK

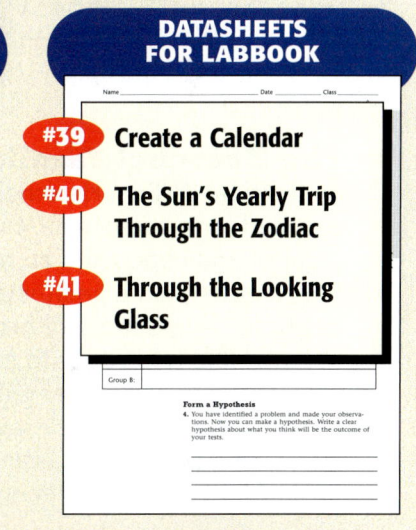

Applications & Extensions

CRITICAL THINKING & PROBLEM SOLVING

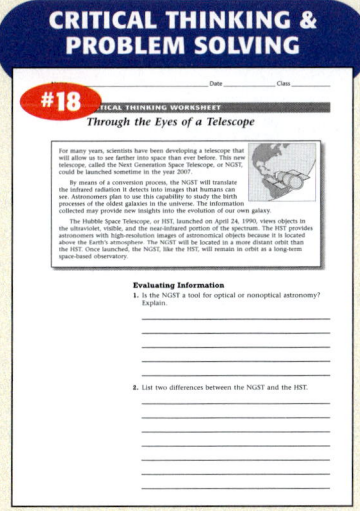

SCIENCE TECHNOLOGY

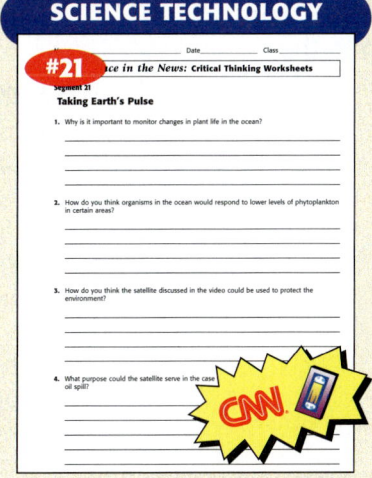

SCIENTISTS IN ACTION

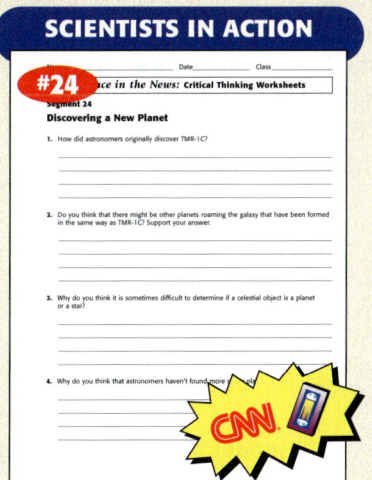

Chapter 18 • Chapter Resources & Worksheets

Chapter Background

SECTION 1

Astronomy—The Original Science

▶ **Maya Calendars**
The Maya of Central America used two calendars, a ceremonial calendar of 260 days and an astronomical calendar of 365 days, divided into 18 months of 20 days each. The Maya created an additional 5-day month for religious ceremony. These interlocking calendars enabled the Maya to predict when eclipses would occur and when Venus would rise.

▶ **The Herschel Family**
By the time William Herschel was 36, he seemed destined for a career as a musician. He was a gifted organist and conducted an orchestra in Bath, England. But Herschel had a great interest in stargazing, and he began to devote more of his time to astronomy. Finding the available telescopes to be inadequate, he set up his own forge and mirror-grinding shop to make large-mirror telescopes. His telescopes were of extremely high quality and power, surpassing even those used at the Royal Observatory, at Greenwich, at that time.

- Herschel was joined by his sister Caroline, and soon the two were conducting systematic telescopic surveys of the skies. In addition to discovering Uranus, Herschel developed new observational techniques; made important discoveries concerning nebulae, star clusters, and double stars; and contributed immeasurably to the cataloging of stars. Herschel's son John continued his father's study of double-star systems and cataloged stars in the Southern Hemisphere.

A model of Galileo's telescope

IS THAT A FACT!

◆ Caroline Herschel made many significant discoveries and is considered to be the first modern female astronomer. She discovered eight comets and three nebulae. In 1828, Britain's Astronomical Society awarded her a gold medal for her collaborations with her brother.

SECTION 2

Mapping the Stars

▶ **Sky Maps**
Some star maps show what the night sky looks like during a particular season in the Northern or Southern Hemisphere. These star maps are circular, and their edges represent the horizon. They are labeled with cardinal directions, and a + represents the zenith. Stars are represented by dots—the larger the dot is, the brighter the star is. To use the map, a stargazer should hold the map overhead and orient it according to the cardinal directions.

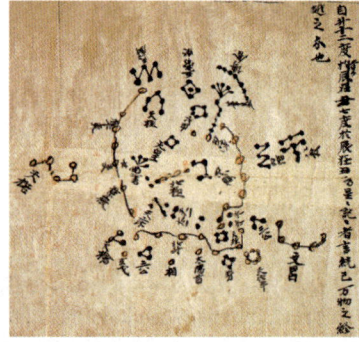

▶ **The Messier Catalog**
The Messier Catalog (1784) is one of the most well-known astronomical catalogs. It was compiled by French astronomer Charles Messier, whom King Louis XV dubbed the "comet ferret." Through the small telescopes available to Messier, comets looked like indistinct blotches. Many of Messier's blurred blotches weren't comets, however, but star clusters, nebulae, and galaxies. After he realized his mistake, Messier began to compile a catalog of these "noncomets" to spare other comet seekers the frustration he experienced.

Chapter 18 • Observing the Sky

IS THAT A FACT!

- Messier's catalog of more than 100 star clusters, nebulae, and galaxies is widely used today by amateur astronomers with small telescopes. The catalog numbers are still used by professional astronomers. The objects on his list, such as the Crab nebula and the Pleiades, retain their Messier designations, M1 and M45, respectively.

SECTION 3

Telescopes—Then and Now

▶ **Linking Radio Telescopes**

To improve image resolution and detect very faint emissions, international teams of astronomers sometimes link telescopes from opposite sides of the world. Recently, scientists have taken this technique a step further with the Very Long Baseline Interferometry (VLBI) Space Observatory Program. In this program, astronomers from around the world link their ground-based radio telescopes with a radio telescope that is orbiting the Earth. Each time the two telescopes link, they function as a single telescope with a width two and one-half times the diameter of the Earth! The VLBI technique has produced images of objects that are billions of light years away.

▶ **X-ray Telescopes**

X-ray telescopes, such as the one aboard the *Einstein Observatory* satellite (launched in 1978), have discovered double-star systems in which one of the stars has collapsed, becoming a neutron star or a black hole. The *Chandra X-ray Observatory* (launched in 1999) has made more detailed observations than any other X-ray telescope.

▶ **Charge Coupled Devices**

Modern professional astronomers who use optical telescopes rarely look through their telescopes. Instead, they view images on computer monitors. This is possible because most modern optical telescopes are equipped with a semiconductor device known as a charge coupled device (CCD), which converts the individual light particles (photons) from celestial objects into electrons. The electrons are detected, counted, and rendered as an image on a computer screen.

▶ **Gamma-ray Telescopes**

Gamma-ray telescopes are designed to detect gamma rays, which behave more like "bullets of energy" than waves. To detect this type of radiation, a gamma-ray telescope is equipped with a particle detector that collects data resulting from the collision of a gamma-ray photon with an atom. The data can be used to determine both the energy of the ray and the direction of the ray's source. The gamma-ray telescope aboard the *Compton Gamma-ray Observatory* satellite (launched in 1991) has detected objects known as gamma-ray bursters—brilliant, brief flashes of tremendous energy that last no more than a few minutes and then disappear.

IS THAT A FACT!

- The Hubble Space Telescope's resolution and sensitivity are so acute that it could detect the light from a firefly 16,000 km away!

For background information about teaching strategies and issues, refer to the *Professional Reference for Teachers*.

Observing the Sky

Pre-Reading Questions

Students may not know the answers to these questions before reading the chapter, so accept any reasonable response.

Suggested Answers

1. Constellations are sections of the sky that contain recognizable star patterns.
2. Some objects in the universe emit invisible radiation. Astronomers use non-optical telescopes, such as X-ray telescopes and radio telescopes, to observe objects they cannot see.

Directed Reading Worksheet 18

Science Puzzlers, Twisters & Teasers Worksheet 18

Guided Reading Audio CD
English or Spanish, Chapter 18

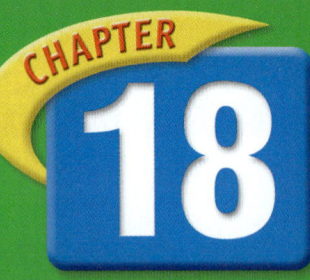

Observing the Sky

Sections

1. **Astronomy—The Original Science** 482
   Internet Connect 488
2. **Mapping the Stars** 489
   QuickLab 490
   Physics Connection .. 493
   MathBreak 494
   Internet Connect 495
3. **Telescopes—Then and Now** 496
   Internet Connect 501

Chapter Review 504
Feature Articles 506, 507
LabBook 706–711

1. What are constellations?
2. How do astronomers observe objects they cannot see?

Eyes to the Sky

This may look like an ordinary building to you, but inside is something that will make you see stars, and it's painless! In this building is the Harlan J. Smith Telescope (HJST). You can find it in one of the darkest places in America. The HJST is part of the McDonald Observatory located in the Davis Mountains of West Texas. Since the late 1960s, astronomers have used this telescope to view stars. In this chapter, you will learn about the different types of stars and how they evolve.

go.hrw.com
For worksheets and other teaching aids, visit the HRW Web site and type in the keyword: **HSTOBS**

www.scilinks.com
Use the *sci*LINKS numbers at the end of each chapter for additional resources on the **NSTA** Web site.

www.cnnfyi.com
Visit the CNN Web site for current events coverage and classroom resources.

START-UP Activity

INDOOR STARGAZING

In this activity, you will measure an object's altitude using a simple instrument called an astrolabe (AS troh LAYB).

Procedure

1. Attach one end of a 12 cm long **piece of string** to the center of the straight edge of a **protractor** with tape. Attach a **paper clip** to the other end of the string.

2. Tape a **soda straw** lengthwise along the straight edge of the protractor. Your astrolabe is complete!

3. Hold the astrolabe in front of your face so you can look along the straw with one eye. The curve of the astrolabe should be pointed toward the floor.

4. Looking along the straw, use your astrolabe to sight one corner of the ceiling.

5. Pinch the string between your thumb and the protractor. Count the number of degrees between the string and the 90° marker on the protractor. This angle is the altitude of the corner. Record this measurement in your ScienceLog.

Analysis

6. How does this activity relate to observing objects in the sky? Explain how you would find the altitude of a star.

START-UP Activity

INDOOR STARGAZING

MATERIALS

For Each Group:
- piece of string (12 cm long)
- protractor
- tape
- paper clip
- soda straw

Teacher's Notes

Have students take more measurements of the corner of the room from different locations. Why did their measurements differ? (The altitude depends on the location of the observer.)

The angle between the string and the 90° marker should fall between 20° and 50°.

Answer to START-UP Activity

6. Answers will vary. Students should note that the astrolabe is an instrument that can also be used to locate objects in the sky, such as stars. Students should also note that it is possible to measure the angle between the horizon and an object in the sky. Students could use the astrolabe they made to measure the altitude of a star.

Chapter 18 • Observing the Sky

SECTION 1

Focus

Astronomy—The Original Science

In this section, students will learn that the units of a calendar are based on the movements of the sun and moon. Students will learn how different cultures based their calendars on different interpretations of astronomical observations. The section then follows the historical development of the calendar we use today. Students will explore the changing science of astronomy from 7,000 years ago through the European Renaissance and up to present times.

Bellringer

Have students suppose that they need to explain the concepts of a *year,* a *month,* and a *day* to a small child. For each concept, have students illustrate the motion of the Earth, moon, and sun. Students should write a caption describing each illustration. **Sheltered English**

1) Motivate

ACTIVITY

Many ancient astronomers attempted to predict and explain eclipses. Even though the ancient Greeks explained how they occur, eclipses were still considered bad portents until the nineteenth century. To help students understand how our relatively small moon can eclipse the sun, have them form small groups and give them a marble and a basketball. The basketball represents the sun and the marble represents the moon. Challenge them to simulate a solar eclipse using the two spheres.

Section 1

Terms to Learn

astronomy   month
calendar   day
year   leap year

What You'll Do

- Identify the units of a calendar.
- Evaluate calendars from different ancient civilizations.
- Explain how our modern calendar developed.
- Summarize how astronomy began in ancient cultures and developed into a modern science.

CROSS-DISCIPLINARY FOCUS

Social Studies Although many societies base their calendars on the movements of the sun or the moon, a calendar's starting date is often linked to cultural or religious traditions. For example, both the Muslim and the Hebrew calendars are based on the phases of the moon, but they differ in a number of significant ways. Have interested students research a calendar used by another culture and find out the cultural significance of that calendar's starting date, the number of days per month, and the number of days per year. Have students give a class presentation about the calendar they studied.

Astronomy—The Original Science

Astronomy is the study of all physical objects beyond Earth. Before astronomy became a science, people in ancient cultures used the seasonal cycles of celestial objects to make calendars and organize their lives. Over time, some people began to observe the sky for less practical reasons—mainly to understand Earth's place in the universe. Today, astronomers all over the world are using new technologies to better understand the universe.

The Stars and Keeping Time

Most ancient cultures probably did not fully understand how celestial objects in our solar system move in relation to each other. However, they did learn the seasonal movements of these objects as they appeared in the Earth's sky and based their calendars on these cycles. People in ancient cultures gradually learned to depend on calendars to keep track of time. For example, by observing the yearly cycle of the sun's movement among the stars, early farmers learned the best times of year to plant and harvest various foods.

After learning the seasonal cycles of celestial objects many civilizations made calendars. One such calendar is shown in **Figure 1**. A **calendar** is a system for organizing time. Most calendars organize time within a single unit called a year. A **year** is the time required for the Earth to orbit the sun once. Within a year are smaller units of time called months. A **month** is roughly the amount of time required for the moon to orbit the Earth once. Within a month are even smaller units of time called days. A **day** is the time required for the Earth to rotate once on its axis.

Ancient Calendars Ancient cultures based their calendars on different observations of the sky. Examine **Figure 2** at the top of the next page to see how different cultures around the world used objects in the sky differently to keep track of time.

Figure 1 *This stone is a calendar used by the Aztecs in pre-colonial America.*

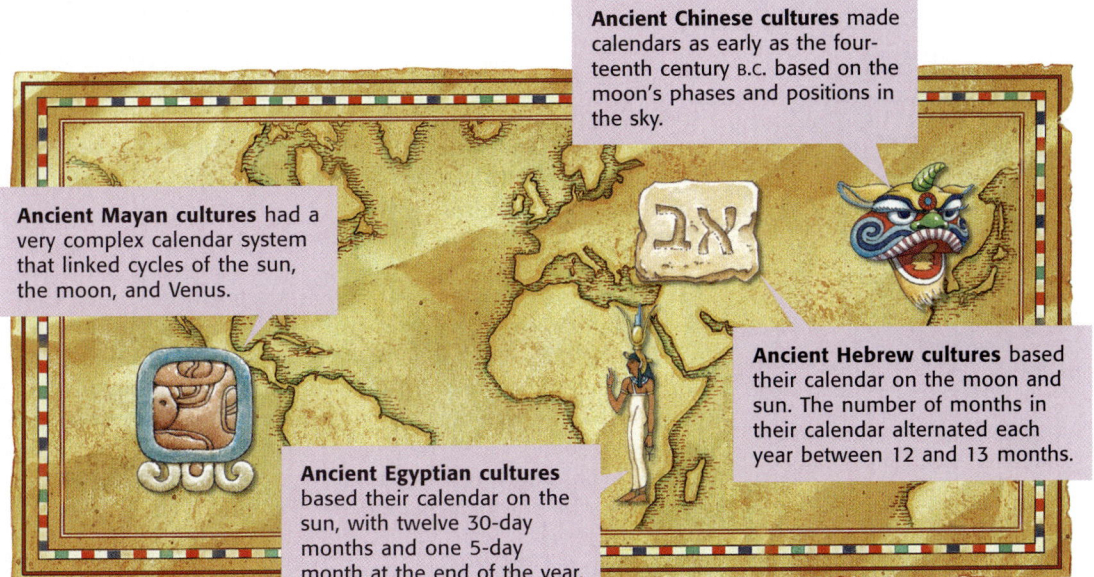

Figure 2 People in ancient cultures based their calendars on different kinds of celestial cycles.

Toward a Modern Calendar The early Roman calendar had exactly 365 days in a year and 7 days in a week. The calendar worked well at first, but gradually the seasons shifted away from their original positions in the year.

It was then determined that there are actually about 365.25 days in a year. To correct this, Julius Caesar created the *Julian calendar*. He began by adding 90 days to the year 46 B.C., which put the seasons back to their original positions. He then added an extra day every 4 years to keep them from shifting again. A year in which an extra day is added to the calendar is called a **leap year**.

In the mid-1500s, people noticed that the Julian calendar was incorrect. Pope Gregory XIII presented this problem to a group of astronomers who determined that there are actually 365.242 days in a year. To solve the problem, a new calendar—the *Gregorian calendar*—was created. The Pope dropped 10 days from the year 1582 and restricted leap years to years that are divisible by 4 but not by 100 (except for years that are divisible by 400). This lowered the number of leap years that occur and made the average length of 1 year closer to 365.242 days. Today most countries use the Gregorian calendar, which scientists calculate will be accurate for another 3,000 years.

Julius Caesar and Pope Gregory XIII aren't the only ones who can decide when to have leap years—you can too! In fact, you can make your own calendar! Turn to page 706 in the LabBook to find out how.

IS THAT A FACT!

Even though the Gregorian calendar was adopted by many countries in 1582, England and its American colonies continued to recognize March 25 as the first day of the year until 1752. In other words, March 24, 1700, was followed by March 25, 1701!

The lunar calendar of the Natchez peoples of the Mississippi River Valley reflected the seasonal rhythms of their culture. The names of the months in their calendar—strawberry month, peach month, maize month, turkey month, and chestnut month—reflect the hunter-gatherer nature of their society. Ask students if they can identify the time period that corresponds to each Natchez month.
Sheltered English

RESEARCH

The ancient Egyptians developed a calendar to help them predict when the Nile River would flood and when they could plant crops. The Egyptians structured their calendar around Sirius, the brightest star in the night sky. Based on the rising of Sirius at dawn, the Egyptians calculated that the year is 365 days long. Have interested students research stories about Sirius from Egyptian mythology and find out more about Egyptian astronomy.

Section 1 • Astronomy—The Original Science

2 Teach, continued

MEETING INDIVIDUAL NEEDS

Advanced Learners There are many theories about why Stonehenge was built. One theory proposes that the great circle of standing stones served as a calendar; another theory argues that it was an observatory for charting the movements of the sun and stars. Perhaps it served both purposes. Invite students to investigate some of the theories about the astronomical significance of Stonehenge. Suggest that students include a diagram in their report that shows how archaeologists think Stonehenge originally looked and how the sun's movement could be tracked by this structure.

Homework

Making Models Ask students to research one of the ancient astronomical sites mentioned in this section and build a scale model of it. Additional sites of interest include the Big Horn Medicine Wheel in Wyoming, the Pyramid of Khufu in Giza, Egypt, or the Anasazi Sun Dagger in Chaco Canyon, New Mexico. Have students share their model with the class and explain the significance of the site. Students may wish to use a flashlight to demonstrate how the structures marked the path of the sun and moon. As an extension, students could create their own sundial or design their own structure to track the movements of the sun.

Early Observers—The Beginnings of Astronomy

Scientists have found evidence for ancient astronomical activities all over the world. Some records are more complete than others. However, they all show that early humans recognized the cycles of celestial objects in the sky.

Nabta The earliest record of astronomical observations is a 6,000 to 7,000-year-old group of stones near Nabta, in southern Egypt. Some of the stones are positioned such that they would have lined up with the sun during the summer solstice 6,000 years ago. The *summer solstice* occurs on the longest day of the year. Artifacts found at the site near Nabta suggest that it was created by African cattle herders. These people probably used the site for many purposes, including trade, social bonding, and ritual. **Figure 3** shows some of the stones at the site near Nabta.

Figure 3 Some stones are still standing at the site near Nabta, in the Sahara Desert.

Stonehenge Another ancient site that was probably used to make observations of the sky is Stonehenge, near Salisbury, England. Stonehenge, shown in **Figure 4,** is a group of stones arranged primarily in circles. Some of the stones are aligned with the sunrise during the summer and winter solstices. People have offered many explanations for the purpose of Stonehenge as well as for who built and used it. Careful studies of the site reveal that it was built over a period of about 1,500 years, from about 3000 B.C. to about 1500 B.C. Most likely, Stonehenge was used as a place for ceremony and ritual. But the complete truth about Stonehenge is still a mystery.

Figure 4 Although its creators have long since gone, Stonehenge continues to indicate the summer and winter solstices each year.

The Babylonians The ancient civilization of Babylon was the heart of a major empire located in present-day Iraq. From about 700 B.C. to about A.D. 50, the Babylonians precisely tracked the positions of planets and the moon. They became skilled at forecasting the movements of these celestial bodies, which enabled them to make an accurate calendar.

Multicultural CONNECTION

One Chinese myth about solar eclipses describes hungry dragons that periodically raid the sky and take bites out of the sun! During solar eclipses, Chinese warriors would beat drums and gongs and shoot arrows into the sky to kill the dragons. The job of Chinese astronomers was to predict when the dragons would become hungry so that warriors could be prepared to save the sun from being completely devoured. Encourage student groups to find out about the mythology of solar eclipses in other cultures. Students may wish to perform these myths as skits for the class.

Ancient Chinese Cultures

As early as 1000 B.C., ancient Chinese cultures could predict eclipses. *Eclipses* occur when the sun, the moon, and the Earth line up in space. The Chinese had also named 800 stars by 350 B.C. The Chinese skillfully tracked and predicted the same motions in the sky as the civilizations that influenced Western astronomy. The Chinese continued to improve their knowledge of the sky at the same time as many other civilizations, as shown in **Figure 5.**

The Ancient Greeks

Like many other civilizations, the ancient Greeks learned to observe the sky to keep track of time. But the Greeks also took a giant leap forward in making astronomy a science. Greek philosophers tried to understand the place of Earth and humans in the universe. Their tools were logic and mathematics, especially geometry. One of the most famous Greek philosophers, Aristotle (ER is TAHT'L), successfully explained the phases of the moon and eclipses. He also correctly argued that the Earth is a sphere—an idea that was not very popular in his time.

Native Americans

Archaeological records show that many of the pre-colonial civilizations in the Americas were skilled in observing the sky. Perhaps the most highly-skilled observers were the Maya, who flourished in the present-day Yucatan about 1,000 years ago. The Maya had complex systems of mathematics and astronomy. Many Mayan buildings, such as the one in **Figure 6,** are aligned with celestial bodies during certain astronomical events.

The Ancient Arabs

After Greek, Roman, and early Christian civilizations weakened, the ancient Arabs inherited much of the Greeks' knowledge of astronomy. The Arabs continued to develop astronomy as a science while Europe fell into the Dark Ages. Today many stars have Arabic names. The Arabs also invented the astrolabe, algebra, and the number system that we use today.

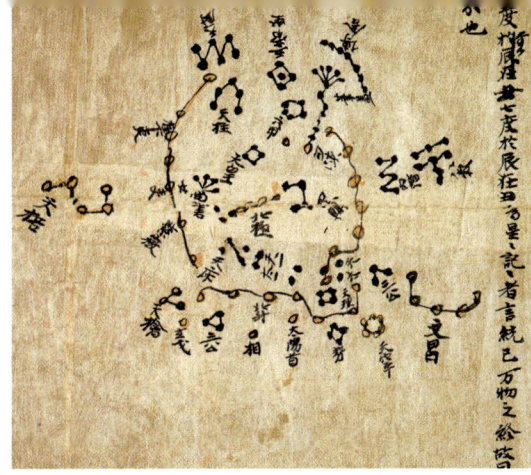

Figure 5 *This ancient Chinese manuscript is the world's oldest existing portable star map. It is more than 1,000 years old.*

Figure 6 *This Mayan building is the Caracol at Chichén Itzá, in the Yucatán. Many parts of the building align with Venus and the sun on certain days.*

Multicultural CONNECTION

Modern astronomy had its beginnings in Arabic and Greek culture. Have students research the following star names and describe their origin:

Betelgeuse, Alnitak, Rigel, Aldebaran, Castor, and Pollux

Ask them to find out the origin and meaning of each star's name and the name's significance. Encourage students to record any other interesting information they find about the stars. (The name *Betelgeuse* is Arabic and means "the armpit of the giant." It refers to the fact that the star marks the general area of the constellation Orion's shoulder. *Alnitak* is Arabic for "belt" and is one of the stars in Orion's belt. *Rigel* is derived from the Arabic words for "left leg of the giant" and marks Orion's left leg or foot. *Aldebaran* means "follower" in Arabic. It appears to follow the star cluster Pleiades across the sky. The names *Castor* and *Pollux* come from Greek mythology; these twin stars form the heads of the twins in the constellation Gemini.)

TOPIC: Early Theories in Astronomy
GO TO: www.scilinks.org
*sci*LINKS NUMBER: HSTE435

SCIENCE HUMOR

Q: Why doesn't the sun have long hair?

A: Eclipse it regularly.

2) Teach, continued

DISCUSSION

The Scientific Mind Johannes Kepler spent much of his life seeking an explanation for the orbits of the planets. A humble man, he often wrote about himself in the third person and was highly self-critical. He once wrote that "that man [Kepler] has in every way a doglike nature. In this man there are two opposite tendencies: always to regret any wasted time and always to waste it willingly." In his writings, Kepler also revealed his inquisitive nature: "He was constantly on the move, ferreting among the sciences, politics, and private affairs . . . he explored various fields of mathematics, as if he were the first man to do so, which later on he found to have already been discovered. He argued with men of every profession for the profit of his mind." Discuss with students what the quotations reveal about Kepler's personality and way of thinking. Have students consider how Kepler's persistence, self-criticism, and open-mindedness may have contributed to his discovery of the laws of planetary motion.

Homework

Research Have students find out why many people were reluctant to accept Copernicus's theory about a sun-centered universe. Have them summarize their findings in a one-page report.

The Who's Who of Early Astronomy

The science of astronomy has come a long way since the early days. The earliest astronomers had no history to learn from—almost everything they knew about the universe came from what they could discover with their own eyes and minds. Not surprisingly, most early astronomers thought that the universe consisted of the sun, moon, and planets, with all the stars occupying the edge of the universe. While they could not have known that our solar system is a very small part of a much larger universe, they had to start somewhere.

Ptolemy In A.D. 140, a Greek astronomer named Claudius Ptolemy (KLAW dee uhs TAHL uh mee) wrote a book that combined all the ancient knowledge of astronomy that he could find. Ptolemy expanded Aristotle's theories with careful mathematical calculations in what was called the *Ptolemaic theory*. As shown in **Figure 7**, Ptolemy thought that the Earth is at the center of the universe—with the sun and the other planets revolving around the Earth.

Even though it was incorrect, the Ptolemaic theory predicted the motions of the planets better than any known method at that time. For more than 1,500 years in Europe, the Ptolemaic theory was the most popular theory for the structure of the universe.

Figure 7 *According to the Ptolemaic theory, the Earth is at the center of the universe.*

Copernicus In 1543, a Polish astronomer named Nicolaus Copernicus (NIK uh LAY uhs koh PUHR ni kuhs) published a new theory that would eventually revolutionize astronomy. According to his theory, which is shown in **Figure 8**, the sun is at the center of the universe and the planets—including the Earth—orbit the sun. While Copernicus was correct about all the planets orbiting the sun, his theory did not immediately replace Ptolemy's theory.

Figure 8 *According to Copernicus's theory, the sun is at the center of the universe.*

Q: What did Copernicus say about Ptolemy's theory of an Earth-centered universe?

A: Ptolemy another one!

Tycho Brahe Danish astronomer Tycho Brahe (TIE koh BRAW uh) used several large tools, such as the one shown in **Figure 9,** to observe the sky. Tycho favored an Earth-centered theory that was different from Ptolemy's. Tycho believed that the other planets revolve around the sun but that the sun and the moon revolve around the Earth. While Tycho's theory was not correct, he did record very precise observations of the planets and stars for several years.

Johannes Kepler After Tycho died, his assistant, Johannes Kepler, continued Tycho's work. Kepler did not agree with Tycho's theory, but he recognized how precise and valuable Tycho's data were. In 1609, after analyzing the data, Kepler announced some new laws of planetary motion. Kepler stated that all the planets revolve around the sun in elliptical orbits and that the sun is not in the exact center of the orbits.

Figure 9 Tycho used the mural quadrant, which is a large quarter-circle on a wall, to measure the positions of stars and planets.

Galileo Galilei In 1609, Galileo became the first person to use a telescope to observe celestial bodies. His telescope is shown in **Figure 10.** Galileo discovered four moons orbiting Jupiter, craters and mountains on the moon, sunspots on the sun, and phases of Venus. These discoveries showed that the planets are not just dots of light—they are physical bodies like the Earth. Galileo favored Copernicus's theory over Ptolemy's.

Figure 10 Galileo's telescope is much simpler than those used by astronomers today.

Isaac Newton Finally, in 1687 a scientist named Sir Isaac Newton explained *why* planets orbit the sun and why moons orbit planets. Newton explained that the force that keeps all of these objects in their orbit is the same one that holds us on the Earth—gravity. Newton's laws of motion and gravitation completed the work of Copernicus, Tycho, Kepler, and Galileo.

Self-Check

Name two astronomers who favored an Earth-centered universe and two astronomers who favored a sun-centered universe. *(See page 726 to check your answer.)*

SCIENTISTS AT ODDS

Tycho Brahe was eccentric and contrary. As a young man, he insulted a fellow student and was challenged to a duel. During the duel, part of his nose was sliced off, and for the rest of his life he wore a metal nose prosthesis. Brahe was also a notoriously bad landlord who cheated and abused the peasants who worked for him. Given his bad temperament, it's not surprising that Brahe withheld vital information from his assistant Johannes Kepler. Kepler gained full access to Brahe's observations after Brahe's death and used them to prove that the planets revolve in elliptical orbits around the sun.

Modern Astronomy

With Galileo's successful use of the telescope and Newton's discoveries about planetary motion, astronomy began to become the modern science that it is today. Gradually, people began to think of stars as more than dots of light at the edge of the universe.

From Fuzzy Patches to an Expanding Universe William Herschel, who discovered Uranus in 1781, used a telescope to study the stars in our galaxy. As he studied these stars, he found small, fuzzy patches in the sky. Herschel did not know what these patches were, but he did record their positions in a catalog.

The invention of photography in the 1800s allowed astronomers to make even better observations of the sky. In 1923, Edwin Hubble used photography to discover that some of the patches Herschel had found are actually other galaxies beyond our own. Before this discovery, scientists thought that the Milky Way galaxy was the entire universe! Hubble also discovered that the universe is expanding. In other words, distant objects in space are moving farther and farther away from each other.

Figure 11 Today computers and telescopes are linked together. Computers not only control telescopes, but they also process the information gathered by the telescopes so that astronomers may better analyze it.

Larger and Better Telescopes Today astronomers still gaze at the sky, trying to assign order to the universe. Larger and better telescopes on Earth and in space, supercomputers, spacecraft, and new models of the universe allow us to study objects both near and far. Many questions about the universe have been answered, but our studies continue to bring new questions to investigate.

internet connect

SCLINKS NSTA
TOPIC: The Stars and Keeping Time, Early Theories in Astronomy
GO TO: www.scilinks.org
sciLINKS NUMBER: HSTE430, HSTE435

REVIEW

1. Which ancient civilization's calendar gave rise to our modern calendar?
2. What advantage did Galileo have over the astronomers that went before him, and how did it help him?
3. **Analyzing Relationships** Is Copernicus's theory completely correct? Why or why not? How does his theory relate to what we know today about the sun's position in our solar system and in the universe?

Section 2
Mapping the Stars

Terms to Learn

constellation
altitude
right ascension
declination
celestial equator
ecliptic
light-year

What You'll Do

- Describe constellations and explain how astronomers use them.
- Explain how to measure altitude.
- Explain right ascension and declination.
- Evaluate the scale of the universe.

Ancient cultures organized the sky by linking stars together in patterns. These patterns reflected the culture's beliefs and legends. Different civilizations often gave the stars names that indicated the stars' positions in their pattern. Today we can see the same star patterns that people in ancient cultures saw. Modern astronomers still use many of the names given to stars centuries ago.

Astronomers can now describe a star's location with precise numbers. These advances have led to a better understanding of just how far away stars are and how big the universe is.

Constellations

When people in ancient cultures linked stars in a section of the sky into a pattern, they named that section of the sky according to the pattern. **Constellations** are sections of the sky that contain recognizable star patterns. Many cultures organized the sky into constellations that honored their gods or reflected objects in their daily lives. Constellations helped people organize the sky and track the apparent motions of planets and stars.

In the Eye of the Beholder . . . Different civilizations had different names for the same constellations. For example, where the Greeks saw a hunter (Orion) in the northern sky, the Japanese saw a drum (*tsuzumi*), as shown in **Figure 12.** Today different cultures still interpret the sky differently.

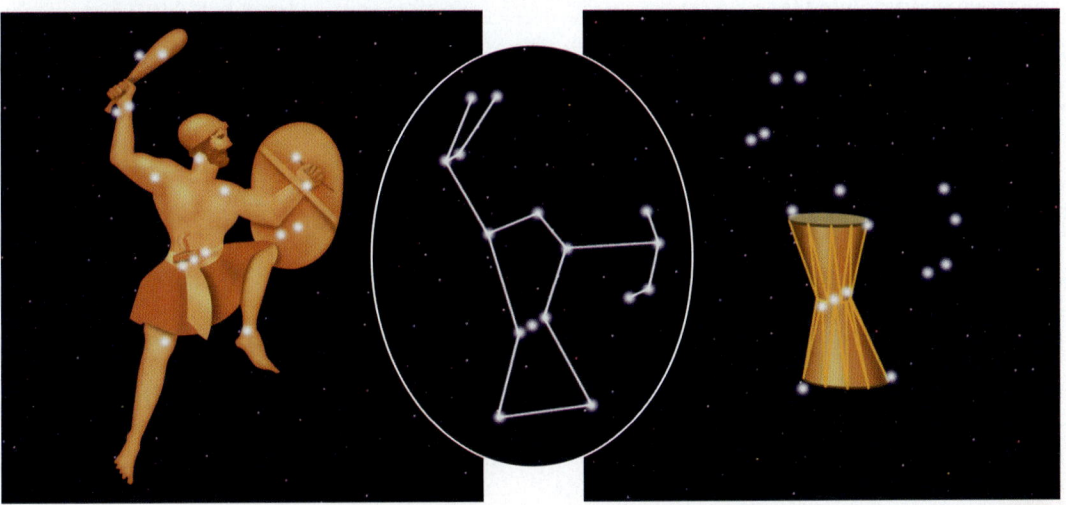

Figure 12 The drawing at left shows that the ancient Greeks saw Orion as a hunter. The drawing at right shows that the Japanese saw the same set of stars as a drum.

2 Teach

Answer to Self-Check

No, the object is within the boundaries of the constellation.

GROUP ACTIVITY

Classroom Planetarium
Divide the class into groups of four. Assign each group a different season, and have the groups locate a sky map for that time of year. Have students copy the map with tracing paper, marking the stars that form constellations and any other celestial objects. Then have groups place a sheet of aluminum foil over a piece of cardboard and tape the tracing paper on top. Have students use a pencil to carefully poke small holes through the tracing paper and aluminum. Students can create larger holes to show planets and other bright objects. After students remove the tracing paper, have them locate the constellations and prepare a guided tour of the night sky in their season. To begin the tour, place the aluminum-foil transparencies on an overhead projector in a darkened room. Be sure to cover the top of the projector completely. As groups give their tours, they can highlight individual constellations by using a piece of colored cellophane.

Safety Caution: Be sure to periodically check the projector for overheating.

Answer to QuickLab

3. The directions are reversed because sky maps are made to be looked at upside down.

Teaching Transparency 180
"Spring Constellations in the Northern Hemisphere"

Self-Check

If a celestial object is said to be "in the constellation of Ursa Minor," does it have to be a part of the stick figure that makes up that constellation? Explain. (See page 726 to check your answer.)

QuickLab

Using a Sky Map

1. Hold your **textbook** over your head with the cover facing upward. Turn the book so that the direction at the bottom of the sky map is the same as the direction you are facing.
2. Notice the location of the constellations in relation to one another.
3. If you look up at the **sky** at night in the spring, you should see the stars positioned as they are on your map.
4. Why are E and W on sky maps the reverse of how they appear on land maps?

MISCONCEPTION ALERT

Students may think that the constellations have always looked the same from Earth. Point out that our solar system and the stars in our galaxy are moving at different speeds as they revolve around the Milky Way. In addition, because the stars are at varying distances from the Earth, they appear to move in the sky at different speeds, a phenomenon known as parallax. Thus, a hundred thousand years ago, the constellations looked much different than they do today.

Regions of the Sky When you think of constellations, you probably think of the stick figures made by connecting bright stars with imaginary lines. To an astronomer, however, a constellation is something more. As you can see in **Figure 13** below, a constellation is an entire region of the sky. Each constellation shares a border with its neighboring constellations. For example, in the same way that the state of Texas is a region of the United States, Ursa Major is a region of the sky. Every star or galaxy in the sky is located within a constellation. Modern astronomers divide the sky into 88 constellations. Around the world, astronomers use the same names for these constellations to make communication easier.

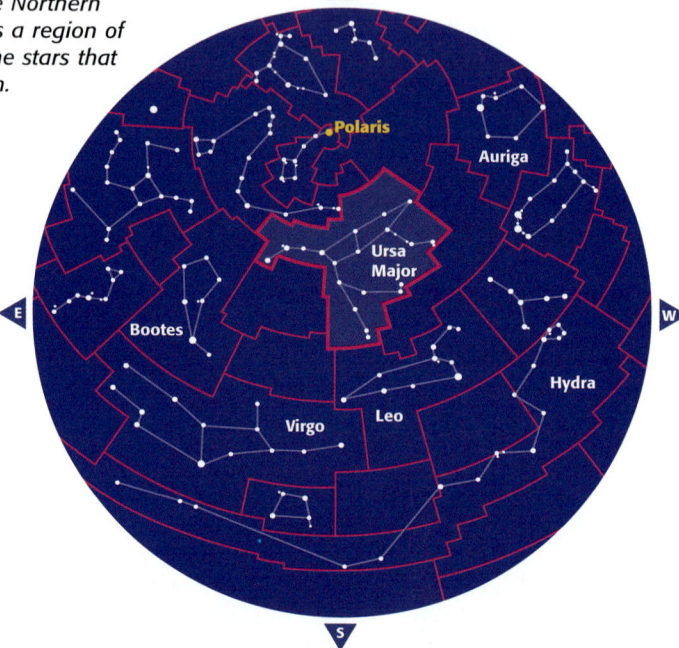

Figure 13 This sky map shows some of the constellations in the Northern Hemisphere. Ursa Major is a region of the sky that includes all the stars that make up that constellation.

Seasonal Changes As we go around the sun each year, the constellations change from season to season. This is one reason that people in ancient cultures were able to keep track of the right time of year to plant and harvest their crops. Notice that the sky map in Figure 13 shows the night sky as seen from the Northern Hemisphere in the spring. This map would not be accurate for the other three seasons. Sky maps for summer, fall, and winter are in the Appendix of this book.

490   Chapter 18 • Observing the Sky

Finding Stars in the Night Sky

You can use what you learned in the Investigate to make your own observations of the sky. Have you ever tried to show another person a star or planet by pointing to it—only to have them miss what you were seeing? With just a few new references, as shown in **Figure 14**, you can tell them exactly where it is. **Figure 15** shows how you can use the astrolabe from the Investigate to make such measurements.

In astronomy, **altitude** is the angle between the object and the horizon.

The **zenith** is an imaginary point in the sky directly above an observer on Earth. The zenith always has an altitude of 90°.

The **horizon** is the line where the sky and the Earth appear to meet.

Figure 14 Altitude, zenith, and horizon are important concepts to know when describing the locations of celestial objects.

Figure 15 With an astrolabe, you can measure the altitude of a star by measuring the angle between your horizon and the star. The altitude of any celestial object depends on where you are and when you look.

ACTIVITY
Tell students that a watch with an hour hand can be used to tell direction during the daytime. Have students hold a watch horizontally with the hour hand pointing directly at the sun. If they halve the distance between the hour hand and the 12 with a toothpick, the toothpick will be pointing south. Ask students how they would adapt this method to work in the Southern hemisphere.

REAL-WORLD CONNECTION
Amateur astronomers can measure the sky with their hands. If you hold your arm extended and make a fist that begins at the horizon, you can gauge roughly 10°. If you open your hand and line up your little finger with the horizon, you have marked off 20°. Of course, the hands of middle-school students may be smaller. Sheltered English

MISCONCEPTION ALERT
Students may be confused by the term *altitude* when used in astronomy. Point out that altitude does not denote height or elevation, but rather the angle between an object, the horizon, and the observer. As the Earth rotates, the altitude of the stars changes. The altitude of an object is also affected by the location of the observer.

Multicultural CONNECTION

The astrolabe that students built at the beginning of this chapter is perhaps the first scientific instrument ever made. It was invented by the ancient Greeks to record the altitude of certain stars and constellations. Arabian astronomers adapted the instrument and made detailed tables of star positions for use in navigation. The exact position of the observer can be calculated by measuring the altitude and azimuth of a star and comparing those measurements to the star tables. Islamic astronomers and mathematicians worked together to create detailed reference tables for navigators and scientists.

 **Teaching Transparency 181** "Finding Stars in the Night Sky"

TOPIC: Constellations
GO TO: www.scilinks.org
*sci*LINKS NUMBER: HSTE440

Section 2 • Mapping the Stars

2) Teach, continued

MISCONCEPTION ALERT

It is a common misconception that each star in a constellation is the same distance from Earth. In fact, most of the stars in a constellation are not near each other in space. They appear to be near each other because of our perspective from Earth. If Earth were in a different location, we would see the same stars in different patterns or we might see different stars altogether.

Homework

Locating Polaris The Big Dipper is an easily recognizable group of stars that can be seen from the mid-northern latitudes all year. If students are unfamiliar with the Big Dipper, draw it on the board or show them a picture of it. Ask students to use a star chart to locate the Big Dipper on a clear night. After students have located the Big Dipper, they can easily find Polaris (the North Star). The two stars that make up the front of the dipper bowl point directly toward Polaris. To find Polaris, students should estimate the distance between the two stars that make up the front of the bowl. Students can pinpoint the North Star by extending an imaginary line that is five times the length of that distance.

Teaching Transparency 182 "Ascension and Declination Lines"

Describing a Star's Position

Finding a star's altitude is one thing, but describing its position in a way that doesn't depend on where you are is another. To do this, astronomers have invented a reference system known as the *celestial sphere*. The celestial sphere surrounds the Earth and is what we look through when we observe the sky. Similar to the way we use latitude and longitude to plot positions on Earth, astronomers use right ascension (RA) and declination (dec) to plot positions in the sky. **Right ascension** is a measure of how far east an object is from the point at which the sun appears on the first day of spring. This point is called the *vernal equinox*. **Declination** is a measure of how far north or south an object is from the celestial equator.

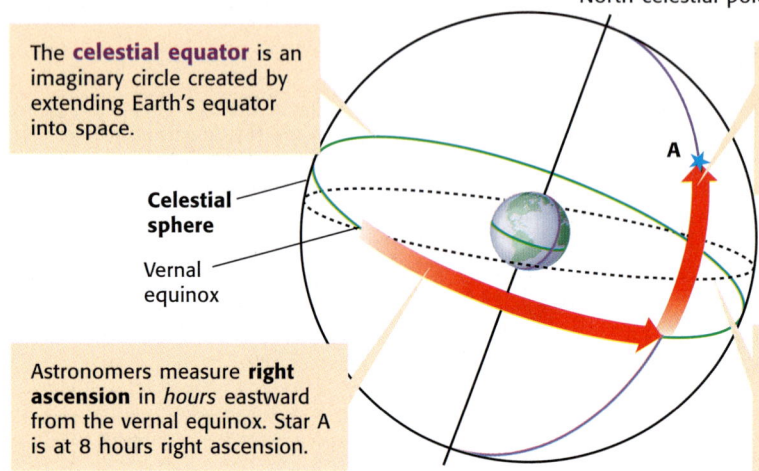

The **celestial equator** is an imaginary circle created by extending Earth's equator into space.

Astronomers measure **right ascension** in *hours* eastward from the vernal equinox. Star A is at 8 hours right ascension.

Astronomers measure **declination** in *degrees* north or south of the celestial equator. Star A is at 50° north declination.

The **ecliptic** is the apparent path the sun takes across the celestial sphere each year, as seen from Earth.

Figure 16 Time-lapse photography traces northern circumpolar stars, which never set below the horizon.

Circumpolar Stars You see different stars in the sky depending on your location, the time of year, and the time of night. Why is this so? As **Figure 16** dramatically illustrates, the Earth rotates once on its axis each day. Because of this, most observers see some stars rise above and set below the horizon much like the sun does each day. Also, the combination of the Earth's motion around the sun and the tilt of Earth's axis causes different stars to be visible during different times of the year. Near the poles, however, stars are circumpolar. *Circumpolar stars* are stars that can be seen at all times of year and all times of night.

IS THAT A FACT!

Polaris has not always been the North Star. Nearly 5,000 years ago, a faint star named Thuban in the constellation Draco held that honor. Because the Earth wobbles on its axis, the location of the North celestial pole changes on a 25,780-year cycle. Some theories argue that the Great Pyramid of Giza was built so its main passageway aligned with Thuban, which—because it did not appear to move in the night sky—symbolized immortality. In 12,000 years, Polaris will be replaced by Vega as the pole star.

The Size and Scale of the Universe

Copernicus noticed that stars never shifted their relative position. If the stars were nearby, he reasoned, their position would appear to shift like the planets' positions do as the Earth travels around the sun. Based on this observation, Copernicus thought that the stars must be very far away from the planets.

Measuring Distance in Space Today we know that Copernicus was correct—the stars are very far away from Earth. In fact, stars are so distant that a new unit of length—the light-year—was created to measure their distance. A **light-year** is a unit of length equal to the distance that light travels through space in 1 year. One light-year is equal to about 9.46 trillion kilometers! **Figure 17** below illustrates how far away some stars that we see really are.

Even after astronomers figured out that stars were very distant, the nature of the universe was hard to understand. Some astronomers thought that our galaxy, the Milky Way, included every object in space. The other galaxies that astronomers found were thought by some to be fuzzy clouds within the Milky Way. In 1935, Edwin Hubble discovered that the Andromeda Galaxy, which is the closest major galaxy to our own, was past the edge of the Milky Way. This discovery confirmed the belief of many astronomers that the universe is much larger than was previously thought.

Physics CONNECTION

Have you ever noticed that when a driver in a passing car blows the horn, the horn's sound gets lower? This is called the *Doppler effect*. It works with both sound and light. As a light source moves away quickly, its light looks redder. This particular Doppler effect is called *red shift*. The farther apart two galaxies are moving, the faster the galaxies are moving apart. From the perspective of each galaxy, the other galaxy looks redder. Because all galaxies except our close neighbors are moving away, the universe must be expanding.

DISCUSSION

Students may assume that because the universe is expanding, every star they see is moving away from Earth. Point out that the only stars visible with the unaided eye are the ones in our galaxy. The Milky Way is not expanding for the same reason that our solar system is not expanding: because gravity holds moving bodies in orbit. Galaxies such as the Milky Way and the Andromeda galaxy are part of a galaxy cluster of 30 galaxies known as the Local Group. The galaxies that make up a galaxy cluster are held together by gravity. The expansion of the universe occurs as galaxy clusters move apart from one another.

If the expansion of the universe were compared to baking a chocolate chip cookie, the chocolate chips would represent galaxy clusters. As the cookie bakes, the dough expands, and the space between chocolate chips increases; the chocolate chips, however, do not change in size.

SCIENTISTS AT ODDS

The Greek astronomer Aristarchus of Samos came up with a method for calculating the distance of heavenly bodies more than 2,200 years ago. He calculated that the moon was much smaller than the sun and therefore much closer to Earth than previously thought. He also suggested that the known planets revolved around the sun and that the stars were very far away. Ironically, Aristarchus was ridiculed for his theory of a sun-centered universe, and his ideas were dismissed by other scientists of the time.

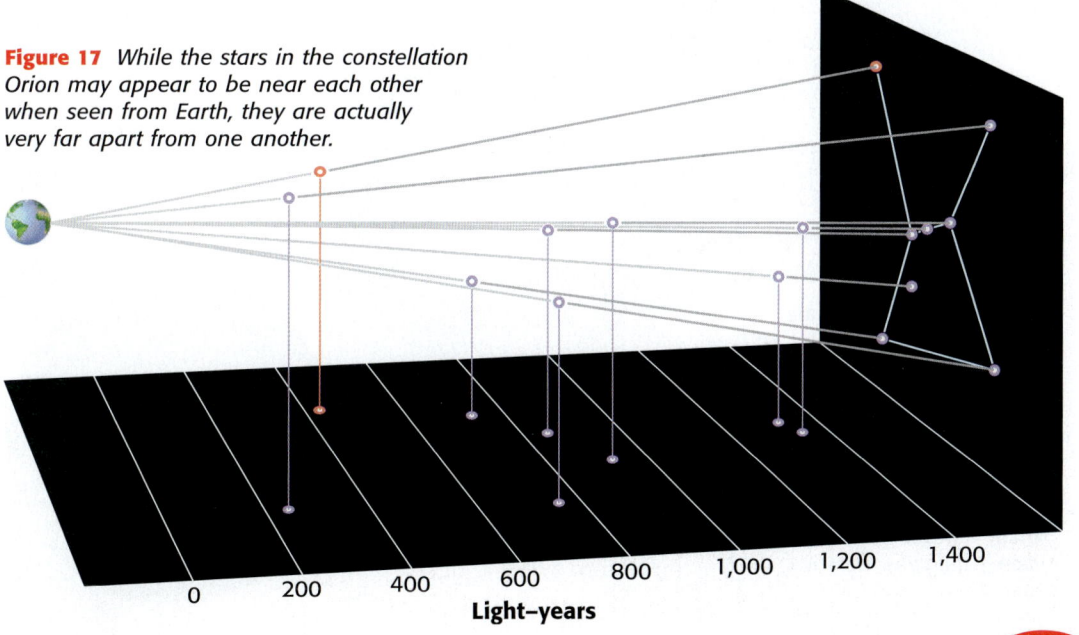

Figure 17 While the stars in the constellation Orion may appear to be near each other when seen from Earth, they are actually very far apart from one another.

As scientists have attempted to map the universe and determine its size and scale, they've discovered that clusters of galaxies are not spread uniformly through the universe. Galaxy clusters seem to be aligned around vast spherical voids as if they were located on the film of a giant soap bubble. Some of the voids are 300 million light-years across. These discoveries have led astronomers to suggest that the universe looks something like a huge conglomeration of soap bubbles!

3) Extend

USING THE FIGURE

After students have examined the images on these two pages, ask them to notice that the first four images in the series are photographs, the next three are illustrations, and the final two are photographs. Lead a discussion on why it is not possible to obtain photographs for every image in a series showing the actual solar system.

GOING FURTHER

Over a week or two, have students use a sky map to identify some of the brighter stars in the night sky. Even if they live in a city, students should be able to locate Betelgeuse, Rigel, and Sirius. In addition, they may be able to spot Venus, Mars, or Jupiter. Students should keep an observer's log in which they record the date; time; sky conditions; instruments used, if any (binoculars are an excellent aid, if available); descriptions and names of stars observed; and drawings of constellations. Students can supplement their logs with astronomical research on the stars they observe.

MATH and MORE

Have students convert the following numbers:

1,200 (1.2×10^3)
150,000 (1.5×10^5)
3.2×10^6 (3,200,000)
790,000,000 (7.9×10^8)
5.6×10^{12} (5,600,000,000,000)

Answers to MATHBREAK

Steps 3–4: 10,000 times farther
Steps 4–5: 1,500 times farther

---

1 Let's start with something familiar, a baseball diamond. You are looking down on home plate from a distance of about 10 m.

2 At 1,000 m away, home plate is hard to see, but now you can see the baseball stadium and the neighborhood it is located in.

3 Moving another 100 times farther away (100 km), you now see the city as a whole in relation to the countryside around it.

4 At 1,000,000 km away, you can see the Earth as a planet, with its companion, the moon.

MATH BREAK

Understanding Scale

From steps 1 to 2 and from steps 2 to 3 in the diagram at right, you increased your distance by a factor of 100. How many times farther away are you in step 4 than you were in step 3? How many times farther away in step 5 than you were in step 4?

Considering Scale in the Universe Today astronomers are studying the most distant objects yet detected in the universe. Every few months, newspapers announce new discoveries as astronomers probe deeper into space. Astronomers still argue about the size of the universe. The farthest objects we can observe are at least 10 billion light-years away.

When thinking about the universe and all the objects in it, it is important to think about scale. For example, stars appear to be very small in the night sky. But we know that most stars are a lot larger than the Earth. Examine the diagram on these two pages to better understand the scale of objects in the universe.

CROSS-DISCIPLINARY FOCUS

Mathematics Calculating the position of objects in the universe involves complex mathematical concepts. Since the first observations of the stars were recorded, mathematics have been used to track their movements and calculate the length of days, months, and years. Math and astronomy evolved together. Today, computers are used to model the structure of the universe, but astronomical discoveries still challenge the ways math is used to describe space and time. General Relativity is just one example of this synthesis. Students may be interested in finding out how astronomy has influenced the development of mathematics, physics, or philosophy.

7 By the time we reach 10 light-years, the sun simply resembles any other star in space.

8 At 1 million light-years, our galaxy would look like the Andromeda galaxy shown here—an island of stars set in the blackness of space.

6 At 150 light-days, the solar system can be seen surrounded by a cloud of comets and other icy debris.

5 Moving 1,500,000,000 km away (83 light-minutes), we can look back at the sun and the inner planets.

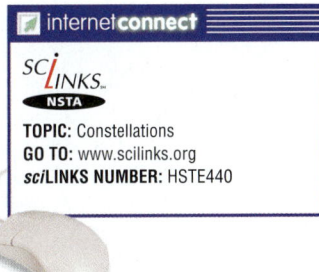

9 When we reach 10 million light-years, our view shows us that the universe is crowded with galaxies, many like our own, and many strangely different.

REVIEW

1. How do constellations relate to patterns of stars? How are constellations like states?
2. How do astronomers plot a star's exact position?
3. **Analyzing Relationships** As shown in the diagram above, there are faraway objects that we can see only with telescopes. There are also objects in the universe that are too small for our unaided eyes to see. How do we detect these small objects?

internetconnect

SC_{*i*}**LINKS**
NSTA
TOPIC: Constellations
GO TO: www.scilinks.org
*sci*LINKS NUMBER: HSTE440

4) Close

Quiz

1. What is the celestial equator? (an imaginary circle extending from Earth's equator into space)
2. What is a circumpolar star? (It is a star that can be seen all year and at all times of night from a given location.)
3. How did Edwin Hubble's discovery that the Andromeda galaxy was far away and outside of our own galaxy contribute to astronomers' knowledge about the size of the universe? (It confirmed many astronomers' theories that the universe was much larger than previously thought.)

ALTERNATIVE ASSESSMENT

Celestial Guidebook Have students develop a guidebook for the novice stargazer that includes a glossary of astronomical terms. Encourage students to include diagrams, illustrations, and analogies to help clarify their entries.

ACTIVITY

Field Trip If there is an observatory or planetarium in your area, plan a field trip for the class. A cloudless night is best. Afterwards, have students record their thoughts and observations in their ScienceLog.

Answers to Review

1. Constellations are sections of the sky that contain easily recognizable patterns of stars. Constellations are similar to states in that both are regions of a much larger area. Like states, constellations share borders with each other.
2. Astronomers measure right ascension and declination to plot a star's exact position.
3. Scientists use microscopes to study objects that are too small for the unaided eye to see.

The Sun's Yearly Trip Through the Zodiac

Teaching Transparency 183
"Considering Scale in the Universe"

Section 2 • Mapping the Stars

SECTION 3

Focus

Telescopes—Then and Now

In this section, students will learn how reflecting and refracting telescopes work and compare their strengths and weaknesses. The section discusses the electromagnetic spectrum and how non-optical telescopes are used to detect radiation that cannot be seen. Students will learn about radio telescopes and other tools astronomers use to study the invisible radiation emitted by celestial objects.

Bellringer

Ask students: Have you ever bent or slowed down light? How? (Students may mention wearing glasses or looking through a microscope.)

1 Motivate

ACTIVITY

Making a Waterdrop Lens
Give pairs of students a 6 × 6 cm square of plastic wrap, and have them place it over some print on a newspaper. Put a drop of water on each piece of plastic. Have students note the shape of the drop and how it magnifies the newsprint. Tell students that the rounded, or convex, waterdrop is a very simple lens, similar in principle to the kinds of lenses used in some telescopes.

 Directed Reading Worksheet 18 Section 3

 **Teaching Transparency 299** "How Your Eyes Work"

Section 3

Terms to Learn
telescope
refracting telescope
reflecting telescope
electromagnetic spectrum

What You'll Do
- Compare and contrast refracting telescopes with reflecting telescopes.
- Explain why the atmosphere is an obstacle to astronomers and how they overcome the obstacle.
- List the types of electromagnetic radiation, other than visible light, that astronomers use to study space.

CONNECT TO PHYSICAL SCIENCE

The human retina contains receptors called *cones* and *rods* which perceive different wavelengths of light. Cones are found in the central part of the retina and perceive color. Rods, located at the outer part of the retina, perceive only black and white. When little light is present, rods perceive detail better than cones. For this reason, stargazers sometimes look at objects by using their peripheral vision rather than looking at an object straight on. This method takes advantage of the rods' ability to detect faint objects in the sky. Use Transparency 299 at left, to discuss the structure of the eye and encourage interested students to test this technique using a telescope, binoculars, or their unaided eyes.

Telescopes—Then and Now

For professional astronomers and amateur stargazers, the telescope is the standard tool for observing the sky. A **telescope** is an instrument that collects *electromagnetic radiation* from the sky and concentrates it for better observation. You will learn more about electromagnetic radiation later in this section.

Optical Astronomy

An optical telescope collects visible light for closer observation. The simplest optical telescope is made with two lenses. One lens, called the *objective lens,* collects light and forms an image at the back of the telescope. The bigger the objective lens, the more light the telescope can gather. The second lens is located in the eyepiece of the telescope. This lens magnifies the image produced by the objective lens. Different eyepieces can be selected depending on the magnification desired.

Without a telescope, you can see about 6,000 stars in the night sky. With an optical telescope, you can see millions of stars and other objects. **Figure 18** shows how much more you can see with an optical telescope.

Figure 18 *The image at left shows a section of the sky as seen with the unaided eye. The image at right shows what the small clusters of stars in the left image look like when seen through a telescope.*

496 Chapter 18 • Observing the Sky

Refracting Telescopes Telescopes that use a set of lenses to gather and focus light are called **refracting telescopes.** The curved objective lens in a refracting telescope bends light that passes through it and focuses the light to be magnified by the eyepiece. **Figure 19** shows how refracting telescopes work. A refracting telescope's size is limited by the objective lens. If the curved lens is too large, the glass sags under its own weight, distorting images. This is why most professional astronomers use *reflecting telescopes.*

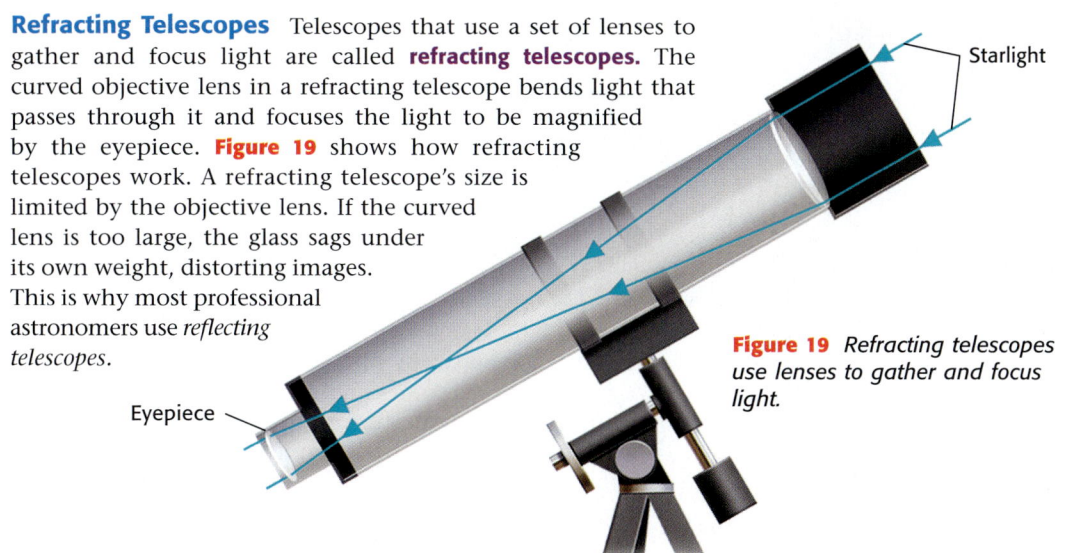

Figure 19 *Refracting telescopes use lenses to gather and focus light.*

Reflecting Telescopes Telescopes that use curved mirrors to gather and focus light are called **reflecting telescopes.** Light enters the telescope and is reflected from a large, curved mirror to a focal point above the mirror. As shown in **Figure 20,** reflecting telescopes use a second mirror in front of the focal point to reflect the light, in this case, through a hole in the side of the telescope. Here the light is collected for observation.

One advantage of reflecting telescopes over refracting telescopes is that mirrors can be made very large, which allows them to gather more light than lenses gather. Also, mirrors are polished on their curved side, preventing light from entering the glass. Therefore, any flaws in the glass do not affect the light. A third advantage is that mirrors reflect all colors of light to the same place, while lenses focus different colors of light at slightly different distances. Reflecting telescopes thus allow all colors of light from an object to be seen in focus at the same time.

LabBook Want to make your own telescope? Turn to page 710 in the LabBook to find out how to build and use a telescope.

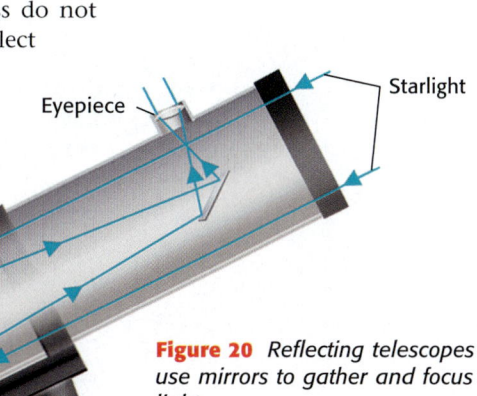

Figure 20 *Reflecting telescopes use mirrors to gather and focus light.*

Homework

Making Observations Binoculars are actually a pair of low-power refracting telescopes, and they can make it possible to see five times as many stars as could be viewed with the naked eye. Students with access to binoculars can make observations of the moon, stars, or planets. A pair of 7 × 35 or 7 × 50 binoculars is best for nighttime observation. The most difficult thing about using binoculars is keeping them steady: suggest that students sit in a comfortable lawn chair and rest their elbows on the armrests. Invite students to share their observations with the class.

2) Teach

READING STRATEGY

Prediction Guide Have students predict whether the following statements are true or false:

- Without a telescope, you can see about 6,000 stars. (true)
- Mirrors are used in some telescopes. (true)
- Telescopes are often located in humid areas because water vapor in the air enhances the visibility of stars. (false)

DEMONSTRATION

Mystery of the Floating Penny Tell students that you can make a penny float on water. Drop a penny in a small bowl. Ask a student to raise the bowl until the penny just disappears from sight. Now slowly pour water into the bowl until the penny "floats" into view. Repeat the demonstration with other students, and ask them if they can solve this mystery. (Students may deduce that light bends or refracts as it passes from air to water; this makes the penny appear to float.)

Explain that light travels at a speed of about 300,000 km/s through air but at only about 225,000 km/s through water and, as it slows down, it bends. Astronomers use the same trick to bend and focus light with curved pieces of glass called lenses.

Through the Looking Glass

Teaching Transparency 184 "Refracting Telescope" "Reflecting Telescope"

Section 3 • Telescopes—Then and Now

2) Teach, continued

DEMONSTRATION

Students may not understand how moisture in the atmosphere can distort the images seen through a telescope. Demonstrate the effect of moisture in the atmosphere with a water spray bottle and a projector. In a darkened room, turn on the projector and shine it on the wall. Spray a mist of water about halfway between the projector and the wall. Ask students to describe what they see. Point out that much of the water in the atmosphere is actually water vapor, which is a gas, but it can cause similar problems for powerful telescopes. **Sheltered English**

MATH and MORE

While astronomers usually refer to a telescope by the diameter of its objective lens or mirror, a telescope's ability to collect light is proportional to the *area* of its main mirror or lens. Have students use the formula for finding a circle's area ($A = \pi r^2$ [$\pi = 3.1416$]) to compare the light-collecting capabilities of a 1 m, 5 m, and 10 m mirror. (For the 1 m mirror: $3.1416 \times 0.25 m^2 = 0.79 m^2$; for the 5 m mirror: $3.1416 \times 6.25 m^2 = 19.64 m^2$; for the 10 m mirror: $3.1416 \times 25 m^2 = 78.54 m^2$. The 5 m mirror can collect 25 times more light than the 1 m mirror; the 10 m mirror can collect 100 times more light than the 1 m mirror and 4 times more than the 5 m mirror.)

Critical Thinking Worksheet 18 "Through the Eyes of a Telescope"

Figure 21 The 36 hexagonal mirrors in each of the Keck Telescopes combine to form a light-reflecting surface that is 10 m across.

Figure 22 The Hubble Space Telescope has provided clearer images of objects in deep space than any ground-based optical telescope.

Very Large Reflecting Telescopes

In some very large reflecting telescopes, several mirrors work together to collect light and deliver it to the same focus. The Keck Telescopes, in Hawaii, shown in **Figure 21**, are twin telescopes that each have 36 hexagonal mirrors working together. Linking several mirrors allows more light to be collected and focused in one spot.

Optical Telescopes and the Atmosphere The light gathered by telescopes on Earth is affected by the atmosphere. Earth's atmosphere causes starlight to shimmer and blur. Also, light pollution from large cities can make the sky look bright, which limits an observer's ability to view faint objects. Astronomers often place telescopes in dry areas to avoid water vapor in the air. Mountaintops are also good places to use a telescope because the air is thinner at higher elevations. The fact that air pollution and light pollution are generally lower on mountaintops also increases the visibility of stars.

Optical Telescopes in Space! To avoid interference by the atmosphere altogether, scientists have put telescopes in space. Although the mirror in the Hubble Space Telescope, shown below in **Figure 22**, is only 2.4 m across, the optical telescope produces images that are as good or better than any images produced by optical telescopes on Earth.

Science Bloopers

When the Hubble Space Telescope was deployed in 1990, it became immediately apparent that the telescope was not operating correctly—images transmitted back to Earth were unfortunately blurred. It was discovered that there was a minute flaw in the telescope's main mirror. The mirror had been ground about 0.0002 cm (about $\frac{1}{50}$ the width of a human hair) flatter than it should have been. Although much of the image distortion was corrected with computer processing, the telescope was much less powerful than originally hoped. During a 1993 repair mission, space shuttle astronauts placed a number of corrective devices on the telescope that made it fully operational.

Non-Optical Astronomy

For thousands of years, humans have observed the universe with their eyes. But scientists eventually discovered that there are more forms of radiation than the kind we can see—*visible light.* In 1800, William Herschel discovered an invisible form of radiation called *infrared radiation.* We sense infrared radiation as heat.

In 1852, James Clerk Maxwell showed that visible light is a form of *electromagnetic radiation.* Each color of visible light represents a different wavelength of electromagnetic radiation. Visible light is just a small part of the electromagnetic spectrum, as shown in **Figure 23.** The **electromagnetic spectrum** is made of all of the wavelengths of electromagnetic radiation. Humans can see radiation only from blue light, which has a short wavelength, to red light, which has a longer wavelength. The rest of the electromagnetic spectrum is invisible to us!

Most electromagnetic radiation is blocked by the Earth's atmosphere. Think of the atmosphere as a screen that lets only certain wavelengths of radiation in. These wavelengths include infrared, visible light, some ultraviolet, and radio. All other wavelengths are blocked.

Activity

Artificial light at night is often needed for safety and security. But it also causes light pollution that interferes with stargazing. Do some research on this problem, and list some possible solutions. What compromises can be made so that people feel safe and stargazers can see objects in the night sky?

TRY at HOME

Figure 23 *Radio waves have the longest wavelengths and gamma rays have the shortest. Visible light is only a small band of the electromagnetic spectrum.*

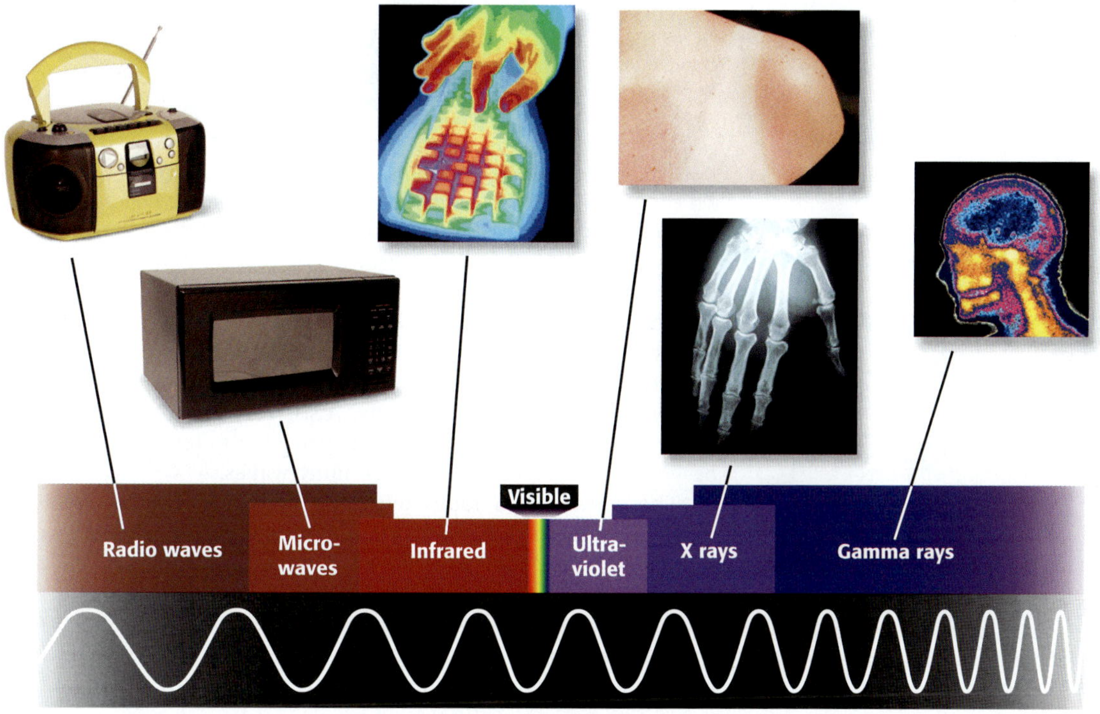

Answer to Activity

Placing special shields over outdoor lights is one simple way to reduce light pollution. The shields keep streets safely illuminated but reduce the amount of light radiated skyward. Invite students to look up the International Dark-Sky Association on the Internet.

Reteaching

To help students comprehend how little of the electromagnetic spectrum is visible to the human eye, have them visualize a piano. Tell them the part of the electromagnetic spectrum that humans can see is comparable to one key on the piano. **Sheltered English**

CONNECT TO LIFE SCIENCE

Human eyes can detect only visible light, but some organisms have eyes more like non-optical telescopes. Insects such as bees, for example, can see ultraviolet radiation. Flowers, in turn, have ultraviolet patterns that direct bees to their center. Have interested students find out what it is like to look at the world through the eyes of a bee or a bioluminescent deep-sea fish. Encourage students to find out about experimental telescope designs that are modeled after the eyes of animals. One example is the Lobster Eye X-ray telescope.

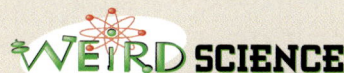

IS THAT A FACT!

Although the sun appears to be yellowish in color, it is radiating energy across the electromagnetic spectrum. When observed with an X-ray telescope, the sun appears nearly black, but sunspots are brilliantly active with magnetic storms and solar flares that release X rays.

WEIRD SCIENCE

Some LEO satellites reflect sunlight off their bodies and dish antennas. These flashes can be many times brighter than any star in the sky and can damage telescope sensors. To find out when these flashes will occur and where they will be visible, look up "Iridium flash" on the Internet.

Teaching Transparency 185, "The Electromagnetic Spectrum"

internetconnect

SCILINKS NSTA
TOPIC: Telescopes
GO TO: www.scilinks.org
***sci*LINKS NUMBER:** HSTE445

3 Extend

BRAIN FOOD
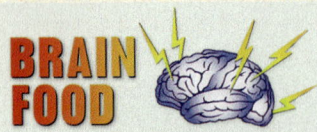

Some astronomers study the universe by heading deep into abandoned mines! These astronomers are looking for evidence of neutrinos (a type of subatomic particle emitted by stars and supernovae). Most neutrinos pass right through the Earth without colliding with any matter. Neutrino observatories are built several kilometers beneath the Earth's surface to shield them from all other types of radiation. The observatories are enormous tanks of extremely pure water or a solution similar to dry cleaning fluid. When a neutrino enters the tank and has a chance collision with an atomic nucleus, photoreceptors detect a faint flash of light and astronomers record a "hit."

GROUP ACTIVITY

Invite pairs of students to construct a simple Newtonian reflecting telescope. The activity works best on a clear night, when the moon is visible. Instruct students to turn off the lights and place a makeup mirror (a curved, focusing mirror) near a window so that the moon and some stars are reflected in it. One student should hold a hand mirror in front of the makeup mirror so that he or she can see a reflection of the makeup mirror in the hand mirror. Then the other student should use a magnifying glass to view the reflection in the hand mirror. Students should be able to see the craters and mountains of the moon.

The Night Sky Through Different Eyes Astronomers are interested in all forms of electromagnetic radiation because different objects radiate at different wavelengths. For each type of radiation, a different type of telescope or detector is needed. For example, infrared telescopes have polished mirrors similar to those of reflecting telescopes, but the detectors are more sensitive to infrared waves than to visible light waves. As you can see in **Figure 24,** the universe looks much different when observed at other wavelengths.

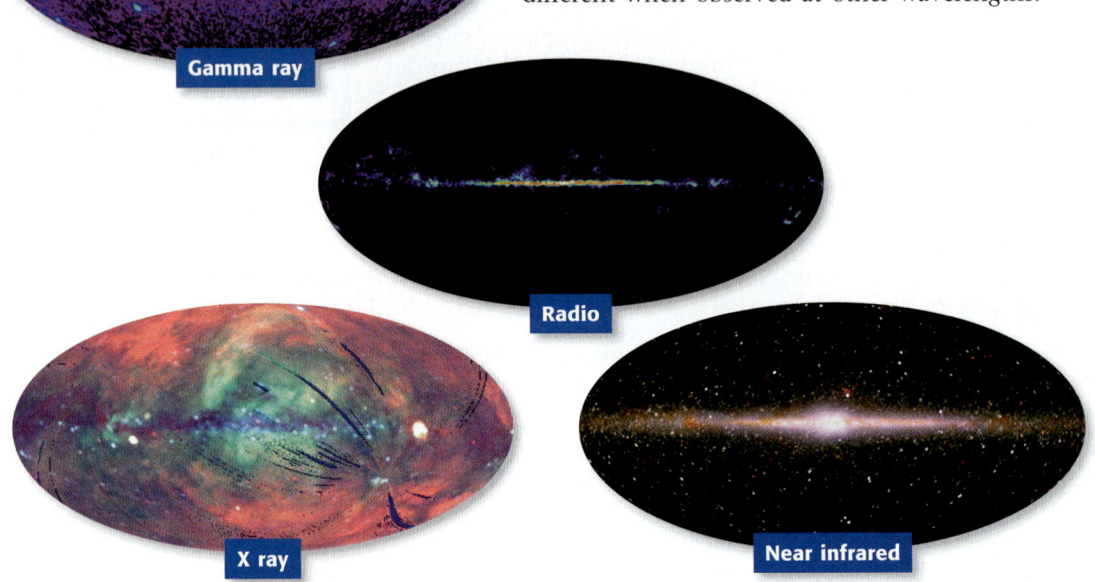

Figure 24 Each image shows the night sky as it would appear if we could see other wavelengths of electromagnetic radiation. The "cloud" that goes across each picture is the Milky Way galaxy.

Figure 25 The Arecibo radio telescope is 305 m across. That is about the length of three football fields arranged end to end!

Radio Telescopes Radio telescopes receive and focus radio waves. Radio telescopes have to be much larger than optical telescopes because radio wavelengths are about 1 million times longer than optical wavelengths. Also, very little radio radiation reaches Earth from objects in space. Radio telescopes must be very sensitive to detect these faint waves.

The surface of a radio telescope does not have to be as flawless as the lens of an optical telescope. In fact, the surface of a radio telescope does not even have to be completely solid. When it was first built, the Arecibo radio telescope, shown in **Figure 25,** was covered with chicken wire! To a radio wave, a surface made of chicken wire is solid because the wavelength is so much longer than the diameter of the holes.

Homework

Research Have students research a non-optical telescope and prepare a report or poster on it. Encourage students to diagram how the telescope works, research the history of the telescope, explain what the telescope was intended for, and report on the discoveries it has enabled. Students can share their research with the class.

WEIRD SCIENCE

Shortly after Marconi invented the radio in the 1890s, people became interested in listening for messages from intelligent life in the universe. In 1901, a reward of 100,000 francs was offered to the first person to communicate with aliens.

Linking Radio Telescopes Together Astronomers can get clearer images of radio waves by using two or more radio telescopes at the same time. When radio telescopes are linked together, they work like a single giant telescope. For example, the Very Large Array (VLA), shown in **Figure 26,** consists of 27 separate telescopes that can be spread out 30 km. When the dishes are spread out to the maximum distance, they work as a single telescope that is 30 km across! The larger the area that linked telescopes cover, the more detailed the collected data are.

Figure 26 The radio telescopes of the Very Large Array near Socorro, New Mexico, work together as one giant telescope.

X-ray Vision Most electromagnetic waves are blocked by the Earth's atmosphere. To detect these blocked waves, scientists have put special telescopes in space. These telescopes include ultraviolet telescopes, infrared telescopes, gamma-ray telescopes, and X-ray telescopes. Each type of telescope is made to receive one type of radiation. For example, **Figure 27** shows a telescope that is designed to detect X rays.

Figure 27 Launched in 1999, the Chandra X-ray Observatory is the most powerful X-ray telescope ever built.

REVIEW

1. Name one way in which refracting telescopes and reflecting telescopes are similar and one way they are different.
2. Name two ways the atmosphere limits what astronomers can detect. What single method do astronomers use to solve both problems?
3. **Summarizing Data** Make two lists—one for electromagnetic wavelengths that commonly penetrate Earth's atmosphere and one for other wavelengths. Which wavelengths can astronomers detect from Earth? How do they detect each wavelength?

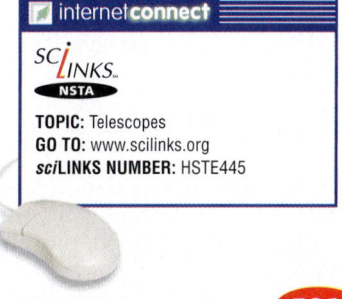

TOPIC: Telescopes
GO TO: www.scilinks.org
sciLINKS NUMBER: HSTE445

Section 3 • Telescopes—Then and Now

Chapter Highlights

VOCABULARY DEFINITIONS

SECTION 1

astronomy the study of all physical objects beyond Earth

calendar a system for organizing time; most calendars organize time within a single unit called a year

year the time required for the Earth to orbit the sun once

month roughly the amount of time required for the moon to orbit the Earth once

day the time required for the Earth to rotate once on its axis

leap year a year in which an extra day is added to the calendar

SECTION 2

constellation a section of the sky that contains a recognizable star pattern

altitude the angle between an object in the sky and the horizon

right ascension a measure of how far east an object is from the point at which the sun appears on the first day of spring

declination a measure of how far north or south an object is from the celestial equator

celestial equator imaginary circle created by extending Earth's equator into space

ecliptic the apparent path the sun takes across the celestial sphere each year

light-year a unit of length equal to the distance that light travels through space in 1 year

Chapter Highlights

SECTION 1

Vocabulary
- **astronomy** (p. 482)
- **calendar** (p. 482)
- **year** (p. 482)
- **month** (p. 482)
- **day** (p. 482)
- **leap year** (p. 483)

Section Notes
- Calendars are based on movements of objects in the sky.
- Many ancient civilizations developed calendars.
- Our modern calendar developed from the Roman calendar.
- There is evidence all around the world for ancient astronomical observations.
- The Ptolemaic theory states that Earth is at the center of the universe, while Copernicus's theory states that the sun is at the center of the universe.
- Isaac Newton was the first scientist to explain why celestial objects move as they do.
- Galileo's use of the telescope brought the technology of astronomy to a new level.

Labs
Create a Calendar (p. 706)

SECTION 2

Vocabulary
- **constellation** (p. 489)
- **altitude** (p. 491)
- **right ascension** (p. 492)
- **declination** (p. 492)
- **celestial equator** (p. 492)
- **ecliptic** (p. 492)
- **light-year** (p. 493)

Section Notes
- Astronomers divide the sky into 88 sections called *constellations*.
- Different constellations are visible from different locations, at different times of the year, and at different times of night.
- Star patterns appear as they do because of Earth's position in space. Most stars that appear close together are actually very far apart.

✓ Skills Check

Math Concepts

KEEPING IT SIMPLE Scientific notation is a way that scientists and others can use large numbers more easily. By using exponents, many place-holding zeros can be eliminated.

For example:
1,000 can be written as 1×10^3, and 1,000,000 can be written as 1×10^6.

Notice that the exponent represents the number of zeros in each number. For more practice with scientific notation, turn to page 743 in the Appendix.

Visual Understanding

OPTICAL ILLUSION Constellations look like they do only because we see them from our location on Earth in patterns we recognize. Look back at Figure 17 on page 493. The constellation Orion would be unrecognizable if seen from the side.

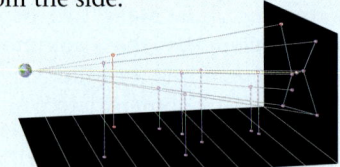

Lab and Activity Highlights

Create a Calendar PG 706

The Sun's Yearly Trip Through the Zodiac PG 708

Through the Looking Glass PG 710

 Datasheets for LabBook (blackline masters for these labs)

SECTION 2

- The north celestial pole, the celestial equator, the zenith, and the horizon are imaginary markers used to locate objects in the sky.
- Right ascension and declination, which are similar to latitude and longitude, give coordinates of objects in the sky.
- Astronomers measure the distance to most objects in the universe in light-years.
- The size and distance of celestial objects detected in the universe can be difficult to determine. Scale must always be considered.

Labs

The Sun's Yearly Trip Through the Zodiac (p. 708)

SECTION 3

Vocabulary
telescope (p. 496)
refracting telescope (p. 497)
reflecting telescope (p. 497)
electromagnetic spectrum (p. 499)

Section Notes

- Telescopes collect and focus electromagnetic radiation.
- Humans can see only visible light. To detect other wavelengths of radiation, astronomers use special telescopes or detectors.
- Types of telescopes include optical, radio, ultraviolet, infrared, X-ray, and gamma-ray.
- Some telescopes are launched into space to avoid the blurring effects of Earth's atmosphere or to collect radiation that can't penetrate Earth's atmosphere.
- Telescopes are often linked together to function as one giant telescope.

Labs

Through the Looking Glass (p. 710)

VOCABULARY DEFINITIONS, continued

SECTION 3

telescope an instrument that collects electromagnetic radiation from the sky and concentrates it for better observation

refracting telescope a telescope that uses a set of lenses to gather and focus light

reflecting telescope a telescope that uses curved mirrors to gather and focus light

electromagnetic spectrum all the wavelengths of electromagnetic radiation

 Blackline masters of these Chapter Highlights can be found in the **Study Guide.**

---

internet connect

 **GO TO:** go.hrw.com

Visit the **HRW** web site for a variety of learning tools related to this chapter. Just type in the keyword:

KEYWORD: HSTOBS

 **GO TO:** www.scilinks.org

Visit the **National Science Teachers Association** on-line Web site for Internet resources related to this chapter. Just type in the sciLINKS number for more information about the topic:

TOPIC: Images from Space	sciLINKS NUMBER: HSTE425
TOPIC: The Stars and Keeping Time	sciLINKS NUMBER: HSTE430
TOPIC: Early Theories in Astronomy	sciLINKS NUMBER: HSTE435
TOPIC: Constellations	sciLINKS NUMBER: HSTE440
TOPIC: Telescopes	sciLINKS NUMBER: HSTE445

Lab and Activity Highlights

LabBank

 Inquiry Labs
Constellation Prize, Lab 13

Whiz-Bang Demonstrations
Refraction Action, Demo 31

Long-Term Projects & Research Ideas,
Celestial Inspiration, Project 46

Chapter Review

Chapter Review Answers

USING VOCABULARY

1. Both reflecting and refracting telescopes are used to study objects in space. Refracting telescopes use lenses to magnify and focus an image. Reflecting telescopes use curved mirrors.
2. Both the celestial equator and the horizon are imaginary lines that help an observer locate objects in space. The celestial equator extends from Earth's equator into space and is always in the same place. The horizon is the line where the Earth and the sky appear to meet; it is determined by the observer's location.
3. Both X rays and microwaves are forms of electromagnetic radiation that the human eye cannot detect. X rays have much shorter wavelengths than microwaves.
4. Both right ascension and declination measure the location of celestial objects. Right ascension refers to how far east along the celestial equator an object is from the point at which vernal equinox occurs. Declination is a measure of how far north or south an object is from the celestial equator.
5. A leap year and a light-year both use the revolution of the Earth around the sun as a reference point. A leap year is a year in which an extra day has been added to the calendar. A light-year is a unit of distance. It refers to the distance that light travels in space during the course of one year.

Chapter Review

USING VOCABULARY

For each set of terms, explain the similarities and differences in their meanings.

1. reflecting telescope/refracting telescope
2. celestial equator/horizon
3. X rays/microwaves
4. right ascension/declination
5. leap year/light-year

UNDERSTANDING CONCEPTS

Multiple Choice

6. The length of a day is based on
   a. the Earth orbiting the sun.
   b. the rotation of the Earth on its axis.
   c. the moon orbiting the Earth.
   d. the rotation of the moon on its axis.

7. Which of the following civilizations directly affected the development of our modern calendar?
   a. The Chinese
   b. The Maya
   c. The Romans
   d. The Polynesians

8. According to __?__, the Earth is at the center of the universe.
   a. the Ptolemaic theory
   b. Copernicus's theory
   c. Galileo's theory
   d. none of the above

9. The first scientist to successfully use a telescope to observe the night sky was
   a. Tycho.   c. Herschel.
   b. Galileo. d. Kepler.

10. Astronomers divide the sky into
    a. galaxies.   c. zeniths.
    b. constellations. d. phases.

11. The stars that you see in the sky depend on
    a. your latitude.
    b. the time of year.
    c. the time of night.
    d. All of the above

12. The altitude of an object in the sky is its angular distance
    a. above the horizon.
    b. from the north celestial pole.
    c. from the zenith.
    d. from the prime meridian.

13. Right ascension is a measure of how far east an object in the sky is from
    a. the observer.
    b. the vernal equinox.
    c. the moon.
    d. Venus.

14. Telescopes that work grounded on the Earth include all of the following except
    a. radio telescopes.
    b. refracting telescopes.
    c. X-ray telescopes.
    d. reflecting telescopes.

504

UNDERSTANDING CONCEPTS
Multiple Choice

6. b	11. d
7. c	12. a
8. a	13. b
9. b	14. c
10. b	15. d

15. Which of the following is true about X-ray and radio radiation from objects in space?
    a. Both types of radiation can be observed with the same telescope.
    b. Separate telescopes are needed to observe each type of radiation, and both telescopes can be on Earth.
    c. Separate telescopes are needed to observe each type of radiation, and both telescopes must be in space.
    d. Separate telescopes are needed to observe each type of radiation, but only one of the telescopes must be in space.

Short Answer

Write one or two sentences to answer the following questions:

16. Explain how right ascension and declination are similar to latitude and longitude.

17. How does a reflecting telescope work?

Concept Mapping

18. Use the following terms to create a concept map: right ascension, declination, celestial sphere, degrees, hours, celestial equator, vernal equinox.

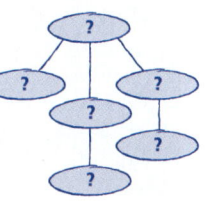

CRITICAL THINKING AND PROBLEM SOLVING

19. Why was it easier for people in ancient cultures to see celestial objects in the sky than it is for most people today?

20. Many forms of radiation do not penetrate Earth's atmosphere. While this limits astronomer's activities, how does it benefit humans in general?

MATH IN SCIENCE

21. How many kilometers away is an object whose distance is 8 light-years?

INTERPRETING GRAPHICS

Examine the sky map below, and answer the questions that follow. (Hint: The star Aldebaran is located at about 4 hours, 30 minutes right ascension, 16 degrees declination.)

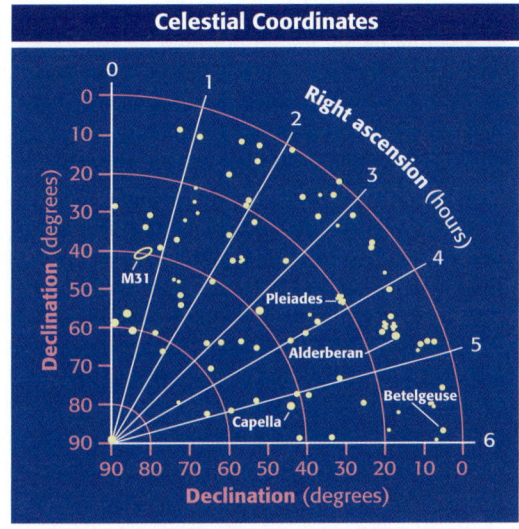

22. What object is located at 5 hr, 55 min right ascension and 7 degrees declination?

23. What are the celestial coordinates for the Andromeda galaxy (M31)? (Round off right ascension to the nearest half-hour.)

 Take a minute to review your answers to the Pre-Reading Questions found at the bottom of page 480. Have your answers changed? If necessary, revise your answers based on what you have learned since you began this chapter.

Short Answer

16. Lines of latitude and longitude divide the Earth into a system of coordinates that can be used to describe a location. Similarly, right ascension and declination allow astronomers to locate objects using coordinates. Both systems are based on spherical objects.

17. Reflecting telescopes use a large mirror to gather and focus light. A second mirror, located in front of the focal point, directs light toward an eyepiece for observation.

Concept Mapping

18. An answer to this exercise can be found at the end of this book.

CRITICAL THINKING AND PROBLEM SOLVING

19. Before the invention of electric lights, there was much less light pollution and atmospheric pollution; therefore, celestial objects were much easier to observe.

20. The Earth's atmosphere absorbs many forms of radiation that are dangerous to humans, including X rays and ultraviolet radiation.

MATH IN SCIENCE

21. $(9.46 \times 10^{12}) \times 8 = 7.57 \times 10^{13}$, or 75.7 trillion kilometers away

INTERPRETING GRAPHICS

22. Betelgeuse
23. 0 hours, 30 minutes right ascension, 40° declination

 Concept Mapping Transparency 18

 Blackline masters of this Chapter Review can be found in the **Study Guide**.

SCIENCE, TECHNOLOGY, AND SOCIETY
Planet or Star?

Background

Dozens of possible planets have been detected outside our solar system. Because these objects are too distant to be observed directly, astronomers gather evidence indirectly. The most common method is to observe slight variations in the light emitted by a star. As a planet orbits a star, its gravity tugs on the star. This causes the star's velocity to change (the "wobble" described in the student page). This wobble is detectable because the star's spectrum changes due to the Doppler effect.

Because most stars are moving away from Earth, the light they emit is shifted towards the red end of the spectrum. When a star's velocity decreases, the red shift decreases; when its velocity increases, the red shift increases. A periodic variation in a star's red shift indicates that it is being pulled by an unseen object. The gravitational attraction of a planet as massive as Jupiter could cause an observable variation in a star's red shift.

Science, Technology, and Society
Planet or Star?

Humans have long wondered if there are inhabited planets in our galaxy or in far-off galaxies. For the first time, NASA's powerful Hubble Space Telescope has photographed what some astronomers believe is a young planet within our own galaxy. This gaseous object, called TMR-1C, is nearly 450 light-years from Earth. Is it really a planet, or is it a star?

Discovering Planets

Scientists have had trouble finding planets beyond our solar system because distant planets are often masked by the light of brighter stars. *Protoplanets,* planets in the process of forming, may be difficult to see because they are often surrounded by clouds of cosmic dust. As a planet revolves around a star, its gravity tugs on the star. This causes the star to move back and forth slightly. If the planet is massive enough, astronomers can see this movement as a "wobble" in the star's motion. Scientists use state-of-the-art technology to detect these minute changes in the star's velocity relative to Earth.

The picture of TMR-1C could be the first photographic evidence that planets exist outside our solar system. Astronomers discovered TMR-1C racing through space at 32,000 km/h in the constellation of Taurus. Scientists believe that TMR-1C was hurled into space by two stars that acted like a giant slingshot. The Hubble Space Telescope's camera used sensitive infrared light to penetrate through the cosmic clouds surrounding TMR-1C. Because TMR-1C is still hot from forming, it emits light, which is picked up by the telescope's camera.

The Birth of a Planet

Scientists believe that it takes millions of years for planets to form. Photographs of TMR-1C, however, have led some researchers to speculate that this process may be much quicker than was previously thought. The stars that ejected TMR-1C are only a few hundred thousand years old. Researchers have not determined for certain whether TMR-1C is a planet. If TMR-1C turns out to be older than these stars, it could not have been ejected from them. If that is the case, TMR-1C may prove to be a *brown dwarf* rather than a planet. Meanwhile, the research continues until scientists know for certain.

▲ TMR-1C is 209 billion km from possible parent stars.

Think About It!

▶ So far, only a few of the many recently discovered planets may be habitable. One such planet, near the star 70 Virginis, is just the right distance from its star for the planet's water to be liquid rather than solid or gaseous. What other features would be necessary for this planet to sustain life as we know it on Earth?

506

Answer to Think About It

Accept all reasonable answers. Have students consider why the other planets in our solar system are not habitable. In addition to liquid water, elements such as carbon are necessary for life. Carbon is essential in forming organic compounds. Organic compounds also require nitrogen and phosphorus.

Students should also consider a planet's orbit. If a planet has an extremely elliptical orbit, it may venture far enough away from its star to cause extreme temperature changes.

Students might also consider a planet's atmospheric composition. The Earth's atmosphere protects organisms from ultraviolet radiation and regulates heat. Our atmosphere is primarily nitrogen, carbon dioxide, and oxygen. These gases can be lethal to humans, however, if they are not in proper proportions.

EYE ON THE ENVIRONMENT

Eyes in the Sky

Have you ever gazed up at the sky on a crystal-clear night? What did you see? You probably noticed the moon and countless twinkling stars. It may surprise you to learn that some of those points of light are not stars at all. A few of them may be phonies.

Phony Stars Exposed

Some of the objects that we think are stars are really satellites circling Earth in low Earth orbit (LEO). The satellites in LEO specialize in observation. You might say that when we watch the sky, satellites are watching us as well. LEO is ideal for observation because of its proximity to Earth's surface.

In order to stay in orbit, satellites in LEO must travel very fast. Traveling at approximately 27,358 km/h, one of these satellites can circle the Earth in only 90 minutes! During these revolutions, some satellites gather weather information, while others might transmit phone calls or observe remote terrain. These "eyes in the sky" can even observe you taking a walk.

Space Junk Explosion

Like many things, satellites do not last forever. They eventually break down and may even explode into hundreds of pieces. Most of the time, these pieces continue to travel in LEO for many years. Some of these pieces are large enough to be catalogued by the United States Space Command. As of January 1, 2000, about 2,647 human-made satellites were recorded orbiting, along with 6,022 pieces of debris, or space junk. This debris poses no immediate threat to astronauts or space shuttles that travel through LEO, but there is the potential that one little piece of space junk could smash into an unwary space traveler with explosive results!

The Satellites Just Keep on Coming

We are dependent on satellites for many everyday tasks. Our ever-increasing quest for knowledge drives us to launch more satellites every year. In the booming satellite industry, there is fierce competition for a position in LEO. Many companies are willing to pay top dollar to ensure their position in space. With LEO quickly becoming a satellite highway, it may soon face a traffic jam.

Satellite Search

▶ Unlike stars, satellites in LEO move noticeably cross the sky. Research different types of satellites that orbit Earth. Look at the night sky, and try to spot some satellites. What kinds of satellites did you find? Present your observations to the class.

Answers to Satellite Search

The best time to see satellites is from May through August, in the early evening and around dawn. A satellite looks like a star or airplane, but it moves across the sky in a straight line, fast enough to see. It will fade out of sight before it reaches the horizon. Satellites can be seen moving from west to east or from pole to pole. Some people report seeing a zigzag pattern of light moving across the sky; this is an optical illusion caused by slight muscle movements of the eyes. The slower the light moves, the higher the satellite is in orbit. This can help students determine what kind of satellite they have spotted. TV broadcasting satellites do not appear to move at all and, therefore, can rarely be detected by human eyes. These satellites travel in geosynchronous Earth orbits at a speed that matches the Earth's rotation.

EYE ON THE ENVIRONMENT
Eyes in the Sky

Teaching Strategy

Encourage students to find out more about the problem of space debris. Suggest that they work in groups to come up with ideas to address this problem.

Chapter Organizer

CHAPTER ORGANIZATION	TIME MINUTES	OBJECTIVES	LABS, INVESTIGATIONS, AND DEMONSTRATIONS
Chapter Opener pp. 508–509	45	National Standards: SAI 1, HNS 1, 3, ES 3c	**Start-Up Activity** Strange Gravity, p. 509
Section 1 A Solar System Is Born	90	▶ Explain the basic process of planet formation. ▶ Compare the inner planets with the outer planets. ▶ Describe the difference between rotation and revolution. ▶ Describe the shape of the orbits of the planets, and explain what keeps them in their orbits. UCP 1, 2, 4, SAI 1, ST 2, HNS 1–3, SPSP 1, 4, 5, ES 3a–3c	**QuickLab,** Staying in Focus, p. 516 GENERAL **Whiz-Bang Demonstrations,** Can You Vote on Venus? Demo 32 BASIC
Section 2 The Sun: Our Very Own Star	90	▶ Describe the basic structure and composition of the sun. ▶ Explain how the sun produces energy. ▶ Describe the surface activity of the sun, and name some of its effects on Earth. ST 2, SPSP 5, HNS 1–3, ES 3a; LabBook SAI 1	**Demonstration,** Observing Sunspots, p. 519 in ATE GENERAL **Discovery Lab,** How Far Is the Sun? p. 712 ADVANCED **Datasheets for LabBook,** How Far Is the Sun? Datasheet 42 ADVANCED
Section 3 The Earth Takes Shape	90	▶ Describe the shape and structure of the Earth. ▶ Explain how the Earth got its layered structure and how this process affects the appearance of Earth's surface. ▶ Explain the development of Earth's atmosphere and the influence of early life on the atmosphere. ▶ Describe how the Earth's oceans and continents were formed. UCP 2, 4, SAI 1, ES 2b	**Demonstration,** p. 524 in ATE GENERAL **QuickLab,** Mixing It Up, p. 525 GENERAL **Long-Term Projects & Research Ideas,** Project 47 ADVANCED

See page T20 for a complete correlation of this book with the **NATIONAL SCIENCE EDUCATION STANDARDS.**

TECHNOLOGY RESOURCES

 Guided Reading Audio CD English or Spanish, Chapter 19

 CNN. Science, Technology & Society, Solar Storms, Segment 22

One-Stop Planner CD-ROM with Test Generator

Chapter 19 • Formation of the Solar System

CLASSROOM WORKSHEETS, TRANSPARENCIES, AND RESOURCES	SCIENCE INTEGRATION AND CONNECTIONS	REVIEW AND ASSESSMENT
Directed Reading Worksheet 19 BASIC **Science Puzzlers, Twisters & Teasers,** Worksheet 19 ADVANCED		
Directed Reading Worksheet 19, Section 1 BASIC **Math Skills for Science Worksheet 32,** Density GENERAL **Transparency 186,** Earth's Rotation and Revolution **Transparency 187,** Ellipse **Transparency 188,** Gravity and the Motion of the Moon **Critical Thinking Worksheet 19,** A Balooney Universe ADVANCED	**Multicultural Connection,** p. 510 in ATE **Biology Connection,** p. 512 **Math and More,** p. 513 in ATE GENERAL **Cross-Disciplinary Focus,** p. 513 in ATE ADVANCED **MathBreak,** Kepler's Formula, p. 516 GENERAL **Math and More,** p. 516 in ATE BASIC **Apply,** p. 517 GENERAL **Cross-Disciplinary Focus,** p. 517 in ATE GENERAL **Scientific Debate:** Mirrors in Space, p. 535	**Self-Check,** p. 511 **Homework,** p. 511 in ATE ADVANCED **Homework,** p. 512 in ATE ADVANCED **Self-Check,** p. 513 **Review,** p. 514 GENERAL **Homework,** p. 517 in ATE GENERAL **Review,** p. 518 GENERAL **Quiz,** p. 518 in ATE GENERAL **Alternative Assessment,** p. 518 in ATE GENERAL
Transparency 189, Structure of the Sun and Its Atmosphere **Directed Reading Worksheet 19,** Section 2 BASIC **Transparency 248,** The Periodic Table of the Elements **Transparency 190,** Fusion of Hydrogen in the Sun **Reinforcement Worksheet 19,** Stay on the Sunny Side GENERAL	**Math and More,** p. 520 in ATE GENERAL **Multicultural Connection,** p. 520 in ATE **Biology Connection,** p. 521 **Connect to Physical Science,** p. 521 in ATE **Cross-Disciplinary Focus,** p. 522 in ATE **Science, Technology, and Society:** Don't Look at the Sun! p. 534 ADVANCED	**Homework,** p. 522 in ATE GENERAL **Review,** p. 523 GENERAL **Quiz,** p. 523 in ATE GENERAL **Alternative Assessment,** p. 523 in ATE GENERAL
Teaching Transparency 122, The Composition of the Earth **Directed Reading Worksheet 19,** Section 3 BASIC **Math Skills for Science Worksheet 12,** Reducing Fractions to Lowest Terms GENERAL **Reinforcement Worksheet 19,** Third Rock from the Sun GENERAL	**Connect to Geology,** p. 525 in ATE ADVANCED **Chemistry Connection,** p. 526 **Math and More,** p. 526 in ATE GENERAL **Environment Connection,** p. 527 **Connect to Life Science,** p. 527 in ATE	**Self-Check,** p. 524 **Review,** p. 529 GENERAL **Quiz,** p. 529 in ATE GENERAL **Alternative Assessment,** p. 529 in ATE GENERAL

 Holt, Rinehart and Winston On-line Resources
go.hrw.com

For worksheets and other teaching aids related to this chapter, visit the HRW Web site and type in the keyword: **HSTSOL**

 **National Science Teachers Association**
www.scilinks.org

Encourage students to use the *sci*LINKS numbers listed in the internet connect boxes to access information and resources on the **NSTA** Web site.

END-OF-CHAPTER REVIEW AND ASSESSMENT

Chapter Review in Study Guide
Vocabulary and Notes in Study Guide
Chapter Tests with Performance-Based Assessment, Chapter 19 Test
Chapter Tests with Performance-Based Assessment, Performance-Based Assessment 19
Concept Mapping Transparency 19

Chapter Resources & Worksheets

Visual Resources

TEACHING TRANSPARENCIES

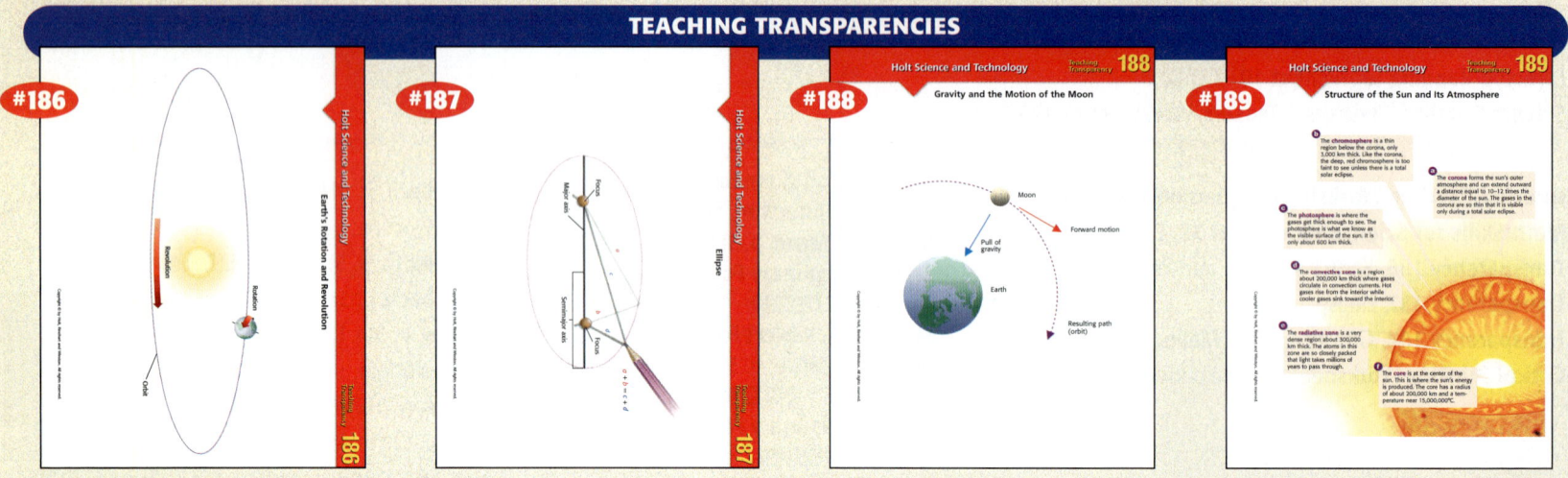

TEACHING TRANSPARENCIES

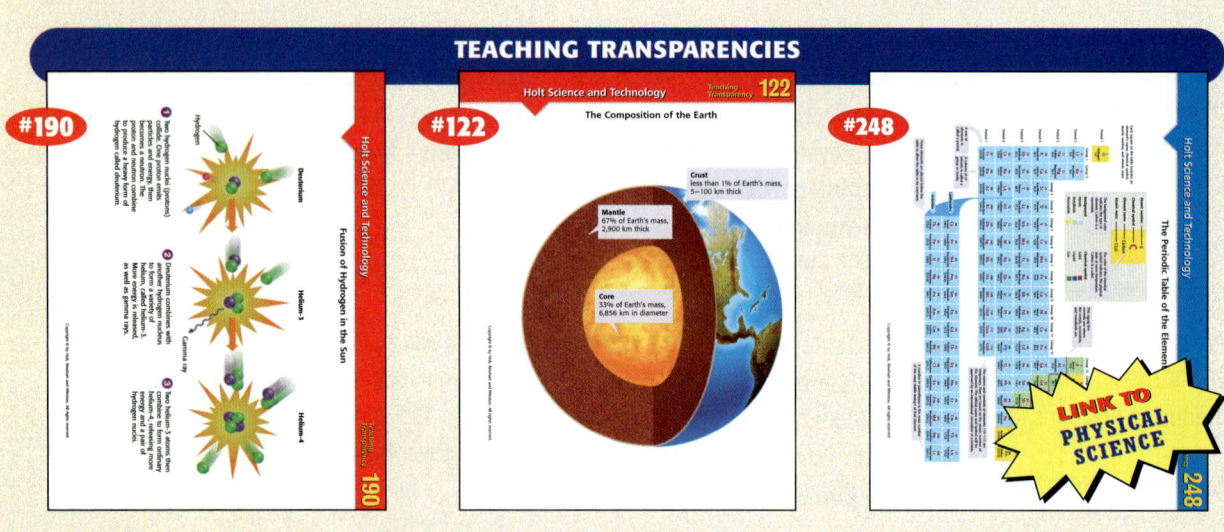

CONCEPT MAPPING TRANSPARENCY

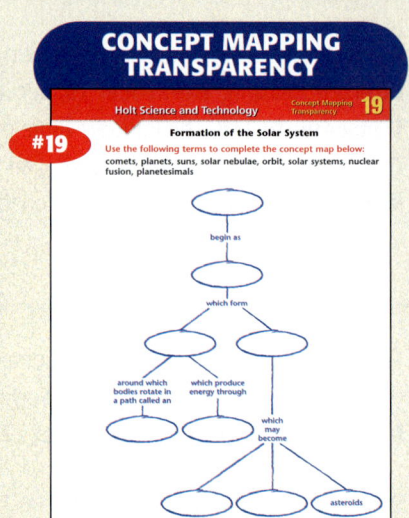

Meeting Individual Needs

DIRECTED READING

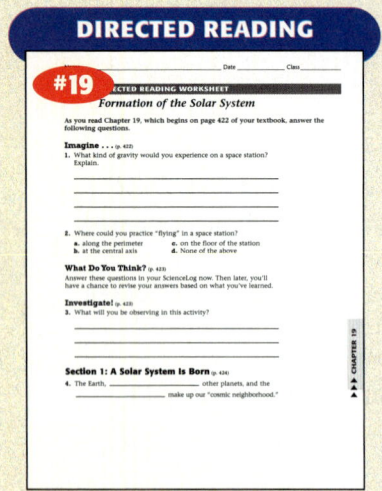

REINFORCEMENT & VOCABULARY REVIEW

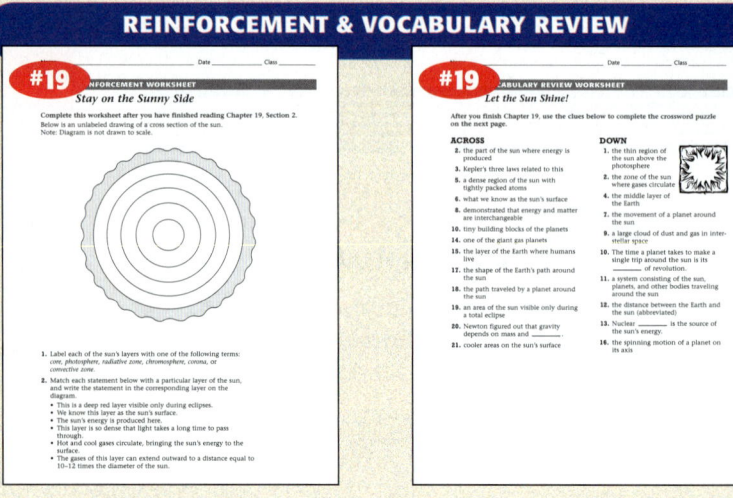

SCIENCE PUZZLERS, TWISTERS & TEASERS

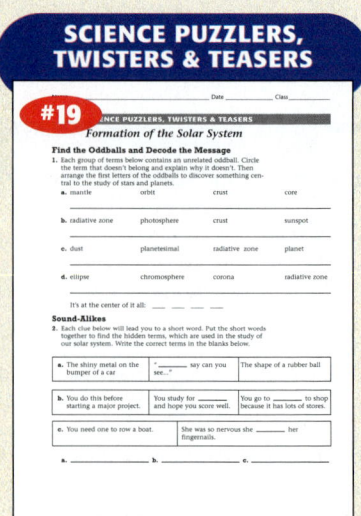

Chapter 19 • Formation of the Solar System

Chapter 19 • Formation of the Solar System

Review & Assessment

STUDY GUIDE

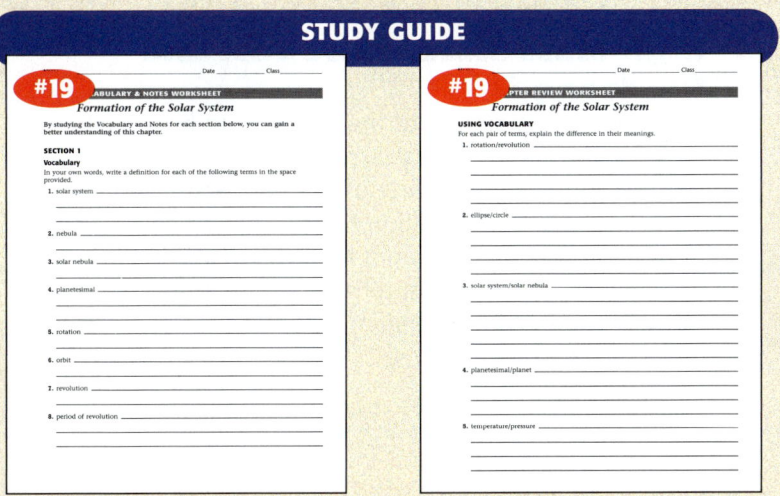

CHAPTER TESTS WITH PERFORMANCE-BASED ASSESSMENT

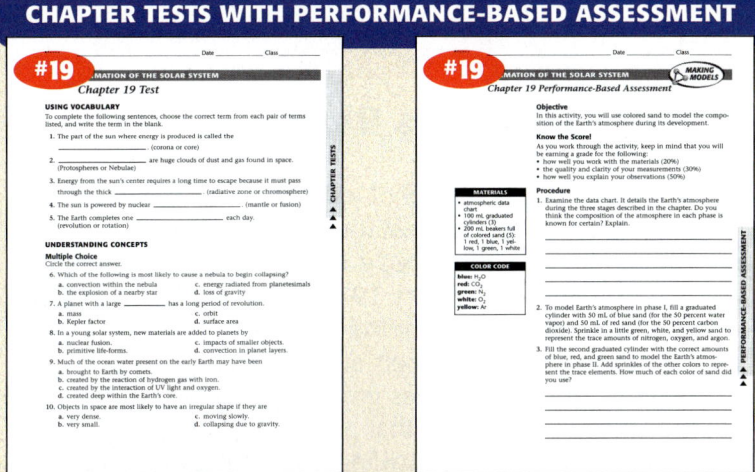

Lab Worksheets

WHIZ-BANG DEMONSTRATIONS

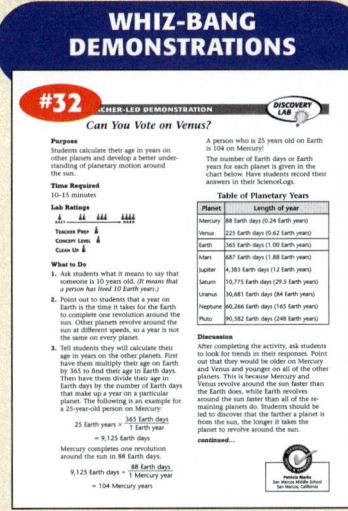

LONG-TERM PROJECTS & RESEARCH IDEAS

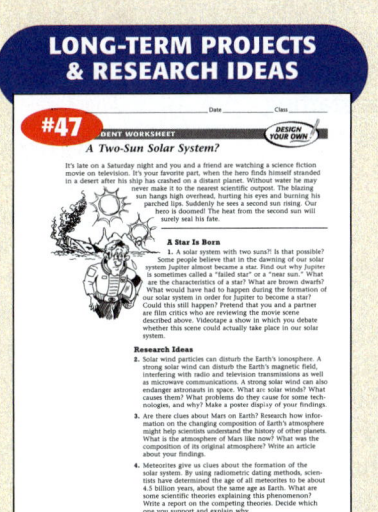

DATASHEETS FOR LABBOOK

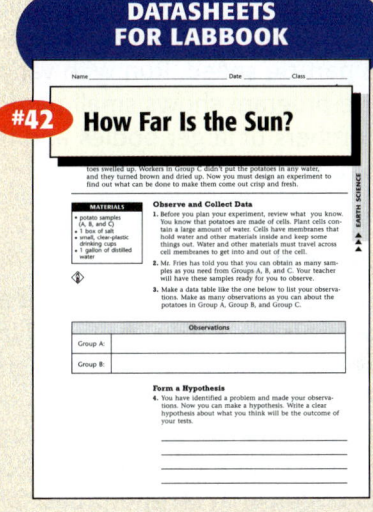

Applications & Extensions

CRITICAL THINKING & PROBLEM SOLVING

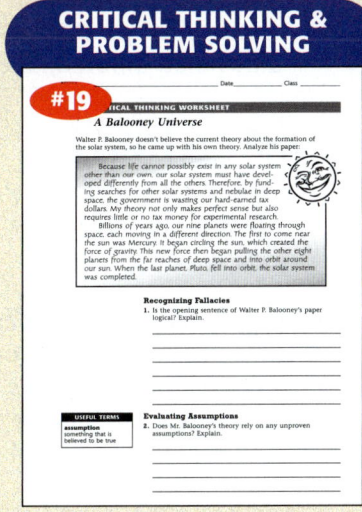

SCIENCE TECHNOLOGY

Chapter 19 • Chapter Resources & Worksheets

507D

Chapter Background

SECTION 1

A Solar System Is Born

▶ **A Computer Model of Planet Building**
The Planetary Science Institute, in Tucson, Arizona, produced a computer program in the late 1970s to test hypotheses about the formation of planetesimals and planets. The program has given credence to the theory that particle collisions within a swirling, collapsing nebula could have led to the creation of our solar system. The program simulates the motion of particles at various distances from the sun and tracks the results of collisions based on actual physical and mechanical properties, such as gas drag and particle speed. Run with various starting conditions, the program shows small particles aggregating into numbers of larger bodies and the eventual production of a system of planets.

▶ **The Orbit of Comets**
Orbits represent the entire closed path of an orbiting body. A planet or asteroid orbit has an elliptical shape. Scientists observe that near the sun comets seem to have a parabolic orbit (shaped like an open-ended ellipse). This could indicate that comets come from the outer reaches of the solar system. Scientists theorize that some comets originate in an enormous spherical cloud surrounding the solar system. This region, named the Oort cloud, may contain 100 billion of these icy bodies. The gravitational pull of another object can knock a comet out of the Oort cloud, after which it is "captured" by the gravity of our sun.

IS THAT A FACT!

▶ A star begins life when fusion reactions start (at about 10 million degrees Celsius). It can burn steadily for billions of years, converting hydrogen to helium in its core. As the hydrogen runs out, the core collapses and heats up. The star's atmosphere expands and cools, and the star becomes a red giant.

▶ **High-Mass Stars: "Live Fast and Die Young"**
Stars with mass similar to that of our sun have a life cycle of 10 to 11 billion years. High-mass stars, with a mass at least 10 times that of our sun, actually burn up much quicker—in 50 million to 100 million years—and burn much brighter. When a high-mass star runs out of fuel, its core collapses, and the star becomes a supernova. A supernova explosion is one of the most violent events in the universe.

SECTION 2

The Sun: Our Very Own Star

▶ **Movement of Energy Within the Sun**
Because the matter in the sun's core is so dense, energy has difficulty escaping. Photons released by nuclear fusion in the sun's core cannot travel more than 1 cm before colliding with another particle. Each time this happens, a photon's energy is scattered in a random direction.

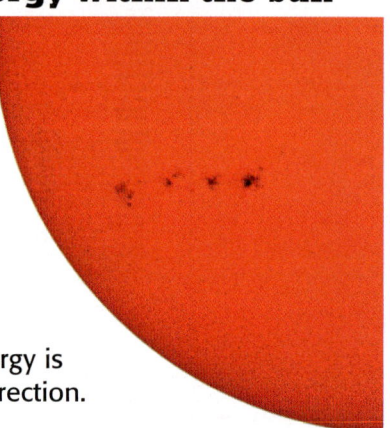

- When energy escapes the core, it travels more rapidly through the convection zone. The energy finally passes into space as visible light, X rays, ultraviolet, infrared, and other types of radiation.

IS THAT A FACT!

▶ It can take millions of years for the energy of a photon to travel from the sun's core to its surface!

▶ **The Sunspot Cycle**
The increasing and decreasing number of sunspots in an 11-year cycle appears to be driven by the magnetic field in the sun's surface layers. The field seems to "wind up" much as a rubber band does (perhaps

Chapter 19 • Formation of the Solar System

because of the difference in rate of rotation between the sun's poles and its equator). This process intensifies the magnetic field; therefore, more sunspots appear, and the sun becomes much more active. Where the sun is most active, giant explosions called solar flares occur.

- Solar flares spew out electrically charged particles that affect human technology on Earth. Despite the great distance between the sun and Earth, solar flares can disrupt TV programs, open electronically controlled garage doors, damage satellites, and even cause power blackouts.

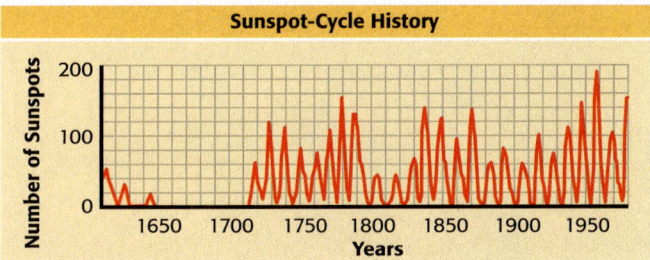

SECTION 3

The Earth Takes Shape

▶ **Evidence of Earth's Origins**

Many different sciences have contributed to our understanding of Earth's origin. Much remains to be discovered through computer models and the study of other planets. The following evidence has shaped the current scientific theories about the formation of Earth and its atmosphere:

- The oldest rocks on Earth are nearly 4 billion years old.

- Some of the oldest rocks are sedimentary in origin, so we know that oceans must have existed early in the history of Earth.

- The sun was cooler when the Earth was forming. We know this from the study of how hydrogen fusion reactions work.

- The Earth must have had a dense atmosphere with greenhouse gases early in its life, or it would have been too cold to have liquid oceans.

- The oldest fossils of primitive life are stromatolites, blue-green algae colonies that originated between 3.7 billion and 3.4 billion years ago. Simple life-forms probably appeared on Earth before this time (between 4.6 billion and 3.9 billion years ago).

- Blue-green algae use photosynthesis to get energy from sunlight to produce oxygen. Evidence from the oxidation of minerals in the rock record indicates that oxygen started to appear in significant concentrations in Earth's atmosphere between 2.5 billion and 2.0 billion years ago.

- Water that formed the oceans came from the early Earth's interior and was released by outgassing during the differentiation process. As the Earth heated and differentiated, water that was chemically bound in minerals was carried to the surface of the planet along with magma. Water vapor was then released to form the early atmosphere. Even at current rates of volcanism, the water vapor released from lava flows would be more than enough to fill the Earth's oceans in 500 million years.

For background information about teaching strategies and issues, refer to the *Professional Reference for Teachers*.

Chapter 19 • Chapter Background **507F**

Chapter 19

Formation of the Solar System

 **Pre-Reading Questions**

Students may not know the answers to these questions before reading the chapter, so accept any reasonable response.

Suggested Answers

1. The gravitational attraction of the sun keeps planets in their orbits.
2. The sun shines because nuclear fusion in its core produces energy.
3. The Earth is round because it became large enough for internal pressure to crush the materials inside it.

 Directed Reading Worksheet 19

 Science Puzzlers, Twisters & Teasers Worksheet 19

 Guided Reading Audio CD English or Spanish, Chapter 19

Formation of the Solar System

Sections

1. A Solar System Is Born 510
   - Biology Connection .. 512
   - Internet Connect 514
   - QuickLab 516
   - MathBreak 516
   - Apply 517
   - Internet Connect 518

2. The Sun: Our Very Own Star 519
   - Biology Connection .. 521
   - Internet Connect 523

3. The Earth Takes Shape 524
   - QuickLab 525
   - Chemistry Connection 526
   - Environment Connection 527
   - Internet Connect 529

Chapter Review 532
Feature Articles 534, 535
LabBook 712–713

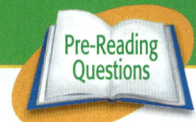 **Pre-Reading Questions**

1. What keeps the planets in their orbits?
2. Why does the sun shine?
3. Why is the Earth round?

---

internet connect

HRW On-line Resources

go.hrw.com

For worksheets and other teaching aids, visit the HRW Web site and type in the keyword: **HSTSOL**

www.scilinks.com

Use the *sci*LINKS numbers at the end of each chapter for additional resources on the **NSTA** Web site.

www.cnnfyi.com

Visit the CNN Web site for current events coverage and classroom resources.

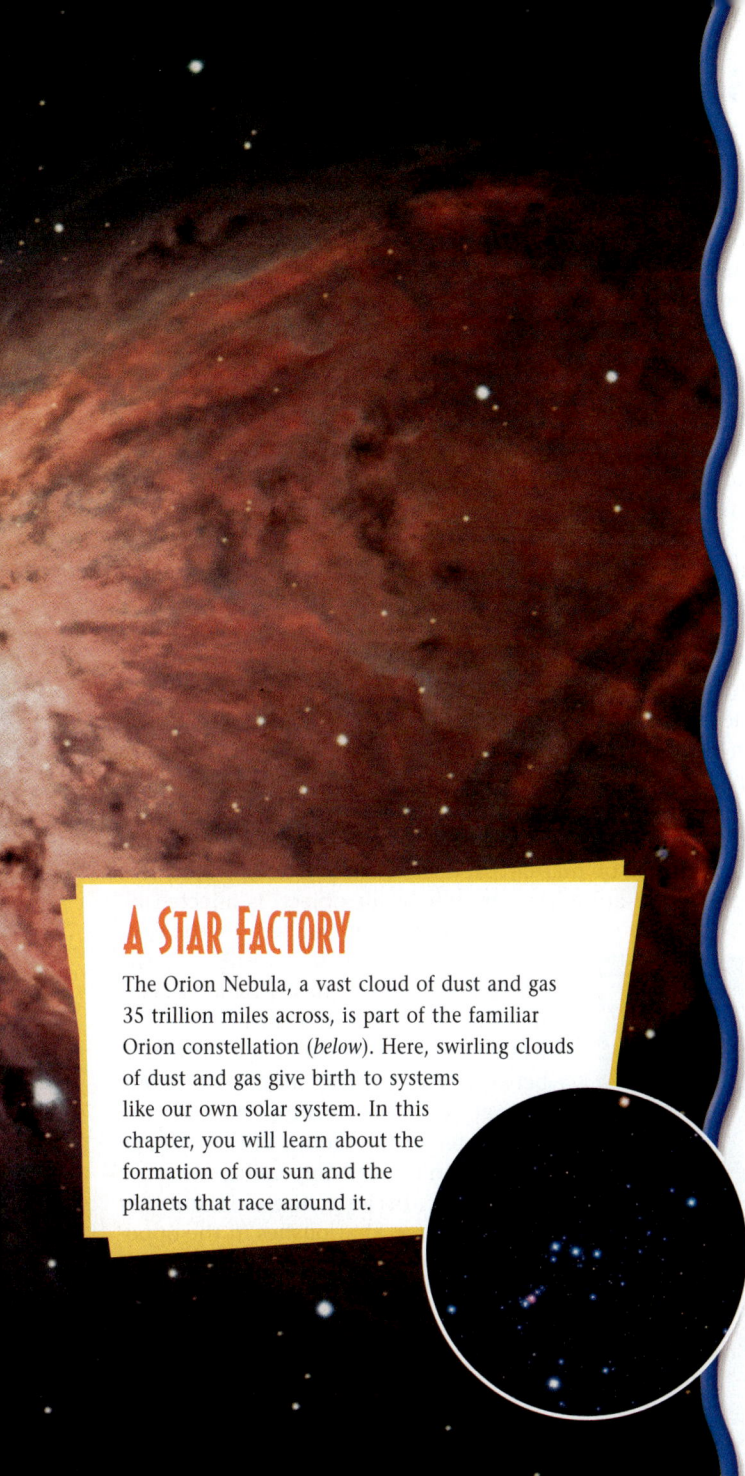

A Star Factory

The Orion Nebula, a vast cloud of dust and gas 35 trillion miles across, is part of the familiar Orion constellation (*below*). Here, swirling clouds of dust and gas give birth to systems like our own solar system. In this chapter, you will learn about the formation of our sun and the planets that race around it.

START-UP Activity

STRANGE GRAVITY

If you drop a heavy object, will it fall faster than a lighter one? According to the law of gravity, the answer is no. In 1971, *Apollo 15* astronaut David Scott stood on the moon and dropped a feather and a hammer. Television audiences were amazed to see both objects strike the moon's surface at the same time. Now you can perform a version of this classic experiment in the classroom.

Procedure

1. Select **two pieces of identical notebook paper.** Crumple one piece of paper into a ball.
2. Place the flat piece of paper on top of a **book** and the paper ball on top of the flat piece of paper.
3. Hold the book waist high, and then drop it to the floor.

Analysis

4. Which piece of paper reached the bottom first? Did either piece of paper fall slower than the book? Explain your observations in your ScienceLog.
5. Now hold the crumpled paper in one hand and the flat piece of paper in the other. Drop both pieces of paper at the same time. What else affected the speed of the falling paper besides gravity? Record your observations in your ScienceLog, and share your ideas with your classmates.

START-UP Activity

STRANGE GRAVITY

MATERIALS
FOR EACH STUDENT: • 2 pieces of notebook paper • book

Teacher's Notes

You might point out to students that when David Scott performed this experiment on the moon's surface, he paid homage to Galileo. While Galileo did predict that the mass of an object does not affect the rate at which the object falls, it is uncertain whether he proved this theory by dropping cannonballs of different masses from the Leaning Tower of Pisa, as legend tells.

Answers to START-UP Activity

4. Both pieces of paper should reach the bottom at the same time. They should have fallen at the same rate as the book. Gravity causes all objects to fall at the same rate, regardless of their mass.
5. The crumpled piece of paper should reach the floor first. While gravity pulled both pieces toward the floor, the crumpled piece of paper hit the ground first because it fell with less air resistance.

Chapter 19 • Formation of the Solar System

SECTION 1

Focus

A Solar System Is Born

This section describes the solar system and explains how it formed from a collapsing nebula. The nebula first formed planetesimals, then planets formed in the outer regions, and finally a star (the sun) formed at the nebula's center. Students will learn why the planets that formed close to the sun are rocky, while those far from the sun are large and gaseous. The section concludes with a discussion of planetary orbits and rotation.

Bellringer

Display this question on the board or an overhead projector:

Could astronauts land on a star in the same way that they landed on the moon? Why or why not? (No; stars are composed of gas, not solid rock like the moon. Stars are also a lot hotter!)

1) Motivate

COOPERATIVE LEARNING

Display a poster of the solar system or a selection of photographs of the planets and the sun. Form student groups, and have each group brainstorm to come up with a list of facts they know about the solar system and some questions they want to answer. Then ask each group to study the display and to note the following:

- what a planet's orbit looks like
- how planets close to the sun differ from those far away

Discuss students' observations and hypotheses about why these conditions exist.

Sheltered English

Section 1

Terms to Learn

solar system
nebula
solar nebula
planetesimal
rotation
orbit
revolution
period of revolution
ellipse
astronomical unit

What You'll Do

- Explain the basic process of planet formation.
- Compare the inner planets with the outer planets.
- Describe the difference between rotation and revolution.
- Describe the shape of the orbits of the planets, and explain what keeps them in their orbits.

Multicultural CONNECTION

Many cultures have myths that describe the creation of the sun. An Australian aboriginal myth explains that people and animals lived in total darkness before the sun appeared. One day an emu egg was thrown into the sky and collided with a pile of dry wood. The wood burst into flame, and a fire burned in the sky. The Great Spirit replenishes the firewood to keep the sun burning. Have interested students find other solar creation myths and make illustrated storyboards of the myths they discover.

A Solar System Is Born

You probably know that Earth is not the only planet orbiting the sun. In fact, it has eight fellow travelers in its cosmic neighborhood. Together these nine planets and the sun are part of the solar system. The **solar system** is composed of the sun (a star) and the planets and other bodies that travel around the sun. But how did our solar system come to be?

The Solar Nebula

All the ingredients for building planets are found in the vast, seemingly empty regions between the stars. But these regions are not really empty—they contain a mixture of gas and dust. The gas is mostly hydrogen and helium, while the dust is made up of tiny grains of elements such as carbon and iron. The dust and gas clump together in huge interstellar clouds called **nebulas** (or *nebulae*), which are so big that light takes many years to cross them! Nebulas, like the one shown in **Figure 1**, are cold and dark. Over time, light from nearby stars interacts with the dust and gas, forming many new chemicals. Eventually, complex molecules similar to those necessary for life form deep within the nebulas. These clouds are the first ingredients of a new planetary system.

Gravity Pulls Matter Together Because these clouds of dust and gas consist of matter, they have mass. *Mass,* which is a measure of the amount of matter in an object, is affected by the force of gravity. But because the matter in a nebula is so spread out, the attraction between the dust and gas particles is very small. If a nebula's density were great enough, then the attraction between the particles might be strong enough to pull everything together into the center of the cloud. But even large clouds don't necessarily collapse toward the center because there is another effect, or force, that pushes in the opposite direction of gravity. You'll soon find out what that force is.

Figure 1 *The Horsehead nebula is a cold, dark cloud of gas and dust as well as a possible site for future star formation.*

---

510 Chapter 19 • Formation of the Solar System

Pressure Pushes Matter Apart *Temperature* is a measure of how fast the particles in an object move around. If the gas molecules in a nebula move very slowly, the temperature is very low and the cloud is cold. If they move fast, the temperature is high and the cloud is warm. Because the cloud has a temperature that is above absolute zero, the gas molecules are moving. There is no particular structure in the cloud, and individual gas molecules can move in any direction. Sometimes they crash into each other. As shown in **Figure 2,** these collisions create a push, or *pressure,* away from the other gas particles. This pressure is what finally balances the gravity and keeps the cloud from collapsing.

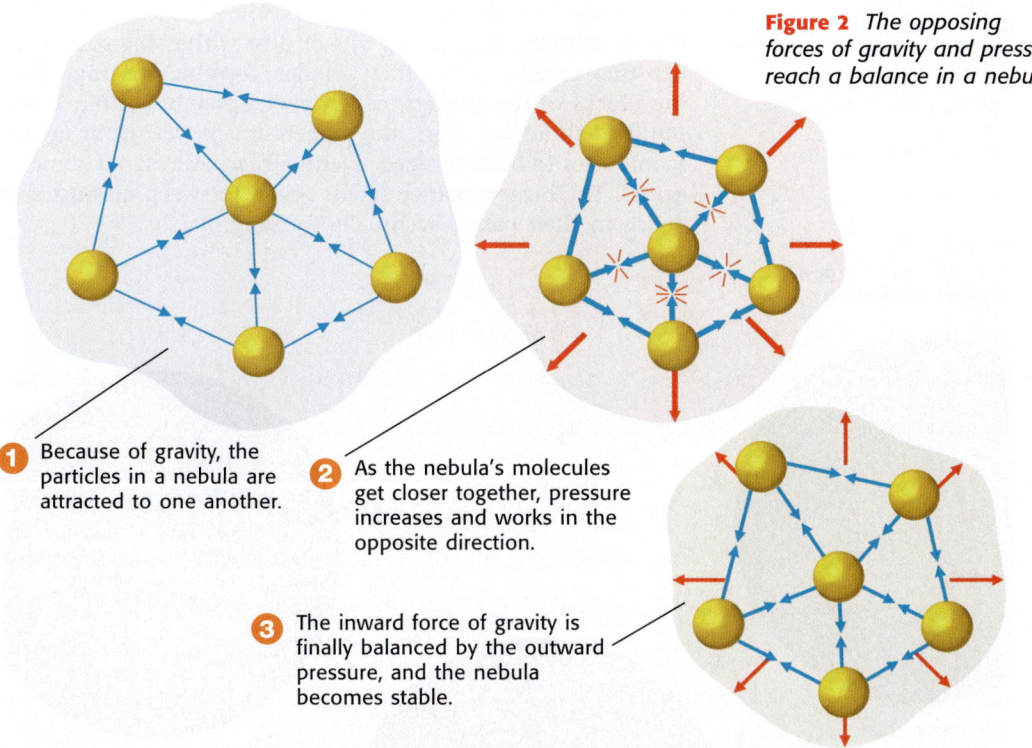

Figure 2 The opposing forces of gravity and pressure reach a balance in a nebula.

① Because of gravity, the particles in a nebula are attracted to one another.

② As the nebula's molecules get closer together, pressure increases and works in the opposite direction.

③ The inward force of gravity is finally balanced by the outward pressure, and the nebula becomes stable.

The Solar Nebula Forms Sometimes something happens to upset this balance. Two nebulas can crash into each other, for example, or a nearby star can explode, causing material from the star to crash into the cloud. These events compress small regions of the cloud so that gravity overcomes the pressure. Gravity then causes the cloud to collapse inward. At this point, the stage is set for the formation of a star and, as in the case of our sun, its planets. The **solar nebula** is the name of the nebula that formed into our own solar system.

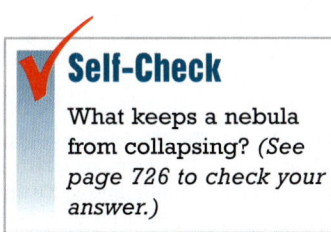

Self-Check

What keeps a nebula from collapsing? *(See page 726 to check your answer.)*

511

2) Teach

USING THE FIGURE

Have students refer to the three steps in **Figure 2** as they explain the force that pulls particles together (gravity) and the force that pushes them apart (pressure due to the collision of particles).

Be sure that students understand the role of temperature in this system. (As temperature increases, particles speed up, collisions increase, and pressure increases.)

DISCUSSION

Have student volunteers describe in their own words an example of a system that is in equilibrium because opposing forces of gravity (pulling) and pressure (pushing) balance one another. (One example is a person sitting in a chair; gravity pulls down with a force equal to the force with which the chair pushes up.)

Homework

Research In October 1995, astronomers discovered the first planet orbiting a star outside of our solar system. The planet is in orbit around the star 51 Pegasi. Astronomers did not directly observe the planet. Instead they observed and measured the wobble in the star's velocity, apparently caused by the gravitational pull of the planet. Since then, astronomers have discovered more planets around other stars. Have students find out how many planets have been discovered and write a brief report comparing what we know about the planets, including our own.

MISCONCEPTION ALERT

Make sure students understand that temperature is a measure of random molecular motion, or vibration, of the particles in a material. This is not the same as the bulk motion of a material. For example, a cold gas or liquid can flow at a fast speed, but this motion does not affect its temperature.

Answers to Self-Check

The balance between gravity and pressure keeps a nebula from collapsing.

Directed Reading Worksheet 19 Section 1

Section 1 • A Solar System Is Born   **511**

2 Teach, continued

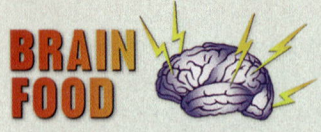

BRAIN FOOD

On Earth a cubic meter of air at sea level has a mass of about 1 kg. Each molecule of air is separated by only one-billionth of a meter (a nanometer). The best artificial vacuums that can be created in laboratories can reduce the number of air molecules in a given volume by a factor of 1 billion. This means that the molecules are one-millionth of a meter apart (a micrometer). How much space is in outer space? In young stellar nurseries, the amount of matter in a cubic meter is smaller by another factor of 1 billion and gas molecules are 1 mm apart! But this is still 10 billion times more dense than interstellar space!

ACTIVITY

Modeling Planetesimal Formation Have students work in pairs. Each pair will need a couple of sheets of wax paper and a small spray bottle with some water tinted by food coloring. Have students spray a little water on a sheet of wax paper. As students observe the wax paper after each spray, they will see large drops form. Discuss whether this is an accurate model of planetesimal formation, and note how gravity, rather than surface tension, causes planetesimals to form.

Biology CONNECTION

Some of the complex molecules created in the cold, dark clouds that eventually form stars and planets contain amino acids. Amino acids are the building blocks of proteins and life. Scientists wonder if some of this material survives in the planetesimals that formed far from the sun—the comets. Could comets have brought life-forming molecules to Earth?

From Planetesimals to Planets

Once the solar nebula started to collapse, things happened quickly, at least on a cosmic time scale. As the dark cloud collapsed, matter in the cloud got closer and closer together. This made the attraction between particles even stronger. The stronger attraction pulled the cloud together, and the gas and dust particles moved at a faster rate, increasing the temperature at the center of the cloud.

As things began to get crowded near the center of the solar nebula, particles of dust and gas in the cloud began to bump into other particles more often. Eventually much of the dust and gas began slowly rotating about the center of the cloud. The rotating solar nebula eventually flattened into a disk.

Planetesimals Sometimes bits of dust within the solar nebula stuck together when they collided, forming the tiny building blocks of the planets, called **planetesimals.** Within a few hundred thousand years, the planetesimals grew from microscopic sizes to boulder-sized, eventually measuring a kilometer across. The biggest planetesimals began to sweep up dust and debris in their paths, eventually forming planets.

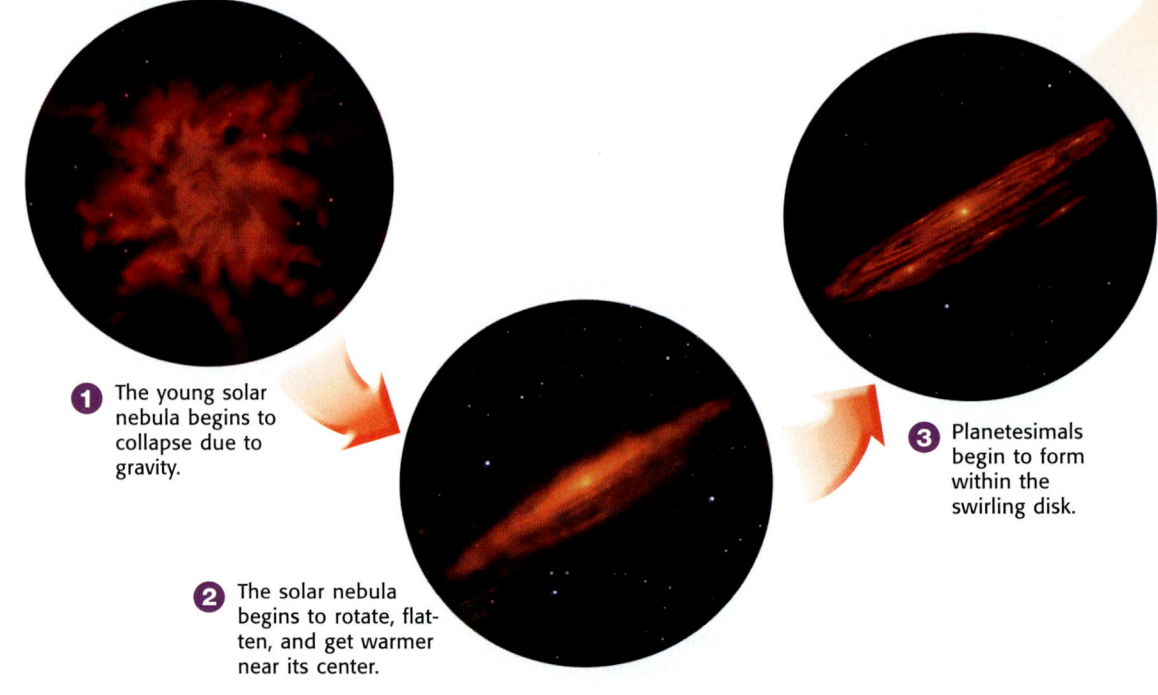

Figure 3 The Process of Solar System Formation

① The young solar nebula begins to collapse due to gravity.

② The solar nebula begins to rotate, flatten, and get warmer near its center.

③ Planetesimals begin to form within the swirling disk.

Homework

Prepare a Presentation Have students find information about the asteroid belt, the Kuiper belt, the Oort cloud, and comets. Ask them to explain one or more of these phenomena using the steps shown in **Figure 3.** Encourage students to find a creative way to present their findings.

IS THAT A FACT!

Scientists think that all Earth-like planetesimals have a thin atmosphere during formation. During the accretion process, this atmosphere is stripped away. If a subsequent atmosphere develops, it comes primarily from gases released during the differentiation of the planet's mantle.

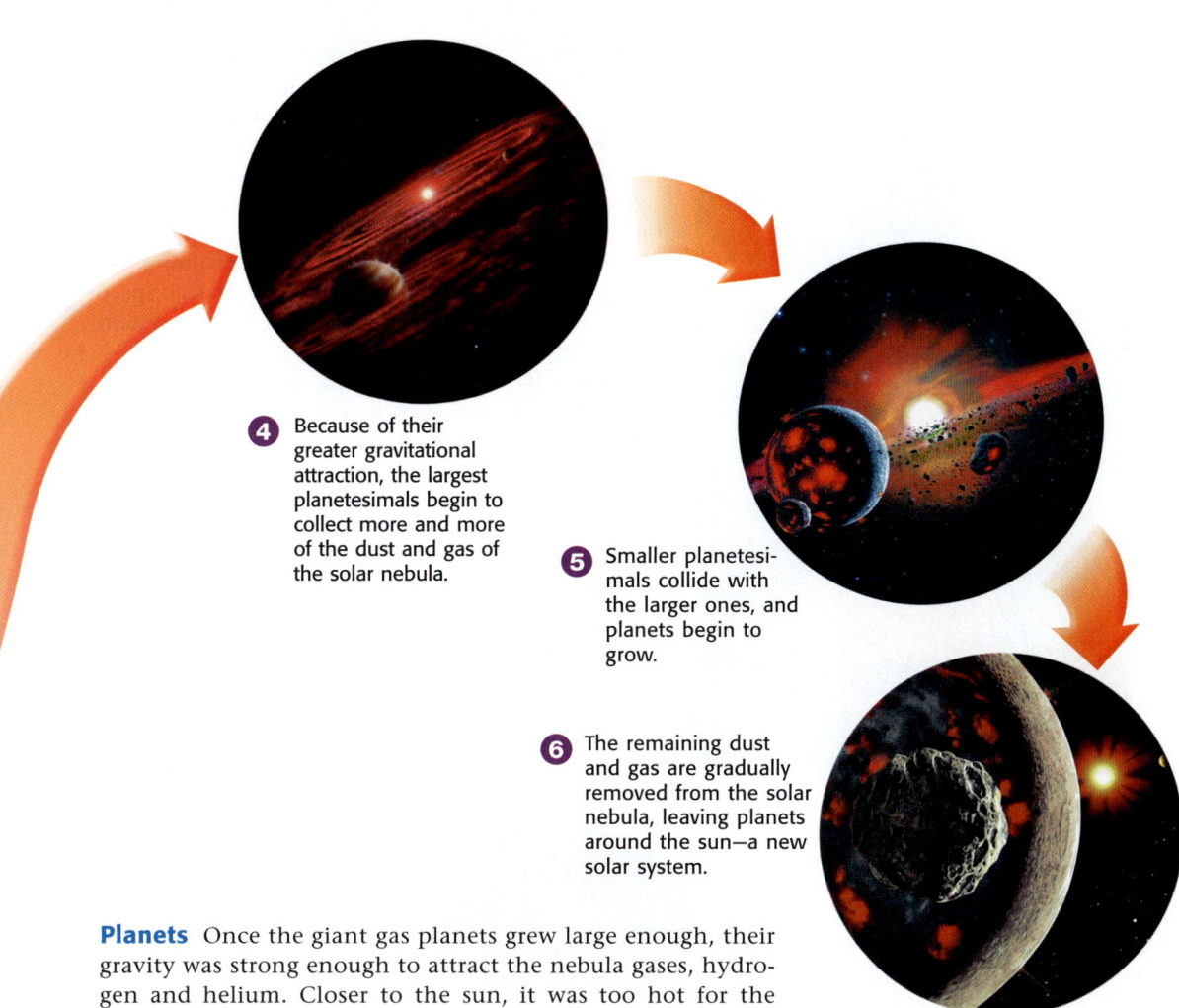

④ Because of their greater gravitational attraction, the largest planetesimals begin to collect more and more of the dust and gas of the solar nebula.

⑤ Smaller planetesimals collide with the larger ones, and planets begin to grow.

⑥ The remaining dust and gas are gradually removed from the solar nebula, leaving planets around the sun—a new solar system.

Planets Once the giant gas planets grew large enough, their gravity was strong enough to attract the nebula gases, hydrogen and helium. Closer to the sun, it was too hot for the gases to remain, so the inner planets are made mostly of rocky material.

Craters and Comets Collisions with smaller planetesimals became more violent as pieces of debris became larger, leaving many craters on the surface of the rocky planets. We see evidence of this today particularly on Mercury, Mars, and our moon.

In the final steps of planet formation, the remaining planetesimals crashed down on the planets or got thrown to the outer edge of the solar nebula by the gravity of the larger planets. Occasionally something, perhaps a passing star, sends them journeying toward the sun. If the planetesimal is icy, we see this visitor as a *comet*.

 **Self-Check**

Why are the giant gas planets so large? *(See page 726 to check your answer.)*

MEETING INDIVIDUAL NEEDS

Learners Having Difficulty
Have students list characteristics of the inner planets and the gas giants. (inner planets: rocky, small, dense, thin atmosphere, few or no moons; gas giants: mostly gas, large, not dense, thick atmosphere, many moons)

Using a diagram of the solar system with the orbits of the planets drawn to scale, guide students to explain what caused these differences. (The inner planets formed close to the sun, where most of the gases burned away and high-temperature solids, such as rock, could condense.)
Sheltered English

MATH and MORE

Density is a measure of the amount of matter in a specific unit of space. Have students answer the questions below, and have them create a bar graph comparing the densities of different planets.

- How many times denser than Jupiter is Mercury? ($\frac{5.43}{1.32} = 4.11$)
- How many times denser than Saturn is Earth? ($\frac{5.52}{0.69} = 8.00$)

Planet	Mean Density (g/cm³)
Mercury	5.43
Venus	5.20
Earth	5.52
Mars	3.93
Jupiter	1.32
Saturn	0.69
Uranus	1.32
Neptune	1.64
Pluto	2.05

 Math Skills Worksheet 32 "Density"

Cross-Disciplinary Focus

History Gerard Peter Kuiper (rhymes with "viper") lived from 1902 to 1973 and is often called the father of modern planetary science. Kuiper made discoveries about Saturn and its largest moon, Titan, as well as about Mars, Uranus, Neptune, Pluto, and Jupiter. Have students find out more about his discoveries.

Answers to Self-Check
The giant gas planets were massive enough for their gravity to attract hydrogen and helium.

2) Teach, continued

GUIDED PRACTICE

Writing Discuss how Boyle's and Charles's laws help us understand the formation of the solar system.

- Boyle's law: at a constant temperature, the volume of a gas is inversely proportional to the pressure.
- Charles's law: at constant pressure, the volume of a gas is directly proportional to the temperature.

Review with students the difference between inverse and direct relationships, and have them give examples. Ask students to explain, in writing, why the temperature of a nebula increases as it becomes denser.

RETEACHING

Draw four large squares on the board, and label them as follows:

1. The Solar Nebula
2. The Nebula Collapsing
3. The Planetesimals Form
4. The Sun and Planets Form

Have volunteers help you sketch each stage of solar-system formation in the appropriate square. Use arrows and phrases to indicate changes in temperature and the balance between gravity and pressure. **Sheltered English**

INDEPENDENT PRACTICE

Concept Mapping Have students construct a concept map that explains the formation of the solar system. Make sure that students correctly identify the physical processes involved at each stage.

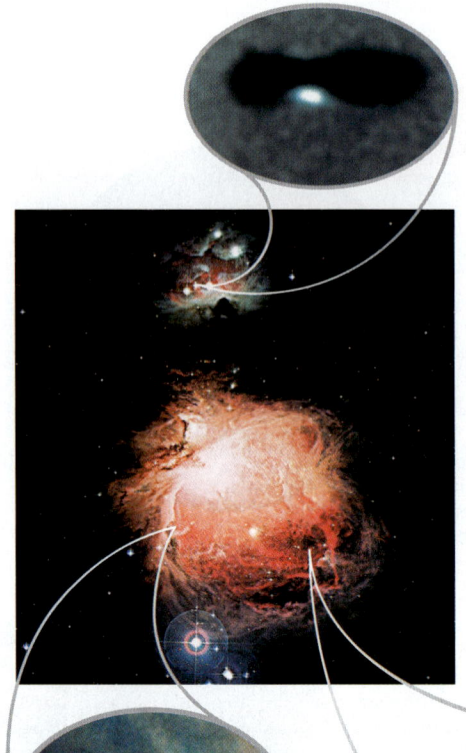

Birth of a Star But what was happening at the middle of the solar nebula? The central part of the solar nebula contained so much mass and had become so hot that hydrogen fusion began. This created so much pressure at the center of the solar nebula that outward pressure balanced the inward force of gravity. At this point, the gas stopped collapsing. As the sun was born, the remaining gas and dust of the nebula were blown into deep space by a strong solar wind, and the new solar system was complete.

From the time the nebula first started to collapse, it took nearly 10 million years for the solar system to form. So how do we know that our ideas of star and planet formation are correct when nobody was around to watch it? Powerful telescopes, such as the Hubble Space Telescope, are now able to show us some of the fine details inside distant nebulas. One such nebula is shown in **Figure 4**. For the first time, scientists can see disks of dust around stars that are in the process of forming.

Figure 4 *The Orion nebula contains several "star nurseries"—disks of gas and dust where new stars form. The insets show newly-formed stars within some of these disks.*

TOPIC: The Planets
GO TO: www.scilinks.org
sciLINKS NUMBER: HSTE455

REVIEW

1. What two forces balance each other to keep a nebula of dust and gas from collapsing or flying apart?
2. Why does the composition of the giant gas planets differ from that of the rocky inner planets?
3. Explain why there is only one planet in each orbit around the sun.
4. **Making Inferences** Why do all the planets go around the sun in the same direction, and why do the planets all lie in a flat plane?

Answers to Review

1. gravity and pressure
2. Giant gas planets were far enough from the sun to collect lighter gases. Close to the sun, it was hot enough that only rocky material and dust were present.
3. The largest planetesimal in an orbit collected all of the material in its path and became a planet.
4. The planets formed from the flattened disk of the nebula, which rotated in one direction. The dust and gas that formed the planets moved in the same direction that the nebula was spinning.

Planetary Motion

The solar system, which is now 4.6 billion years old, is not simply a collection of stationary planets and other bodies around the sun. Each one moves according to strict physical laws. The ways in which the Earth moves, for example, cause seasons and even day and night.

Rotation and Revolution How does the motion of the Earth cause day and night? The answer has to do with the Earth's spinning on its axis, or **rotation.** As the Earth rotates, only one-half of the Earth faces the sun at any given time. The half facing the sun is light (day), and the half facing away from the sun is dark (night).

In addition to rotating on its axis, the Earth also travels around the sun in a path called an **orbit.** This motion around the sun along its orbit is called **revolution.** The other planets in our solar system also revolve around the sun. The amount of time it takes for a single trip around the sun is called a **period of revolution.** The period for the Earth to revolve around the sun is 365 days. Mercury orbits the sun in 88 days.

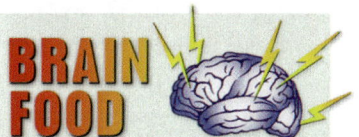

BRAIN FOOD

All planets *revolve* around the sun in the same direction. If you could look down on the solar system from above the sun's north pole, you would see all the planets revolving in a counterclockwise direction. Not all planets *rotate* in the same direction, however. Venus, Uranus, and Pluto rotate backward compared with the rest of the planets.

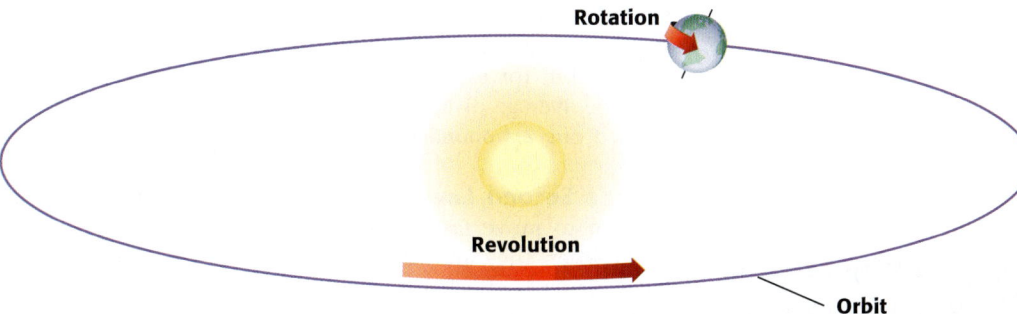

Figure 5 *A planet rotates on its own axis and revolves around the sun in a path called an orbit.*

Planetary Orbits But why do the planets continue to revolve around the sun? Does something hold them in their orbit? Why doesn't gravity pull the planets toward the sun? Or why don't they fly off into space? To answer these questions, we need to go back in time to look at the discoveries made by the scientists of the 1500s and 1600s.

Danish astronomer Tycho Brahe (TIE koh BRAW uh) carefully observed the positions of the planets for over a quarter of a century. When he died in 1601, his young assistant, Johannes Kepler, inherited all of his records. Kepler set out to understand the motions of the planets and to make a simple description of the solar system.

2) Teach, continued

QuickLab

MATERIALS
- string, about 12 cm long
- unlined paper
- 2 thumbtacks
- pencil

Safety Caution: Students should use care with thumbtacks to avoid injuring themselves or damaging the surface on which they work. Have them put a piece of cardboard under their sheet of paper.

Answer to QuickLab
4. The closer together the foci are, the more circular the ellipse is.

MATH and MORE

Have students use a ruler to measure segments *a*, *b*, *c*, and *d* in **Figure 6** and then test Kepler's first law of motion. Point out that the illustration shows the string at two distinct points in its description of an ellipse.

Teaching Transparency 187
"Ellipse"

 **internet**connect

SC**LINKS**
NSTA
TOPIC: The Planets
GO TO: www.scilinks.org
*sci*LINKS NUMBER: HSTE455

TOPIC: Kepler's Laws
GO TO: www.scilinks.org
*sci*LINKS NUMBER: HSTE460

QuickLab

Staying in Focus
1. Take a short piece of **string**, and pin both ends to a **piece of paper** with two **thumbtacks**.
2. Keeping the string stretched tight at all times, use a **pencil** to trace out the path of an ellipse.
3. Change the distance between the thumbtacks to change the shape of the ellipse.
4. How does the position of the thumbtacks (foci) affect the ellipse?

TRY at HOME

MATH BREAK

Kepler's Formula
Kepler's third law can be expressed with the formula

$$P^2 = a^3$$

where *P* is the period of revolution and *a* is the semimajor axis of an orbiting body. For example, Mars's period is 1.88 years, and its semimajor axis is 1.523 AU. Therefore, $1.88^2 = 1.523^3 = 3.53$. If astronomers know either the period or the distance, they can figure the other one out.

Kepler's First Law of Motion Kepler's first discovery, or *first law of motion*, came from his careful study of the movement of the planet Mars. He discovered that the planet did not move in a circle around the sun, but in an elongated circle called an *ellipse*. An **ellipse** is a closed curve in which the sum of the distances from the edge of the curve to two points (called *foci*) inside the ellipse is always the same, as shown in **Figure 6**.

Figure 6 Parts of an Ellipse

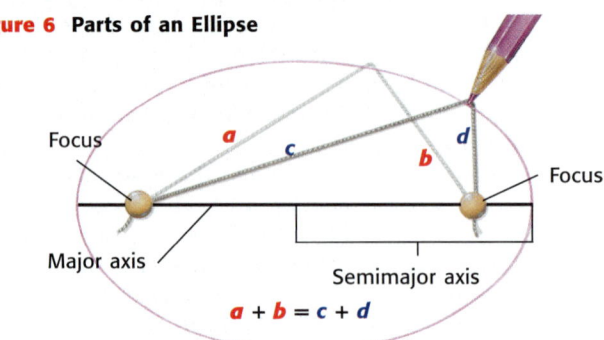

$$a + b = c + d$$

The maximum length of an ellipse is called its *major axis*, and half of this distance is the *semimajor axis*, which is usually used to give the size of an ellipse. The semimajor axis of Earth's orbit, for example, is 150 million kilometers. It represents the average distance between the Earth and the sun and is called one **astronomical unit**, or one AU.

Kepler's Second Law Kepler also discovered that the planets seem to move faster when they are close to the sun and slower when they are farther away. To illustrate this, imagine that a planet is attached to the sun by a string. The string will sweep out the same area in equal amounts of time. To keep the area of *A*, for example, equal to the area of *B*, the planet must move farther around its orbit in the same amount of time. This is Kepler's *second law of motion.*

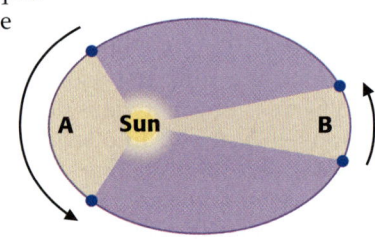

Kepler's Third Law Kepler's *third law of motion* compares the period of a planet's revolution with its semimajor axis. By doing some mathematical calculations, Kepler was able to demonstrate that by knowing a planet's period of revolution, the planet's distance from the sun can be calculated.

Science Bloopers

Johannes Kepler was obsessed with trying to describe the geometric harmony of the universe. He believed that there were five perfect geometric solids that fit precisely between the six known planets and that this pattern contained the divine meaning of the solar system. Although Kepler was wrong, his efforts to prove this idea enabled him to discover the elliptical orbit of the planets.

Newton's Law of Universal Gravitation

Kepler wondered what caused the planets closest to the sun to move faster than the planets farther away, but he never got an answer. It was Sir Isaac Newton who finally put the puzzle together. He did this with his ideas about *gravity*. Newton didn't understand *why* gravity worked or what caused it. Even today, modern scientists do not fully understand gravity. But Newton was able to combine the work of earlier scientists to explain *how* the force of attraction between matter works.

An Apple One Day Newton reasoned that small objects fall toward the Earth because the Earth and the objects are attracted to each other by the force of gravity. But because the Earth has so much more mass than a small object, say an apple, only the object appears to move.

Newton thus developed his *law of universal gravitation*, which states that the force of gravity depends on the product of the masses of the objects divided by the square of the distance between them. In other words, if two objects are moved twice as far apart, the gravitational attraction between them will decrease by a factor of $2 \times 2 = 4$, as shown in **Figure 7**. If the objects are moved 10 times as far apart, the gravitational attraction will decrease by a factor of $10 \times 10 = 100$.

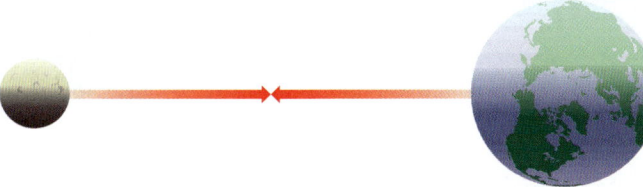

Figure 7 If two objects are moved twice as far apart, the gravitational attraction between them will be four times less.

Newton's Law and Satellites

Space engineers that plan the paths of orbiting satellites must be able to calculate the height of the most appropriate orbit and the location of the satellite at each moment. To do this, they must take into account both Kepler's laws of motion and Newton's law of universal gravitation. Try this exercise: If the mass of the Earth were twice its actual mass, by how much would the gravity increase on a satellite in orbit around Earth? If the satellite were suddenly moved three times farther away, would Earth's gravitational pull on the satellite increase or decrease? By how much?

When you consider the motion of the Earth's rotation, the Earth's revolution around the sun, and the sun's movement around the Milky Way galaxy, you are actually traveling more than 900,000 km/h just standing still.

Answers to APPLY

If Earth's mass were doubled, the effect of gravity on a satellite would be doubled. If the satellite were moved three times farther away, gravity would decrease by nine times ($3 \times 3 = 9$).

3 Extend

CROSS-DISCIPLINARY FOCUS

Writing — Language Arts While Kepler described the orbits of planets, Sir Isaac Newton (1642–1727) showed *why* they orbit. His law of universal gravitation explains why planets do not fly off into space:

- Every object in the universe attracts every other object in the universe with a force dependent on its mass and the square of the distance between them.

Newton's law of inertia explains why planets do not fall into the sun:

- An object remains in a state of rest or motion unless acted upon by an outside force.

Have students use these ideas to compose a letter to Kepler explaining why the planets stay in orbit.

Homework

The Dutch astronomer and mathematician Christiaan Huygens (1629–1695) discovered Saturn's largest moon, Titan, in 1655. He knew that Saturn and Titan take 30 Earth years to orbit the sun and observed that the Titanians' lives "must be very different from ours, having such tedious winters." Have students write a short story describing life on another planet and provide information on the planet's climate and the length of its days and years.

Section 1 • A Solar System Is Born   **517**

4 Close

Quiz

1. Explain the imbalance that creates a solar nebula. *(In a nebula, gravity and gas pressure are balanced. If an outside force, such as an explosion, causes the particles to move closer together, gravity may then trigger the collapse of the cloud.)*

2. Why does the center of a collapsing nebula form a star? *(Pressure is so intense among the crowded particles that atoms fuse, giving off enormous amounts of energy.)*

3. How do planets form? *(Particles swirling in a cloud of dust and gas stick together, forming planetesimals, which accumulate more matter and finally form planets.)*

Alternative Assessment

 Have students write a story in their ScienceLog that would explain to a seventeenth-century astronomer how the sun and the planets of our solar system formed. A seventeenth-century astronomer would not know, by name, nebulas or planetesimals. Students should share their stories with the class.

 Teaching Transparency 188
"Gravity and the Motion of the Moon"

Critical Thinking Worksheet 19
"A Balooney Universe"

518 Chapter 19 • Formation of the Solar System

Activity

When the space shuttle is in orbit, we see the astronauts floating around as they work. Many people talk about this as a "zero-g" environment, meaning no gravity. Is this correct? Are shuttle astronauts affected by gravity? Do research to find out what happens when objects are in orbit around Earth.

TRY at HOME

Falling Down and Around How did Newton explain the orbit of the moon around the Earth? After all, according to gravity, the moon should come crashing into the Earth. And this is what the moon would do if it were not moving at a high velocity. In fact, if it were not for gravity, the moon would simply shoot off away from the Earth.

To understand this better, imagine twirling a ball on the end of a string. As long as you hold the string, the ball will orbit your hand. As soon as you let go of the string, the ball will fly off in a straight path. This same principle applies to the moon. But instead of a hand holding a string, gravity is keeping the moon from flying off in a straight path. **Figure 8** shows how this works. This same principle holds true for all bodies in orbit, including the Earth and other planets in our solar system.

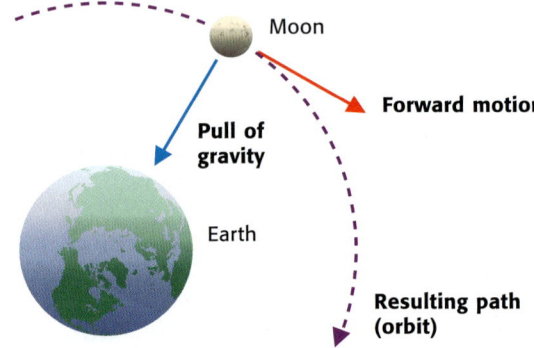

Figure 8 *Gravity is actually causing the moon to fall toward the Earth, changing what would be a straight-line path. The resulting path is a curved orbit.*

TOPIC: Kepler's Laws
GO TO: www.scilinks.org
sciLINKS NUMBER: HSTE460

REVIEW

1. On what properties does the force of gravity between two objects depend?

2. Will a planet or comet be moving faster in its orbit when it is farther from or closer to the sun? Explain.

3. How does gravity keep a planet moving in an orbit around the sun?

4. **Applying Concepts** Suppose a certain planet had two moons, one of which was twice as far from the planet as the other. Which moon would complete one revolution of the planet first? Explain.

518

Answers to Review

1. mass and distance

2. According to Kepler's second law, a planet sweeps out equal areas in equal amounts of time. When the planet is close to the sun, it must travel a longer distance along its orbit to sweep out the same amount of area. Because speed is distance traveled per unit of time, the planet will travel faster when it is close to the sun.

3. The motion of a planet is balanced between falling toward the sun and moving in a straight line past the sun. The resultant path is a curved orbit around the sun.

4. The closer moon would finish first. Kepler's third law states that period of revolution is related to the distance of an orbiting body from the object it orbits (its semimajor axis).

Section 2

The Sun: Our Very Own Star

Terms to Learn

corona
chromosphere
photosphere
convective zone
radiative zone
core
nuclear fusion
sunspot

What You'll Do

- Describe the basic structure and composition of the sun.
- Explain how the sun produces energy.
- Describe the surface activity of the sun, and name some of its effects on Earth.

There is nothing special about our sun, other than the fact that it is close enough to the Earth to give us light and warmth. Otherwise, the sun is similar to most of the other stars in our galaxy. It is basically a large ball of gas made mostly of hydrogen and helium held together by gravity. But let's take a closer look.

The Structure of the Sun

Although it may look like the sun has a solid surface, it does not. When we see a picture of the sun, we are really seeing through the sun's outer atmosphere, down to the point where the gas becomes so thick we cannot see through it anymore. As shown in **Figure 9,** the sun is composed of several layers.

Figure 9 Structure of the Sun and Its Atmosphere

a The **corona** forms the sun's outer atmosphere and can extend outward a distance equal to 10–12 times the diameter of the sun. The gases in the corona are so thin that it is visible only during a total solar eclipse.

b The **chromosphere** is a thin region below the corona, only 3,000 km thick. Like the corona, the deep, red chromosphere is too faint to see unless there is a total solar eclipse.

c The **photosphere** is where the gases get thick enough to see. The photosphere is what we know as the visible surface of the sun. It is only about 600 km thick.

d The **convective zone** is a region about 200,000 km thick where gases circulate in convection currents. Hot gases rise from the interior while cooler gases sink toward the interior.

e The **radiative zone** is a very dense region about 300,000 km thick. The atoms in this zone are so closely packed that light can take millions of years to pass through.

f The **core** is at the center of the sun. This is where the sun's energy is produced. The core has a radius of about 200,000 km and a temperature near 15,000,000°C.

IS THAT A FACT!

During an eclipse in 1868, a French astronomer named Pierre Janssen detected a new element in the chromosphere of the sun that was unknown on Earth. The new element, called helium (named after the Greek word for the sun, *helios*) was not discovered on Earth until 1895.

WEIRD SCIENCE

Even though the temperature of the corona can reach 2 million degrees Celsius, particles in the corona are so far apart that they don't transfer much thermal energy. A spaceship could enter the sun's corona and not burn up, despite the high temperature.

SECTION 2

Focus

The Sun: Our Very Own Star

This section describes the structure of the sun. Students will learn early theories about the source of the sun's energy and why nuclear fusion is the accepted model today. Finally, students will learn how the sun's surface activity affects the Earth.

Bellringer

Have students write about the following quotation by Henry Thoreau:

The sun is but a morning star.

1) Motivate

DEMONSTRATION

Observing Sunspots Clamp a pair of binoculars in a ring stand and cut a hole in a piece of cardboard that fits around the eyepiece of one binocular lens. Darken the classroom and orient the binoculars toward the sun. Hold a mirror in the shadow of the cardboard and project an image of the sun onto a wall. Focus the image and have students identify sunspots and other features of the sun.

Safety Caution: Do not look at the sun through the binoculars.

Teaching Transparency 189 "Structure of the Sun and Its Atmosphere"

Directed Reading Worksheet 19 Section 2

2) Teach

USING THE FIGURE

Refer students to **Figure 9** on the previous page. Have students find dictionary definitions for the name of each of the sun's layers and write an additional caption that explains why that name is appropriate for that particular layer. Sheltered English

READING STRATEGY

Prediction Guide Before students read the section on energy production in the sun, ask them what they think the major source of the sun's energy is.

a. It burns fuel, releasing energy.
b. Gravity is causing it to collapse, releasing energy.
c. Intense pressure is fusing atoms, releasing energy.
d. all of the above

(c)

How Far Is the Sun? PG 712

MATH and MORE

Have students create a line graph showing the differences in the temperature of the sun's layers from the core to the corona.

core: 15,000,000°C
radiative zone: 8,000,000°C
convective zone: 500,000°C
photosphere: 6,000°C
chromosphere: 4,000°–50,000°C
corona: 2,000,000°C

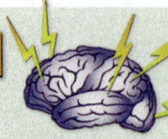
BRAIN FOOD
Despite the large size of Jupiter and Saturn, the sun itself contains over 99 percent of all the matter in the solar system.

Energy Production in the Sun

The sun has been shining on the Earth for about 4.6 billion years. How can it stay hot for so long? And what makes it shine? Over the years, several theories have been proposed to answer these questions. Because the sun is so bright and hot, many people thought that it was burning fuel to create the energy. But the amount of energy that is released during burning would not be enough to power the sun. If the sun were simply burning, it would last for only 10,000 years.

Burning or Shrinking? It eventually became clear that burning wouldn't last long enough to keep the sun shining. Scientists began to think that the sun was slowly shrinking due to gravity and that perhaps this would release enough energy to heat the sun. While the release of gravitational energy is more powerful than burning, it is still not enough to power the sun. If all of the sun's gravitational energy were released, the sun would last for only 45 million years. We know that dinosaurs roamed the Earth more than 65 million years ago, so this couldn't be the explanation. Something even more powerful was needed.

Some type of burning fuel was first thought to be the source of the sun's energy.

Figure 10 Ideas about the source of the sun's energy have changed over time.

A shrinking sun was another explanation for solar energy.

The sun is difficult to study because it is far away from Earth. Just how far? You might be able to figure it out by turning to page 712 in the LabBook.

Multicultural CONNECTION

Ancient cultures imagined the sun as a glorious god. The Greeks called their sun god *Helios* and depicted him driving a flaming chariot across the sky. For the Egyptians, *Ra* was a sun god and the creator and controller of the universe. The Japanese considered their emperor to be a descendant of their sun goddess, *Amaterasu*.

Nuclear Fusion At the beginning of the twentieth century, Albert Einstein demonstrated that matter and energy are interchangeable. Matter can be converted to energy according to his famous formula: $E = mc^2$, where E is energy, m is mass, and c is the speed of light. Because the speed of light is so large, even a small amount of matter can produce a large amount of energy. This idea paved the way for an understanding of a very powerful source of energy. **Nuclear fusion** is the process by which two or more nuclei with small masses (such as hydrogen) join together, or fuse, to form a larger, more massive nucleus (such as helium). During the process, energy is produced—a lot of it!

Einstein's equation changed ideas about the sun's energy source by equating mass and energy.

At the time Darwin introduced his theory of evolution, scientists thought that the sun was a few million years old at most. Some scientists argued that evolution—which takes place over billions of years—was therefore impossible because the sun could not have been shining that long. The nuclear fusion that fuels the sun, however, gives it a lifespan of at least 10 billion years!

Atomic Review

Let's do a little review. *Atoms* are the smallest particles of matter that keep their chemical identity. An atom consists of a *nucleus* surrounded by one or more *electrons,* which have a negative charge. A nucleus is made up of two types of particles—*protons,* with a positive charge, and *neutrons,* with no charge. The positively charged protons in the nucleus are balanced by an equal number of negatively charged electrons. The number of protons and electrons gives the atom its chemical identity. A helium atom, for example, has two protons and two electrons.

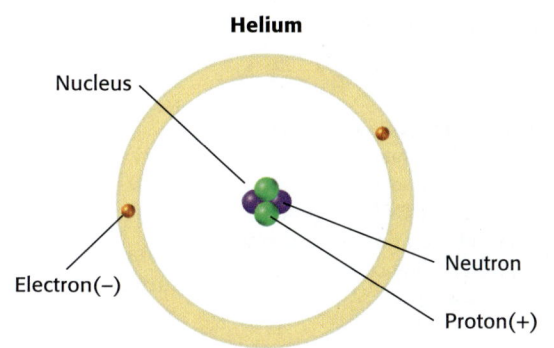

Helium
Nucleus
Electron(−)
Neutron
Proton(+)

BRAIN FOOD

Stars are the crucibles in which the heavy elements of the universe are forged. The calcium in our bones and the iron in our blood originated in stars—we are made of "star stuff." The big bang produced mainly helium and hydrogen, the fuel that powers stars. All other elements in the universe are produced during the life cycle of stars. Our sun is massive enough to create elements as heavy as oxygen, and red giants can produce elements as heavy as sodium. Elements heavier than iron are synthesized only when extremely massive supergiants become supernovae.

3) Extend

DEBATE

Nuclear Fusion: Feasible Energy Source for Earth?
Nuclear fusion is a reaction that produces tremendous amounts of energy. If that energy could be harnessed, nuclear fusion would provide a practically unlimited energy source. Nuclear fusion, however, requires such high temperatures and pressures that it has not been a feasible source of energy on Earth. Scientists have attempted to duplicate solar fusion using magnetic fields and lasers, but the research is very expensive. Do its potential benefits outweigh the burden of this expense? Why or why not? Who should fund the research? Why? Ask students to research the most recent fusion studies and to debate these questions.

GOING FURTHER

Writing The magnetic cycle of the sun produces sunspots, prominences, solar flares, and solar wind. Have students read further and prepare a report on what causes these phenomena and how they affect Earth's atmosphere. Students may also wish to investigate the links between sunspot cycles and climate change on Earth.

Homework

Concept Mapping Have students create a concept map that explains the process of solar nuclear fusion.

Teaching Transparency 190 "Fusion of Hydrogen in the Sun"

Figure 11 *Like charges repel, just like similar poles on a pair of magnets.*

Fusion in the Sun Under normal conditions, the nuclei of hydrogen atoms never get close enough to combine. This is because they are positively charged, and like charges repel each other, as shown in **Figure 11**. In the center of the sun, however, the temperature and pressure are very high because of the huge amount of matter within the core. This gives the hydrogen nuclei enough energy to overcome the repulsive force, allowing the conversion of hydrogen to helium, as shown in **Figure 12**.

Figure 12 Fusion of Hydrogen in the Sun

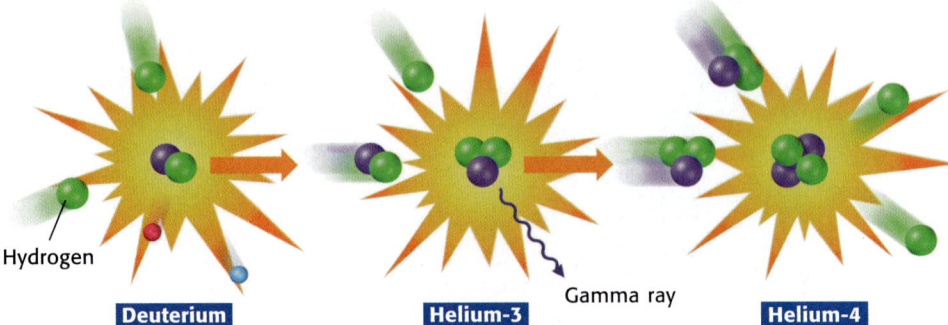

Hydrogen — Deuterium — Helium-3 — Gamma ray — Helium-4

1 Two hydrogen nuclei (protons) collide. One proton emits particles and energy, then becomes a neutron. The proton and neutron combine to produce a heavy form of hydrogen called *deuterium*.

2 Deuterium combines with another hydrogen nucleus to form a variety of helium called helium-3. More energy is released, as well as gamma rays.

3 Two helium-3 atoms then combine to form ordinary helium-4, releasing more energy and a pair of hydrogen nuclei.

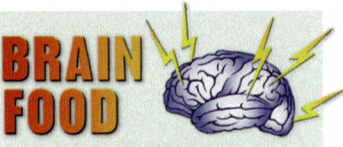

BRAIN FOOD
The energy released during the nuclear fusion of 1 g of hydrogen is equal to about 100 tons of TNT! Each second, the sun converts about 5 million tons of matter into pure energy.

The energy produced in the core of the sun takes millions of years to reach the sun's surface. In the radiative zone, the matter is so crowded that the light and energy keep getting blocked and sent off in different directions. Eventually the energy reaches the convective zone, where hot gases carry it up to the photosphere relatively quickly. From there the energy leaves the sun as light, taking only 8.3 minutes to reach Earth.

Activity on the Sun's Surface

The photosphere, or the visible surface of the sun, is a very dynamic place. As energy from the sun's interior reaches the surface, it causes the gas to boil and churn, a result of the rising and sinking of gases in the convective zone below.

CROSS-DISCIPLINARY FOCUS

Health Explain that atoms of the same element with varying numbers of neutrons are called *isotopes*. Isotopes that are unstable are called *radioactive*. Radioactive isotopes are useful in treating some cancers. Have students talk with a local oncologist or the local American Cancer Society chapter to find out more about such treatments.

IS THAT A FACT!

We have learned from observing sunspots that the sun rotates. Because the sun is made of gases, it rotates faster at its equator than at its poles. Sunspots at the equator take about 25 days to go around, while sun spots near the poles take about 35 days.

Sunspots The circulation of the gases within the sun, in addition to the sun's own rotation, produces magnetic fields that reach out into space. But these magnetic fields also tend to slow down the activity in the convective zone. This causes areas on the photosphere above to be slightly cooler than surrounding areas. These areas show up as sunspots. **Sunspots** are cooler, dark spots on the sun, as shown in **Figure 13.**

The number of sunspots and their location on the sun change in a regular cycle. Records of the number of sunspots have been kept ever since the invention of the telescope. In **Figure 14,** the sunspot cycle is shown, with the exception of the years 1645–1715, when sunspots were not observed.

Solar Flares The magnetic fields that cause sunspots also cause disturbances in the solar atmosphere. Giant storms on the surface of the sun, called *solar flares,* have temperatures of up to 5 million degrees Celsius. Solar flares send out huge streams of particles from the sun. These particles interact with the Earth's upper atmosphere, causing spectacular light shows called *auroras.* Solar flares can interrupt radio communications on Earth. They can also affect satellites in orbit. Scientists are trying to find ways to predict solar activity and give advanced warning of such events.

Figure 13 Sunspots mark cooler areas on the sun's surface. They are related to changes in the magnetic properties of the sun.

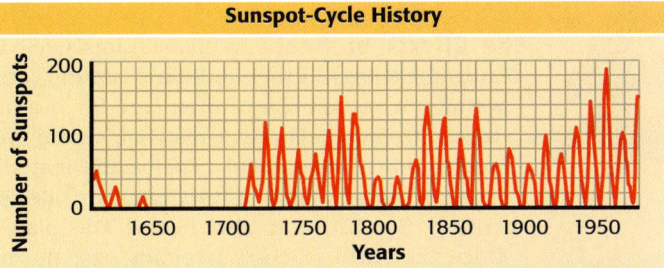

Figure 14 This graph shows the number of sunspots that have occurred each year since Galileo's first observations, in 1610.

REVIEW

1. According to modern understanding, what is the source of the sun's energy?
2. If nuclear fusion in the sun's core suddenly stopped today, would the sky be dark in the daytime tomorrow? Why?
3. **Interpreting Illustrations** In Figure 12, the nuclear fusion process ends up with one helium-4 nucleus and two free protons. What might happen to the two protons next?

internet connect

SCILINKS
NSTA

TOPIC: The Sun
GO TO: www.scilinks.org
*sci*LINKS NUMBER: HSTE465

Answers to Review

1. nuclear (hydrogen) fusion
2. No; it would take millions of years for the last energy made in the core to reach the surface of the sun.
3. The two free protons (hydrogen nuclei) might collide, starting the process again.

4) Close

Quiz

1. How do you know that gravity does not produce the sun's energy? (If all of the sun's gravitational energy were released, the sun would last only 45 million years; the solar system is at least 4.6 billion years old.)
2. What happens during nuclear fusion? (Hydrogen nuclei fuse, forming helium atoms and releasing huge amounts of energy.)
3. How does energy produced by nuclear fusion move from the sun's core to space? (It moves very slowly through the radiative zone, circulates through the convective zone, and passes through the photosphere and into the chromosphere and corona.)

ALTERNATIVE ASSESSMENT

Have students explain, orally or in writing, how energy released from the collision of two protons in the sun's core warms a car seat on Earth. Students should account for the following:

- nuclear fusion
- the movement of energy through the radiative and convective zones
- Earth's atmosphere
- the amount of time this process takes

 Reinforcement Worksheet 19 "Stay on the Sunny Side"

SECTION 3

Focus

The Earth Takes Shape

This section explores the formation of Earth and explains how gravity and rising temperatures caused the planet to become spherical and separate into layers of different density. Students will learn about the stages in the development of Earth's atmosphere and how our atmosphere sustains life today. The section concludes with a discussion of how oceans and continents formed.

Bellringer

Tell students that the Earth is approximately 4.6 billion years old. The first fossil evidence of life on Earth has been dated to nearly 3.5 billion years ago.

Have them write a paragraph in their ScienceLog describing what Earth might have been like during the first billion years of its existence.

1 Motivate

DEMONSTRATION

Heat water in a beaker until it boils, and ask students to describe what is happening. (Water vapor is released from the heated liquid.)

Explain that gases released from Earth's molten surface helped create its first atmosphere. Explain that the gases in our atmosphere are held by gravity, and ask students to speculate why there is very little hydrogen or helium in our atmosphere if these are the most abundant elements in the universe. (These gases are so light that Earth's gravity cannot trap them.) Sheltered English

---

Section 3

The Earth Takes Shape

Terms to Learn
crust   core
mantle

What You'll Do

◆ Describe the shape and structure of the Earth.
◆ Explain how the Earth got its layered structure and how this process affects the appearance of Earth's surface.
◆ Explain the development of Earth's atmosphere and the influence of early life on the atmosphere.
◆ Describe how the Earth's oceans and continents were formed.

Investigating the early history of the Earth is not easy because no one was there to study it directly. Scientists develop ideas about what happened based on their knowledge of chemistry, biology, physics, geology, and other sciences. Astronomers are also gathering evidence from other stars where planets are forming to better understand how our own solar system formed.

The Solid Earth Takes Form

As scientists now understand it, the Earth formed from the accumulation of planetesimals. This would have taken place within the first 10 million years of the collapse of the solar nebula—the blink of an eye on the cosmic time scale!

The Effects of Gravity When a young planet is still small, it can have an irregular shape, like a potato. As more matter builds up on the young planet, the force of gravity increases and the material pushing toward the center of the planet gets heavier. When a rocky planet, such as Earth, reaches a diameter of about 350 km, pressure from all this material becomes greater than the strength of the rock. At this point, the planet starts to become spherical in shape as the rock in the center is crushed by gravity.

The Effects of Heat As planetesimals fell to Earth, the energy of their motion made the Earth warmer. A second source of energy for heating the Earth was radioactive material, which was present in the solar nebula. Radioactive material radiates energy, and as this energy collected within the Earth, it also heated the planet. Once the Earth reached a certain size, the interior could not cool off as fast as its temperature rose, and the rocky material inside began to melt. As you will see on the next page, the effects of heat and gravity contributed to the formation of the Earth's layers.

Figure 15 *The Earth has not always looked as inviting as it does today.*

Self-Check

Why is the Earth spherical in shape, while most asteroids and comets are not? *(See page 726 to check your answer.)*

Answer to Self-Check

Earth has enough mass that gravitational pressure crushed and melted rocks during its formation. The force of gravity pulled this material toward the center, forming a sphere. Asteroids are not massive enough for their interiors to be crushed or melted.

The Earth and Its Layers Have you ever dropped pebbles into water or tried mixing oil and vinegar together for a salad? What happens? The heavier material (either solid or liquid) sinks, and the lighter material floats to the top. This is because of gravity. The material with a higher density is more strongly attracted and falls to the bottom. The same thing happened in the young Earth. As its rocks melted, the heavy elements, such as nickel and iron, sank to the center of the Earth, forming what we call the *core*. Lighter materials floated to the surface. This process is illustrated in **Figure 16**.

Figure 16 Earth's Materials Separate into Layers

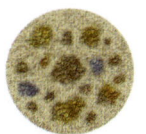
All materials in the early Earth are randomly mixed.

Rocks melt, and dense materials separate and sink.

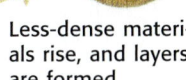
Less-dense materials rise, and layers are formed.

QuickLab
Mixing It Up
Have you ever mixed oil and water and watched what happened? Try this.
1. Pour 50 mL of **water** into a 150 mL **beaker**.
2. Add 50 mL of **cooking oil** to the water. Stir vigorously.
3. Let the mixture stand undisturbed for a few minutes.
4. What happens to the oil and water?
5. How does this relate to the interior of the early Earth?

The Earth's Interior The Earth is divided into three distinct layers according to the composition of its materials. These layers are shown in **Figure 17**. Geologists map the interior of the Earth by measuring how sound waves pass through the planet during earthquakes and underground explosions.

Figure 17 The interior of the Earth consists of three layers.

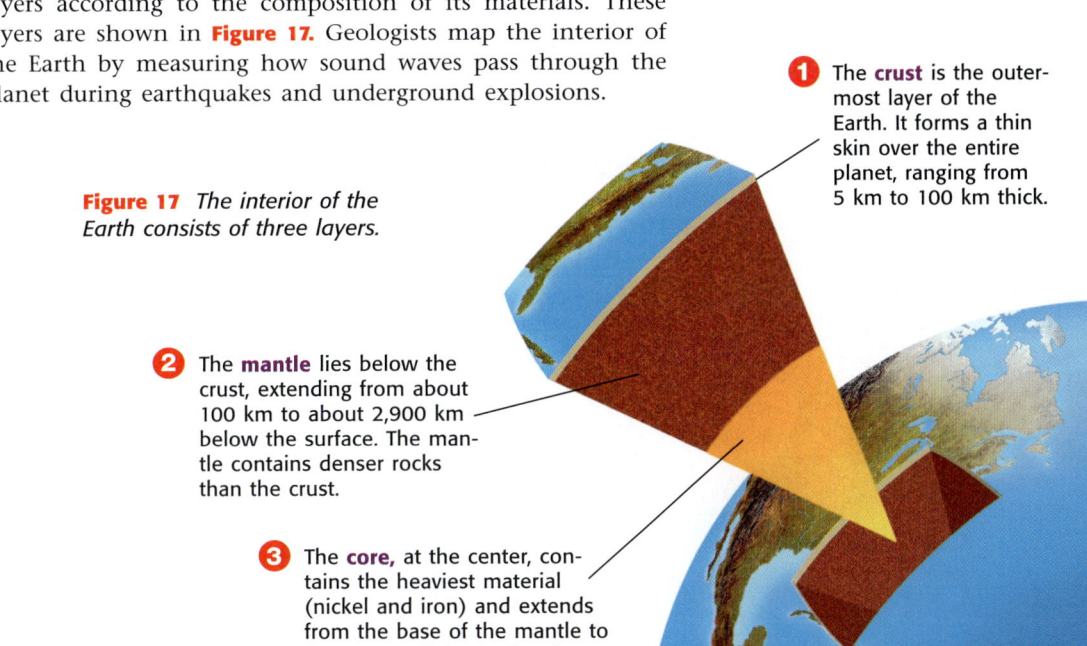

① The **crust** is the outermost layer of the Earth. It forms a thin skin over the entire planet, ranging from 5 km to 100 km thick.

② The **mantle** lies below the crust, extending from about 100 km to about 2,900 km below the surface. The mantle contains denser rocks than the crust.

③ The **core**, at the center, contains the heaviest material (nickel and iron) and extends from the base of the mantle to the center of the Earth—almost 6,400 km below the surface.

Science Bloopers
Impact craters have left scars on planets and moons throughout the solar system. In 1826, an eccentric Bavarian astronomer named Franz von Paula Gruithuisen was one of the first to suggest that lunar craters were caused by meteorite impacts. However, he also asserted that other lunar features were built by a race of moon creatures called Selenites, and his theory of crater formation was not taken seriously. Students will enjoy reading and reporting on other imaginative descriptions of the moon by authors such as Jules Verne. Even astronomer Johannes Kepler wrote about creatures living on the moon.

② Teach

QuickLab
MATERIALS
For Each Group:
- 50 mL water
- 150 mL beaker
- 50 mL cooking oil

Answers to QuickLab
4. The oil floats on top of the water.
5. The water, which is denser than oil, sinks to the bottom in the same way that iron and nickel sank to the center of the Earth.

CONNECT TO GEOLOGY

Have students use the transparency listed below to compare Mars with the core of Earth in terms of diameter and mass. The Earth's core is 33 percent of Earth's mass. Although Mars has approximately the same volume as Earth's core, its mass is only 11 percent of Earth's mass. Ask students to compare the density of Mars with the density of the Earth's core and to explain the differences they note. (Mars is less dense than the core of the Earth. This is because Earth's core formed as a result of differentiation, and denser elements sank to the core.) Sheltered English

Teaching Transparency 122 "The Composition of the Earth"

Directed Reading Worksheet 19 Section 3

Section 3 • The Earth Takes Shape **525**

② Teach, continued

INDEPENDENT PRACTICE

Poster Project Have students create a series of drawings and captions showing how Earth's atmosphere first formed and how it changed over time. Encourage students to use creative approaches, such as comic-strip frames, to communicate the concepts. **Sheltered English**

MATH and MORE

Remind students that ratios are a means of comparing two values using division. Have students calculate the ratio of oxygen to nitrogen in Earth's present atmosphere. (They can round percentages to the nearest tenth.)

21:78 rounds to 20:80
20:80 = 2:8 or 1:4
The ratio is one part oxygen to four parts nitrogen.

 Math Skills Worksheet 12 "Reducing Fractions to Lowest Terms"

TOPIC: The Layers of the Earth
GO TO: www.scilinks.org
sciLINKS NUMBER: HSTE470

TOPIC: The Oceans
GO TO: www.scilinks.org
sciLINKS NUMBER: HSTE475

Chemistry CONNECTION

The Cassini Mission to Saturn (launched in October 1997) will study the chemistry of Saturn's moon Titan. Titan's atmosphere, like Earth's, is composed mostly of nitrogen, but it also contains many hydrogen-rich compounds. Scientists want to study how molecules essential to life may form in this atmosphere.

The Atmosphere Evolves

Other than the presence of life, one of the biggest differences between the Earth of today and the Earth of 4.6 billion years ago is the character of its atmosphere. Earth's atmosphere today is composed of 21 percent oxygen, 78 percent nitrogen, and about 1 percent argon (with tiny amounts of many other gases). But it has not always been this way. Read on to discover how the Earth's atmosphere has changed through time.

Earth's First Atmosphere Earth's early atmosphere was very different from the atmosphere of today. In the 1950s, laboratory experiments on the origins of life were based on the hypothesis that Earth's early atmosphere was largely made up of methane, ammonia, and water. And because the solar nebula was rich in hydrogen, many scientists thought that Earth's first atmosphere also contained a lot of hydrogen compounds.

New Evidence New evidence is changing the way we think about Earth's first atmosphere. For one thing, 85 percent of the Earth's matter probably came from material similar to *meteoroids*—planetesimals made of rock. The other 15 percent probably came from the outer solar system in the form of *comets*—planetesimals made of ice.

Volcanic Gases During the final stages of formation, the Earth was hit many times by planetesimals, and the surface was very hot, even molten in places, as illustrated in **Figure 18.** The ground would have been venting large amounts of gas released from the heated minerals. The composition of meteorites tells us that much of that gas would have been water vapor and carbon dioxide. These two gases are also commonly released during volcanic eruptions. Earth's first atmosphere was probably a steamy atmosphere made of water vapor and carbon dioxide.

Figure 18 This is an artist's view of what Earth's surface may have looked like shortly after Earth's formation.

Q: Have you heard about the new restaurant on the moon?

A: great food, lousy atmosphere

---

526 Chapter 19 • Formation of the Solar System

The Role of Impacts Planetesimal impacts may have helped release gases from the Earth. In addition, they may have also helped to knock some of those gases back into space. Because planetesimals travel very fast, their impacts can speed up gas molecules in the atmosphere enough for them to overcome gravity and escape into space.

Heavier elements, such as iron, that were on the surface of the Earth also reacted chemically with water, giving off hydrogen—the lightest element. And because the early Earth was very warm, this hydrogen also had enough energy to escape.

Comets brought in a range of elements, such as carbon, hydrogen, oxygen, and nitrogen. They may also have brought water that eventually helped form the oceans, as shown in **Figure 19.**

Figure 19 *Comets may have brought some of the water that formed Earth's early oceans.*

Earth's Second Atmosphere After the Earth cooled off and the core formed, it became possible for the Earth's second atmosphere to take shape. This atmosphere formed from gases contributed by both volcanoes and comets. Volcanoes, like the one in **Figure 20,** produced large amounts of water vapor, along with chlorine, nitrogen, sulfur, and large amounts of carbon dioxide. This carbon dioxide kept the planet much warmer than it is today.

Figure 20 *As this volcano in Hawaii shows, a large amount of gas is released during an eruption.*

Because carbon dioxide is a very good *greenhouse gas*—one that traps thermal energy—scientists have tried to estimate how much carbon dioxide the Earth must have had in its second atmosphere in order to keep it as warm as it was. For example, if all of the carbon dioxide that is now tied up in the rocks and minerals of the ocean floor were released, it would make an atmosphere of carbon dioxide 60 times as thick as our present atmosphere.

3) Extend

READING STRATEGY

Activity Before students read this page, ask them to write down what they know about ultraviolet rays from the sun. (Students may note that UV rays help the body form vitamin D but that they also cause sunburn, snow blindness, cataracts, and skin cancer.)

Have students share their facts and discuss the ways people protect themselves from UV radiation.

Ask students what effect they think UV rays would have if Earth had no atmosphere to absorb them. Have students assess their ideas after they have finished reading this section. **Sheltered English**

DEBATE

Life on Earth: Could It Happen Again? Ask students to imagine that life on Earth is completely destroyed. Encourage students to debate whether life could evolve again with our current atmosphere. Students should consider conditions on primitive Earth as well as the requirements for life as we know it.

Earth's Current Atmosphere How did this early atmosphere change to become the atmosphere we know today? It happened with the help of solar ultraviolet (UV) radiation, the very thing that we worry about now for its cancer-causing ability. Solar UV light is dangerous because it has a lot of energy and can break molecules apart in the air or in your skin. Today we are shielded from most of the sun's ultraviolet rays by Earth's protective ozone layer. But Earth's early atmosphere had no ozone, and many molecules were broken apart in the atmosphere. The pieces were later washed out into shallow seas and tide pools by rain. Eventually a rich supply of these pieces of molecules collected in protected areas, forming a rich organic solution that is sometimes called a "primordial soup."

The Source of Oxygen Although there was no ozone, water offered protection from the effects of ultraviolet radiation. In these sheltered pools of water, complex molecules may have been able to form. Then, sometime between 4.6 and 3.9 billion years ago, life began on Earth. By 3.7 to 3.4 billion years ago, living organisms had evolved that were able to photosynthesize energy from sunlight and produce oxygen as a byproduct. These early life-forms are still around today, as shown in **Figure 21.**

Figure 21 Fossilized algae (left) are among the earliest signs of life discovered. Today's stromatolites (right) are mats of microorganisms thought to be similar to the first life on Earth.

Eventually, between 2.5 and 2.0 billion years ago, the amount of oxygen started to increase rapidly—reaching about 20 percent of the amount we have in the atmosphere today. As plants began to cover the land, oxygen levels increased because plants produce oxygen during photosynthesis. Therefore, it was the emergence of life that completely changed our atmosphere into the one we have today.

MISCONCEPTION ALERT

Primordial means "original," coming from the Latin for "first order." Students may think that the early oceans were the primordial "soup" from which life arose. Recent work suggests that life may have actually begun in a hydrothermal vent system where organisms evolved that could derive energy from chemosynthesis.

WEIRD SCIENCE

Could life exist on Jupiter? Portions of its atmosphere have water, moderate temperatures, and gases that could sustain life. Carl Sagan and Edwin E. Salpeter have postulated the existence of floating organisms that synthesize food from Jupiter's atmosphere, providing food for other organisms.

Oceans and Continents

It is hard to say exactly when the first oceans appeared on Earth, but they probably formed early, as soon as the Earth was cool enough for rain to fall and remain on the surface. We know that Earth's second atmosphere had plenty of water vapor. After millions of years of rainfall, water began to cover the Earth, and by 4 billion years ago, a giant global ocean covered the planet. For the first few hundred million years of the Earth's history, there were no continents.

So how and when did the continents appear? Continental crust material is very light compared with material in the mantle. The composition of the granite and other rocks making up the continents tells geologists that the rocks of the crust have melted and cooled many times in the past. Each time the rocks melted, the heavier elements sank, leaving the lighter ones to rise to the surface. This process is illustrated in **Figure 22.**

The Growth of Continents After a while, some of the rocks were light enough that they no longer sank, and they began to pile up on the surface. This was the beginning of the earliest continents. After gradually thickening, the continents slowly rose above the surface of the ocean. These scattered young continents didn't stay in the same place, however, because the slow convection in the mantle pushed them around. By around 2.5 billion years ago, continents really started to grow. By 1.5 billion years ago, the upper mantle had cooled and become denser and heavier, so it was easier for the colder parts of it to sink. Then the real continental action, or *plate tectonics*, began.

TOPIC: The Layers of the Earth, The Oceans
GO TO: www.scilinks.org
sciLINKS NUMBER: HSTE470, HSTE475

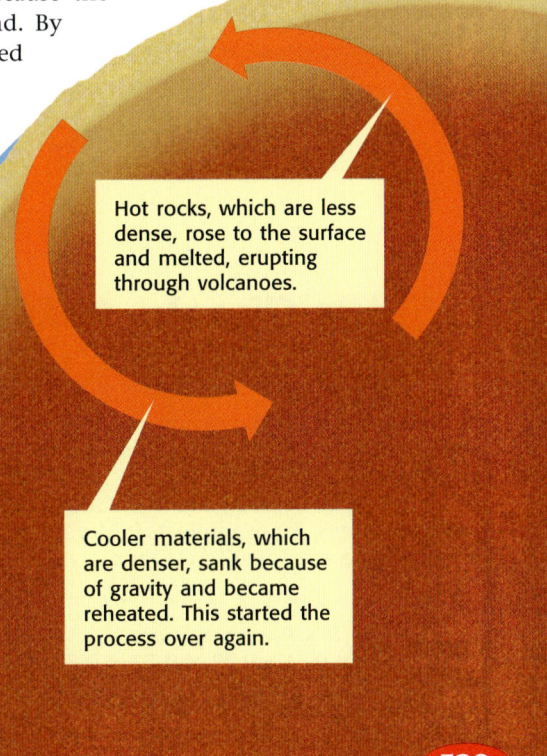

Figure 22 The slow convective motion in the Earth's mantle was the engine that caused mantle rock to rise and sink, forming the continents.

Hot rocks, which are less dense, rose to the surface and melted, erupting through volcanoes.

Cooler materials, which are denser, sank because of gravity and became reheated. This started the process over again.

REVIEW

1. Why did the Earth separate into distinct layers?
2. How did the Earth's atmosphere change composition to become today's nitrogen and oxygen atmosphere?
3. Which are older, oceans or continents? Explain.
4. **Drawing Conclusions** If the Earth were not hot inside, would we have moving continents (plate tectonics)? Explain.

4 Close

Quiz

1. Why was there a large amount of water vapor in Earth's second atmosphere? (Volcanic eruptions produced large amounts of water vapor. Comets crashing into the forming Earth also brought water.)
2. How and when did oxygen become abundant in Earth's atmosphere? (Sometime between 3.7 and 3.4 million years ago, life-forms evolved that could produce oxygen through photosynthesis; over millions of years, oxygen levels increased.)
3. How has the relationship between ozone and life on Earth changed since the time of Earth's early atmosphere? (The absence of ozone in Earth's early atmosphere allowed molecules to be broken apart by UV radiation. These broken-down molecules combined to form the complex molecules that gave rise to life. Currently, the ozone layer protects life on Earth from the harmful effects of UV radiation.)

ALTERNATIVE ASSESSMENT

Have students review this section and write facts about each stage of Earth's development on 3 × 5 in. cards. Mix the cards as a deck. Students should form teams and play a quiz game. Teams will earn points by assigning the correct fact to the correct stage of the Earth's development.

 **Reinforcement Worksheet 19** "Third Rock from the Sun"

Answers to Review

1. Melting inside the Earth allowed heavy material to sink to the center and lighter materials to rise to the surface.
2. The Earth's first atmosphere contained methane, ammonia, and water. Later, volcanoes added carbon dioxide, chlorine, nitrogen, and sulfur. Comets brought carbon, hydrogen, nitrogen, and oxygen. Solar energy created new chemicals that led to the formation of living organisms. These organisms greatly changed the composition of the atmosphere by adding oxygen.
3. Oceans are older because they formed as soon as the Earth was cool enough to allow rain to collect. Continents formed later as lighter materials separated from the Earth's mantle and rose above sea level.
4. No; convection in the mantle causes crustal movement and plate tectonics.

Chapter Highlights

VOCABULARY DEFINITIONS

SECTION 1

solar system the system composed of the sun (a star) and the planets and other bodies that travel around the sun

nebula a large cloud of dust and gas in interstellar space; the location of star formation

solar nebula the nebula that formed into the solar system

planetesimal the tiny building blocks of the planets that formed as dust particles stuck together and grew in size

rotation the spinning motion of a body on its axis

orbit the elliptical path a body takes as it travels around another body in space; the motion itself

revolution the elliptical motion of a body as it orbits another body in space

period of revolution the time it takes for one body to make one complete orbit, or *revolution*, around another body in space

ellipse a closed curve in which the sum of the distances from the edge of the curve to two points inside the ellipse is always the same

astronomical unit (AU) the average distance between the Earth and the sun, or approximately 150,000,000 km

Chapter Highlights

SECTION 1

Vocabulary
solar system (p. 510)
nebula (p. 510)
solar nebula (p. 511)
planetesimal (p. 512)
rotation (p. 515)
orbit (p. 515)
revolution (p. 515)
period of revolution (p. 515)
ellipse (p. 516)
astronomical unit (p. 516)

Section Notes
- The solar system formed out of a vast cloud of cold gas and dust called a nebula.
- Gravity and pressure were balanced, keeping the cloud unchanging until something upset the balance. Then the nebula began to collapse.
- Collapse of the solar nebula caused heating in the center. As material crowded closer together, planetesimals began to form.
- The central mass of the nebula became the sun. Planets formed from the surrounding disk of material.
- It took about 10 million years for the solar system to form, and it is now 4.6 billion years old.
- The orbit of one body around another has the shape of an ellipse.
- Planets move faster in their orbits when they are closer to the sun.
- The square of the period of revolution of the planet is equal to the cube of its semimajor axis.
- Gravity depends on the masses of the interacting objects and the square of the distance between them.

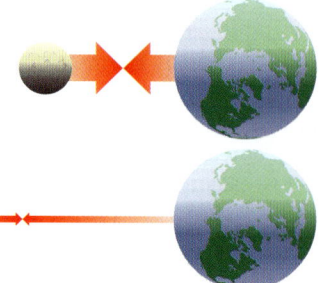

✓ Skills Check

Math Concepts

SQUARES AND CUBES Let's take another look at Kepler's third law of motion. Expanding the formula $P^2 = a^3$ to $P \times P = a \times a \times a$ may be an easier way to consider the calculation. The period of Venus, for example, is 0.61 years, and its semimajor axis is 0.72 AU. Thus,

$$P^2 = a^3$$
$$P \times P = a \times a \times a$$
$$0.61 \times 0.61 = 0.72 \times 0.72 \times 0.72$$
$$0.37 = 0.37$$

Visual Understanding

LIKE AN ONION The sun is formed of six different layers of gas. From the inside out, the layers are the core, radiative zone, convective zone, photosphere, chromosphere, and corona. Look back at Figure 9 on page 519 to review the characteristics of each layer.

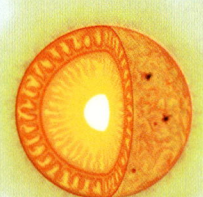

Lab and Activity Highlights

How Far Is the Sun? PG 712

Datasheets for LabBook
(blackline masters for this lab)

SECTION 2

Vocabulary

corona (p. 519)
chromosphere (p. 519)
photosphere (p. 519)
convective zone (p. 519)
radiative zone (p. 519)
core (p. 519)
nuclear fusion (p. 521)
sunspot (p. 523)

Section Notes

- The sun is a gaseous sphere made primarily of hydrogen and helium.
- The sun produces energy in its core by a process called nuclear fusion.
- Magnetic changes within the sun cause sunspots and solar flares.

Labs

How Far Is the Sun? (p. 712)

SECTION 3

Vocabulary

crust (p. 525)
mantle (p. 525)
core (p. 525)

Section Notes

- The Earth is divided into three main layers—crust, mantle, and core.
- Materials with different densities separated because of melting inside Earth. Heavy elements sank to the center because of Earth's gravity.
- Earth's original atmosphere formed from the release of gases brought to Earth by meteorites and comets.
- Earth's second atmosphere arose from volcanic eruptions and impacts by comets. The composition was largely water and carbon dioxide.
- The presence of life dramatically changed Earth's atmosphere, adding free oxygen.
- Earth's oceans formed shortly after the Earth did, when it had cooled off enough for rain to fall.
- Continents formed when lighter materials gathered on the surface and rose above sea level.

VOCABULARY DEFINITIONS, continued

SECTION 2

corona the sun's outer atmosphere, which can extend outward a distance equal to 10–12 times the diameter of the sun

chromosphere a thin region of the sun's atmosphere between the corona and the photosphere; too faint to see unless there is a total solar eclipse

photosphere the layer of the sun at which point the gases get thick enough to see; the surface of the sun

convective zone a region of the sun where gases circulate in convection currents, bringing the sun's energy to the surface

radiative zone a very dense region of the sun in which the atoms are so closely packed that light can take millions of years to pass through

core the center of the sun where the sun's energy is produced

nuclear fusion the process by which two or more nuclei with small masses join together, or fuse, to form a larger, more massive nucleus, along with the production of energy

sunspot an area on the photosphere of the sun that is cooler than surrounding areas, showing up as a dark spot

SECTION 3

crust the thin, outermost layer of the Earth, or the uppermost part of the lithosphere

mantle the layer of the Earth between the crust and the core

core the central, spherical part of the Earth below the mantle

---

internetconnect

GO TO: go.hrw.com

GO TO: www.scilinks.org

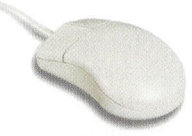

Visit the **HRW** Web site for a variety of learning tools related to this chapter. Just type in the keyword:

KEYWORD: HSTSOL

Visit the **National Science Teachers Association** on-line Web site for Internet resources related to this chapter. Just type in the sciLINKS number for more information about the topic:

TOPIC: The Planets	sciLINKS NUMBER: HSTE455
TOPIC: Kepler's Laws	sciLINKS NUMBER: HSTE460
TOPIC: The Sun	sciLINKS NUMBER: HSTE465
TOPIC: The Layers of the Earth	sciLINKS NUMBER: HSTE470
TOPIC: The Oceans	sciLINKS NUMBER: HSTE475

Lab and Activity Highlights

LabBank

Whiz-Bang Demonstrations, Can You Vote on Venus? Demo 32

Long-Term Projects & Research Ideas, A Two-Sun Solar System, Project 47

Vocabulary Review Worksheet 19

Blackline masters of these Chapter Highlights can be found in the **Study Guide.**

Chapter Review Answers

USING VOCABULARY

1. Rotation is the spinning of a body on its axis. Revolution is the movement of a smaller body around a larger body.
2. An ellipse is a closed curve in which the sum of the distances from the edge of the curve to two points inside the ellipse is always the same. A circle is an ellipse with only one focus.
3. The solar system is composed of the sun, its planets, and other bodies in orbit around the sun. The solar nebula was an interstellar cloud of gas and dust that eventually became the solar system.
4. A planetesimal is a tiny building block of a planet. A planet is a large object made of planetesimals.
5. Temperature is a measure of the average kinetic energy of randomly moving particles in an object. Pressure is a force or push.
6. The photosphere is the layer of the sun that we can see, or the surface of the sun. The corona is the sun's outer atmosphere that can be seen only during a solar eclipse.
7. radiative zone
8. Rotation
9. plate tectonics

UNDERSTANDING CONCEPTS

Multiple Choice
10. d
11. a
12. a
13. c
14. b
15. c
16. a
17. a

Chapter Review

USING VOCABULARY

For each pair of terms, explain the difference in their meanings.

1. rotation/revolution
2. ellipse/circle
3. solar system/solar nebula
4. planetesimal/planet
5. temperature/pressure
6. photosphere/corona

To complete the following sentences, choose the correct term from each pair of terms below.

7. It takes millions of years for light energy to travel through the sun's __?__. (*radiative zone* or *convective zone*)
8. __?__ of the Earth causes night and day. (*Rotation* or *Revolution*)
9. Convection in Earth's mantle causes __?__. (*plate tectonics* or *nuclear fusion*)

UNDERSTANDING CONCEPTS

Multiple Choice

10. Impacts in the early solar system
    a. brought new materials to the planets.
    b. released energy.
    c. dug craters.
    d. All of the above

11. Which type of planet will have a higher overall density?
    a. one that forms close to the sun
    b. one that forms far from the sun

12. Which process releases the most energy?
    a. nuclear fusion
    b. burning
    c. shrinking due to gravity

13. Which of the following planets has the shortest period of revolution?
    a. Pluto   c. Mercury
    b. Earth   d. Jupiter

14. Which gas in Earth's atmosphere tells us that there is life on Earth?
    a. hydrogen   c. carbon dioxide
    b. oxygen   d. nitrogen

15. Which layer of the Earth has the lowest density?
    a. the core
    b. the mantle
    c. the crust

16. What is the term for the speed of gas molecules?
    a. temperature   c. gravity
    b. pressure   d. force

17. Which of the following objects is least likely to have a spherical shape?
    a. a comet   c. the sun
    b. Venus   d. Jupiter

 Concept Mapping Transparency 19

 Blackline masters of this Chapter Review can be found in the **Study Guide**.

Short Answer

18. An external force, perhaps from a collision with another nebula or from a nearby exploding star, pushed inward on the nebula. This force was strong enough to overcome the pressure of the nebula and trigger its collapse.
19. The square of the period of revolution is equal to the cube of the semimajor axis: $P \times P = a \times a \times a$. (Students' drawings should resemble Figure 6.)

532 Chapter 19 • Formation of the Solar System

Short Answer

18. Why did the solar nebula begin to collapse to form the sun and planets if the forces of pressure and gravity were balanced?

19. How is the period of revolution related to the semimajor axis of an orbit? Draw an ellipse and label the semimajor axis.

20. How did our understanding of the sun's energy change over time?

Concept Mapping

21. Use the following terms to create a concept map: solar nebula, solar system, planetesimals, sun, photosphere, core, nuclear fusion, planets, Earth.

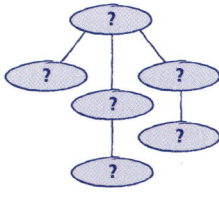

CRITICAL THINKING AND PROBLEM SOLVING

Write one or two sentences to answer the following questions:

22. Explain why nuclear fusion works inside the sun but not inside Jupiter, which is also made mostly of hydrogen and helium.

23. Why is it less expensive to launch an interplanetary spacecraft from the international space station in Earth's orbit than from Earth itself?

24. Soon after the formation of the universe, there was only hydrogen and helium. Heavier elements, such as carbon, oxygen, silicon, and all the matter that makes up the heavier minerals and rocks in the solar system, were made inside an earlier generation of stars. Do you think the first generation of stars had any planets like Earth, Venus, Mercury, and Mars? Explain.

MATH IN SCIENCE

25. Suppose astronomers discover a new planet orbiting our sun. The orbit has a semimajor axis of 2.52 AU. What is the planet's period of revolution?

26. If the planet in the previous question is twice as massive as the Earth but is the same size, how much would a person who weighs 100 lb on Earth weigh on this planet?

INTERPRETING GRAPHICS

Examine the illustration below, and answer the questions that follow.

27. Do you think this is a rocky, inner planet or a gas giant?

28. Did this planet form close to the sun or far from the sun? Explain.

29. Does this planet have an atmosphere? Why or why not?

Take a minute to review your answers to the Pre-Reading Questions found at the bottom of page 508. Have your answers changed? If necessary, revise your answers based on what you have learned since you began this chapter.

---

20. At first, people thought the sun was burning fuel. Later, scientists thought that the sun releases energy because it is shrinking. Finally, nuclear fusion was identified as the source of the sun's energy.

Concept Mapping

21. An answer to this exercise can be found at the end of this book.

CRITICAL THINKING AND PROBLEM SOLVING

22. The mass of Jupiter is too small. The pressure in Jupiter's core is not high enough to reach the temperatures needed to initiate nuclear fusion. Fusion requires temperatures of 10 million degrees and masses about 75 times that of Jupiter.

23. The spacecraft is moving with the space station as it orbits Earth, so the spacecraft will not have to provide as much speed to escape Earth's gravity. This takes less fuel and is less expensive.

24. No; Earth, Venus, Mercury, and Mars formed mostly from rocky material. The only type of planet that could have orbited the first generation of stars is a gas giant.

MATH IN SCIENCE

25. Using Kepler's third law of motion, $P \times P = a \times a \times a$, where a = 2.52 AU gives a value of 16 for one side of the equation. Since $4 \times 4 = 16$ AU, the period of revolution must be 4 years.

26. Because the planet is twice as massive as Earth, the person would weigh twice as much, or 200 lb.

INTERPRETING GRAPHICS

27. It is a rocky inner planet.
28. It probably formed close to the sun. The planet is rocky, with a relatively thin atmosphere, and the sun is visible as a disk in the sky rather than as a pinpoint of light.
29. Yes; there are clouds in the sky, and the surface of the planet has been weathered.

SCIENCE, TECHNOLOGY, AND SOCIETY
Don't Look at the Sun!

Background
The McMath-Pierce solar telescope has a 91.5 m focal length. Such a long focal length allows us to see a lot of details on a sunspot. The facility that houses the telescope looks like an upside-down V. The vertical side of this V is 30 m tall and contains the heliostat. The sun strikes the heliostat, which is a large, flat, rotating mirror. After sunlight strikes the heliostat, it travels 50 m underground to another mirror, which reflects it back to the observation room. In the observation room, the light is broken down into its different wavelengths by a spectrograph. The spectrograph also photographs the image that results from this process.

The McMath-Pierce telescope is also used to study the spectra of planets, comets, and other stars. Spectrography gives us important information about these objects, such as the location of magnetic fields and the temperature, pressure, and density of the gases surrounding the object.

Science, Technology, and Society
Don't Look at the Sun!

You know you are not supposed to look at the sun, right? But how can we learn anything about the sun if we can't look at it? By using a solar telescope, of course! Where would you find one of these, you ask? Well, if you travel about 70 km southwest of Tucson, Arizona, you will arrive at Kitt Peak National Observatory, where you will find three of them. One telescope in particular has gone to great lengths to give astronomers extraordinary views of the sun!

Top Selection
In 1958, Kitt Peak was chosen from more than 150 mountain ranges to be the site for a national observatory. Located in the Sonoran Desert, Kitt Peak is a part of lands belonging to the Tohono O'odham nation. The McMath-Pierce Facility houses the three largest solar telescopes in the world. Astronomers come from around the globe to use these telescopes. The largest of the three, called the McMath-Pierce telescope, creates an image of the sun that is almost 1 m wide!

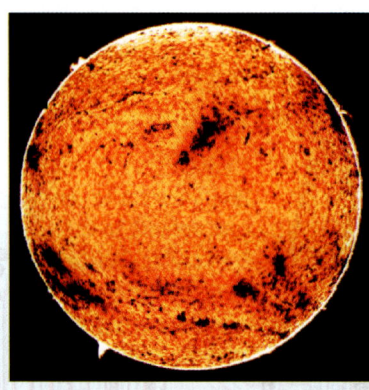

▲ This is an image of the sun as viewed through the McMath-Pierce solar telescope.

Too Hot to Handle
Have you ever caught a piece of paper on fire using only a magnifying glass and the rays from the sun? Sunlight that has been focused can produce a great amount of thermal energy—enough to start a fire. Now imagine a magnifying glass 1.6 m in diameter focusing the sun's rays. The resulting heat could melt metal. This is what would happen to a conventional telescope if it were pointed directly at the sun.

To avoid a meltdown, the McMath-Pierce solar telescope uses a mirror that produces a large image of the sun. This mirror directs the sun's rays down a diagonal shaft to another mirror 50 m underground. This mirror is adjustable to focus the sunlight. The sunlight is then directed to a third mirror, which directs the light to an observing room and instrument shaft.

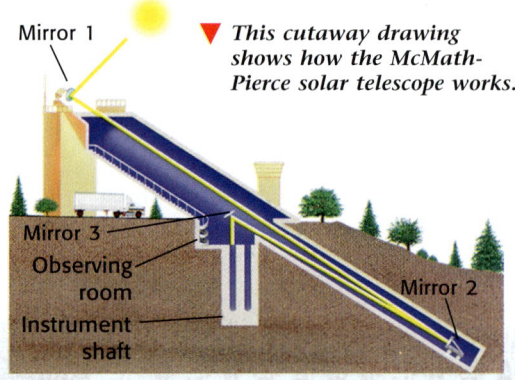

▼ This cutaway drawing shows how the McMath-Pierce solar telescope works.

Scope It Out
▶ Kitt Peak Observatory also has optical telescopes, which differ from solar telescopes. Do some research to find out how optical telescopes work and what the ones at Kitt Peak are used for.

Answer to Scope It Out
There are two types of optical telescopes—reflecting and refracting. A reflecting telescope uses a mirror to collect and reflect the light. This mirror is at the back of a tube. A secondary mirror brings the light into focus. A refracting telescope uses glass lenses to magnify and focus an image. Although the large telescopes built today are reflectors, earlier telescopes were refractors. The telescope Galileo built was a refracting telescope, while the one Newton built was a reflecting telescope. Students should visit the official Kitt Peak Web site to discover what objects its optical telescopes are currently being used to study.

SCIENTIFIC DEBATE

Mirrors in Space

People who live in areas that do not get much sunshine are more prone to health problems such as depression and alcoholism. The people of Siberia, Russia, experience a shortage of sunshine during the winter, when the sun shines only 6 hours on certain days. Could there be a solution to this problem?

A Mirror From *Mir*

In February 1999, the crew of the space station *Mir* was scheduled to insert a large, umbrellalike mirror into orbit. The mirror was designed to reflect sunlight to Siberia. Once placed into orbit, however, problems arose and the crew was unable to unfold the mirror. Had things gone as planned, the beam of reflected sunlight was expected to be 5 to 10 times brighter than the light from the moon. If the first mirror had worked, this would have opened the door for Russia to build many more mirrors that are larger in diameter. These larger mirrors would have been launched into space to lengthen winter days, provide additional heat, and even reduce the amount of electricity used for lighting. The idea of placing mirrors in space, however, caused some serious concerns about the effects it could have.

Overcrowding

The first mirror was about 30 m in diameter. Because it was put in Low Earth Orbit (LEO), the light beam would have been obstructed by the Earth's horizon as the mirror made its orbit. As a result, it would have reflected light on a single area for only about 30 seconds. In order to shine light on Siberia on a large scale, hundreds of larger mirrors would have to be used. But using this many mirrors could result in collisions with satellites that share LEO.

Damage to Ecosystems

It is very difficult to determine what effects extra daylight would have on Siberian ecosystems. Many plants and animals have cycles for various biological functions, such as feeding, sleeping, moving, and reproducing. Extra light and increased temperatures could adversely affect these cycles. Birds might migrate so late that they wouldn't survive the trip across the colder climates because food would be scarce. Plants might sprout too soon and freeze. Arctic ice might melt and cause flooding.

Light Pollution

Astronomers may also be affected by orbiting mirrors. Already astronomers must plan their viewing times to avoid the passing of bright planets and satellites. More sunlight directed toward the Earth would increase light pollution and could make seeing into space more difficult. A string of several hundred mirrors shining light toward the Earth would likely cause additional light pollution in certain locations as the mirrors passed overhead.

What's the Current Status?

▶ Find out more about the Russian project and where it stands now. If you had to decide whether to pursue this project, what would you decide? Why?

▲ The end of a winter day in Siberia

SCIENTIFIC DEBATE
Mirrors in Space

Background

Another application of the technology used in the space mirror is the "solar sail." A solar sail is simply a flat, reflective membrane that catches energy particles in the solar wind. Perhaps in the future spaceships will use solar sails to propel them through the solar system.

Answer to What's the Current Status?

The group responsible for the space-mirror project is a company based in Russia called the Space Regatta Consortium. Unfortunately, this company is having economic trouble, so the ultimate goal of the project may never be realized. Students' responses will vary. Accept all reasonable answers.

Chapter Organizer

CHAPTER ORGANIZATION	TIME MINUTES	OBJECTIVES	LABS, INVESTIGATIONS, AND DEMONSTRATIONS
Chapter Opener pp. 536–537	45	National Standards: SAI 1, HNS 1, 3, ES 3a	**Start-Up Activity** Measuring Space, p. 537
Section 1 The Nine Planets	90	▶ List the names of the planets in the order they orbit the sun. ▶ Describe three ways in which the inner and outer planets are different from each other. UCP 1, 3, SAI 1, ST 2, SPSP 5, HNS 1, 3, ES 1c, 3a, 3b; LabBook UCP 2, SAI 1, ST 1	**Demonstration,** p. 540 in ATE GENERAL **Making Models,** Why Do They Wander? p. 714 ADVANCED **Datasheets for LabBook,** Why Do They Wander? Datasheet 43 ADVANCED
Section 2 Moons	135	▶ Describe the current theory for the origin of Earth's moon. ▶ Describe what causes the phases of Earth's moon. ▶ Explain the difference between a solar eclipse and a lunar eclipse. UCP 1–3, SAI 1, HNS 1, 3, ES 3a–3c; LabBook UCP 2, SAI 1, ST 1, ES 3b	**QuickLab,** Clever Insight, p. 552 GENERAL **Interactive Explorations CD-ROM,** Space Case GENERAL A *Worksheet* is also available in the *Interactive Explorations Teacher's Edition.* **Making Models,** Eclipses, p. 716 GENERAL **Datasheets for LabBook,** Eclipses, Datasheet 44 GENERAL **Discovery Lab,** Phases of the Moon, p. 717 BASIC **Datasheets for LabBook,** Phases of the Moon, Datasheet 45 BASIC
Section 3 Small Bodies in the Solar System	90	▶ Explain why comets, asteroids, and meteoroids are important to the study of the formation of the solar system. ▶ Compare the different types of asteroids with the different types of meteoroids. ▶ Describe the risks to life on Earth from cosmic impacts. UCP 1, ES 2a, 3a, 3b	**Demonstration,** p. 557 in ATE GENERAL **Labs You Can Eat,** Meteorite Delight, Lab 17 ADVANCED **Whiz-Bang Demonstrations,** Crater Creator, Demo 33 BASIC **Whiz-Bang Demonstrations,** Space Snowballs, Demo 34 BASIC **Long-Term Projects & Research Ideas,** Project 48 ADVANCED

See page T20 for a complete correlation of this book with the **NATIONAL SCIENCE EDUCATION STANDARDS.**

TECHNOLOGY RESOURCES

 Guided Reading Audio CD English or Spanish, Chapter 20

 One-Stop Planner CD-ROM with Test Generator

 CNN Scientists in Action, Future Mars Astronauts, Segment 25

 Interactive Explorations CD-ROM CD 2, Exploration 7, Space Case

Chapter 20 • A Family of Planets

Chapter 20 • A Family of Planets

CLASSROOM WORKSHEETS, TRANSPARENCIES, AND RESOURCES	SCIENCE INTEGRATION AND CONNECTIONS	REVIEW AND ASSESSMENT
Directed Reading Worksheet 20 BASIC **Science Puzzlers, Twisters & Teasers,** Worksheet 20 ADVANCED		**Homework,** p. 537 in ATE GENERAL
Transparency 191, The Inner Planets **Directed Reading Worksheet 20,** Section 1 BASIC **Math Skills for Science Worksheet 4,** A Shortcut for Multiplying Large Numbers GENERAL **Science Skills Worksheet 26,** Grasping Graphing GENERAL **Transparency 191,** The Outer Planets **Critical Thinking Worksheet 20,** Martian Holiday ADVANCED	**Math and More,** p. 539 in ATE GENERAL **Connect to Environmental Science,** p. 540 in ATE GENERAL **Math and More,** p. 542 in ATE GENERAL **Physics Connection,** p. 543 **Cross-Disciplinary Focus,** p. 543 in ATE GENERAL **Cross-Disciplinary Focus,** p. 544 in ATE ADVANCED **Connect to Meteorology,** p. 544 in ATE **Apply,** p. 547 GENERAL **Connect to Environmental Science,** p. 547 in ATE	**Homework,** p. 540 in ATE GENERAL **Review,** p. 543 GENERAL **Review,** p. 548 GENERAL **Quiz,** p. 548 in ATE GENERAL **Alternative Assessment,** p. 548 in ATE ADVANCED
Directed Reading Worksheet 20, Section 2 BASIC **Transparency 223,** Two Motions Combine to Form Projectile Motion **Transparency 192,** Formation of the Moon **Transparency 193,** Phases of the Moon **Transparency 194,** Solar Eclipse and Lunar Eclipse **Reinforcement Worksheet 20,** The Planets of Our Solar System BASIC **Reinforcement Worksheet 20,** Lunar and Solar Eclipses BASIC	**Physics Connection,** p. 550 **Math and More,** pp. 550, 552 in ATE GENERAL **MathBreak,** Orbits Within Orbits, p. 553 GENERAL **Cross-Disciplinary Focus,** p. 553 in ATE ADVANCED **Connect to Life Science,** p. 554 in ATE **Holt Anthology of Science Fiction,** *The Mad Moon* ADVANCED	**Homework,** p. 550 in ATE GENERAL **Homework,** p. 552 in ATE GENERAL **Review,** p. 553 GENERAL **Homework,** p. 554 in ATE ADVANCED **Self-Check,** p. 555 **Review,** p. 556 GENERAL **Quiz,** p. 556 in ATE GENERAL **Alternative Assessment,** p. 556 in ATE GENERAL
Directed Reading Worksheet 20, Section 3 BASIC	**Cross-Disciplinary Focus,** p. 561 in ATE **Scientific Debate:** Is Pluto Really a Planet? p. 566 GENERAL	**Review,** p. 561 GENERAL **Quiz,** p. 561 in ATE GENERAL **Alternative Assessment,** p. 561 in ATE GENERAL

 **Holt, Rinehart and Winston On-line Resources**
go.hrw.com
For worksheets and other teaching aids related to this chapter, visit the HRW Web site and type in the keyword: **HSTFAM**

 **National Science Teachers Association**
www.scilinks.org
Encourage students to use the *sci*LINKS numbers listed in the internet connect boxes to access information and resources on the **NSTA** Web Site.

END-OF-CHAPTER REVIEW AND ASSESSMENT

Chapter Review in Study Guide
Vocabulary and Notes in Study Guide
Chapter Tests with Performance-Based Assessment, Chapter 20 Test
Chapter Tests with Performance-Based Assessment, Performance-Based Assessment 20
Concept Mapping Transparency 20

Chapter Resources & Worksheets

Visual Resources

TEACHING TRANSPARENCIES

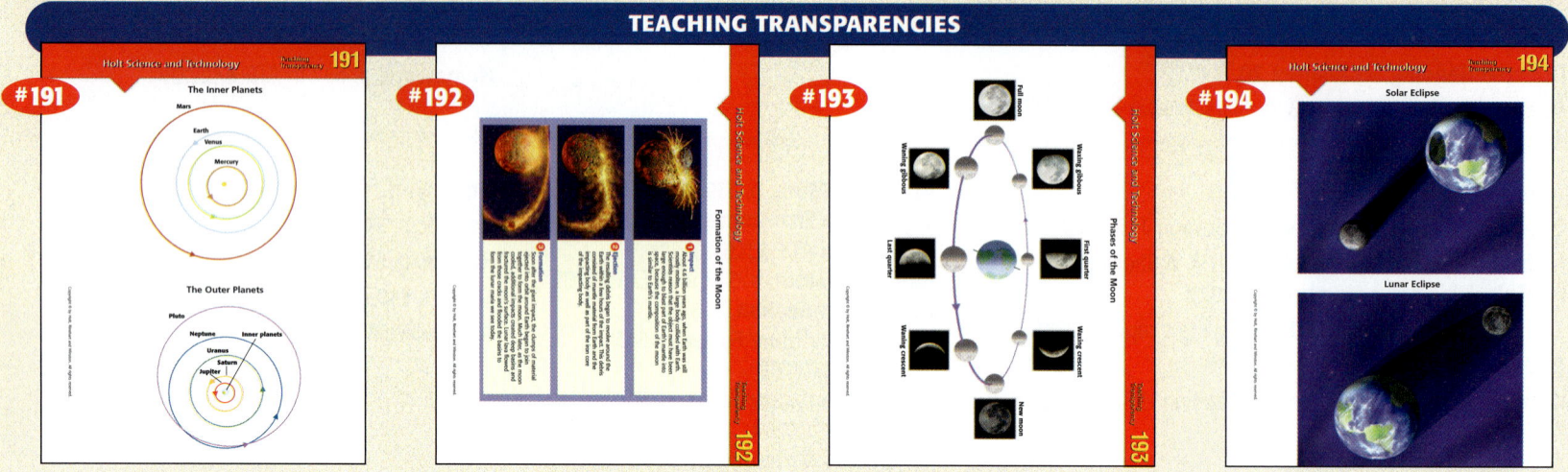

TEACHING TRANSPARENCIES

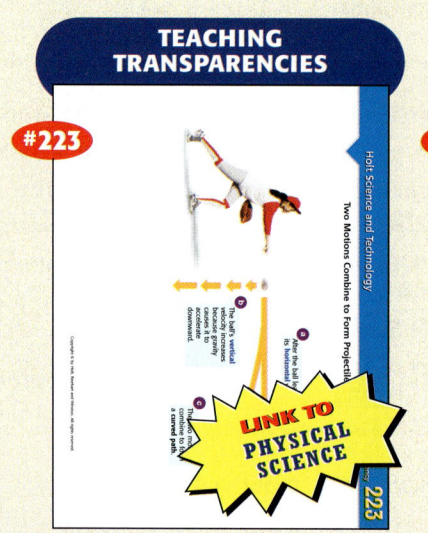

CONCEPT MAPPING TRANSPARENCY

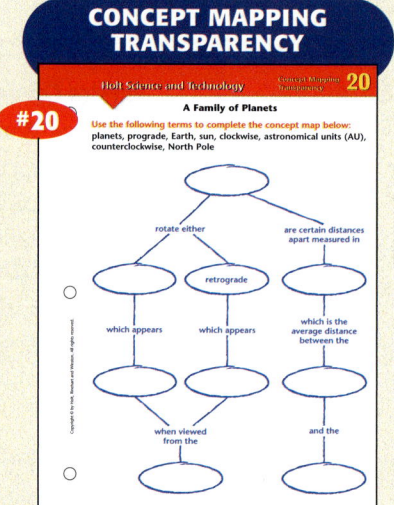

Meeting Individual Needs

DIRECTED READING

REINFORCEMENT & VOCABULARY REVIEW

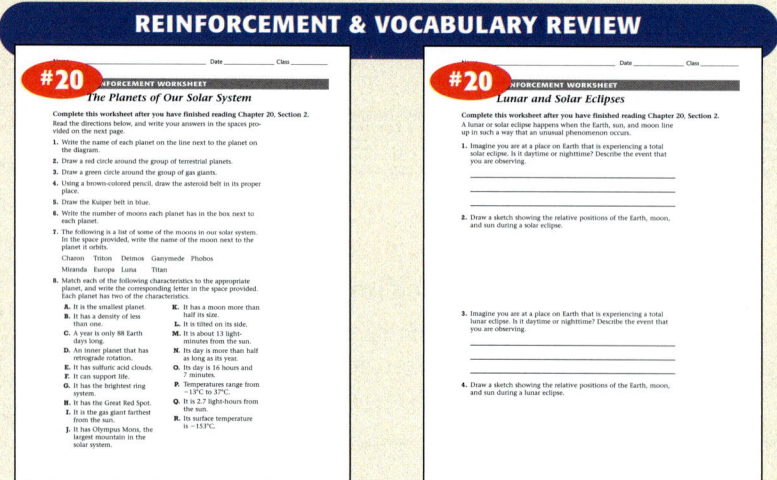

SCIENCE PUZZLERS, TWISTERS & TEASERS

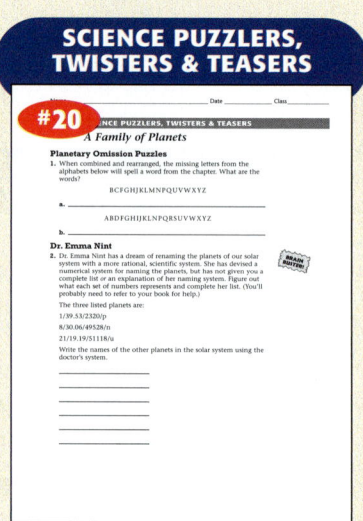

535C Chapter 20 • A Family of Planets

Chapter 20 • A Family of Planets

Review & Assessment

STUDY GUIDE
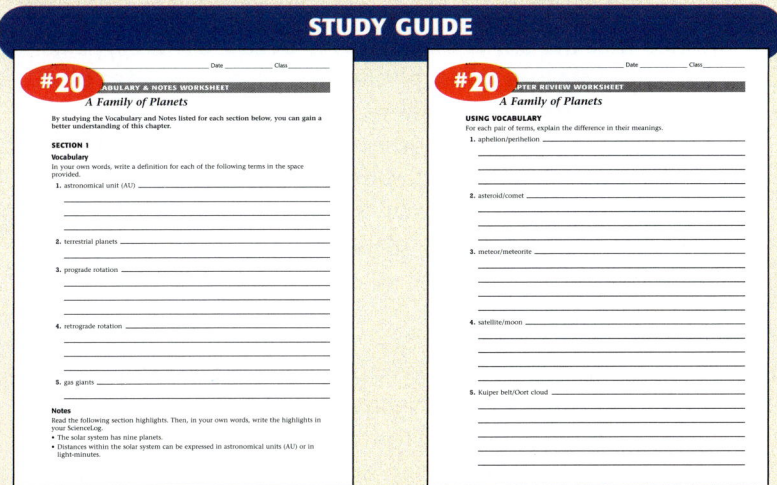

CHAPTER TESTS WITH PERFORMANCE-BASED ASSESSMENT
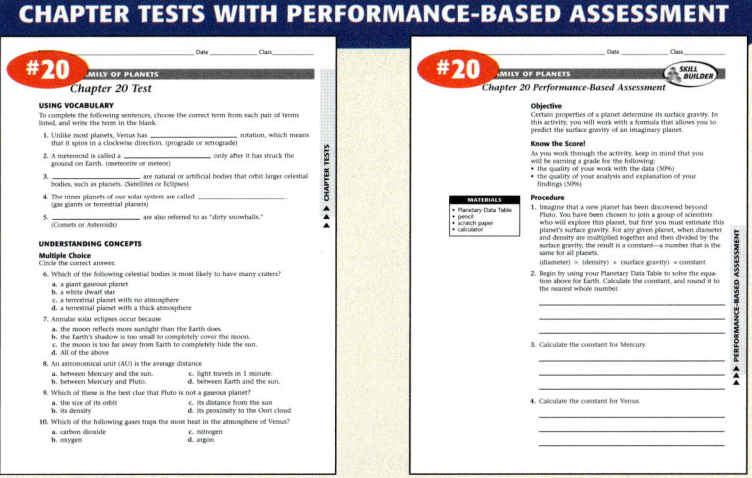

Lab Worksheets

LABS YOU CAN EAT
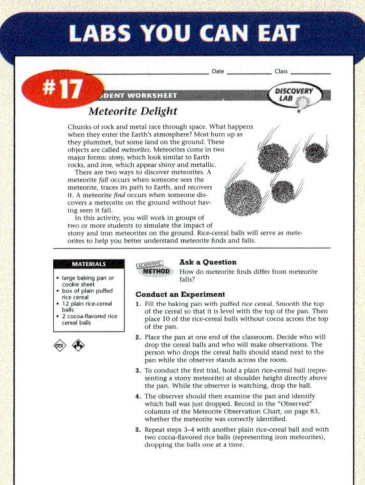

WHIZ-BANG DEMONSTRATIONS
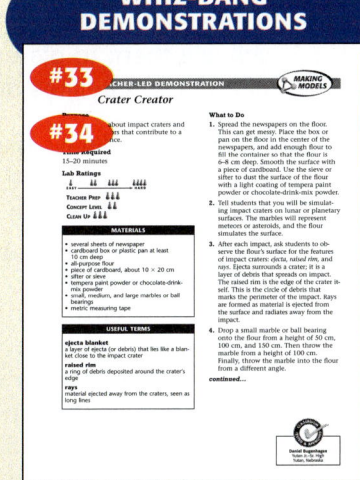

LONG-TERM PROJECTS & RESEARCH IDEAS
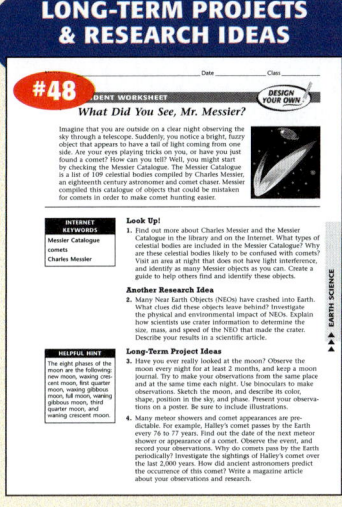

DATASHEETS FOR LABBOOK
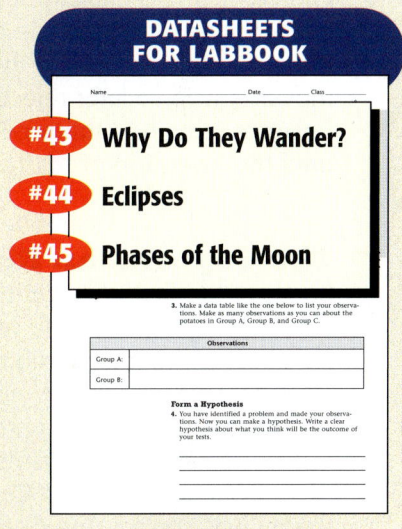

Applications & Extensions

CRITICAL THINKING & PROBLEM SOLVING
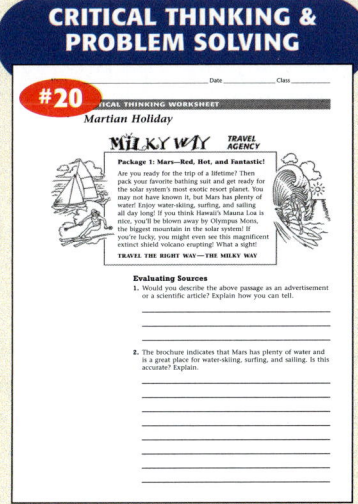

SCIENTISTS IN ACTION
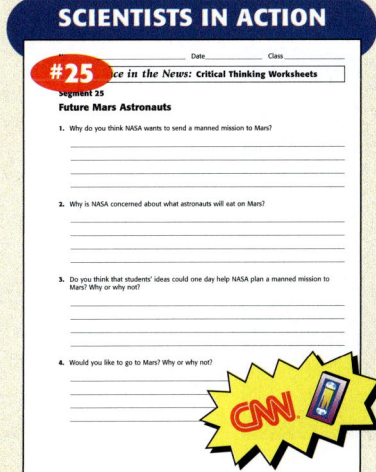

INTERACTIVE EXPLORATIONS
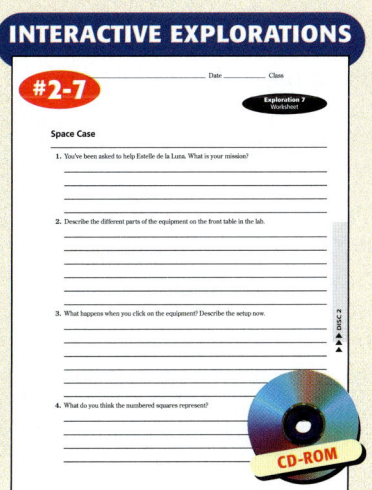

Chapter 20 • Chapter Resources & Worksheets

Chapter Background

Section 1

The Nine Planets

▶ **Ptolemy**

In the second century A.D., the astronomer Claudius Ptolemy formulated the first scientific theory that the Earth was the center of the universe. He argued that everything in the universe revolves around or falls toward Earth's center. In Ptolemy's model, the stars moved in a rotating sphere, and the motion of planets, moons, and comets was explained by a series of large and small circles turning inside one another. Although Ptolemy's theories about the mechanism of planetary movement were later rejected, his basic model of the universe remained the predominant scientific theory until the invention of the telescope in 1609.

▶ **The Copernican Revolution**

Some of the first observations Galileo made with the newly invented telescope were of Jupiter and its moons. He observed that the moons of Jupiter revolve around Jupiter and not Earth. He also discovered that Venus has phases, like our moon has. This evidence helped Galileo argue that Ptolemy's model of the solar system must be wrong and that Copernicus's heliocentric theory was correct. The Copernican revolution had a profound social impact and provided impetus for the Age of Enlightenment.

▶ **A Day on Mercury**

Imagine waking up in the middle of winter just before dawn to find the outside temperature a frigid −173°C! As you watch the sun slowly rise over the next several days, you notice that it appears three times as big as it does from Earth. You also notice that the sky is black. This is because Mercury has an extremely thin atmosphere, so it doesn't scatter blue light, like Earth's atmosphere does. Forty-four Earth days later, it would be noon on Mercury and the middle of summer as well. The temperature would be a toasty 427°C. The range of Mercury's surface temperatures is the most extreme of any planet in the solar system.

IS THAT A FACT!

- The planet Mercury has been known and studied for more than 2,000 years. Its wanderings may have been noted by Hypatia (415–370 B.C.), an Egyptian mathematician and philosopher and the first known female astronomer. Hypatia was also a student of Plato.

- Although Kepler's laws of motion were formulated almost 400 years ago, space scientists and engineers still use them to plan and calculate the flight paths of artificial satellites orbiting the Earth.

- Pluto is not always the farthest planet from the sun. Pluto's orbit around the sun takes 248 Earth years to complete. Because of its highly elliptical orbit, for about 20 years it is actually closer to the sun than Neptune is. The last time Pluto was closer to the sun than Neptune was from 1979 to 1999. The next time will be in the twenty-third century.

Section 2

Moons

▶ **The Origin of the Moon**

At a conference on satellites in 1974, William Hartmann and Donald Davis first presented the leading modern hypothesis of how the moon formed. This theory, called the impact model, stated the following:

535E Chapter 20 • A Family of Planets

Chapter 20 • A Family of Planets

- A smaller planetary body forming at about the same time as Earth collided with Earth late in Earth's formation. The collision blew rocky debris into orbit around Earth. That debris aggregated to form the moon.

▶ Support for the Impact Model
The impact model has held up for the following reasons:

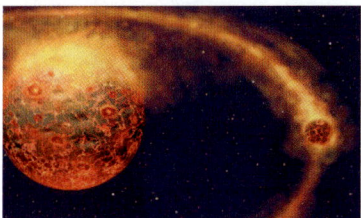

- **Composition** The terrestrial planets in our solar system, such as the Earth, all formed from the solar nebula and therefore tend to have similar ratios of common elements, such as iron. The moon, however, is relatively iron deficient. This means that the differentiation of Earth into distinct layers must have been happening *before* the formation of the moon. Because the iron-deficient composition of the moon closely matches that of the Earth's mantle, the internal differentiation of the Earth is a plausible mechanism for the present composition of the moon. Also, the oxygen-isotope composition of the moon is the same as Earth's. Other solar-system bodies have different oxygen-isotope compositions.

- **Orbital Properties** Computer simulations show that it is nearly impossible for an object with the mass of Earth to capture an object with as much mass as the moon. Instead they show that, although it would be a rare event, it is possible that a glancing blow from a Mars-sized object could throw enough Earth material into orbit to form the moon. The present size, distance, and orbital speed of the moon can all be accounted for by the impact theory.

▶ Earth Tides
As the moon revolves around the Earth, it causes tides—even on land! The distance from the center of Earth to its surface increases by a few centimeters as the moon passes overhead. This change is not as noticeable as ocean tides, but it can be detected by very sensitive instruments.

IS THAT A FACT!
■ Four moons in the solar system are larger than Earth's moon: Jupiter's Ganymede, Callisto, and Io, and Saturn's Titan. Earth's moon is special because it is very large relative to the planet it orbits. Pluto's moon, Charon, however, is more that half the size of Pluto.

SECTION 3

Small Bodies in the Solar System

▶ The Oort Cloud
To explain the origin of comets, a Dutch astronomer named Jan Oort suggested in the 1950s that a spherical cloud of comets surrounds the solar system. He estimated that the cloud is 40,000–100,000 AU from the sun and that trillions of icy bodies may be contained within it.

▶ The Kuiper Belt
The Dutch-American astronomer Gerard Kuiper proposed in 1949 that a belt of icy bodies must lie beyond the orbits of Pluto and Neptune to explain the source

of short-period comets (comets with a relatively short orbit). Kuiper argued that comets were icy planetesimals that formed during the condensation of our solar nebula. Because the icy bodies are so far from any large planet's gravitational field (30–100 AU), they can remain on the fringe of the solar system. Some theorists speculate that the large moons Triton and Charon were once members of the Kuiper belt before being captured by Neptune and Pluto. These moons and short-period comets have similar physical and chemical properties.

For background information about teaching strategies and issues, refer to the *Professional Reference for Teachers*.

A Family of Planets

Pre-Reading Questions

Students may not know the answers to these questions before reading the chapter, so accept any reasonable response.

Suggested Answers

1. Planets and moons are large and spherical. Comets, asteroids, and meteoroids are smaller and generally have irregular shapes. Planets can be large or small and gaseous or rocky. Most comets are icy bodies within the Oort cloud and the Kuiper belt. Asteroids are rocky bodies, most of which are within the asteroid belt. Meteoroids are thought to be the debris left over from asteroid collisions.

2. The number of impact craters on a planet's surface tells us how old the surface is. A planet with few craters has a young surface, indicating that its rocks are recycled. Flowing water leaves characteristic marks, such as stream channels, on a planet's surface.

Directed Reading Worksheet 20

Science Puzzlers, Twisters & Teasers Worksheet 20

Guided Reading Audio CD
English or Spanish, Chapter 20

A Family of Planets

Sections

1. The Nine Planets 538
   - Physics Connection .. 543
   - Apply 547
   - Internet Connect 548

2. Moons 549
   - Physics Connection .. 550
   - QuickLab 552
   - MathBreak 553
   - Internet Connect 556

3. Small Bodies in the Solar System 557
   - Internet Connect 561

Chapter Review 564
Feature Articles 566, 567
LabBook 714–717

Pre-Reading Questions

1. What are the differences between planets, moons, asteroids, comets, and meteoroids?
2. How can surface features tell us about a planet's history?

536

Close Neighbors in Space

Can you identify the objects in this illustration? The planets and other objects of the solar system appear almost close enough to run into each other. From this perspective, you can easily observe the mysterious and beautiful differences between the planets—in terms of their visible properties. In this chapter, you will study the properties of planets, moons, comets, asteroids, and meteoroids—and learn about eclipses, the moon's phases, and measuring interplanetary distances.

internet connect

HRW On-line Resources
go.hrw.com
For worksheets and other teaching aids, visit the HRW Web site and type in the keyword: **HSTFAM**

www.scilinks.com
Use the *sci*LINKS numbers at the end of each chapter for additional resources on the **NSTA** Web site.

www.cnnfyi.com
Visit the CNN Web site for current events coverage and classroom resources.

536 Chapter 20 • A Family of Planets

START-UP Activity

MEASURING SPACE

Earth's distance from the sun is about 150 million kilometers, or 1 AU. *AU* stands for astronomical unit, which is the average distance between Earth and the sun. Do the following exercise to get a better idea of your solar neighborhood.

Procedure

1. Plant a **stake with a flag attached** at the goal line of a **football field**. This stake represents the sun. Then use the table to plant **9 more stakes with flags** representing the position of each planet.

Analysis

2. After you have positioned all the "planets," what do you notice about how the planets are spaced?

Interplanetary Distances		
Planet	Distance from sun in AU	Scaled distance in yards
Mercury	0.39	1.0
Venus	0.72	1.8
Earth	1.00	2.5
Mars	1.52	3.9
Jupiter	5.20	13.3
Saturn	9.58	24.4
Uranus	19.20	48.9
Neptune	30.05	76.6
Pluto	39.24	100

START-UP Activity

MEASURING SPACE

MATERIALS
For Each Group: • 10 stakes • 10 flags

Teacher's Notes

The planetary data presented in this chapter are the most current available at the time of publication. Because of the vast size of the solar system, instrument limitations, and differences in methods of gathering data, the values given have varying margins of error. As measuring precision increases, these values are updated. Therefore, other sources may show different values for the same statistics.

Answer to START-UP Activity

2. The inner four planets are close together compared with the outer planets.

SECTION 1

Focus

The Nine Planets
This section begins with an explanation of the units used to measure astronomical distances. Then the section discusses each planet in our solar system.

Bellringer
Ask students to write about the following scenario:

Suppose that you were in charge of gathering the materials and supplies needed to live on Mars for a month. What materials would you need? What would you eat? How would you breathe? Where would you live?

1) Motivate

ACTIVITY
Remind students that the gravitational force between objects depends on their masses and the square of the distance between the objects. Weight, measured in *newtons*, is the measurement of the gravitational force acting on a mass. Have students make a chart showing what their weight would be on the different planets. Remind students that their mass will not change. Have them start by calculating their weight on Mercury. As they read about the surface gravity on each planet, have them add to their chart.

Teaching Transparency 191
"The Inner Planets"

Directed Reading Worksheet 20 Section 1

Section 1

Terms to Learn
- astronomical unit (AU)
- terrestrial planets
- prograde rotation
- retrograde rotation
- gas giants

What You'll Do
- List the names of the planets in the order they orbit the sun.
- Describe three ways in which the inner and outer planets are different from each other.

The Nine Planets

Ancient people knew about the existence of planets and could predict their motions. But it wasn't until the seventeenth century, when Galileo used the telescope to study planets and stars, that we began our first exploration of these alien worlds. Since the former Soviet Union launched *Sputnik 1*—the first artificial satellite—in 1957, over 150 successful missions have been launched to moons, planets, comets, and asteroids. **Figure 1** shows how far we have come since Galileo's time.

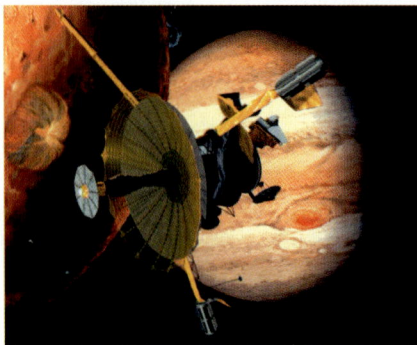

Figure 1 Galileo Galilei (left) discovered Jupiter's four largest moons using the newly invented telescope in 1610. The Galileo spacecraft (right) arrived at Jupiter on December 7, 1995.

Galileo Galilei

Measuring Interplanetary Distances

As you have seen, one way scientists measure distances in space is by using the astronomical unit. The **astronomical unit (AU)** is the average distance between the Earth and the sun. Another way to measure distances in space is by the distance light travels in a given amount of time. Light travels at about 300,000 km per second in space. This means that in 1 second, light travels a distance of 300,000 km—or about the distance you would cover if you traveled around Earth 7.5 times.

In 1 minute, light travels nearly 18,000,000 km! This distance is also called 1 *light-minute*. For example, it takes light from the sun 8.3 minutes to reach Earth, so the distance from the Earth to the sun is 8.3 light-minutes. Distances within the solar system can be measured in light-minutes and light-hours, but the distances between stars are measured in light-years!

Figure 2 One astronomical unit equals about 8.3 light-minutes.

Sun — 1 Light-minute — 1 Astronomical unit — Earth

MISCONCEPTION ALERT
Tell students that the diameters of the Earth and the sun are not to scale in **Figure 2**. If they were, the sun would be a little less than 2 mm across and the Earth would be too small to see. The lengths of the light-minute and the AU, however, are to scale. Ask students why the AU is the *average* distance between the Earth and sun. (The Earth's orbit is elliptical, therefore the distance between the Earth and the sun is continually changing.)

The Inner Planets

The solar system is divided into two groups of planets—the inner planets and the outer planets. As you learned from the Investigate, the inner planets are more closely spaced than the outer planets. Other differences between the inner and outer planets are their sizes and the materials of which they are made. The inner planets are called **terrestrial planets** because they are like Earth—small, dense, and rocky. The outer planets, except for icy Pluto, are much larger and are made mostly of gases.

Mercury—Closest to the Sun If you were to visit the planet Mercury, you would find a very strange world. For one thing, on Mercury you would weigh only 38 percent of what you weigh on Earth. The weight you experience on Earth is due to *surface gravity,* which is less on less massive planets. Also, a day on Mercury is almost 59 Earth days long! This is because Mercury spins on its axis much more slowly than Earth does. The spin of an object in space is called *rotation.* The amount of time it takes for an object to rotate once is called its *period of rotation.*

Another curious thing about Mercury is that its year is only 88 Earth days long. As you know, a year is the time it takes for a planet to go around the sun once. The motion of a body as it *orbits* another body in space is called *revolution.* The time it takes for an object to revolve around the sun once is called its *period of revolution.* Every 88 Earth days, or 1.5 Mercurian days, Mercury completes one revolution around the sun.

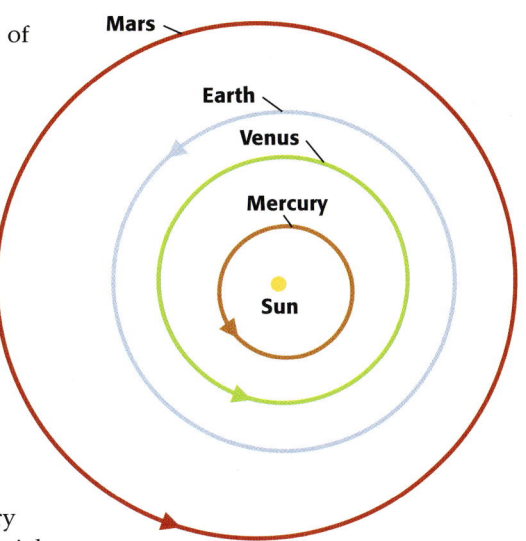

Figure 3 *The lines show orbits of the inner planets. The arrows indicate the direction of motion and the location of each planet on January 1, 2005.*

Figure 4 *This image of Mercury was taken by the* Mariner 10 *spacecraft on March 24, 1974, from a distance of 5,380,000 km.*

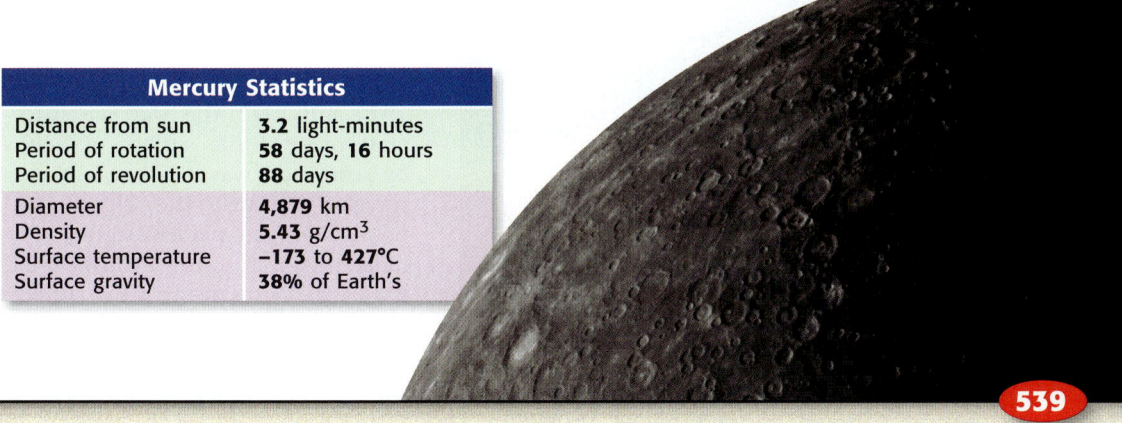

Mercury Statistics	
Distance from sun	3.2 light-minutes
Period of rotation	58 days, 16 hours
Period of revolution	88 days
Diameter	4,879 km
Density	5.43 g/cm^3
Surface temperature	−173 to 427°C
Surface gravity	38% of Earth's

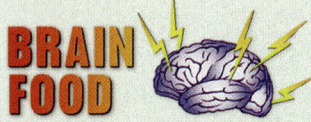

Inform students that the density value given in statistics boxes is the bulk density for each planet. Different layers of planets have different densities. The cores are denser than the surface layers, for example. Although Mercury is about 29 percent smaller than Mars, its surface gravity is about the same. What does this tell us about the two planets? Because the force of gravity depends on how massive an object is and because Mercury is smaller than Mars, Mercury must have a higher density than Mars. Astronomers speculate that Mercury has more iron, a relatively dense element, in its core than Mars does.

---

2 Teach

READING STRATEGY

Mnemonics Have students create a mnemonic device to help them remember the order of the planets:

Mercury, **V**enus, **E**arth, **M**ars, **J**upiter, **S**aturn, **U**ranus, **N**eptune, and **P**luto

MISCONCEPTION ALERT

Tell students that planets, asteroids, comets, and moons shine because sunlight is reflected off their surfaces. Most photographs shown in astronomy books are false-color images. Chances are, if the caption does not state that the image is true-color, it probably is not what your eye would see. False-color images serve a valuable function—they bring out details of the object that the human eye would not ordinarily be able to see.

MATH and MORE

If light travels 18,000,000 km in 1 minute, how far away is Earth from the sun if it takes sunlight 8.3 minutes to reach Earth?

(18,000,000 km/minute × 8.3 minutes = 149,400,000 km)

How far is Mercury from the sun if it takes sunlight 3.2 minutes to reach its surface? (57,600,000 km)

Remind students that these numbers are rounded and are therefore imprecise.

Math Skills Worksheet 4 "A Shortcut for Multiplying Large Numbers"

Section 1 • The Nine Planets

2 Teach, continued

DEMONSTRATION

As you discuss the inner planets and Jupiter with students, keep a stopwatch on your desk. Tell them to imagine that they will be traveling at the speed of light to each planet they are learning about. For example, 3 minutes into your discussion of Mercury, tell students that light from the sun has reached this planet. It will take 43 minutes, or an entire class period, to reach Jupiter. When students leave class, they can set their watches to mark their planetary journey throughout the rest of the day.

CONNECT TO ENVIRONMENTAL SCIENCE

The greenhouse effect caused by the concentration of carbon dioxide in Venus's atmosphere creates surface temperatures hot enough to melt lead. Could an increased greenhouse effect cause Earth's atmosphere to become more like Venus's? Earth's current atmosphere is primarily nitrogen and oxygen. Deforestation and fossil fuel use have caused CO_2 levels in our atmosphere to rise steadily since the industrial revolution. Scientists have already noticed a possible global warming trend, and they are concerned that it could have far-reaching effects on Earth's biological systems. Have students write a short story describing how Earth's atmosphere could become more like the atmosphere of Venus. How would life change? What would happen if Earth's atmosphere was more like the atmosphere of Mars?

Figure 5 *This image of Venus was taken by* Mariner 10 *on February 5, 1974. The uppermost layer of clouds consists of sulfuric acid.*

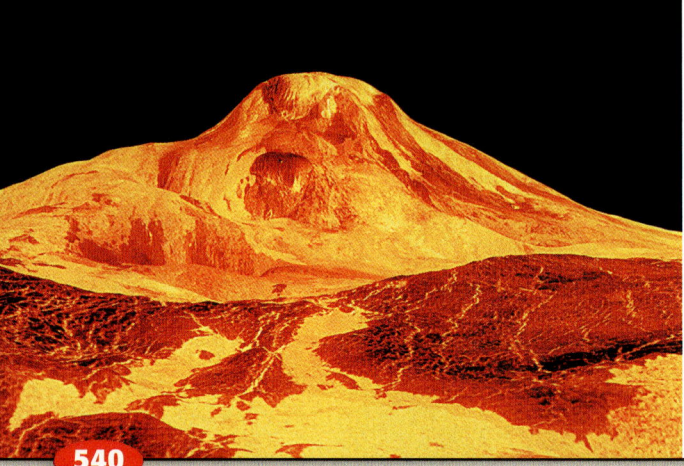

Figure 6 *This false-color image of a volcano on the surface of Venus was made with radar data gathered by the* Magellan *spacecraft. Bright areas indicate massive lava flows.*

Venus Statistics

Distance from sun	6.0 light-minutes
Period of rotation	243 days, (R)*
Period of revolution	224 days, 17 hours
Diameter	12,104 km
Density	5.24 g/cm³
Surface temperature	464°C
Surface gravity	91% of Earth's

*R = retrograde rotation

Venus—Earth's Twin? In many ways Venus is more similar to Earth than is any other planet—they have about the same size, mass, and density. But in other ways Venus is very different from Earth. Unlike on Earth, on Venus the sun rises in the west and sets in the east. This is because Venus rotates in the opposite direction that Earth rotates. Earth is said to have **prograde rotation,** because when viewed from above its north pole, Earth appears to spin in a *counterclockwise* direction. If a planet spins in a *clockwise* direction, it is said to have **retrograde rotation.**

The Atmosphere of Venus At 90 times the pressure of Earth's atmosphere, the atmosphere of Venus is the densest of the terrestrial planets. It consists mostly of carbon dioxide, but it also contains some of the most corrosive acids known. The carbon dioxide in the atmosphere traps thermal energy from sunlight in a process known as the *greenhouse effect*. This is why the surface temperature is so high. With an average temperature of 464°C, Venus has the hottest surface of any planet in the solar system.

Mapping Venus's Surface Between 1990 and 1992, the *Magellan* spacecraft mapped the surface of Venus by using radar waves. The radar waves traveled through the clouds and bounced off the planet's surface. The radar image in **Figure 6** shows that, like Earth, Venus has an active surface.

Homework

Using Maps Interestingly, most of the features of Venus are named after female scientists, historical figures, and goddesses. Many of Mercury's craters are named after artists and musicians, and most craters of the moon are named after famous scientists. Have students use maps of the inner planets to learn more about their features and the origin of their names.

IS THAT A FACT!

Venus is the second-brightest object in the night sky, after the moon. Venus is often called the morning star or the evening star because it always rises and sets with the sun. Also, the planet rotates much more slowly than Earth. A Venusian day is longer than a Venusian year!

Earth—An Oasis in Space As viewed from space, Earth is like a sparkling blue oasis suspended in a black sea. Constantly changing weather patterns create the swirls of clouds that blanket the blue and brown sphere we call home. Why did Earth have such good fortune while its two nearest neighbors, Venus and Mars, are unsuitable for life as we know it?

Water on Earth Earth is fortunate enough to have formed at just the right distance from the sun. The temperatures are warm enough to prevent most of its water from freezing but cool enough to keep it from boiling away. Liquid water was the key to the development of life on Earth. Water provides a means for much of the chemistry that living things depend on for survival.

The Earth from Space You might think the only goal of space exploration is to make discoveries beyond Earth. But NASA has a program to study Earth using satellites—just as we study other planets. The goal of this project, called the Earth Science Enterprise, is to study the Earth as a system and to determine the effects humans have in changing the global environment. By studying Earth from space, we hope to understand how different parts of the global system—such as weather, climate, and pollution—interact.

Figure 7 Earth is the only planet we know of that supports life.

Figure 8 This image of Earth was taken on December 7, 1972, by the crew of the *Apollo 17* spacecraft while on their way to the moon.

Earth Statistics	
Distance from sun	8.3 light-minutes
Period of rotation	23 hours, 56 minutes
Period of revolution	365 days, 6 hours
Diameter	12,756 km
Density	5.52 g/cm^3
Surface temperature	–13 to 37°C
Surface gravity	100% of Earth's

RETEACHING

Discuss with students why Earth is referred to in their text as an oasis. Ask students what an oasis is. (An oasis is a hospitable place in an otherwise inhospitable area.)

Then ask them how Earth qualifies as an oasis in space. Tell them to focus on the importance of Earth's distance from the sun and the presence of large amounts of liquid water on Earth's surface. Earth's mass also plays an important role because it allows the planet to "hold" the gases around it that constitute Earth's life-sustaining atmosphere.

MEETING INDIVIDUAL NEEDS

Writing Have students research the Mars Arctic Research Station, the first fully simulated Mars base. The project will allow scientists to test technology that might be used during a manned expedition to Mars. A large impact crater on Devon Island, in the Arctic Circle, was selected for the reseach station because a polar desert on Earth closely matches the Martian environment. Have students compile their findings in a short report.

MISCONCEPTION ALERT

Earth is not a perfect sphere. The diameter of Earth as measured from the North Pole to the South Pole is 44 km less than the diameter as measured at the equator. None of the other planets or stars are perfectly spherical either. Therefore, all of the planetary diameters given in this chapter are equatorial diameters.

WEIRD SCIENCE

The Earth and its moon revolve around the sun like a "double planet." They can be thought of as the unequal ends of a weighted barbell. The center of gravity for the Earth-moon system, called the *barycenter*, is actually 1,700 km below the Earth's surface. This barycenter is what follows the curved line of Earth's orbit. Around this center of gravity, the moon and Earth wobble as they circle the sun.

internetconnect

SCI LINKS — NSTA
TOPIC: Studying Earth from Space
GO TO: www.scilinks.org
sciLINKS NUMBER: HSTE485

Section 1 • The Nine Planets **541**

2) Teach, continued

MATH and MORE

Have students use the planetary statistics tables to make a comparative bar graph of each planet's distance to the sun and its *average* surface temperature. Challenge students to draw conclusions about the relationship between the two statistics. Is there a linear relationship between the two? **(no)**

Why is Mercury colder than Venus even though it is 3 light-minutes closer to the sun? **(Mercury does not have an atmosphere dense enough to trap solar radiation.)**

Science Skills Worksheet 26 "Grasping Graphing"

USING THE FIGURE

The southern icecap of Mars is just visible in the lower right part of the image in **Figure 9**. Have students describe the differences between Mercury, Venus, Mars, and Earth. Ask them to refer to **Figure 10** to answer the following question:

What evidence suggests that there was once water on Mars?

MISCONCEPTION ALERT

Students may believe that the planets always have the same brightness. Actually, planets appear brighter when they are closer to Earth. For example, as Mars and Earth orbit the sun, the distance between the two planets varies from about 75 million kilometers to about 375 million kilometers. This change causes the apparent brightness of Mars to vary by a factor of 25.

542 Chapter 20 • A Family of Planets

Mars Statistics	
Distance from sun	**12.7** light-minutes
Period of rotation	**24** hours, **37** minutes
Period of revolution	**1** year, **322** days
Diameter	**6,794** km
Density	**3.93** g/cm^3
Surface temperature	**−123** to **37**°C
Surface gravity	**38%** of Earth's

Figure 9 *This* Viking *orbiter image shows the eastern hemisphere of Mars. The large circular feature in the center is the impact crater Schiaparelli, with a diameter of 450 km.*

Mars—The Red Planet Other than Earth, Mars is perhaps the most studied planet in the solar system. Much of our knowledge of Mars has come from information gathered by the *Viking 1* and *Viking 2* spacecraft that landed on Mars in 1976 and from the *Pathfinder* spacecraft that landed on Mars in 1997.

The Atmosphere of Mars Because of its thin atmosphere and its great distance from the sun, Mars is a cold planet. Mid-summer temperatures recorded by the *Pathfinder* lander ranged from −13°C to −77°C. The atmosphere of Mars is so thin that the air pressure at the planet's surface is roughly equal to the pressure 30 km above Earth's surface—about three times higher than most planes fly. The pressure is so low that any liquid water would quickly boil away. The only water you'll find on Mars is in the form of ice.

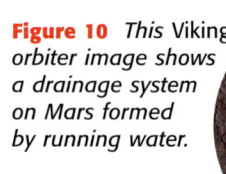

Figure 10 *This* Viking *orbiter image shows a drainage system on Mars formed by running water.*

Water on Mars Even though liquid water cannot exist on Mars's surface today, there is strong evidence that it did exist there in the past! **Figure 10** shows a region on Mars with features that look like dry river beds on Earth. This means that in the past Mars might have been a warmer place with a thicker atmosphere. Where is the water now?

Science Bloopers

In the late 1800s, Giovanni Schiaparelli (1835–1910), an Italian astronomer, was studying Mars. He thought that he saw straight lines crisscrossing the surface of the red planet. He called these lines *canali*. In Italian this means "channels," but the word was erroneously translated to English as "canals." Partly because of this misconception, for nearly 100 years, many people believed that Mars had supported intelligent beings at some time in its past—beings that had built canals. This belief was disproved in the 1960s, when a spacecraft sent to Mars found no canals.

Mars has two polar icecaps that contain both frozen water and frozen carbon dioxide, but this cannot account for all the water. Looking closely at the walls of some Martian craters, scientists have found that the debris surrounding the craters looks as if it were made by a mud flow rather than by the movement of dry material. Where does this suggest some of the "lost" Martian water went? Many scientists think it is frozen beneath the Martian soil.

Martian Volcanoes Mars has a rich volcanic history. Unlike on Earth, where volcanoes occur in many places, Mars has only two large volcanic systems. The largest, the Tharsis region, stretches 8,000 km across the planet. The largest mountain in the solar system, Olympus Mons, is an extinct shield volcano similar to Mauna Kea, on the island of Hawaii. Mars is not only smaller and cooler than Earth, but it also has a slightly different chemical composition. Those factors may have prevented the Martian crust from moving around as Earth's crust has, so the volcanoes kept building up in the same spots. Images and data sent back by probes like the *Sojourner* rover, shown in **Figure 11**, are helping to explain Mars's mysterious past.

Figure 11 *The* Sojourner *rover, part of the Mars Pathfinder mission, is shown here creeping up to a rock named Yogi to measure its composition. The dark panel on top of the rover collected the solar energy used to power its motor.*

REVIEW

1. What three characteristics do the inner planets have in common?
2. List three differences and three similarities between Venus and Earth.
3. **Analyzing Relationships** Mercury is closest to the sun, yet Venus has a higher surface temperature. Explain why this is so.

Physics CONNECTION

At sea level on Earth's surface, water boils at 100°C, but if you try to boil water on top of a high mountain, you will find that the boiling point is lower than 100°C. This is because the atmospheric pressure is less at high altitude. The atmospheric pressure on the surface of Mars is so low that liquid water can't exist at all!

Why Do They Wander?

MISCONCEPTION ALERT

As Mars moves eastward through Earth's night sky, it appears to gradually slow to a stop and then reverse its direction for several weeks. Then it resumes its normal west-to-east motion through the sky. This curious looped path puzzled astronomers in the past. Today we know that Earth passes Mars as the two planets orbit the sun, and thus Mars seems to move backward for a time. This is called *retrograde motion*, not to be confused with *retrograde rotation*.

CROSS-DISCIPLINARY FOCUS

Literature Percival Lowell (1855–1916), an American astronomer, wrote several books on the existence of an advanced civilization on Mars. Unfortunately, what Lowell observed were optical illusions caused by Earth's atmosphere and by dust storms and natural features on the surface of Mars. Lowell's books had a profound effect on the writings of H. G. Wells (1866–1946) and Edgar Rice Burroughs (1875–1950). Have interested students read and report on *War of the Worlds*, by Wells, or *A Princess of Mars*, by Burroughs.

TOPIC: The Nine Planets
GO TO: www.scilinks.org
*sci*LINKS NUMBER: HSTE480

Answers to Review

1. Answers will vary. Sample answer: The inner planets are small and dense, and they are made of rocky material.
2. Similarities include size, density, mass, surface gravity, and bulk composition.

   Some differences are that Venus has retrograde rotation, Venus's surface temperature is much hotter, and Venus's atmosphere is much denser. (Also, Venus's atmosphere has a much more acidic composition, and the conditions on Venus are unsuitable for life.)
3. Unlike Mercury, Venus has a thick atmosphere that traps energy from the sun.

2) Teach, continued

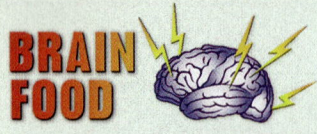

Some astronomers think of Jupiter as a small star that never reached maturity. In fact, the Galileo probe mentioned in the text found that the relative amounts of hydrogen and helium in Jupiter's atmosphere are very similar to those in the sun. Jupiter's 30,000°C core temperature is not high enough to initiate the fusion reactions that occur in the sun's core however. Had Jupiter been about 75 times more massive, it would have been hot enough to initiate nuclear reactions and become a second star in our solar system.

CROSS-DISCIPLINARY FOCUS

Writing — Language Arts In 1980, Carl Sagan wrote in *Cosmos*, "The Earth is a place. It is by no means the only place. It is not even a typical place. No planet or star or galaxy can be typical, because the Cosmos is mostly empty. The only typical place is within the vast, cold, universal vacuum, the everlasting night of intergalactic space, a place so strange and desolate that, by comparison, planets and stars and galaxies seem achingly rare and lovely." Ask students to think about Sagan's quote and write a paragraph or poem about the emptiness of space.

Teaching Transparency 191 "The Outer Planets"

The Outer Planets

The outer planets differ significantly in composition and size from the inner planets. All of the outer planets, except for Pluto, are gas giants. **Gas giants** are very large planets that don't have any known solid surfaces—their atmospheres blend smoothly into the denser layers of their interiors, very deep beneath the outer layers.

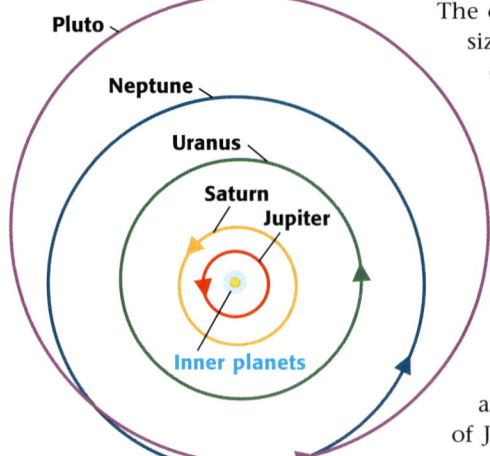

Figure 12 This view of the solar system shows the orbits and positions of the outer planets on January 1, 2005.

Jupiter—A Giant Among Giants Like the sun, Jupiter is made primarily of hydrogen and helium. The outer part of Jupiter's atmosphere is made of layered clouds of water, methane, and ammonia. The beautiful colors in **Figure 13** are probably due to trace amounts of organic compounds. Another striking feature of Jupiter is the Great Red Spot, which is a long-lasting storm system that has a diameter of about one and a half times that of Earth! At a depth of about 10,000 km, the pressure is high enough to change hydrogen gas into a liquid. Deeper still, the pressure changes the liquid hydrogen into a metallic liquid state. Unlike most planets, Jupiter radiates much more energy into space than it receives from the sun. This is because energy is continuously transported from Jupiter's interior to its outer atmospheric layers, where it is radiated into space.

NASA Missions to Jupiter There have been five NASA missions to Jupiter—two Pioneer missions, two Voyager missions, and the recent Galileo mission. The *Voyager 1* and *Voyager 2* spacecraft sent back images that revealed a thin faint ring around the planet, as well as the first detailed images of its moons. The *Galileo* spacecraft reached Jupiter in 1995 and released a probe that plunged into Jupiter's atmosphere. The probe sent back data on the atmosphere's composition, temperature, and pressure.

Figure 13 This *Voyager 2* image of Jupiter was taken at a distance of 28.4 million kilometers. Io, one of Jupiter's largest moons, can also be seen in this image.

Jupiter Statistics	
Distance from sun	43.3 light-minutes
Period of rotation	9 hours, 56 minutes
Period of revolution	11 years, 313 days
Diameter	142,984 km
Density	1.33 g/cm^3
Temperature	−153°C
Gravity	236% of Earth's

CONNECT TO METEOROLOGY

All planets with atmospheres have weather. Jupiter's Great Red Spot appears to be very similar to a hurricane system on Earth, but it has lasted for centuries, driven by the planet's internal energy. Have students write a humorous but accurate weather forecast for one of the planets with an atmosphere.

IS THAT A FACT!

The solar system has two main bodies—the sun and Jupiter. In terms of mass, the rest of the solar system is insignificant! Jupiter has one-thousandth the mass of the sun but is roughly 317 times more massive than Earth, and Jupiter's volume is 1,321 times that of Earth.

Saturn Statistics	
Distance from sun	1.3 light-hours
Period of rotation	10 hours, 39 minutes
Period of revolution	29 years, 155 days
Diameter	120,536 km
Density	0.69 g/cm^3
Temperature	–185°C
Gravity	92% of Earth's

USING THE TABLE

Have students compare the density of Saturn with the densities of other planets, including Earth. Then have them compare the density of Saturn with the density of water. What conclusions can they draw from this information? **(If Saturn were put in an ocean large enough, Saturn would float.)**

Saturn—Still Forming Saturn, the second largest planet in the solar system, has roughly 764 times the volume of Earth and is 95 times more massive. Its overall composition, like Jupiter's, is mostly hydrogen and helium, with methane, ammonia, and ethane in the upper atmosphere. Saturn's interior is probably very similar to that of Jupiter. Like Jupiter, Saturn gives off a lot more energy than it receives from the sun. Scientists believe that, in Saturn's case, the extra energy is caused by helium raining out of the atmosphere and sinking to the core. In essence, Saturn is still forming!

The Rings of Saturn Although all of the gas giants have rings, Saturn's rings are the largest. Saturn's rings start near the top of Saturn's atmosphere and extend out 136,000 km, yet they are only a few hundred meters thick. The rings consist of icy particles that range in size from a few centimeters to several meters across. **Figure 15** shows a close-up view of Saturn's rings.

NASA Goes to Saturn Launched in 1997, the *Cassini* spacecraft is designed to study Saturn's rings, its moons, and its atmosphere. It will return more than 300,000 color images, beginning in 2004.

Figure 14 This *Voyager 2* image of Saturn was taken from 21 million kilometers away. The dot you see below the rings is the shadow of Tethys, one of Saturn's moons.

Figure 15 The different colors in this *Voyager 2* image of Saturn's rings show differences in the chemical composition.

USING THE FIGURE

Ask students to measure the circumfrence of Saturn in **Figure 14** and ask them to hypothesize why Saturn appears to bulge around its equator. Tell students that there are two clues in the Saturn Statistics table. Point out that Saturn's low density (0.69 g/cm^3) and its fast period of rotation (10 hours and 30 minutes) cause the gaseous planet to bulge along its equator.

BRAIN FOOD

When Galileo saw Saturn's rings through a telescope in 1610, he supposedly exclaimed, "Saturn has ears!" Point out to students that *Voyager 2* counted more than 100,000 ringlets in Saturn's ring system. The ring particles range from the size of a dust speck to the size of a house. Ask students to find out more about the Cassini mission to Saturn, including what kind of information the Cassini color images will provide.

IS THAT A FACT!

Saturn has the most violent winds of any planet in our solar system. At Saturn's equator, the wind blows at nearly 1,700 km/h—not exactly good weather for playing outside.

WEIRD SCIENCE

Although Saturn has a similar composition to Jupiter, it appears less colorful. This is because its colder atmosphere causes thick, white ammonia clouds to condense, blocking our view.

Section 1 • The Nine Planets

2) Teach, continued

READING STRATEGY

Prediction Guide Before students read this page, ask them if they agree with the following statements. Students will learn the answers as they continue to explore Section 1.

- Uranus was discovered in the eighteenth century. (true)
- The orbits of the moons of Uranus are almost perpendicular to the planet's orbit around the sun. (true)

USING THE FIGURE

Using **Figure 17,** point out that because Uranus has an 82.1° tilt, its poles point toward the sun during part of its year. In contrast, Venus's 2.7° tilt means that, as with most planets, its poles never point directly toward the sun. Students can simulate these axial tilts using a globe and an object to represent the sun. As students revolve around the sun, have them tilt the globe to represent the axial tilts of Venus, Earth (23.5°), and Uranus. Point out the times that Uranus's poles point toward the sun. For consistency, the "axial tilts" of the planets are often described as angles less than 90°. In contrast, *obliquity* values for planets, which also measure the tilt of a planet's axis, are greater than 90° for planets with retrograde rotation. These planets are thought to have tipped over after colliding with other massive bodies shortly after they formed. In essence, their "rotational north poles" now point "south" in space. This is why the obliquity values for Venus, Uranus, and Pluto are 177.3°, 97.9°, and 122.5°, respectively.

Figure 16 *This image of Uranus was taken by* Voyager 2 *at a distance of 9.1 million kilometers.*

Uranus Statistics	
Distance from sun	2.7 light-hours
Period of rotation	17 hours, 14 minutes (R)*
Period of revolution	83 years, 274 days
Diameter	51,118 km
Density	1.27 g/cm³
Temperature	–214°C
Gravity	89% of Earth's

*R = retrograde rotation

Uranus—A Small Giant Uranus (YOOR uh nuhs) was discovered by the English amateur astronomer William Herschel in 1781. Viewed through a telescope, Uranus looks like a featureless blue-green disk. The atmosphere is mainly hydrogen and methane gas, which absorbs the red part of sunlight very strongly. Uranus and Neptune are much smaller than Jupiter and Saturn, and yet they have similar densities. This suggests that they have lower percentages of light elements and more water in their interiors.

A Tilted Planet Uranus has about 63 times the volume of Earth and is nearly 15 times as massive. One especially unusual quality of Uranus is that it is tipped over on its side—the axis of rotation is tilted by almost 90° and lies almost in the plane of its orbit. **Figure 17** shows how far Uranus's axis is inclined. For part of a Uranus year, one pole points toward the sun while the other pole is in darkness. At the other end of Uranus's orbit the poles are reversed. Scientists suggest that early in its history, Uranus got hit by a massive object that tipped the planet over.

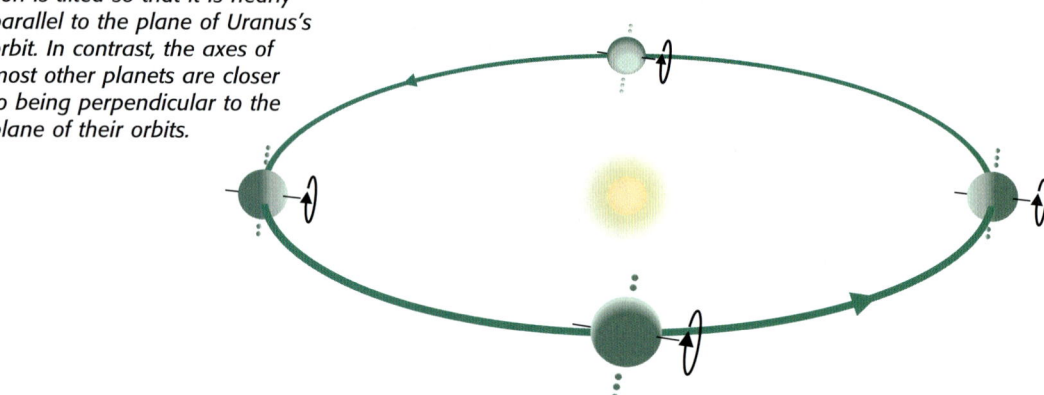

Figure 17 *Uranus's axis of rotation is tilted so that it is nearly parallel to the plane of Uranus's orbit. In contrast, the axes of most other planets are closer to being perpendicular to the plane of their orbits.*

Science Bloopers

Uranus was discovered in 1781 by an English music teacher named William Herschel. Herschel originally named the planet *Georgium Sidus,* Latin for George's Star, after England's King George III. No one outside of England liked the name. A few years later, an astronomer named J. E. Bode suggested the name Uranus because it would continue the tradition of naming the planets after Greek or Roman gods.

Surviving Space

Imagine that it is the year 2120 and you are the pilot of an interplanetary spacecraft on your way to explore Pluto. In the middle of your journey, your navigation system malfunctions, giving you only one chance to land safely. You will not be able to make it to your original destination or back to Earth, so you must choose one of the other planets to land on. Your equipment includes two years' supply of food, water, and air. You will be stranded on the planet you choose until a rescue mission can be launched from Earth. Which planet will you choose to land on? How would your choice of this planet increase your chances of survival? Explain why you did not choose each of the other planets.

Neptune—The Blue World Irregularities in the orbit of Uranus suggested to early astronomers that there must be another planet beyond Uranus whose gravitational force causes Uranus to move off its predicted path. By using the predictions of the new planet's orbit, astronomers discovered the planet Neptune in 1846.

The Atmosphere of Neptune The *Voyager 2* spacecraft sent back images that gave us much new information about the nature of Neptune's atmosphere. Although the composition of Neptune's atmosphere is nearly the same as that of Uranus's atmosphere, Neptune's atmosphere contains belts of clouds that are much more visible. At the time of *Voyager 2*'s visit, Neptune had a Great Dark Spot, similar to the Great Red Spot on Jupiter. And like the interiors of Jupiter and Saturn, Neptune's interior releases energy to its outer layers. This helps the warm gases rise and the cool gases sink, setting up the wind patterns in the atmosphere that create the belts of clouds. *Voyager 2* images also revealed that Neptune has a set of very narrow rings.

Figure 18 This *Voyager 2* image of Neptune, taken at a distance of more than 7 million kilometers, shows the Great Dark Spot as well as some bright cloud bands.

Neptune Statistics	
Distance from sun	4.2 light-hours
Period of rotation	16 hours, 7 minutes
Period of revolution	163 years, 265 days
Diameter	49,528 km
Density	1.64 g/cm³
Temperature	–225°C
Gravity	112% of Earth's

CONNECT TO ENVIRONMENTAL SCIENCE

Since the *Voyager* spacecraft passed Neptune's moon Triton in 1989, scientists have noticed an interesting trend in Triton's atmosphere. Images from the Hubble Space Telescope taken in 1998 indicate that Triton is going through a rapid period of global warming. As Triton warms, frozen nitrogen on its surface melts and contributes nitrogen gas to its thin atmosphere. This process has happened so rapidly that the atmospheric pressure of Triton has doubled in less than 10 years! Scientists hope to use the global warming trends on Triton to understand warming patterns on Earth. Because Triton is a much simpler world than Earth—with a thinner atmosphere, a surface of frozen nitrogen, and no oceans—it is a good place to study environmental change.

3 Extend

Answers to APPLY
Answers will vary. No matter which planet students choose, they should have a logical explanation for their choice.

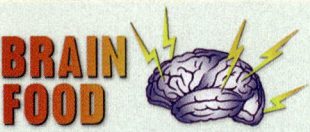

Point out that Neptune was discovered in 1846 by the British astronomer John Adams and the French astronomer Joseph Leverrier. The discovery of Neptune was a triumph for modern physics. Using Newton's laws of motion and gravity, the astronomers accurately predicted Neptune's position. They found discrepancies in Uranus's motion that could not be explained by its gravitational interactions with the sun and the other known planets. Have students look up Newton's laws of motion and gravity. Then ask them to explain, in their own words, how deviations in one planet's orbit could indicate the presence of an unknown planet.

GROUP ACTIVITY

Packing for Space Have students make a list of the resources they would need to live in space. Remind them that it is very expensive to bring items from Earth because it takes a tremendous amount of energy to reach the velocity needed to escape the Earth's gravity. If an item could not be brought from Earth, have students suggest another planet where they could find that resource.

Pluto Statistics	
Distance from sun	5.5 light-hours
Period of rotation	6 days, 9 hours (R)*
Period of revolution	248 years
Diameter	2,390 km
Density	2.05 g/cm^3
Surface temperature	−236°C
Surface gravity	6% of Earth's

*R = retrograde rotation

Figure 19 This Hubble Space Telescope image is one of the clearest ever taken of Pluto (left) and its moon, Charon.

Pluto—A Double Planet? Pluto is the farthest planet from the sun. It is also the smallest planet—less than half the size of Mercury. Another reason Pluto is unusual is that its moon, Charon (KER uhn), is more than half its size! In fact, Charon is the largest satellite relative to its planet in the solar system. **Figure 19** shows Pluto and Charon together.

From Earth, it is hard to separate the images of Pluto and Charon because they are so far away. **Figure 20** shows just how far away from the sun Pluto and Charon really are—from the surface of Pluto the sun appears to be only a very distant, bright star.

From calculations of Pluto's density, we know that it must be made of rock and ice. A very thin atmosphere of methane has been detected. While Pluto is covered by nitrogen ice, Charon is covered by water ice. Pluto is the only planet that has not been visited by a NASA mission, but plans are underway to finally visit this world and its moon in 2010.

Figure 20 An artist's view of the sun and Charon from Pluto shows just how little light and heat Pluto receives from the sun.

internetconnect

TOPIC: The Nine Planets
GO TO: www.scilinks.org
sciLINKS NUMBER: HSTE480

REVIEW

1. How are the gas giants different from the terrestrial planets?
2. What is so unusual about Uranus's axis of rotation?
3. What conclusion can you draw about a planet's properties just by knowing how far it is from the sun?
4. **Applying Concepts** Why is the word *surface* not included in the statistics for the gas giants?

Section 2

Moons

Terms to Learn
- satellite
- phases
- eclipse

What You'll Do
- Describe the current theory for the origin of Earth's moon.
- Describe what causes the phases of Earth's moon.
- Explain the difference between a solar eclipse and a lunar eclipse.

Satellites are natural or artificial bodies that revolve around larger bodies like planets. Except for Mercury and Venus, all of the planets have natural satellites called *moons*.

Luna: The Moon of Earth

We know that Earth's moon—also called *Luna*—has a different overall composition from the Earth because its density is much less than Earth's. This tells us that the moon has a lower percentage of heavy elements than the Earth has. The composition of lunar rocks brought back by Apollo astronauts suggests that the composition of the moon is similar to that of the Earth's mantle.

The Surface of the Moon The explorations of the moon's surface by the Apollo astronauts have given us insights about other planets and moons of the solar system. For example, the lunar rocks brought back during the Apollo missions were found to be about 4.6 billion years old. Because these rocks have hardly changed since they formed, we know the solar system itself is about 4.6 billion years old.

In addition, we know that the surfaces of bodies that have no atmospheres preserve a record of almost all the impacts they have had with other objects. As shown in **Figure 22**, the moon's history is written on its face! Because we now know the age of the moon, we can count the number of impact craters on the moon and use that number to calculate the rate of cratering that has occurred since the birth of our solar system. By knowing the rate of cratering, scientists are able to use the number of craters on the surface of any body to estimate how old its surface is—without having to bring back rock samples!

Figure 21 Apollo 17 *astronaut Harrison Schmidt—the first geologist to walk on the moon—samples the lunar soil.*

Figure 22 *This image of the moon was taken by the* Galileo *spacecraft while on its way to Jupiter. The large dark areas are lava plains called* maria.

Moon Statistics	
Period of rotation	27 days, 8 hours
Period of revolution	27 days, 8 hours
Diameter	3,476 km
Density	3.34 g/cm³
Surface temperature	−170 to 134°C
Surface gravity	17% of Earth's

The first astronauts to land on the moon were quarantined after their mission. NASA wanted to make sure that the astronauts didn't bring back any disease-causing organisms from the moon.

Directed Reading Worksheet 20 Section 2

TOPIC: The Earth's Moon
GO TO: www.scilinks.org
***sci*LINKS NUMBER:** HSTE490

2) Teach

READING STRATEGY

Prediction Guide Before students read this page, ask them: Where did the moon come from? What evidence is there to support this theory? As students read the rest of this section, have them construct a chart that describes some of the major moons in our solar system and their possible origin.

MATH and MORE

Every second, the moon travels 1 km in its orbit, but during that second, it also falls about 14 mm toward the Earth. Because of the moon's velocity and the pull of gravity, it travels along a path that follows the curved surface of the Earth. This condition, known as free fall, keeps the moon in orbit around the Earth. Explain to students that the condition of free fall, or weightlessness, does not mean that there is no gravity. The Earth's gravity acts on the moon in the same way it acts on an apple that falls out of a tree. The difference is that the moon, unlike the apple, is moving forward much, much faster than it is falling. Use the transparency listed below to discuss the moon's orbit.

Teaching Transparency 223
"Two Motions Combine to Form Projectile Motion"
LINK TO PHYSICAL SCIENCE

Teaching Transparency 192
"Formation of the Moon"

Physics
CONNECTION

Did you know that the moon is falling? It's true. Because of gravity, every object in orbit around Earth is falling toward the planet. But the moon is also moving forward at the same time. The combination of the moon's forward motion and its falling motion results in the moon's curved orbit around Earth.

Lunar Origins Before rock samples from the Apollo missions confirmed the composition of the moon, there were three popular explanations for the formation of the moon: (1) it was a separate body captured by Earth's gravity, (2) it formed at the same time and from the same materials as the Earth, and (3) the newly formed Earth was spinning so fast that a piece flew off and became the moon. Each idea had problems. If the moon were captured by Earth's gravity, it would have a completely different composition from that of Earth, which is not the case. On the other hand, if the moon formed at the same time as the Earth or as a spin off of the Earth, the moon would have exactly the same composition as Earth, which it doesn't.

The current theory is that a large, Mars-sized object collided with Earth while the Earth was still forming. The collision was so violent that part of the Earth's mantle was blasted into orbit around Earth to form the moon. This theory is consistent with the composition of the lunar rocks brought back by the Apollo missions.

Formation of the Moon

❶ Impact
About 4.6 billion years ago, when Earth was still mostly molten, a large body collided with Earth. Scientists reason that the object must have been large enough to blast part of Earth's mantle into space, because the composition of the moon is similar to Earth's mantle.

❷ Ejection
The resulting debris began to revolve around the Earth within a few hours of the impact. This debris consisted of mantle material from Earth and the impacting body as well as part of the iron core of the impacting body.

❸ Formation
Soon after the giant impact, the clumps of material ejected into orbit around Earth began to join together to form the moon. Much later, as the moon cooled, additional impacts created deep basins and fractured the moon's surface. Lunar lava flowed from those cracks and flooded the basins to form the lunar maria we see today.

Homework

Moon Journal Have students keep a record of the moon for 2 weeks. Have them make drawings of what they see, label the phase, and record the time of day and the position of the moon when they observed it. Emphasize that students should observe the moon from the same place and time each night and use the same landmark for observation. Students could use newspapers or a calendar to determine the current phase of the moon and the time the moon rises and sets during that phase. If you live near a body of water with tides, have students compare the times of high tides with the times that the moon rises.

550 Chapter 20 • A Family of Planets

Phases of the Moon From Earth, one of the most noticeable aspects of the moon is its continually changing appearance. Within a month, its Earthward face changes from a fully lit circle to a thin crescent and then back to a circle. These different appearances of the moon result from its changing position with respect to the Earth and the sun. As the moon revolves around the Earth, the amount of sunlight on the side of the moon that faces the Earth changes. The different appearances of the moon due to its changing position are called **phases**. The phases of the moon are shown in **Figure 23**.

The moon's appearance changes every night. To find out how this occurs, turn to page 717 in your LabBook.

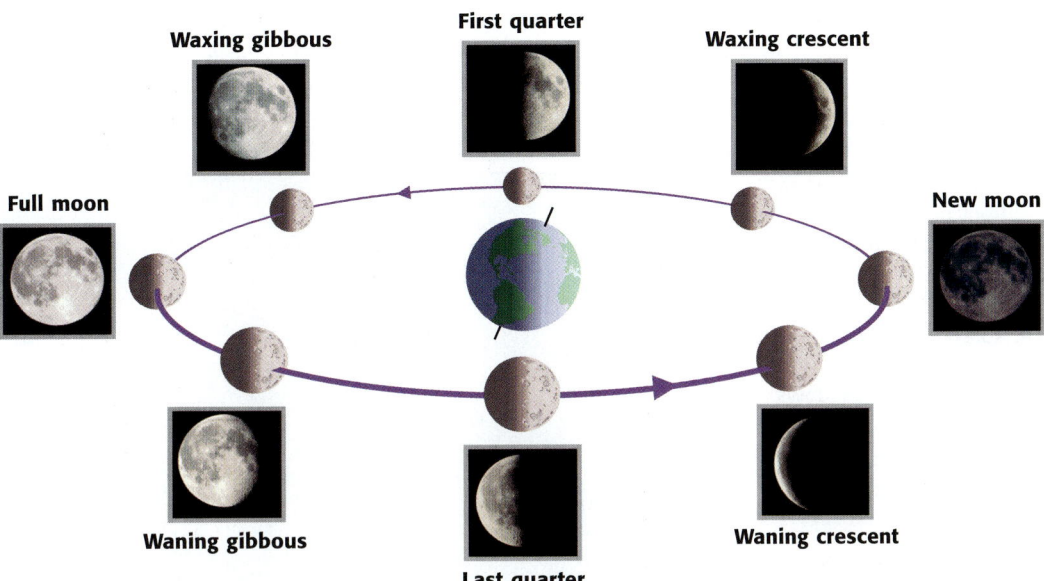

Figure 23 *The relative positions of the moon, sun, and Earth determine which phase the moon is in. The photo insets show how the moon looks from Earth at each phase.*

Waxing and Waning When the moon is *waxing*, it means that the sunlit fraction we can see from Earth is getting larger. When it is *waning*, the sunlit fraction is getting smaller. Notice in Figure 23 that even as the phases of the moon change, the total amount of sunlight the moon gets remains the same. Half the moon is always in sunlight, just as half the Earth is always in sunlight. But because the period of rotation for the moon is the same as its period of revolution, on Earth we always see the same side of the moon. If you lived on the far side of the moon, you would see the sun for half of each lunar day, but you would never see the Earth!

IS THAT A FACT!

Waxing means "growing," while *waning* means "shrinking." In the first quarter of a lunar phase, the moon is one quarter of the way through its cycle of phases. At this point, sunlight is shining on the right half of the moon. During the last quarter, sunlight is shining on the left half of the moon.

2 Teach, continued

QuickLab

MATERIALS
- heavy white paper
- 2 spherical objects
- objects with other shapes
- lamp

Safety Caution: Strongly caution students against looking directly at the sun (especially through binoculars or a telescope). Explain that doing so can result in permanent damage to their eyes or even blindness.

Answer to QuickLab
5. Spherical objects always cast a curved shadow.

MATH and MORE

To better understand the uniqueness of a solar eclipse on Earth, have students calculate the following: What is the ratio of the moon's diameter (3,476 km) to the sun's diameter (1,392,000 km)? **(1:400)**

What is the ratio of their distances from Earth if the moon is about 384,000 km from Earth and the sun is about 150,000,000 km from Earth? **(1:390)**

Help students understand that because the Earth is nearly 400 times closer to the moon than to the sun and because the sun is 400 times larger than the moon, the moon and sun appear to be the same size in the sky.

Eclipses PG 716

QuickLab

Clever Insight

Pythagoras (540–510 B.C.) and Aristotle (384–322 B.C.) used observations of lunar eclipses and a little logic to figure out that Earth is a sphere. Can you?

1. Cut out a circle of **heavy white paper.** This will represent Earth.
2. Find **two spherical objects** and several other **objects** with different shapes.
3. Hold each object up in front of a **lamp** (representing the sun) so that its shadow falls on the white paper circle.
4. Rotate your objects in all directions, and record the shapes of the shadows they make.
5. Which objects always cast a curved shadow?

NEVER look directly at the sun! You can permanently damage your eyes.

Teaching Transparency 194
"Solar Eclipse"
"Lunar Eclipse"

Eclipses An **eclipse** occurs when the shadow of one celestial body falls on another. A *lunar eclipse* happens when the Earth comes between the sun and the moon, and the shadow of the Earth falls on the moon. A *solar eclipse* happens when the moon comes between the Earth and the sun, and the shadow of the moon falls on part of Earth.

Solar Eclipses By a remarkable coincidence, the moon in the sky appears to be nearly the same size as the sun. So during a solar eclipse, the disk of the moon almost always covers the disk of the sun. However, because the moon's orbit is not completely circular, sometimes the moon is farther away from the Earth, and a thin ring of sunlight shows around the outer edge of the moon. This type of solar eclipse is called an *annular eclipse*. **Figure 24** illustrates the position of the Earth and the moon during a solar eclipse.

Figure 24 Because the shadow of the moon on Earth is small, a solar eclipse can be viewed from only a few locations.

Figure 25 This is an image of the sun's corona during the February 26, 1998, eclipse in the Caribbean. The solar corona is visible only when the entire disk of the sun is blocked by the moon.

Homework

Naming the Full Moon Students may be surprised to learn that every full moon has a name. The most familiar moon is the harvest moon, which occurs in the fall. Have students find out about other full moons, such as the hunter's moon or the sap moon, and report on the origins of the names.

Chapter 20 • A Family of Planets

Lunar Eclipses As you can see in **Figure 26,** the view during a lunar eclipse is also spectacular. Earth's atmosphere acts like a lens and bends some of the sunlight into the Earth's shadow, and the interaction of the sunlight with the molecules in the atmosphere filters out the blue light. With the blue part of the light removed, most of the remaining light that illuminates the moon is red.

Figure 26 *Because of atmospheric effects on Earth, the moon can have a reddish color during a lunar eclipse.*

Figure 27 *During a lunar eclipse, the moon passes within the Earth's shadow.*

The Moon's Orbit Is Tilted! From our discussion of the moon's phases, you might now be asking the question, "Why don't we see solar and lunar eclipses every month?" The answer is that the moon's orbit around the Earth is tilted—by about 5°—with respect to the orbit of the Earth around the sun. This tilt is enough to place the moon out of Earth's shadow for most full moons and the Earth out of the moon's shadow for most new moons.

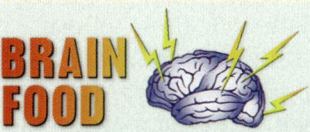

MATH BREAK

Orbits Within Orbits

The average distance between the Earth and the moon is about 384,400 km. As you have read, the average distance between the Earth and the sun is 1 AU, or about 150,000,000 km. Assume that the orbit of the Earth around the sun and the orbit of the moon around the Earth are perfectly circular. Using the distances given above, calculate the maximum and minimum distances between the moon and the sun.

REVIEW

1. What evidence suggests that Earth's moon formed from a giant impact?
2. Why do we always see the same side of the moon?
3. How are lunar eclipses different from solar eclipses?
4. **Analyzing Methods** How does knowing the age of a lunar rock help astronomers estimate the age of the surface of a planet like Mercury?

CONNECT TO LIFE SCIENCE

One of the most debated questions among scientists is whether there is life on other planets. Life as we know it requires liquid water. If liquid water exists on other planets or their moons, it is possible that there are also living organisms there. Scientists have been studying a group of organisms called extremophiles for clues about what extraterrestrial life might be like. Extremophiles are organisms that live in extreme environments, such as deep-ocean volcanic vents, hot springs, or highly acidic or basic environments. Scientists hope that by studying these organisms, they will have a better idea about where to look for life elsewhere in the solar system. Some of the most likely places to search for evidence of life are Mars and some of the moons of Jupiter. Have interested students find out about the status of NASA projects that are searching for extraterrestrial life and about organisms classified as extremophiles.

USING SCIENCE FICTION

Students will enjoy reading Stanley Weinbaum's "The Mad Moon" in the *Holt Anthology of Science Fiction*. Discuss the author's description of Jupiter's moon Io. How does the author's description compare with what we now know about Io? Have students use the story as inspiration to write their own description of a human colony on one of Jupiter's moons.

The Moons of Other Planets

The moons of the other planets range in size from very small to as large as terrestrial planets. All of the gas giants have multiple moons, and scientists are still discovering new moons. Some moons have very elongated, or elliptical, orbits, and some even revolve around their planet backward! Many of the very small moons may be captured asteroids. As we are learning from recent space missions, moons can be some of the most bizarre and interesting places in the solar system!

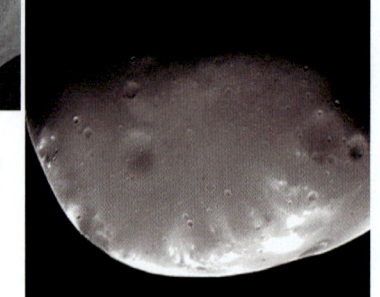

Figure 28 Above is Mars's largest moon, Phobos, which is 28 km long. At right is the smaller moon, Deimos, which is 16 km long.

The Moons of Mars Mars's two moons, Phobos and Deimos, are both small satellites that have irregular shapes. The two moons have very dark surfaces that reflect even less light than asphalt does. The surface materials are very similar to those found in asteroids, and scientists speculate that these two moons are probably captured asteroids.

The Moons of Jupiter Jupiter has dozens of known moons. The four largest—Ganymede, Callisto, Io, and Europa—were discovered in 1610 by Galileo and are known as the Galilean satellites. The largest moon, Ganymede, is even larger than the planet Mercury! Many of the smaller satellites are probably captured asteroids.

Moving outward from Jupiter, the first Galilean satellite is Io (IE oh), a truly bizarre world. Io is caught in a gravitational tug-of-war between Jupiter and Io's nearest neighbor, the moon Europa. This constant tugging stretches Io a little, causing it to heat up. Because of this, Io is the most volcanically active body in the solar system!

Recent pictures of the moon Europa support the idea that liquid water may lie beneath the moon's icy surface. This has many scientists wondering if life could have evolved in the subterranean oceans of Europa.

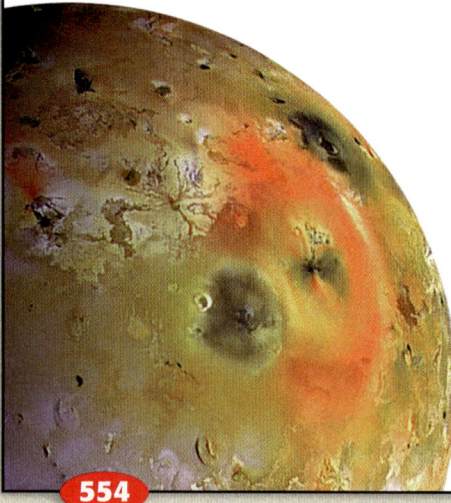

Figure 29 At left is a Galileo image of Jupiter's innermost moon, Io. At right is a Galileo image of Jupiter's fourth largest moon, Europa.

Homework

Have students research the moons of a planet other than Earth and write a short paper about them. Suggest that they compare the moons with each other and with Earth's moon and then research the possible reasons for the differences they find.

MISCONCEPTION ALERT

Students may think the moon is larger when it is close to the horizon. The moon appears larger because the observer's reference point is the skyline. The same phenomenon makes the sun appear larger. Challenge students to devise a way to verify this for themselves. Remind them not to look directly at the sun.

The Moons of Saturn Like Jupiter, Saturn also has dozens of moons. Most of these moons are small bodies made mostly of water ice with some rocky material. The largest satellite, Titan, was discovered in 1655 by Christiaan Huygens. In 1980, the *Voyager 1* spacecraft flew past Titan and discovered a hazy orange atmosphere, as shown in **Figure 30.** Titan's atmosphere is similar to what Earth's atmosphere may have been like before life began to evolve. In 1997, NASA launched the *Cassini* spacecraft to study Saturn and its moons, including Titan. By studying Titan, scientists hope to answer some of the questions about how life began on Earth.

Figure 30 Titan is one of only two moons that have a thick atmosphere. Titan's hazy orange atmosphere is made of nitrogen plus several other gases, such as methane.

Self-Check

What is one major difference between Titan and the early Earth that would suggest that there probably isn't life on Titan? *(See page 726 to check your answer.)*

The Moons of Uranus Uranus has more than 20 moons. Like the moons of Saturn, the four largest moons are made of ice and rock and are heavily cratered. The little moon Miranda, shown in **Figure 31,** has some of the most unusual features in the solar system. Miranda's surface includes smooth, cratered plains as well as regions with grooves and cliffs up to 20 km high. Current ideas suggest that Miranda may have been hit and broken apart in the past but was able to come together again, leaving a patchwork surface.

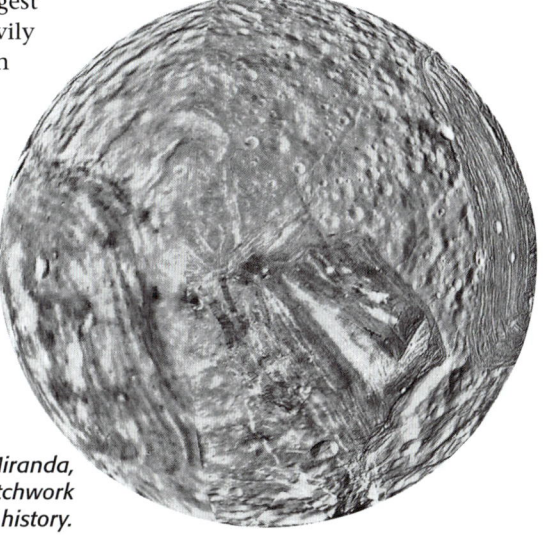

Figure 31 This *Voyager 2* image shows Miranda, the most unusual moon of Uranus. Its patchwork terrain indicates that it has had a violent history.

IS THAT A FACT!

Io, one of Jupiter's moons, is well known for the volcanoes on its surface. These volcanoes, which are the hottest in the solar system, regularly erupt yellow and red clouds of sulfur up to 300 km above the surface!

internet connect

TOPIC: The Moons of Other Planets
GO TO: www.scilinks.org
sciLINKS NUMBER: HSTE495

3) Extend

BRAIN FOOD

Like planets, most moons are spherical in shape. Ask the class why this is the case. Why aren't some moons square, tube shaped, or pyramidal? Tell them that the force of gravity and the origin of celestial bodies have something to do with the answer. Lead them to the conclusion that as the mass of an object increases, the gravitational force that it exerts also increases. When a rocky object reaches a diameter of about 350 km, the gravitational force becomes greater than the strength of the material and the moon starts to become spherical.

Answer to Self-Check

The surface of Titan is much colder than the surface of the Earth. (In fact, the temperature is close to −178°C!)

RESEARCH

NASA is planning several missions to explore the moons of different planets. Have students select one of NASA's projects and find out the details of what was discovered or what NASA hopes to find. Have students imagine that they are scientists working on the project, and have them write a press release with the details of the project.

4) Close

Quiz

Have students complete the following sentences:

1. A naturally formed planetary satellite is a _____ . (moon)
2. As Earth's moon waxes, the sunlit fraction we see from Earth becomes _____ . (larger)
3. When the moon is waning, the sunlit fraction is becoming _____ . (smaller)
4. If you lived on the far side of the moon, you would never see _____ . (Earth)
5. The two moons of Mars are believed to be captured _____ . (asteroids)
6. The four largest moons of Jupiter were discovered by _____ . (Galileo)
7. Two moons with atmospheres are _____ (Triton) and _____ . (Titan)

ALTERNATIVE ASSESSMENT

 Provide students with construction paper, glue, scissors, and markers. Have them use these materials to make models of the nine planets and their moons.

 Reinforcement Worksheet 20
"The Planets of Our Solar System"

 Reinforcement Worksheet 20
"Lunar and Solar Eclipses"

 Interactive Explorations CD-ROM "Space Case"

The Moons of Neptune Neptune has eight known moons, only one of which is large. This moon, Triton, revolves around the planet in a *retrograde,* or "backward," orbit, suggesting that it may have been captured by Neptune's gravity. Triton has a very thin atmosphere made mostly of nitrogen gas. The surface of Triton consists mainly of frozen nitrogen and methane. *Voyager 2* images revealed that it is geologically active. "Ice volcanoes," or geysers, were seen ejecting nitrogen gas high into the atmosphere. The other seven moons of Neptune are small, rocky worlds much like the smaller moons of Saturn and Jupiter.

Figure 32 This *Voyager 2* image shows Neptune's largest moon, Triton. The polar icecap currently facing the sun may have a slowly evaporating layer of nitrogen ice, adding to Triton's thin atmosphere.

The Moon of Pluto Pluto's only known moon, Charon, was discovered in 1978. Charon's period of revolution is the same as Pluto's period of rotation—about 6.4 days. This means that one side of Pluto always faces Charon. In other words, if you stood on the surface of Pluto, Charon would always occupy the same place in the sky. Imagine Earth's moon staying in the same place every night! Because Charon's orbit around Pluto is tilted with respect to Pluto's orbit around the sun, as seen from Earth, Pluto is sometimes eclipsed by Charon. But don't hold your breath; this happens only once every 120 years!

REVIEW

1. What makes Io the most volcanically active body in the solar system?
2. Why is Saturn's moon Titan of so much interest to scientists studying the origins of life on Earth?
3. What two properties of Neptune's moon Triton make it unusual?
4. **Identifying Relationships** Charon always stays in the same place in Pluto's sky, but the moon always moves across Earth's sky. What causes this difference?

internet connect
SC/LINKS NSTA
TOPIC: The Moons of Other Planets
GO TO: www.scilinks.org
*sci*LINKS NUMBER: HSTE495

Answers to Review

1. Io is caught in the middle of a gravitational "tug of war" between Jupiter and its other large moons.
2. Titan has a thick atmosphere of nitrogen, which scientists think is very similar to that of the early Earth.
3. Triton has a thin atmosphere of nitrogen, and it has a retrograde orbit around Neptune. Most moons have a prograde orbit and no atmosphere.
4. Pluto's period of rotation is the same as Charon's period of revolution. The Earth's period of rotation is much shorter than the moon's period of revolution.

Section 3

Small Bodies in the Solar System

Terms to Learn
comet
asteroid
asteroid belt
meteoroid
meteorite
meteor

What You'll Do
- Explain why comets, asteroids, and meteoroids are important to the study of the formation of the solar system.
- Compare the different types of asteroids with the different types of meteoroids.
- Describe the risks to life on Earth from cosmic impacts.

In addition to planets and moons, the solar system contains many other types of objects, including comets, asteroids, and meteoroids. As you will see, these objects play an important role in the study of the origins of the solar system.

Comets

A **comet** is a small body of ice, rock, and cosmic dust loosely packed together. Because of their composition, some scientists refer to comets as "dirty snowballs." Comets originate from the cold, outer solar system. Nothing much has happened to them since the birth of the solar system some 4.6 billion years ago. Because comets are probably the leftovers from the process of planet formation, each comet is a sample of the early solar system. Scientists want to learn more about comets in order to piece together the chemical and physical history of the solar system.

Comet Tails When a comet passes close enough to the sun, solar radiation heats the water ice so that the comet gives off gas and dust in the form of a long tail, as shown in **Figure 33**. Sometimes a comet has two tails—an *ion tail* and a *dust tail*. The ion tail consists of electrically charged particles called *ions*. The solid center of a comet is called its *nucleus*. Comet nuclei can range in size from less than half a kilometer to more than 100 km in diameter. **Figure 34** shows the different features of a comet when it passes close to the sun.

Figure 33 *Comet Hale-Bopp appeared in North American skies in the spring of 1997.*

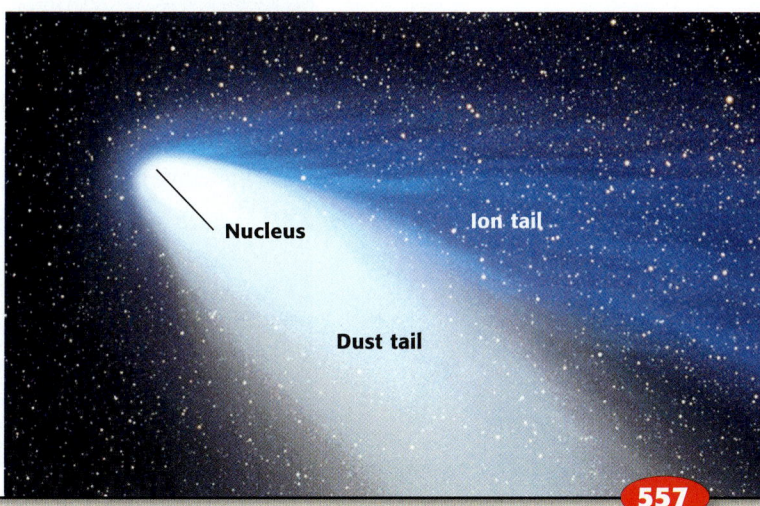

Figure 34 *This image shows the physical features of a comet when it is close to the sun. The nucleus of a comet is hidden by brightly lit gases and dust.*

IS THAT A FACT!
When the comet Shoemaker-Levy 9 broke apart and fell into Jupiter, some of the fragments generated explosions that produced fireballs larger than Earth.

2 Teach

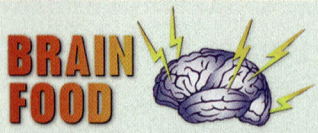

In the past, the primary distinction between a comet and an asteroid was that comets have ices and asteroids do not. The development of sophisticated telescopes and remote-sensing instruments has challenged this distinction. There is evidence that some asteroids may contain ices and that some asteroids develop comet tails. Also, some comets have stopped producing tails and are beginning to look more like asteroids! In general, comets contain enough ice to become "active" and develop a tail, and asteroids do not. Asteroids range in size from a few kilometers to about 1,000 km across, while comet nuclei are rarely larger than 100 km.

USING THE FIGURE

As you discuss **Figure 36,** point out to students that the Kuiper belt is like the asteroid belt—it is circular and relatively flat, lying close to the plane of the planets' orbits. The Oort cloud, on the other hand, is spherical and surrounds the entire solar system. The average period of revolution for a comet is about 10 million years. Comets that originate in the Oort cloud do not necessarily orbit the sun in the plane of the planets' orbits—most of them have inclined orbits. They can also have either retrograde or prograde orbits.

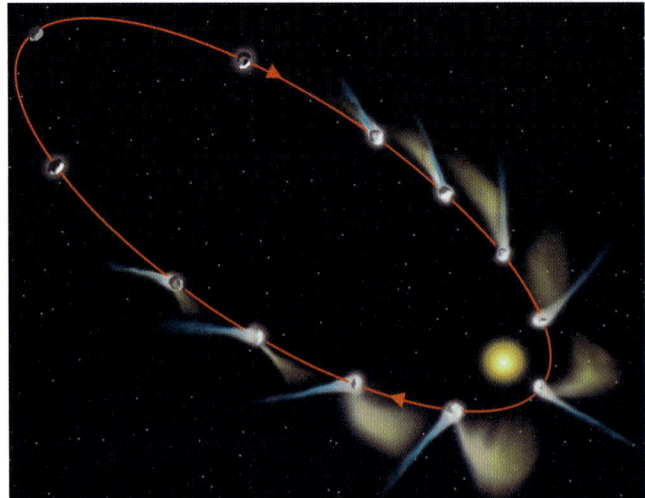

Figure 35 *When a comet's highly elliptical orbit carries it close to the sun, it can develop one or two tails. As shown here, the ion tail is blue and the dust tail is yellow.*

Comet Orbits All orbits are *ellipses*—circles that are somewhat stretched out of shape. Whereas the orbits of most planets are nearly circular, comet orbits are highly elliptical—they are very elongated.

Notice in **Figure 35** that a comet's ion tail always points directly away from the sun. This is because the ion tail is blown away from the sun by the solar wind, which also consists of ions. The dust tail tends to follow the comet's orbit around the sun and does not always point away from the sun. When a comet is close to the sun its tail can extend millions of kilometers through space!

Comet Origins Where do comets come from? Many scientists think they may come from a spherical region, called the *Oort* (ohrt) *cloud,* that surrounds the solar system. When the gravity of a passing planet or star disturbs part of this cloud, comets can be pulled in toward the sun. Another recently discovered region where comets exist is called the *Kuiper* (KIE per) *belt,* which is the region outside the orbit of Neptune. These two regions where comets orbit are shown in **Figure 36.**

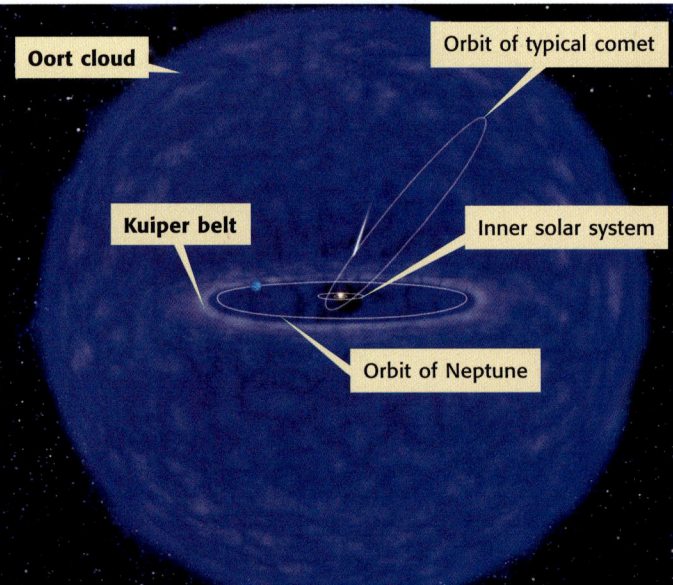

Figure 36 *The Kuiper belt is a disk-shaped region that extends outward from the orbit of Neptune. The Oort cloud is a spherical region far beyond the orbit of Pluto.*

MISCONCEPTION ALERT

Students may be surprised to learn that comets don't have a tail during most of their orbit. It is only when they near the sun that they warm up and release a tail made of gas and dust. The comet nucleus has an irregular shape. Sometimes gas leaves the comet's surface unevenly in "jets." This can have an effect similar to that of a miniature rocket engine, pushing a comet slightly off course and making it difficult to find during its next orbit.

558 Chapter 20 • A Family of Planets

Asteroids

Asteroids are small, rocky bodies in orbit around the sun. They range in size from a few meters to more than 900 km in diameter. Asteroids have irregular shapes, although some of the larger ones are spherical. Most asteroids orbit the sun in a wide region between the orbits of Mars and Jupiter, called the **asteroid belt**. Like comets, asteroids are thought to be material left over from the formation of the solar system.

Types of Asteroids Asteroids can have a variety of compositions, depending on where they are located within the asteroid belt. In the outermost region of the asteroid belt, asteroids have dark reddish brown to black surfaces, which may indicate that they are rich in organic material. A little closer to the sun, asteroids have dark gray surfaces, indicating that they are rich in carbon. In the innermost part of the asteroid belt are light gray asteroids that have either a stony or metallic composition. **Figure 38** shows some examples of what some of the asteroids may look like.

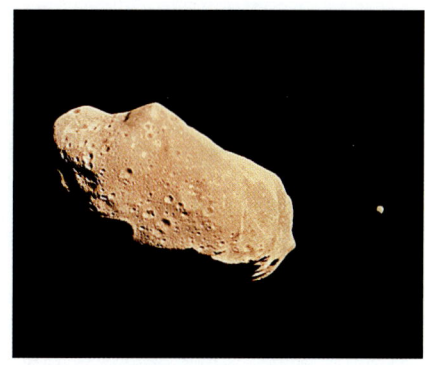

Figure 37 The asteroid Ida has a small companion asteroid that orbits it called Dactyl. Ida is about 52 km long.

Figure 38 The asteroid belt is a disk-shaped region located between the orbits of Mars and Jupiter.

RETEACHING
Draw a diagram of a comet on the board. Ask volunteers to label the parts and to describe the composition of each part. **Sheltered English**

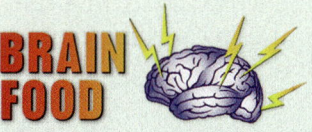

The orbits of some asteroids cross Earth's orbit. Every few million years, one of these asteroids hits the Earth. If an asteroid is larger than 10 km across, its impact can have catastrophic global effects. In the first few seconds of an impact event, both the impactor and part of the target become liquid and an impact crater forms. Shock waves spread out from the site, and debris is ejected high into the atmosphere. About 65 million years ago, a large asteroid struck the Earth on the Yucatan Peninsula. This event may have led to the mass extinction of the dinosaurs. In 1994, the world watched with awe as parts of the comet Shoemaker-Levy 9 collided with Jupiter, causing enormous explosions. This event has led NASA to devote more of its resources to finding and tracking asteroids whose orbits cross Earth's. Have students find out more about NASA's asteroid-tracking program.

In 1908, an object thought to be a comet about 60 m in diameter exploded less than 10 km above a remote part of Siberia. The blast flattened trees in an area greater than 2,000 km² and left no crater.

IS THAT A FACT!
Comets are fairly fragile; some break apart on their own, or the gravity of a planet can pull them apart. This is what happened in the case of comet Shoemaker-Levy 9, which passed too close to Jupiter. When it returned in 1994, fragments of the comet crashed into Jupiter's atmosphere.

INDEPENDENT PRACTICE
Concept Mapping Have students create a concept map using at least six vocabulary words in this chapter. Tell them that their map should illustrate logical connections between the terms they choose.

3) Extend

MEETING INDIVIDUAL NEEDS

Learners Having Difficulty
List the terms *meteoroid*, *meteor*, and *meteorite* on the board. For each of the terms, have students define the word, use it in a sentence, and draw an illustration. (A meteoroid is a small rocky body orbiting the sun. A meteor is the bright streak of light we see when a meteoroid enters our atmosphere. A meteorite is a meteoroid that does not burn completely and lands on the Earth's surface.) **Sheltered English**

ACTIVITY

Collecting Micrometeorites
Earth's atmosphere is constantly bombarded with microscopic meteorites that are too small to burn up. These micrometeorites float in the atmosphere and eventually settle to the ground. The best time to collect micrometeorites is after a meteor shower. Clean a small glass dish, and place it outside to collect rainwater. If you live in an area with little rain, fill the dish with distilled water and place it outside for several days. Place a small, strong magnet in a small plastic bag, and sweep the covered magnet slowly through the water, along the bottom and sides of the dish. Place the covered magnet in a second pan of distilled water, and remove the magnet, shaking the bag in the water to dislodge any particles. Evaporate the water over a hot plate, and drag a magnetized needle across the sides and bottom of the dish. Tap the needle onto a microscope slide, and examine the sediment with a microscope—any rounded and pitted metallic particles are probably micrometeorites.

560 Chapter 20 • A Family of Planets

Meteoroids

A **meteoroid** is a small, rocky body orbiting the sun. Meteoroids are similar to asteroids, but they are much smaller. In fact, most meteoroids probably come from asteroids. If a meteoroid enters Earth's atmosphere and strikes the ground, it is then called a **meteorite**. When a meteoroid falls into Earth's atmosphere, it is usually traveling at such a high speed that its surface heats up and melts. As it burns up, the meteoroid glows red hot and gives off an enormous amount of light. From the ground, we see a spectacular streak of light, or a shooting star. The bright streak of light caused by a meteoroid or comet dust burning up in the atmosphere is called a **meteor**.

Meteor Showers Many of the meteors that we see come from very small (dust-sized to pebble-sized) rocks and can be seen on almost any night if you are far enough away from the city to avoid the glare of its lights. At certain times of the year, you can see large numbers of meteors, as shown in **Figure 39**. These events are called *meteor showers*. Meteor showers occur when Earth passes through the dusty debris left behind in the orbit of a comet.

Types of Meteorites Like their relatives the asteroids, meteorites have a variety of compositions. The three major types of meteorites—stony, metallic, and stony-iron—are shown in **Figure 40**. Many of the stony meteorites probably come from carbon-rich asteroids and may contain organic materials and water. Scientists use meteorites to study the early solar system. Like comets and asteroids, meteoroids are some of the building blocks of planets.

The total mass of meteorites that fall to Earth each year is between 10,000 and 1 million metric tons!

Figure 39 Meteors are the streaks of light caused by meteoroids as they burn up in Earth's atmosphere.

Figure 40 There are three major types of meteorites.

Stony meteorite
rocky material

Metallic meteorite
iron and nickel

Stony-iron meteorite
rocky material, iron, and nickel

SCIENTISTS AT ODDS

As late as the 1800s, scientists were skeptical that meteorites originate in space—despite records from the Chinese, Romans, and Greeks describing stones falling from the sky. In 1803, meteorites fell in France. A physicist documented the event, finally convincing scientists that meteorites fall from the sky.

WEIRD SCIENCE

In 1954, Mrs. E. Hulitt Hodge, of Alabama, was struck by a meteorite as she was taking her afternoon nap. Bruised, but not badly injured, she is one of only two people known to have been struck by a meteorite.

The Role of Impacts in the Solar System

Planets and moons that have no atmosphere have many more impact craters than those that do have atmospheres. Look at **Figure 41.** The Earth's moon has many more impact craters than the Earth because it has no atmosphere or tectonic activity. Fewer objects land on Earth because Earth's atmosphere acts like a shield. Smaller bodies burn up before they ever reach the surface. On the moon, there is nothing to stop them! Also, most craters left on Earth have been erased due to weathering, erosion, and tectonic activity.

Figure 41 The surface of the moon preserves a record of billions of years of cosmic impacts.

Impacts on Earth Objects smaller than about 10 m across usually burn up in the atmosphere, causing a meteor. Larger objects are more likely to strike Earth's surface. In order to estimate the risk of cosmic impacts, we need to consider how often large impacts occur.

The number of large objects that could collide with Earth is relatively small. Scientists estimate that impacts powerful enough to cause a natural disaster might occur once every few thousand years. An impact large enough to cause a global catastrophe—such as the extinction of the dinosaurs—is estimated to occur once every 30 million to 50 million years on average.

REVIEW

1. Why is the study of comets, asteroids, and meteoroids important in understanding the formation of the solar system?
2. Why do a comet's two tails often point in different directions?
3. Describe one reason asteroids may become a natural resource in the future.
4. **Analyzing Viewpoints** Do you think the government should spend money on programs to search for asteroids and comets with Earth-crossing orbits? Discuss why.

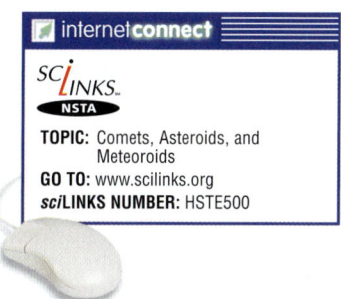

internet connect
TOPIC: Comets, Asteroids, and Meteoroids
GO TO: www.scilinks.org
sciLINKS NUMBER: HSTE500

Chapter Highlights

VOCABULARY DEFINITIONS

SECTION 1

astronomical unit (AU) the average distance between the Earth and the sun, or approximately 150,000,000 km

terrestrial planets the small, dense, rocky planets of the inner solar system

prograde rotation the counterclockwise spin of a planet or moon as seen from above the planet's north pole

retrograde rotation the clockwise spin of a planet or moon as seen from above the planet's north pole

gas giants the large, gaseous planets of the outer solar system

SECTION 2

satellite a natural or artificial body that revolves around a planet

phases the different appearances of the moon due to varying amounts of sunlight on the side of the moon that faces the Earth; results from the changing relative positions of the moon, Earth, and the sun

eclipse an event in which the shadow of one celestial body falls on another

Chapter Highlights

SECTION 1

Vocabulary
- astronomical unit (AU) *(p. 538)*
- terrestrial planets *(p. 539)*
- prograde rotation *(p. 540)*
- retrograde rotation *(p. 540)*
- gas giants *(p. 544)*

Section Notes
- The solar system has nine planets.
- Distances within the solar system can be expressed in astronomical units (AU) or in light-minutes.
- The inner four planets, called the terrestrial planets, are small and rocky.
- The outer planets, with the exception of Pluto, are gas giants.
- By learning about the properties of the planets, we get a better understanding of global processes on Earth.

Labs
Why Do They Wander? *(p. 714)*

SECTION 2

Vocabulary
- satellite *(p. 549)*
- phases *(p. 551)*
- eclipse *(p. 552)*

Section Notes
- Earth's moon probably formed from a giant impact on Earth.
- The moon's phases are caused by the moon's orbit around the Earth. At different times of the month, we view different amounts of sunlight on the moon because of the moon's position relative to the sun and the Earth.
- Lunar eclipses occur when the Earth's shadow falls on the moon.

✓ Skills Check

Math Concepts

INTERPLANETARY DISTANCES The distances between planets are so vast that scientists have invented new units of measurement to describe them. One of these units is the astronomical unit (AU). One AU is equal to the average distance between the Earth and the sun—about 150 million kilometers. If you wanted to get to the sun from the Earth in 10 hours, you would have to travel at a rate of 15,000,000 km/h!

$$\frac{150 \text{ million kilometers}}{15 \text{ million kilometers/hour}} = 10 \text{ hours}$$

Visual Understanding

AXIAL TILT A planet's axis of rotation is an imaginary line that runs through the center of the planet and comes out its north and south poles. The tilt of a planet's axis is the angle between the planet's axis and the plane of the planet's orbit around the sun.

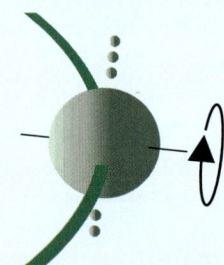

Lab and Activity Highlights

Why Do They Wander? PG 714

Eclipses PG 716

Phases of the Moon PG 717

 **Datasheets for LabBook** (blackline masters for these labs)

SECTION 2

- Solar eclipses occur when the moon is between the sun and the Earth, causing the moon's shadow to fall on the Earth.
- The plane of the moon's orbit around the Earth is tilted by 5° relative to the plane of the Earth's orbit around the sun.

Labs
Eclipses (p. 716)
Phases of the Moon (p. 717)

SECTION 3

Vocabulary
comet (p. 557)
asteroid (p. 559)
asteroid belt (p. 559)
meteoroid (p. 560)
meteorite (p. 560)
meteor (p. 560)

Section Notes
- Comets are small bodies of water ice and cosmic dust left over from the formation of the solar system.
- When a comet is heated by the sun, the ices convert to gases that leave the nucleus and form an ion tail. Dust also comes off a comet to form a second kind of tail called a dust tail.
- All orbits are ellipses—circles that have been stretched out.
- Asteroids are small, rocky bodies that orbit the sun between the orbits of Mars and Jupiter.
- Meteoroids are small, rocky bodies that probably come from asteroids.
- Meteor showers occur when Earth passes through the dusty debris along a comet's orbit.
- Impacts that cause natural disasters occur once every few thousand years, but impacts large enough to cause global extinctions occur once every 30 million to 50 million years.

VOCABULARY DEFINITIONS, continued

SECTION 3

comet a small body of ice, rock, and cosmic dust loosely packed together that gives off gas and dust in the form of a tail as it passes close to the sun

asteroid a small, rocky body that revolves around the sun

asteroid belt the region of the solar system most asteroids occupy; roughly between the orbits of Mars and Jupiter

meteoroid a very small, rocky body that revolves around the sun

meteorite a meteoroid that reaches the Earth's surface without burning up completely

meteor a streak of light caused when a meteoroid or comet dust burns up in the Earth's atmosphere before it reaches the ground

 Vocabulary Review Worksheet 20

 Blackline masters of these Chapter Highlights can be found in the **Study Guide**.

---

internet connect

 **GO TO:** go.hrw.com

 **GO TO:** www.scilinks.org

Visit the **HRW** Web site for a variety of learning tools related to this chapter. Just type in the keyword:

KEYWORD: HSTFAM

Visit the **National Science Teachers Association** on-line Web site for Internet resources related to this chapter. Just type in the *sci*LINKS number for more information about the topic:

TOPIC: The Nine Planets	*sci*LINKS NUMBER: HSTE480
TOPIC: Studying Earth from Space	*sci*LINKS NUMBER: HSTE485
TOPIC: The Earth's Moon	*sci*LINKS NUMBER: HSTE490
TOPIC: The Moons of Other Planets	*sci*LINKS NUMBER: HSTE495
TOPIC: Comets, Asteroids, and Meteoroids	*sci*LINKS NUMBER: HSTE500

563

Lab and Activity Highlights

LabBank

 Labs You Can Eat, Meteorite Delight, Lab 17

 Long-Term Projects & Research Ideas, What Did You See, Mr. Messier? Project 48

Whiz-Bang Demonstrations
- Crater Creator, Demo 33
- Space Snowballs, Demo 34

Interactive Explorations CD-ROM
CD 2, Exploration 7, "Space Case"

Chapter 20 • Chapter Highlights

Chapter Review

Chapter Review Answers

USING VOCABULARY

1. The terrestrial planets are the small, rocky planets of the inner solar system. The gas giants are the large, gaseous planets of the outer solar system.
2. Asteroids are small bodies made of rocky material, while comets are small bodies made of ices and cosmic dust.
3. A meteor is a streak of light caused by a meteoroid burning up in the atmosphere. A meteorite is a meteoroid that has passed through the atmosphere and struck the ground.
4. A satellite is any object that revolves around another object, including artificial satellites, while a moon is a naturally formed satellite.
5. Both the Kuiper belt and the Oort cloud are regions where comets exist, but the Oort cloud is a spherical region outside the orbit of Pluto, while the Kuiper belt is a disk-shaped region beyond the orbit of Neptune.
6. AU
7. meteoroid
8. revolve
9. impacts

UNDERSTANDING CONCEPTS

Multiple Choice

10. d	13. a	16. d
11. d	14. a	17. a
12. c	15. d	18. b

Short Answer

19. Solar eclipses occur during the new moon. During the new moon, the side of the moon that faces the Earth is in darkness because the moon is between the sun and the Earth. This is the same arrangement that causes a solar eclipse.
20. We see evidence of them in meteors and meteorites.
21. Venus, Uranus, and Pluto

Chapter Review

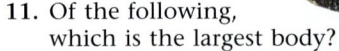

USING VOCABULARY

For each pair of terms, explain the difference in their meaning.

1. terrestrial planet/gas giant
2. asteroid/comet
3. meteor/meteorite
4. satellite/moon
5. Kuiper belt/Oort cloud

To complete the following sentences, choose the correct term from each pair of terms listed below:

6. The average distance between the sun and the Earth is 1 __?__. (*light-minute* or *AU*)
7. A small rock in space is called a __?__. (*meteor* or *meteoroid*)
8. The time it takes for the Earth to __?__ around the sun is one year. (*rotate* or *revolve*)
9. Most lunar craters are the result of __?__. (*volcanoes* or *impacts*)

UNDERSTANDING CONCEPTS

Multiple Choice

10. When do annular eclipses occur?
    a. every solar eclipse
    b. when the moon is closest to the Earth
    c. only during full moon
    d. when the moon is farthest from the Earth

11. Of the following, which is the largest body?
    a. the moon   c. Mercury
    b. Pluto   d. Ganymede

12. Which is not true about impacts?
    a. They are very destructive.
    b. They can bring water to dry worlds.
    c. They only occurred as the solar system formed.
    d. They can help us do remote geology.

13. Which of these planets does not have any moons?
    a. Mercury   c. Uranus
    b. Mars   d. none of the above

14. What is the most current theory for the formation of Earth's moon?
    a. The moon formed from a collision between another body and the Earth.
    b. The moon was captured by the Earth.
    c. The moon formed at the same time as the Earth.
    d. The moon formed by spinning off from the Earth early in its history.

15. Liquid water cannot exist on the surface of Mars because
    a. the temperature is too hot.
    b. liquid water once existed there.
    c. the gravity of Mars is too weak.
    d. the atmospheric pressure is too low.

16. Which of the following planets is not a terrestrial planet?
    a. Mercury   c. Earth
    b. Mars   d. Pluto

17. All of the gas giants have ring systems.
    a. true   b. false

18. A comet's ion tail consists of
    a. dust.   c. light rays.
    b. electrically charged particles of gas. d. comet nuclei.

Concept Mapping

22. 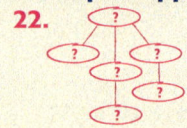 An answer to this exercise can be found at the end of this book.

 Concept Mapping Transparency 20

564   Chapter 20 • A Family of Planets

Short Answer

19. Do solar eclipses occur at the full moon or at the new moon? Explain why.

20. How do we know there are small meteoroids and dust in space?

21. Which planets have retrograde rotation?

Concept Mapping

22. Use the following terms to create a concept map: solar system, terrestrial planets, gas giants, moons, comets, asteroids, meteoroids.

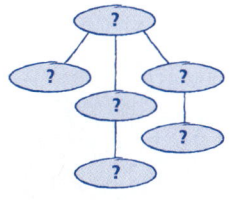

CRITICAL THINKING AND PROBLEM SOLVING

23. Even though we haven't yet retrieved any rock samples from Mercury's surface for radiometric dating, we know that the surface of Mercury is much older than that of Earth. How do we know this?

24. Where in the solar system might we search for life, and why?

25. Is the far side of the moon always dark? Explain your answer.

26. If we could somehow bring Europa as close to the sun as the Earth is, 1 AU, what do you think would happen?

MATH IN SCIENCE

27. Suppose you have an object that weighs 200 N (45 lbs.) on Earth. How much would that same object weigh on each of the other terrestrial planets?

INTERPRETING GRAPHICS

The graph below shows density versus mass for Earth, Uranus, and Neptune. Mass is given in Earth masses—the mass of Earth equals one. The relative volumes for the planets are shown by the size of each circle.

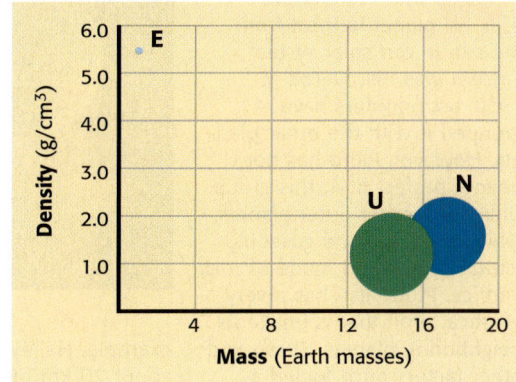

Density vs. Mass for Earth, Uranus, and Neptune

28. Which planet is denser, Uranus or Neptune? How can you tell?

29. You can see that although Earth has the smallest mass, it has the highest density. How can Earth be the densest of the three when Uranus and Neptune have so much more mass?

Reading Check-up

Take a minute to review your answers to the Pre-Reading Questions found at the bottom of page 536. Have your answers changed? If necessary, revise your answers based on what you have learned since you began this chapter.

CRITICAL THINKING AND PROBLEM SOLVING

23. Mercury's surface is covered with impact craters that record the planet's history. The Earth's surface has only a few craters, indicating that the rocks on Earth's surface are continually recycled. (The two planets are approximately the same age.)

24. The search for life should include areas where liquid water is present because all life we know of depends on liquid water for survival.

25. No; the far side of the moon gets just as much sunlight as the near side. As the moon revolves around the Earth, it also rotates, which gives it night and day.

26. Answers will vary. If Europa was closer to the sun, it would heat up considerably. Europa is made mostly of ice, so much of its surface would probably melt to form oceans and an atmosphere.

MATH IN SCIENCE

27. Students will have to refer back to the tables in the chapter as well as understand which planets are terrestrial.
    Mercury 0.38 × 200 N = 76 N
    Venus   0.91 × 200 N = 182 N
    Mars   0.38 × 200 N = 76 N

INTERPRETING GRAPHICS

28. Neptune is denser. It has a higher density value on the chart. (Also, Neptune has both a smaller volume and more mass, giving it a greater density than Uranus.)

29. The masses of Neptune and Uranus occupy a much larger volume than the mass of the Earth. (Density is the amount of mass that exists within a given volume of space.)

Blackline masters of this Chapter Review can be found in the **Study Guide**.

SCIENTIFIC DEBATE

Is Pluto Really a Planet?

Background

Classifying Pluto can be problematic. Pluto simply does not fit in with the inner terrestrial planets or the outer gas giants. It seems that Pluto is a planet in a class all its own. There is much speculation about the origin of Pluto. Pluto's orbit is so inclined that it is doubtful that it formed from the primordial disk-shaped solar nebula that spawned the other planets. Pluto in many ways resembles Neptune's moon Triton. Pluto and Triton are similar in size, and both rotate in a direction counter to the other planets.

Some scientists believe that there was a collision between Pluto and Triton and that the force of the collision ejected Pluto from the Neptune system.

Another theory proposes that Pluto formed from the accretion of cometlike bodies at the beginning of the solar system, similar to the way the terrestrial planets originated from rocky planetesimals.

Is Pluto Really a Planet?

We have all learned that Pluto is the planet farthest from the sun in our solar system. Since it was discovered in 1930, astronomers have grouped it with the outer planets. However, Pluto has not been a perfect fit in this group. Unlike the other outer planets, which are large and gaseous, Pluto is small and made of rock and ice. Pluto also has a very elliptical orbit that is unlike its neighboring planets. These and other factors once fueled a debate as to whether Pluto should be classified as a planet.

◀ A composite drawing of Pluto, Charon, Triton, and Halley's comet

Kuiper Belt

In the early 1990s, astronomers discovered a belt of comets outside the orbit of Neptune. The belt was named the Kuiper Belt in honor of Gerard Kuiper, a Dutch-born American astronomer. So what does this belt have to do with Pluto? Given its proximity to Pluto, some astronomers thought Pluto might actually be a large comet that escaped the Kuiper Belt.

Comet?

Comets are basically dirty snowballs made of ice and cosmic dust. Pluto is about 30 percent ice and 70 percent rock. This is much more rock than is in a normal comet. Also, at 2,390 km in diameter, Pluto is much larger than a comet. For example, Halley's comet is only about 20 km in diameter. Even so, Pluto's orbit is very similar to that of a comet. Both have orbits that are very elliptical.

Escaped Moon?

Pluto and its moon, Charon, have much in common with Neptune's moon, Triton. All three have atmospheres made of nitrogen and methane, which suggests that they share a similar origin. And because Triton has a "backward" orbit compared with Neptune's other moons, it may have been captured by Neptune's gravity. Some astronomers thought Pluto might also have been captured by Neptune but broke free by some cataclysmic event.

New Category of Planet?

Some astronomers suggested that perhaps we should create a new subclass of planets, such as the ice planets, to add to the gas-giant and terrestrial classification we currently use. Pluto would be the only planet in this class, but scientists think we are likely to find others.

As there are more new discoveries, astronomers will likely continue to debate these issues. To date, however, Pluto is still officially considered a planet. This decision is firmly grounded by the fact that Pluto has been called a planet since its discovery.

You Decide

▶ Do some additional research about Pluto, the Kuiper Belt, and comets. What do you think Pluto should be called?

Answer to You Decide

Answers will vary. Students should be able to support their views with the information gathered from additional research.

Science Fiction

"The Mad Moon"
by Stanley Weinbaum

The third largest satellite of Jupiter, called Io, can be a hard place to live. Although living comfortably is possible in the small cities at the polar regions, most of the moon is hot, humid, and jungle-like. There is also *blancha*, a kind of tropical fever that causes hallucinations, weakness, and vicious headaches. Without proper medication a person with *blancha* can go mad or even die.

Just 2 years ago, Grant Calthorpe was a wealthy hunter and famous sportsman. Then the gold market crashed, and he lost his entire fortune. What better way for an experienced hunter and explorer to get a fresh start than to set out for a little space travel? The opportunity to rekindle his fortune by gathering ferva leaves so that they can be converted into useful human medications lures Calthorpe to Io.

There he meets the loonies—creatures with balloon heads and silly grins atop *really* long necks. The three-legged parcat Oliver quickly becomes Calthorpe's pet and helps him cope with the loneliness and the slinkers. The slinkers, well, they would just as soon *not* have Calthorpe around at all, but they are pretty good at making even this famous outdoorsman wonder why he ever took this job.

In "The Mad Moon," you'll discover a dozen adventures with Grant Calthorpe as he struggles to stay alive—and sane. Read Stanley Weinbaum's story "The Mad Moon" in the *Holt Anthology of Science Fiction.* Enjoy your trip!

Further Reading You can check out some of Stanley Weinbaum's best-known short stories in the following reprinted collections:

The Best of Stanley G. Weinbaum, Ballantine Books, Inc., 1978

The Black Flame, Tachyon Publications, 1995

SCIENCE FICTION
"The Mad Moon"
by Stanley Weinbaum

Even the bravest of human adventurers may not be prepared to deal with the madness on Jupiter's third habitable moon . . .

Teaching Strategy

Reading Level This story can be enjoyed by students of all levels, but it is one of the more challenging stories in the *Holt Anthology of Science Fiction.*

Background

About the Author In 1934, Stanley Weinbaum published his first science fiction story, "A Martian Odyssey." Many people read the story about alien life on Mars and enjoyed its author's lighthearted style. Weinbaum quickly wrote several other works that audiences adored. His writing demonstrated his fascination with alien life-forms and with unusual human characters.

Before becoming a writer, Weinbaum studied chemical engineering. During the Great Depression, writers sold stories for just a few pennies; yet Weinbaum gave up his science career to be a writer. Sadly, he died of cancer in 1935, less than 2 years after his first story was published. Although his list of works is short, many believe he is one of the best science fiction writers of all time.

Chapter 20 • Science Fiction

Chapter Organizer

CHAPTER ORGANIZATION	TIME MINUTES	OBJECTIVES	LABS, INVESTIGATIONS, AND DEMONSTRATIONS
Chapter Opener pp. 568–569	45	National Standards: SAI 1, ST 2, SPSP 5, HNS 1	**Start-Up Activity** Exploring Galaxies, p. 569
Section 1 Stars	135	▶ Describe how color indicates temperature. ▶ Compare absolute magnitude with apparent magnitude, and discuss how each measures brightness. ▶ Describe the difference between the apparent motion of stars and the real motion of stars. UCP 1, 3, SAI 1, SPSP 5; LabBook UCP 2, 3, SAI 1	**Demonstration,** Light Pollution, p. 570 in ATE **BASIC** **Demonstration,** p. 571 in ATE **GENERAL** **QuickLab,** Not All Thumbs! p. 575 **GENERAL** **Skill Builder,** Red Hot, or Not? p. 718 **BASIC** **Skill Builder,** I See the Light! p. 720 **ADVANCED** **Datasheets for LabBook,** Datasheets 46 and 47 **ADVANCED** **Whiz-Bang Demonstrations,** Where Do the Stars Go? Demo 35 **BASIC**
Section 2 The Life Cycle of Stars	90	▶ Describe the quantities that are plotted in the H-R diagram. ▶ Explain how stars at different stages in their life cycle appear on different parts of the H-R diagram. UCP 1–3, 5, SAI 1, HNS 1, 2	**QuickLab,** Plotting Pairs, p. 577 **GENERAL**
Section 3 Galaxies	90	▶ Identify the various types of galaxies from pictures. ▶ Describe the contents of galaxies. ▶ Explain why looking at distant galaxies reveals what early galaxies looked like. UCP 1, 5, SAI 1, ST 1, 2, HNS 1, 2, SPSP 5	
Section 4 Formation of the Universe	90	▶ Describe the big bang theory. ▶ Explain evidence used to show support for the big bang theory. ▶ Explain how the expansion of the universe is explained by the big bang theory. UCP 1–3, 5, SAI 1	**Long-Term Projects & Research Ideas,** Project 49 **ADVANCED**

See page **T20** for a complete correlation of this book with the **NATIONAL SCIENCE EDUCATION STANDARDS.**

TECHNOLOGY RESOURCES

 Guided Reading Audio CD English or Spanish, Chapter 21

 One-Stop Planner CD-ROM with Test Generator

CNN. Scientists in Action, Neutrino Breakthrough, Segment 4
Deep Space Photographers, Segment 26

Chapter 21 • The Universe Beyond

CLASSROOM WORKSHEETS, TRANSPARENCIES, AND RESOURCES	SCIENCE INTEGRATION AND CONNECTIONS	REVIEW AND ASSESSMENT
Directed Reading Worksheet 21 BASIC **Science Puzzlers, Twisters & Teasers,** Worksheet 21 ADVANCED		
Directed Reading Worksheet 21, Section 1 BASIC **Transparency 291,** The Electromagnetic Spectrum **Math Skills for Science Worksheet 10,** Arithmetic with Positive and Negative Numbers GENERAL **Math Skills for Science Worksheet 44,** Distances in Space GENERAL **Transparency 195,** Finding the Distance to Stars with Parallax	**Physics Connection,** p. 571 **Biology Connection,** p. 572 **MathBreak,** Starlight, Star Bright, p. 573 **Cross-Disciplinary Focus,** p. 573 in ATE **Environment Connection,** p. 574 **Multicultural Connection,** p. 574 in ATE **Math and More,** p. 574 in ATE BASIC **Math and More,** p. 575 in ATE GENERAL	**Homework,** p. 570 in ATE GENERAL **Self-Check,** p. 574 **Review,** p. 576 GENERAL **Quiz,** p. 576 in ATE GENERAL **Alternative Assessment,** p. 576 in ATE BASIC
Directed Reading Worksheet 21, Section 2 BASIC **Transparency 196,** The H-R Diagram: A **Transparency 197,** The H-R Diagram: B **Reinforcement Worksheet 21,** Diagramming the Stars BASIC	**Cross-Disciplinary Focus,** p. 579 in ATE GENERAL **Cross-Disciplinary Focus,** p. 580 in ATE ADVANCED **Weird Science:** Holes Where Stars Once Were, p. 594 ADVANCED	**Review,** p. 581 GENERAL **Quiz,** p. 581 in ATE GENERAL **Alternative Assessment,** p. 581 in ATE GENERAL
Directed Reading Worksheet 21, Section 3 BASIC	**Cross-Disciplinary Focus,** p. 582 in ATE GENERAL **Multicultural Connection,** p. 583 in ATE **Careers:** Astrophysicist—Jocelyn Bell-Burnell, p. 595 GENERAL	**Review,** p. 585 GENERAL **Quiz,** p. 585 in ATE GENERAL **Alternative Assessment,** p. 585 in ATE GENERAL
Directed Reading Worksheet 21, Section 4 BASIC **Transparency 198,** The Big Bang Theory **Critical Thinking Worksheet 21,** Fleabert and the Amazing Watermelon Seed ADVANCED	**Multicultural Connection,** p. 587 in ATE **Apply,** p. 588 GENERAL	**Homework,** p. 588 in ATE GENERAL **Review,** p. 589 GENERAL **Quiz,** p. 589 in ATE GENERAL **Alternative Assessment,** p. 589 in ATE GENERAL

END-OF-CHAPTER REVIEW AND ASSESSMENT

Chapter Review in Study Guide
Vocabulary and Notes in Study Guide
Chapter Tests with Performance-Based Assessment, Chapter 21 Test
Chapter Tests with Performance-Based Assessment, Performance-Based Assessment 21
Concept Mapping Transparency 21

internetconnect

 Holt, Rinehart and Winston On-line Resources
go.hrw.com
For worksheets and other teaching aids related to this chapter, visit the HRW Web site and type in the keyword: **HSTUNV**

 **National Science Teachers Association**
www.scilinks.org
Encourage students to use the sciLINKS numbers listed in the internet connect boxes to access information and resources on the **NSTA** Web site.

Chapter 21 • Chapter Organizer **567B**

Chapter Resources & Worksheets

Visual Resources

TEACHING TRANSPARENCIES

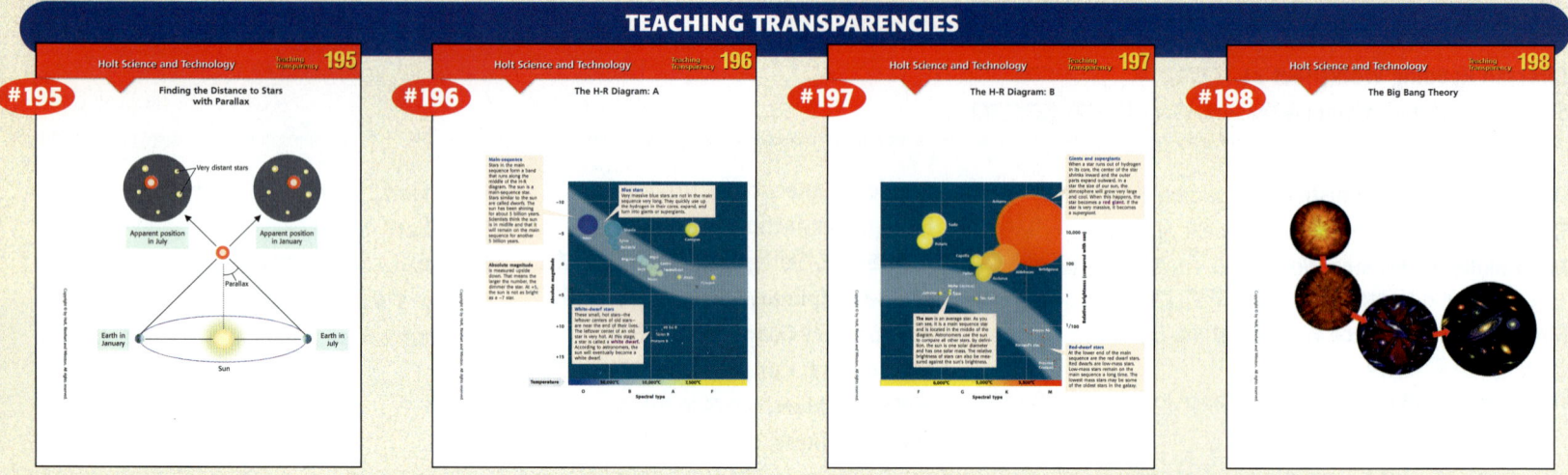

#195 Finding the Distance to Stars with Parallax
#196 The H-R Diagram: A
#197 The H-R Diagram: B
#198 The Big Bang Theory

TEACHING TRANSPARENCIES

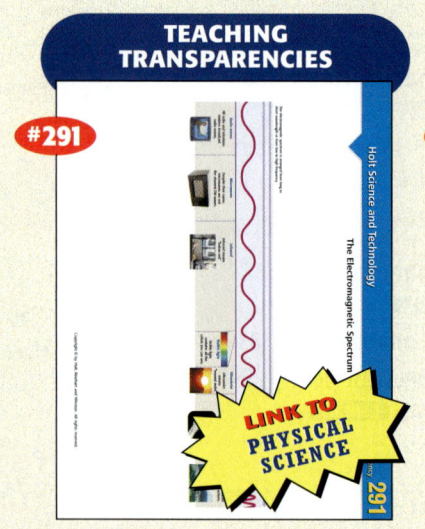

#291 The Electromagnetic Spectrum — LINK TO PHYSICAL SCIENCE

CONCEPT MAPPING TRANSPARENCY

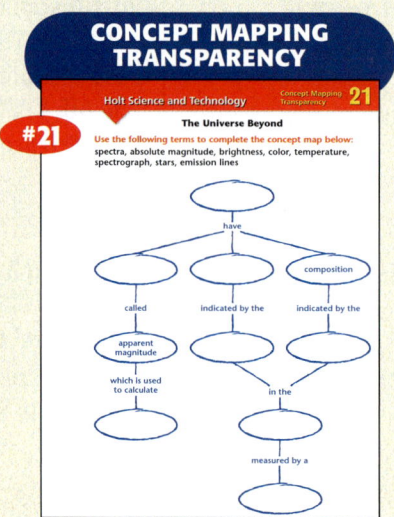

#21 The Universe Beyond

Meeting Individual Needs

DIRECTED READING

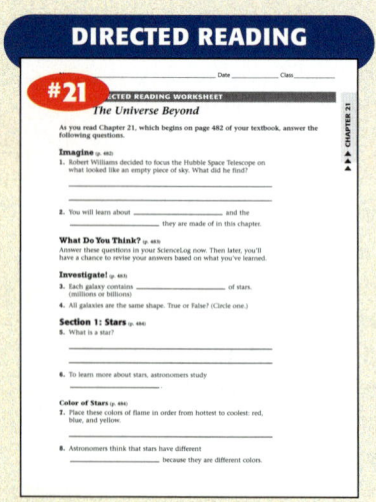

#21 Diagramming the Stars

REINFORCEMENT & VOCABULARY REVIEW

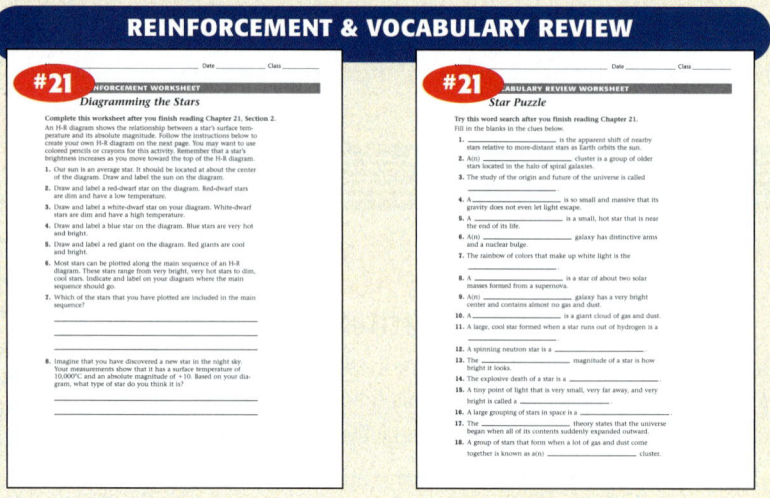

#21 Reinforcement Worksheet
#21 Vocabulary Review Worksheet — Star Puzzle

SCIENCE PUZZLERS, TWISTERS & TEASERS

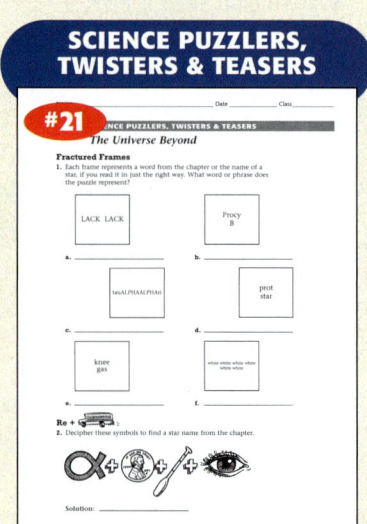

#21 The Universe Beyond

567C Chapter 21 • The Universe Beyond

Chapter 21 • The Universe Beyond

Review & Assessment

STUDY GUIDE

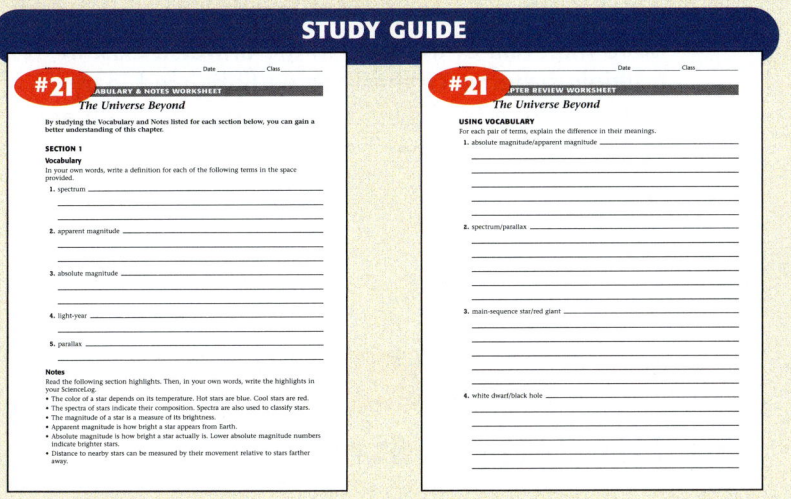

CHAPTER TESTS WITH PERFORMANCE-BASED ASSESSMENT

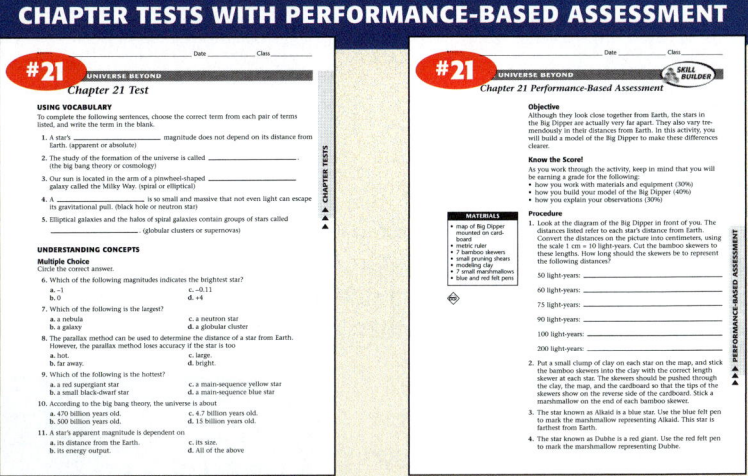

Lab Worksheets

WHIZ-BANG DEMONSTRATIONS

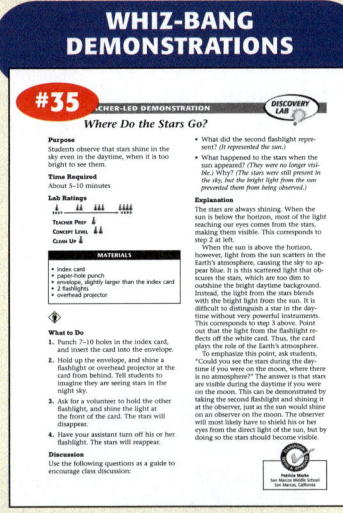

LONG-TERM PROJECTS & RESEARCH IDEAS

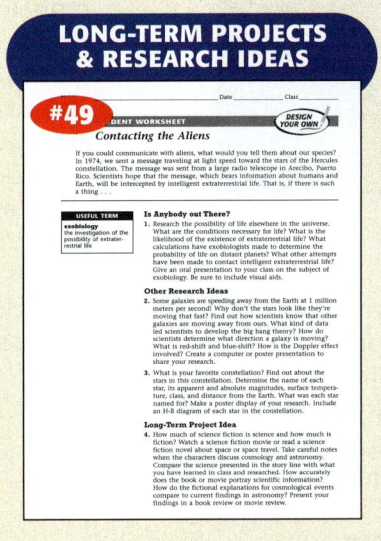

DATASHEETS FOR LABBOOK

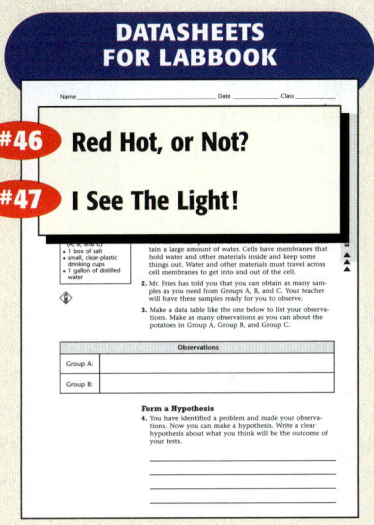

Applications & Extensions

CRITICAL THINKING & PROBLEM SOLVING

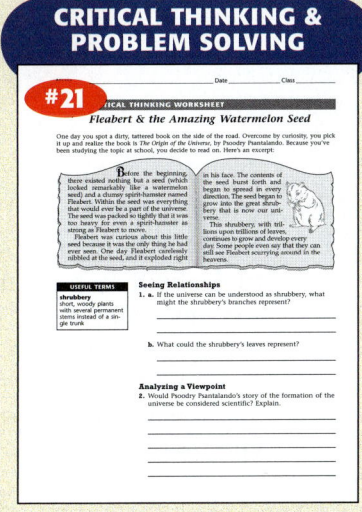

SCIENTISTS IN ACTION

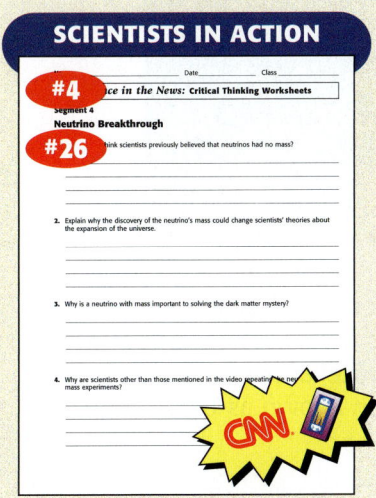

Chapter 21 • Chapter Resources & Worksheets

Chapter Background

SECTION 1

Stars

▶ **Space Distances**
After the sun, the star closest to Earth is Proxima Centauri, located more than 4 light-years away. To travel an equivalent distance, a person would have to walk around the Earth more than 944 million times!

- Four space probes—*Voyagers 1* and *2* and *Pioneers 10* and *11*—are currently en route to interstellar space, traveling at a rate of approximately 40,000 km/h (25,000 mph). Even at this astounding speed, it would take 150,000 years before the probes would reach Proxima Centauri.

IS THAT A FACT!

▶ Although stars appear to twinkle in the sky, they actually shine with a steady light. They appear to twinkle because their light is distorted when it passes through the Earth's atmosphere. If you were standing on the moon, where there is no atmosphere, the stars would appear to shine steadily.

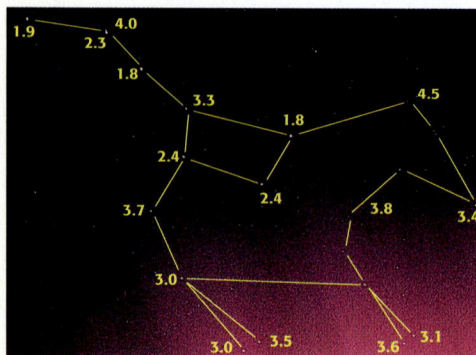

▶ The Big Dipper is not a constellation; it is an *asterism*, a familiar pattern of stars that may or may not be part of one of the 88 constellations. The Big Dipper is part of the constellation known as Ursa Major, or Big Bear.

▶ More than half of the stars in the universe exist in multiple systems. Of these, three-fifths are binary systems, three-tenths are triplets, and one-tenth are groups of four or more.

SECTION 2

The Life Cycle of Stars

▶ **The Birth of a Star**
Like humans, stars undergo a life cycle that consists of birth, infancy, maturity, old age, and death. In space, clouds of gas and dust abound; drawn together by gravity, they eventually form a *protostar*. This fledgling star gives off no visible light and must undergo many changes before it is recognizable as a star. In a process that takes millions of years, the protostar contracts. This shrinkage causes an enormous buildup of pressure and heat. When its temperature reaches 10 million degrees Celsius, the protostar stops contracting, and the process of nuclear fusion begins. Once this hydrogen-fusing process is initiated, the star is born!

IS THAT A FACT!

▶ From the time our sun emerged as a protostar, it took about 10 million years to become a main-sequence star. A star with one-tenth the mass of the sun would mature in 100 million years, and a star with three times the mass of the sun would mature in 1 million years. Stars with greater mass are hotter and take less time to mature.

567E Chapter 21 • The Universe Beyond

Chapter 21 • The Universe Beyond

SECTION 3

Galaxies

▶ **Observing Spiral Galaxies**
Most spiral galaxies appear very thin when seen edge-on. The thickness of the spiral disk is only about one-fifth to one-twentieth the width of the disk. When seen edge-on, spiral galaxies resemble straight lines with a bulge in the middle. The relative size and shape of the bulge is an important clue to determining the type of galaxy.

▶ **How Many Stars Are in a Galaxy?**
To estimate the number of stars in a galaxy, astronomers consider the sun as one unit of mass. Large spiral galaxies, for example, have a mass of 1 billion to 1 trillion solar masses. If the average star is one solar mass—or each star is like the sun—this means these galaxies have more than 1 billion stars. Dwarf elliptical galaxies have only a few million solar masses, about one-thousandth the mass of a spiral galaxy. Giant elliptical galaxies have more mass than large spiral galaxies.

IS THAT A FACT!
- The word *galaxy* comes from the Greek word *gala*, meaning "milk." This is because, when seen from afar, galaxies have a milky-white appearance.

SECTION 4

Formation of the Universe

▶ **Top-Down or Bottom-Up?**
No one is certain how large-scale structures in the universe emerged. Some scientists support the top-down theory. This theory explains that areas of the universe with large-scale objects (the size of clusters and superclusters) were the first to collapse into gaseous, pancake-like shapes. Galaxies condensed from these structures.

- Other scientists support the *bottom-up theory*. This theory argues that areas of the universe with small-scale objects (the size of galaxies or smaller) were the first to form. Due to the gravitational forces, these areas aggregated into clusters and superclusters.

▶ **Life on Other Planets?**
Many scientists believe that in our galaxy alone there are hundreds of millions of planets similar to Earth. These planets may be able to support carbon-based life. Thus far, scientists do not have the technology to explore this possibility.

IS THAT A FACT!
- The William Herschel telescope, on La Palma, in the Canary Islands, is one of the world's biggest telescopes. With its 4.2 m mirror, it could detect a single candle burning 160,000 km away.
- In 1998, astronomers detected a gamma-ray burst that for 2 seconds was as bright as the entire universe. The cause of this vast energy release is unknown.

For background information about teaching strategies and issues, refer to the *Professional Reference for Teachers*.

CHAPTER 21

The Universe Beyond

 **Pre-Reading Questions**

Students may not know the answers to these questions before reading the chapter, so accept any reasonable response.

Suggested Answers

1. Stars shine because nuclear reactions in their core produce large amounts of energy. This energy leaves the stars as light.
2. A galaxy is a large collection of stars in space.
3. According to the big bang theory, the universe began when all the contents of the universe, which were gathered in a small location, began to expand in all directions. Answers will vary to the last parts of this item. Scientists are in disagreement on this subject. Students may have interesting points of view.

 Directed Reading Worksheet 21

 Science Puzzlers, Twisters & Teasers Worksheet 21

 Guided Reading Audio CD
English or Spanish, Chapter 21

CHAPTER 21

The Universe Beyond

Sections

1. **Stars** 570
   - Physics Connection .. 571
   - Biology Connection .. 572
   - MathBreak 573
   - Environment Connection 574
   - QuickLab 575
   - Internet Connect 576

2. **The Life Cycle of Stars** 577
   - QuickLab 577
   - Internet Connect 581

3. **Galaxies** 582
   - Internet Connect 585

4. **Formation of the Universe** 586
   - Apply 588

   Chapter Review 592
   Feature Articles 594, 595
   LabBook 718–721

 **Pre-Reading Questions**

1. Why do stars shine?
2. What is a galaxy?
3. How did the universe begin, and how will it end? or will it?

Galaxies Galore

If you had a telescope, what would you look for? In the 1920s, astronomer Edwin Hubble chose to look for galaxies much like the NGC 3031 galaxy shown here. Basically, a galaxy is a large group of stars. In 1995 the Hubble Space Telescope was used to develop the single image called the Hubble Deep Field shown below. The segment of sky in that image contains nearly 2,000 galaxies! In this chapter, you will learn about the different types of galaxies.

Hubble Deep Field image

internet connect

 **HRW On-line Resources**
go.hrw.com
For worksheets and other teaching aids, visit the HRW Web site and type in the keyword: **HSTUNV**

 **sciLINKS NSTA**
www.scilinks.com
Use the sciLINKS numbers at the end of each chapter for additional resources on the **NSTA** Web site.

 **CNNfyi.com**
www.cnnfyi.com
Visit the CNN Web site for current events coverage and classroom resources.

EXPLORING GALAXIES IN THE UNIVERSE

Galaxies are large groupings of millions of stars. But not all galaxies are the same. In this activity, you will explore some of these differences.

Procedure

1. Look at the different galaxies in the Hubble Deep Field image on page 96. (The bright spot with spikes is a star that is much closer to Earth; you can ignore it.)

2. Can you find different types of galaxies? In your ScienceLog, make sketches of at least three different types. Make up a name that describes each type of galaxy.

3. In your ScienceLog, construct a chart to classify, compare, and describe the different characteristics you see in these galaxies.

Analysis

4. Why did you classify the galaxies the way you did?

5. Compare your types of galaxies with those of your classmates. Are there similarities?

EXPLORING GALAXIES IN THE UNIVERSE

Answers to START-UP Activity

4. Answers will vary.
5. There should be many similarities between the galaxies, but the galaxy names may not be similar.

Chapter 21 • The Universe Beyond **569**

SECTION 1

Focus

Stars

In this section, students learn that the color of a star indicates its temperature and that the star's spectrum indicates the elements in its atmosphere. They learn that stars are classified not only according to temperature but also by brightness. The section explores the difference between apparent magnitude and absolute magnitude and the difference between apparent motion and actual motion of stars.

Bellringer

On the board, write the following questions:

- What are stars made of?
- How do stars differ from one another?
- Do stars move?

Have students review their responses after completing this section.

1) Motivate

DEMONSTRATION

Light Pollution Demonstrate how ambient light affects the number of visible stars using a slide projector, a piece of aluminum foil, and a flashlight. Poke small holes in the foil, and in a dark room, project light through the foil. Tell students that they might see this number of stars on a dark night. Ask students to count the stars. Then shine the flashlight on the screen, and ask students to count the stars again. Discuss the natural and artificial sources of ambient light with students. **Sheltered English**

570 Chapter 21 • The Universe Beyond

SECTION 1

Terms to Learn

spectrum
apparent magnitude
absolute magnitude
light-year
parallax

What You'll Do

- Describe how color indicates temperature.
- Compare absolute magnitude with apparent magnitude, and discuss how each measures brightness.
- Describe the difference between the apparent motion of stars and the real motion of stars.

Stars

Most stars look like faint dots of light in the night sky. But stars are actually huge, hot, brilliant balls of gas trillions of kilometers away from Earth. How do astronomers learn about stars when they are too far away to visit? They study starlight!

Color of Stars

Look closely at the flames on the candle and the Bunsen burner shown here. Which one has the hotter flame? How can you tell? Although artists may speak of *red* as a "hot" color, to a scientist, *red* is a "cool" color. The blue flame of the Bunsen burner is much hotter than the yellow flame of the candle. In the same way, the candle's yellow flame is hotter than the red glowing embers of a campfire.

If you look carefully at the night sky, you might notice the different colors of some familiar stars. Betelgeuse (BET uhl jooz), which is red, and Rigel (RIE juhl), which is blue, are the stars that form two corners of the constellation Orion, shown in **Figure 1**. This constellation is easy to see in the evenings during the winter months. Because these two stars are different colors, we can infer that they have different temperatures.

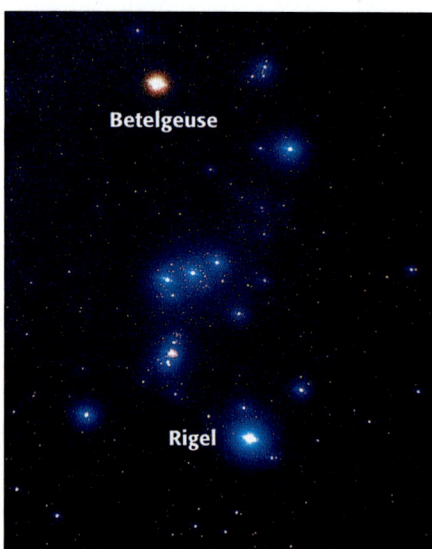

Figure 1 Because Betelgeuse is red and Rigel is blue, astronomers know that Rigel is the hotter star.

Composition of Stars

When you look at white light through a glass prism, you see a rainbow of colors called a **spectrum.** The spectrum consists of millions of colors, including the ones we recognize as red, orange, yellow, green, blue, indigo, and violet. A hot solid object, like the glowing wire inside a light bulb, gives off a *continuous spectrum*—one that shows all the colors. Astronomers use an instrument called a *spectrograph* to spread starlight out into its colors, just as you might use a prism to spread sunlight. Stars, however, don't have continuous spectra. Because they are not solid objects, stars give off spectra that are different from those of light bulbs.

570

Homework

SpaceLog As students read this chapter, have them keep a SpaceLog at home. Encourage them to observe the night sky for 10 minutes every night and record their observations. Students can annotate their SpaceLog with photographs and articles from magazines or newspapers that relate to what they are learning in this chapter.

Hot, Dense Gas Stars are made of various gases that are so dense that they act like a hot solid. For this reason, the "surface" of a star, or the part that we see, gives off a continuous spectrum. But the light we see passes through the star's "atmosphere," which is made of cooler gases than the star itself. A star therefore produces a spectrum with various lines in it. To understand what these lines are, let's look at something you might be more familiar with than stars.

Making an ID Many restaurants use neon signs to attract customers. The gas in a neon sign glows orange-red when an electric current flows through it. If we were to look at the sign with an astronomer's spectrograph, we would not see a continuous spectrum. Instead we would see *emission lines*. Emission lines are bright lines that are made when certain wavelengths of light are given off, or emitted, by hot gases. Only some colors in the spectrum show up, while all of the other colors are missing. Every tube of neon gas, for example, emits light with the same emission lines. Each element has its own unique set of emission lines. Emission lines are like fingerprints for the elements. You can see some of these "fingerprints" in **Figure 2.**

Physics CONNECTION

Police use spectrographs to "fingerprint" cars. Automobile manufacturers put trace elements in the paint of cars. Each make of car has its own special paint and therefore its own combination of trace elements. When a car is involved in a hit-and-run accident, the police can identify the make of the car by the paint that is left behind.

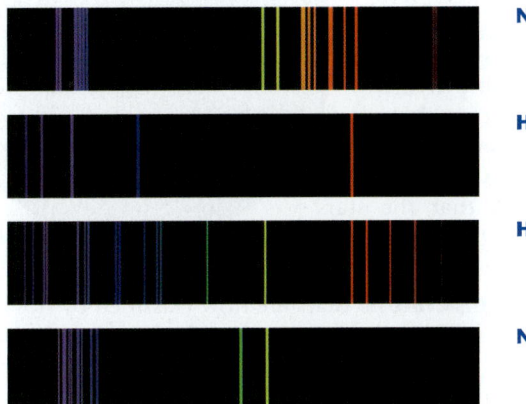

Ne (neon)

H (hydrogen)

He (helium)

Na (sodium)

Figure 2 *Neon gas produces its own characteristic pattern of emission lines, as do hydrogen, helium, and sodium.*

Trapping the Light The spectrum produced by a star is not continuous, nor is it made of bright lines similar to those of the elements you saw above. Because a star's atmosphere is cooler than the star itself, the gases in its atmosphere absorb some of the star's light. The cooler gases in a star's atmosphere remove certain colors of light from the continuous spectrum of the hot star. In fact, the colors that the atmosphere absorbs are the same colors it would emit if heated.

To learn more about the color and temperature of stars, turn to page 718 in the LabBook.

IS THAT A FACT!

Sometimes it is difficult to differentiate between stars and planets in the night sky. If it twinkles, it's probably a star. Planets, because of their proximity to Earth, appear as tiny disks shining with a steady light. Venus is an easy planet to spot; it can often be seen shining brightly in the west, immediately after the sun sets. Venus can also be seen in the morning, accompanying the rising sun. Venus is then called "the morning star."

② Teach, continued

MEETING INDIVIDUAL NEEDS

Advanced Learners When electrons become excited or absorb energy, they are boosted to a higher energy level. When the electrons return to their normal energy level, they release energy at specific wavelengths. The specific wavelength emitted depends on the amount of energy the electron releases when it returns to its normal energy level. This wavelength is unique for each element. By studying the wavelength emitted, scientists can determine the elements that are present in a substance. Have students research which elements and compounds scientists have found by studying starlight, and have students reproduce some of the spectra in their ScienceLog.

USING THE FIGURE

As you discuss **Figures 2** and **3** with students, use Teaching Transparency 291 to show students what a continuous spectrum is. Have them compare this transparency with the emission spectra shown in the text. Students should find that the absorption spectrum in **Figure 3** matches the emission spectrum for hydrogen in **Figure 2**.

Teaching Transparency 291
"The Electromagnetic Spectrum"
LINK TO PHYSICAL SCIENCE

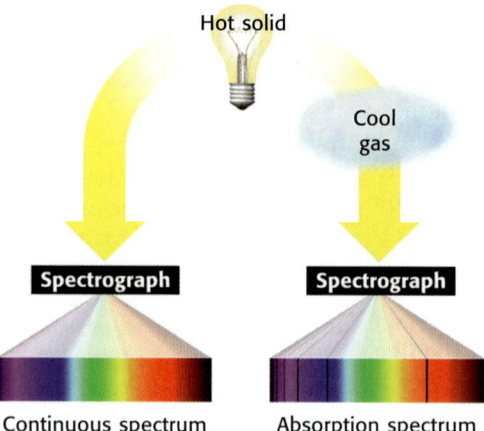

Figure 3 *An absorption spectrum (right) is produced when light passes through a cooler gas. Notice the dark lines in the spectrum.*

Our eyes are not sensitive to colors when light levels are low. There are two types of light-sensitive cells inside the eye: rods and cones. Rods are good at distinguishing shades of light and dark as well as shape and movement. Cones are good for distinguishing colors. Cones, however, do not work well in low light. This is why it is hard to distinguish between star colors.

Cosmic Detective Work If light from a hot solid passes through a cooler gas, it produces an *absorption spectrum*—a continuous spectrum with dark lines where less light gets through. Take a look at **Figure 3**. Can you identify the element in the gas by comparing the position of the dark lines in its spectrum with the bright lines in Figure 2?

An astronomer's spectrum of a star shows an absorption spectrum. The pattern of lines shows some of the elements that are in the star's atmosphere. If a star were made of just one element, it would be simple to identify the element. But stars are a mixture of things, and all the different sets of lines for its elements appear together in a star's spectrum. Sorting out the patterns is often a puzzle.

Classifying Stars

In the 1800s, people started to collect the spectra of lots of stars and tried to classify them. At first, letters were assigned to each type of spectra. Stars with spectra that had very noticeable hydrogen patterns were classified as A type stars. Other stars were classified as B, and so on. Later, scientists realized that the stars were classified in the wrong order.

Differences in Temperature Stars are now classified by how hot they are. We see the temperature differences as colors. The original class O stars are blue—they are very hot, the hottest of all stars. If you arrange the letters in order of temperature, they are no longer in alphabetical order. The resulting order of star classes—OBAFGKM—is shown in the table on the next page.

If you see a certain pattern of absorption lines in a star, you know that a certain element or molecule is in the star or its atmosphere. But the absence of a pattern doesn't mean the element isn't there; the temperature might not be high enough or low enough to produce absorption lines.

572

Science Bloopers

The composition of the sun has been the subject of much speculation. In the nineteenth century, some scientists thought the sun was made of pure anthracite coal, because coal was one of the best heat-generating fuels of the time. But given the energy output of the sun, coal would have lasted only about 10,000 years. It took the discovery of radiation and nuclear energy for scientists to develop the current model of the sun's composition and structure.

Types of Stars

Class	Color	Surface temperature (°C)	Elements detected	Examples of stars
O	blue	above 30,000	helium	10 Lacertae
B	blue-white	10,000–30,000	helium and hydrogen	Rigel, Spica
A	blue-white	7,500–10,000	hydrogen	Vega, Sirius
F	yellow-white	6,000–7,500	hydrogen and heavier elements	Canopus, Procyon
G	yellow	5,000–6,000	calcium and other metals	the sun, Capella
K	orange	3,500–5,000	calcium and molecules	Arcturus, Aldebaran
M	red	less than 3,500	molecules	Betelgeuse, Antares

Differences in Brightness With only their eyes to aid them, ancient astronomers also came up with a system to classify stars based on their brightness. They called the brightest stars in the sky *first magnitude* stars and the faintest stars *sixth magnitude* stars. But when they began to use telescopes, astronomers were able to see many stars that had previously been too faint to see. Rather than replace the old system of magnitudes, they added to it—positive numbers for dimmer stars and negative numbers for brighter stars. For example, with large telescopes, astronomers can see stars as dim as 29th magnitude. And the brightest star in the sky, Sirius, has a magnitude of −1.4.

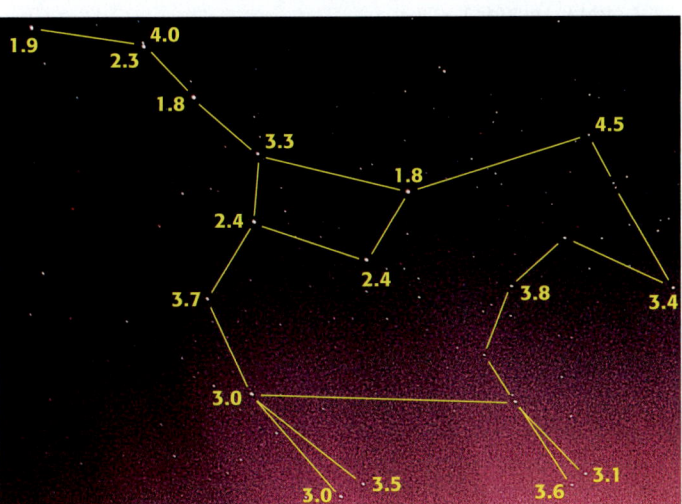

Figure 4 The constellation Ursa Major, or the Great Bear, contains both bright and faint stars. Numbers indicate their relative brightness. What is the magnitude of the brightest star?

MATH BREAK

Starlight, Star Bright

Magnitude is used to indicate how bright one object is compared with another. Five magnitudes equal a factor of 100 times in brightness. The brightest blue stars, for example, have an absolute magnitude of −10. The sun is about +5. How much brighter is a blue star than the sun? Since each five magnitudes is a factor of 100 and the blue star and the sun are 15 magnitudes different, the blue star must be 100 × 100 × 100 times brighter than the sun. This is 1,000,000 (one million) times!

IS THAT A FACT!

The brightness of astronomical objects other than stars is measured in star magnitudes as well. For example, Venus shines with an apparent magnitude of −4.6, while the full moon shines with an apparent magnitude of −12.5. With practice, the human eye can discern differences in brightness to one-tenth of a magnitude!

② Teach, continued

Multicultural CONNECTION

Writing The constellation that includes the familiar Big Dipper or Big Bear is called Ursa Major. The ancient Greeks were probably the first to equate the constellation with a bear. Have students find out about the mythologies of other constellations. Students can also find their own constellation in the night sky, name it, and write a legend about it.

Answer to Self-Check
The two stars would have the same apparent magnitude.

MATH and MORE

Encourage students to compare the apparent magnitude of stars. Point out that a decrease in apparent magnitude by a factor of 1 indicates that a star is 2.5 times brighter than the star it is being compared with. Tell them that the star Rigel has an apparent magnitude of 0.18, while Pollux has an apparent magnitude of 1.16. Have them calculate how much brighter Rigel looks than Pollux.
(1.16 − 0.18 = 0.98)
Students should find that Rigel appears about 2.5 times brighter than Pollux.

Math Skills Worksheet 10 "Arithmetic with Positive and Negative Numbers"

internetconnect
TOPIC: Stars
GO TO: www.scilinks.org
sciLINKS NUMBER: HSTE510

How Bright Is That Star?

If you look at a row of street lights along a highway, like those shown in **Figure 5**, do they all look exactly the same? Does the light you are standing under look the same as a light several blocks away? Of course not! The nearest ones look bright, and the farthest ones look dim.

Apparent Magnitude How bright a light looks, or appears, is called **apparent magnitude**. If you measure the brightness of a street light with a light meter, you will find that its brightness depends on the square of the distance between them. For example, a light that is 10 m away will appear four (2 × 2 or 2^2) times as bright as a light that is 20 m away. The same light will appear nine (3 × 3 or 3^2) times as bright as a light that is 30 m away.

Figure 5 You can estimate how far away each street light is by looking at its apparent brightness. Does this work with stars?

Self-Check
If two identical stars are located the same distance away from Earth, what can you say about their apparent magnitudes? *(See page 726 to check your answer.)*

Environment CONNECTION

And speaking of street lights . . . Someone looking at the night sky in a city would not see as many stars as someone looking at the sky in the country. Light pollution is a big problem for astronomers and backyard stargazers alike. Certain types of lighting can help reduce glare, but there will continue to be a conflict between lighting buildings at night and seeing the stars.

But unlike street lights, some stars are brighter than others because of their size or energy output, not their distance from Earth. So how can you tell the difference?

Absolute Magnitude Astronomers use a star's apparent magnitude (how bright it seems to be) and its distance from Earth to calculate its absolute magnitude. **Absolute magnitude** is the actual brightness of a star. In other words, if all stars could be placed the same distance away, their absolute magnitudes would be the same as their apparent magnitudes and the brighter stars would look brighter. The sun, for example, has an absolute magnitude of +4.8—pretty ordinary for a star. But because the sun is so close to Earth, its apparent magnitude is −26.8, making it the brightest object in the sky.

MISCONCEPTION ALERT

Students may think that stars with negative absolute magnitude values are fainter than those with positive numbers. Point out that *decreasing* numbers indicate *increasing* brightness.

Distance to the Stars

Because they are so far away, astronomers use light-years to give the distances to the stars. A **light-year** is the distance that light travels in one year. Because the speed of light is about 300,000 km/s, it travels almost 9.5 trillion kilometers in one year. Obviously it would be easier to give the distance to the North Star as 431 light-years than 4,080,000,000,000,000 km. But how do astronomers measure a star's distance?

To get a clue, take a look at the QuickLab at right. Just as your thumb appeared to move, stars near the Earth seem to move compared with more-distant stars as Earth revolves around the sun, as shown in **Figure 6.** This apparent shift in position is called **parallax.** While this shift can be seen only through telescopes, using parallax and simple trigonometry (a type of math), astronomers can find the actual distance to stars that are close to Earth.

QuickLab

Not All Thumbs!

1. Hold your **thumb** in front of your face at arm's length.
2. Close one **eye** and focus on an **object** some distance behind your thumb.
3. Slowly move your **head** back and forth a small amount, and notice how your thumb seems to be moving compared with the background you are looking at.
4. Now move your thumb in close to your face and move your head the same amount. Notice how much more your thumb moves.

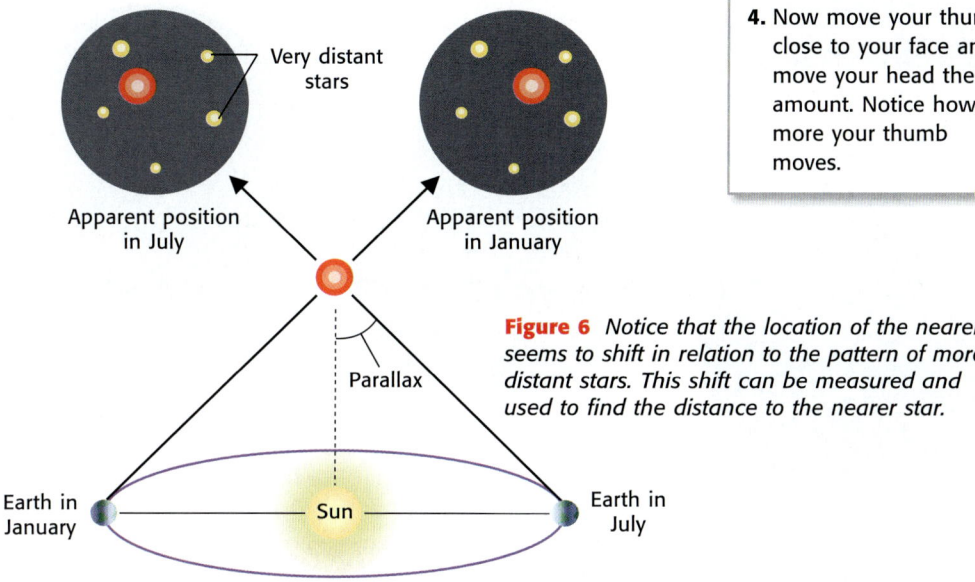

Figure 6 *Notice that the location of the nearer star seems to shift in relation to the pattern of more-distant stars. This shift can be measured and used to find the distance to the nearer star.*

Motions of Stars

As you know, the Earth rotates on its axis. As the Earth turns, different parts of its surface face the sun. This is why we have days and nights. The Earth also revolves around the sun. At different times of the year, you see different stars in the night sky. This is because the side of Earth that is away from the sun at night faces a different part of the universe.

To learn more about parallax, turn to page 720 in the LabBook.

575

IS THAT A FACT!

The trigonometric technique students used in the QuickLab is called triangulation. It is the same method used by ancient Egyptians and Greeks to measure distances. It also was used to map the city of Paris!

3) Extend

QuickLab

Teacher Notes: Explain the concept of parallax by asking students to imagine they are in a car traveling on a road lined with trees. Ask students to imagine looking out the window and to describe the apparent motion of the trees. (Students may answer that the trees closest to the car appear to move faster than those farther away.)

Tell students that they can determine the distance to a tree or a star if they can measure its apparent motion.

MATH and MORE

The textbook lists the distance light travels in a year as 9.5 trillion kilometers. Have students verify this by doing the calculation themselves. Ask students to calculate the distance light travels in 1 day. (approximately 26 million kilometers)

Math Skills Worksheet 44 "Distances in Space"

I See the Light!

Teaching Transparency 195 "Finding the Distance to Stars with Parallax"

Section 1 • Stars **575**

4) Close

Quiz

1. How does apparent magnitude differ from absolute magnitude? (Apparent magnitude is the measure of how bright a star appears from Earth, while absolute magnitude is a measure of the brightness of stars as if they were all the same distance away.)

2. What is parallax? (It is an apparent shift in position that occurs when stars nearest Earth seem to move relative to more-distant stars as Earth revolves around the sun.)

3. How is the distance from Earth to a star measured? (Scientists determine the distance to a star by using parallax and trigonometry.)

4. How is the apparent movement of the stars in the night sky different from the movement of the stars within a constellation? (The stars in the night sky rise and set as the Earth rotates. The stars in the constellation are all moving relative to one another. It takes thousands of years to observe their movement.)

ALTERNATIVE ASSESSMENT

Have students illustrate in their ScienceLog the way the distance to a star is measured. Students can explain their illustration to a partner.

Figure 7 As Earth rotates on its axis, stars set in the western horizon.

Apparent Motion Because of Earth's rotation, the sun appears to move across the sky. Likewise, if you look at the night sky long enough, the stars also appear to move. In fact, at night we can observe that the whole sky is rotating above us. As shown in **Figure 7**, the rest of the stars appear to rotate around Polaris, the North Star, which is directly above Earth's north pole. Because of Earth's rotation, all of the stars in the sky appear to make one complete circle around Polaris every 24 hours.

Actual Motion You now know that the apparent motion of the sun and stars in our sky is due to Earth's rotation. But each star is also really moving in space. Because stars are so distant, however, their real motion is hard to observe. If you could watch stars over thousands of years, their movement would be obvious. As shown in **Figure 8**, you would see that familiar star patterns slowly change their shapes.

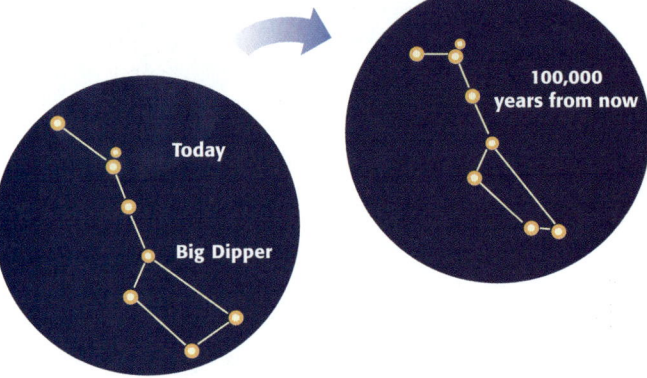

Figure 8 Over time, the shapes of the constellations and other star groups change.

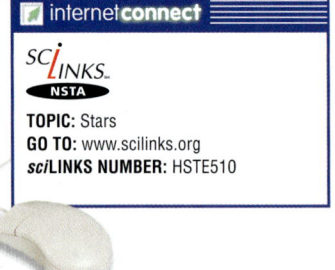

internet connect

SCILINKS
NSTA

TOPIC: Stars
GO TO: www.scilinks.org
sciLINKS NUMBER: HSTE510

REVIEW

1. Is a yellow star, such as the sun, hotter or cooler than an orange star? Explain.

2. Suppose you see two stars that have the same apparent magnitude. If one star is actually four times as far away as the other, how much brighter is the farther star?

3. **Interpreting Illustrations** Look back at Figure 7. How many hours passed between the first image and the second image? How can you tell?

Answers to Review

1. A yellow star is hotter than an orange star. Hotter temperatures are indicated by colors toward the blue end of the spectrum. Yellow is closer to blue than orange is.

2. The farther star would be 4^2, or 16, times brighter.

3. About 6 hours have passed. The stars would make a complete circle (360°) in 24 hours. In the illustrations, they have turned 90° in 6 hours.

Section 2

Terms to Learn

H-R diagram
main sequence
white dwarf
red giant
supernova
neutron star
pulsar
black hole

What You'll Do

- Describe the quantities that are plotted in the H-R diagram.
- Explain how stars at different stages in their life cycle appear on different parts of the H-R diagram.

The Life Cycle of Stars

Just like people, stars are born, grow old, and eventually die. But unlike people, stars exist for billions of years. They are born when clouds of gas and dust come together and become very hot and dense. As stars get older, they lose some of their material. Usually this is a gradual change, but sometimes it happens in a big explosion. Either way, when a star dies, much of its material returns to space. There some of it combines with more gas and dust to form new stars. How do scientists know these things about stars? Read on to find out.

The Diagram That Did It!

In 1911, a Danish astronomer named Ejnar Hertzsprung (IE nahr HUHRTZ sprung) compared the temperature and brightness of stars on a graph. Two years later, American astronomer Henry Norris Russell made some similar graphs. Although they used different data, these astronomers had similar results. The combination of their ideas is now called the *Hertzsprung-Russell,* or *H-R, diagram.* The **H-R diagram** is a graph showing the relationship between a star's surface temperature and its absolute magnitude. Russell's original diagram is shown in **Figure 9**.

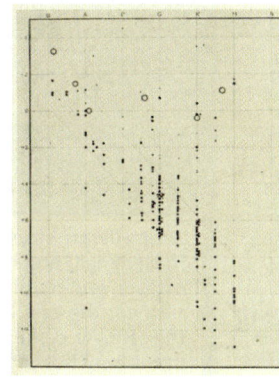

Figure 9 *Notice that a pattern begins to appear from the lower right to the upper left of the graph. Although it may not look like much, this graph began a revolution in astronomy.*

QuickLab

Plotting Pairs

Compare your classmates by making a graph of two different characteristics that each student has. Choose variables that you can assign a number to, such as age and shoe size.

1. Decide on two variables.
2. Collect the data from your classmates.
3. Construct your graph, plotting one variable against the other.
4. Do you see a pattern in your graph? What does the graph tell you about how the two variables you chose are related?

Over the years, the H-R diagram has become a tool for studying the nature of stars. It not only shows how stars are classified by temperature and brightness but also is a good way to illustrate how stars change over time. Turn the page to see a modern version of this diagram.

IS THAT A FACT!

Most of the stars near our solar system are not as bright as the sun. How do we know this? When the 100 stars nearest Earth are arranged on the H-R diagram, we can see that almost all of them fall in the region of the red dwarfs. The sun is a brighter type G main-sequence star.

Directed Reading Worksheet 21 Section 2

2) Teach

GROUP ACTIVITY

Divide the class into small groups, and provide each group with a piece of newsprint paper and markers. Direct each group to use these materials to create a flowchart describing the life of a star. Encourage them to refer to the H-R diagram as they work. Their chart should indicate that stars are formed when gas and dust are drawn together by gravity and nuclear fusion begins; that they enter the main sequence when they mature; and that they then may become a red giant, a supergiant, or eventually a white dwarf. Have students label their charts and write a descriptive caption for each stage.

USING THE FIGURE

Remind students that the lower a star's magnitude is, the brighter the star is. By looking at the H-R diagram, students should be able to identify the sun as a main-sequence, yellowish dwarf star with medium brightness and a surface temperature of about 6,000°C. Have students describe other stars in the diagram in a similar manner.

The H-R Diagram

Look closely at the diagram on these two pages. Temperature is given along the bottom of the diagram. Absolute magnitude, or brightness, is given along the left side. Hot (blue) stars are located on the left, and cool (red) stars are on the right. Bright stars are at the top, and faint stars are at the bottom. The brightest stars are a million times brighter than the sun. The faintest are 1/10,000 as bright as the sun. As you can see, there seems to be a band of stars going from the top left to the bottom right corner. This diagonal pattern of stars is called the **main sequence.** A star spends most of its lifetime as a main-sequence star and then changes into one of the other types of stars shown here.

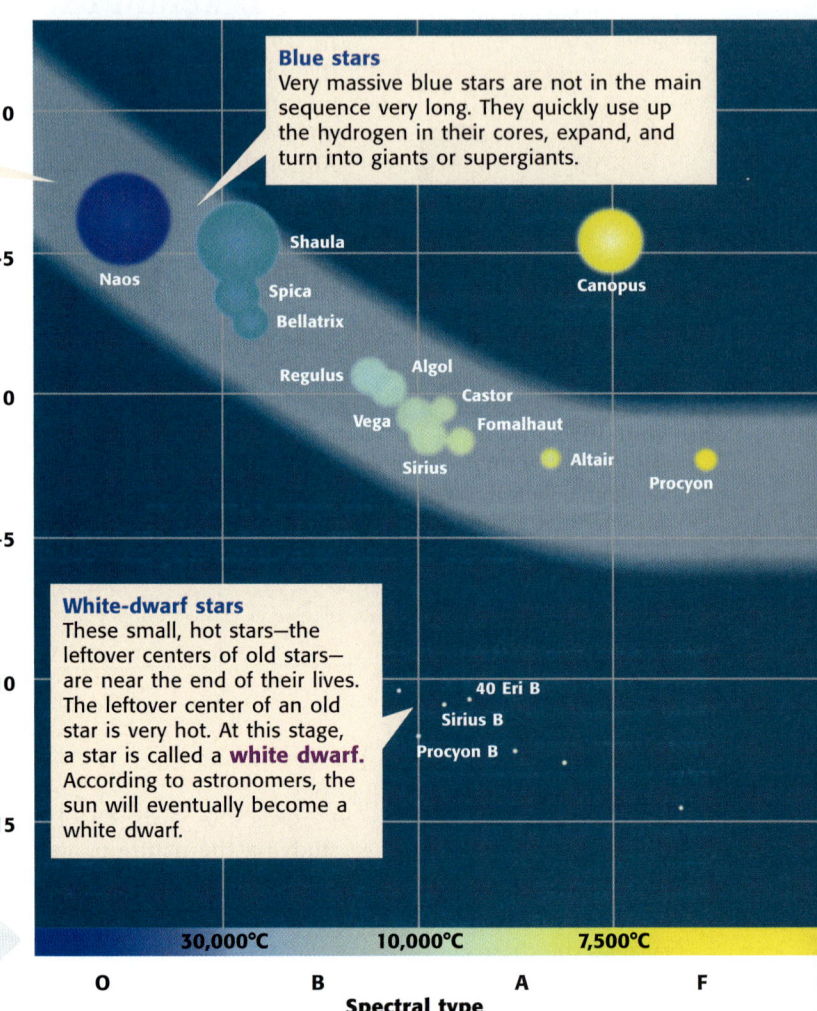

Main-sequence Stars in the main sequence form a band that runs along the middle of the H-R diagram. The sun is a main-sequence star. Stars similar to the sun are called *dwarfs*. The sun has been shining for about 5 billion years. Scientists think the sun is in midlife and that it will remain on the main sequence for another 5 billion years.

Absolute magnitude is measured upside down. That means the larger the number, the dimmer the star. At +5, the sun is not as bright as a −7 star.

Blue stars Very massive blue stars are not in the main sequence very long. They quickly use up the hydrogen in their cores, expand, and turn into giants or supergiants.

White-dwarf stars—These small, hot stars—the leftover centers of old stars—are near the end of their lives. The leftover center of an old star is very hot. At this stage, a star is called a **white dwarf.** According to astronomers, the sun will eventually become a white dwarf.

IS THAT A FACT!

Our sun probably took about 10 million years to enter the main sequence. It has been shining for about 5 billion years. In another 5 billion years, our sun will burn up all of its hydrogen and change from a yellow dwarf to a red giant. The sun's diameter will increase beyond the orbit of Venus and possibly even beyond the Earth's orbit. Current models suggest, however, that life on Earth will be long since extinct. In one billion years, the surface temperature of the sun will have increased by one percent. This change will probably make Earth an uninhabitable planet.

All stars begin as a ball of gas and dust in space as gravity pulls the gas and dust together into a sphere. As the sphere becomes denser, it gets hotter. When it is hot enough in the center, hydrogen turns into helium in a process called nuclear fusion and lots of energy is given off. A star is born!

Stars spend most of their lives on the main-sequence. Small-mass stars tend to be located at the lower right end of the main-sequence; more massive stars are found at the left end. As main-sequence stars age, they move up and to the right on the H-R diagram to become giants or supergiants. Such stars can then lose their atmospheres, leaving small cores behind, which end up in the lower left corner of the diagram as white dwarfs.

Giants and supergiants
When a star runs out of hydrogen in its core, the center of the star shrinks inward and the outer parts expand outward. In a star the size of our sun, the atmosphere will grow very large and cool. When this happens, the star becomes a **red giant.** If the star is very massive, it becomes a *supergiant.*

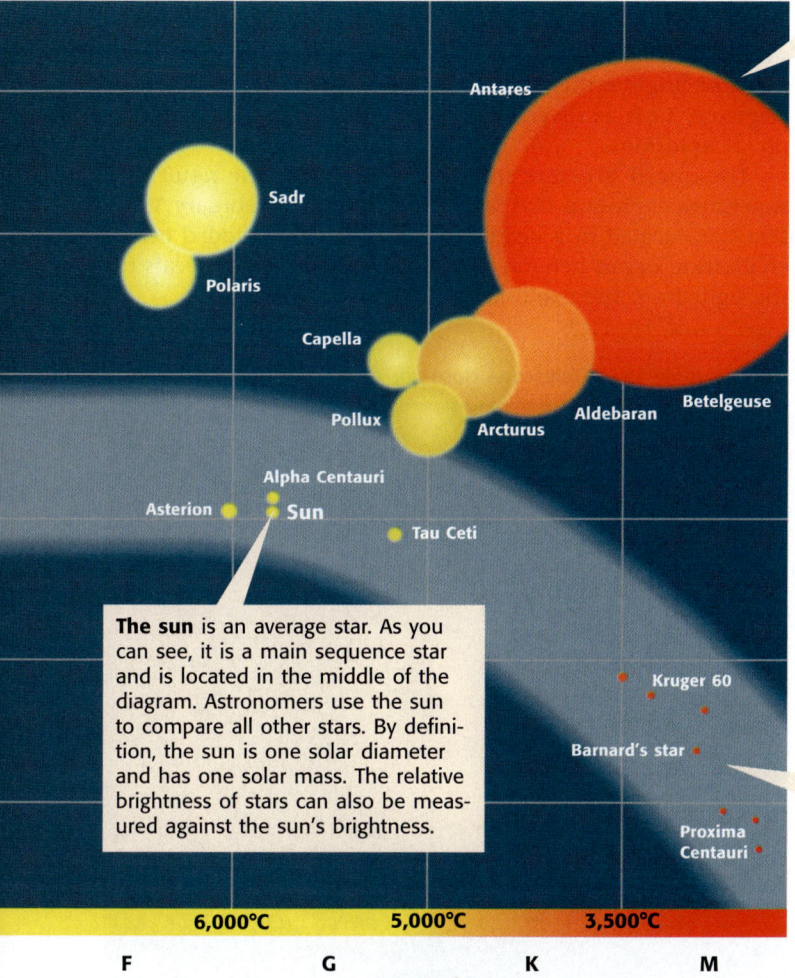

The sun is an average star. As you can see, it is a main sequence star and is located in the middle of the diagram. Astronomers use the sun to compare all other stars. By definition, the sun is one solar diameter and has one solar mass. The relative brightness of stars can also be measured against the sun's brightness.

Red-dwarf stars
At the lower end of the main sequence are the red dwarf stars. Red dwarfs are low-mass stars. Low-mass stars remain on the main sequence a long time. The lowest mass stars may be some of the oldest stars in the galaxy.

MEETING INDIVIDUAL NEEDS

Learners Having Difficulty
Have students locate where on the H-R diagram each of the following stars would be found:

	Magnitude	Temperature
Star A	+10	10,000°C
Star B	−2	5,000°C
Star C	+3	7,000°C
Star D	−9	3,500°C

Which star is a giant? (B)
Which star is a dwarf? (A)
Which star is a supergiant? (D)
Which star is most like the sun? (C)

CROSS-DISCIPLINARY FOCUS

Language Arts Divide the class into small groups, and challenge each group to create a crossword puzzle using the vocabulary and concepts from this section. Have them work together to write clues and to construct the puzzle. Then allow groups to exchange and solve the puzzles. Sheltered English

Teaching Transparency 196
"The H-R Diagram: A"

Teaching Transparency 197
"The H-R Diagram: B"

WEIRD SCIENCE

When a star the size of the sun becomes a white dwarf the size of Earth, the white dwarf is much denser than our planet. In fact, a teaspoon of the matter that makes up a white dwarf would weigh several metric tons on Earth!

Section 2 • The Life Cycle of Stars

3) Extend

CROSS-DISCIPLINARY FOCUS

History Encourage students to research the astral events of 1987, known as "the year of the supernova." Have them prepare a brief report and share their findings with the class. (In 1987, for the first time in almost 400 years, people on Earth witnessed the death of a star without using a telescope. The supernova was located in a satellite galaxy of the Milky Way called the Large Magellanic Cloud and was visible only from the Southern Hemisphere.)

MEETING INDIVIDUAL NEEDS

Advanced Learners Encourage students to research what happens as a red giant or supergiant ages. Direct them to focus on the physical changes that occur, preparing a brief report or poster describing the reactions that allow an old star to spend several million years alternately approaching and receding from the main sequence. (As a red giant or supergiant ages, its helium core contracts and grows hotter while its burning hydrogen mantle expands and cools. As a result, the star grows bigger and brighter. When the core reaches a temperature of 100 million degrees Celsius, its helium converts to carbon through nuclear fusion. Over the next several million years, the star alternately approaches and recedes from the main sequence.)

TOPIC: Supernovas
GO TO: www.scilinks.org
sciLINKS NUMBER: HSTE515

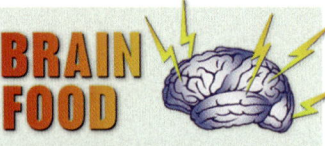

BRAIN FOOD

Many of the elements in your body were made during supernova explosions and then scattered into space. In other words, you are made of "starstuff"!

When Stars Get Old

While stars may stay on the main sequence for a long time, they don't stay there forever. Average stars, such as the sun, turn into red giants and then white dwarfs. But when massive stars get old, they may leave the main sequence in a more spectacular fashion. Stars much larger than the sun may explode with such violence that they turn into a variety of strange new objects. Let's take a look at some of these objects.

Supernovas Massive blue stars use up their hydrogen much faster than stars like the sun. This means they make a lot more energy, which makes them very hot and therefore blue! And compared with other stars, they don't last long. At the end of its life, a blue star may explode in a tremendous flash of light called a *supernova*. A **supernova** is basically the death of a large star by explosion. A supernova explosion is so powerful that it can be brighter than an entire galaxy for several days. Heavy elements, such as silver, gold, and lead, are formed by supernova explosions.

The ringed structure shown in **Figure 10** is the result of a supernova explosion that was first observed in February 1987. The star, located in a nearby galaxy, actually exploded before civilization began here on Earth, but it took 169,000 years for the light from the explosion to reach our planet!

Before (1984)

During (1987)

Figure 10 Supernova 1987A was the first supernova visible to the unaided eye in 400 years. The first image shows what the original star must have looked like only a few hours before the explosion. Today its remains form a double ring of gas and dust, shown at right.

After (Hubble Space Telescope close-up, 1994)

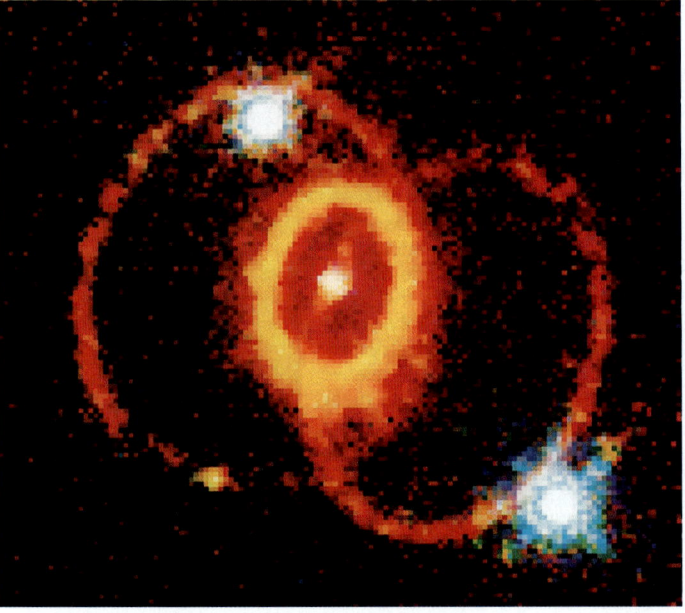

580

IS THAT A FACT!

The Crab Nebula is an expanding cloud of gas created by a supernova explosion. It was first observed by Chinese astronomers in 1054; the nebula was so bright it could be seen during the day for several weeks.

SCIENCE HUMOR

When pulsars were first recorded, their regular pulses of energy were unlike anything else in the universe. Astronomers thought they might be signals transmitted by intelligent beings. Jokingly, pulsars were called LGM—an acronym for Little Green Men.

Neutron Stars So what happens to a star that becomes a supernova? The leftover materials in the center of a supernova are squeezed together to form a star of about two solar masses. But the star is only about 20 km in diameter. The particles inside the star become neutrons, so this star is called a **neutron star.** A neutron star is so dense that if you brought a teaspoon of it back to Earth, it would weigh nearly a billion metric tons!

Pulsars If a neutron star is spinning, it is called a **pulsar.** A pulsar sends out beams of radiation that also spin around very rapidly. These beams are much like the beams from a lighthouse. The beams are detected as rapid clicks or pulses by radio telescopes.

Black Holes Sometimes the leftovers of a supernova are so massive that they collapse to form a *black hole*. A **black hole** is an object with more than three solar masses squeezed into a ball only 10 km across—100 football fields long. A black hole's gravity is so strong that not even light can escape. That is why it is called a *black* hole. Contrary to some movie depictions, a black hole doesn't gobble up other stars. But if a star is nearby, some gas or dust from the star will spiral into the black hole, as shown in **Figure 11,** giving off X rays. It is by these X rays that astronomers can detect the existence of black holes.

Figure 11 *A black hole's gravity is so strong that it can pull in material from a nearby star, as shown in this artist's drawing.*

REVIEW

1. Are blue stars young or old? How can you tell?
2. In main-sequence stars, what is the relationship between brightness and temperature?
3. Arrange the following in order of their appearance in the life cycle of a star: white dwarf, red giant, main-sequence star. Explain your answer.
4. **Applying Concepts** Given that there are more low-mass stars than high-mass stars in the universe, do you think there are more white dwarfs or more black holes? Explain.

internet connect

SC/LINKS
NSTA

TOPIC: Supernovas
GO TO: www.scilinks.org
sciLINKS NUMBER: HSTE515

581

SECTION 3

Focus

Galaxies

In this section students learn the differences between the three types of galaxies—spiral, elliptical, and irregular. Students also learn that galaxies have features known as nebulas, open clusters, and globular clusters. Finally, two different theories about the origin of galaxies are presented.

Bellringer

Show students a photograph of a spiral galaxy. Ask them to describe the evidence they see that indicates that the galaxy is rotating. Ask students, "What other objects have you seen that look similar? Do they rotate?"
`Sheltered English`

1) Motivate

DISCUSSION

Point out to students that galaxies can be thought of as star factories. Encourage them to identify the raw materials used by the "factory" to produce stars (clouds of gas and dust) and to describe how stars are assembled. (The gases and dust are drawn together by gravity, eventually forming stars.)

Tell students that the clouds of gases scattered throughout a galaxy often achieve a width of 200 light-years, and encourage them to speculate whether star formation is an ongoing process. (They should recognize that the process is ongoing because of the abundance of raw materials.)

Tell students that in this section they will learn about the different kinds of star factories, their contents, and theories about how they came to be.

582   Chapter 21 • The Universe Beyond

Section 3

Terms to Learn

galaxy   nebula
spiral galaxy   open cluster
elliptical galaxy globular cluster
irregular galaxy quasar

What You'll Do

- Identify the various types of galaxies from pictures.
- Describe the contents of galaxies.
- Explain why looking at distant galaxies reveals what early galaxies looked like.

Galaxies

Stars don't exist alone in space. They belong to larger groups that are held together by the attraction of gravity. The most common groupings are galaxies. **Galaxies** are large groupings of stars in space. Galaxies come in a variety of sizes and shapes. The largest galaxies contain more than a trillion stars. Some of the smaller ones have only a few million. Astronomers don't count the stars, of course; they estimate from the size and brightness of the galaxy how many sun-sized stars the galaxy might have.

Types of Galaxies

Look again at the Hubble Deep Field image at the beginning of this chapter. You'll notice many different types of *galaxies*. Edwin Hubble, the astronomer for whom the Hubble Space Telescope is named, began to classify galaxies in the 1920s, mostly by their shapes. We still use the galaxy names that Hubble originally assigned.

Figure 12 *The Milky Way galaxy is thought to be a spiral galaxy similar to the galaxy in Andromeda, shown here.*

Spiral Galaxies Spiral galaxies are what most people think of when you say *galaxy*. **Spiral galaxies** have a bulge at the center and very distinctive spiral arms. Hot blue stars in the spiral arms make the arms in spiral galaxies appear blue. The central region appears yellow because it contains cooler stars. **Figure 12** shows a spiral galaxy tilted, so you can see its pinwheel shape. Other spiral galaxies appear to be "edge-on." It is hard to tell what type of galaxy we are in because the gas, dust, and stars keep us from having a good view. It is like trying to figure out what pattern a marching band is making while you are in the band. Observing other galaxies and making measurements inside our galaxy lead astronomers to think that Earth is in a spiral galaxy.

582

CROSS-DISCIPLINARY FOCUS

Writing **History** Encourage students to research the work of an early twentieth century astronomer such as Sir Arthur Stanley Eddington (1882–1944). Eddington, an eminent British astronomer, was the first to propose that "spiral-structure nebulae" were actually separate galaxies, like the Milky Way. His ideas were published in 1914 in his book *Stellar Movements and the Structure of the Universe*. Ask them to prepare a brief report and be prepared to share their findings with the class.

Elliptical Galaxies About one-third of all galaxies are simply massive blobs of stars, as shown in **Figure 13.** Many look like spheres, while others are more elongated. Because we don't know how they are oriented, some of these galaxies could be cucumber shaped, with the round end facing us. These galaxies are called *elliptical galaxies*. **Elliptical galaxies** have very bright centers and very little dust and gas. Because there is so little gas, there are no new stars forming, and therefore elliptical galaxies contain only old stars. Some elliptical galaxies, like M87, at right, are huge and are therefore called *giant elliptical galaxies.* Others are much smaller and are called *dwarf elliptical galaxies.* There are probably lots of dwarf ellipticals, but because they are small and faint, they are very hard to detect.

Figure 13 *Unlike the Milky Way, the galaxy known as M87 has no spiral arms.*

Irregular Galaxies When Hubble first classified galaxies, he had a group of leftovers. He named them "irregulars." **Irregular galaxies** are galaxies that don't fit into any other class. As their name suggests, their shape is irregular. Many of these galaxies, such as the Large Magellanic Cloud, shown in **Figure 14,** are close companions of large spiral galaxies, whose gravity may be distorting the shape of their smaller neighbors.

Figure 14 *The Large Magellanic Cloud, an irregular galaxy, is located within our own galactic neighborhood.*

Activity

Now that you know the names Edwin Hubble gave to different shapes of galaxies, look at the names you gave the galaxies in the Hubble Deep Field activity at the beginning of this chapter. Rename your types with the Hubble names. Look for examples of spirals, ellipticals, and irregular galaxies.

TRY at HOME

IS THAT A FACT!

Earth is about $\frac{2}{3}$ of the distance from the center of the Milky Way to its edge. Our solar system revolves around the galaxy every 200 million years. The last time the solar system was in its current position was during the Triassic period, when dinosaurs first appeared on Earth!

Directed Reading Worksheet 21 Section 3

2) Teach

MEETING INDIVIDUAL NEEDS

Learners Having Difficulty
Help students differentiate between the types of galaxies by having them divide a large sheet of paper into thirds and draw a spiral, an ellipse, and an irregular shape. Have students list under each drawing other objects and one galaxy that have that shape. **Sheltered English**

BRAIN FOOD

Challenge students to explain why the shape of galaxies indicates that stars are revolving around a center. (Students should recognize that galaxies would not have their characteristic shapes if they were not continuously rotating.)

What would happen if the stars stopped orbiting the center of a galaxy? (In the absence of movement, gravity would pull all of the stars and dust into a more spherical shape.)

Which galaxy shape is most similar to orbits in our solar system? (Spiral galaxies most resemble the orbital paths in our solar system.)

Multicultural CONNECTION

Many cultures have created legends about the Milky Way. The ancient Chinese believed that the Milky Way was a heavenly silver river, while early Scandinavians thought it was the path that souls took to reach heaven. American Indian legends say the stars of the Milky Way were campfires that guided souls to paradise.

Section 3 • Galaxies

3) Extend

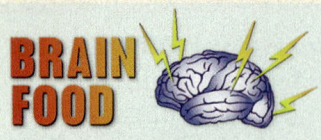

BRAIN FOOD

Sometimes entire galaxies collide and form new galaxies. It is theorized that these collisions result in elliptical or irregular galaxies. The Milky Way and our closest neighboring spiral galaxy, Andromeda, are moving toward each other at 500,000 km per hour. Even at this speed, the galaxies will not collide for another 5 billion years.

Discussion

Tell students that the material that exists between a galaxy's stars is called interstellar medium. Ask them to hypothesize about what makes up interstellar medium. **(They should recognize that nebulae—giant clouds of gas and dust—make up interstellar medium.)**

Challenge students to compare irregular, spiral, and elliptical galaxies and determine how much interstellar medium each has. **(Irregular and spiral galaxies have more interstellar medium than elliptical galaxies have.)**

TOPIC: Galaxies
GO TO: www.scilinks.org
sciLINKS NUMBER: HSTE520

Contents of Galaxies

Galaxies are composed of billions and billions of stars. But besides the stars and the planetary systems many of them probably have, there are larger features within galaxies that are made up of stars or the material of stars. Among these are gas clouds and star clusters.

Gas Clouds The Latin word for "cloud" is *nebula*. In space, **nebulas** (or *nebulae*) are giant clouds of gas and dust. Some types of nebulas glow by themselves, while others absorb light and hide stars. Still others reflect starlight, producing some amazing images. Some nebulas are regions where new stars form. **Figure 15** shows part of the Eagle nebula. Spiral galaxies generally contain nebulas, but elliptical galaxies don't.

Globular Clusters **Globular clusters** are groups of older stars. A globular cluster looks like a ball of stars, as shown in **Figure 16.** There may be 20,000 to 100,000 stars in an average globular cluster. Globular clusters are located in a spherical *halo* that surrounds spiral galaxies such as the Milky Way. Globular clusters are also common around giant elliptical galaxies.

Open Clusters **Open clusters** are groups of stars that are usually located along the spiral disk of a galaxy. Newly formed open clusters have many bright blue stars, as shown in **Figure 17.** There may be a few hundred to a few thousand stars in an open cluster.

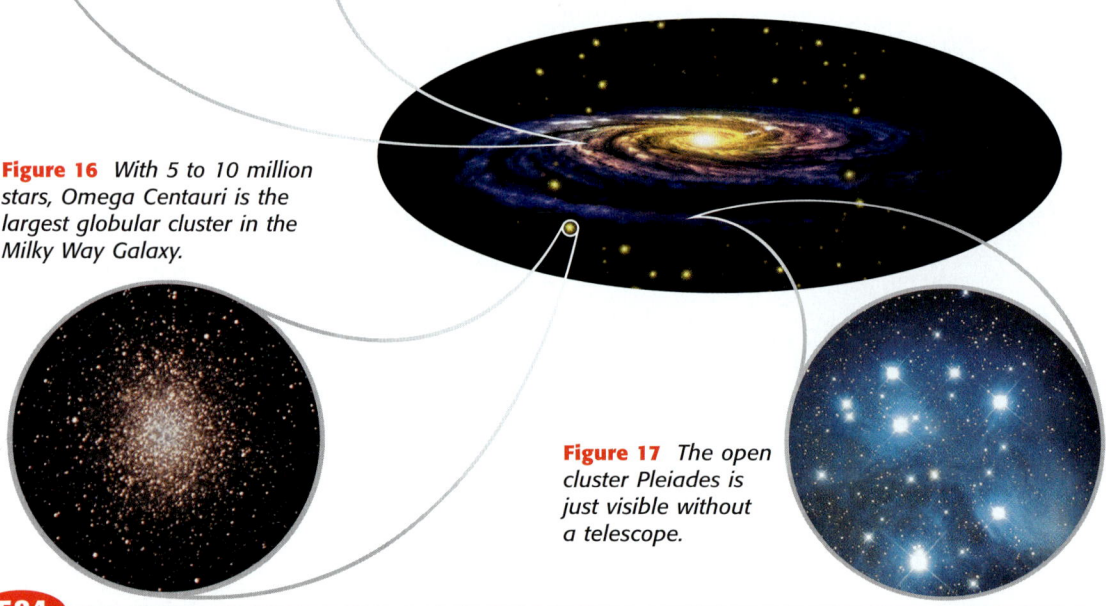

Figure 15 Part of a nebula in which stars are born is shown above. The finger-like shape to the left of the bright star is slightly wider than our solar system.

Figure 16 With 5 to 10 million stars, Omega Centauri is the largest globular cluster in the Milky Way Galaxy.

Figure 17 The open cluster Pleiades is just visible without a telescope.

SCIENTISTS AT ODDS

When the American astronomer Harlow Shapley mapped globular clusters in the universe, he found that they formed an enormous spherical system surrounding the Milky Way and, more importantly, that Earth was not at its center. This discovery led to a heated astronomical debate over whether other spiral nebulae in the distant universe are part of our galaxy or are separate "island universes." This led to the 1920 Shapley-Curtis debate at the National Academy of Sciences. The debate was resolved in 1924, when observations by Edwin Hubble showed that these "nebulae" were so far away that they must be distinct galaxies.

584 Chapter 21 • The Universe Beyond

Origin of Galaxies

How did galaxies form in the first place? To answer this question, astronomers must travel back in time, exploring the early universe through telescopes. Scientists investigate the early universe by observing objects that are extremely far away in space. Because it takes time for light to travel through space, looking through a telescope is like looking back in time. The farther out one looks, the further back in time one travels.

Looking at distant galaxies reveals what early galaxies looked like. This helps give scientists an idea of how galaxies evolve through time and perhaps what caused them to form in the first place. Scientists have already found some very strange looking objects in the early universe.

Quasars Among the most distant objects are **quasars,** which look like tiny points of light. But because they are very far away, they must be extremely bright for their size. Quasars are among the most powerful energy sources in the universe. They may be young galaxies with massive black holes at their centers. Some scientists think that what we see as quasars are galaxies in the process of forming. In **Figure 18,** you can see a quasar that is 6 billion light-years away. You are seeing it as it was 6 billion years ago—long before the Earth even existed!

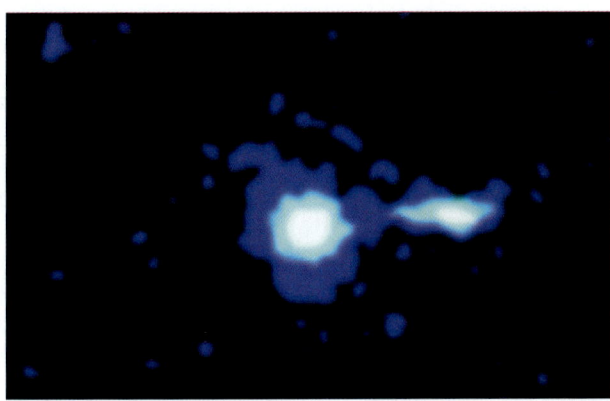

Figure 18 The quasar known as PKS 0637-752 is as powerful as 10 trillion suns.

REVIEW

1. Arrange these galaxies in order of decreasing size: spiral, giant elliptical, dwarf elliptical, irregular.
2. Describe the difference between an elliptical galaxy and a globular cluster.
3. **Analyzing Relationships** Suppose the quasar in Figure 18 suddenly underwent some dramatic change. How long would we have to wait to see this change? Explain.

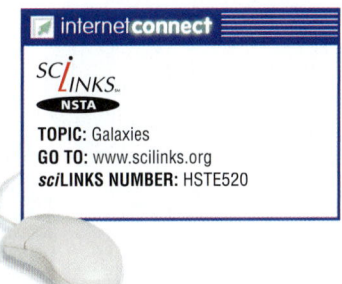

TOPIC: Galaxies
GO TO: www.scilinks.org
sciLINKS NUMBER: HSTE520

SECTION 4

Focus

Formation of the Universe

In this section, students learn that cosmology is the study of the origin and future of the universe. They learn about various interpretations of the big bang theory and about evidence supporting the theory. Finally, they learn about repeating patterns in the structure of the universe.

🔔 Bellringer

Discuss the four images in **Figure 19** with students. Have students describe the differences between each image. The first image represents the initial explosion, and the following images represent the expansion of the universe and the formation of the galaxies.

1) Motivate

ACTIVITY

The Expanding Universe Have students draw several dots on an uninflated balloon with a permanent marker and label them with letters. Ask them to measure the distances between the dots and record the information in their ScienceLog. Then have students blow up their balloon and tie the end. The students should then measure the distances between the dots again. Ask them to explain how this represents the expansion of the universe. (As the universe expands, the distance between every star and galaxy increases.) Can one dot represent the center of the universe? (no)

After students have finished this section, have them reevaluate this model and assess its accuracy.

Section 4

Terms to Learn

cosmology
big bang theory
cosmic background radiation

What You'll Do

◆ Describe the big bang theory.
◆ Explain evidence used to show support for the big bang theory.
◆ Explain how the expansion of the universe is explained by the big bang theory.

Figure 19 *The big bang caused the universe to expand in all directions.*

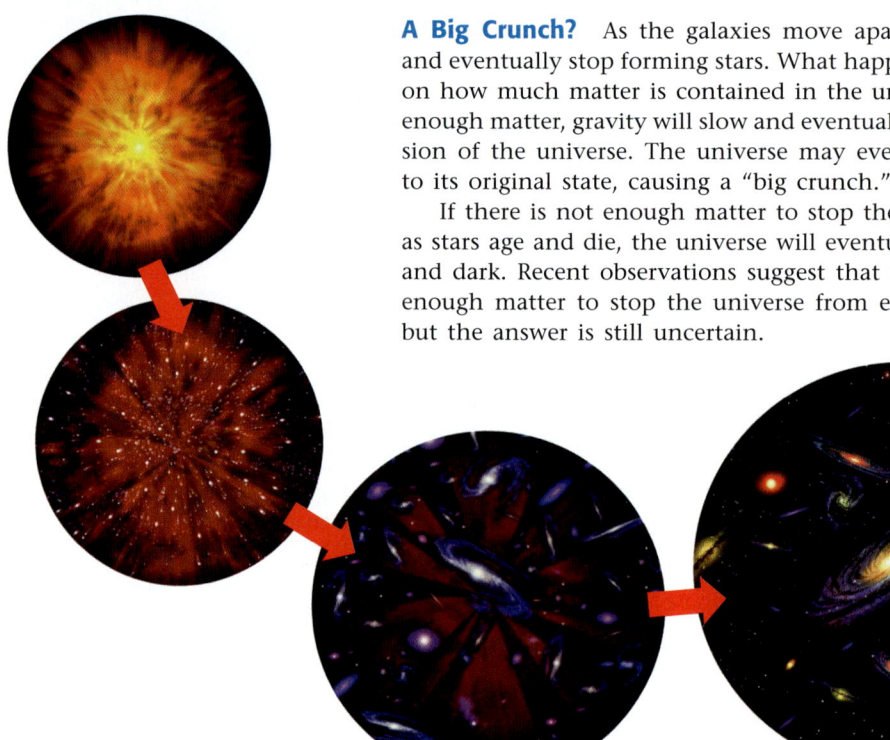

 **Teaching Transparency 198** "The Big Bang Theory"

 Directed Reading Worksheet 21 Section 4

Formation of the Universe

So far you've learned about the contents of the universe. But what about its history? How did the universe begin? How might it end? Questions like these are a special part of astronomy called *cosmology*. **Cosmology** is the study of the origin and future of the universe. Like other scientific theories, theories about the beginning and end of the universe must be tested by observations or experiments.

The Big Bang Theory

One of the most important theories in cosmology is the big bang theory. The **big bang theory** states that the universe began with a tremendous explosion. According to the theory, 12 to 15 billion years ago, all the contents of the universe were gathered together under extreme pressure, temperature, and density in a very tiny spot. Then, for some reason, it rapidly expanded. In the early moments of the universe, some of the expanding energy turned into matter that eventually became the galaxies, as shown in **Figure 19**.

A Big Crunch? As the galaxies move apart, they get older and eventually stop forming stars. What happens next depends on how much matter is contained in the universe. If there is enough matter, gravity will slow and eventually stop the expansion of the universe. The universe may even start collapsing to its original state, causing a "big crunch."

If there is not enough matter to stop the expansion, then as stars age and die, the universe will eventually become cold and dark. Recent observations suggest that there may not be enough matter to stop the universe from expanding forever, but the answer is still uncertain.

IS THAT A FACT!

Scientists believe that the universe formed about 12–15 billion years ago. To count to 15 billion, a person would have to count one number every second, day, and night for 480 years!

586 Chapter 21 • The Universe Beyond

Supporting the Theory So how do we know if the big bang really happened? In 1964, two scientists, using the antenna shown in **Figure 20,** accidentally found radiation coming from all directions in space. One explanation for this radiation is that it is **cosmic background radiation** left over from the big bang.

Think about what happens when an oven door is left open after the oven has been used. Thermal energy is transferred throughout the kitchen and the oven cools. Eventually the room and the oven are the same temperature. According to the big bang theory, thermal energy from the original explosion was distributed in every direction as the universe expanded. This cosmic background radiation—corresponding to a temperature of −270°C—now fills all of space.

Figure 20 Robert Wilson (left) and Arno Penzias (right) discovered the cosmic background radiation, giving a big boost to the big bang theory.

Universal Expansion

Today, the big bang theory is widely accepted by astronomers. But where did the idea of a big bang come from? The answer is found in deep space. No matter what direction we look, galaxies are moving away from us, as shown in **Figure 21.** This observation may make it seem like our galaxy is the center of the universe, with all other galaxies moving away from our own. But this is not the case. Careful measurements have shown that all distant galaxies are moving away from all other galaxies.

With the discovery that the universe is expanding, scientists began to wonder what it would be like to watch the universe evolve backwards through time. In reverse, the universe would appear to be contracting, not expanding. All matter would eventually come together to a single point. Thinking about what would happen if all of the matter in the universe were squeezed into such a small space led scientists to the big bang theory.

Figure 21 The big bang theory explains the expansion of the universe we observe as galaxies move outward in all directions.

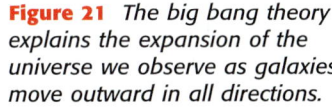

Make sure students realize that the big bang was not an explosion that happened "somewhere in space." Space and time did not exist before the big bang; they came into being with the big bang. Just before expansion, the universe was compressed in an infinitely dense ball. There was no "space" outside this ball. Thus, we are not receding away from the bang; rather, the explosion continues to expand. We aren't moving away from the point of the big bang because the big bang is happening everywhere.

2 Teach

READING STRATEGY

Prediction Guide Before students read this section, have them write a paragraph describing how they think the universe formed. Have them evaluate their responses after reading the section.

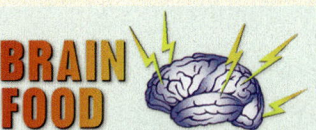

How do scientists know that galaxies are moving apart? They don't see the movement but rather see a shift toward the red end of the spectrum in the light from the stars making up the galaxies. This occurs because, as galaxies move away, the light waves that reach Earth are stretched out, making them appear to have longer wavelengths. This phenomenon is caused by the Doppler effect. For the same reason, the siren of an ambulance sounds higher in pitch when it is approaching than when it is receding.

Multicultural CONNECTION

The ancient Greeks believed that the universe began with Chaos (space), which produced Gaea (Earth). Gaea gave birth to Uranus (the starry heavens) as a cover for herself and then gave birth to the mountains, fields, seas, plants, and animals. Encourage students to learn how other cultures have explained the origin of the universe.

3) Extend

INDEPENDENT PRACTICE

Writing Students can work independently to summarize, in writing, the big bang theory, including the evidence that supports it. Encourage students to investigate other theories of the origin of the universe. Direct them to select three such theories, summarizing their key points in a table.

DISCUSSION

Remind students that one way to determine the age of the universe is to divide the distance to other galaxies by the speed at which they are moving away from us. Tell students that while scientists do not know the exact age of the universe, they believe it formed about 12–15 billion years ago.

Have students consider how many light-years away a celestial object would be if it existed during the formation of the universe. (It would have to be 12–15 billion light-years away.)

Homework

Universal Address Have students use reference materials to find out their universal address:

Name
Street address
City, State
Country
Continent
Planet
Solar system
Galaxy
Galaxy group
Galaxy cluster
Local supercluster
The universe

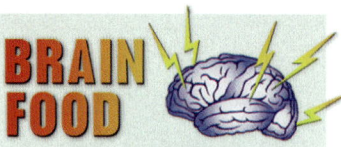

Objects in very distant space look "younger" than they really are. In fact, we cannot even be sure they still exist. If a distant galaxy disappeared, for example, people on Earth wouldn't know about it for billions of years.

A Raisin-Bread Model

Imagine a loaf of raisin bread before it is baked. Inside the dough, each raisin is a certain distance from every other raisin. As the dough gets warm and rises, it expands and all of the raisins begin to move away from each other. No matter which raisin you observe, the other raisins are moving farther from it.

The universe itself is like the rising bread dough—it is expanding in all directions. And like the raisins, every distant galaxy is moving away from our galaxy as well as every other galaxy. In other words, there isn't any way to find the "center" of the universe.

How Old Is the Universe?

One way scientists can measure the age of the universe is by measuring the distance to the farthest galaxies. Because light travels at a certain speed, the amount of time it takes light to travel this distance is a measure of the age of the universe. Another way to estimate the age of the universe is to calculate the ages of old, nearby stars. Because the universe must be at least as old as the oldest stars it contains, their ages provide a clue to the age of the universe. But according to these calculations, some stars are older than the universe itself! Astronomers continue to search for evidence that will solve this puzzle.

Graphing Expansion

Suppose you decide to make some raisin bread. You would form a lump of dough, as shown in the top image. The lower image represents dough that has been rising for 2 hours. Look at raisin **B** in the top image. Measure how far it is from each of the other raisins—**A, C, D, E, F,** and **G**—in millimeters. Now measure how far each raisin has moved away from **B** in the lower image. Make a graph of speed (in units of mm/h) versus original distance (in mm). Remember that speed equals distance divided by time. For example, if raisin **E** was originally 15 mm from raisin **B** and is now 30 mm away, it moved 15 mm in 2 hours. Its speed is therefore 7.5 mm/h. Repeat the procedure, starting with raisin **D**. Plot your results on the same graph, and compare the two results. What can you conclude from the information you graphed?

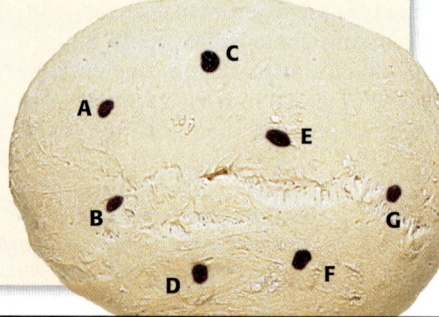

Students may have difficulty understanding that due to the great distances between the Earth and stars, the light they see actually was emitted from the star in the distant past. If a star is 100 light-years away, it takes 100 years for the light to travel that distance.

Answer to APPLY

The farther a raisin is from raisin **B** (or any other raisin), the faster it is moving away from that raisin. The same is true for galaxies in the expanding universe. **Note:** Student graphs should resemble the graph in the Chapter Review under Interpreting Graphics.

Structure of the Universe

The universe is an amazing place. From our home on planet Earth, it stretches out farther than we can see with our most sensitive instruments. It contains a variety of objects, some of which you have just learned about. But these objects are not simply scattered through the universe at random. The universe has a structure that is repeated over and over again.

A Cosmic Repetition You already know that the Earth is a planet. But planets are part of planetary systems. Our solar system is the one we are most familiar with, but recently planets have been detected in orbit around other stars. Scientists think that planetary systems are actually quite common in the universe. Stars are grouped in larger systems, ranging from star clusters to galaxies. Galaxies themselves are arranged in groups that are bound together by gravity. Even galaxy groups form galaxy clusters and superclusters, as shown in **Figure 22**.

Multiple Universes? Farther than the eye can see, the universe continues with this pattern, with great collections of galaxy clusters and vast empty regions of space in between. But is the universe itself alone? Some cosmologists think that our universe is only one of a great many other universes, perhaps similar to ours or perhaps not. At present, we cannot observe other universes. But someday, who knows? Maybe students in future classrooms will have much more to study!

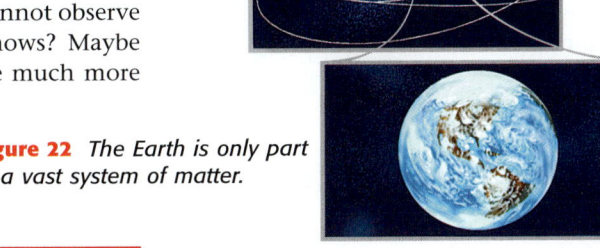

Figure 22 The Earth is only part of a vast system of matter.

REVIEW

1. Name one observation that supports the big bang theory.
2. How does the big bang theory explain the observed expansion of the universe?
3. **Understanding Technology** Large telescopes gather more light than small telescopes gather. Why are large telescopes used to study very distant galaxies?

4) Close

Quiz

1. What is cosmic background radiation? (It is the radiation that comes from all directions in space and is left over from the big bang.)
2. How is the structure of the universe repeated? (There are great collections of galaxy clusters—made up of similar components—with vast regions of empty space in between.)

ALTERNATIVE ASSESSMENT

Board Game To reinforce chapter concepts, divide the class into small groups and challenge each group to create a board game. The game should lead players through the universe, encountering the features they have learned about in this chapter. Provide each group with a piece of poster board, plain index cards, and markers. Have them use the index cards to write clues directing players' movements through the "universe." For example, they might write, "If you can describe what a star is made of, move ahead to the nebula. If not, lose a turn." Have students create written rules and exchange their games.

Critical Thinking Worksheet 21
"Fleabert and the Amazing Watermelon Seed"

Answers to Review

1. The existence of cosmic background radiation supports the big bang theory. The observable expansion of the universe also supports the big bang theory.
2. According to the big bang theory, the expansion of the universe was the result of a massive explosion of all matter and energy.
3. Very distant galaxies are very faint. Only large telescopes can gather enough light to detect them.

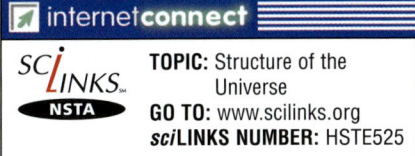

internetconnect
TOPIC: Structure of the Universe
GO TO: www.scilinks.org
sciLINKS NUMBER: HSTE525

Section 4 • Formation of the Universe

Chapter Highlights

VOCABULARY DEFINITIONS

SECTION 1

spectrum the rainbow of colors produced when white light passes through a prism or spectrograph

apparent magnitude how bright a light appears to an observer

absolute magnitude the actual brightness of a star

light-year a unit of length equal to the distance that light travels through space in 1 year

parallax an apparent shift in the position of an object when viewed from different locations

SECTION 2

H-R diagram Hertzsprung-Russell diagram; a graph that shows the relationship between a star's surface temperature and its absolute magnitude

main sequence a diagonal pattern of stars on the H-R diagram

white dwarf a small, hot star near the end of its life; the leftover center of an old star

red giant a star that expands and cools once it runs out of hydrogen fuel

supernova the death of a large star by explosion

neutron star a star in which all the particles have become neutrons; the collapsed remains of a supernova

pulsar a spinning neutron star that emits rapid pulses of light

black hole an object with more than three solar masses squeezed into a ball only 10 km across whose gravity is so strong that not even light can escape

Chapter Highlights

SECTION 1

Vocabulary
spectrum (p. 570)
apparent magnitude (p. 574)
absolute magnitude (p. 574)
light-year (p. 575)
parallax (p. 575)

Section Notes
- The color of a star depends on its temperature. Hot stars are blue. Cool stars are red.
- The spectra of stars indicate their composition. Spectra are also used to classify stars.
- The magnitude of a star is a measure of its brightness.
- Apparent magnitude is how bright a star appears from Earth.
- Absolute magnitude is how bright a star actually is. Lower absolute magnitude numbers indicate brighter stars.
- Distance to nearby stars can be measured by their movement relative to stars farther away.

Labs
Red Hot, or Not? (p. 718)
I See the Light! (p. 720)

SECTION 2

Vocabulary
H-R diagram (p. 577)
main sequence (p. 578)
white dwarf (p. 578)
red giant (p. 579)
supernova (p. 580)
neutron star (p. 581)
pulsar (p. 581)
black hole (p. 581)

Section Notes
- New stars form from the material of old stars that have gone through their life cycles.
- The H-R diagram relates the temperature and brightness of a star. It also illustrates the life cycle of stars.
- Most stars are main-sequence stars. Red giants and white dwarfs are later stages in a star's life cycle.
- Massive stars become supernovas. Their cores turn into neutron stars or black holes.

✓ Skills Check

Math Concepts

SQUARING THE DIFFERENCE The difference in brightness (apparent magnitude) between a pair of similar stars depends on the difference in their distances from Earth. Compare a star that is 10 light-years away with a star that is 5 light-years away. One star is twice as close, so it is $2 \times 2 = 4$ times brighter than the other star. The star that is 5 light-years away is also 3^2, or 9, times brighter than one that is 15 light-years away.

Visual Understanding

READING BETWEEN THE LINES The composition of a star is determined by the absorption spectra it displays. Dark lines in the spectrum of a star indicate which elements are present. Look back at Figure 3 to review.

Lab and Activity Highlights

Red Hot, or Not?   PG 718

I See the Light!   PG 720

Datasheets for LabBook
(blackline masters for these labs)

SECTION 3

Vocabulary
- galaxy (p. 582)
- spiral galaxy (p. 582)
- elliptical galaxy (p. 583)
- irregular galaxy (p. 583)
- nebula (p. 584)
- open cluster (p. 584)
- globular cluster (p. 584)
- quasar (p. 585)

Section Notes
- Edwin Hubble classified galaxies according to their shape. Major types include spiral, elliptical, and irregular galaxies.
- A nebula is a cloud of gas and dust. New stars are born in some nebulas.
- Open clusters are groups of stars located along the spiral disk of a galaxy. Globular star clusters are found in the halos of spiral galaxies and in elliptical galaxies.
- Because light travels at a certain speed, observing distant galaxies is like looking back in time. Scientists look at distant galaxies to learn what early galaxies looked like.

SECTION 4

Vocabulary
- cosmology (p. 586)
- big bang theory (p. 586)
- cosmic background radiation (p. 587)

Section Notes
- The big bang theory states that the universe began with an explosion about 12 to 15 billion years ago.
- Cosmic background radiation fills the universe with radiation that is left over from the big bang. It is supporting evidence for the big bang theory.
- Observations show that the universe is expanding outward. There is no measurable center and no apparent edge.
- All matter in the universe is a part of larger systems, from planets to superclusters of galaxies.

VOCABULARY DEFINITIONS, continued

SECTION 3

galaxy a large grouping of stars in space

spiral galaxy a galaxy with a bulge in the center and very distinctive spiral arms

elliptical galaxy a spherical or elongated galaxy with a bright center and very little dust and gas

irregular galaxy a galaxy that does not fit into any other category; one with an irregular shape

nebula a large cloud of dust and gas in interstellar space; the location of star formation

open cluster a group of stars that are usually located along the spiral disk of a galaxy

globular cluster a group of older stars that looks like a ball of stars

quasar "quasi-stellar" object; a star-like source of light that is extremely far away; one of the most powerful sources of energy in the universe

SECTION 4

cosmology the study of the origin and future of the universe

big bang theory the theory that states the universe began with a tremendous explosion

cosmic background radiation radiation left over from the big bang that fills all of space

internet connect

GO TO: go.hrw.com

Visit the **HRW** Web site for a variety of learning tools related to this chapter. Just type in the keyword:

KEYWORD: HSTUNV

GO TO: www.scilinks.org

Visit the **National Science Teachers Association** on-line Web site for Internet resources related to this chapter. Just type in the *sci*LINKS number for more information about the topic:

TOPIC:	*sci*LINKS NUMBER:
The Hubble Space Telescope	HSTE505
Stars	HSTE510
Supernovas	HSTE515
Galaxies	HSTE520
Structure of the Universe	HSTE525

591

 Vocabulary Review Worksheet 21

 Blackline masters of these Chapter Highlights can be found in the **Study Guide.**

Lab and Activity Highlights

LabBank

Whiz-Bang Demonstrations, Where Do the Stars Go? Demo 35

Long-Term Projects & Research Ideas, Contacting the Aliens, Project 49

Chapter 21 • Chapter Highlights   **591**

Chapter Review Answers

USING VOCABULARY

1. Absolute magnitude is the actual brightness of a star, or how bright it would appear if all stars were the same distance from Earth. Apparent magnitude is how bright a star appears from Earth.
2. A spectrum is made when white light is broken into its colors by a prism or spectrograph. Parallax is a measure of the apparent shift in position of an object due to a difference in the location from which it is viewed.
3. A main-sequence star is a star that is stable and uses fusion to produce energy. A red giant became a giant star when its fusion stopped and its outer layers expanded.
4. A white dwarf is the leftover core of a small star at the end of its life. A black hole is the leftover core of a massive star at the end of its life.
5. An elliptical galaxy is composed mostly of older stars, and it contains very little dust or gas. It is shaped like a sphere or an elongated oval. A spiral galaxy has a bulge with cooler stars; spiral arms with hot blue stars, gas, and dust; and a halo of stars and globular clusters.
6. The big bang occurred when all the matter and energy of the universe suddenly expanded. The cosmic background radiation is the radiation coming from all directions in space. It may be evidence of the big bang.

UNDERSTANDING CONCEPTS

Multiple Choice

7. c
8. d
9. b
10. d
11. c
12. a
13. c

Chapter Review

USING VOCABULARY

For each pair of terms, explain the difference in their meanings.

1. absolute magnitude/apparent magnitude
2. spectrum/parallax
3. main-sequence star/red giant
4. white dwarf/black hole
5. elliptical galaxy/spiral galaxy
6. big bang/cosmic background radiation

UNDERSTANDING CONCEPTS

Multiple Choice

7. The majority of stars in our galaxy are
   a. blue.
   b. white dwarfs.
   c. main-sequence stars.
   d. red giants.

8. Which would be seen as the brightest star in the following group?
   a. Alcyone—apparent magnitude of 3
   b. Alpheratz—apparent magnitude of 2
   c. Deneb—apparent magnitude of 1
   d. Rigel—apparent magnitude of 0

9. A cluster of stars forms in a nebula. There are red stars, blue stars, yellow stars, and white stars. Which stars are most like the sun?
   a. red   c. blue
   b. yellow   d. white

10. Individual stars are moving in space. How long will it take to see a noticeable difference without using a telescope?
    a. 24 hours   c. 100 years
    b. 1 year   d. 100,000 years

11. You visited an observatory and looked through the telescope. You saw a ball of stars through the telescope. What type of object did you see?
    a. a spiral galaxy
    b. an open cluster
    c. a globular cluster
    d. an irregular galaxy

12. In which part of a spiral galaxy do you expect to find nebulas?
    a. the spiral arms
    b. the central region
    c. the halo
    d. all parts of the galaxy

13. Which statement about the big bang theory is accurate?
    a. The universe will never end.
    b. New matter is being continuously created in the universe.
    c. The universe is filled with radiation coming from all directions in space.
    d. We can locate the center of the universe.

Concept Mapping Transparency 21

Blackline masters of this Chapter Review can be found in the **Study Guide**.

592   Chapter 21 • The Universe Beyond

Short Answer

14. Describe how the apparent magnitude of a star varies with its distance from Earth.

15. Name six types of astronomical objects in the universe. Arrange them by size.

16. Which contains more stars on average, a globular cluster or an open cluster?

17. What does the big bang theory have to say about how the universe will end?

Concept Mapping

18. Use the following terms to create a concept map: black hole, neutron star, main-sequence star, red giant, nebula, white dwarf.

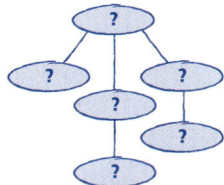

CRITICAL THINKING AND PROBLEM SOLVING

Write one or two sentences to answer the following questions:

19. If a certain star displayed a large parallax, what could you say about its distance from Earth?

20. Two M-type stars have the same apparent magnitude. Their spectra show that one is a red giant and the other is a red-dwarf star. Which one is farther from Earth? Explain your answer.

21. Look back at the H-R diagram in Section 2. Why do astronomers use absolute magnitudes to plot the stars? Why don't they use apparent magnitudes?

22. While looking at a galaxy through a nearby university's telescope, you notice that there are no blue stars present. What kind of galaxy is it most likely to be?

MATH IN SCIENCE

23. An astronomer observes two stars of about the same temperature and size. Alpha Centauri B is about 4 light-years away, and Sigma^2 Eridani A is about 16 light-years away. How much brighter does Alpha Centauri B appear?

INTERPRETING GRAPHICS

The following graph illustrates the Hubble law relating the distances of galaxies and their speed away from us.

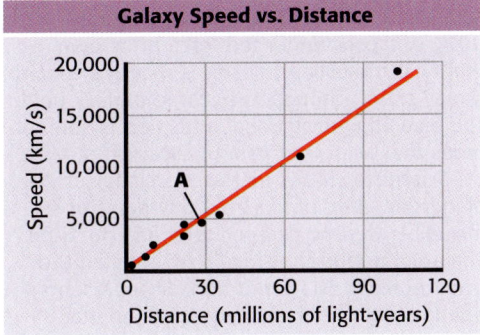

24. Look at the galaxy marked **A** in the graph. What is its speed and distance?

25. If a new galaxy with a speed of 15,000 km/s were found, at what distance would you expect it to be?

 Take a minute to review your answers to the Pre-Reading Questions found at the bottom of page 568. Have your answers changed? If necessary, revise your answers based on what you have learned since you began this chapter.

Short Answers

14. The apparent magnitude decreases as distance increases.
15. Answers may vary. Possible answers include globular cluster, nebula, spiral arm, nuclear bulge, halo, spiral galaxy, elliptical galaxy, and galaxy cluster.
16. On average, globular clusters contain more stars.
17. If there is enough matter in the universe, gravity will slow or stop the expansion, perhaps even pulling everything back into a "big crunch." If there is not enough matter, everything will continue to expand outward, get older, cool down, and become dark.

Concept Mapping

18.  An answer to this exercise can be found at the end of this book.

CRITICAL THINKING AND PROBLEM SOLVING

19. The star would be relatively close to Earth.
20. The red giant is farther away. If it were the same distance as the red dwarf (or closer), it would be much brighter than the red dwarf.
21. Absolute magnitude is a physical property of the star. Apparent magnitude varies according to a star's distance and absolute magnitude.
22. The galaxy is most likely an elliptical galaxy because it lacks the gas and dust needed for star formation. Blue stars are young stars.

MATH IN SCIENCE

23. Alpha Centauri B is 16 times as bright because it is 4 times closer.

INTERPRETING GRAPHICS

24. Its speed is about 5,000 km/s, and its distance is about 30 million light-years.
25. almost 90 million light-years

Weird Science
Holes Where Stars Once Were

Background

Scientists theorize that two types of stars can turn into black holes. When an extremely large star (about 8 to 25 times as massive as the sun) runs out of fuel and dies, it usually explodes as a supernova. A star that is more than 25 times as massive as the sun may collapse without exploding. If the core of either type of star is at least three times more massive than the sun, the core will collapse under its own gravity and become a black hole.

Many scientists also think that black holes may have formed at the center of many galaxies in the early universe. As a galaxy forms, gases and stars rotate around its center in a swirling mass. Some of this matter may become so closely packed in the center of the forming galaxy that it eventually condenses into a single lump. The gravity of the resulting mass causes it to condense even further until it is so dense that it forms a black hole. These black holes typically are millions or even billions of times as massive as the sun.

WEIRD SCIENCE

HOLES WHERE STARS ONCE WERE

An invisible phantom lurks in outer space, ready to swallow up everything that comes near it. Once trapped in its grasp, matter is stretched, torn, and crushed into oblivion. Does this sound like a horror story? Guess again! Scientists call it a black hole.

Born of a Collapsing Star

As a star runs out of fuel, it cools and eventually collapses under the force of its own gravity. If the collapsing star is massive enough, it may shrink enough to become a black hole. The resulting gravitational attraction is so enormous that even light cannot escape!

Scientists predict that at the center of the black hole is a *singularity,* a tiny point of incredible density, temperature, and pressure. The area around the singularity is called the *event horizon.* The event horizon represents the boundary of the black hole. Anything that crosses the event horizon, including light, will eventually be pulled into the black hole. As matter comes near the event horizon, the matter begins to swirl in much the same way that water swirls down a drain.

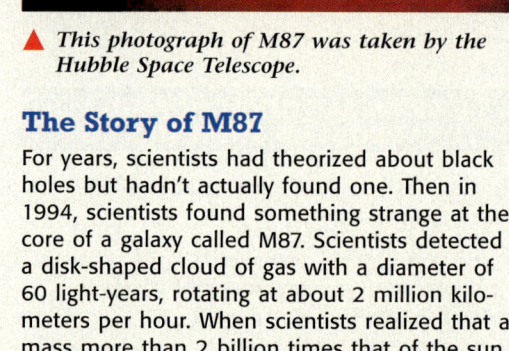

▲ *This photograph of M87 was taken by the Hubble Space Telescope.*

The Story of M87

For years, scientists had theorized about black holes but hadn't actually found one. Then in 1994, scientists found something strange at the core of a galaxy called M87. Scientists detected a disk-shaped cloud of gas with a diameter of 60 light-years, rotating at about 2 million kilometers per hour. When scientists realized that a mass more than 2 billion times that of the sun was crammed into a space no bigger than our solar system, they knew that something was pulling in the gases at the center of the galaxy.

Many astronomers think that black holes, such as the one in M87, lie at the heart of many galaxies. Some scientists suggest that there is a giant black hole at the center of our own Milky Way galaxy. But don't worry. The Earth is too far away to be caught.

Modeling a Black Hole

▶ Make a model to show how a black hole pulls in the matter surrounding it. Indicate the singularity and event horizon.

▲ *The Hubble Space Telescope*

Answers to Modeling a Black Hole
Encourage students to use a variety of materials and to clearly mark the important parts of the black hole with toothpicks or flags.

CAREERS

ASTROPHYSICIST

Jocelyn Bell-Burnell became fascinated with astronomy at an early age. As a research student at Cambridge University, Bell-Burnell discovered pulsars, celestial objects that emit radio waves at short and regular intervals. Today Bell-Burnell is a leading expert in the field of astrophysics and the study of stars. She is currently head of the physics department at the Open University, in Milton Keynes, England.

At Cambridge University in 1967, Bell-Burnell and her adviser, Antony Hewish, completed work on a gigantic radio telescope designed to pick up signals from quasars. Bell-Burnell's job was to operate the telescope and analyze the "chart paper" recordings of the telescope on a graph. Each day, the telescope recorded 29.2 m of chart paper! After a month of operating the telescope, Bell-Burnell noticed a few "bits of scruff" that she could not explain—they were very short, pulsating radio signals. The signals were only 6.3 mm long, and they occurred only once every 4 days. What Bell-Burnell had accidentally found was a needle in a cosmic haystack!

LGM 1

Bell-Burnell and Hewish struggled to find the source of this mysterious new signal. They double-checked the equipment and began eliminating all of the possible sources of the signal, such as satellites, television, and radar. Because they could not rule out that the signal was coming from aliens, Bell-Burnell and Hewish called it LGM 1. Can you guess why? LGM stood for "Little Green Men"!

The Answer: Neutron Stars

Shortly after finding the first signal, Bell-Burnell discovered yet another strange, pulsing signal within the vast quantity of chart paper. This signal was similar to the first, except that it came from the other side of the sky. To Bell-Burnell, this second signal was exciting because it meant that her first signal was not of local origin and that she had stumbled on a new and unknown signal from space! By January 1968, Bell-Burnell had discovered two more pulsating signals. In March of that year, her findings were published, to the amazement of the scientific community. The scientific press coined the term *pulsars,* from pulsating radio stars. Bell-Burnell and other scientists reached the conclusion that her "bits of scruff" were caused by rapidly spinning neutron stars!

Star Tracking

▶ Pick out a bright star in the sky, and keep a record of its position in relation to a reference point, such as a tree or building. Each night, record what time the star appears at this point in the sky. Do you notice a pattern?

▲ *An artist's depiction of a pulsar*

CAREERS
Astrophysicist— Jocelyn Bell-Burnell

Background

One of the most fascinating properties of neutron stars is their incredible mass. Most neutron stars are only about 10 to 16 km in diameter, but their mass can be equal to the mass of our sun! The mass of a neutron star is so great that if you could stand on its surface and drop a coin, the coin would hit the ground at half the speed of light!

In 1991, two planets were discovered near a pulsar in the Virgo constellation. This discovery was remarkable because planets had not been detected beyond our solar system, and it suggested that there may be more planets in the universe than astronomers had previously imagined. It is extremely doubtful, however, that these two planets support life because the nearby neutron star bombards them with lethal radiation.

Answer to Star Tracking
This exercise helps students learn to make accurate astronomical observations over an extended period of time. Students should discover that the stars move in accordance with sidereal time, or "star time," in which a day lasts 23 hours and 56 minutes.

Chapter Organizer

CHAPTER ORGANIZATION	TIME MINUTES	OBJECTIVES	LABS, INVESTIGATIONS, AND DEMONSTRATIONS
Chapter Opener pp. 596–597	45	National Standards: UCP 2, SAI 1, ST 1, 2, SPSP 5, HNS 1, 3	**Start-Up Activity** Rocket Fun, p. 597
Section 1 Rocket Science	45	▶ Outline the early development of rocket technology. ▶ Explain how a rocket works. ▶ Explain the difference between orbital velocity and escape velocity. UCP 2–5, SAI 1, ST 2, SPSP 5, HNS 1, 3; LabBook SAI 1, ST 1	**Demonstration,** p. 598 in ATE GENERAL **Design Your Own,** Water Rockets Save the Day! p. 722 GENERAL **Datasheets for LabBook,** Water Rockets Save the Day! Datasheet 48 GENERAL **Whiz-Bang Demonstrations,** Rocket Science, Demo 36 GENERAL
Section 2 Artificial Satellites	90	▶ Describe how the launch of the first satellite started the space race. ▶ Explain why some orbits are better than others for communications satellites. ▶ Describe how the satellite program has given us a better understanding of the Earth as a global system. UCP 3, 4, SAI 1, ST 2, SPSP 5, HNS 1, 3	**Inquiry Labs,** Crash Landing, Lab 14 BASIC
Section 3 Space Probes	90	▶ Describe some of the discoveries made by space probes. ▶ Explain how space-probe missions help us better understand the Earth. ▶ Describe how future space-probe missions will differ from the original missions to the planets. UCP 4, 5, ST 2, SPSP 5, HNS 1, 3	**Long-Term Projects and Research Ideas,** Project 50 ADVANCED
Section 4 Living and Working in Space	90	▶ Summarize the benefits of the manned space program. ▶ Explain how large projects such as the Apollo program and the *International Space Station* developed. ▶ Identify future possibilities for human exploration of space. UCP 4, 5, SAI 1, ST 2, SPSP 5, HNS 1, 3; LabBook UCP 2, SAI 1, ST 1, 2	**Demonstration,** O-Ring Failure, p. 614 in ATE GENERAL **Making Models,** Reach for the Stars, p. 724 GENERAL **Datasheets for LabBook,** Reach for the Stars, Datasheet 49 GENERAL **Inquiry Labs,** Space Fitness, Lab 15 ADVANCED **EcoLabs and Field Activities,** There's a Space for Us, EcoLab 16 ADVANCED

See page T20 for a complete correlation of this book with the **NATIONAL SCIENCE EDUCATION STANDARDS.**

TECHNOLOGY RESOURCES

 Guided Reading Audio CD English or Spanish, Chapter 22

 One-Stop Planner CD-ROM with Test Generator

 CNN. Science, Technology & Society, Mars Pathfinder, Segment 28 Surveying the Red Planet, Segment 29 **Scientists in Action,** Growing Plants in Space, Segment 16

Chapter 22 • Exploring Space

CLASSROOM WORKSHEETS, TRANSPARENCIES, AND RESOURCES	SCIENCE INTEGRATION AND CONNECTIONS	REVIEW AND ASSESSMENT
Directed Reading Worksheet 22 BASIC **Science Puzzlers, Twisters & Teasers,** Worksheet 22	**Multicultural Connection,** p. 597 in ATE	
Directed Reading Worksheet 22, Section 1 BASIC **Transparency 199,** How Rockets Work **Reinforcement Worksheet 22,** Ronnie Rocket BASIC	**Multicultural Connection,** p. 598 in ATE **Cross-Disciplinary Focus,** p. 599 in ATE **Connect to Physical Science,** p. 601 in ATE **MathBreak,** It's Just Rocket Science, p. 601 GENERAL	**Homework,** p. 600 in ATE GENERAL **Review,** p. 601 GENERAL **Quiz,** p. 601 in ATE GENERAL **Alternative Assessment,** p. 601 in ATE GENERAL
Directed Reading Worksheet 22, Section 2 BASIC	**Multicultural Connection,** p. 603 in ATE GENERAL **Real-World Connection,** p. 603 in ATE BASIC **Apply,** p. 603 GENERAL **Environment Connection,** p. 604 **Connect to Physical Science,** p. 604 in ATE	**Self-Check,** p. 603 **Homework,** p. 605 in ATE BASIC **Review,** p. 605 GENERAL **Quiz,** p. 605 in ATE GENERAL **Alternative Assessment,** p. 605 in ATE GENERAL
Directed Reading Worksheet 22, Section 3 BASIC **Transparency 200,** The Position of Space Probes **Transparency 251,** Forming Positive and Negative Ions **Critical Thinking Worksheet 22,** Spacecraft R' Us ADVANCED **Reinforcement Worksheet 22,** Probing Space BASIC	**Connect to Physical Science,** p. 608 in ATE **Cross-Disciplinary Focus,** p. 608 in ATE ADVANCED **Cross-Disciplinary Focus,** p. 609 in ATE GENERAL **Connect to Physical Science,** p. 610 in ATE **Biology Connection,** p. 611 **Holt Anthology of Science Fiction:** Why I Left Harry's All-Night Hamburgers ADVANCED	**Homework,** p. 610 in ATE BASIC **Review,** p. 611 GENERAL **Quiz,** p. 611 in ATE GENERAL **Alternative Assessment,** p. 611 in ATE GENERAL
Directed Reading Worksheet 22, Section 4 BASIC	**Multicultural Connection,** p. 613 in ATE **Connect to Physical Science,** p. 613 in ATE **Connect to Life Science,** p. 613 in ATE **Biology Connection,** p. 614 **Math and More,** p. 614 in ATE BASIC **Cross-Disciplinary Focus,** p. 616 in ATE ADVANCED **Across the Sciences:** International Space Station, p. 622	**Homework,** p. 613 in ATE GENERAL **Homework,** p. 614 in ATE GENERAL **Review,** p. 617 GENERAL **Quiz,** p. 617 in ATE GENERAL **Alternative Assessment,** p. 617 in ATE BASIC

 Holt, Rinehart and Winston On-line Resources
go.hrw.com
For worksheets and other teaching aids related to this chapter, visit the HRW Web site and type in the keyword: **HSTEXP**

 **National Science Teachers Association**
www.scilinks.org
Encourage students to use the *sci*LINKS numbers listed in the internet connect boxes to access information and resources on the **NSTA** Web site.

END-OF-CHAPTER REVIEW AND ASSESSMENT

Chapter Review in Study Guide
Vocabulary and Notes in Study Guide
Chapter Tests with Performance-Based Assessment, Chapter 22 Test
Chapter Tests with Performance-Based Assessment, Performance-Based Assessment 22
Concept Mapping Transparency 22

Chapter 22 • Chapter Organizer   **595B**

Chapter Resources & Worksheets

Visual Resources

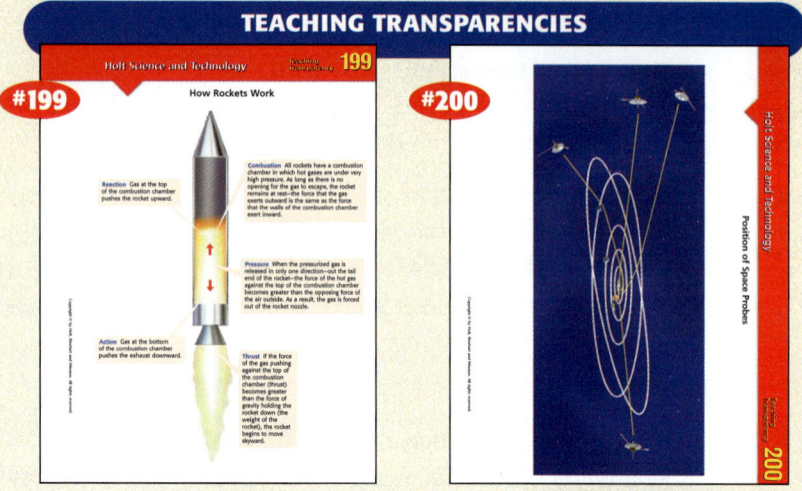

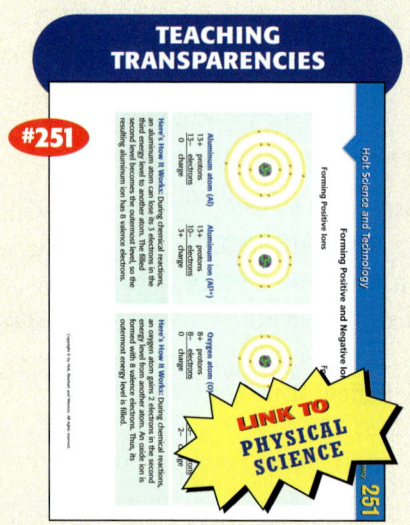

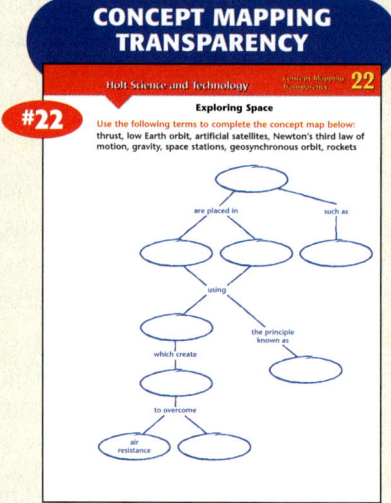

Meeting Individual Needs

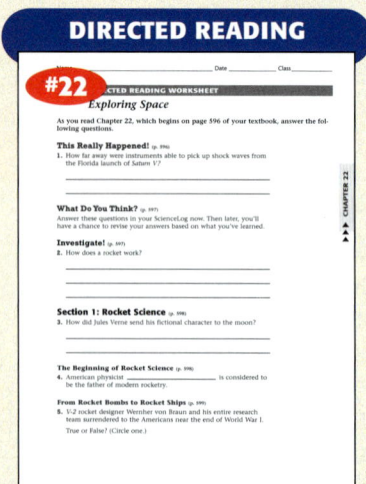

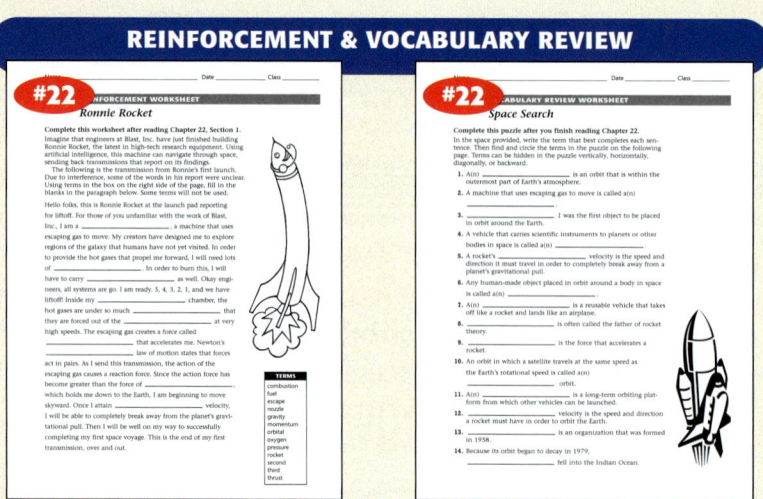

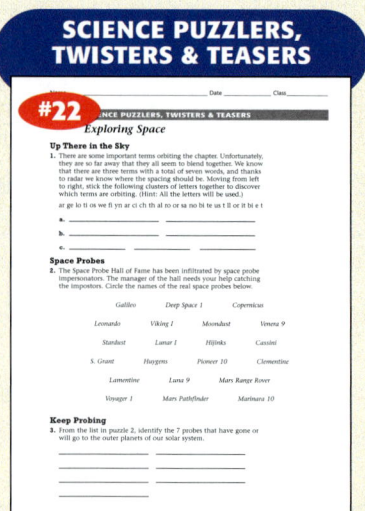

Chapter 22 • Exploring Space

Chapter 22 • Exploring Space

Review & Assessment

STUDY GUIDE
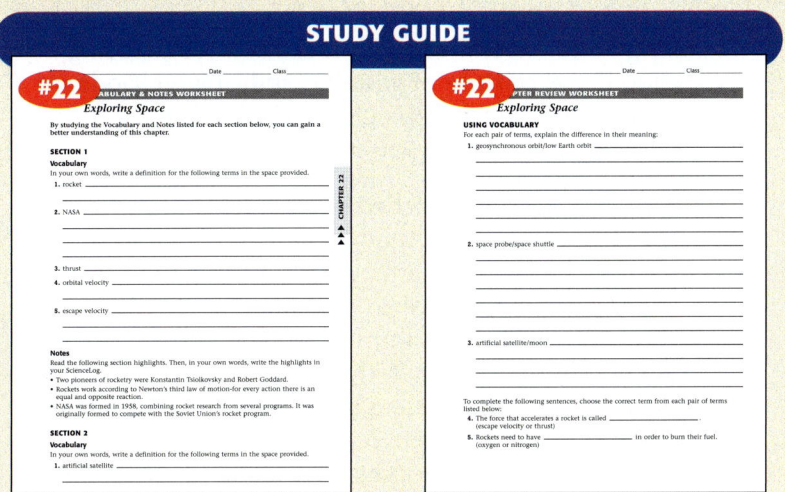

CHAPTER TESTS WITH PERFORMANCE-BASED ASSESSMENT
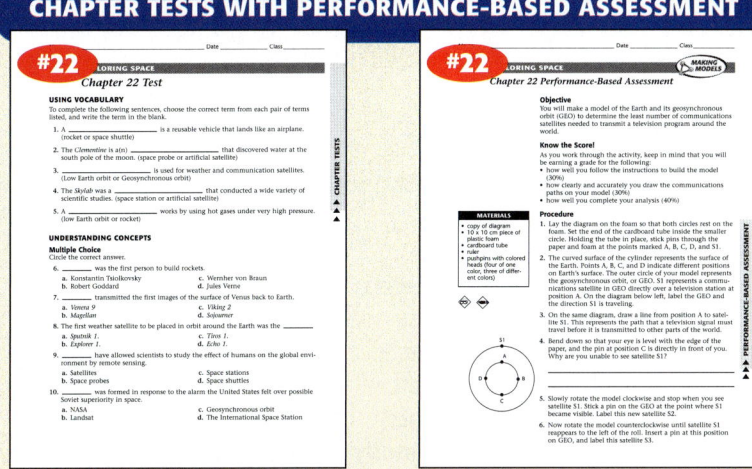

Lab Worksheets

INQUIRY LABS
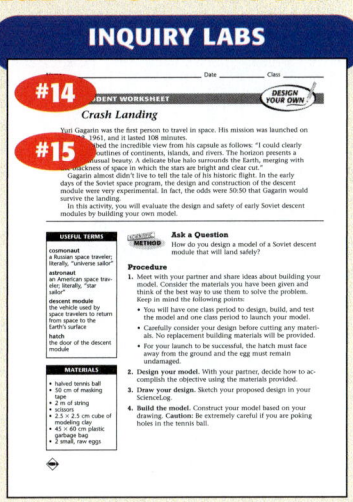

ECOLABS & FIELD ACTIVITIES
LONG-TERM PROJECTS & RESEARCH IDEAS

WHIZ-BANG DEMONSTRATIONS

DATASHEETS FOR LABBOOK
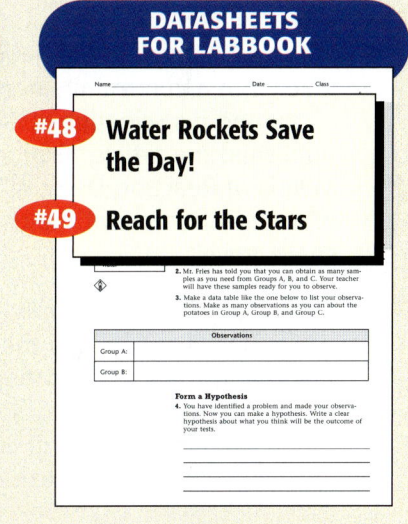

Applications & Extensions

CRITICAL THINKING & PROBLEM SOLVING
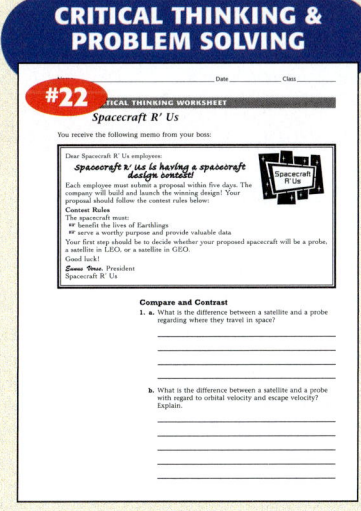

SCIENCE TECHNOLOGY
SCIENTISTS IN ACTION
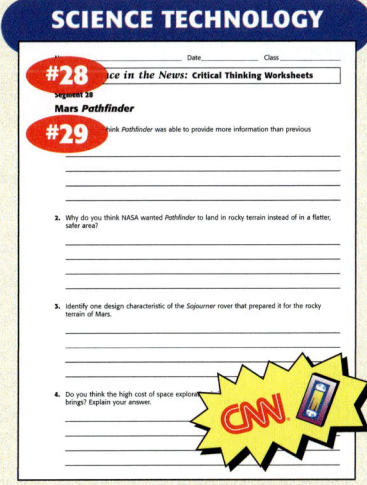

Chapter 22 • Chapter Resources & Worksheets   595D

Chapter Background

SECTION 1
Rocket Science

▶ **Konstantin Tsiolkovsky (1857–1935)**
As a youth, Konstantin Tsiolkovsky, the father of rocket theory, demonstrated a keen interest in science and mathematics. At age 9, a bout of scarlet fever left him partially deaf, and he spent much of his time studying on his own. After studying chemistry, astronomy, mathematics, and mechanics in Moscow, Tsiolkovsky got a job in 1876 as a mathematics teacher in a community north of Moscow. There he continued his scientific pursuits. In 1903, Tsiolkovsky published the article "Exploration of Cosmic Space by Means of Reaction Devices," the culmination of years of theorization about the use of rocket engines for space travel.

- In later years, Tsiolkovsky elaborated on his earlier theories, developing a theory of rocket propulsion and anticipating a number of technologies used in contemporary space exploration, including multistage boosters and the use of chemical propellants to achieve enough thrust to overcome Earth's gravity.

▶ **Robert Goddard (1882–1945)**
In his youth, Robert Goddard was an enthusiastic reader of science fiction tales of space travel, and at an early age he wrote a paper titled "The Navigation of Space." In 1912, Goddard developed a mathematical theory of rocket propulsion. He achieved a major breakthrough in 1915 when he proved that rocket engines would work in a vacuum and thus could be used for space travel.

- In 1919, Goddard published his research in the landmark paper "A Method of Reaching Extreme Altitudes," in which he argued that rockets could be used to escape Earth's gravity. Some people found Goddard's theories ludicrous. The *New York Times,* for example, scoffed at Goddard and questioned his scientific qualifications. Goddard, undeterred, continued to design and experiment with rockets. In 1926, using a liquid fuel mixture of gasoline and oxygen, Goddard launched his first liquid-fueled rocket, which ascended to a height of nearly 13 m in 2.5 seconds.

- In 1929, Goddard launched his first rocket to carry scientific instruments. The rocket rose about 30 m and then crashed to Earth, where it caught fire. People living nearby called the state fire marshal, who banned Goddard from doing any further rocket tests in Massachusetts. With a Guggenheim grant of $50,000, Goddard set up a test site in an unpopulated area outside of Roswell, New Mexico. He launched increasingly complex rockets that featured innovations such as steering systems, fuel pumps, and cooling mechanisms.

IS THAT A FACT!

▶ At his death in 1945, Goddard's immense contributions to rocket technology were still relatively unknown. By 1960, however, the U.S. Department of Defense and NASA had fully recognized Goddard's achievements and paid his estate $1 million for the use of his 214 patented rocket-componentry designs. A year later, NASA named the Goddard Space Flight Center in Greenbelt, Maryland, in his honor.

SECTION 2
Artificial Satellites

▶ **The Echo Satellites**
The United States launched its first communications satellite, *Echo I,* into orbit on August 12, 1960. *Echo I* was surprisingly simple in its design, consisting of an aluminum-coated plastic balloon that inflated to a diameter of 30 m when it reached orbit. From a low

Chapter 22 • Exploring Space

Earth orbit, *Echo I* reflected radio signals back to Earth until 1968. The United States placed a larger aluminized balloon satellite, *Echo II*, in orbit on January 25, 1964. *Echo II* remained functional until 1969.

IS THAT A FACT!

■ The *Echo II* satellite was part of the first cooperative space effort between the United States and the Soviet Union, when a radio signal from an observatory in England reflected off *Echo II* and was received in the Soviet Union.

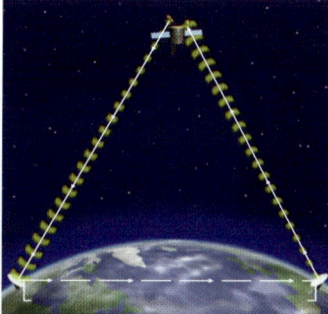

SECTION 3

Space Probes

▶ **Soviet Lunar Probes**
Although Soviet cosmonauts never landed on the moon, their *Luna* space probes gathered a remarkable amount of lunar data using robotics and remotely controlled devices. In 1966 the *Luna 9* became the first space probe to make a soft landing on the moon (previous probes crash-landed, and one shot past the moon into space). On impact, *Luna 9*'s egg-shaped instrument capsule rolled itself upright and automatically stabilized itself with four spring-loaded mechanisms. *Luna 9* sent the first television images of the lunar landscape back to Earth.

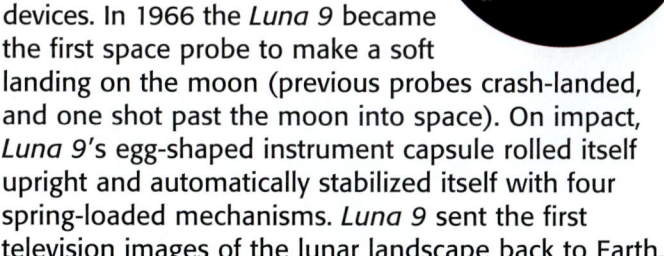

• Perhaps the most impressive of the Soviets' lunar space probes were *Luna 17* and *Luna 18*, which carried the eight-wheeled heavy-duty lunar rovers *Lunokhod 1* and *2*. From Earth, the vehicles were directed around treacherous craters to cover vast expanses of the moon's surface. The rovers took photos, collected soil samples, and carried out other tests. *Lunokhod 1* traveled over the moon's surface for 11 months and even recorded a solar eclipse, during which the temperature plunged 230°C.

SECTION 4

Living and Working in Space

▶ **The Daily Routine Aboard Skylab**
Measuring 36 m long and 6.4 m high, *Skylab* was luxuriously large in comparison with earlier spacecraft and had both working quarters and a living space. The living area included private sleeping quarters, a galley, a shower, and a suction toilet. Crew members carried out hundreds of astronomical and medical experiments.

• Astronauts were required to document everything they ate; measure the girth of their limbs, waists, and necks to check for muscle-tone loss; and wear electrodes while exercising so that their vital signs could be monitored. Astronauts did enjoy diversions such as "astrobatics"; in fact, *Skylab* astronaut Charles "Pete" Conrad commented, "We never went anywhere straight. We always did a somersault or a flip on the way."

IS THAT A FACT!

■ By the time of the Skylab missions, the infamous spacebars and tubes of gooey "spacefood" had been replaced with much more recognizable and palatable frozen, canned, and dehydrated foods. With more than 80 food items to choose from, a crew might whip up a breakfast of scrambled eggs, sausage, strawberries, bread and jam, orange juice, and coffee and finish out the day with a dinner of filet mignon, potato salad, and ice cream.

For background information about teaching strategies and issues, refer to the *Professional Reference for Teachers*.

Exploring Space

Pre-Reading Questions

Students may not know the answers to these questions before reading the chapter, so accept any reasonable response.

Suggested Answers

1. A satellite is any object in orbit around a planet or other body in the universe. A space probe is a human-made vehicle that carries scientific instruments to study objects in the universe.

2. Answers will vary. Students may note how technology developed for the space program has been adapted for life on Earth. They may also describe how scientific studies of planets and moons in our solar system have helped us understand the Earth's environment.

3. Answers will vary. Students may explain how the space stations such as *Skylab* and *Mir* have prepared astronauts to live and work in space. They may also note that the *International Space Station* is the next space station planned.

 Directed Reading Worksheet 22

 Science Puzzlers, Twisters & Teasers Worksheet 22

 Guided Reading Audio CD English or Spanish, Chapter 22

Exploring Space

Sections

1. **Rocket Science** 598
   Math Break 601
   Internet Connect 601

2. **Artificial Satellites** 602
   Apply 603
   Environment
      Connection 604
   Internet Connect 605

3. **Space Probes** 606
   Biology Connection .. 611
   Internet Connect 611

4. **Living and Working
   in Space** 612
   Biology Connection .. 614
   Internet Connect 617

   Chapter Review 620
   Feature Articles 622, 623
   LabBook 722–725

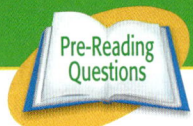 **Pre-Reading Questions**

1. What's the difference between a satellite and a space probe?
2. How has the space program benefited our daily lives?
3. How are humans preparing to live in space?

A Shuttle to Outer Space

The space shuttle was developed to take people into outer space. Because the shuttle can be reused, it lowers the cost of space launches by up to 90 percent. The lower cost of getting to outer space has opened a new era of space exploration in which space missions are more common. From these missions, scientists are able to gather important information that will eventually help humans adapt to living and working in space. In this chapter, you will see how technology and space exploration are connected and how they both impact us on Earth.

internet connect

 **HRW On-line Resources**
go.hrw.com
For worksheets and other teaching aids, visit the HRW Web site and type in the keyword: **HSTEXP**

 **www.scilinks.com**
Use the *sci*LINKS numbers at the end of each chapter for additional resources on the **NSTA** Web site.

 **www.cnnfyi.com**
Visit the CNN Web site for current events coverage and classroom resources.

START-UP Activity

ROCKET FUN

Rockets are used to send people into space. Rockets work by forcing hot gas out one end of a tube. As this gas escapes in one direction, the rocket moves in the opposite direction. While you may have let a full balloon loose many times before, here you will use a balloon to learn about the principles of rocket propulsion.

Procedure

1. Thread a **string** through a **drinking straw,** and tie the string between two things that won't move, such as chairs. Make sure that the string is tight.

2. Blow into a large **balloon** until it is the size of a grapefruit. Hold the neck of the balloon closed.

3. **Tape** the balloon to the straw so that the opening of the balloon points toward one end of the string.

4. Move the balloon and straw to one end of the string, and then release the neck of the balloon. Record what happens in your ScienceLog.

5. Fill the balloon until it is almost twice the size it was in step 2, and repeat steps 3 and 4. Again record your observations.

Analysis

6. What happened during the second test that was different from the first? Can you figure out why?

START-UP Activity

ROCKET FUN

MATERIALS

FOR EACH GROUP:
- string
- drinking straw
- large balloon
- tape

Teacher's Notes

Discuss the limitations of using a balloon to model a launch vehicle. If the balloon were to "launch" something, what improvements should be made? (Students may suggest that the balloon would need to be more powerful and able to sustain thrust for a longer period of time. In addition, the balloon would need a steering or guidance device.)

Answer to START-UP Activity

6. Sample answer: The balloon went faster and farther because the air inside it was under greater pressure. In addition, the balloon had to expel more air in the second trial.

Chapter 22 • Exploring Space

SECTION 1

Focus

Rocket Science

In this section, students learn about the contributions Konstantin Tsiolkovsky, Robert Goddard, and Wernher von Braun made to early rocket technology. Students also learn about the establishment of NASA and the development of rockets powerful enough to launch spacecraft into space. The section concludes with a discussion of the principles of rocket propulsion.

Bellringer

Ask students the question:
Why can't a commercial airplane be used for space exploration? (Students may reason that commercial airplanes cannot carry enough fuel for space exploration, that their engines are not powerful enough to escape Earth's gravity, and that they cannot withstand the extreme cold of space or the heat of reentry into Earth's atmosphere. Point out that jet engines rely on air for propulsion and fuel combustion, and that there is no air in space.) **Sheltered English**

1 Motivate

DEMONSTRATION

Attach a pre-stretched balloon over the mouth of a plastic bottle, and put the bottle in a bucket. Pour hot (but not boiling) water into the bucket. Explain that as the gases in the balloon become hot, they expand, causing the balloon to inflate. Explain that the expansion of hot gases is powerful enough to launch rockets into space. As rocket fuel burns, the heated gases inside the rocket expand. As the gases escape through the rocket nozzle, the rocket reacts by moving in the opposite direction—skyward.

SECTION 1

Terms to Learn
rocket
NASA
thrust
orbital velocity
escape velocity

What You'll Do
- Outline the early development of rocket technology.
- Explain how a rocket works.
- Explain the difference between orbital velocity and escape velocity.

Rocket Science

How would you get to the moon? Before the invention of rockets, people could only dream of going into outer space. Science fiction writers, such as Jules Verne, were able to dress those dreams in scientific clothing by using what seemed like reasonable means of getting into space. For example, in a story he wrote in 1865, some of Verne's characters rode a capsule to the moon shot from a giant 900 ft long cannon.

But, as growing knowledge about the heavens was stimulating the imagination of writers and readers alike, an invention was slowly being developed that would become the key to exploring space. This was the rocket. A **rocket** is a machine that uses escaping gas to move.

The Beginning of Rocket Science

Around the year 1900, a Russian high school teacher named Konstantin Tsiolkovsky (KAHN stan teen TSEE uhl KAHV skee) began trying to understand the reasoning behind the motion of rockets. Tsiolkovsky's inspiration came from the fantastic, imaginative stories of Jules Verne. Tsiolkovsky believed that rockets were the key to space exploration. In his words, "The Earth is the cradle of mankind. But one does not have to live in the cradle forever." Tsiolkovsky is considered the father of rocket theory.

Although Tsiolkovsky explained how rockets work, he never built any rockets himself. That was left to American physicist Robert Goddard, who became known as the father of modern rocketry.

Modern Rocketry Gets a Boost Goddard, shown in **Figure 1,** conducted many rocket experiments in Massachusetts from 1915 to 1930. He then moved to New Mexico, where deserts provided enough room to conduct his tests safely. Between 1930 and 1941, Goddard tested more than 150 rocket engines, and by the time of World War II, his work was receiving much attention, most notably from the United States military.

Figure 1 Robert Goddard tests one of his early rockets.

Multicultural CONNECTION

Many nations have taken an active role in space exploration. China launched its first satellite in 1970, and by late 1980, it was launching Western communications satellites in its advanced booster rockets. Before achieving launch capability in 1980, India had a number of satellites launched by the United States and the Soviet Union. An Indian astronaut took part in a *Soyuz* visit to the *Salyut 7* space station in 1984. In 1993, Brazil launched its first satellite. The satellite measures air pollution and collects data from 500 sensors along the Amazon River basin. Encourage interested students to find out more about the space programs of other countries.

598 Chapter 22 • Exploring Space

From Rocket Bombs to Rocket Ships

During World War II, Germany developed the V-2 rocket, shown in **Figure 2,** and used it to bomb England. The design for the V-2 rocket came from Wernher von Braun, a young Ph.D. student whose research was being supported by the German military. In 1945, near the end of the war, von Braun and his entire research team surrendered to the advancing Americans. The United States thus gained 127 of the best German rocket scientists, and rocket research in the United States boomed in the 1950s.

Figure 2 *The V-2 rocket is the direct ancestor of all modern space vehicles.*

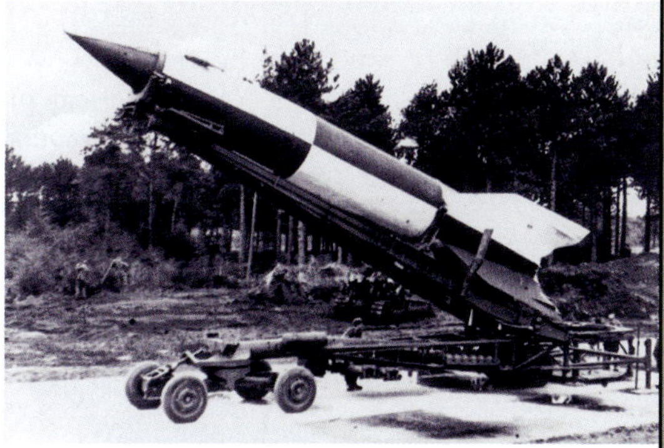

The Birth of NASA The end of World War II marked the beginning of the Cold War—the arms race between the United States and the Soviet Union. The Soviet Union was made up of Russia and 15 other countries, forming a superpower that supported a military rivaling that of the United States.

On July 29, 1958, in response to the alarm Americans felt over a possible Soviet superiority in space, the National Aeronautics and Space Administration, or **NASA,** was formed. This organization combined all of the separate rocket-development teams in the United States. Their combined efforts led to the development of a series of rockets, including the Saturn V rocket and those used to launch the space shuttle, as shown in **Figure 3.**

Figure 3 *Some of the space vehicles developed by NASA during its first 40 years are shown here to scale.*

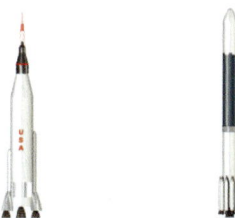

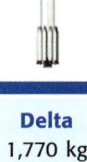

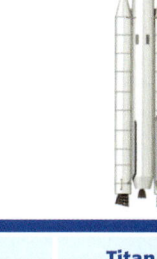

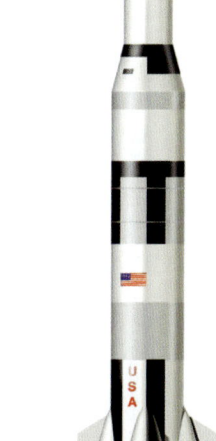

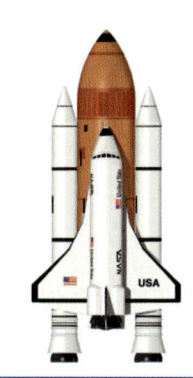

Mercury-Atlas	Delta	Titan IV	Saturn V	Space shuttle and boosters
1,400 kg payload	1,770 kg payload	18,000 kg payload	129,300 kg payload	29,500 kg payload
29 m tall	36 m tall	62 m tall	111 m tall	56 m tall

2 Teach

CROSS-DISCIPLINARY FOCUS

History Make sure students understand that the term *cold war* describes a period of tense or strained political relations without actual military aggression. You might explain to students that after World War II, the United States and its allies followed very different political and economic policies from the Soviet Union and its allies. The two powers viewed each other with suspicion and fear. Both countries responded by spending tremendous amounts of money to increase their military strength. An arms race led to the proliferation of nuclear weapons, which increased tensions further with the fear that nuclear war could destroy all of humanity. For both sides, space exploration became a yardstick of national superiority and played an important role in the development of military weapons.

CROSS-DISCIPLINARY FOCUS

PORTFOLIO

Language Arts The works of Jules Verne inspired both Goddard and Tsiolkovsky to develop rocket theory. Have interested students read sections from Jules Verne's *From the Earth to the Moon* or *Around the Moon.* Suggest that students compare Verne's descriptions of spaceships and how they were powered with what they are learning in this section. Ask them to consider how accurately Verne predicted the future of space travel. Have students summarize their thoughts in a written book report. Students may also wish to find out about the influence of H. G. Wells on the development of space science.

SCIENCE HUMOR

Robert Goddard experienced several spectacular failures while trying to develop the liquid-fuel rocket. Several rockets exploded on the launch pad before ever lifting off. After one failed test, Goddard dryly commented, "Well, there goes $10,000 up in smoke."

Directed Reading Worksheet 22 Section 1

internetconnect

SCI LINKS. NSTA

TOPIC: Rocket Technology
GO TO: www.scilinks.org
***sci*LINKS NUMBER:** HSTE530

3) Extend

Water Rockets Save the Day! PG 722

Meeting Individual Needs

Learners Having Difficulty
Explain Newton's third law by asking students to imagine firefighters directing a hose at a fire. The reason why firefighters brace their bodies as they hold the hose is that the force of the water causes the nozzle to move backward in *reaction*.

But how can a gas move a heavy, solid rocket? Imagine a cannon shooting a cannon ball. You know the cannon ball goes far and fast in the direction it is shot. The cannon, which has a lot more mass than the ball, recoils backward at a much slower speed and in the opposite direction as the cannon ball travels. In the same manner, when a rocket is launched, the hot gases within the rocket rush out of the exhaust nozzle at high speeds. The rocket reacts by moving upward at a slower speed.

Homework

Poster Project Have students make a series of sketches that show the evolution of rocket design. Encourage them to use poster board so they can make scale models to compare the size of the spacecraft. Have students write a brief description of the function of each spacecraft. Alternately, have students write a report on the life of Konstantin Tsiolkovsky, Robert Goddard, or Wernher von Braun.

Teaching Transparency 199
"How Rockets Work"

600 Chapter 22 • Exploring Space

How Rockets Work

As you saw in the Investigate, rockets work on a simple physical principle. This principle, known as *Newton's third law of motion,* states that for every action there is an equal reaction in the opposite direction. For example, the air rushing backward from a balloon (the action) is paired with the forward motion of the balloon itself (the reaction).

In the case of rockets, however, the equality between the action and the reaction may not be obvious. This is because the mass of a rocket—which includes all of the fuel it carries—is much more than the mass of the hot gases as they come out of the exhaust nozzle. Because the hot gases are under extreme pressure, however, they exert a tremendous amount of force. The force that accelerates a rocket is called **thrust.** To learn more about how this works, look at **Figure 4.**

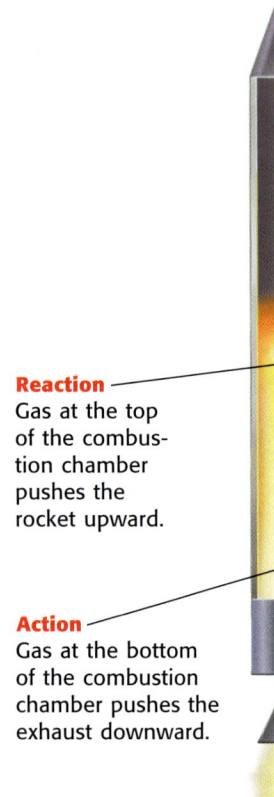

Figure 4 *Rockets work according to Newton's third law of motion.*

Reaction
Gas at the top of the combustion chamber pushes the rocket upward.

Action
Gas at the bottom of the combustion chamber pushes the exhaust downward.

Combustion All rockets have a combustion chamber in which hot gases are under very high pressure. As long as there is no opening for the gas to escape, the rocket remains at rest. In this state, the force that the gas exerts outward is the same as the force that the walls of the combustion chamber exert inward.

Pressure When the pressurized gas is released in only one direction—out the tail end of the rocket—the force of the hot gas against the top of the combustion chamber becomes greater than the opposing force of the air outside. As a result, the gas is forced out of the rocket nozzle.

Thrust If the force of the gas pushing against the top of the combustion chamber (thrust) becomes greater than the force of gravity holding the rocket down (the weight of the rocket), the rocket begins to move skyward.

MISCONCEPTION ALERT

Rockets don't move by pushing against air in the atmosphere. The reaction to the force and direction of the exhaust causes a rocket to move. That is why rockets can accelerate in the vacuum of space, where there is nothing to push against. In fact, rockets accelerate more efficiently in space, where there is no friction to slow them down.

IS THAT A FACT!

As a rocket moves away from Earth, the gravitational pull and the air resistance exerted on the rocket decrease. In addition, the rocket's mass decreases as it burns fuel. Thus, rockets accelerate as they travel from Earth's surface. The space shuttle accelerates from zero to 27,000 km/h in a little over 8 minutes!

How Fast Is Fast Enough? It is not enough for a rocket to have sufficient thrust to just move upward. It must have enough thrust to achieve *orbital velocity*. **Orbital velocity** is the speed and direction a rocket must have in order to orbit the Earth. The lowest possible speed a rocket may go and still orbit the Earth is about 8 km/s.

For Earth, all speeds less than about 8 km/s are *suborbital*. If the rocket goes any slower, it will fall back to Earth. If a rocket travels fast enough, however, it can attain *escape velocity*. **Escape velocity** is the speed and direction a rocket must travel in order to completely break away from a planet's gravitational pull. As you can see in **Figure 5,** the speed a rocket must attain to escape the Earth is about 11 km/s.

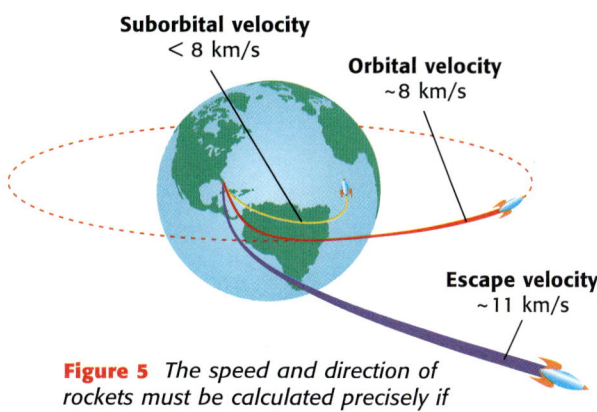

Figure 5 The speed and direction of rockets must be calculated precisely if they are to attain orbit.

You Need More Than Rocket Fuel . . . Rockets burn fuel to provide the thrust that propels them forward. But in order for something to burn, oxygen must be present. The earliest rocket fuel was gunpowder, which burns because oxygen is present in the atmosphere. Goddard was the first to use liquid fuel for rockets, which also burns in the presence of oxygen. But while oxygen is plentiful at the Earth's surface, in the upper atmosphere and in outer space, there is little or no oxygen. For this reason, rockets that go into outer space must carry enough oxygen with them to be able to burn their fuel. Otherwise the escaping gas would not create enough thrust to propel the rocket forward.

REVIEW

1. What force must we overcome to reach outer space?
2. How does a rocket engine work?
3. What is the difference between orbital velocity and escape velocity?
4. **Making Inferences** How did World War II help us get into space exploration earlier than we otherwise would have?

MATH BREAK

It's Just Rocket Science

As a burning gas (g) rushes out the back of a rocket (r), it provides thrust to move the rocket. The mass (m) and speed (v) of the gas and rocket are given by the following equation:

$$m_g \times v_g = m_r \times v_r$$

If the mass of a rocket is 100,000 kg, the speed of the gas leaving the rocket is 1,000 m/s, and the mass of the gas leaving the rocket is 1,000 kg, how fast will the rocket move?

internetconnect

SC_{*INKS.*}
NSTA

TOPIC: Rocket Technology
GO TO: www.scilinks.org
*sci*LINKS NUMBER: HSTE530

SECTION 2

Focus

Artificial Satellites

In this section, students learn about the first artificial satellites. They will learn about different kinds of satellites, what they are used for, and which orbits they are placed in. Students also learn how remote sensing devices have helped us understand Earth as a global system. Finally, students will learn about current developments in satellite technology.

Bellringer

Ask students to list the ways they benefit from satellite technology. (Students might mention the Global Positioning System, satellite television, cellular phones, or accurate weather forecasts.)

Ask students to write two paragraphs describing the ways satellite technology affects their lives.

1 Motivate

ACTIVITY

Students may think that satellites and the Space Shuttle orbit far above Earth. Actually, satellites orbiting in LEO are only around 300 km above Earth. To give students an idea of how low this orbit really is, have students find two cities on a globe that are 300 km apart. For example, the distance from Boston to New York is about 300 km. Have students mark the distance on a piece of string and then turn the string perpendicular to the surface of the globe—LEO is only 4 percent of Earth's diameter. You may wish to contrast this altitude with a GEO orbit, which is 35,862 km high.

Section 2

Terms to Learn
artificial satellite
low Earth orbit
geosynchronous orbit

What You'll Do

- Describe how the launch of the first satellite started the space race.
- Explain why some orbits are better than others for communications satellites.
- Describe how the satellite program has given us a better understanding of the Earth as a global system.

Figure 6 *Sputnik 1 was the first artificial satellite successfully placed in Earth orbit.*

Directed Reading Worksheet 22 Section 2

TOPIC: Artificial Satellites
GO TO: www.scilinks.org
sciLINKS NUMBER: HSTE540

Artificial Satellites

In 1955, President Dwight D. Eisenhower announced that the United States would launch an artificial satellite as part of America's contribution to international space science. An **artificial satellite** is any human-made object placed in orbit around a body in space, such as Earth. The Soviets were also working on a satellite program—and launched their satellite first!

The Space Race Begins

On October 4, 1957, a Soviet satellite became the first object to be placed in orbit around the Earth. *Sputnik 1*, shown in **Figure 6**, carried instruments to measure the properties of Earth's upper atmosphere. Less than a month later, the Soviets launched *Sputnik 2*. This satellite carried a dog named Laika.

Two months later, the U.S. Navy attempted to launch its own satellite by using a Vanguard rocket, which was originally intended for launching weather instruments into the atmosphere. To the embarrassment of the United States, the rocket rose only 1 m into the air and exploded.

The U.S. Takes a Close Second In the meantime, the U.S. Army was also busy modifying its military rockets to send a satellite into space, and on January 31, 1958, *Explorer 1*, the first United States satellite, was successfully launched. The space race was on!

Explorer 1, shown in **Figure 7**, carried scientific instruments to measure cosmic rays and small dust particles and to record temperatures of the upper atmosphere. *Explorer 1* discovered the Van Allen radiation belts around the Earth. These are regions in the Earth's magnetic field where charged particles from the sun have been trapped.

Figure 7 *From left to right, NASA scientists William Pickering, James Van Allen, and Wernher von Braun show off a model of the first successfully launched American artificial satellite, Explorer 1.*

SCIENCE HUMOR

When the first American satellite exploded on the launch pad on December 6, 1957, the London *Daily Herald* poked fun at the embarrassing incident by printing the headline "Oh, What a Flopnik!" comparing it to the successful Soviet Sputnik missions.

Into the Information Age

The first United States weather satellite, *Tiros 1*, was launched in April 1960 and gave meteorologists their first look at the Earth and its clouds from above. Weather satellites have given us an understanding of how storms develop and change by helping us study wind patterns and ocean currents. You now can see weather satellite images on your television at almost any time of the day or night or download them from the Internet.

Just a few months after *Tiros 1* began returning signals to Earth, the United States launched its first communications satellite, *Echo 1*. This satellite bounced signals from the ground to other areas on Earth, as shown in **Figure 8**. Within 3 years, sophisticated communications-satellite networks were sending TV signals from continent to continent.

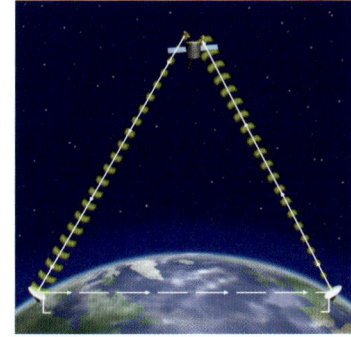

Figure 8 Satellites can send signals beyond the curve of the Earth's surface, enabling communication around the world.

Choose Your Orbit

All of the early satellites were placed in **low Earth orbit** (LEO), a few hundred kilometers above the Earth's surface. This location, while considered space, is still within the outermost part of Earth's atmosphere. A satellite in LEO travels around the Earth very quickly, which can place it out of contact much of the time.

Science fiction writer Arthur C. Clarke suggested a much higher orbit than LEO for weather and communications satellites. In this orbit, called a **geosynchronous orbit** (GEO), a satellite travels around the Earth at a speed that exactly matches the rotational speed of the Earth. This keeps the satellite positioned above the same spot on Earth at all times. Today there are many communications satellites in GEO. Ground stations are in continuous contact with these satellites, so your television program or phone call is not interrupted.

Self-Check

The space station being built by the United States and other countries is in LEO. What is one advantage of this location? *(See page 726 to check your answer.)*

Anything GOES

The height above the Earth's surface for a geosynchronous orbit is 35,862 km. Today, a network of Geostationary Operational Environment Satellites (GOES) provides us with an international network of weather satellites. What would happen if a GOES satellite were placed in LEO rather than in GEO? How would that adversely affect the information the satellite was able to collect?

Multicultural CONNECTION

INTELSAT is an international not-for-profit communications satellite cooperative representing more than 140 nations. Decisions about the system's upkeep and future are reached by consensus among the member nations. INTELSAT satellites relay telephone calls, television broadcasts, and other telecommunications data. During the 1998 Winter Olympics, INTELSAT linked people from China, Germany, South Africa, the United States, Australia, and Japan to form an international 2,000-member chorus. Have groups of students work together to write a proposal to launch a satellite that would benefit the global community.

3) Extend

Going Further

Satellites such as those in the Landsat program are deployed in polar orbits; that is, they orbit Earth from pole to pole. Have students find out why polar orbits are best for mapping purposes. (One reason is that as the Landsat satellites orbit the Earth, the Earth rotates beneath them. In this way, the satellites can survey the entire planet without changing their orbit.)

Ask them to write a brief explanation of the advantages of polar orbits and to draw a diagram showing the path a satellite in a polar orbit would take. Students might also include depictions of satellites in other types of orbits.

CONNECT TO PHYSICAL SCIENCE

What causes objects to heat up as they enter our atmosphere? People generally assume that friction from high-speed collisions with air molecules generates this thermal energy. Actually, friction plays a minor role compared with pressure. As an object such as a spacecraft enters our atmosphere, it compresses a layer of air about a meter deep beneath it. Imagine a snow plow pushing a mound of snow before it. As the layer of air beneath the spacecraft reaches tremendous pressures, it transfers thermal energy to the surface of the spacecraft by conduction, causing it to glow red-hot. If students have ever inflated a bike tire using a well-oiled pump, they have observed this effect: the repeated compression of air causes the pump to become hot. For this reason, LEO satellites orbit in the outer reaches of Earth's atmosphere at a point where air pressure is insignificant.

Environment CONNECTION

After more than 40 years of space launches, the space near Earth is getting cluttered with "space junk." The United States Space Command—a new branch of the military—tracks nearly 10,000 pieces of debris larger than a few centimeters. Left uncontrolled, all this debris may become a problem for space vehicles in the future!

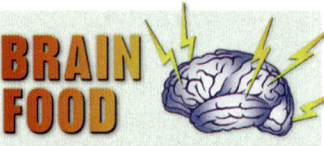

BRAIN FOOD

Not all satellites look down on Earth. Among the most important satellites to astronomers, for example, are the Hubble Space Telescope and the Chandra X-ray Observatory, both of which look out toward the stars.

Results of the Satellite Programs

Satellites gather information by *remote sensing*. Remote sensing is the gathering of images and data from high above the Earth's surface. The images and data help us investigate the Earth's surface by measuring the light and other forms of energy that reflect off Earth. Some satellites use radar, which bounces high-frequency radio waves off the surface of objects and measures the returned signal.

Military Satellites
The United States military, which has a keen interest in satellites for defense and spying purposes, recognized that LEO was a perfect location for placing powerful telescopes that could be turned toward the Earth to photograph activities on the ground anywhere in the world.

The period from the late 1940s to the late 1980s is known as the Cold War. During that time, the United States and the former Soviet Union built up their military forces in order to ensure that neither nation became more powerful than the other. Both countries monitored each other using spy satellites. **Figure 9** shows an image of part of the United States taken by a Soviet spy satellite during the Cold War.

The military also launches satellites into GEO to aid in navigation and to serve as early warning systems against missiles launched toward the United States. Even though the Cold War is over, spy satellites continue to play an important role in the United States's military defense.

Figure 9 *This image was taken in 1989 by a Soviet spy satellite in LEO about 220 km above the city of San Francisco. Can you identify any objects on the ground?*

WEIRD SCIENCE

Geosynchronous satellites generally have a life span of 5–13 years. Because there are a limited number of locations around the equator in which geosynchronous satellites may orbit, "dead" satellites must be disposed of in some way. Currently, satellites use their remaining propellant to navigate into a higher "graveyard orbit." Once in a graveyard orbit, a dead satellite circles Earth every 2–5 days and does not interfere with operating satellites in geosynchronous orbits.

Eyes on the Environment

Satellites have given us a new vantage point for looking at the Earth. By getting above the Earth's atmosphere and looking down, we have been able to study the Earth in ways that were never before possible.

One of the most successful remote-sensing projects was the Landsat program, which began in 1972 and continues today. It has given us the longest continuous record of Earth's surface as seen from space. The newest Landsat satellite (number 7) was launched in 1999. It will gather images in several frequencies—from visible light that we can see to infrared. The Landsat program has produced millions of images that are being used to identify and track global and regional changes on Earth, as shown in **Figure 10.**

Remote sensing has allowed scientists to perform large-scale mapping, look at changes in patterns of vegetation growth, map the spread of urban development, help with mineral exploration, and study the effect of humans on the global environment.

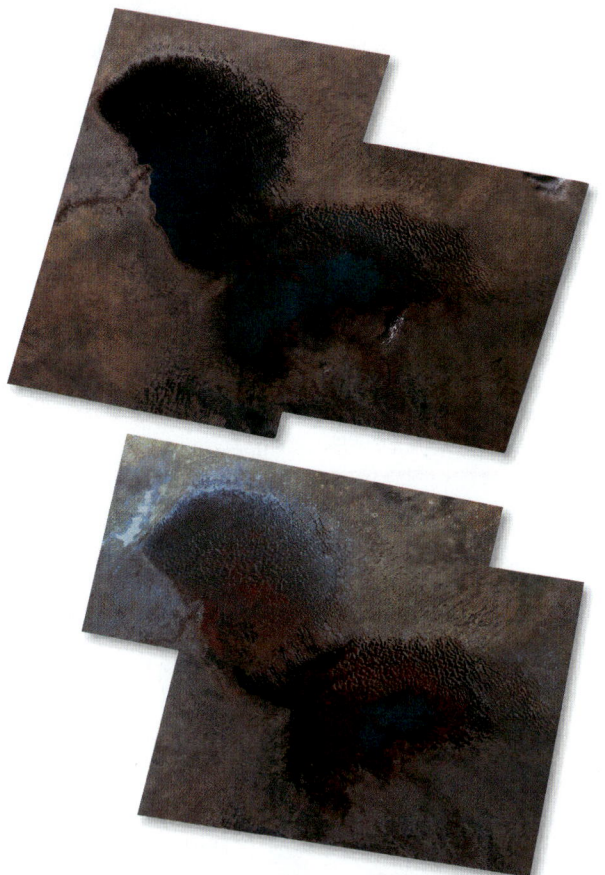

Figure 10 *These Landsat images of Lake Chad, Africa, show how environmental changes can be monitored from orbit. The top image was taken in 1973, and the bottom image was taken in 1987. Can you tell what changed?*

REVIEW

1. What types of satellites did the United States first place in orbit?
2. List two ways that satellites have benefited human society.
3. **Applying Concepts** The Hubble Space Telescope is located in LEO. Will the telescope move faster or slower around the Earth compared with a geosynchronous weather satellite? Explain.

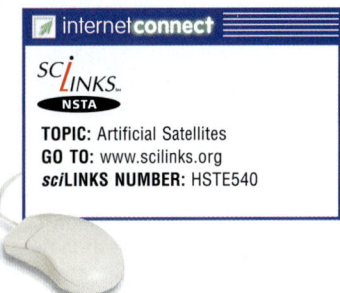

internetconnect

SC**LINKS** NSTA
TOPIC: Artificial Satellites
GO TO: www.scilinks.org
sciLINKS NUMBER: HSTE540

Answers to Review

1. The first satellites launched by the United States carried scientific instruments to low Earth orbit.
2. Answers will vary. Satellites have improved communications and helped us study the Earth from space.
3. The Hubble Space telescope moves faster than a geosynchronous satellite. To maintain a LEO orbit, an object must travel very fast.

4) Close

Quiz

1. What is an artificial satellite? (any human-made object placed in orbit around a body in space)
2. What was the name of the first satellite to be placed in orbit, and what nation launched it? (The Soviet Union launched *Sputnik 1*.)
3. What is a geosynchronous orbit? (In a geosynchronous orbit, a satellite travels at a speed that matches the rotational speed of the Earth; it completes one orbit in the same length of time that Earth completes one rotation.)

ALTERNATIVE ASSESSMENT

Have students construct a timeline showing the development of artificial satellite technology from 1957 to the present.

Homework

Making Observations Have students go outside on a clear evening and look for satellites. Satellites do not produce their own light; they reflect sunlight and "Earthshine" off their surfaces. The best time to view satellites is about an hour after sunset or an hour before sunrise. Encourage students to lie on the ground or sit in a reclining chair and scan the skies for satellites. Students can use binoculars if they are available. A satellite will look like a star moving across the sky in a straight line. It will fade out of sight before it reaches the horizon. Satellites can be seen moving from west to east or from pole to pole. Geosynchronous satellites are difficult to detect because they do not appear to move at all.

Section 2 • Artificial Satellites

SECTION 3

Focus

Space Probes

The section describes some of the discoveries made by the earliest space probes. Students will also learn about the data gathered by recent probes that have visited the inner and outer planets. The section discusses how space probe missions to other planets have helped us understand more about the Earth. Finally, students will learn about a new approach to space exploration—"faster, cheaper, and better."

Bellringer

Ask students to consider the following question:

> Does exploring other planets benefit us here on Earth? Why or why not?

1) Motivate

ACTIVITY

Design Your Own Space Mission Have students imagine that they could send a space probe anywhere in the solar system. In their ScienceLogs, have students write a paragraph about where they would send their probe, what kind of instruments it would carry, what kind of data it would collect, and what its primary mission would be. Invite volunteers to read their paragraphs to the class and to elaborate on their choices. Sheltered English

Directed Reading Worksheet 22 Section 3

Section 3

Terms to Learn
space probe

What You'll Do
- Describe some of the discoveries made by space probes.
- Explain how space-probe missions help us better understand the Earth.
- Describe how future space-probe missions will differ from the original missions to the planets.

Space Probes

The 1960s and early 1970s are known as the golden era of space exploration. The Soviets were the first to successfully launch a space probe. A **space probe** is a vehicle that carries scientific instruments to planets or other bodies in space. Unlike satellites, which stay in Earth orbit, space probes travel away from Earth. The early space probes gave us our first close encounters with the other planets and their moons.

Visits to Our Planetary Neighborhood

Because the Earth's moon and the inner planets of the solar system are so much closer to us than any other celestial bodies, they were the first to be targeted for exploration by the Soviet Union and the United States. Launched by the Soviets, *Luna 1* was the first space probe. In January of 1959, it flew past the moon. Two months later, an American space probe—*Pioneer 4*—accomplished the same feat. Follow along the next few pages to learn about space-probe missions since *Luna 1*.

The Moon

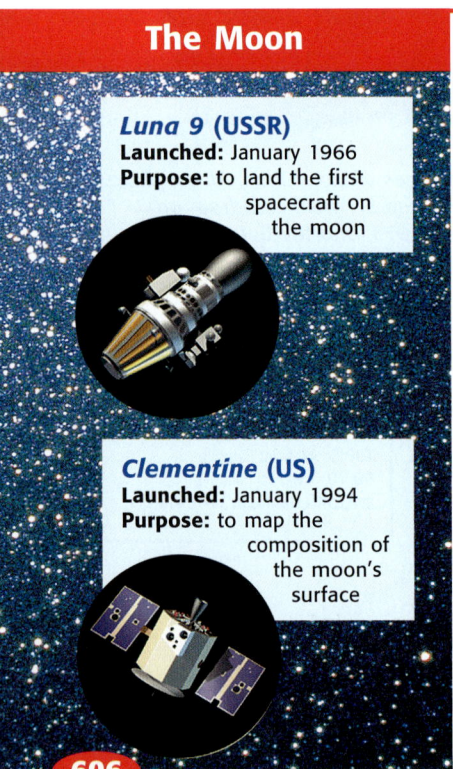

Luna 9 (USSR)
Launched: January 1966
Purpose: to land the first spacecraft on the moon

Clementine (US)
Launched: January 1994
Purpose: to map the composition of the moon's surface

The Luna 9 and Clementine Missions *Luna 9*, a Soviet probe, made the first soft landing on the moon's surface. During the next 10 years, there were more than 30 lunar missions made by the Soviet Union and the United States. Thousands of images of the moon's surface were taken.

In 1994, the probe *Clementine* discovered possible signs of water at the south pole of the moon. The image below was taken by the *Clementine* space probe and shows the area surrounding the south pole of the moon. You can see that some of the craters at the pole are permanently in shadow. Elsewhere on the moon, sunlight would cause any ice to vaporize. Ice may have been left by comet impacts. If this frozen water exists, it will be very valuable to humans seeking to colonize the moon.

Lunar South Pole

IS THAT A FACT!

The level of navigational accuracy required to have a space probe reach another planet is comparable to throwing a baseball from Los Angeles so accurately that it would fly through a predetermined window in New York City's Empire State Building!

The Venera 9 Mission The Soviet Union landed the first probe on Venus. The probe, called *Venera 9*, parachuted into Venus's atmosphere and transmitted the first images of the surface. *Venera 9* found that surface temperature and atmospheric pressure on Venus are much higher than on Earth. It also found that the chemistry of the surface rocks is similar to that of rocks on Earth. Perhaps most importantly, *Venera 9* and earlier missions showed us a planet with a severe greenhouse effect. Scientists study Venus's atmosphere to learn about how greenhouse gases released into Earth's atmosphere trap thermal energy.

The Magellan Mission In 1989, the United States launched the *Magellan* probe, which used radar to map 98 percent of the surface of Venus. The Magellan mission showed that, in many ways, the geology of Venus is similar to that of Earth. Venus has features that suggest some type of plate tectonics occurs, as it does on Earth. Venus also has volcanoes, some of which may have been active recently. The diagram at below left shows the *Magellan* probe using radar to penetrate the thick cloud layer. The radar data were then transmitted back to Earth, where computers were able to use the data to generate three-dimensional maps like the one at below right.

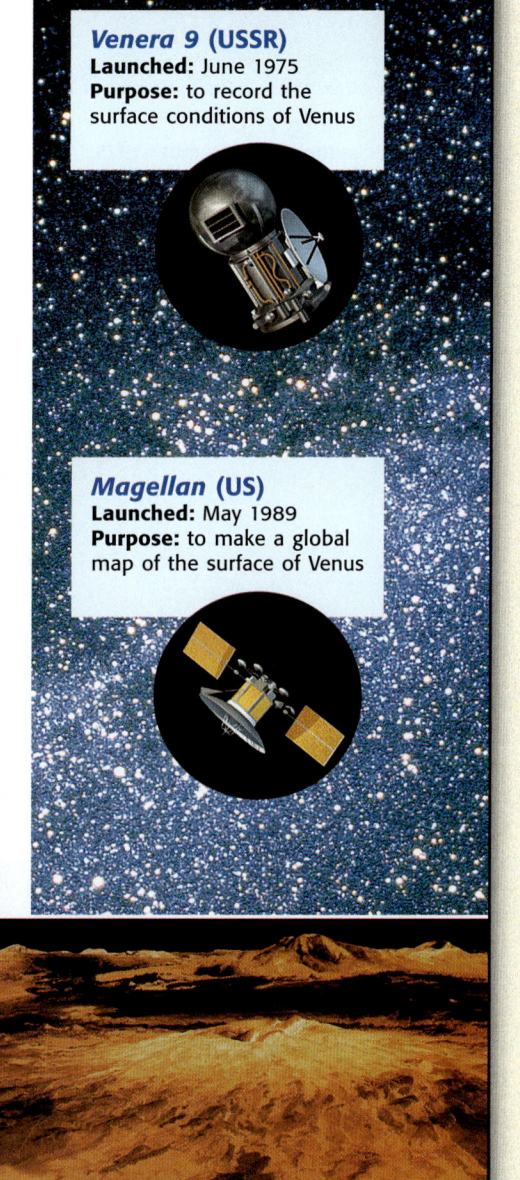

Venus

Venera 9 (USSR)
Launched: June 1975
Purpose: to record the surface conditions of Venus

Magellan (US)
Launched: May 1989
Purpose: to make a global map of the surface of Venus

2 Teach

USING THE FIGURE
Have students study the images of space probes in this section. Then have students design and draw their own version of a space probe. Have them outline their probe's mission and give the probe an appropriate name. **Sheltered English**

ACTIVITY
Designing a Mission Patch Astronauts Gordon Cooper and Charles "Pete" Conrad, members of the 1965 *Gemini 5* mission, began a NASA tradition by designing a patch to be worn on their spacesuits that symbolized the purpose of their mission. As students read about the space-probe missions described in the section, have them choose one and then create a patch design that commemorates the purpose and accomplishments of that mission. Students might also include a motto on their patches. Patch designs are available on the NASA Web site.

USING SCIENCE FICTION
Have students read "Why I left Harry's All-Night Hamburgers" by Lawrence-Watt Evans in the *Holt Anthology of Science Fiction*.

Science Bloopers
For the first half of the twentieth century, a popular theory suggested that every planet had once supported life or would support it in the future. The theory was based on the idea that the sun has gradually cooled since its formation. Thus, Mars had once harbored life; it was currently Earth's turn, and Venus would be next.

Some scientists thought that Venus might already be home to primitive life-forms equivalent to those of Earth's Cambrian period. However, the 1962 *Mariner 2* flyby showed that Venus was a constant 464°C. We also know now that the sun is becoming hotter, not cooler.

② Teach, continued

DISCUSSION

Ask students to discuss the advantages and disadvantages of using small space probes to explore the solar system and beyond. In what other types of situations do scientists use probes? Have students find out the amount of time it took for each probe to reach its destination. Remind students that if astronauts had been on these missions, the time would have to be doubled to allow for their return to Earth. **Sheltered English**

CONNECT TO PHYSICAL SCIENCE

Voyagers 1 and *2, Galileo,* and *Ulysses,* have used a maneuver called a *gravity assist* to explore the solar system. In a gravity assist, spacecraft make use of a planet's gravitational pull to accelerate, slow down, or change direction. Accomplishing such maneuvers using gravity is a triumph of Newtonian physics, and it saves a tremendous amount of fuel. A slingshot analogy is sometimes used to describe gravity assists because of the way the spacecraft swings around the planet and is released, slingshotting out into space in a new flight path. *Voyagers 1* and *2* gained momentum with gravity assists from Jupiter, Saturn, Uranus, and Neptune. The *Ulysses* space probe obtained a gravity assist from Jupiter that sent it into a highly inclined trajectory, which eventually placed it in a polar orbit around the sun.

internetconnect
SCI LINKS TOPIC: Space Probes
NSTA GO TO: www.scilinks.org
sciLINKS NUMBER: HSTE545

Mars

Viking 2 (US)
Launched: September 1975
Purpose: to search for life on the surface of Mars

Mars Pathfinder (US)
Launched: December 1996
Purpose: to use inexpensive technology to study the surface of Mars

The Viking Missions In 1975, the United States sent a pair of probes—*Viking 1* and *Viking 2*—to Mars. Because the surface of Mars is more like the Earth's surface than that of any other planet, one of the main goals of the Viking missions was to look for signs of life. The probes contained instruments designed to collect soil samples and test them for evidence of life. However, no hard evidence was found. The Viking missions did find evidence that Mars was once much warmer and wetter than it is now. The probes sent back images of dry water channels on the planet's surface. This discovery led scientists to ask even more questions about Mars. Why and when did the Martian climate change?

The Mars Pathfinder Mission More than 20 years later, in 1997, the surface of Mars was visited again by a NASA space probe. The goal of the Mars Pathfinder mission was to show that Martian exploration is possible at a lower cost than that of the larger Viking mission. The *Mars Pathfinder* successfully landed on Mars and deployed the *Sojourner* rover, which traveled across the planetary surface for almost 3 months, collecting data and recording images of the Martian surface, as shown at left.

CROSS-DISCIPLINARY FOCUS

History On January 23, 1967, the United Nations Outer Space Treaty was signed. The treaty guarantees all nations the freedom to explore and use space. The treaty emphasizes a humanistic and pacifist philosophy, which governs the actions of countries as they explore outer space, the moon, and other celestial objects. Have students research this treaty and outline its major points.

The Pioneer and Voyager Missions The *Pioneer 10* and *Pioneer 11* space probes were the first to visit the outer planets. Among other things, these probes sampled the *solar wind*—the flow of particles coming from the sun. The Pioneer probes also found that the dark belts on Jupiter are warmer than the light belts and that these dark belts provide deeper views into Jupiter's atmosphere. In June of 1983, *Pioneer 10* became the first space probe to travel past the orbit of Pluto, the outermost planet.

The Voyager space probes were the first to detect Jupiter's faint rings, and *Voyager 2* was the first space probe to fly by the four gas giant planets—Jupiter, Saturn, Uranus, and Neptune. The paths of the Pioneer and Voyager space probes are shown below. Today they are all near the edge of the solar system and are still sending back information.

The Outer Solar System

Pioneer 10 (US)
Launched: March 1972
Purpose: to study Jupiter and the outer solar system

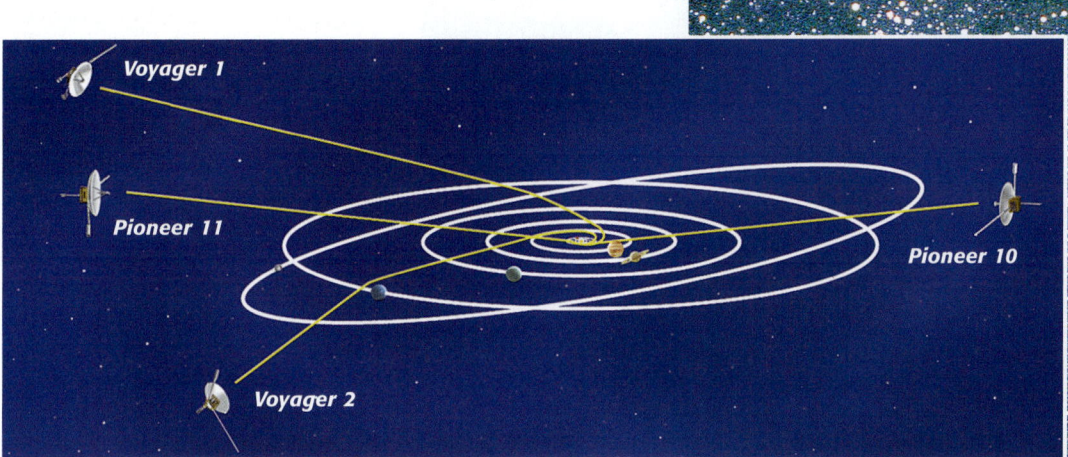

Galileo (US)
Launched: October 1989
Purpose: to study Jupiter and its moons

The Galileo Mission The *Galileo* space probe arrived at Jupiter in 1995. While *Galileo* itself began a long tour of Jupiter's moons, it sent a smaller probe into Jupiter's atmosphere to measure composition, density, temperature, and cloud structure. During its tour, *Galileo* gathered data that allowed scientists to study the geology of Jupiter's major moons and to examine Jupiter's magnetic properties more closely. The moons of Jupiter proved to be far more exciting than the earlier Pioneer and Voyager images had suggested. The *Galileo* probe discovered that two of Jupiter's moons have magnetic fields and that one of its moons, Europa, may have an ocean of liquid water lying under its icy surface.

IS THAT A FACT!

In order to keep *Voyager 2's* cameras steady as the probe passed by the gas giants, NASA engineers had to keep the probe from spinning. In fact, they devised a way to reduce the probe's spin to a speed 30 times slower than that of an hour hand on a clock!

Teaching Transparency 200
"Position of Space Probes"

CROSS-DISCIPLINARY FOCUS

History When the *Voyager* space probes were launched in 1977, each carried two gold-plated phonograph records with a variety of sounds and music intended as a message for intelligent life in the universe. The probes also carried a variety of images and written messages. Share the following list with students and discuss the kinds of historical, scientific, and cultural information that the *Voyagers* carry:

- Greetings from Earth spoken in 55 different languages, ranging from ancient Sumerian to English
- Printed messages from U.S. President Jimmy Carter and U.N. Secretary General Kurt Waldheim
- The sound of surf, wind, thunder, birdcalls, cricket chirps, and a whale "song"
- Musical selections ranging from bagpipe music from Azerbaijan to "Johnny B. Goode" by Chuck Berry
- A diagram of the solar system; drawings of a man and a woman
- A variety of images, ranging from the Great Wall of China to rush-hour traffic in India to a house in New England

Have students suppose that the *Voyagers* are being launched today. Discuss how they might add to, revise, or update the information aboard the probes. Ask students:

What information would you consider most important? What important events or discoveries have occurred since 1977? What kinds of music or images would you want beings beyond our solar system to know about?

3 Extend

Debate

Faster, Cheaper, Better? Some scientists believe that the traditional space probe projects are obsolete. These projects are expensive and require considerable support staff to receive and interpret the data. Because future funding is uncertain, these projects could fold long before the probe reaches its destination. Other scientists feel that large, complex probes are the best way to explore the solar system. Larger probes can carry more equipment and gather more information than smaller, cheaper probes. Have students form two groups to research this debate. Student groups should present their findings as if they were NASA scientists going before Congress to secure funding for their projects.

Homework

Space Probe Profiles After reviewing the section, have students select one space probe they'd like to know more about. Have them create a profile of their probe that includes pictures of the probe and information about its mission and discoveries.

Going Further

Deep Space 1 carries 81 kg of xenon gas propellant, which is enough to operate the thruster at one-half throttle for over 20 months. Use Teaching Transparency 251 to show students how the xenon ions that propel the probe are formed.

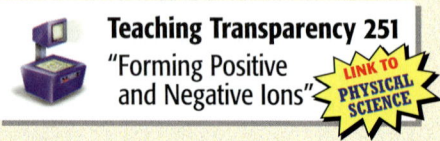

Teaching Transparency 251 "Forming Positive and Negative Ions" LINK TO PHYSICAL SCIENCE

Space Probes—A New Approach

NASA has a vision for missions that are "faster, cheaper, and better." The original space probes were very large, complex, and costly. Probes such as *Voyager 2* and *Galileo* took years to develop and carry out. One new program, called Discovery, seeks proposals for smaller science programs. The missions are supposed to bring faster results at much lower costs. The first six approved Discovery missions included sending small space probes to asteroids, another Mars landing, studies of the moon, the return of comet dust to Earth, collecting samples of the solar wind, and a tour of three comets.

Stardust—Comet Detective

Launched in 1999, the *Stardust* space probe is a NASA Discovery mission and the first to focus only on a comet. As shown in **Figure 11**, it will arrive at the comet in 2004 and gather samples of the comet's dust tail, returning them to Earth in 2006. It will be the first time that material from beyond the orbit of the moon has been brought back to Earth. The comet dust should help scientists better understand the evolution of the sun and the planets.

Figure 11 *Stardust will visit a comet and collect samples of its dust tail.*

Deep Space 1—The New Kid in Town
Another NASA project is the New Millennium program. Its purpose is to test new and risky technologies so that they can be used with confidence in the years to come. *Deep Space 1*, shown in **Figure 12**, undertook the first mission of this program. It is a space probe with an ion-propulsion system. Rather than burning chemical fuel, an ion rocket uses charged particles that exit the vehicle at high speed. An ion rocket still follows Newton's third law of motion, but it does so using a different source of propulsion.

Figure 12 *Deep Space 1 uses a revolutionary type of propulsion—an ion drive.*

CONNECT TO PHYSICAL SCIENCE

NASA's *Deep Space 1* probe features a revolutionary ion-propulsion engine 10 times more efficient than chemical thrusters. Inside the probe, xenon gas is bombarded with electrons which ionize it. (Ions are electrically-charged atoms.) Positively-charged ions are drawn toward a high voltage grid at the open end of the engine and are expelled into space at a speed of 30 km/s. This may sound fast, but the thrust generated by *Deep Space 1* is 10,000 times weaker than that generated by a typical space probe. Although this thrust is equivalent to the weight of one sheet of paper on Earth, the probe will gradually accelerate to incredible speeds over many months. One engineer described this new method of propulsion as "acceleration with patience."

The Last of the Big Boys On October 15, 1997, the *Cassini* space probe was launched on a 7-year journey to Saturn. This is the last of the large old-style missions. The *Cassini* space probe will make a grand tour of Saturn's system of moons, much as *Galileo* toured Jupiter's system. As shown in **Figure 13,** a smaller probe, called the *Huygens probe,* will detach itself from *Cassini* and descend into the atmosphere of Saturn's moon Titan to study its chemistry.

Biology CONNECTION

The atmosphere of Titan, Saturn's largest moon, may be similar to Earth's early atmosphere. Scientists hope to study the chemistry of Titan's atmosphere for clues to how life developed on Earth.

Figure 13 *An artist's view of* Cassini *at Saturn, with* Huygens *falling toward Saturn's moon Titan.*

Future Missions Proposals for future missions include a first-ever space-probe visit to Pluto, an orbiter for Jupiter's moon Europa that will use radar to determine whether it has a liquid ocean, and a possible Mercury orbiter to survey the planet closest to the sun. These are just a few of the many exciting international missions planned for the future—opening up a new golden era of planetary exploration.

REVIEW

1. List three discoveries that have been made by space probes.
2. Which two planets best help us understand Earth's environment? Explain.
3. What are the advantages of the new Discovery program over the older space-probe missions?
4. **Inferring Conclusions** Why did we need space probes to discover water channels on Mars or ice on Europa?

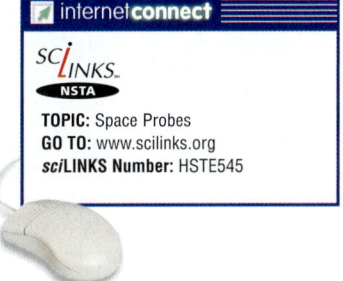

TOPIC: Space Probes
GO TO: www.scilinks.org
***sci*LINKS Number:** HSTE545

Answers to Review

1. Sample answer: The *Viking* missions sent images of dry water channels on the surface of Mars. *Venera 9* recorded information about the surface and atmosphere of Venus. *Galileo* discovered that two of Jupiter's moons have magnetic fields.
2. Venus and Mars; both planets have surface features that are similar to Earth. In addition, the high levels of CO_2 in Venus's atmosphere produce a severe greenhouse effect. This may help us understand the greenhouse effect on Earth.
3. The Discovery program will produce results quickly and inexpensively.
4. Answers will vary. Students should note that the conditions on Mars and Europa are extreme, and that the danger and expense of sending humans is great.

RESEARCH

The *Voyagers* are expected to continue gathering interplanetary and possibly interstellar data until about 2020, when their nuclear-powered energy supplies will run out. Have students research the *Voyagers'* latest discoveries and write an update on the spacecrafts' findings.

4) Close

Quiz

1. How is a space probe different from a satellite? (A space probe is a vehicle that carries scientific instruments to planets or other bodies in space. Unlike satellites, probes travel away from Earth rather than orbiting it. Students may also note that some probes become satellites of other planets.)
2. What was the main goal of the Viking missions? (to look for signs of life on Mars)
3. What new type of propulsion system is being tested with the *Deep Space 1* probe? (an ion-propulsion system)

ALTERNATIVE ASSESSMENT

Have students find photographs of a space probe and construct a model of it. Encourage students to be creative in their choice of materials and to write a paragraph describing the probe, the function of its parts, and its mission.

Critical Thinking Worksheet 22 "Spacecraft R' Us"

SECTION 4

Focus

Living and Working in Space

This section explores how the political rivalry between the Soviet Union and the United States led to the Apollo program and the first crewed mission to the moon. The section discusses how reusable space shuttles have revolutionized space travel and research. Students also learn about space stations such as *Skylab* and *Mir* and future plans for the *International Space Station*.

Bellringer

Ask students to write a postcard from a space station orbiting Earth. They should describe the station, their mission, and their day-to-day lives.

1 Motivate

DISCUSSION

A "Walk" on the Moon Read students *Apollo 12* astronaut Alan Bean's description of his 1969 moon walk:

"Once on the Moon's surface you'll quickly discover that walking is pretty difficult, while running is easy. . . . You'll feel as light on your feet as you could possibly expect—lighter even. . . . After pushing off on one foot, there will be a long wait until you land on the other, exactly like running in slow motion. . . . As you run, you'll feel as if you're leaping long, impossible distances. And in fact you are."

Discuss some of the other ways that life on the moon would be different from life on Earth. Have students write a ScienceLog entry in the style of Bean's account.

612   Chapter 22 • Exploring Space

Section 4

Terms to Learn
space shuttle
space station

What You'll Do
- Summarize the benefits of the manned space program.
- Explain how large projects such as the Apollo program and the *International Space Station* developed.
- Identify future possibilities for human exploration of space.

Living and Working in Space

Although sending human explorers into space was an early goal of the space program, it had to come in small steps. The first steps were to test the control of spacecraft with rocket-powered airplanes. Test flights in high-speed aircraft through the upper atmosphere became the beginnings of the Mercury program. The goal of the Mercury program was to put a man in orbit and to test his ability to function in space. Test flights began in 1959, but the dates for manned flight kept getting delayed because of unreliable rockets.

Human Space Exploration

On April 12, 1961, a Soviet cosmonaut named Yuri Gagarin became the first human to orbit the Earth. The United States didn't achieve its first suborbital flight until May 5, 1961, when Alan Shepard reached space but not orbit. Because the Soviets were first once again, they appeared to be winning the Cold War. As a result, many Americans began to consider the military advantages of a strong presence in space. On May 25, 1961, an announcement was made that would set the tone for American space policy for the next 10 years.

Figure 14 In 1962, John Glenn flew aboard Friendship 7, the first NASA spacecraft to orbit the Earth.

> "I believe that this nation should commit itself to achieving the goal, before this decade is out, of landing a man on the moon and returning him safely to the Earth. No single space project in this period will be more impressive to mankind, or more important for the long-range exploration of space; and none will be so difficult or expensive to accomplish."
>
> — John F. Kennedy, President of the United States

Many people were expecting the simple announcement of an accelerated space program, but Kennedy's proclamation took everyone by surprise—especially the leaders at NASA. Go to the moon? The United States had not even achieved Earth orbit yet! But the American people took the challenge seriously, and by February 1962, a new spaceport site in Florida was purchased, a manned space-center site was bought, and John Glenn, shown in **Figure 14,** was successfully launched into orbit around the Earth.

SCIENCE HUMOR

As *Apollo 11* approached the moon, a special mechanism kept it rotating slowly. Had it not been rotating, the side of the spacecraft exposed to the sun would have quickly overheated. The *Apollo* astronauts comically referred to this rotisserie-like movement as the "barbecue mode."

After Neil Armstrong hopped off the ladder onto the moon's surface and made his historic speech, "Buzz" Aldrin followed. As the shorter astronaut stepped onto the moon, he joked, "That may have been a small step for Neil, but it was a pretty big one for me."

The Dream Comes True On July 20, 1969, the President's challenge was met. The *Apollo 11* landing module—the *Eagle,* shown in **Figure 15**—landed on the moon. Astronaut Neil Armstrong became the first human to set foot on a world other than Earth, forever changing the way we view ourselves and our planet.

Although the primary reason for the Apollo program was political (national pride), the Apollo missions also contributed to the advancement of science and technology. *Apollo 11* returned nearly 22 kg of moon rocks to Earth for study. Its crew also put devices on the moon to monitor moonquake activity and the solar wind. The results from these samples and studies completely changed our view of the solar system.

The Space Shuttle

The dream of human space flight and Kennedy's challenge were great for getting us into space, but they could not be the motivation for the continued political support of space exploration. The huge rockets required for launching spacecraft into orbit were just too expensive.

Early in the manned program, Wernher von Braun had suggested that a reusable space transportation system would be needed. Proposals for reusable launch vehicles were made in the 1950s and 1960s, but the Kennedy challenge overshadowed other efforts, and these ideas were not given serious attention. Finally in 1972, President Richard Nixon announced a space shuttle program to the American public, saying that this would be an economical way to get into space regularly. A **space shuttle** is a reusable vehicle that takes off like a rocket and lands like an airplane, as shown in **Figure 16.**

Figure 15 *Astronaut Neil Armstrong took this photo of Edwin "Buzz" Aldrin as he was about to become the second human being to step onto the moon.*

Figure 16 Columbia *was one of NASA's original shuttles.*

CONNECT TO PHYSICAL SCIENCE

Make sure that students understand that rocket engines are powered by combustion. Combustion requires oxygen, so rockets must carry both fuel and an oxidizer into space. Because their volume as gases would be too great to be practical as rocket fuel, oxygen and hydrogen must be stored as liquids in pressurized fuel tanks.

CONNECT TO LIFE SCIENCE

During the second crewed mission to the moon (*Apollo 12,* November 14–24, 1969), astronauts retrieved some pieces of the space probe *Surveyor.* Amazingly, the pieces of *Surveyor* harbored bacteria from Earth that survived for two and a half years in the moon's dry, near-vacuum environment!

2) Teach

READING STRATEGY

Prediction Guide Have students predict whether the following statements are true or false:
- The space shuttle can be used only once. (false)
- Both the United States and the Soviet Union have launched space stations. (true)
- Many nations are collaborating on an international space station. (true)

Homework

Oral History Project Have students interview adults who remember the 1969 moon landing. Have students draft questions about the event and how the nation reacted to that historic moment. The National Geographic video *For All Mankind* will serve as an excellent introduction to this project. If possible, have students tape-record the interviews and then transcribe them. As an extension, student groups could compile and edit their interviews for a presentation or discussion about the cultural and scientific significance of the first crewed moon landing.

Multicultural CONNECTION

The first black person in space was a Cuban cosmonaut named Arnaldo Tamayo-Mendez. In 1980, he flew aboard *Soyuz 38* to the Soviet space station *Salyut 6.* Have interested students research the contributions that other ethnic groups have made to space programs.

Directed Reading Worksheet 22 Section 4

Section 4 • Living and Working in Space

② Teach, continued

DEMONSTRATION

O-Ring Failure The day of the *Challenger* disaster was unseasonably cold for Florida, with temperatures below freezing. The investigation that followed the tragedy traced the explosion to the failure of O-ring seals that were designed to prevent hot exhaust gases from leaking out of the spacecraft's rocket boosters. The rings had stiffened as a result of the cold temperatures and had failed to seal effectively. As a result, one of the rocket boosters leaked, leading to a catastrophic explosion 73 seconds after liftoff. To demonstrate how the cold weather contributed to the O-ring failure, place a rubber washer or gasket in a glass of ice water for a few minutes and then allow students to examine how inflexible it becomes.

GROUP ACTIVITY

Have students find out about the experiments conducted on *Skylab* or *Mir*. Groups should focus on biological, medical, space manufacturing, or astronomical experiments. Have groups share their findings in an oral presentation.

MATH and MORE

When fueled, the space shuttle has a mass of about 2 million kilograms. About 80 percent of this weight is propellant (fuel and oxidizer). Have students calculate the weight of the space shuttle's propellant.

(2,000,000 kg × 0.8 = 1,600,000 kg)

Figure 17 Future space planes may provide inexpensive transportation not only between Earth and outer space but around the world.

When a human body stays in space for long periods of time without having to work against gravity, the bones lose mass and muscles become weaker. Long space-station missions, which can last for months, are very important in order to study whether humans can survive voyages to Mars and other planets. These missions will last for several years.

The first shuttle was launched on April 12, 1981, and was followed by two dozen successful missions until 1986, when tragedy struck. On January 28, 1986, the booster rocket on the space shuttle *Challenger* exploded just after takeoff, killing all seven of its astronauts. On board was Christa McAuliffe, who would have been the first teacher in space. All shuttle flights were suspended until this disaster could be explained. Finally in 1988, the space shuttle program resumed with the return of shuttle *Discovery* to space.

Commuter Shuttle? Currently efforts are underway to make space travel easier and cheaper. NASA is working to develop a space plane that will fly like a normal airplane through the atmosphere but will be equipped with rocket engines for use in the vacuum of space. Once in operation, space planes, such as the *X-33* shown in **Figure 17,** may lower the cost of getting material to LEO by 90 percent. Research is now being done on the next generation of space vehicles. New types of rockets and rocket fuels, as well as other means of sending vehicles into space, are being considered.

Space Stations—People Working in Space

On April 19, 1971, the Soviets became the first to successfully place a manned space station in low Earth orbit. A **space station** is a long-term orbiting platform from which other vehicles can be launched or scientific research can be carried out. In June of the same year, a crew of three Soviet cosmonauts entered *Salyut 1* to conduct a 23-day mission. By 1982, the Soviets had put up a total of seven space stations. Because of this experience, the Soviet Union became the world leader in space-station development and in the study of the effects of weightlessness on humans. Their discoveries will be important for future manned flights to other planets—journeys that will take years to complete.

Homework

Many space technology innovations are made by private companies and individuals. Several awards are currently offered for the first private group to launch an inexpensive rocket into space. Ask students to find out more about the role of private companies in the future of space exploration and suggest that they learn about experimental projects such as the Roton rocket.

As astronaut William Pogue exercised on *Skylab*, he reported that his sweat "just sort of slithered around" instead of pooling on the floor beneath him. After exercising, he corralled the hovering sweat with a towel so that it wouldn't interfere with the spacecraft's equipment!

A Home Away from Home *Skylab,* the United States's first space station, was a science and engineering lab that orbited the Earth in LEO at a height of 435 km. The lab, shown in **Figure 18,** was used to conduct a wide variety of scientific studies, including astronomy, biological experiments, and experiments in space manufacturing. Three different crews spent a total of 171 days on board *Skylab*.

All objects in LEO, including *Skylab,* eventually spiral toward Earth. Even at several hundred kilometers above the Earth, there is still a very small amount of atmosphere. The atmosphere slows down any object in orbit unless something periodically pushes the object in the opposite direction. *Skylab*'s orbit began to decay in 1979. A space shuttle was supposed to return the lab to a higher orbit, but delays in the shuttle program prevented the rescue of *Skylab,* and it fell into the Indian Ocean.

Figure 18 *Skylab, in orbit above Earth, was lifted into space by a Saturn V rocket.*

From Russia with Peace In 1986, the Soviets began to launch the pieces for a much more ambitious space station called *Mir* (meaning "peace"). The Soviets, and later the Russians, used *Mir* to conduct astronomy experiments, provide biological and Earth orbital observations, and study manufacturing technologies in space. When completed, *Mir* had seven modules and measured 33 m long and 27 m wide.

Astronauts from the United States and other countries eventually became visitors to *Mir,* as shown in **Figure 19.** Almost continuously inhabited between 1987 and 1999, *Mir* became the inspiration to build the next generation of space station—the International Space Station.

Working in space requires the use of special tools, such as the space shuttle's robot arm. Turn to page 724 in the LabBook to extend your own reach.

Figure 19 *Mir provided an opportunity for American astronauts and Russian cosmonauts to live and work together in space.*

SCIENCE HUMOR

The news that *Skylab* would re-enter the atmosphere and plummet to Earth generated mild panic among some people. Despite NASA's assurances that the debris would fall in oceans or unpopulated areas, a few quick profits were made from the sale of hard hats billed as "Skylab Survival Kits." Much of the debris fell into the Indian Ocean, but some charred fragments were found strewn across the Australian Outback, prompting Australian officials to present the United States with a $400 fine for littering!

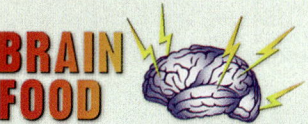

What happens to the trash that is generated on a space station? Even a small space station such as *Mir* generates trash. Transporting it back to Earth is a costly endeavor. Tossing the garbage out into orbit could be a hazard for other satellites or spacecraft. The *Mir* periodically filled a used cargo ship with trash and sent it in a rapidly decaying orbit into the Earth's atmosphere. When it entered the atmosphere it burned up. Ask students if they can think of other ways to safely dispose of, or recycle, space trash.

Reach for the Stars

MISCONCEPTION ALERT

Students may presume that astronauts experience weightlessness because there is no gravity in space. Astronauts in a typical orbit 296 km above Earth are still affected by Earth's gravity; in fact, gravity is what keeps the spacecraft in orbit. The reason the astronauts have the sensation of weightlessness is that they are in a constant state of free fall as they orbit Earth. This apparent weightlessness is similar to what sky divers experience when they jump from airplanes.

TOPIC: Space Exploration and Space Stations
GO TO: www.scilinks.org
sciLINKS NUMBER: HSTE550

Section 4 • Living and Working in Space **615**

3) Extend

DEBATE

Space Exploration: Does Its Expense Outweigh Its Benefits? Encourage students to debate the costs of space exploration versus its potential benefits to humankind. Students should recognize that although space exploration is very expensive, it is difficult to measure or to predict how much could be gained by exploration. The space industry also employs many people, including scientists and laborers who build the rockets. On the other hand, there are many immediate problems on Earth, such as hunger, disease, homelessness, and illiteracy.

CROSS-DISCIPLINARY FOCUS

Social Studies Discuss how the political and economic changes of the mid- to late 1980s led to the collapse of the Soviet Union. Tell students that the 1975 Apollo-Soyuz Test Project was the result of a 1972 U.S.-Soviet agreement to conduct a joint venture in space. Remind them, however, that it took 20 years before such cooperation became commonplace. You might tell students that in 1995 the U.S. space shuttle *Atlantis* engaged in several dockings with *Mir* in preparation for future American-Russian collaborations on the *International Space Station*. Ask students if they think that such an event could have occurred if the political situation in Russia had not changed. Have students prepare a timeline of the important political, social, and scientific events of the age of space exploration.

Science CONNECTION

Working together to live in space? To learn more about the latest station in orbit, turn to page 622.

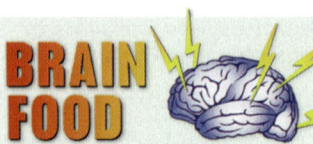

BRAIN FOOD

It will take more than 40 shuttle flights and 6 years to lift into space the 400 tons of materials needed for the construction of the *International Space Station*.

The International Space Station

In 1993, a design for a new space station was proposed that called for international involvement and a collaboration between the newly formed Russian Republic and the United States. The new space station is called the *International Space Station (ISS)*. A drawing of the station when completed is shown in **Figure 20.**

The station is being assembled in LEO with materials brought up on the space shuttle or by Russian rockets. The United States is providing lab modules, the supporting truss, solar panels for power, living quarters, and a biomedical laboratory. The Russians are contributing a service module, docking modules, life support and research modules, and transportation to and from the station. Other components will come from Japan, Canada, and several European countries.

The *ISS* will provide many benefits—some of which we cannot even predict. What we do know is that it will be a good place to perform space-science experiments and perhaps to invent new technologies. Hopefully the *ISS* will also promote cooperation among countries and continue the pioneering spirit of the first astronauts and cosmonauts.

Figure 20 *This artist's view of the* International Space Station *shows what the station will look like once it is completed.*

IS THAT A FACT!

The *International Space Station* is the largest and most complex space project ever undertaken; it is more than four times larger than the *Mir* space station. The completed station will be nearly 110 m wide and 90 m long. It will have a mass of about 470,000 kg, and almost one acre of solar panels will power six scientific labs on the station.

The Moon, Mars, and Beyond

We may eventually need resources and living space beyond what Earth can provide. Space can provide abundant mineral resources. One interesting resource is a rare form of helium that can be found on the moon. Used as a fuel for nuclear reactors, it leaves no radioactive waste!

We have seen that there are also many scientific benefits to space exploration. For example, the far side of the moon can be 100 times darker than any observatory site on Earth. The moon also could be a wonderful place to locate factories that require a vacuum to process materials, as shown in **Figure 21.** A base in Earth orbit can produce materials that require low gravity. A colony or base on the moon or on Mars could be an important link to bringing space resources to Earth. The key will be to make these missions economically worthwhile.

Activity

Technological improvements intended for space exploration have often led to the invention of new products that improve our lives here on Earth. NASA has a special program that transfers these new ideas and technology to the public. Find out more about NASA's technology transfers on the Internet and about how many everyday technologies had their beginnings in the space program.

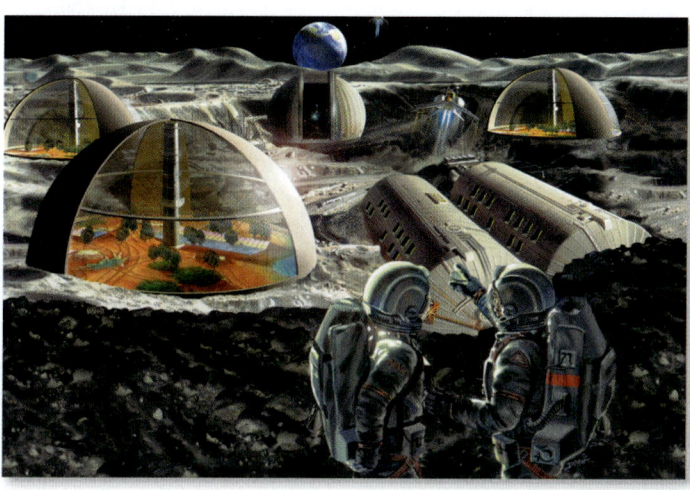

Figure 21 *Humans may eventually colonize the moon for scientific, economic, and perhaps even recreational reasons.*

REVIEW

1. How was the race to explore our solar system influenced by the Cold War?
2. How did missions to the moon benefit space science?
3. How will space stations help in the exploration of space?
4. **Making Inferences** Why did the United States quit sending people to the moon after the Apollo program ended?

TOPIC: Space Exploration and Space Stations
GO TO: www.scilinks.org
sciLINKS NUMBER: HSTE550

Answers to Review

1. Answers will vary. Students should note that Cold War tensions greatly accelerated the space programs of the United States and the Soviet Union.
2. Answers will vary. The Apollo missions helped us understand the geology of the moon and measure the solar wind.
3. Answers will vary. Space stations will serve as refueling, construction and research stations.
4. Answers will vary. Without a political reason to go to the moon, the United States government decided that the Apollo program was too expensive to continue.

Answers to Activity

Suggest that students use their findings to construct a "Space Age Spin-Offs" comic book that describes how a few items developed in the space program have made their way into our daily lives.

GOING FURTHER

Have a round-table discussion in which students impersonate the following people after having researched their lives and careers:

Robert Goddard, Konstantin Tsiolkovsky, Yuri Gagarin, John Glenn, Rita Mae Jemison, Valentina Tereshkova, Alexi Leonov, Edward White, Chuck Yeager, or Helen Sharman.

Have students discuss the history of the space program and then speculate on future innovations and developments.

4 Close

Quiz

1. What kind of vehicle has been proposed that would make space travel cheaper? (a space plane)
2. What is a space station? (It is a long-term orbiting platform from which other space vehicles can launch and where scientific research can be conducted.)
3. What resources might space someday provide? (minerals, living space, factory sites)

ALTERNATIVE ASSESSMENT

 **Make a Poster** Have students make a poster that shows a day in the life of a space traveler. Events during the day might include making breakfast, exercising, conducting experiments, calling home, and relaxing.

Chapter Highlights

VOCABULARY DEFINITIONS

SECTION 1

rocket a machine that uses escaping gas to move

NASA National Aeronautics and Space Administration; founded to combine all of the separate rocket-development teams in the United States

thrust the force that accelerates a rocket

orbital velocity the speed and direction a rocket must have in order to orbit the Earth

escape velocity the speed and direction a rocket must travel in order to completely break away from a planet's gravitational pull

SECTION 2

artificial satellite any human-made object placed in orbit around a body in space

low Earth orbit an orbit located a few hundred kilometers above the Earth's surface

geosynchronous orbit an orbit in which a satellite travels at a speed that matches the rotational speed of the Earth exactly, keeping the satellite positioned above the same spot on Earth at all times

Chapter Highlights

SECTION 1

Vocabulary
- rocket (p. 598)
- NASA (p. 599)
- thrust (p. 600)
- orbital velocity (p. 601)
- escape velocity (p. 601)

Section Notes
- Two pioneers of rocketry were Konstantin Tsiolkovsky and Robert Goddard.
- Rockets work according to Newton's third law of motion—for every action there is an equal and opposite reaction.
- NASA was formed in 1958, combining rocket research from several programs. It was originally formed to compete with the Soviet Union's rocket program.

Labs
Water Rockets Save the Day! (p. 722)

SECTION 2

Vocabulary
- artificial satellite (p. 602)
- low Earth orbit (p. 603)
- geosynchronous orbit (p. 603)

Section Notes
- The Soviet Union launched the first Earth-orbiting satellite in 1957. The first United States satellite went up in 1958.

- Low Earth orbits (LEOs) are located a few hundred kilometers above the Earth's surface. Satellites in geosynchronous orbits (GEOs) have an orbit period of 24 hours and remain over one spot.
- Satellite programs are used for weather observations, communications, mapping the Earth, and tracking ocean currents, crop growth, and urban development.
- One great legacy of the satellite program has been an increase in our awareness of the Earth's fragile environment.

✓ Skills Check

Math Concepts

THE ROCKET EQUATION Suppose the mass of a certain rocket is 1,000 kg and the mass of the gas leaving the rocket is 100 kg. If the speed that the gas leaves the rocket is 50 m/s, the rocket will move at a speed of 5 m/s. Rearranging the rocket equation:

$$m_g \times v_g = m_r \times v_r$$

as $\quad v_r = m_g \times v_g / m_r$

gives $\quad v_r = \dfrac{100 \text{ kg} \times 50 \text{ m/s}}{1,000 \text{ kg}} = 5 \text{ m/s}$

Visual Understanding

GLOBAL COMMUNICATION As you saw on page 603, satellites can relay television, radio, and telephone signals around the world. Because they remain in GEO, these satellites are always above the same spot on Earth, letting them relay our signals without interruption.

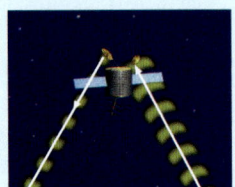

Lab and Activity Highlights

Water Rockets Save the Day! PG 722

Reach for the Stars PG 724

 Datasheets for LabBook (blackline masters for these labs)

SECTION 3

Vocabulary
space probe (p. 606)

Section Notes
- Planetary exploration with space probes began with missions to the moon. The next targets of exploration were the inner planets: Venus, Mercury, and Mars.
- The United States has been the only country to explore the outer solar system, beginning with the Pioneer and Voyager missions.
- Space-probe science has given us information about how planets form and develop, helping us better understand our own planet Earth.

SECTION 4

Vocabulary
space shuttle (p. 613)
space station (p. 614)

Section Notes
- The great race to get a manned flight program underway and to reach the moon was politically motivated.

- The United States beat the Soviets to a manned moon landing with the Apollo moon flights in 1969.
- During the 1970s, the United States focused on developing the space shuttle. The Soviets focused on developing orbiting space stations.
- The United States, Russia, and 14 other international partners are currently developing the *International Space Station*.
- Because of scientific, economic, and even recreational reasons, humans may eventually live and work on other planets and moons.

Labs
Reach for the Stars (p. 724)

VOCABULARY DEFINITIONS, continued

SECTION 3
space probe a vehicle that carries scientific instruments to planets or other bodies in space

SECTION 4
space shuttle a reusable vehicle that takes off like a rocket and lands like an airplane

space station a long-term orbiting platform from which other vehicles can be launched or scientific research can be carried out

 Blackline masters of these Chapter Highlights can be found in the **Study Guide**.

---

internetconnect

GO TO: go.hrw.com

Visit the **HRW** Web site for a variety of learning tools related to this chapter. Just type in the keyword:

KEYWORD: HSTEXP

SCILINKS NSTA

GO TO: www.scilinks.org

Visit the **National Science Teachers Association** on-line Web site for Internet resources related to this chapter. Just type in the *sci*LINKS number for more information about the topic:

TOPIC:	Rocket Technology	*sci*LINKS NUMBER: HSTE530
TOPIC:	The History of NASA	*sci*LINKS NUMBER: HSTE535
TOPIC:	Artificial Satellites	*sci*LINKS NUMBER: HSTE540
TOPIC:	Space Probes	*sci*LINKS NUMBER: HSTE545
TOPIC:	Space Exploration and Space Stations	*sci*LINKS NUMBER: HSTE550

Lab and Activity Highlights

LabBank

 Whiz-Bang Demonstrations, Rocket Science, Demo 36

Inquiry Labs
- Crash Landing, Lab 14
- Space Fitness, Lab 15

 EcoLabs & Field Activities, There's a Space for Us, EcoLab 16

Long-Term Projects & Research Ideas, Space Voyage, Project 50

Chapter Review

USING VOCABULARY

For each pair of terms, explain the difference in their meaning:

1. geosynchronous orbit/low Earth orbit
2. space probe/space shuttle
3. artificial satellite/moon

To complete the following sentences, choose the correct term from each pair of terms listed below:

4. The force that accelerates a rocket is called __?__. *(escape velocity* or *thrust)*
5. Rockets need to have __?__ in order to burn their fuel. *(oxygen* or *nitrogen)*

UNDERSTANDING CONCEPTS

Multiple Choice

6. The father of modern rocketry is considered to be
   a. K. Tsiolkovsky.
   b. R. Goddard.
   c. W. von Braun.
   d. D. Eisenhower.

7. Rockets work according to Newton's
   a. first law of motion.
   b. second law of motion.
   c. third law of motion.
   d. law of universal gravitation.

8. The first artificial satellite to orbit the Earth was
   a. *Pioneer 4.*
   b. *Explorer 1.*
   c. *Voyager 2.*
   d. *Sputnik 1.*

9. Satellites are able to transfer TV signals across and between continents because satellites
   a. are located in LEOs.
   b. relay signals past the horizon.
   c. travel quickly around Earth.
   d. can be used during the day and night.

10. GEOs are better orbits for communications because satellites in GEO
    a. remain in position over one spot.
    b. are farther away from Earth's surface.
    c. do not revolve around the Earth.
    d. are only a few hundred kilometers high.

11. Which space probe discovered evidence of water at the moon's south pole?
    a. *Luna 9*
    b. *Viking 1*
    c. *Clementine*
    d. *Magellan*

12. When did humans first set foot on the moon?
    a. 1949
    b. 1959
    c. 1969
    d. 1979

13. Which one of these planets has not yet been visited by space probes?
    a. Mercury
    b. Neptune
    c. Mars
    d. Pluto

14. Of the following, which space probe is about to leave our solar system?
    a. *Galileo*
    b. *Magellan*
    c. *Mariner 10*
    d. *Pioneer 10*

15. Based on space-probe data, which of the following is the most likely place in our solar system to find liquid water?
    a. the moon
    b. Mars
    c. Europa
    d. Venus

Short Answer

16. Answers will vary. Sample answer: Newton's third law states that for every action, there is an equal reaction in the opposite direction. A rocket's combustion chamber contains gases that are under extreme pressure. As the gases escape through the rocket nozzle, the rocket reacts by moving in the opposite direction.

17. Answers will vary. One disadvantage of LEO is that a satellite cannot maintain constant communication with a ground station because it is orbiting faster than the Earth rotates.

Short Answer

16. Describe how Newton's third law of motion relates to the movement of rockets.

17. What is one disadvantage that objects in LEO have?

18. Why did the United States develop the space shuttle?

19. During which period were spy satellites first used?

Concept Mapping

20. Use the following terms to create a concept map: orbital velocity, thrust, LEO, artificial satellites, escape velocity, space probes, GEO, rockets.

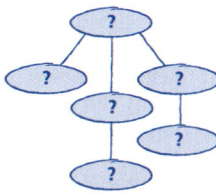

CRITICAL THINKING AND PROBLEM SOLVING

Write one or two sentences to answer the following questions:

21. What is the difference between speed and velocity?

22. Why must rockets that travel in outer space carry oxygen with them?

23. How will data from space probes help us understand the Earth's environment?

24. Why is it necessary for several nations to work together to create the *ISS*?

MATH IN SCIENCE

25. In order to escape Earth's gravity, a rocket must travel at least 11 km/s. This is pretty fast! If you could travel to the moon at this speed, how many hours would it take you to get there? (The moon is about 384,000 km away from Earth.) Round your answer to the nearest whole number.

INTERPRETING GRAPHICS

The map below was made using satellite data. It indicates the different amounts of chlorophyll in the ocean. Chlorophyll, in turn, identifies the presence of marine plankton. The blues and purples show the smallest amount of chlorophyll, and the reds and oranges show the most. Examine the map, and answer the questions that follow:

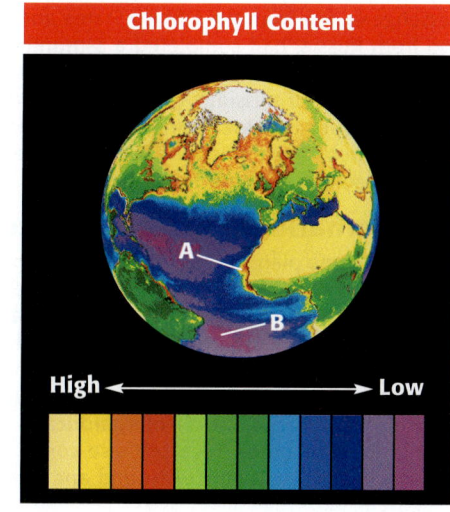

Chlorophyll Content

High ← → Low

26. At which location, **A** or **B**, are more plankton concentrated?

27. What do you conclude about the conditions in which plankton prefer to live?

Reading Check-up

Take a minute to review your answers to the Pre-Reading Questions found at the bottom of page 596. Have your answers changed? If necessary, revise your answers based on what you have learned since you began this chapter.

621

---

18. Answers will vary. One reason the United States developed the space shuttle is that it is reusable.
19. Spy satellites were first used during the Cold War.

Concept Mapping

20. 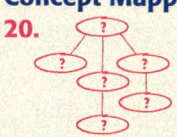 An answer to this exercise can be found at the end of this book.

CRITICAL THINKING AND PROBLEM SOLVING

21. Speed is a measure of how fast an object travels. Velocity is the speed and direction an object travels.
22. Rockets must carry oxygen with them because there is little or no oxygen in the Earth's upper atmosphere or in outer space. Without oxygen, rocket fuel cannot burn.
23. Answers will vary. Space probes enable us to study the atmosphere and surface of other bodies in the solar system. Scientists use this data to understand changes in Earth's environment.
24. Answers will vary. Building the *ISS* together gives different countries a common goal and encourages international cooperation. In addition, the cost of the *ISS* will be shared by many countries.

MATH IN SCIENCE

25. $\frac{384,000 \text{ km}}{11 \text{ km/s}} = 34,909$ seconds

    $34,909 \text{ s} \times \frac{1 \text{ min}}{60 \text{ s}} \times \frac{1 \text{ h}}{60 \text{ min}} = 9.7 \text{ h} = 10$ hours

INTERPRETING GRAPHICS

26. A
27. Answers will vary. Sample answer: Plankton populations tend to be concentrated in coastal waters. (Students may note that upwelling at continental margins provides the nutrients that plankton populations need in order to live.)

Across the Sciences

EARTH SCIENCE • LIFE SCIENCE

International Space Station

On a June day in 1995, the space shuttle *Atlantis* docked at the Russian space station, *Mir,* and picked up three passengers. These passengers, one from the United States and two from Russia, had completed a 3-month stay at the space station. This mission was the first in a series of missions to develop construction techniques for assembling the *International Space Station.* These missions are considered to be phase one of the process.

An International Place in Space

Sixteen nations plan to build the *International Space Station (ISS)* by the year 2004. These nations are the United States, Russia, Canada, Brazil, Japan, Denmark, Germany, France, Italy, Belgium, the Netherlands, Switzerland, the United Kingdom, Spain, Norway, and Sweden.

The *ISS* will be made up of cylindrical rooms called *modules.* Each of these components will be built on the ground and then assembled 274 km above Earth. The current plan calls for more than 40 space flights to carry the parts of the space station into orbit. Once the *ISS* is completed, a seven-member crew will be able to live and work there.

Life Aboard

One of the strange things about living in space is the reduced effect of gravity known as *free fall.* Everything inside the space station that is not fastened down, including the astronauts, will float! The designers of the *ISS*'s habitation module have come up with some intriguing solutions to this problem. For example, each astronaut will sleep in a sack similar to a sleeping bag that is fastened to the module. The sack will keep the astronauts from floating around while they sleep. Astronauts will shower with a hand-held nozzle that squirts water onto their body. Afterward, the water droplets will be vacuumed up so that they won't float around. Other problems being studied include how to prepare and serve food, how to design an effective toilet, and how to dispose of waste.

Ready to Go

Phase two began with the actual construction of the *ISS* in orbit. In November and December of 1998, two modules, *Zarya* and *Unity,* were launched into orbit. In early 2000, a three-person crew began living on board—the first of many crews expected to inhabit the *International Space Station.*

Address the Gravity of a Situation

▶ Create a sketch for a device that will help the space-station crew cope with free fall. Pick a problem to solve such as brushing teeth, getting exercise, or washing hair.

▲ Parts of the *International Space Station* are being assembled in space.

Science Fiction

"Why I Left Harry's All-Night Hamburgers"

by Lawrence Watt-Evans

At 16, he needed a job. His dad was out of work and his family needed money. Right around the corner from his house was Harry's All-Night Hamburgers. With a little persistence, he talked Harry into giving him a job.

He worked from midnight to 7:30 A.M. so he could still go to school. He was the counterman, waiter, busboy, and janitor, all in one. Harry's was pretty quiet most nights, especially because the interstate was 8 mi away and nobody wanted to drive to Harry's. Most of the time, the customers were pretty normal.

There were some, though, who were unusual. For instance, one guy came in dressed for Arctic winter, even though it was April and it was 60°F outside. Then there were the folks who parked a very strange vehicle right out in the parking lot for anyone to see.

Pretty soon, the captivated waiter starts asking questions. What he learns startles and fascinates him. Soon he's thinking about leaving Harry's. Find out why by reading "Why I Left Harry's All-Night Hamburgers," by Lawrence Watt-Evans, in the *Holt Anthology of Science Fiction*.

Further Reading If you liked this story, check out more of Lawrence Watt-Evans's work, such as the following:

Crosstime Traffic, Del Rey Books, November 1992

Denner's Wreck, Avon, April 1988

Shining Steel, Avon, June 1986

SCIENCE FICTION
"Why I Left Harry's All-Night Hamburgers"
by Lawrence Watt-Evans

Flying saucers in the parking lot? Just how alien and strange are the late-night visitors to Harry's burger joint? And why does the teenager who works the night shift want to leave?

Teaching Strategy

Reading Level Students of all reading levels should find this story enjoyable. However, the class may benefit from a discussion of some of the concepts and themes introduced in the story.

Background

About the Author Lawrence Watt-Evans's memorable characters and stories have earned him high honors in the fields of science fiction and fantasy writing. Readers of *Isaac Asimov's Science Fiction Magazine* nominated "Why I Left Harry's All-Night Hamburgers" for the best short story of 1987. The next year that story earned Watt-Evans the Hugo Award and was nominated for the Nebula Award. Check out "Windwagon Smith and the Martians" and other stories in *Crosstime Traffic*.

Lawrence Watt-Evans currently lives in Maryland. He and his wife have two children and several pets, including a cat, a snake, and a hamster. You can learn more about Lawrence Watt-Evans by visiting his Web site, which is filled with illustrations from his book covers, notes on his own writing, and suggestions of his favorite works.

Contents

Safety First! **626**

Chapter 1 The World of Earth Science
Using the Scientific Method 630

Chapter 2 Maps as Models of the Earth
Round or Flat? 632
Orient Yourself! 634
Topographic Tuber 636

Chapter 3 Minerals of the Earth's Crust
Mysterious Minerals 638
Is It Fool's Gold?—A Dense Situation .. 640

Chapter 4 Rocks: Mineral Mixtures
Crystal Growth 642
Let's Get Sedimental 645
Metamorphic Mash 647

Chapter 5 Energy Resources
Make a Water Wheel 648
Power of the Sun 650

Chapter 6 The Rock and Fossil Record
How DO You Stack Up? 652

Chapter 7 Plate Tectonics
Convection Connection 656
Oh, the Pressure! 657

Chapter 8 Earthquakes
Quake Challenge 660
Earthquake Waves 662

Chapter 9 Volcanoes
Some Go "Pop," Some Do Not 664
Volcano Verdict 666

Chapter 10
Weathering and Soil Formation
Great Ice Escape 668
Rockin' Through Time 669

Chapter 11 The Flow of Fresh Water
Water Cycle—What Goes Up 670
Clean Up Your Act 672

Chapter 12
Agents of Erosion and Deposition
Dune Movement 676
Gliding Glaciers 677
Creating a Kettle 679

Chapter 13 Exploring the Oceans
Probing the Depths 680
Investigating an Oil Spill 682

Chapter 14
The Movement of Ocean Water
Up from the Depths 684
Turning the Tides 686

Chapter 15 The Atmosphere
Boiling Over! 688
Go Fly a Bike! 690
Under Pressure! 692

Chapter 16 Understanding Weather
Watching the Weather 694
Let It Snow! 697
Gone with the Wind 698

Chapter 17 Climate
Global Impact 700
For the Birds 701
Biome Business 704

Chapter 18 Observing the Sky
Create a Calendar 706
The Sun's Yearly Trip Through
  the Zodiac 708
Through the Looking Glass 710

Chapter 19
Formation of the Solar System
How Far Is the Sun? 712

Chapter 20 A Family of Planets
Why Do They Wander? 714
Eclipses 716
Phases of the Moon 717

Chapter 21 The Universe Beyond
Red Hot, or Not? 718
I See the Light! 720

Chapter 22 Exploring Space
Water Rockets Save the Day! 722
Reach for the Stars 724

Exploring, inventing, and investigating are essential to the study of science. However, these activities can also be dangerous. To make sure that your experiments and explorations are safe, you must be aware of a variety of safety guidelines.

You have probably heard of the saying, "It is better to be safe than sorry." This is particularly true in a science classroom where experiments and explorations are being performed. Being uninformed and careless can result in serious injuries. Don't take chances with your own safety or with anyone else's.

Following are important guidelines for staying safe in the science classroom. Your teacher may also have safety guidelines and tips that are specific to your classroom and laboratory. Take the time to be safe.

Safety Rules!

Start Out Right

Always get your teacher's permission before attempting any laboratory exploration. Read the procedures carefully, and pay particular attention to safety information and caution statements. If you are unsure about what a safety symbol means, look it up or ask your teacher. You cannot be too careful when it comes to safety. If an accident does occur, inform your teacher immediately, regardless of how minor you think the accident is.

Safety Symbols

All of the experiments and investigations in this book and their related worksheets include important safety symbols to alert you to particular safety concerns. Become familiar with these symbols so that when you see them, you will know what they mean and what to do. It is important that you read this entire safety section to learn about specific dangers in the laboratory.

If you are instructed to note the odor of a substance, wave the fumes toward your nose with your hand. Never put your nose close to the source.

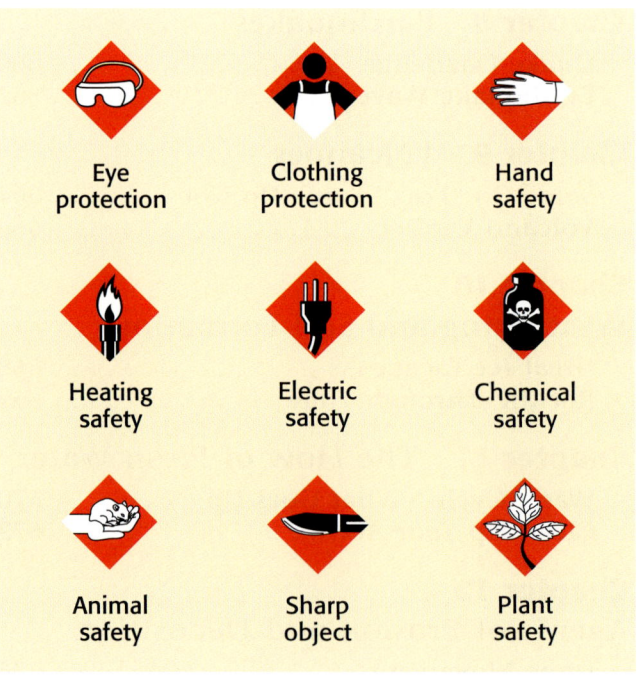

Eye protection Clothing protection Hand safety
Heating safety Electric safety Chemical safety
Animal safety Sharp object Plant safety

626 LabBook Safety First!

Eye Safety

Wear safety goggles when working around chemicals, acids, bases, or any type of flame or heating device. Wear safety goggles any time there is even the slightest chance that harm could come to your eyes. If any substance gets into your eyes, notify your teacher immediately, and flush your eyes with running water for at least 15 minutes. Treat any unknown chemical as if it were a dangerous chemical. Never look directly into the sun. Doing so could cause permanent blindness.

Avoid wearing contact lenses in a laboratory situation. Even if you are wearing safety goggles, chemicals can get between the contact lenses and your eyes. If your doctor requires that you wear contact lenses instead of glasses, wear eye-cup safety goggles in the lab.

Safety Equipment

Know the locations of the nearest fire alarms and any other safety equipment, such as fire blankets and eyewash fountains, as identified by your teacher, and know the procedures for using them.

Be extra careful when using any glassware. When adding a heavy object to a graduated cylinder, tilt the cylinder so the object slides slowly to the bottom.

Neatness

Keep your work area free of all unnecessary books and papers. Tie back long hair, and secure loose sleeves or other loose articles of clothing, such as ties and bows. Remove dangling jewelry. Don't wear open-toed shoes or sandals in the laboratory. Never eat, drink, or apply cosmetics in a laboratory setting. Food, drink, and cosmetics can easily become contaminated with dangerous materials.

Certain hair products (such as aerosol hair spray) are flammable and should not be worn while working near an open flame. Avoid wearing hair spray or hair gel on lab days.

Sharp/Pointed Objects

Use knives and other sharp instruments with extreme care. Never cut objects while holding them in your hands. Place objects on a suitable work surface for cutting.

Safety First! LabBook **627**

Heat

Wear safety goggles when using a heating device or a flame. Whenever possible, use an electric hot plate as a heat source instead of an open flame. When heating materials in a test tube, always angle the test tube away from yourself and others. In order to avoid burns, wear heat-resistant gloves whenever instructed to do so.

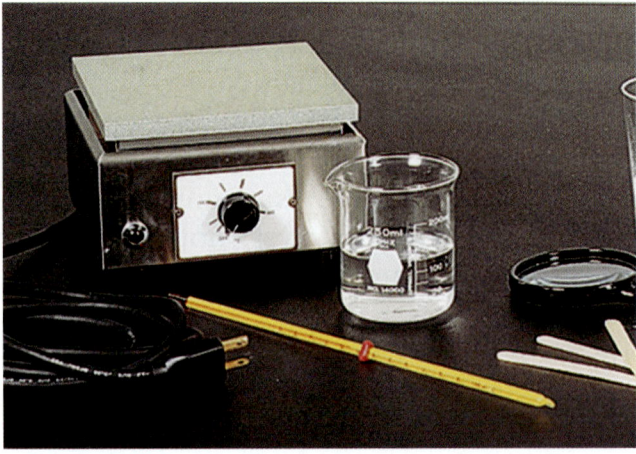

Electricity

Be careful with electrical cords. When using a microscope with a lamp, do not place the cord where it could trip someone. Do not let cords hang over a table edge in a way that could cause equipment to fall if the cord is accidentally pulled. Do not use equipment with damaged cords. Be sure your hands are dry and that the electrical equipment is in the "off" position before plugging it in. Turn off and unplug electrical equipment when you are finished.

Chemicals

Wear safety goggles when handling any potentially dangerous chemicals, acids, or bases. If a chemical is unknown, handle it as you would a dangerous chemical. Wear an apron and safety gloves when working with acids or bases or whenever you are told to do so. If a spill gets on your skin or clothing, rinse it off immediately with water for at least 5 minutes while calling to your teacher.

Never mix chemicals unless your teacher tells you to do so. Never taste, touch, or smell chemicals unless you are specifically directed to do so. Before working with a flammable liquid or gas, check for the presence of any source of flame, spark, or heat.

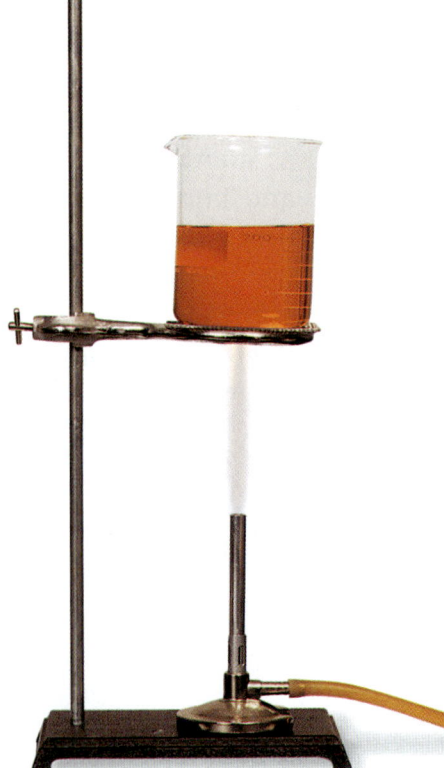

Animal Safety

Always obtain your teacher's permission before bringing any animal into the school building. Handle animals only as your teacher directs. Always treat animals carefully and with respect. Wash your hands thoroughly after handling any animal.

Plant Safety

Do not eat any part of a plant or plant seed used in the laboratory. Wash hands thoroughly after handling any part of a plant. When in nature, do not pick any wild plants unless your teacher instructs you to do so.

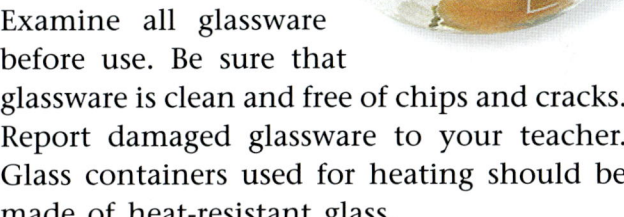

Glassware

Examine all glassware before use. Be sure that glassware is clean and free of chips and cracks. Report damaged glassware to your teacher. Glass containers used for heating should be made of heat-resistant glass.

Using the Scientific Method
Teacher's Notes

Time Required
One 45-minute class period

Lab Rating

TEACHER PREP
STUDENT SET-UP
CONCEPT LEVEL
CLEAN UP

MATERIALS
The materials listed on the student page are enough for a pair of students. Students can also work in groups of four. In that case, two students should assume the role of model builders, and the two others should assume the role of core samplers.

Safety Caution
Remind students to review all safety cautions and icons before beginning this lab activity.

Lab Notes
Provide each student group with three pieces of $\frac{1}{2}$ in. PVC pipe cut slightly longer than the height of their models.

Jan Nelson
East Valley Middle School
East Helena, Montana

630   Chapter 1 • LabBook

Using Scientific Methods

 **MAKING MODELS**

Using the Scientific Method

Geologists often use a technique called *core sampling* to learn what underground rock layers look like. This technique involves drilling several holes in the ground in different places and taking samples of the underground rock or soil. Geologists then compare the samples from each hole to construct a diagram that shows the bigger picture.

In this activity, you will model the process geologists use to diagram underground rock layers. You will first use modeling clay to form a rock-layer model. You will then exchange models with a classmate, take core samples, and draw a diagram of your classmate's layers.

Materials
- 3 colored pencils or markers
- nontransparent pan or box
- modeling clay in three colors
- 1/2 in. PVC pipe
- plastic knife

Ask a Question
1. Can unseen features be revealed by sampling parts of the whole?

Form a Hypothesis
2. Form a hypotheses on whether taking core samples from several locations will give a good indication of the entire hidden feature.

Test the Hypothesis
3. To test your hypothesis, you will take core samples from a model of underground rock layers, draw a diagram of the entire rock-layer sequence, and then compare your drawing with the actual model.

Build a Model
The model rock layers should be formed out of view of the classmates who will be taking the core samples.

4. Form a plan for your rock layers, and sketch the layers in your ScienceLog. Your sketch should include the three colors in several layers of varying thicknesses.

630

5. In the pan or box, mold the clay into the shape of the lowest layer in your sketch.

6. Repeat step 5 for each additional layer of clay. You now have a rock-layer model. Exchange models with a classmate.

Collect Data

7. Choose three places on the surface of the clay to drill holes. The holes should be far apart and in a straight line. (You do not need to remove the clay from the pan or box.)

8. Use the PVC pipe to "drill" a vertical hole in the clay at one of the chosen locations by slowly pushing the pipe through all the layers of clay. Slowly remove the pipe.

9. Remove the core sample from the pipe by gently pushing the clay out of the pipe with an unsharpened pencil.

10. Draw the core sample in your ScienceLog, and record your observations. Be sure to use a different color of pencil or marker for each layer.

11. Repeat steps 8–10 for the next two core samples. Make sure your drawings are side by side in your ScienceLog in the same order as the samples in the model.

Analyze the Results

12. Look at the pattern of rock layers in each of your core samples. Think about how the rock layers between the core samples might look. Then construct a diagram of the rock layers.

13. Complete your diagram by coloring the rest of the rock layers.

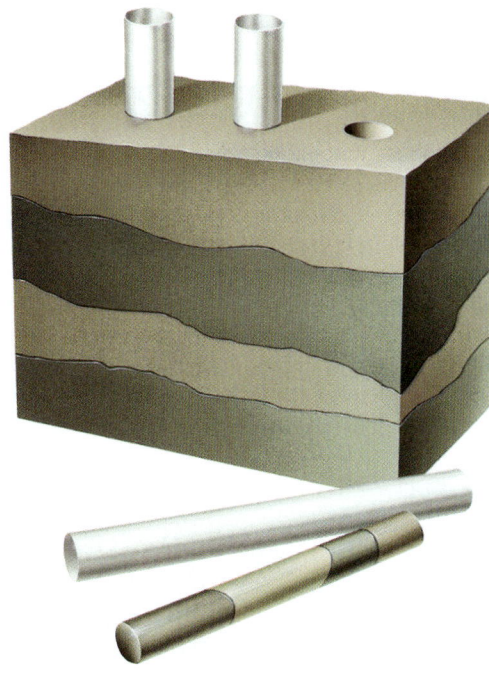

Draw Conclusions

14. Use the plastic knife to cut the clay model along a line connecting the three holes and remove one side of the model. The rock layers should now be visible.

15. How well does your rock-layer diagram match the model? Explain.

16. Is it necessary to revise your diagram from step 13? If so, how?

17. Do your conclusions support your hypothesis? Why or why not?

Going Further
What are two ways that the core-sampling method could be improved?

Answers

15. The rock-layer diagram provides a general overview of the layers. It may not be as specific as the model or provide all the details from the model.

16. Answers will vary. If the model is significantly different than the diagram, students should modify their diagram.

17. Answers will depend on student hypotheses.

Going Further

Answers will vary. Sample answers: More core samples could be taken, the core samples could be taken in specific areas, the core samples could be larger or closer together, or smaller areas could be combined for an overall picture of the layers.

 Datasheets for LabBook Datasheet 1

 Science Skills Worksheet 10 "Doing a Lab Write-up"

 Science Skills Worksheet 24 "Using Models to Communicate"

Round or Flat?
Teacher's Notes

Time Required

One 45-minute class period

Lab Ratings

TEACHER PREP ▲▲
STUDENT SET-UP ▲▲▲
CONCEPT LEVEL ▲▲▲
CLEAN UP ▲

MATERIALS

The materials listed on the student page are enough for a group of 3–4 students.

Safety Caution

Remind students to review all safety cautions before beginning this lab activity.

Preparation Notes

Obtain inflated basketballs from your school's physical education instructor. It may be necessary to ask students to bring basketballs from home. Begin the activity by reminding students that *circumference* is the distance around a circle or sphere.

You may also need to review the use of protractors with students before performing this activity.

Using Scientific Methods

Round or Flat?

Eratosthenes thought he could measure the circumference of the Earth. He came up with the idea while reading that a deep vertical well in southern Egypt was entirely lit up by the sun at noon once each year. He realized that for this to happen, the sun must be directly over the well at that moment! But at the same moment, in a city just north of this well, a tall monument cast a shadow. Eratosthenes reasoned that the sun could not be directly over both the monument and the well at noon on the same day. In this experiment, you will test his idea and see for yourself how his experiment works.

SKILL BUILDER

Materials

- basketball
- 2 books or notebooks
- modeling clay
- 2 unsharpened pencils
- metric ruler
- meterstick
- masking tape
- flashlight or small lamp
- string, 10 cm long
- protractor
- tape measure
- calculator (optional)

Ask a Question

1. How could I use Eratosthenes' experiment to measure the size of the Earth?

Conduct an Experiment

2. Set the basketball on a table, and place a book or notebook on either side to hold the ball in place. The ball represents the Earth.

3. Use modeling clay to attach a pencil to the "equator" of the ball so that it sticks directly outward.

4. Attach the second pencil to the ball 5 cm above the first pencil. This second pencil should also stick directly outward, as shown on the next page.

Lab Notes

Explain that Eratosthenes' experiment worked because he set up a ratio. It may be necessary to review ratios before performing this activity. The formula Eratosthenes used is as follows:

$$\frac{\text{Distance around ball}}{\text{Distance between sticks}} = \frac{360° \text{ in the sphere}}{\text{Angle of shadow with stick}}$$

5. Using a meterstick, mark a position 1 m away from the ball with masking tape. Label it "sun." Place the flashlight here.

6. When your teacher turns out the lights, turn on your flashlight, and point it so that the pencil on the equator does not cast a shadow. Ask a partner to hold the flashlight in this position. The second pencil should cast a shadow on the ball.

7. Tape one end of the string to the top of the second pencil. Hold the other end of the string against the ball at the far edge of the shadow. Make sure that the string is taut, but be careful not to pull the pencil over.

8. Use a protractor to measure the angle between the string and the pencil. Record this angle in your ScienceLog.

9. Use the following formula to calculate the *experimental circumference* of the ball:

$$\text{Circumference} = \frac{360° \times 5 \text{ cm}}{\text{angle between pencil and string}}$$

Record this circumference in your ScienceLog.

10. Wrap the tape measure around the ball's "equator" to measure the *actual circumference* of the ball. Record this circumference in your ScienceLog.

Analyze the Results

11. In your ScienceLog, compare the experimental circumference with the actual circumference.

12. What could have caused your experimental circumference to be different from the actual value?

13. What are some of the advantages and disadvantages of taking measurements this way?

Draw Conclusions

14. Was this an effective method for Eratosthenes to measure the Earth's circumference? Explain your answer.

Lab Notes

Students may be interested to learn that they can calculate the circumference of the Earth by performing Eratosthenes' experiment in partnership with other schools around the world. The experiment is conducted twice a year during the fall and spring equinoxes. To find out more, have students search for "Eratosthenes' experiment" on the Internet.

Answers

11. Students are likely to find that the experimental and actual circumference are not equal, but the two values should be close.

12. Answers may vary. Factors that affect this measurement include a slant of the pencils and human error in measurement.

13. Because it is impossible to use a tape measure to determine the circumference of the Earth, this procedure offers a good approximation. One disadvantage is that the measurements are not exact.

14. Yes, because it gives a value that is close to the actual value.

Datasheets for LabBook
Datasheet 2

Science Skills Worksheet 12
"Working with Hypotheses"

Barry L. Bishop
San Rafael Junior High
Ferron, Utah

Orient Yourself!
Teacher's Notes

Time Required
Two 45-minute class periods, one period to learn the use of a compass and the second to follow the orienteering course

Lab Ratings

TEACHER PREP 🧪🧪🧪
STUDENT SET-UP 🧪
CONCEPT LEVEL 🧪🧪🧪
CLEAN UP 🧪

MATERIALS
The materials listed on the student page are enough for a group of 3–4 students.

Preparation Notes
Find a suitable outdoor location for a simple orienteering course, and choose five control points for students to map. For example, you may wish to use several pieces of equipment in the playground, the flagpole, a tree, and a small hill. Be sure to mark each control point with either a specific color or a code word that students can collect or note on their maps when they reach each point.

Next, draw a map that includes the control points and the cardinal directions. Label a sixth spot as the starting point. Each group of students will need a copy of this map.

DESIGN YOUR OWN

Orient Yourself!

You have been invited to attend an orienteering event with your neighbors. In orienteering events, participants use maps and compasses to find their way along a course. There are several control points that each participant must reach. The object is to reach each control point and then the finish line. Orienteering events are often timed competitions. In order to find the fastest route through the course, the participants must read the map and use their compass correctly. Being the fastest runner does not necessarily guarantee finishing first. You also must choose the most direct route to follow.

Your neighbors participate in several orienteering events each year. They always come home raving about how much fun they had. You would like to join them, but you will need to learn how to use your compass first.

Materials
- magnetic compass
- course map
- ruler
- 2 colored pencils or markers

Procedure

1. Together as a class, go outside to the orienteering course your teacher has made.

2. Hold your compass flat in your hand. Turn the compass until the N is pointing straight in front of you. (The needle in your compass will always point north.) Turn your body until the needle lines up with the N on your compass. You are now facing north.

3. Regardless of which direction you want to face, you should always align the end of the needle with the N on your compass. If you are facing south, the needle will be pointing directly toward your body. When the N is aligned with the needle, the S will be directly in front of you, and you will be facing south.

4. Use your compass to face east. Align the needle with the N. Where is the E? Turn to face that direction. When the needle and the N are aligned and the E is directly in front of you, you are facing east.

5. In an orienteering competition, you will need to know how to determine which direction you are traveling. Now, face any direction you choose.

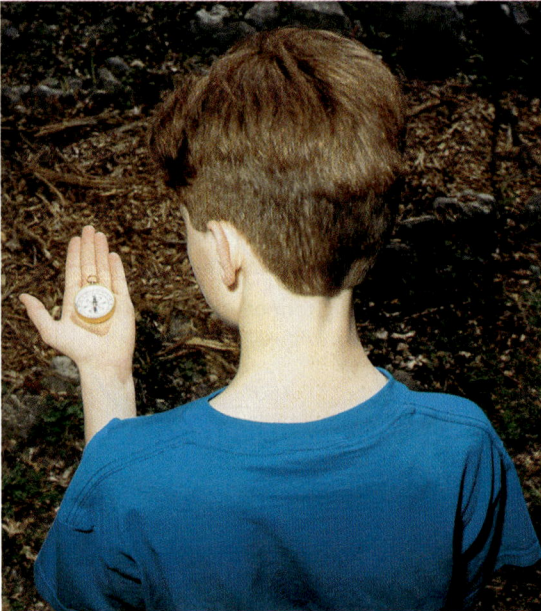

Before groups begin exploring the orienteering course, have students perform steps 1–6 individually. It may take as much as an entire class period for students to feel confident using a compass.

David Jones
Andrew Jackson Middle School
Cross Lanes, West Virginia

6. Do not move, but rotate the compass to align the needle on your compass with the N. What direction are you facing? You are probably not facing directly north, south, east, or west. If you are facing between north and west, you are facing northwest. If you are facing between north and east, you are facing northeast.

7. Find a partner or partners to follow the course your teacher has made. Get a copy of the course map from your teacher. It will show several control points. You must stop at each one. You will need to follow this map to find your way through the course. Find and stand at the starting point.

8. Face the next control point on your map. Rotate your compass to align the needle on your compass with the N. What direction are you facing?

9. Use the ruler to draw a line on your map between the two control points. Write the direction between the starting point and the next control point on your map.

10. Walk toward the control point. Keep your eyes on the horizon, not on your compass. You might need to go around obstacles such as a fence or building. Use the map to find the easiest way around.

11. Record the color or code word you find at the control point next to the control point symbol on your map.

12. Repeat steps 8–11 for each control point. Follow the points in order as they are labeled. For example, determine the direction from control point 1 to control point 2. Be sure to include the direction between the final control point and the starting point.

Analysis

13. The object of an orienteering competition is to arrive at the finish line first. The maps provided at these events do not instruct the participants to follow a specific path. In one form of orienteering, called "score orienteering," competitors may find the control points in any order. Look at your map. If this course were used for a score-orienteering competition, would you change your route? Explain.

14. If there is time, follow the map again. This time, use your own path to find the control points. Draw this path and the directions on your map in a different color. Do you believe this route was faster? Why?

Going Further

Do some research to find out about orienteering events in your area. The Internet and local newspapers may be good sources for the information. Are there any events that you would like to attend?

Answers

13. Answers will vary. Students should realize that the path shown on the map did not instruct them to follow the most direct route. They should propose a more direct route to follow. Their proposal should include the direction from one control point to the next.

14. This route should be faster. Students should realize that in an orienteering event, participants generally need to determine the quickest route. Some students may also realize that the quickest route is not necessarily the most direct. For example, there may be obstacles in the way (like hills or lakes) that could slow participants down. Orienteering maps include these landmarks.

 Datasheets for LabBook Datasheet 3

 Science Skills Worksheet 13 "Designing an Experiment"

Chapter 2 • LabBook

Topographic Tuber
Teacher's Notes

Time Required
One 45-minute class period

Lab Ratings

TEACHER PREP 🔺🔺
STUDENT SET-UP 🔺🔺🔺
CONCEPT LEVEL 🔺🔺🔺
CLEAN UP 🔺🔺

MATERIALS
The materials listed on the student page are enough for groups of 2–3 students. Modeling clay may be used in place of the potatoes. Students can mold the clay into a variety of shapes and compare their topographic maps.

Preparation Notes
It may be easier for students to see the waterline if you add a few drops of food coloring to the water before they add it to the container.

Before the activity, select several oddly shaped root vegetables from your local grocery store. Choose vegetables that have varied contour and shape. Sweet potatoes, for example, are available year-round and have many irregular shapes. If you cannot find naturally occurring root vegetables that have odd shapes, shape potatoes with a knife and peeler. You will then need to cut the potatoes in half lengthwise.

Using Scientific Methods

Topographic Tuber

Imagine that you live on top of a tall mountain and often look down on the lake below. Every summer, an island appears. You call it Sometimes Island because it goes away again during heavy fall rains. This summer you begin to wonder if you could make a topographic map of Sometimes Island. You don't have fancy equipment to make the map, but you have an idea. What if you place a meterstick with the 0 m mark at the water level in the summer? Then as the expected fall rains come, you could draw the island from above as the water rises. Would this idea really work?

Materials
- clear plastic storage container with transparent lid
- transparency marker
- metric ruler
- potato, cut in half
- water
- tracing paper

Ask a Question
1. How do I make a topographic map?

Conduct an Experiment
2. Place a mark at the storage container's base. Label this mark "0 cm" with a transparency marker.
3. Measure and mark 1 cm increments up the side of the container until you reach the top of the container. Label these marks "1 cm," "2 cm," "3 cm," and so on.
4. The scale for your map will be 1 cm = 10 m. Draw a line 2 cm long in the bottom right-hand corner of the lid. Place hash marks at 0 cm, 1 cm, and 2 cm. Label these marks "0 m," "10 m," and "20 m."
5. Place the potato flat side down in the center of the container.
6. Place the lid on the container, and seal it.
7. Viewing the potato from above, use the transparency marker to trace the outline of the potato where it rests on the bottom of the container. The floor of the container corresponds to the summer water level in the lake.

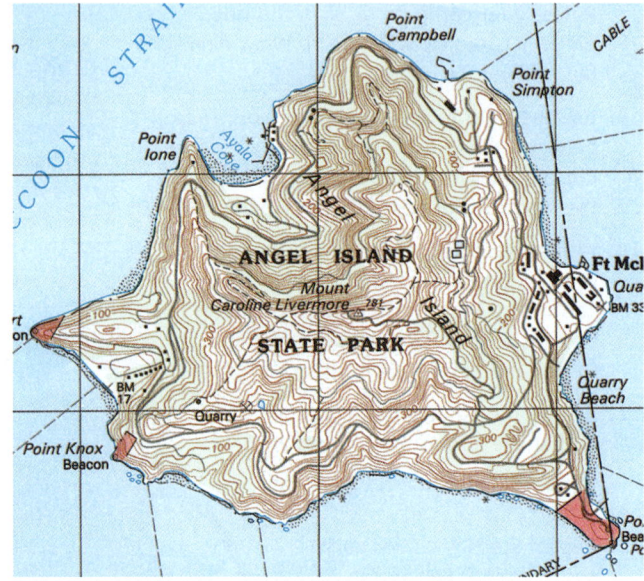

Lab Notes
Only islands that are at sea level begin at an elevation of 0 m. In order to calculate the elevation of an island that forms in a lake, you must also consider the elevation of the lake.

Michael E. Kral
West Hardin Middle School
Cecilia, Kentucky

8. Label this contour 0 m. (For this activity, assume that the water level in the lake during the summer is the same as sea level.)

9. Pour water into the container until it reaches the line labeled "1 cm."

10. Again place the lid on the container, and seal it. Part of the potato will be sticking out above the water. Viewing the potato from above, trace the part of the potato that touches the top of the water.

11. Label the elevation of the contour line you drew in step 10. According to the scale, the elevation is 10 m.

12. Remove the lid. Carefully pour water into the container until it reaches the line labeled "2 cm."

13. Place the lid on the container, and seal it. Viewing the potato from above, trace the part of the potato that touches the top of the water at this level.

14. Use the scale to calculate the elevation of this line. Label the elevation on your drawing.

15. Repeat steps 12–14, adding 1 cm to the depth of the water each time. Stop when the potato is completely covered.

16. Remove the lid, and set it on a tabletop. Place tracing paper on top of the lid. Trace the contours from the lid onto the paper. Label the elevation of each contour line. Congratulations! You have just made a topographic map!

Analyze the Results

17. What is the contour interval of this topographic map?

18. By looking at the contour lines, how can you tell which parts of the potato are steeper?

19. What is the elevation of the highest point on your map?

Draw Conclusions

20. Do all topographic maps have a 0 m elevation contour line as a starting point? How would this affect a topographic map of Sometimes Island? Explain your answer.

21. Would this method of measuring elevation be an effective way to make a topographic map of an actual area on Earth's surface? Why or why not?

Going Further
Place all of the potatoes on a table or desk at the front of the room. Your teacher will mix up the potatoes as you trade topographic maps with another group. By reading the topographic map you just received, can you pick out the matching potato?

Answers

17. The contour interval of the topographic map is 10 m.

18. Steeper parts of the potato will have contour lines that are closer together.

19. Answers will vary. Elevation is indicated by numbers on the contour lines.

20. No; topographic maps do not necessarily start with a 0 m elevation contour line. It is possible to make a topographic map of Sometimes Island showing its contours but it is impossible to know the island's elevation above sea level.

21. No; flooding an island is not an effective way of mapping it.

 Datasheets for LabBook Datasheet 4

Mysterious Minerals
Teacher's Notes

Time Required
One 45-minute class period

Lab Ratings

TEACHER PREP △△
STUDENT SET-UP △△
CONCEPT LEVEL △△
CLEAN UP △

MATERIALS
The materials listed on the student page are sufficient for each student. Students may also work in groups of 3–4. You will need one streak plate per student or group. A class should be able to share 3–5 streak plates.

Safety Caution
Remind students to review all safety cautions and icons before beginning this lab activity. Students need to be careful with glass microscope slides. Broken slides are likely to have sharp edges. Caution students not to taste the mineral samples.

Preparation Notes
Explain to students that they are not determining the absolute hardness of the mineral samples. Instead they are comparing the hardness of the samples with that of glass.

Your sample minerals should include pyrite, galena, hematite, magnetite, orthoclase (feldspar), quartz, muscovite, gypsum, hornblende (amphibole), garnet, biotite, and graphite.

Mysterious Minerals

Imagine sitting on a rocky hilltop, gazing at the ground below you. You can see dozens of different types of rocks. How can scientists possibly identify the countless variations? It's a mystery!

In this activity you'll use your powers of observation and a few simple tests to determine the identities of rocks and minerals. Take a look at the Mineral Identification Key on the next page. That key will help you use clues to discover the identity of several minerals.

Materials
- several sample minerals
- glass microscope slides
- streak plate
- safety gloves
- iron filings

Procedure

1. In your ScienceLog, create a data chart like the one below.

2. Choose one mineral sample, and locate its column in your data chart.

3. Follow the Mineral Identification Key to find the identity of your sample. When you are finished, record the mineral's name and primary characteristics in the appropriate column in your data chart.
   Caution: Put on your gloves when scratching the glass slide.

4. Select another mineral sample, and repeat steps 3 and 4 until your data table is complete.

Analysis

5. Were some minerals easier to identify than others? Explain.

6. A streak test is a better indicator of a mineral's true color than visual observation. Why isn't a streak test used to help identify every mineral?

7. In your ScienceLog, summarize what you learned about the various characteristics of each mineral sample you identified.

Mineral Summary Chart						
Characteristics	1	2	3	4	5	6
Mineral name						
Luster						
Color						
Streak						
Hardness						
Cleavage						
Special properties						

Answers

5. Students will find that some minerals required fewer steps to identify than others. For example, pyrite and galena are identified in two steps. Students may also find that they recognize some of the minerals and that the identification key is there merely to verify the identity.

6. For a mineral to leave a streak on the streak plate, the plate must be harder than the mineral. Therefore, extremely hard minerals do not leave a streak. Alternatively, some minerals that are softer than a streak plate leave behind a colorless streak.

7. Answers will vary.

Mineral Identification Key

1. **a.** If your mineral has a metallic luster, **GO TO STEP 2.**
   b. If your mineral has a nonmetallic luster, **GO TO STEP 3.**

2. **a.** If your mineral is black, **GO TO STEP 4.**
   b. If your mineral is yellow, it is **PYRITE.**
   c. If your mineral is silver, it is **GALENA.**

3. **a.** If your mineral is light in color, **GO TO STEP 5.**
   b. If your mineral is dark in color, **GO TO STEP 6.**

4. **a.** If your mineral leaves a red-brown line on the streak plate, it is **HEMATITE.**
   b. If your mineral leaves a black line on the streak plate, it is **MAGNETITE.** Test your sample for its magnetic properties by holding it near some iron filings.

5. **a.** If your mineral scratches the glass microscope slide, **GO TO STEP 7.**
   b. If your mineral does not scratch the glass microscope slide, **GO TO STEP 8.**

6. **a.** If your mineral scratches the glass slide, **GO TO STEP 9.**
   b. If your mineral does not scratch the glass slide, **GO TO STEP 10.**

7. **a.** If your mineral shows signs of cleavage, it is **ORTHOCLASE FELDSPAR.**
   b. If your mineral does not show signs of cleavage, it is **QUARTZ.**

8. **a.** If your mineral shows signs of cleavage, it is **MUSCOVITE.** Examine this sample for twin sheets.
   b. If your mineral does not show signs of cleavage, it is **GYPSUM.**

9. **a.** If your mineral shows signs of cleavage, it is **HORNBLENDE.**
   b. If your mineral does not show signs of cleavage, it is **GARNET.**

10. **a.** If your mineral shows signs of cleavage, it is **BIOTITE.** Examine your sample for twin sheets.
    b. If your mineral does not show signs of cleavage, it is **GRAPHITE.**

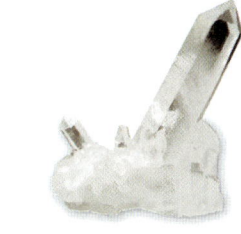

Going Further
Using your textbook and other reference books, research other methods of identifying different types of minerals. Based on your findings, create a new identification key. Give it to a friend along with a few sample minerals, and see if your friend can unravel the mystery!

Lab Notes
Each test in this lab tells the student more about the sample and narrows the possibilities. For example, the fact that a particular mineral sample does not have a streak eliminates hematite as a possibility but indicates that quartz is a possibility.

- It is possible for minerals that are softer than glass to leave a mark on glass. If the glass wipes clean and no scratch remains, then students will know that the mineral is softer than glass.
- Garnet is typically red but it can also be pale green.

Datasheets for LabBook
Datasheet 5

Going Further
Scientists test minerals for their density, crystal form, reaction to acids, optical properties, fluorescence, and radioactivity. Students should create an identification key that is very similar to the one provided in the lab, but their key should include different characteristics.

David Jones
Andrew Jackson Middle School
Cross Lanes, West Virginia

Is It Fool's Gold?— A Dense Situation

Teacher's Notes

Time Required
One 45-minute class period

Lab Ratings

TEACHER PREP 🧪🧪
STUDENT SET-UP 🧪🧪🧪
CONCEPT LEVEL 🧪🧪
CLEAN UP 🧪🧪

MATERIALS
Materials listed on the student page are sufficient for a group of 2–4 students. If your mineral samples are small, the change in volume may be difficult to detect. In that case, replace the beaker in steps 6–7 with a graduated cylinder.

Preparation Notes
Students may need to review density and specific gravity prior to performing this activity.

Lab Notes
- Density is conventionally described as g/cm^3, not g/mL.
- Because specific gravity is the ratio of a substance's density to the density of water ($1 g/cm^3$), the value will be the same for density. The difference is that specific gravity is a number, and density is a number with the units g/cm^3.
- Due to impurities, the density of some minerals is given in ranges. The density of pure gold is $19.3 g/cm^3$; lower numbers indicate the presence of impurities. The density of pure silver is $10.5 g/cm^3$; depending on impurities, that number can be higher or lower.
- Ideally, the values for specific gravity and density obtained in this lab will be identical. Discrepancies will likely result from differences in precision. Students should learn that all scientific measurements involve some margin of error.

Using Scientific Methods

Is It Fool's Gold?—A Dense Situation

Have you heard of fool's gold? Maybe you've seen a piece of it. This notorious mineral was often passed off as real gold. There are, however, simple tests you can do to keep from being tricked. Minerals can be identified by their properties. Some properties, such as color, vary between different samples of the same mineral. Other properties, such as density and specific gravity, remain consistent from one sample to another. In this activity, you will try to verify the identity of some mineral samples.

Materials
- spring scale
- ring stand
- pyrite sample
- galena sample
- balance
- string
- 400 mL beaker
- 400 mL of water

Ask a Question
1. How can I determine if an unknown mineral is not gold or silver?

Make Observations
2. Copy the data table below into your ScienceLog. Use it to record your observations.

Observation Chart		
Measurement	Galena	Pyrite
Mass in air (g)		
Weight in air (N)		
Beginning volume of water (mL)		
Final volume of water (mL)		
Volume of mineral (mL)		
Weight in water (N)		

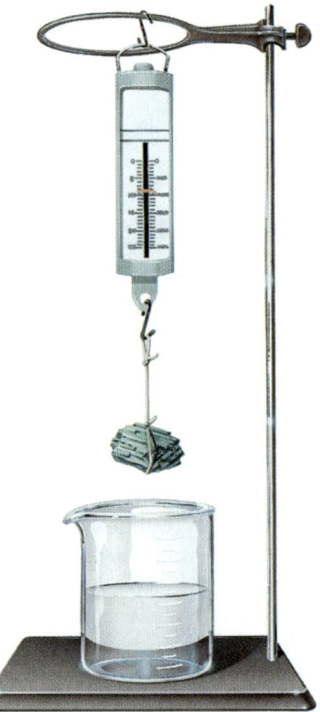

3. Find the mass of each sample by laying the mineral on the balance. Record the mass of each in your data table.

4. Attach the spring scale to the ring stand.

5. Tie a string around the sample of galena, leaving a loop at the loose end. Suspend the galena from the spring scale, and find its weight in air. Do not remove the sample from the spring scale yet. Enter these data in your data table.

Norman Holcomb
Marion Local Schools
Maria Stein, Ohio

6. Fill a beaker halfway with water. Record the beginning volume of water in your data table.

7. Carefully lift the beaker around the galena until the mineral is completely submerged. Be careful not to splash any water out of the beaker! Be sure the mineral does not touch the beaker.

8. Record the new volume and weight in your data table.

9. Subtract the original volume of water from the new volume to find the amount of water displaced by the mineral. This is the volume of the mineral sample itself. Record this value in your data table.

10. Repeat steps 5–9 for the sample of pyrite.

Analyze the Results

11. Copy the data table below into your ScienceLog. **Note:** 1 mL = 1 cm³

12. Use the following equations to calculate the density and specific gravity of each mineral, and record your answers in your data table.

$$\text{Density} = \frac{\text{mass in air}}{\text{volume}}$$

$$\text{Specific gravity} = \frac{\text{weight in air}}{\text{weight in air} - \text{weight in water}}$$

Mineral	Density (g/cm³)	Specific gravity
Silver	10.5	10.5
Galena		
Pyrite		
Gold	19.3	19.3

DO NOT WRITE IN BOOK

Draw Conclusions

13. The density of pure gold is 19.3 g/cm³. How can you use this information to prove that your sample of pyrite is not gold?

14. The density of pure silver is 10.5 g/cm³. How can you use this information to prove that your sample of galena is not silver?

15. If you found a gold-colored nugget, how could you find out if the nugget was real gold or fool's gold?

Answers

12.

Mineral	Density (g/cm³)	Specific gravity
Silver	10.5	10.5
Galena	7.4–7.6	7.4–7.6
Pyrite	5	5
Gold	19.3	19.3

13. Because the density of the sample is not 19.3 g/cm³, it is not gold.

14. Because the density of the sample is not 10.5 g/cm³, it is not pure silver. (The sample could contain silver mixed with other minerals.)

15. Sample answer: You could find the density and specific gravity of the gold-colored nugget. If it is pure gold, the density will be 19.3 g/cm³ and the specific gravity will be 19.3, but you would have to perform more tests to prove it was gold. If the sample has a density of 5 g/cm³ and a specific gravity of 5, then it is likely to be pyrite (fool's gold).

Datasheets for LabBook
Datasheet 6

Crystal Growth
Teacher's Notes

Time Required
Two 45-minute class periods

Lab Ratings

TEACHER PREP 🧪🧪
STUDENT SET-UP 🧪🧪🧪
CONCEPT LEVEL 🧪🧪
CLEAN UP 🧪🧪

MATERIALS
The materials listed are enough for a group of 4–5 students working cooperatively. Using a higher proportion of magnesium sulfate crystals to water will take significantly longer.

Safety Caution
Remind students to review all safety cautions and icons before beginning this lab activity.

Preparation Notes
Samples of igneous rocks may be obtained locally or through various science supply catalogs.

Gordon Zibelman
Drexel Hill Middle School
Drexel Hill, Pennsylvania

Using Scientific Methods

SKILL BUILDER

Crystal Growth

Magma forms deep below the Earth's surface at depths of 25 to 160 km and at extremely high temperatures. Some magma reaches the surface and cools quickly. Other magma gets trapped in cracks or magma chambers beneath the surface and cools very slowly. When magma cools slowly, large, well-developed crystals form. On the other hand, when magma erupts onto the surface, thermal energy is lost rapidly to the air or water. There is not enough time for large crystals to grow. The size of the crystals found in igneous rocks gives geologists clues about where and how the crystals formed.

In this experiment, you will demonstrate how the rate of cooling affects the size of crystals in igneous rocks by cooling crystals of magnesium sulfate at two different rates.

Make a Prediction

1. Suppose you have two solutions that are identical in every way except for temperature. How will the temperature of a solution affect the size of the crystals and the rate at which they form?

Make Observations

2. Put on your gloves, apron, and goggles.

3. Fill the beaker halfway with tap water. Place the beaker on the hot plate, and let it begin to warm. The temperature of the water should be between 40°C and 50°C.
Caution: Make sure the hot plate is away from the edge of the lab table.

4. Examine two or three crystals of the magnesium sulfate with your magnifying lens. In your ScienceLog, describe the color, shape, luster, and other interesting features of the crystals.

5. Draw a sketch of the magnesium sulfate crystals in your ScienceLog.

Conduct an Experiment

6. Use the pointed laboratory scoop to fill the test tube about halfway with the magnesium sulfate. Add an equal amount of distilled water.

Materials

- heat-resistant gloves
- 400 mL beaker
- 200 mL of tap water
- hot plate
- Celsius thermometer
- magnesium sulfate ($MgSO_4$) (Epsom salts)
- magnifying lens
- pointed laboratory scoop
- medium test tube
- distilled water
- watch or clock
- aluminum foil
- test-tube tongs
- dark marker
- masking tape
- basalt
- pumice
- granite

7. Hold the test tube in one hand, and use one finger from your other hand to tap the test tube gently. Observe the solution mixing as you continue to tap the test tube.

8. Place the test tube in the beaker of hot water, and heat it for approximately 3 minutes.
   Caution: Be sure to direct the opening of the test tube away from you and other students.

9. While the test tube is heating, shape your aluminum foil into two small boatlike containers by doubling the foil and turning up each edge.

10. If all the magnesium sulfate is not dissolved after 3 minutes, tap the test tube again, and heat it for 3 more minutes.
    Caution: Use the test-tube tongs to handle the hot test tube.

11. With a marker and a piece of masking tape, label one of your aluminum boats "Sample 1," and place it on the hot plate. Turn the hot plate off.

12. Label the other aluminum boat "Sample 2," and place it on the lab table.

13. Using the test-tube tongs, remove the test tube from the beaker of water, and evenly distribute the contents to each of your foil boats. Carefully pour the hot water in the beaker down the drain. Do not move or disturb either of your foil boats.

Make Observations

14. Copy the table below into your ScienceLog. Using the magnifying lens, carefully observe the foil boats. Record the time it takes for the first crystals to appear.

Crystal-Formation Table			
Crystal formation	Time	Size and appearance of crystals	Sketch of crystals
Sample 1			
Sample 2			

DO NOT WRITE IN BOOK

Lab Notes
Some volcanic rocks contain both large and small crystals. This is because the magma cooled for a period of time before erupting. This period of time was long enough for some minerals to crystallize but too short for other minerals to form.

Datasheets for LabBook
Datasheet 7

Chapter 4 • LabBook **643**

Answers

17. Answers will vary. A correct prediction would state that a cool solution will produce crystals more quickly than a warm solution. A correct prediction would also state that the crystals produced in a warm solution will be much larger than those produced in a cool solution.

18. Because the original crystals were small, students may conclude that they formed quickly.

20. Accept all reasonable sketches.

21. See the chart at the bottom of the page.

Going Further

Volcanic rocks that form in the air as the result of a violent volcanic eruption would cool quickly and have small crystals. Volcanic rocks that form from lava oozing out of a volcano would cool more slowly and have larger crystals.

Science Skills Worksheet 27 "Interpreting Your Data"

---

15. If crystals have not formed in the boats before class is over, carefully place the boats in a safe place. You may then record the time in days instead of in minutes.

16. When crystals have formed in both boats, use your magnifying lens to examine the crystals carefully.

Analyze the Results

17. Was your prediction correct? Explain.

18. Compare the size and shape of the crystals in Samples 1 and 2 with the size and shape of the crystals you examined in step 4. How long do you think the formation of the original crystals must have taken?

Draw Conclusions

19. Granite, basalt, and pumice are all igneous rocks. The most distinctive feature of each is the size of their crystals. Different igneous rocks form when magma cools at different rates. Examine a sample of each with your magnifying lens.

20. Copy the table below into your ScienceLog, and sketch each rock sample.

21. Use what you have learned in this activity to explain how each rock sample formed and how long it took for the crystals to form. Record your answers in your table.

Igneous Rock Observations			
	Granite	Basalt	Pumice
Sketch			
How did the rock sample form?			
Rate of cooling			

Going Further
Describe the size and shape of the crystals you would expect to find when a volcano erupts and sends material into the air and when magma oozes down the volcano's slope.

21.

	Granite	Basalt	Pumice
How did the rock sample form?	when magma cools slowly beneath the Earth's surface	when lava cools quickly on the Earth's surface	when magma is ejected from a volcano during a violent eruption
Rate of cooling	cools slowly; large crystals	cools quickly; small crystals	cools very quickly; very small or no crystals

Let's Get Sedimental

How do we determine if sedimentary rock layers are undisturbed? The best way is to be sure that the top of the layer still points up. This activity will show you how to read rock features that say, in effect, "This side up." Then you can look for the signs at a real outcrop.

Procedure

1. Thoroughly mix the sand, gravel, and soil together, and fill the plastic container about one-third full of the mixture.

2. Add water until the container is two-thirds full. Twist the cap back onto the container, and shake the container vigorously until all of the sediment is mixed in the rapidly moving water.

3. Place the container on a tabletop. Using the scissors, carefully cut the top off the container a few centimeters above the water, as shown at right. This will promote evaporation.

4. Do not disturb the container. Allow the water to evaporate. (You may accelerate the process by carefully using the dropper pipet to siphon off some of the clear water after allowing the container to sit for at least 24 hours.)

5. Immediately after you set the bottle on the desk, describe what you see from above and through the sides of the bottle. Do this at least once each day. Record your observations in your ScienceLog.

6. After the sediment has dried and hardened, describe its surface in your ScienceLog.

7. Carefully lay the container on its side, and cut a strip of plastic out of the side to expose the sediments in the bottle. You may find it easier if you place pieces of clay on either side of the bottle to stabilize it.

Materials

- sand
- gravel
- soil (clay-rich, if available)
- 3 L mixing bowl
- plastic pickle jar or 3 L plastic soda bottle with a cap
- water
- scissors
- dropper pipet
- magnifying lens

645

Helen Schiller
Northwood Middle School
Taylors, South Carolina

Lab Notes

This lab illustrates the sedimentary (depositional) process of *sorting*. When sediment is suspended in water, the largest, heaviest particles will settle out first, followed by the finer, lighter particles. This process allows scientists and students studying sedimentary rock layers to determine the original orientation of the rock.

Let's Get Sedimental
Teacher's Notes

Time Required
Two 45-minute class periods

Lab Ratings

TEACHER PREP	🧪
STUDENT SET-UP	🧪🧪
CONCEPT LEVEL	🧪🧪
CLEAN UP	🧪🧪🧪

MATERIALS

The materials listed are enough for a group of 3–4 students. You may substitute smaller plastic bottles. The amount of sand, gravel, and soil depends on the size of the jar. Each group will need enough of these materials to fill the bottle two-thirds full with a mixture of sand, gravel, and soil.

Safety Caution
Remind students to review all safety cautions and icons before beginning this lab activity. Students should be extremely careful when cutting the sides from the plastic bottles.

Preparation Notes
If the students use larger plastic bottles, it may take several days for the sediment to dry completely. It may be a good idea to ask the students to follow steps 1–5 as an introduction to the chapter. The class can then finish the procedure when the sediment has dried and you have covered all of the concepts in this lab.

Chapter 4 • LabBook

Answers

9. Answers will vary. Students should understand that the finest sediments should be at the top layers. This sequence can indicate the top of a sedimentary outcrop. If the layers are not in this order, the rock may have been disturbed.

10. Students might find mud cracks and peels on the top layer. Geologists would not expect to find these features in the bottom of an undisturbed column of sedimentary rock.

11. If features that geologists expect to find only in the top layer are found elsewhere, this indicates that the column has been disturbed. Geologists carefully study the layers for these features so they can determine their original order.

12. Each layer should show finer particles at the top. This pattern can only be seen from the side.

13. Students should see the same grading effect at the boundaries. The changes within each layer will be gradual, but the changes between different layers in the "rock" column may be more dramatic.

Going Further

- Answers will vary. Students should realize that finding the bottom of a layer in an undisturbed column would indicate which direction was down at the time of deposition.

- Students should realize that the bottom of the new layer would match the surface features of the column in their container. Any cracks, for example, would be filled with the new sediment.

8. Brush away the loose material from the sediment, and gently blow on the surface until it is clean. Examine the surface, and record your observations in your ScienceLog.

Analysis

9. Do you see anything through the side of the bottle that could help you determine if a sedimentary rock is undisturbed? Explain.

10. What structures do you see on the surface of the sediment that you would not expect to find at the bottom?

11. Explain how these features might be used to identify the top of the sedimentary bed in a real outcrop and to decide if the bed has been disturbed.

12. Did you see any structures on the side of the container that might indicate which direction is up?

13. After removing the side of the bottle, use the magnifying lens to examine the boundaries between the gravel, sand, and silt. What do you see? Do the size and type of sediment change quickly or gradually?

Going Further

Explain why the following statement is true: "If the top of a layer can't be found, finding the bottom of it works just as well."

Imagine that a layer was deposited directly above the layers in your container. Describe the bottom of this layer.

 Datasheets for LabBook
Datasheet 8

646 Chapter 4 • LabBook

Metamorphic Mash

Metamorphism is a complex process that takes place deep within the Earth, where the temperature and pressure would turn a human into a crispy pancake. The effects of this extreme temperature and pressure are obvious in some metamorphic rocks. One of these effects is the reorganization of mineral grains within the rock. In this activity, you will investigate the process of metamorphism without being charred, flattened, or buried.

Procedure

1. Flatten the clay into a layer about 1 cm thick. Sprinkle the surface with sequins.
2. Roll the corners of the clay toward the middle to form a neat ball.
3. Carefully use the plastic knife to cut the ball in half. In your ScienceLog, describe the position and location of the sequins inside the ball.
4. Put the ball back together, and use the sheets of cardboard or plywood to flatten the ball until it is about 2 cm thick.
5. Using the plastic knife, slice open the slab of clay in several places. In your ScienceLog, describe the position and location of the sequins in the slab.

Analysis

6. What physical process does flattening the ball represent?
7. Describe any changes in the position and location of the sequins that occurred as the clay ball was flattened into a slab.
8. How are the sequins oriented in relation to the force you put on the ball to flatten it?
9. Do you think the orientation of the mineral grains in a foliated metamorphic rock tells you anything about the rock? Defend your answer.

Going Further

Suppose you find a foliated metamorphic rock that has grains running in two distinct directions. Use what you have learned in this activity to offer a possible explanation for this observation.

Materials

- modeling clay
- sequins or other small flat objects
- plastic knife
- small pieces of very stiff cardboard or plywood

Dwight Patton
Carrol T. Welch Middle School
Horizon City, Texas

Going Further
Answers will vary. Two pressures acting on the rock at different times must have pushed on the rock in different directions.

Metamorphic Mash
Teacher's Notes

Time Required
One 45-minute class period

Lab Ratings

TEACHER PREP 🧪
STUDENT SET-UP 🧪🧪
CONCEPT LEVEL 🧪🧪
CLEAN UP 🧪🧪

MATERIALS
The materials listed in the student page are enough for one student.

Safety Caution
Remind students to review all safety cautions and icons before beginning this lab activity.

Answers

3. The sequins should be lying in a random pattern. Any layering is the result of rolling the ball.
5. The sequins are all horizontal.
6. It represents the pressure that creates metamorphic rock.
7. Before the ball was flattened, the sequins were in a random pattern. Once the ball was flattened, they lined up perpendicular to the pressure.
8. The sequins are aligned perpendicular to the force.
9. Because the grains line up at right angles to the pressure, they are perpendicular to the strongest stress.

Datasheets for LabBook
Datasheet 9

Make A Water Wheel
Teacher's Notes

Time Required
One or two 45-minute class periods

Lab Ratings

- TEACHER PREP 🔬
- STUDENT SET-UP 🔬🔬🔬
- CONCEPT LEVEL 🔬
- CLEAN UP 🔬🔬

MATERIALS
The materials listed are best for a group of 3–4 students.

Safety Caution
Remind students to review all safety cautions and icons before beginning this lab activity.

Preparation Notes
One week before the activity, have students bring in empty, 1 gal plastic milk and distilled-water jugs. (Be sure that the milk jugs are thoroughly rinsed.) You can also get these from a plastic recycling drop-off center. Do not use plastic jugs that once contained harmful chemicals. Also have students bring in empty 2 L soda bottles. Obtain corks from a craft store, or collect them yourself. Some restaurants will save corks for you from opened wine bottles if you ask ahead of time. You may wish to have extra corks on hand; some corks become dry, brittle, and crumbly. Skewers can be obtained at a grocery store; they usually come in packages of 200 and are inexpensive. Pick off the rough fibers from the skewers to reduce the friction.

Using Scientific Methods

Make a Water Wheel

Lift Enterprises is planning to build a water wheel that will lift objects like a crane does. City planners feel that this would make very good use of the energy supplied by the river that flows through town. Development of the water wheel is in the early stages. The president of the company has asked you to modify the basic water-wheel design so that the final product will lift objects more quickly.

Ask a Question
1. What factors influence the rate at which a water wheel lifts a weight?

Form a Hypothesis
2. In your ScienceLog, change the question above into a statement giving your "best guess" as to what factors will have the greatest effect on your water wheel.

Build a Model
3. Measure and mark a 5 × 5 cm square on an index card. Cut the square out of the card.
4. Fold the square in half to form a triangle.
5. Measure and mark a line 8 cm from the bottom of the plastic jug. Use scissors to cut along this line. (Your teacher may need to use a safety razor to start this cut for you.) Keep both sections of the jug.
6. Use the permanent marker to trace four triangles onto the flat parts of the top section of the plastic jug. Use the paper triangle you made in step 4 as a template. Cut the triangles out of the plastic to form four fins.
7. Use a thumbtack to attach one corner of each plastic fin to the round edge of the cork, as shown at right. Make sure the fins are equally spaced around the cork.
8. Press a thumbtack into one of the flat sides of the cork. Jiggle the thumbtack to widen the hole in the cork, and then remove the thumbtack.
9. Repeat step 8 on the other side of the cork.

SKILL BUILDER

Materials
- index card
- metric ruler
- scissors
- safety razor (for teacher)
- large plastic milk jug
- permanent marker
- 5 thumbtacks
- cork
- glue
- 2 wooden skewers
- hole punch
- modeling clay
- transparent tape
- 20 cm of thread
- coin
- 2 L bottle filled with water
- watch or clock that indicates seconds

Lab Notes
If the coin is lowered instead of raised in step 16, instruct students to unwrap the thread, wrap it in the other direction around the clay, and repeat step 16. You may wish to have a class competition to see which wheel can lift the weight the fastest.

Tracy Jahn
Berkshire Jr.–Sr. High
Canaan, New York

10. Place a drop of glue on the end of a skewer, and insert the skewer into one of the holes in the end of the cork. Insert the second skewer into the hole in the other end.

11. Use a hole punch to carefully punch two holes in the bottom section of the plastic jug. Punch each hole 1 cm from the top edge of the jug, directly across from one another.

12. Carefully push the skewers through the holes, and suspend the cork in the center of the jug.

13. Attach a small ball of clay to the end of each skewer. The clay balls should be the same size.

14. Tape one end of the thread to one skewer on the outside of the jug next to the clay ball. Wrap the thread around the clay ball three times. (As the water wheel turns, the thread should continue to wrap around the clay. The other ball of clay balances the weight and helps to keep the water wheel turning smoothly.)

15. Tape the free end of the thread to a coin. Wrap the thread around the coin once, and tape it again. You are now ready to test your hypothesis.

Test the Hypothesis

16. Slowly and carefully pour water from the 2 L bottle onto the fins so that the water wheel spins. What happens to the coin? Record your observations in your ScienceLog.

17. Lower the coin back to the starting position. Add more clay to the skewer to increase the diameter of the wheel. Repeat step 16. Did the coin rise faster or slower this time?

18. Lower the coin back to the starting position. Modify the shape of the clay, and repeat step 16. Does the shape of the clay affect how quickly the coin rises? Explain your answer.

19. What happens if you remove two of the fins from opposite sides? What happens if you add more fins? Modify your water wheel to find out.

20. Experiment with another fin shape. How does a different fin shape affect how quickly the coin rises?

Analyze the Results

21. What factors influence how quickly you can lift the coin?

Draw Conclusions

22. What recommendations would you make to Lift Enterprises to improve its water wheel?

Answers

16. The coin rises.
17. The coin rises faster with more clay.
18. If the clay is shaped so that the thread has to wrap around a bulge, the coin will rise faster. If the clay is shaped so that the thread has to wrap around a narrow part, the coin will rise slower.
19. Fewer fins cause the wheel to turn slower, and the coin rises slower. More fins cause the wheel to turn faster, and the coin rises faster.
20. Generally, fins that catch more water will cause the wheel to turn faster, and the coin will rise faster.
21. The shape and amount of clay and the number and shape of the fins influence how quickly the wheel lifts the coin.
22. Answers will vary. Recommendations could include the following: more fins, fin shapes that catch more water, and wrapping the rope or cable around a large diameter.

Datasheets for LabBook
Datasheet 10

Power of the Sun
Teacher's Notes

Time Required

One or two 45-minute class periods

Lab Ratings

TEACHER PREP 🧪🧪
STUDENT SET-UP 🧪
CONCEPT LEVEL 🧪🧪
CLEAN UP 🧪

MATERIALS

The materials listed for this lab are enough for a group of 2–3 students.

Safety Caution

Remind students to review all safety cautions and icons before beginning this lab activity. Instruct students to not look directly at the sun. Also caution them not to squeeze the aluminum too hard around the thermometer to avoid crushing the thermometer bulb. Also tell students not to force the thermometers through the holes if the holes are too small.

Preparation Notes

Prepare the lids by punching a hole in the center of each lid with a nail and hammer. Flatten the jagged edges against the inside of the lid with the hammer. Each hole should be big enough to accommodate a thermometer. Cut 2 × 8 cm strips of aluminum from the bottom of a pie plate. Make sure there are no sharp burrs left on the edges of the strips. Before beginning this lab, you may wish to review the concept of ratios with students.

Power of the Sun

The sun radiates energy in every direction. Like the sun, the energy radiated by a light bulb spreads out in all directions. But how much energy an object receives depends on how close that object is to the source. As you move farther from the source, the amount of energy you receive decreases. For example, if you measure the amount of energy that reaches you from a light and then move three times farther away, you will discover that nine times less energy will reach you at your second position. Energy from the sun travels as light energy. When light energy is absorbed by an object it is converted into thermal energy. *Power* is the rate at which one form of energy is converted to another, and it is measured in *watts*. Because power is related to distance, nearby objects can be used to measure the power of far-away objects. In this lab you will calculate the power of the sun using an ordinary 100-watt light bulb.

Materials

- protective gloves
- aluminum strip, 2 × 8 cm
- pencil
- black permanent marker
- Celsius thermometer
- mason jar, cap, and lid with hole in center
- modeling clay
- desk lamp with a 100 W bulb and removable shade
- metric ruler
- watch or clock that indicates seconds
- scientific calculator

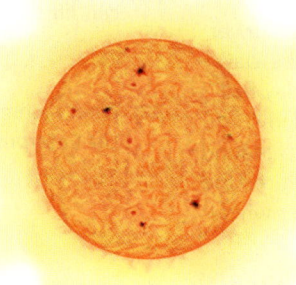

Procedure

1. Gently shape the piece of aluminum around a pencil so that it holds on in the middle and has two wings, one on either side of the pencil.

2. Bend the wings outward so that they can catch as much sunlight as possible.

3. Use the marker to color both wings on one side of the aluminum strip black.

4. Remove the pencil and place the aluminum snugly around the thermometer near the bulb.
   Caution: Do not press too hard—you do not want to break the thermometer! Wear protective gloves when working with the thermometer and the aluminum.

5. Carefully slide the top of the thermometer through the hole in the lid. Place the lid on the jar so that the thermometer bulb is inside the jar, and screw down the cap.

6. Secure the thermometer to the jar lid by molding clay around the thermometer on the outside of the lid. The aluminum wings should be in the center of the jar.

7. Read the temperature on the thermometer. Record this as room temperature.

8. Place the jar on a windowsill in the sunlight. Turn the jar so that the black wings are angled toward the sun.

9. Watch the thermometer until the temperature reading stops rising. Record the temperature in your ScienceLog.

10. Remove the jar from direct sunlight, and allow it to return to room temperature.

Gordon Zibelman
Drexel Hill Middle School
Drexel Hill, Pennsylvania

11. Remove any shade or reflector from the lamp. Place the lamp at one end of a table.
12. Place the jar about 30 cm from the lamp. Turn the jar so that the wings are angled toward the lamp.
13. Turn on the lamp, and wait about 1 minute.
14. Move the jar a few centimeters toward the lamp until the temperature reading starts to rise. When the temperature stops rising, compare it with the reading you took in step 9.
15. Repeat step 14 until the temperature matches the temperature you recorded in step 9.
16. If the temperature reading rises too high, move the jar away from the lamp and allow it to cool. Once the reading has dropped to at least 5°C below the temperature you recorded in step 9, you may begin again at step 12.
17. When the temperature in the jar matches the temperature you recorded in step 9, record the distance between the center of the light bulb and the thermometer bulb in your ScienceLog.

Analysis

18. The thermometer measured the same amount of energy absorbed by the jar at the distance you measured to the lamp. In other words, your jar absorbed as much energy from the sun at a distance of 150 million kilometers as it did from the 100 W light bulb at the distance you recorded in step 17.

19. Use the following formula to calculate the power of the sun (be sure to show your work):

$$\frac{\text{power of the sun}}{(\text{distance to the sun})^2} = \frac{\text{power of the lamp}}{(\text{distance to the lamp})^2}$$

Hint: (distance)² means that you multiply the distance by itself. If you found that the lamp was 5 cm away from the jar, for example, the (distance)² would be 25.

Hint: Convert 150,000,000 km to 15,000,000,000,000 cm.

20. Review the discussion of scientific notation in the Math Refresher found in the Appendix at the back of this book. You will need to understand this technique for writing large numbers in order to compare your calculation with the actual figure. For practice, convert the distance to the sun given in step 19 to scientific notation.

    15,000,000,000,000 cm = 1.5 × 10$^{\underline{?}}$ cm

21. The sun emits 3.7 × 10²⁶ W of power. Compare your answer in step 19 with this value. Was this a good way to calculate the power of the sun? Explain.

Answers

19. Answers will vary. Ask students to show their calculations.
20. 15,000,000,000,000 cm = 1.5 × 10¹³ cm
21. Answers will vary. If students performed the lab correctly, their numbers should be close to 3.7 × 10²⁶ W.

Datasheets for LabBook
Datasheet 11

Math Skills Worksheet 25
"What Is Scientific Notation?"

Math Skills Worksheet 26
"Multiplying and Dividing in Scientific Notation"

How DO You Stack Up?
Teacher's Notes

Time Required

Two 45-minute class periods

Lab Ratings

TEACHER PREP
STUDENT SET-UP
CONCEPT LEVEL
CLEAN UP

MATERIALS

The materials listed on the student page are enough for each group. The activity works best if the class is divided into five groups.

Safety Caution

Remind students to review all safety cautions and icons before beginning this lab activity.

How DO You Stack Up?

DISCOVERY LAB

According to the *law of superposition,* in undisturbed sequences of sedimentary rock, the oldest layers are on the bottom. Geologists use this principle to determine the relative age of the rocks in a small area. Geologists can also use fossils in the rocks to date the rocks. When geologists find similar rock sequences and fossils in different areas, they can match parts of the sequences. Each new area they examine helps improve and expand our picture of the rock record. When enough areas around the world are examined, geologists then build a geologic column that shows a general history of the Earth and a relative age for each rock.

In this activity, you will model what geologists do by drawing stratigraphic sections for different rock outcrops. Then, along with your classmates, you will create a part of the geologic column, showing the geologic history of the area that contains all of the outcrops.

Materials

- metric ruler
- pencil
- colored pencils or crayons
- white paper
- scissors

Procedure

1. After your teacher assigns you to one of five groups, look at the illustration of the section for Outcrop 1 at right. Copy this section onto a blank piece of paper. Follow the specific instructions in steps 2–6 concerning rock color and texture and the contact between layers—bedding planes or unconformities. Use the Rock and Fossil Key on the next page to determine the color and texture of each layer.

2. Use a metric ruler and a pencil to draw a box 3 cm wide and 9 cm tall. With colored pencils, sketch a layer of conglomerate (A1) on the bottom of the box. It should reach from side to side and be 2 cm tall.

3. Use a black crayon or pencil to add B3 and C3 fossils to the conglomerate layer. The top of this layer is a bedding plane, so it should be a straight line.

4. Draw a 2 cm layer of sandstone (B1) with B3 fossils above the conglomerate layer. The top of the layer is an unconformity, so use a wavy line to represent the break in rock-layer sequence.

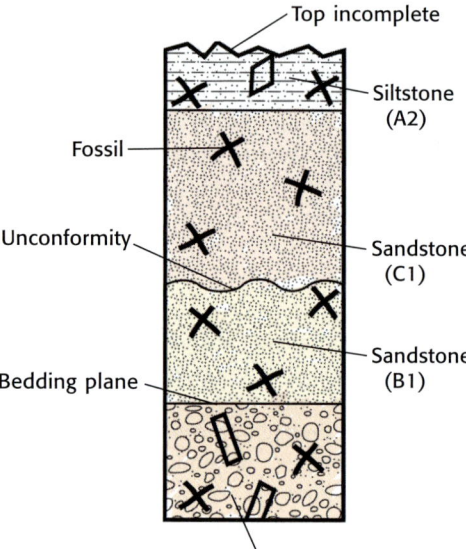

Section for Outcrop 1

- Top incomplete
- Siltstone (A2)
- Fossil
- Sandstone (C1)
- Unconformity
- Sandstone (B1)
- Bedding plane
- Conglomerate (A1)

Dwight Patton
Carroll T. Welch Middle School
Horizon City, Texas

652 Chapter 6 • LabBook

5. Add a 3 cm layer of another sandstone (C1) with B3 fossils. The top of this layer is another bedding plane.

6. Add a 1 cm layer of siltstone (A2) containing B3 and C4 fossils. The top of this layer is incomplete, so draw a jagged edge at the top. Write the outcrop number (1) at the top of the section.

	Outcrop 1			
Layer	Rock type	Fossils	Thickness	Upper contact
top	siltstone (A2)	B3, C4	1 cm	incomplete
	sandstone (C1)	B3	3 cm	bedding plane
	sandstone (B1)	B3	2 cm	unconformity
bottom	conglomerate (A1)	B3, C3	2 cm	bedding plane

7. Compare the section you drew with the chart above. You will need to follow a similar chart to draw your own stratigraphic section. Be sure you understand how the section and chart for Outcrop 1 are related before you continue.

8. After your teacher assigns an outcrop to your group, find the chart on the following page that corresponds to your outcrop's section. As a group, use the chart to draw the section.

9. Sketch your section in a column that is 3 cm wide. The height of each rock layer is given in the chart for your section. Include the rock color, the rock type, and the types of fossils, as indicated in the chart and the Rock and Fossil Key at right. Pay close attention to the type of contact between the layers. (Assume that the bottom of the lowest layer is a bedding plane.)

10. When you finish your section, check to make sure it represents the information in the chart and key correctly. Write the outcrop number at the top of your section.

11. Make four more copies of your section, and pass them out to the other groups in your class. Ultimately, each group should have six sections, including the section for Outcrop 1.

Rock and Fossil Key

	A	B	C
1			
2			
3		✕	▯
4	△	⬡	◇
5	ҩ	☐	◯

Preparation Notes
You may need to review correlation and the law of superposition before performing this activity. Also be certain that your students understand what an index fossil is.

Thicknesses of layers given in the lab are the thicknesses on the stratigraphic sections only. The rock layers represented by the sections would probably be much thicker. However, the relative thicknesses of the layers are represented in the measurements given (i.e., a layer that is 4 cm thick is twice as thick as a layer that is 2 cm thick).

Lab Notes
Explain that the geologic column for the entire Earth is constructed from smaller columns similar to the hypothetical column in this lab. Stratigraphic sections are pieced together to form short columns, and short columns are pieced together to form longer columns. All columns put together make up the geologic column for the entire Earth.

Datasheets for LabBook
Datasheet 12

Chapter 6 • LabBook

A Sample Geologic Column

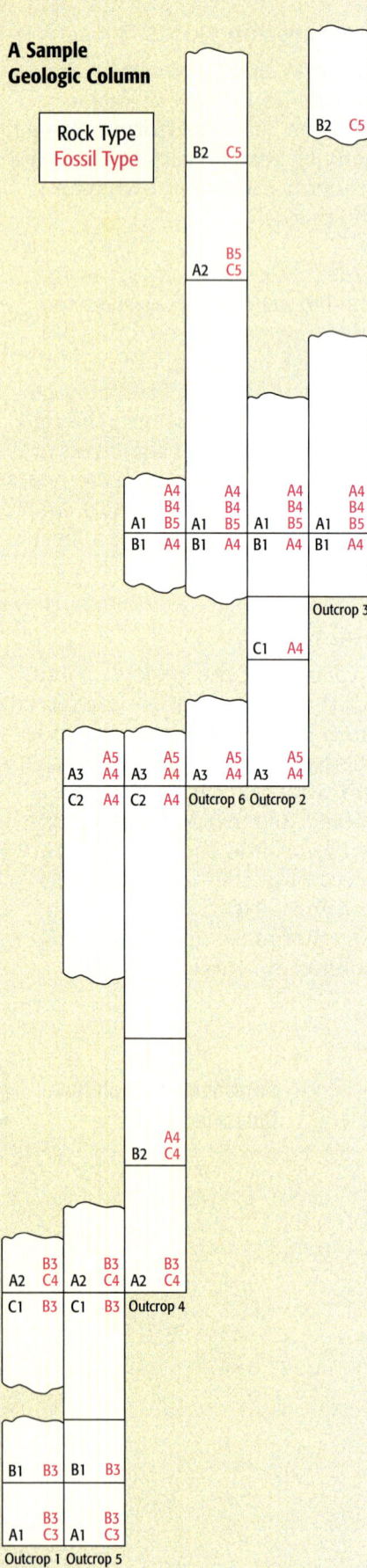

Outcrop 2

Layer	Rock type	Fossils	Thickness	Upper contact
top	conglomerate (A1)	A4, B4, B5	4 cm	incomplete
↑	sandstone (B1)	A4	2 cm	bedding plane
	sandstone (C1)	A4	2 cm	bedding plane
bottom	limestone (A3)	A4, A5	3 cm	bedding plane

Outcrop 3

Layer	Rock type	Fossils	Thickness	Upper contact
top	shale (B2)	C5	4 cm	incomplete
↑	conglomerate (A1)	A4, B4, B5	6 cm	unconformity
bottom	sandstone (B1)	A4	2 cm	bedding plane

Outcrop 4

Layer	Rock type	Fossils	Thickness	Upper contact
top	conglomerate (A1)	A4, B4, B5	1 cm	incomplete
↑	sandstone (B1)	A4	1 cm	bedding plane
	limestone (A3)	A4, A5	1 cm	unconformity
	shale (C2)	A4	6 cm	bedding plane
	shale (B2)	A4, C4	4 cm	bedding plane
bottom	siltstone (A2)	B3, C4	4 cm	bedding plane

Outcrop 5

Layer	Rock type	Fossils	Thickness	Upper contact
top	limestone (A3)	A4, A5	1 cm	incomplete
↑	shale (C2)	A4	4 cm	bedding plane
	siltstone (A2)	B3, C4	3 cm	unconformity
	sandstone (C1)	B3	4 cm	bedding plane
	sandstone (B1)	B3	2 cm	bedding plane
bottom	conglomerate (A1)	B3, C3	2 cm	bedding plane

Outcrop 6

Layer	Rock type	Fossils	Thickness	Upper contact
top	shale (B2)	C5	3 cm	incomplete
↑	siltstone (A2)	B5, C5	4 cm	bedding plane
	conglomerate (A1)	A4, B4, B5	8 cm	bedding plane
	sandstone (B1)	A4	2 cm	bedding plane
bottom	limestone (A3)	A4, A5	2 cm	unconformity

Answers

16. There are 12 layers in the completed geologic column.

17. The oldest layer in this column is conglomerate A1. This rock layer contains B3 and C3 fossils and is 2 cm thick. The youngest rock layer is shale B2. This layer contains C5 fossils, and its thickness is at least 4 cm.

18. C3, A5, and B4 fossils can be used as index fossils for single layers. The bottom layer (A1) contains C3 fossils. The layer of limestone (A3) contains A5 fossils, and the younger layer of conglomerate (A1) contains B4 fossils. These fossils are considered index fossils because they occur in a narrow range of geologic time.

Note for Question 18: Index fossils are not always restricted to a single rock layer, but the shorter the column occupied by an index fossil, the more useful the index fossil is.

12. Cut the sections out of the paper. Don't cut off the outcrop numbers! In different sections, find layers that have the same rocks and contain the same fossils. Line the sections up next to each other by matching similar layers. Don't be surprised if layers don't look exactly the same. This happens in the real world, too.

13. If unconformities appear in any of the sections, there may be some rock layers missing. You may need to examine other sections to find out what fits between the layers above and below the unconformities. To leave space for these layers, cut the sections along the unconformities.

14. When you find layers that match, you should be able to do one of three things with the other sections—add rock layers to the bottom of your matched sections, add rock layers to the top of your matched sections, or slip missing rock layers between unconformities. Remember to determine whether any of the fossils are index fossils for certain layers.

15. After several tries, you should be able to create the part of the geologic column that corresponds to the area containing the six outcrops. The part of the column will show rock types and fossils for all the known layers in the area.

Analysis

16. How many layers are found in this part of the geologic column?

17. Which is the oldest layer in your column? Which rock layer is the youngest? Describe these layers in terms of rock type and the fossils they contain.

18. Which (if any) fossils can be used as index fossils for a single layer? Which layer or layers contain each of these fossils? Why are these fossils considered index fossils?

19. Fossils may also be used to distinguish similar layers from one another. Name two layers in your column that are distinguished only by the fossils they contain. Which fossil(s) identifies each layer?

20. List the fossils in your column from oldest to youngest. Label the oldest and youngest fossils.

21. Look at the unconformities in the sections for Outcrops 3 and 4. Which rock layers are partially or completely missing from each section? Explain how you know this.

19. There are two layers of sandstone (B1). These can be distinguished by their fossils. The older layer contains B3 fossils, and the younger layer contains A4 fossils. There are two other layers of sandstone (C1) that can be distinguished by their fossils. The older layer contains B3 fossils, and the younger layer contains A4 fossils. Students may also compare the two layers of conglomerate (A1), the two layers of siltstone (A2), or the two layers of shale (B2).

20. The relative age of the fossils in this column, from oldest to youngest, is: C3, B3, C4, A4, A5, B4, B5, and C5.

21. The following layers are partially or completely missing from the section for Outcrop 3:

    Shale B2 (containing fossil C5)
    Siltstone A2 (containing fossils B5 and C5)
    Conglomerate A1 (containing fossils A4, B4, and B5)

    The following layers are partially or completely missing from the section for Outcrop 4:

    Sandstone B1 (containing fossil A4)
    Sandstone C1 (containing fossil A4)
    Limestone A3 (containing fossils A4 and A5)

    The missing layers from the sections for outcrops 3 and 4 are identified by comparing the layers in the outcrops with the complete geologic column.

Students should create a geologic column that contains the information shown in the table at left.

LAYER	ROCK TYPE	FOSSILS	THICKNESS	CONTACT
top	shale (B2)	C5	≥ 4 cm	incomplete
	siltstone (A2)	B5, C5	4 cm	bedding plane
	conglomerate (A1)	A4, B4, B5	8 cm	bedding plane
	sandstone (B1)	A4	2 cm	bedding plane
	sandstone (C1)	A4	2 cm	bedding plane
	limestone (A3)	A4, A5	3 cm	bedding plane
	shale (C2)	A4	6 cm	bedding plane
	shale (B2)	A4, C4	4 cm	bedding plane
	siltstone (A2)	B3, C4	4 cm	bedding plane
	sandstone (C1)	B3	4 cm	bedding plane
	sandstone (B1)	B3	2 cm	bedding plane
bottom	conglomerate (A1)	B3, C3	2 cm	bedding plane

Convection Connection
Teacher's Notes

Time Required
One 45-minute class period

Lab Ratings

TEACHER PREP 🔺
STUDENT SET-UP 🔺🔺🔺
CONCEPT LEVEL 🔺🔺
CLEAN UP 🔺🔺

MATERIALS
The materials listed on the student page are enough for a group of 2–3 students.

Safety Caution
Remind students to review all safety cautions and icons before beginning this lab activity.

Preparation Notes
Because of the volume of water being used, you may wish to set up the blocks and hot plates ahead of time. Also, breezes and drafts may move the craft sticks, so eliminate or reduce as many of these variables as possible.

 Datasheets for LabBook
Datasheet 13

Terry J. Rakes
Elmwood Jr. High
Rogers, Arkansas

Convection Connection

Some scientists think convection currents within the Earth's mantle are responsible for the movement of tectonic plates. Because these convection currents cannot be observed, scientists use models to simulate the process. In this activity, you will make your own model to simulate tectonic-plate movement.

Procedure

1. Place two hot plates side by side in the center of your lab table. Be sure they are away from the edge of the table.
2. Place the pan on top of the hot plates. Slide the wooden blocks under the pan to support the ends. Make sure the pan is level and secure.
3. Fill the pan with cold water. The water should be at least 4 cm deep. Turn on the hot plates, and put on your gloves.
4. After a minute or two, tiny bubbles will begin to rise in the water above the hot plates. Gently place two craft sticks on the water's surface.
5. Use the pencil to align the sticks parallel to the short ends of the pan. The sticks should be about 3 cm apart and near the center of the pan.
6. As soon as the sticks begin to move, place a drop of food coloring in the water at the center of the pan. Observe what happens to the food coloring.
7. With the help of a partner, hold one thermometer bulb just under the water at the center of the pan. Hold the other two thermometers just under the water near the ends of the pan. Record the temperatures.
8. When you are finished, turn off the hot plates. After the water has cooled, carefully empty the water into a sink.

Analysis

9. Based on your observations of the motion of the food coloring, how does the temperature of the water affect the direction the water moves?
10. How does the motion of the craft sticks relate to the motion of the water?
11. How does this model relate to plate tectonics and the movement of the continents?

Materials
- heat-resistant gloves
- 2 small hot plates
- rectangular aluminum pan
- wooden blocks
- cold water
- 2 craft sticks
- pencil
- metric ruler
- food coloring
- 3 thermometers

Answers
9. The warmer water rises, and the cooler water sinks.
10. The hot water flowed outward from the center of the pan. This movement pushed the sticks away from each other and toward the edges of the pan. (In some cases, the sticks may move together.)
11. Convection currents within the Earth's mantle may move tectonic plates in the same way the convecting water moved the craft sticks. The convection currents in this model were created by the hot plates warming the water. In the mantle, convection currents are caused by heat from deep within the Earth.

Using Scientific Methods

Oh, the Pressure!

When scientists want to understand natural processes, such as mountain formation, they often make models to help them. Models are useful in studying how rocks react to the forces of plate tectonics. In a short amount of time, a model can demonstrate geological processes that take millions of years. Do the following activity to find out how folding and faulting occur in the Earth's crust.

Materials

- modeling clay in 4 different colors
- 5 × 15 cm strip of poster board
- soup can or rolling pin
- newspaper
- colored pencils
- plastic knife
- 5 × 5 cm squares of poster board (2)

Ask a Question

1. How do synclines, anticlines, and faults form?

Conduct an Experiment

2. Use modeling clay of one color to form a long cylinder, and place the cylinder in the center of the glossy side of the poster-board strip.

3. Mold the clay to the strip. Try to make the clay layer the same thickness all along the strip; you can use the soup can or rolling pin to even it out. Pinch the sides of the clay so that it is the same width and length as the strip. Your strip should be at least 15 cm long and 5 cm wide.

Daniel Bugenhagen
Yutan Jr.–Sr. High
Yutan, Nebraska

Oh, the Pressure!
Teacher's Notes

Time Required
One 45-minute class period

Lab Ratings

EASY ──────────── HARD

TEACHER PREP 🧪🧪🧪
STUDENT SET-UP 🧪🧪
CONCEPT LEVEL 🧪🧪🧪
CLEAN UP 🧪🧪🧪

MATERIALS
The materials listed on the student page are enough for a group of 3–4 students.

Safety Caution
Remind students to review all safety cautions and icons before beginning this lab activity.

Lab Notes
Homemade modeling dough may be substituted for modeling clay in this activity. In step 3, students may find it easier to trim each layer of clay with the plastic knife before stacking the layers together.

 Datasheets for LabBook
Datasheet 14

Chapter 7 • LabBook **657**

Preparation Notes

Homemade Modeling Dough (optional) The night before the activity, prepare enough modeling dough for each class using the recipe below. The recipe provides enough dough for each group. Combine the following ingredients in a large saucepan over low heat in the order that they are listed:

- 2 cups cold water
- $\frac{1}{3}$ cup cooking oil
- 1 cup salt
- 4 teaspoons cream of tartar
- 2 cups flour
- Food coloring

Constantly stir the mixture until the modeling dough forms a ball. Turn the modeling dough out onto a floured surface. Use a ruler to divide the dough into fourths. When the dough cools slightly, add 15–20 drops of food coloring to each quarter. Fold and knead to evenly distribute the color throughout the dough. Place the dough in an airtight container, such as an 8 oz yogurt container. If you freeze it, the modeling dough will last for months.

Just before the activity, cover all workspaces with newspaper and secure the newspapers in place. If the dough gets dry, rinse your hands and continue to mold the dough.

4. Flip the strip over on the newspaper your teacher has placed across your desk. Carefully peel the strip from the modeling clay.

5. Repeat steps 2–4 with the other colors of modeling clay. Each member of your group should have a turn molding the clay. Each time you flip the strip over, stack the new clay layer on top of the previous one. When you are finished, you should have a block of clay made of four layers.

6. Lift the block of clay and hold it parallel to and just above the tabletop. Push gently on the block from opposite sides, as shown below.

7. Use the colored pencils to draw the results of step 6 in your ScienceLog. Use the terms *syncline* and *anticline* to label your diagram. Draw arrows to show the direction that each edge of the clay was pushed.

8. Repeat steps 2–5 to form a second block of clay.

9. Cut the second block of clay in two at a 45° angle as seen from the side of the block.

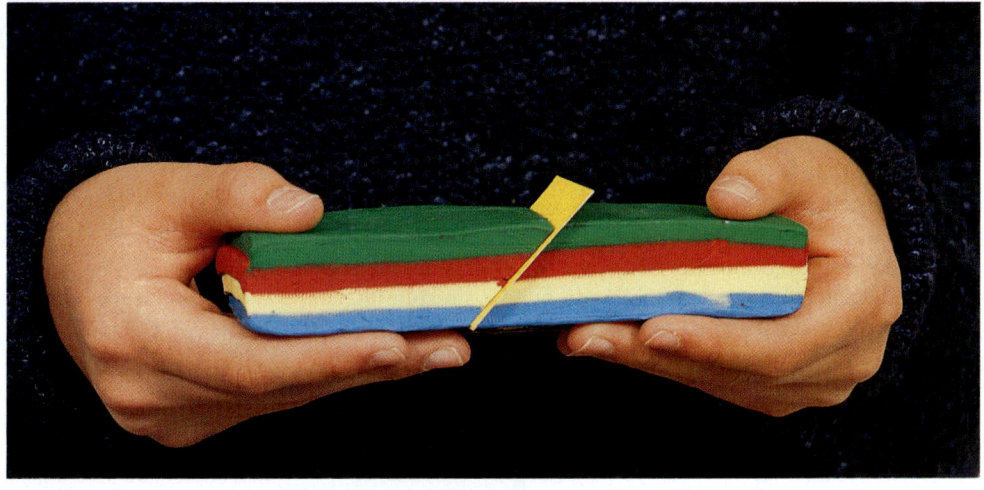

10. Press one poster-board square on the angled end of each of the block's two pieces. The poster board represents a fault. The two angled ends represent a hanging wall and a footwall. The model should resemble the one in the photograph above.

11. Keeping the angled edges together, lift the blocks and hold them parallel to and just above the tabletop. Push gently on the two blocks until they move. Record your observations in your Sciencelog.

12. Now hold the two pieces of the clay block in their original position, and slowly pull them apart, allowing the hanging wall to move downward. Record your observations.

Analyze the Results

13. What happened to the first block of clay in step 6? What kind of force did you apply to it?

14. What happened to the pieces of the second block of clay in step 11? What kind of force did you apply to them?

15. What happened to the pieces of the second block of clay in step 12? Describe the forces that acted on the block and how the pieces of the block reacted.

Draw Conclusions

16. Summarize how the forces you applied to the blocks of clay relate to the way tectonic forces affect rock layers. Be sure to use the terms *fold, fault, anticline, syncline, hanging wall, footwall, tension,* and *compression* in your summary.

Lab Notes
Students should realize that stress is equivalent to pressure or force. Explain to them that rocks can undergo stress without deforming. When the stress becomes too much, the rocks become folded or faulted. This deformation is also called *strain*. Stress and the result of stress (strain) are two different things.

Answers
13. The first block got shorter and taller. The layers of clay became folded due to compression.

14. One of the pieces (the hanging wall) slid above the other piece (the footwall) due to compression.

15. One of the pieces (the footwall) moved up relative to the other piece (the hanging wall) as tension was released.

16. The conclusion should be a complete summary of this activity, indicating the direction of pressure at each step. Any diagrams should be correctly labeled, and students should demonstrate a good understanding of the terms *fold, fault, anticline, syncline, hanging wall, footwall, tension,* and *compression.*

Chapter 7 • LabBook

Quake Challenge
Teacher's Notes

Time Required
One 45-minute class period

Lab Ratings

- TEACHER PREP
- STUDENT SET-UP
- CONCEPT LEVEL
- CLEAN UP

MATERIALS
The materials listed on the student page are enough for two students.

Safety Caution
Remind students to review all safety cautions and icons before beginning this lab activity.

Preparation Notes
Make the gelatin 24 hours in advance to ensure that it has set sufficiently. Cut the gelatin squares ahead of time, and place each square on a piece of wax paper. For steps 8 and 9, you will need to create a gelatin square large enough to place all the student structures on. This allows each group's structure to be evaluated on its own merit. Keep the gelatin refrigerated until it's ready to be used.

Helen Schiller
Northwood Middle School
Taylors, South Carolina

660 Chapter 8 • LabBook

Using Scientific Methods

Quake Challenge

DESIGN YOUR OWN

In many parts of the world, it is important that buildings be built with earthquakes in mind. Each building must be designed so that the structure is protected during an earthquake. Architects have improved the design of buildings a lot since 1906, when an earthquake destroyed much of San Francisco. In this activity you will use marshmallows and toothpicks to build a structure that can withstand a simulated earthquake. In the process, you will discover some of the ways a building can be built to withstand an earthquake.

Materials
- 10 marshmallows
- 10 toothpicks
- square of gelatin, approximately 8 × 8 cm
- paper plate

Ask a Question
1. What features help a building withstand an earthquake? How can I use this information to build my structure?

Form a Hypothesis
2. Brainstorm with a classmate to design a structure that will resist the simulated earthquake. Sketch your design in your ScienceLog. Write two or three sentences to describe your design.

Test the Hypothesis
3. Follow your design to build a structure using the toothpicks and marshmallows.
4. Set your structure on a square of gelatin.
5. Shake the square of gelatin to test whether your building will remain standing during a quake. Do not pick up the gelatin.
6. If your first design does not work well, change it until you find a design that does. Try to determine why your building is falling so that you can improve your design each time.
7. Sketch your final design in your ScienceLog.
8. After you have tested your final design, place your structure on the gelatin square on your teacher's desk.

9. When every group has added a structure to the teacher's gelatin, your teacher will simulate an earthquake by shaking the gelatin. Watch to see which buildings withstand the most severe quake.

Analyze the Results

10. Which buildings were still standing after the final earthquake? What features made them more stable?

11. How would you change your design to make your structure more stable?

Communicate Results

12. This was a simple model of a real-life problem for architects. Based on this activity, what advice would you give to those who design buildings in earthquake-prone areas?

Answers

10. Answers will vary. Sample answer: Structures that had a wide base generally withstood the earthquake. Structures that incorporated triangles into the design also were successful.

11. Answers will vary. Accept all reasonable answers.

12. Buildings designed in earthquake-prone areas should have wide and flexible foundations. The building should also be reinforced to prevent collapsing.

**Datasheets for LabBook
Datasheet 15**

Earthquake Waves
Teacher's Notes

Time Required
One 45-minute class period

Lab Ratings

TEACHER PREP ▲
STUDENT SET-UP ▲▲
CONCEPT LEVEL ▲▲▲▲
CLEAN UP ▲

MATERIALS
The materials listed in the student page are enough for two students.

Safety Caution
Remind students to review all safety cautions and icons before beginning this lab activity.

Preparation Notes
Be sure that students understand how to calculate the distance from each city to the epicenter of the earthquake in step 6. These distances must be correct to accurately determine the epicenter of the earthquake on the map.

Emphasize to students that the circles on the map must intersect or come very close to intersecting in order to determine the epicenter of the earthquake. If the circles do not come close to intersecting, tell students that they must check their calculations.

Earthquake Waves

The energy from an earthquake travels as seismic waves in all directions through the Earth. Seismologists can use the properties of certain types of seismic waves to find the epicenter of an earthquake.

P waves travel more quickly than S waves and are always detected first. The average speed of P waves in the Earth's crust is 6.1 km/s. The average speed of S waves in the Earth's crust is 4.1 km/s. The difference in arrival time between P waves and S waves is called *lag time*.

In this activity you will use the S-P-time method to determine the location of an earthquake's epicenter.

SKILL BUILDER

Materials
- calculator (optional)
- compass
- metric ruler

Procedure

1. The illustration below shows seismographic records made in three cities following an earthquake. These traces begin at the left and show the arrival of P waves at time zero. The second set of waves on each record represents the arrival of S waves.

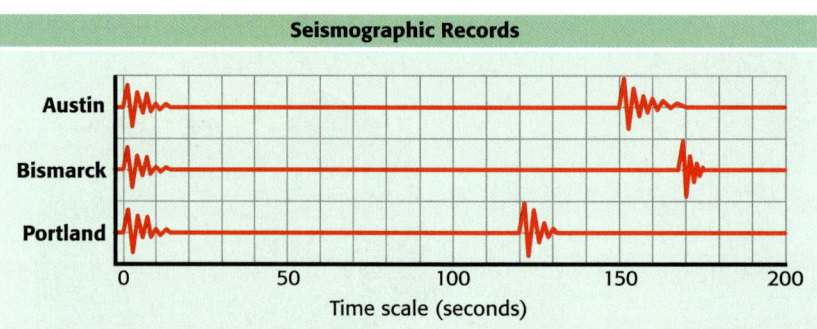

2. Copy the data table on the next page into your ScienceLog.

3. Use the time scale provided with the seismographic records to find the lag time between the P waves and the S waves for each city. Remember, the lag time is the time between the moment when the first P wave arrives and the moment when the first S wave arrives. Record this data in your table.

4. Use the following equation to calculate how long it takes each wave type to travel 100 km:

   100 km ÷ average speed of the wave = time

Janel Guse
West Central Middle School
Hartford, South Dakota

662 Chapter 8 • LabBook

5. To find lag time for earthquake waves at 100 km, subtract the time it takes P waves to travel 100 km from the time it takes S waves to travel 100 km. Record the lag time in your ScienceLog.

6. Use the following formula to find the distance from each city to the epicenter:

$$\text{distance} = \frac{\text{measured lag time (s)} \times 100 \text{ km}}{\text{lag time for 100 km (s)}}$$

In your Data Table, record the distance from each city to the epicenter.

7. Trace the map below into your ScienceLog.

8. Use the scale to adjust your compass so that the radius of a circle with Austin at the center is equal to the distance between Austin and the epicenter of the earthquake.

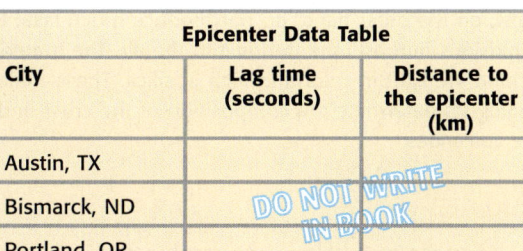

Epicenter Data Table		
City	Lag time (seconds)	Distance to the epicenter (km)
Austin, TX		
Bismarck, ND	DO NOT WRITE IN BOOK	
Portland, OR		

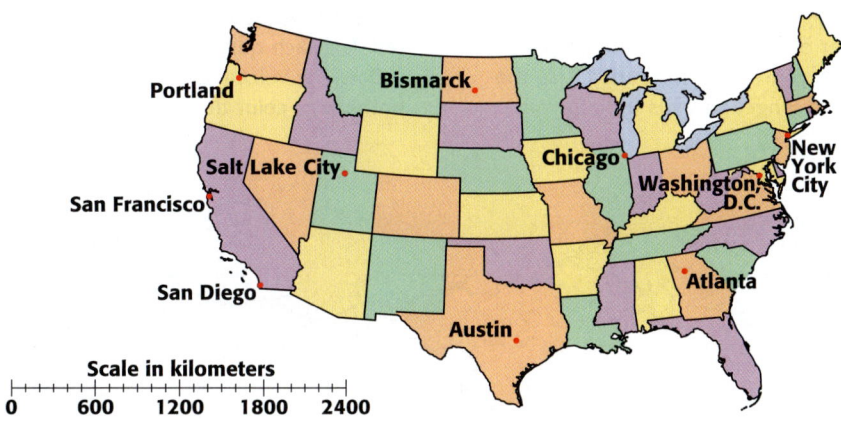

9. Put the point of your compass at Austin on your copy of the map, and draw a circle.

10. Repeat steps 8 and 9 for Bismarck and Portland. The epicenter of the earthquake is located near the point where the three circles meet.

Analysis

11. Which city is closest to the epicenter?

12. Why do seismologists need measurements from three different locations to find the epicenter of an earthquake?

Answers

3. Austin: 150 seconds
   Bismarck: 168 seconds
   Portland: 120 seconds

6. Austin: 1,875 km; Bismarck: 2,100 km; Portland: 1,500 km

11. San Diego, California

12. Seismologists need measurements from three different cities to ensure that the location is accurate. The first two circles intersect in two places. When a third circle is used, all three circles intersect in only one place.

Datasheets for LabBook
Datasheet 16

Science Skills Worksheet 26
"Grasping Graphing"

Chapter 8 • LabBook

Some Go "Pop," Some Do Not
Teacher's Notes

Time Required
One 45-minute class period

Lab Ratings

- TEACHER PREP 🧪🧪
- STUDENT SET-UP 🧪
- CONCEPT LEVEL 🧪🧪🧪
- CLEAN UP 🧪

MATERIALS
The materials listed on the student page are enough for one student. Students may wish to use tracing paper in step 1.

Preparation Notes
From the unit, students should be aware that volcanoes with a high water and silica content tend to erupt explosively. They should use this information to analyze the data in this activity. You may also wish to inform students that, in general, quietly erupting volcanoes are derived from basaltic magma, while explosively erupting volcanoes are derived from granitic magma. Remind students that oceanic crust is basaltic and low in silica, while continental crust is granitic and high in silica.

Students may need some practice finding locations using latitude and longitude. If necessary, guide them through the steps needed to locate the first volcano on the chart.

Some Go "Pop," Some Do Not

Volcanic eruptions range from mild to violent. When volcanoes erupt, the materials left behind provide information to scientists studying the Earth's crust. Mild, or nonexplosive, eruptions produce thin, runny lava that is low in silica. During nonexplosive eruptions, lava simply flows down the side of the volcano. Explosive eruptions, on the other hand, do not produce much lava. Instead, the explosions hurl ash and debris into the air. The materials left behind are light in color and high in silica. These materials help geologists determine the composition of the crust underneath the volcanoes.

DISCOVERY LAB

Materials
- graph paper
- metric ruler
- red, yellow, and orange colored pencils or markers

TRY at HOME

Procedure

1. Copy the map below onto graph paper. Take care to line the grid up properly.

2. Locate each volcano from the list on the next page by drawing a circle with a diameter of about 1 cm in the proper location on your copy of the map. Use the latitude and longitude grids to help you.

3. Review all the eruptions for each volcano. For each explosive eruption, color the circle red. For each quiet volcano, color the circle yellow. For volcanoes that have erupted in both ways, color the circle orange.

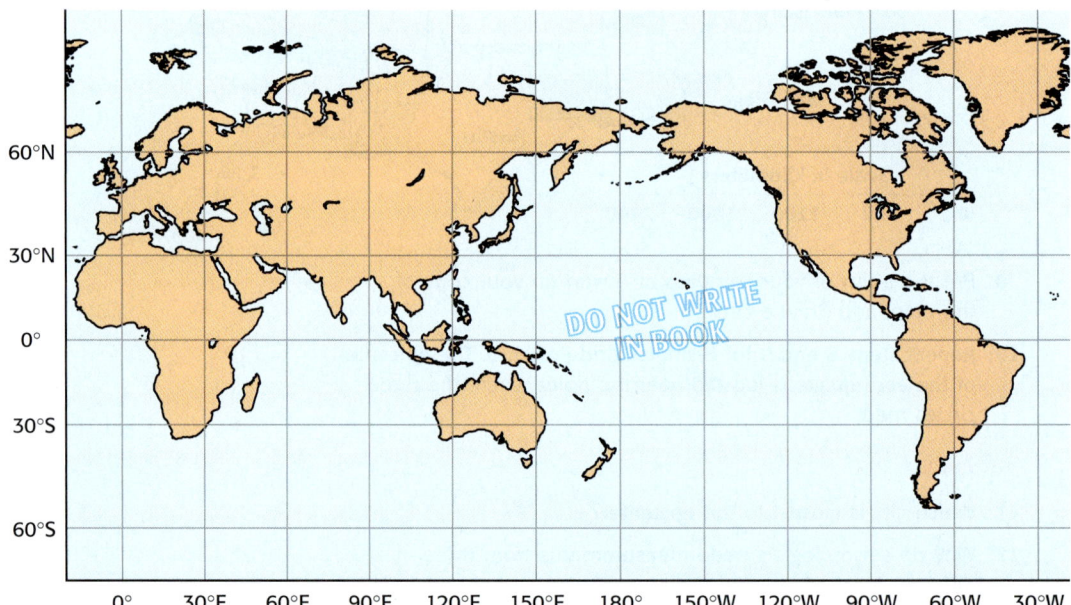

Lab Notes
In a very simple way, this lab models how the composition of magma can evolve. For example, basaltic (mafic) magma can evolve into granitic (felsic) magma through chemical differentiation processes. Scientists often use measurements of trace elements in the resulting rock to "fingerprint" the source of magma from which volcanic rocks formed.

C. John Graves
Monforton Middle School
Bozeman, Montana

Volcanic Activity Chart

Volcano name	Location	Description
Mount St. Helens	46°N 122°W	An explosive eruption blew the top off the mountain. Light-colored ash covered thousands of square kilometers. Another eruption sent a lava flow down the southeast side of the mountain.
Kilauea	19°N 155°W	One small eruption sent a lava flow along 12 km of highway.
Rabaul caldera	4°S 152°E	Explosive eruptions have caused tsunamis and have left 1–2 m of ash on nearby buildings.
Popocatépetl	19°N 98°W	During one explosion, Mexico City closed the airport for 14 hours because huge columns of ash made it too difficult for pilots to see. Eruptions from this volcano have also caused damaging avalanches.
Soufriere Hills	16°N 62°W	Small eruptions have sent lava flows down the hills. Other explosive eruptions have sent large columns of ash into the air.
Long Valley caldera	37°N 119°W	Explosive eruptions have sent ash into the air.
Okmok	53°N 168°W	Recently, there have been slow lava flows from this volcano. Twenty-five hundred years ago, ash and debris exploded from the top of this volcano.
Pavlof	55°N 161°W	Eruption clouds have been sent 200 m above the summit. Eruptions have sent ash columns 10 km into the air. Occasionally, small eruptions have caused lava flows.
Fernandina	42°N 12°E	Eruptions have ejected large blocks of rock from this volcano.
Mount Pinatubo	15°N 120°E	Ash and debris from an explosive eruption destroyed homes, crops, and roads within 52,000 km² around the volcano.

Analysis

4. According to your map, where are volcanoes that always have nonexplosive eruptions located?
5. Where are volcanoes that always erupt explosively located?
6. Where are volcanoes that erupt in both ways located?
7. If volcanoes get their magma from the crust below them, what can you say about the silica content of Earth's crust under the oceans?
8. What is the composition of the crust under the continents? How do we know?
9. What is the source of materials for volcanoes that erupt in both ways? How do you know?
10. Do the locations of volcanoes that erupt in both ways make sense based on your answers to questions 7 and 8? Explain.

Going Further

Volcanoes are present on other planets. If a planet had only nonexplosive volcanoes on its surface, what would we be able to infer about the planet? If a planet had volcanoes that ranged from nonexplosive to explosive, what might that tell us about the planet?

Answers

4. Nonexplosive volcanoes are usually located on oceanic crust.
5. Explosive volcanoes are usually located on continental crust.
6. Volcanoes that erupt in both ways are usually located near boundaries between oceanic and continental crust.
7. The crust under the oceans must be low in silica. Students may also know that the crust is likely to be made of basalt.
8. Continental crust is generally high in silica. Students may also know that the crust is likely to be made of granite.
9. The volcanoes that erupt in both ways must be near the boundary between the oceanic crusts and the continental crusts. The crust must have both basalt and granite.
10. The volcanoes that erupt in both ways are located near the boundaries between continents and oceans. Students should understand that two different crusts must meet in these areas and that both granitic (felsic) and basaltic (mafic) magma is generated.

Going Further

Answers should reflect the idea that the crust on planets with nonexplosive volcanoes must be low in silica compared to Earth. Students may also realize that planets that have only nonexplosive volcanoes must have basaltic crust. If a planet has all three types of volcanoes, it must have both basaltic and granitic crust.

Datasheets for LabBook
Datasheet 17

Volcano Verdict
Teacher's Notes

Time Required
One 45-minute class period

Lab Ratings

TEACHER PREP ▲▲
STUDENT SET-UP ▲▲▲
CONCEPT LEVEL ▲▲
CLEAN UP ▲▲

MATERIALS
The materials listed in the student page are sufficient for a pair of students.

Safety Caution
Remind students to review all safety cautions and icons before beginning this lab activity. Students should wear goggles and aprons for this activity.

Preparation Notes
You may want to combine this activity with an activity involving a tiltmeter. Emphasize to students that a gas-emissions tester is just one tool used by volcanologists. These scientists must compare the data gathered through many tests before drawing any conclusions. Other tools include seismographs or satellites that record infrared images of volcanoes over a period of time.

Volcano Verdict

You will need to pair up with a partner for this exploration. You and your partner will act as geologists who work in a city located near a volcano. City officials are counting on you to predict when the volcano will erupt next. You and your partner have decided to use limewater as a gas-emissions tester. You will use this tester to measure the levels of carbon dioxide emitted from a simulated volcano. The more active the volcano is, the more carbon dioxide it releases.

Materials

- 1 L of limewater
- 9 oz clear plastic cup
- graduated cylinder
- 100 mL of water
- 140 mL of white vinegar
- 16 oz drink bottle
- modeling clay
- flexible drinking straw
- 15 mL of baking soda
- 2 sheets of bathroom tissue
- coin
- box or stand for plastic cup

Procedure

1. Put on your safety goggles, and carefully pour limewater into the plastic cup until the cup is three-fourths full. This is your gas-emissions tester.

2. Now build a model volcano. Begin by pouring 50 mL of water and 70 mL of vinegar into the drink bottle.

3. Form a plug of clay around the short end of the straw, as shown below. The clay plug must be large enough to cover the opening of the bottle. Be careful not to get the clay wet.

4. Sprinkle 5 mL of baking soda along the center of a single section of bathroom tissue. Then roll the tissue and twist the ends so that the baking soda can't fall out.

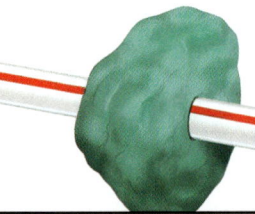

Lab Notes

Scientists base their predictions of eruptions on several different kinds of evidence. If a variety of evidence indicates an eruption is imminent, they will recommend evacuation. They are much less likely to make this kind of recommendation if only one kind of evidence suggests an eruption is possible.

Gordon Zibelman
Drexel Hill Middle School
Drexel Hill, Pennsylvania

5. Drop the tissue into the drink bottle, and immediately put the short end of the straw inside the bottle, making a seal with the clay.

6. Put the other end of the straw into the limewater, as shown at right.

7. You have just taken your first measurement of gas levels from the volcano. Record your observations in your ScienceLog.

8. Imagine that it is several days later and you need to test the volcano again to collect more data. Before you continue, toss a coin. If it lands heads up, go to step 9a. If it lands tails up, go to step 9b. Write the step you take in your ScienceLog.

9a. Repeat steps 1–7. This time add 2 mL of baking soda to the vinegar and water. **Note:** You must use fresh water, vinegar, and limewater. Describe your observations in your ScienceLog. Go to step 10.

9b. Repeat steps 1–7. This time add 8 mL of baking soda to the vinegar and water. **Note:** You must use fresh water, vinegar, and limewater. Describe your observations in your ScienceLog. Go to step 10.

Analysis

10. How do you explain the difference in the appearance of the limewater from one trial to the next?

11. What do your measurements indicate about the activity in the volcano?

12. Based on your results, do you think it would be necessary to evacuate the city?

13. How would a geologist use a gas-emissions tester to forecast volcanic eruptions?

Answers

10. Students should realize that carbon dioxide makes the limewater cloudy. If more carbon dioxide is released, the limewater becomes cloudier.

11. The answer to this question depends on which steps the students followed. If the students performed step 9a and used 2 mL of baking soda in the second trial, they should conclude that the volcano is not likely to erupt in the immediate future because it released less gas during the second trial. If the students performed step 9b with 8 mL of baking soda, on the other hand, they should conclude that the volcano is likely to erupt. More gas was released during the second trial, and therefore the pressure must be building.

12. If the students followed step 9a, they should conclude that the city does not need to be evacuated. If they performed step 9b, they should conclude that the city may need to be evacuated.

13. A geologist would use a gas-emissions tester in conjunction with other tests to determine if pressure is building within a volcano. As the pressure builds, the volcano is more likely to erupt.

Datasheets for LabBook
Datasheet 18

Great Ice Escape
Teacher's Notes

Time Required
Two 45-minute class periods

Lab Ratings

TEACHER PREP 🧪🧪🧪
STUDENT SET-UP 🧪🧪
CONCEPT LEVEL 🧪
CLEAN UP 🧪🧪

MATERIALS
The materials listed on the student page are enough for 1–3 students. If a freezer is unavailable, students may perform this activity at home.

Safety Caution
Remind students to review all safety cautions and icons before beginning this lab activity. Warn them that when a plastic jar cracks, the pieces could be very sharp.

Preparation Notes
You should perform this lab ahead of time in order to make certain that your plastic jars will break. Be sure to use hard plastic jars. If these jars bend or "give," they may not break. Be sure the students fill the jars to overflowing.

David M. Sparks
Redwater Junior High School
Redwater, Texas

Using Scientific Methods

Great Ice Escape

DISCOVERY LAB

Did you know that ice acts as a natural wrecking ball? Even rocks don't stand a chance against the power of ice. When water trapped in rock freezes, a process called *ice wedging* occurs. The water volume increases, and the rock cracks to "get out of the way." This expansion can fragment a rock into several pieces. In this exercise you will see how this natural wrecker works, and you will try to stop the great ice escape.

Ask a Question
1. If a plastic jar is filled with water, is there a way to prevent the jar from breaking when the water freezes?

Conduct an Experiment
2. Fill three identical jars to overflowing with water, and close two of them securely.
3. Measure the height of the water in the unsealed container. Record the height in your ScienceLog.
4. Tightly wrap one of the closed jars with tape, string, or other items to reinforce the jar. These items must be removable. The unwrapped, sealed jar will serve as your control.
5. Place all three jars in resealable sandwich bags, and leave them in the freezer overnight. (Make sure the open jar does not spill.)
6. Remove the jars from the freezer, and carefully remove the wrapping from the reinforced jar.

Make Observations
7. Did your reinforced jar crack? Why or why not?
8. What does each jar look like? Record your observations in your ScienceLog.
9. In your ScienceLog, record the height of the ice in the unsealed jar. How does the new height compare with the height you measured in step 3?

Analyze the Results
10. Do you think it is possible to stop the ice from breaking the sealed jars? Why or why not?
11. How could ice wedging affect soil formation?

Materials
- 3 small, identical hard-plastic jars with screw-on lids, such as spice containers
- water
- metric ruler
- tape, strings, rubber bands, and other items to bind or reinforce the jars
- 3 resealable sandwich bags
- freezer

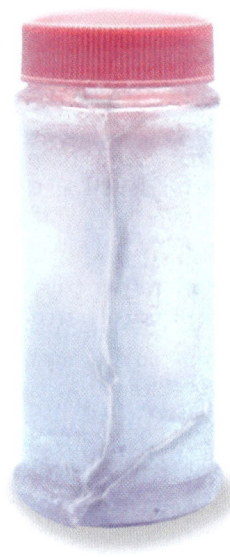

Answers
7. Answers will vary.
8. Sample answer: Ice is protruding from the top of the unsealed jar. Both sealed jars are cracked. The unwrapped jar cracked more severely.
9. Answers will vary, but students should observe that the height of the water has increased.
10. No; the expanding ice cannot be confined. If it can shatter a rock, it can break plastic.
11. Ice wedging breaks up large rocks into smaller pieces that are further weathered chemically and physically. The processes of weathering create soil.

 **Datasheets for LabBook**
Datasheet 19

Rockin' Through Time

Wind, water, and gravity constantly change rocks. As wind and water rush over the rocks, the rocks may be worn smooth. As rocks bump against one another, their shapes change. The form of mechanical weathering that occurs as rocks collide and scrape together is called **abrasion**. In this activity, you will shake some pieces of limestone to model the effects of abrasion.

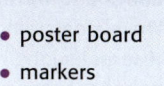

Procedure

1. Copy the chart below onto a piece of poster board. Allow enough space to place rocks in each square.
2. Lay three of the limestone pieces on the poster board in the area marked "0 shakes." Be careful not to bump the poster board once you have added the rocks.
3. Place the remaining 21 rocks in the 3 L bottle. Then fill the bottle halfway with water. Close the lid securely.
4. Shake the bottle vigorously 100 times.
5. Remove three rocks from the bottle, and place them on the poster board in the area marked "100 shakes."
6. Repeat steps 4 and 5 six times until all of the rocks have been added to the board.

Analysis

7. Describe the surface of the rocks that you placed in the area marked "0 shakes." Are they smooth or rough?
8. How did the shapes of the rocks change as you performed this activity?
9. Why did the rocks change?
10. What did the water look like at the beginning of the activity?
11. How did the water change during the activity? Why did it change?
12. What would happen if you did this experiment with a much harder rock, like gneiss?
13. How do the results of this experiment compare with what happens in a river?

Materials

- poster board
- markers
- 24 pieces of limestone, all about the same size
- 3 L plastic wide-mouth bottle with lid
- tap water

Rocks Table

0 shakes	100 shakes
200 shakes	300 shakes
400 shakes	500 shakes
600 shakes	700 shakes

Larry Tackett
Andrew Jackson Middle School
Cross Lanes, West Virginia

13. As pebbles and small particles are carried along with the river's water, they bounce and grind against other rocks. Eventually, the rocks become smooth.

 Datasheets for LabBook
Datasheet 20

Rockin' Through Time
Teacher's Notes

Time Required
One 45-minute period

Lab Ratings

EASY ———→ HARD

Teacher Prep 🧪🧪
Student Set-Up 🧪
Concept Level 🧪🧪
Clean Up 🧪

MATERIALS
The materials listed on the student page are adequate for groups of 4–5 students.

Safety Caution
Remind students to review all safety cautions and icons before beginning this lab activity. Be sure to use plastic bottles in this activity.

Answers

7. The surfaces of the rocks are rough and jagged.
8. As the rocks were shaken more, they became much smoother.
9. The rocks became smoother because the edges broke off of them when they collided in the jar.
10. At the beginning of this activity, the water was clear.
11. As the activity progressed, the water became increasingly dirty. This happened because particles broke away from the rocks and were suspended in the water.
12. If a harder rock were used, similar results would require longer and harder shaking.

Chapter 10 • LabBook   **669**

Water Cycle— What Goes Up . . .
Teacher's Notes

Time Required
One 45-minute class period

Lab Rating

TEACHER PREP 🧪
STUDENT SET-UP 🧪🧪
CONCEPT LEVEL 🧪🧪
CLEAN UP 🧪

MATERIALS
The materials listed on the student page are enough for a group of 4–5 students.

Safety Caution

Remind students to review all safety cautions and icons before beginning this lab activity. Students should be cautioned when using a hot plate. Care should also be exercised in using the glassware. Appropriate methods should be used to dispose of broken glass.

Norman Holcomb
Marion Local Schools
Maria Stein, Ohio

Water Cycle— What Goes Up . . .

Why does a bathroom mirror "fog up"? What happens when water "dries up"? Where does rain come from, and why doesn't it just "run out"? These questions relate to the major parts of the water cycle—condensation, evaporation, and precipitation. In this activity, you will make a model of the water cycle and watch water as it moves through the model.

Procedure

1. Use the graduated cylinder to pour 50 mL of water into the beaker. Note the water level in the beaker.

2. Put on your gloves, and place the beaker securely on the hot plate. Turn on the heat to medium, and bring the water to a boil.

3. While waiting for the water to boil, practice picking up and handling the glass plate or watch glass with the tongs. Hold the glass plate a few centimeters above the beaker, and tilt it so that the lowest edge of the glass is still above the beaker.

4. Observe the glass plate as the water in the beaker heats. In your ScienceLog, write down the changes you see in the beaker, in the air above the beaker, and on the glass plate held over the beaker. Write down any changes you see in the water.

5. Continue until you have observed steam rising off the water, the glass plate above the beaker becoming foggy, and water dripping from the glass plate.

6. Carefully set the glass plate on a counter or other safe surface as directed by your teacher.

7. Turn off the hot plate, and allow the beaker to cool. Move the hot beaker with gloves or tongs if directed to do so by your teacher.

8. Copy the illustration shown on the next page into your ScienceLog. On your sketch, draw and label the water cycle as it occurred in your model. Include arrows and labels for condensation, evaporation, and precipitation.

Materials
- graduated cylinder
- 50 mL of tap water
- heat-resistant gloves
- beaker
- hot plate
- glass plate or watch glass
- tongs or forceps

Analysis

9. Compare the water level in the beaker now with the water level at the beginning of the experiment. Was there a change? Explain why or why not.

10. If you had used a scale or balance to measure the mass of the water in the beaker before and after this activity, would the mass have changed? Why or why not?

11. How is your model similar to the Earth's water cycle? On your sketch of the illustration above, label where the processes shown in the model mimic the Earth's water cycle.

12. When you finished this experiment, the water in the beaker was still hot. What stores much of the energy in the Earth's water cycle?

Going Further
As rainwater runs over the land, the rainwater picks up minerals and salts. Do these minerals and salts evaporate, condense, and precipitate as part of the water cycle? Where do they go?

If the average global temperature on Earth gets warmer, how would you expect sea levels to change, and why? What if the average global temperature cools?

671

LabBook

Answers
8. Answer is at the bottom of the page.
9. The water level is less at the end of the experiment than at the beginning of the experiment because some of the water escaped in the form of steam.
10. The mass would have changed slightly. Because some of the steam escaped, the mass of the water in the beaker would be reduced.
11. The model is similar to the Earth's water cycle because precipitation, condensation, and evaporation occurred. Accept all reasonable depictions of the water cycle.
12. Much of the energy in the water cycle is stored in bodies of water such as the oceans. Energy is also stored in the atmosphere and the Earth's land surface.

Going Further
- No; minerals and salts are not part of the water cycle. As water evaporates, minerals and salts are left behind as deposits.
- If the average global temperature gets warmer, the sea level may rise because the polar icecaps would melt. If the average global temperature gets cooler, the sea level may decrease as more water is frozen.

8. Student sketches should resemble the water cycle illustrated below:

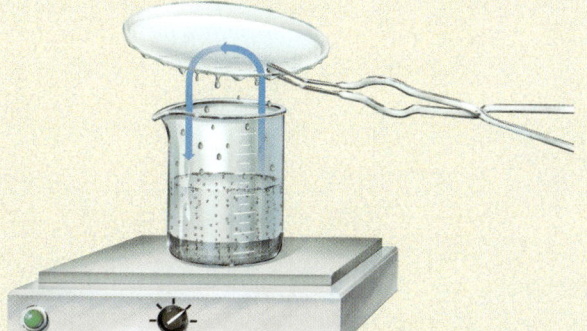

Datasheets for LabBook
Datasheet 21

Science Skills Worksheet 23
"Science Drawing"

Chapter 11 • LabBook **671**

Clean Up Your Act
Teacher's Notes

Time Required
Two 45-minute class periods

Lab Rating
EASY ———————→ HARD

TEACHER PREP 🧪🧪🧪
STUDENT SET-UP 🧪🧪🧪
CONCEPT LEVEL 🧪🧪🧪
CLEAN UP 🧪🧪🧪

MATERIALS

The materials listed on the student page are enough for a group of 4–5 students. To keep results consistent with all lab groups, each group should have the same size gravel and the same size sand. Also, the layers of sand and gravel should be the same dimensions in each group.

Safety Caution

Remind students to review all safety cautions and icons before beginning this lab activity. Caution students not to taste any of the liquids in this lab.

Kenneth Creese
White Mountain Jr. High
Rock Springs, Wyoming

672 Chapter 11 • LabBook

Using Scientific Methods

DISCOVERY LAB

Clean Up Your Act

When you wash dishes, the family car, the bathroom sink, or your clothes, you wash them with water. But have you ever wondered how water gets clean? Two major methods of purifying water are filtration and evaporation. In this activity you will use both of these methods to test how well they remove pollutants from water. You will test detritus (decaying plant matter), soil, vinegar, and detergent. Your teacher may also ask you to test other pollutants.

Form a Hypothesis

1. Form a hypothesis about whether filtration and evaporation will clean each of the four pollutants from the water and how well they might do it. Then use the procedures below to test your hypothesis.

Part A: Filtration

Filtration is a common method of removing various pollutants from water. It requires very little energy—gravity pulls water down through the layers of filter material. See how well this energy-efficient method works to clean your sample of polluted water.

Conduct an Experiment

2. Put on your gloves and goggles. Use scissors to cut the bottom out of the empty soda bottle carefully.

3. Carefully punch four or five small holes through the plastic cap of the bottle using a small nail and hammer. Screw the plastic cap onto the bottle.

4. Turn the bottle upside down, and set its neck in a ring on a ring stand, as shown on the next page. Put a handful of gravel into the inverted bottle. Add a layer of activated charcoal, followed by thick layers of sand and gravel. Place a 400 mL beaker under the neck of the bottle.

5. Fill each of the large beakers with 1,000 mL of clean water. Set one beaker aside to serve as the control. Add three or four spoonfuls of each of the following pollutants to the other beaker: detritus, soil, household vinegar, and dishwashing detergent.

Materials

Part A
- scissors
- plastic 2 L soda bottle with cap
- hammer and small nail
- gravel
- activated charcoal
- sand

Part B
- Erlenmeyer flask
- one-hole rubber stopper with a glass tube
- 1.5 m of plastic tubing
- heat-resistant gloves
- hot plate
- sealable plastic sandwich bag
- ice

Parts A and B
- ring stand with ring
- 400 mL beaker
- 1,000 mL beakers (2)
- 2,000 mL of water
- detritus (grass and leaf clippings)
- soil
- household vinegar
- dishwashing detergent
- hand lens
- 2 plastic spoons
- pH test strips

Collect Data

6. Copy the table below into your ScienceLog, and record your observations for each beaker in the columns labeled "Before cleaning."

7. Observe the color of the water in each beaker.

8. Use a hand lens to examine the water for visible particles.

9. Smell the water, and note any unusual odors.

10. Stir the water in each beaker rapidly with a plastic spoon, and check for suds. Use a different spoon for each sample.

11. Use a pH test strip to find the pH of the water.

12. Gently stir the clean water, and then pour half of it through the filtration device.

13. Observe the water in the collection beaker for color, particles, odors, suds, and pH. Be patient. It may take several minutes for the water to travel through the filtration device.

14. Record your observations in the appropriate "After filtration" column in your table.

15. Repeat steps 12–14 using the polluted water.

Preparation Notes

Varying the thickness of the layers can contribute to a variation in the results. Specify the thickness of each layer so that the results between groups are comparable. The layers could be the following dimensions: 7 cm of gravel, 2.5 cm of charcoal, 10 cm of sand, and 10 cm of gravel. You may adjust the layers according to your class size or the size of the bottles.

For variation, try different sizes of gravel or different textures of sand. Both will affect how many particles travel through the filter. If you place a few drops of food coloring in the water, students can watch the progress of the water as it passes through the filter.

You may decide that it is easier and safer for you to perform step 2 of Part A, cutting the soda bottles, before class. You may also wish to perform steps 19–22 of Part B ahead of time. Some students may find it difficult to attach the plastic tubing to the glass tube or to slide the glass tube into the rubber stopper.

Results Table						
	Before cleaning (clean water)	Before cleaning (polluted water)	After filtration (clean water)	After filtration (polluted water)	After evaporation (clean water)	After evaporation (polluted water)
Color						
Particles						
Odor						
Suds						
pH						

Datasheets for LabBook
Datasheet 22

Chapter 11 • LabBook

Answers

16. The filtered water was lighter in color than the unfiltered water. The water was still not as clear as the clean water. The color of the clean water stayed about the same.

17. No; the filtration method did not remove all of the particles from the polluted water. Many of the particles passed through the filter, but there were fewer particles than before the filtration.

18. The pH of the water changed slightly. The final pH of the polluted water was not the same as the clean water. After the polluted water was filtered, its pH was still slightly more acidic than the clean water.

Analyze the Results

16. How did the color of the polluted water change after the filtration? Did the color of the clean water change?

17. Did the filtration method remove all of the particles from the polluted water? Explain.

18. How much did the pH of the polluted water change? Did the pH of the clean water change? Was the final pH of the polluted water the same as the pH of the clean water before cleaning? Explain.

Part B: Evaporation

Cleaning water by evaporation is more expensive than cleaning water by filtration. Evaporation requires more energy, which can come from a variety of sources. In this activity, you will use an electric hot plate as the energy source. See how well this method works to clean your sample of polluted water.

Conduct an Experiment

19. Fill an Erlenmeyer flask with about 250 mL of the clean water, and insert the rubber stopper and glass tube into the flask.

20. Wearing goggles and gloves, connect about 1.5 m of plastic tubing to the glass tube.

21. Set the flask on the hot plate, and run the plastic tubing up and around the ring and down into a clean, empty 400 mL collection beaker.

22. Fill the sandwich bag with ice, seal the bag, and place the bag on the ring stand. Be sure the plastic bag and the tubing touch, as shown below.

23. Bring the water in the flask to a slow boil. As the water vapor passes by the bag of ice, the vapor will condense and drip into the collection beaker.

674   Chapter 11 • LabBook

Collect Data

24. Observe the water in the collection beaker for color, particles, odor, suds, and pH. Record your observations in the appropriate "After evaporation" column in your data table.
25. Repeat steps 23–24 using the polluted water.

Analyze the Results

26. How did the color of the polluted water change after evaporation? Did the color of the clean water change after evaporation?
27. Did the evaporation method remove all of the particles from the polluted water? Explain.
28. How much did the pH of the polluted water change? Did the pH of the final clean water change? Was the final pH of the polluted water the same as the pH of the clean water before it was cleaned? Explain.

Draw Conclusions (Parts A and B)

29. Which method—filtration or evaporation—removed the most pollutants from the water? Explain your reasoning.
30. Describe any changes that occurred in the clean water during this experiment.
31. What do you think are the advantages and disadvantages of each method?
32. Explain how you think each material (sand, gravel, and charcoal) used in the filtration system helped clean the water.
33. List areas of the country where you think each method of purification would be the most and the least beneficial. Explain your reasoning.

Going Further
Do you think either purification method would remove oil from water? If time permits, repeat your experiment using several spoonfuls of cooking oil as the pollutant.

Filtration is only one step in the purification of water at water-treatment plants. Research other methods used to purify public water supplies.

Answers
26. After the evaporation process, the polluted water was clear. The color of the clean water did not change.
27. No particles were visible in the treated water after the evaporation method. The particles in the polluted water were left behind when the water evaporated.
28. Answers may vary, depending on the clean-water source. Generally, the pH of the two samples should be very close or the same.
29. The evaporation method removed the most pollutants from the water. The pollutants were left behind when the water evaporated.
30. The clean water picked up some particles as it traveled through the filter. It was not as clean after the filtration as it had been before the filtration.
31. The advantages of the filtration method include: it is easy to do; it can treat large amounts of water; and it works relatively quickly. The filtration method doesn't remove all of the pollutants, however.

    The evaporation method removed more of the pollutants, but it is time consuming and expensive, particularly with large volumes of water.
32. Answers will vary. The sand filtered out some of the larger particles and some of the soap. The gravel also removed the large particles. The charcoal removed most of the smaller particles, the odors, and some of the soap.
33. Answers will vary.

Going Further
- Oil is removed from the water in both methods. The filtration method is relatively quicker than the evaporation method.
- Other methods of water purification include: reverse osmosis; settling ponds; chemical additives, such as chlorine; and other filtration layers. Students may also find out about bioremediation and the use of bacteria and plants to clean polluted water.

Dune Movement
Teacher's Notes

Time Required
30 minutes

Lab Ratings

TEACHER PREP 🧪
STUDENT SET-UP 🧪🧪
CONCEPT LEVEL 🧪
CLEAN UP 🧪🧪

MATERIALS
The materials listed in the student page are enough for two students.

Safety Caution
Remind students to review all safety cautions and icons before beginning this lab activity.

Preparation Notes
You might want to have students do this activity outside, in an area where an electrical outlet is available.

 Datasheets for LabBook Datasheet 23

Larry Tackett
Andrew Jackson Middle School
Cross Lanes, West Virginia

Dune Movement

 **MAKING MODELS**

Wind moves the sand by a process called *saltation*. The sand skips and bounces along the ground in the direction the wind is blowing. As the sand is blown across the beach, the dunes change. In this activity, you will investigate the effect wind has on a model sand dune.

Procedure

1. Use the marker to draw and label vertical lines 5 cm apart along one side of the box.
2. Fill the box about halfway with sand. Brush the sand into a dune shape about 10 cm from the end of the box.
3. Use the lines you drew along the edge of the box to measure the location of the dune's peak to the nearest centimeter.
4. Slide the box into the paper bag until only about half the box is exposed, as shown below.
5. Put on your safety goggles and filter mask. Hold the hair dryer so that it is level with the peak of the dune and about 10–20 cm from the open end of the box.
6. Turn on the hair dryer at the lowest speed, and direct the air toward the model sand dune for 1 minute.
7. Record the new location of the model dune in your ScienceLog.
8. Repeat steps 5 and 6 three times. After each trial, measure and record the location of the dune's peak.

Analysis

9. How far did the dune move during each trial?
10. How far did the dune move overall?
11. How might the dune's movement be affected if you were to turn the hair dryer to the highest speed?

Going Further
Flatten the sand. Place a barrier, such as a rock, in the sand. Position the hair dryer level with the top of the sand's surface. How does the rock affect the dune's movement?

Materials

- marker
- metric ruler
- shallow cardboard box
- fine sand
- paper bag, large enough to hold half the box
- filter mask
- hair dryer
- watch or clock that indicates seconds

676

Answers

9. Answers will vary. A typical answer would be about 0.5 to 1.0 cm.
10. Answers will vary. A typical answer would be about 5 to 10 cm.
11. Answers will vary. The sand could be blown until it hits the bag or the dune could move farther. Students may also have predicted that more sand would be blown out of the box.

Going Further
The dune forms on the downwind side of the barrier. The rock slows the migration of the dune.

Gliding Glaciers

A glacier is large moving mass of ice. Glaciers are responsible for shaping many of the Earth's natural features. Glaciers are set in motion by the pull of gravity. As a glacier moves it changes the landscape, eroding the surface over which it passes.

Slip-Sliding Away

The material that is carried by a glacier erodes the Earth's surface, gouging out grooves called *striations*. Different materials have varying effects on the landscape. By creating a model glacier, you will demonstrate the effects of glacial erosion by various materials.

Procedure

1. Fill one margarine container with sand to a depth of 1 cm. Fill another margarine container with gravel to a depth of 1 cm. Leave the third container empty. Fill the containers with water.
2. Put the three containers in a freezer, and leave them overnight.
3. Retrieve the containers from the freezer, and remove the three ice blocks from the containers.
4. Use a rolling pin to flatten the modeling clay.
5. Hold the plain ice block firmly with a towel, and press as you move it along the length of the clay. Do this three times. In your ScienceLog, sketch the pattern the ice block makes in the clay.
6. Repeat steps 4 and 5 with the ice block that contains sand. Sketch the pattern this ice block makes in the clay.
7. Repeat steps 4 and 5 with the ice block that contains gravel. Sketch the pattern this ice block makes in the clay.

Materials

- 3 empty margarine containers
- sand
- gravel
- metric ruler
- water
- freezer
- rolling pin
- modeling clay
- small towel
- 3 bricks
- 3 pans
- 50 mL graduated cylinder
- timer

Datasheets for LabBook
Datasheet 24

Gliding Glaciers
Teacher's Notes

Time Required
Two 45-minute class periods plus a 15-minute activity ahead of time

Lab Ratings

EASY ———————————— HARD

Teacher Prep 🧪🧪
Student Set-Up 🧪🧪
Concept Level 🧪🧪🧪
Clean Up 🧪🧪

MATERIALS
The materials listed in the student page are enough for one student or a pair of students. These materials could also be used in larger groups. To reduce the amount of materials, students could use ice cubes and smaller amounts of clay, sand, and gravel.

Preparation Notes
Students should review the entire section on glaciers in this chapter prior to performing this activity. For the second part of the lab, students might have to refreeze ice blocks overnight or make three more ice blocks. If new ice blocks are made, the sand and gravel can be omitted.

Bert Sherwood
Socorro Middle School
El Paso, Texas

Lab Notes

This part of the lab models how the weight of glacial ice causes the ice at the bottom of the glacier to melt. This is one way that glaciers move. You may wish to explain this concept by discussing how ice skates work. Ice skates glide smoothly because they distribute a skater's weight on two thin blades. The weight of a skater applied to such a small surface area causes the ice beneath the blades of the skate to melt and quickly re-freeze. Like glaciers, ice skaters glide on a thin layer of water.

Answers

8. Answers will vary. Small amounts of the surface material may become mixed with the ice.
9. Answers will vary. Small amounts of the material in the ice may be deposited on the clay surface.
10. Answers will vary. Answers may include moraines, striations, and outwash plains.
11. Accept all reasonable, justified answers. Alpine glaciers leave rugged features behind as they flow. Continental glaciers smooth the landscape.
17. The ice block with two bricks on it produced the most water.
18. The bricks represent layers of ice.
19. The bottom of the ice block melted first due to the weight of the bricks on top of it.
20. Students should conclude that glaciers that are heavier melt faster. This, in turn, causes glaciers to move faster.

Analysis

8. Did any material from the clay become mixed with the material in the ice blocks? Explain.
9. Was any material deposited on the clay surface? Explain.
10. What glacial features are represented in your clay model?
11. Compare the patterns formed by the three model glaciers. Do the patterns look like features carved by alpine glaciers or by continental glaciers? Explain.

Slippery When Wet

As the layers of ice build up and the glacier gets larger, the glacier will eventually begin to melt. The water from the melted ice allows the glacier to move forward. In this activity, you'll learn about the effect of pressure on the melting rate of a glacier.

Procedure

12. Place one ice block upside down in each pan.
13. Place one brick on top of one of the ice blocks. Place two bricks on top of another ice block. Leave the third ice block alone.
14. After 15 minutes, remove the bricks from the ice blocks.

Going Further

Replace the clay with different materials, such as soft wood or sand. How does each ice block affect the different surface materials? What types of surfaces do the different materials represent?

15. Measure the amount of water that has melted from each ice block using the graduated cylinder.
16. Record your findings in your ScienceLog.

Analysis

17. Which ice block produced the most water?
18. What did the bricks represent?
19. What part of the ice block melted first? Explain.
20. How could you relate this investigation to the melting rate of glaciers? Explain.

Using Scientific Methods

Creating a Kettle

As glaciers recede, they leave huge amounts of rock material behind. Sometimes receding glaciers form moraines by depositing some of the rock material in ridges. At other times, glaciers leave chunks of ice that form depressions called *kettles*. These depressions may form ponds or lakes. In this activity, you will create your own kettle and discover how they are formed by glaciers.

Materials

- small tub
- sand
- 4–5 ice cubes of various sizes
- metric ruler

Ask a Question

1. How are kettles formed?

Conduct an Experiment

2. Fill the tub three-quarters full with sand.
3. In your ScienceLog, describe the size and shape of the ice cubes.
4. Push the ice cubes to various depths in the sand.
5. Put the tub where it won't be disturbed overnight.

Make Observations

6. Look for the ice cubes the next day. Closely observe the sand around the area where you left each ice cube.
7. What happened to the ice cubes?
8. Use a metric ruler to measure the depth and diameter of the indentation left by the ice cubes.

Analyze the Results

9. How does this model relate to the size and shape of a natural kettle?
10. In what ways are your model kettles similar to real ones? How are they different?

Draw Conclusions

11. Based on your model, what can you conclude about the formation of kettles by receding glaciers?

Datasheets for LabBook
Datasheet 25

Janel Guse
West Central Middle School
Hartford, South Dakota

Creating a Kettle
Teacher's Notes

Time Required
One 45-minute class period plus 30 minutes during a second day

Lab Ratings

EASY ———————————→ HARD

- **TEACHER PREP** 🧪
- **STUDENT SET-UP** 🧪
- **CONCEPT LEVEL** 🧪
- **CLEAN UP** 🧪

MATERIALS

The materials listed on the student page are enough for a group of 4–5 students.

Answers

9. Answers will vary. The model is similar. The simulated kettle is the size of the ice cube. A real kettle hole is the size of the block of ice that breaks off a glacier. Its shape is determined by the shape of the ice.

10. Answers will vary. **Similarities:** The ice cube in the lab melted slowly to form a depression. Similarly, blocks of ice left behind by glaciers melt slowly to form kettles. **Differences:** The materials and debris surrounding the model hole are different from that surrounding a real kettle. In addition, a real kettle would not be as uniform as the shape of the model hole.

11. Accept all reasonable responses. Kettles form from the slow melting of ice left behind when a glacier recedes.

Chapter 12 • LabBook

Probing the Depths
Teacher's Notes

Time Required
One 45-minute class period

Lab Ratings

TEACHER PREP 🧪
STUDENT SET-UP 🧪🧪
CONCEPT LEVEL 🧪🧪
CLEAN UP 🧪

MATERIALS

The materials listed on the student page are enough for each student or for a group of 2–4 students.

Safety Caution
Remind students to review all safety cautions and icons before beginning this lab activity.

Preparation Notes
You may wish to ask students to provide their own shoe boxes. It may be safer and easier if you punch the holes along the center of the lids for the students prior to class. You may use corrugated cardboard instead of modeling clay. If you do, shape the cardboard into steps and ridges to model changes in depth. With this type of model, students should use the eraser end of an unsharpened pencil to measure depths.

Probing the Depths

In the 1870s, the crew of the ship the HMS *Challenger* used a wire and a weight to discover and map some of the deepest places in the world's oceans. Scientists tied a wire to a weight and dropped the weight overboard. When the weight reached the bottom of the ocean, they hauled the weight back up to the surface and measured the length of the wet wire. In this way, they were eventually able to map the ocean floor.

In this activity, you will model this traditional method of mapping by making a map of an ocean-floor model.

Materials
- modeling clay
- shoe box and lid
- scissors
- 8 unsharpened pencils
- metric ruler

Procedure

1. Use the clay to make a model ocean floor in the shoe box. Give the floor some mountains and valleys.

2. Cut eight holes in a line along the center of the lid. The holes should be just big enough to slide a pencil through. Close the box.

3. Exchange boxes with another student or group of students. Do not look into the box.

4. Copy the data table below into your ScienceLog. Also make a copy of the graph on the next page.

Ocean Depth Chart				
Hole position	Original length of probe	Amount of probe showing	Depth in centimeters	Depth in meters (cm × 200)
1				
2				
3				
4				
5				
6				
7				
8				

DO NOT WRITE IN BOOK

5. Measure the length of the probe (pencil) in centimeters. Record the length in your data table.

Tracy Jahn
Berkshire Jr.-Sr. High
Canaan, New York

6. Gently insert the probe into the first hole position in the box until it touches the bottom. Do not force the probe down; this could affect your reading.

7. Making sure the probe is straight up and down, measure the length of probe showing above the lid. Record your data in the data table.

8. Use the following formula to calculate the depth in centimeters:

$$\text{original length of probe} - \text{amount of probe showing} = \text{depth in cm}$$

9. Use the scale 1 cm = 200 m to convert the depth in centimeters to meters to better represent real ocean depths. Add the data to your table.

10. Transfer the data to your graph for position 1.

11. Repeat steps 6–10 for the additional positions in the box.

12. After plotting all the points onto your graph, connect the points with a smooth curve.

13. Put a pencil in each of the holes in the shoe box. Compare the rise and fall of the set of pencils with your graph.

Analysis

14. What was the depth of your deepest point? your shallowest point?

15. Did your graph resemble the ocean-floor model, as shown by the pencils? If not, why not?

16. What difficulties might scientists have when measuring the real ocean floor? Do they ever get to "open the box"? Explain.

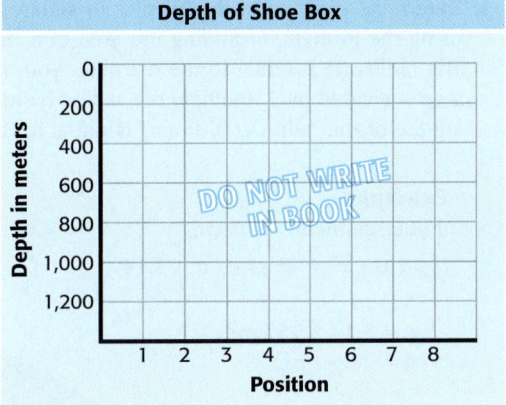

LabBook

Answers

14. Answers will vary.

15. Answers will vary. Accept all reasonable responses. Discrepancies between the model and the graph may be attributed to incorrectly plotting the points, failing to keep the probe vertical, or pushing the probe into the clay.

16. Scientists may encounter many difficulties in measuring the ocean floor. Students may note that the extreme depths of the ocean make it difficult to map the ocean floor accurately. Students may also note that scientists are often unable to "open the box" to check their measurements; that is, the ocean is too deep in places and too vast to fully explore.

Datasheets for LabBook
Datasheet 26

Science Skills Worksheet 25
"Introduction to Graphs"

Investigating an Oil Spill
Teacher's Notes

Time Required
One 45-minute class period

Lab Ratings

TEACHER PREP 🧪🧪🧪
STUDENT SET-UP 🧪
CONCEPT LEVEL 🧪🧪
CLEAN UP 🧪🧪🧪

MATERIALS
The materials listed on the student page are sufficient for a group of 2–4 students. You may also choose to perform this activity as a demonstration to limit the use of machine oil.

Safety Caution
Remind students to review all safety cautions and icons before beginning this lab activity. Machine oil releases a strong odor. Use it only in well-ventilated areas.

Preparation Notes
Light machine oil may be replaced by cooking oil to demonstrate the same principle. If you choose to use machine oil, be sure there is sufficient ventilation in your classroom.

Disposal Information
Always follow federal, state, and local guidelines when disposing of oil. Pour cooking oil into a container of sand and put it in the trash.

Investigating an Oil Spill

Have you ever wondered why it is important to bring used motor oil to a recycling center rather than simply pouring it down the nearest drain or sewer? Or have you ever wondered why an oil spill of only a few thousand liters into an ocean containing many millions of liters of water can cause so much damage? The reason has to do with the fact that a little oil goes a long way.

Observing Oil and Water

You may have heard the expression "Oil and water don't mix." This is true—oil dropped on water will spread out thinly over the surface of the water. In this activity, you'll learn exactly how far oil can spread when it is in contact with water.

Procedure

1. Fill the pan two-thirds full with water. Be sure to wear your goggles and gloves.

2. Using the pipet, carefully add one drop of oil to the water in the middle of the pan.
   Caution: Machine oil is poisonous. Keep materials that have contacted oil out of your mouth and eyes.

3. Observe what happens to the drop of oil for the next few seconds. Record your observations in your ScienceLog.

4. Using a metric ruler, measure the diameter of the oil slick to the nearest centimeter.

5. Determine the area of the oil slick in square centimeters by using the formula for finding the area of a circle ($A = \pi r^2$). The radius (r) is equal to the diameter you measured in step 4 divided by 2. Multiply the radius by itself to get the square of the radius (r^2). Pi (π) is equal to 3.14.

   Example
   If your diameter is 10 cm,
   $r = 5$ cm, $r^2 = 25$ cm^2, $\pi = 3.14$
   $A = \pi r^2$
   $A = 3.14 \times 25$ cm^2
   $A = 78.5$ cm^2

6. Record your answers in your ScienceLog.

Materials
- safety gloves
- large pan (at least 22 cm in diameter)
- water
- pipet
- 15 mL light machine oil
- metric ruler
- graduated cylinder
- calculator (optional)

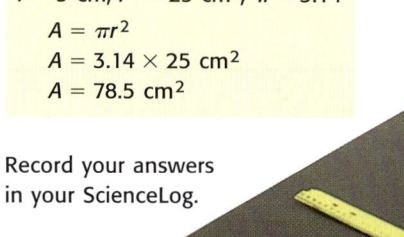

David Sparks
Redwater Jr. High
Redwater, Texas

Analysis

7. What happened to the drop of oil when it came in contact with the water? Did this surprise you?

8. What total surface area was covered by the oil slick? (Be sure to show your calculations.)

9. What does this experiment tell you about the density of oil compared with the density of water? Explain.

Finding the Number of Drops in a Liter

"It's only a few drops," you may think as you spill something toxic on the ground. But those drops eventually add up. Just how many drops does it take to make a difference? In this activity, you'll learn just what an impact a few drops can have.

Procedure

10. Using a clean pipet, count the number of water drops it takes to fill the graduated cylinder to 10 mL. Be sure to add the drops slowly so you get an accurate count.

11. Since there are 1,000 mL in a liter, multiply the number of drops in 10 mL by 100. This gives you the number of drops in a liter.

Analysis

12. How many drops of water from your pipet does it take to fill a 1 L container?

13. What would happen if someone spilled 4 L of oil into a lake?

Going Further
Find out how much oil supertankers contain. Can you imagine the size of an oil slick that would form if one of these tankers spilled its oil?

Going Further
Can you devise a way to clean the oil from the water? Get permission from your teacher before testing your cleaning method.

Do you think oil behaves the same way in ocean water? Devise an experiment to test your hypothesis.

Answers

7. When the drop of oil touched the water, it spread out. This may surprise some students, who might expect the two substances to mix or the oil to sink.

8. Answers will vary. Students should show their work to illustrate that they understand the mathematical principles involved.

9. This experiment shows that oil is less dense than water. For this reason, oil floats on water.

Going Further

- Answers will vary. One possibility is to use detergent to change the surface tension and remove the oil.

- To test the behavior of oil in ocean water, students could repeat the activity, using cold salt water instead of tap water. They could also rock the pan back and forth to simulate waves.

12. Answers will vary. The answer depends on the number of drops the students count in 10 mL of water. They should show their work to illustrate that they understand the mathematical principles involved.

13. The oil would spread to cover a large area. Students will not be able to determine the exact area for such an oil slick, but they should understand that the oil will spread significantly and pollute much of the lake.

 Datasheets for LabBook Datasheet 27

Up from the Depths
Teacher's Notes

Time Required
One 45-minute class period

Lab Ratings

TEACHER PREP 🧪
STUDENT SET-UP 🧪🧪🧪
CONCEPT LEVEL 🧪🧪
CLEAN UP 🧪🧪

MATERIALS
The materials listed on the student page are enough for a group of 4–5 students. Note that the food coloring is used only to distinguish the water layers. Any two colors will work. You may find it simpler to make a roll of plastic wrap available to the class. Groups can then take a piece when they reach the appropriate steps.

Safety Caution
Remind students to review all safety cautions and icons before beginning this lab activity.

Answers
13. The warm, red water remained on top of the cold, blue water. There was very little mixing (if any), and there was no turning over.

15. The cold, blue water did not remain on top of the warm, red water. There was very little mixing (if any), and the water turned over.

Using Scientific Methods

Up from the Depths

Every year, the water in certain parts of the ocean "turns over." This means that the water at the bottom rises to the top and the water at the top falls to the bottom. This yearly change brings fresh nutrients from the bottom of the ocean to the fish living near the surface. That makes it a great time for fishing! However, the water in some parts of the ocean never turns over. You will use this activity to find out why.

Some parts of the ocean are warmer at the bottom, and some are warmer at the top. Sometimes the saltiest water is at the bottom; sometimes it is not. You will investigate how these factors help determine whether the water will turn over.

Ask a Question
1. Why do some parts of the ocean turn over, while others do not?

Conduct an Experiment
2. Label the beakers 1 through 5. Fill beakers 1 through 4 with tap water.
3. Add a drop of blue food coloring to the water in beakers 1 and 2. Stir.
4. Place beaker 1 in the bucket of ice for 10 minutes.
5. Add a drop of red food coloring to the water in beakers 3 and 4. Stir.
6. Set beaker 3 on a hot plate turned to a low setting for 10 minutes.
7. Add one spoonful of salt to the water in beaker 4, and stir.
8. While beaker 1 is cooling and beaker 3 is heating, copy the data table on the next page into your ScienceLog.

Materials
- 400 mL beakers (5)
- tap water
- blue and red food coloring
- spoon
- bucket of ice
- watch or clock
- hot plate
- heat-resistant gloves
- 4 pieces of plastic wrap, approximately 30 × 20 cm
- salt

Gordon Zibelman
Drexel Hill Middle School
Drexel Hill, Pennsylvania

Observations Chart

Mixture of water	Observations
Warm water placed above cold water	
Cold water placed above warm water	DO NOT WRITE IN BOOK
Salty water placed above fresh water	
Fresh water placed above salty water	

9. Pour half of the water in beaker 1 into beaker 5. Return beaker 1 to the bucket of ice.

10. Tuck a sheet of plastic wrap into beaker 5 so that the plastic rests on the surface of the water and lines the upper half of the beaker.

11. Put on your gloves. Slowly pour half of the water in beaker 3 into the plastic-lined upper half of beaker 5 to form two layers of water. Return beaker 3 to the hot plate, and remove your gloves.

12. Very carefully pull on one edge of the plastic wrap and remove it so that the warm, red water rests on the cold, blue water.
    Caution: The plastic wrap may be warm.

Make Observations

13. Wait about 5 minutes, and then observe the layers in beaker 5. Did one layer remain on top of the other? Was there any mixing or turning over? Record your observations in your data table.

14. Empty and rinse beaker 5 with clean tap water.

15. Repeat the procedure in steps 9–14, this time with warm, red water from beaker 3 on the bottom and cold, blue water from beaker 1 on top. (Use gloves when pouring warm water.)

16. Again repeat the procedure used in steps 9–14, this time with blue tap water from beaker 2 on the bottom and red, salty water from beaker 4 on top.

17. Repeat the procedure used in steps 9–14 a third time, this time with red, salty water from beaker 4 on the bottom and blue tap water from beaker 2 on top.

Analyze the Results

18. Compare the results of all four trials. Explain why the water turned over in some of the trials but not in all of them.

Draw Conclusions

19. What is the effect of temperature and salinity on the density of water?

20. What makes the temperature of ocean water decrease? What could make the salinity of ocean water increase?

21. What explanations can you give for the fact that some parts of the ocean turn over in the spring, while some do not?

Going Further
Suggest a method for setting up a model that tests the combined effects of temperature and salinity on the density of water. Consider using more than two water samples and dyes.

16. The red, salty water did not remain on top of the blue tap water. There was little mixing, and the water turned over.

17. The blue tap water remained on top of the red, salty water. There was little mixing, and the water did not turn over.

18. In each case, the denser water sank to the bottom. Cold water is denser than warm water. When put in a beaker with warm water, the cold water either stayed at the bottom or sank to the bottom. Salt water is denser than fresh water. When put in a beaker with fresh water, the salt water either stayed at the bottom or sank to the bottom.

19. The density of water increases as its temperature decreases— cold water is denser than warm water. The density of water increases as its salinity increases—salt water is denser than fresh water.

20. The temperature of water can decrease due to seasonal temperature fluctuations or cold wind blowing across the water's surface. Currents can also carry cooler water to an area. The salinity of water can increase when evaporation occurs or when ice forms on the water's surface. These processes leave salts behind and make the remaining water more dense.

21. Parts of the ocean that turn over do so because their density changes due to variations in salinity or temperature. Parts of the ocean that do not turn over must not experience significant variations in salinity or temperature.

Going Further

The following combinations could be used:

Top	Bottom
Salt/cold	Fresh/warm
Salt/warm	Fresh/cold
Fresh/cold	Salt/warm
Fresh/warm	Salt/cold

Datasheets for LabBook
Datasheet 28

Turning the Tides
Teacher's Notes

Time Required

One 45-minute class period

Lab Ratings

TEACHER PREP 🔺🔺
STUDENT SET-UP 🔺🔺🔺
CONCEPT LEVEL 🔺🔺🔺
CLEAN UP 🔺

MATERIALS

The materials listed on the student page are enough for a group of 2–4 students.

Safety Caution

Remind students to review all safety cautions and icons before beginning this lab activity. Students should wear safety goggles. Be sure that students have enough space to spin the system.

Preparation Notes

You will need to put a mark at the center of all of the cardboard disks. Students will need to draw the radius of the circle from the center to the edge of the disk. Encourage students to draw this line along the corrugations of the cardboard. Otherwise, several other steps will be made more difficult. The cardboard disks are not to scale with the Earth and moon. They are used to show how a two-body system, such as the Earth-moon system, rotates. The disks must be different sizes. The large disks could be 10 cm in diameter, and the smaller disks could be 5 cm in diameter.

Turning the Tides

Daily tides are caused by two "bulges" on the ocean's surface—one on the side of the Earth facing the moon and the other on the opposite side. The bulge on the side facing the moon is caused by the moon's gravitational pull on the water. But the bulge on the opposite side is slightly more difficult to explain. Whereas the moon pulls the water on one side of the Earth, the combined rotation of the Earth and the moon "pushes" the water on the opposite side of the Earth. In this activity, you will model the motion of the Earth and the moon to investigate the tidal bulge on the side of Earth facing away from the moon.

Procedure

1. Draw a line from the center of each disk along the folds in the cardboard to the edge of the disk. This line is the radius.

2. Place a drop of white glue on one end of the dowel. Lay the larger disk flat, and align the dowel with the line for the radius you drew in step 1. Insert about 2.5 cm of the dowel into the edge of the disk.

3. Add a drop of glue to the other end of the dowel, and push that end into the smaller disk, again along its radius. The setup should look like a large two-headed lollipop, as shown below. This is a model of the Earth-moon system.

4. Staple the string to the edge of the large disk on the side opposite the dowel. Staple the cardboard square to the other end of the string. This smaller piece of cardboard represents the Earth's oceans that face away from the moon.

5. Place the tip of the pencil at the center of the large disk, as shown in the figure on the next page, and spin the model. You may poke a small hole in the bottom of the disk with your pencil, but DO NOT poke all the way through the cardboard. Record your observations in your ScienceLog. **Caution:** Be sure you are at a safe distance from other people before spinning your model.

Materials

- 2 disks of corrugated cardboard, one large and one small, with centers marked
- white glue
- piece of dowel, 1/4 in. in diameter and 36 cm long
- 5 cm length of string
- stapler with staples
- 1 × 1 cm piece of cardboard
- sharp pencil

Tracy Jahn
Berkshire Jr.-Sr. High
Canaan, New York

6. Now find your model's *center of mass*. This is the point at which the model can be balanced on the end of the pencil. **Hint:** It might be easier to find the center of mass using the eraser end. Then use the sharpened end of the pencil to balance the model. This balance point should be just inside the edge of the larger disk.

7. Place the pencil at the center of mass, and spin the model around the pencil. Again, you may wish to poke a small hole in the disk. Record your observations in your ScienceLog.

Analysis

8. What happened when you tried to spin the model around the center of the large disk? This model, called the Earth-centered model, represents the incorrect view that the moon orbits the center of the Earth.

9. What happened when you tried to spin the model around its center of mass? This point, called the *barycenter*, is the point around which both the Earth and the moon rotate.

10. In each case, what happened to the string and cardboard square when the model was spun?

11. Which model—the Earth-centered model or the barycentric model—explains why the Earth has a tidal bulge on the side opposite the moon? Explain.

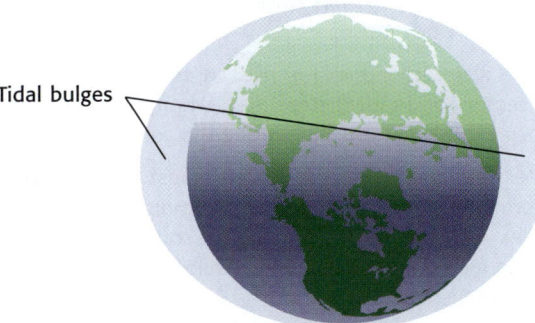

Moon   Tidal bulges   Earth

Answers

8. Answers will vary. Sample answer: When I tried to spin the model around the center of the large disk, I could not get the model to balance on the pencil.

9. Answers will vary. Sample answer: I was able to balance the model at the barycenter. The model spun, and the small piece of cardboard on the string swung outward.

10. Answers will vary. Sample answer: The cardboard square hung down when I tried to swing the model around the center of the large disk; I was unable to make the model spin. When I spun the model around its barycenter, the square swung away from the model.

11. The barycentric model explains why the Earth has a bulge on the side opposite the moon. The side of the Earth opposite the side facing the moon acts in much the same way the small square of cardboard does in this model. As the Earth-moon system rotates, the side of the Earth facing away from the moon bulges outward.

 Datasheets for LabBook Datasheet 29

Boiling Over!
Teacher's Notes

Time Required
One 45-minute class period

Lab Ratings

- TEACHER PREP 🧪
- STUDENT SET-UP 🧪🧪🧪
- CONCEPT LEVEL 🧪🧪
- CLEAN UP 🧪🧪

MATERIALS
The materials listed on the student page are enough for a group of 3–4 students.

Safety Caution
Remind students to review all safety cautions and icons before beginning this lab activity.

Preparation Notes
Begin the activity by leading a discussion of how thermometers work. Have students observe a regular thermometer. Ask students what parts are involved to make a thermometer work. (a receptacle containing the fluid referred to as the bulb, a tube, and air in the tube)

 Datasheets for LabBook
Datasheet 30

Using Scientific Methods

 DESIGN YOUR OWN

Boiling Over!

Safety Industries, Inc., would like to offer the public safer alternatives to the mercury thermometer. Many communities have complained that the glass thermometers are easy to break, and people are concerned about mercury poisoning. As a result, we would like your team of inventors to come up with a workable prototype that uses water instead of mercury. Safety Industries would like to offer a contract to the team that comes up with the best substitute for a mercury thermometer. In this activity, you will design and test your own water thermometer. Good luck!

Ask a Question
1. What conditions cause the liquid to rise in a thermometer? How can I use this information to build a thermometer?

Form a Hypothesis
2. Brainstorm with a classmate to design a thermometer that requires only water. Sketch your design in your ScienceLog. Write a one-sentence hypothesis that describes how your thermometer will work.

Test the Hypothesis
3. Follow your design to build a thermometer using only materials from the materials list. Like a mercury thermometer, your thermometer will need a bulb and a tube. However, the liquid in your thermometer will be water.
4. To test your design, place the aluminum pie pan on a hot plate. Carefully pour water into the pan until it is halfway full. Allow the water to heat.
5. Put on your gloves, and carefully place the "bulb" of your thermometer in the hot water. Observe the water level in the tube. Does it rise?
6. If the water level does not rise, adjust your design as necessary, and repeat steps 3–5. When the water level does rise, sketch your final design in your ScienceLog.
7. After you finalize your design, you must calibrate your thermometer with a laboratory thermometer by taping an index card to the thermometer tube so that the entire part of the tube protruding from the "bulb" of the thermometer touches the card.

Materials
- heat-resistant gloves
- aluminum pie pan
- hot plate
- water
- assorted containers, such as plastic bottles, soda cans, film canisters, medicine bottles, test tubes, balloons, and yogurt containers with lids
- assorted tubes, such as clear inflexible plastic straws or 5 mm diameter plastic tubing, 30 cm long
- modeling clay
- food coloring
- pitcher
- transparent tape
- index card
- Celsius thermometer
- a paper cone-shaped filter or funnel
- 2 large plastic-foam cups
- ice cubes
- metric ruler

Daniel Bugenhagen
Yutan Jr.–Sr. High
Yutan, Nebraska

8. Place the cone-shaped filter or funnel into the plastic-foam cup. Carefully pour hot water from the hot plate into the filter or funnel. Be sure that no water splashes or spills.

9. Place your own thermometer and a laboratory thermometer in the hot water. Mark the water level on the index card as it rises. Observe and record the temperature on the laboratory thermometer, and write this value on the card beside the mark.

10. Repeat steps 8–9 with warm water from the faucet.

11. Repeat steps 8–9 with ice water.

12. Divide the markings on the index card into equally sized increments, and write the corresponding temperatures on the index card.

Analyze the Results

13. How effective is your thermometer at measuring temperature?

14. Compare your thermometer design with other students' designs. How would you modify your design to make your thermometer measure temperature even better?

Draw Conclusions

15. Take a class vote to see which design should be chosen for a contract with Safety Industries. Why was this thermometer chosen? How did it differ from other designs in the class?

Answers
13. Answers will vary. Accept all reasonable responses.
14. Answers will vary. Accept all reasonable responses.
15. Accept all reasonable responses.

 Science Skills Worksheet 1 "Being Flexible"

 Science Skills Worksheet 5 "Using Logic"

General Design

A water thermometer has a receptacle containing water and air with a tube protruding from the receptacle. A trick to getting the water thermometer to work well is to allow a lot of air in the "bulb" because air expands more than water. As the air heats, it expands, pushing the water upward in the tube. One way to build such a thermometer is to put a straw in a soda can and to seal the opening of the can with modeling clay so that water can escape only by moving upward, out of the straw. It is important that student thermometers are tightly sealed. A sample design is shown below.

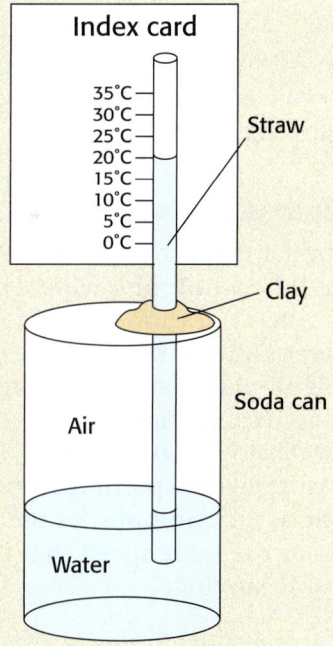

Chapter 15 • LabBook

Go Fly a Bike!
Teacher's Notes

Time Required
One 45-minute class period

Lab Ratings

- TEACHER PREP — easy
- STUDENT SET-UP — medium
- CONCEPT LEVEL — medium
- CLEAN UP — easy

MATERIALS
The materials listed on the student page are enough for a group of 3–4 students.

Safety Caution
Remind students to review all safety cautions and icons before beginning this lab activity.

Preparation Notes
Conduct this activity on a day when the wind is blowing, but not when the wind speed is greater than 50 km/h. Use straight, plastic straws. Before the activity, explain that an *anemometer* is a device that measures wind speed. It works because the wind pushes the cups at the same speed that the wind is moving.

 Datasheets for LabBook
Datasheet 31

Using Scientific Methods

DISCOVERY LAB

Go Fly a Bike!

Your friend Daniel just invented a bicycle that can fly! Trouble is, the bike can fly only when the wind speed is between 3 m/s and 10 m/s. If the wind is not blowing hard enough, the bike won't get enough lift to rise into the air, and if the wind is blowing too hard, the bike is difficult to control. Daniel needs to know if he can fly his bike today. Can you build a device that can estimate how fast the wind is blowing?

Ask a Question
1. How can I construct a device to measure wind speed?

Construct an Anemometer
2. Cut off the rolled edges of all five paper cups. This will make them lighter, so that they can spin more easily.
3. Measure and place four equally spaced markings 1 cm below the rim of one of the paper cups.
4. Use the hole punch to punch a hole at each mark so that the cup has four equally spaced holes. Use the sharp pencil to carefully punch a hole in the center of the bottom of the cup.
5. Push a straw through two opposite holes in the side of the cup.
6. Repeat step 5 for the other two holes. The straws should form an X.
7. Measure 3 cm from the bottom of the remaining paper cups, and mark each spot with a dot.
8. At each dot, punch a hole in the paper cups with the hole punch.
9. Color the outside of one of the four cups.
10. Slide a cup on one of the straws by pushing the straw through the punched hole. Rotate the cup so that the bottom faces to the right.

Materials
- scissors
- 5 small paper cups
- metric ruler
- hole punch
- 2 straight plastic straws
- colored marker
- small stapler
- thumbtack
- sharp pencil with an eraser
- modeling clay
- masking tape
- watch or clock that indicates seconds

Terry J. Rakes
Elmwood Jr. High
Rogers, Arkansas

11. Fold the end of the straw, and staple it to the inside of the cup directly across from the hole.
12. Repeat steps 10–11 for each of the remaining cups.
13. Push the tack through the intersection of the two straws.
14. Push the eraser end of a pencil through the bottom hole in the center cup. Push the tack as far as it will go into the end of the eraser.
15. Push the sharpened end of the pencil into some modeling clay to form a base. This will allow the device to stand up without being knocked over, as shown at right.
16. Blow into the cups so that they spin. Adjust the tack so that the cups can freely spin without wobbling or falling apart. Congratulations! You have just constructed an anemometer.

Conduct an Experiment

17. Find a suitable area outside to place the anemometer vertically on a surface away from objects that would obstruct the wind, such as buildings and trees.
18. Mark the surface at the base of the anemometer with masking tape. Label the tape "starting point."
19. Hold the colored cup over the starting point while your partner holds the watch.
20. Release the colored cup. At the same time, your partner should look at the watch or clock. As the cups spin, count the number of times the colored cup crosses the starting point in 10 seconds.

Analyze the Results

21. How many times did the colored cup cross the starting point in 10 seconds?
22. Divide your answer in step 21 by 10 to get the number of revolutions in 1 second.

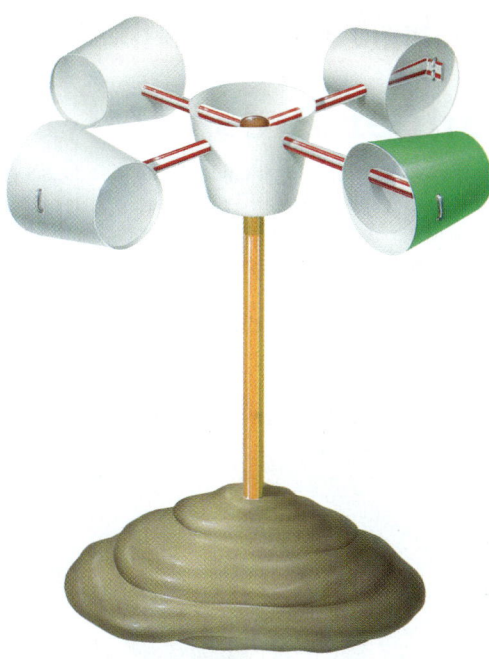

23. Measure the diameter of your anemometer (the distance between the outside edges of two opposite cups) in centimeters. Multiply this number by 3.14 to get the circumference of the circle made by the cups of your anemometer.
24. Multiply your answer from step 23 by the number of revolutions per second (step 22). Divide that answer by 100 to get wind speed in meters per second.
25. Compare your results with those of your classmates. Did you get the same result? What could account for any slight differences in your results?

Draw Conclusions

26. Could Daniel fly his bicycle today? Why or why not?

Answers
21. Answers will vary, depending on the wind speed.
22. Answers will vary according to each student's response to question 21.
23. Answers will vary according to the length of the straws and the size of the cups used.
24. Answers will vary.
25. Each group's anemometer should provide similar results. Differences may be caused by inconsistent wind speed. If students did not answer question 21 accurately, their results will be slightly different from other groups.
26. If the wind speed is between 3 and 10 m/s, Daniel could fly his bicycle. Otherwise, the weather would be too windy or too still for the bicycle to work.

Under Pressure!
Teacher's Notes

Time Required
One 45-minute class period plus 15 minutes each day for 3–4 days

Lab Ratings

TEACHER PREP ▲▲
STUDENT SET-UP ▲▲▲
CONCEPT LEVEL ▲▲▲
CLEAN UP ▲▲

MATERIALS
The materials listed on the student page are enough for a group of 2–4 students.

Safety Caution
Remind students to review all safety cautions and icons before beginning this lab activity.

Do not allow students to make a mercury barometer. Mercury fumes are dangerous.

Preparation Notes
A few weeks before the activity, collect daily weather newspaper clippings. A week before the activity, have students bring in large coffee cans. Jars can substitute for coffee cans in this experiment. For more accurate results, make sure students place their barometers in a shaded area.

Using Scientific Methods

Under Pressure!

You are planning a picnic with your friends, so you look in the newspaper for the weather forecast. The temperature this afternoon should be in the low 80s. This sounds quite comfortable! But you notice that the newspaper's forecast also includes the barometer reading. What does the reading tell you? In this activity, you will build your own barometer and discover what this instrument can tell you.

Materials
- balloon
- scissors
- large empty coffee can with 10 cm diameter
- masking tape or rubber band
- drinking straw
- transparent tape
- index card

Ask a Question
1. How can I construct a device that measures changes in atmospheric pressure?

Conduct an Experiment
2. Stretch and inflate the balloon. Let the air out. This will allow your barometer to be more sensitive to changes in atmospheric pressure.
3. Cut off the end of the balloon that you put in your mouth to inflate it. Stretch the balloon snugly over the mouth of the coffee can. Attach the balloon to the can with the tape or the rubber band.
4. Cut one end of the straw at an angle to form a pointer.
5. Place the straw with the pointer pointed away from the center of the stretched balloon so that 5 cm of the end of the straw hangs over the edge of the can, as shown on the next page. Tape the straw to the balloon.
6. Tape the index card to the can near the straw. Congratulations! You have just constructed a barometer!

 Datasheets for LabBook Datasheet 32

 Science Skills Worksheet 2 "Using Your Senses"

Terry J. Rakes
Elmwood Jr. High
Rogers, Arkansas

7. Find a suitable area outside to place the barometer. Record the location of the straw for 3–4 days by marking it on the index card.

Analyze the Results

8. What factors affect how your barometer works? Explain your answer.

9. What does an upward movement of the straw indicate?

10. What does a downward movement of the straw indicate?

Draw Conclusions

11. Compare your results with the barometric pressures listed in your local newspaper. What kind of weather is associated with high pressure? What kind of weather is associated with low pressure?

Going Further

Now you can calibrate your barometer! Gather the weather section from your local newspaper for the same 3 or 4 days that you were testing your barometer. Find the barometer reading in the newspaper for each day, and record it beside that day's mark on your index card. Divide the markings on the index card into regular increments, and write the corresponding barometric pressures on the card.

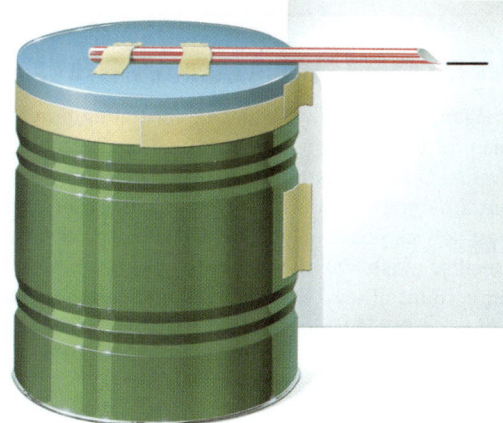

Answers

8. Temperature and pressure will affect how the barometer works. Assuming that the can is sealed without leaks, as the temperature outside increases, the temperature of the can increases, and this increases the pressure of the enclosed gas. The rubber bulges upward making the straw point down. As the temperature outside decreases, the temperature of the can decreases, and this decreases the pressure of the enclosed gas. The rubber bulges downward making the straw point up. Therefore, falling temperature produces the same effect as a rising barometric pressure, and rising temperature produces the same effect as a decreasing barometric pressure.

9. An upward movement of the straw means that the atmospheric pressure is increasing. Pressure is pushing on top of the balloon, causing the pointer to rise.

10. A downward movement of the straw means that the atmospheric pressure is decreasing.

11. Clear, dry days are associated with high pressure. Cloudy, rainy, or humid days are associated with low pressure. A sudden drop in air pressure usually indicates that a storm is on the way.

Chapter 15 • LabBook

Watching the Weather
Teacher's Notes

Time Required
One 45-minute class period

Lab Ratings

TEACHER PREP ▲
STUDENT SET-UP ▲▲
CONCEPT LEVEL ▲▲
CLEAN UP ▲

MATERIALS

There are no materials required in this lab. Have students complete the lab individually.

Gordon Zibelman
Drexel Hill Middle School
Drexel Hill, Pennsylvania

694   Chapter 16 • LabBook

Watching the Weather

Imagine that you own a private consulting firm that helps people plan for big occasions, such as weddings, parties, and celebrity events. One of your duties is making sure the weather doesn't put a damper on your clients' plans. In order to provide the best service possible, you have taken a crash course in reading weather maps. Will the celebrity golf match have to be delayed on account of rain? Will the wedding ceremony have to be moved inside so the blushing bride doesn't get soaked? It is your job to say "yea" or "nay."

Procedure

1. Study the station model and legend shown on the next page. You will use the legend to interpret the weather map on the final page of this activity.

2. Weather data is represented on a weather map by a station model. A station model is a small circle that shows the location of the weather station along with a set of symbols and numbers around the circle that represent the data collected at the weather station. Study the table below.

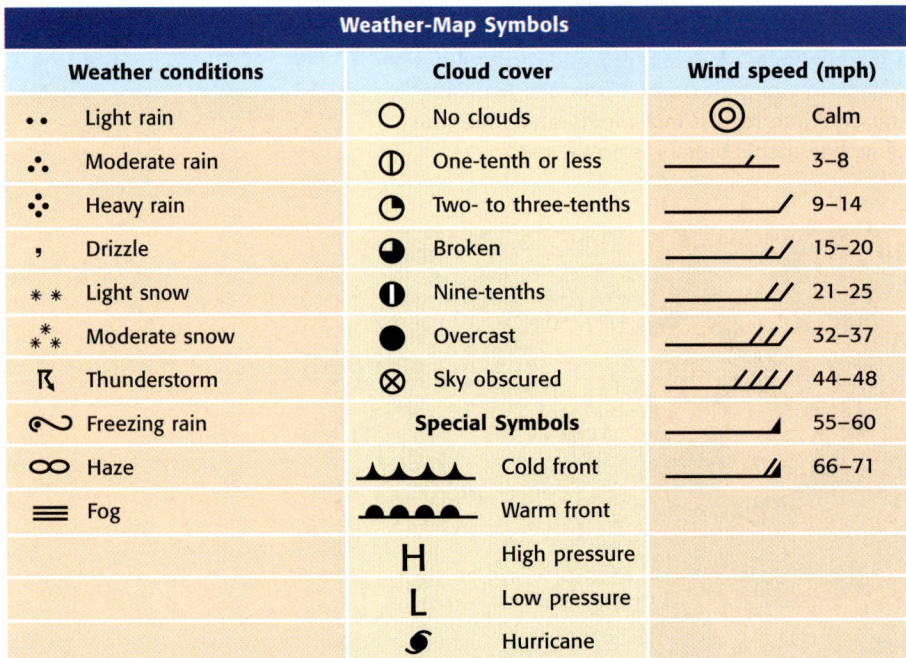

694

Station Model

Wind speed is represented by whole and half tails.

A line indicates the direction the wind is coming from.

Air temperature

A symbol represents the current weather conditions. If there is no symbol, there is no precipitation.

Dew point temperature

Shading indicates the cloud coverage.

Atmospheric pressure in millibars (mbar). This number has been shortened on the station model. To read the number properly you must follow a few simple rules.
- If the first number is greater than 5, place a 9 in front of the number and a decimal point between the last two digits.
- If the first number is less than or equal to 5, place a 10 in front of the number and a decimal point between the last two digits.

Lab Notes

You may want to go over the different weather symbols with students and discuss how to convert the abbreviated form of atmospheric pressure to its actual measure. Before the lab, have students review the different kinds of fronts. Students may enjoy creating a weather report based on the weather report provided in this lab. Students can present this report to the class as a "live" studio show or through a video tape they create in their own time.

Datasheets for LabBook
Datasheet 33

Interpreting Station Models

The station model below is for Boston, Massachusetts. The current temperature in Boston is 42°F, and the dew point is 39°F. The barometric pressure is 1011.0 mbar. The sky is overcast, and there is a moderate rainfall. The wind is coming from the southwest at 15–20 mph.

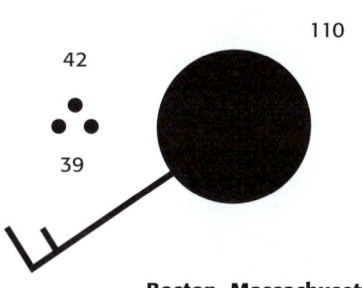

Boston, Massachusetts

Chapter 16 • LabBook   **695**

Answers

3. It's the winter. A cold front is coming through. Temperatures are low where the cold front has passed.

4. The temperature is 42°F. The dewpoint is 36°F. There is broken cloud cover, light rain, and the wind is from the northwest at 3–8 mph. The barometric pressure is 1024.6 mb.

5. As the cold front approaches, the wind is generally from the south, the barometric pressure is low, and temperatures are warmer. As the cold front passes, the wind is from the northwest, the pressure rises, and temperatures are much cooler.

6. The temperature is 45°F. The barometric pressure is 965.4 mb, the dewpoint is 38°F, the sky is obscured, there is a thunderstorm, and the wind is from the south at 21–25 mph.

Analysis

3. Based on the weather for the entire United States, what time of year is it? Explain your answer.

4. Interpret the station model for Salem, Oregon. What is the temperature, dew point, cloud coverage, wind direction, wind speed, and atmospheric pressure? Is there any precipitation? If so, what kind?

5. What is happening to wind direction, temperature, and pressure as the cold front approaches? as it passes?

6. Interpret the station model for Amarillo, Texas.

Let It Snow!

While an inch of rain might be good for your garden, 7 or 8 cm could cause an unwelcome flood. But what about snow? How much snow is too much? A blizzard might drop 40 cm of snow overnight. Sure it's up to your knees, but how does this much snow compare with rain? This activity will help you find out.

Materials

- 150 mL of shaved ice
- 100 mL beaker
- metric ruler
- heat-resistant gloves
- hot plate
- graduated cylinder

Procedure

1. Pour 50 mL of shaved ice into your beaker. Do not pack the ice into the beaker. This ice will represent your snowfall.
2. Use the ruler to measure the height of the snow in the beaker.
3. Turn on the hot plate to a low setting.
   Caution: Wear heat-resistant gloves and goggles when working with the hot plate.
4. Place the beaker on the hot plate, and leave it there until all of the snow melts.
5. Pour the water into the graduated cylinder, and record the height and volume of the water in your ScienceLog.
6. Repeat steps 1–5 two more times.

Analysis

7. What was the difference in height before and after the snow melted in each of your three trials? What was the average difference?
8. Why did the volume change after the ice melted?
9. In this activity, what was the ratio of snow height to water height?
10. Use the ratio you found in step 9 to calculate how much water 50 cm of this snow would produce. Use the following equation to help.

$$\frac{\text{measured height of snow}}{\text{measured height of water}} = \frac{50 \text{ cm of snow}}{? \text{ cm of water}}$$

11. Why is it important to know the water content of a snowfall?

Going Further

Shaved ice isn't really snow. Research to find out how much water real snow would produce. Does every snowfall produce the same ratio of snow height to water depth?

Walter Woolbaugh
Manhattan School System
Manhattan, Montana

Going Further

Every snowfall does not produce the same ratio of snow height to water depth. The ratio of snow height to water depth is dependent on several variables, including whether the snow is wet or dry.

Let It Snow!
Teacher's Notes

Time Required
One 45-minute class period

Lab Ratings

EASY ——— HARD

- **Teacher Prep** 🧪
- **Student Set-Up** 🧪🧪
- **Concept Level** 🧪
- **Clean Up** 🧪

MATERIALS
The materials listed are best for a group of 3–4 students.

Safety Caution
Remind students to review all safety cautions and icons before beginning this lab activity.

Answers

7. Answers will vary according to the water content of the ice or snow sample.
8. The volume changed because the water changed from a solid to a liquid.
9. Answers will vary.
10. Answers will vary
11. Answers will vary. The water content of a snowfall—whether it is relatively wet or relatively dry—affects how much flooding may occur as the snow melts. A "wetter" snow has more water per volume and may cause more flooding than a "drier" snow.

Datasheets for LabBook
Datasheet 34

Chapter 16 • LabBook

Gone with the Wind
Teacher's Notes

Time Required
One 45-minute class period

Lab Ratings

TEACHER PREP 🧪🧪
STUDENT SET-UP 🧪🧪
CONCEPT LEVEL 🧪🧪
CLEAN UP 🧪

> **MATERIALS**
> This activity works best in groups of 2–3 students.

Safety Caution
Remind students to review all safety cautions and icons before beginning this lab activity.

Preparation Notes
You might want to watch your local weather station in order to schedule this experiment on a windy day. Use a magnetic compass to find magnetic north. Then use masking tape or chalk to mark the sidewalk or parking lot with an arrow pointing toward magnetic north. Before the activity, ask students if they have ever seen a weather vane. Also have them list several reasons why knowing the wind direction might be helpful.

Using Scientific Methods

MAKING MODELS

Gone with the Wind

Pilots at the Fly Away Airport need your help—fast! Last night, lightning destroyed the orange windsock. This windsock helped pilots measure which direction the wind was blowing. But now the windsock is gone with the wind, and an incoming airplane needs to land. The pilot must know what direction the wind is blowing and is counting on you to make a device that can measure wind direction.

Materials
- paper plate
- drawing compass
- metric ruler
- protractor
- index card
- scissors
- stapler
- straight plastic straw
- sharpened pencil
- thumbtack or pushpin
- magnetic compass
- small rock

Ask a Question
1. How can I measure wind direction?

Conduct an Experiment
2. Find the center of the plate by tracing around its edge with a drawing compass. The pointed end of the compass should poke a small hole in the center of the plate.
3. Use a ruler to draw a line across the center of the plate.
4. Use a protractor to help you draw a second line through the center of the plate. This new line should be at a 90° angle to the line you drew in step 3.
5. Moving clockwise, label each line *N, E, S,* and *W.*
6. Use a protractor to help you draw two more lines through the center of the plate. These lines should be at a 45° angle to the lines you drew in steps 3 and 4.
7. Moving clockwise from *N*, label these new lines *NE, SE, SW,* and *NW*. The plate now resembles the face of a magnetic compass. This will be the base of your wind-direction indicator. It will help you read the direction of the wind at a glance.

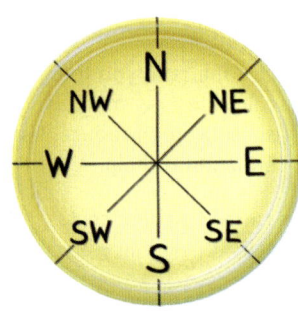

Walter Woolbaugh
Manhattan School System
Manhattan, Montana

8. Measure and mark a 5 × 5 cm square on an index card. Cut the square out of the card. Fold the square in half to form a triangle.

9. Staple an open edge of the triangle to the straw so that one point of the triangle touches the end of the straw.

10. Hold the pencil at a 90° angle to the straw. The eraser should touch the balance point of the straw. Push a thumbtack or pushpin through the straw and into the eraser. The straw should spin without falling off.

11. Find a suitable area outside to measure the wind direction. The area should be clear of trees and buildings.

12. Press the sharpened end of the pencil through the center hole of the plate and into the ground. The labels on your paper plate should be facing the sky, as shown below.

13. Use a compass to find magnetic north. Rotate the plate so that the *N* on the plate points north. Place a small rock on top of the plate so that it does not turn.

14. Watch the straw as it rotates. The triangle will point in the direction the wind is blowing.

Analyze the Results

15. From what direction is the wind coming?

16. In what direction is the wind blowing?

Draw Conclusions

17. Would this be an effective way for pilots to measure wind direction? Why or why not?

18. What improvements would you suggest to Fly Away Airport to measure wind direction more accurately?

Going Further
Use this tool to measure and record wind direction for several days. What changes in wind direction occur as a front approaches? as a front passes?

Review magnetic declination in the chapter titled "Maps as Models of the Earth." How might magnetic declination affect your design for a tool to measure wind direction?

Answers

15. Answers will vary.
16. Answers will vary.
17. Answers will vary. Accept all reasonable responses.
18. Answers will vary. Accept all reasonable responses.

Going Further

Answers will vary. (Wind direction varies according to the type of front that is moving through.)

Answers will vary. Sample answer: You have to adjust the weather vane to account for the difference between magnetic north and true north. The adjustment will vary depending on where you live.

Datasheets for LabBook
Datasheet 35

Science Skills Worksheet 24
"Using Models to Communicate"

Global Impact
Teacher's Notes

Time Required
One 45-minute class period

Lab Ratings

TEACHER PREP 🧪
STUDENT SET-UP 🧪🧪🧪
CONCEPT LEVEL 🧪🧪
CLEAN UP 🧪

MATERIALS
The materials listed in the student page are enough for each student.

Preparation Notes
This activity requires graphing skills. Students may need a review of graphing, analyzing data from a graph, and calculating the slope of a graph.

Datasheets for LabBook
Datasheet 36

Science Skills Worksheet 26
"Grasping Graphing"

Janel Guse
West Central Middle School
Hartford, South Dakota

700   Chapter 17 • LabBook

Global Impact

For years scientists have debated the topic of global warming. Is the temperature of the Earth actually getting warmer? Sample sizes are a very important factor in any scientific study. In this activity, you will examine a chart to determine if the data indicate any trends. Be sure to notice how much the trends seem to change as you analyze different sets of data.

Materials
- 4 colored pencils
- metric ruler

Procedure

1. Look at the chart below. It shows average global temperatures recorded over the last 100 years.

2. Draw a graph in your ScienceLog. Label the horizontal axis "Time," and mark the grid in 5-year intervals. Label the vertical axis "Temperature (°C)," with values ranging from 13°C to 15°C.

3. Starting with 1900, use the numbers in red to plot the temperature in 20-year intervals. Connect the dots with straight lines.

4. Using a ruler, estimate the overall slope of temperatures, and draw a red line to represent the slope.

5. Using different colors, plot the temperatures at 10-year intervals and 5-year intervals on the same graph. Connect each set of dots, and draw the average slope for each set.

Analysis

6. Examine your completed graph, and explain any trends you see in the graphed data. Was there an increase or a decrease in average temperature over the last 100 years?

7. What differences did you see in each set of graphed data? what similarities?

8. What conclusions can you draw from the data you graphed in this activity?

9. What would happen if your graph were plotted in 1-year intervals? Try it!

Average Global Temperatures

Year	°C	Year	°C	Year	°C	Year	°C	Year	°C	Year	°C
1900	14.0	1917	13.6	1934	14.0	1951	14.0	1968	13.9	1985	14.1
1901	13.9	1918	13.6	1935	13.9	1952	14.0	1969	14.0	1986	14.2
1902	13.8	1919	13.8	1936	14.0	1953	14.1	1970	14.0	1987	14.3
1903	13.6	1920	13.8	1937	14.1	1954	13.9	1971	13.9	1988	14.4
1904	13.5	1921	13.9	1938	14.1	1955	13.9	1972	13.9	1989	14.2
1905	13.7	1922	13.9	1939	14.0	1956	13.8	1973	14.2	1990	14.5
1906	13.8	1923	13.8	1940	14.1	1957	14.1	1974	13.9	1991	14.4
1907	13.6	1924	13.8	1941	14.1	1958	14.1	1975	14.0	1992	14.1
1908	13.7	1925	13.8	1942	14.1	1959	14.0	1976	13.8	1993	14.2
1909	13.7	1926	14.1	1943	14.0	1960	14.0	1977	14.2	1994	14.3
1910	13.7	1927	14.0	1944	14.1	1961	14.1	1978	14.1	1995	14.5
1911	13.7	1928	14.0	1945	14.0	1962	14.0	1979	14.1	1996	14.4
1912	13.7	1929	13.8	1946	14.0	1963	14.0	1980	14.3	1997	14.4
1913	13.8	1930	13.9	1947	14.1	1964	13.7	1981	14.4	1998	14.5
1914	14.0	1931	14.0	1948	14.0	1965	13.8	1982	14.1	1999	
1915	14.0	1932	14.0	1949	13.9	1966	13.9	1983	14.3	2000	
1916	13.8	1933	13.9	1950	13.8	1967	14.0	1984	14.1	2001	

Answers

6. Students will notice that the temperatures fluctuated over the last 100 years but have gradually increased in the last 30 years.

7. The larger the sample size, the more precise your analysis will be. You notice that in the larger samples, temperatures are constantly fluctuating. A smaller sample doesn't always adequately display what is really happening with the data. For instance, the average temperature for a certain year might not be representative for the entire decade. The smaller the data set, the more your outcome is subject to error. There were very few similarities among the graphs.

8. You can conclude that a larger data set gives you a more complete picture of what is happening. Global temperatures have gradually increased in the twentieth century.

9. Global temperatures would appear to fluctuate more.

Using Scientific Methods

DISCOVERY LAB

For the Birds

You and a partner have a new business building birdhouses. But your first clients have told you that birds do not want to live in the birdhouses you have made. The clients want their money back unless you can solve the problem. You need to come up with a solution right away!

You remember reading an article about microclimates in a science magazine. Cities often heat up because the pavement and buildings absorb so much solar radiation. Maybe the houses are too warm! How can the houses be kept cooler?

You decide to investigate the roofs; after all, changing the roofs would be a lot easier than building new houses. In order to help your clients and the birds, you decide to test different roof colors and materials to see how these variables affect a roof's ability to absorb the sun's rays.

One partner will test the color, and the other partner will test the materials. You will then share your results and make a recommendation together.

Materials

- 4 pieces of cardboard
- black, white, and light-blue tempera paint
- 4 Celsius thermometers
- watch or clock
- beige or tan wood
- beige or tan rubber

For the Birds
Teacher's Notes

Time Required
One 45-minute class period

Lab Ratings

TEACHER PREP 🧪
STUDENT SET-UP 🧪🧪
CONCEPT LEVEL 🧪🧪
CLEAN UP 🧪🧪

MATERIALS
The materials listed on the student page are enough for a group of 4–5 students.

Safety Caution
Remind students to review all safety cautions and icons before beginning this lab activity.

Part A: Color Test

Ask a Question

1. What color would be the best choice for the roof of a birdhouse?

Form a Hypothesis

2. In your ScienceLog, write down the color you think will keep a birdhouse coolest.

Test the Hypothesis

3. Paint one piece of cardboard black, another piece white, and a third light blue.

4. After the paint has dried, take the three pieces of cardboard outside, and place a thermometer on each piece.

5. In an area where there is no shade, place each piece at the same height so that all three receive the same amount of sunlight. Leave the pieces in the sunlight for 15 minutes.

6. Leave a fourth thermometer outside in the shade to measure the temperature of the air.

Datasheets for LabBook
Datasheet 37

Larry Tackett
Andrew Jackson Middle School
Cross Lanes, West Virginia

Answers

8. Sample answer: No, the thermometers recorded different temperatures. The black and blue pieces of cardboard, particularly the black one, caused the temperature to increase.

9. Sample answer: The temperature of the black cardboard was much higher than the outside temperature. Students should find that the temperature of the other colors was also different from the outside temperature.

10. Students' answers will vary. Accept all reasonable responses.

7. In your ScienceLog, record the reading of the thermometer on each piece of cardboard. Also record the outside temperature.

Analyze the Results

8. Did each of the three thermometers record the same temperature after 15 minutes? Explain.

9. Were the temperature readings on each of the three pieces of cardboard the same as the reading for the outside temperature? Explain.

Draw Conclusions

10. How do your observations compare with your hypothesis?

Part B: Material Test

Ask a Question

11. Which material would be the best choice for the roof of a birdhouse?

Form a Hypothesis

12. In your ScienceLog, write down the material you think will keep a birdhouse coolest.

Test the Hypothesis

13. Take the rubber, wood, and the fourth piece of cardboard outside, and place a thermometer on each.

14. In an area where there is no shade, place each material at the same height so that they all receive the same amount of sunlight. Leave the materials in the sunlight for 15 minutes.

15. Leave a fourth thermometer outside in the shade to measure the temperature of the air.

16. In your ScienceLog, record the temperature of each material. Also record the outside temperature.

702 Chapter 17 • LabBook

Analyze the Results

17. Did each of the thermometers on the three materials record the same temperature after 15 minutes? Explain.

18. Were the temperature readings on the rubber, wood, and cardboard the same as the reading for the outside temperature? Explain.

Draw Conclusions

19. How do your observations compare with your hypothesis?

Sharing Information (Parts A and B)

Communicate Results

After you and your partner have finished your investigations, take a few minutes to share your results. Then work together to design a new roof.

20. Which material would you use to build the roofs for your birdhouses? Why?

21. Which color would you use to paint the new roofs? Why?

Going Further

Make three different-colored samples for each of the three materials. When you measure the temperatures for each sample, how do the colors compare for each material? Is the same color best for all three materials? How do your results compare with what you concluded in steps 20 and 21 of this activity? What's more important, color or material?

Answers

17. Sample answer: No, the temperatures were different. The temperature of the rubber was higher than that of the other two materials.

18. Sample answer: No, the temperature of the rubber was higher than the outside temperature. Accept all other reasonable answers for the other materials.

19. Answers will vary. Accept all reasonable answers.

20. Sample answer: The wood would be the coolest. The cardboard would be a possible alternative.

21. The white roof would be the coolest. A light blue roof would be a possible alternative.

Going Further

Answers will vary. Accept all reasonable interpretations of the data collected.

Science Skills Worksheet 11
"Understanding Variables"

Chapter 17 • LabBook

Biome Business
Teacher's Notes

Time Required
One 45-minute class period

Lab Ratings

TEACHER PREP ▲
STUDENT SET-UP ▲
CONCEPT LEVEL ▲▲▲
CLEAN UP ▲

MATERIALS

Student groups will need a general map to identify their biome location.

Preparation Notes

Remind students not to use seasonal terms such as spring and fall because some of the biomes in the Southern Hemisphere may experience seasons opposite those of the Northern Hemisphere.

 Datasheets for LabBook
Datasheet 38

David Sparks
Redwater Jr. High
Redwater, Texas

704 Chapter 17 • LabBook

Biome Business

You have just been hired as an assistant to a world-famous botanist. Your duties include collecting vegetation samples to study the effects of human activity on different plant species. Unfortunately, you were hired at the last minute, and no one has explained tomorrow's plan to you. You have been provided with climatographs for three biomes. A *climatograph* is a graph that shows the temperature and precipitation patterns for an area for a year.

You can use the information provided in the graphs to determine the type of climate in each biome. You also have a general map of the biomes, but nothing is labeled. Using this information, you must figure out what the environment will be like so that you can prepare yourself.

In this activity you will use climatographs and maps to determine where you will be traveling. You can find the exact locations by tracing the general maps and matching them to Figure 10 in the Climate chapter. Good luck!

Procedure

1. Look at each climatograph. The shaded areas show the average precipitation for the biome. The red line shows the average temperature.

2. Use the climatographs to determine the climate patterns for each biome. Compare the maps with the general map in Figure 10 to find the exact location of each region.

Analysis

3. Describe the precipitation patterns of each biome by answering the following questions:
   a. When does it rain the most in this biome?
   b. Do you think the biome is relatively dry, or do you think it rains a lot?

4. Describe the temperature patterns of each biome by answering the following questions:
   a. What are the warmest months of the year?
   b. Does the biome seem to have temperature cycles, like seasons, or is the temperature almost always the same?
   c. Do you think the biome is warm or cool? Explain.

5. Name each biome.

6. Where is each biome located?

Biome A

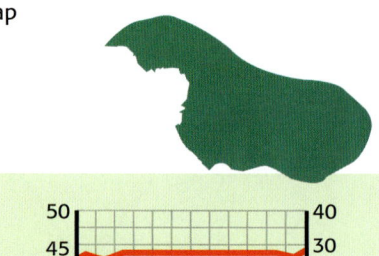

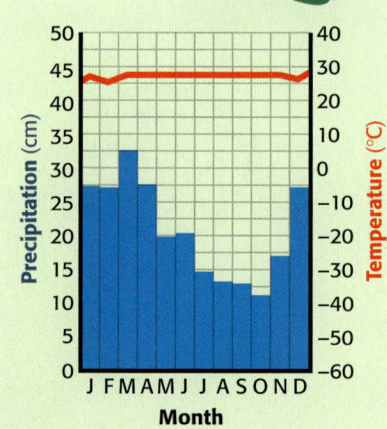

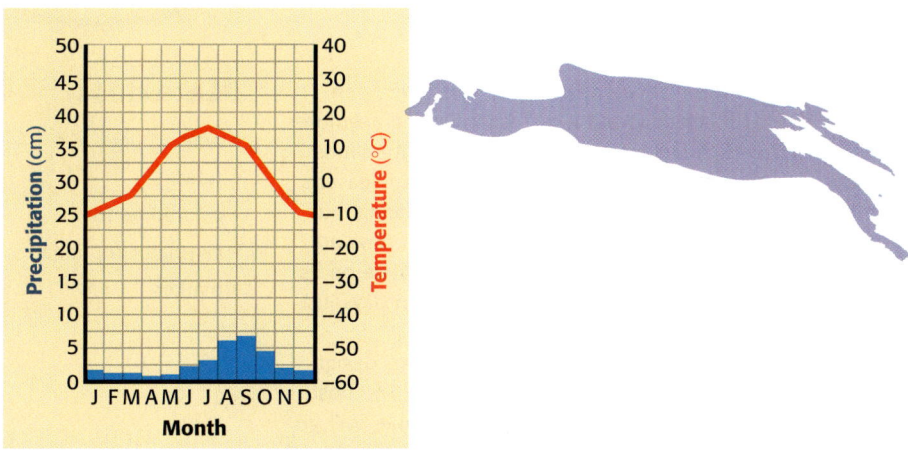

Biome B

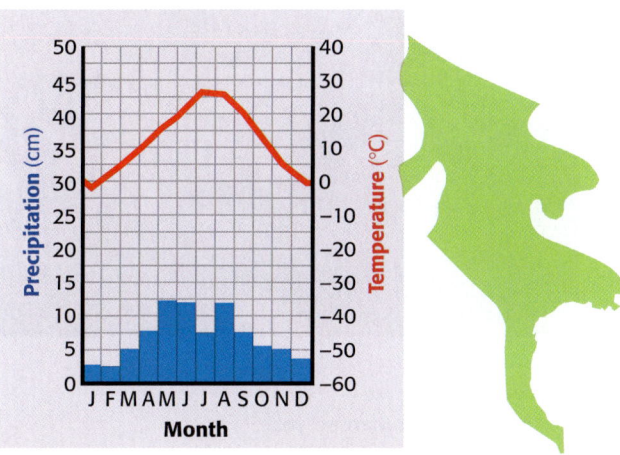

Biome C

Going Further

In a cardboard box no bigger than a shoe box, build a model of one of the biomes that you investigated. Include things to represent the biome, such as the plants and animals that inhabit the area. Use magazines, photographs, colored pencils, plastic figurines, clay, or whatever you like. Be creative!

Answers

3. a. In Biome A, the rain falls throughout the year but is heaviest in March.
   In Biome B, the rain is heaviest in September.
   In Biome C, the rain is heaviest in May, June, and August.

   b. Biome A is very rainy and wet. Biomes B and C are relatively dry, but some months are rainier than others.

4. a. Biome A has a relatively constant temperature throughout the year.
   Biomes B and C experience their warmest months from June to August.

   b. Biome A has a constant temperature throughout the year.
   Biomes B and C experience seasonal cycles.

   c. Biome A is warm and the temperature is high year-round. Biome B has a cooler climate and the climatograph shows cooler temperatures year-round.
   Biome C has a moderate climate in the early and late months of the year, but the temperature is quite hot in the middle months of the year.

5. Biome A = a tropical rain forest
   Biome B = a taiga
   Biome C = a temperate grassland

6. Biome A = the west coast of Africa near the equator
   Biome B = northern Asia
   Biome C = midwestern United States

Chapter 17 • LabBook

Create a Calendar
Teacher's Notes

Time Required

One 45-minute class period

Lab Ratings

TEACHER PREP 🔬🔬
STUDENT SET-UP 🔬
CONCEPT LEVEL 🔬🔬🔬
CLEAN UP 🔬

MATERIALS

The materials listed on the student page are enough for a group of 2–3 students.

Preparation Notes

This activity will require math skills. As a class, you may need to review how to multiply fractions.

As an extension activity, students may research the rotation and revolution of other planets. Students can then create a calendar for one of the other planets.

Michael E. Kral
West Hardin Middle School
Cecilia, Kentucky

706   Chapter 18 • LabBook

Using Scientific Methods

Create a Calendar

Imagine that you live in the first colony on Mars. You have been trying to follow the Earth calendar, but it just isn't working anymore. Mars takes almost 2 Earth years to revolve around the sun—almost 687 Earth days to be exact! That means that there are two seasons each Earth calendar year. One year, you get winter and spring, but the next year, you get only summer and fall! And Martian days are longer than Earth days. Mars takes 24.6 Earth hours to rotate on its axis. Even though they are similar, Earth days and Martian days just don't match. This won't do!

Several groups of Mars pioneers have been chosen to design a new calendar that will be based on the Martian year. The best design will be chosen as the Martian calendar. The winner will go down in history as the founder of the modern Martian calendar. Your calendar should include months, weeks, and days.

Materials
- poster board
- ruler
- colored pencils
- calculator (optional)
- marker

Ask a Question

1. How can I create a calendar for Mars that includes months, weeks, and days?

Conduct an Experiment

2. Use the following formulas to determine the number of Martian days there are in a Martian year:

$$\frac{687 \text{ Earth days}}{1 \text{ Martian year}} \times \frac{24 \text{ Earth hours}}{1 \text{ Earth day}} = \text{Earth hours per Martian year}$$

$$\text{Earth hours per Martian year} \times \frac{1 \text{ Martian day}}{24.6 \text{ Earth hours}} = \text{Martian days per Martian year}$$

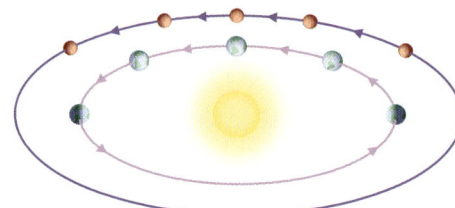

3. Decide how to divide your calendar into Martian months, weeks, and days. Will you have a leap day, a leap week, a leap month, or a leap year? How often will it occur?

4. Choose names for the months and days of your calendar. In your ScienceLog, explain why you chose each name. If you have time, explain how you would number the Martian years. For instance, would the first year correspond to a certain Earth year?

5. Follow your design to create your own calendar for Mars. Draw the calendar on your piece of poster board. Make sure it is brightly colored and easy to follow.

6. Present your calendar to the class. Explain how you chose your months, weeks, and days.

Analyze the Results

7. What advantages does your calendar design have? Are there any disadvantages to your design?

8. Which student or group created the most original calendar? Which design was the most useful? Explain.

9. What might you do to improve your calendar?

Draw Conclusions

10. Take a class vote to decide which design should be chosen as the new calendar for Mars. Why was this calendar chosen? How did it differ from other designs?

11. Why is it useful to have a calendar that matches the cycles of the planet you live on?

Answers

7. Answers will vary. Accept all reasonable responses.
8. Answers will vary. Accept all reasonable responses.
9. Answers will vary. Accept all reasonable responses. Students may suggest simplifying their design.
10. Answers will vary. Accept all reasonable responses.
11. Answers will vary. Accept all reasonable responses.

Datasheets for LabBook
Datasheet 39

Chapter 18 • LabBook **707**

The Sun's Yearly Trip Through the Zodiac
Teacher's Notes

Time Required
Two 45-minute class periods

Lab Ratings

- TEACHER PREP 🧪🧪🧪
- STUDENT SET-UP 🧪🧪
- CONCEPT LEVEL 🧪🧪🧪
- CLEAN UP 🧪

MATERIALS

The materials listed on the student pages are enough for a group of 12 students. However, you may choose to use this activity as a demonstration for the entire class.

Preparation Notes

One week before the activity, collect large cardboard boxes. Designate a large, clear area for the activity, such as a gym, cafeteria, playground, or large classroom. You may wish to get a basketball from the physical education instructor, or ask students to bring basketballs from home. Folding chairs work best for this activity because of their portability.

Review the terms *clockwise* and *counterclockwise* to ensure consistency of student results.

Using Scientific Methods

The Sun's Yearly Trip Through the Zodiac

During the course of a year, the sun appears to move through a circle of twelve constellations in the sky. The twelve constellations make up a "belt" in the sky called the *zodiac.* Each month, the sun appears to be in a different constellation. The ancient Babylonians developed a 12-month calendar based on the idea that the sun moved through this circle of constellations as it revolved around the Earth. They believed that the constellations of stars were fixed in position and that the sun and planets moved past the stars. Later, Copernicus developed a model of the solar system in which the Earth and the planets revolve around the sun. But how can Copernicus's model of the solar system be correct when the sun appears to move through the zodiac?

Materials
- 12 chairs
- 12 index cards
- roll of masking tape
- inflated ball
- large cardboard box

Ask a Question

1. If the sun is at the center of the solar system, why does it appear to move with respect to the stars in the sky?

Conduct an Experiment

2. Set the chairs in a large circle so that the backs of the chairs all face the center of the circle. Make sure that the chairs are equally spaced, like the numbers on the face of a clock.

3. Write the name of each constellation in the zodiac on the index cards. You should have one card for each constellation.

4. Stand inside the circle with the masking tape and the index cards. Moving counterclockwise, attach the cards to the backs of the chairs in the following order: Aries, Taurus, Gemini, Cancer, Leo, Virgo, Libra, Scorpio, Sagittarius, Capricorn, Aquarius, and Pisces.

5. Use masking tape to label the ball "Sun."

6. Place the large closed box in the center of the circle. Set the roll of masking tape flat on top of the box.

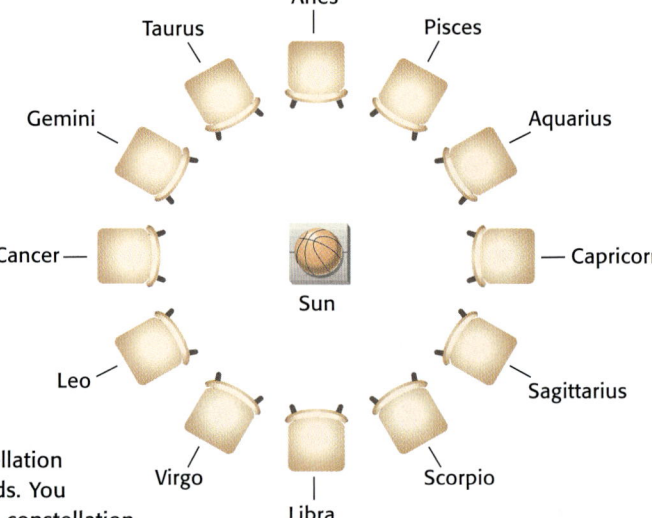

Joseph W. Price
H.M. Browne Junior High
Washington, D.C.

7. Place the ball on top of the roll of masking tape so that the ball stays in place.

8. Stand inside of the circle of chairs. You will represent the Earth. As you move around the ball, you will model the Earth's orbit around the sun. Notice that even though only the "Earth" is moving, as seen from the Earth, the sun appears to move through the entire zodiac!

9. Stand in front of the chair labeled "Aries." Look at the ball representing the sun. Then look past the ball to the chair at the opposite side of the circle. Where in the zodiac does the sun appear to be?

10. Move to the next chair on your right (counterclockwise). Where does the sun appear to be? Is it in the same constellation? Explain your answer.

11. Repeat step 10 until you have observed the position of the sun from each chair in the circle.

Analyze the Results

12. Did the sun appear to move through the 12 constellations, even though the Earth was orbiting around the sun? How can you explain this?

Draw Conclusions

13. How does Copernicus's model of the solar system explain the apparent movement of the sun through the constellations of the zodiac?

Datasheets for LabBook
Datasheet 40

Background

Begin the activity by asking students if they are familiar with the constellations of the Zodiac. Have they seen them depicted in a list or in a circle? How did the mythology of the Zodiac begin? (The 12 familiar signs of the Zodiac were adopted by the Babylonians about 3,000 years ago. The word *zodiac* means "circle," and the Babylonians thought that the sun and the planets moved in a circle through 12 fixed constellations in the night sky.)

Ask each student group to list as many Zodiac constellations as they can remember on the chalkboard. The constellations and their corresponding signs are as follows: Aries (the ram), Taurus (the bull), Gemini (the twins), Cancer (the crab), Leo (the lion), Virgo (the virgin), Libra (the scales), Scorpio (the scorpion), Sagittarius (the hunter), Capricorn (the mountain goat), Aquarius (the water bearer), and Pisces (the fish).

Answers

12. When students stand in front of a chair, the sun appears to be in the constellation opposite the chair. As they move outside the circle counterclockwise, the sun appears to shift through the constellations counterclockwise. As the Earth (the student) orbits the sun (the ball), the sun never appears in the same constellation because of the Earth's perspective relative to the fixed constellations.

13. In Copernicus' heliocentric model of the solar system, the Earth orbits the sun. As the Earth moves around the sun, the position of the sun in relation to the constellations changes.

Chapter 18 • LabBook

Through the Looking Glass
Teacher's Notes

Time Required
One 45-minute class period

Lab Ratings

EASY — HARD

TEACHER PREP 🔬🔬
STUDENT SET-UP 🔬🔬🔬
CONCEPT LEVEL 🔬🔬
CLEAN UP 🔬

MATERIALS
The materials listed on the student page are enough for a group of 2–3 students.

Safety Caution
Remind students to review all safety cautions and icons before beginning this lab activity. Students should never look at the sun through their telescopes. Caution students not to focus sunlight through their telescopes because it could start a fire.

Preparation Notes
One week before the activity, ask students to collect wrapping-paper and toilet-paper cardboard tubes to bring to class. Obtain two double-convex lenses for each group of students.

You may wish to experiment with the lenses before class to determine how far the paper must be to form an image. If you add another lens to the telescope, you can make the image right side up, but light is lost as it passes through the third lens.

Through the Looking Glass

SKILL BUILDER

Have you ever looked toward the horizon or up into the sky and wished you could see farther? Think a telescope might help? Astronomers use huge telescopes to study the universe. You can build your very own telescope to get a glimpse of what astronomers see with their incredible equipment.

Procedure

1. Use modeling clay to form a base to hold one of the lenses upright on your desktop. When the lights are turned off, your teacher will turn on a lamp at the front of the classroom. Rotate your lens so that the light from the lamp passes through it.

2. Hold the construction paper so that the light passing through the lens lands on the paper. Slowly move the paper closer to or farther from the lens until you see the sharpest image of the light on the paper. Hold the paper in this position.

3. With the metric ruler, measure the distance between the lens and the paper. Record this distance in your ScienceLog.

4. How far is the paper from the lens? This distance, called the *image distance,* is how far the paper has to be from the lens in order for the image to be in focus.

5. Repeat steps 1–4 with the other lens.

Materials
- masking tape
- 2 convex lenses, 3 cm in diameter
- desk lamp
- sheet of construction paper
- metric ruler
- cardboard wrapping-paper tube
- cardboard toilet-paper tube
- scissors
- modeling clay

710

Michael E. Kral
West Hardin Middle School
Cecilia, Kentucky

6. From one end of the long cardboard tube, measure and mark the image distance of the lens with the longer image distance. Place a mark 2 cm past this line toward the other end of the tube, and label the mark "cut."

7. From one end of the short cardboard tube, measure and mark the image distance of the lens with the shorter image distance. Place a mark 2 cm past this line toward the other end of the tube, and label the mark "cut."

8. Shorten the tubes by cutting along the marks labeled "cut."

9. Tape the lens with the longer image distance to one end of the longer tube. Tape the other lens to one end of the shorter tube. Slip one tube inside the other. Be sure the lenses are at each end of this new, longer tube.

10. Congratulations! You have just constructed a telescope! To use your telescope, look through the short tube (the eyepiece), and point the long end at various objects in the room. You can focus the telescope by adjusting its length. Are the images right side up, or upside down? Observe birds, insects, trees, or other outside objects.
Caution: Never look directly at the sun! This could cause permanent blindness.

Analysis

11. Which type of telescope did you just construct—a refracting telescope or a reflecting telescope? What makes it one type and not the other?

12. Would upside-down images negatively affect astronomers looking at stars through their telescopes? Explain your answer.

Background

Begin the activity by discussing the components of a telescope. Simple telescopes, like the one Galileo made, consist of two lenses and a tube. To provide a clear image, the tube should be as long as the sum of the image distances of the two lenses. Some students may have difficulty knowing when the image is in focus. Explain to these students that they should focus the light bulb's filament on the paper.

Answers

11. a refracting telescope; Refracting telescopes use lenses, while reflecting telescopes use mirrors and lenses.

12. Answers will vary. Accept all reasonable responses.

Datasheets for LabBook
Datasheet 41

Chapter 18 • LabBook   **711**

How Far Is the Sun?
Teacher's Notes

Time Required

One 45-minute class period

Lab Ratings

TEACHER PREP 🧪🧪
STUDENT SET-UP 🧪
CONCEPT LEVEL 🧪🧪🧪🧪
CLEAN UP 🧪

MATERIALS
The materials listed on the student page are enough for a group of 2–3 students.

Safety Caution

Remind students to review all safety cautions and icons before beginning this lab activity. Also caution students never to look directly at the sun.

Preparation Notes

Conduct this activity on a sunny day. This lab works best in the late afternoon because the sun is lower in the sky. The sunlight should come through the window at an angle as close to perpendicular as possible. It may help to lower the blinds so that the sunlight will pass through a narrow opening.

Some sample data is provided in the table below.

Diameter of image (cm)	Distance from hole to image (cm)
2 cm	214 cm

Using Scientific Methods

DISCOVERY LAB

How Far Is the Sun?

It doesn't slice, it doesn't dice, but it can give you an idea of how big our universe is! You can build your very own stellar-distance measuring device from household items. Amaze your friends by figuring out how many metersticks can be placed between Earth and the sun.

Materials

- poster board
- scissors
- square of aluminum foil
- thumbtack
- masking tape
- index card
- meterstick
- metric ruler

Ask a Question

1. If it were possible, how many metersticks could I place between the sun and the Earth?

Conduct an Experiment

2. Measure and cut a 4 × 4 cm square from the middle of the poster board. Tape the foil square in the center of the poster board.

3. Carefully prick the foil with a thumbtack to form a tiny hole in the center. Congratulations—you have just constructed your very own stellar-distance measuring device!

4. Tape the device to a window facing the sun so that sunlight shines directly through the pinhole.
   Caution: Do not look directly into the sun.

5. Place one end of the meterstick against the window and beneath the foil square, and steady the meterstick with one hand.

Daniel Bugenhagen
Yutan Jr.–Sr. High
Yutan, Nebraska

6. With the other hand, hold the index card close to the pinhole. You should be able to see a circular image on the card. This is an image of the sun.

7. Move the card back until the image is large enough to measure. Be sure to keep the image on the card sharply focused. Reposition the meterstick so that it touches the bottom of the card.

8. Ask your partner to measure the diameter of the image on the card with the metric ruler. Record the diameter of the image in your ScienceLog.

9. Record the distance between the window and the index card by reading the point at which the card rests on the meterstick.

10. Calculate the distance between the Earth and the sun using the following formula:

$$\text{Distance between the sun and Earth} = \text{sun's diameter} \times \frac{\text{distance to the image}}{\text{image's diameter}}$$

1 cm = 10 mm
1 m = 100 cm
1 km = 1,000 m

Hint: The sun's diameter is 1,392,000,000 m.

Analyze the Results

11. According to your calculations, how far is the sun from the Earth? Don't forget to convert your measurements to meters.

Draw Conclusions

12. You could put 150 billion metersticks between the Earth and the sun. Compare this with your result in step 11. Do you think that this is a good way to measure the Earth's distance from the sun? Support your answer.

Background

On the board, draw the diagram at the bottom of the page and explain that this activity uses triangles and proportions to find the distance to the sun. Because the sun forms the image on the paper, there must be a proportionate relationship between the triangles in the diagram. The hole divides the proportions, so the distance between the image and the hole is related to the distance between the sun and the hole.

Answers

11. Answers will vary, but based on the sample data and the formula provided, the sun is 148,944,000,000 m from the Earth. The sun is actually 149,600,000,000 m away.

12. Answers will vary. Accept all well-supported answers. According to the sample data, the calculated value was within 0.5 percent of the actual value. So it is generally a good way to measure the distance from the Earth to the sun.

Datasheets for LabBook
Datasheet 42

Math Skills Worksheet 17
"Using Proportions and Cross-Multiplication"

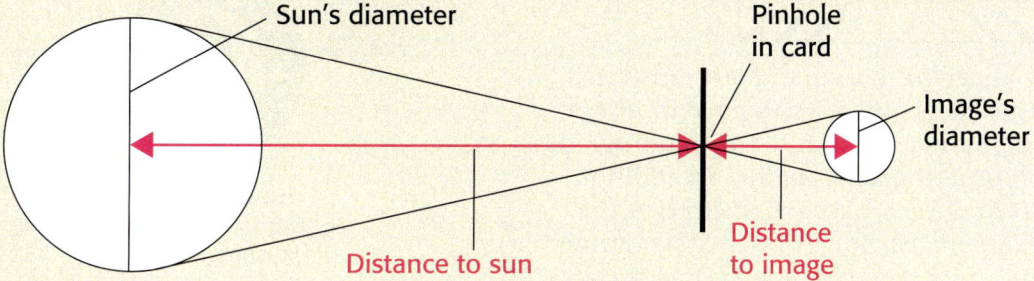

Chapter 19 • LabBook

Why Do They Wander?
Teacher's Notes

Time Required
This activity will take approximately 30 minutes. But it may take as much as one 45-minute class period to instruct students on how to use a compass.

Lab Ratings

TEACHER PREP 🔺🔺
STUDENT SET-UP 🔺
CONCEPT LEVEL 🔺🔺🔺🔺
CLEAN UP 🔺

MATERIALS
The materials listed on the student page are enough for 1–2 students. The compasses, rulers, and colored pencils may be shared among several groups.

Safety Caution
Remind students to review all safety cautions and icons before beginning this lab activity.

Preparation Notes
Students may need instruction on how to use a drawing compass. You may need to demonstrate the proper use of a compass. This activity works best when students work individually or in pairs. Each group will need a compass, a piece of white paper, and a metric ruler. The compasses, rulers, and colored pencils may be shared among several groups.

Using Scientific Methods

MAKING MODELS

Why Do They Wander?

Before the discoveries of Nicholas Copernicus in the early 1500s, most people thought that the planets and the sun revolve around the Earth and that the Earth was the center of the solar system. But Copernicus observed that the sun is the center of the solar system and that all the planets, including Earth, revolve around the sun. He also explained a puzzling aspect of the movement of planets across the night sky.

If you watch a planet every night for several months, you'll notice that it appears to "wander" among the stars. While the stars remain in fixed positions relative to each other, the planets appear to move independently of the stars. First Mars travels to the left, then it goes back to the right a little, and finally it reverses direction and travels again to the left. No wonder the early Greeks called the planets wanderers!

In this lab you will make your own model of part of the solar system to find out how Copernicus's model of the solar system explained this zigzag motion of the planets.

Materials
- drawing compass
- white paper
- metric ruler
- colored pencils

Ask a Question
1. Why do the planets appear to move back and forth in the Earth's night sky?

Conduct an Experiment
2. Use the compass to draw a circle with a diameter of 9 cm on the paper. This circle will represent the orbit of the Earth around the sun. (Note: The orbits of the planets are actually slightly elliptical, but circles will work for this activity.)

3. Using the same center point, draw a circle with a diameter of 12 cm. This circle will represent the orbit of Mars.

4. Using a blue pencil, draw three parallel lines in a diagonal across one end of your paper, as shown at right. These lines will help you plot the path Mars appears to travel in Earth's night sky. Turn your paper so that the diagonal lines are at the top of the page.

5. Place 11 dots on your Earth orbit, as shown on the next page, and number them 1 through 11. These dots will represent Earth's position from month to month.

MISCONCEPTION ALERT

The apparent motion of Mars illustrated in this lab is called "retrograde motion." It should not be confused with retrograde orbit or retrograde rotation. In addition, this lab does not accurately portray the actual *positions* of Earth and Mars during their orbits, it merely shows how their relative positions change.

Joseph W. Price
H. M. Browne Junior High
Washington, D.C.

6. Now place 11 dots along the top of your Mars orbit, as shown below. Number the dots as shown. These dots will represent the position of Mars at the same time intervals. Notice that Mars travels slower than Earth.

7. Use a green line to connect the first dot on Earth's orbit to the first dot on Mars's orbit, and extend the line all the way to the first diagonal line at the top of your paper. Place a green dot where this green line meets the first blue diagonal line, and label the green dot *1*.

8. Now connect the second dot on Earth's orbit to the second dot on Mars's orbit, and extend the line all the way to the first diagonal at the top of your paper. Place a green dot where this line meets the first blue diagonal line, and label this dot *2*.

9. Continue drawing green lines from Earth's orbit through Mars's orbit and finally to the blue diagonal lines. Pay attention to the pattern of dots you are adding to the diagonal lines. When the direction of the dots changes, extend the green line to the next diagonal, and add the dots to that line instead.

10. When you are finished adding green lines, draw a red line to connect all the dots on the blue diagonal lines in the order you drew them.

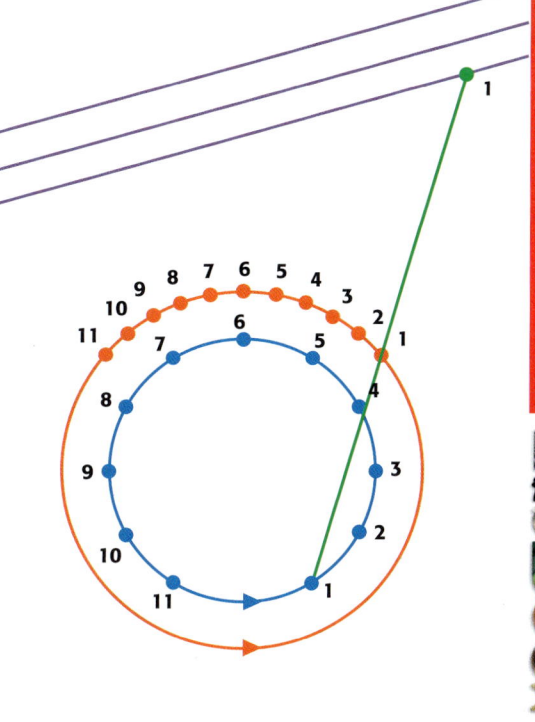

Analyze the Results

11. What do the green lines connecting points along Earth's orbit and Mars's orbit represent?

12. What does the red line connecting the dots along the diagonal lines look like? How can you explain this?

Draw Conclusions

13. What does this demonstration show about the motion of Mars?

14. Why do planets appear to move back and forth across the sky?

15. Were the Greeks justified in calling the planets wanderers? Explain.

Answers

11. The lines connecting Earth's orbit and Mars's orbit represent the students' line of sight as they stand on Earth and look at Mars.

12. The line along the diagonals changed direction at the fifth and seventh points. This happened because Mars was behind Earth in its orbit. To a person on Earth, it would look as if Mars changed direction at those moments.

13. When Earth catches up to Mars, Mars appears to reverse its direction. As Earth passes Mars, Mars appears to revert to its original direction.

14. Planets appear to move back and forth because they travel around the sun at different speeds and at different distances. When the Earth overtakes a slower planet, such as Mars, that planet appears to move backwards in Earth's sky.

15. Answers may vary. Accept all well-supported responses. Although the planets do not actually wander, it does appear as if they do to people on Earth. Students may consider this enough justification for calling the planets wanderers.

715

Lab Notes

Plan View Versus Sky View: It is important to note that the circles represent a plan view of part of the solar system, while the diagonal lines represent a view of the apparent motion of Mars in Earth's night sky. Students are asked to jump from line to line as they draw their dots in order to show them the apparent path of Mars in the sky.

Note on Scale: Notice that, according to the drawing, it appears that for less than half of its orbit, Mars travels more than a year of Earth's time. In fact, an Earth year is actually more than half of a Martian year. Mars's period of revolution is 1.88 Earth years. The drawing on this page is not to scale in this respect; if it were to scale, the wandering motion of the planets could not be depicted on one page.

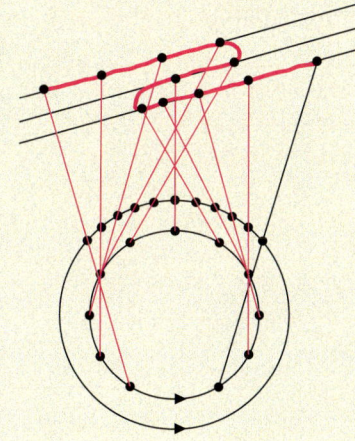

Datasheets for LabBook
Datasheet 43

Eclipses
Teacher's Notes

Time Required
One 45-minute class period

Lab Ratings

TEACHER PREP 🧪
STUDENT SET-UP 🧪🧪
CONCEPT LEVEL 🧪🧪🧪
CLEAN UP 🧪

MATERIALS

The materials listed on the student page are enough for each student or for students working in groups of 2–3.

Answers

6. The flashlight represents the sun.
7. As viewed from Earth, step 4 modeled a lunar eclipse.
8. As viewed from the moon, step 4 modeled a solar eclipse.
9. As viewed from Earth, step 5 modeled a solar eclipse.
10. As viewed from the moon, step 5 modeled an eclipse of Earth.
11. There would be a lunar and a solar eclipse each month. This is because the model shows Earth and the moon orbiting in exactly the same plane around the sun. However, the planes are usually above or below the shadow of the other, so an eclipse does not always occur.

 **MAKING MODELS**

Eclipses

As the Earth and the moon revolve around the sun, they both cast shadows into space. An eclipse occurs when one planetary body passes through the shadow of another. You can demonstrate how an eclipse occurs by using clay models of planetary bodies.

Materials
- modeling clay
- metric ruler
- sheet of notebook paper
- small flashlight

Procedure

1. Make two balls out of the modeling clay. One ball should have a diameter of about 4 cm and will represent the Earth. The other should have a diameter of about 1 cm and will represent the moon.

2. Place the two balls about 15 cm apart on the sheet of paper. (You may want to prop the smaller ball up on folded paper or on clay so that the centers of the two balls are at the same level.)

3. Hold the flashlight approximately 15 cm away from the large ball. The flashlight and the two balls should be in a straight line. Keep the flashlight at about the same level as the clay. When the whole class is ready, your teacher will turn off the lights.

4. Turn on your flashlight. Shine the light on the larger ball, and sketch your model in your ScienceLog. Include the beam of light in your drawing.

5. Move the flashlight to the opposite side of the paper. The flashlight should now be approximately 15 cm away from the smaller clay ball. Repeat step 4.

Analysis

6. What does the flashlight in your model represent?
7. As viewed from Earth, what event did your model represent in step 4?
8. As viewed from the moon, what event did your model represent in step 4?
9. As viewed from Earth, what event did your model represent in step 5?
10. As viewed from the moon, what event did your model represent in step 5?
11. According to your model, how often would solar and lunar eclipses occur? Is this accurate? Explain.

 Datasheets for LabBook
Datasheet 44

Joseph W. Price
H. M. Browne Junior High
Washington, D.C.

Phases of the Moon

It's easy to see when the moon is full. But you may have wondered exactly what happens when the moon appears as a crescent or when you cannot see the moon at all. Does the Earth cast its shadow on the moon? In this activity, you will discover how and why the moon appears as it does in each phase.

DISCOVERY LAB

LabBook

Materials

- globe
- light source
- plastic-foam ball

Procedure

1. Place your globe near the light source. Be sure that the north pole is tilted toward the light. Rotate the globe so that your state faces the light.
2. Using the ball as your model of the moon, move the moon between the Earth (the globe) and the sun (the light). The side of the moon that faces the Earth will be in darkness. Write your observations of this new-moon phase in your ScienceLog.
3. Continue to move the moon in its orbit around the Earth. When part of the moon is illuminated by the light, as viewed from Earth, the moon is in the crescent phase. Add your observations to your ScienceLog.
4. If you have time, you may draw your own moon-phase diagram.

Analysis

5. About 2 weeks after the new moon appears, the entire moon is visible in the sky. Move the ball to show this event.
6. What other phases can you add to your diagram? For example, when does the quarter moon appear?
7. Explain why the moon sometimes appears as a crescent to viewers on Earth.

Joseph W. Price
H. M. Browne Junior High
Washington, D.C.

7. When the moon is in a direct line between Earth and the sun, the side of the moon facing Earth is dark. This is the new moon phase. During this phase, there is no illuminated area of the moon visible from Earth. As the moon continues to move in its orbit around Earth, part of its illuminated half becomes visible. When a sliver of the moon is visible from Earth, the moon enters a crescent phase.

Phases of the Moon
Teacher's Notes

Time Required
One 45-minute class period

Lab Ratings

EASY ─────────► HARD

- TEACHER PREP ▲▲
- STUDENT SET-UP ▲▲
- CONCEPT LEVEL ▲
- CLEAN UP ▲

MATERIALS

The materials listed on the student page are enough for a group of 3–4 students. You can use a lamp or a flashlight as the light source.

Answers

5. At full moon, Earth is between the sun and the moon. To represent this phase, students should move the plastic-foam ball to the opposite side of the globe from the light source.

6. Students should demonstrate their understanding of the phases and the events that create them. The first-quarter moon occurs halfway between the new moon and the full moon phases, and the last-quarter moon occurs between the full moon and the new moon. In the model, students should move the plastic-foam ball one-quarter of the way around the globe and three-quarters of the way around the globe. These positions represent the first quarter phase and last quarter phase.

Datasheets for LabBook
Datasheet 45

Red Hot, or Not?
Teacher's Notes

Time Required
One 45-minute class period

Lab Ratings

- TEACHER PREP 🧪🧪
- STUDENT SET-UP 🧪🧪
- CONCEPT LEVEL 🧪
- CLEAN UP 🧪

MATERIALS

The materials listed on this page are enough for a group of 3–4 students.

Safety Caution

Remind students to review all safety cautions and icons before beginning this lab activity. Be sure the students disconnect the wires at each step. If they are left connected, they can get very hot.

Lab Notes

Students may find it difficult to hold the wires to the light bulb. In that case, you may use a light socket. Any miniature incandescent light bulb can be used as the flashlight bulb.

Red Hot, or Not?

DISCOVERY LAB

When you look at the night sky, some stars are brighter than others. Some are even different colors from what you might expect. For example, one star in the constellation Orion glows red; and Sirius, the brightest star in the sky, glows a bluish white. Astronomers use these colors to estimate the temperature of the stars. In this activity, you will experiment with a light bulb and some batteries to discover what the color of a glowing object reveals about the temperature of the object.

Materials
- electrical tape
- 2 conducting wires
- weak D cell
- flashlight bulb
- 2 fresh D cells

Procedure

1. Tape one end of a conducting wire to the positive pole of the weak D cell. Tape one end of the second conducting wire to the negative pole.

2. Touch the free end of each wire to the light bulb. Hold one of the wires against the bottom tip of the light bulb. Hold the second wire against the side of the metal portion of the bulb. The bulb should light.

3. In your ScienceLog, record the color of the filament in the light bulb. Carefully touch your hand to the bulb. Observe the temperature of the bulb. Record your observations in your ScienceLog.

Kathy McKee
Hoyt Middle School
Des Moines, Iowa

718   Chapter 21 • LabBook

4. Repeat steps 1–3 with one of the two fresh D cells.

5. Use the electrical tape to connect the two fresh D cells in a continuous circuit so that the positive pole of the first cell is connected to the negative pole of the second cell.

6. Repeat steps 1–3 with both fresh D cells in combination.

Analysis

7. How did the color of the filament change in the three trials? How did the temperature change?

8. What information does the color of a star provide?

9. What color are stars with relatively high surface temperatures? What color are stars with relatively low surface temperatures?

10. Arrange the following stars in order from highest to lowest surface temperature: Sirius is bluish white. Aldebaran is orange. Procyon is yellow-white. Capella is yellow. Betelgeuse (BET uhl jooz) is red.

Answers

7. With the weaker cell, the filament should burn with a dull red color. The filament burns bright red or orange with the stronger cell. With two fresh D cells, the filament becomes almost white. The temperature increases from one trial to the next.

8. Cooler objects emit red light. As an object becomes hotter, its color gradually changes from red to orange to white. Therefore, the color of the light emitted from the stars helps scientists determine the relative temperatures of stars.

9. Stars with relatively high surface temperatures are white or blue. Stars with relatively low surface temperatures are red or orange.

10. The order of the stars from highest to lowest surface temperature is as follows: Sirius, Procyon, Capella, Aldebaran, and Betelgeuse.

 Datasheets for LabBook Datasheet 46

I See the Light!
Teacher's Notes

Time Required

One to two 45-minute class periods

Lab Ratings

EASY ——————→ HARD

TEACHER PREP 🔺🔺
STUDENT SET-UP 🔺🔺🔺
CONCEPT LEVEL 🔺🔺🔺🔺
CLEAN UP 🔺

MATERIALS

The materials listed on the student page are enough for a group of 1–2 students.

Safety Caution

Remind students to review all safety cautions and icons before beginning this lab activity. Remind students to be careful about traffic hazards around your school's flagpole.

Preparation Notes

Students may need an introduction to angles and the use of protractors. Be sure they understand how to use protractors *before* you perform this activity. Students may feel uneasy with the mathematics. Explain that astronomers use trigonometry, which is the measurement of triangles, to calculate distances to nearby stars. By using the TAN function on a calculator, the length of the unknown leg of the triangle formed by the sun, Earth, and a star can be found. If students are unfamiliar with the TAN function, they may prefer to use the table at right.

I See the Light!

How do you find the distance to an object you can't reach? You can do it by measuring something you can reach, finding a few angles, and using mathematics. In this activity, you'll practice measuring the distances of objects here on Earth. When you get used to it, you can take your skills to the stars!

Procedure

1. Draw a line 4 cm away from the edge of one side of the piece of poster board. Fold the poster board along this line.

2. Tape the protractor to the poster board with its flat edge against the fold, as shown in the photo below.

3. Use a sharp pencil to carefully punch a hole through the poster board along its folded edge at the center of the protractor.

4. Thread the string through the hole, and tape one end to the underside of the poster board. The other end should be long enough to hang off the far end of the poster board.

5. Carefully punch a second hole in the smaller area of the poster board halfway between its short sides. The hole should be directly above the first hole and should be large enough for the pencil to fit through. This is the viewing hole of your new parallax device. This device will allow you to measure the distance of faraway objects.

6. Find a location outside that is at least 50 steps away from a tall, narrow object, such as the school's flagpole or a tall tree. (This object will represent background stars.) Set the meterstick on the ground with one of its long edges facing the flagpole.

7. Ask your partner, who represents a nearby star, to take 10 steps toward the flagpole, starting at the left end of the meterstick. You will be the observer. When you stand at the left end of the meterstick, which represents the location of the sun, your partner's nose should be lined up with the flag pole.

SKILL BUILDER

Materials

- 16 × 16 cm piece of poster board
- metric ruler
- protractor
- scissors
- sharp pencil
- 30 cm string
- transparent tape
- meterstick
- metric measuring tape
- scientific calculator

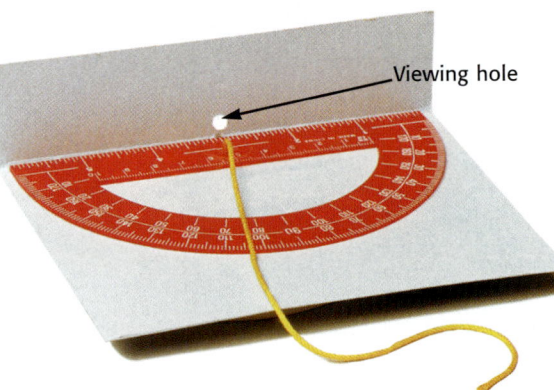

Viewing hole

8. Move to the other end of the meterstick, which represents the location of Earth. Does your partner appear to the left or right of the flagpole? Record your observations in your ScienceLog.

9. Hold the string so that it runs straight from the viewing hole to the 90° mark on the protractor. Using one eye, look through the viewing hole along the string and point the device at your partner's nose.

Angle	Tangent	Angle	Tangent
1°	0.0175	6°	0.1051
2°	0.0349	7°	0.1228
3°	0.0524	8°	0.1405
4°	0.0699	9°	0.1584
5°	0.0875	10°	0.1763

Susan Gorman
North Ridge Middle School
North Richmond Hills, Texas

10. Holding the device still, slowly move your head until you can see the flagpole through the viewing hole. Move the string so that it lines up between your eye and the flagpole. Make sure the string is taut, and hold it tightly against the protractor.

11. Read and record the angle made by the string and the string's original position at 90° (count the number of degrees between 90° and the string's new position).

12. Use the measuring tape to find and record the distance from the left end of the meterstick to your partner's nose.

13. Now find a place outside that is at least 100 steps away from the flagpole. Set the meterstick on the ground as before, and repeat steps 7–12.

Analysis

14. The angle you recorded in step 11 is called the *parallax angle*. The distance from one end of the meterstick to the other is called the *baseline*. With this angle and the length of your baseline, you can calculate the distance to your partner.

15. To calculate the distance (d) to your partner, use the following equation:

$$d = b/\tan A$$

In this equation, A is the parallax angle and b is the length of the baseline (1 m). (Tan A means the tangent of angle A, which you will learn more about in high school math classes.)

16. To find d, enter 1 (the length of your baseline in meters) into the calculator, press the "divide" key, enter the value of A (the parallax angle you recorded), then press the "tan" key. Finally, press the "equals" key.

17. Record this result in your ScienceLog. It is the distance in meters between the left end of the meterstick and your partner. You may want to use a table like the one shown at right.

18. How close is this calculated distance to the distance you measured in step 12?

19. Repeat steps 15–17 using the angle you found when the flagpole was 100 steps away.

Conclusions

20. At which position, 50 steps or 100 steps from the flagpole, did your calculated distance better match the actual distance as measured in step 12?

21. What do you think would happen if you were even farther from the flagpole?

22. When astronomers use parallax, their "flagpole" is the very distant stars. How might this affect the accuracy of their parallax readings?

Distance by Parallax Versus Measuring Tape

	At 50 steps	At 100 steps
Parallax angle		
Distance (calculated)	DO NOT WRITE IN BOOK	
Distance (measured)		

Lab Notes

If the school's flagpole is not in a convenient spot, a tall tree or lamp post will work. If students have difficulty keeping the device still while moving their head, you might have them try steadying the device on a tripod or on the end of a meterstick.

Some students may have difficulty understanding the relationship between measuring stars with parallax and the parallax effects on measurements (e.g., reading a dial off to the side can give a different value). The viewing hole in the parallax device used in this activity reduces such errors. Thus, the parallax effect in this activity measures only faraway distances.

Students should realize that as the distance to a reference point (such as a flagpole or background stars) increases, the angle measured by the parallax device becomes closer to the actual parallax angle. Therefore, students should find that their calculation of the distance to their partner should be more accurate when they move 100 steps from the tree.

They should also realize that astronomers use the "fixed stars," which are essentially at optical infinity, as a reference.

Answers

18. Answers will vary but should approximate the actual distance given in meters.
19. Answers will vary due to differences in technique.
20. At 100 steps, the distance calculated should be closer to the distance measured.
21. Accuracy should increase.
22. Their calculations should be very close to the actual distance (if it could be measured).

Datasheets for LabBook
Datasheet 47

Water Rockets Save the Day!
Teacher's Notes

Time Required

Two 45-minute class periods

Lab Ratings

| EASY | | | HARD |

TEACHER PREP 🧪🧪🧪
STUDENT SET-UP 🧪🧪🧪
CONCEPT LEVEL 🧪🧪
CLEAN UP 🧪🧪

The materials listed in this lab are enough for one student. Students can also work in groups of 3–4.

Safety Caution

Remind students to review all safety cautions and icons before beginning this lab activity. Make sure that students are several meters away from the launch site when the rockets are being launched.

Alyson Mike
East Valley Middle School
East Helena, Montana

Using Scientific Methods

Water Rockets Save the Day!

Imagine that for the big Fourth of July celebration you and your friends had planned a full day of swimming, volleyball, and fireworks at the lake. You've just learned however, that the city passed a law that bans all fireworks within city limits. But you are not one to give up so easily on having fun. Last year at summer camp you learned how to build water rockets. And you kept the launcher in your garage all this time! With a little bit of creativity, you and your friends are going to celebrate with a splash!

DESIGN YOUR OWN

Materials

- 2 L soda bottle with cap
- foam board
- modeling clay
- duct tape
- scissors
- water
- bucket, 5-gal
- rocket launcher
- watch or clock that indicates seconds

Ask a Question

1. How can I use water and a soda bottle to build a rocket?

Conduct an Experiment

2. Decide how you want your rocket to look. Draw a sketch in your ScienceLog.

3. Using only the materials listed, decide how to build your rocket. Describe your design in your ScienceLog. Keep in mind that you will need to leave the opening of your bottle clear. It will be placed over a rubber stopper on the rocket launcher.

4. Fins are often used to stabilize rockets. Do you want fins on your water rocket? Decide on the best shape for the fins, and then decide how many fins your rocket needs. Use the foam board to construct the fins.

Preparation Notes

Each student or group of students will need a 2 L soda bottle to construct their rocket. You can ask students a week or two ahead of time to save any 2 L soda bottles they have at home.

Water rockets require a launcher that you will need to make or purchase in advance. Launchers are the key to a successful and safe liftoff. They can be purchased at most hobby shops or from Science Kit®. You can expect to spend at least $20 for a launcher or launcher kit at a hobby shop. You need only one launcher for your class. When buying a launcher, make sure the launcher is compatible with your rocket bottle size.

If you wish to construct the launcher yourself, research one of the many water rocket Web sites on the Internet. This is a popular hobby, and good information on the subject is not hard to find.

5. Your rocket must be heavy enough to fly along a controlled pathway. Consider using clay in the body of your rocket to provide some additional weight and stability.

6. Pour water into your rocket until it is one-third to one-half full.

7. Your teacher will provide the launcher and assist you during blastoff. Attach your rocket to the launcher by placing its opening on the rubber stopper.

8. When the rocket is in place, clear the immediate area and begin pumping air into your rocket. Watch the pump gauge, and take note of how much pressure is needed for liftoff.
   Caution: Be sure to step back from the launch site. You should be several meters away from the bottle when you launch it.

9. Use the watch to time your rocket's flight. (How long was your rocket in the air?)

10. Make small changes in your rocket design that you think will improve the rocket's performance. Consider using different amounts of water and clay or experimenting with different fins. You may also want to compare your design with those of your classmates.

Analyze the Results

11. How did your rocket perform? If you used fins, do you think they helped your flight? Explain.

12. What do you think propelled your rocket? Use Newton's third law of motion to justify your answer.

13. How did the amount of water in your rocket affect the launch?

Draw Conclusions

14. What modifications made your rocket fly for the longest time? How did the design help the rockets fly so far?

15. Which group's rockets were the most stable? How did the design help the rockets fly straight?

16. How can you improve your design to make your rocket perform even better?

Newton's third law of motion: For every action there is an equal and opposite reaction.

Answers

11. Answers will vary. Fins might help stabilize the rocket when it is in flight.

12. Answers will vary. Students should note that the water in the bottle was under pressure. When the rocket was released, the water escaped out of the opening. The bottle reacted by moving in the opposite direction—upward.

13. Answers will vary. Water is the propellant for the rocket. Pressurized air provides the force to launch the rocket. The amount of water in a rocket determines how much space air can occupy. The ideal rocket should expel all of the water at the maximum pressure.

14. Answers will vary. Modifying the fins, adjusting the water-to-air ratio, increasing the air pressure inside the rocket, and changing the amount of modeling clay used should affect the duration of the rocket's flight.

15. Answers will vary.

16. Answers will vary.

Datasheets for LabBook
Datasheet 48

Reach for the Stars
Teacher's Notes

Time Required

Two 45-minute class periods

Lab Ratings

Teacher Prep 🔺
Student Set-Up 🔺🔺🔺
Concept Level 🔺🔺
Clean Up 🔺🔺

MATERIALS

The materials listed in this lab are enough for 3–4 students.

Safety Caution

Remind students to review all safety cautions and icons before beginning this lab activity.

Alyson Mike
East Valley Middle School
East Helena, Montana

Using Scientific Methods

Reach for the Stars

MAKING MODELS

Have you ever thought about living and working in space? Well, in order for you to do so, you would have to learn to cope with the new environment and surroundings. At the same time astronauts are adjusting to the topsy-turvy conditions of space travel, they are also dealing with special tools used to repair and build space stations. In this activity, you will get the chance to model one tool that might help astronauts work in space.

Materials

- cardboard box
- scissors
- metric ruler
- hole punch
- 2 paper brads
- metal wire
- 2 jumbo paper clips
- plastic-foam ball

Ask a Question

1. How can I build a piece of equipment that models how astronauts work in space?

Conduct an Experiment

2. Cut three strips from the cardboard box. Each strip should be about 5 cm wide. The strips should be at least 20 cm long but not longer than 40 cm.

3. Punch holes near the center of each end of the three cardboard strips. The holes should be about 3 cm from the end of each strip.

4. Lay the strips end to end along your table. Slide the second strip toward the first strip so that a hole in the first strip lines up with a hole in the second strip. Slip a paper brad through the holes and bend its ends out to attach the cardboard strips.

5. Use another brad to attach the third cardboard strip to the free end of the second strip. Now you have your mechanical arm. The paper brads create joints where the cardboard strips meet.

6. Straighten the wire, and slide it through the hole in one end of your mechanical arm. Bend about 3 cm of the wire in a 90° angle so that it will not slide back out of the hole.

7. Now try to move the arm by holding the free ends of the cardboard and wire. The arm should bend and straighten at the joints. If it is difficult to move your mechanical arm, adjust the design. Consider loosening the brads, for example.

8. Now your mechanical arm needs a hand. Otherwise, it won't be able to pick things up! Straighten one paper clip, and slide it through the hole where you attached the wire in step 6. Bend one end of the paper clip to form a loop around the cardboard and the other end to form a hook. You will use this hook to pick things up.

9. Bend a second paper clip into a U-shape. Stick the straight end of this paper clip into the foam ball. Leave the ball on your desk.

10. Move your mechanical arm so that you can lift the foam ball. The paper-clip hook on the mechanical arm will have to catch the paper clip on the ball.

Analyze the Results

11. Did you have any trouble moving the mechanical arm in step 7? What adjustments did you make?

12. Did you have trouble picking up the foam ball? What might have made this easier?

Draw Conclusions

13. What improvements could you make to your mechanical arm that might make it easier to use?

14. How would a tool like this one help astronauts work in space?

Going Further

Adjust the design for your mechanical arm. Can you find a way to lift objects other than the foam ball? For example, can you lift heavier objects or objects that do not have a loop attached? How?

Research the tools that astronauts use on space stations and on the space shuttle. How do their tools help them work in the special conditions of space?

Answers

11. Answers will vary. Students may have loosened the paper brads.

12. Answers will vary. Altering the paper-clip loop on the ball or changing the shape of the hook on the arm could make the task easier.

13. Answers will vary. Students may suggest using different materials, changing the length of different arm segments, or mounting the arm on a secure base.

14. Answers will vary. This device could help astronauts manipulate objects outside a spacecraft without having to go on a spacewalk. Also, if the arm were mechanized, it could allow astronauts to move massive objects with precision.

Going Further

Answers will vary.

Datasheets for LabBook
Datasheet 49

Self-Check Answers

Chapter 2—Maps as Models of the Earth

Page 36: The Earth rotates around the geographic poles.

Page 47: If the lines are close together, then the mapped area is steep. If the lines are far apart, the mapped area has a gradual slope or is flat.

Chapter 3—Minerals of the Earth's Crust

Page 69: These minerals form wherever salt water has evaporated.

Chapter 4—Rocks: Mineral Mixtures

Page 88: From fastest-cooled to slowest-cooled, the rocks in Figure 10 are: basalt, rhyolite, gabbro, and granite.

Page 96: A rock can come into contact with magma and also be subjected to pressure underground.

Chapter 5—Energy Resources

Page 123: Both devices harness energy from falling water.

Chapter 6—The Rock and Fossil Record

Page 148: Coprolites and tracks are trace fossils because they are evidence of animal activity rather than fossilized organisms.

Chapter 7—Plate Tectonics

Page 183: When folding occurs, sedimentary rock strata bend but do not break. When faulting occurs, sedimentary rock strata break along a fault, and the fault blocks on either side move relative to each other.

Chapter 8—Earthquakes

Page 199: Convergent motion creates reverse faults, while divergent motion creates normal faults. Convergent motion produces deep, strong earthquakes, while divergent motion produces shallow, weak earthquakes.

Chapter 9—Volcanoes

Page 231: Solid rock may become magma when pressure is released, when the temperature rises above its melting point, or when its composition changes.

Chapter 10—Weathering and Soil Formation

Page 248: Water expands as it freezes. This expansion exerts a force great enough to crack rock.

Chapter 11—The Flow of Fresh Water

Page 274: If a river slowed down, the suspended load would be deposited.

Page 278: Answers will vary. A river might slow where there is a bend, where the gradient decreases, or where the river empties into a large body of water.

Page 282: The impermeable rock layer in the aquifer traps the water in the permeable layer below. This creates the pressure needed to form an artesian spring.

Chapter 12—Agents of Erosion and Deposition

Page 299: A large wave has more erosive energy than a small wave because a large wave releases more energy when it breaks.

Page 305: Deflation hollows form in areas where there is little vegetation because there are no plant roots to anchor the sediment in place.

Page 311: When a moving glacier picks up speed or flows over a high point, a crevasse may form. This occurs because the ice cannot stretch quickly while it is moving, and it cracks.

Chapter 13—Exploring the Oceans

Page 331: If North America and South America continue to drift westward and Asia continues to drift eastward, the continents will eventually collide on the other side of the Earth.

Page 339: Rift valleys form where tectonic plates pull apart, and ocean trenches form where one oceanic plate is forced underneath a continental plate or another oceanic plate.

Chapter 14—The Movement of Ocean Water

Page 365: Because he was traveling from Peru to a Polynesian island to the west, Heyerdahl would have noticed the wind blowing from the east.

Chapter 15—The Atmosphere

Page 394: As you climb a mountain, the air becomes less dense because there are fewer air molecules. So even though cold air is generally more dense than warm air, it is less dense at higher elevations.

Chapter 16—Understanding Weather

Page 424: Evaporation occurs when liquid water changes into water vapor and returns to the air. Humidity is the amount of water vapor in the air.

Chapter 17—Climate

Page 454: Australia has summer during our winter months, December–March.

Page 460: Because of its dryness, desert soil is poor in organic matter, which fertilizes the soil. Without this natural fertilizer, crops would not be able to grow.

Page 468: The Earth's elliptical orbit causes seasonal differences. When the Earth's orbit is more elliptical, summers are hotter because the Earth is closer to the sun and receives more solar radiation. Winters are cooler because the Earth is farther from the sun and receives less solar radiation.

Chapter 18—Observing the Sky

Page 487: Ptolemy and Tycho Brahe thought that the universe was Earth-centered. Copernicus and Galileo thought the universe was sun-centered.

Page 490: No, the object is within the boundaries of the constellation.

Chapter 19—Formation of the Solar System

Page 511: The balance between pressure and gravity keeps a nebula from collapsing.

Page 513: The giant gas planets were massive enough for their gravity to attract hydrogen and helium.

Page 524: The Earth has enough mass that gravitational pressure crushed and melted rocks during its formation. The force of gravity pulled this material toward the center, forming a sphere. Asteroids are not massive enough for their interiors to be crushed or melted.

Chapter 20—A Family of Planets

Page 555: The surface of Titan is much colder than the surface of the Earth.

Chapter 21—The Universe Beyond

Page 574: The two stars would have the same apparent magnitude.

Chapter 22—Exploring Space

Page 603: It requires much less fuel to reach LEO.

Self-Check Answers

CONTENTS

Concept Mapping 730
SI Measurement 731
Temperature Scales 732
Measuring Skills 733
Scientific Method 734
Making Charts and Graphs 737
Math Refresher 740
Periodic Table of the Elements 744
Physical Science Refresher 746
Physical Laws and Equations 748
Properties of Common Minerals 750
Sky Maps 752

Concept Mapping: A Way to Bring Ideas Together

What Is a Concept Map?

Have you ever tried to tell someone about a book or a chapter you've just read and found that you can remember only a few isolated words and ideas? Or maybe you've memorized facts for a test and then weeks later discovered you're not even sure what topics those facts covered.

In both cases, you may have understood the ideas or concepts by themselves but not in relation to one another. If you could somehow link the ideas together, you would probably understand them better and remember them longer. This is something a concept map can help you do. A concept map is a way to see how ideas or concepts fit together. It can help you see the "big picture."

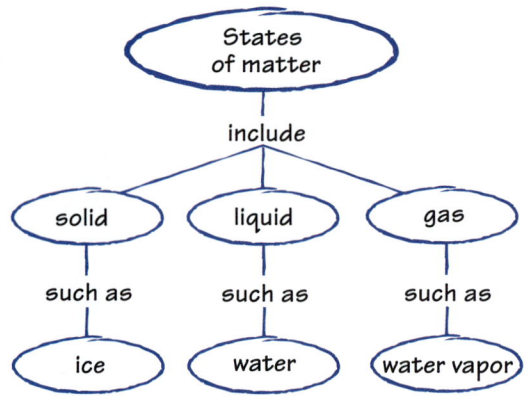

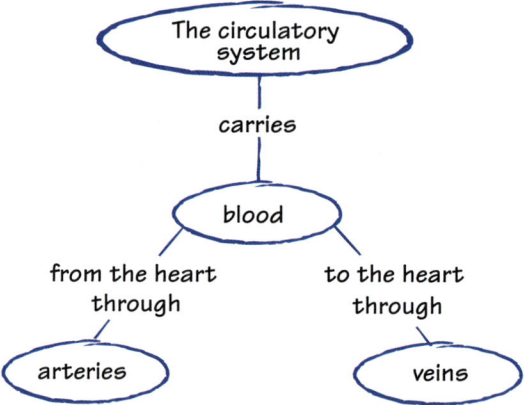

How to Make a Concept Map

❶ Make a list of the main ideas or concepts.

It might help to write each concept on its own slip of paper. This will make it easier to rearrange the concepts as many times as necessary to make sense of how the concepts are connected. After you've made a few concept maps this way, you can go directly from writing your list to actually making the map.

❷ Arrange the concepts in order from the most general to the most specific.

Put the most general concept at the top and circle it. Ask yourself, "How does this concept relate to the remaining concepts?" As you see the relationships, arrange the concepts in order from general to specific.

❸ Connect the related concepts with lines.

❹ On each line, write an action word or short phrase that shows how the concepts are related.

Look at the concept maps on this page, and then see if you can make one for the following terms:

plants, water, photosynthesis, carbon dioxide, sun's energy

One possible answer is provided at right, but don't look at it until you try the concept map yourself.

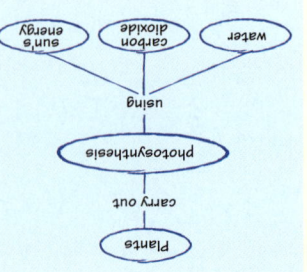

730   Appendix

SI Measurement

The International System of Units, or SI, is the standard system of measurement used by many scientists. Using the same standards of measurement makes it easier for scientists to communicate with one another.

SI works by combining prefixes and base units. Each base unit can be used with different prefixes to define smaller and larger quantities. The table below lists common SI prefixes.

\	SI Prefixes		
Prefix	**Abbreviation**	**Factor**	**Example**
kilo-	k	1,000	kilogram, 1 kg = 1,000 g
hecto-	h	100	hectoliter, 1 hL = 100 L
deka-	da	10	dekameter, 1 dam = 10 m
		1	meter, liter
deci-	d	0.1	decigram, 1 dg = 0.1 g
centi-	c	0.01	centimeter, 1 cm = 0.01 m
milli-	m	0.001	milliliter, 1 mL = 0.001 L
micro-	μ	0.000 001	micrometer, 1 μm = 0.000 001 m

SI Conversion Table		
SI units	**From SI to English**	**From English to SI**
Length		
kilometer (km) = 1,000 m	1 km = 0.621 mi	1 mi = 1.609 km
meter (m) = 100 cm	1 m = 3.281 ft	1 ft = 0.305 m
centimeter (cm) = 0.01 m	1 cm = 0.394 in.	1 in. = 2.540 cm
millimeter (mm) = 0.001 m	1 mm = 0.039 in.	
micrometer (μm) = 0.000 001 m		
nanometer (nm) = 0.000 000 001 m		
Area		
square kilometer (km^2) = 100 hectares	1 km^2 = 0.386 mi^2	1 mi^2 = 2.590 km^2
hectare (ha) = 10,000 m^2	1 ha = 2.471 acres	1 acre = 0.405 ha
square meter (m^2) = 10,000 cm^2	1 m^2 = 10.765 ft^2	1 ft^2 = 0.093 m^2
square centimeter (cm^2) = 100 mm^2	1 cm^2 = 0.155 in.^{2}	1 in.^{2} = 6.452 cm^2
Volume		
liter (L) = 1,000 mL = 1 dm^3	1 L = 1.057 fl qt	1 fl qt = 0.946 L
milliliter (mL) = 0.001 L = 1 cm^3	1 mL = 0.034 fl oz	1 fl oz = 29.575 mL
microliter (μL) = 0.000 001 L		
Mass		
kilogram (kg) = 1,000 g	1 kg = 2.205 lb	1 lb = 0.454 kg
gram (g) = 1,000 mg	1 g = 0.035 oz	1 oz = 28.349 g
milligram (mg) = 0.001 g		
microgram (μg) = 0.000 001 g		

Temperature Scales

Temperature can be expressed using three different scales: Fahrenheit, Celsius, and Kelvin. The SI unit for temperature is the kelvin (K). Although 0 K is much colder than 0°C, a change of 1 K is equal to a change of 1°C.

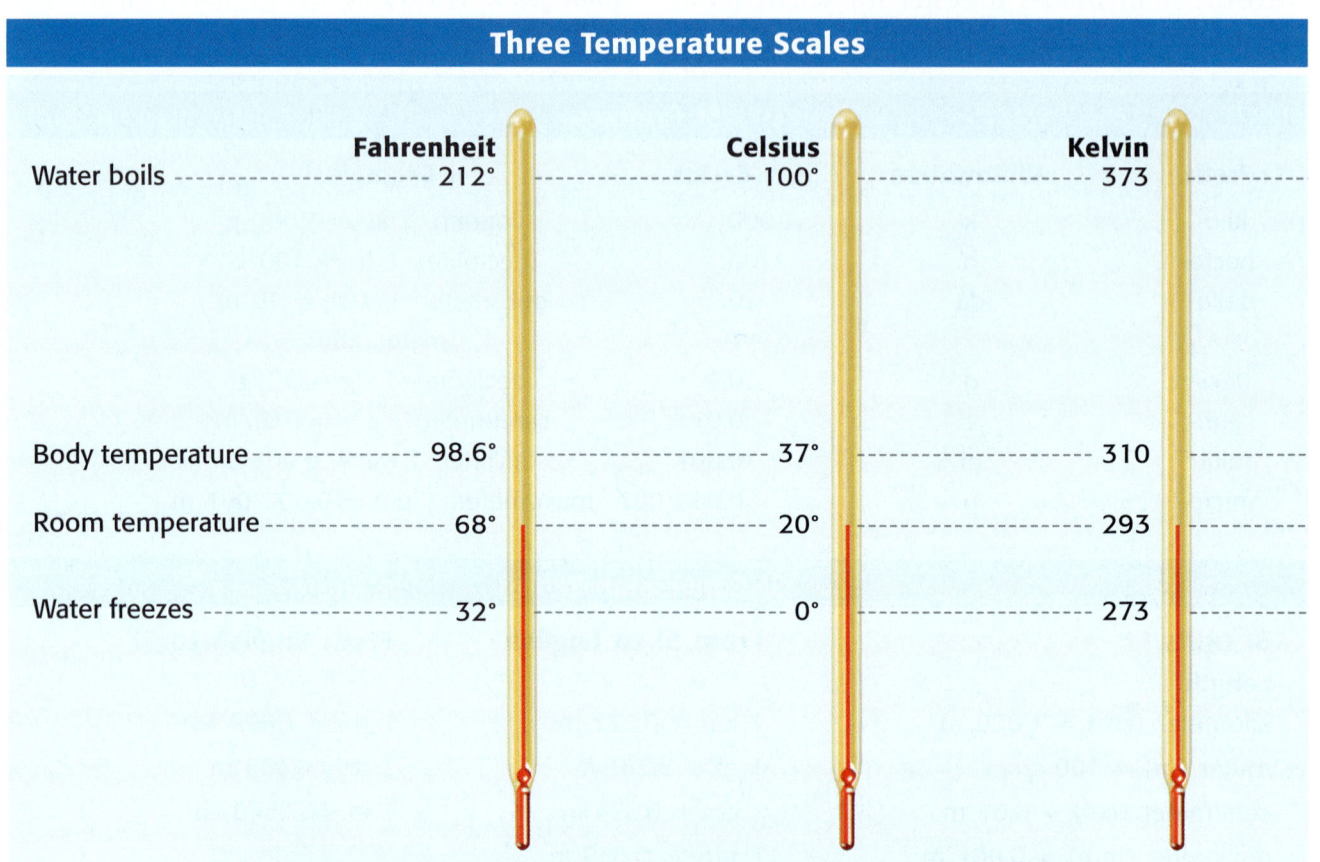

Three Temperature Scales

	Fahrenheit	Celsius	Kelvin
Water boils	212°	100°	373
Body temperature	98.6°	37°	310
Room temperature	68°	20°	293
Water freezes	32°	0°	273

Temperature Conversions Table

To convert	Use this equation:	Example
Celsius to Fahrenheit °C → °F	$°F = \left(\frac{9}{5} \times °C\right) + 32$	Convert 45°C to °F. $°F = \left(\frac{9}{5} \times 45°C\right) + 32 = 113°F$
Fahrenheit to Celsius °F → °C	$°C = \frac{5}{9} \times (°F - 32)$	Convert 68°F to °C. $°C = \frac{5}{9} \times (68°F - 32) = 20°C$
Celsius to Kelvin °C → K	$K = °C + 273$	Convert 45°C to K. $K = 45°C + 273 = 318 K$
Kelvin to Celsius K → °C	$°C = K - 273$	Convert 32 K to °C. $°C = 32 K - 273 = -241°C$

Measuring Skills

Using a Graduated Cylinder

When using a graduated cylinder to measure volume, keep the following procedures in mind:

1. Make sure the cylinder is on a flat, level surface.
2. Move your head so that your eye is level with the surface of the liquid.
3. Read the mark closest to the liquid level. On glass graduated cylinders, read the mark closest to the center of the curve in the liquid's surface.

Using a Meterstick or Metric Ruler

When using a meterstick or metric ruler to measure length, keep the following procedures in mind:

1. Place the ruler firmly against the object you are measuring.
2. Align one edge of the object exactly with the zero end of the ruler.
3. Look at the other edge of the object to see which of the marks on the ruler is closest to that edge. **Note:** Each small slash between the centimeters represents a millimeter, which is one-tenth of a centimeter.

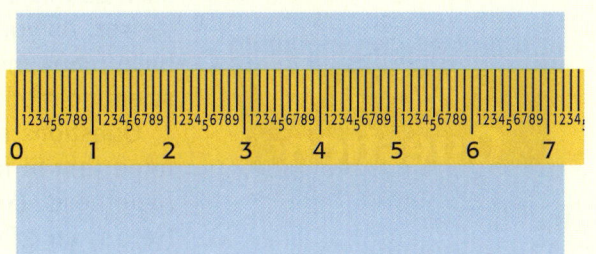

Using a Triple-Beam Balance

When using a triple-beam balance to measure mass, keep the following procedures in mind:

1. Make sure the balance is on a level surface.
2. Place all of the countermasses at zero. Adjust the balancing knob until the pointer rests at zero.
3. Place the object you wish to measure on the pan. **Caution:** Do not place hot objects or chemicals directly on the balance pan.
4. Move the largest countermass along the beam to the right until it is at the last notch that does not tip the balance. Follow the same procedure with the next-largest countermass. Then move the smallest countermass until the pointer rests at zero.
5. Add the readings from the three beams together to determine the mass of the object.
6. When determining the mass of crystals or powders, use a piece of filter paper. First find the mass of the paper. Then add the crystals or powder to the paper and remeasure. The actual mass of the crystals or powder is the total mass minus the mass of the paper. When finding the mass of liquids, first find the mass of the empty container. Then find the mass of the liquid and container together. The mass of the liquid is the total mass minus the mass of the container.

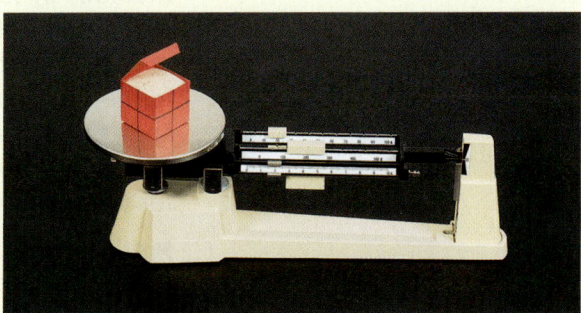

Appendix **733**

Scientific Method

The series of steps that scientists use to answer questions and solve problems is often called the **scientific method.** The scientific method is not a rigid procedure. Scientists may use all of the steps or just some of the steps of the scientific method. They may even repeat some of the steps. The goal of the scientific method is to come up with reliable answers and solutions.

Six Steps of the Scientific Method

1 Ask a Question Good questions come from careful **observations.** You make observations by using your senses to gather information. Sometimes you may use instruments, such as microscopes and telescopes, to extend the range of your senses. As you observe the natural world, you will discover that you have many more questions than answers. These questions drive the scientific method.

Questions beginning with *what, why, how,* and *when* are very important in focusing an investigation, and they often lead to a hypothesis. (You will learn what a hypothesis is in the next step.) Here is an example of a question that could lead to further investigation.

Question: How does acid rain affect plant growth?

2 Form a Hypothesis After you come up with a question, you need to turn the question into a **hypothesis.** A hypothesis is a clear statement of what you expect the answer to your question to be. Your hypothesis will represent your best "educated guess" based on your observations and what you already know. A good hypothesis is testable. If observations and information cannot be gathered or if an experiment cannot be designed to test your hypothesis, it is untestable, and the investigation can go no further.

Here is a hypothesis that could be formed from the question, "How does acid rain affect plant growth?"

Hypothesis: Acid rain causes plants to grow more slowly.

Notice that the hypothesis provides some specifics that lead to methods of testing. The hypothesis can also lead to predictions. A **prediction** is what you think will be the outcome of your experiment or data collection. Predictions are usually stated in an "if . . . then" format. For example, **if** meat is kept at room temperature, **then** it will spoil faster than meat kept in the refrigerator. More than one prediction can be made for a single hypothesis. Here is a sample prediction for the hypothesis that acid rain causes plants to grow more slowly.

Prediction: If a plant is watered with only acid rain (which has a pH of 4), then the plant will grow at half its normal rate.

734 Appendix

3 **Test the Hypothesis** After you have formed a hypothesis and made a prediction, you should test your hypothesis. There are different ways to do this. Perhaps the most familiar way is to conduct a **controlled experiment.** A controlled experiment tests only one factor at a time. A controlled experiment has a **control group** and one or more **experimental groups.** All the factors for the control and experimental groups are the same except for one factor, which is called the **variable.** By changing only one factor, you can see the results of just that one change.

Sometimes, the nature of an investigation makes a controlled experiment impossible. For example, dinosaurs have been extinct for millions of years, and the Earth's core is surrounded by thousands of meters of rock. It would be difficult, if not impossible, to conduct controlled experiments on such things. Under such circumstances, a hypothesis may be tested by making detailed observations. Taking measurements is one way of making observations.

4 **Analyze the Results** After you have completed your experiments, made your observations, and collected your data, you must analyze all the information you have gathered. Tables and graphs are often used in this step to organize the data.

5 **Draw Conclusions** Based on the analysis of your data, you should conclude whether or not your results support your hypothesis. If your hypothesis is supported, you (or others) might want to repeat the observations or experiments to verify your results. If your hypothesis is not supported by the data, you may have to check your procedure for errors. You may even have to reject your hypothesis and make a new one. If you cannot draw a conclusion from your results, you may have to try the investigation again or carry out further observations or experiments.

6 **Communicate Results** After any scientific investigation, you should report your results. By doing a written or oral report, you let others know what you have learned. They may want to repeat your investigation to see if they get the same results. Your report may even lead to another question, which in turn may lead to another investigation.

Scientific Method in Action

The scientific method is not a "straight line" of steps. It contains loops in which several steps may be repeated over and over again, while others may not be necessary. For example, sometimes scientists will find that testing one hypothesis raises new questions and new hypotheses to be tested. And sometimes, testing the hypothesis leads directly to a conclusion. Furthermore, the steps in the scientific method are not always used in the same order. Follow the steps in the diagram below, and see how many different directions the scientific method can take you.

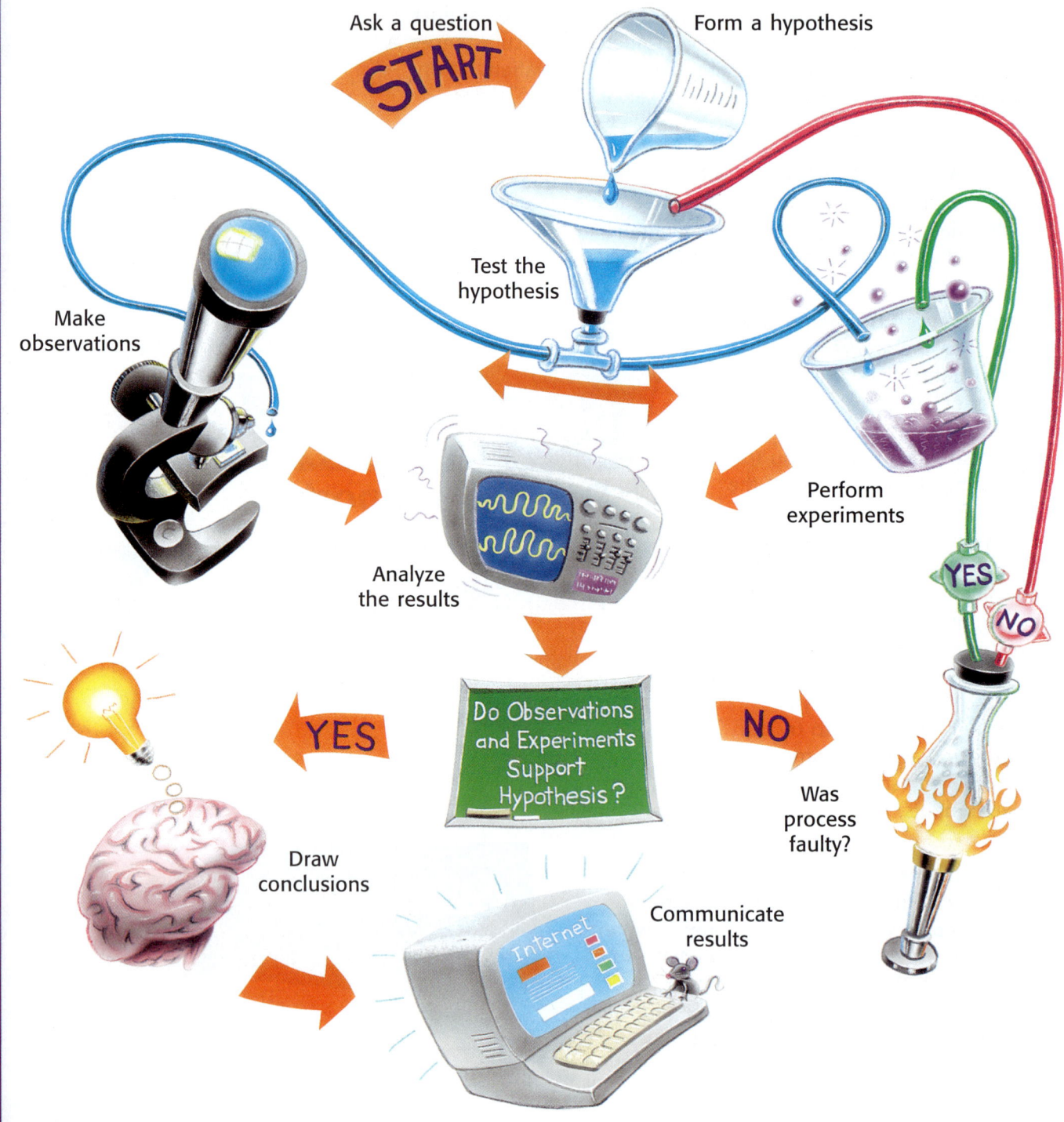

Making Charts and Graphs

Circle Graphs

A circle graph, or pie chart, shows how each group of data relates to all of the data. Each part of the circle represents a category of the data. The entire circle represents all of the data. For example, a biologist studying a hardwood forest in Wisconsin found that there were five different types of trees. The data table at right summarizes the biologist's findings.

Wisconsin Hardwood Trees	
Type of tree	Number found
Oak	600
Maple	750
Beech	300
Birch	1,200
Hickory	150
Total	3,000

How to Make a Circle Graph

① In order to make a circle graph of this data, first find the percentage of each type of tree. To do this, divide the number of individual trees by the total number of trees and multiply by 100.

$$\frac{600 \text{ oak}}{3{,}000 \text{ trees}} \times 100 = 20\%$$

$$\frac{750 \text{ maple}}{3{,}000 \text{ trees}} \times 100 = 25\%$$

$$\frac{300 \text{ beech}}{3{,}000 \text{ trees}} \times 100 = 10\%$$

$$\frac{1{,}200 \text{ birch}}{3{,}000 \text{ trees}} \times 100 = 40\%$$

$$\frac{150 \text{ hickory}}{3{,}000 \text{ trees}} \times 100 = 5\%$$

② Now determine the size of the pie shapes that make up the chart. Do this by multiplying each percentage by 360°. Remember that a circle contains 360°.

20% × 360° = 72°   25% × 360° = 90°
10% × 360° = 36°   40% × 360° = 144°
5% × 360° = 18°

③ Then check that the sum of the percentages is 100 and the sum of the degrees is 360.

20% + 25% + 10% + 40% + 5% = 100%
72° + 90° + 36° + 144° + 18° = 360°

④ Use a compass to draw a circle and mark its center.

⑤ Then use a protractor to draw angles of 72°, 90°, 36°, 144°, and 18° in the circle.

⑥ Finally, label each part of the graph, and choose an appropriate title.

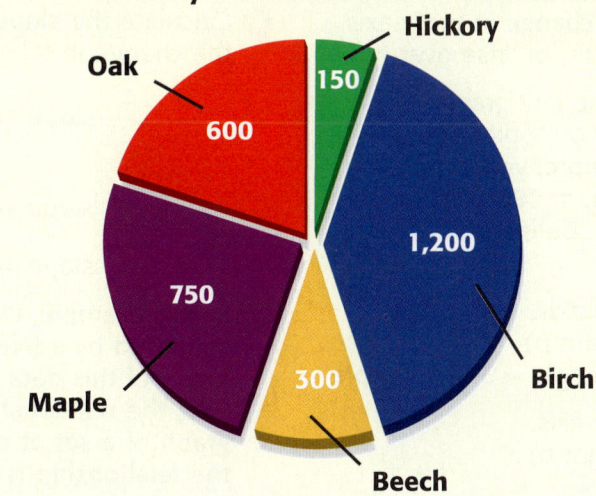

A Community of Wisconsin Hardwood Trees

Appendix **737**

Line Graphs

Line graphs are most often used to demonstrate continuous change. For example, Mr. Smith's science class analyzed the population records for their hometown, Appleton, between 1900 and 2000. Examine the data at left.

Because the year and the population change, they are the *variables*. The population is determined by, or dependent on, the year. Therefore, the population is called the **dependent variable**, and the year is called the **independent variable**. Each set of data is called a **data pair**. To prepare a line graph, data pairs must first be organized in a table like the one at left.

Population of Appleton, 1900–2000

Year	Population
1900	1,800
1920	2,500
1940	3,200
1960	3,900
1980	4,600
2000	5,300

How to Make a Line Graph

1. Place the independent variable along the horizontal (x) axis. Place the dependent variable along the vertical (y) axis.
2. Label the x-axis "Year" and the y-axis "Population." Look at your largest and smallest values for the population. Determine a scale for the y-axis that will provide enough space to show these values. You must use the same scale for the entire length of the axis. Find an appropriate scale for the x-axis too.
3. Choose reasonable starting points for each axis.
4. Plot the data pairs as accurately as possible.
5. Choose a title that accurately represents the data.

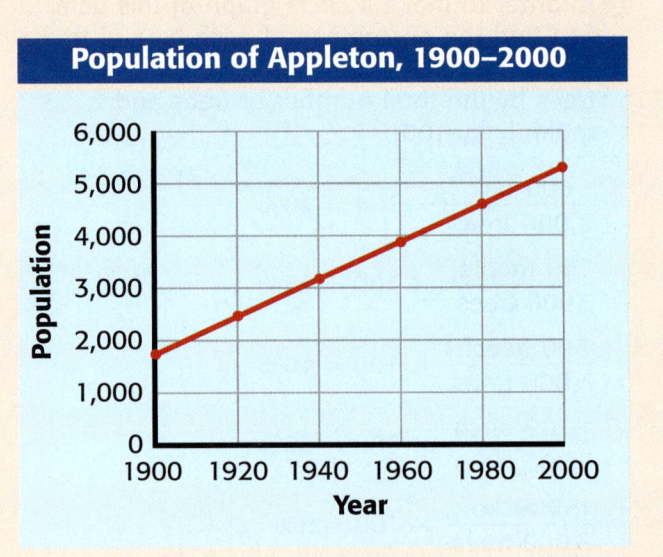

How to Determine Slope

Slope is the ratio of the change in the y-axis to the change in the x-axis, or "rise over run."

1. Choose two points on the line graph. For example, the population of Appleton in 2000 was 5,300 people. Therefore, you can define point *a* as (2000, 5,300). In 1900, the population was 1,800 people. Define point *b* as (1900, 1,800).
2. Find the change in the y-axis.
   (y at point *a*) − (y at point *b*)
   5,300 people − 1,800 people = 3,500 people
3. Find the change in the x-axis.
   (x at point *a*) − (x at point *b*)
   2000 − 1900 = 100 years
4. Calculate the slope of the graph by dividing the change in y by the change in x.

$$\text{slope} = \frac{\text{change in } y}{\text{change in } x}$$

$$\text{slope} = \frac{3{,}500 \text{ people}}{100 \text{ years}}$$

$$\text{slope} = 35 \text{ people per year}$$

In this example, the population in Appleton increased by a fixed amount each year. The graph of this data is a straight line. Therefore, the relationship is **linear**. When the graph of a set of data is not a straight line, the relationship is **nonlinear**.

Using Algebra to Determine Slope

The equation in step 4 may also be arranged to be:

$y = kx$

where y represents the change in the y-axis, k represents the slope, and x represents the change in the x-axis.

$$\text{slope} = \frac{\text{change in } y}{\text{change in } x}$$

$$k = \frac{y}{x}$$

$$k \times x = \frac{y \times x}{x}$$

$$kx = y$$

Bar Graphs

Bar graphs are used to demonstrate change that is not continuous. These graphs can be used to indicate trends when the data are taken over a long period of time. A meteorologist gathered the precipitation records at right for Hartford, Connecticut, for April 1–15, 1996, and used a bar graph to represent the data.

Precipitation in Hartford, Connecticut April 1–15, 1996

Date	Precipitation (cm)	Date	Precipitation (cm)
April 1	0.5	April 9	0.25
April 2	1.25	April 10	0.0
April 3	0.0	April 11	1.0
April 4	0.0	April 12	0.0
April 5	0.0	April 13	0.25
April 6	0.0	April 14	0.0
April 7	0.0	April 15	6.50
April 8	1.75		

How to Make a Bar Graph

1. Use an appropriate scale and a reasonable starting point for each axis.
2. Label the axes, and plot the data.
3. Choose a title that accurately represents the data.

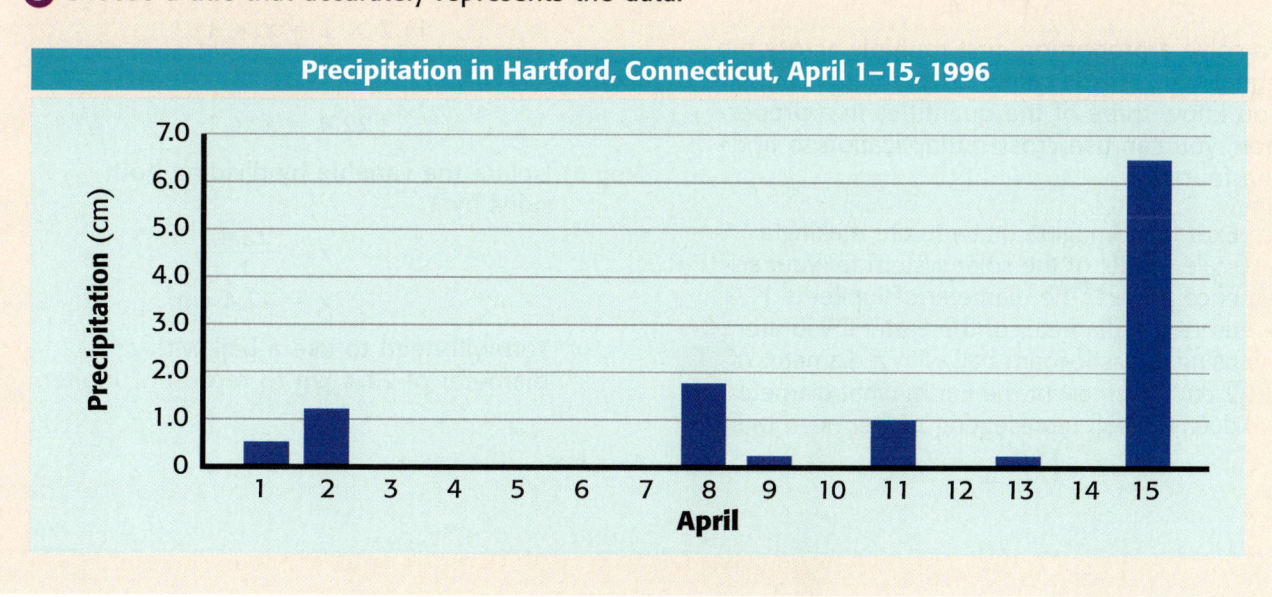

Math Refresher

Science requires an understanding of many math concepts. The following pages will help you review some important math skills.

Averages

An **average**, or **mean**, simplifies a list of numbers into a single number that *approximates* their value.

Example: Find the average of the following set of numbers: 5, 4, 7, and 8.

Step 1: Find the sum.

$$5 + 4 + 7 + 8 = 24$$

Step 2: Divide the sum by the amount of numbers in your set. Because there are four numbers in this example, divide the sum by 4.

$$\frac{24}{4} = 6$$

The average, or mean, is **6**.

Ratios

A **ratio** is a comparison between numbers, and it is usually written as a fraction.

Example: Find the ratio of thermometers to students if you have 36 thermometers and 48 students in your class.

Step 1: Make the ratio.

$$\frac{36 \text{ thermometers}}{48 \text{ students}}$$

Step 2: Reduce the fraction to its simplest form.

$$\frac{36}{48} = \frac{36 \div 12}{48 \div 12} = \frac{3}{4}$$

The ratio of thermometers to students is **3 to 4**, or $\frac{3}{4}$. The ratio may also be written in the form 3:4.

Proportions

A **proportion** is an equation that states that two ratios are equal.

$$\frac{3}{1} = \frac{12}{4}$$

To solve a proportion, first multiply across the equal sign. This is called cross-multiplication. If you know three of the quantities in a proportion, you can use cross-multiplication to find the fourth.

Example: Imagine that you are making a scale model of the solar system for your science project. The diameter of Jupiter is 11.2 times the diameter of the Earth. If you are using a plastic-foam ball with a diameter of 2 cm to represent the Earth, what diameter does the ball representing Jupiter need to be?

$$\frac{11.2}{1} = \frac{x}{2 \text{ cm}}$$

Step 1: Cross-multiply.

$$\frac{11.2}{1} \diagdown\!\!\!\!\diagup \frac{x}{2}$$

$$11.2 \times 2 = x \times 1$$

Step 2: Multiply.

$$22.4 = x \times 1$$

Step 3: Isolate the variable by dividing both sides by 1.

$$x = \frac{22.4}{1}$$

$$x = 22.4 \text{ cm}$$

You will need to use a ball with a diameter of **22.4 cm** to represent Jupiter.

Percentages

A **percentage** is a ratio of a given number to 100.

Example: What is 85 percent of 40?

Step 1: Rewrite the percentage by moving the decimal point two places to the left.

.85

Step 2: Multiply the decimal by the number you are calculating the percentage of.

0.85 × 40 = 34

85 percent of 40 is **34.**

Decimals

To **add** or **subtract decimals,** line up the digits vertically so that the decimal points line up. Then add or subtract the columns from right to left, carrying or borrowing numbers as necessary.

Example: Add the following numbers: 3.1415 and 2.96.

Step 1: Line up the digits vertically so that the decimal points line up.

$$\begin{array}{r} 3.1415 \\ + \ 2.96 \ \ \ \\ \hline \end{array}$$

Step 2: Add the columns from right to left, carrying when necessary.

$$\begin{array}{r} 1\ 1\ \ \ \ \ \\ 3.1415 \\ + \ 2.96\ \ \ \\ \hline 6.1015 \end{array}$$

The sum is **6.1015.**

Fractions

Numbers tell you how many; **fractions** tell you *how much of a whole.*

Example: Your class has 24 plants. Your teacher instructs you to put 5 in a shady spot. What fraction does this represent?

Step 1: Write a fraction with the total number of parts in the whole as the denominator.

$$\frac{?}{24}$$

Step 2: Write the number of parts of the whole being represented as the numerator.

$$\frac{5}{24}$$

$\frac{5}{24}$ of the plants will be in the shade.

Reducing Fractions

It is usually best to express a fraction in simplest form. This is called *reducing* a fraction.

Example: Reduce the fraction $\frac{30}{45}$ to its simplest form.

Step 1: Find the largest whole number that will divide evenly into both the numerator and denominator. This number is called the greatest common factor (GCF).

factors of the numerator 30: 1, 2, 3, 5, 6, 10, **15,** 30

factors of the denominator 45: 1, 3, 5, 9, **15,** 45

Step 2: Divide both the numerator and the denominator by the GCF, which in this case is 15.

$$\frac{30}{45} = \frac{30 \div 15}{45 \div 15} = \frac{2}{3}$$

$\frac{30}{45}$ reduced to its simplest form is $\frac{2}{3}$.

Appendix

Adding and Subtracting Fractions

To **add** or **subtract fractions** that have the **same denominator,** simply add or subtract the numerators.

Examples:

$$\frac{3}{5} + \frac{1}{5} = ? \text{ and } \frac{3}{4} - \frac{1}{4} = ?$$

Step 1: Add or subtract the numerators.

$$\frac{3}{5} + \frac{1}{5} = \frac{4}{} \text{ and } \frac{3}{4} - \frac{1}{4} = \frac{2}{}$$

Step 2: Write the sum or difference over the denominator.

$$\frac{3}{5} + \frac{1}{5} = \frac{4}{5} \text{ and } \frac{3}{4} - \frac{1}{4} = \frac{2}{4}$$

Step 3: If necessary, reduce the fraction to its simplest form.

$$\frac{4}{5} \text{ cannot be reduced, and } \frac{2}{4} = \frac{1}{2}.$$

To **add** or **subtract fractions** that have **different denominators,** first find the least common denominator (LCD).

Examples:

$$\frac{1}{2} + \frac{1}{6} = ? \text{ and } \frac{3}{4} - \frac{2}{3} = ?$$

Step 1: Write the equivalent fractions with a common denominator.

$$\frac{3}{6} + \frac{1}{6} = ? \text{ and } \frac{9}{12} - \frac{8}{12} = ?$$

Step 2: Add or subtract.

$$\frac{3}{6} + \frac{1}{6} = \frac{4}{6} \text{ and } \frac{9}{12} - \frac{8}{12} = \frac{1}{12}$$

Step 3: If necessary, reduce the fraction to its simplest form.

$$\frac{4}{6} = \frac{2}{3}, \text{ and } \frac{1}{12} \text{ cannot be reduced.}$$

Multiplying Fractions

To **multiply fractions,** multiply the numerators and the denominators together, and then reduce the fraction to its simplest form.

Example:

$$\frac{5}{9} \times \frac{7}{10} = ?$$

Step 1: Multiply the numerators and denominators.

$$\frac{5}{9} \times \frac{7}{10} = \frac{5 \times 7}{9 \times 10} = \frac{35}{90}$$

Step 2: Reduce.

$$\frac{35}{90} = \frac{35 \div 5}{90 \div 5} = \frac{7}{18}$$

Dividing Fractions

To **divide fractions,** first rewrite the divisor (the number you divide *by*) upside down. This is called the reciprocal of the divisor. Then you can multiply and reduce if necessary.

Example:

$$\frac{5}{8} \div \frac{3}{2} = ?$$

Step 1: Rewrite the divisor as its reciprocal.

$$\frac{3}{2} \rightarrow \frac{2}{3}$$

Step 2: Multiply.

$$\frac{5}{8} \times \frac{2}{3} = \frac{5 \times 2}{8 \times 3} = \frac{10}{24}$$

Step 3: Reduce.

$$\frac{10}{24} = \frac{10 \div 2}{24 \div 2} = \frac{5}{12}$$

Scientific Notation

Scientific notation is a short way of representing very large and very small numbers without writing all of the place-holding zeros.

Example: Write 653,000,000 in scientific notation.

Step 1: Write the number without the place-holding zeros.

$$653$$

Step 2: Place the decimal point after the first digit.

$$6.53$$

Step 3: Find the exponent by counting the number of places that you moved the decimal point.

$$6.53000000$$

The decimal point was moved eight places to the left. Therefore, the exponent of 10 is positive 8. Remember, if the decimal point had moved to the right, the exponent would be negative.

Step 4: Write the number in scientific notation.

$$\mathbf{6.53 \times 10^8}$$

Area

Area is the number of square units needed to cover the surface of an object.

Formulas:
Area of a square = side × side
Area of a rectangle = length × width
Area of a triangle = $\frac{1}{2}$ × base × height

Examples: Find the areas.

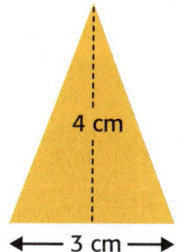

Triangle
Area = $\frac{1}{2}$ × base × height
Area = $\frac{1}{2}$ × 3 cm × 4 cm
Area = **6 cm²**

Rectangle
Area = length × width
Area = 6 cm × 3 cm
Area = **18 cm²**

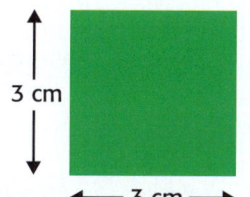

Square
Area = side × side
Area = 3 cm × 3 cm
Area = **9 cm²**

Volume

Volume is the amount of space something occupies.

Formulas:
Volume of a cube = side × side × side

Volume of a prism = area of base × height

Examples:
Find the volume of the solids.

Cube
Volume = side × side × side
Volume = 4 cm × 4 cm × 4 cm
Volume = **64 cm³**

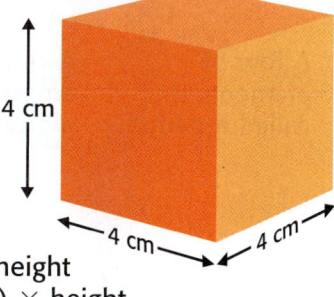

Prism
Volume = area of base × height
Volume = (area of triangle) × height
Volume = $\left(\frac{1}{2} \times 3 \text{ cm} \times 4 \text{ cm}\right) \times 5$ cm
Volume = 6 cm² × 5 cm
Volume = **30 cm³**

Periodic Table of the Elements

Each square on the table includes an element's name, chemical symbol, atomic number, and atomic mass.

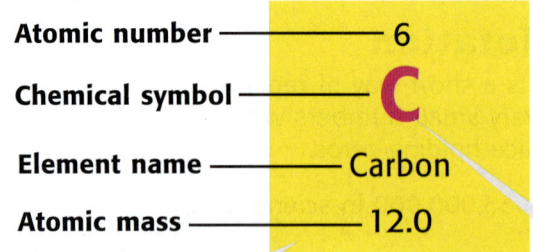

Atomic number — 6
Chemical symbol — C
Element name — Carbon
Atomic mass — 12.0

The background color indicates the type of element. Carbon is a nonmetal.

The color of the chemical symbol indicates the physical state at room temperature. Carbon is a solid.

Background
- Metals
- Metalloids
- Nonmetals

Chemical symbol
- Solid
- Liquid
- Gas

Period	Group 1	Group 2	Group 3	Group 4	Group 5	Group 6	Group 7	Group 8	Group 9
Period 1	1 H Hydrogen 1.0								
Period 2	3 Li Lithium 6.9	4 Be Beryllium 9.0							
Period 3	11 Na Sodium 23.0	12 Mg Magnesium 24.3							
Period 4	19 K Potassium 39.1	20 Ca Calcium 40.1	21 Sc Scandium 45.0	22 Ti Titanium 47.9	23 V Vanadium 50.9	24 Cr Chromium 52.0	25 Mn Manganese 54.9	26 Fe Iron 55.8	27 Co Cobalt 58.9
Period 5	37 Rb Rubidium 85.5	38 Sr Strontium 87.6	39 Y Yttrium 88.9	40 Zr Zirconium 91.2	41 Nb Niobium 92.9	42 Mo Molybdenum 95.9	43 Tc Technetium (97.9)	44 Ru Ruthenium 101.1	45 Rh Rhodium 102.9
Period 6	55 Cs Cesium 132.9	56 Ba Barium 137.3	57 La Lanthanum 138.9	72 Hf Hafnium 178.5	73 Ta Tantalum 180.9	74 W Tungsten 183.8	75 Re Rhenium 186.2	76 Os Osmium 190.2	77 Ir Iridium 192.2
Period 7	87 Fr Francium (223.0)	88 Ra Radium (226.0)	89 Ac Actinium (227.0)	104 Rf Rutherfordium (261.1)	105 Db Dubnium (262.1)	106 Sg Seaborgium (263.1)	107 Bh Bohrium (262.1)	108 Hs Hassium (265)	109 Mt Meitnerium (266)

A row of elements is called a period.

A column of elements is called a group or family.

Lanthanides

58 Ce Cerium 140.1	59 Pr Praseodymium 140.9	60 Nd Neodymium 144.2	61 Pm Promethium (144.9)	62 Sm Samarium 150.4

Actinides

90 Th Thorium 232.0	91 Pa Protactinium 231.0	92 U Uranium 238.0	93 Np Neptunium (237.0)	94 Pu Plutonium 244.1

These elements are placed below the table to allow the table to be narrower.

Appendix

TOPIC: Periodic Table
GO TO: go.hrw.com
KEYWORD: HN0 Periodic

Visit the HRW Web site to see the most recent version of the periodic table.

This zigzag line reminds you where the metals, nonmetals, and metalloids are.

The names and symbols of elements 110–112 are temporary. They are based on the atomic number of the element. The official name and symbol will be approved by an international committee of scientists.

Group 10	Group 11	Group 12	Group 13	Group 14	Group 15	Group 16	Group 17	Group 18
								2 **He** Helium 4.0
			5 **B** Boron 10.8	6 **C** Carbon 12.0	7 **N** Nitrogen 14.0	8 **O** Oxygen 16.0	9 **F** Fluorine 19.0	10 **Ne** Neon 20.2
			13 **Al** Aluminum 27.0	14 **Si** Silicon 28.1	15 **P** Phosphorus 31.0	16 **S** Sulfur 32.1	17 **Cl** Chlorine 35.5	18 **Ar** Argon 39.9
28 **Ni** Nickel 58.7	29 **Cu** Copper 63.5	30 **Zn** Zinc 65.4	31 **Ga** Gallium 69.7	32 **Ge** Germanium 72.6	33 **As** Arsenic 74.9	34 **Se** Selenium 79.0	35 **Br** Bromine 79.9	36 **Kr** Krypton 83.8
46 **Pd** Palladium 106.4	47 **Ag** Silver 107.9	48 **Cd** Cadmium 112.4	49 **In** Indium 114.8	50 **Sn** Tin 118.7	51 **Sb** Antimony 121.8	52 **Te** Tellurium 127.6	53 **I** Iodine 126.9	54 **Xe** Xenon 131.3
78 **Pt** Platinum 195.1	79 **Au** Gold 197.0	80 **Hg** Mercury 200.6	81 **Tl** Thallium 204.4	82 **Pb** Lead 207.2	83 **Bi** Bismuth 209.0	84 **Po** Polonium (209.0)	85 **At** Astatine (210.0)	86 **Rn** Radon (222.0)
110 **Uun** Ununnilium (271)	111 **Uuu** Unununium (272)	112 **Uub** Ununbium (277)						

63 **Eu** Europium 152.0	64 **Gd** Gadolinium 157.3	65 **Tb** Terbium 158.9	66 **Dy** Dysprosium 162.5	67 **Ho** Holmium 164.9	68 **Er** Erbium 167.3	69 **Tm** Thulium 168.9	70 **Yb** Ytterbium 173.0	71 **Lu** Lutetium 175.0
95 **Am** Americium (243.1)	96 **Cm** Curium (247.1)	97 **Bk** Berkelium (247.1)	98 **Cf** Californium (251.1)	99 **Es** Einsteinium (252.1)	100 **Fm** Fermium (257.1)	101 **Md** Mendelevium (258.1)	102 **No** Nobelium (259.1)	103 **Lr** Lawrencium (262.1)

A number in parentheses is the mass number of the most stable isotope of that element.

Physical Science Refresher

Atoms and Elements

Every object in the universe is made up of particles of some kind of matter. **Matter** is anything that takes up space and has mass. All matter is made up of elements. An **element** is a substance that cannot be separated into simpler components by ordinary chemical means. This is because each element consists of only one kind of atom. An **atom** is the smallest unit of an element that has all of the properties of that element.

Atomic Structure

Atoms are made up of small particles called subatomic particles. The three major types of subatomic particles are **electrons, protons,** and **neutrons.** Electrons have a negative electric charge, protons have a positive charge, and neutrons have no electric charge. The protons and neutrons are packed close to one another to form the **nucleus.** The protons give the nucleus a positive charge. Electrons are most likely to be found in regions around the nucleus called **electron clouds.** The negatively charged electrons are attracted to the positively charged nucleus. An atom may have several energy levels in which electrons are located.

Atomic Number

To help in the identification of elements, scientists have assigned an **atomic number** to each kind of atom. The atomic number is the number of protons in the atom. Atoms with the same number of protons are all the same kind of element. In an uncharged, or electrically neutral, atom there are an equal number of protons and electrons. Therefore, the atomic number equals the number of electrons in an uncharged atom. The number of neutrons, however, can vary for a given element. Atoms of the same element that have different numbers of neutrons are called **isotopes.**

Periodic Table of the Elements

In the periodic table, the elements are arranged from left to right in order of increasing atomic number. Each element in the table is in a separate box. An atom of each element has one more electron and one more proton than an atom of the element to its left. Each horizontal row of the table is called a **period.** Changes in chemical properties of elements across a period correspond to changes in the electron arrangements of their atoms. Each vertical column of the table, known as a **group,** lists elements with similar properties. The elements in a group have similar chemical properties because their atoms have the same number of electrons in their outer energy level. For example, the elements helium, neon, argon, krypton, xenon, and radon all have similar properties and are known as the noble gases.

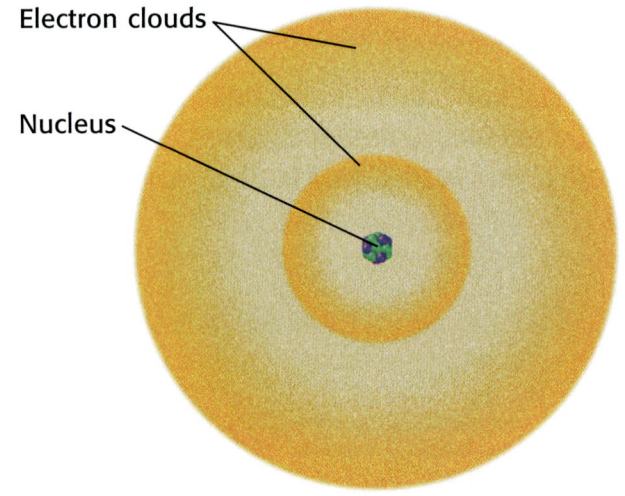

Electron clouds

Nucleus

Molecules and Compounds

When two or more elements are joined chemically, the resulting substance is called a **compound.** A compound is a new substance with properties different from those of the elements that compose it. For example, water, H_2O, is a compound formed when hydrogen (H) and oxygen (O) combine. The smallest complete unit of a compound that has the properties of that compound is called a **molecule.** A chemical formula indicates the elements in a compound. It also indicates the relative number of atoms of each element present. The chemical formula for water is H_2O, which indicates that each water molecule consists of two atoms of hydrogen and one atom of oxygen. The subscript number is used after the symbol for an element to indicate how many atoms of that element are in a single molecule of the compound.

Acids, Bases, and pH

An ion is an atom or group of atoms that has an electric charge because it has lost or gained one or more electrons. When an acid, such as hydrochloric acid, HCl, is mixed with water, it separates into ions. An **acid** is a compound that produces hydrogen ions, H^+, in water. The hydrogen ions then combine with a water molecule to form a hydronium ion, H_3O^+. A **base,** on the other hand, is a substance that produces hydroxide ions, OH^-, in water.

To determine whether a solution is acidic or basic, scientists use pH. The **pH** is a measure of the hydronium ion concentration in a solution. The pH scale ranges from 0 to 14. The middle point, pH = 7, is neutral, neither acidic nor basic. Acids have a pH less than 7; bases have a pH greater than 7. The lower the number is, the more acidic the solution. The higher the number is, the more basic the solution.

Chemical Equations

A chemical reaction occurs when a chemical change takes place. (In a chemical change, new substances with new properties are formed.) A chemical equation is a useful way of describing a chemical reaction by means of chemical formulas. The equation indicates what substances react and what the products are. For example, when carbon and oxygen combine, they can form carbon dioxide. The equation for the reaction is as follows:

$$C + O_2 \rightarrow CO_2.$$

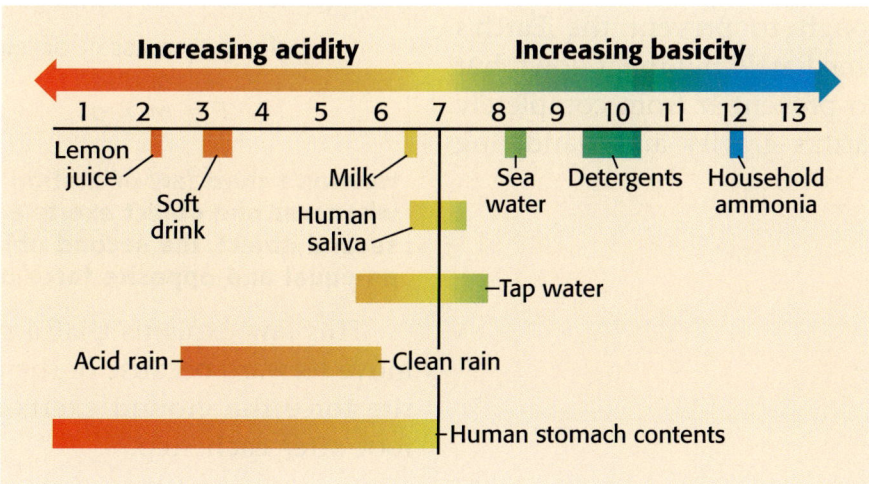

Physical Laws and Equations

Law of Conservation of Energy

The law of conservation of energy states that energy can be neither created nor destroyed.

The total amount of energy in a closed system is always the same. Energy can be changed from one form to another, but all the different forms of energy in a system always add up to the same total amount of energy, no matter how many energy conversions occur.

Law of Universal Gravitation

The law of universal gravitation states that all objects in the universe attract each other by a force called gravity. The size of the force depends on the masses of the objects and the distance between them.

The first part of the law explains why a bowling ball is much harder to lift than a table-tennis ball. Because the bowling ball has a much larger mass than the table-tennis ball, the amount of gravity between the Earth and the bowling ball is greater than the amount of gravity between the Earth and the table-tennis ball.

The second part of the law explains why a satellite can remain in orbit around the Earth. The satellite is carefully placed at a distance great enough to prevent the Earth's gravity from immediately pulling it down but small enough to prevent it from completely escaping the Earth's gravity and wandering off into space.

Newton's Laws of Motion

Newton's first law of motion states that an object at rest remains at rest and an object in motion remains in motion at constant speed and in a straight line unless acted on by an unbalanced force.

The first part of the law explains why a football will remain on a tee until it is kicked off or until a gust of wind blows it off.

The second part of the law explains why a bike's rider will continue moving forward after the bike tire runs into a crack in the sidewalk and the bike comes to an abrupt stop until gravity and the sidewalk stop the rider.

Newton's second law of motion states that the acceleration of an object depends on the mass of the object and the amount of force applied.

The first part of the law explains why the acceleration of a 4 kg bowling ball will be greater than the acceleration of a 6 kg bowling ball if the same force is applied to both.

The second part of the law explains why the acceleration of a bowling ball will be larger if a larger force is applied to it.

The relationship of acceleration (a) to mass (m) and force (F) can be expressed mathematically by the following equation:

$$\text{acceleration} = \frac{\text{force}}{\text{mass}} \quad \text{or} \quad a = \frac{F}{m}$$

This equation is often rearranged to the form:

$$\text{force} = \text{mass} \times \text{acceleration}$$
$$\text{or}$$
$$F = m \times a$$

Newton's third law of motion states that whenever one object exerts a force on a second object, the second object exerts an equal and opposite force on the first.

This law explains that a runner is able to move forward because of the equal and opposite force the ground exerts on the runner's foot after each step.

Useful Equations

Average speed

$$\text{Average speed} = \frac{\text{total distance}}{\text{total time}}$$

Example: A bicycle messenger traveled a distance of 136 km in 8 hours. What was the messenger's average speed?

$$\frac{136 \text{ km}}{8 \text{ h}} = 17 \text{ km/h}$$

The messenger's average speed was **17 km/h.**

Average acceleration

$$\text{Average acceleration} = \frac{\text{final velocity} - \text{starting velocity}}{\text{time it takes to change velocity}}$$

Example: Calculate the average acceleration of an Olympic 100 m dash sprinter who reaches a velocity of 15 m/s south at the finish line. The race was in a straight line and lasted 10 s.

$$\frac{15 \text{ m/s} - 0 \text{ m/s}}{10 \text{ s}} = 1.5 \text{ m/s/s}$$

The sprinter's average acceleration is **1.5 m/s/s south.**

Net force

Forces in the Same Direction
When forces are in the same direction, add the forces together to determine the net force.

Example: Calculate the net force on a stalled car that is being pushed by two people. One person is pushing with a force of 13 N northwest and the other person is pushing with a force of 8 N in the same direction.

$$13 \text{ N} + 8 \text{ N} = 21 \text{ N}$$

The net force is **21 N northwest.**

Forces in Opposite Directions
When forces are in opposite directions, subtract the smaller force from the larger force to determine the net force.

Net force (cont'd)

Example: Calculate the net force on a rope that is being pulled on each end. One person is pulling on one end of the rope with a force of 12 N south. Another person is pulling on the opposite end of the rope with a force of 7 N north.

$$12 \text{ N} - 7 \text{ N} = 5 \text{ N}$$

The net force is **5 N south.**

Density

$$\text{Density} = \frac{\text{mass}}{\text{volume}}$$

Example: Calculate the density of a sponge with a mass of 10 g and a volume of 40 mL.

$$\frac{10 \text{ g}}{40 \text{ mL}} = 0.25 \text{ g/mL}$$

The density of the sponge is **0.25 g/mL.**

Pressure

Pressure is the force exerted over a given area. The SI unit for pressure is the pascal, which is abbreviated Pa.

$$\text{Pressure} = \frac{\text{force}}{\text{area}}$$

Example: Calculate the pressure of the air in a soccer ball if the air exerts a force of 10 N over an area of 0.5 m^2.

$$\text{Pressure} = \frac{10 \text{ N}}{0.5 \text{ m}^2} = 20 \text{ N/m}^2 = 20 \text{ Pa}$$

The pressure of the air inside of the soccer ball is **20 Pa.**

Concentration

$$\text{Concentration} = \frac{\text{mass of solute}}{\text{volume of solvent}}$$

Example: Calculate the concentration of a solution in which 10 g of sugar is dissolved in 125 mL of water.

$$\frac{10 \text{ g of sugar}}{125 \text{ mL of water}} = 0.08 \text{ g/mL}$$

The concentration of this solution is **0.08 g/mL.**

Properties of Common Minerals

Silicate Minerals

Mineral	Color	Luster	Streak	Hardness
Beryl	deep green, pink, white, bluish green, or light yellow	vitreous	none	7.5–8
Chlorite	green	vitreous to pearly	pale green	2–2.5
Garnet	green or red	vitreous	none	6.5–7.5
Hornblende	dark green, brown, or black	vitreous or silky	none	5–6
Muscovite	colorless, gray, or brown	vitreous or pearly	white	2–2.5
Olivine	olive green	vitreous	none	6.5–7
Orthoclase	colorless, white, pink, or other colors	vitreous to pearly	white or none	6
Plagioclase	blue gray to white	vitreous	white	6
Quartz	colorless or white; any color when not pure	vitreous or waxy	white or none	7

Nonsilicate Minerals

Native Elements

Mineral	Color	Luster	Streak	Hardness
Copper	copper-red	metallic	copper-red	2.5–3
Diamond	pale yellow or colorless	vitreous	none	10
Graphite	black to gray	submetallic	black	1–2

Carbonates

Mineral	Color	Luster	Streak	Hardness
Aragonite	colorless, white, or pale yellow	vitreous	white	3.5–4
Calcite	colorless or white to tan	vitreous	white	3

Halides

Mineral	Color	Luster	Streak	Hardness
Fluorite	light green, yellow, purple, bluish green, or other colors	vitreous	none	4
Halite	colorless or gray	vitreous	white	2.5–3

Oxides

Mineral	Color	Luster	Streak	Hardness
Hematite	reddish brown to black	metallic to earthy	red to red-brown	5.6–6.5
Magnetite	iron black	metallic	black	5–6

Sulfates

Mineral	Color	Luster	Streak	Hardness
Anhydrite	colorless, bluish, or violet	vitreous to pearly	white	3–3.5
Gypsum	white, pink, gray, or colorless	vitreous, pearly, or silky	white	1–2.5

Sulfides

Mineral	Color	Luster	Streak	Hardness
Galena	lead gray	metallic	lead gray to black	2.5
Pyrite	brassy yellow	metallic	greenish, brownish, or black	6–6.5

Density (g/cm³)	Cleavage, Fracture, Special Properties	Common Uses
2.6–2.8	1 cleavage direction; irregular fracture; some varieties fluoresce in ultraviolet light	gemstones, ore of the metal beryllium
2.6–3.3	1 cleavage direction; irregular fracture	
4.2	no cleavage; conchoidal to splintery fracture	gemstones, abrasives
3.2	2 cleavage directions; hackly to splintery fracture	
2.7–3	1 cleavage direction; irregular fracture	electrical insulation, wallpaper, fireproofing material, lubricant
3.2–3.3	no cleavage; conchoidal fracture	gemstones, casting
2.6	2 cleavage directions; irregular fracture	porcelain
2.6–2.7	2 cleavage directions; irregular fracture	ceramics
2.6	no cleavage; conchoidal fracture	gemstones, concrete, glass, porcelain, sandpaper, lenses
8.9	no cleavage; hackly fracture	wiring, brass, bronze, coins
3.5	4 cleavage directions; irregular to conchoidal fracture	gemstones, drilling
2.3	1 cleavage direction; irregular fracture	pencils, paints, lubricants, batteries
2.95	2 cleavage directions; irregular fracture; reacts with hydrochloric acid	minor source of barium
2.7	3 cleavage directions; irregular fracture; reacts with weak acid, double refraction	cements, soil conditioner, whitewash, construction materials
3.2	4 cleavage directions; irregular fracture; some varieties fluoresce or double refract	hydrochloric acid, steel, glass, fiberglass, pottery, enamel
2.2	3 cleavage directions; splintery to conchoidal fracture; salty taste	tanning hides, fertilizer, salting icy roads, food preservation
5.25	no cleavage; splintery fracture; magnetic when heated	iron ore for steel, gemstones, pigments
5.2	2 cleavage directions; splintery fracture; magnetic	iron ore
2.89–2.98	3 cleavage directions; conchoidal to splintery fracture	soil conditioner, sulfuric acid
2.2–2.4	3 cleavage directions; conchoidal to splintery fracture	plaster of Paris, wallboard, soil conditioner
7.4–7.6	3 cleavage directions; irregular fracture	batteries, paints
5	no cleavage; conchoidal to splintery fracture	dyes, inks, gemstones

Appendix

Sky Maps

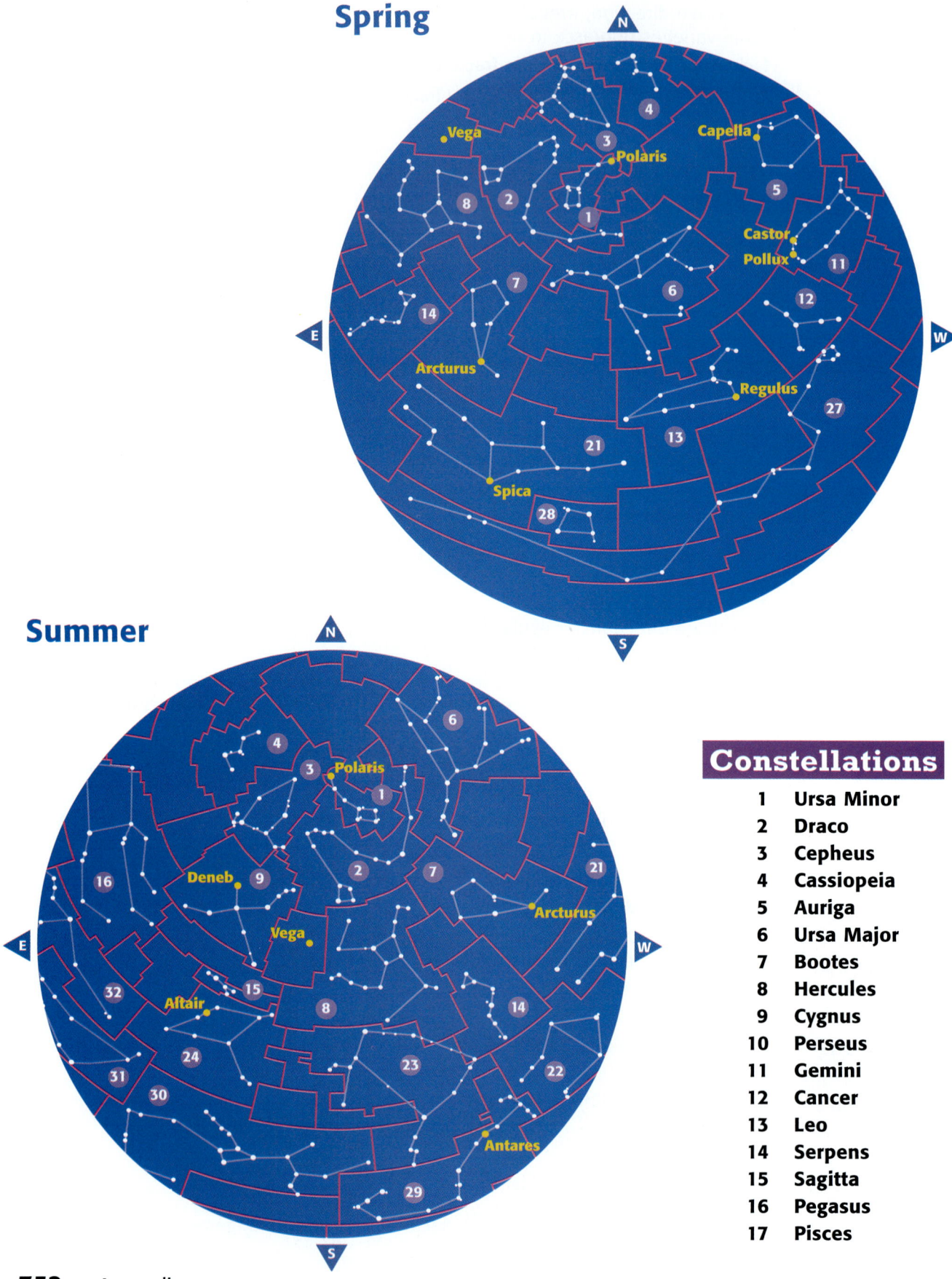

Constellations

1. Ursa Minor
2. Draco
3. Cepheus
4. Cassiopeia
5. Auriga
6. Ursa Major
7. Bootes
8. Hercules
9. Cygnus
10. Perseus
11. Gemini
12. Cancer
13. Leo
14. Serpens
15. Sagitta
16. Pegasus
17. Pisces

Appendix

Autumn

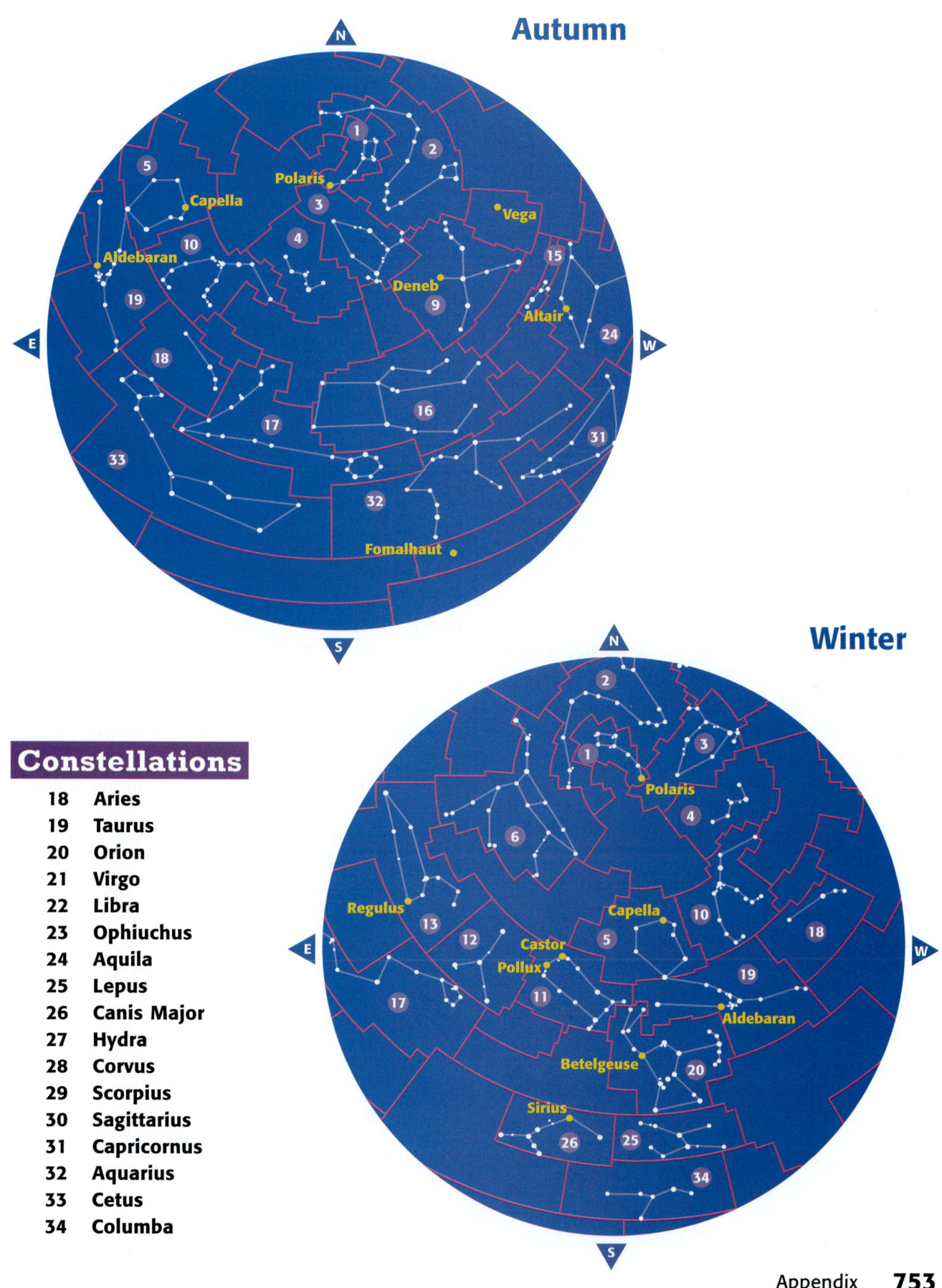

Winter

Constellations

- 18 Aries
- 19 Taurus
- 20 Orion
- 21 Virgo
- 22 Libra
- 23 Ophiuchus
- 24 Aquila
- 25 Lepus
- 26 Canis Major
- 27 Hydra
- 28 Corvus
- 29 Scorpius
- 30 Sagittarius
- 31 Capricornus
- 32 Aquarius
- 33 Cetus
- 34 Columba

Appendix 753

Glossary

A

abrasion the grinding and wearing down of rock surfaces by other rock or sand particles (247, 306)

absolute dating the process of establishing the age of an object, such as a fossil or rock layer, by determining the number of years it has existed (142)

absolute magnitude the actual brightness of a star (574)

abyssal (uh BIS uhl) **plain** the broad, flat portion of the deep-ocean basin (338)

acid precipitation precipitation that contains acids due to air pollution (116, 249, 411)

aerial photograph a photograph taken from the air (43)

air mass a large body of air that has similar temperature and moisture throughout (430)

air pressure the measure of the force with which air molecules push on a surface (393)

alluvial (uh LOO vee uhl) **fan** fan-shaped deposits of alluvium that form on dry land (279)

alluvium (uh LOO vee uhm) rock and soil deposited by streams (277)

altitude the height of an object above the Earth's surface (393); in astronomy, the angle between an object in the sky and the horizon (491)

anemometer (AN uh MAHM uht uhr) a device used to measure wind speed (441)

annular (AN yoo luhr) **eclipse** a solar eclipse during which the outer ring of the sun can be seen around the moon (552)

anticline a bowl-shaped fold in sedimentary rock layers (182)

apparent magnitude how bright a light appears to an observer (574)

aquifer (AHK wuh fuhr) a rock layer that stores and allows the flow of ground water (280)

arête (uh RAYT) a jagged ridge that forms between two or more cirques cutting into the same mountain (313)

artesian (ahr TEE zhuhn) **spring** a spring that forms where cracks occur naturally in the cap rock and the pressurized water in the aquifer flows through the cracks to the surface (282)

artificial satellite any human-made object placed in orbit around a body in space (602)

asteroid a small, rocky body that revolves around the sun (559)

asteroid belt the region of the solar system most asteroids occupy; roughly between the orbits of Mars and Jupiter (559)

asthenosphere (as THEN uh SFIR) the soft layer of the mantle on which pieces of the lithosphere move (168)

astronomical unit (AU) the average distance between the Earth and the sun, or approximately 150,000,000 km (516, 538)

astronomy the study of all physical objects beyond Earth (9, 482)

atmosphere a mixture of gases that surrounds a planet, such as Earth (392)

atom the smallest part of an element that has all of the properties of that element (61)

azimuthal (AZ i MYOOTH uhl) **projection** a map projection that is made by transferring the features of the globe onto a plane (42)

B

barometer an instrument used to measure air pressure (441)

beach an area of the shoreline made up of material deposited by waves (300)

bedrock the layer of rock beneath soil (255)

benthic environment the ocean floor and all the organisms that live on or in it; also known as the bottom environment (343)

benthos organisms that live on or in the ocean floor (342)

big bang theory the theory that states the universe began with a tremendous explosion (586)

biomass organic matter, such as plants, wood, and waste, that contains stored energy (124)

biome a large region characterized by a specific type of climate and the plants and animals that live there (458)

black hole an object with more than three solar masses squeezed into a ball only 10 km across whose gravity is so strong that not even light can escape (581)

breaker a heightened water wave that begins to tumble downward, or break, upon nearing the shore (374)

C

caldera (kahl DER uh) a circular depression that forms when a magma chamber empties and causes the ground above to sink (229)

calendar a system for organizing time; most calendars organize time within a single unit called a year (482)

cardinal directions north, south, east, and west (35)

cast an object created when sediment fills a mold and becomes rock (148)

catastrophism a principle that states that all geologic change occurs suddenly (135)

celestial equator imaginary circle created by extending Earth's equator into space (492)

channel the path a stream follows (273)

chemical weathering the chemical breakdown of rocks and minerals into new substances (249)

chromosphere (KROH muh SFIR) a thin region of the sun's atmosphere between the corona and the photosphere; too faint to see unless there is a total solar eclipse (519)

cinder cone volcano a small, steeply sloped volcano that forms from moderately explosive eruptions of pyroclastic material (228)

circumpolar stars stars that can be seen at all times of the year and all times of the night (492)

cirque (suhrk) a bowl-like depression where glacial ice cuts back into mountain walls (313)

cirrus (SIR uhs) **clouds** thin, feathery white clouds found at high altitudes (427)

cleavage (KLEEV ij) the tendency of a mineral to break along flat surfaces (65)

climate the average weather conditions in an area over a long period of time (452)

cloud a collection of millions of tiny water droplets or ice crystals (426)

coal a solid fossil fuel formed underground from buried, decomposed plant material (112)

comet a small body of ice, rock, and cosmic dust loosely packed together that gives off gas and dust in the form of a tail as it passes close to the sun (557)

composite volcano a volcano made of alternating layers of lava and pyroclastic material; also called *stratovolcano* (228)

composition the makeup of a rock; describes either the minerals or elements present in it (85)

compound a pure substance made of two or more elements that have been chemically joined, or bonded together (61)

compression the type of stress that occurs when an object is squeezed (181)

condensation the change of state from a gas to a liquid (335, 425)

conduction the transfer of thermal energy from one material to another by direct contact; conduction can also occur within a substance (399)

conic (KAHN ik) **projection** a map projection that is made by transferring the features of the globe onto a cone (42)

constellation a section of the sky that contains a recognizable star pattern (489)

continental drift the theory that continents can drift apart from one another and have done so in the past (173)

continental margin the portion of the Earth's surface beneath the ocean that is made of continental crust (338)

continental rise the base of the continental slope (338)

continental shelf the flattest part of the continental margin (338)

continental slope the steepest part of the continental margin (338)

contour interval the difference in elevation between one contour line and the next (47)

contour lines lines that connect points of equal elevation (46)

convection the transfer of thermal energy by the circulation or movement of a liquid or a gas (399)

convective zone a region of the sun where gases circulate in convection currents, bringing the sun's energy to the surface (519)

convergent boundary the boundary between two colliding tectonic plates (178)

coprolites (KAHP roh LIETS) preserved feces, or dung, from animals (148)

core the central, spherical part of the Earth below the mantle (167, 525); *also* the center of the sun where the sun's energy is produced (519)

Coriolis (KOHR ee OH lis) **effect** the curving of moving objects from a straight path due to the Earth's rotation (366, 403)

corona the sun's outer atmosphere, which can extend outward a distance equal to 10–12 times the diameter of the sun (519)

cosmic background radiation radiation left over from the big bang that fills all of space (587)

cosmology the study of the origin and future of the universe (586)

crater a funnel-shaped pit around the central vent of a volcano (229)

creep the extremely slow movement of material downslope (319)

crest the highest point of a wave (372)

crevasse (kruh VAS) a large crack that forms where a glacier picks up speed or flows over a high point (311)

crust the thin, outermost layer of the Earth, or the uppermost part of the lithosphere (166, 525)

crystal the solid, geometric form of a mineral produced by a repeating pattern of atoms (61)

cumulus (KYOO myoo luhs) **clouds** puffy, white clouds that tend to have flat bottoms (426)

D

day the time required for the Earth to rotate once on its axis (482)

deciduous (dee SIJ oo uhs) describes trees that lose their leaves when the weather becomes cold (462)

declination a measure of how far north or south an object is from the celestial equator (492)

deep current a streamlike movement of ocean water far below the surface (368)

deep-ocean basin the portion of the Earth's surface beneath the ocean that is made of oceanic crust (338)

deflation the lifting and removal of fine sediment by wind (305)

deformation the change in the shape of rock in response to stress (197)

delta a fan-shaped deposit of alluvium at the mouth of a stream, where the stream empties into a large body of water (278)

density the amount of matter in a given space; mass per unit volume (66)

deposition the process by which material is dropped or settles (277)

desalination the process of evaporating sea water so that the water and the salt separate (349)

dew point the temperature to which air must cool to be completely saturated (425)

differential weathering the process by which softer, less weather-resistant rocks wear away, leaving harder, more weather-resistant rocks behind (252)

discharge the amount of water a stream or river carries in a given amount of time (273)

divergent boundary the boundary between two tectonic plates that are moving away from each other (179)

divide an area of higher ground that separates drainage basins (272)

drainage basin the land drained by a river system, which includes the main river and all of its tributaries (272)

dune a mound of wind-deposited sand (306)

E

eclipse an event in which the shadow of one celestial body falls on another (552)

ecliptic the apparent path the sun takes across the celestial sphere (492)

ecosystem a community of organisms and their nonliving environment (10)

elastic rebound the sudden return of elastically deformed rock to its original shape (197)

electromagnetic spectrum all the wavelengths of electromagnetic radiation (499)

element a pure substance that cannot be separated or broken down into simpler substances by ordinary chemical means (60)

elevation the height of an object above sea level; the height of surface landforms above sea level (46, 456)

ellipse a closed curve in which the sum of the distances from the edge of the curve to two points inside the ellipse is always the same (516)

elliptical galaxy a spherical or elongated galaxy with a bright center and very little dust and gas (583)

El Niño periodic change in the location of warm and cool surface waters in the Pacific Ocean (371)

energy resource a natural resource that humans use to produce energy (111)

eon the largest division of geologic time (153)

epicenter the point on the Earth's surface directly above an earthquake's starting point (202)

epoch (EP uhk) the fourth-largest division of geologic time (153)

equator a circle halfway between the poles that divides the Earth into the Northern and Southern Hemispheres (37)

era the second-largest division of geologic time (153)

erosion the removal and transport of material by wind, water, or ice (260, 270)

escape velocity the speed and direction a rocket must travel in order to completely break away from a planet's gravitational pull (601)

evaporation the change of state from a liquid to a vapor (335)

evergreens trees that keep their leaves year-round (462)

extrusive (eks TROO siv) the type of igneous rock that forms when lava or pyroclastic material cools and solidifies on the Earth's surface (90)

F

fault a break in the Earth's crust along which blocks of the crust slide relative to one another due to tectonic forces (183, 196)

fault block a block of the Earth's crust on one side of a fault (183)

fault-block mountain a mountain that forms when faulting causes large blocks of the Earth's crust to drop down relative to other blocks (186)

felsic (FEL SIK) describes relatively light-colored, light-weight igneous rocks that are rich in silicon, aluminum, sodium, and potassium (88)

flood plain an area along a river formed from sediments deposited by floods (279)

focus the point inside the Earth where an earthquake begins (202)

folded mountain a mountain that forms when rock layers are squeezed together and pushed upward (185)

folding the bending of rock layers due to stress in the Earth's crust (182)

foliated the texture of metamorphic rock in which the mineral grains are aligned like the pages of a book (98)

footwall the fault block that is below a fault (183)

fossil any naturally preserved evidence of life (146)

fossil fuel a nonrenewable energy resource that forms in the Earth's crust over millions of years from the buried remains of once-living organisms (111)

fracture the tendency of a mineral to break along curved or irregular surfaces (65)

front the boundary that forms between two different air masses (432)

G

galaxy a large grouping of stars in space (582)

gap hypothesis states that sections of active faults that have had relatively few earthquakes are likely to be the sites of strong earthquakes in the future (207)

gas giants the large, gaseous planets of the outer solar system (544)

gasohol a mixture of gasoline and alcohol that is burned as a fuel (124)

geologic column an ideal sequence of rock layers that contains all the known fossils and rock formations on Earth arranged from oldest to youngest (138)

geologic time scale a scale that divides Earth's 4.6-billion-year history into distinct intervals of time (152)

geology the study of the solid Earth (6)

geosynchronous orbit an orbit in which a satellite travels at a speed that matches the rotational speed of the Earth exactly, keeping the satellite positioned above the same spot on Earth at all times (603)

geothermal energy energy from within the Earth (125)

glacial drift all material carried and deposited by glaciers (314)

glacier an enormous mass of moving ice (309)

global warming a rise in average global temperatures (18, 400, 470)

globular cluster a group of older stars that looks like a ball of stars (584)

gradient a measure of the change in elevation over a certain distance (273)

greenhouse effect the natural heating process of a planet, such as the Earth, by which gases in the atmosphere trap thermal energy (400, 470, 540)

ground water water that is located within rocks below the Earth's surface (280)

H

half-life for a particular radioactive sample, the time it takes for one-half of the sample to decay (143)

hanging valley a small glacial valley that joins the deeper main valley (313)

hanging wall the fault block that is above a fault (183)

hardness the resistance of a mineral to being scratched (66)

horizon the line where the sky and the Earth appear to meet (491)

horn a sharp, pyramid-shaped peak that forms when three or more cirque glaciers erode a mountain (313)

hot spot a place on Earth's surface that is directly above a column of rising magma called a mantle plume (233)

H-R diagram Hertzsprung-Russell diagram; a graph that shows the relationship between a star's surface temperature and its absolute magnitude (577)

humidity the amount of water vapor or moisture in the air (423)

humus (HYU muhs) very small particles of decayed plant and animal material in soil (255)

hurricane a large, rotating tropical weather system with wind speeds of at least 119 km/h (437)

hydroelectric energy electricity produced by falling water (123)

hypothesis a possible explanation or answer to a question (14)

I

ice age a period during which ice collects in high latitudes and moves toward lower latitudes (467)

iceberg a large piece of ice that breaks off an ice shelf and drifts into the ocean (310)

ice wedging the mechanical weathering process in which water seeps into cracks in rock, freezes, then expands, opening the cracks even wider (246)

igneous rock rock that forms from the cooling of magma (84)

index contour a darker, heavier contour line that is usually every fifth line and is labeled by elevation (47)

index fossil a fossil of an organism that lived during a relatively short, well-defined time span; a fossil that is used to date the rock layers in which it is found (150)

inner core the solid, dense center of the Earth (169)

intrusive (in TROO siv) the type of igneous rock that forms when magma cools and solidifies beneath Earth's surface (89)

irregular galaxy a galaxy that does not fit into any other category; one with an irregular shape (583)

isobars lines that connect points of equal air pressure (443)

isotopes atoms of the same element that have the same number of protons but have different numbers of neutrons (142)

J

jet streams narrow belts of high-speed winds that blow in the upper troposphere and the lower stratosphere (406)

K

Kuiper (KIE per) **Belt** the region of the solar system outside the orbit of Neptune that is occupied by small, icy, cometlike bodies (558)

L

landslide a sudden and rapid movement of a large amount of material downslope (317)

latitude the distance north or south from the equator; measured in degrees (37, 453)

lava magma that flows onto the Earth's surface (84, 222)

leaching the process by which rainwater dissolves and carries away the minerals and nutrients in topsoil (256)

leap year a year in which an extra day is added to the calendar (483)

light-minute a unit of length equal to the distance light travels in space in 1 minute, or 18,000,000 km (538)

lightning the large electrical discharge that occurs between two oppositely charged surfaces (435)

light-year a unit of length equal to the distance that light travels through space in 1 year (493, 575)

lithosphere (LITH oh SFIR) the outermost, rigid layer of the Earth that consists of the crust and the rigid upper part of the mantle (168)

load the materials carried in a stream's water (274)

loess (LOH ES) thick deposits of windblown, fine-grained sediments (308)

longitude the distance east or west from the prime meridian; measured in degrees (38)

longshore current the movement of water near and parallel to the shoreline (301)

low Earth orbit an orbit located a few hundred kilometers above the Earth's surface (603)

lunar eclipse an event in which the shadow of the Earth falls on the moon (552)

luster the way the surface of a mineral reflects light (64)

M

mafic (MAYF ik) describes relatively dark-colored, heavy igneous rocks that are rich in iron, magnesium, and calcium (88)

magma the hot liquid that forms when rock partially or completely melts; may include mineral crystals (83)

magnetic declination the angle of correction for the difference between geographic north and magnetic north (36)

magnetic reversal the process by which the Earth's north and south magnetic poles periodically change places (176)

main sequence a diagonal pattern of stars on the H-R diagram (578)

mantle the layer of the Earth between the crust and the core (167, 525)

map a model or representation of the Earth's surface (34)

mass the amount of matter that something is made of; its value does not change with the object's location (24)

mass movement the movement of any material downslope (316)

mechanical weathering the breakdown of rock into smaller pieces by physical means (246)

Mercator projection a map projection that is made by transferring the features of the globe onto a cylinder (41)

mesosphere literally, the "middle sphere"—the strong, lower part of the mantle between the asthenosphere and the outer core (169); *also* the coldest layer of the atmosphere (396)

metamorphic rock rock that forms when the texture and composition of preexisting rock changes due to heat or pressure (84)

meteor a streak of light caused when a meteoroid or comet dust burns up in the Earth's atmosphere before it reaches the ground (560)

meteorite a meteoroid that reaches the Earth's surface without burning up completely (560)

meteoroid a very small, rocky body that revolves around the sun (560)

meteorology the study of the entire atmosphere (8)

meter the basic unit of length in the SI system (23)

microclimate a small region with unique climatic characteristics (466)

mid-ocean ridge a long mountain chain that forms on the ocean floor where tectonic plates pull apart; usually extends along the center of ocean basins (175, 339)

mineral a naturally formed, inorganic solid with a crystalline structure (60)

model a representation of an object or system (19)

Moho a place within the Earth where the speed of seismic waves increases sharply; marks the boundary between the Earth's crust and mantle (211)

mold a cavity in the ground or rock where a plant or animal was buried (148)

monocline a fold in sedimentary rock layers in which the layers are horizontal on both sides of the fold (182)

month roughly the amount of time required for the moon to orbit the Earth once (482)

moon a natural satellite of a planet (549)

mudflow the rapid movement of a large mass of mud, rock, and soil mixed with a large amount of water that flows downhill (318)

N

NASA National Aeronautics and Space Administration; founded to combine all of the separate rocket-development teams in the United States (599)

natural gas a gaseous fossil fuel (112)

natural resource any natural substance, organism, or energy form that living things use (108)

neap tides tides with minimum daily tidal range that occur during the first and third quarters of the moon (380)

nebula (NEB yuh luh) a large cloud of dust and gas in interstellar space; the location of star formation (510, 584)

nekton (NEK TAHN) free-swimming organisms of the ocean (342)

neutron star a star in which all the particles have become neutrons; the collapsed remains of a supernova (581)

nonfoliated the texture of metamorphic rock in which mineral grains show no alignment (98)

nonpoint-source pollution pollution that comes from many sources and that cannot be traced to specific sites (285, 352)

nonrenewable resource a natural resource that cannot be replaced or that can be replaced only over thousands or millions of years (109)

nonsilicate mineral a mineral that does not contain compounds of silicon and oxygen (63)

normal fault a fault in which the hanging wall moves down relative to the footwall (183)

nuclear energy the form of energy associated with changes in the nucleus of an atom; an alternative energy resource (118)

nuclear fusion the process by which two or more nuclei with small masses join together, or fuse, to form a larger, more massive nucleus, along with the production of energy (521)

O

observation any use of the senses to gather information (14)

oceanography the study of the ocean (7)

ocean trench a seemingly bottomless crack in the deep-ocean basin that forms where one oceanic plate is forced underneath a continental plate or another oceanic plate (339)

Oort (ort) **cloud** a spherical region of space that surrounds the solar system in which distant comets revolve around the sun (558)

open cluster a group of stars that are usually located along the spiral disk of a galaxy (584)

orbit the elliptical path a body takes as it travels around another body in space; the motion itself (515)

orbital velocity the speed and direction a rocket must have in order to orbit the Earth (601)

ore a mineral deposit large enough and pure enough to be mined for a profit (70)

outer core the liquid layer of the Earth's core that lies beneath the mantle and surrounds the inner core (169)

oxidation a chemical reaction in which an element combines with oxygen to form an oxide (251)

ozone a gas molecule that is made up of three oxygen atoms and that absorbs ultraviolet radiation from the sun (395)

P

parallax an apparent shift in the position of an object when viewed from different locations (575)

parent rock rock that is the source of soil (255)

pelagic (pi LAJ ik) **environment** the entire volume of water in the ocean and the marine organisms that live above the ocean floor; also known as the water environment (345)

period the third-largest division of geologic time (153)

period of revolution the time it takes for one body to make one complete orbit, or *revolution*, around another body in space (515, 539)

period of rotation the time it takes for an object to rotate once (539)

permeability (PUHR mee uh BIL uh tee) a rock's ability to let water pass through it (280)

permineralization a process in which minerals fill in pore spaces of an organism's tissues (146)

petrification a process in which an organism's tissues are completely replaced by minerals (146)

petroleum an oily mixture of flammable organic compounds from which liquid fossil fuels and other products are separated; crude oil (111)

phases the different appearances of the moon due to varying amounts of sunlight on the side of the moon that faces the Earth; results from the changing relative positions of the moon, Earth, and the sun (551)

photosphere the layer of the sun at which point the gases get thick enough to see; the surface of the sun (519)

planetesimal (PLAN i TES i muhl) the tiny building blocks of the planets that formed as dust particles stuck together and grew in size (512)

plankton microscopic organisms that float at or near the ocean's surface (342)

plate tectonics the theory that the Earth's lithosphere is divided into tectonic plates that move around on top of the asthenosphere (177)

point-source pollution pollution that comes from one particular source area (285)

polar easterlies wind belts that extend from the poles to 60° latitude in both hemispheres (405)

polar zone the northernmost and southernmost climate zones (464)

porosity (poh RAHS uh tee) the amount of open space between individual rock particles (280)

precipitation solid or liquid water that falls from the air to the Earth (335, 428)

prevailing winds winds that blow mainly from one direction (455)

primary pollutants pollutants that are put directly into the air by human or natural activity (409)

prime meridian the line of longitude that passes through Greenwich, England; represents 0° longitude (38)

prograde rotation the counterclockwise spin of a planet or moon as seen from above the planet's north pole (540)

psychrometer (sie KRAHM uht uhr) an instrument used to measure relative humidity (424)

pulsar a spinning neutron star that emits rapid pulses of light (581)

P waves the fastest type of seismic wave; can travel through solids, liquids, and gases; also known as pressure waves and primary waves (200)

pyroclastic material fragments of rock that are created by explosive volcanic eruptions (225)

Q

quasar (KWAY ZAHR) a "quasi-stellar" object; a starlike source of light that is extremely far away; one of the most powerful sources of energy in the universe (585)

R

radiation the transfer of energy as electromagnetic waves, such as visible light or infrared waves (398); *also* energy transferred as waves or particles (118)

radiative zone a very dense region of the sun in which the atoms are so closely packed that light can take millions of years to pass through (519)

radioactive decay a process in which radioactive isotopes tend to break down into stable isotopes of other elements (142)

radiometric dating determining the absolute age of a sample based on the ratio of parent material to daughter material (143)

recharge zone the ground surface where water enters an aquifer (281)

reclamation the process of returning land to its original state after mining is completed (71)

recycling the process by which used or discarded materials are treated for reuse (110)

red giant a star that expands and cools once it runs out of hydrogen fuel (579)

reference point a fixed place on the Earth's surface from which direction and location can be described (35)

reflecting telescope a telescope that uses curved mirrors to gather and focus light (497)

refracting telescope a telescope that uses a set of lenses to gather and focus light (497)

relative dating determining whether an object or event is older or younger than other objects or events (137)

relative humidity the amount of moisture the air contains compared with the maximum amount it can hold at a particular temperature (423)

relief the difference in elevation between the highest and lowest points of an area being mapped (47)

remote sensing gathering information about something without actually being nearby (43)

renewable resource a natural resource that can be used and replaced over a relatively short time (109)

residual soil soil that remains above the bedrock from which it formed (255)

retrograde orbit the clockwise revolution of a satellite around a planet as seen from above the north pole of the planet (556)

retrograde rotation the clockwise spin of a planet or moon as seen from above the planet's or moon's north pole (540)

reverse fault a fault in which the hanging wall moves up relative to the footwall (183)

revolution the elliptical motion of a body as it orbits another body in space (515, 539)

rift a deep crack that forms between tectonic plates as they separate (232)

rift valley a valley that forms in a rift zone between diverging tectonic plates (339)

right ascension a measure of how far east an object is from the point at which the sun appears on the first day of spring (492)

rock a solid mixture of crystals of one or more minerals or other materials (80)

rock cycle the process by which one rock type changes into another rock type (82)

rocket a machine that uses escaping gas to move (598)

rock fall a group of loose rocks that fall down a steep slope (317)

rotation the spinning motion of a body on its axis (515, 539)

S

salinity a measure of the amount of dissolved salts and other solids in a given amount of liquid (332)

saltation the movement of sand-sized particles by a skipping and bouncing action in the direction the wind is blowing (304)

satellite a natural or artificial body that revolves around a planet (549)

scientific method a series of steps that scientists use to answer questions and solve problems (13)

sea-floor spreading the process by which new oceanic lithosphere is created at mid-ocean ridges as older materials are pulled away from the ridge (175)

seamount an individual mountain of volcanic material on the abyssal plain (339)

secondary pollutants pollutants that form from chemical reactions that occur when primary pollutants come in contact with other primary pollutants or with naturally occurring substances, such as water vapor (409)

sedimentary rock rock that forms when sediments are compacted and cemented together (84)

seismic (SIEZ mik) gap an area along a fault where relatively few earthquakes have occurred (207)

seismic waves waves of energy that travel through the Earth (200)

seismogram a tracing of earthquake motion created by a seismograph (202)

seismograph an instrument located at or near the surface of the Earth that records seismic waves (202)

seismology the study of earthquakes (196)

septic tank a large, underground tank that collects and cleans waste water from a household (287)

sewage treatment plant a factory that cleans waste materials out of water that comes from sewers or drains (286)

shadow zone an area on the Earth's surface where no direct seismic waves from a particular earthquake can be detected (211)

shield volcano a large, gently sloped volcano that forms from repeated, nonexplosive eruptions of lava (228)

shoreline the boundary between land and a body of water (298)

silica a compound of silicon and oxygen atoms (224)

silicate mineral a mineral that contains a combination of the elements silicon and oxygen (62)

smog a photochemical fog produced by the reaction of sunlight and air pollutants (117)

soil a loose mixture of small mineral fragments and organic material (255)

soil conservation the various methods by which humans take care of the soil (259)

solar eclipse an event in which the shadow of the moon falls on the Earth's surface (552)

solar energy energy from the sun (119)

solar nebula the nebula that formed into the solar system (511)

solar system the system composed of the sun (a star) and the planets and other bodies that travel around the sun (510)

space probe a vehicle that carries scientific instruments to planets or other bodies in space (606)

space shuttle a reusable vehicle that takes off like a rocket and lands like an airplane (613)

space station a long-term orbiting platform from which other vehicles can be launched or scientific research can be carried out (614)

specific gravity the ratio of an object's density to the density of water (66)

spectrum the rainbow of colors produced when white light passes through a prism or spectrograph (570)

spiral galaxy a galaxy with a bulge in the center and very distinctive spiral arms (582)

spring tides tides with maximum daily tidal range that occur during the new and full moons (380)

station model a small circle showing the location of a weather station along with a set of symbols and numbers surrounding it that represent weather data (442)

storm surge a local rise in sea level near the shore that is caused by strong winds from a storm, such as a hurricane (377)

strata layers of sedimentary rock that form from the deposition of sediment (91)

stratification the layering of sedimentary rock (94)

stratified drift rock material that has been sorted and deposited in layers by water flowing from the melted ice of a glacier (314)

stratosphere the atmospheric layer above the troposphere (395)

stratus (STRAT uhs) **clouds** clouds that form in layers (426)

streak the color of a mineral in powdered form (65)

stress the amount of force per unit area that is put on a given material (181)

strike-slip fault a fault in which the two fault blocks move past each other horizontally (184)

strip mining a process in which rock and soil are stripped from the Earth's surface to expose the underlying materials to be mined (115)

subduction zone the region where an oceanic plate sinks down into the asthenosphere at a convergent boundary, usually between continental and oceanic plates (178)

sunspot an area on the photosphere of the sun that is cooler than surrounding areas, showing up as a dark spot (523)

supernova the death of a large star by explosion (580)

superposition a principle that states that younger rocks lie above older rocks in undisturbed sequences (137)

surf the area between the breaker zone and the shore (374)

surface current a streamlike movement of water that occurs at or near the surface of the ocean (365, 457)

surface gravity the percentage of your Earth weight you would experience on another planet; the weight you would experience on another planet (539)

S waves the second-fastest type of seismic wave; cannot travel through materials that are completely liquid; also known as shear waves and secondary waves (200)

swells rolling waves that move in a steady procession across the ocean (375)

syncline a trough-shaped fold in sedimentary rock layers (182)

T

tectonic plate a piece of the lithosphere that moves around on top of the asthenosphere (170)

telescope an instrument that collects electromagnetic radiation from the sky and concentrates it for better observation (496)

temperate zone the climate zone between the Tropics and the polar zone (462)

temperature a measure of how hot (or cold) something is (25)

tension the type of stress that occurs when forces act to stretch an object (181)

terrestrial planets the small, dense, rocky planets of the inner solar system (539)

texture the sizes, shapes, and positions of the grains that a rock is made of (86)

theory a unifying explanation for a broad range of hypotheses and observations that have been supported by testing (19)

thermocline a layer of ocean water extending from 300 m below sea level to about 700 m below sea level in which water temperature drops with increased depth faster than it does in other zones of the ocean (333)

thermometer a tool used to measure air temperature (440)

thermosphere the uppermost layer of the atmosphere (396)

thrust the force that accelerates a rocket (600)

thunder the sound that results from the rapid expansion of air along a lightning strike (435)

thunderstorms small, intense weather systems that produce strong winds, heavy rain, lightning, and thunder (434)

tidal bore a body of water that rushes up through a narrow bay, estuary, or river channel during the rise of high tide, causing a very sudden tidal rise (381)

tidal range the difference between levels of ocean water at high tide and low tide (380)

tides daily movements of ocean water that change the level of the ocean's surface (378)

till unsorted rock material that is deposited directly by glacial ice when it melts (315)

topographic map a map that shows the surface features of the Earth (46)

topsoil the top layer of soil that generally contains humus (256)

tornado a small, rotating column of air that has high wind speeds and low central pressure and that touches the ground (436)

trace fossil any naturally preserved evidence of an animal's activity (148)

trade winds the winds that blow from 30° latitude to the equator (404)

transform boundary the boundary between two tectonic plates that are sliding past each other horizontally (179)

transported soil soil that has been blown or washed away from its parent rock (255)

tributary a smaller stream or river that flows into a larger one (272)

tropical zone the warm zone located around the equator (459)

troposphere (TROH poh SFIR) the lowest layer of the atmosphere (395)

trough (trahf) the lowest point of a wave (372)

true north the geographic North Pole (36)

tsunami a wave that forms when a large volume of ocean water is suddenly moved up or down (376)

U

unconformity a surface that represents a missing part of the geologic column (140)

uniformitarianism a principle that states that the same geologic processes shaping the Earth today have been at work throughout Earth's history (134)

upwelling a process in which cold, nutrient-rich water from the deep ocean rises to the surface and replaces warm surface water (371)

U-shaped valley a valley that forms when a glacier erodes a river valley from its original V shape to a U shape (313)

V

vent a hole in the Earth's crust through which magma rises to the surface (224)

volcano a mountain that forms when molten rock, called magma, is forced to the Earth's surface (222)

volume the amount of space that something occupies or the amount of space that something contains (23)

W

water cycle the continuous movement of water from water sources into the air, onto land, into and over the ground, and back to the water sources; a cycle that links all of the Earth's solid, liquid, and gaseous water together (270, 335, 422)

watershed the land drained by a river system, which includes the main river and all of its tributaries (272)

water table an underground boundary where the zone of aeration and the zone of saturation meet (280)

wave height the vertical distance between a wave's crest and its trough (372)

wavelength the distance between two adjacent wave crests or wave troughs (372)

wave period the time between the passage of two wave crests (or troughs) at a fixed point (373)

weather the condition of the atmosphere at a particular time and place (422, 452)

weather forecast a prediction of future weather conditions over the next 3 to 5 days (440)

weathering the breakdown of rock into smaller and smaller pieces by mechanical or chemical means (246)

westerlies wind belts found in both the Northern and Southern Hemispheres between 30° and 60° latitude (405)

whitecap a white, foaming wave with a very steep crest that breaks in the open ocean before the wave gets close to the shore (375)

white dwarf a small, hot star near the end of its life; the leftover center of an old star (578)

wind moving air (402)

wind energy energy in wind (122)

windsock a device used to measure wind direction (441)

wind vane a device used to measure wind direction (441)

Y

year the time required for the Earth to orbit the sun once (482)

Z

zenith an imaginary point in the sky directly above an observer on Earth (491)

Spanish Glossary

A

abrasion/corrosión erosión y desgaste de las superficies de las rocas causadas por otras rocas o partículas de arena (247, 306)

absolute dating/datación absoluta el proceso de establecer la edad de un objeto, como un fósil o una capa de roca, determinando el número de años que ha existido (142)

absolute magnitude/magnitud absoluta el brillo real de una estrella (574)

abyssal plain/llanura abismal la parte ancha y plana de la cuenca de lo más profundo del océano (338)

acid precipitation/precipitación ácida precipitación que contiene ácido por la contaminación del aire (116, 249, 411)

aerial photograph/fotografía aérea fotografía tomada desde el aire (43)

air mass/masa de aire gran masa de aire que tiene temperatura y humedad similares en toda su extensión (430)

air pressure/presión del aire la medida de la fuerza con la que las moléculas de aire empujan una superficie (393)

alluvial fan/abanico aluvial depósitos de aluvión en forma de abanico que se forman en la tierra seca (279)

alluvium/aluvión rocas y tierra depositadas por las corrientes (277)

altitude/altitud la altura de un objeto por encima de la superficie de la tierra; en astronomía, la distancia angular entre un objeto en el cielo y el horizonte (491)

anemometer/anemómetro aparato usado para medir la velocidad del viento (441)

annular eclipse/eclipse anular eclipse de sol durante el cual el anillo exterior del sol se puede ver alrededor de la luna (552)

anticline/anticlinal un pliegue con forma de bol en capas de roca sedimentaria (182)

apparent magnitude/magnitud aparente el brillo que una luz parece tener para un observador (574)

aquifer/acuífero capa rocosa que almacena agua subterránea y que permite que ésta fluya (280)

arete/arista un risco serrado que se forma entre dos o más excavaciones naturales que se insertan en la misma montaña (313)

artesian spring/manantial artesiano un manantial que se forma en donde las grietas ocurren naturalmente en la roca, y el agua bajo presión en el acuífero fluye a través de estas grietas a la superficie (282)

artificial satellite/satélite artificial cualquier objeto hecho por los humanos puesto en órbita alrededor de un cuerpo en el espacio (602)

asteroid/asteroide un cuerpo pequeño y rocoso que da vueltas alrededor del sol (559)

asteroid belt/cinturón de asteroides región del sistema solar ocupado por la mayoría de los asteroides; aproximadamente entre las órbitas de Marte y Júpiter (559)

asthenosphere/astenosfera la capa parcialmente derretida del manto superior en el cual se mueven las placas tectónicas de la litosfera (168)

astronomical unit/unidad astronómica la distancia promedio entre la Tierra y el sol, o aproximadamente 150,000,000 km (516, 538)

astronomy/astronomía el estudio de todos los objetos físicos más allá de la Tierra (9, 482)

atmosphere/atmósfera mezcla de gases que rodea a un planeta como la Tierra (392)

atom/átomo la partícula más pequeña en la que se puede dividir un elemento y aún retener todas las propiedades de aquel elemento (61)

azimuthal projection/proyección en acimut proyección de un mapa que se hace transfiriendo el contenido del globo a un plano (42)

B

barometer/barómetro instrumento que se usa para medir la presión del aire (441)

beach/playa área de la costa formada por materiales depositados por las olas (300)

bedrock/ lecho de roca, la capa de roca bajo la tierra (255)

benthic environment/ambiente bentónico el fondo del océano y todos los organismos que viven en él o sobre él; también se conoce como el medio ambiente del fondo (343)

benthos/bentos organismos que viven en el fondo del océano o sobre él (342)

big bang theory/teoría de la gran explosión la teoría que establece que el universo comenzó con una tremenda explosión (586)

biomass/biomasa materia orgánica, como plantas, madera, y desechos, que contiene energía almacenada (124)

biome/bioma región grande caracterizada por un tipo de clima específico y por las plantas y animales que viven allí (458)

black hole/agujero negro objeto con más de tres masas solares comprimidas en una bola de sólo 10 km de diámetro cuya gravedad es tan fuerte que ni siquiera la luz puede escapar (581)

breaker/rompimiento de olas donde una ola de agua muy grande comienza a rodar hacia abajo, o a romper, al acercarse a la costa (374)

C

caldera/caldera depresión circular que se forma cuando se vacía una cámara de magma y hace que la tierra que está encima se hunda (229)

calendar/calendario sistema para organizar el tiempo; la mayoría de los calendarios organizan el tiempo en una unidad llamada año (482)

cardinal directions/puntos cardinales norte, sur, este, y oeste (35)

cast/vaciado objeto creado cuando los sedimentos llenan un molde y éste se vuelve roca (148)

catastrophism/catastrofismo principio que declara que todos los cambios geológicos ocurren súbitamente (135)

celestial equator/ecuador celeste círculo imaginario creado al extender el ecuador de la Tierra al espacio (492)

channel/cauce la trayectoria de una corriente (273)

chemical weathering/acción geológica atmosférica química la desintegración química de las rocas y los minerales en sustancias nuevas (249)

chromosphere/cromosfera una fina región de la atmósfera solar entre la corona y la fotosfera, demasiado tenue para ser visible, a no ser que haya un eclipse total de sol (519)

cinder cone volcano/volcán de cono de ceniza un volcán pequeño, de paredes abruptas, que se forma de erupciones moderadamente explosivas de material piroclástico (228)

circumpolar stars/estrellas circunpolares la estrellas que se pueden ver durante todo el año y en todo momento durante la noche (492)

cirque/excavación natural una depresión en forma de bol donde el hielo de los glaciares se inserta en las paredes de la montaña (313)

cirrus clouds/cirrus nubes finas, blancas y parecidas al plumón que se encuentran a grandes altitudes (427)

cleavage/plano de fractura la tendencia de un mineral de romperse a lo largo de superficies planas (65)

climate/clima las condiciones promedio del tiempo en un área durante un período largo (452)

cloud/nube colección de millones de gotitas de agua o cristales de hielo diminutos (426)

coal/carbón combustible fósil sólido que se forma de manera subterránea de materiales vegetales enterrados y descompuestos (112)

comet/cometa un pequeño cuerpo de hielo y roca cósmica poco compacta que despide gases y polvo en forma de cola al pasar cerca del sol (557)

composite volcano/volcán mixto volcán formado por capas alternadas de lava y material piroclástico; también conocido como estratovolcano (228)

composition/composición lo que forma la roca; describe ya sea los minerales o los elementos presentes (85)

compound/compuesto sustancia pura formada por dos o más elementos que se han unido o enlazado químicamente (61)

compression/compresión la clase de presión que ocurre cuando un objeto es compactado (181)

condensation/condensación el cambio de estado de gas a líquido (335, 425)

conduction/conducción la transferencia de calor de un material a otro por contacto directo; la conducción también puede ocurrir dentro de una sustancia (399)

conic projection/proyección cónica proyección de un mapa que se hace al transferir los contenidos del globo a un cono (42)

constellation/constelación sección del cielo que contiene una posición de las estrellas que puede ser reconocida (489)

continental drift/deriva continental la teoría de que los continentes pueden separarse uno de otro y que lo han hecho en el pasado (173)

continental margin/margen continental la porción de la superficie de la Tierra bajo el océano formada por la corteza continental (338)

continental rise/elevación continental la base de la pendiente continental (338)

continental shelf/cuesta continental la parte más llana del margen continental (338)

continental slope/pendiente continental la parte más escarpada del margen continental (338)

contour interval/intervalo de las curvas de nivel la diferencia en elevación entre una línea de contorno y la siguiente (47)

contour lines/curvas de nivel líneas que conectan puntos de igual elevación (46)

convection/convección la transferencia de calor por la circulación o el movimiento de un líquido o un gas (399)

convective zone/zona de convección región del sol en que los gases circulan en corrientes convectivas, llevando la energía del sol a la superficie (519)

convergent boundary/límite convergente el límite entre dos placas tectónicas en colisión (178)

coprolites/coprolito excremento o bosta de animales, preservados (148)

core/núcleo la parte central, esférica, de la tierra bajo el manto (167, 525); también, el centro del sol donde se produce la energía solar (519)

Coriolis effect/efecto de Coriolis la manera en que se curva de una línea recta la trayectoria de los objetos en movimiento a causa de la rotación de la Tierra (366, 403)

corona/corona la atmósfera exterior del sol, que se puede extender hacia afuera en una distancia igual a 10 a 12 veces el diámetro del sol (519)

cosmic background radiation/radiación cósmica de fondo radiación que dejó la Gran Explosión, que llena todo el espacio (587)

cosmology/cosmología el estudio del origen y el futuro del universo (586)

crater/cráter un pozo con forma de embudo alrededor de la chimenea central de un volcán (229)

creep/arrastre movimiento muy lento de material cuesta abajo (319)

crest/cresta el punto más alto de una ola (372)

crevasse/grieta quebradura enorme que se forma donde un glaciar se acelera o fluye sobre una altura (311)

crust/corteza la capa fina y exterior de la Tierra, o la capa superior de la litosfera (166, 525)

crystal/cristal la forma sólida y geométrica de un mineral, producida por un modelo de átomos que se repite (61)

cumulus clouds/cúmulos nubes blancas y algodonosas que tienden a tener la superficie inferior plana (426)

D

day/día el tiempo que lleva para que la Tierra rote una vez sobre su eje (482)

deciduous/caducifolio describe a los árboles que pierden las hojas cuando comienza a hacer frío (462)

declination/declinación medida de la posición de un objeto al norte o al sur del ecuador celeste (492)

deep current/corriente submarina movimiento del agua del océano muy por debajo de la superficie (368)

deep-ocean basin/cuenca profunda del océano la porción de la superficie de la tierra bajo el océano que está formada por la corteza oceánica (338)

deflation/deflación cuando el viento levanta y traslada el sedimento fino (305)

deformation/deformación el cambio en la forma de las rocas en respuesta al estrés (197)

delta/delta depósito de aluvión en forma de abanico en la desembocadura de una corriente de agua, donde la corriente fluye en una gran masa de agua (278)

density/densidad la cantidad de materia en un espacio dado; masa por unidad de volumen (66)

deposition/depósito proceso por el cual el material se deposita o se asienta (277)

desalination/desalinización proceso de evaporación del agua de mar para que el agua y la sal se separen (349)

dew point/punto de rocío la temperatura a la cual el aire debe enfriarse para estar completamente saturado (425)

differential weathering/diferencial de acción geológica atmosférica proceso por el cual las rocas más blandas y menos resistentes a los elementos se desintegran, mientras que las rocas más resistentes perduran (252)

discharge/descarga el volumen de agua que transporta una corriente (273)

divergent boundary/límite divergente el límite entre dos placas tectónicas que se separan (179)

divide/cresta divisoria área de tierras más altas que separa cuencas de drenaje (272)

drainage basin/cuenca de drenaje la tierra drenada por un sistema fluvial que incluye el río principal y todos sus afluentes (272)

dune/duna un montículo de arena depositada por el viento (306)

E

eclipse/eclipse suceso en el que la sombra de un cuerpo celeste se proyecta sobre otro (552)

ecliptic/eclíptico el trayecto aparente del sol a través de la esfera celeste (492)

ecosystem/ecosistema comunidad de organismos y su medio ambiente que no está vivo (10)

elastic rebound/rebote elástico el regreso súbito a su forma original de las rocas deformadas elásticamente (197)

electromagnetic spectrum/espectro electromagnético todas las longitudes de onda de la radiación electromagnética (499)

element/elemento sustancia pura que no puede separarse o dividirse en sustancias simples por procemientos químicos comunes (60)

elevation/altitud la altura de un objeto sobre el nivel del mar, y la altura de los accidentes geográficos sobre el nivel del mar (46, 456)

ellipse/elipse curva cerrada en que la suma de las distancias del borde de la curva a dos puntos dentro de la elipse son siempre iguales (516)

elliptical galaxy/galaxia elíptica galaxia esférica o alargada con un centro brillante y muy poco polvo y gas (583)

El Niño/El Niño cambio periódico en la situación de aguas superficiales cálidas y frías en el Océano Pacífico (371)

energy resource/recurso energético recurso natural que los humanos usan para producir energía (111)

eon/eón la división más grande del tiempo geológico (153)

epicenter/epicentro lugar en la superficie de la Tierra directamente sobre el punto donde comienza un terremoto (202)

epoch/época la cuarta división más grande del tiempo geológico (153)

equator/ecuador círculo a medio camino entre los polos, que divide la Tierra en los hemisferios norte y sur (37)

era/era la segunda división más grande del tiempo geológico (153)

erosion/erosión cuando el viento, el agua, o el hielo levantan y transportan materiales (260, 270)

escape velocity/velocidad de escape la velocidad y dirección en que debe viajar un cohete para separarse por completo del arrastre gravitacional de un planeta (601)

evaporation/evaporación el cambio de estado de líquido a vapor (335)

evergreens/perennifolio árboles que conservan sus hojas todo el año (462)

extrusive/extrusivo el tipo de roca ígnea que se forma cuando la lava o el material piroclástico se enfría y se solidifica sobre la corteza terrestre (90)

F

fault/falla grieta en la corteza terrestre a lo largo de la cual los bloques de corteza se deslizan con respecto a otros bloques; la falla se debe a las fuerzas tectónicas (183, 196)

fault block/bloque de falla bloque de corteza terrestre a un lado de una falla (183)

fault-block mountain/montaña de bloque de falla montaña que se forma cuando las fallas hacen que grandes bloques de corteza terrestre se hundan con respecto a otros bloques (186)

felsic/félsica describe a las rocas ígneas de color relativamente claro, y livianas, ricas en silicio, aluminio, sodio, y potasio (88)

flood plain/llanura aluvial área a lo largo de un río formada por los sedimentos depositados por las inundaciones (279)

focus/foco punto dentro de la Tierra donde comienza un terremoto (202)

folded mountain/montaña de plegamiento montaña que se forma cuando las capas de roca se comprimen y son empujadas hacia arriba (185)

folding/plegamiento cuando las capas rocosas se doblan por presiones en la corteza terrestre (182)

foliated/foliada la textura de las rocas metamórficas en las que los granos minerales están alineados como las páginas de un libro (98)

footwall/pared baja el bloque de falla que está debajo de una falla (183)

fossil/fósil cualquier evidencia de vida que se ha preservado naturalmente (146)

fossil fuel/combustible fósil recurso no renovable de energía que se forma en la corteza terrestre a través de millones de años de los restos enterrados de organismos que una vez estuvieron vivos (111)

fracture/fractura la tendencia de un mineral a quebrarse a lo largo de superficies curvas o irregulares (65)

front/frente la línea divisoria que se forma entre dos masas de aire diferentes (432)

G

galaxy/galaxia agrupación grande de estrellas en el espacio (582)

gap hypothesis/hipótesis de brecha establece que las secciones de fallas activas que han tenido relativamente pocos terremotos probablemente van a ser los lugares donde ocurran terremotos fuertes en el futuro (207)

gas giants/gigantes de gases planetas grandes y gaseosos en el sistema solar (544)

gasohol/gasohol mezcla de gasolina y alcohol que se quema como combustible (124)

geologic column/columna estratigráfica secuencia ideal de capas rocosas que contienen todos los fósiles y formaciones rocosas conocidos en la Tierra, ordenados del más antiguo al más moderno (138)

geologic time scale/escala de tiempo geológico escala que divide la historia de 4.6 millones de millones de años de la Tierra en distintos intervalos de tiempo (152)

geology/geología el estudio de la Tierra sólida (6)

geosynchronous orbit/órbita geosíncrona órbita en la que viaja un satélite a una velocidad que iguala exactamente a la velocidad de rotación de la Tierra, manteniendo en todo momento al satélite en posición sobre el mismo punto de la Tierra (603)

geothermal energy/energía geotérmica energía producida por el calor dentro de la corteza terrestre (125)

Spanish Glossary

glacial drift/sedimento glaciar todo el material transportado y depositado por los glaciares (314)

glacier/glaciar enorme masa de hielo en movimiento (309)

global warming/calentamiento global un aumento en las temperaturas promedio mundiales (18, 400, 470)

globular cluster/agrupación globular grupo de estrellas antiguas que parece una bola de estrellas (584)

gradient/declive medida del cambio en sobre una cierta distancia (273)

greenhouse effect/efecto invernadero el proceso natural de calentamiento de un planeta, como la Tierra, por el que los gases en la atmósfera atrapan el calor (400, 470, 540)

ground water/agua subterránea agua almacenada dentro de la roca bajo la superficie de la Tierra (280)

H

half-life/vida media para una muestra radioactiva específica, el tiempo que lleva para que una mitad de la muestra se desintegre (143)

hanging valley/valle colgante pequeño valle glaciar que se une al valle principal más profundo (313)

hanging wall/pared colgante el bloque de falla que está sobre una falla (183)

hardness/dureza la resistencia de un mineral a ser raspado (66)

horizon/horizonte la línea donde el cielo y la Tierra parecen unirse (491)

horn/cuerno pico agudo, con forma de pirámide, que se forma cuando tres o más excavaciones naturales erosionan una montaña (313)

hot spot/punto caliente lugar en la superficie de la Tierra que está directamente sobre la columna magma que sube, llamada columna del manto (233)

H-R diagram/diagrama H-R diagrama Herzprung-Russell; gráfica que muestra la relación entre la temperatura de la superficie de una estrella y su magnitud absoluta (577)

humidity/humedad la cantidad de vapor de agua o de condensación en el aire (423)

humus/humus partículas muy pequeñas de materiales descompuestos de plantas y animales en la tierra (255)

hurricane/huracán gran sistema climático tropical en rotación, con viento a velocidades de por lo menos 119 km/h (437)

hydroelectric energy/energía hidroeléctrica electricidad producida por caídas de agua (123)

hypothesis/hipótesis posible explicación o respuesta a una pregunta (14)

I

ice age/era glacial período en que el hielo se junta en latitudes altas y se mueve hacia las latitudes bajas (467)

iceberg/témpano gran trozo de hielo que se separa de una plataforma de hielo y se desliza al océano (310)

ice wedging/témpano de hielo el proceso de desgaste mecánico en que el agua se filtra en grietas en la roca, se congela, y luego se expande, ensanchando las grietas (246)

igneous rock/roca ígnea roca que se forma al enfriarse el magma (84)

index contour/índice de las curvas de nivel una línea de contorno oscura y más gruesa que generalmente se da cada quinta línea y está marcada por la elevación (47)

index fossil/fósil indicador fósil de un organismo que vivió durante un período relativamente corto y bien definido; se usa para fechar las capas de roca en que se encontró (150)

inner core/núcleo interior el centro de la tierra, que es sólido y denso (169)

intrusive/intrusiva tipo de roca ígnea que se forma cuando el magma se enfría y se solidifica bajo la superficie de la Tierra (89)

irregular galaxy/galaxia irregular galaxia que no entra en ninguna otra categoría; que tiene una forma irregular (583)

isobars/isobaras líneas que conectan puntos con igual presión del aire (443)

isotopes/isótopos átomos del mismo elemento que tienen igual número de protones pero diferentes números de neutrones (142)

J

jet streams/corrientes en chorro cinturones angostos de vientos de alta velocidad que soplan en la troposfera superior y en la estratosfera inferior (406)

K

Kuiper Belt/Cinturón de Kuiper la región del sistema solar fuera de la órbita de Neptuno, ocupada por cuerpos pequeños, helados, y parecidos a los cometas (558)

L

landslide/desprendimiento de tierras movimiento cuesta abajo, súbito, de una gran cantidad de material (317)

latitude/latitud distancia al norte o al sur del ecuador; se mide en grados (37, 453)

lava/lava magma que fluye a la superficie de la Tierra (84, 222)

leaching/lixiviación proceso por el que el agua de lluvia se disuelve y se lleva los materiales y los nutrientes en la superficie de la tierra (256)

leap year/año bisiesto año en el que se agrega un día al calendario (483)

light-minute/minuto-luz unidad de longitud igual a la distancia que recorre la luz en el espacio en un minuto, o sea 18,000,000 km (538)

lightning/rayo la descarga eléctrica grande que ocurre entre dos superficies con cargas opuestas (435)

light-year/año luz unidad de longitud igual a la distancia que recorre la luz a través del espacio en un año (493, 575)

lithosphere/litosfera la capa rígida, exterior de la Tierra, que consiste de la corteza y de la capa rígida superior del manto (168)

load/carga los materiales que lleva una corriente de agua (274)

loess/loess los depósitos densos de sedimentos de grano fino arrastrados por el viento (308)

longitude/longitud la distancia al este o al oeste del primer meridiano; se mide en grados (38)

longshore current/deriva litoral el movimiento del agua cerca de la costa y paralelo a ella (301)

low Earth orbit/órbita terrestre baja una órbita situada a unos pocos cientos de kilómetros sobre la superficie de la Tierra (603)

lunar eclipse/eclipse de luna fenomeno durante el cual la sombra de la Tierra se proyecta sobre la superficie de la luna (552)

luster/brillo la manera en que la superficie de un mineral refleja la luz (64)

M

mafic/máfica describe rocas ígneas pesadas y de color relativamente oscuro que son ricas en hierro, magnesio, y calcio (88)

magma/magma el líquido caliente que se forma cuando la roca se derrite total o parcialmente; puede incluir cristales minerales (83)

magnetic declination/desviación magnética el ángulo de corrección para la diferencia entre el norte geográfico y el norte magnético (36)

magnetic reversal/inversión magnética proceso por el cual cambian de lugar los polos magnéticos del norte y del sur de la Tierra (176)

main sequence/secuencia principal el patrón diagonal de estrellas en el diagrama H-R (578)

mantle/manto capa de la Tierra entre la corteza y el centro (167, 525)

map/mapa modelo o representación de la superficie de la Tierra (34)

mass/masa la cantidad de materia de que está hecho algo; su valor no cambia con la posición del objeto (24)

mass movement/movimiento de masa el movimiento cuesta abajo de cualquier material (316)

mechanical weathering/acción geológica atmosférica mecánica la desintegración de las rocas a trozos más pequeños por medios físicos (246)

Mercator projection/proyección de Mercator mapa de proyección que resulta cuando los contenidos del globo se transfieren a un cilindro (41)

mesosphere/mesosfera literalmente, la "esfera media" – la parte inferior, rígida, del manto entre la astenosfera y el centro exterior (169); también es la capa más fría de la atmósfera (396)

metamorphic rock/roca metamórfica roca que se forma cuando la textura o la composición de la roca pre-existente cambia a causa del calor o la presión (84)

meteor/meteoro rayo de luz causado cuando el polvo de un meteoroide o de un cometa se quema en la atmósfera de la Tierra antes de llegar al suelo (560)

meteorite/meteorito un meteoroide que llega a la superficie de la Tierra sin haberse consumido por completo (560)

meteoroid/meteoroide un cuerpo rocoso, muy pequeño, que da vueltas alrededor del sol (560)

meteorology/meteorología el estudio de la totalidad de la atmósfera (8)

meter/metro la unidad básica de longitud en el sistema SI (23)

microclimate/microclima una pequeña región con características climáticas únicas (466)

mid-ocean ridge/dorsal intra-oceánica una larga cadena de montañas que se forma en el fondo del océano, donde se separan las placas tectónicas; usualmente se extiende a lo largo del centro de las cuencas oceánicas (175, 339)

mineral/mineral sólido inorgánico con estructura cristalina que se forma naturalmente (60)

model/modelo representación de un objeto o sistema (19)

Moho/Moho lugar dentro de la Tierra donde la velocidad de las ondas sísmicas aumenta en gran forma; marca el límite entre la corteza terrestre y el manto (211)

mold/molde cavidad en el suelo o la roca donde estaba enterrado un animal o una planta (148)

monocline/monoclinal pliegue en las capas de roca sedimentaria en que las capas son horizontales a ambos lados del pliegue (182)

month/mes aproximadamente, la cantidad de tiempo en que la luna completa una vez la órbita de la Tierra (482)

moon/luna el satélite natural de un planeta (549)

mudflow/alud de fango el movimiento rápido de una gran masa de roca o barro y tierra mezclado con una gran cantidad de agua, que fluye cuesta abajo (318)

N

NASA/NASA Administración Nacional de Aeronáutica y del Espacio; fundada para combinar todos los equipos separados dedicados al desarrollo de cohetes en los Estados Unidos (599)

natural gas/gas natural un combustible fósil gaseoso (112)

natural resource/recurso natural cualquier sustancia natural; organismo, o forma de energía que usan los seres vivientes (108)

neap tides/mareas muertas mareas con rangos diarios mínimos que ocurren durante la luna creciente y la luna menguante (380)

nebula/nebulosa una gran nube de polvo y gas en el espacio interestelar; el lugar donde se forman las estrellas (510, 584)

nekton/necton los organismos en el océano que nadan en forma independiente (342)

neutron star/estrella de neutrón estrella en la que todas las partículas se han vuelto neutrones; restos de una supernova comprimida (581)

nonfoliated/no foliada la textura de la roca metamórfica en la que los granos de mineral no muestran ninguna alineación (98)

nonpoint-source pollution/polución con punto de orígen contaminación que viene de muchas fuentes y cuyo origen no se puede trazar a puntos específicos (285, 352)

nonrenewable resource/recurso no renovable un recurso natural que no se puede remplazar, o que puede remplazarse solamente después de miles o millones de años (109)

nonsilicate mineral/mineral no silíceo mineral que no contiene compuestos de silicio y oxígeno (63)

normal fault/falla normal falla en la que la pared colgante se mueve hacia abajo en relación con la pared baja (183)

nuclear energy/energía nuclear forma de energía asociada con los cambios en el núcleo de un átomo; un recurso energético alternativo (118)

nuclear fusion/fusión nuclear proceso por el cual dos o más núcleos con masas pequeñas se unen, o se fusionan, para formar un núcleo más grande y masivo, y para producir energía (521)

O

observation/observación usar cualquiera de los sentidos para reunir información (14)

oceanography/oceanografía el estudio del océano (7)

ocean trench/zanja oceánica una fractura aparentemente sin fondo en la cuenca profunda del océano, que se forma cuando una placa oceánica se ve forzada a deslizarse bajo una placa continental u otra placa oceánica (339)

Oort cloud/nube Oort región esférica del espacio que rodea el sistema solar en la que los cometas distantes dan vuelta alrededor del sol (558)

open cluster/agrupación abierta grupo de estrellas que en general están situadas a lo largo del disco espiral de una galaxia (584)

orbit/órbita la trayectoria elíptica seguida por un cuerpo al viajar alrededor de otro cuerpo en el espacio; el mismo movimiento (515)

orbital velocity/velocidad orbital la velocidad y dirección en que debe viajar un cohete para permanecer en órbita alrededor de la Tierra (601)

ore/mena un depósito de minerales lo suficientemente grande y puro para que se explote con ganancia (70)

outer core/núcleo exterior la capa líquida del centro de la Tierra situada bajo el manto, que envuelve el interior del centro (169)

oxidation/oxidación una reacción química en la cual un elemento se combina con oxígeno para formar un óxido (251)

ozone/ozono molécula de gas formada por tres átomos de oxígeno y que absorbe la radiación ultravioleta del sol (395)

P

parallax/paralaje cambio aparente en la posición de un objeto cuando se mira desde posiciones diferentes (575)

parent rock/ roca madre, la roca que da origen a la tierra (255)

pelagic environment/ambiente pelágico el volumen completo de agua en el océano y los organismos marinos que viven sobre el fondo del océano; también se conoce como el medio ambiente marino (345)

period/período la tercera divisió del tiempo geológico (153)

period of revolution/período de translación el tiempo que lleva para que un cuerpo celeste complete una órbita, o revolución, alrededor de otro cuerpo en el espacio (515, 539)

period of rotation/período de rotación el tiempo que lleva para que un ojeto rote una vuelta completa (539)

permeability/permeabilidad la capacidad de la roca de dejar pasar el agua a través de sí misma (280)

permineralization/permineralización proceso en que los minerales llenan los espacios de los poros en los tejidos de un organismo (146)

petrification/petrificación proceso en el que los tejidos de un organismo son completamente remplazados por minerales (146)

petroleum/petróleo crudo mezcla aceitosa de compuestos orgánicos inflamables de los que se separan los combustibles fósiles líquidos y otros productos (111)

phases/fases las diferentes maneras en que aparece la luna según la cantidad de luz solar que recibe el lado de la luna que se enfrenta a la Tierra; los resultados de las posiciones relativas cambiantes de la luna, la Tierra y el sol (551)

photosphere/fotosfera la capa del sol al punto en que los gases se vuelven lo suficientemente densos para ser visibles; la superficie del sol (519)

planetesimal/planetesimal los pequeñísimos bloques que constituyen los planetas, que se forman al juntarse y crecer las partículas de polvo (512)

plankton/plancton organismos microscópicos que flotan en la superficie del océano o cerca de ella (342)

plate tectonics/tectónica de placas la teoría de que la litosfera de la Tierra está dividida en placas tectónicas que se mueven sobre la astenosfera (177)

point-source pollution/polución con punto de orígen contaminación que viene de una fuente en un área en particular (285)

polar easterlies/vientos polares del este cinturones de viento que se extienden desde los polos a 60 grados de latitud en ambos hemisferios (405)

polar zone/zona polar las zonas climáticas más al norte y más al sur (464)

porosity/porosidad la cantidad de espacio abierto entre las partículas individuales de roca (280)

precipitation/precipitación agua sólida o líquida que cae del aire a la Tierra (335, 428)

prevailing winds/vientos dominantes vientos que soplan principalmente de una dirección (455)

primary pollutants/contaminantes primarios contaminantes puestos en el aire por la actividad natural o de los humanos (409)

prime meridian/primer meridiano la línea de longitud que pasa a través de Greenwich, en Inglaterra; representa 0 grados de longitud (38)

prograde rotation/rotación prógrada la rotación contraria al movimiento de las agujas del reloj de un planeta o luna, observado desde arriba del polo norte de ese planeta (540)

psychrometer/psicrómetro instrumento usado para medir la humedad relativa (424)

pulsar/púlsar estrella de neutrón que rota y emite rápidos pulsos de luz (581)

P waves/ondas P el tipo más rápido de onda sísmica; puede pasar a través de sólidos, líquidos, y gases; también se las llama ondas de presión y ondas primarias (200)

pyroclastic material/material piroclástico fragmentos de roca creados por erupciones volcánicas explosivas (225)

Q

quasar/cuásar un objeto "casi estelar"; una fuente estelar de luz que está extremadamente alejada; una de las fuentes de energía más poderosas en el universo (585)

R

radiation/radiación energía que se transfiere en forma de ondas electromagnéticas, como la luz visible o las ondas infrarrojas (398)

radiative zone/zona radiactiva una región muy densa del sol en la que los átomos estan comprimidos tan cerca uno de otro que puede llevar millones de años para que la luz la atraviese (519)

radioactive decay/desintegración radioactiva proceso en que los isótopos radioactivos tienden a desintegrarse en isótopos estables de otros elementos (142)

radiometric dating/datación radiométrica determinar la edad absoluta de una muestra basándose en la proporción de material original a material hijo (143)

recharge zone/zona de recarga la superficie en la tierra en que el agua entra a un acuífero (281)

reclamation/recuperación proceso de volver la tierra a su condición original luego de haber completado una explotación minera (71)

recycling/reciclaje proceso por el cual los materiales usados o desechados se procesan para volver a ser usados (110)

red giant/gigante roja una estrella que se expande y que se enfría una vez que se le acaba el combustible hidrógeno (579)

reference point/punto de referencia un lugar fijo en la superficie de la Tierra desde donde se pueden describir la dirección y la posición (35)

reflecting telescope/telescopio de reflexión telescopio que usa espejos curvos para juntar y enfocar la luz (497)

refracting telescope/telescopio de refracción telescopio que usa una serie de lentes para juntar y enfocar la luz (497)

relative dating/datación relativa determinar si un objeto o un suceso es más antiguo o más moderno que otros objetos o sucesos (137)

relative humidity/humedad relativa la cantidad de humedad que contiene el aire comparada con la cantidad máxima que puede contener a una temperatura específica (423)

relief/relieve la diferencia en elevación entre los puntos más altos y más bajos de un área de la que se está trazando un mapa (47)

remote sensing/reconocimiento remoto juntar información sobre algo sin estar cerca en realidad (43)

renewable resource/recurso renovable recurso natural que puede usarse y remplazarse en un período de tiempo relativamente corto (109)

residual soil/tierra residual la tierra que permanece sobre la capa de roca de la que se formó (255)

retrograde orbit/órbita retrógrada la revolución en el sentido de las agujas del reloj de un satélite alrededor de un planeta, observada de arriba del polo norte del planeta (556)

retrograde rotation/rotación retrógrada la rotación en el sentido de las agujas del reloj de un planeta o luna, observada de arriba del polo norte del planeta o de la luna (540)

reverse fault/falla inversa falla en que la pared colgante se mueve hacia arriba con respecto a la pared baja (183)

revolution/translación el movimiento elíptico de un cuerpo celeste al hacer órbita alrededor de otro cuerpo en el espacio (515, 539)

rift/falla profunda fractura que se forma entre las placas tectónicas al separarse éstas (232)

rift valley/valle de grietas valle que se forma en una zona de fisura entre placas tectónicas que se separan (339)

right ascension/ascensión recta medida de la distancia al este de un objeto desde el punto en el que aparece el sol el primer día de primavera (492)

rock/roca una mezcla sólida de cristales de un mineral o más, o de otros materiales (80)

rock cycle/ciclo de la roca el proceso por el que un tipo de roca se convierte en otro tipo de roca (82)

rocket/cohete máquina que usa el escape de gas para moverse (598)

rock fall/desprendimiento de rocas grupo de rocas que se desprenden y caen por una cuesta empinada (317)

rotation/rotación el movimiento giratorio de un cuerpo sobre su eje (515, 539)

S

salinity/salinidad la medida de la cantidad de sales y otros sólidos disueltos en una cantidad de líquido dada (332)

saltation/saltación movimiento de partículas del tamaño de granos de arena por una acción de rebote en la dirección en que sopla el viento (304)

satellite/satélite un cuerpo natural o artificial que da vueltas alrededor de un planeta (549)

scientific method/método científico serie de pasos que usan los científicos para encontrar respuestas para preguntas y soluciones para problemas (13)

sea-floor spreading/expansión de los fondos oceánicos el proceso por el que se forman nuevas litosferas oceánicas en las cordilleras en el medio del océano cuando los materiales más antiguos se separan de las cordilleras (175)

seamount/monte de mar montaña individual formada por materiales volcánicos en la llanura abisal (339)

secondary pollutants/contaminantes secundarios contaminantes que se forman por reacciones químicas que ocurren cuando los contaminantes primarios entran en contacto con sustancias que ocurren naturalmente, como el vapor de agua (409)

sedimentary rock/roca sedimentaria roca que se forma cuando los sedimentos se comprimen y se cementan (84)

seismic gap/brecha sísmica área a lo largo de una falla donde han ocurrido relativamente pocos terremotos (207)

seismic waves/ondas sísmicas ondas de energía que se trasladan a través de la Tierra (200)

seismogram/sismograma trazado del movimiento de un terremoto creado por un sismógrafo (202)

seismograph/sismógrafo instrumento colocado en la superficie de la tierra o cerca de ella, que registra las ondas sísmicas (202)

seismology/sismología el estudio de los terremotos (196)

septic tank/tanque séptico un tanque grande, subterráneo, que junta y limpia las aguas servidas de una casa (287)

sewage treatment plant/planta de tratamiento de aguas de cloaca fábrica que limpia materiales de desecho del agua que viene de las cloacas o los caños (286)

shadow zone/zona de sombra área en la superficie de la Tierra donde no se pueden detectar ondas sísmicas directas de un terremoto dado (211)

shield volcano/volcán en escudo un volcán grande, con cuestas poco empinadas, que se forma con erupciones no explosivas repetidas de lava (228)

shoreline/zona litoral el límite entre la costa y una masa de agua (298)

silica/sílice compuesto de átomos de silicio y oxígeno (224)

silicate mineral/mineral silíceo mineral que contiene una combinación de los elementos silicio y oxígeno (62)

smog/smog niebla fotoquímica producida por la reacción de la luz solar y los contaminantes en el aire (117)

soil/suelo mezcla suelta de pequeños fragmentos de minerales y materia orgánica (255)

soil conservation/conservación del suelo los varios métodos por los cuales los humanos cuidan la tierra (259)

solar eclipse/eclipse solar incidente en el cual la sombra de la luna se proyecta sobre la superficie de la Tierra (552)

solar energy/energía solar energía del sol (119)

solar nebula/nebulosa solar nébula que se formó dentro del sistema solar (511)

solar system/sistema solar sistema compuesto del sol (una estrella) y de planetas y otros cuerpos celestes que se trasladan alrededor del sol (510)

space probe/sonda espacial vehículo que lleva instrumentos científicos a los planetas o a otros cuerpos en el espacio (606)

space shuttle/transbordador espacial vehículo que puede volverse a usar que despega como un cohete y aterriza como un avión (613)

space station/estación espacial una plataforma que está en órbita por un tiempo largo, de la que se pueden lanzar otros vehículos o donde se puede hacer investigación científica (614)

specific gravity/gravedad específica la razón de la densidad de un objeto a la densidad del agua (66)

spectrum/espectro el arco iris de colores que se produce cuando la luz blanca pasa a través de un prisma o espectrógrafo (570)

spiral galaxy/galaxia espiral galaxia con un bulto en el centro y brazos espirales muy distintivos (582)

spring tides/aguas vivas mareas con rangos diarios máximos que ocurren durante la luna nueva y la luna llena (380)

station model/modelo de estación un pequeño círculo que muestra la posición de una estación meteorológica junto con un grupo de símbolos y números que lo rodean que representan información sobre el tiempo (442)

storm surge/oleada de tormenta una subida local en el nivel del mar cerca de la costa causada por los vientos fuertes de una tormenta, como un huracán (377)

strata/estratos capas de roca sedimentaria que se forman del depósito de sedimentos (91)

stratification/estratificación las capas de roca sedimentaria que se superponen (94)

stratified drift/sedimento estratificado material rocoso que ha sido dividido y depositado en capas por el agua que fluye del hielo derretido de un glaciar (314)

stratosphere/estratosfera la capa atmosférica sobre la troposfera (395)

stratus clouds/nubes estratos nubes que se forman en capas (426)

streak/color de la raya el color de un mineral en polvo (65)

stress/exfuerzo la cantidad de fuerza por unidad de área que se ejerce sobre un material dado (181)

strike-slip fault/falla de desplazamiento horizontal falla en la que los dos bloques de falla se mueven más allá uno de otro en forma horizontal (184)

strip mining/minería a cielo abierto proceso en que la roca y la tierra se quitan de la superficie de la Tierra para exponer los materiales que están abajo que van a ser extraídos (115)

subduction zone/zona de subducción la región donde una placa oceánica se hunde en la astenosfera en un límite convergente, usualmente entre las placas continentales y las oceánicas (178)

sunspot/mancha solar área en la fotosfera del sol que es más fría que las áreas que la rodean, y parece una mancha oscura (523)

supernova/supernova la muerte de una estrella grande causada por una explosión (580)

superposition/superposición principio que establece que las rocas más nuevas descansan sobre rocas más antiguas en secuencias inalteradas (137)

surf/oleaje área entre la rompiente y la costa (374)

surface current/corriente superficial movimiento de agua parecido a la corriente que ocurre en la superficie del océano o cerca de ella (365, 457)

surface gravity/gravedad de la superficie el porcentaje de tu peso en la Tierra que experimentarías en otro planeta; el peso que experimentarías en otro planeta (539)

S waves/ondas S el tipo de onda sísmica que está en segundo lugar en cuanto a velocidad; no puede trasladarse a través de materiales completamente líquidos; también conocidas como ondas cortantes y ondas secundarias (200)

swells/marejada olas ondulantes que se mueven en una procesión estable a través del océano (375)

syncline/sinclinal un pliegue con forma de hondonada en las capas de roca sedimentaria (182)

T

tectonic plate/tectónica de placas un trozo de la litosfera que se mueve sobre la astenosfera (170)

telescope/telescopio instrumento que junta radiación electromagnética del cielo y la concentra para mejor observación (496)

temperate zone/zona templada la zona climática entre los trópicos y la zona polar (462)

temperature/temperatura medida de cuán caliente o frío es algo (25)

tension/tensión la clase de presión que ocurre cuando las fuerzas actúan para estirar un objeto (181)

terrestrial planets/planetas terrestres los planetas pequeños, densos y rocosos del interior del sistema solar (539)

texture/textura el tamaño, la forma y la posición de los granos que forman la roca (86)

theory/teoría explicación unificadora para una variedad de hipótesis y observaciones que han sido apoyadas con la experimentación (19)

thermocline/termoclino una capa de agua del océano que se extiende entre 300 m y aproximadamente 700 m bajo el nivel del mar en que la temperatura del agua baja con más rapidez al aumentar la profundidad de lo que lo hace en otras zonas del océano (333)

thermometer/termómetro instrumento usado para medir la temperatura del aire (440)

thermosphere/termosfera la capa superior de la atmosfera (396)

thrust/propulsión la fuerza que acelera un cohete (600)

thunder/trueno el sonido que resulta de la rápida expansión de aire a lo largo de un rayo (435)

thunderstorms/tormentas sistemas de tormentas pequeños e intensos que producen vientos fuertes, lluvia torrencial, relámpagos, y truenos (434)

tidal bore/oleada masa de agua que avanza a través de una bahía, un estuario o canal de río pequeños durante la subida de la marea alta, causando una subida muy súbita de la marea (381)

tidal range/rango de marea la diferencia entre los niveles del agua del océano durante la marea alta y la marea baja (380)

tides/mareas movimientos diarios del agua del océano que cambian el nivel de la superficie (378)

till/sedimento desordenado materia rocosa no separada, depositada directamente por el hielo glacial cuando se derrite (315)

topographic map/plano topográfico mapa que muestra los accidentes geográficos de la Tierra (46)

topsoil/capa superior del suelo la capa exterior de tierra que generalmente contiene el humus (256)

tornado/tornado una columna de aire pequeña y rotativa que tiene vientos de alta velocidad y presión central baja y que toca la tierra (436)

trace fossil/fósil vestigio cualquier evidencia de la actividad de un animal que se ha preservado naturalmente (148)

trade winds/vientos alisios los vientos que soplan entre los 30 grados de latitud y el ecuador (404)

transform boundary/límite transformante el límite entre dos placas tectónicas que se deslizan horizontalmente (179)

transported soil/tierra transportada la tierra que ha sido arrastrada por viento o por agua lejos de su roca original (255)

tributary/tributario una corriente o un río más pequeño que desemboca en uno más grande (272)

tropical zone/zona tropical la zona cálida situada alrededor del ecuador (459)

troposphere/troposfera la capa más baja de la atmósfera (395)

trough/seno el punto más bajo de una ola (372)

true north/norte real el Polo Norte geográfico (36)

tsunami/tsunami una ola que se forma cuando un gran volumen de agua del océano súbitamente se mueve hacia abajo o hacia arriba (376)

U

unconformity/disconformidad superficie que representa una parte de la columna geologica que falta en una secuencia de capas rocosas (140)

uniformitarianism/uniformismo principio que establece que los mismos procesos geológicos que hoy en día dan forma a la Tierra han estado presentes a través de la historia de la Tierra (134)

upwelling/corriente ascendente proceso en el cual el agua fría y llena de nutrientes de las profundidades del océano sube a la superficie y remplaza el agua cálida de la superficie (371)

U-shaped valley/valle con forma de U valle que se forma cuando un glaciar erosiona un valle de su forma original en V a una U (313)

V

vent/respiradero agujero en la corteza terrestre a través del cual sube el magma a la superficie (224)

volcano/volcán montaña que se forma cuando la roca derretida, llamada magma, es forzada a la superficie de la Tierra (222)

volume/volumen la cantidad de espacio que ocupa algo, o la cantidad de espacio que algo contiene (23)

W

water cycle/ciclo hidrológico el movimiento continuo del agua de fuentes de agua al aire, a la tierra, adentro y arriba del suelo, y de vuelta a las fuentes; ciclo que une a toda el agua de la Tierra, en su forma sólida, líquida, y gaseosa (270, 335, 422)

watershed/cuenca el terreno drenado por un sistema fluvial, que incluye el río principal y todos sus afluentes (272)

water table/nivel hidrostático un límite subterráneo donde la zona de aireación y la zona de saturación se unen (280)

wave height/altitud de onda la distancia vertical entre la cresta de una ola y su seno (372)

wavelength/longitud de onda dos crestas o senos de onda adyacentes (372)

wave period/período de onda el tiempo entre el pasaje de dos crestas (o senos) de onda por un punto fijo (373)

weather/tiempo atmosférico la condición de la atmósfera en un momento y lugar específicos (422, 452)

weather forecast/pronóstico meteorológico predicción de las condiciones futuras del tiempo para los próximos 3 a 5 días (440)

weathering/acción geológica atmosférica la desintegración de la roca en trozos cada vez más pequeños por medios mecánicos o químicos (246)

westerlies/vientos del oeste cinturones de viento que se encuentran en los hemisferios norte y sur entre 30 y 60° (405)

whitecap/cabrilla una ola con cresta blanca, espumosa, y muy profunda, que rompe en el océano abierto antes de acercarse a la costa (375)

white dwarf/enana blanca una estrella pequeña y caliente que se acerca al final de su vida; el centro que queda de una estrella antigua (578)

wind/viento aire en movimiento (402)

wind energy/energía eólica energía que se encuentra en el viento (122)

windsock/manga de viento aparato que se usa para medir la dirección del viento (441)

wind vane/veleta aparato usado para medir la dirección del viento (441)

Y

year/año el tiempo que toma para que la Tierra recorra una vez la órbita del sol (482)

Z

zenith/zenit punto imaginario en el cielo directamente sobre un observador en la Tierra (491)

Index

A **boldface** number refers to an illustration on that page.

A

aa (lava), 225, **225**
abrasion, 247, **247**, 306
absolute dating, 142
absolute magnitude, 574
absorption spectra, 572, **572**
abyssal plain, 338, **338**
abyssal zone, 344, **344**
acceleration, average, 749
acid(s)
    amino, 512
    defined, 747
    sulfuric, 116
    weathering by, 249–250
acid precipitation, 116, **116,** **249,** 249–250, 411, **411**
active tendon system, **208**
Adopt-a-Beach program, 355, **355**
aeration zone, 280, **280**
aerial photographs, 43, 55
aftershocks, 207
agriculture, water usage in, 289
air, 408, **455**. *See also* air pollution; atmosphere
    weathering by, 251
air masses, **430,** 430–433, **433**
air pollution
    car exhaust and, 117, **117, 409,** 410, 471
    cure for, 419
    health effects of, 412, **412**
    indoor, 410
    particulates in, 418
    remediation of, 412–413, 419
    sources of, 410
    types of, 409, **409**
air pressure, 393, **393, 394, 402,** 402–407, **443**
air temperature, 394, **394**
Alamogordo (New Mexico), 388
Alaskan Volcano Observatory, 240
alcohol fuels, 124
Aldrin, Edwin "Buzz," **613**
algae, **528**
algal blooms, 387, **387**
alluvial fans, 279, **279**
alluvium, 277–279
alpine glaciers, 309, **309,** 312, 313
alternative energy resources, 118–125
altitude, 393, 481, **491**
Alvin (minisub), 7, **7,** 337, **337**
Amazon River basin, 272
amber, 147, **147**
amethyst, 64
amino acids, 512
ammonites, **148,** 150, **150**
Amundsen, Roald, 3
Andrews, Roy Chapman, 3
Andromeda (galaxy), **582**
anemometers, 441, **441**
angle of repose, 316, **316**
anglerfish, **345**
Anguilla, 325
anhydrite, 750
animals
    earthquakes and, 218
    weathering by, 248, **248**
annelids, 266
annular eclipses, 552, **552**
Antarctic glaciers, 310, **310**
anthracite, **114**
anticlines, 182, **182**
apatite, **66**
Apollo 11, 613
Apollo 13, **479**
Appalachian Mountains, **185,** 186, **186,** 193, 242
apparent magnitude, 574
aqualung, 327, 360
aquanauts, 328
Aquarius (undersea laboratory), 328, **328**
aquifers, 280–281, **281,** 282, **282,** 289, **289.** *See also* ground water
Arabic astronomy, **478,** 485
aragonite, 750
Archaeopteryx, **57**
Archean eon, **152,** 155
Arctic Ocean, **330**
area
    calculation of, 743
    defined, 743
Arecibo radio telescope, **500**
arêtes, **313**
Aristotle, 485, 486
Armstrong, Neil, 613
artesian springs, 282, **282**
artificial satellites, 507, **602–603,** 602–605
ash, volcanic, 226, **226,** 227, **227**
asphalt, 111
asteroid collisions, 136, **136**
asteroids, 559, **559**
asthenosphere, 168–169, **168–169, 172, 175, 177**
astrolabe, 481, **481, 491**
astronomical units (AU), 516, 537, 538, **538,** 553
astronomy, 6, 9, 482–488
astrophysics, 595
Atlantic Ocean, **330**
Atlantis (space shuttle), 622
atmosphere, 390–413. *See also* air; weather
    composition, 392–393
    formation of, 526–528
    heating of, 398–401
    layers of, **394,** 394–397
    of moons, 555–556
    of other planets, 540, 542, 544–546, 548
    pollution of, 408–413, 419. *See also* air pollution
    pressure and temperature, **393,** 393–394, **394, 402,** 402–403, 440, 543
    telescopes and, 498
    water vapor in, 395, 422–426, 428
    weather and, 441–442
atmospheric pressure, 543
atomic bomb, **388**
atomic nucleus, 521, 522
atomic number, 746
atoms, 61, 746
    model of, **19**
    structure of, **521**
Audubon, John James, **389**
auroras, 397, **397,** 523
averages, defined, 740
axis, 516, 546, **546**
azimuthal projections, 42, **42**
Aztec calendar, **482**

B

Babylonian astronomy, 484
Babylonian maps, **32**
ballooning, 390
Barney Bay (Anguilla), 325, **325**
barometers, 441

barrier spits, **301**
basalt, **88**
base isolators, **208**
bases, 747
basin, deep-ocean, 338
batholiths, **89**
bathyal zone, 344, **344**
bathymetric profile, **340**
bats, 283
bauxite, **71**
Bay of Fundy (Canada), **381**
beaches, **300**, 300–301, 325
bed loads, **274**
Bell-Burnell, Jocelyn, 595
benthic environment, 343
benthos, **342**, 343, **343**
Berg, Wally, 164
Bermuda Triangle, 362, **362**
beryl, 71, 750
Betelgeuse, 570, **570**, 573, **579**
big bang theory, **586**, 586–587
Big Dipper, **573, 576**
biomass, 124
biomes, 458–466, **458–466**
biosphere, 169
biotite, **62**
birthstones, 97
bituminous coal, **114**
black holes, 581, **581**, 585, 594
black smokers, 7, 344
blocks, volcanic, 226, **226**
Blue Lagoon (Iceland), 192, **192**
Bluestein, Howard, 8
boiling point, 543
bombs
    atomic, **388**
    volcanic, 226, **226**
boulders, 324
boundaries
    convergent, 178, **178**, 185, 233, **233**
    divergent, 179, **179**, 232, **232**
    transform, 179, **179**
Boyle's law, 29
Bradbury, Ray, 449
Brahe, Tycho, 487, **487**, 515
Brandt, George, 57
breakers, 374, **374**
breccia, **92**
breezes, **406**, 406–407, **407**
brown dwarfs, 506
bubonic plague, 476
Bunker Hill, 243
burial mounds, 144, **144**
butane, 112
butterflies, 99

C

Cairo (Illinois), **243**
calcite, **63, 66, 67, 97,** 250, 750
calcium, 92
    in stars, 573
calcium carbonate, 92, 283. See also limestone
calderas, 229, **229**
calendars, **478, 482,** 482–483
California Current, **370**
Calypso II, 360, **360**
Candlestick Park (San Francisco), 219
Canyonlands National Park (Utah), **276**
Cape Cod (Massachusetts), **301**
Capitol Reef National Park, **251**
cap rocks, 282, **282**
carbon, 114
carbon-14 dating, 145
carbonate minerals, **63,** 750
carbon dioxide
    in Earth's early atmosphere, 526–527
    greenhouse effect and, 400, **400,** 470–471, 527
    igneous rock and, **87**
    in volcanoes, 235
cardinal directions, 35
careers in science
    astronomer, 9
    astrophysicist, 595
    cartographer, 11
    ecologist, 10
    environmental scientist, 11
    geochemist, 10
    geographer, 11
    geophysicist, 31
    meteorologist, 8, 448, 477
    oceanographer, 7
    paleontologist, 6, 14, 161
    seismologist, 6, 196, 386
    volcanologist, 6
    watershed planner, 55
Carlsbad Caverns (New Mexico), **242, 283**
cars
    electric, 419, **419**
    fuels for, 106, 112, 124
    pollution from, 117, 409, **409,** 413, **413**
    solar, 106, **106**
cartography, 11
Cassini (space probe), 545, 611, **611**

casts, fossil, 148, **148**
catastrophism, 135–136
CAT scans, 160, **160**
caves, 6, **6, 283,** 283–284, **302**
celestial equator, 492, **492**
celestial sphere, 492, **492**
Celsius scale, **22,** 25, 232, 732
Cenozoic era, **152,** 154, **154, 155**
Ceres (asteroid), **559**
CFCs, 388
chalcopyrite, 71
Challenger (space shuttle), 614
Challenger, HMS, 326
Chandra X-ray Observatory, **501,** 604
channels, 273
chaparrals, **458, 462,** 463, **463**
Charbeneau, Nancy, 55
Charon (moon), 548, **548,** 556, 566, **566**
chemical equations, 747
chemical reactions, **67**
Chernobyl accident, 119, 389
Chinese astronomy, **478,** 485, **485**
Chinese calendar, **483**
chlorine, 332
chlorite, **97,** 750
chlorofluorocarbons (CFCs), **388**
chromite, 71
chromosphere, **519**
cinder cone volcanoes, 228, **228**
Ciparis, August, 220, **220**
circumpolar stars, 492, **492**
cirques, **313**
clams, **344**
Clarke, Arthur C., 603
clastic sedimentary rock, 92
Clean Air Act of 1970, 412
Clean Water Act of 1972, 354
cleavage, 65, **65,** 751
Clementine (space probe), 606, **606**
Cleopatra's Needle, **242**
climate, 452–471. See also weather
    changes in, 227, 467–471, 477
    elevation and, 450, 456
    global warming, 18, 20–21, 400–401, 470–471
    ice ages and, **467,** 467–469
    latitude and, 453, **453**
    microclimates, 466
    models, 19–21, 477
    mountains and, 456, **456**

Index **781**

oceans and, 336, **336**
prevailing winds, 455, **455, 456**
soils and, 257–258
surface currents and, **370,** 370–371, 457, **457**
volcanoes and, 227, 469, **469**
weathering and, 254
zones, 458, **458,** 459, 462, 464
clouds, **426,** 426–428, **427**
formation of, 426–427
funnel clouds, 436, **436**
height of, **427**
types of, 426–427, **426–427**
coal, 112
distribution of, **115**
formation of, 114, **114**
problems with, 116, **116**
types of, **114**
cobalt, 57
coelacanth, **327**
cold air masses, 431, **432**
cold fronts, **432, 443**
Cold War, 599, 604, 612
collisions, plate, **178,** 233
color (of minerals), 64, 750
color television, **163**
Columbia (space shuttle), **613**
Columbia River plateau, 229
combustion chamber, **600**
comet(s)
description of, 557, **557**
Hale-Bopp, **471**
Halley's, **2**
impacts of, 527, **527,** 561
life on Earth and, 512
orbit of, 558, **558**
planet formation and, 513, 526–527, **527,** 566
compact discs, **163**
compasses, 36–37
compass rose, **35, 45**
composite volcanoes, 228
composition, 85
compounds, defined, 61, 747
compression, 181
computerized axial tomography (CAT), 160
concentration, calculation of, 749
concept mapping, 730
conceptual models, 19
conchoidal fracture, **65**
condensation, **271, 335, 422, 425,** 425–426
conduction, 399, **399**

conglomerates, **86**
conic projections, 42, **42**
conifers, 466
conservation of energy, law of, 748
conservation of natural resources, 110
constellations, 489–490, **489–490,** 576, **576**
contact metamorphism, 96, **96**
continental collisions, 165
continental crust, 166, **166, 167, 168,** 171, **171,** 233
continental deflections, 366, **366**
Continental Divide, 272, **272**
continental drift, **163, 173,** 173–176, 193, 469
continental glaciers, 309, 310, **310,** 312, **312**
continental margin, 338, **338**
continental polar (cP) air masses, **430**
continental rise, **338**
continental shelf, **338**
continental slope, **338**
continental tropical (cT) air masses, **430**
continents, formation of, 529, **529**
contour interval, 47, **47**
contour lines, 46, **46,** 49
contour plowing, 261, **261**
controlled experiments, 15, 735
convection
in the atmosphere, 399, **399**
in Earth's mantle, 529, **529**
plate tectonics and, **177**
convection cells, 403, **403**
convection currents, 399, **399**
convective zone, **519**
convergent boundaries, 178, **178,** 185, 233, **233**
convergent motion, **198–199**
conversion tables, SI, 731
Cook Inlet (Alaska), 350
Copernicus, Nicolaus, 56, 486, **486,** 493
copper, 750
coprolites, 148, **148**
coral, 93, **93,** 328, 343, **343**
core
of Earth, 30, 167, **167, 168–169,** 525, **525**
of sun, **519**
Coriolis effect, 366, **366,** 403, **403**

corona, **519, 552**
corundum, **63, 66,** 71
cosmic background radiation, 587
cosmology, 586
Cousteau, Jacques, **327,** 360
cover crops, 261
craters, 229, **229**
creep, 319, **319**
crest, 372, **372**
crevasses, 311, **311**
crop rotation, 261
cross-beds, **94**
cross braces, **208**
crude oil, 111
crust (of the Earth), **525**
continental, 166, **166, 167,** 171, **171, 233**
deformations of, **181,** 181–187, **182, 183, 184,** 197, **197**
oceanic, 166, **166,** 171, **171,** 175, **178–179, 232,** 233, **233,** 234
crystals
formation of, **68–69**
in minerals, 61
Cullinan diamond, **71**
currents
climate and, 370, **370,** 457, **457**
convection, 399, **399**
deep, **368,** 368–369, **369**
longshore, **300,** 301, 320, 375, **375**
ocean, 364–371
surface, **365,** 365–367, **366, 367**
cyclones, 437. *See also* hurricanes

D

Dactyl (asteroid), **559**
Dante II, **163,** 240, **240**
Darwin, Charles, 135, 521
Davis, William Morris, 275
Death Valley (California), 324, **324**
deciduous trees, 462
decimals, 741
declination (stellar), 492, **492**
deep currents, 368–369, **368–369**
Deep Flight (minisub), 337, **337**
deep mining, 70

deep-ocean basin, 338–339, **338–339**
Deep Space 1 (space probe), 610, **610**
deflation, 305, **305**
deflation hollows, 305, **305**
deforestation, 471, **471**
deformation, 181, **181**, 197
Deimos (moon), 554, **554**
deltas, 278, 295
density
    of air, **455**
    calculation of, 749
    Earth's formation and, 525, **525**
    of ice, 246
    mantle convection and, **529**
    of minerals, 66
    of the moon, 549
    of ocean currents, 368, **368**
    planetary, 539–548
deposition
    in caves, 283
    glacial, **314**, 314–315, **315**
    gravity and, 316–319, **316–319**
    by streams and rivers, 277–279, **278, 279**
    waves, **300**, 300–301, **301**
    wind, 306–308, **307, 308**
depression (contour lines), 49, **49**
desalination, 349
desert pavement, 305, **305**
deserts
    temperate, **458, 462,** 464, **464**
    tropical, **458, 459,** 460, **460**
    weathering in, 257, **257**
desert tortoises, 307, **307**
deuterium, **522**
Devils Tower, 252, **252**
dew point, 425
diamonds, 65, **65, 66, 71,** 750
    artificial, 56
diesel fuel, 111
differential weathering, 252
dikes, **89**
Dillo Dirt, 352
dinosaur eggs, **3**
dinosaurs, 4, **12,** 12–16, **16–17,** 160–161, **243,** 418
directions, cardinal, 35
discharge, stream, 273
disconformities, 141, **141**
Discovery (space shuttle), 614
disease, 286
dissolution, weathering by, 249

dissolved loads, **274**
dissolved solids, 332, **332, 368.** *See also* salt
divergent boundaries, 179, **179,** 232, **232**
divides, 272
dodo, **56**
doldrums, 405
dolphins, **345**
Doppler effect, 493
Doppler radar, 442, **442**
drainage basins, 272
Drake, Edwin, 131, **131**
drift nets, 346, **346**
drilling for oil, 131, 348
dripstone, 283, **283**
droughts, 306
drumlin, 243
dry-bulb thermometer, 424
dunes, 306–307, **307**
Dust Bowl, 267, 306, **306**
dust storms, 306, **306**
dwarf elliptical galaxies, 583
dwarf stars, **578–579**

E

Eagle (lunar landing module), 613, **613**
Eagle nebula, 584, **584**
Earth. *See also* atmosphere; maps; plate tectonics
    composition, 166–167, **166–167**
    continent formation on, 529, **529**
    core of, 30, **30,** 167, **167, 168–169**
    crust of, 166, **166,** 167, 171, **171, 232,** 525
    formation of, 524–525
    geologic time scale, **152,** 152–154, **155**
    interior of, 167, **167,** 525, **525**
    latitude, **453,** 453–454, **454**
    mantle of, 167, **167,** 230
    maps of, 40–42, **41, 42**
    orbital changes and climate, 468, **468**
    orbit of, 515, **515,** 516, **539**
    rotation of, 515, **515**
    size of, 35
    from space, 541, **541**
    structure of, 168–169, **168–169,** 172, **172**
    surface of, **526,** 561

    tectonic plates, 164–187, **170,** 193
    tides and, 378–381, **379, 380**
Earth Day, **3**
earthquakes, 194–213
    animals and, 218
    causes of, 197, **197**
    damage by, 194, **194,** 197, **207,** 207–208
    Earth's interior and, 211
    epicenter of, **202,** 202–203, **203**
    focus of, 202, **202**
    forecasting, **206,** 206–207, **207**
    Great Hanshin, 194, **194,** 213
    hazard levels and, 205, **205**
    Kobe, Japan, 194, **194**
    location of, 196, **196,** 202–203, **202–203**
    Loma Prieta (California), 207, 219
    magnitude of, 204, **204**
    on other cosmic bodies, 212–213
    plate motion and, **178–179,** 179, **198–199**
    prediction of, **206,** 206–207, **207**
    preparation for, **209,** 209–210
    strength of, 204, **204,** 206
    tsunamis and, **376,** 376–377, 386
    types of, 198–199, **198–199**
Earth's rotation and magnetic fields, 30
earthworms, 266
Echo 1 (satellite), 603
eclipses, 485, 552–553, **552–553**
ecliptic, **492**
ecology, 10
ecosystems, 10
    threats to, 295
Effigy Mounds National Monument (Iowa), 144, **144**
Egyptian calendar, **483**
Einstein, Albert, 521
elastic rebound, 197, **197**
electric cars, 419, **419**
electricity
    for cars, 413, 419, **419**
    from geothermal energy, 125, **125**
    from hydroelectric energy, 123, **123**

from nuclear energy, 118–119, **118–119**
from solar energy, 119–121, **119–121**
from tidal energy, 350, **350**
from wind energy, 122, **122,** 405, **405**
electromagnetic fields, 218
electromagnetic spectrum, 499, **499**
electromagnetic waves, 31
electron clouds, 746, **746**
electrons, 521, **521**
elements. See also periodic table
  in atomic models, 746
  defined, 746
  in minerals, 60–61, 63
  origin of, 580
  in stars, 573
elevation, 46–47, 254, 450, 456
ellipses, 516, **516,** 558, **558**
elliptical galaxies, 583, **583**
elliptical orbits, 516, **516,** 558, **558**
El Niño, 371, **371,** 476
emission lines, **571,** 571–572
Enchanted Rock (Llano, Texas), **89**
energy
  in the atmosphere, 398–399
  from fossil fuels, 111–115
  geothermal, 125, **125**
  gravitational, 520
  hydroelectric, 123, **123**
  nuclear, 118–119
  resources, 111–125
  solar, 119–121, **119–121**
  of the sun, 520–522, **522**
  tidal, 350, **350**
  transfer of, 398–399, **398–399**
  wave, 298–299, 350
  wind, 122, **122,** 405, **405**
energy, resources, 111–125
English Channel, **327**
Environmental Protection Agency (EPA), 351, 412
environmental science, 11
eons, 153
EPA, 351, 412–413
epicenters, **202,** 202–203, **203**
epochs, 153
equator, 35, **35,** 37, **37**
equinox, vernal 492, **492**
eras, 153
Eratosthenes, 35

erosion
  in caves, 283
  glacial, **312–313,** 312–314, **314**
  mass movement and, **316,** 316–319, **317, 318, 319**
  the rock cycle and, **82–83**
  shoreline, 296, **301,** 301–303, **302–303,** 375
  soil, **260,** 260–261, 267
  streams and rivers, 270, **270,** 273–276, **274**
  unconformities and, 140, **140**
  wind, **304,** 304–306, **305**
eruptions, volcanic
  effects of, 227–229, **227–229**
  explosive, 223, **223,** 227, 228
  nonexplosive, 222, **222,** 228
escape velocity, 601, **601**
Europa (moon), 241, **241,** 554, **554**
evaporation, **271,** 332, **335, 368, 422**
Everest, Mount (Nepal), **56, 164,** 164–165
evergreens, 462
evolution, theory of, 135, 521
Exeter Cathedral (England), 81
experiments, controlled, 15, 735
Explorer 1 (satellite), 602, **602**
extrusive igneous rocks, 90
Exxon Valdez spill, 116, 353

F

Fahrenheit, Gabriel, 389
Fahrenheit–Celsius conversion, 232, 236, 732
Fahrenheit scale, 25, **25,** 732, **732**
fallout, volcanic, 227
fault-block mountains, 186, **186, 187**
fault blocks, 183, **183**
faults, 139, **139,** 183–184, **183–184,** 196, **198**
feldspar, **62**
felsic composition, 88, **88**
fingernail growth, 401
first law of motion (Newton's), 748
fish farming, 347, **347**
fishing, 346, **346**
fission, 118, **118**
fissures, 90, 229
flood plains, 276, 279, **279**

flow of water, 268–289
  deposits from, 277–279, **278, 279**
  ground water, **280–282,** 280–284
  river systems, 272–276
  streams, 272–276
fluorescence, **67**
fluorite, **63, 66, 67,** 750
focus (of an earthquake), 202, **202**
fog, 426
folded mountains, 185, **185, 186**
folding, 182, **182**
folds, 139, **139**
foliated metamorphic rock, 98
fool's gold, 64
footwalls, 183, **183**
force(s)
  calculation of, 749
  in mass movement, 316–319
Ford, Henry, 163
forests, temperate, **458,** 462, **462**
forty-niners, **57**
Fossett, Steve, 390
fossil fuels, 111–117
  extraction of, 115, **115**
  formation of, **113,** 113–114, **114**
  location of, 115, **115**
  problems with, **116,** 116–117, **117,** 411–412
  as solar energy, 120
  types of, 111–112, 601, 610
fossiliferous limestone, 93
fossils, **2, 81,** 93, **93,** 146–150, 160, 173
fractionation, **111**
fractions, 741–742
fracture, 65, **65,** 751
frankincense, 54
Franklin, Benjamin, **389**
free fall, 622
fresh water, 361
freshwater supply, 349
Fronk, Robert, 6
fronts, 432–433, **432–433, 443**
fuel, rocket, 601, 610. See also fossil fuels
fuel oil, 111
Fuji, Mount (Japan), 228, **228**
fulgurites, 76, **76**
Fundy, Bay of, **381**
funnel clouds, 436, **436**
fusion, 119, 521, 522, **522, 579**

G

gabbro, **88**
Gagarin, Yuri, 612
galaxies, 568, **582–584**, 582–585
galena, **63, 71,** 750
Galileo (space probe), **538,** 544, 609, **609**
Galileo Europa Mission, 241
Galileo Galilei, 388, 487, 509, **538,** 554
gamma rays, **499, 500**
gamma ray telescopes, 501
Ganymede, 554
gap hypothesis, 206–207, **207**
garnet, **97,** 750
garnet schist, **95**
gas clouds, 510, **510–511,** 584, **584.** See also nebulas
gases
　emission lines of, 571, **571**
　greenhouse, 400, 527
　natural, 112–113, 184, 348
　solar, **519,** 522–523
　volcanic, 235, **235**
gas giants, 544–550
gasohol, 124
gasoline, 58, **58,** 65, 97, 111
gems, 71
gemstones, 58, 65, 97
geochemistry, 10
geographic information system (GIS), 55, 324
geographic poles, 36, **36**
geography, 11, 456, **456**
geologic column, 138, **138**
geologic time scale, **152,** 152–154, **155**
geology, 6, 134
geophysicist, 31
Geosat, 341
Geostationary Operational Environment Satellites (GOES), 603
geosynchronous orbits (GEOs), 603
geothermal energy, 125, **125,** 192
geysers, 125, 294
Geysers, The (California), 125
giant elliptical galaxies, 583, **583**
Gillette, David D., 14–17, **17**
GIS, 55, 324
glacial drift, 314–315

glacial periods, 467, **467**
glaciers
　continental drift and, 174, **174,** 469
　deposition and, **314,** 314–315, **315**
　erosion by, **312–313,** 312–314, **314**
　interglacial periods, 467–468
　landforms carved by, 312–313, **312–313**
　movement of, 311
　speed of, 311
　types of, 309–310, **309–310**
glass scalpels, 105, **105**
glaze ice, 428, **428**
Glenn, John, **479,** 612, **612**
global positioning system (GPS), 38, **38,** 164, 180, **180,** 324
global warming, 18, 20–21, 400–401, 470–471, 556. See also climate
global winds, 365, **404,** 404–406
globes, 40
globular clusters, 584, **584**
glossopteris, 173
gneiss, 98, **98**
Gobi Desert, 3
Goddard, Robert, 598, **598,** 601
gold
　density of, 66
　purity of, 70
　in sea water, 332
　structure of, 61, **61**
Gold Rush (California), **57,** 278, **278**
Gondwana, 174
GPS (global positioning system), 38, **38,** 164, 180, **180,** 324
gradient, 273, **273**
graduated cylinder, 23–24, **24,** 733, **733**
grams, 22, 24
Grand Canyon (Arizona), **91,** 151, **151, 243,** 270, **270**
granite, **62,** 85, 88, 249, **249**
graph
　types of, 737–739, **737–739**
　time-distance, 203, **203**
graphite, 750
grasslands, temperate, **458, 462,** 463, **463**
gravity
　artificial, 508–509

atmosphere and, 393
black holes and, 581, 594
energy production in the sun and, 520
erosion and deposition and, 316–319, **316–319**
free fall and, 622
law of universal gravitation, 517
on the moon, 549
in nebulas, 510–511, **511**
Newton's law, **517,** 517–518, **518**
orbits and, 518, **518**
planet formation and, 512–513, **512–513**
on planets, 539–548
star formation and, 514
surface, 539
tides and, 378–380, **379, 380**
weathering and, 254
zero, 518
Great Basin Desert, **464**
Great Hanshin earthquake, 194, **194,** 213
Great Lakes, 243
Great Red Spot, 439
Greek astronomy, 485
Gregorian calendar, 483
greenhouse effect, 20, **20, 400,** 400–401, 470, **470,** 527, 540
Grimm, Bob, 31
groundspeed, 407
ground water
　acids in, 250
　aquifers, **280,** 280–281, **281**
　mineral formation and, **68–69**
　use of, 288, **288**
groups, elements, 746
Gulf of Mexico, **333**
Gulf Stream, 336, **336,** 365, **370,** 457
gypsum, **63, 66,** 750

H

HABs, 387, **387**
hadal zone, 344, **344**
Hadean eon, **152,** 155
hail, 429, **429,** 435
Hale-Bopp (comet), **557**
half-life, 143, **143**
halide minerals, 63, 750
halite, **61, 65,** 750
Halley, Edmond, 2

Halley's comet, 2
hanging valleys, **313**
hanging walls, 183, **183**
hardness, 66, **66,** 750
harmful algal blooms (HABs), 387, **387**
Hawaiian Islands, 228, 233–234, 377
headlands, **302–303**
health, human, 412, **412**
Hebrew calendar, **483**
Hektor (asteroid), **559**
heliostats, **121**
helium
 emission lines of, **571**
 in fusion process, 522, **522**
 on the moon, 617
 in stars, 573
hematite, **65, 97,** 750
hemispheres, 37–38
Herschel, William, 488, 499, 546
Hertzsprung, Ejnar, 577
Hertzsprung-Russell (H-R) diagrams, 577, **578–579**
Hewish, Anthony, 595
Heyerdahl, Thor, 364
hieroglyphics, 3
Hillary, Edmund, 56
Hilo (Hawaii) tsunami, 377
Himalaya Mountains, 165
HMS *Challenger,* 326
holdfasts, 343
Hong Kong, **243**
Hoover Dam, 57
horizon
 soil, 256, **256**
 visual, **491**
hornblende, 750
Horner, Jack, 161
horns, **313**
Horsehead nebula, **510**
horse latitudes, 405
hot-air balloons, 390, **390**
hot spots, 233–234, **234,** 237
hot springs, 294
Hubble, Edwin, **479,** 488, 493, 583
Hubble Deep Field, 568, **568,** 583
Hubble Space Telescope (HST), **3,** 480, **480,** 498, **498,** 568, **568,** 594
human health, 412, **412**
humidity, **423,** 423–424
humus, 255, **256**
Hurricane Andrew, 8, **8**

Hurricane Elena, **448**
Hurricane Fran, **437**
Hurricane Luis, 325
Hurricane Mitch, **402, 439**
hurricanes, 8, **8,** 325, **402, 437,** 437–439, **438, 448**
Hutton, James, 134
Huygens (space probe), 611
Huygens, Christiaan, 555
hydrocarbons, 112
hydroelectric dams, 57, 123, **123**
hydroelectric energy, 123, **123**
hydrogen,
 emission lines of, **571**
 in the fusion process, 522, **522**
 in stars, 573
hydrograph, **293**
hydrothermal vents, 7
hypotheses, 4
 formation of, 14
 testing of, 15

I

ice ages, 389, **467,** 467–469
icebergs, **243,** 310, **310,** 361, **361**
Iceland, 192
ice sheets, 310, **310,** 361. *See also* glaciers
ice shelves, 310, **310**
ice wedging, 246, **246**
Ida (asteroid), **559**
igneous rock, 79, 83, **83, 84,** 87–90, **88–90**
 composition of, 88, **88**
 extrusive, 90, **90**
 formations, 89, **89**
 intrusive, 89, **89**
 origins of, 87
 texture of, 88, **88**
index contour, 47, **47**
index fossils, 150, **150**
Indian Ocean, **330**
infiltration, **271**
infrared radiation, 499, **499, 500**
inner core, 30, **30,** 168, **169, 172, 211**
interglacial periods, 468
International Space Station (ISS), 616, **616,** 622, **622**
International System of Units (SI), **22,** 22–25, 731

interstellar clouds. *See* nebulas
intertidal zone, 343, **343**
intrusions, 139, **139**
intrusive igneous rocks, 89, **89**
Io (moon), **162, 544,** 554, **554,** 567
ion drive, 610
ionosphere, 397, **397**
ions, 747
irregular galaxies, 583, **583**
isobars, 443, **443**
isotopes, **142,** 142–145
ISS (*International Space Station*), 616, **616,** 622, **622**

J

Japan, earthquake in, 194, **194**
jet fuel, 111
jet streams, 406, **406**
Jones, Brian, 389
Journey to the Center of the Earth, **162**
Julian calendar, 483
Jupiter, 439, **536,** 544, **544,** 554, 567, 609

K

kamikaze, **388**
Kanamori, Hiroo, 386
kangaroo rats, 460
Keck telescopes, **498**
kelp, 347
Kelvin temperature scale, **22,** 25, 732
Kennedy, John F., 612
Kepler, Johannes, 487, 515–516
Kepler's laws of motion, 516, **516**
kerosene, 111
kettles, 314, **314**
Kilauea (Hawaii), **222**
Kilimanjaro, Mount (Kenya), 450, **450,** 456
Kitt Peak National Observatory, 534
Kitty Hawk, North Carolina, 479
knapper, 105
Kobe (Japan) earthquake, 194, **194**
Kon-Tiki, 364, **364**
Krakatau, 162
Kuiper, Gerard, 566
Kuiper belt, 558, **558,** 566

L

La Brea tar pits, 147, **147**
laccoliths, **89**
lahars, 318, **318**
land breezes, **406**
Landsat satellites, 605, **605**
landslides, 317, **317**
lapilli, 226, **226**
Large Magellanic cloud, 583, **583**
lateral moraines, **315**
latitude, **37,** 37–39, **39**
    climate and, 453, **453**
    defined, 37
    seasons and, 454, **454**
Laurasia, **174**
lava, 84
    flows, 90, **90,** 222, **222,** 224
    plateaus, 90, **229**
    types, 225, **225**
Lavoisier, Antoine, 389
law
    of conservation of energy, 748
    of motion, Kepler's, 516, **516**
    of motion, Newton's, 748
    of universal gravitation, 517, 748
LBJ Library (Austin, Texas), **81**
leaching, **256,** 257. *See also* soil; weathering
leap year, 483
Lecomte, Ben, 327
legend, **45**
length, units, **22,** 23
lenses (telescope), 496
LEO (low Earth orbit), 507, 603
Libby, Willard F., **57**
lichens, 250, **250**
life on Earth, 512, 528, **528**
light
    absorption spectrum, 572, **572**
    emission lines, 571, **571**
    eyes and, 572
    pollution, 574
    spectrum, 570–572
light-minute, 538
lightning, 76, **76,** 434, 435, **435**
light-year, 493, **493,** 575
lignite, **114**
limestone, **85,** 92–93, **92–93,** 99, 283, **283**
    caves, 250, **250**
    types of, 92–93, **92–93**

Lindbergh, Charles, 327
liters, **22,** 23
lithosphere, 168, **168–169,** 172, 175
    continental, **177, 178**
    oceanic, **177, 179**
loads, 274, **274**
local winds, 404, 406
loess, 308, **308**
Loma Prieta earthquake (California), 207, **207,** 219
longitude, 37–39, **38, 39**
longshore currents, 301, 375, **375**
Louisiana, 325
low Earth orbit (LEO), 507, 603
Luna 9 (space probe), 606, **606**
lunar eclipses, 552–553, **553**
luster of minerals, 64, **64,** 750
Lyell, Charles, 135
Lyme disease, 476

M

M81 (galaxy), 583, **583**
M87 (galaxy), 594, **594**
Machu Picchu, Peru, **80**
mafic composition, 88, **88**
Magellan (space probe), 607, **607**
Magellanic clouds, 583, **583**
magma. *See also* volcanoes
    chamber, **224,** 229, **229**
    composition, 224
    formation, **230,** 230–231, **231**
    metamorphism and, 95–96, **96**
    rock formation, **83,** 88
magnetic declination, 36–37, **37**
magnetic field(s)
    of Earth, 30
    of sun, 523, **523**
magnetic poles, 3, 36, **36**
magnetic reversals, 176, **176**
magnetism, 36, **67,** 176, **176**
magnetite, 62, **63, 67,** 750
magnitude
    of earthquakes, 204, **204**
    of stars, 573–574, 577, **578–579**
main-sequence stars, **578–579**
Maisasaura, 161
Mammoth Cave (Kentucky), **250**
manganese nodules, 349, **349**

mantle (of the Earth), 167, **167,** 230, 525, **525,** 529, **529**
mantle plumes, 233–234, **234**
map legends, 45, **45**
map projections, 41–42, **41–42**
maps
    directions on, **45**
    early, 32, **32**
    information on, **44–45**
    latitude and longitude, 37–39, **37–39**
    legend, 45, **45**
    modern mapmaking, 43
    projections, 41–42, **41–42**
    scale, **44**
    topographic, **46,** 46–49, **47, 48**
    weather, 442–443, **443**
map scale, **44**
marble, 99, **99**
margin, continental, 338, **338**
Mariana Trench, 185, 339
Marine Protection, Research, and Sanctuaries Act of 1992, 354
Marine Sulphur Queen, 362
maritime polar (mP) air masses, **430, 431**
maritime tropical (mT) air masses, **430, 431**
Mars, 31, 213, 278, 516, **536, 542,** 542–543, **543,** 554, 608, **608**
Mars Pathfinder (space probe), 608, **608**
Martinique, 220, **220**
mass, **22,** 24, 510, 517, 731
mass damper, **208**
mass movement, **316,** 316–319, **317, 318, 319**
mathematical models, 19–21
matter, 746
Mauna Kea (Hawaii), 228, **228**
Mayan astronomy, 485, **485**
Mayan calendar, **483**
McAuliffe, Christa, 614
meanders, **275,** 276, **276**
measurement systems, 22–25
measurement units, 731
medial moraines, **315**
medical waste, 351
Mediterranean Sea, **333**
Mercator projections, 41, **41**
Mercury (planet), **536,** 539, **539**
mercury thermometer, 389
meridians, 38, **38**
mesosaurus, **173**

Index   **787**

mesosphere
    of the atmosphere, **394,** 396
    of the Earth, 168–169, **168–169, 172, 177, 179**
Mesozoic era, **152,** 154, **154, 155**
Messina, Paula, 324, **324**
metallic luster, 64, **64**
metamorphic rock, 79, 82, **82, 84, 95,** 95–99, **97–99**
    composition of, 97, **97**
    foliated, 98, **98**
    nonfoliated, 99, **99**
    origins of, 95–96, **96**
    textures of, 98, **98, 99**
metamorphism, **68,** 95–96, **96**
    contact, 96, **96**
    regional, 96, **96**
metamorphosis, 99
meteor, 560, **560**
meteorites, **81,** 526, **560,** 560–561
meteoroids, 560
meteorologist, 8, 440, 448, 477, **477**
meteorology, 8
meters (units), 23
meter stick, 733
methane (natural gas), 112–113, 184, 348
metric system, 22
mica, **62, 65, 97**
microclimates, 466
microwaves, **499**
Mid-Atlantic Ridge, 175, **175,** 192
mid-ocean ridges, 175, **175, 177, 179,** 232, 339, **339**
Milankovitch, Milutin, 389, 468
Milankovitch theory, 468, **468**
Milky Way galaxy, 582, 584, **584**
minerals, 58–71
    color of, 64, 750
    common uses of, **71,** 751
    density of, 66, 751
    formation of, **68–69**
    hardness of, 66, **66,** 750
    identification of, 64–67
    luster of, 64, **64,** 750
    metamorphism and, 97, **97**
    mining of, 70, **70**
    on ocean floor, 349, **349**
    overview of, 60–63
    properties of, 750–751
    in rocks, 85, **85**
    special properties of, 67, **67,** 751
    streak of, 65, **65,** 750
    types of, 62–63, **62–63**

mining, 70, **115,** 115–116, **116**
Mir (space station), 535, 615, **615,** 622
Miranda (moon), 555, **555**
mirrors, 534–535
Mississippi River, **243,** 295, **295**
    basin, 272, **272,** 277–278, **279**
    delta, 295, **295**
Mitchell, Cristy, 448
models
    of climate, 19–21, 477
    scientific, 19, 20–21
Moho, 211, **211**
Mohs' hardness scale, 66, **66**
Mojave Desert (California), **121**
molds (fossil), 148, **148**
molecules, 747
monoclines, 182, **182**
Montserrat, 162
moon (Luna)
    colonization of, 617
    earthquakes on, 212, **212**
    eclipses and, 552–553, **552–553**
    orbit of, 518, **518,** 550, **551**
    origin of, **550,** 550–551
    phases of, 551, **551**
    rocks from, 144
    surface of, 549, **549, 561**
    and tides, 378–380, **379, 380**
moon rocks, 144
moons of other planets, 554–556
moraines, 315, **315**
motion
    Kepler's laws of, 516, **516**
    Newton's laws of, 748
mountain breezes, 407, **407**
mountains
    Appalachian, **185, 186,** 193, 242
    climate and, 450, **450,** 456, **456, 458**
    fault-block, 186, **186**
    floating, 171
    folded, 185, **185–186**
    formation of, **185,** 185–187, **186, 187**
    Himalaya, 165
    volcanic, 187
Mount Everest (Nepal), **56, 164,** 164–165
Mount Fuji (Japan), 228, **228**
Mount Kilimanjaro (Kenya), 450, **450,** 456
Mount Pelée (Martinique), 220, **220,** 222

Mount Pinatubo (Philippines), 227, **227**
Mount Redoubt, (Alaska), **223**
Mount Rushmore (South Dakota), **242**
Mount Spurr (Alaska), 240
Mount St. Helens (Washington), 162, **223,** 418, **469**
mudflows, 318, **318**
mud pots, 294, **294**
mummification, 147
mural quadrant, **487**
muscovite, **97,** 750

N

Nabataeans, 104
Nabta astronomy, 484, **484**
NASA, **479,** 599, 617
National Aeronautics and Space Administration (NASA), **479,** 599, 617
National Oceanic and Atmospheric Administration (NOAA), 442
national parks
    Canyonlands (Utah), **276**
    Carlsbad Caverns (New Mexico), **242, 283**
    Yellowstone (Wyoming), 294, **294**
National Weather Service (NWS), 442, 448
Native-American astronomy, 485
native elements, 750
natural gas, 112–113, **113,** 184, 348
natural resources, 108–110
    conservation of, 110
neap tides, 380, **380**
nebulas
    galaxies and, 584, **584**
    solar system formation and, 510–514, **510–514**
nekton, 342
neon, emission lines of, 571, **571**
Neptune, **536,** 547, **547,** 556, **558**
neritic zone, 345, **345**
neutrons, 521, **521, 522,** 746
neutron stars, 581, 595, **595**
Newton, Sir Isaac, **479,** 487, 517–518

788   Index

Newton's laws of motion, 600, 748
Nile River, **278**
nitrogen, **392**
Nixon, Richard, 613
nodules, manganese, 349, **349**
nonfoliated metamorphic rock, 99, **99**
nonmetallic luster, 64, **64**
nonpoint-source pollution, 285, **285**, 352, **352**
nonrenewable resources, 109–110, **110**, 288, 348
nonsilicate minerals, 63, 750
Norgay, Tenzing, 56
normal faults, **183**, 183–184, **184**
Northern Hemisphere, 37, 366, 438
northern lights, **397**
North Pole, 35, **35, 36,** 37
nuclear energy, 118–119
nuclear fission, 118, **118**
nuclear fusion, 119, 521, 522, **522, 579**
nuclear waste, 118, **118**
nucleus, 746

O

objective lenses, 496
observation, 14
obsidian scalpels, 105, **105**
occluded fronts, **433**
ocean currents, 364–371, **365, 367, 369–370,** 457, **457**
oceanic crust, 166, **166,** 171, **171, 175, 178–179, 232,** 233, **234**
oceanic zone, 345, **345**
oceanography, 7
oceans, 328–355. See also currents; ocean waves
　climate and, 336, **336,** 457, **457**
　desalination and, 349
　divisions of, 330, **330**
　floor of, 233, 337–341, **338–339, 341**
　formation of, 527, **527,** 529, **529**
　as a global thermostat, 336
　history of, 331, **331**
　life in, **342,** 342–345, **343–345**
　mapping of, **340,** 340–341, **341**
　pollution of, **351,** 351–355, **352, 353**
　resources from, 346–350, **346–350**
　sea-floor spreading and, **175,** 175–176
　sea-level changes and, 468, 471
　temperature zones in, 333, **333**
　tides and, 378–381, **379–381**
　water characteristics of, **332,** 332–334, **333**
　water cycle and, 335, **335**
ocean trenches, 339, **339**
ocean waves
　anatomy of, 372, **372**
　deposits by, 300–301, **300–301**
　depth and, 374, **374**
　energy of, 298–299
　formation and movement of, **372,** 372–373, **373**
　landforms created by, 302–303
　speed of, 373, **373**
　types of, 373–376, **374–376**
　wave period, 299, 373, **373**
　wave trains, 299, **299**
octopuses, **344**
Ogallala aquifer, 289, **289**
oil, 348, **348,** 353, **353.** See also petroleum
　drilling of, 131
　first well, 131
　spills, 353, **353**
Old Faithful, 294
olivine, 167, 750
Olympic games, **3**
Omega Centauri, **584**
Oort cloud, 558, **558**
open clusters, 584, **584**
open-pit mining, 70, **70**
optical properties, **67**
orbital velocity, 601, **601**
orbits
　elliptical, 516, **516**
　gravity and, 518, **518**
　rotation and revolution, 515, **515**
ore, 70
organic sedimentary rock, 92, 93, **93**
Orion (constellation), 489, **489,** 570, **570**
Orion nebula, **514**
orthoclase, **66,** 750
outer core, 30, **30,** 169, **169,** 172

outwash plains, 314, **314**
oxidation, 251
oxides
　atmospheric, 410
　mineral, 63, 750
oxygen, **392,** 527–529
ozone, 395, **395,** 409, **409,** 411
ozone hole, 389, 411, **411**
ozone layer, 388, 395

P

Pacific Ocean, **330, 331**
pahoehoe, 225, **225**
Painted Desert (Arizona), **305**
paint pots, 294
paleontology, 6, 161
Paleozoic era, **152,** 153, **153, 155**
pampas, 463
Pangaea, 174, **174, 331,** 469, **469**
Panthalassa, 174, **174, 331**
parallax, 575, **575**
parallels, 37. See also meridians
parent rock, 255, **256**
Paricutín volcano (Mexico), **2,** 228, **228**
particulates, 418
peat, **114**
pegmatites, **69**
pelagic environment, 345, **345**
Pelée, Mount (Martinique), 220, **220,** 222
Penzias, Arno, **587**
percentages, defined, 741
percolation, **271**
period, 746
　geologic, 153
　of planetary revolutions, 515–516, 539
　of planetary rotations, 539
　of a wave, 299, 373, **373**
periodic table, **744–745**
permafrost, 465. See also tundra
permeability, 113, 280–281
permineralization, 146
Petra (Jordan), 104, **104**
petrification, 146, **146**
petroleum, 111, **111,** 113, **113,** 115, **115,** 348, **348**
petroleum geology, 348, **348**
pH, 747
Phacops, 150, **150**
Phanerozoic eon, **152, 155**
Phobos (moon), 554, **554**

Index **789**

phosphates, 349
photochemical fog, 117
photosphere, **519**, 522–523
photosynthesis, 145, 528
phyllite, 98, **98**
physical states, change in, 426
phytoplankton, **342**
Piccard, Bertrand, 389
Piccard, Jacques, **327**
Pickering, William, **602**
Pikes Peak (Colorado), **47**
pillow lava, 225, **225**
Pinatubo, Mount (Philippines), 227, **227**
Pioneer 4 (space probe), 606
Pioneer 10 and 11 (space probes), 609, **609**
pistol-butt tree shapes, 319, **319**
placer deposits, 278
plagioclase, 750
planetary system. *See* solar system
planetesimals, 512–513, **512–513**, 524, 526–527
planets, 536–548. *See also* orbits; *individual planets*
   distance from sun, 537, **537**, 538
   early observation of, 536
   formation of, 512–513, **512–513**
   gas giants, 544–547, **544–547**
   motion, **515**, 515–516
   new, 506
   relative sizes of, **536–537**
   rings of, 545, **545**, 547
   terrestrial, 539–543
plankton, **342**
plants, weathering by, 248, **248**
plastics, recycling of, 130, **130**
plate boundaries
   convergent, 178, **178**, 185, **199**, 233, **233**
   divergent, 179, **179, 199**, 232, **232**
   transform, 179, **179, 199**
plate tectonics, 164–187
   boundaries, 178–179, **178–179, 185, 198–199**
   causes of, 177, **177**, 529
   climate change and, 469, **469**
   continental drift and, **173**, 173–175, **174, 175**
   earthquakes and, 196, **196**

magma formation and, 232–233, **232–233**
mountain building and, **185**, 185–187, **186, 187**
plates, **170**, 170–171, 178–179, **178–179, 196**
tracking, 180, **180**
Pleiades, 584, **584**
Pluto, **536**, 548, **548**, 556, 566, **566**
plutons, **69**, 89, **89**
point-source pollution, 285
polar air masses, **430, 431**
polar climate zones, **464**, 464–466
polar easterlies, 404–405
polar icecaps, **18**, 285, 471
polarity, **176**
polar zones, **464**, 464–466
poles (of the Earth), 35, **35**, 36, **36**
pollution
   air, 117, 408–413, **410–411**
   from mining, 71
   of oceans, **351**, 351–355, **352, 353**
   point-source/nonpoint-source, 285, 351–353
   water, 285–287
porosity, 280
potassium-argon dating, 145
prairies, 463, **463**
precipitation
   acid, 116, **116**, 411, **411**
   global warming and, **18**, 471
   types of, 428–429, **428–429**
   water cycle, **271, 335**, 422
   winds and, 455, **455, 456**
prefixes, SI, 731
pressure
   atmospheric, 393, **393, 394, 402**, 402–403, 443, **443**, 543
   belts, 403, **403**
   calculation of, 749
   igneous rock and, **87**
   metamorphic rock and, **95–98**, 95–99
   in nebulas, 511, **511**
   rocket engines and, **600**
pressure waves, 200, **200**. *See also* P waves
prevailing winds, 455, **455**
primary pollutants, 409, **409**
primary treatment, 286, **286**
primary waves, 200, **200**. *See also* P waves

prime meridian, 38, **38**
primordial soup, 528. *See also* life on Earth
prograde rotation, 540
propane, 112
properties of common minerals, 750–751
proportions, defined, 740
Proterozoic eon, **152**, 155
protons, 521, **521, 522**, 746
protoplanets, 506
psychrometers, 424, **424**
Ptolemy, Claudius, 486, **486**
Puget Sound (Washington), 206
pulsars, 581, 595, **595**
pumice, 90, **90**
P waves, **200**, 200–203, **201, 203, 211**
pyramids at Giza, **80**
pyrite, 64, 750
pyroclastic material, 225–226, **225–226**
pyrrhotite, **67**
Pytheas, 378

Q

quartz, **62**, 64, **66, 85**, 750
quartzite, **85**, 99, **99**
quasars, 585, **585**

R

radar, 442
radar imaging, 540
radiation
   cosmic background, 587
   of energy, 398–399, **399**
radiation balance, 401
radiative zone, **519**
radioactive carbon, 57
radioactive decay, 142–143, **142–143**
radioactive wastes, 118
radioactivity, **67, 119,** 524
radiometric dating, **142**, 142–145, **143, 145**
radio telescopes, 9, **9**, 500–501, **500–501**
radio waves, 397, **499**
radium, **67**
rain forest destruction, 20
rain forests, tropical, **458**, 459, **459**
rain gauges, 429, **429**

rain shadow, **456**
ratios, defined, **740**
raw sewage, 286, 352
recharge zone, 281
reclamation, mining, 71
recycling, 110
    plastics, 130
red-dwarf stars, **579**
red giants, **579**
Redoubt, Mount (Alaska), **223**
Red Rocks Amphitheater (Colorado), 78
red shift, 493
red tides, 387, **387**
reef, coral, 343
reference points, 35
reflecting telescopes, **497**, 497–498, **498**
refracting telescopes, 497, **497**
relative dating, 137–141
relative humidity, **423**, 423–424, **424**
relief, 47
remote sensing, 43, 54, 55, 604–605, **604–605**. See also satellite images
renewable resources, 109
resources
    alternative, 118–125
    conservation of, 110
    fossil fuels, 111–117
    nonrenewable, 109, 348
    from oceans, 346–350
    recycling, 110
    renewable, 109
retrograde orbit, 556
retrograde rotation, 540
reverse faults, **183**, 183–184, **184**
reverse polarity, **176**
revolution, planetary, **515**, 515–516, 539–548
Reykjavik (Iceland), 192
Rhinodrilus, 266
rhyolite, **88**
Richter, Charles, 163, 204
Richter scale, 204, **204**
Ride, Sally, **478**
rift, 232
rift valleys, 339, **339**
Rigel, 570, **570**, 573
right ascension, 492, **492**
Ring of Fire, 187, 231, **231**
ripple marks, **94**
rise, continental, 338, **338**
rivers, 270–279, **270–279**
robot, 240

rock, 78–99. See also plate tectonics
    cap, 282, **282**
    city of, 104
    classification of, **85**, 85–86, **86**
    composition of, 85, **85**, 88, **88**, **92**, 92–93, 97, **97**
    cycle, **82–83**, 84, **84**, 91
    dancing, 324
    definition, 80
    disturbed layers in, 139, **139**
    elastic rebound of, 197, **197**
    faulting, **183**, 183–184, **184**, **197–199**
    folding, 182, **182**
    fossil dating of, 150
    geologic time and, 151–155, **152**
    igneous, 79, **83**, 84, **87**, 87–90, **88–90**
    metamorphic, 79, **82**, 84, 95–99, **95–99**
    minerals in, 85, **85**
    parent, 255, **256**
    plutonic, 89
    radiometric dating, **142**, 142–145, **143**
    relative dating, 137–141
    river, 247
    sedimentary, 79, **82**, 84, **86**, 91–94, **91–94**
    texture, 86, **86**, 88, **88**, 98, **98**
    types of, 79, 82
    unconformities in, 140–141, **140–141**
    value of, 80–81
rock cycle, **82–83**, 84, **84**, 91
rockets
    development of, 598–599
    fuel for, 601, 610
    physics of, 600, **600**
    types of, 599, **599**
rocket science, 598–601, **600**, **601**
rock falls, 317, **317**
rose quartz, 64
Rosetta stone, **3**
Ross Ice Shelf, 310, **310**
rotation
    of Earth and magnetic fields, 30
    planetary, 515, **515**, 539–548
    retrograde, 540
rubies, 71
runoff, **271**, 422

Rushmore, Mount (South Dakota), **242**
Russell, Henry Norris, 577
rust, 251

S

safety rules, 25, 626–629
Sahara Desert, 54, **54**, **455**, 460
salinity, **332**, 332–333, **333**, 368
salt
    halite, **61**, **65**
    ocean currents and, **368**
    in ocean water, **332**, 332–333, **333**
saltation, 304, **304**
Salyut 1 (space station), 614
San Andreas Fault (California), 179–180, **207**
sandbars, **301**
sandblasting, 244, **244**
sandstone, **86**, 99
San Francisco, 163, **207**, 219, 476
sapphires, 71
Sargasso Sea, **333**
satellites. See also moons of other planets
    artificial, 507, **602–603**, 602–605
    images from, 235, 341, **341**, 442, 604, **604**, 605
    natural, 549
    remote sensing and, 54, 604–605, **604–605**
    weather, 2, 8, **8**, 603
saturation, 423
saturation zone, 280, **280**
Saturn, **388**, 526, **536**, 545, **545**, 555, 611
Saturn V (rocket), 596, **596**, 599
savanna, tropical, **458–459**, 461, **461**
scale, on maps, **44**
scale models, 168
scalpels, **80**, 105, **105**
schist, **95**, 98, **98**
science fiction, 598
scientific method, 12–17, **13**, 734–736
scientific notation, 743
scrubbers, 413
sea anemones, 343
sea arches, **302**
sea breezes, **406**

sea caves, 302
sea cliffs, 301, **301, 302–303**
sea-floor spreading, **175,** 175–176, 193, 232, **232**
sea-level changes, 15, **18,** 471
seamounts, 339, **339**
Seasat, 341
seasons, 454, **454,** 490
sea stacks, **302**
seaweed, 347
secondary pollutants, 409, **409**
secondary treatment, 286, **286**
secondary waves, 200. *See also* S waves
second law of motion (Newton's), 748
sedimentary rock, 79, **82, 84, 86,** 91–94
   chemical, **92,** 92–93, **93**
   clastic, 92, **92**
   composition of, 92
   organic, 92, 93, **93**
   origins of, 91
   structures, 94, **94**
sediments, 82, 113, 277–279, **278–279,** 295
seismic engineering, 208, **208**
seismic gaps, 206–207, **207**
seismic waves, 172, **200,** 200–201, **201, 203, 211**
seismograms, **202,** 202–203, **203**
seismographs, **162,** 172, 202, **202,** 234, **234**
seismology, 6, 196
Seismosaurus hallorum, 12, **12,** 16–17, **16–17**
septic tanks, 287, **287**
severe weather, 434–439
sewage, **286,** 286–287, 352
sewage treatment plants, 286
shadow zone, **211**
shale, 98, **98**
shear waves, 200, **200.** *See also* S waves
Sheele, Karl, 389
shelf, continental, 338, **338**
Shepard, Alan, 612
shield volcanoes, 228, **228**
shoreline, 298
Siberia, 535
sidewinder adder, 308, **308**
Sierra Nevada (California), **456**
silica, 76, 224
silicate minerals, 62, **62,** 750
sills, **89**
siltstone, **86**

sinkholes, 284, **284**
SI prefixes, 22, 731
SI units, **22,** 22–25, 731
Skylab, 596, 615, **615**
slab pull, **177**
slate, 98, **98**
sleet, 428
slope
   continental, 338, **338**
   graphing and, 738
   mass movement and, 316–319
sludge dumping, 352
slumps, 317, **317**
smog, 117, **408,** 409, **409.** *See also* air pollution
smoking, 412
snow, 428–429
sodium, emission lines of, **571**
sodium chloride. *See* salt
SOHO, 213, **213**
soil
   climate and, 257–258
   conservation of, 259–261
   earthworms and, 266
   erosion, **260,** 260–261, 267
   fertility of, 226, 277, **277,** 279, 308, **308**
   humus, 255, **256**
   importance of, 259–260
   layers, 256, **256**
   sources of, 255
   transported, 255, **255**
   water storage and, 260
Sojourner (Martian rover), **57,** 608
solar cars, 106, **106**
solar cells, 120, **120**
solar collectors, 121, **121**
solar eclipses, **552,** 552–553. *See also* sun
solar energy, 106–107, 119–121, 398–399, **398–399,** 402, 451
solar flares, 213, 523
solar nebula, 511. *See also* nebulas
solar radiation, 398–399, **398–399,** 468, **468**
solar system. *See also* comets; moons; planets
   asteroid belt, 559, **559**
   formation of, **512,** 512–514, **513**
   impacts in, 561
   Kuiper belt, 558, **558**
   meteoroids, 560, **560**

   moons of other planets, 554–556
   Oort cloud, 558, **558**
Solar Two, 121
solar wind, 514, 558, 609
solstices, 484
sonar, 340, **340**
Soufriere Hills volcano (Montserrat), 163
Southern Hemisphere, 37, 366, 438, **454**
South Pole, 35, **35, 36,** 37
space exploration, human, 612–614
space junk, 507, 604
space probes, 606–611, **606–611**
space shuttles, **599, 613,** 613–614, 622
space stations, 614–616, **615, 616, 622**
space travel, 547
spadefoot toads, **460**
specific gravity, 66
spectra, 570–572
   absorption, 572, **572**
   continuous, 570, 572, **572**
spectrographs, 570, **572**
speed
   average, 749
   of glaciers, 311
   of ocean waves, 373, **373**
   of seismic waves, 172, 200–201, **201, 211,** 437, 439
   of wind, 437, 439, 441, **443**
spiral galaxies, 582, **582**
springs, 281–282, **282**
spring tides, 380, **380**
S-P-time method, 203, **203**
Spurr, Mount (Alaska), 240
Sputnik 1 and *2* (satellites), 602, **602**
stalactites, 6, **6, 283**
stalagmites, 6, **6, 283**
Stardust (space probe), 610, **610**
starfish, 343
stars, 570–581. *See also* sun
   brightness of, 573–574, 577, **578–579**
   color of, 570, **570,** 573
   composition of, 570–573
   distance to, 493, **493,** 575, **575**
   formation of, 514, **514**
   galaxies and, 582–584, **584**

life cycle of, 577–581, **578–579**
locating, 491–492, **491–492**
magnitude of, 573–574, 577, **578–579**
motion of, 575–576
spectra of, 570–572
temperature of, 572–573, 577, **578–579**
stationary fronts, 432, **433, 443**
station models, 442, **443**
steel scalpels, 105
Steno, Nicolaus, 2
steppes, 463
St. Helens, Mount (Washington), 162, **223,** 418, **469**
Stonehenge, 484, **484**
stone tools, **80**
storm surge, 377, 439
St. Pierre (Martinique), 220, **220**
strata, 91
stratification, 94, **94**
stratified drift, 314, **314**
stratosphere, **394,** 395
stratovolcanoes, 228, **228**
streak, 65, **65,** 750
stream erosion, 273–274
stress, 181, 197
striations, 314, **314**
strike-slip faults, 184, **184, 198**
strip mining, 70, 115, **115,** 116
subduction zones, **178,** 233, **233**
sublittoral zone, 343, **343**
submetallic luster, 64, **64**
suborbital velocity, 601, **601**
subscripts, 747
subsoil, **256**
succulents, **460**
sulfate minerals, 63, 750
sulfide minerals, 63, 750
sulfur dioxide, 116, 235, 411
sulfuric acid, **540**
summer solstice, 484
sun, 519–523. *See also* stars
   directions and, 37
   eclipses and, **552,** 552–553
   energy production in, 520–522, **522**
   latitude and, 453–454
   life cycle of, **578–579**
   magnitude of, 574
   nuclear fusion in, 521–522, **522**
   observing, 534
   seismic activity, 213, **213**
   solar energy, 106–107, 119–121, 398–399, **398–399,** 402
   solar flares, 213, 523
   solar radiation, 398–399, **398–399,** 468, **468**
   structure, 519, **519**
   surface activity, 522–523
   ultraviolet radiation from, 528
sunblock, 395
sunspots, 523, **523**
supergiants, **579**
supernovas, 580, **580**
superposition, **137,** 137–138
surf, 299, 374, **374.** *See also* ocean waves
surface area, 253, **253**
surface currents, 365, **365, 367,** 457
surface gravity, 539
surface mining, 70
suspended load, **274**
sustainable farming, 267
S waves, **200,** 200–203, **201, 203, 211**
swells, 375, **375**
Sylbaris, Ludger, 220, **220**
symbols, safety, **25, 626**
synclines, 182, **182**
Système International (SI), 22, 731. *See also* International System of Units

T

Tabei, Junko, **56**
taiga, **458, 465,** 466, **466**
talc, **66**
talus slopes, **317**
tar pits, 147, **147**
taste, **67**
technology transfers, 617
tectonic plates, **170,** 170–171, 177–179, **178–179,** 180, **196.** *See also* plate tectonics
telescopes
   Hubble Space, 568, **568,** 594, **594**
   McMath-Pierce, 534, **534**
   non-optical, 499–501, **500, 501**
   optical, 496–498, **496–498**
   radio, 9, **9,** 500–501, **500–501**
   solar, 534
   X-ray, **500,** 501, **501**
television, **163**
temperate deserts, **458,** 464, **464**
temperate forests, **458,** 462, **462**
temperate grasslands, **458,** 463, **463**
temperate zones, **458, 462,** 462–464
temperature
   atmospheric, 394, **394,** 395, 396, 400–401
   building roofs and, 466
   conversions, 232, 732
   definition, 25
   igneous rock and, **87**
   of magma, 232
   measurement, 440
   metamorphic rock, 95–97
   in nebulas, 511
   of ocean currents, 367, **367, 368**
   of ocean water, **333,** 333–334, **334,** 336, **336**
   relative humidity and, 423, **423,** 424
   scales, 25, 732
   of stars, 572–573, 577, **578–579**
   table of conversions, 732
   units, **22,** 25
tension, 181
terminal moraines, 315, **315**
terraces, 276
terracing, 261, **261**
terrestrial planets, 539
Tetons, 187, **187**
texture, 86
theories, 19
thermal vent communities, **7, 326, 344**
thermocline, **333**
thermometers, 25, **389,** 424, **424,** 440, **440**
thermosphere, **394, 396,** 396–397
third law of motion (Newton's), 748
thrust, **600**
thunder, 435
thunderstorms, **434,** 434–435
tidal bore, 381
tidal energy, 350, **350**
tidal range, 380, **381**
tidal waves. *See* tsunamis
tides, 378–381, **379–381**
till, glacial, 315, **315**
tilting, 139, **139**

Index **793**

tiltmeters, 234
time-distance graph, 203, **203**
timekeeping, 482–483
Tiros 1 (satellite), 2, 603
Titan (moon), 526, 555, **555,** 611
Titanic, 310
tobacco smoking, 412
topaz, **66**
topographic maps, **46,** 46–49, **47, 48**
topography, 46, 55, 381
topsoil, 256, **256,** 260–261, 267
Tornado Alley, 420
tornadoes, 8, 420, **436,** 436–437
Torrington, John, 465
Toscanelli (mapmaker), **32**
trace fossils, 148, **148**
trade winds, **404,** 404–405
transform boundaries, 179, **179, 198**
transform motion, **179, 198**
transpiration, **422**
trash
  dumping, 351, **351**
  recycling, 110, 130
trees, **459,** 462, 466, 471, **471**
Trefry, John, 7
trenches, ocean, 339, **339**
tributaries, 272
trilobites, 150, **150**
triple-beam balance, 733
Triton (moon), 556, **556**
tropical air masses, **430**
tropical deserts, **458,** 460, **460**
tropical rain forest, **458,** 459, **459**
tropical savanna, **458,** 461, **461**
tropical zones, **458, 459,** 459–461
tropic of Cancer, 459
tropic of Capricorn, 459
tropites, 150, **150**
troposphere, **394,** 395, **395, 396**
trough, 372, **372**
true north, 36
Tsiolkovsky, Konstantin, 598
tsunami earthquakes, 386
tsunamis, **376,** 376–377, 386
tube worms, 7, **344**
tundra, **458,** 465, **465**
Tycho Brahe, 487, **487,** 515
typhoons, **388,** 437. *See also* hurricanes
Tyrannosaurus rex, 161

U

Ubar, 54
ultraviolet (UV) radiation, **499,** 528
ultraviolet rays, 328, 395
unconformities, 140–141, **140–141**
undertow, 374, **374**
uniformitarianism, **134,** 134–135, 149
United States
  earthquake risk in, 205, **205**
  fossil fuel reserves in, 115, **115**
  ocean pollution and, 354–355, **355**
United States Space Command, 604
units
  astronomical, 516, 537, 538, **538**
  SI, **22,** 22–25, 731
  of time, 482
Unity (space-station module), 622
universal gravitation, law of, 517, 748
universe
  age of, 588
  expansion of, **587,** 587–588
  formation of, 586–588
  size and scale of, **493,** 493–495, **494–495**
  structure of, 589, **589**
upper mantle, **232.** *See also* asthenosphere; lithosphere
upwelling, 371
uranium, **67,** 118
uranium-lead dating, 144
Uranus, **536,** 546, **546,** 555
Ursa Major, 490, **490,** 573, **573**
USGS, 46
U-shaped valleys, **313**
UV radiation, 528

V

valley breezes, 407, **407**
valley glaciers, 309
Van Allen, James, **602**
Van Allen radiation belts, 602
variables, 15, 735
veldt, 463
Venera 9 (space probe), 607, **607**
vents, 224, **224, 229**
Venus, 515, **536,** 540, **540,** 607
vernal equinox, 492, **492**
Verne, Jules, 162, 598
Very Large Array (VLA), 501, **501**
Vesta (asteroid), **559**
Viking 1 and *2,* (space probes), 608, **608**
volcanic
  ash, 226, **226**
  batholiths, **89**
  blocks, 226, **226**
  bombs, 226, **226**
  dikes, **89**
  eruptions, 222, **222,** 223, **223,** 224–229, **229**
  laccoliths, **89**
  necks, **89,** 252
  plutons, **69,** 89, **89**
  sills, **89**
volcanoes. *See also* magma
  air pollution and, 418
  climate change and, 469, **469**
  cross sections, 224, **224,** 228, **228**
  defined, 222
  Earth's early atmosphere and, 527, **527**
  effects, 220, **220,** 227–229, **227–229**
  explosive eruptions, 223, **223,** 224
  extinct, dormant, and active, 234
  formation, **230,** 230–235, **232, 233, 234**
  Fuji (Japan), 228, **228**
  gases in, 235, **235**
  lava, 90, **90,** 222, **222,** 225, **225**
  location of, **231,** 231–234
  mudflows, 318, **318**
  nonexplosive eruptions, 222, **222**
  on other planets, **540,** 543
  Paricutín (Mexico), **2**
  Pelée (Martinique), 220, **220,** 222
  Pinatubo (Philippines), 227, **227**
  predictions, 234–235
  pyroclastic materials, 225–226, **226**
  Soufriere Hills (Montserrat), 163
  Spurr (Alaska), 240
  St. Helens (Washington), 162, **223,** 418, **469**

types of, 228, **228**
vents, **167,** 224, **224,** 229
volcanology, 6
volume, **22,** 23–24, **24**
   calculation of, 24, 743
   defined, 23, 743
von Braun, Wernher, 599, **602,** 613
Voyager 1 and *2* (space probes), **478,** 609, **609**

W

War of the Worlds, The, **479**
warm air masses, 431, **432**
warm fronts, **432, 443**
waste, nuclear, 118, **118**
water. *See also* flow of water; ground water; oceans
   in the atmosphere, 393, 422–429
   cycle, 270, **271,** 335, **335,** 422, **422**
   desalination, 349
   flow of, 269–270
   hydroelectric energy, 123, **123**
   in magma, 224, 233
   origin of Earth's, 526–527, **527**
   pollution, 285, 351–353
   storage in soils, 260
   table, 280, **280, 282**
   treatment, **286,** 286–287
   uses of, **287,** 287–289, **288**
   vapor, 395, 422–426, 428
   weathering by, 247, **247**
water cycle, 270, **271,** 335, **335,** 422, **422**
water pollution, 285, 351–353
watershed, 272
waterspouts, 362, 437
water table, 280, **280, 282**
water vapor, 395, 422–426, 428
Watt-Evans, Lawrence, 623
wave-cut terraces, **303**
wave erosion, 301–302, **302–303**
wave height, 372, **372,** 374
wavelength, 372–374, **372–374,** 376
wave period, 299, 373, **373**
waves. *See also* ocean waves
   crest of, 372, **372**
   energy of, 298–299, 350
   erosion by, 301–303
   height of, 372, **372**
   period of, 320, 373, **373**
   radio, 397
   seismic, 172, **200,** 200–203, **201, 203,** 211, **211,** 212–213
   speed of, 373, **373**
   trough of, 372, **372**
   wavelength of, 372–374, **372–374,** 376
wave speed, 373, **373**
wave trains, 299, **299**
weather, 420–443. *See also* climate; precipitation
   air masses and fronts, **430,** 430–433, **432–433, 443**
   climate and, 452
   clouds, **426,** 426–428, **427, 435**
   condensation, 425–426
   forecasting, 440–443
   humidity, **423,** 423–424
   hurricanes, 8, **8, 402,** 437–439, **437–439**
   maps, 442–443, **443**
   thunderstorms, **434,** 434–435
   tornadoes, 8, **8,** 420, **436,** 436–437
   water cycle and, 422, **422**
   water vapor and, 422–429
weather balloon, 442, **442**
weathering, 91
   chemical, 249–251, **249–251**
   climate and, 254
   differential, 252
   elevation and, 254
   gravity and, 254
   mechanical, 246–248, **246–248**
   surface area and, 253, **253**
weather satellites, 2, 442, 603
Wegener, Alfred, 163, 173–175, 193, **193**
Weinbaum, Stanley, 567
wells, 281–282, **282**
Wells, H. G., **479**
westerlies, 404–405
wet-bulb thermometers, 424, **424**
wetlands, 295, 325
whaling, **326**
whitecaps, 375, **375**
white-dwarf stars, **578,** 578–579
Williams, Robert, 568
Williamson, Jack, 77
Wilson, Robert, **587**
wind, 402. *See also* ocean waves
   chill, **417**
   deposition, 306–308, **307, 308**
   energy, 122, **122,** 405
   erosion, **304,** 304–306, **305**
   global, 365, 402–407, **404**
   on Jupiter, 439
   local, **406,** 406–407, **407**
   prevailing, **404,** 404–405, 455, **455, 456**
   solar, 514, 558, 609
   speed, 441, **443**
   types of, **404,** 404–407, **406–407**
   upper atmosphere, 396
   weathering by, 247, **247**
windsocks, 441, **441**
wind vanes, 441
Winter Park sinkhole (Florida), **284**
winter solstice, 484
Wright brothers, 479

X

X-15, **2**
X-33, **614**
X rays, **499**
X-ray telescopes, **500,** 501, **501**

Y

Yakima River (Washington), 293
Yellowstone National Park (Wyoming), 294, **294**
Yogi, 57

Z

Zarya (space-station module), 622
zenith, **491**
zone of aeration, 280, **280**
zone of saturation, 280, **280**
zones, climate
   polar, 458, **464,** 464–466
   temperate, **458, 462,** 462–464, **464**
   tropical, **458, 459,** 459–461, **460, 461**
zooplankton, **342**

Credits

Abbreviations used: (t) top, (c) center, (b) bottom, (l) left, (r) right, (bkgd) background

ILLUSTRATIONS

All work, unless otherwise noted, contributed by Holt, Rinehart & Winston.

Table of Contents: Page ix(tr), MapQuest.com; ix(bl), Uhl Studios, Inc.; x(t), Patrick Gnan; xi(tl), Mike Wepplo/Das Group; xi(bl), Marty Roper/Planet Rep; xii(cl), Yuan Lee; xii(bl), Marty Roper/Planet Rep; xiv(tl), Marty Roper/Planet Rep; xv(tl), Paul DiMare; xv(cr), Dan McGeehan/Koralick Associates.

Chapter One: Page 4(br), Barbara Hoopes-Ambler; 7(br), Craig Attebery/Jeff Lavaty Artist Agent; 9(b), David Schleinkofer; 10(tl), Robert Hynes; 12(b), Barbara Hoopes-Ambler; 14, Carlyn Iverson, 15, Carlyn Iverson, 16(tl, cl), Carlyn Iverson; 16–17(b), Christy Krames; 18, Uhl Studios, Inc.; 19(br), Stephen Durke/Washington Artists; 20(c), Jared Schneidman Design; 25(tr), Stephen Durke/Washington Artists; 26(c), Christy Krames; 28(cr), Geoff Smith/Scott Hull; 29(br), Sidney Jablonski; 30(c), Uhl Studios, Inc.

Chapter Two: Page 35(bl), John White/The Neis Group; 37, MapQuest.com; 38(tl), MapQuest.com; 39(t), MapQuest.com; 41, MapQuest.com; 42, MapQuest.com.

Chapter Three: Page 60(bl), Gary Locke; 61, Stephen Durke/Washington Artists; 68–69(bkgd), Uhl Studios, Inc.; 70(bl), Jared Schneidman Design.

Chapter Four: Pages 82–83, Uhl Studios, Inc.; 85(b), Sidney Jablonski; 87, Keith Locke; 88(l), Uhl Studios, Inc.; 89(b), Uhl Studios, Inc.; 92(br), Robert Hynes; 96(b), Uhl Studios, Inc.; 97(t), Stephen Durke/Washington Artists; 97(b), Uhl Studios, Inc.; 100(br), Sidney Jablonski; 103(cr), Sidney Jablonski.

Chapter Five: Page 106(tl), Uhl Studios, Inc.; 108(b), Uhl Studios, Inc.; 113(bl), Uhl Studios, Inc.; 114(l), Uhl Studios, Inc.; 115(t), MapQuest.com; 118(cl), Stephen Durke/Washington Artists; 121(tr), John Huxtable/Black Creative; 125(br), Uhl Studios, Inc.; 126(br), John Huxtable/Black Creative; 126(cr), Uhl Studios, Inc.; 129(cr), Sidney Jablonski.

Chapter Six: Page 132(t), Nenad Jakesevic; 134(b), Uhl Studios, Inc.; 136(c), Barbara Hoopes-Ambler; 138(b), Jared Schneidman Design; 139, Uhl Studios, Inc.; 140(b), Jared Schneidman Design; 141, Uhl Studios, Inc.; 142(b), Stephen Durke/Washington-Artists' Represents; 147(br), Will Nelson/Sweet Reps; 148–149(c), Frank Ordaz; 150(cr), Uhl Studios, Inc.; 159(tr), Joe LeMonnier.

Unit Three: Page 163(cr), Terry Kovalcik.

Chapter Seven: Page 166(b), Uhl Studios, Inc.; 167(br), Uhl Studios, Inc.; 168–169, Uhl Studios, Inc.; 170(c), Uhl Studios, Inc.; 171(c), Uhl Studios, Inc.; 172(tl), Uhl Studios, Inc.; 173(tr), Uhl Studios, Inc.; 173(bl), MapQuest.com; 174, MapQuest.com; 175, Uhl Studios, Inc.; 176(cl), Stephen Durke/Washington Artists; 176(cr), Uhl Studios, Inc.; 177(b), Uhl Studios, Inc.; 178–179(b), Uhl Studios, Inc.; 182(tl), Uhl Studios, Inc.; 183(tr), Marty Roper/Planet Rep; 183(cr), Uhl Studios, Inc.; 183(br), Uhl Studios, Inc.; 185(tr), Uhl Studios, Inc.; 186(t), Tony Morse/Ivy Glick; 186(bl), Uhl Studios, Inc.; 188, Uhl Studios, Inc.; 189(cr), Marty Roper/Planet Rep.

Chapter Eight: Page 194(tr), Tony Morse/Ivy Glick; 196(b), MapQuest.com; 197(b), Uhl Studios, Inc.; 198(b), Uhl Studios, Inc.; 198–199, Uhl Studios, Inc.; 200, Uhl Studios, Inc.; 201(cl), Uhl Studios, Inc.; 202(bl), Uhl Studios, Inc.; 203(tr), Sidney Jablonski; 205(b), MapQuest.com; 207(t), Jared Schneidman Design; 208, Uhl Studios, Inc.; 211(b), Uhl Studios, Inc.; 212, Sidney Jablonski; 214(br), Sidney Jablonski; 214(cl), Uhl Studios, Inc.; 216(br), Uhl Studios, Inc.; 217(cr), Sidney Jablonski.

Chapter Nine: Page 224(tl), Uhl Studios, Inc.; 228(l), Patrick Gnan; 229(tr), Uhl Studios, Inc.; 230(b), Uhl Studios, Inc.; 231(tr), Stephen Durke/Washington Artists; 231(bl), MapQuest.com; 232, Uhl Studios, Inc.; 233, Uhl Studios, Inc.; 234(t), Uhl Studios, Inc.; 239(tr), Ross, Culbert and Lavery.

Unit Four: Page 243(tl), MapQuest.com.

Chapter Ten: Page 246(b), Uhl Studios, Inc.; 248(br), Will Nelson/Sweet Reps; 249(r), Stephen Durke/Washington Artists; 252(b), Stephen Durke/Washington Artists; 253, Stephen Durke/Washington Artists; 256(r), Will Nelson/Sweet Reps; 260(t), Uhl Studios, Inc.

Chapter Eleven: Page 271, Mike Wepplo/Das Group; 272(bc), MapQuest.com; 274, Uhl Studios, Inc.; 277(b), Marty Roper/Planet Rep; 280(c), Stephen Durke/Washington Artists; 281(c), MapQuest.com; 281(br), Geoff Smith/Scott Hull; 282, Stephen Durke/Washington Artists; 286(b), John Huxtable/Black Creative; 287(cl), John Huxtable/Black Creative; 287(b), Sidney Jablonski; 289(c), MapQuest.com; 290(c), Mike Wepplo/Das Group; 293(cr), Sidney Jablonski.

Chapter Twelve: Page 296(t), Paul DiMare; 300(bl), Uhl Studios, Inc.; 302–303, Mike Wepplo/Das Group; 304(b), Dean Fleming; 304(cl), Keith Locke; 306(bl), Geoff Smith/Scott Hull; 307(c), Uhl Studios, Inc.; 313(b), Robert Hynes; 323(tr), Sidney Jablonski.

Chapter Thirteen: Page 328(t), Rainey Kirk/The Neis Group; 331, MapQuest.com; 332(tl), Ross, Culbert and Lavery; 333(tr), MapQuest.com; 333(b), Ross, Culbert and Lavery; 335(b), Mike Wepplo/Das Group; 338–339, Uhl Studios, Inc.; 340(b), Uhl Studios, Inc.; 341(br), Ross, Culbert and Lavery; 342, Yuan Lee; 350(tl), Jared Schneidman Design; 353(br), Mark Heine; 357(c), Jared Schneidman Design; 358(c), Bill Mayer; 358(tr), MapQuest.com; 359(tr), Ross, Culbert and Lavery.

Chapter Fourteen: Page 362(t), John Huxtable/Black Creative; 362(bl), Tony Morse/Ivy Glick; 364(tr), Dean Fleming; 365(tr), Stephen Durke/Washington Artists; 365(bl), MapQuest.com; 366, MapQuest.com; 367(c), MapQuest.com; 368, Stephen Durke/Washington Artists; 369, Jared Schneidman Design; 370, MapQuest.com; 372, Jared Schneidman Design; 373, Dean Fleming; 374, Dean Fleming; 376(tc), Uhl Studios, Inc.; 377(t), MapQuest.com; 378(c), Marty Roper/Planet Rep; 379, Sidney Jablonski; 380, Sidney Jablonski; 382(br), Dean Fleming; 382(c), Stephen Durke/Washington Artists; 383(c), Marty Roper/Planet Rep; 385(cr), Sidney Jablonski.

Unit Six: Page 388(bl), John Huxtable/Black Creative; 388(br), Annie Bissett; 389(cl), Terry Kovalcik.

Chapter Fifteen: Page 392(b), Sidney Jablonski; 393(br), Stephen Durke/Washington Artists; 394(b), Stephen Durke/Washington Artists; 395(c), Stephen Durke/Washington Artists; 396, Stephen Durke/Washington Artists; 398(b), Uhl Studios, Inc.; 399(b), Uhl Studios, Inc.; 400(c), John Huxtable/Black Creative; 402(bl), Uhl Studios, Inc.; 402(bl), Stephen Durke/Washington Artists; 403(tr), Uhl Studios, Inc.; 403(tr), Stephen Durke/Washington Artists; 404(b), Uhl Studios, Inc.; 404(b), Stephen Durke/Washington Artists; 406, Stephen Durke/Washington Artists; 407, Stephen Durke/Washington Artists; 409(b), John Huxtable/Black Creative; 415(c), Stephen Durke/Washington Artists.

Chapter Sixteen: Page 422(b), Robert Hynes; 427(b), Stephen Durke/Washington Artists; 428(tl), Stephen Durke/Washington Artists; 430(b), MapQuest.com; 432, Stephen Durke/Washington Artists; 433, Stephen Durke/Washington Artists; 435(br), Paul DiMare; 438(b), Paul DiMare; 440(tr), Dan McGeehan/Koralick Associates; 443(cr), MapQuest.com; 447(cr), MapQuest.com.

Chapter Seventeen: Page 450(tr), Will Nelson/Sweet Reps; 453(br), Uhl Studios, Inc.; 453(br), Stephen Durke/Washington Artists; 454(c), Craig Attebery/Jeff Lavaty Artist Agent; 455(tc), Stephen Durke/Washington Artists; 456(b), Uhl Studios, Inc.; 457(c), MapQuest.com; 458(cl), Stephen Durke/Washington Artists; 458(b), MapQuest.com; 459(tr), Stephen Durke/Washington Artists; 459(c), MapQuest.com; 462(tr), Stephen Durke/Washington Artists; 462(c), MapQuest.com; 464(bl), Stephen Durke/Washington Artists; 465(t), MapQuest.com; 467(bl), MapQuest.com; 467(tr), Marty Roper/Planet Rep; 468, Sidney Jablonski; 469(c), Uhl Studios, Inc.; 469(br), MapQuest.com; 470(b), Marty Roper/Planet Rep; 472(t), Craig Attebery/Jeff Lavaty Artist Agent; 472(cr), Stephen Durke/Washington Artists; 474(tr), Terry Kovalcik; 475(cr), Sidney Jablonski.

Chapter Eighteen: Page 483(t), Nenad Jakesevic; 486, Dan McGeehan/Koralick Associates; 489, Stephen Durke/Washington Artists; 490(c), Sidney Jablonski; 491(tr), Stephen Durke/Washington Artists; 492(t), Stephen Durke/Washington Artists; 493(b), Stephen Durke/Washington Artists; 495, Paul DiMare; 497, Uhl Studios, Inc.

Chapter Nineteen: Page 508(l), Stephen Durke/Washington Artists; 511(c), Stephen Durke/Washington Artists; 512–513, Paul DiMare; 515(c), Sidney Jablonski; 516(t), Mark Heine; 516(br), Sidney Jablonski; 518(c), Sidney Jablonski; 519(br), Uhl Studios, Inc.; 520, Marty Roper/Planet Rep; 521(c), Marty Roper/Planet Rep; 521(b), Stephen Durke/Washington Artists; 522, Stephen Durke/Washington Artists; 523(b), Sidney Jablonski; 525, Uhl Studios, Inc.; 526(bl), Paul DiMare; 527(tr), Paul DiMare; 529(br), Uhl Studios, Inc.

Chapter Twenty: Page 536(tl), Uhl Studios, Inc.; 538(b), Sidney Jablonski; 539(tr), Sidney Jablonski; 544(tl), Sidney Jablonski; 546(b), Sidney Jablonski; 547(tr), Dan McGeehan/Koralick Associates; 548(cl), Paul DiMare; 550, Stephen Durke/Washington Artists; 551(c), Sidney Jablonski; 552(c), Paul DiMare; 553(c), Paul DiMare; 558(tl), Stephen Durke/Washington Artists; 558(br), Paul DiMare; 559, Craig Attebery/Jeff Lavaty Artist Agent; 562(br), Sidney Jablonski; 563(cl), Stephen Durke/Washington Artists.

Chapter Twenty-One: Page 568(br), Craig Attebery/Jeff Lavaty Artist Agent; 571(c), Stephen Durke/Washington Artists; 572(tl), Stephen Durke/Washington Artists; 575(c), Sidney Jablonski; 576(tl), Sidney Jablonski; 576(c), Stephen Durke/Washington Artists; 578–579, Stephen Durke/Washington Artists; 587(br), Craig Attebery/Jeff Lavaty Artist Agent; 589(r), Craig Attebery/Jeff Lavaty Artist Agent; 593(cr), Sidney Jablonski.

Chapter Twenty-Two: Page 599(b), Stephen Durke/Washington Artists; 600(l), John Huxtable/Black Creative; 603(tr), Stephen Durke/Washington Artists; 606, Stephen Durke/Washington Artists; 607, Stephen Durke/Washington Artists; 608, Stephen Durke/Washington Artists; 609(b), Craig Attebery/Jeff Lavaty Artist Agent; 609(tr), Stephen Durke/Washington Artists; 609(br), Stephen Durke/Washington Artists; 611(tl), Paul DiMare; 617(c), Paul DiMare.

LabBook: Page 631(tr), Mark Heine; 632(cl), Marty Roper/Planet Rep; 640(br), Mark Heine; 645, Mark Heine; 648(br), Mark Heine; 650(c), Uhl Studios, Inc.; 662(c), Sidney Jablonski; 663(c), MapQuest.com; 664(b), MapQuest.com; 666(t), Marty Roper/Planet Rep; 667(tr), Ralph Garafola/Lorraine Garafola Represents; 671(t), Mark Heine; 673(tr), Mark Heine; 680(tr), Dean Fleming; 683(br), Geoff Smith/Scott Hull; 686(b), Mark Heine; 687(b), Sidney Jablonski; 691(tr), Mark Heine; 693(tr), Mark Heine; 696(t), MapQuest.com; 698(tl), Dan McGeehan/Koralick Associates; 698(br), Mark Heine; 701(cr), Marty Roper/Planet Rep; 704(br), Sidney Jablonski; 704(cr), MapQuest.com; 705(tl), Sidney Jablonski; 705(tr), MapQuest.com; 705(cl), Sidney Jablonski; 705(cr), MapQuest.com; 706(b), Sidney Jablonski; 708(cr), Sidney Jablonski; 712, Marty Roper/Planet Rep; 723(tr), Geoff Smith/Scott Hull.

Appendix: Page 729(cl), Blake Thornton/Rita Marie; 732(c), Terry Guyer; 736(b), Mark Mille/Sharon Langley; 744, Kristy Sprott; 745, Kristy Sprott; 746(bl), Stephen

Durke/Washington Artists; 747(tl), Stephen Durke/Washington Artists; 747(c), Stephen Durke/Washington Artists; 747(b), Bruce Burdick; 752–753, Sidney Jablonski.

PHOTOGRAPHY

Cover and Title Page: (tl), Jack Dykinga/Tony Stone Images; (tr), Barry Rosenthal/ FPG International; (bl), David Parker/Science Photo Library/Photo Researchers, Inc.; (Earth on cover, title page), Geospace/Science Photo Library/Photo Researchers, Inc., (owl on cover, spine, back, title page), Kim Taylor/Bruce Coleman, Inc.

Sam Dudgeon/HRW Photo: Page v(br), vi(bl), vii(cl), viii(tl), ix(cl), xi(tr), xiii(cl), xiv(bl), xvii(b), xviii(br), xx, 5, 23(cl), 35(tr), 38(bl), 46(tr), 59(b), 60, 62(cr), 65(tr, bl), 66(bl), 67(tc, cl), 68(c), 69(b), 73(cl), 74(tl), 84, 85(c), 86(cl), 92(c), 95(cl), 97(brt), 98(cl, bl, bc), 105(c), 107, 110(tr), 117(cr, c), 119(b), 124(tl), 135(tl, br, tr, bl), 137(bl), 143(all), 164(tr, tl), 181(c), 195, 209(tr), 210(br), 244(tl, cr, tr, bc), 266, 269(br), 288(bl), 297, 316(bc, br), 329(tl, tr), 391, 395(bc), 412, 421, 423, 424, 429(br), 440, 451, 499(radio, oven), 508(joggers), 509, 569(br), 577(cl), 588(all), 597, 624(cl, tr, br), 626, 627(bc), 628(br, cl), 629(tl, b), 633, 634, 635, 637, 639(hematite, br), 641(tr, br), 642, 643(all), 646(tr), 647(all), 649, 651, 656, 658, 659, 661(all), 664(tr), 667, 668, 669(bl), 676, 678, 679, 681, 682, 689, 690, 692, 693, 699, 702, 707, 713, 714, 716, 717, 719, 720, 721, 725, 729(br, tr), 733(br).

Table of Contents: Page v(tr), E. R. Degginger/Color-Pic, Inc; v(cr), K. Segerstrom/ USGS; vi(tl), Jean Miele/The Stock Market; vii(tr), Mike Husar/DRK Photo; vii(bl), Walter H. Hodge/Peter Arnold, Inc.; viii(cr), Thomas R. Taylor/Photo Researchers, Inc.; viii(bl), American Museum of Natural History; x(tl), Tom Bean/DRK Photo; x(bl), Tom Walker/Tony Stone Images; xii(tr), James B. Wood; xii(bl), Norbert Wu; xii(bc), James Wilson/Woodfin Camp & Associates; xiii(bl), TOMS/NASA; xv(bl), World Perspective/ Tony Stone Images; xvi(tl), I M House/Tony Stone Images; xvi(bl, bc), NASA; xix, Peter Van Steen/HRW Photo; xxi(br), G.R. Roberts Photo Library.

Unit One: Page 2(tl), Ed Reschke/Peter Arnold, Inc.; 2(tr), Uwe Fink/ University of Arizona, Department of Planetary Sciences, Lunar & Planetary Laboratory; 2(cr), USGS; 2(bl), Smithsonian Air and Space Museum; 2(tl), T. A. Wiewandt/DRK Photo; 3(tl), Hulton Getty Images/Liaison Agency; 3(tr), Adam Woolfitt/British Museum/Woodfin Camp & Associates, Inc.; 3(cl), Francois Gohier; 3(bl), Jason Laure/Woodfin Camp & Associates, Inc.; 3(br), NASA.

Chapter One: Page 4(inset), Dr. David Gillette; 4(t), Peter Van Steen/HRW Photo; 6(bl), S. Schwabe/The Rob Palmer Blue Holes Foundation; 6(tr), Earth Imaging/Tony Stone Images; 8(tl), Marit Jentof-Nilsen and Fritz Hasler–NASA Goddard Laboratory for Atmospheres; 8(bl), Howard B. Bluestein; 9(tr), Jean Miele/The Stock Market; 10(bc, br), Andy Christiansen/HRW Photo; 11(tr), Mark Howard/Westfall Eco Images; 11(cr), Annie Griffiths/Corbis; 15(tr), Brian Parker/Tom Stack & Associates; 17, Paul Fraughton/ HRW Photo; 19(tr), NASA; 21, Victoria Smith/HRW Photo; 23(tr), Otis Imboden/ National Geographic Image Collection; 23(cr), Alan Schein/The Stock Market; 24(tl), Andy Christiansen/HRW Photo; 24(bl, br), Peter Van Steen/HRW Photo; 28(cl), Visuals Unlimited/Ken Lucas; 31(tl), Michael Lyon/HRW Photo; 31(br), NASA.

Chapter Two: Page 32(bkgd), USGS; 32(bl), Victor Boswell/National Geographic Society Image Collection; 32(cr), Scala/Art Resource, NY; 34, Royal Geographical Society, London, UK/The Bridgeman Art Library; 36, Tom Van Sant/The Stock Market; 40(cl, b), Andy Christiansen/HRW Photo; 43, Aerial Images, Inc. and SOVINFORM-SPUTNIK; 44(bl), 45(br), The American Map Corporation/ADC The Map People; 46(bl), 47(bl, cr), 48, USGS; 51, Tom Van Sant/The Stock Market; 52(bl), Andy Christiansen/HRW Photo; 52(tr), Vladimir Pcholkin/FPG International; 53, USGS; 54, JPL/NASA; 55(tl), Andy Christiansen/HRW Photo; 55(br), Courtesy Lower Colorado River Authority, Austin, TX.

Unit Two: 56(tl), Science Photo Library/Photo Researchers, Inc.; 56(tr), Visuals Unlimited/Science VU; 56(bl), NASA/International Stock; 56(bc), UPI/Corbis; 56(br), Thomas Laird/Peter Arnold, Inc; 57(tr), SuperStock; 57(cr), Francois Gohier; 57(cl), AP/Wide World Photos; 57(br), NASA/Science Photo Library/Photo Researchers, Inc.

Chapter Three: Page 58(t), E. R. Degginger/Color-Pic, Inc.; 58(t), Mike Husar/ DRK Photo; 59(tr), Inga Spence/Tom Stack & Associates; 61(br), Dr. Rainer Bode/ Bode-Verlag Gmb; 62(bl), Pat Lanza/Bruce Coleman Inc.; 62(cl, c), E. R. Degginger/ Color-Pic, Inc.; 63(top to bottom), (top four), E. R. Degginger/Color-Pic, Inc.; SuperStock; Visuals Unlimited/Ken Lucas; 64(tr), Liaison Agency; (tl), Jane Burton/Bruce Coleman, Inc.; Luster Chart (row 1), E. R. Degginger/Color-Pic, Inc.; John Cancalosi 1989/DRK Photo; (row 2), Biophoto Associates/Photo Researchers, Inc.; Dr. E. R. Degginger/ Bruce Coleman Inc.; (row 3), E. R. Degginger/Color-Pic, Inc.; Biophoto Associates/ Photo Researchers, Inc.; (row 4), E. R. Degginger/Color-Pic, Inc.; 65(br), Tom Pantages; 65(c), E. R. Degginger/Color-Pic, Inc.; 65(cl), Erica and Harold Van Pelt/American Museum of Natural History; 66(1), Visuals Unlimited/Ken Lucas; 66(2, 4, 5, 6), E. R. Degginger/Color-Pic, Inc.; 66(3), Visuals Unlimited/Dane S. Johnson; 66(7), Carlyn Iverson/Absolute Science Illustration and Photography; 66(8), Mark A. Schneider/ Visuals Unlimited; 66(9), Charles D. Winters/Photo Researchers, Inc.; 66(10), Bard Wrisley/Liaison Agency; 67(tl, bc), E. R. Degginger/Color-Pic, Inc.; 67(tr), Sam Dudgeon/ HRW Photo Courtesy Science Stuff, Austin, TX; 67(cr), Tom Pantages Photography; 67(br), Victoria Smith/HRW Photo; 68(b), E. R. Degginger/Color-Pic, Inc.; 68(tl), Victoria Smith/HRW Photo, Courtesy Science Stuff, Austin, TX; 69(cr, t), E. R. Degginger/Color-Pic, Inc.; 70(c), Wernher Krutein/Liaison Agency; 70(inset), Kosmatsu Mining Systems; 70, Index Stock Photography, Inc.; 71, Historic Royal Palaces; 73(inset), Kosmatsu Mining Systems; 73(tr), Wernher Krutein/Liaison Agency; 74(bl), E. R. Degginger/ Color-Pic, Inc.; 76(bl), Peter Menzel; 76(bl), Ralph Wetmore/Tony Stone Images.

Chapter Four: Page 78(t), Ron Ruhoff/Stock Imagery; 78(c), Kreg Photography courtesy Denver Theatres & Arenas; 79, Victoria Smith/HRW Photo; 80(c), Kenneth Garrett; 80(bc), Fergus O'Brian/FPG International; 80(br), Peter Cummings/Tom Stack & Associates; 80(bl), Historical Collections, National Museum of Health and Medicine, AFIP; 81(bl), A. F. Kersting; 81(br), Andy Christiansen/HRW Photo; 81(c), Breck P. Kent; 81(cr), NASA/Science Photo Library/Photo Researchers, Inc.; 85(granite), Pat Lanza/ Bruce Coleman Inc.; 85(br,cr), E. R. Degginger/Color-Pic, Inc.; 85(cl), Walter H. Hodge/ Peter Arnold; 85(bl), Sp. Harry Taylor/Dorling Kindersley; 85(bc), Breck P. Kent; 86(c), Dorling Kindersley; 86(cr bc), Breck P. Kent; 88(br), E. R. Degginger/Color-Pic, Inc.; 88(cl, bl, cr), Breck P. Kent; 89(tr), Laurence Parent; 90(cl), Breck P. Kent; 90(cr), Peter Frenck/Bruce Coleman, Inc.; 91(br), Robert Glusic/Natural Selection; 92(tl), Breck P. Kent/Animals Animals/Earth Scenes; 92(breccia), Breck P. Kent; 92(cl), Joyce Photographics/Photo Researchers, Inc.; 92(cr), E. R. Degginger/Color-Pic, Inc.; 92(br), Breck P. Kent; 93(br), Ed Cooper; 93, Stephen Frink/Corbis; 93(bl), Breck P. Kent; 93(c), SuperStock; 94(cr), Franklin P. OSF/Animals Animals/Earth Scenes; 94(tl), Breck P. Kent; 95(bl), E. R. Degginger/Color-Pic, Inc.; 95(br), George Wuerthner; 97(tl), Visuals Unlimited/Dane S. Johnson; 97(tlc), Carlyn Iverson/Absolute Science Illustration and Photography; 97(tlb), Breck P. Kent; 97(tr), Breck P. Kent/Animals Animals/Earth Scenes; 97(brc), Tom Pantages; 97(br), Breck P. Kent/Animals Animals/Earth Scenes; 98(tl), Ken Karp/HRW Photo; 98(br), Breck P. Kent; 99(tl), E. R. Degginger/Color-Pic, Inc.; 99(bl), Ray Simmons/ Photo Researchers, Inc.; 99(tc), The Natural History Museum, London; 99(bc), Breck P. Kent; 100, E. R. Degginger/Color-Pic, Inc.; 101, Doug Sokell/Tom Stack & Associates; 104(c), Wolfgang Kaehler/Liaison International.

Chapter Five: Page 106(t), Greg Vaughn/Tom Stack & Associates; 106(t, b, bl), Kaku Kurita/ Liaison Agency; 106(br), Mark Burnett/Photo Researchers, Inc.; 106(t), Florida Institute of Technology; 108(c), Andy Christiansen/HRW Photo; 108(l), John Blaustein/Liaison Agency; 108(r), Mark Lewis/Tony Stone Images; 109(tc), James Randklev/Tony Stone Images; 109(tr), Bruce Hands/Tony Stone Images; 109(br), John Zoiner Photographer; 109(bl), Ed Malles/Liaison Agency; 110(cl), Andy Christiansen/ HRW Photo; 111, Telegraph Colour Library/FPG International; 112(cr, bl), John Zoiner; 114(t), Paolo Koch/Photo Researchers, Inc.; 114(t), Horst Schafer/Peter Arnold, Inc.; 114(b), Brian Parker/Tom Stack & Associates; 114(b), C. Kuhn/Image Bank; 115(bl), Mark A. Leman/Tony Stone Images; 115(br), Tim Eagan/Woodfin Camp & Associates; 116(tr), Adam Hart-Davis/Science Photo Library/Photo Researchers, Inc.; 116(bl), James Stanfield/National Geographic Image Collection; 117(tc, tr), Victoria Smith/ HRW Photo; 118(bl), Sylvain Coffie/Tony Stone Images; 119(tr), Tom Myers/Photo Researchers, Inc.; 120(c), Alex Bartel/Science Photo Library/Photo Researchers, Inc.; 120(bl), Joyce Photographics/Photo Researchers,Inc.; 121(bl), Hank Morgan/Science Source/Photo Researchers, Inc.; 122, Mark Lewis/Liaison International; 123(tr), Craig Sands/National Geographic Image Collection; 123(cl), Tom Bean; 124(cr), G.R. Roberts Photo Library; 128(tl), John Blaustein/Liaison Agency; 128(tr), Tom Myers/Photo Researchers, Inc.; 130(t), SuperStock; 130(c), Bedford Recycled Plastic Timbers; 130(b), Kay Park-Rec Corp.; 131, Culver Pictures, Inc.

Chapter Six: Page 132(tl, c), Louis Psihoyos/Matrix International; 133(cr), M. C. Chamberlain/DRK Photo; 133(br), Bill Patterson, Sr./Patterson Graphics, Inc.; 137(br), Andy Christiansen/HRW Photo; 144, Tom Till/DRK Photo; 145, Courtesy Charles S. Tucek/University of Arizona at Tucson; 146(bl), Francois Gohier/Photo Researchers, Inc.; 146(cr), 147(tr), E. R. Degginger/Color-Pic, Inc.; 148(cl), Breck P. Kent; 148(bl), The G.R. "Dick" Roberts Photo Library; 149(c, cr), Brian Exton; 150(tr), Thomas R. Taylor/ Photo Researchers, Inc.; 151(br), Mike Buchheit Photography; 153, 154(all), American Museum of Natural History; 158(tl), Runk/Schoenberger/Grant Heilman Photography; 158(cr), Tony Stone Images; 160(c), Andrew Leitch/©1992 The Walt Disney Co. Reprinted with the permission of Discover Magazine; 161(br, tl), Louie Psihoyos/Matrix.

Unit Three: Page 162(c), Charles Scribner's Sons NY, 1906; 162(br), Steve Winter/ National Geographic Society; 162(bl), USGS/NASA/Science Source/Photo Researchers, Inc.; 163(tl), FPG International; 163(tr), Culver Pictures Inc.; 163(cl), Lambert/Archive Photos; 163(bl), Randy Duchaine/The Stock Market; 163(br), The Robotics Institute Carnegie Mellon University.

Chapter Seven: Page 164(inset), Wally Berg; 164(b), Alex Stewart/The Image Bank; 165, Peter Van Steen/HRW Photo; 167(tr), James Wall/Animals Animals/Earth Scenes; 167(bl), World Perspective/Tony Stone Images; 180(cl), ESA/CE/Eurocontrol/ Science Photo Library/Photo Researchers, Inc.; 180(tl), NASA; 182(br), Visuals Unlimited/ SylvesterAllred; 182(bl), 184(br), The G. R. "Dick" Roberts Photo Library; 184(tl), Tom Bean; 184(tr), Landform Slides; 185(bl), William Manning/The Stock Market; 187, Michelle & Tom Grimm/Tony Stone Images; 190, NASA/Photo Researchers, Inc.; 192, Bob Krist; 193, Martin Schwarzbach/Photo Deutsches Museum Munchen.

Chapter Eight: Page 194(b), Haruyoshi Yamaguchi/Sygma; 197, Joe Dellinger/ NOAA/National Geophysical Data Center; 202(cl), Bob Paz/Caltech; 203, Earth Images/ Tony Stone Images; 206, Peter Cade/Tony Stone Images; 207, A. Ramey/Woodfin Camp & Associates; 209(bl), Paul Chesley/Tony Stone Images; 210(tl), Ken Lax; 213(cr), NASA; 213(tr), SOHO (ESA & NASA); 215, A. Ramey/Woodfin Camp & Associates; 216(tl), Chuck O'Rear/Corbis; 218(c), Novaswan/FPG International; 219(cr), David Madison/Bruce Coleman, Inc.

Chapter Nine: Page 220(t), David Hardy/Science Photo Library/Photo Researchers, Inc.; 220(cr), Circus World Museum, Baraboo, Wisconsin; 221, Victoria Smith/HRW Photo; 222(cl), Robert W. Madden/National Geographic Society; 222(cr), Douglas Peebles Photography; 222(bc), Ken Sakamoto/Black Star; 223(b), Breck P. Kent/Earth Scenes; 223(tr), Joyce Warren/USGS Photo Library; 225(cr), Jim Yuskavitch; 225(bl), Karl Weatherly; 225(bc), Tui De Roy/Minden Pictures; 225(br), B. Murton/Southampton Oceanography Centre/Science Photo Library/Photo Researchers, Inc.; 226(tl), Tom Bean/DRK Photo; 226(t), Francois Gohier/Photo Researchers, Inc.; 226(c), Visuals Unlimited/Glenn Oliver; 226(b), E. R. Degginger/Color-Pic, Inc.; 227, Alberto Garcia/ SABA; 228(tl), Visuals Unlimited/Jeff Greenberg; 228(cl), Krafft/Explorer/Science Source/Photo Researchers, Inc.; 228(bl), SuperStock; 234(bl), Andrew Rafkind/Tony Stone Images; 235(tr), Game McGimsey/USGS Alaska Volcano Observatory; 235(br), Gilles Bassignac/Liaison Agency; 236(c), Robert W. Madden/National Geographic Society; 238(tl), Krafft/Explorer/Science Source/Photo Researchers, Inc.; 238(bl), Karl Weatherly; 240(c), The Robotics Institute Carnegie Mellon University; 241(bl), NASA/Science Photo Library/Photo Researchers, Inc.

Unit Four: Page 242(tl), The Age of Reptiles, a mural by Rudolph F. Zallinger. ©1996, 1975,1985,1989, Peabody Museum of Natural History, Yale University,

New Haven, Connecticut, USA.; 242(c), Tom Bean/Tony Stone Images; 242(bl), Dr. John Murphy; 242(br), Mike Roemer/Liaison Agency; 243(tr), John Eastcott/YVA Momatiuk/DRK Photo; 243(cr), Peter Essick/Aurora & Quanta; 243(tl), Stock Montage, Inc.; 243(bl), Price, R.-Survi OSF/Animals Animals/Earth Scenes; 243(br), David Wong/South China Morning Post; 243(inset), Ed Horn/Telegraph Colour Library/FPG International.

Chapter Ten: Page 244(bkgd), Corbis Images/HRW Library Photo; 245(bc, br), Andy Christiansen/HRW Photo; 246, SuperStock; 247(tr), Index Stock Photography; 247(bl), Visuals Unlimited/Martin G. Miller; 247(br), Grant Heilman/Grant Heilman Photography; 248, Andy Christiansen/HRW Photo; 249(bl), Alan Briere/SuperStock; 250(bl), C. Campbell/Corbis; 251(cr), Bob Krueger/Photo Researchers, Inc.; 251(cl), SuperStock; 252(b), B. Ross/Corbis; 254, Steven Ferry/HRW Photo; 255(cl), Visuals Unlimited/John D. Cunningham; 255(br), The G. R. "Dick" Roberts Photo Library; 257(tr), Tim Laman/Adventure Photo & Film; 257(br), Bill Ross/Corbis; 258(c), Lee Rentz/Bruce Coleman, Inc.; 258(tl), Bruce Coleman, Inc.; 259(br), Tom Walker/Tony Stone Images; 259(cl), Grant Heilman Photography, Inc.; 259(bl), Charlton Photos, Inc.; 260(bl), Grant Heilman/Grant Heilman Photography; 261(cr), Mark Lewis and Adventure Photo & Film; 261(cl), Paul Chesley/Tony Stone Images; 262(br), B. Ross/Corbis; 263, Tom Walker/Tony Stone Images; 264(bl), Visuals Unlimited/Mark A. Schneider; 264(tr), SuperStock; 267, Donald Specker/Animals Animals/Earth Scenes.

Chapter Eleven: Pages 268–269(t), Andy Christiansen/HRW Photo; 270, Tom Bean/DRK Photo; 273(br), Ed Reschke/Peter Arnold, Inc.; 273(bl), Jim Work/Peter Arnold, Inc.; 275(br), Frans Lanting/Minden Pictures; 275(tr), Laurence Parent; 276(tl), The G.R. "Dick" Roberts Photo Library; 276(cl), Galen Rowell/Peter Arnold, Inc.; 278(tl), The Huntington Library/SuperStock; 278(cr), Earth Satellite Corporation/Science Photo Library/Photo Researchers, Inc.; 279(tr), Visuals Unlimited/Martin G. Miller; 279(cr), Earth Satellite Corporation; 283, Rich Reid/Animals Animals/Earth Scenes; 284, Leif Skoogfers/Woodfin Camp & Associates; 285(bl), Laurence B. Aiuppy/FPG International; 285(tr), Wayne Lynch/DRK Photo; 288(tl), Arthus Bertrand/Explorer/Photo Researchers, Inc.; 291(c), Rich Reid/Animals Animals/Earth Scenes; 292(bl), Donald Nausbaum/Tony Stone Images; 292(tr), TSA/Tom Stack & Associates; 294, Jeff and Alexa Henry; 295, C. C. Lockwood/DRK Photo.

Chapter Twelve: Page 296(inset), Ken Lubas/LA Times; 298, Aaron Chang/The Stock Market; 299(tr), Philip Long/Tony Stone Images; 299(bl), SuperStock; 300(tl), Don Herbert/FPG International; 300(cl), Jonathan Weston/Adventure Photo & Film; 300(tl), SuperStock; 301(cl), NASA; 301(br), Index Stock; 301(tl), Index Stock; 302(tl), The G.R. "Dick" Roberts Photo Library; 302(br), Jeff Foott/DRK Photo; 302(bl), Jeff Foott/Tom Stack & Associates; 303(tl), Breck P. Kent; 303(cr), John S. Shelton; 305(tl), Breck P. Kent; 305(b), Tom Bean; 306, Brown Brothers; 307(br), Mickey Gibson/Animals Animals/Earth Scenes; 308(cr), Walter H. Hodge/Peter Arnold, Inc.; 308(cl), Michael Fogden/Bruce Coleman, Inc.; 309, Tom Bean/DRK Photo; 310(bl), Tui De Roy/The Roving Tortoise Photography; 310(cr), Barbara Gerlach/DRK Photo; 311, Didier Givois/Photo Researchers, Inc.; 312(b), Tony Stone Images; 312(cl), Visuals Unlimited/Glenn M. Oliver; 314(br), Tom Bean; 314, Breck P. Kent; 315, Tom Bean; 317(cr), Visuals Unlimited/A. J. Copley; 317(bl), The G.R. "Dick" Roberts Photo Library; 318(tr), Jebb Harris/Orange County Register/SAPA; 319(b), Mike Yamashita/Woodfin Camp & Associates; 319(cl), Visuals Unlimited/John D. Cunningham; 319(cr), J&B Photographers/Animals Animals/Earth Scenes; 320, Brown Brothers; 321, Didier Givois Agence Vandystadt/Photo Researchers, Inc.; 322(bl), Michael Fredericks/Animals Animals/Earth Scenes; 322(tr), Face of the Earth/Tom Stack & Associates; 324(cl), Richard Sisk/Panoramic Images; 324(c), Jane Stevens/Courtesy Paula Messina; 325(cr, tr), Gillian Cambers/UNESCO/Coping with beach erosion, Coastal Management Sourcebooks.

Unit Five: Page 326(tl), Herman Melville: Classics Illustrated/Kenneth Spencer Research Library; 326(c), Visuals Unlimited/D. Foster/WHOI; 326(br), Mark Votier/Sygma; 327(br), Dennis J. Sigrist, International Tsunami Center, Honolulu, Hawaii/National Geophysical Data Center; 327(tl), National Air and Space Museum/Smithsonian; 327(cr), Saola/Wallet-Rosenfeld/Liaison Agency; 327(c), Hulton-Deutsch Collection/Corbis; 327(bl), Jeremy Horner/Corbis; 327(bc), Bassignac/Deville/Gaillar/Liaison Agency.

Chapter Thirteen: Page 328(bc), NOAA/National Undersea Research Center, University North Carolina, Wilmington/Tom & Theresa Stack; 328(tr), Peter Scoones/Woodfin Camp & Associates; 330, Tom Van Sant, Geosphere Project/Planetary Visions/Science Photo Library; 334, U.S. Navy; 336(cl), Rosentiel School of Marine and Atmospheric Science, University of Miami; 337(br), James Wilson/Woodfin Camp & Associates; 337(bl), Norbert Wu; 341, NOAA/NSDS; 343(br), Mike Bacon/Tom Stack & Associates; 343(cr), Jim Zipp/Photo Researchers, Inc.; 344(tl), James B. Wood; 344(cl), Al GIddings/Al Giddings Images; 344(bl), JAMESTEC; 345(tr), E. R. Degginger/Color-Pic, Inc.; 345(cr), Nobert Wu; 346, Paolo Curto/UP/Bruce Coleman, Inc.; 347(br), Bryan and Cherry Alexander Photography; 347(cl), Breg Vaughn/Tom Stack & Associates; 348(cr), TGS-NOPEC Geophysical Company; 349(bl), Institute of Oceanographic Sciences/NERC/Science Photo Library/Photo Researchers, Inc.; 349(bc), Charles D. Winters/Photo Researchers, Inc.; 351(b), E. R. Degginger/Color-Pic, Inc.; 352(cl), Photo Edit; 352(bc), Andy Christiansen/HRW Photo; 352(br), Ron Chapple/FPG International; 353(tr), Ben Osborne/Tony Stone Images; 353(bl), Courtesy Mobil; 354(bkgd), Andy Christiansen/HRW Photo; 355(tl, tr), Courtesy Texas General Land Office Adopt-A-Beach Program; 356, James Wilson/Woodfin Camp & Associates; 360, Gilles Bassignac/Liaison Agency; 361, SuperStock.

Chapter Fourteen: Page 364(cr), Hulton Getty/Liaison Agency; 371, Lacy Atkins/San Francisco Examiner/AP/Wide World Photos; 375(tr), CC Lockwood/Bruce Coleman, Inc.; 375(bl), Darrell Wong/Tony Stone Images; 375(br), August Upitis/FPG International; 381(tl, tr), VOSCAR/The Maine Photographer; 383(cl), Art Resource, NY; 384(tl), Warren Bolster/Tony Stone Images; 384(br), Fred Whitehead/Animals Animals/Earth Scenes; 386(tl), Todd Bigelow/HRW Photo; 386(br), Warren Bolster/Tony Stone Images; 387(tc), J. A. L. Cooke/Oxford Scientific Films/Animals Animals/Earth Scenes; 387(tr), Visuals Unlimited/David M. Williams.

Unit Six: Page 388(tl), Ronald Sheridan/Ancient Art & Architecture Collection; 388–389(t), NASA; 389(c), The Huntington Library, Art Collections, and Botanical Gardens, San Marino, California/SuperStock; 389(bc), Lawrence Livermore Laboratory/Photo Researchers, Inc.

Chapter Fifteen: Page 390(c), SuperStock; 390(inset), Paul Wager/Brisbane Courier Mail/AP/Wide World Photos; 390(bkgd), Michael Melford/Image Bank; 393, Peter Van Steen/HRW Photo; 395(tr), SuperStock; 396(b), Image Copyright ©(2001) PhotoDisc, Inc.; 397, Johnny Johnson/DRK Photo; 401, Renee Lynn/Photo Researchers, Inc.; 402(tr), Jaime Puebla/AP/Wide World Photos; 405(tr), A&L Sinibaldi/Tony Stone Images; 405(cl), Luc Marescot/Liaison Agency; 406(tl), NASA/Science Photo Library/Photo Researchers, Inc.; 408, Byron Augustin/Tom Stack & Associates; 409(tc), Argus Potoarchiv/Peter Arnold, Inc.; 409(cr), Bruce Forster/Tony Stone Images; 409(tr), David Weintraub/Photo Researchers, Inc; 410(tl), Robert Ginn/PhotoEdit; 410(cr), Phil Schofield/Picture Quest; 411(cl), Jean Lauzon/Publiphoto/Photo Researchers, Inc.; 411(cr), David Woodfall/Tony Stone Images; 411(br), NASA; 413(tl), SuperStock; 413(tr), Chromosohm/Sohm/Photo Researchers, Inc.; 416(bl), Telegraph Colour Library/FPG International; 416(tr), Salaber/Liaison Agency; 418(c), Bill Thompson/Woodfin Camp & Associates, Inc.; 419(tr), Steve Winter/Black Star.

Chapter Sixteen: Page 420(bkgd), Ted S. Warren/Austin American-Statesman/Liaison Agency; 420(c), Duane A. Laverty/Waco(TX) Tribune Harold; 425, Victoria Smith/HRW Photo; 426(cl), Eric Sandler/Liaison Agency; 426(bl), NOAA; 427(tr), Joyce Photographics/Photo Researchers, Inc.; 428(cl), Muridsany et Perennou/Science Source/Photo Researchers, Inc.; 428(br), Jim Mone/AP/Wide World Photos; 429(tr), Gene E. Moore; 431(br), Image Copyright ©2001 PhotoDisc, Inc.; 431(tr), Rod Planck/Tom Stack & Associates; 434, Kent Wood/Peter Arnold, Inc.; 435(br), Jean-Loup Charmet/Science Photo Library/Photo Researchers, Inc.; 436(all), Howard B. Bluestein/Photo Researchers, Inc.; 437(tr), Red Huber/Orlando Sentinel/SYGMA; 437(bl), NASA; 438(tl), NASA/Science Photo Library/Photo Researchers, Inc.; 439, Victor R. Caivano/AP/Wide World Photos; 441(cl), David Hwang/Mazer Corp.; 441(br), G.R. Roberts Photo Library; 442(cr), David R. Frazier/Photolibrary; 442(tl), Tom Bean; 444–445, The American Map Corporation/ADC The Map People; 446(tr), Clyde H. Smith/Peter Arnold, Inc.; 447, Jean-Loup Charmet/Science Photo Library/Photo Researchers, Inc.; 448(br), Salaber/Liaison Agency; 448(tl), Michael Lyon.

Chapter Seventeen: Page 450(bl), Gunter Ziesler/Peter Arnold, Inc.; 450(br), Richard Packwood/Oxford Scientific Films/Animals Animals/Earth Scenes; 452(bkgd), Tom Van Sant, Geosphere Project/Planetary Visions/Science Photo Library/Photo Researchers, Inc.; 452(tl), G.R. Roberts Photo Library; 452(tr), Index Stock; 452(c), Yva Momatiuk & John Eastcott; 452(bl), Gary Retherford/Photo Researchers, Inc.; 452(br), SuperStock; 453(tc), Michael Newman/Photo Edit; 453(tr), Kim Heacox/DRK Photo; 455(b), Tom Van Sant, Geosphere Project/Planetary Visions/Science Photo Library/Photo Researchers, Inc.; 456(bl), Larry Ulrich Photography; 456(br), Paul Wakefield/Tony Stone Images; 459(bc), Michael Fogden/Bruce Coleman, Inc.; 460(c), Larry Ulrich Photography; 460(l), Thomas A. Wiewandt; 461, Nadine Zuber/Photo Researchers, Inc.; 462, Carr Clifton/Minden Pictures; 463(tl), Tom Bean/Tony Stone Images; 463(bc), Fred Hirschmann; 464(c), Steven Simpson/FPG International; 465, Harry Walker/Alaska Stock; 466, SuperStock; 469(tr), Roger Werth/Woodfin Camp & Associates; 471(tr), Jacques Jangoux/Tony Stone Images; 471(cr), Leverett Bradley/Tony Stone Images; 473, Danilo G. Donadoni/Bruce Coleman Inc.; 474(bl), Richard Pharaoh/International Stock; 476, George Bernard/Animals Animals/Earth Scenes; 477, Hank Morgan/Photo Researchers, Inc.

Unit Seven: Page 478(tl), Astronomical Society of Pacific/Peter Arnold, Inc; 478(cr, bl), NASA/JPL; 479(tl), Alfred Pasieka/Peter Arnold, Inc.; 479(tc), Hulton Getty/Liaison Agency; 479(cr), Warren Faidley/NASA/International Stock; 479(c, bc), NASA; 479(cl), Raven/Explorer/Photo Researchers, Inc; 479(tr), Hulton Getty/Liaison Agency; 479(inset), NASA/Liaison Agency.

Chapter Eighteen: Page 480(inset), NASA/Science Photo Library/Photo Researchers, Inc.; 480(bkgd), Jim Ballard/Tony Stone Images; 481, Peter Van Steen/HRW Photo; 482, George Holton/Photo Researchers, Inc.; 484(tl), J. McKim Mallville/University of Colorado; 484(cl), Telegraph Colour Library/FPG; 485(tr), The British Library Picture Library; 485(br), David L. Brown/Tom Stack & Associates; 487(tr), The Bridgeman Art Library; 487(bl), Scala/Art Resource; 488, Roger Ressmeyer/Corbis; 491(br), Peter Van Steen/HRW Photo; 491(bkgd), Johnny Johnson/Index Stock; 492(bl), A. J. Copley/Visuals Unlimited; 494(tl), Jim Cummings/FPG International/PNI; 494(cl), Mike Yamashita/Woodfin Camp/PNI; 494(c, br), NASA; 495(tr), Jerry Lodriguss/Photo Researchers, Inc.; 495(cr), Tony & Daphne Hallas/Science Photo Library/Photo Researchers, Inc.; 496(bl-bkgd), David Nunuk/Science Photo Library/Photo Researchers, Inc.; 496(br-bkgd), Jerry Lodriguss; 496(bl, br), Peter Van Steen/HRW Photo; 498(tl), Simon Fraser/Science Photo Library/Photo Researchers, Inc.; 498(b), NASA; 498(inset), Roger Ressmeyer/Corbis Images; 499(keyboard), Chuck O'Rear/Woodfin Camp & Associates, Inc.; 499(sunburn), Andy Christiansen/HRW Photo; 499(x-ray), David M. Dennis/Tom Stack & Associates; 499(head), Michael Scott/Photo Researchers, Inc.; 500(all NASA except bl), David Parker/Science Photo Library/Photo Researchers, Inc.; 501(tr), Larry Mulvehill/Photo Researchers, Inc.; 501(cr), Harvard-Smithsonian Center for Astrophysics; 502(c), George Holton/Photo Researchers, Inc.; 503(cr), HRW Photo by Daniel Schaefer; 504, Jerry Lodriguss/Photo Researchers, Inc.; 506, NASA; 507, Benjamin Shearn/FPG.

Chapter Nineteen: Page 510, David Malin/Anglo-Australian Observatory/Royal Observatory, Edinburgh; 514(tl), Royal Observatory, Edinberg/AATB/Science Photo Library/Photo Researchers, Inc; 514(insets), NASA/Liaison Agency; 517(bl), Michael Freeman/Bruce Coleman; 523, John Bova/Photo Researchers, Inc; 524, Earth Imaging/Tony Stone Images; 527(bl), SuperStock; 528(bl), Breck P. Kent/Animals Animals/Earth Scenes; 528(br), John Reader/Science Photo Library/Photo Researchers, Inc; 533, John T. Whatmough/JTW Incorporated; 534(bl), NSO/NASA; 535, Dean Congerngs/National Geographic Society Image Collection.

Chapter Twenty: Page 536(Mercury), NASA; 536(Venus), NASA/Peter Arnold, Inc; 536(Earth), Paul Morrell/Tony Stone Images; 536(Jupiter), Reta Beebe (New Mexico State University)/NASA; 536(Mars), USGS/TSADO/Tom Stack & Associates; 537(Saturn, Uranus, Neptune, Pluto), NASA; 538(l), Hulton Getty/Liaison Agency; 538(tr), NASA;

539, NASA/Mark S. Robinson; 540(tl), NASA; 540(bl), Mark Marten/NASA/Science Source/Photo Researchers, Inc.; 541(tl), Frans Lanting/Minden Pictures; 541(br), 542(c) NASA; 542(tl), World Perspective/Tony Stone Images; 542–543(b), NASA; 543(cr), NASA; 544, NASA/Peter Arnold, Inc.; 545(all), 546(tl), 547, 548(tl), 549(l, br), NASA; 551(all), John Bova/Photo Researchers, Inc.; 552(bl), Fred Espenak; 553(tr), Jerry Lodriguss/Photo Researchers, Inc.; 554(all), 555(tr) NASA; 555(br), USGS/Science Photo Library/Photo Researchers, Inc.; 556, World Perspectives/Tony Stone Images; 557(cl), Bob Yen/Liaison Agency; 557(br), Bill & Sally Fletcher/Tom Stack & Associates; 559(tr), NASA/Science Photo Library/Photo Researchers, Inc.; 560(bc), Breck P. Kent/Animals Animals/Earth Scenes; 560(bl), E. R. Degginger/Bruce Coleman Inc.; 560(br), Ken Nichols/Institute of Meteorites; 560(cl), Dennis Wilson/Science Photo Library/Photo Researchers, Inc.; 561, 562, NASA.

Chapter Twenty-One: Page 568(t), NASA/Science Source/Photo Researchers, Inc.; 569(tr), David Malin/Anglo-Australian Observatory; 570(tc), Phil Degginger/Color-Pic, Inc.; 570(bl), John Sanford/Astrostock; 570(tr), E. R. Degginger/Color-Pic, Inc.; 572(cr), Allan Morton/Science Photo Library/Photo Researchers, Inc.; 573, Magrath Photography/Science Photo Library/Photo Researchers, Inc.; 574, Andre Gallant/Image Bank; 577(c), Astrophysics Library, Princeton University; 580(br), Dr. Christopher Burrows, ESA/STScI/NASA; 580(cl, bl), Anglo-Australian Telescope Board; 581, David Hardy/Science Photo Library/Photo Researchers Inc.; 582, Bill & Sally Fletcher/Tom Stack & Associates; 583(bl), Dennis Di Cicco/Peter Arnold, Inc.; 583(tr), David Malin/Anglo-Australian Observatory; 584(tr), I M House/Tony Stone Images; 584(br), Bill & Sally Fletcher/Tom Stack & Associates; 584(bl), Jerry Lodriguss/Photo Researchers, Inc; 585, NASA/CXC/Smithsonian Astrophysical Observatory; 587(tr), Pictures Unlimited, Inc; 590, John Sanford/Astrostock; 591, I M House/Tony Stone Images; 592(tr), David Nunuk/Science Photo Library/Photo Researchers Inc; 594(all), NASA; 595(tl), The Open University.

Chapter Twenty-Two: Page 596, Harvey Lloyd/Peter Arnold, Inc.; 598(tr), Gustav Dore/Hulton Getty/Liaison Agency; 598(bl), NASA; 599(tr), Hulton Getty Images/Liaison Agency; 602(cr), Brian Parker/Tom Stack & Associates; 602(b), NASA; 603(br), Hesler, Chester, Jentoff-Nilsen/ NASA Goddard Lab of Atmospheres & Nielsen, U. of Hawaii; 604, Aerial Images, Inc. and SOVINFORMSPUTNIK; 605(tr, cr), EROS Data Center/USGS; 606(tr), NASA; 606(br), 607(br),TSADO/JPL/Tom Stack & Associates; 607(bl), NASA/Liaison Agency; 607(bkgd), Jim Ballard/Tony Stone Images; 608(c), NASA; 608(bl), JPL/NASA/Liaison Agency; 608(bkgd), 609(bkgd), Jim Ballard/Tony Stone Images; 610(tl, bl), JPL/NASA; 612, SuperStock; 613(tr, b), 614, NASA; 614(bkgd), Telegraph Colour Library/FPG International; 615(tr), NASA/Science Photo Library/Photo Researchers, Inc.; 615(bl), 616 NASA; 618(cl), Hesler, Chester, Jentoff-Nilsen/ NASA Goddard Lab of Atmospheres & Nielsen, U. of Hawaii; 619(all), 620(bl), NASA; 620(cr), Zvi Har'El/Jules Vern; 621, Dr. Gene Feldman, NASA GSFC/Photo Researchers, Inc.

LabBook/Appendix: "LabBook Header", "L", Corbis Images; "a", Letraset Phototone; "b", and "B", HRW; "o", and "k", images ©2001 PhotoDisc/HRW; Page 624(c), Scott Van Osdol/HRW Photo; 627(tr), John Langford/HRW Photo; 627(cl), Michelle Bridwell/HRW Photo; 627(br), Image ©2001 PhotoDisc, Inc./HRW; 628(bl), Stephanie Morris/HRW Photo; 629(tr), Jana Birchum/HRW Photo; 630, Victoria Smith/HRW Photo; 636, USGS; 639(tr), Victoria Smith/Courtesy of Science Stuff, Austin, TX/HRW Photo; 639(galena), Ken Lucas/Visuals Unlimited Inc.; 639(cr), Charlie Winters/HRW Photo; 641(bc), Russell Dian/HRW Photo; 644, Andy Christiansen/HRW Photo; 646(b), James Tallon/Outdoor Exposures; 655, Jonathan Blair/Corbis Images; 657, Tom Bean; 660, NOAA/NGDC; 662, Andy Christiansen/HRW Photo; 670, 674, Victoria Smith/HRW Photo; 675, Andy Christiansen/HRW Photo; 678, NASA; 684, Andy Christiansen/HRW Photo; 687, Victoria Smith/HRW Photo; 695, Kuni Stringer/AP/Wide World Photos; 696, Victoria Smith/HRW Photo; 697, Jay Malonson/AP/Wide World Photos; 703, Andy Christiansen/HRW Photo; 709, 710, 711, Peter Van Steen/HRW Photo; 718, John Sanford/Astrostock; 722, Jeff Hunter/The Image Bank; 724, NASA/Tony Stone Images; 733(tr), Peter Van Steen/HRW Photo.

Feature Borders: Unless otherwise noted below, all images copyright ©2001 PhotoDisc/HRW.

Across the Sciences: all images by HRW; *Careers:* (sand bkgd and Saturn), Corbis Images; (DNA), Morgan Cain & Associates; (scuba gear), ©1997 Radlund & Associates for Artville; *Eureka:* copyright ©2001 PhotoDisc/HRW; *Eye on the Environment:* (clouds and sea in bkgd), HRW; (bkgd grass, red eyed frog), Corbis Images; (hawks, pelican), Animals Animals/Earth Scenes; (rat), Visuals Unlimited/John Grelach; (endangered flower), Dan Suzio/PhotoResearchers, Inc.; *Health Watch:* (dumbbell), Sam Dudgeon/HRW Photo; (aloe vera, EKG), Victoria Smith/HRW Photo; (basketball), ©1997 Radlund & Associates for Artville; (shoes, bubbles), Greg Geisler; *Scientific Debate:* Sam Dudgeon/HRW Photo; *Science Fiction:* (saucers), Ian Christopher/Greg Geisler; (book), HRW; (bkgd), Stock Illustration Source; *Science Technology and Society:* (robot), Greg Geisler; *Weird Science:* (mite), David Burder/Tony Stone; (atom balls), J/B Woolsey Associates; (walking stick, turtle), EclectiCollection.

ANNOTATED TEACHER'S EDITION CREDITS

TE Front Matter: Page T1, Louis Psihoyos/Matrix International; T2(cl), Image copyright ©2001 PhotoDisc/HRW; T3, Trevor Wood/Tony Stone Images; T4, Image copyright ©2001 PhotoDisc, Inc./HRW; T5, Soames Summerhays/Photo Researchers, Inc.; T6, Image copyright ©2001 PhotoDisc, Inc./HRW; T7, Sam Dudgeon/HRW; T8–T9, E. R. Degginger/Color-Pic and DRK Photo; T10(tl), Bruce Coleman, Inc.; T11(bl), Ron Ruhoff/Stock Imagery; T12, Image copyright ©2001 PhotoDisc/HRW; T13, The Stock Market; T14, NASA; T15, Sam Dudgeon/HRW Photo; T16(br), Corbis Images/HRW; T17(br), SuperStock.

Master Materials List: Unless otherwise noted all images © 2001 PhotoDisc/HRW: Page xxii(CD), HRW Photo; xxiii(beans), Corbis Images; (gelatin,marshmallows), Sam Dudgeon/HRW; (paint), Andy Christiansen/HRW; xxiv(salt), Corbis Images;(ball), ©1997 Radlund & Assoc. for Artville; xxv(coin), EyeWire, Inc; (hammer), Sam Dudgeon/HRW; xxvi(minerals,bl), HRW Photos; (coins), EyeWire, Inc xxvii(tr), Robert Wolf/HRW.

Lab Approval Portraits: All photos courtesy of the reviewers.

TE Background Illustrations: Page 3F(cr), Stephen Durke/Washington Artists; (bl), David Schleinkofer; 57E(tl), HRW; 77E(bl), Dan Stuckenschneider/Uhl Studios, Inc; 77F(cr), Dan Stuckenschneider/Uhl Studios, Inc; 105F(c), HRW; 105F(tr), Dan Stuckenschneider/Uhl Studios, Inc; 163E(tl), Dan Stuckenschneider/Uhl Studios, Inc; (bl), MapQuest.com; 163F(tl), Dan Stuckenschneider/Uhl Studios, Inc; 219E(tr), Dan Stuckenschneider/Uhl Studios, Inc; (br), Dan Stuckenschneider/Uhl Studios, Inc; 219F(bl), MapQuest.com; 243E(br), Stephen Durke/Washington Artists; 361E(bl), MapQuest.com; 361F(cr), Marty Roper/Planet Rep; 389E(cr), John Huxtable; 389F(tl), Stephen Durke/Washington Artists; 419E(br), MapQuest.com; 449E(cl), MapQuest.com; (cr), Stephen Durke/Washington Artists; (br), Marty Roper/Planet Rep; 449F(cl), MapQuest.com; 507E(tl), Paul DiMare; 507F(tl), HRW; (bl), Paul DiMare; 535F(tl), Stephen Durke/Washington Artists; 595F(tl,cl), Stephen Durke/Washington Artists.

TE Background Photography: Page 3E(tr), Marit Jentof-Nilsen and Fritz Hasler/NASA Goddard Laboratory for Atmospheres; (bl), S. Schwabe/The Rob Palwer Blue Holes Foundation; 3F(tl), Earth Imaging/Tony Stone Images; 31E(tl,bl), Andy Christiansen/HRW Photo; (br), Aerial Images, Inc. and SOVINFORMSPUTNIK; 31F(tl), Sam Dudgeon/HRW Photo; (cr), USGS; (bl), USGS; 57E(cr), E. R. Degginger/Color-Pi; 57F(cl), Erica and Harold Van Pelt/American Museum of Natural History; (cr), E. R. Degginger/Color-Pic; (bl), Index Stock Photography; 77E(tl), Peter Cummings/Tony Stone Images; (bl), Sam Dudgeon/HRW Photo; (bc), Breck P. Kent; (br), Dorling Kindersley; 77F(tl), Peter Frenck/Bruce Coleman, Inc.; (br), E. R. Degginger/Color-Pic; 105E(tl), James Randklev/Tony Stone Images; (cr), Mark A. Leman/Tony Stone Images; (bl), Andy Christiansen/HRW Photo; 105F(cl), Sylvain Coffie/Tony Stone Images; (br), G.R. Dick Roberts; 131E, Mike Bucheit Photography; 131F(bl), E. R. Degginger/Color-Pic, Inc., 131F(cr), Breck P. Kent; 163F(cr), Visuals Unlimited/Sylvester Allred; (bl), ESA/CE/Eurocontral/Science Photo Library/Photo Researchers; 193E(cr), Bob Paz/Caltech; 193F(tr), Astronomy Online; (tr inset), SOHO/ESA/NASA; (cl), A. Ramey/Woodfin Camp & Associates 211E(br), Sam Dudgeon/HRW photo; 211F(tl), John Langford/HRW photo; 219E(cl), Robert W. Madden/National Geographic Society; 219F(tr), Andrew Rafkind/Tony Stone Images; (cr), Gilles Bassignac/Liaison International; 243E(cl), SuperStock, 243E(br), B. Ross/Westlight/Corbis; 243F, Paul Chesley/Tony Stone Images; 267E(tl), Galen Rowell/Peter Arnold; (cr), Earth Satellite Corporation/Science Photo Library; (bl), Laurence Parent; 295E(cr), SuperStock; (bl), NASA; (cr), Brown Brothers; 295F(tl), Didier Givois Agence Vandystadt/Photo Researchers; (cr), A. J. Copley/Visuals Unlimited; (bl), Colin Monteath/Hedgehog House New Zealand; 327E(cl), James Wilson/Woodfin Camp & Associates; (br), NOAA/NSDS; (tr), E. R. Degginger/Color-Pic, Inc.; 327F(tl), Norbert Wu; (br), Ben Osborne/Tony Stone Images; 361E(tl), Hulton Getty/Liaison International; (br), August Upitis/FPG International; 361F(bl), Darrell Wong/Tony Stone Images; 389E(cl), Image copyright ©2001 PhotoDisc; (bl), SuperStock; 389F(tr), David Weintraub/Photo Researchers; (bl), NASA/Science Photo Library/Photo Researchers; 419E(tr), Gene E. Moore; (cl), Eric Sandler/Liaison Agency; 419F(tr), NASA/Science Photo Library/Photo Researchers; (cl), Howard Bluestein/Photo Researchers; 449F(tr), Jaques Janqoux/Tony Stone Images; (br), Leverett Bradley/Tony Stone Images; 479E(tl), George Holton/Photo Researchers, Inc., (bl), Scala/Art Resource, NY, (br), The British Library Picture Library; 479F(cl), Larry Mulvehill/Photo Researchers, Inc, (tr), Roger Ressmeyer/Corbis, (br), NASA; 507E, David Malin/Anglo-Australian Observatory/Royal Observatory, Edinburgh, (br), John Bova/Photo Researchers, Inc.; 507F(cr), John Reader/Science Photo Library/Photo Researchers, Inc.; 535E(tl), NASA, (bl), NASA/Mark S. Robinson, (cr), NASA; 535F(bl), John Bova/Photo Researchers, Inc., (cr), Bill & Sally Fletcher/Tom Stack and Associates; 567E(tl), John Sanford/Astrostock, (bl), Magrath Photography/Science Photo Library/Photo Researchers, Inc., (br), I M House/Tony Stone Images; 567F(tl), Bill & Sally Fletcher/Tom Stack & Associates, (br), David Hardy/Science Photo Library/Photo Researchers, Inc.; 595E(tl), Sovfoto/Eastfoto, (cr), NASA; 595F(cr), NASA/Science Photo Library/Photo Researchers, Inc.

Answers to Concept Mapping Questions

The following pages contain sample answers to all of the concept mapping questions that appear in the Chapter Reviews. Because there is more than one way to do a concept map, your students' answers may vary.

CHAPTER 1 The World of Earth Science

17.

CHAPTER 2 Maps as Models of the Earth

21.

CHAPTER 3 Minerals of the Earth's Crust

17.

CHAPTER 4 Rocks: Mineral Mixtures

19.

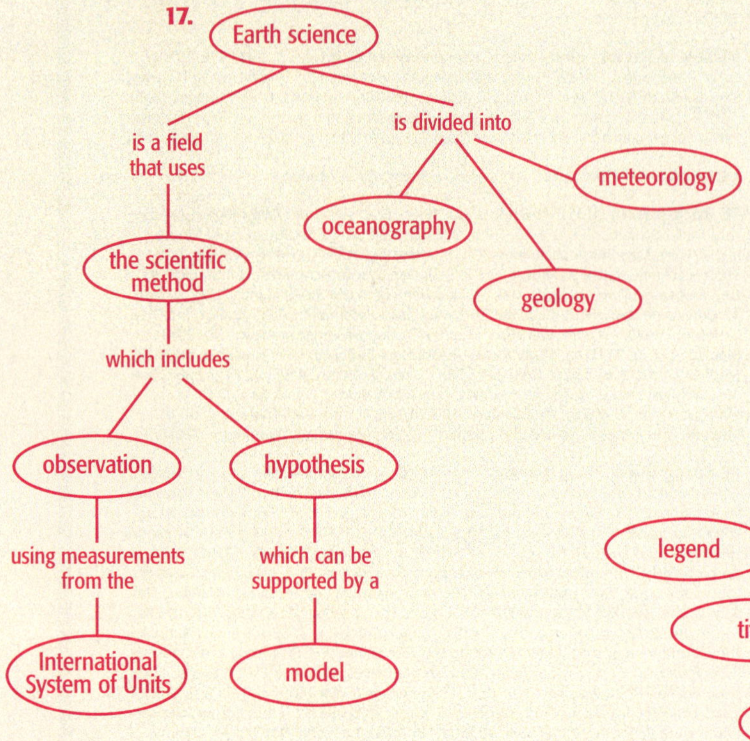

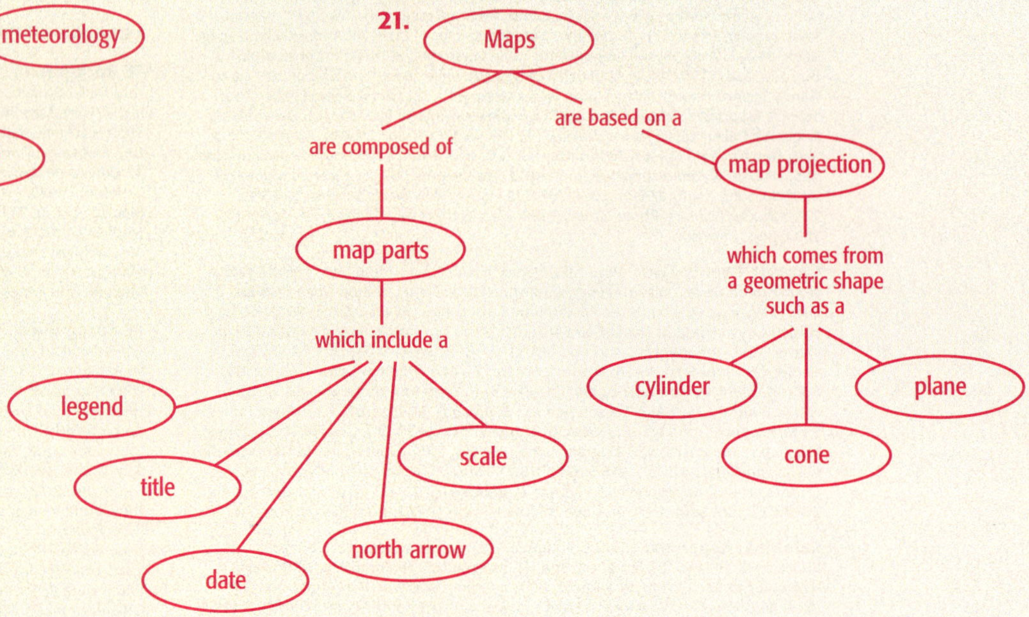

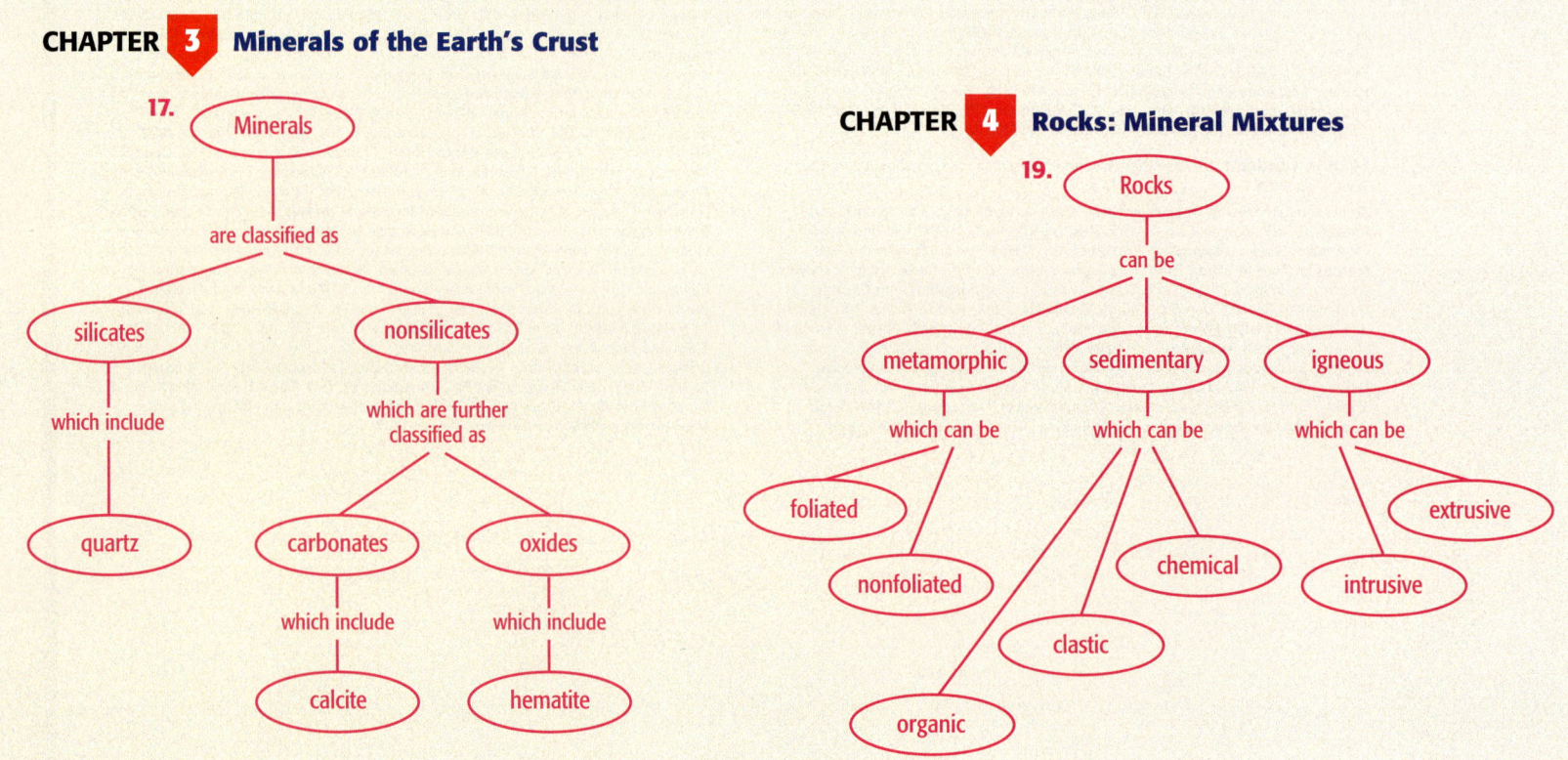

CHAPTER 5 Energy Resources

18.
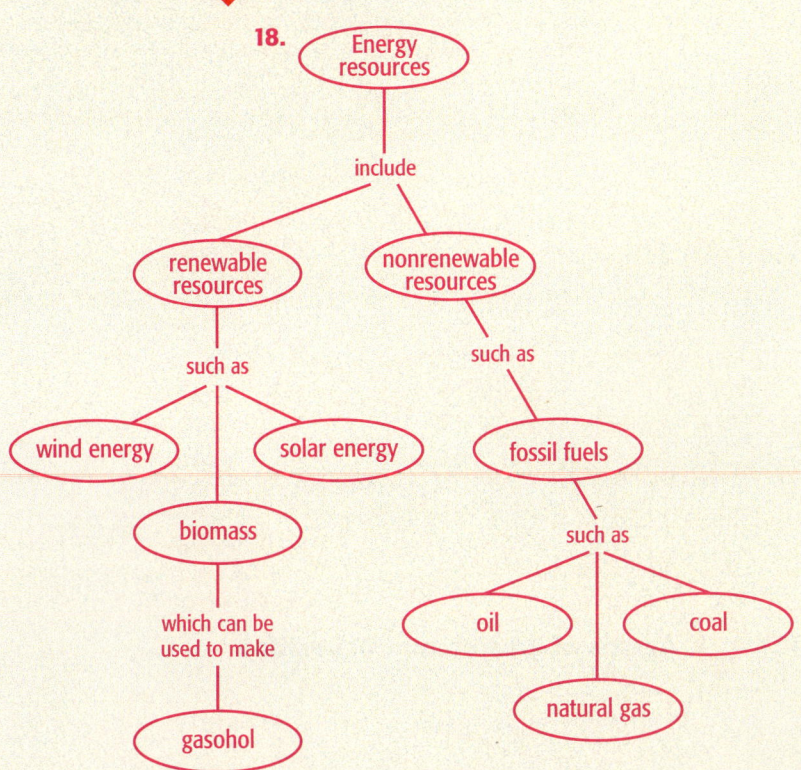

CHAPTER 6 The Rock and Fossil Record

17.
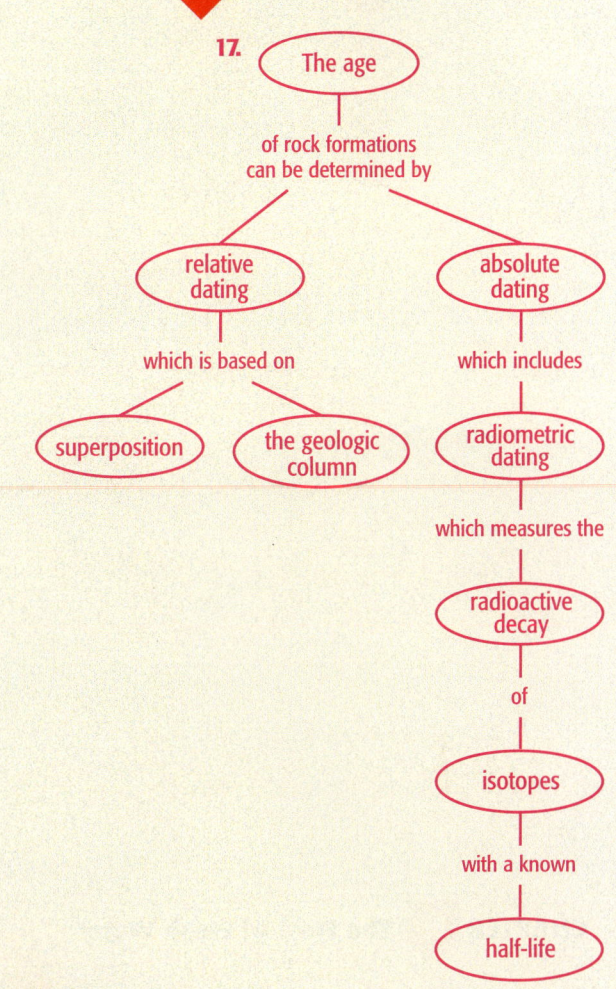

CHAPTER 7 Plate Tectonics

21.
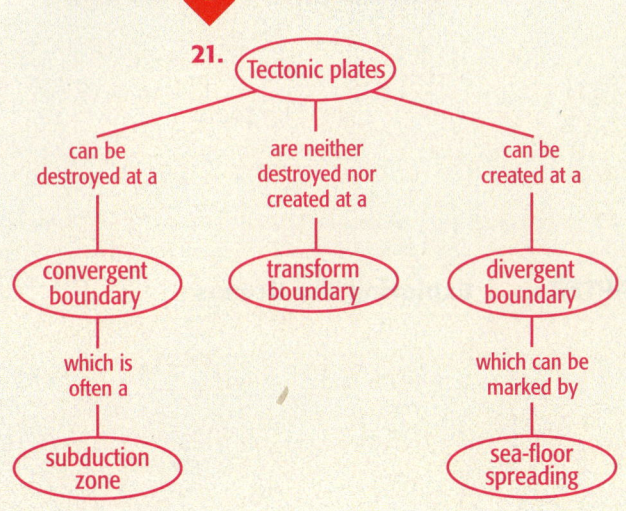

CHAPTER 8 Earthquakes

15.
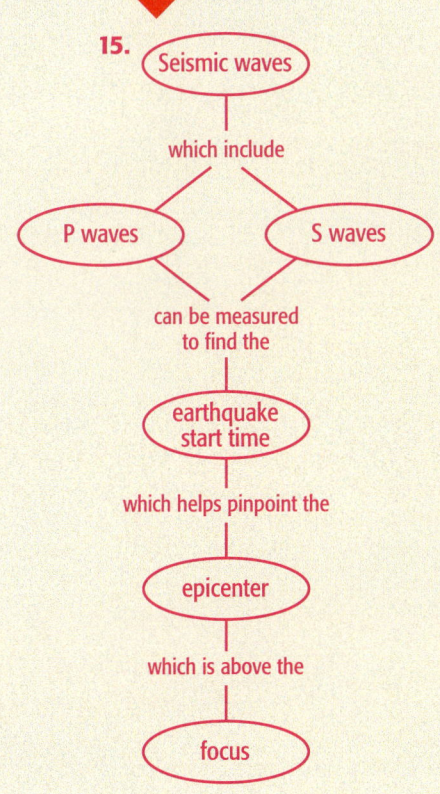

CHAPTER 9 Volcanoes

17.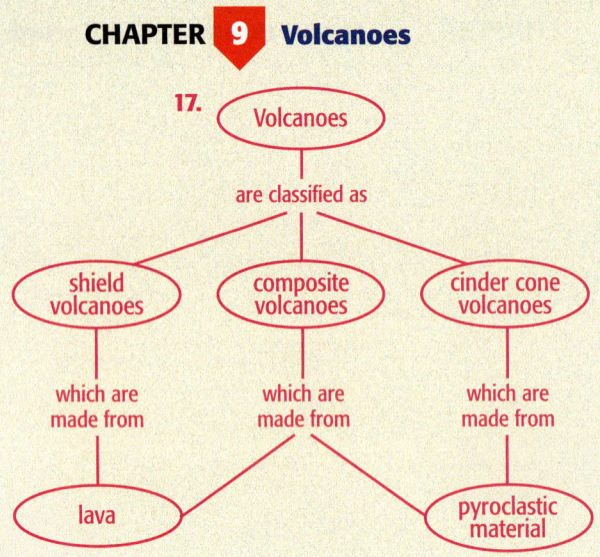

CHAPTER 10 Weathering and Soil Formation

20.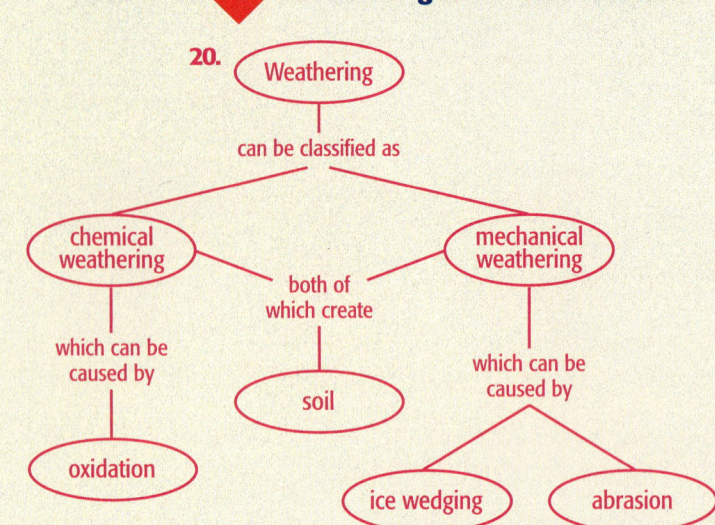

CHAPTER 12 Agents of Erosion and Deposition

23.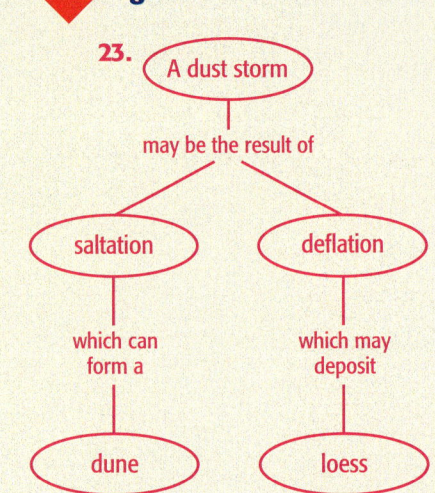

CHAPTER 11 The Flow of Fresh Water

19.

CHAPTER 13 Exploring the Oceans

19.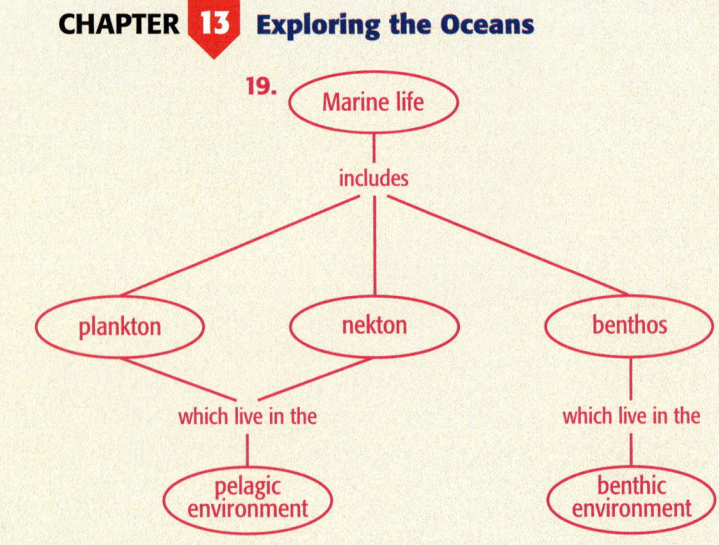

CHAPTER 14 The Movement of Ocean Water

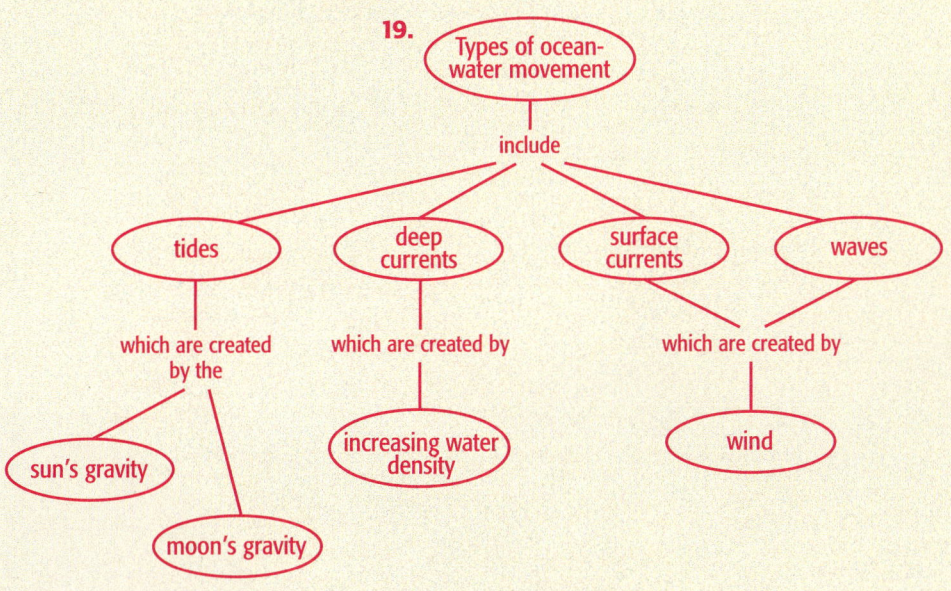

CHAPTER 15 The Atmosphere

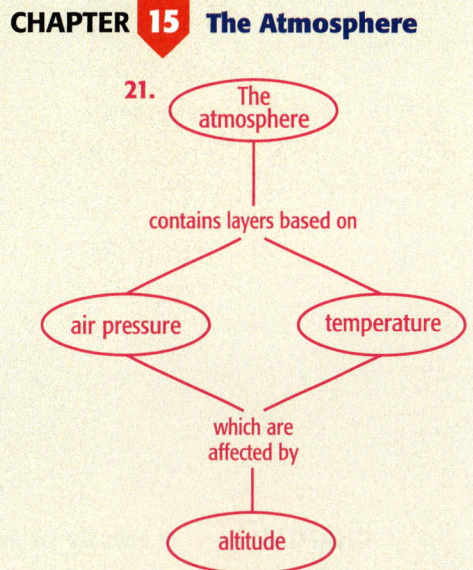

CHAPTER 16 Understanding Weather

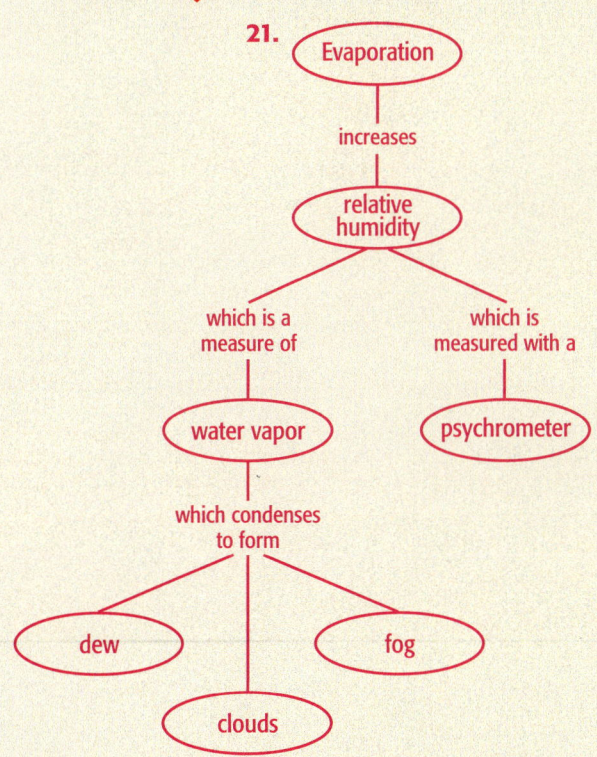

CHAPTER 17 Climate

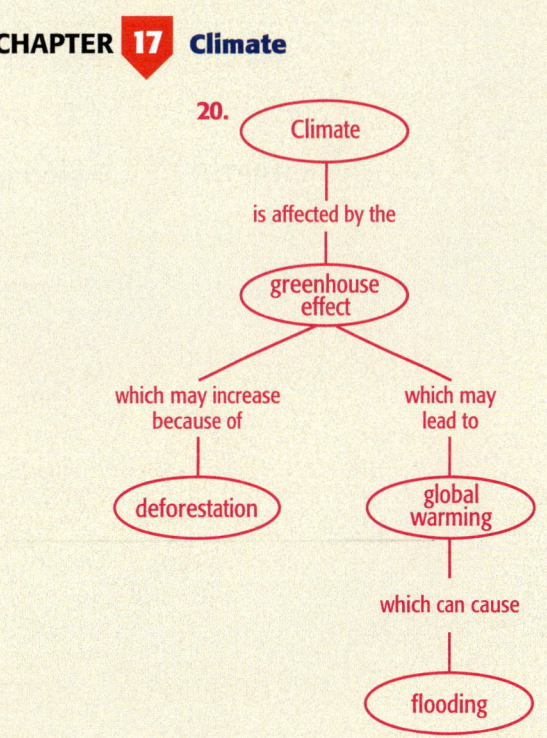

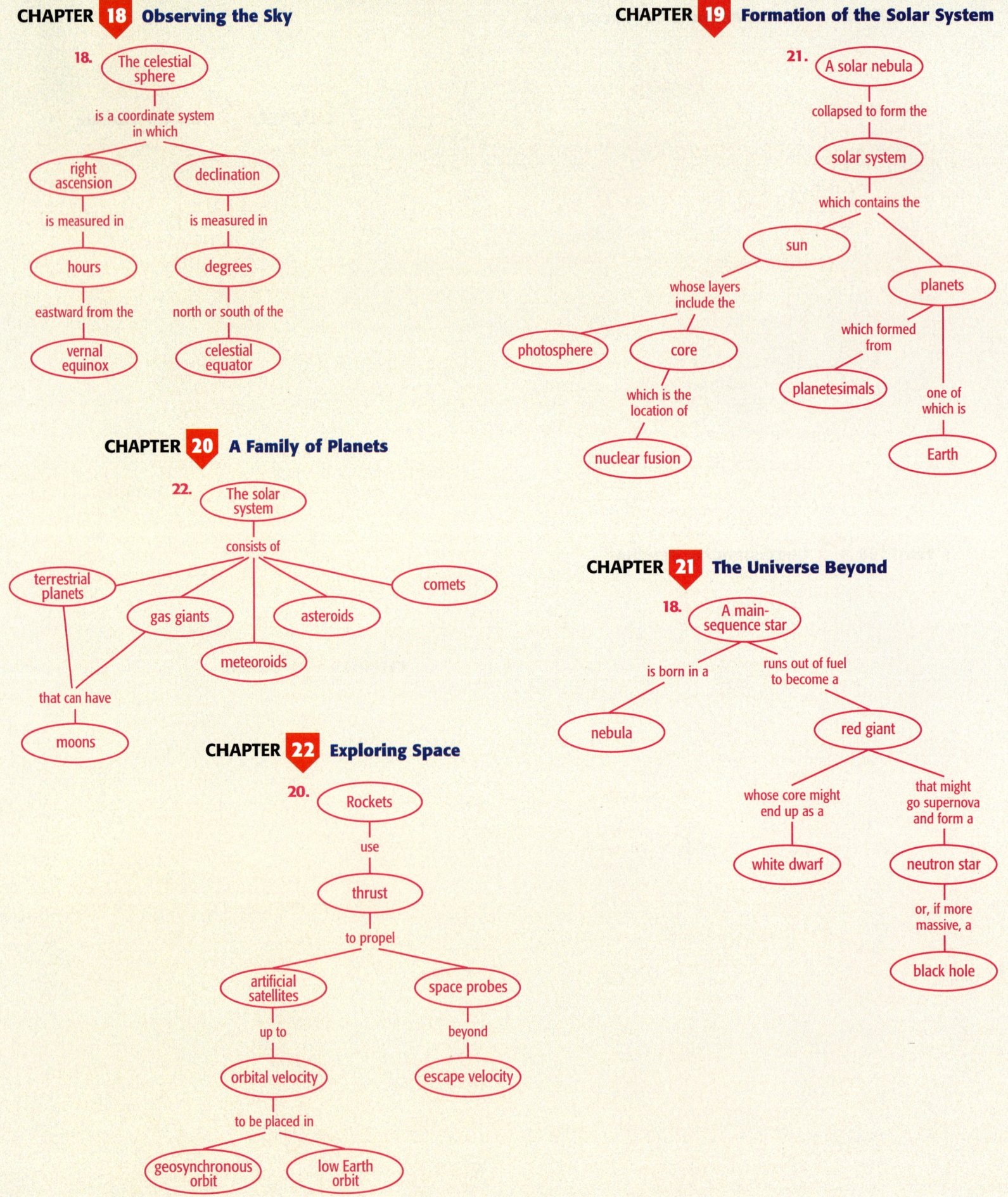